CLYMER® MANUALS

HARLEY-DAVIDSON

FXD TWIN CAM 88 • 1999-2005

WHAT'S IN YOUR TOOLBOX?

YouTube

Disclaimer

More information available at haynes.com
Phone: 805-498-6703

Haynes Group Limited
Sparkford Nr Yeovil
Somerset BA22 7JJ England

Haynes North America, Inc.
2801 Townsgate Road, Suite 340
Thousand Oaks, CA 91361 USA

ISBN-10: 0-89287-986-6
ISBN-13: 978-0-89287-986-1
Library of Congress: 2005907848

Technical Photography: Ed Scott, assistance provided by Jordan Engineering, Oceanside, California
Dyna Glide Twin Cam 88 FXDX for technical photographs provided by
San Diego Harley-Davidson, San Diego, California (www.sandiegoharley.com)
Twin Cam 88 engine provided by Patrick Racing, Garden Grove, California (www.patrickracing.com)

Printed in India

M425-3, 11X2, 13-608

ABCDEFGHI

Common spark plug conditions

NORMAL

Symptoms: Brown to grayish-tan color and slight electrode wear. Correct heat range for engine and operating conditions.
Recommendation: When new spark plugs are installed, replace with plugs of the same heat range.

WORN

Symptoms: Rounded electrodes with a small amount of deposits on the firing end. Normal color. Causes hard starting in damp or cold weather and poor fuel economy.
Recommendation: Plugs have been left in the engine too long. Replace with new plugs of the same heat range. Follow the recommended maintenance schedule.

CARBON DEPOSITS

Symptoms: Dry sooty deposits indicate a rich mixture or weak ignition. Causes misfiring, hard starting and hesitation.
Recommendation: Make sure the plug has the correct heat range. Check for a clogged air filter or problem in the fuel system or engine management system. Also check for ignition system problems.

ASH DEPOSITS

Symptoms: Light brown deposits encrusted on the side or center electrodes or both. Derived from oil and/ or fuel additives. Excessive amounts may mask the spark, causing misfiring and hesitation during acceleration.
Recommendation: If excessive deposits accumulate over a short time or low mileage, install new valve guide seals to prevent seepage of oil into the combustion chambers. Also try changing gasoline brands.

OIL DEPOSITS

Symptoms: Oily coating caused by poor oil control. Oil is leaking past worn valve guides or piston rings into the combustion chamber. Causes hard starting, misfiring and hesitation.
Recommendation: Correct the mechanical condition with necessary repairs and install new plugs.

GAP BRIDGING

Symptoms: Combustion deposits lodge between the electrodes. Heavy deposits accumulate and bridge the electrode gap. The plug ceases to fire, resulting in a dead cylinder.
Recommendation: Locate the faulty plug and remove the deposits from between the electrodes.

TOO HOT

Symptoms: Blistered, white insulator, eroded electrode and absence of deposits. Results in shortened plug life.
Recommendation: Check for the correct plug heat range, over-advanced ignition timing, lean fuel mixture, intake manifold vacuum leaks, sticking valves and insufficient engine cooling.

PREIGNITION

Symptoms: Melted electrodes. Insulators are white, but may be dirty due to misfiring or flying debris in the combustion chamber. Can lead to engine damage.
Recommendation: Check for the correct plug heat range, over-advanced ignition timing, lean fuel mixture, insufficient engine cooling and lack of lubrication.

HIGH SPEED GLAZING

Symptoms: Insulator has yellowish, glazed appearance. Indicates that combustion chamber temperatures have risen suddenly during hard acceleration. Normal deposits melt to form a conductive coating. Causes misfiring at high speeds.
Recommendation: Install new plugs. Consider using a colder plug if driving habits warrant.

DETONATION

Symptoms: Insulators may be cracked or chipped. Improper gap setting techniques can also result in a fractured insulator tip. Can lead to piston damage.
Recommendation: Make sure the fuel anti-knock values meet engine requirements. Use care when setting the gaps on new plugs. Avoid lugging the engine.

MECHANICAL DAMAGE

Symptoms: May be caused by a foreign object in the combustion chamber or the piston striking an incorrect reach (too long) plug. Causes a dead cylinder and could result in piston damage.
Recommendation: Repair the mechanical damage. Remove the foreign object from the engine and/or install the correct reach plug.

CONTENTS

QUICK REFERENCE DATA

MOTORCYCLE INFORMATION

MODEL:______________________________ YEAR:______________

VIN NUMBER:______________________________

ENGINE SERIAL NUMBER:______________________________

CARBURETOR SERIAL NUMBER OR I.D. MARK:______________________________

TIRE INFLATION PRESSURE (COLD)*

Model	kPa	psi
Front wheels		
Rider only	207	30
Rider and one passenger	207	30
Rear wheels		
Rider only	248	36
Rider and one passenger	276	40

*Tire pressure for original equipment tires. Aftermarket tires may require different inflation pressure.

ENGINE OIL SPECIFICATIONS

Type	HD rating	Viscosity	Operating temperature
HD Multi-grade	HD360	SAE 10W/40	Below 40° F
HD Multi-grade	HD360	SAE 20W/50	Above 40° F
HD Regular heavy	HD360	SAE 50	Above 60° F
HD Extra heavy	HD360	SAE 60	Above 80° F

ENGINE AND PRIMARY DRIVE/TRANSMISSION OIL CAPACITIES

Oil tank refill capacity	
With oil filter change	2.5 U.S. qts. (2.4 L)
After engine rebuild	2.9 U.S. qts. (2.7 L)
Primary chain case	26 oz. (768 mL)
Transmission	
Oil change	20-24 U.S. oz. (591-709 mL)
Rebuild (dry)	24 U.S. oz. (709 mL)

RECOMMENDED LUBRICANTS AND FLUIDS

Brake fluid	DOT 5 silicone
Front fork oil	HD Type E or an equivalent
Fuel	91 pump octane or higher leaded or unleaded
Transmission	HD Transmission Lubricant or an equivalent
Primary chaincase	HD Primary Chaincase Lubricant or an equivalent

MAINTENANCE AND TUNE-UP TORQUE SPECIFICATIONS

Item	ft.-lb.	in.-lb.	N•m
Air filter			
Backplate screws	–	20-40	2-5
Cover screw	–	36-60	4-7
Clutch adjusting			
screw locknut	–	72-120	8-14
Clutch inspection			
cover screws	–	84-108	9-12
Crankcase oil plug	–	120-144	14-16
Engine oil drain plug	14-21	–	19-28
Front fork cap bolt	11-22	–	15-30
Primary drive chain			
Inspection cover screws	–	84-108	10-12
Chain adjuster shoe nut	21-29	–	28-39
Oil tank drain plug	14-21	–	19-28
Front axle nut	50-55	–	68-75
Rear axle nut	60-65	–	81-88
Transmission drain plug	14-21	–	19-28
Upper fork bridge			
pinch bolts			
FXDWG	30-35	–	41-47
All models			
except FXDWG	25-30	–	34-41
Spark plug	11-18	–	15-24

FRONT FORK OIL CAPACITY AND OIL LEVEL DIMENSION

Model	Capacity oz. (ml)	Oil level dimension in. (mm)
1999 models		
FXDWG	10.2 (302)	–
All models except FXDWG	9.2 (272)	–
2000-on models		
FXD, FXDI	10.6 (314)	6.69 (169.9)
FXDC, FXDCI	10.6 (314)	6.69 (169.9)
FXDL (2000-2001 models)	10.7 (316)	7.20 (182.0)
FXDL, FXDLI (2002-on)	10.6 (314)	6.69 (169.9)
FXDS-CONV	11.5 (341)	6.10 (154.9)
FXDWG, FXDWGI	12.0 (356)	7.28 (184.9)
FXDX, FXDXI, FXDXT	NA	
FXDP	NA	

*NA = Information not available from the manufacturer.

MAINTENANCE AND TUNE-UP SPECIFICATIONS

Item	Specification
Engine compression	90 psi (620 kPa)
Spark plugs	HD No. 6R12*
Gap	0.038-0.043 in. (0.097-1.09 mm)
Idle speed	950-1050 rpm
Ignition timing	Non-adjustable
Drive belt deflection	5/16-3/8 in. (8-10 mm)
Brake pad minimum thickness	
1999	1/16 in. (1.6 mm)
2000-on	0.04 in. (1.02 mm)
Clutch cable free play	1/16-1/8 in. (1.6-3.2 mm)

*Harley-Davidson recommends that no other type of spark plug be substituted for the recommended H-D type.

REPLACEMENT BULBS

Item	Size (all 12 volt) × quantity
Headlamp	55/60
Position lamp*	3.9
Indicator lamps	
FXDL, FXDLI	1.1 × 4
FXDP	2.1 × 4
All models except FXDL and FXDP	2.2 × 3
Fuel gauge	
FXDL, FXDLI, FXDWG, FXDWGI	2.7
FXD, FXDI, FXDC, FXDCI, FXDX, FXDXI, FXDX-CONV, FXDXT	3.7
FXDP	NA
Front turn signal/running light	27/7 × 2
Front turn signal*	21 × 2
Rear turn signal	27 × 2
Rear turn signal	21 × 2
Tail/brake lamp	7/27
Tail/brake lamp*	5/21

*Indicates bulb specification for HD International models.

MODEL DESIGNATION

FXD/FXDI Dyna Super Glide (1999-2005)
FXDX/FXDXI Dyna Super Glide Sport (1999-2005)
FXDL/FXDLI Dyna Low Rider (1999-2005)
FXDS-CONV Dyna Super Glide Convertible (1999-2000)
FXDWG/FXDWGI Dyna Wide Glide (1999-2005)
FXDXT Dyna Super Glide T-Sport (1999-2003)
FXDC/FXDCI Dyna Super Glide Custom (2005)
FXDP (2001-2004)

CHAPTER ONE

GENERAL INFORMATION

This detailed and comprehensive manual covers the Harley-Davidson Dyna Glide Twin Cam 88 model from 1999-on. Procedures and specifications unique to 2002-2005 models are covered in the Supplement at the end of the manual. The text provides complete information on maintenance, tune-up, repair and overhaul. Hundreds of photos and drawings guide the reader through every job.

A shop manual is a reference tool and as in all Clymer manuals, the chapters are thumb tabbed for easy reference. Important items are indexed at the end of the book. All procedures, tables and figures are designed for the reader who may be working on the vehicle for the first time. Frequently used specifications and capacities from individual chapters are summarized in the *Quick Reference Data* at the front of the book.

Tables 1-9 are at the end of this chapter.

Table 1 lists model designation.

Table 2 lists general vehicle dimensions.

Table 3 lists vehicle weight.

Table 4 lists decimal and metric equivalents.

Table 5 lists conversion tables.

Table 6 lists general torque specifications.

Table 7 lists technical abbreviations.

Table 8 lists American tap and drill sizes.

Table 9 lists special tools.

MANUAL ORGANIZATION

All dimensions and capacities are expressed in metric and U.S. standard units of measurement.

This chapter provides general information on shop safety, tool use, service fundamentals and shop supplies. The tables at the end of the chapter include general vehicle information.

Chapter Two provides methods for quick and accurate diagnosis of problems. Troubleshooting procedures present typical symptoms and logical methods to pinpoint and repair the problem.

Chapter Three explains all routine maintenance necessary to keep the vehicle running well. Chapter Three also includes recommended tune-up procedures, eliminating the need to constantly consult the chapters on the various assemblies.

Subsequent chapters describe specific systems such as engine, transmission, clutch, drive system, fuel and exhaust systems, suspension and brakes. Each disassembly, repair and assembly procedure is discussed in step-by-step form.

Some of the procedures in this manual specify special tools. In most cases, the tool is illustrated in use. Well-equipped mechanics may be able to substitute similar tools or fabricate a suitable replacement. However, in some cases, the specialized equipment or expertise needed may make it impractical for the home mechanic to attempt the procedure. When necessary, such operations are identified in the text with the recommendation to have a dealership or specialist perform the task. It may be less expensive to have a professional perform these jobs, especially when considering the cost of the equipment.

WARNINGS, CAUTIONS AND NOTES

The terms, WARNING, CAUTION and NOTE have specific meanings in this manual.

A WARNING emphasizes areas where injury or even death could result from negligence. Mechanical damage may also occur. WARNINGS *are to be taken seriously*.

A CAUTION emphasizes areas where equipment damage could result. Disregarding a CAUTION could cause permanent mechanical damage, though injury is unlikely.

A NOTE provides additional information to make a step or procedure easier or clearer. Disregarding a NOTE could cause inconvenience, but would not cause equipment damage or personal injury.

SAFETY

Professional mechanics can work for years and never sustain a serious injury or mishap. Follow these guidelines and practice common sense to safely service the vehicle.

1. Do not operate the vehicle in an enclosed area. The exhaust gasses contain carbon monoxide, an odorless, colorless, and tasteless poisonous gas. Carbon monoxide levels build quickly in small enclosed areas and can cause unconsciousness and death in a short time. Make sure the work area is properly ventilated or operate the vehicle outside.
2. *Never* use gasoline or any extremely flammable liquid to clean parts. Refer to *Cleaning Parts* and *Handling Gasoline Safely* in this chapter.
3. *Never* smoke or use a torch in the vicinity of flammable liquids, such as gasoline or cleaning solvent.
4. If welding or brazing on the vehicle, remove the fuel tank, carburetor and shocks to a safe distance at least 50 ft. (15 m) away.
5. Use the correct type and size of tools to avoid damaging fasteners.
6. Keep tools clean and in good condition. Replace or repair worn or damaged equipment.
7. When loosening a tight fastener, be guided by what would happen if the tool slips.
8. When replacing fasteners, make sure the new fasteners are of the same size and strength as the original ones.
9. Keep the work area clean and organized.
10. Wear eye protection *anytime* the safety of the eyes is in question. This includes procedures involving drilling, grinding, hammering, compressed air and chemicals.
11. Wear the correct clothing for the job. Tie up or cover long hair so it can not get caught in moving equipment.
12. Do not carry sharp tools in clothing pockets.
13. Always have an approved fire extinguisher available. Make sure it is rated for gasoline (Class B) and electrical (Class C) fires.
14. Do not use compressed air to clean clothes, the vehicle or the work area. Debris may be blown into the eyes or skin. *Never* direct compressed air at anyone. Do not allow children to use or play with any compressed air equipment.
15. When using compressed air to dry rotating parts, hold the part so it can not rotate. Do not allow the force of the air to spin the part. The air jet is capable of rotating parts at extreme speed. The part may be damaged or disintegrate, causing serious injury.
16. Do not inhale the dust created by brake pad and clutch wear. These particles may contain asbestos. In addition, some types of insulating materials and gaskets may contain asbestos. Inhaling asbestos particles is hazardous to health.

17. Never work on the vehicle while someone is working under it.

18. When placing the vehicle on a stand, make sure it is secure before walking away.

Handling Gasoline Safely

Gasoline is a volatile flammable liquid and is one of the most dangerous items in the shop. Because gasoline is used so often, many people forget that it is hazardous. Only use gasoline as fuel for gasoline internal combustion engines. Keep in mind, when working on a vehicle, gasoline is always present in the fuel tank, fuel line and carburetor. To avoid a disastrous accident when working around the fuel system, carefully observe the following precautions:

1. *Never* use gasoline to clean parts. See *Cleaning Parts* in this chapter.

2. When working on the fuel system, work outside or in a well-ventilated area.

3. Do not add fuel to the fuel tank or service the fuel system while the vehicle is near open flames, sparks or where someone is smoking. Gasoline vapor is heavier than air, it collects in low areas and is more easily ignited than liquid gasoline.

4. Allow the engine to cool completely before working on any fuel system component.

5. When draining the carburetor, catch the fuel in a plastic container and then pour it into an approved gasoline storage device.

6. Do not store gasoline in glass containers. If the glass breaks, a serious explosion or fire may occur.

7. Immediately wipe up spilled gasoline with rags. Store the rags in a metal container with a lid until they can be properly disposed of, or place them outside in a safe place for the fuel to evaporate.

8. Do not pour water onto a gasoline fire. Water spreads the fire and makes it more difficult to put out. Use a class B, BC or ABC fire extinguisher to extinguish the fire.

9. Always turn off the engine before refueling. Do not spill fuel onto the engine or exhaust system. Do not overfill the fuel tank. Leave an air space at the top of the tank to allow room for the fuel to expand due to temperature fluctuations.

Cleaning Parts

Cleaning parts is one of the more tedious and difficult service jobs performed in the home garage. There are many types of chemical cleaners and solvents available for shop use. Most are poisonous and extremely flammable. To prevent chemical exposure, vapor buildup, fire and serious injury, observe each product warning label and note the following:

1. Read and observe the entire product label before using any chemical. Always know what type of chemical is being used and whether it is poisonous and/or flammable.

2. Do not use more than one type of cleaning solvent at a time. If mixing chemicals is called for, measure the proper amounts according to the manufacturer.

3. Work in a well-ventilated area.

4. Wear chemical-resistant gloves.

5. Wear safety glasses.

6. Wear a vapor respirator if the instructions call for it.

7. Wash hands and arms thoroughly after cleaning parts.

8. Keep chemical products away from children and pets.

9. Thoroughly clean all oil, grease and cleaner residue from any part that must be heated.

10. Use a nylon brush when cleaning parts. Metal brushes may cause a spark.

11. When using a parts washer, only use the solvent recommended by the manufacturer. Make sure the parts washer is equipped with a metal lid that will lower in case of fire.

Warning Labels

Most manufacturers attach information and warning labels to the vehicle. These labels contain instructions that are important to personal safety when operating, servicing, transporting and storing the vehicle. Refer to the owner's manual for the description and location of labels. Order replacement labels from the manufacturer if they are missing or damaged.

SERIAL NUMBERS

Serial numbers are stamped on various locations on the frame, engine, transmission and carburetor. Record these numbers in the *Quick Reference Data* section in the front of the book. Have these numbers available when ordering parts.

The frame serial number (**Figure 1**) is stamped on the right side of the frame down tube.

The VIN number label (**Figure 2**) is located just below the frame number on the right side frame down tube.

Engine serial number is stamped on a pad on the left side of the crankcase (**Figure 3**), as well as the right side of the crankcase (**Figure 4**).

The transmission serial number (**Figure 5**) is stamped on a pad on the right side of the transmission case next to the side door.

The carburetor serial number (**Figure 6**) is located on the side of the carburetor body next to the accelerator pump linkage.

Table 1 lists model designation.

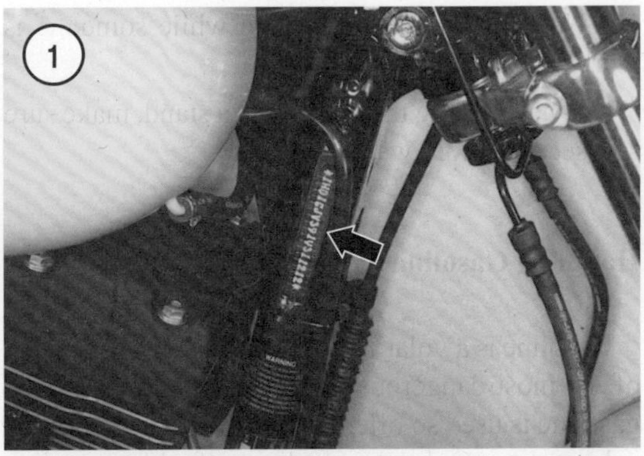

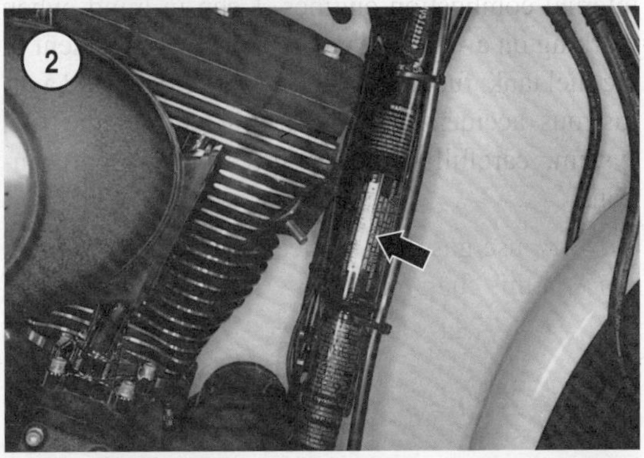

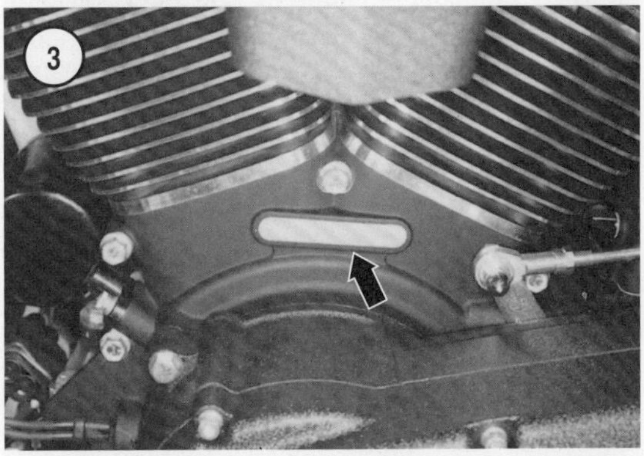

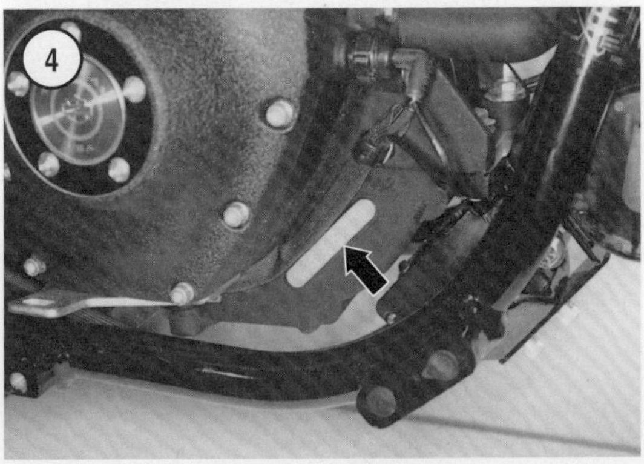

FASTENERS

Proper fastener selection and installation is important to ensure that the vehicle operates as designed and can be serviced efficiently. The choice of original equipment fasteners is not arrived at by chance. Make sure that replacement fasteners meet all the same requirements as the originals.

Threaded Fasteners

Threaded fasteners secure most of the components on the vehicle. Most are tightened by turning them clockwise (right-hand threads). If the normal rotation of the component being tightened would loosen the fastener, it may have left-hand threads. If a left-hand threaded fastener is used, it is noted in the text.

Two dimensions are required to match the threads of the fastener: the number of threads in a given distance and the outside diameter of the threads.

Two systems are currently used to specify threaded fastener dimensions: the U.S. Standard system and the metric system (**Figure 7**). Pay particular attention when working with unidentified fasteners; mismatching thread types can damage threads.

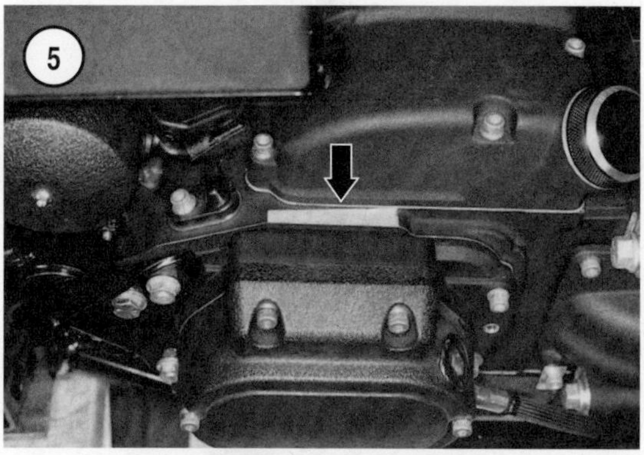

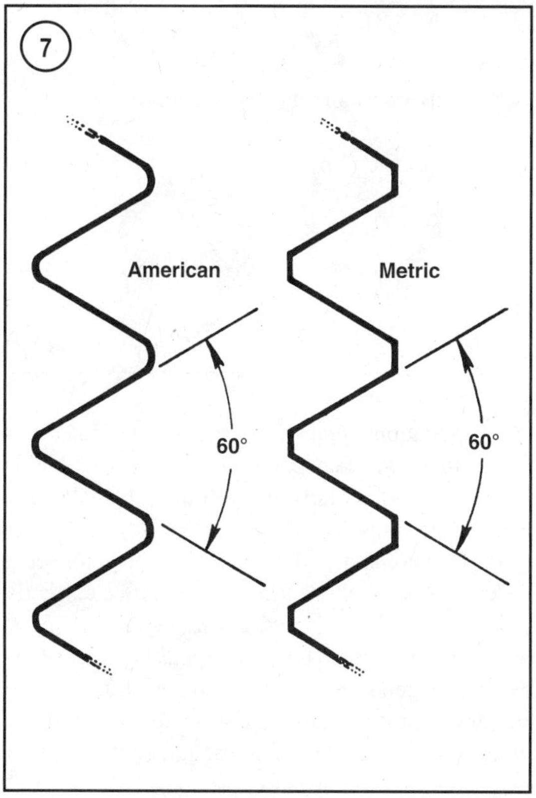

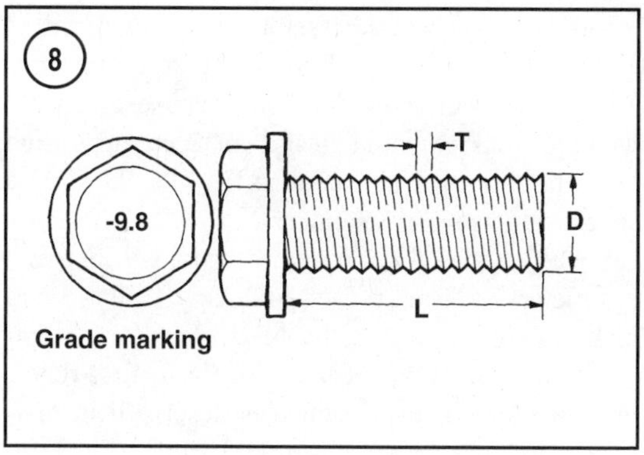

NOTE
To ensure that the fastener threads are not mismatched or cross-threaded, start all fasteners by hand. If a fastener is hard to start or turn, determine the cause before tightening with a wrench.

The length (L, **Figure 8**), diameter (D) and distance between thread crests (pitch) (T) classify metric screws and bolts. A typical bolt may be identified by the numbers, 8—1.25 × 130. This indicates the bolt has diameter of 8 mm, the distance between thread crests is 1.25 mm and the length is 130 mm. Always measure bolt length as shown in **Figure 8** to avoid purchasing replacements of the wrong length.

The numbers located on the top of the fastener (**Figure 8**) indicate the strength of metric screws and bolts. The higher the number, the stronger the fastener is. Unnumbered fasteners are the weakest.

Many screws, bolts and studs are combined with nuts to secure particular components. To indicate the size of a nut, manufacturers specify the internal diameter and the thread pitch.

The measurement across two flats on a nut or bolt indicates the wrench size.

WARNING
Do not install fasteners with a strength classification lower than what was originally installed by the manufacturer. Doing so may cause equipment failure and/or damage.

Torque Specifications

The materials used in the manufacture of the vehicle may be subjected to uneven stresses if the fasteners of the various subassemblies are not installed and tightened correctly. Fasteners that are improperly installed or work loose can cause extensive damage. It is essential to use an accurate torque wrench, described in this chapter, with the torque specifications in this manual.

Specifications for torque are provided in Newton-meters (N•m), foot-pounds (ft.-lb.) and inch-pounds (in.-lb.). Refer to **Table 6** for general torque specifications. To use **Table 6**, first determine the size of the fastener as described in *Fasteners* in this chapter. Torque specifications for specific components are at the end of the appropriate chapters. Torque wrenches are covered in the *Basic Tools* section.

Self-Locking Fasteners

Several types of bolts, screws and nuts incorporate a system that creates interference between the two fasteners. Interference is achieved in various ways. The most common type is the nylon insert nut and a dry adhesive coating on the threads of a bolt.

Self-locking fasteners offer greater holding strength than standard fasteners, which improves their resistance to vibration. Most self-locking fasteners cannot be reused. The materials used to form the lock become distorted after the initial installation and removal. It is a good practice to discard and replace self-locking fasteners after their removal. Do not replace self-locking fasteners with standard fasteners.

Washers

There are two basic types of washers: flat washers and lockwashers. Flat washers are simple discs with a hole to fit a screw or bolt. Lockwashers are used to prevent a fastener from working loose. Washers can be used as spacers and seals, or to help distribute fastener load and to prevent the fastener from damaging the component.

As with fasteners, when replacing washers make sure the replacement washers are of the same design and quality.

Cotter Pins

A cotter pin is a split metal pin inserted into a hole or slot to prevent a fastener from loosening. In certain applications, such as the rear axle on an ATV or motorcycle, the fastener must be secured in this way. For these applications, a cotter pin and castellated (slotted) nut is used.

9

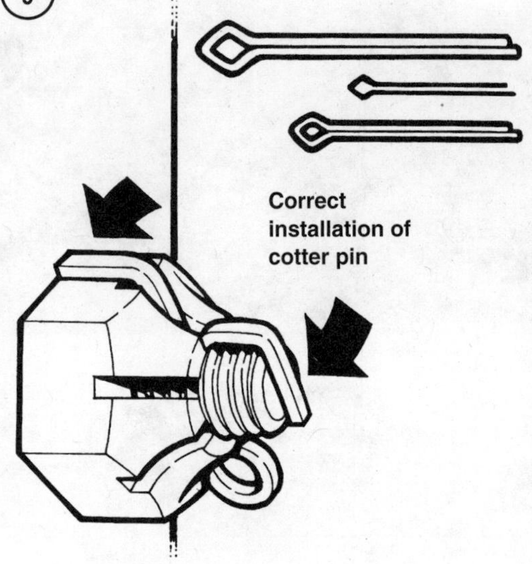

10

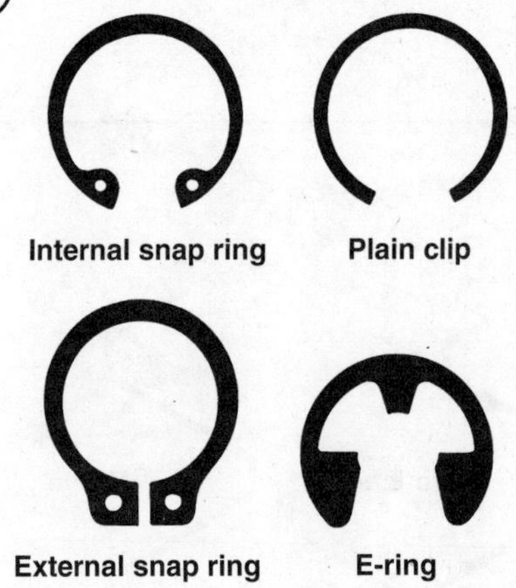

To use a cotter pin, first make sure the diameter is correct for the hole in the fastener. After correctly tightening the fastener and aligning the holes, insert the cotter pin through the hole and bend the ends over the fastener (**Figure 9**). Unless instructed to do so, never loosen a torqued fastener to align the holes. If the holes do not align, tighten the fastener just enough to achieve alignment.

11

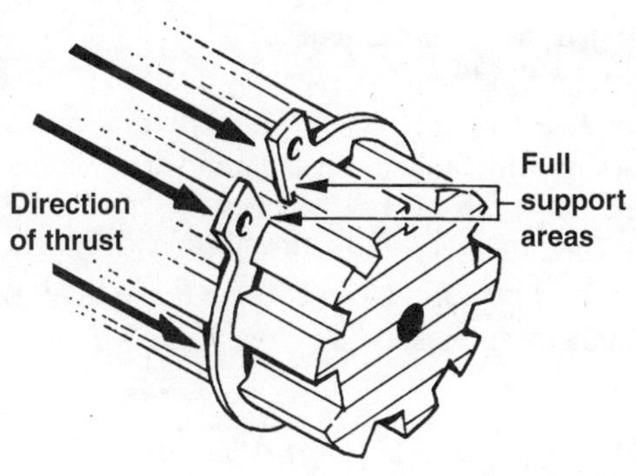

12

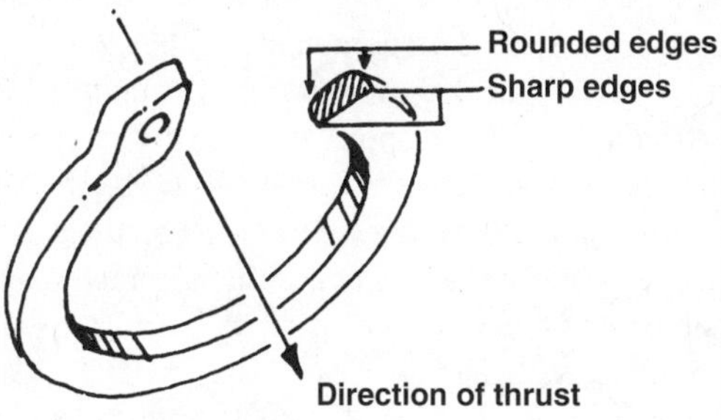

Cotter pins are available in various diameters and lengths. Measure length from the bottom of the head to the tip of the shortest pin.

Snap rings and E-clips

Snap rings (**Figure 10**) are circular-shaped metal retaining clips. They are required to secure parts and gears in place on parts such as shafts, pins or rods. External type snap rings are used to retain items on shafts. Internal type snap rings secure parts within housing bores. In some applications, in addition to securing the component(s), snap rings of varying thickness also determine endplay. These are usually called selective snap rings.

Two basic types of snap rings are used: machined and stamped snap rings. Machined snap rings (**Figure 11**) can be installed in either direction, since both faces have sharp edges. Stamped snap rings (**Figure 12**) are manufactured with a sharp edge and a round edge. When installing a stamped snap ring in a thrust application, install the sharp edge facing away from the part producing the thrust.

E-clips and circlips are used when it is not practical to use a snap ring. Remove E-clips with a flat blade screwdriver by prying between the shaft and E-clip. To install an E-clip, center it over the shaft groove and push or tap it into place.

Observe the following when installing snap rings:

1. Remove and install snap rings with snap ring pliers. See *Snap Ring Pliers* in this chapter.
2. In some applications, it may be necessary to replace snap rings after removing them.
3. Compress or expand snap rings only enough to install them. If overly expanded, they lose their retaining ability.
4. After installing a snap ring, make sure it seats completely.
5. Wear eye protection when removing and installing snap rings.

SHOP SUPPLIES

Lubricants and Fluids

Periodic lubrication helps ensure a long service life for any type of equipment. Using the correct type of lubricant is as important as performing the lubrication service, although in an emergency the wrong type is better than none. The following section describes the types of lubricants most often required. Make sure to follow the manufacturer's recommendations for lubricant types.

Engine oils

Engine oil is classified by two standards: the American Petroleum Institute (API) service classification and the Society of Automotive Engineers (SAE) viscosity rating. This information is on the oil container label. Two letters indicate the API service classification. The number or sequence of numbers and letter (10W-40 for example) is the oil's viscosity rating. The API service classification and the SAE viscosity index are not indications of oil quality.

The service classification indicates that the oil meets specific lubrication standards. The first letter in the classification (*S*) indicates that the oil is for gasoline engines. The second letter indicates the standard the oil satisfies. The classification started with the letter *A* and is currently at the letter *J*.

Always use an oil with a classification recommended by the manufacturer. Using an oil with a different classification can cause engine damage.

Viscosity is an indication of the oil's thickness. Thin oils have a lower number while thick oils have a higher number. Engine oils fall into the 5- to 50-weight range for single-grade oils.

Most manufacturers recommend multigrade oil. These oils perform efficiently across a wide range of operating conditions. Multigrade oils are identified by a *W* after the first number, which indicates the low-temperature viscosity.

Engine oils are most commonly mineral (petroleum) based; however, synthetic and semi-synthetic types are used more frequently. When selecting engine oil, follow the manufacturer's recommendation for type, classification and viscosity when selecting engine oil.

Greases

Grease is lubricating oil with thickening agents added to it. The National Lubricating Grease Institute (NLGI) grades grease. Grades range from No. 000 to No. 6, with No. 6 being the thickest. Typical multipurpose grease is NLGI No. 2. For specific applications, manufacturers may recommend water-resistant type grease or one with an additive such as molybdenum disulfide (MoS_2).

Brake fluid

Brake fluid is the hydraulic fluid used to transmit hydraulic pressure (force) to the wheel brakes. Brake fluid is classified by the Department of Transportation (DOT). Current designations for brake fluid are DOT 3, DOT 4 and DOT 5. This classification appears on the fluid container.

Each type of brake fluid has its own definite characteristics. The Harley-Davidson Dyna Glide uses the silicone based DOT 5 brake fluid. Do not intermix DOT 3 or DOT 4 type brake fluid as this may cause brake system failure since the DOT 5 brake fluid is not compatible with other brake fluids. When adding brake fluid, *only* use the fluid recommended by the manufacturer.

Brake fluid will damage any plastic, painted or plated surface it contacts. Use extreme care when working with brake fluid and remove any spills immediately with soap and water.

Hydraulic brake systems require clean and moisture free brake fluid. Never reuse brake fluid. Keep containers and reservoirs properly sealed.

WARNING

Never put a mineral-based (petroleum) oil into the brake system. Mineral oil will cause rubber parts in the system to swell and break apart, resulting in complete brake failure.

Cleaners, Degreasers and Solvents

Many chemicals are available to remove oil, grease and other residue from the vehicle. Before using cleaning solvents, consider how they will be used and disposed of, particularly if they are not water-soluble. Local ordinances may require special procedures for the disposal of many types of cleaning chemicals. Refer to *Safety and Cleaning Parts* in this chapter for more information on their use.

Use brake parts cleaner to clean brake system components when contact with petroleum-based products will damage seals. Brake parts cleaner leaves no residue. Use electrical contact cleaner to clean electrical connections and components without leaving any residue. Carburetor cleaner is a powerful solvent used to remove fuel deposits and varnish from fuel system components. Use this cleaner carefully, as it may damage finishes.

Generally, degreasers are strong cleaners used to remove heavy accumulations of grease from engine and frame components.

Most solvents are designed to be used in a parts washing cabinet for individual component cleaning. For safety, use only nonflammable or high flash point solvents.

Gasket Sealant

Sealants are used in combination with a gasket or seal and are occasionally alone. Follow the manufacturer's recommendation when using sealants.

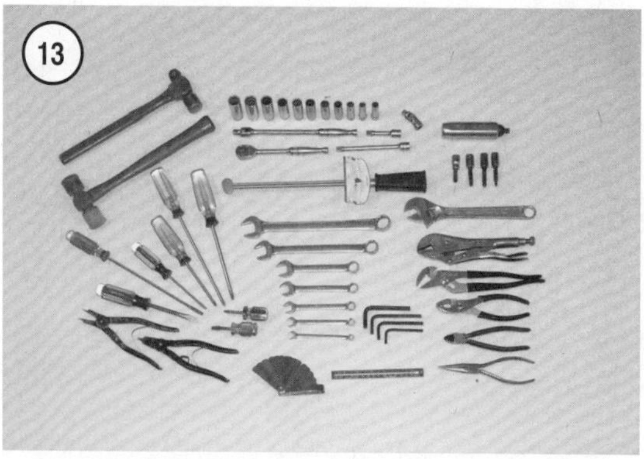

Use extreme care when choosing a sealant different from the type originally recommended. Choose sealants based on their resistance to heat, various fluids and their sealing capabilities.

One of the most common sealants is RTV, or room temperature vulcanizing sealant. This sealant cures at room temperature over a specific time period. This allows the repositioning of components without damaging gaskets.

Moisture in the air causes the RTV sealant to cure. Always install the tube cap as soon as possible after applying RTV sealant. RTV sealant has a limited shelf life and will not cure properly if the shelf life has expired. Keep partial tubes sealed and discard them if they have surpassed the expiration date.

Applying RTV sealant

Clean all old gasket residue from the mating surfaces. Remove all gasket material from blind threaded holes; it can cause inaccurate bolt torque. Spray the mating surfaces with aerosol parts cleaner and then wipe with a lint-free cloth. The area must be clean for the sealant to adhere.

Apply RTV sealant in a continuous bead 2-3 mm (0.08-0.12 in.) thick. Circle all the fastener holes unless otherwise specified. Do not allow any sealant to enter these holes. Assemble and tighten the fasteners to the specified torque within the time frame recommended by the RTV sealant manufacturer.

Gasket Remover

Aerosol gasket remover can help remove stubborn gaskets. This product can speed up the removal process and prevent damage to the mating surface that may be caused by using a scraping tool. Most of these types of products are very caustic. Follow the gasket remover manufacturer's instructions for use.

Threadlocking Compound

A threadlocking compound is a fluid applied to the threads of fasteners. After tightening the fastener, the fluid dries and becomes a solid filler between the threads. This makes it difficult for the fastener to work loose from vibration, or heat expansion and contraction. Some threadlocking compounds also provide a seal against fluid leakage.

Before applying threadlocking compound, remove any old compound from both thread areas and clean them with aerosol parts cleaner. Use the compound sparingly. Excess fluid can run into adjoining parts.

Threadlocking compounds are available in different strengths. Follow the particular manufacturer's recommendations regarding compound selection. Two manufacturers of threadlocking compound are ThreeBond and Loctite. They both offer a wide range of compounds for various strength, temperature and repair applications.

BASIC TOOLS

Most of the procedures in this manual can be carried out with simple hand tools and test equipment familiar to the home mechanic. Always use the correct tools for the job at hand. Keep tools organized and clean. Store them in a tool chest with related tools organized together.

Quality tools are essential. The best are constructed of high-strength alloy steel. These tools are light, easy to use and resistant to wear. Their working surface is devoid of sharp edges and the tool is carefully polished. They have an easy-to-clean finish and are comfortable to use. Quality tools are a good investment.

When purchasing tools to perform the procedures covered in this manual, consider the tools' potential frequency of use. If a tool kit is just now being started, consider purchasing a basic tool set (**Figure 13**) from a large tool supplier. These sets are available in many tool combinations and offer substantial savings when compared to individually purchased tools. As work experience grows and tasks become more complicated, specialized tools can be added.

Screwdrivers

Screwdrivers of various lengths and types are mandatory for the simplest tool kit. The two basic types are the slotted tip (flat blade) and the Phillips tip. These are available in sets that often include an assortment of tip sizes and shaft lengths.

As with all tools, use a screwdriver designed for the job. Make sure the size of the tip conforms to the size and shape of the fastener. Use them only for driving screws. Never use a screwdriver for prying or chiseling metal. Repair or replace worn or damaged screwdrivers. A worn tip may damage the fastener, making it difficult to remove.

Wrenches

Open-end, box-end and combination wrenches (**Figure 14**) are available in various types and sizes.

The number stamped on the wrench refers to the distance between the work areas. This size must match the size of the fastener head.

The box-end wrench is an excellent tool because it grips the fastener on all sides. This reduces the chance of the tool slipping. The box-end wrench is designed with either a 6- or 12-point opening. For stubborn or damaged fasteners, the 6-point provides superior holding ability by contacting the fastener across a wider area at all six edges. For general use, the 12-point works well. It allows the wrench to be removed and reinstalled without moving the handle over such a wide arc.

An open-end wrench is fast and works best in areas with limited overhead access. It contacts the fastener at only two points, and is subject to slipping under heavy force, or if the tool or fastener is worn. A box-end wrench is preferred in most instances, especially when breaking loose and applying the final tightness to a fastener.

The combination wrench has a box end on one end and an open end on the other. This combination makes it a very convenient tool.

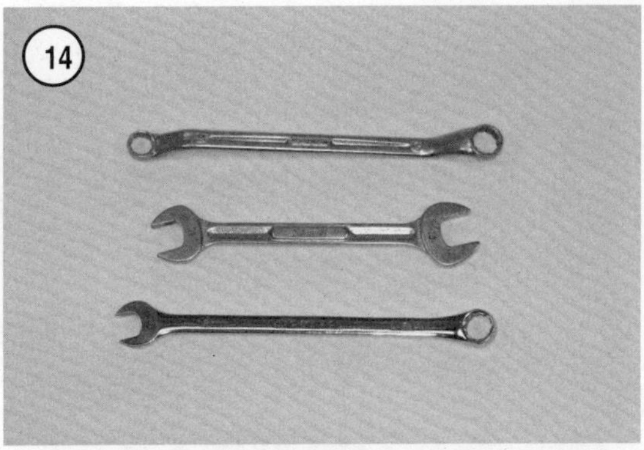

14

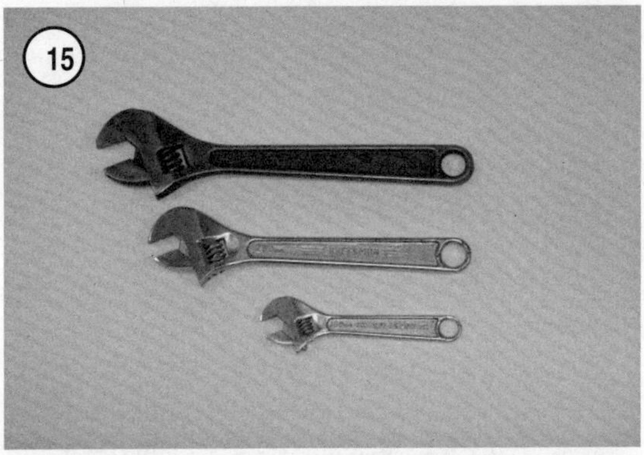

15

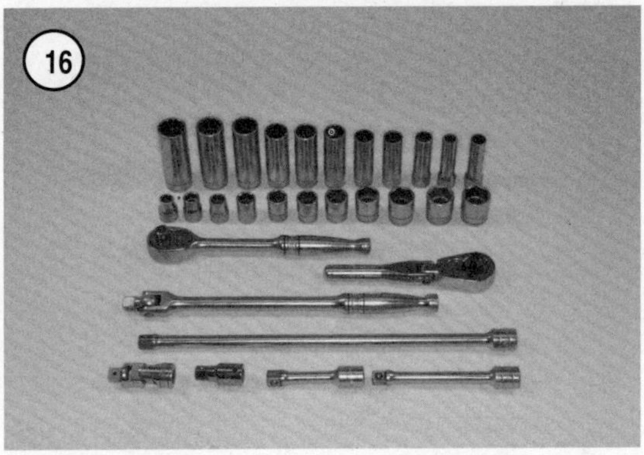

16

Adjustable Wrenches

An adjustable wrench or Crescent wrench (**Figure 15**) can fit nearly any nut or bolt head that has clear access around its entire perimeter. Adjustable wrenches are best used as a backup wrench to keep a large nut or bolt from turning while the other end is being loosened or tightened with a box-end or socket wrench.

Adjustable wrenches contact the fastener at only two points, making them more likely to slip off the fastener. The fact that one jaw is adjustable and may

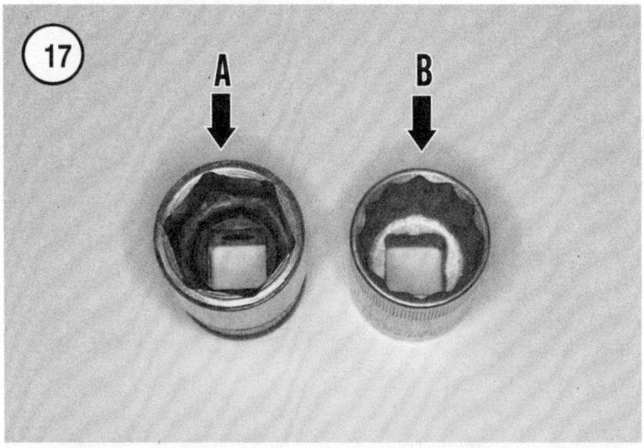

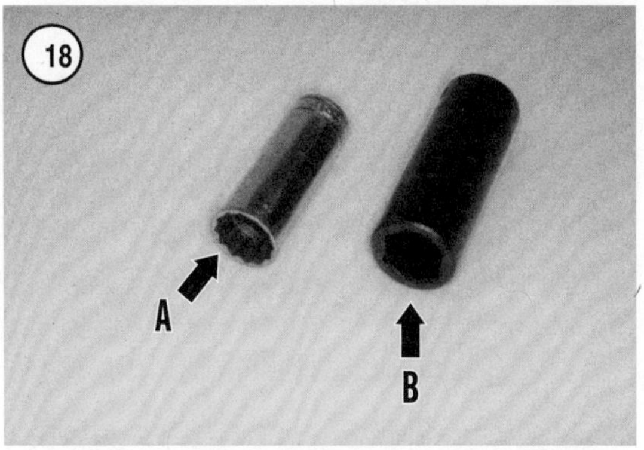

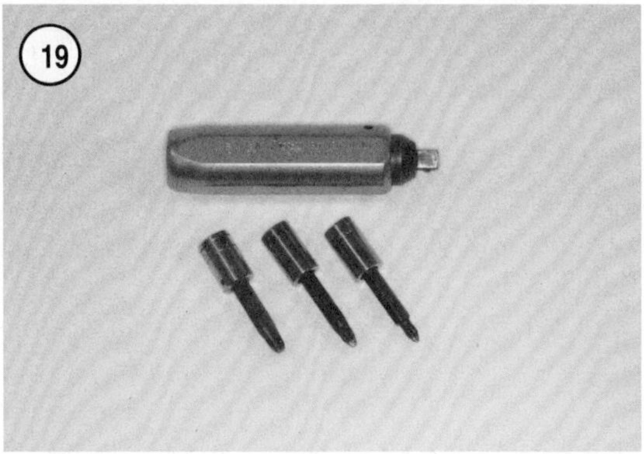

loosen only aggravates this shortcoming. Make certain that the solid jaw is the one transmitting the force.

Socket Wrenches, Ratchets and Handles

Sockets that attach to a ratchet handle (**Figure 16**) are available with 6-point (A, **Figure 17**) or 12-point (B) openings and different drive sizes. The drive size indicates the size of the square hole that accepts the ratchet handle. The number stamped on the socket is the size of the work area and must match the fastener head.

As with wrenches, a 6-point socket provides superior holding ability, while a 12-point socket needs to be moved only half as far to reposition it on the fastener.

Sockets are designated for either hand or impact use. Impact sockets are made of thicker material for more durability. Compare the size and wall thickness of a 19-mm hand socket (A, **Figure 18**) and the 19-mm impact socket (B). Use impact sockets when using an impact driver or air tools. Use hand sockets with hand-driven attachments.

WARNING
Do not use hand sockets with air or impact tools, as they may shatter and cause injury. Always wear eye protection when using impact or air tools.

Various handles are available for sockets. The speed handle is used for fast operation. Flexible ratchet heads in varying lengths allow the socket to be turned with varying force, and at odd angles. Extension bars allow the socket setup to reach difficult areas. The ratchet is the most versatile. It allows the user to install or remove the nut without removing the socket.

Sockets combined with any number of drivers make them undoubtedly the fastest, safest and most convenient tool for fastener removal and installation.

Impact Driver

An impact driver provides extra force for removing fasteners, by converting the impact of a hammer into a turning motion. This makes it possible to remove stubborn fasteners without damaging them. Impact drivers and interchangeable bits (**Figure 19**) are available from most tool suppliers. When using a socket with an impact driver make sure the socket is designed for impact use. Refer to *Socket Wrenches, Ratchets and Handles* in this section.

WARNING
Do not use hand sockets with air or impact tools as they may shatter and cause injury. Always wear eye protection when using impact or air tools.

Allen Wrenches

Allen or setscrew wrenches (**Figure 20**) are used on fasteners with hexagonal recesses in the fastener head. These wrenches are available in L-shaped bar, socket and T-handle types. A metric set is required when working on most vehicles. Allen bolts are sometimes called socket bolts.

Torque Wrenches

A torque wrench is used with a socket, torque adapter or similar extension to tighten a fastener o a measured torque. Torque wrenches come in several drive sizes (1/4, 3/8, 1/2 and 3/4) and have various methods of reading the torque value. The drive size indicates the size of the square drive that accepts the socket, adapter or extension. Common methods of reading the torque value are the deflecting beam, the dial indicator and the audible click (**Figure 21**).

When choosing a torque wrench, consider the torque range, drive size and accuracy. The torque specifications in this manual provide an indication of the range required.

A torque wrench is a precision tool that must be properly cared for to remain accurate. Store torque wrenches in cases or separate padded drawers within a toolbox. Follow the manufacturer's instructions for their care and calibration.

Torque Adapters

Torque adapters or extensions extend or reduce the reach of a torque wrench. The torque adapter shown in **Figure 22** is used to tighten a fastener that cannot be reached due to the size of the torque wrench head, drive, and socket. If a torque adapter changes the effective lever length (**Figure 23**), the torque reading on the wrench will not equal the actual torque applied to the fastener. It is necessary to recalibrate the torque setting on the wrench to compensate for the change of lever length. When a torque adapter is used at a right angle to the drive head, calibration is not required, since the effective length has not changed.

To recalculate a torque reading when using a torque adapter, use the following formula, and refer to **Figure 23**.

TW = TA × L

L + A = E

TW is the torque setting or dial reading on the wrench.

TA is the torque specification and the actual amount of torque that will be applied to the fastener.

A is the amount that the adapter increases (or in some cases reduces) the effective lever length as measured along the centerline of the torque wrench (**Figure 23**).

L is the lever length of the wrench as measured from the center of the drive to the center of the grip.

20

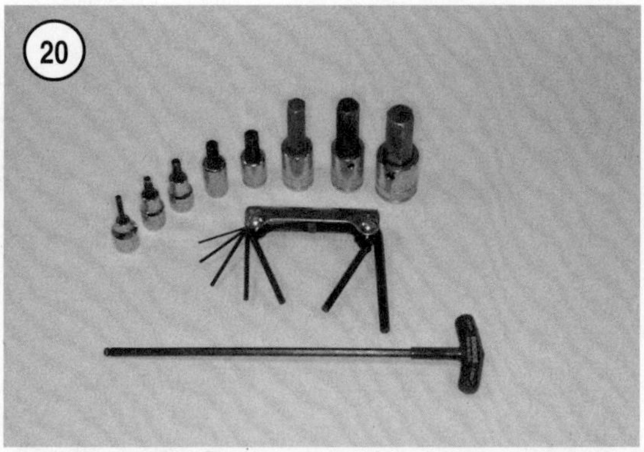

21

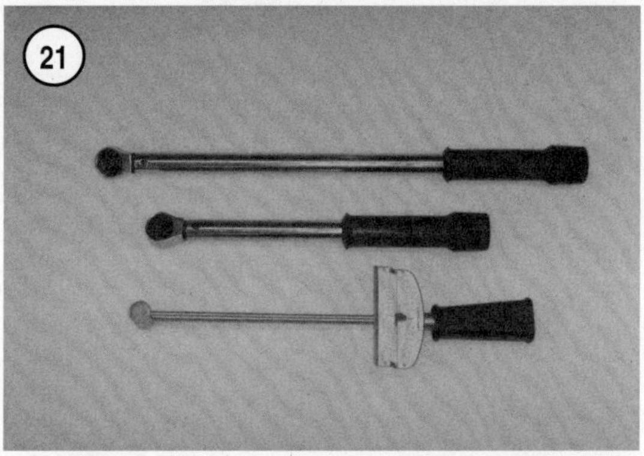

22

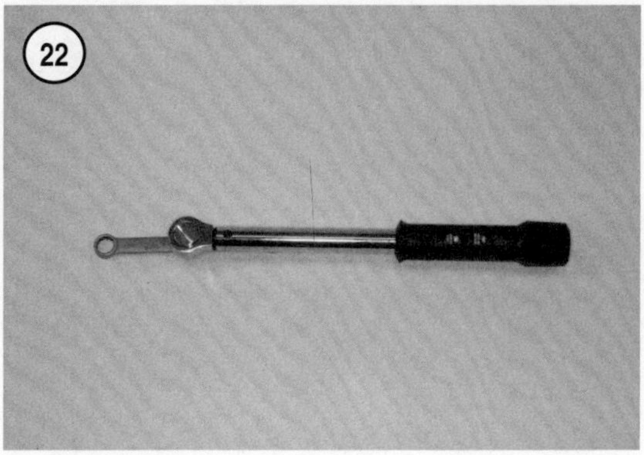

23 **HOW TO MEASURE TORQUE WRENCH EFFECTIVE LENGTH**

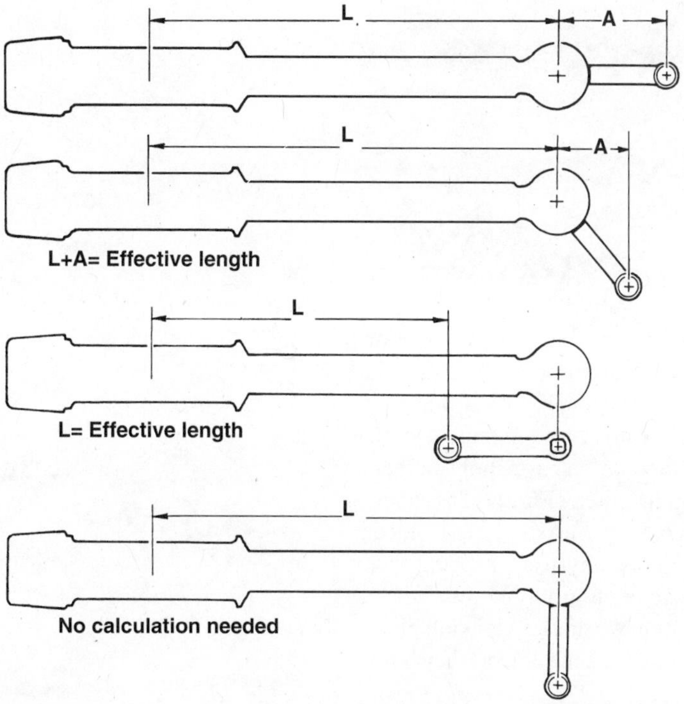

24

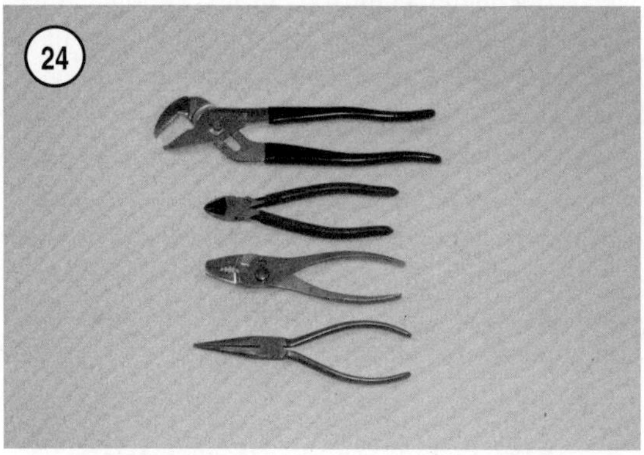

25

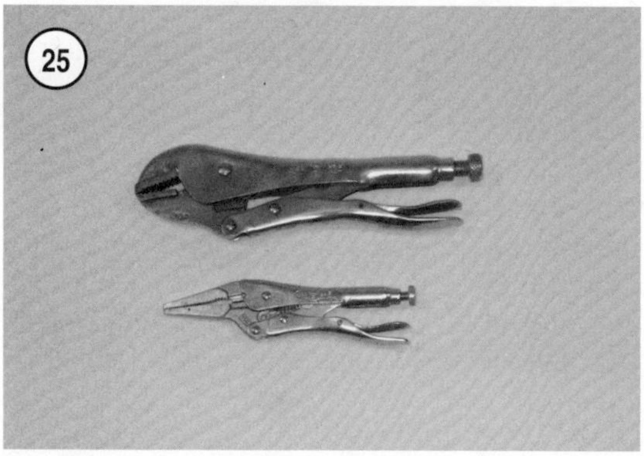

The effective length is the sum of L and A (**Figure 23**).

Example:

TA = 20 ft.-lb.

A = 3 in.

L = 14 in.

E = 17 in.

$$TW = \frac{20 \times 14}{14 + 3} = \frac{280}{17} = 16.5 \text{ ft. Lb.}$$

In this example, the torque wrench would be set to the recalculated torque value (TW = 16.5 ft.-lb.).

When using a beam-type wrench, tighten the fastener until the pointer aligns with 16.5 ft.-lb. In this example, although the torque wrench is preset to 16.5 ft.-lb., the actual torque is 20 ft.-lb.

Pliers

Pliers come in a wide range of types and sizes. Pliers are useful for holding, cutting, bending, and crimping. Do not use them to turn fasteners. **Figure 24** and **Figure 25** show several types of useful pli-

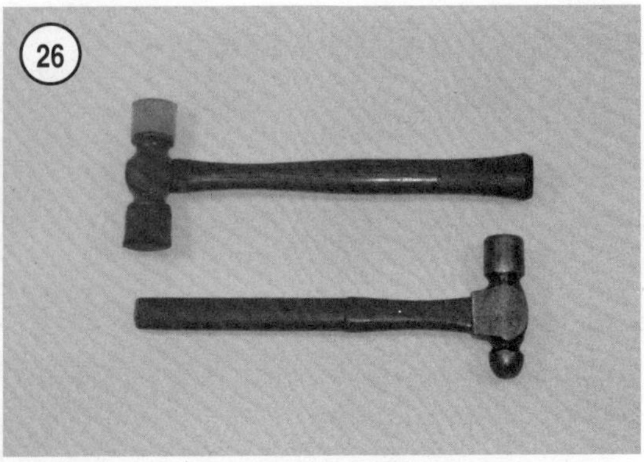

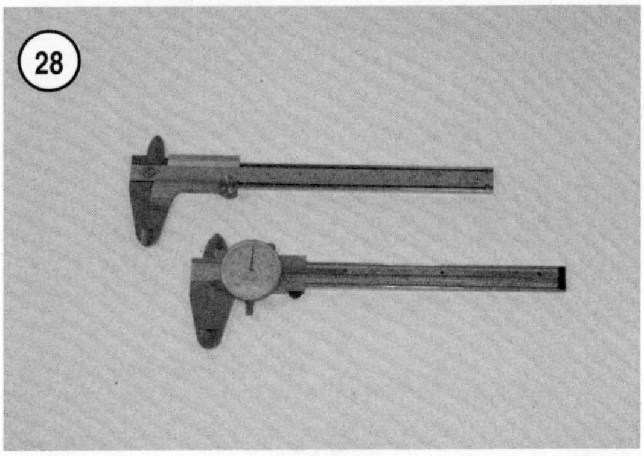

ers. Each design has a specialized function. Slip-joint pliers are general-purpose pliers used for gripping and bending. Diagonal cutting pliers are needed to cut wire and can be used to remove cotter pins. Needlenose pliers are used to hold or bend small objects. Locking pliers (**Figure 25**), sometimes called Vise-grips, are used to hold objects very tightly. They have many uses, ranging from holding two parts together to gripping the end of a broken stud. Use caution when using locking pliers, as the sharp jaws will damage the objects they hold.

Snap Ring Pliers

Snap ring pliers are specialized pliers with tips that fit into the ends of snap rings to remove and install them.

Snap ring pliers are available with a fixed action (either internal or external) or convertible (one tool works on both internal and external snap rings). They may have fixed tips or interchangeable ones of various sizes and angles. For general use, select a convertible type pliers with interchangeable tips.

WARNING
Snap rings can slip and fly off when removing and installing them. Also, the snap ring pliers tips may break. Always wear eye protection when using snap ring pliers.

Hammers

Various types of hammers (**Figure 26**) are available to fit a number of applications. A ball-peen hammer is used to strike another tool, such as a punch or chisel. Soft-faced hammers are required when a metal object must be struck without damaging it. *Never* use a metal-faced hammer on engine and suspension components, as damage will occur in most cases.

Always wear eye protection when using hammers. Make sure the hammer face is in good condition and the handle is not cracked. Select the correct hammer for the job and make sure to strike the object squarely. Do not use the handle or the side of the hammer to strike an object.

PRECISION MEASURING TOOLS

The ability to accurately measure components is essential to successfully rebuild an engine. Equipment is manufactured to close tolerances, and obtaining consistently accurate measurements is essential to determining which components require replacement or further service.

Each type of measuring instrument is designed to measure a dimension with a certain degree of accuracy and within a certain range. When selecting the measuring tool, make sure it is applicable to the task.

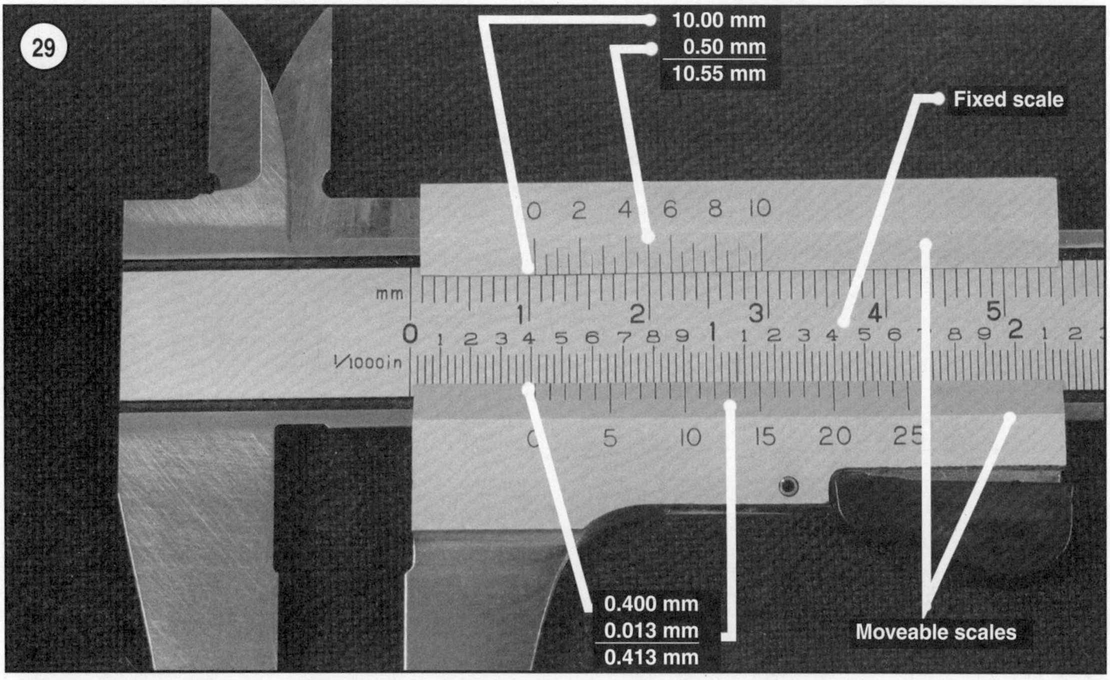

As with all tools, measuring tools provide the best results if cared for properly. Improper use can damage the tool and result in inaccurate results. If any measurement is questionable, verify the measurement using another tool. A standard gauge is usually provided with measuring tools to check accuracy and calibrate the tool if necessary.

Precision measurements can vary according to the experience of the person performing the procedure. Accurate results are only possible if the mechanic possesses a feel for using the tool. Heavy-handed use of measuring tools will produce less accurate results. Hold the tool gently by the fingertips so the point at which the tool contacts the object is easily felt. This feel for the equipment will produce more accurate measurements and reduce the risk of damaging the tool or component. Refer to the following sections for specific measuring tools.

Feeler Gauge

The feeler or thickness gauge (**Figure 27**) is used for measuring the distance between two surfaces.

A feeler gauge set consists of an assortment of steel strips of graduated thickness. Each blade is marked with its thickness. Blades can be of various lengths and angles for different procedures.

A common use for a feeler gauge is to measure valve clearance. Wire (round) type gauges are used to measure spark plug gap.

Calipers

Calipers (**Figure 28**) are excellent tools for obtaining inside, outside and depth measurements. Although not as precise as a micrometer, they allow reasonable precision, typically to within 0.05 mm (0.001 in.). Most calipers have a range up to 150 mm (6 in.).

Calipers are available in dial, vernier or digital versions. Dial calipers have a dial readout that provides convenient reading. Vernier calipers have marked scales that must be compared to determine the measurement. The digital caliper uses an LCD to show the measurement.

Properly maintain the measuring surfaces of the caliper. There must not be any dirt or burrs between the tool and the object being measured. Never force the caliper closed around an object; close the caliper around the highest point so it can be removed with a slight drag. Some calipers require calibration. Always refer to the manufacturer's instructions when using a new or unfamiliar caliper.

To read a vernier caliper refer, to **Figure 29**. The fixed scale is marked in 1 mm increments. Ten indi-

30

DECIMAL PLACE VALUES*

0.1	Indicates 1/10 (one tenth of an inch or millimeter)
0.010	Indicates 1/100 (one one-hundreth of an inch or millimeter)
0.001	Indicates 1/1,000 (one one-thousandth of an inch or millimeter)

*This chart represents the values of figures placed to the right of the decimal point. Use it when reading decimals from one-tenth to one one-thousandth of an inch or millimeter. It is not a conversion chart (for example: 0.001 in. is not equal to 0.001 mm).

vidual lines on the fixed scale equal 1 cm. The moveable scale is marked in 0.05 mm (hundredth) increments. To obtain a reading, establish the first number by the location of the 0 line on the movable scale in relation to the first line to the left on the fixed scale. In this example, the number is 10 mm. To determine the next number, note which of the lines on the movable scale align with a mark on the fixed scale. A number of lines will seem close, but only one will align exactly. In this case, 0.50 mm is the reading to add to the first number. The result of adding 10 mm and 0.50 mm is a measurement of 10.50 mm.

Micrometers

A micrometer is an instrument designed for linear measurement using the decimal divisions of the inch or meter (**Figure 30**). While there are many types and styles of micrometers, most of the procedures in this manual call for an outside micrometer. The outside micrometer is used to measure the outside diameter of cylindrical forms and the thickness of materials.

A micrometer's size indicates the minimum and maximum size of a part that it can measure. The usual sizes (**Figure 31**) are 0-1 in. (0-25 mm), 1-2 in. (25-50 mm), 2-3 in. (50-75 mm) and 3-4 in. (75-100 mm).

Micrometers that cover a wider range of measurements are available. These use a large frame with interchangeable anvils of various lengths. This type of micrometer offers a cost savings; however, its overall size may make it less convenient.

31

Reading a Micrometer

When reading a micrometer, numbers are taken from different scales and added together. The following sections describe how to read the measurements of various types of outside micrometers.

For accurate results, properly maintain the measuring surfaces of the micrometer. There cannot be any dirt or burrs between the tool and the measured object. Never force the micrometer closed around an object. Close the micrometer around the highest point so it can be removed with a slight drag. **Figure 32** shows the markings and parts of a standard inch micrometer. Be familiar with these terms before using a micrometer in the following sections.

Standard inch micrometer

The standard inch micrometer is accurate to one-thousandth of an inch or 0.001. The sleeve is marked in 0.025 in. increments. Every fourth sleeve

32

STANDARD INCH MICROMETER

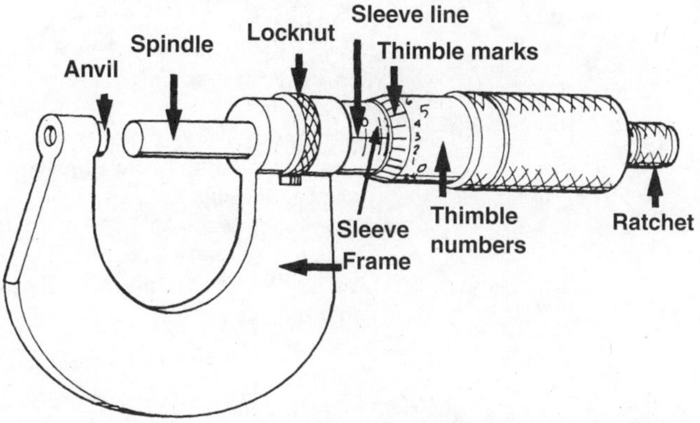

33

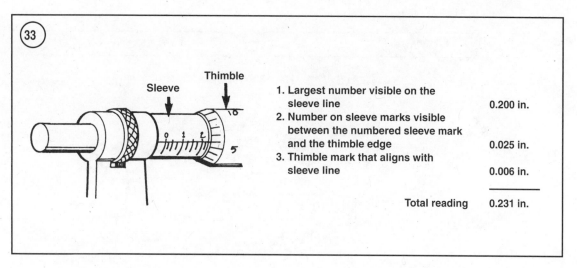

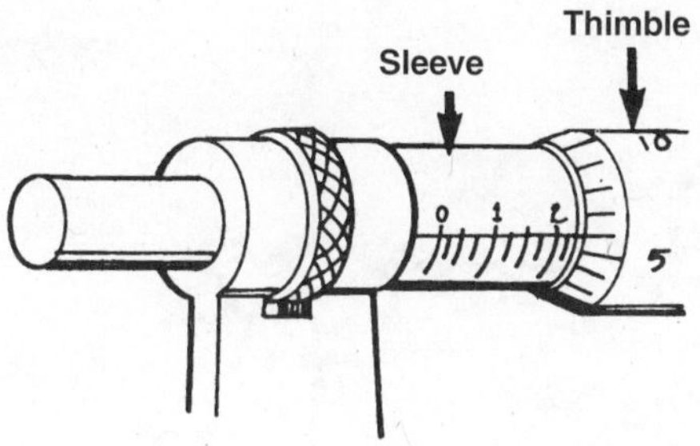

1. Largest number visible on the sleeve line	0.200 in.
2. Number on sleeve marks visible between the numbered sleeve mark and the thimble edge	0.025 in.
3. Thimble mark that aligns with sleeve line	0.006 in.
Total reading	0.231 in.

mark is numbered 1, 2, 3, 4, 5, 6, 7, 8, 9. These numbers indicate 0.100, 0.200, 0.300, and so on.

The tapered end of the thimble has twenty-five lines marked around it. Each mark equals 0.001 in. One complete turn of the thimble will align its zero mark with the first mark on the sleeve or 0.025 in.

When reading a standard inch micrometer, perform the following steps while referring to **Figure 33**.

1. Read the sleeve and find the largest number visible. Each sleeve number equals 0.100 in.

2. Count the number of lines between the numbered sleeve mark and the edge of the thimble. Each sleeve mark equals 0.025 in.

3. Read the thimble mark that aligns with the sleeve line. Each thimble mark equals 0.001 in.

NOTE

If a thimble mark does not align exactly with the sleeve line, estimate the amount between the lines. For accurate readings in ten-thousandths of an inch (0.0001 in.), use a vernier inch micrometer.

4. Add the readings from Steps 1-3.

Vernier inch micrometer

A vernier inch micrometer is accurate to one ten-thousandth of an inch or 0.0001 in. It has the same marking as a standard inch micrometer with an additional vernier scale on the sleeve (**Figure 34**).

34

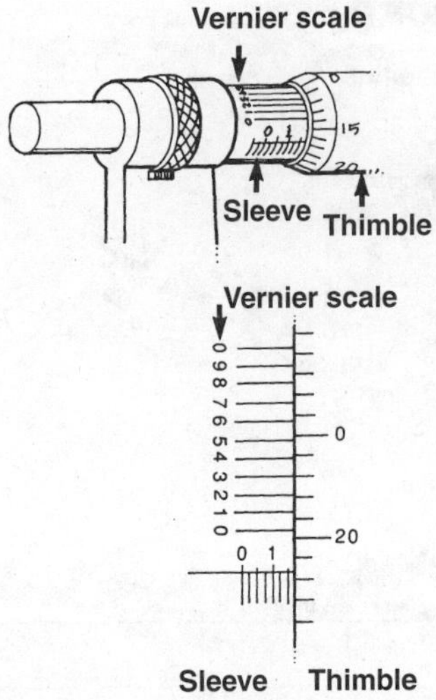

1. Largest number visible on sleeve line	0.100 in.
2. Number of sleeve marks visible between the numbered sleeve mark and the thimble edge	0.050 in.
3. Thimble is between 0.018 and 0.019 in. on the sleeve line	0.018 in.
4. Vernier line coinciding with thimble line	0.0003 in.
Total reading	0.1683 in.

35

STANDARD METRIC MICROMETER

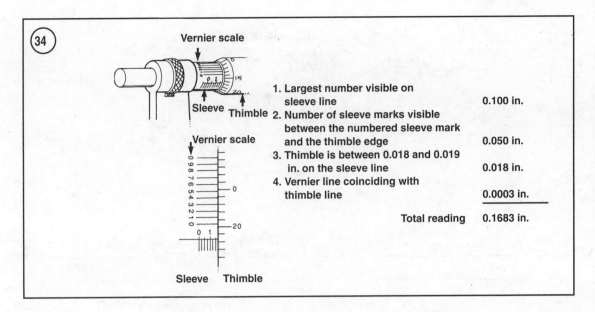

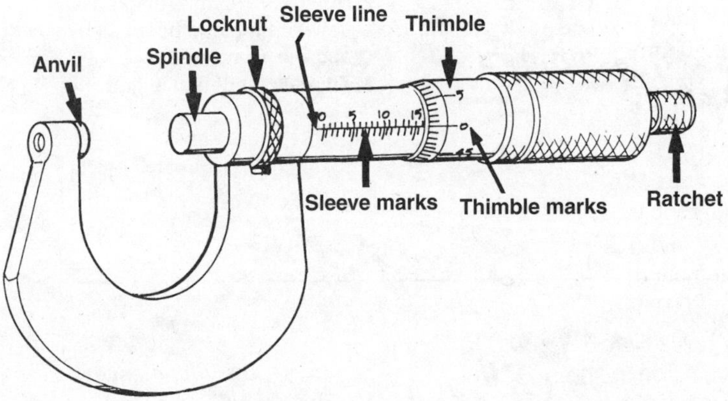

The vernier scale consists of 11 lines marked 1-9 with a 0 on each end. These lines run parallel to the thimble lines and represent 0.0001 in. increments.

When reading a vernier inch micrometer, perform the following steps while referring to **Figure 34**.

1. Read the micrometer in the same way as a standard micrometer. This is the initial reading.

2. If a thimble mark aligns exactly with the sleeve line, reading the vernier scale is not necessary. If they do not align, read the vernier scale in Step 3.

3. Determine which vernier scale mark aligns with one thimble mark. The vernier scale number is the amount in ten-thousandths of an inch to add to the initial reading from Step 1.

Metric micrometer

The standard metric micrometer (**Figure 35**) is accurate to one one-hundredth of a millimeter (0.01-mm). The sleeve line is graduated in millimeter and half millimeter increments. The marks on the upper half of the sleeve line equal 1.00 mm. Every fifth mark above the sleeve line is identified with a number. The number sequence depends on

36

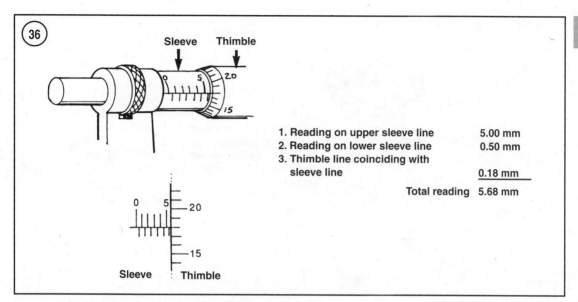

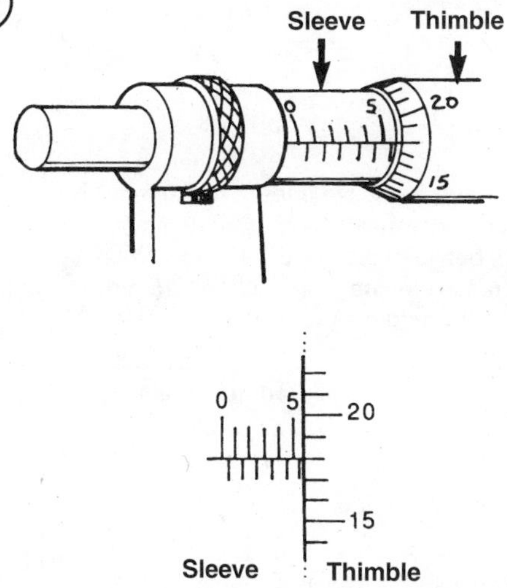

1. Reading on upper sleeve line	5.00 mm
2. Reading on lower sleeve line	0.50 mm
3. Thimble line coinciding with sleeve line	0.18 mm
Total reading	5.68 mm

the size of the micrometer. A 0-25 mm micrometer, for example, will have sleeve marks numbered 0 through 25 in 5 mm increments. This numbering sequence continues with larger micrometers. On all metric micrometers, each mark on the lower half of the sleeve equals 0.50 mm.

The tapered end of the thimble has 50 lines marked around it. Each mark equals 0.01 mm. One complete turn of the thimble aligns its 0 mark with the first line on the lower half of the sleeve line or 0.50 mm.

When reading a metric micrometer, add the number of millimeters and half-millimeters on the sleeve line to the number of one one-hundredth millimeters on the thimble. Perform the following steps while referring to **Figure 36**.

1. Read the upper half of the sleeve line and count the number of lines visible. Each upper line equals 1 mm.
2. See if the half-millimeter line is visible on the lower sleeve line. If so, add 0.50 mm to the reading in Step 1.
3. Read the thimble mark that aligns with the sleeve line. Each thimble mark equals 0.01 mm.

NOTE
If a thimble mark does not align exactly with the sleeve line, estimate the amount between the lines. For accurate readings in two-thousandths of a millimeter (0.002 mm), use a metric vernier micrometer.

4. Add the readings from Steps 1-3.

Metric vernier micrometer

A metric vernier micrometer (**Figure 37**) is accurate to two-thousandths of a millimeter (0.002 mm). It has the same markings as a standard metric micrometer with the addition of a vernier scale on the sleeve.

The vernier scale consists of five lines marked 0, 2, 4, 6, and 8. These lines run parallel to the thimble lines and represent 0.002-mm increments.

When reading a metric vernier micrometer, perform the following steps and refer to **Figure 37**.

1. Read the micrometer in the same way as a standard metric micrometer. This is the initial reading.
2. If a thimble mark aligns exactly with the sleeve line, reading the vernier scale is not necessary. If they do not align, read the vernier scale in Step 3.
3. Determine which vernier scale mark aligns exactly with one thimble mark. The vernier scale number is the amount in two-thousandths of a millimeter to add to the initial reading from Step 1.

Micrometer Adjustment

Before using a micrometer, check its adjustment as follows.

1. Clean the anvil and spindle faces.

2A. To check a 0-1 in. or 0-25 mm micrometer:

   a. Turn the thimble until the spindle contacts the anvil. If the micrometer has a ratchet stop, use it to ensure that the proper amount of pressure is applied.

37

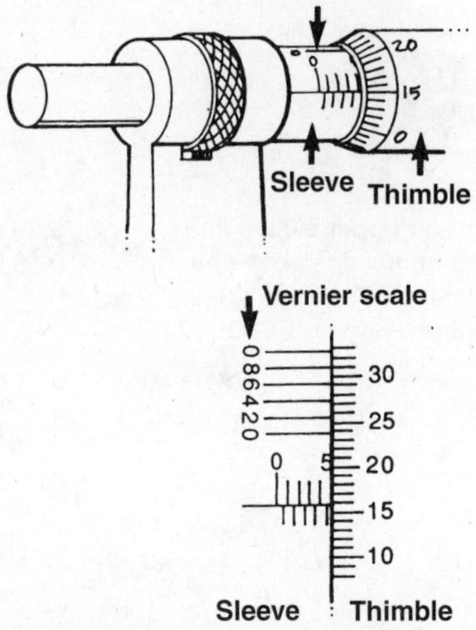

1. Reading on upper sleeve line	4.0 mm
2. Reading on lower sleeve line	0.5 mm
3. Thimble is between 0.15 and 0.16 mm on the sleeve line	0.15 mm
4. Vernier line coinciding with thimble line	0.008 mm
Total reading	4.658 mm

38

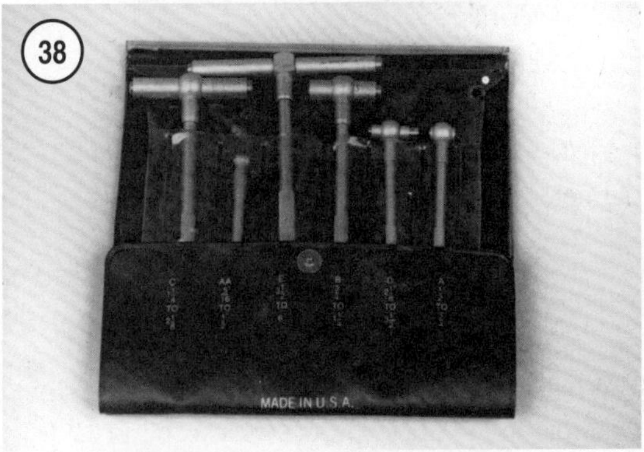

39

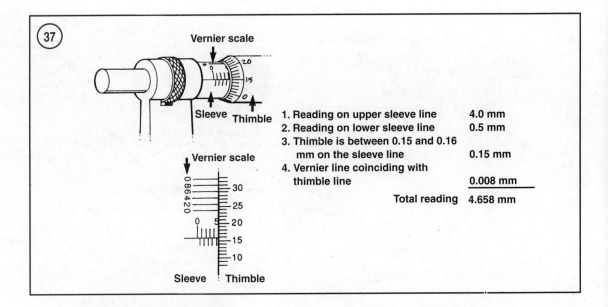

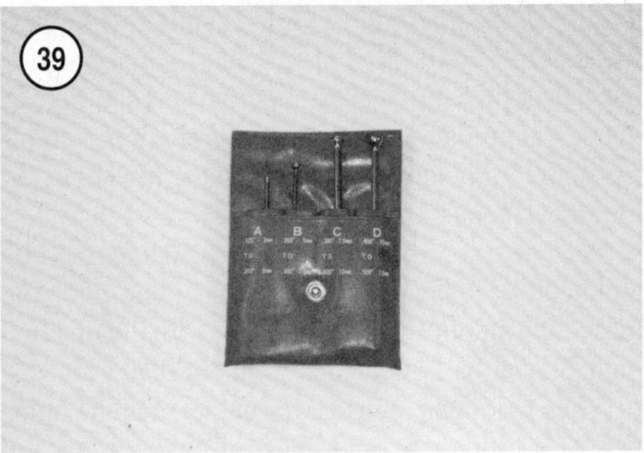

b. If the adjustment is correct, the 0 mark on the thimble will align exactly with the 0 mark on the sleeve line. If the marks do not align, the micrometer is out of adjustment.

c. Follow the manufacturer's instructions to adjust the micrometer.

2B. To check a micrometer larger than 1 in. or 25 mm use the standard gauge supplied by the manufacturer. A standard gauge is a steel block, disc or rod that is machined to an exact size.

a. Place the standard gauge between the spindle and anvil, and measure its outside diameter or length. If the micrometer has a ratchet stop, use it to ensure that the proper amount of pressure is applied.

b. If the adjustment is correct, the 0 mark on the thimble will align exactly with the 0 mark on the sleeve line. If the marks do not align, the micrometer is out of adjustment.

c. Follow the manufacturer's instructions to adjust the micrometer.

Micrometer Care

Micrometers are precision instruments. They must be used and maintained with great care. Note the following:

1. Store micrometers in protective cases or separate padded drawers in a toolbox.
2. When in storage, make sure the spindle and anvil faces do not contact each other or an other object. If they do, temperature changes and corrosion may damage the contact faces.
3. Do not clean a micrometer with compressed air. Dirt forced into the tool will cause wear.
4. Lubricate micrometers with WD-40 to prevent corrosion.

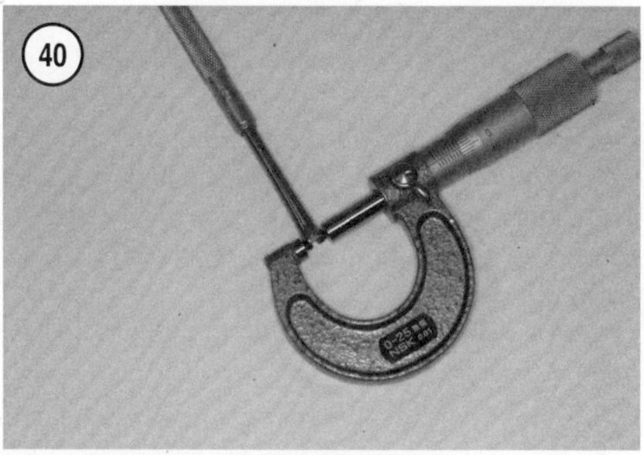

40

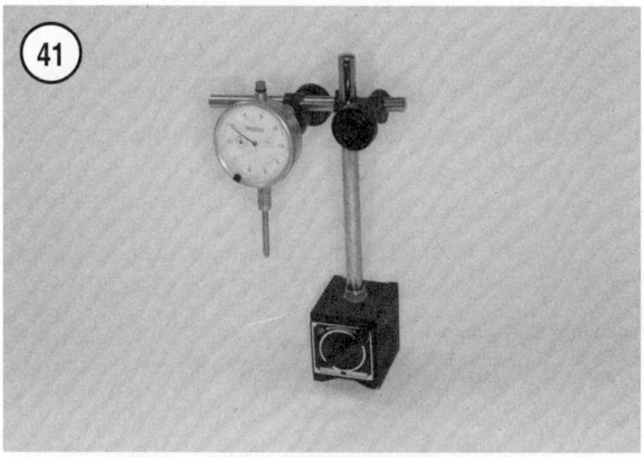

41

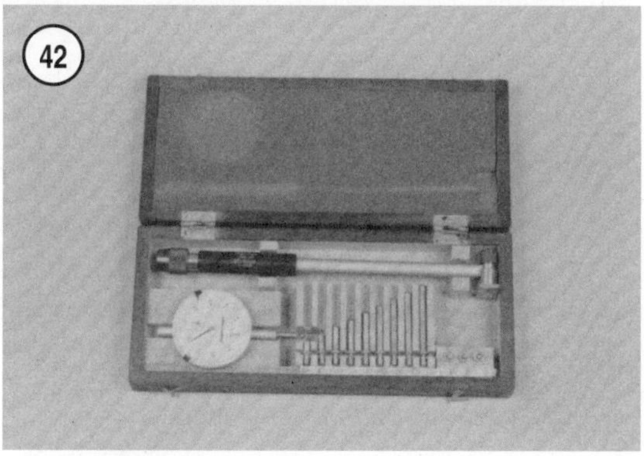

42

Telescoping and Small Bore Gauges

Use telescoping gauges (**Figure 38**) and small hole gauges (**Figure 39**) to measure bores. Neither gauge has a scale for direct readings. An outside micrometer must be used to determine the reading.

To use a telescoping gauge, select the correct size gauge for the bore. Compress the movable post and carefully insert the gauge into the bore. Carefully move the gauge in the bore to make sure it is centered. Tighten the knurled end of the gauge to hold the movable post in position. Remove the gauge and measure the length of the posts. Telescoping gauges are typically used to measure cylinder bores.

To use a small-bore gauge, select the correct size gauge for the bore. Carefully insert the gauge into the bore. Tighten the knurled end of the gauge to carefully expand the gauge fingers to the limit within the bore. Do not overtighten the gauge, as there is no built-in release. Excessive tightening can damage the bore surface and damage the tool. Remove the gauge and measure the outside dimension (**Figure 40**). Small hole gauges are typically used to measure valve guides.

Dial Indicator

A dial indicator (**Figure 41**) is a gauge with a dial face and needle used to measure variations in dimensions and movements. Measuring brake rotor runout is a typical use for a dial indicator.

Dial indicators are available in various ranges and graduations and with three basic types of mounting bases: magnetic, clamp, or screw-in stud. When purchasing a dial indicator, select the magnetic stand type with a continuous dial.

Cylinder Bore Gauge

A cylinder bore gauge is similar to a dial indicator. The gauge set shown in **Figure 42** consists of a dial indicator, handle, and different length adapters (anvils) to fit the gauge to various bore sizes. The bore gauge is used to measure bore size, taper and out-of-round. When using a bore gauge, follow the manufacturer's instructions.

Compression Gauge

A compression gauge (**Figure 43**) measures combustion chamber (cylinder) pressure, usually in psi or kg/cm^2. The gauge adapter is either inserted or screwed into the spark plug hole to obtain the reading. Disable the engine so it will not start and hold the throttle in the wide-open position when performing a compression test. An engine that does not have adequate compression cannot be properly tuned. See Chapter Three.

43

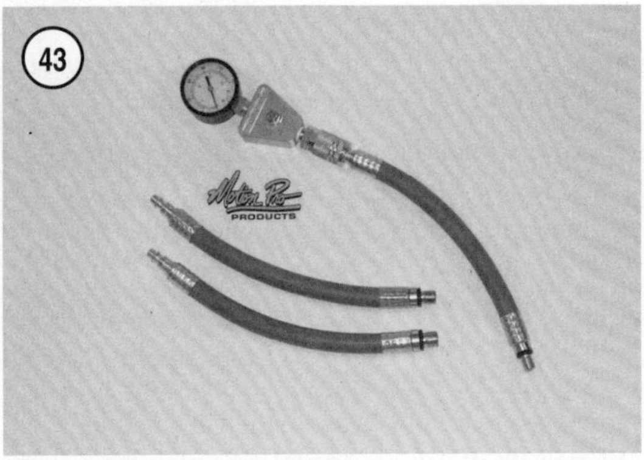

44

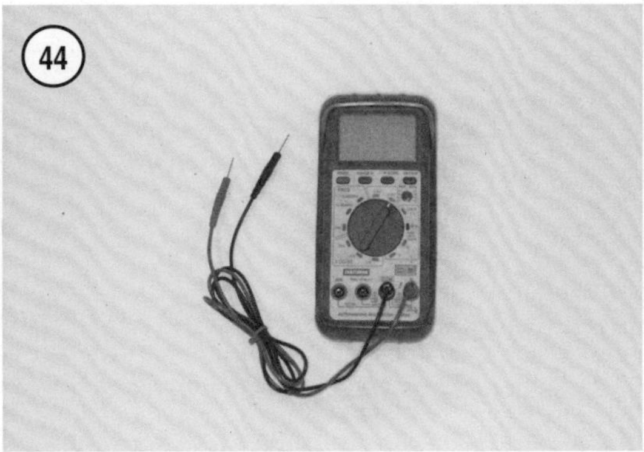

Multimeter

A multimeter (**Figure 44**) is an essential tool for electrical system diagnosis. The voltage function indicates the voltage applied or available to various electrical components. The ohmmeter function tests circuits for continuity, or lack of continuity, and measures the resistance of a circuit.

Some manufacturers' specifications for electrical components are based on results using a specific test meter. Results may vary if a meter not recommend by the manufacturer is used. Such requirements are noted when applicable.

Ohmmeter (analog) calibration

Each time an analog ohmmeter is used or if the scale is changed, the ohmmeter must be calibrated.

Digital ohmmeters do not require calibration.

1. Make sure the meter battery is in good condition.
2. Make sure the meter probes are in good condition.
3. Touch the two probes together and observe the needle location on the ohms scale.

The needle must align with the 0 mark to obtain accurate measurements.

4. If necessary, rotate the meter ohms adjust knob until the needle and 0 mark align.

ELECTRICAL SYSTEM FUNDAMENTALS

A thorough study of the many types of electrical systems used in today's vehicles is beyond the scope of this manual. However, a basic understanding of electrical basics is necessary to perform simple diagnostic tests.

Voltage

Voltage is the electrical potential or pressure in an electrical circuit and is expressed in volts. The more pressure (voltage) in a circuit, the more work that can be performed.

Direct current (DC) voltage means the electricity flows in one direction. All circuits powered by a battery are DC circuits.

Alternating current (AC) means that the electricity flows in one direction momentarily then switches to the opposite direction. Alternator output is an example of AC voltage. This voltage must be changed or rectified to direct current to operate in a battery powered system.

Measuring voltage

Unless otherwise specified, perform all voltage tests with the electrical connectors attached. When measuring voltage, select the meter range that is one scale higher than the expected voltage of the circuit to prevent damage to the meter. To determine the actual voltage in a circuit, use a voltmeter. To simply check if voltage is present, use a test light.

NOTE
When using a test light, either lead can be attached to ground.

1. Attach the negative meter test lead to a good ground (bare metal). Make sure the ground is not insulated with a rubber gasket or grommet.
2. Attach the positive meter test lead to the point being checked for voltage (**Figure 45**).
3. Turn on the ignition switch. The test light should light or the meter should display a reading. The reading should be within one volt of battery voltage.

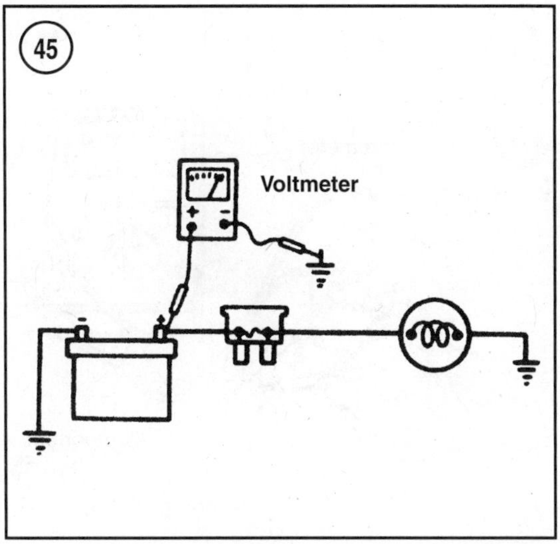

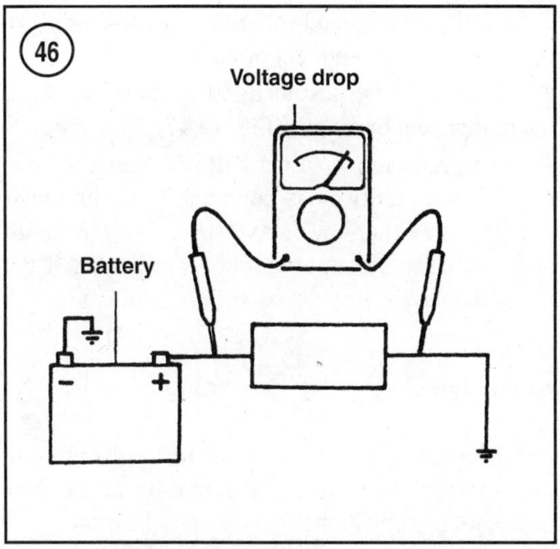

If the voltage is less, there is a problem in the circuit.

Voltage drop test

Resistance causes voltage to drop. This resistance can be measured in an active circuit by using a voltmeter to perform a voltage drop test. A voltage drop test compares the difference between the voltage available at the start of a circuit to the voltage at the end of the circuit while the circuit is operational. If the circuit has no resistance, there will be no voltage drop. The greater the resistance, the greater the voltage drop will be. A voltage drop of one volt or more indicates excessive resistance in the circuit.

1. Connect the positive meter test lead to the electrical source (where electricity is coming from).
2. Connect the negative meter test lead to the electrical load (where electricity is going). See **Figure 46**.
3. If necessary, activate the component(s) in the circuit.
4. A voltage reading of 1 volt or more indicates excessive resistance in the circuit. A reading equal to battery voltage indicates an open circuit.

Resistance

Resistance is the opposition to the flow of electricity within a circuit or component and is measured in ohms. Resistance causes a reduction in available current and voltage.

Resistance is measured in an inactive circuit with an ohmmeter. The ohmmeter sends a small amount of current into the circuit and measures how difficult it is to push the current through the circuit.

An ohmmeter, although useful, is not always a good indicator of a circuit's actual ability under operating conditions. This is due to the low voltage (6-9 volts) that the meter uses to test the circuit. The voltage in an ignition coil secondary winding can be several thousand volts. Such high voltage can cause the coil to malfunction, even though it tests acceptable during a resistance test.

Resistance generally increases with temperature. Perform all testing with the component or circuit at room temperature. Resistance tests performed at high temperatures may indicate high resistance readings and result in the unnecessary replacement of a component.

Measuring resistance and continuity testing

CAUTION

*Only use an ohmmeter on a circuit that has no voltage present. The meter will be damaged if it is connected to a live circuit. An analog meter must be calibrated each time it is used or the scale is changed. See **Multimeter** in this chapter.*

A continuity test can determine if the circuit is complete. This type of test is performed with an ohmmeter or a self-powered test lamp.

1. Disconnect the negative battery cable.

2. Attach one test lead (ohmmeter or test light) to one end of the component or circuit.
3. Attach the other test lead to the opposite end of the component or circuit (**Figure 47**).
4. A self-powered test light will come on if the circuit has continuity or is complete. An ohmmeter will indicate either low or no resistance if the circuit has continuity. An open circuit is indicated if the meter displays infinite resistance.

47

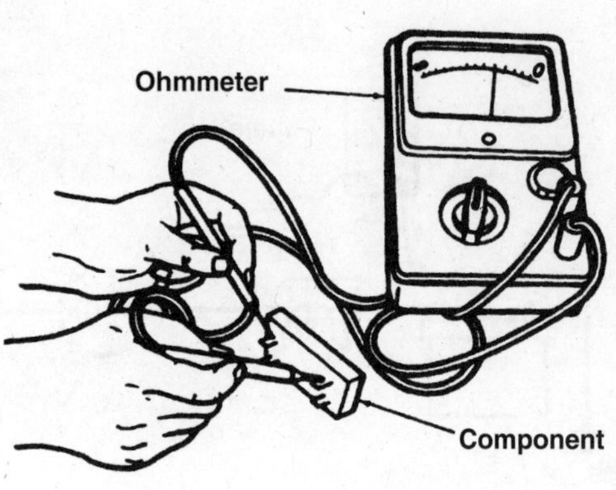

Amperage

Amperage is the unit of measure for the amount of current within a circuit. Current is the actual flow of electricity. The higher the current, the more work that can be performed up to a given point. If the current flow exceeds the circuit or component capacity, the system will be damaged.

Measuring amps

An ammeter measures the current flow or amps of a circuit (**Figure 48**). Amperage measurement requires that the circuit be disconnected and the ammeter be connected in series to the circuit. Always use an ammeter that can read higher than the anticipated current flow to prevent damage to the meter. Connect the red test lead to the electrical source and the black test lead to the electrical load.

SPECIAL TOOLS

Some of the procedures in this manual require special tools (**Table 9**). These are described in the appropriate chapter and are available from either the manufacturer or a tool supplier.

In many cases, an acceptable substitute may be found in an existing tool kit. Another alternative is to make the tool. Many schools with a machine shop curriculum welcome outside work that can be used as practical shop applications for students.

BASIC SERVICE METHODS

Most of the procedures in this manual are straightforward and can be performed by anyone reasonably competent with tools. However, consider personal capabilities carefully before attempting any operation involving major disassembly of the engine.

1. Front, in this manual, refers to the front of the vehicle. The front of any component is the end closest to the front of the vehicle. The left and right sides refer to the position of the parts as viewed by the rider sitting on the seat facing forward.
2. Whenever servicing an engine or suspension component, secure the vehicle in a safe manner.
3. Tag all similar parts for location and mark all mating parts for position. Record the number and thickness of any shims as they are removed. Identify parts by placing them in sealed and labeled plastic sandwich bags.
4. Tag disconnected wires and connectors with masking tape and a marking pen. Do not rely on memory alone.
5. Protect finished surfaces from physical damage or corrosion. Keep gasoline and other chemicals off painted surfaces.
6. Use penetrating oil on frozen or tight bolts. Avoid using heat where possible. Heat can warp, melt or affect the temper of parts. Heat also damages the finish of paint and plastics.
7. When a part is a press fit or requires a special tool for removal, the information or type of tool is identified in the text. Otherwise, if a part is difficult to remove or install, determine the cause before proceeding.
8. To prevent objects or debris from falling into the engine, cover all openings.
9. Read each procedure thoroughly and compare the illustrations to the actual components before

48

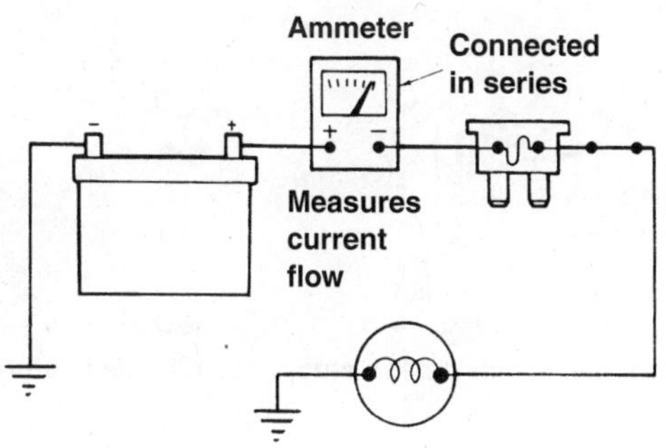

starting the procedure. Perform the procedure in sequence.

10. Recommendations are occasionally made to refer service to a dealership or specialist. In these cases, the work can be performed more economically by the specialist than by the home mechanic.

11. The term *replace* means to discard a defective part and replace it with a new part. *Overhaul* means to remove, disassemble, inspect, measure, repair and/or replace parts as required to recondition an assembly.

12. Some operations require the use of a hydraulic press. If a press is not available, have these operations performed by a shop equipped with the necessary equipment. Do not use makeshift equipment that may damage the vehicle.

13. Repairs are much faster and easier if the vehicle is clean before starting work. Degrease the vehicle with a commercial degreaser; follow the directions on the container for the best results. Clean all parts with cleaning solvent as they are removed.

CAUTION

Do not direct high-pressure water at steering bearings, carburetor hoses, wheel bearings, suspension and electrical components, or drive belt. The water will force the grease out of the bearings and possibly damage the seals.

14. If special tools are required, have them available before starting the procedure. When special tools are required, they will be described at the beginning of the procedure.

15. Make diagrams of similar-appearing parts. For instance, crankcase bolts are often not the same lengths. Do not rely on memory alone. It is possible that carefully laid out parts will become disturbed, making it difficult to reassemble the components correctly without a diagram.

16. Make sure all shims and washers are reinstalled in the same location and position.

17. Whenever rotating parts contact a stationary part, look for a shim or washer.

18. Use new gaskets if there is any doubt about the condition of old ones.

19. If self-locking fasteners are used, replace them with new ones. Do not install standard fasteners in place of self-locking ones.

20. Use grease to hold small parts in place if they tend to fall out during assembly. Do not apply grease to electrical or brake components.

Removing Frozen Fasteners

If a fastener cannot be removed, several methods may be used to loosen it. First, apply penetrating oil such as Liquid Wrench or WD-40. Apply it liberally and let it penetrate for 10-15 minutes. Rap the fastener several times with a small hammer. Do not hit it hard enough to cause damage. Reapply the penetrating oil if necessary.

For frozen screws, apply penetrating oil as described, then insert a screwdriver in the slot and rap the top of the screwdriver with a hammer. This loosens the rust so the screw can be removed in the normal way. If the screw head is too damaged to use this method, grip the head with locking pliers and twist the screw out.

Avoid applying heat unless specifically instructed, as it may melt, warp or remove the temper from parts.

Removing Broken Fasteners

If the head breaks off a screw or bolt, several methods are available for removing the remaining portion. If a large portion of the remainder projects out, try gripping it with locking pliers. If the pro-

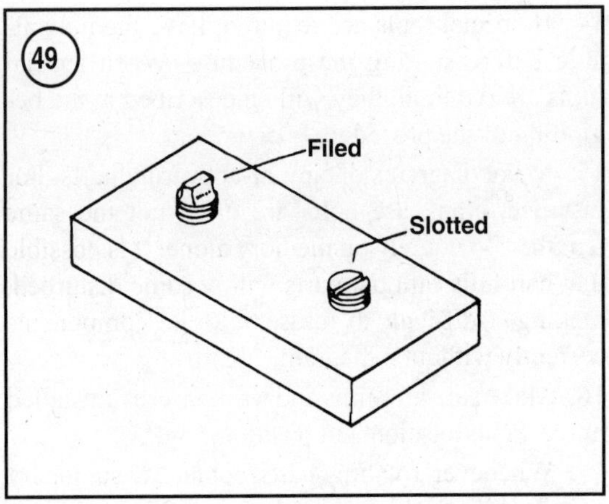
49
Filed
Slotted

jecting portion is too small, file it to fit a wrench or cut a slot in it to fit a screwdriver (**Figure 49**).

If the head breaks off flush, use a screw extractor. To do this, centerpunch the exact center of the remaining portion of the screw or bolt. Drill a small hole in the screw and tap the extractor into the hole. Back the screw out with a wrench on the extractor (**Figure 50**).

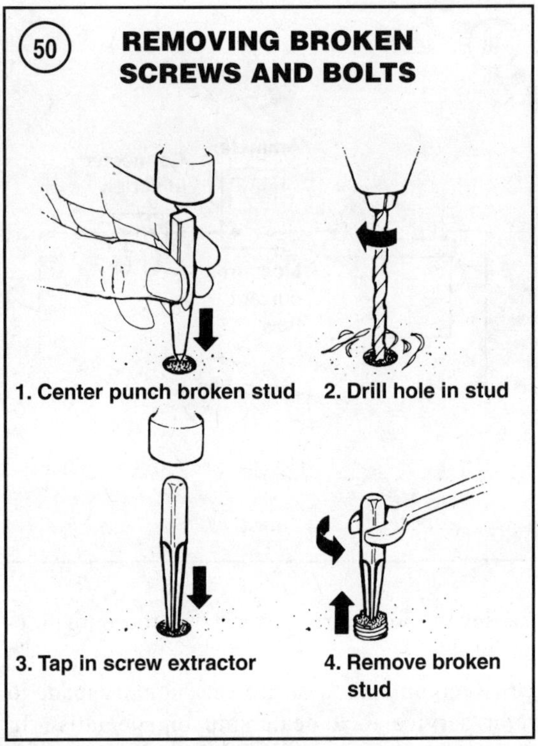
50
REMOVING BROKEN SCREWS AND BOLTS
1. Center punch broken stud
2. Drill hole in stud
3. Tap in screw extractor
4. Remove broken stud

Repairing Damaged Threads

Occasionally, threads are stripped through carelessness or impact damage. Often the threads can be repaired by running a tap (for internal threads on nuts) or die (for external threads on bolts) through the threads (**Figure 51**). To clean or repair spark plug threads, use a spark plug tap.

If an internal thread is damaged, it may be necessary to install a Helicoil or some other type of thread insert. Follow the manufacturer's instructions when installing their insert.

If it is necessary to drill and tap a hole, refer to **Table 8** for American tap and drill sizes.

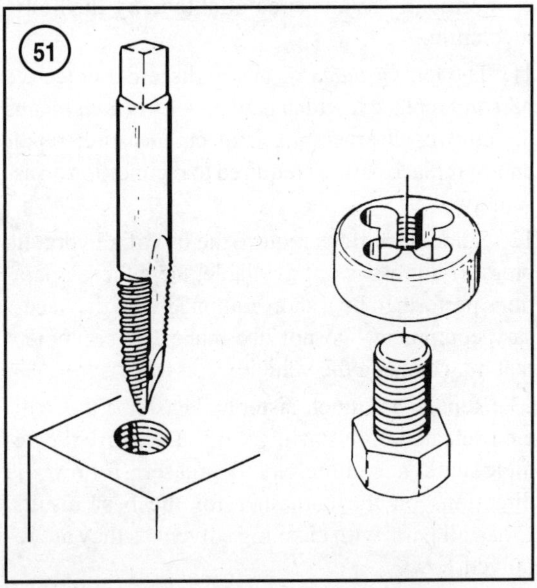
51

Stud Removal/Installation

A stud removal tool is available from most tool suppliers. This tool makes the removal and installation of studs easier. If one is not available, thread two nuts onto the stud and tighten them against each other. Remove the stud by turning the lower nut (**Figure 52**).

1. Measure the height of the stud above the surface.
2. Thread the stud removal tool onto the stud and tighten it, or thread two nuts onto the stud.
3. Remove the stud by turning the stud remover or the lower nut.
4. Remove any threadlocking compound from the threaded hole. Clean the threads with an aerosol parts cleaner.
5. Install the stud removal tool onto the new stud or thread two nuts onto the stud.

52

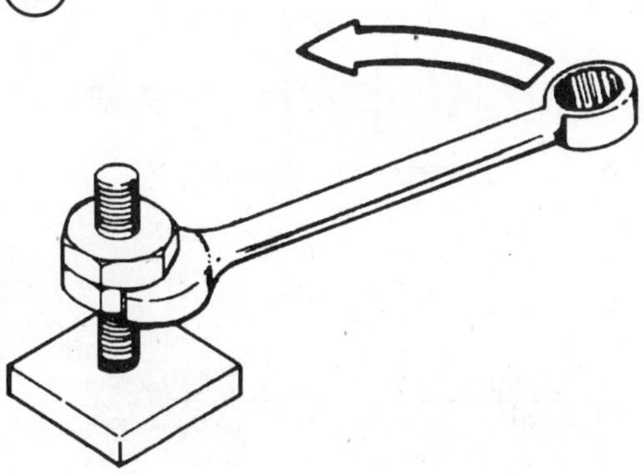

53

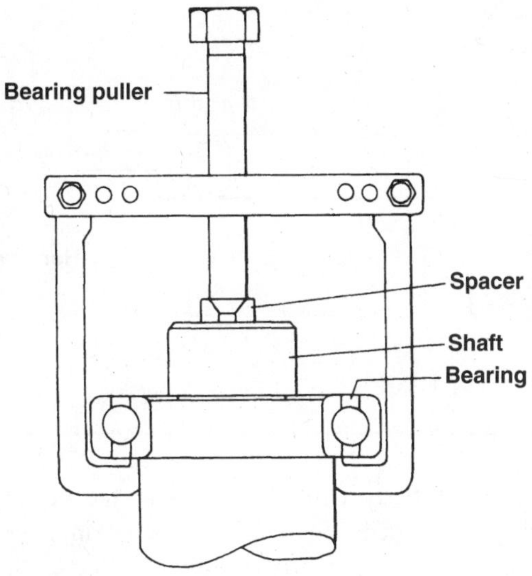

6. Apply threadlocking compound to the threads of the stud.

7. Install the stud and tighten with the stud removal tool or the top nut.

8. Install the stud to the height noted in Step 1 or its torque specification.

9. Remove the stud removal tool or the two nuts.

Removing Hoses

When removing stubborn hoses, do not exert excessive force on the hose or fitting. Remove the hose clamp and carefully insert a small screwdriver or pick tool between the fitting and hose. Apply a spray lubricant under the hose and carefully twist the hose off the fitting. Clean the fitting of any corrosion or rubber hose material with a wire brush. Clean the inside of the hose thoroughly. Do not use any lubricant when installing the hose (new or old). The lubricant may allow the hose to come off the fitting, even with the clamp secure.

Bearings

Bearings are used in the engine and transmission assembly to reduce power loss, heat and noise resulting from friction. Because bearings are precision parts, they must be maintained by proper lubrication and maintenance. If a bearing is damaged, replace it immediately. When installing a new bearing, take care to prevent damaging it. Bearing replacement procedures are included in the individual chapters where applicable; however, use the following sections as a guideline.

NOTE

Unless otherwise specified, install bearings with the manufacturer's mark or number facing outward.

Removal

While bearings are normally removed only when damaged, there may be times when it is necessary to remove a bearing that is in good condition. However, improper bearing removal will damage the bearing and maybe the shaft or case half. Note the following when removing bearings.

1. When using a puller to remove a bearing from a shaft, take care that the shaft is not damaged. Always place a piece of metal between the end of the shaft and the puller screw. In addition, place the puller arms next to the inner bearing race. See **Figure 53**.

2. When using a hammer to remove a bearing from a shaft, do not strike the hammer directly against the shaft. Instead, use a brass or aluminum rod between the hammer and shaft (**Figure 54**) and make sure to

54

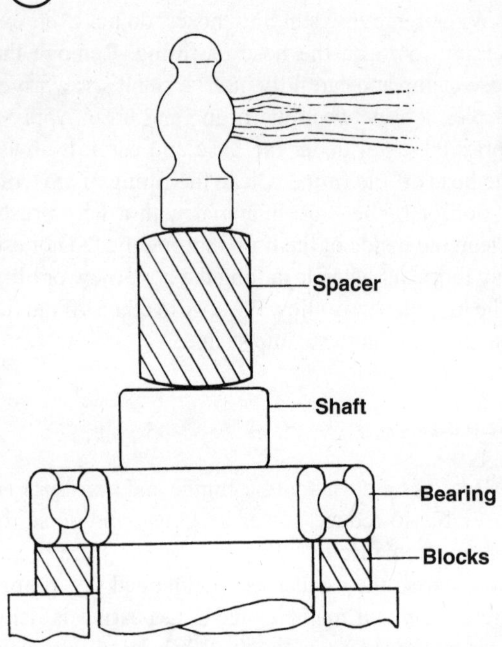

support both bearing races with wooden blocks as shown.

3. A hydraulic press is the ideal method of bearing removal. Note the following when using a press:
   a. Always support the inner and outer bearing races with a suitable size wooden or aluminum ring (**Figure 55**). If only the outer race is supported, pressure applied against the balls and/or the inner race will damage them.
   b. Always make sure the press arm (**Figure 55**) aligns with the center of the shaft. If the arm is not centered, it may damage the bearing and/or shaft.
   c. The moment the shaft is free of the bearing, it will drop to the floor. Secure or hold the shaft to prevent it from falling.

Installation

1. When installing a bearing in a housing, apply pressure to the *outer* bearing race (**Figure 56**). When installing a bearing on a shaft, apply pressure to the *inner* bearing race (**Figure 57**).
2. When installing a bearing as described in Step 1, some type of driver is required. Never strike the bearing directly with a hammer or the bearing will be damaged. When installing a bearing, use a piece of pipe or a driver with a diameter that matches the bearing race. **Figure 58** shows the correct way to use a socket and hammer to install a bearing.
3. Step 1 describes how to install a bearing in a case half or over a shaft. However, when installing a bearing over a shaft and into a housing at the same time, a tight fit will be required for both outer and inner bearing races. In this situation, install a spacer underneath the driver tool so that pressure is applied evenly across both races. See **Figure 59**. If the outer race is not supported as shown in **Figure 59**, the balls will push against the outer bearing race and damage it.

55

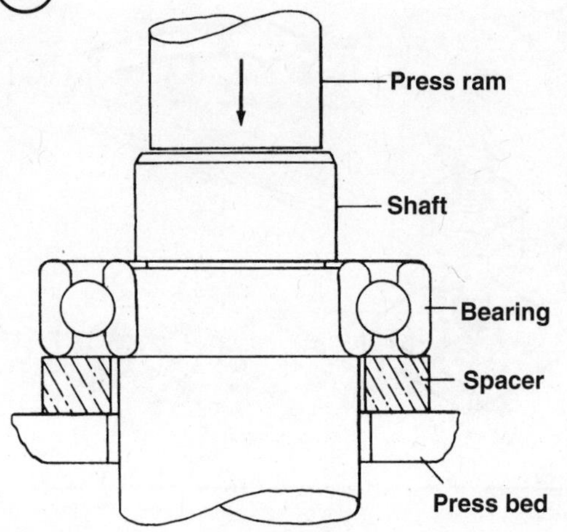

56

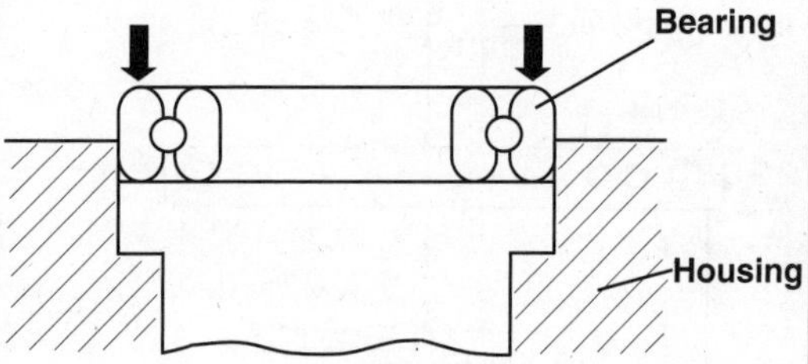

57

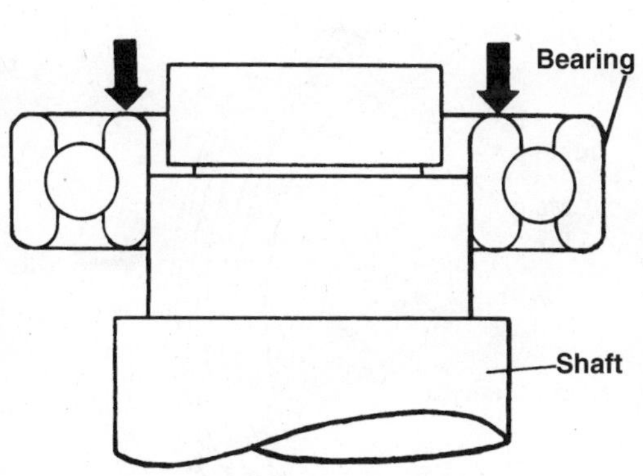

58

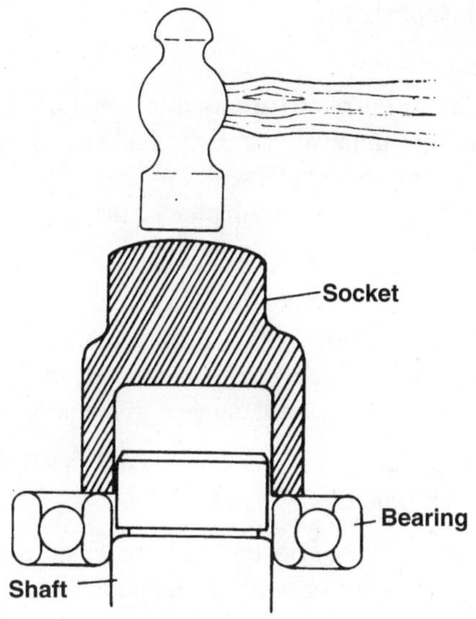

59

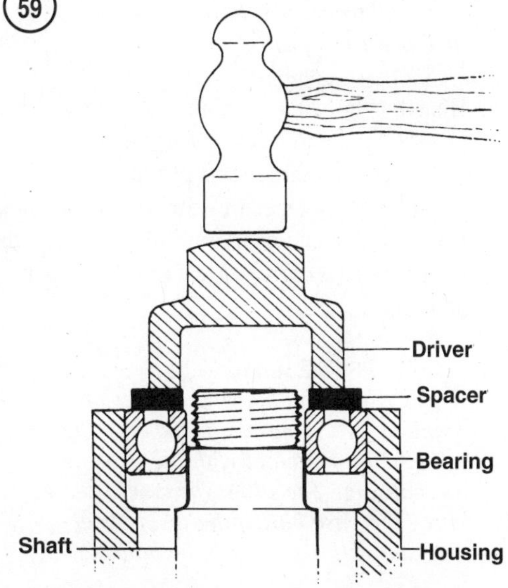

Interference Fit

1. Follow this procedure when installing a bearing over a shaft. When a tight fit is required, the bearing inside diameter will be smaller than the shaft. In this case, driving the bearing on the shaft using normal methods may cause bearing damage. Instead, heat the bearing before installation. Note the following:

   a. Secure the shaft so it is ready for bearing installation.

   b. Clean all residues from the bearing surface of the shaft. Remove burrs with a file or sandpaper.

   c. Fill a suitable pot or beaker with clean mineral oil. Place a thermometer rated above 120° C (248° F) in the oil. Support the thermometer so that it does not rest on the bottom or side of the pot.

   d. Remove the bearing from its wrapper and secure it with a piece of heavy wire bent to hold it in the pot. Hang the bearing in the pot so it does not touch the bottom or sides of the pot.

   e. Turn the heat on and monitor the thermometer. When the oil temperature rises to approximately 120° C (248° F), remove the bearing from the pot and quickly install it. If necessary, place a socket on the inner bearing race and tap the bearing into place. As the bearing chills, it will tighten on the shaft, so installation must be done quickly. Make sure the bearing is installed completely.

2. Follow this step when installing a bearing in a housing. Bearings are generally installed in a housing with a slight interference fit. Driving the bearing into the housing using normal methods may damage the housing or cause bearing damage. Instead, heat the housing before the bearing is installed. Note the following:

CAUTION

Before heating the housing in this procedure, wash the housing thoroughly with detergent and water. Rinse and rewash the cases as required to remove all traces of oil and other chemical deposits.

a. Heat the housing to approximately 212° F (100° C) in an oven or on a hot plate. An easy way to check that it is the proper temperature is to place tiny drops of water on the housing; if they sizzle and evaporate immediately, the temperature is correct. Heat only one housing at a time.

CAUTION
Do not heat the housing with a propane or acetylene torch. Never bring a flame into contact with the bearing or housing. The direct heat will destroy the case hardening of the bearing and will likely warp the housing.

b. Remove the housing from the oven or hot plate, and hold onto the housing with a kitchen potholder, heavy gloves or heavy shop cloth. It is hot!

NOTE
Remove and install the bearings with a suitable size socket and extension.

c. Hold the housing with the bearing side down and tap the bearing out. Repeat for all bearings in the housing.
d. Before heating the bearing housing, place the new bearing in a freezer if possible. Chilling a bearing slightly reduces its outside diameter while the heated bearing housing assembly is slightly larger due to heat expansion. This will make bearing installation easier.

NOTE
Always install bearings with the manufacturer's mark or number facing outward.

e. While the housing is still hot, install the new bearing(s) into the housing. Install the bearings by hand, if possible. If necessary, lightly tap the bearing(s) into the housing with a socket placed on the outer bearing race (**Figure 56**). Do not install new bearings by driving on the inner-bearing race. Install the bearing(s) until it seats completely.

60

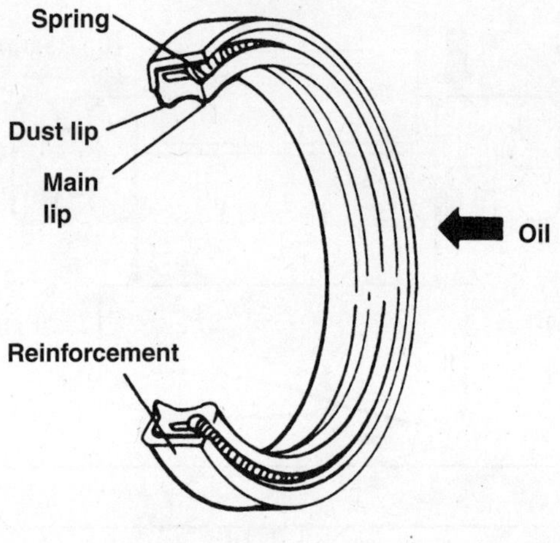

Seal Replacement

Seals (**Figure 60**) are used to contain oil, water, grease or combustion gasses in a housing or shaft. Improper removal of a seal can damage the housing or shaft. Improper installation of the seal can damage the seal. Note the following:

1. Prying is generally the easiest and most effective method of removing a seal from a housing. However, always place a rag underneath the pry tool (**Figure 61**) to prevent damage to the housing.

2. Pack waterproof grease in the seal lips before the seal is installed.

3. In most cases, install seals with the manufacturer's numbers or marks face out.

4. Install seals with a socket placed on the outside of the seal as shown in **Figure 62**. Drive the seal squarely into the housing. Never install a seal by hitting against the top of the seal with a hammer.

STORAGE

Several months of non-use can cause a general deterioration of the vehicle. This is especially true in areas of extreme temperature variations. This deterioration can be minimized with careful preparation for storage. A properly stored vehicle will be much easier to return to service.

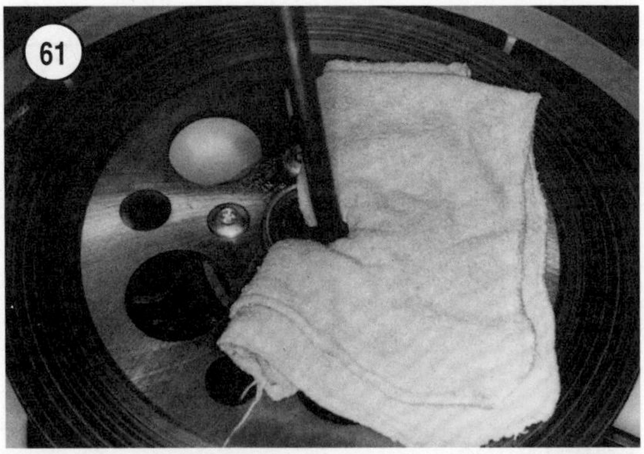

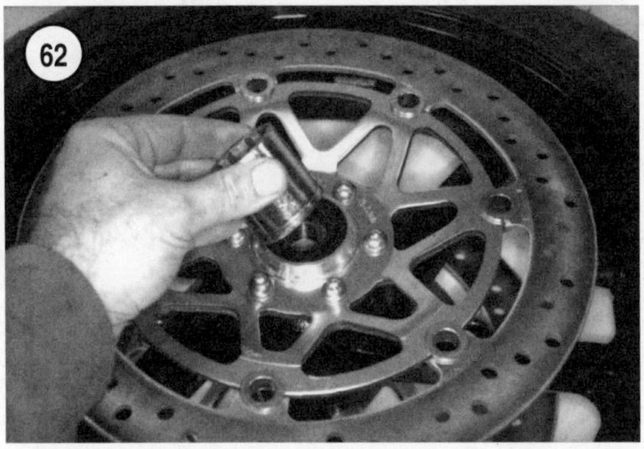

Storage Area Selection

When selecting a storage area, consider the following:

1. The storage area must be dry. A heated area is best, but not necessary. It should be insulated to minimize extreme temperature variations.
2. If the building has large window areas, mask them to keep sunlight off the vehicle.
3. Avoid buildings in industrial areas where corrosive emissions may be present. Avoid areas close to saltwater.
4. Consider the area's risk of fire, theft or vandalism. Check with an insurer regarding vehicle coverage while in storage.

Preparing the Vehicle for Storage

The amount of preparation a vehicle should undergo before storage depends on the expected length of non-use, storage area conditions and personal preference. Consider the following list the minimum requirement:

1. Wash the vehicle thoroughly. Make sure all dirt, mud and road debris are removed.
2. Start the engine and allow it to reach operating temperature. Drain the engine oil and transmission oil, regardless of the riding time since the last service. Fill the engine and transmission with the recommended type of oil.
3. Drain all fuel from the fuel tank, run the engine until all the fuel is consumed from the lines and carburetor.
4. Remove the spark plugs and pour a teaspoon of engine oil into the cylinders. Place a rag over the openings and slowly turn the engine over to distribute the oil. Reinstall the spark plugs.
5. Remove the battery. Store the battery in a cool and dry location.
6. Cover the exhaust and intake openings.
7. Reduce the normal tire pressure by 20%.
8. Apply a protective substance to the plastic and rubber components, including the tires. Make sure to follow the manufacturer's instructions for each type of product being used.
9. Place the vehicle on a stand or wooden blocks, so the wheels are off the ground. If this is not possible, place a piece of plywood between the tires and the ground. Inflate the tires to the recommended pressure if the vehicle can not be elevated.
10. Cover the vehicle with old bed sheets or something similar. Do not cover it with any plastic material that will trap moisture.

Returning the Vehicle to Service

The amount of service required when returning a vehicle to service after storage depends on the length of non-use and storage conditions. In addition to performing the reverse of the above procedures, make sure the brakes, clutch, throttle and engine stop switch work properly before operating the vehicle. Refer to Chapter Three and evaluate the service intervals to determine which areas require service.

Tables 1-9 are on the following pages

Table 1 MODEL DESIGNATION

1999-2000
FXDS-CONV Dyna Convertable
1999-on
FXD Dyna Super Glide
FXDX Dyna Super Glide Sport
FXDL Dyna Low Rider
FXDWG Dyna Wide Glide
FXDXT Dyna Glide T-Sport
FXDP Dyna Defender (law enforcement model)

Table 2 GENERAL DIMENSIONS

Item/model	in.	mm
Wheelbase		
FXDWG	66.10	1678.95
FXDS-CONV	63.88	1622.55
FXDL	65.60	1666.24
FXD	62.80	1592.12
FXDX	63.88	1622.55
FXDXT T-Sport	63.90	1623.10
FXDP	64.00	1625.60
Overall length		
FXDWG	94.50	2400.30
FXDS-CONV	92.88	2359.15
FXDL	94.00	2387.60
FXD	91.00	2311.40
FXDX	92.88	2359.15
FXDXT T-Sport	92.60	2359.70
FXDP	91.60	2326.60
Overall width		
FXDWG	33.50	850.90
FXDS-CONV	28.95	735.33
FXDL	28.50	723.90
FXD	28.50	723.90
FXDX	33.00	838.20
FXDXT T-Sport	33.00	838.20
FXDP	33.50	850.90
Road clearance		
FXDWG	5.62	142.75
FXDS-CONV	5.75	146.05
FXDL	5.38	136.65
FXD	5.38	136.65
FXDX	5.75	146.05
FXDXT T-Sport	5.90	149.60
FXDP	5.50	139.70
Overall height		
FXDWG	47.50	1206.50
FXDS-CONV	59.25	1504.95
FXDL	47.50	1206.50
FXD	47.50	1206.50
FXDX	51.25	1301.75
FXDXT T-Sport	51.25	1301.75
FXDP	47.50	1206.50
Saddle height		
FXDWG	26.75	679.45
FXDS-CONV	27.75	704.85

(continued)

1

Table 2 GENERAL DIMENSIONS (continued)

Item/model	in.	mm
Saddle height (continued)		
FXDL	26.50	673.10
FXD	26.50	673.10
FXDX	27.00	685.80
FXDXT T-Sport	27.25	692.20
FXDP	31.00	787.40

Table 3 VEHICLE WEIGHT (DRY)

Model	lbs.	kg
FXDWG	612.0	277.8
FXDS-CONV	640.0	290.6
FXDL	614.0	278.8
FXD	612.0	277.8
FXDX	619.0	281.1
FXDXT T-Sport	619.0	281.1
FXDP	697.4	316.3

Table 4 DECIMAL AND METRIC EQUIVALENTS

Fractions	Decimal in.	Metric mm	Fractions	Decimal in.	Metric mm
1/64	0.015625	0.39688	33/64	0.515625	13.09687
1/32	0.03125	0.79375	17/32	0.53125	13.49375
3/64	0.046875	1.19062	35/64	0.546875	13.89062
1/16	0.0625	1.58750	9/16	0.5625	14.28750
5/64	0.078125	1.98437	37/64	0.578125	14.68437
3/32	0.09375	2.38125	19/32	0.59375	15.08125
7/64	0.109375	2.77812	39/64	0.609375	15.47812
1/8	0.125	3.1750	5/8	0.625	15.87500
9/64	0.140625	3.57187	41/64	0.640625	16.27187
5/32	0.15625	3.96875	21/32	0.65625	16.66875
11/64	0.171875	4.36562	43/64	0.671875	17.06562
3/16	0.1875	4.76250	11/16	0.6875	17.46250
13/64	0.203125	5.15937	45/64	0.703125	17.85937
7/32	0.21875	5.55625	23/32	0.71875	18.25625
15/64	0.234375	5.95312	47/64	0.734375	18.65312
1/4	0.250	6.35000	3/4	0.750	19.05000
17/64	0.265625	6.74687	49/64	0.765625	19.44687
9/32	0.28125	7.14375	25/32	0.78125	19.84375
19/64	0.296875	7.54062	51/64	0.796875	20.24062
5/16	0.3125	7.93750	13/16	0.8125	20.63750
21/64	0.328125	8.33437	53/64	0.828125	21.03437
11/32	0.34375	8.73125	27/32	0.84375	21.43125
23/64	0.359375	9.12812	55/64	0.859375	22.82812
3/8	0.375	9.52500	7/8	0.875	22.22500
25/64	0.390625	9.92187	57/64	0.890625	22.62187
13/32	0.40625	10.31875	29/32	0.90625	23.01875
27/64	0.421875	10.71562	59/64	0.921875	23.41562
7/16	0.4375	11.11250	15/16	0.9375	23.81250
29/64	0.453125	11.50937	61/64	0.953125	24.20937
15/32	0.46875	11.90625	31/32	0.96875	24.60625
31/64	0.484375	12.30312	63/64	0.984375	25.00312
1/2	0.500	12.70000	1	1.00	25.40000

Table 5 CONVERSION TABLES

Multiply	By:	To get the equivalent of:
Length		
Inches	25.4	Millimeter
Inches	2.54	Centimeter
Miles	1.609	Kilometer
Feet	0.3048	Meter
Millimeter	0.03937	Inches
Centimeter	0.3937	Inches
Kilometer	0.6214	Mile
Meter	0.0006214	Mile
Fluid volume		
U.S. quarts	0.9463	Liters
U.S. gallons	3.785	Liters
U.S. ounces	29.573529	Milliliters
Imperial gallons	4.54609	Liters
Imperial quarts	1.1365	Liters
Liters	0.2641721	U.S. gallons
Liters	1.0566882	U.S. quarts
Liters	33.814023	U.S. ounces
Liters	0.22	Imperial gallons
Liters	0.8799	Imperial quarts
Milliliters	0.033814	U.S. ounces
Milliliters	1.0	Cubic centimeters
Milliliters	0.001	Liters
Torque		
Foot-pounds	1.3558	Newton-meters
Foot-pounds	0.138255	Meters-kilograms
Inch-pounds	0.11299	Newton-meters
Newton-meters	0.7375622	Foot-pounds
Newton-meters	8.8507	Inch-pounds
Meters-kilograms	7.2330139	Foot-pounds
Volume		
Cubic inches	16.387064	Cubic centimeters
Cubic centimeters	0.0610237	Cubic inches
Temperature		
Fahrenheit	(F -32°) × 0.556	Centigrade
Centigrade	(C × 1.8) + 32	Fahrenheit
Weight		
Ounces	28.3495	Grams
Pounds	0.4535924	Kilograms
Grams	0.035274	Ounces
Kilograms	2.2046224	Pounds
Pressure		
Pounds per square inch	0.070307	Kilograms per square centimeter
Kilograms per square centimeter	14.223343	Pounds per square inch
Kilopascals	0.1450	Pounds per square inch
Pounds per square inch	6.895	Kilopascals
Speed		
Miles per hour	1.609344	Kilometers per hour
Kilometers per hour	0.6213712	Miles per hour

Table 6 GENERAL TORQUE SPECIFICATIONS (FT.-LB.)[1]

Type[2]	1/4	5/16	3/8	7/16	1/2	9/16	5/8	3/4	7/8	1
SAE 2	6	12	20	32	47	69	96	155	206	310
SAE 5	10	19	33	54	78	114	154	257	382	587
SAE 7	13	25	44	71	110	154	215	360	570	840
SAE 8	14	29	47	78	119	169	230	380	600	700

1. Convert ft.-lb. specification to N•m by multiplying by 1.3558.
2. Fastener strength of SAE bolts can be determined by the bolt head grade markings. Unmarked bolt heads and cap screws are usually mild steel. More grade markings indicate higher fastener quality.

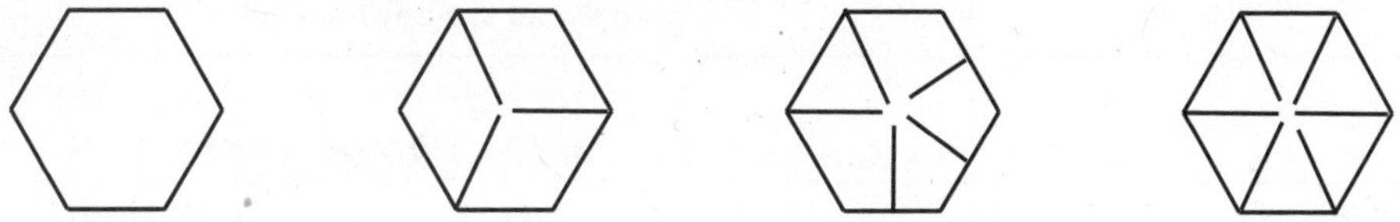

SAE 2 SAE 5 SAE 7 SAE 8

Table 7 TECHNICAL ABBREVIATIONS

ABDC	After bottom dead center
ATDC	After top dead center
BBDC	Before bottom dead center
BDC	Bottom dead center
BTDC	Before top dead center
C	Celsius (Centigrade)
cc	Cubic centimeters
cid	Cubic inch displacement
CDI	Capacitor discharge ignition
CKP	Crankshaft position sensor
CMP	Camshaft position sensor
cu. in.	Cubic inches
ECM	Electronic control module
ET	Engine temperature sensor
F	Fahrenheit
ft.	Feet
ft.-lb.	Foot-pounds
gal.	Gallons
H/A	High altitude
hp	Horsepower
IAC	Idle air control valve
IAT	Intake air temperature sensor
in.	Inches
in.-lb.	Inch-pounds
I.D.	Inside diameter
kg	Kilograms
kgm	Kilogram meters
km	Kilometer
kPa	Kilopascals
L	Liter
m	Meter
MAG	Magneto
MAP	Manifold absolute pressure
ml	Milliliter
mm	Millimeter

(continued)

Table 7 TECHNICAL ABBREVIATIONS (continued)

N•m	Newton-meters
O.D.	Outside diameter
OE	Original equipment
oz.	Ounces
psi	Pounds per square inch
PTO	Power take off
pt.	Pint
qt.	Quart
rpm	Revolutions per minute
TP	Throttle position sensor
TSM	Turn signal module
TSSM	Turn signal security module

Table 8 AMERICAN TAP AND DRILL SIZES

Tap thread	Drill size	Tap thread	Drill size
#0-80	3/64	1/4-28	No. 3
#1-64	No. 53	5/16-18	F
#1-72	No. 53	5/16-24	I
#2-56	No. 51	3/8-16	5/16
#2-64	No. 50	3/8-24	Q
#3-48	5/64	7/16-14	U
#3-56	No. 46	7/16-20	W
#4-40	No. 43	1/2-13	27/64
#4-48	No. 42	1/2-20	29/64
#5-40	No. 39	9/16-12	31/64
#5-44	No. 37	9/16-18	33/64
#6-32	No. 36	5/8-11	17/32
#6-40	No. 33	5/18-18	37/64
#8-32	No. 29	3/4-10	21/32
#8-36	No. 29	3/4-16	11/16
#10-24	No. 25	7/8-9	49/64
#10-32	No. 21	7/8-14	13/16
#12-24	No. 17	1-8	7/8
#12-28	No. 15	1-14	15/16
1/4-20	No. 8		

Table 9 SPECIAL TOOLS*

Description	Manufacturer	Part No.
Connecting rod bushing tool	JIMS	1051
Connecting rod clamp	H-D	H-D 95952-33B
Connecting rod bushing hone	H-D	H-D 422569
Wrist pin bushing reamer tool	JIMS	1726-3
Cylinder torque plates	JIMS	1287
Inner cam bearing removal tool	JIMS	1279
Inner cam bearing installer	JIMS	1278
Cam chain tensioner tool	JIMS	1283
Cam/crank sprocket lock tool	JIMS	1285
Camshaft remover and installer	JIMS	1277
Cam bearing puller	JIMS	1280
Twin Cam 88 engine stand	JIMS	1022
Crankshaft bearing tool	JIMS	1275
Crankshaft guide	JIMS	1288
Crankshaft bushing tool	JIMS	1281

(continued)

Table 9 SPECIAL TOOLS (continued)*

Description	Manufacturer	Part No.
Crank assembly removing tool	JIMS	1047-TP
Hard cap	JIMS	1048
Motor sprocket shaft seal install tool	JIMS	39361-69
Big twin Timken bearing remover	JIMS	1709
Big twin sprocket shaft bearing installation tool	JIMS	97225-55
Sprocket shaft bearing race tool set	JIMS	94547-80A
Race and bearing install tool handle	JIMS	33416-80
Timken bearing race installer	JIMS	2246
Snap ring installer and removal tool	JIMS	1710
Belt tension gauge	H-D	H-D 35381
Cylinder head stand	JIMS	39782
Chamfering cone	JIMS	2078
Driver handle	H-D	H-D 34740
Drive sprocket lock	JIMS	2260
Fork seal/cap installer	JIMS	2046
Fork oil level gauge	Motion Pro	08-0121
Steering head bearing race installer	JIMS	1725
Hydraulic brake bleeder	Mityvac	–
Mainshaft bearing race puller and installer	JIMS	34902-84
Transmission main drive gear tool set	JIMS	35316-80
Transmission main drive gear bearing tool	JIMS	37842-91
Transmission bearing remover set	JIMS	1078
Transmission pawl adjuster	H-D	H-D 39618
Transmission shaft installer	JIMS	2189
Countershaft sprocket nut wrench	JIMS	946600-37A
Retaining ring pliers	H-D	J-5586
Rocker arm bushing reamer	JIMS	94804-57
Spark tester	Motion Pro	08-0122
Sprocket shaft bearing cone installer	H-D	H-D 997225-55B
Vacuum hose identifier kit	Lisle	74600
Valve seal installation tool	H-D	H-D 34643A
Valve seat cutter set	H-D	H-D 35758A
Valve guide installer sleeve	H-D	H-D 34741
Valve guide reamer	H-D	H-D 39932
Valve guide reamer T-handle	H-D	H-D 39847
Valve guide reamer	H-D	H-D H-D 39964
Valve guide hone	H-D	H-D 34723
Valve guide brush	H-D	H-D 34751
Wheel bearing race remover and installer	JIMS	33461-80

*For special tools specific to 2002-on models, see Table 4 in Supplement.

CHAPTER TWO

TROUBLESHOOTING

Diagnosing mechanical problems is relatively simple if an orderly procedure is used. The first step in any troubleshooting procedure is to define the symptoms closely and then localize the problem.

Subsequent steps involve testing and analyzing those areas that could cause the symptoms. A haphazard approach may eventually solve the problem, but it can be very costly with wasted time and unnecessary parts replacement.

Proper lubrication, maintenance and periodic tune-ups as described in Chapter Three will reduce the necessity for troubleshooting. Even with the best of care, however, the motorcycle may require troubleshooting.

Never assume anything; do not overlook the obvious. If the engine will not start, the engine stop switch or start button may be shorted out or damaged. When trying to start the engine, it may be flooded.

If the engine suddenly quits, consider the easiest, most accessible system first. If the engine sounded as if it ran out of fuel, make sure there is fuel in the tank and that it is reaching the carburetor. Make sure the fuel shutoff valve (**Figure 1**) is turned to the ON position.

If a quick check does not reveal the problem, proceed with one of the troubleshooting procedures described in this chapter. Gather as many symptoms as possible to aid in determining where to start. For ex-

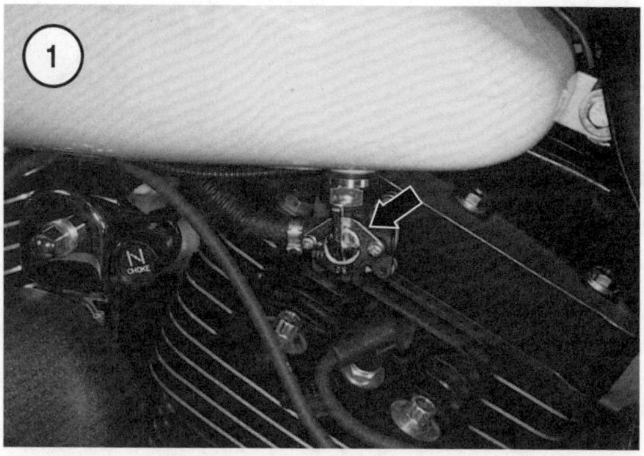

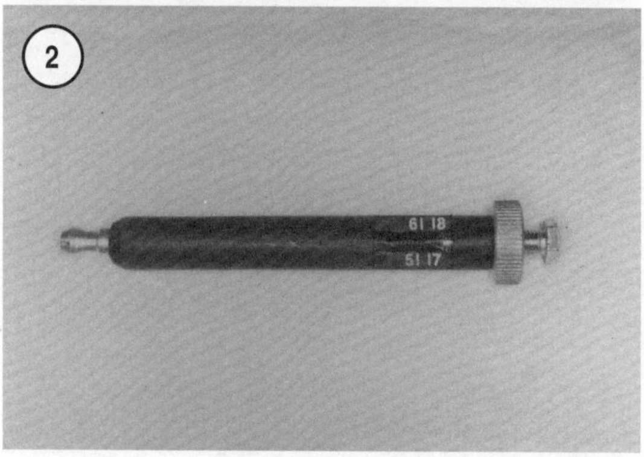

ample, note whether the engine lost power gradually or all at once, what color smoke came from the exhaust, etc.

After defining the symptoms, follow the procedure that most closely relates to the condition(s). Guessing at the cause of the problem may provide a solution, but it can easily lead to wasted time and unnecessary parts replacement.

Expensive equipment or complicated test gear is not required to determine whether repairs can be attempted at home. A few simple checks could save a large repair bill and lost time while the motorcycle sits in a dealership's service department. On the other hand, be realistic and do not attempt repairs beyond personal capabilities. Dealership service departments tend to charge heavily when working on equipment that has been abused. Some will not even take on such a job. Use common sense to avoid getting involved in a procedure that cannot be completed satisfactorily.

If the decision has been made to refer troubleshooting to a repair facility, describe problems accurately and fully.

Table 1 and **Table 2** list electrical specifications. **Tables 1-3** are located at the end of this chapter.

OPERATING REQUIREMENTS

An engine needs three basics to run properly: correct fuel/air mixture, compression and a spark at the right time. If one basic requirement is missing, the engine will not run. Four-stroke engine operating principles are described in Chapter Four under *Engine Principles*.

If the motorcycle has been sitting for any time and refuses to start, check and clean the spark plugs. If the plugs are not fouled, look to the fuel delivery system. This includes the fuel tank, fuel shutoff valve, fuel filter and fuel lines. If the motorcycle sat for a while with fuel in the carburetor, fuel deposits may have gummed up carburetor jets and air passages. Gasoline tends to lose its potency after standing for long periods. Condensation may contaminate it with water. Drain the old gas and try starting with a fresh tankful.

STARTING THE ENGINE

Engine Fails to Start (Spark Test)

Perform the following spark test to determine if the ignition system is operating properly.

CAUTION

Before removing the spark plugs in Step 1, clean all dirt and debris away from the plug base. Dirt that falls into the cylinder will cause rapid engine wear.

1. Refer to Chapter Three and disconnect the spark plug wire and remove the spark plug.

NOTE

A spark tester is a useful tool for testing the spark output. ***Figure 2*** *shows the Motion Pro Ignition System Tester (part No. 08-122). This tool is inserted in the spark plug cap and its base is grounded against the cylinder head. The tool's air gap is adjustable, and it allows the visual inspection of the spark while testing the intensity of the spark. This tool is available through motorcycle repair shops.*

2. Cover the spark plug hole with a clean shop cloth to lessen the chance of gasoline vapors being emitted from the hole.
3. Insert the spark plug (**Figure 3**), or spark tester (**Figure 4**), into its plug cap and ground the spark plug base against the cylinder head. Position the spark plug so the electrode is visible.

NOTE

If a spark plug is used, perform the procedure with a new spark plug.

WARNING

Mount the spark plug, or tester, away from the spark plug hole in the cylinder so the spark cannot ignite the gasoline vapors in the cylinder. If the engine is flooded, do not perform this test. The firing of the spark plug can ignite fuel that is ejected through the spark plug hole.

4. Turn the ignition switch to the ON position.

WARNING

*Do **not** hold the spark plug, wire or connector, or a serious electrical shock may result.*

5. Turn the engine over with the electric starter. A crisp blue spark should be evident across the spark plug electrode or spark tester terminals. If there is strong sunlight on the plug, shade the plug by hand to better see the spark.
6. If the spark is good, check for one or more of the following possible malfunctions:
   a. Obstructed fuel line or fuel filter.
   b. Low compression or engine damage.
   c. Flooded engine.
7. If the spark is weak or if there is no spark, refer to *Engine is Difficult to Start* in this chapter.

NOTE

If the engine backfires during starting attempts, the ignition timing may be incorrect due to a defective ignition component. Refer to Ignition Timing in Chapter Three for more information.

Engine is Difficult to Start

Check for one or more of the following possible malfunctions:

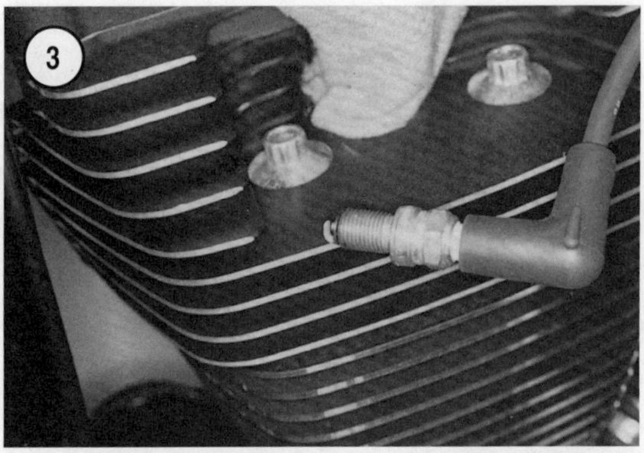

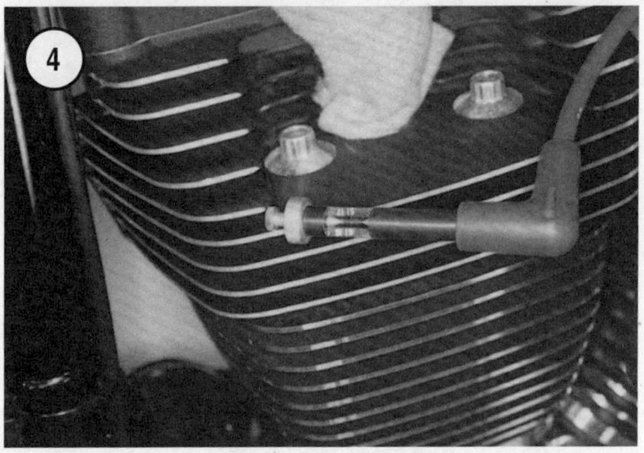

1. Fouled spark plug(s).
2. Improperly adjusted enrichener valve.
3. Intake manifold air leak.
4. A plugged fuel tank filler cap.
5. Clogged carburetor fuel line.
6. Contaminated fuel system.
7. An improperly adjusted carburetor.
8. A defective ignition module.
9. A defective ignition coil.
10. Damaged ignition coil primary and secondary wires (**Figure 5**).
11. Incorrect ignition timing.
12. Low engine compression.
13. Engine oil too heavy (winter temperatures).
14. Discharged battery.
15. A defective starter motor.
16. Loose or corroded starter and/or battery cables.
17. A loose ignition sensor and module electrical connector.
18. Incorrect pushrod length (intake and exhaust valve pushrods interchanged).

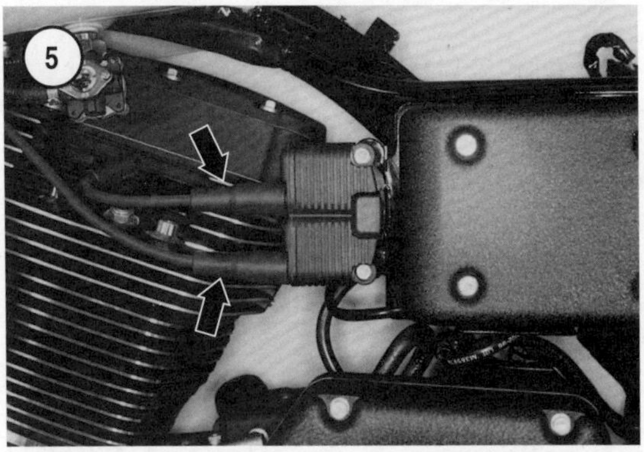

Engine Will Not Crank

Check for one or more of the following possible malfunctions:

1. Ignition switch turned OFF.
2. A defective ignition switch.
3. Run switch in OFF position.
4. A defective engine run switch.
5. Loose or corroded starter and battery cables (solenoid chatters).
6. Discharged or defective battery.
7. A defective starter motor.
8. A defective starter solenoid.
9. A defective starter shaft pinion gear.
10. Slipping overrunning clutch assembly.
11. A seized piston(s).
12. Seized crankshaft bearings.
13. A broken connecting rod.

ENGINE PERFORMANCE

In the following check list, it is assumed that the engine runs, but is not operating at peak performance. This will serve as a starting point from which to isolate a performance malfunction.

Fouled Spark Plugs

If the spark plugs continually foul, check for the following:

1. Severely contaminated air filter element.
2. Incorrect spark plug heat range. See Chapter Three.
3. Rich fuel mixture.
4. Worn or damaged piston rings.
5. Worn or damaged valve guide oil seals.
6. Excessive valve stem-to-guide clearance.
7. Incorrect carburetor float level.

Engine Runs but Misfires

1. Fouled or improperly gapped spark plugs.
2. Damaged spark plug cables.
3. Incorrect ignition timing.
4. Defective ignition components.
5. An obstructed fuel line or fuel shutoff valve.
6. Obstructed fuel filter.
7. Clogged carburetor jets.
8. Loose battery connection.
9. Wiring or connector damage.
10. Water or other contaminants in fuel.
11. Weak or damaged valve springs.
12. Incorrect camshaft/valve timing.
13. A damaged valve(s).
14. Dirty electrical connections.
15. Intake manifold or carburetor air leak.
16. A plugged carburetor vent hose.
17. Plugged fuel tank vent system.

Engine Overheating

1. Incorrect carburetor adjustment or jet selection.
2. Incorrect ignition timing or defective ignition system components.
3. Improper spark plug heat range.
4. Damaged or blocked cooling fins.
5. Low oil level.
6. Oil not circulating properly.
7. Leaking valves.
8. Heavy engine carbon deposits.

Engine Runs Roughly with Excessive Exhaust Smoke

1. Clogged air filter element.
2. Incorrect rich carburetor adjustment.
3. Choke not operating correctly.
4. Water or other contaminants in fuel.
5. Clogged fuel line.
6. Spark plugs fouled.
7. A defective ignition coil.
8. A defective ignition module or sensor(s).
9. Loose or defective ignition circuit wire.
10. Short circuits from damaged wire insulation.
11. Loose battery cable connections.
12. Incorrect camshaft/valve timing.

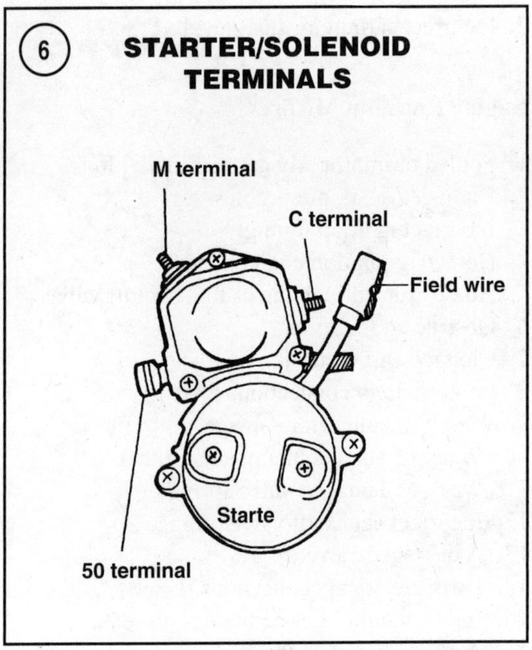

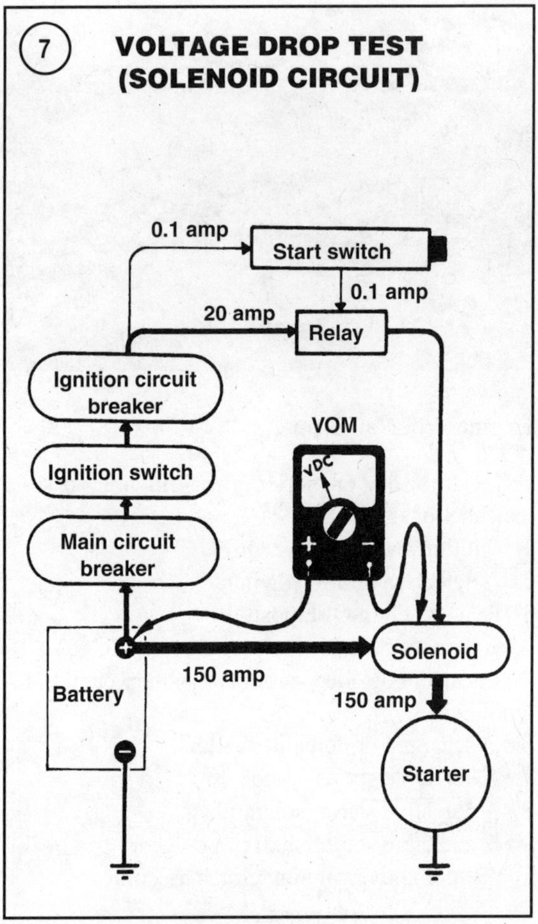

13. Intake manifold or air filter air leaks.

Engine Loses Power

1. Incorrect carburetor (lean) adjustment.
2. Engine overheating.
3. Incorrect ignition timing.
4. Incorrectly gapped spark plugs.
5. An obstructed muffler.
6. Dragging brake(s).

Engine Lacks Acceleration

1. Incorrect carburetor adjustment.
2. Clogged fuel line.
3. Incorrect ignition timing.
4. Dragging brake(s).

Valve Train Noise

1. A bent pushrod(s).
2. A defective hydraulic lifter(s).
3. A bent valve.
4. Rocker arm seizure or damage (binding on shaft).
5. Worn or damaged camshaft gear bushing(s).
6. Worn or damaged camshaft gear(s).

ELECTRIC STARTING SYSTEM

The starting system consists of the battery, starter motor, starter relay, solenoid, start switch, starter mechanism and related wiring.

When the ignition switch is turned on and the start button is pushed in, current is transmitted from the battery to the starter relay. When the relay is activated, it in turn activates the starter solenoid that mechanically engages the starter with the engine.

Starting system problems are most often related to a loose or corroded electrical connection.

Refer to **Figure 6** for starter motor and solenoid terminal identification.

Troubleshooting Preparation

Before troubleshooting the starting system, check the following:

1. Make sure the battery is fully charged.

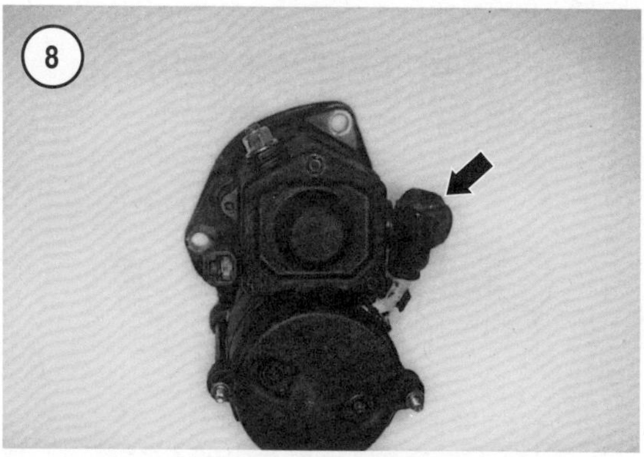

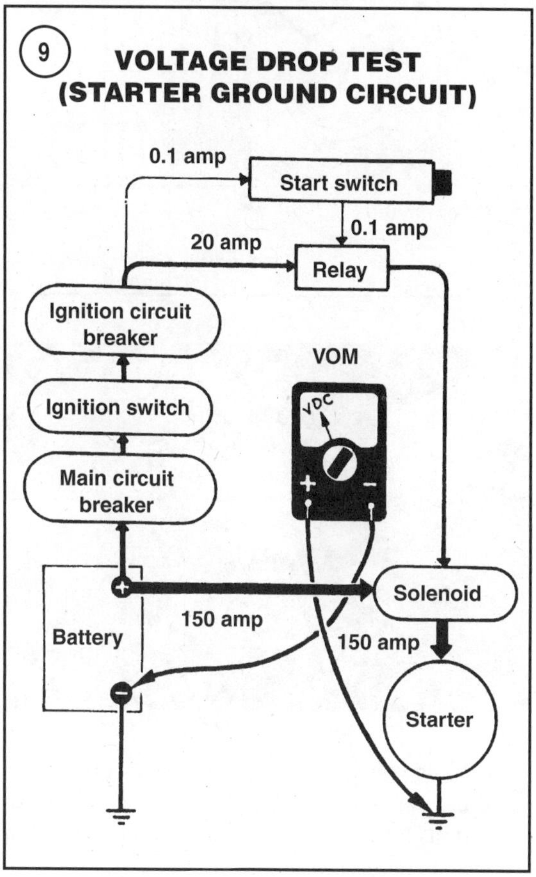

2. Battery cables are the proper size and length. Replace damaged or undersized cables.

3. All electrical connections are clean and tight. High resistance caused from dirty or loose connectors can affect voltage and current levels.

4. The wiring harness is in good condition, with no worn or frayed insulation or loose harness sockets.

5. The fuel tank is filled with an adequate supply of fresh gasoline.

6. The spark plugs are in good condition and properly gapped.

7. The ignition system is working correctly.

Voltage Drop Test

Before performing the steps listed under *Troubleshooting*, perform this voltage drop test. These steps will help find weak or damaged electrical components that may be causing the starting system problem. A voltmeter is required to test voltage drop.

1. To check voltage drop in the solenoid circuit, connect the positive voltmeter lead to the positive battery terminal; connect the negative voltmeter lead to the solenoid (**Figure 7**).

NOTE

The voltmeter lead must not touch the starter-to-solenoid terminal. ***Figure 8*** *shows the solenoid terminal with the starter/solenoid removed to better illustrate the step.*

2. Turn the ignition switch on and push the starter button while reading the voltmeter scale. Note the following:

   a. The circuit is operating correctly if the voltmeter reading is 2 volts or less. A voltmeter reading of 12 volts indicates an open circuit.
   b. A voltage drop of more than 2 volts shows a problem in the solenoid circuit.
   c. If the voltage drop reading is correct, continue with Step 3.

3. To check the starter motor ground circuit, connect the negative voltmeter lead to the negative battery terminal; connect the positive voltmeter lead to the starter motor housing (**Figure 9**).

4. Turn the ignition switch on and push the starter button while reading the voltmeter scale. The voltage drop must not exceed 0.2 volts. If it does, check the ground connections between the meter leads.

5. If the problem is not found, refer to *Troubleshooting* in the following section.

NOTE

Steps 3 and 4 check the voltage drop across the starter motor ground circuit. Repeat this test to check any ground circuit in the starting circuit. To do so, leave the negative voltmeter lead connected to the battery and con-

nect the positive voltmeter lead to the ground in question.

Troubleshooting

The basic starter related troubles are:

1. Starter motor does not spin.
2. Starter motor spins but does not engage.
3. The starter motor will not disengage after the start button is released.
4. Loud grinding noises when starter motor turns.
5. Starter motor stalls or spins too slowly.

Perform the steps listed under *Troubleshooting Preparation*. The following test results must be within 1/2 volt of battery voltage.

CAUTION

Never operate the starter motor for more than 30 seconds at a time. Allow the starter to cool before reusing it. Failing to allow the starter motor to cool after continuous starting attempts can damage the starter.

Starter motor does not spin

1. Turn the ignition switch on and push the starter button while listening for a click at the starter relay in the electrical panel. Turn the ignition switch off and note the following:
   a. If the starter relay clicks, test the starter relay as described under *Component Testing* in this section. If the starter relay test readings are correct, continue with Step 2.
   b. If the solenoid clicks, go to Step 3.
   c. If there was no click, go to Step 6.
2. Check the wiring connectors between the starter relay and solenoid. Note the following:
   a. Repair any dirty, loose fitting or damaged connectors or wiring.
   b. If the wiring is okay, remove the starter motor as described in Chapter Eight. Perform the solenoid and starter motor bench tests described in this section.
3. Perform a voltage drop test between the battery and solenoid terminals as described under *Voltage Drop Tests* in this section. The normal voltage drop is less than 2 volts. Note the following:
   a. If the voltage drop is less than 2 volts, perform Step 4.

10 STARTER JUMP TEST

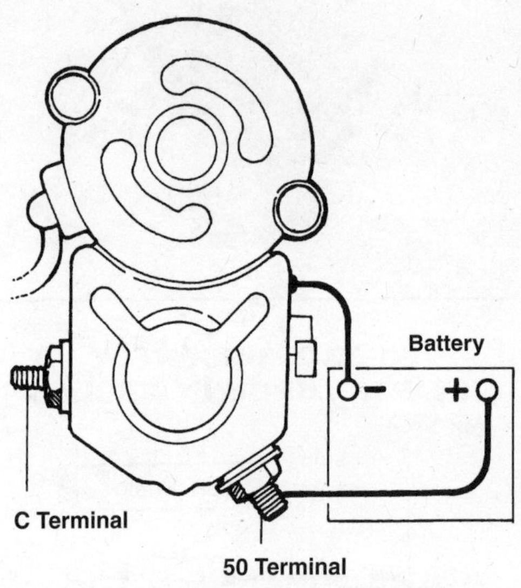

11

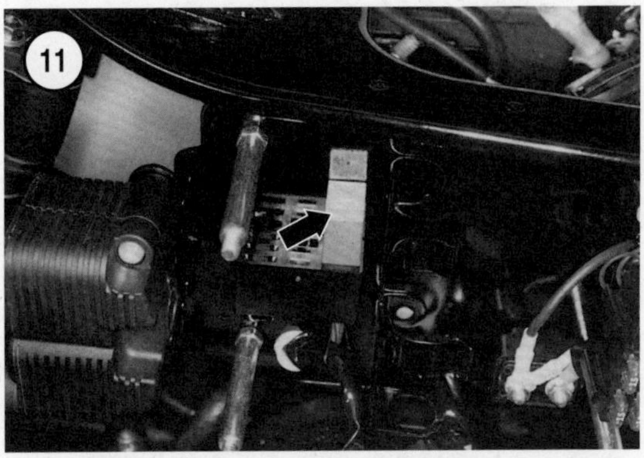

   b. If the voltage drop is more than 2 volts, check the solenoid and battery wires and connections for dirty or loose fitting terminals; clean and repair as required.
4. Remove the starter motor as described in Chapter Eight. Momentarily connect a fully charged 12-volt battery to the starter motor as shown in **Figure 10**. If the starter motor is operational, it will turn when connected to the battery. Disconnect the battery and note the following:
   a. If the starter motor turns, perform the solenoid pull-in and hold-in tests as described under *Solenoid Testing (Bench Tests)* in this section.

   b. If the starter motor does not turn, disassemble the starter motor as described in Chapter Eight, and check it for opens, shorts and grounds.

5. If the problem is not evident after performing Steps 3 and 4, check the starter shaft to see if it is binding at the jackshaft. Check the jackshaft for binding or damage. Refer to *Starter Jackshaft* in Chapter Five.

6. If there is no click when performing Step 1, measure voltage between the starter button and the starter relay. The voltmeter must read battery voltage. Note the following:
   a. If battery voltage is noted, continue with Step 7.
   b. If there is no voltage, go to Step 8.

7. Check the starter relay ground at the starter relay (**Figure 11**). Note the following:
   a. If the starter relay is properly grounded, test the starter relay as described in this section.
   b. If the starter relay is not grounded, check the ground connection. Repair the ground connection, then retest.

8. Check for voltage at the starter button. Note the following:
   a. If there is voltage at the starter button, test the starter relay as described in this section.
   b. If there is no voltage at the starter button, check continuity across the starter button. If there is voltage leading to the starter button but no voltage leaving the starter button, replace the button switch and retest. If there is no voltage leading to the starter button, check the starter button wiring for dirty or loose-fitting terminals or damaged wiring; clean and/or repair as required.

Starter motor spins but does not engage

If the starter motor spins but the pinion gear does not engage the ring gear, perform the following:

1. Remove the outer primary cover as described in Chapter Five.
2. Check the pinion gear (A, **Figure 12**) mounted on the end of the jackshaft. If the teeth are chipped or worn, inspect the clutch ring gear (B, **Figure 12**) for the same problems. Note the following:
   a. If the pinion gear and ring gear are damaged, service these parts as described in Chapter Five.
   b. If the pinion gear and ring gear are not damaged, continue with Step 3.
3. Remove and disassemble the starter motor as described in Chapter Eight. Then check the overrunning clutch assembly (**Figure 13**) for:
   a. Roller damage (**Figure 14**).
   b. Compression spring damage (A, **Figure 15**).
   c. Excessively worn or damaged pinion teeth.
   d. Pinion does not run in overrunning direction.
   e. Damaged clutch shaft splines (B, **Figure 15**).

f. Damaged overrunning clutch assembly (**Figure 16**).

4. Replace worn or damaged parts as required.

Starter motor will not disengage after the start button is released

1. A sticking solenoid, caused by a worn solenoid compression spring (A, **Figure 15**), can cause this problem. Replace the solenoid if damaged.
2. On high-mileage vehicles, the pinion gear (A, **Figure 12**) can jam on a worn clutch ring gear (B, **Figure 12**). Unable to return, the starter will continue to run. This condition usually requires ring gear replacement.
3. Check the start switch and starter relay (**Figure 11**) for internal damage. Test the start switch as described under *Switches* in Chapter Eight. Test the starter relay as described in this chapter.

Loud grinding noises when the starter motor turns

Incorrect pinion gear and clutch ring gear engagement (**Figure 12**) or a broken overrunning clutch mechanism (**Figure 16**) can cause this problem. Remove and inspect the starter motor as described in Chapter Eight.

Starter motor stalls or spins too slowly

1. Perform a voltage drop test between the battery and solenoid terminals as described under *Voltage Drop Tests* in this section. The normal voltage drop is less than 2 volts. Note the following:
   a. If the voltage drop is less than 2 volts, continue with Step 2.
   b. If the voltage drop exceeds 2 volts, check the solenoid and battery wires and connections for dirty or loose-fitting terminals; clean and repair as required.
2. Perform a voltage drop test between the solenoid terminals and the starter motor as described under *Voltage Drop Tests* in this section. The normal voltage drop is less than 2 volts. Note the following:
   a. If the voltage drop is less than 2 volts, continue with Step 3.
   b. If the voltage drop exceeds 2 volts, check the solenoid and starter motor wires and connections for dirty or loose-fitting terminals; clean and repair as required.

15

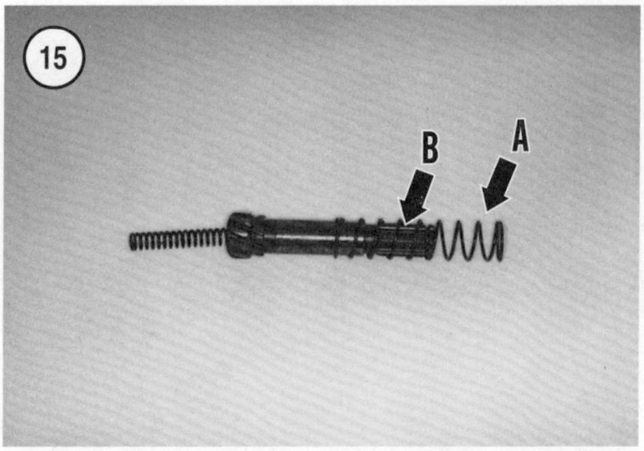

16

17

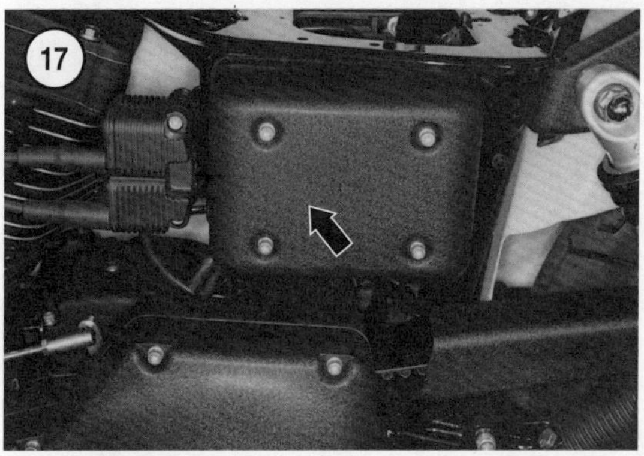

3. Perform a voltage drop test between the battery ground wire and the starter motor as described under *Voltage Drop Tests* in this section. The normal voltage drop is less than 0.2 volts. Note the following:
   a. If the voltage drop is less than 0.2 volts, continue with Step 4.
   b. If the voltage drop exceeds 0.2 volts, check the battery ground wire connections for dirty or loose-fitting terminals; clean and repair as required.

18

19

20

STARTER RELAY

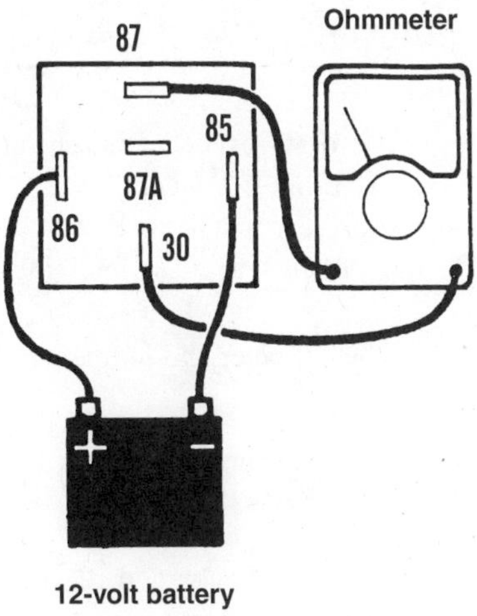

4. Perform the *Starter Current Draw Test* in this section. Note the following:
   a. If the current draw is excessive, check for a damaged starter motor or starter drive assembly. Remove the starter motor as described in Chapter Eight and perform the *Free Running Current Draw Test* in this section.
   b. If the current draw reading is correct, continue with Step 5.
5. Remove the outer primary cover as described in Chapter Five. Check the pinion gear (A, **Figure 12**). If the teeth are chipped or worn, inspect the clutch ring gear (B, **Figure 12**) for the same problem.
   a. If the pinion gear and ring gear are damaged, service these parts as described in Chapter Five.
   b. If the pinion gear and ring gear are not damaged, continue with Step 6.
6. Remove and disassemble the starter motor as described in Chapter Eight. Check the disassembled starter motor for opens, shorts and grounds.

Component Testing

The following sections describe how to test individual starting system components. Refer to Chapter Eight for starter service.

Starter Relay Removal/Testing/Installation

Check the starter relay operation with an ohmmeter, jumper wires and a fully charged 12-volt battery.

NOTE
Do not loosen the electrical panel screws. They are trapped within the mounting pin and do not have to be removed.

1. Carefully pull out and remove the electric panel cover (**Figure 17**).
2. Remove the nuts securing the outer panel (**Figure 18**) and remove the outer panel.
3. Disconnect and remove the starter relay (**Figure 19**) from the starting circuit.
4. Connect an ohmmeter and 12-volt battery between the relay terminals shown in **Figure 20**. This setup will energize the relay for testing.

5. Check for continuity through the relay contacts using an ohmmeter while the relay coil is energized. The correct reading is 0 ohms. If resistance is excessive or if there is no continuity, replace the relay.
6. If the starter relay passes this test, reconnect the relay.
7. Install the outer panel (**Figure 18**) and tighten the nuts.
8. Correctly position the electrical panel cover with the *This side down* label facing down (**Figure 21**).
9. Carefully push the electric panel cover (**Figure 17**) back into position. Push it on until it bottoms.

Starter Motor Current Draw Tests

The following current draw test measures current (amperage) that the starter circuit requires to crank the engine. Refer to **Table 1** for current draw specifications.

A short circuit in the starter motor or a damaged pinion gear assembly can cause excessive current draw. If the current draw is low, suspect an undercharged battery or an open circuit in the starting circuit.

Current draw test (starter motor mounted on the engine)

NOTE
This test requires a fully charged battery and an inductive ammeter.

1. Shift the transmission into NEUTRAL.
2. Disconnect the two spark plug caps from the spark plugs. Then ground the plug caps with two extra spark plugs. Do *not* remove the spark plugs from the cylinder heads.
3. Connect an inductive ammeter between the starter motor terminal and positive battery terminal (**Figure 22**). Connect a jumper cable from the negative battery terminal to ground (**Figure 22**).
4. Turn the ignition switch on and press the start button for approximately 10 seconds. Note the ammeter reading.

NOTE
The current draw is high when the start button is first pressed, then it will drop and stabilize at a lower reading. Refer to the lower stabilized reading during this test.

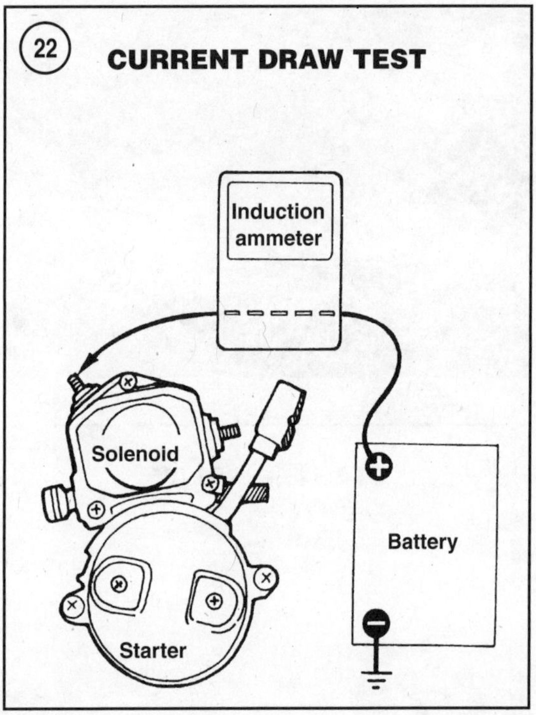

5. If the current draw exceeds the current draw specification in **Table 1**, check for a defective starter or starter drive mechanism. Remove and service these components as described in Chapter Eight.
6. Disconnect the ammeter and jumper cables.

Current draw test (starter motor removed from the engine)

This test requires a fully charged 12-volt battery, an inductive ammeter, a jumper wire (14 gauge minimum) and 3 jumper cables (6 gauge minimum).

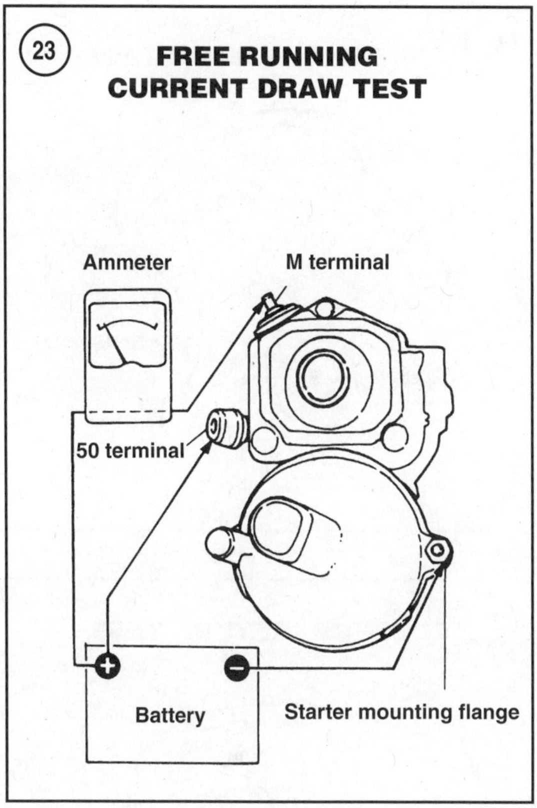

1. Remove the starter motor as described in Chapter Eight.

NOTE
The solenoid must be installed on the starter motor during the following tests.

2. Mount the starter motor in a vise with soft jaws.
3. Connect the 14-gauge jumper cable between the positive battery terminal and the solenoid 50 terminal (**Figure 23**).
4. Connect a jumper cable (6-gauge minimum) between the positive battery terminal and the ammeter (**Figure 23**).
5. Connect the second jumper cable between the ammeter and the M terminal on the starter solenoid (**Figure 23**).
6. Connect the third jumper cable between the battery ground terminal and the starter motor mounting flange (**Figure 23**).
7. Read the ammeter, the correct ammeter reading is 90 amps. A damaged pinion gear assembly will cause an excessively high current draw reading. If the current draw reading is low, check for an undercharged battery or an open field winding or armature in the starter motor.

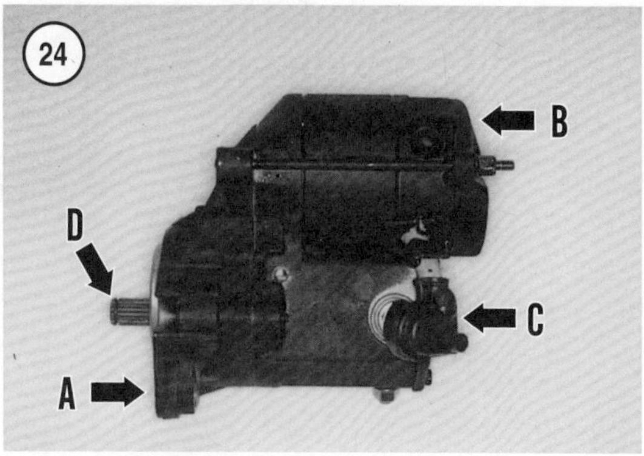

Solenoid Testing (Bench Tests)

This test requires a fully charged 12-volt battery and three jumper wires.

1. Remove the starter motor (A, **Figure 24**) as described in Chapter Nine.

NOTE
*The solenoid (B, **Figure 24**) must be installed on the starter motor during the following tests. Do not remove it.*

2. Disconnect the C field wire terminal (C, **Figure 24**) from the solenoid before performing the following tests. Insulate the end of the wire terminal so that it cannot short out on any of the test connectors.

CAUTION
Because battery voltage is being applied directly to the solenoid and starter in the following tests, do not leave the jumper cables connected to the solenoid for more than 3-5 seconds; otherwise, the voltage will damage the solenoid.

NOTE
Thoroughly read the following procedure to familiarize and understand the procedures and test connections. Then perform the tests in the order listed and without interruption.

3. Perform the solenoid pull-in test as follows:

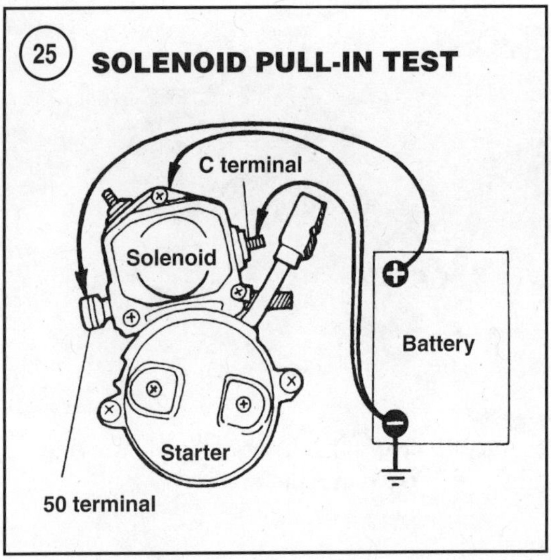

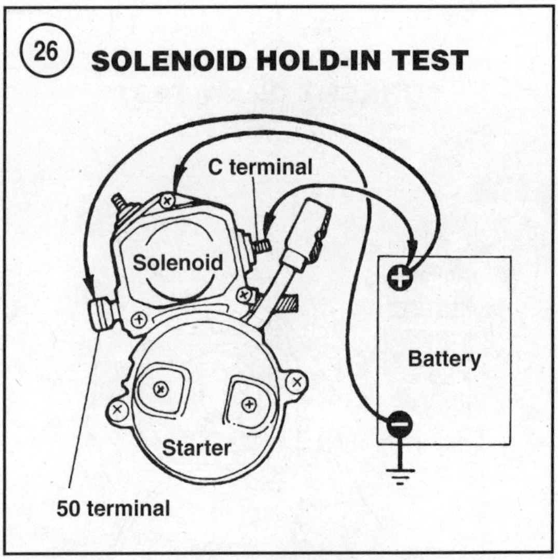

a. Connect 1 jumper wire from the negative battery terminal to the solenoid C terminal (**Figure 25**).

b. Connect 1 jumper wire from the negative battery terminal to the solenoid housing (ground) (**Figure 25**).

c. Touch a jumper wire from the positive battery terminal to the starter 50 terminal (**Figure 25**). The pinion shaft (D, **Figure 24**) must pull into the housing.

d. Leave the jumper wires connected and continue with Step 4.

4. To perform the solenoid hold-in test, perform the following:

a. With the pinion shaft pulled in (Step 3), disconnect the C terminal jumper wire from the negative battery terminal and connect it to the positive battery terminal (**Figure 26**). The pinion shaft will remain in the housing. If the pinion shaft returns to its out position, replace the solenoid.

b. Leave the jumper wires connected and continue with Step 5.

5. To perform the solenoid return test, perform the following:

a. Disconnect the jumper wire from the starter 50 terminal (**Figure 27**); the pinion shaft must return to its out position.

b. Disconnect all of the jumper wires from the solenoid and battery.

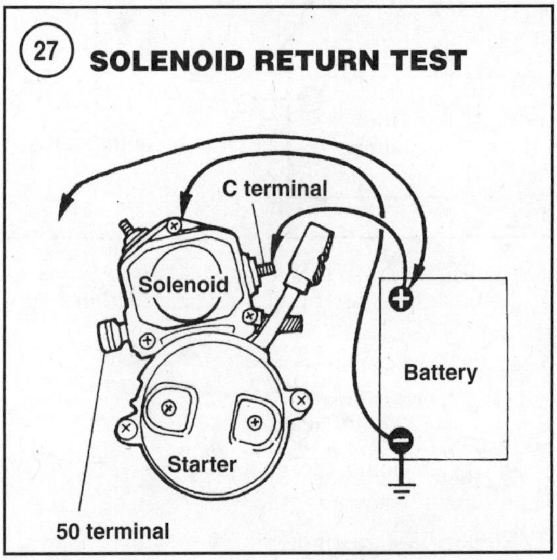

6. Replace the solenoid if the starter shaft failed to operate as described in Steps 3-5. See *Solenoid Replacement* in Chapter Eight.

CHARGING SYSTEM

The charging system consists of the battery, alternator and a solid state rectifier/voltage regulator.

The alternator generates alternating current (AC) which the rectifier converts to direct current (DC). The regulator maintains the voltage to the battery at a constant level despite variations in engine speed and load.

28

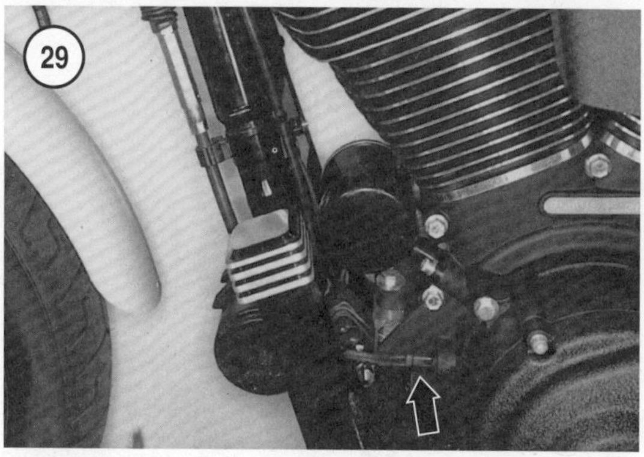

29

A malfunction in the charging system generally causes the battery to remain undercharged.

Service Precautions

Before servicing the charging system, observe the following precautions to prevent damage to any charging system component.

1. Never reverse battery connections.
2. Do not short across any connection.
3. Never start the engine with the alternator disconnected from the voltage regulator/rectifier, unless instructed to do so during testing.
4. Never attempt to start or run the engine with the battery disconnected.
5. Never attempt to use a high-output battery charger to help start the engine.
6. Before charging the battery, remove it from the motorcycle as described in Chapter Eight.
7. Never disconnect the voltage regulator/rectifier connector with the engine running. The voltage regulator/rectifier (**Figure 28**) is mounted on the front frame down tubes.
8. Do not mount the voltage regulator/rectifier unit in another location.
9. Make sure the negative battery terminal is connected to the engine and frame.

Troubleshooting

If the battery is discharged, perform the following procedure.

1. Test the battery as described in Chapter Eight. Charge the battery if required. If the battery will hold a charge, continue with Step 2.
2. Perform the regulator ground test.

Testing

If charging system trouble is suspected, first check the battery charge. Clean and test the battery as described in Chapter Eight. If the battery is fully charged, test the charging system as follows.

If the battery discharges while riding the motorcycle, perform the *Voltage Regulator/Rectifier Test*. Also refer to *Current Drain Test (Battery Discharges While Riding the Motorcycle)*.

If the battery discharges while the motorcycle is not running, perform the *Current Drain Test (Battery Discharges While the Motorcycle is Not Running)* test.

Voltage Regulator Ground Test

The voltage regulator base (**Figure 28**) must be grounded to the frame for proper operation.

1. Switch an ohmmeter to the R×1 scale.
2. Connect one ohmmeter lead to a good engine or frame ground and the other ohmmeter lead to the regulator base. Read the ohmmeter scale. The correct reading is 0 ohm. Note the following:
   a. If there is low resistance (0 ohm), the voltage regulator is properly grounded.
   b. If there is high resistance, remove the voltage regulator and clean its frame mounting points.
3. Check that the voltage regulator connector plug (**Figure 29**) is clean and tightly connected.

Voltage Regulator Bleed Test

This test requires a 12-volt test lamp. This tool relies on the vehicle's battery to supply power to the component being tested.

1. Disconnect the voltage regulator connector from the engine crankcase (**Figure 29**).

NOTE
Do not disconnect the wire from the voltage regulator to the 30-amp circuit breaker.

2. Connect one test lamp probe to a good frame or engine ground.
3. Connect the other test lamp probe to one of the voltage regulator pins, then to the other pin.
4. If the test lamp lights, replace the voltage regulator.
5. If the voltage regulator passes this test, reconnect the voltage regulator connector at the engine crankcase.

Current Drain Test (Battery Discharges While the Motorcycle is Not Running)

Accessory items that require voltage when the engine is not running will eventually drain the battery. Perform the following steps to check current drain when the ignition switch and all of the lights are turned off. A drain that exceeds 3 milliamperes (mA) will discharge the battery. This test requires a fully charged 12-volt battery.

1. Disconnect the negative battery cable from the battery.
2. Connect an ammeter between the negative battery terminal and the battery ground cable as shown in **Figure 30**.
3. With the ignition switch, lights and all accessories turned off, read the ammeter. If the current drain exceeds 3 mA, continue with Step 4.
4. Refer to the wiring diagram at the end of the manual, for the model being worked on. Check the charging system wires and connectors for shorts or other damage.
5. Unplug each electrical connector separately and check for a change in the meter reading. If the meter reading changes after disconnecting a connector, the damaged circuit has been found. Check the electrical connectors carefully before testing the individual component.
6. After completing the test, disconnect the ammeter and reconnect the negative battery cable.

30 CHECKING CURRENT DRAW WITH IGNITION SWITCH OFF

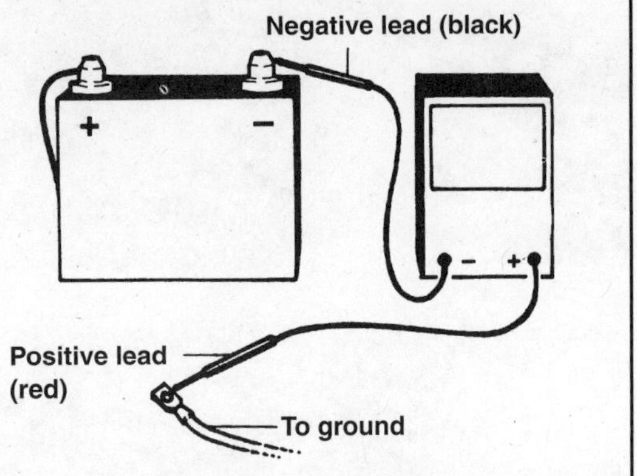

31 LOAD TEST

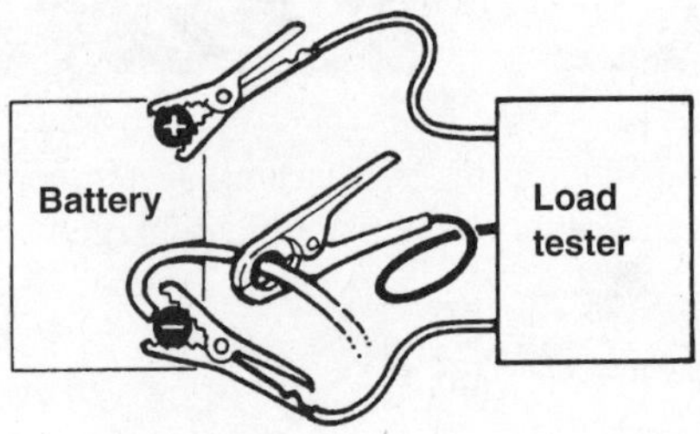

Current Drain Test (Battery Discharges While Riding the Motorcycle)

This test measures the current draw or load of the motorcycle's electrical system. A load tester is required for this test. Perform this test if the battery keeps being discharged, yet the charging system is working correctly.

The charging system is designed to provide current to meet the demands of the original equipment

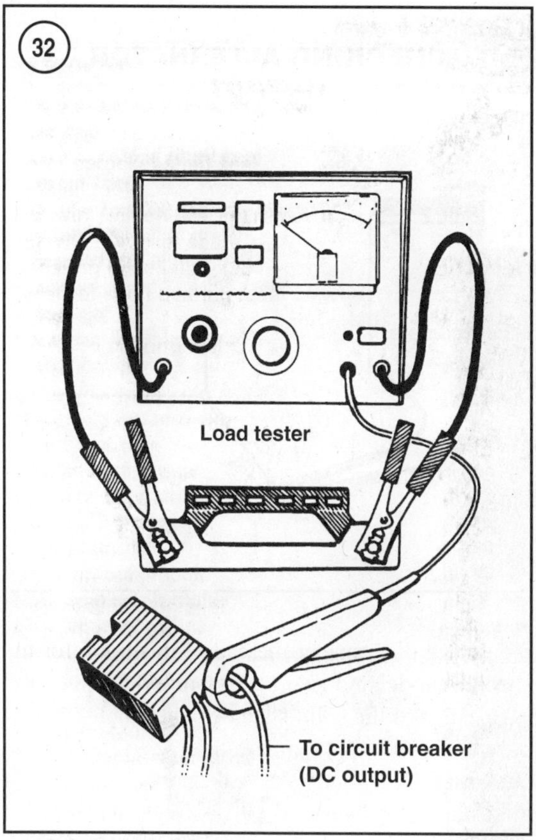

(OE) installed on the motorcycle. If aftermarket accessories have been installed, the increased current demand may exceed the charging systems capacity and result in a discharged battery.

NOTE

When using a load tester, read and follow its manufacturer's instructions. To prevent tester damage from overheating, do not leave the load switch ON for more than 20 seconds at a time.

1. Connect a load tester to the battery as shown in **Figure 31**.
2. Turn the ignition switch ON (but do not start the engine). Then turn on *all* electrical accessories and switch the headlight beam to HIGH.
3. Read the ampere reading (current draw) on the load tester and compare it to the test results obtained in the *Charging System Output Test* in this chapter. The charging system output test results (current reading) must exceed the current draw by 3.5 amps for the battery to remain sufficiently charged.
4. If aftermarket accessories have been added to the motorcycle, disconnect them and repeat Step 2. If the current draw is now within the specification, the problem is with the additional accessories.
5. If no accessories have been added to the motorcycle, a short circuit may be causing the battery to discharge.

2

Charging System Output Test

This test requires a load tester.

1. To perform this test, the battery must be fully charged.

NOTE

When using a load tester, read and follow its manufacturer's instructions. To prevent tester damage from overheating, do not leave the load switch ON for more than 20 seconds at a time.

2. Connect the load tester negative and positive leads to the battery terminals. Then place the load tester's induction pickup over the wire connecting the 30 amp circuit breaker to the voltage regulator (**Figure 32**).
3. Start the engine and slowly bring the speed up to 2000 rpm while reading the load tester scale. With the engine running at 3000 rpm, operate the load tester switch until the voltage scale reads 13.0 volts. The tester must show an alternator current output reading of 26-32 amps.
4. With the engine still running at 3000 rpm, turn the load switch off and read the load tester voltage scale. Battery voltage must not exceed 15 volts. Turn the engine off and disconnect the load tester from the motorcycle.
5. Perform the *Stator Test* described in this chapter. If the stator tests acceptable a defective voltage regulator/rectifier (**Figure 28**) or a wiring short circuit is indicated.

Make sure to eliminate the possibility of a poor connection or damaged wiring before replacing the voltage regulator/rectifier.

Stator Test

1. With the ignition switch turned OFF, disconnect the regulator/rectifier connector from the crankcase (**Figure 29**).

33

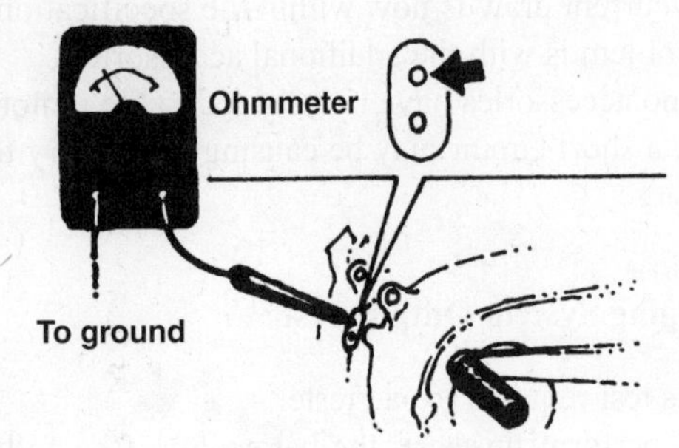

34

CHECKING ALTERNATOR OUTPUT

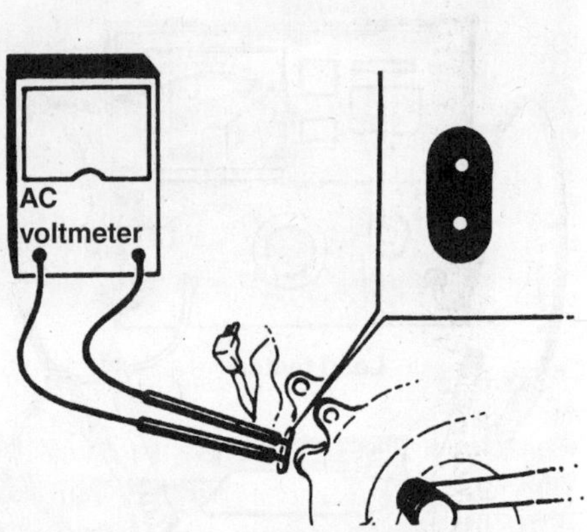

2. Switch an ohmmeter to its R×1 scale. Then connect it between either stator socket, at the crankcase, and ground (**Figure 33**). The correct ohmmeter reading is infinity. Any other reading suggests a grounded stator. Repeat this test for the other stator socket.
3. Switch an ohmmeter to its R×1 scale. Then connect it between both stator sockets (at the crankcase). The correct ohmmeter reading is 0.1-0.2 ohm. If resistance is not as specified, replace the stator.
4. Check stator AC voltage output as follows:
   a. Connect an AC voltmeter across the stator pins as shown in **Figure 34**.
   b. Start the engine and slowly increase engine speed. The correct voltmeter reading is 16-20 volts AC per each 1000 rpm. For example, if the engine is running at 2000 rpm, the correct AC output reading is 32-40 volts AC.

NOTE

Figure 35 *is shown with the engine removed to better illustrate the step.*

   c. If the AC voltage output reading is below the specified range, the trouble is probably a defective stator (**Figure 35**) or rotor. If these parts are not damaged, perform the *Charging System Output Test* in this section.
5. Reconnect the regulator/rectifier connector.

IGNITION SYSTEM

All models are equipped with a transistorized ignition system. This solid state system uses no contact breaker points or other moving parts. Refer to the wiring diagrams at the end of this book for the specific model and year being worked on.

Because of the solid state design, problems with the transistorized system are rare. If a problem occurs, it generally causes a weak spark or no spark at all. An ignition system with a weak spark or no spark is relatively easy to troubleshoot. It is difficult, however, to troubleshoot an ignition system that only malfunctions when the engine is hot or under load.

All models are equipped with an on-board diagnostic system. Troubleshooting this system by non Harley-Davidson personnel is limited to trouble code retrieval.

Retrieving the trouble code(s) will indicate where a fault(s) has occurred. Further testing requires several Harley-Davidson special tools that are available *only* to H-D dealers.

If a fault has occurred, have the diagnostic procedures performed at a H-D dealership.

NOTE

The H-D Scanalyzer and Breakout Box are not available for purchase.

Ignition System Precautions

Certain measures must be taken to protect the ignition system.

1. Never disconnect any of the electrical connectors while the engine is running.

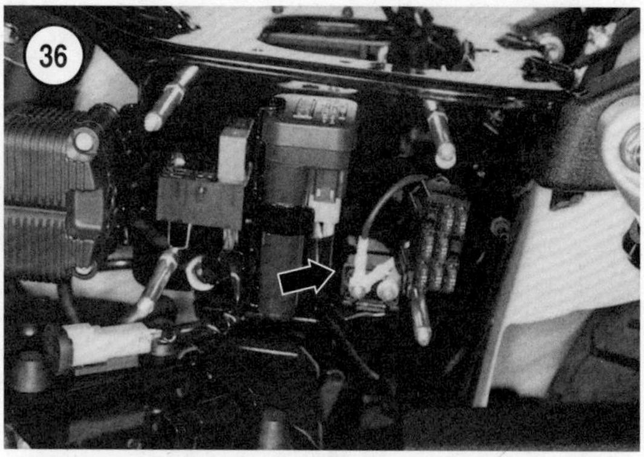

2. Apply dielectric grease to all electrical connectors prior to reconnecting them. This will help seal out moisture.
3. Make sure all electrical connectors are free of corrosion and are completely coupled to each other.
4. The ignition module must always be mounted securely to the backside of the electrical panel.

Troubleshooting Preparation

1. Refer to the wiring diagram for the specific model being worked on at the end of this book when performing the following.
2. Check the wiring harness for visible signs of damage.
3. Make sure all connectors are properly attached to each other and locked in place.
4. Check all electrical components for a good ground to the engine.
5. Check all wiring for short circuits or open circuits.
6. Check for a damaged ignition circuit breaker (**Figure 36**) located behind the electric panel.
7. Make sure the fuel tank has an adequate supply of fresh gasoline.
8. Check spark plug cable routing and their connections at the spark plugs. If there is no spark or only a weak one, repeat the test with new spark plugs. If the condition remains the same with new spark plugs and if all external wiring connections are good, the problem is most likely in the ignition system. If a strong spark is present, the problem is probably not in the ignition system. Check the fuel system.
9. Remove the spark plugs and examine them as described in Chapter Three.

Diagnostic Trouble Codes

The Dyna-Glide on-board diagnostic system identifies faults and stores this information as a two-digit diagnostic trouble code. If more than one fault is found it also sets that fault.

If a trouble code has been set, the check-engine light will come on. During normal operation, the check engine light will illuminate for approximately four seconds when the ignition is turned ON. The check-engine light then turns off and remains off. If a diagnostic trouble code(s) has been set, the check-engine light turns on for four seconds, turns off, and then turns back on for eight seconds or remains on beyond the eight second period.

Trouble codes are retrieved by counting the number of times the check-engine light flashes.

Diagnostic Trouble Codes (Retrieving)

Diagnostic trouble codes are displayed as a series of flashes at the check-engine light on the speedometer face. To retrieve the stored codes, a jumper wire made of 18-gauge wire and two Deutsch sockets (H-D part No. 72191-94), as shown in **Figure 37**, are required

To retrieve the diagnostic trouble code(s), perform the following:

1. Remove the seat as described in Chapter Thirteen.

NOTE
Do not loosen the electrical panel screws. They are trapped within the mounting pin and do not have to be removed.

37

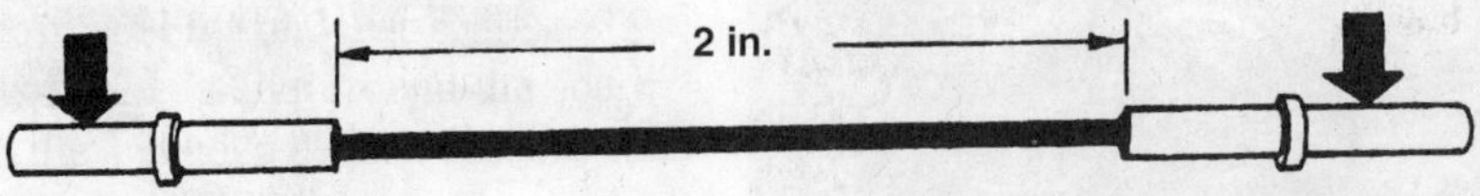

2. Carefully pull out and remove the electric panel cover (**Figure 17**).

3. Remove the nuts securing the outer panel (**Figure 18**) and remove the outer panel.

4. Remove the data link connector (A, **Figure 38**) from the holder on the electrical panel.

5. Remove the protective cover (B, **Figure 38**) from the data link connector.

6. Install the jumper wire onto pins No. 1 (light green/red) and No. 2 (black) on the data link connector (**Figure 39**).

7. Turn the ignition switch to the ON position. After approximately eight seconds, the different systems enter the diagnostic codes.

   a. The check engine light begins with a ready signal, which is a series of six rapid flashes, approximately three per second. The ready signal indicates that the check engine light is ready to flash a diagnostic trouble code.
   b. This is followed by a two-second pause.
   c. The system then flashes the first digit of the stored diagnostic trouble code. The check-engine light will illuminate for one second and then turn off for one second. Count the number of flashes and record the number. For example, two blinks indicates the first digit is two.
   d. The system will pause for two seconds and then flash the second digit of the diagnostic trouble code. Count the number of flashes, and record this number. For example, five blinks indicates the second digit is five. This indicates that the first trouble code is twenty five, or a problem with the rear ignition coil.
   e. If more than one trouble code is present, the system will pause for two seconds and then flash the ready signal, which is a series of six rapid flashes. It is now ready to flash the next trouble code.

38

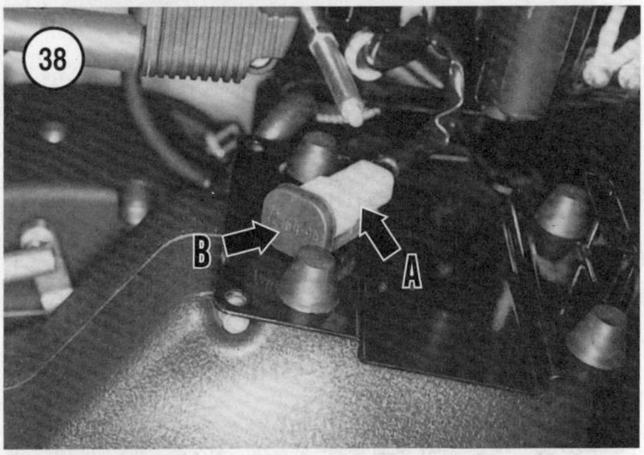

39

   f. The system will pause for two seconds, and then flashes the first digit of the next diagnostic trouble code, followed by the second digit.

8. The system displays the stored codes, sequentially, one at a time, until each diagnostic trouble code has been displayed. The system then repeats. The check-engine light will continue to flash out stored codes until the jumper wire is disconnected. When the codes repeat, this indicates that all stored codes have been displayed. Turn the ignition switch to the OFF position and remove the jumper wire from the data link connector.

9. Refer to **Table 3** for diagnostic trouble codes, and check the component indicated. If multiple codes have been sent, troubleshoot the lowest numbered code first. The source of subsequent codes may be the same malfunction that has caused the first.

10. Install the protective cover onto the data link connector (B, **Figure 38**) and fit the data link connector (A, **Figure 38**) onto the holder on the electrical panel.

11. Install the outer panel (**Figure 18**) and tighten the nuts.

12. Correctly position the electrical panel cover with the *This side down* label facing down (**Figure 21**).

13. Carefully push the electric panel cover (**Figure 17**) back into position. Push it on until it bottoms.

14. Install the seat.

Diagnostic Trouble Codes (Clearing)

The trouble codes can only be cleared by a Harley-Davidson dealership.

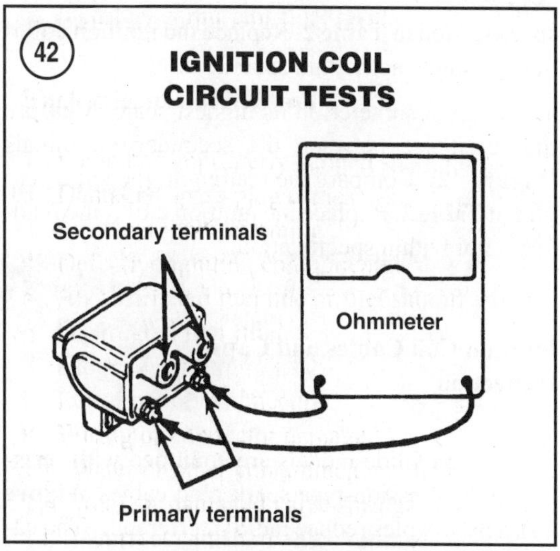

Ignition Module Testing and Replacement

If the ignition module is suspected of being defective, have it tested by a H-D dealership before purchasing a replacement. The cost of the test will not exceed the cost of replacing an ignition module that may not repair the problem. Most parts suppliers will not accept returns on electrical components.

Ignition Coil Testing

Use an ohmmeter to check the ignition coil secondary and primary resistance. Test the coil twice: first when it is cold (room temperature) and then at normal operating temperature. If the engine will not start, heat the coil with a hair dryer, then test with the ohmmeter.

1. Remove the seat as described in Chapter Thirteen.

2. Disconnect the secondary (**Figure 40**) and primary wire connector (**Figure 41**) from the ignition coil.

NOTE

When switching between ohmmeter scales in the following tests, always cross the test leads and zero the needle to assure a correct reading (analog meter only).

3. Set an ohmmeter on R × 1. Measure the ignition coil primary resistance between the coil primary terminals (**Figure 42**). Compare the reading to the

specification in **Table 2**. Replace the ignition coil if the reading is not within specification.

4. Set the ohmmeter on its highest scale. Measure the resistance between the secondary terminals (**Figure 42**). Compare the reading to the specification in **Table 2**. Replace the ignition coil if the reading is not within specification.

Ignition Coil Cables and Caps Inspection

All Dyna Glide models are equipped with resistor- or suppression-type spark plug cables (**Figure 43**). These cables reduce radio interference. The cable's conductor consists of a carbon-impregnated fabric core material instead of solid wire.

If a plug cable becomes damaged, either due to corrosion or conductor breaks, its resistance increases. Excessive cable resistance will cause engine misfire and other ignition or driveability problems.

When troubleshooting the ignition system, inspect the spark plug cables (**Figure 44**) for:

1. Corroded or damaged connector ends.
2. Breaks in the cable insulation that could allow arcing.
3. Split or damaged plug caps that could allow arcing to the cylinder heads.

Replace damaged or questionable spark plug cables.

FUEL SYSTEM

Many riders automatically assume that the carburetor is at fault when the engine does not run properly. While fuel system problems are not uncommon, carburetor adjustment is seldom the answer. In many cases, adjusting will only compound the problem by making the engine run worse.

Begin fuel system troubleshooting with the fuel tank and work through the system, reserving the carburetor as the final point. Most fuel system problems result from an empty fuel tank, a plugged fuel filter or fuel valve, sour fuel, a dirty air filter or clogged carburetor jets.

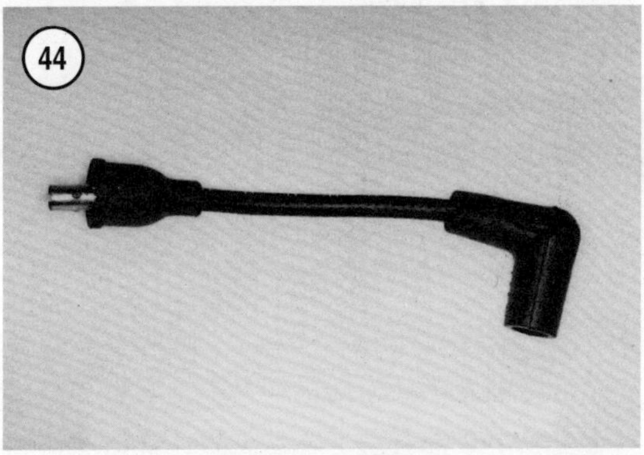

Identifying Carburetor Conditions

Refer to the following conditions to identify whether the engine is running lean or rich.

Rich

1. Fouled spark plugs.
2. Engine misfires and runs rough under load.
3. Excessive exhaust smoke as the throttle is increased.
4. An extreme rich condition results in a choked or dull sound from the exhaust and an inability to clear the exhaust with the throttle held wide open.

Lean

1. Blistered or very white spark plug electrodes.
2. Engine overheats.
3. Slow acceleration, engine power is reduced.
4. Flat spots on acceleration that are similar in feel to when the engine starts to run out of gas.
5. Engine speed fluctuates at full throttle.

45 **FUEL LEVEL SYSTEM**

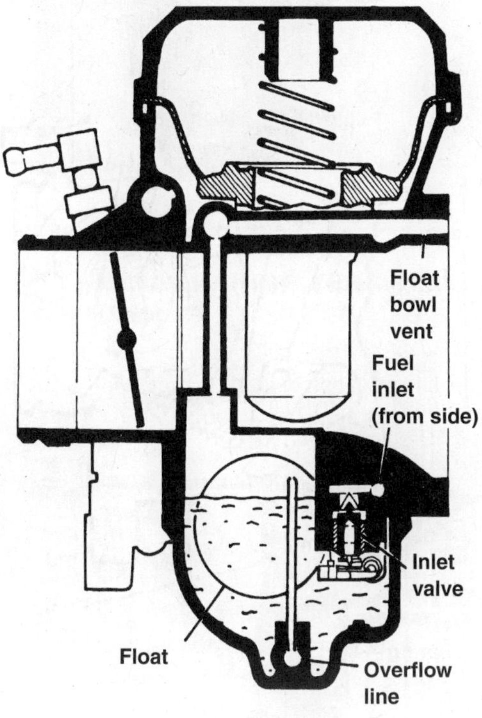

Troubleshooting

Isolate fuel system problems to the fuel tank, fuel shutoff valve and filter, fuel hoses, external fuel filter (if used) or carburetor. The following procedures assume that the ignition system is working properly and is correctly adjusted.

Fuel level system

The fuel level system is shown in **Figure 45**. Proper carburetor operation depends on a constant and correct carburetor fuel level. As fuel is drawn from the float bowl during engine operation, the float level in the bowl drops. As the float drops, the fuel valve moves away from its seat and allows fuel to flow through the seat into the float bowl. Fuel entering the float bowl will cause the float to rise and push against the fuel valve. When the fuel level reaches a predetermined level, the fuel valve is pushed against the seat to prevent the float bowl from overfilling.

If the fuel valve fails to close, the engine will run too rich or flood with fuel. Symptoms of this problem are rough running, excessive black smoke and poor acceleration. This condition will sometimes clear up when the engine is run at wide-open throttle, as the fuel is being drawn into the engine before the float bowl can overfill. As the engine speed is reduced, however, the rich-running condition returns.

Several things can cause fuel overflow. In most instances, it can be as simple as a small piece of dirt trapped between the fuel valve and seat or an incorrect float level. If fuel is flowing out of the overflow tube connected to the bottom of the float bowl, the fuel valve inside the carburetor is being held open. First check the position of the fuel shutoff valve lever. Turn the fuel shutoff valve lever OFF. Then *lightly* tap on the carburetor float bowl and turn the fuel shutoff valve lever ON. If the fuel flow stops running out of the overflow tube, whatever was holding the fuel valve off of its seat has been dislodged. If fuel continues to flow from the overflow tube, remove and service the carburetor. See Chapter Seven.

NOTE

Fuel will not flow from the vacuum-operated fuel shutoff valve until the engine is running.

Starting enrichment (choke) system

A cold engine requires a rich mixture to start and run properly. On all models, a cable-actuated starter enrichment valve is used for cold starting.

If the engine is difficult to start when cold, check the starting enrichment (choke) cable adjustment described in Chapter Three.

Accelerator pump system

During sudden throttle openings the diaphragm type accelerator pump system (**Figure 46**) provides additional fuel to the engine. Without this system the carburetor would not be able to provide a sufficient amount of fuel.

The system consists of a spring loaded neoprene diaphragm that is compressed during sudden acceleration by the pump lever. This movement causes the diaphragm to force fuel from the pump chamber, through a check valve and into the carburetor venturi. The diaphragm spring returns the diaphragm to the uncompressed position, which allows the chamber to refill with fuel.

If the engine hesitates during sudden acceleration, check the operation of the accelerator pump system. Carburetor Service is covered in Chapter Seven.

Vacuum-operated fuel shutoff valve testing

All models are equipped with a vacuum-operated fuel shutoff valve. A vacuum hose is connected between the fuel shutoff valve diaphragm and the carburetor. When the engine is running, vacuum is applied to the fuel shutoff valve through this hose. For fuel to flow through the fuel valve, a vacuum must be present with the fuel shutoff valve handle in the ON or RES position. The following steps troubleshoot the fuel shutoff valve by applying a vacuum from a separate source. A Miti-Vac hand-operated vacuum pump (**Figure 47**), gas can, drain hose that is long enough to reach from the fuel valve to the gas can, and hose clamp are required for this test.

WARNING
Gasoline is highly flammable. When servicing the fuel system in the following sections, work in a well-ventilated area. Do not expose gasoline and gasoline vapors to sparks or other ignition sources.

1. Disconnect the negative battery cable.
2. Visually check the amount of fuel in the tank. Add fuel if necessary.
3. Turn the fuel shutoff valve to the OFF position (A, **Figure 48**) and disconnect the fuel hose (B, **Figure 48**) from the fuel shutoff valve. Plug the open end of the hose.
4. Connect the drain hose to the fuel shutoff valve and secure it with a hose clamp. Insert the end of the drain hose into a gas can.

WARNING
Do not perform this test if there are open flames or sparks in the area.

46

ACCELERATOR PUMP SYSTEM

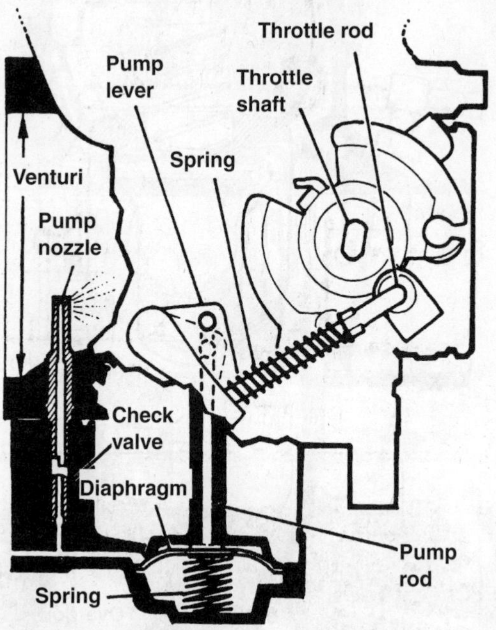

5. Disconnect the vacuum hose (**Figure 49**) from the fuel shutoff valve.
6. Connect a hand-operated vacuum pump to the fuel shutoff valve vacuum hose nozzle.
7. Turn the fuel shutoff valve lever (A, **Figure 48**) to the ON position.

CAUTION
In Step 8, do not apply more than 25 in. (635 mm) Hg vacuum or the fuel shutoff valve diaphragm will be damaged.

8. Apply 25 in. Hg of vacuum to the valve. Fuel must flow through the fuel shutoff valve when the vacuum is applied.
9. With the vacuum still applied, turn the fuel shutoff valve lever (A, **Figure 48**) to the RES position. Fuel must continue to flow through the valve.

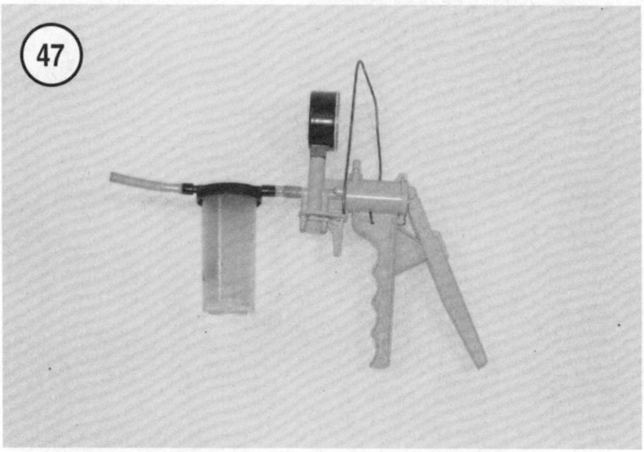

47

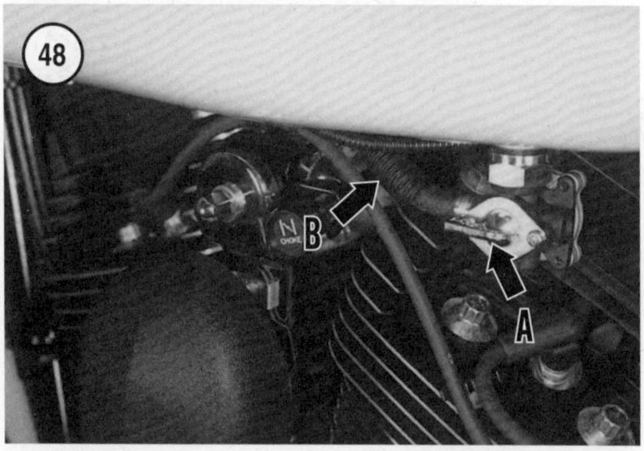

48

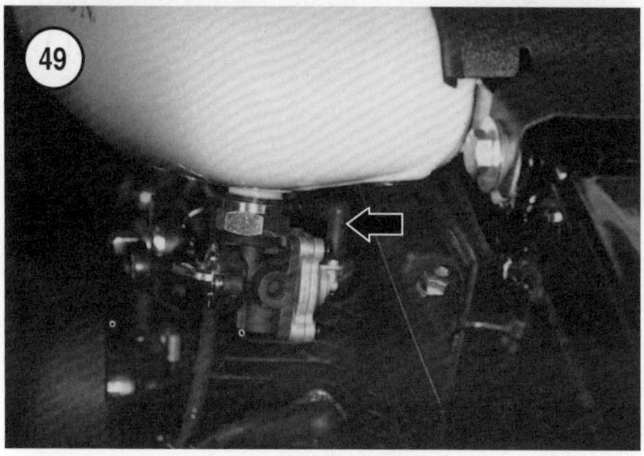

49

10. Release the vacuum and check that fuel flow stops.

11. Repeat Steps 8-10 five times and check that fuel flows with vacuum applied and stops flowing when the vacuum is released.

12. Turn the fuel shutoff valve OFF. Disconnect the vacuum pump and drain hoses.

13. Reconnect the fuel hose (B, **Figure 48**) onto the fuel shutoff valve.

14. If the fuel valve failed this test, replace the fuel shutoff valve as described in Chapter Seven.

ENGINE NOISES

1. *Knocking or pinging during acceleration* can be caused by using a lower octane fuel than recommended or a poor grade of fuel. Incorrect carburetor jetting and an incorrect (hot) spark plug heat range can cause pinging. Refer to *Spark Plug Heat Range* in Chapter Three. Check also for excessive carbon buildup in the combustion chamber or a defective CDI unit.

2. *Slapping or rattling noises at low speed or during acceleration* can be caused by excessive piston-to-cylinder wall clearance. Check also for a bent connecting rod(s) or worn piston pin and/or piston pin hole in the piston(s).

3. *Knocking or rapping while decelerating* is usually caused by excessive rod bearing clearance.

4. *Persistent knocking and vibration or other noises* are usually caused by worn main bearings. If the main bearings are in good condition, consider the following:

   a. Loose engine mounts.
   b. Cracked frame.
   c. Leaking cylinder head gasket(s).
   d. Exhaust pipe leakage at cylinder head(s).
   e. Stuck piston ring(s).
   f. Broken piston ring(s).
   g. Partial engine seizure.
   h. Excessive connecting rod bearing clearance.
   i. Excessive connecting rod side clearance.
   j. Excessive crankshaft runout.

5. *Rapid on-off squeal* indicates a compression leak around the cylinder head gasket or spark plug.

6. *Valve train noise*- Check for the following:

   a. Bent pushrod(s).
   b. Defective lifter(s).
   c. Valve sticking in guide.
   d. Worn cam gears and/or cam.
   e. Damaged rocker arm or shaft. Rocker arm may be binding on shaft.

ENGINE LUBRICATION

An improperly operating engine lubrication system will quickly lead to serious engine damage. Check the engine oil level weekly as described in Chapter Three. Oil pump service is covered in Chapter Four.

Oil Light

The oil light, mounted on the indicator light panel (**Figure 50**, typical), will come on when the ignition switch is turned ON before starting the engine. After the engine is started, the oil light will turn off when the engine speed is above idle.

If the oil light does not come on when the ignition switch is turned to ON and the engine is not running, check for a burned out oil light bulb as described in Chapter Eight. If the bulb is working, check the oil pressure switch (**Figure 51**) as described in Chapter Eight.

If the oil light remains on when the engine speed is above idle, turn the engine off and check the oil level in the oil tank. If the oil level is satisfactory, the oil may not be returning to the tank from the return line. Check for a clogged or damaged return line or a damaged oil pump. If the motorcycle is being operated in conditions where the ambient temperature is below freezing, ice and sludge may be blocking the oil feed pipe. This condition will prevent the oil from circulating properly.

Oil Consumption High or Engine Smokes Excessively

1. Worn valve guides.
2. Worn valve guide seals.
3. Worn or damaged piston rings.
4. Oil pan overfilled.
5. Oil filter restricted.
6. Leaking cylinder head surfaces.

Oil Fails to Return to Oil Tank

1. Oil lines or fittings restricted or damaged.
2. Oil pump damaged or operating incorrectly.
3. Oil pan empty.
4. Oil filter restricted.
5. Damaged oil feed pump.

Engine Oil Leaks

1. Clogged air filter breather hose.
2. Restricted or damaged oil return line to oil tank.
3. Loose engine parts.
4. Damaged gasket sealing surfaces.
5. Oil tank overfilled.

50

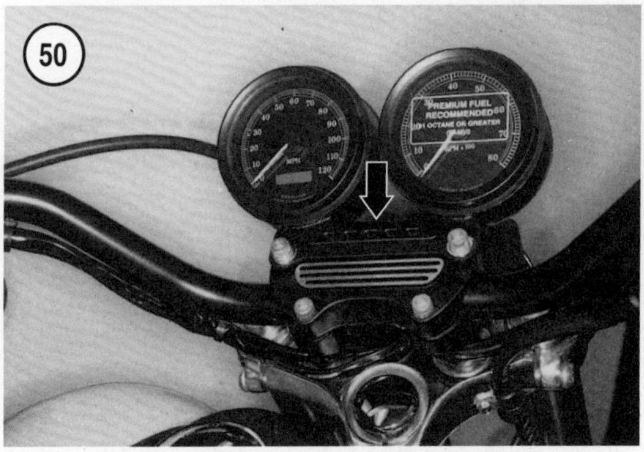

6. Restricted oil filter.
7. Plugged air filter-to-breather system hose.

CLUTCH

All clutch troubles, except adjustments, require partial clutch disassembly to identify and repair the problem. Refer to Chapter Five for clutch service procedures.

Clutch Chatter or Noise

This problem is usually caused by worn or warped friction and steel plates.

Clutch Slippage

1. Incorrect clutch adjustment.
2. Worn friction plates.
3. Weak or damaged diaphragm spring.
4. Damaged pressure plate.

Clutch Dragging

1. Incorrect clutch adjustment.
2. Warped clutch plates.
3. Worn or damaged clutch shell or clutch hub.
4. Worn or incorrectly assembled clutch ball and ramp mechanism.
5. Incorrect primary chain alignment.
6. Weak or damaged diaphragm spring.

TRANSMISSION

Transmission symptoms are sometimes hard to distinguish from clutch symptoms. Refer to Chapter Six for transmission service procedures.

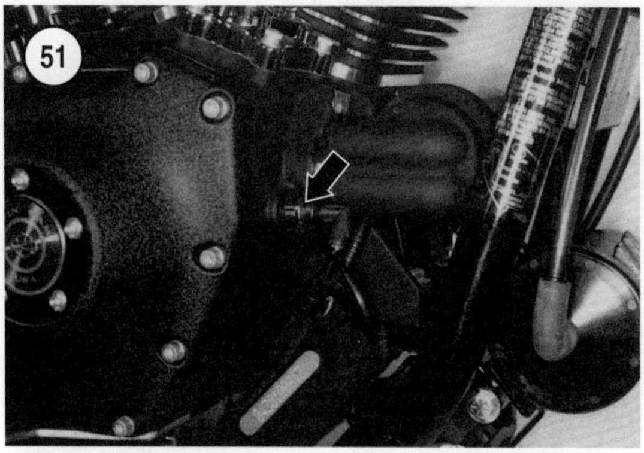

Jumping Out of Gear

1. Worn or damaged shifter parts.
2. Incorrect shifter rod adjustment.
3. Incorrect shifter drum adjustment.
4. Severely worn or damaged gears and/or shift forks.

Difficult Shifting

1. Worn or damaged shift forks.
2. Worn or damaged shifter clutch dogs.
3. Weak or damaged shifter return spring.
4. Clutch drag.

Excessive Gear Noise

1. Worn or damaged bearings.
2. Worn or damaged gears.
3. Excessive gear backlash.

LIGHTING SYSTEM

If bulbs burn out frequently, check for excessive vibration, loose connections that permit sudden current surges, or the installation of the wrong type of bulb.

Most light and ignition problems are caused by loose or corroded ground connections. Check these prior to replacing a bulb or electrical component.

EXCESSIVE VIBRATION

Excessive vibration is usually caused by loose engine mounting hardware. A bent axle shaft or a loose suspension component will cause high-speed vibration problems. Vibration can also be caused by the following conditions:

1. Cracked or broken frame.
2. Severely worn primary chain.
3. Tight primary chain links.
4. Loose, worn or damaged engine stabilizer link.
5. Loose or damaged rubber mounts.
6. Improperly balanced wheel(s).
7. Defective or damaged wheel(s).
8. Defective or damaged tire(s).
9. Internal engine wear or damage.
10. Loose or worn steering head bearings.
11. Loose swing arm pivot shaft nut.

FRONT SUSPENSION AND STEERING

Poor handling may be caused by improper tire inflation pressure, a damaged or bent frame or front steering components, worn wheel bearings or dragging brakes. Possible causes for suspension and steering malfunctions are listed below.

Irregular or Wobbly Steering

1. Loose wheel axle nut(s).
2. Loose or worn steering head bearings.
3. Excessive wheel bearing play.
4. Damaged cast wheel.
5. Spoked wheel out of alignment.
6. Unbalanced wheel assembly.
7. Incorrect wheel alignment.
8. Bent or damaged steering stem or frame at steering neck.
9. Tire incorrectly seated on rim.
10. Excessive front end loading from non-standard equipment.

Stiff Steering

1. Low front tire air pressure.
2. Bent or damaged steering stem or frame.
3. Loose or worn steering head bearings.

Stiff or Heavy Fork Operation

1. Incorrect fork springs.
2. Incorrect fork oil viscosity.
3. Excessive amount of fork oil.

4. Bent fork tubes.

Poor Fork Operation

1. Worn or damage fork tubes.
2. Fork oil capacity low due to leaking fork seals.
3. Bent or damaged fork tubes.
4. Contaminated fork oil.
5. Incorrect fork springs.
6. Heavy front end loading from non-standard equipment.

Poor Rear Shock Absorber Operation

1. Weak or worn springs.
2. Damper unit leaking.
3. Shock shaft worn or bent.
4. Incorrect rear shock springs.
5. Rear shocks adjusted incorrectly.
6. Heavy rear end loading from non-standard equipment.
7. Incorrect loading.

BRAKE PROBLEMS

All models are equipped with front and rear disc brakes. Good brakes are vital to the safe operation of any vehicle. Perform the maintenance specified in Chapter Three to minimize brake system problems. Brake system service is covered in Chapter Twelve. When refilling the front and rear master cylinders, use only DOT 5 silicone-based brake fluid.

Insufficient Braking Power

Worn brake pads or disc, air in the hydraulic system, glazed or contaminated pads, low brake fluid level, or a leaking brake line or hose can cause this problem. Visually check for leaks. Check for worn brake pads. Check also for a leaking or damaged primary cup seal in the master cylinder. Bleed and adjust the brakes. Rebuild a leaking master cylinder or brake caliper. Brake drag will result in excessive heat and brake fade. See *Brake Drag* in this section.

Spongy Brake Feel

This problem is generally caused by air in the hydraulic system. Bleed and adjust the brakes.

Brake Drag

Check the brake adjustment while checking for insufficient brake pedal and/or hand lever free play. Also check for worn, loose or missing parts in the brake calipers. Check the brake disc for excessive runout.

Brakes Squeal or Chatter

Check brake pad thickness and disc condition. Check that the caliper anti-rattle springs are properly installed and in good condition. Clean off any dirt on the pads. Loose components can also cause this. Check for:
1. Warped brake disc
2. Loose brake disc.
3. Loose caliper mounting bolts.
4. Loose front axle nut.
5. Worn wheel bearings.
6. Damaged hub.

Table 1 STARTER MOTOR TEST SPECIFICATIONS

Minimum no-load speed @ 11.5 volts	3000 rpm
Maximum no-load current @ 11.5 volts	90 amps
Current draw	
Normal	160-180 amps
Maximum	200 amps
Brush length (minimum)	0.433 in. (11.0 mm)
Commutator diameter (minimum)	1.141 in. (28.981 mm)

Table 2 ELECTRICAL SPECIFICATIONS

Item	Specification
Battery capacity	12 volts, 19 amp hour
Alternator	
AC voltage output	16-20 VAC per 1000 rpm
Stator coil resistance	0.1-0.2 ohms
Voltage regulator	
Voltage output @ 3600 rpm	14.3-14.7 @ 75 degrees F (24 degrees C)
Amps @ 3600 rpm	32 amps
Ignition coil	
Primary resistance	0.5-0.7 ohms
Secondary resistance	5500-7500 ohms

Table 3 DIAGNOSTIC TROUBLE CODES

Diagnostic Code No.	Fault Condition
12	MAP sensor
16	Battery voltage
24	Front cylinder ignition coil
25	Rear cylinder ignition coil
35	Tachometer
41	Crankshaft position sensor
42	Camshaft position sensor (1999-2000)
44	Bank angle sensor
52	RAM failure
53	ROM failure
54	EPROM failure
55	Ignition module failure
56	Camshaft position sensor and crankshaft position sensor timing

NOTE: Refer to the Supplement at the back of this manual for information unique to 2002-on models.

CHAPTER THREE

LUBRICATION, MAINTENANCE AND TUNE-UP

The service life and operation of the Harley-Davidson depends on the maintenance it receives. This is easy to understand once it is realized that a motorcycle, even in normal use, is subjected to tremendous heat, stress and vibration. When neglected, any motorcycle becomes unreliable and dangerous to ride.

All motorcycles require attention before and after riding them. The time spent on basic maintenance and lubrication will give the utmost in safety and performance. Minor problems found during these inspections are simple and inexpensive to correct. If they are not found and corrected at this time, they can lead to major, more expensive problems.

Start by doing simple tune-up, lubrication and maintenance procedures. Tackle more involved jobs after becoming more familiar with the machine.

Perform critical maintenance tasks and checks weekly. Perform others at specific time or mileage intervals or if certain symptoms appear. The Tune-up section at the end of this chapter lists procedures that affect drivability and performance. If a procedure requires more than minor disassembly, it is covered in a subsequent chapter.

Periodic maintenance intervals are listed in **Table 1** at the end of the chapter. Subsequent tables provide capacities, recommendations and specifications.

ROUTINE SAFETY CHECKS

Perform the following safety checks before the first ride of the day.

General Inspection

1. Inspect the engine, transmission and primary drive for oil leakage.
2. Check the tires for embedded stones. Pry them out with a suitable tool.

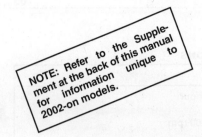

1

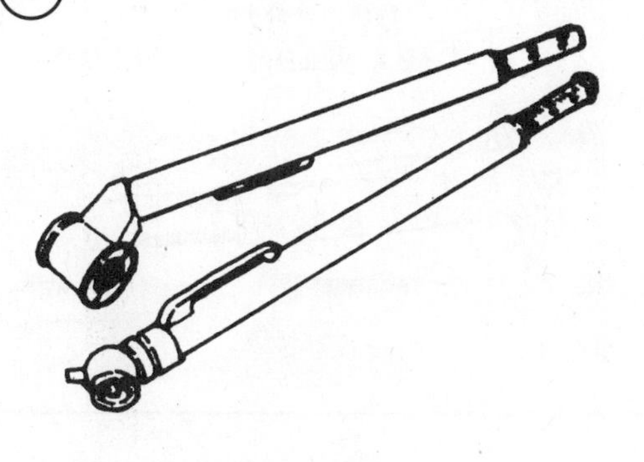

3. Check tire pressure (**Table 2**) when the tires are cold. Refer to *Tires and Wheels* in this chapter for more information.
4. Make sure ALL lights work.
5. Inspect the fuel lines and fittings for leakage.
6. Check the fuel level in the fuel tank. Top off, if required.
7. Check the operation of the front and rear brakes. Add DOT 5 brake fluid to the front and rear master cylinders as required.
8. Check clutch operation. If necessary, adjust the clutch as described in this chapter.
9. Check the throttle operation. The hand throttle must move smoothly with no roughness, sticking or tightness. The throttle must snap back when released. Adjust throttle free play, if necessary, as described in this chapter.
10. Check the rear brake pedal. It must move smoothly.
11. Inspect the front and rear suspension. Make sure they have a good solid feel with no looseness.
12. Check the exhaust system for leakage or damage.

CAUTION
When checking the tightness of the exposed fasteners on the Dyna Glide, do not check the cylinder head bolts without following the specific cylinder head tightening sequence described in Chapter Four.

Lights and Horn

With the engine running, check the following.

1. Pull the front brake lever and check that the brake light comes on.
2. Push the rear brake pedal down and check that the brake light comes on soon after the pedal has been depressed.
3. Make sure the headlight and taillight are on.
4. Move the dimmer switch up and down between the high and low positions, and make sure both headlight elements are working.
5. Push the turn signal switch to the left and right positions and make sure all four turn signal lights are working.
6. Check that all accessory lights work properly, if so equipped.
7. Check the horn button operation.
8. If the horn or any light fails to work properly, refer to Chapter Eight.

MAINTENANCE INTERVALS

The recommended service intervals are listed in **Table 1**. Strict adherence to these recommendations will go a long way toward ensuring long service from the motorcycle. To prevent rust damage when operating the motorcycle in areas of high humidity or when riding near the ocean, increase the lubrication service intervals.

This chapter describes most of the services shown in **Table 1**. The remaining chapters cover those procedures that require more than minor disassembly or adjustment.

TIRES AND WHEELS

Tire Pressure

Check the tire pressure often to maintain tire profile, traction, and handling and to get the maximum life out of the tire. Carry a tire gauge (**Figure 1**) in the motorcycle's tool kit. **Table 2** lists the cold tire pressures for the tires.

NOTE
After checking and adjusting the air pressure, reinstall the air valve caps. These caps prevent debris from collecting in the valve stems and causing air leakage or incorrect tire pressure readings.

Tire Inspection

The tires take a lot of punishment, so inspect them periodically for excessive wear, deep cuts and imbedded objects such as stones or nails. If a nail or other object is found in a tire, mark its location with a light crayon prior to removing it. This will help locate the hole for repair.

Refer to Chapter Nine for tire changing and repair information. Check local traffic regulations concerning minimum tread depth. Measure with a tread depth gauge (**Figure 2**) or a small ruler. As a guideline, replace tires when the tread depth is 5/16 in. (8.0 mm.) or less.

Laced Wheel Spoke Tension

Check the laced wheels for loose or damaged spokes, on models so equipped. Refer to Chapter Nine for spoke service.

Rim Inspection

On both cast and laced wheels, check the wheel rims for cracks and other damage. If damaged, a rim can make the motorcycle handle poorly. Refer to Chapter Nine for wheel service.

PERIODIC LUBRICATION

Engine Oil Level Check

Check the engine oil level with the dipstick/oil filler cap located in the transmission/oil tank case cover. The dipstick and oil filler cap (**Figure 3**) is located on the right side top surface of transmission cover.

NOTE
Check both vent hoses and interconnecting oil hoses for swelling, cracks or damage and replace immediately. Check each hose connection and make sure the hose clamps are secure.

1. Start and run the engine for approximately 10 minutes or until the engine has reached normal operating temperature. Then turn the engine off and allow the oil to settle in the tank.
2. Place the motorcycle on a level surface and park it on its jiffy stand.

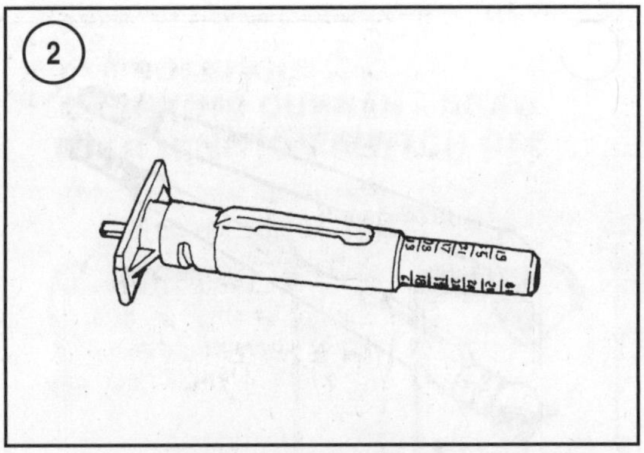

CAUTION
Holding the motorcycle straight up will result in an incorrect oil level reading.

3. Wipe the area around the oil filler cap with a clean rag. Then pull the oil filler cap (**Figure 3**) out of the transmission case. Wipe the dipstick off with a clean rag and reinsert it all the way into the oil tank until it bottoms. Withdraw the filler cap again and check the oil level on the dipstick. The oil level should be at the FULL HOT mark on the dipstick (**Figure 4**). If the oil level is even with, or below the ADD QUART mark, continue with Step 4. If the oil level is correct, go to Step 5.
4. To correct the oil level, add the recommended engine oil listed in **Table 3**.

CAUTION
Do not overfill the oil level in the transmission or the oil filler cap will pop out when the oil gets hot.

5. Check the O-ring (**Figure 5**) for cracks or other damage. Replace the O-ring if necessary.

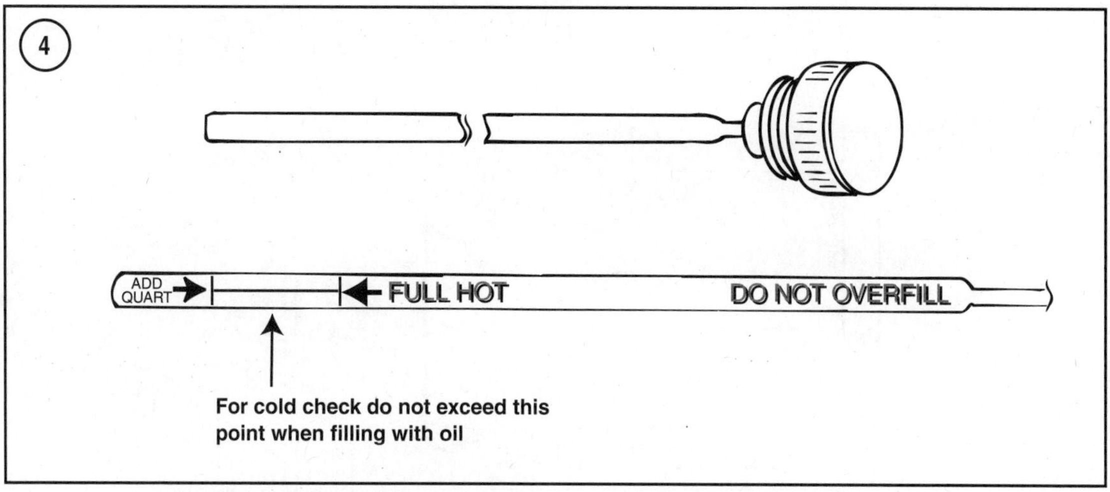

6. Reinstall the oil filler cap and push it down until it bottoms.

Engine Oil and Filter Change

Regular oil and filter changes will contribute more to engine longevity than any other maintenance performed. **Table 1** lists the recommended oil and filter change interval. This assumes that the motorcycle is operated in moderate climates. The time interval is more important than the mileage interval because combustion acids, formed by gasoline and water vapor, will contaminate the oil even if the motorcycle is not run for several months. If the motorcycle is operated under dusty conditions, the oil will become contaminated more quickly and should be changed more frequently than recommended.

Use a motorcycle oil with an API classification of *SF* or *SG*. The classification is printed on the container. Always try to use the same brand of oil at each change. Refer to **Table 3** for correct oil viscosity to use under anticipated ambient temperatures, not engine oil temperature. Using oil additives is not recommended as they may cause clutch slippage.

WARNING
Contact with oil may cause skin cancer. Wash hands with soap and water as soon as possible after handling engine oil.

CAUTION
Do not use the current SH and SJ rated automotive oils in motorcycle engines. The SH and SJ rated oils contain friction modifiers that reduce frictional losses on engine components. Specifically designed for automotive engines, these oils can damage motorcycle engines and clutches.

NOTE
The engine oil tank is an integral part of the transmission case and is connected to the rear of the crankcase with two hoses. The oil level dipstick is located on the upper right side of the transmission/oil tank case ***(Figure 3)****.*

NOTE
Never dispose of motor oil in the trash, on the ground or down a storm drain. Many service stations and oil retailers will accept used oil for recycling. Do not combine other fluids with motor oil to be recycled. To lo-

6

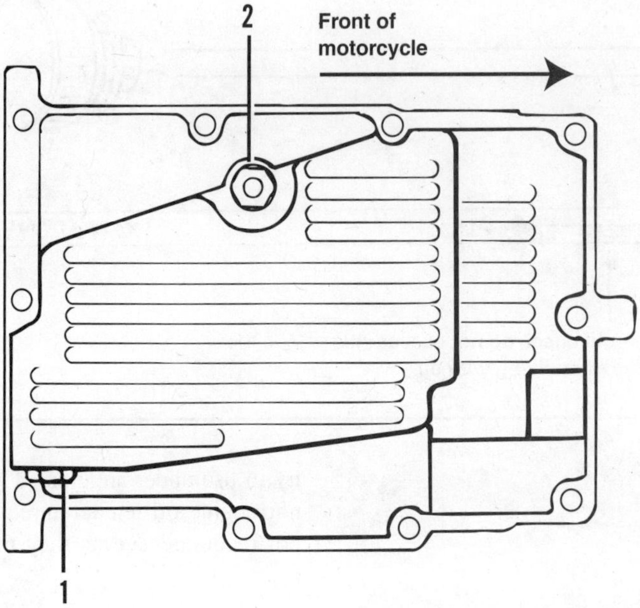

1. Engine drain plug
2. Transmission drain plug

cate a recycling facility, contact the American Petroleum Institute (API) at ***www.recycleoil.org****.*

1. Start and run the engine for approximately 10 minutes or until the engine has reached normal operating temperature. Then turn the engine off and allow the oil to settle in the transmission case. Support the motorcycle so that the oil can drain completely.

NOTE
Before removing the oil filler cap, clean off all dirt and debris around it.

2. Remove the oil filler cap (**Figure 3**) as this will speed up the flow of oil.

NOTE
The transmission/oil tank case is equipped with two drain plugs. Make sure to remove only the engine oil drain plug (1, ***Figure 6****). Do not remove the transmission drain plug (2,* ***Figure 6****).*

3. Place a drain pan underneath the transmission/oil tank pan and remove the engine oil drain

7

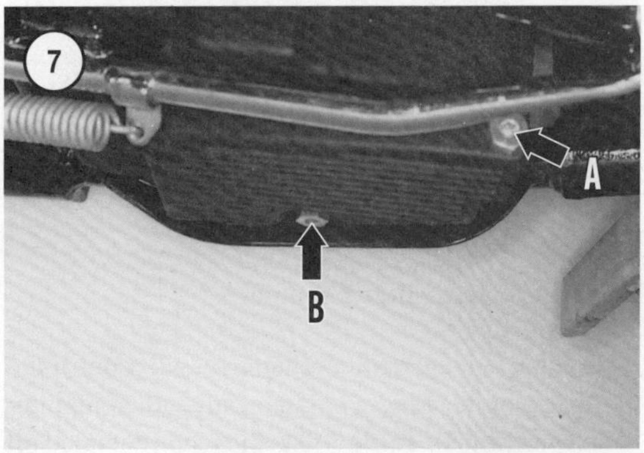

8

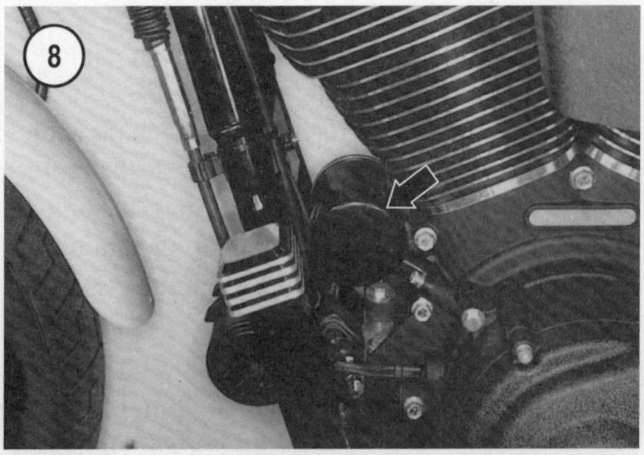

9

10

11

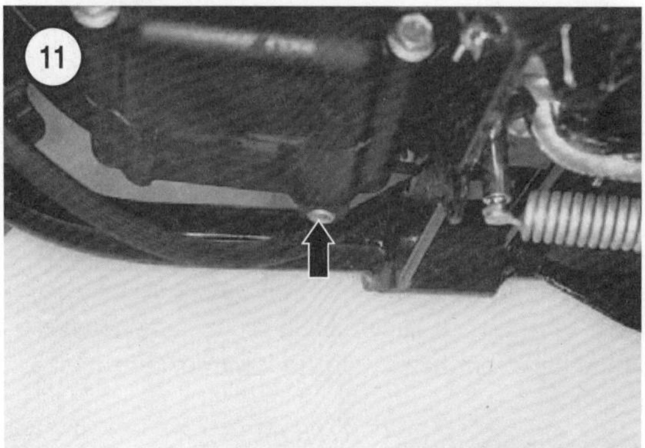

plug and O-ring (A, **Figure 7**) from the side of the pan.

4. Allow the oil to drain completely.

5. To replace the oil filter (**Figure 8**), perform the following:

 a. Temporarily install the drain bolt and O-ring and tighten finger-tight. Then move the drain pan underneath the oil filter.

 b. At the front of the engine, install a socket type oil filter wrench squarely over the oil filter and loosen it by turning it *counterclockwise.* Quickly remove the oil filter as oil will begin to run out.

 c. Hold the filter over the drain pan and pour out the remaining oil. Place the filter in a plastic bag, seal it and dispose of it properly.

 d. Remove the drain plug and gasket. Wipe the drain plug sealing surface on the oil pan with a clean, lint-free cloth.

 e. Coat the neoprene gasket (**Figure 9**) on the new filter with clean oil.

CAUTION

Tighten the oil filter by hand. Do not overtighten.

 f. Screw the oil filter onto its mount by hand and tighten until the filter gasket just touches the sealing surface, then tighten the filter by hand an additional 1/2 to 3/4 turn.

6. Replace the engine oil drain plug O-ring (**Figure 10**) if leaking or damaged.

7. Lubricate the O-ring with clean engine oil before installing it. Then screw in the drain plug and O-ring and tighten to the torque specification in **Table 6**.

8. While the engine is drained of oil, inspect the oil plug (**Figure 11**) at the base of the right side crankcase for leakage. If leakage has occurred, remove the oil plug, clean the threads thoroughly in solvent and dry. Apply Loctite Pipe Sealant, or an equivalent, to the threads and reinstall the oil plug. Tighten the plug to the specification in **Table 6**.

CAUTION

*Do not overfill the engine in Step 9. **Table 4** lists two engine oil refill capacities. One capacity is for an oil and filter change and the other is for after rebuilding the engine. If too much oil is added, the oil filler cap will be forced out of the transmission case cover when the oil gets hot.*

9. Add the correct viscosity (**Table 3**) and quantity (**Table 4**) of oil into the transmission/oil tank case. Insert the oil filler cap into the case and push it down until it bottoms.

NOTE

*After oil has been added, the oil level will register above the FULL HOT dipstick mark (**Figure 4**) until the engine runs and the filter fills with oil.*

To obtain a correct reading after adding oil and installing a new oil filter, follow the procedure in Step 10.

10. After changing the engine oil and filter, check the oil level as follows:
   a. Start and run the engine for 1 minute, then shut it off.
   b. Check the oil level on the dipstick as described in this chapter.
   c. If the oil level is correct, it will register in the dipstick's safe operating level range. If so, *do not* top off or add oil to bring it to the FULL HOT level on the dipstick.
11. Check the oil filter and drain plug for leaks.
12. Dispose the used oil properly.

Transmission Oil Level Check

Table 1 lists the recommended transmission oil inspection intervals. When checking the transmission oil level, do not allow any dirt or debris to enter the transmission/oil tank case opening.

WARNING

Contact with oil may cause skin cancer. Wash oil from hands with soap and water as soon as possible after handling engine oil.

NOTE

The transmission oil tank is an integral part of the transmission case. The oil level checking dipstick is located on the forward portion of the clutch release cover attached to the side of the transmission/oil tank case.

1. Ride the motorcycle for approximately 10 minutes and shift through all five gears until the transmission oil has reached normal operating temperature. Turn the engine off and allow the oil to settle in the tank. Park the motorcycle on a level surface and have an assistant support it so that it is standing straight up.

CAUTION

Do not check the oil level with the motorcycle supported on its jiffy stand or the reading will be incorrect.

2. Clean the area around the transmission filler cap/dipstick (**Figure 12**).

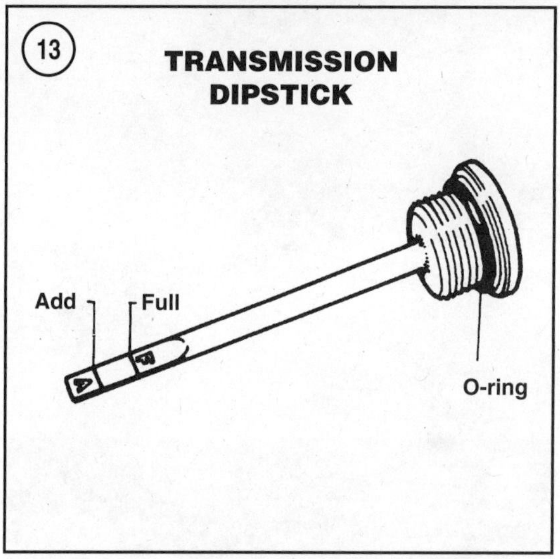

3. Wipe the dipstick and reinsert it back into the clutch release cover housing; do not screw the cap/dipstick into place. Rest it on the housing and then withdraw it. The oil level is correct when it registers between the two dipstick marks (**Figure 13**).

CAUTION

Do not add engine oil. Add only the recommended transmission oil listed in ***Table 5****.*

4. If the oil level is low, add the recommended type of Harley-Davidson Transmission Oil, or equivalent, listed in **Table 5**. Do not overfill.
5. Inspect the filler cap O-ring. Replace if worn or damaged.
6. Install the oil filler cap/dipstick and tighten it securely.
7. Wipe any spilled oil off the clutch release cover housing.

Transmission Oil Change

Table 1 lists the recommended transmission oil change intervals.

1. Ride the motorcycle for approximately 10 minutes and shift through all five gears until the transmission oil has reached normal operating temperature. Turn off the engine and allow the oil to settle in the tank. Park the motorcycle on a level surface and have an assistant support it so that it is standing straight up.
2. Clean the area around the transmission filler cap/dipstick (**Figure 12**). Unscrew it and remove the cap.

NOTE
The oil tank pan is equipped with two drain plugs. Make sure to remove the transmission oil drain plug (B, ***Figure*** *7) and not the engine oil drain plug (A,* ***Figure*** *7).*

3. Place a drain pan underneath the transmission/oil tank pan and remove the transmission oil drain plug and O-ring (B, **Figure** 7).

WARNING
If any oil spills onto the ground, wipe it up immediately before it contacts the rear tire.

4. Check the drain plug O-ring (**Figure 10**) for damage and replace if necessary.
5. The drain plug is magnetic. Check the plug (**Figure 10**) for metal debris that may indicate transmission damage, then wipe the plug off. Replace the plug if damaged.
6. Install the transmission drain plug and gasket (B, **Figure** 7) and tighten to the specification in **Table 6**.

CAUTION
Do not add engine oil. Add only the recommended transmission oil in ***Table 5****. Make sure to add the oil to the correct oil filler hole.*

7. Refill the transmission through the oil filler cap/dipstick hole with the recommended quantity (**Table 4**) and type (**Table 5**) transmission oil.
8. Install the transmission filler cap/dipstick cap and O-ring (**Figure 12**) and tighten securely.
9. Remove the oil drain pan from underneath the transmission oil pan and dispose of the oil as outlined under *Engine Oil and Filter Change* in this chapter.
10. Ride the motorcycle until the transmission oil reaches normal operating temperature. Then shut the engine off.
11. Check the transmission drain plug for leaks.
12. Check the transmission oil level as described in this chapter. Readjust the level if necessary.

Primary Chaincase Oil Level Check

The primary chaincase oil lubricates the clutch, primary chain and sprockets. **Table 1** lists the intervals for checking the chaincase oil level. When checking the primary chaincase oil level, do not allow any dirt or debris to enter the housing.

1. Park the motorcycle on a level surface and support it so that it is standing straight up. Do not support it on the jiffy stand.

CAUTION
Do not check the oil level with the motorcycle supported on its jiffy stand or the reading will be incorrect.

2. Remove the screws securing the clutch inspection cover and O-ring (**Figure 14**). Remove the cover.
3. The oil level is correct when it is even with the bottom of the clutch opening or at the bottom of the clutch diaphragm spring (**Figure 15**).

CAUTION
Do not add engine oil. Add only the recommended primary chaincase lubricant listed in ***Table 5****.*

4. If necessary, add Harley-Davidson Primary Chaincase Lubricant, or equivalent, through the opening (**Figure 16**) to correct the level.
5. Install the clutch inspection cover O-ring (**Figure 17**) onto the primary chain case cover.
6. Install the clutch inspection cover and tighten the screws to the torque specification in **Table 6**.

Primary Chaincase Oil Change

Table 1 lists the recommended primary chaincase lubricant replacement intervals.
1. Ride the motorcycle for approximately 10 minutes and shift through all five gears until the transmission oil has reached normal operating temperature. Turn off the engine and allow the oil to settle. Park the motorcycle on a level surface and have an assistant support it so that it is standing straight up. Do not support it with its jiffy stand.
2. Place a drain pan under the chaincase and remove the drain plug (**Figure 18**).
3. Allow the oil to drain for at least 10 minutes.
4. The drain plug is magnetic. Check the plug for metal debris that may indicate primary drive component or clutch damage, then wipe the plug off. Replace the plug if damaged.
5. Reinstall the drain plug and tighten securely.
6. Remove the screws securing the clutch inspection cover and O-ring (**Figure 14**). Remove the cover.

CAUTION
*Do not add engine oil. Add only the recommended primary chaincase lubricant listed in **Table 5**.*

7. Refill the primary chaincase through the clutch opening (**Figure 16**) with the recommended quantity (**Table 4**) and type (**Table 5**) primary chaincase oil. Do not overfill. The oil level must be even with the bottom of the clutch opening or at the bottom of the clutch diaphragm spring (**Figure 15**).
8. Install the clutch inspection cover O-ring (**Figure 17**) onto the primary chain case cover.
9. Install the clutch inspection cover and tighten the screws to the specification in **Table 6**.
10. Ride the motorcycle until the primary chaincase oil reaches normal operating temperature. Then shut the engine off and recheck the oil level.
11. Check the primary chaincase drain plug for leaks.

15

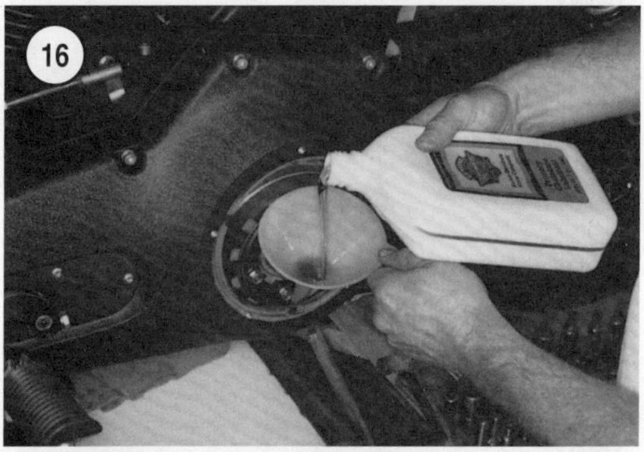
16

17

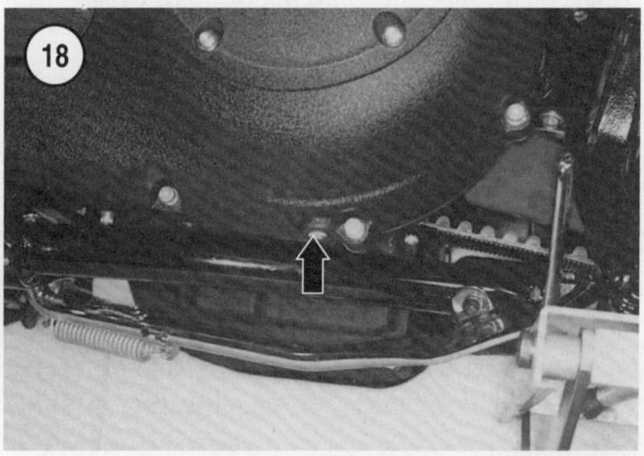
18

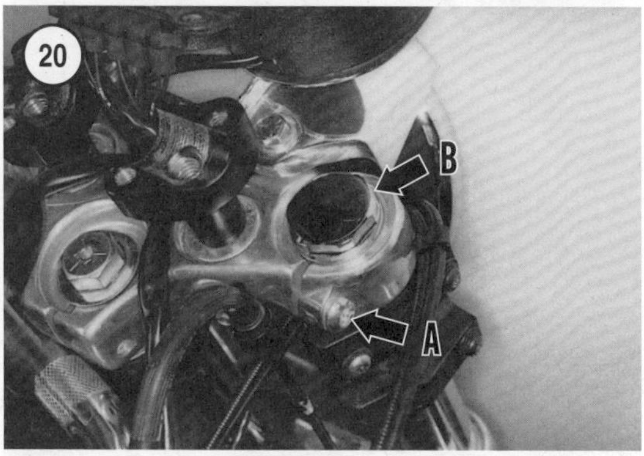

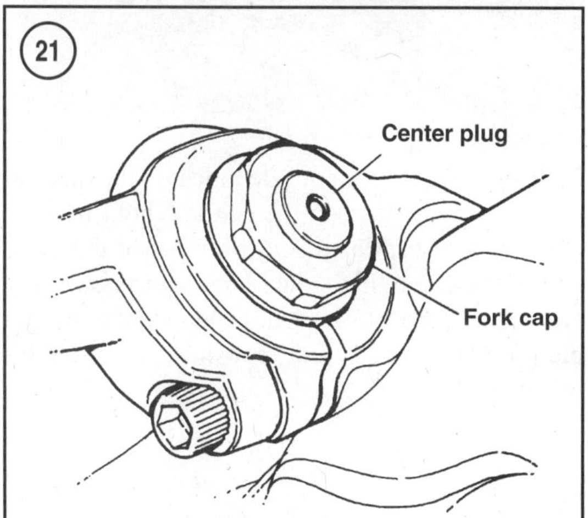

Front Fork Oil Change (Except FXDX and FXDXT Models)

NOTE

The cartridge fork installed on FXDX and FXDXT models must be partially disassembled for fork oil replacement. Refer to Front Fork Disassembly and Assembly (FXDX and FXDXT Models) in Chapter Ten.

Table 1 lists the factory recommended fork oil change intervals.

1. Place a drain pan beside one fork tube, then remove the drain screw and washer (**Figure 19**, typical) from the slider.
2. Straddle the motorcycle and apply the front brake lever. Push down on the fork and release. Repeat to force as much oil out of the fork tube as possible.

CAUTION

Do not allow the fork oil to come in contact with any of the brake components.

3. Replace the drain screw washer if damaged.
4. Repeat Steps 1-3 for the opposite fork tube.
5. Raise and secure the front end so that the front wheel clears the ground. Make sure both fork tubes are fully extended.
6. Loosen the upper fork bridge bolt (A, **Figure 20**) on each side.

NOTE

If the handlebars interfere with fork top cap removal in Step 7, partially remove the handlebars as described in Chapter Ten.

7A. On models with a center plug, perform the following:

a. Loosen the center plug and remove it (**Figure 21**).
b. Install the drain screw and washer and tighten securely.

7B. On all other models, perform the following:

a. Loosen the top cap (B, **Figure 20**) and remove it with the spacer and oil seal.
b. Install the drain screw and washer and tighten securely.

8. Insert a small funnel into the fork tube opening.
9. Fill the fork tube with the correct viscosity and quantity of fork oil. Refer to **Table 5** and **Table 7**. Remove the small funnel.

10A. On models with a center plug, install the fork tube plug into the fork tube and tighten securely.

10B. On all other models, install the top cap and the O-ring seal and tighten to the torque specification listed in **Table 6**.

11. Tighten the upper fork bridge bolt (A, **Figure 20**) on each side to the torque specification in **Table 6**.
12. Repeat for the opposite fork tube.
13. If partially removed, install the handlebar as described in Chapter Ten.
14. Road test the motorcycle and check for leaks.

Control Cables

Lubricate the control cables at the intervals specified in **Table 1** or when they become stiff or sluggish. At this time, inspect each cable for fraying and cable sheath damage. Cables are relatively inexpensive and should be replaced if faulty. Lubricate the cables with a cable lubricant.

CAUTION
If the original equipment cables have been replaced with nylon-lined cables, do not lubricate them as described in this procedure. Oil and most cable lubricants will cause the cable liner to expand, pushing the liner against the cable sheath. Nylon-lined cables are normally used dry. When servicing nylon-lined and other aftermarket cables, follow the manufacturer's instructions.

CAUTION
Do not use chain lube to lubricate control cables.

CAUTION
The starting enrichment valve (choke) cable is designed to operate with a certain amount of cable resistance. Do ***not*** *lubricate the enrichener cable or its conduit.*

1A. Disconnect the clutch cable ends as described under *Clutch Cable Replacement* in Chapter Five.
1B. Disconnect both throttle cable ends as described under *Throttle and Idle Cable Replacement* in Chapter Seven.
2. Attach a lubricator tool to the cable following its manufacturer's instructions (**Figure 22**).

NOTE
Place a shop cloth at the end of the cable to catch all excess lubricant.

22

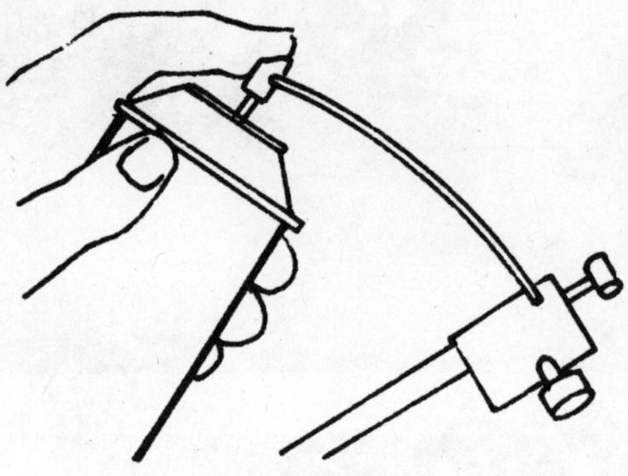

23

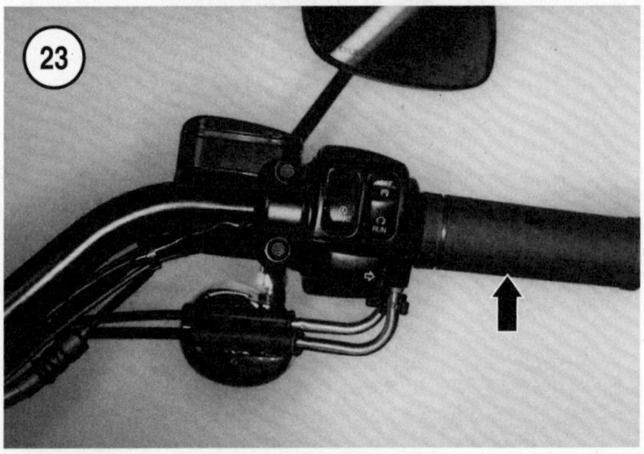

3. Insert the lubricant nozzle tube into the lubricator, press the button on the can and hold it down until the lubricant begins to flow out of the other end of the cable. If the lubricant squirts out from around the lubricator, it is not clamped it to the cable properly. Loosen and reposition the cable lubricator.

NOTE
If the lubricant does not flow out of the other end of the cable, check the cable for fraying, bending or other damage. Replace damaged cables.

4. Remove the lubricator tool and wipe off both ends of the cable.
5A. Reconnect the clutch cable ends as described under *Clutch Cable Replacement* in Chapter Five.
5B. Reconnect both the throttle cable ends as described under *Throttle and Idle Cable Replacement* in Chapter Seven.

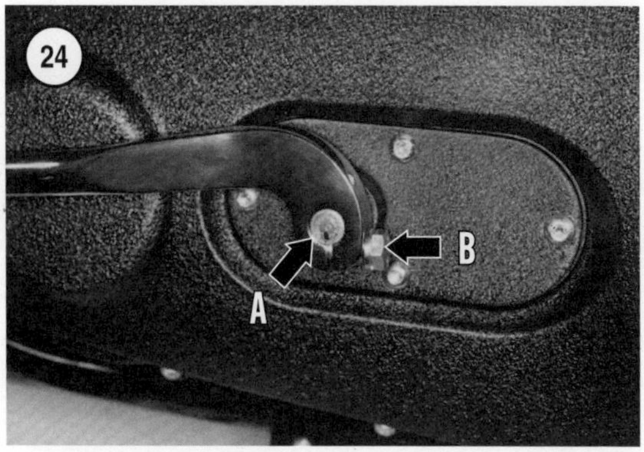

6. Adjust the cables as described in this chapter.

Throttle Control Grip Lubrication

Table 1 lists the recommended throttle control grip lubrication intervals. To remove and install the throttle grip (**Figure 23**), refer to *Throttle and Idle Cable Replacement* in Chapter Seven. Lubricate the throttle control grip (where it contacts the handlebar) with graphite.

Steering Head Lubrication

Lubricate the steering head bearings at the intervals specified in **Table 1**. Complete lubrication requires removal of the steering head assembly. Refer to Chapter Ten.

Wheel Bearings (1999 Models)

Lubricate the wheel bearings at the intervals specified in **Table 1**. Complete lubrication requires removal of the wheel bearing assemblies. Refer to Chapter Nine.

Swing Arm Bearings

Lubricate the swing arm at the interval in **Table 1**. Refer to Chapter Eleven for procedures.

Front Brake Lever Pivot Pin Lubrication

Inspect the front brake lever pivot pin for lubrication at the intervals specified in **Table 1**. If the pin is dry, lubricate it with a light weight oil. To service the pivot pin, refer to *Front Master Cylinder* in Chapter Twelve.

Clutch Lever Pivot Pin Lubrication

Inspect the clutch lever pivot pin for adequate lubrication at the intervals specified in **Table 1**. If the pin is dry, lubricate it with a light weight oil. To service the pivot pin, refer to *Clutch Cable Replacement* in Chapter Five.

PERIODIC MAINTENANCE

This section describes the periodic inspection, adjustment and replacement of various operational items on the Dyna Glide. Perform these procedures at the intervals in **Table 1**, or earlier, if necessary.

Primary Chain Adjustment

As the primary chain stretches and wears, its free play movement increases. Excessive free play will cause premature chain and sprocket wear and increase chain noise. If the free play is adjusted too tight, the chain will wear prematurely.

NOTE
On models so equipped, always disarm the optional TSSM security system prior to disconnecting the battery or the siren will sound.

1. Disconnect the negative battery cable as described in Chapter Eight.
2. Support the motorcycle with the rear wheel off the ground.

NOTE
Note the location of the inspection cover screws. There are two different length screws and they must be reinstalled in the correct location.

3A. On all models except FXDWG, perform the following:

   a. Make an alignment mark (A, **Figure 24**) on the outer shift lever and the end of the inner shift lever shaft.

b. Remove the clamping bolt (B, **Figure 24**) and remove the outer shift lever.
c. Remove the screws and the inspection cover and gasket (**Figure 25**) from the primary chaincase cover.

3B. On FXDWG models, remove the primary chain inspection cover and gasket.

4. Turn the primary chain to find the tightest point on the chain. Measure chain free play at this point.

NOTE
***Figure 26** is shown with the primary chain case removed to better illustrate the steps.*

5. Check primary chain free play at the upper chain run midway between the sprockets (**Figure 26**). The correct primary chain free play specifications are:
a. Cold engine: 5/8 to 7/8 in. (16-22 mm).
b. Hot engine: 3/8 to 5/8 in. (10-16 mm).

If the primary chain free play is incorrect, continue with Step 6. If the free play is correct, go to Step 7.

6A. On 1999-2000 models, perform the following:
a. Loosen the primary chain adjuster shoe nut (**Figure 27**).
b. Move the shoe assembly up or down to correct free play.
c. Tighten the primary chain adjuster shoe nut to the torque specification in **Table 6**, then recheck free play.

6B. On 2001 models, perform the following:
a. Loosen the primary chain adjuster shoe nut (A, **Figure 28**).
b. Move the shoe assembly up or down to correct free play.
c. Tighten the primary chain adjuster shoe nut (A, **Figure 28**) to the torque specification in **Table 6**, then recheck free play.

7. Install the primary chain inspection cover and a *new* gasket (B, **Figure 28**). Tighten the cover screws to the specification in **Table 6**.

8. Lower the motorcycle to the ground.

Final Drive Belt
Deflection and Alignment

Inspect drive belt deflection and rear axle alignment at the intervals specified in **Table 1**. If the drive belt is severely worn, or if it is wearing incor-

25
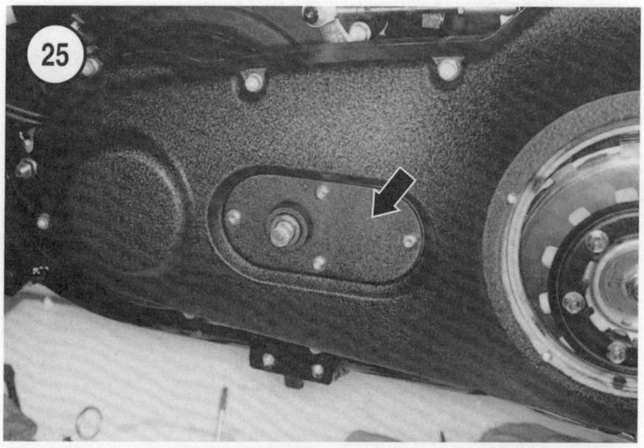

26
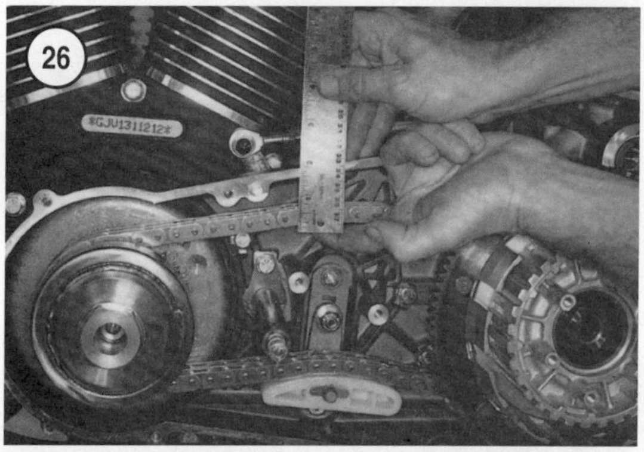

27

28
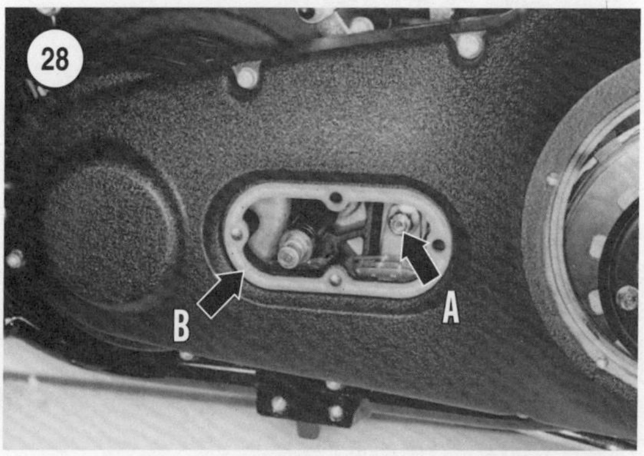

29 DRIVE BELT DEFLECTION

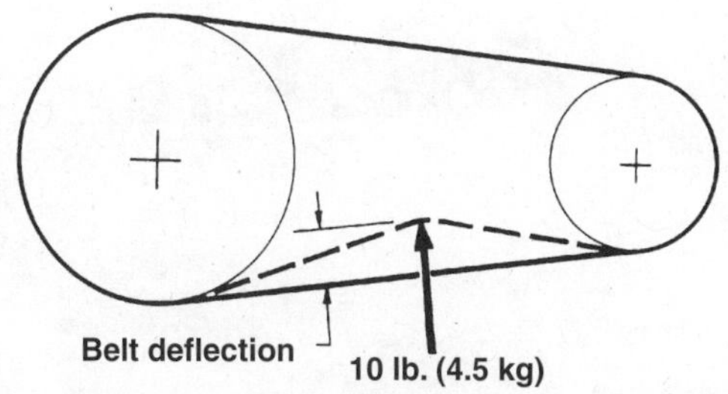

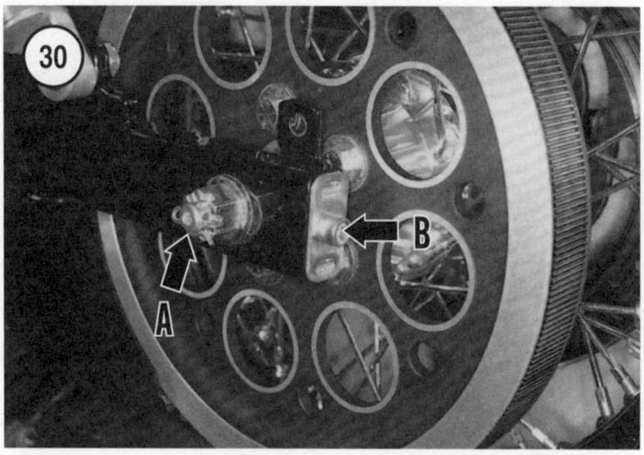

31 REAR AXLE ALIGNMENT TOOL

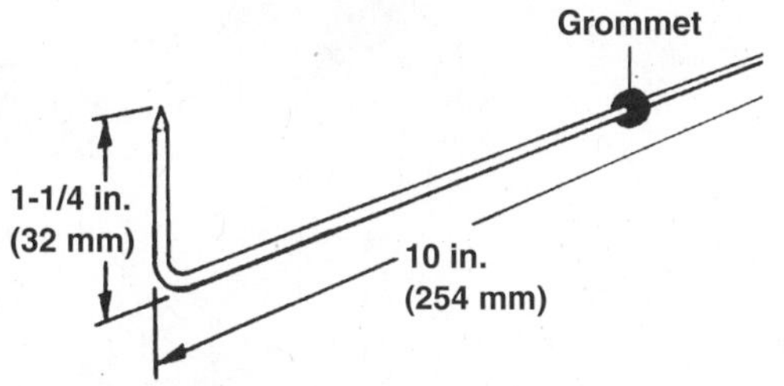

rectly, refer to Chapter Eleven for inspection and replacement procedures.

NOTE
Check the drive belt deflection and axle alignment when the belt is cold.

1. Support the motorcycle with the rear wheel off the ground. Then turn the rear wheel and check the drive belt for its tightest point. When this point is located, turn the wheel so that the belt's tight spot is on the lower belt run, midway between the front and rear sprockets.
2. Lower the motorcycle to the ground.
3. Position the motorcycle so that both wheels are on the ground. When checking and adjusting drive belt deflection in the following steps, have an assistant sit on the seat facing forward.

NOTE
Use the Harley-Davidson belt tension gauge (part No. HD-35381) or equivalent to apply pressure against the drive belt in Step 4.

4. Apply a force of 10 lb. (4.5 kg) to the middle of the lower belt strand while measuring the belt's deflection measurement at the same point (**Figure 29**). Compare the belt deflection measurement with the specification in **Table 8**. If the belt deflection measurement is incorrect, continue with Step 5. If the deflection measurement is correct, go to Step 8.
5. Support the motorcycle with the rear wheel off the ground.
6. Remove the spring clip and loosen the rear axle nut (A, **Figure 30**).
7. Turn each axle adjuster (B, **Figure 30**) in equal amounts to adjust belt deflection while maintaining rear wheel alignment. Recheck drive belt deflection as described in Step 4.
8. When the drive belt deflection measurement is correct, check axle alignment as follows:
   a. To make the alignment tool shown in **Figure 31**, refer to *Vehicle Alignment* in Chapter Nine.
   b. Support the motorcycle with the rear wheel off the ground.
   c. Insert the alignment tool into the swing arm index holes. Then hold it parallel to the rear axle and slide the grommet on the tool until it aligns with the axle center point (**Figure 32**).
   d. Remove the alignment tool without disturbing the position of the grommet and insert the tool into the opposte side of the swing arm. Compare the axle center point with the position of the grommet. Axle alignment is correct if the two measurements are within 0.32 in. (0.8 mm) of each other.
   e. If the axle alignment is incorrect, adjust the axle with the axle adjusters (B, **Figure 30**) while maintaining the correct drive belt deflection measurement.

3

9. When the drive belt deflection and axle alignment adjustments are correct, tighten the rear axle nut (A, **Figure 30**) to the torque specification in **Table 6**. Install the spring clip through the axle nut and rear axle.
10. Lower the rear wheel to the ground.

Brake Pad Inspection

1. Without removing the front or rear brake calipers, inspect the brake pads (**Figure 33**) for damage.
2. Measure the thickness of each brake pad lining (**Figure 34**) with a ruler. Replace the brake pad if its thickness is worn to the minimum thickness in **Table 8**. Replace the brake pads as described in Chapter Twelve.

Disc Brake Fluid Level

1. To check the front master cylinder, perform the following:
   a. Turn the handlebar so the master cylinder is level.
   b. Observe the brake fluid level by looking at the sight glass (A, **Figure 35**) on the master cylinder reservoir top cover. If the fluid level is correct, the sight glass will appear dark purple. If the level is low, the sight glass will have a lightened or clear appearance.
2. To check the rear master cylinder, perform the following:
   a. Support the motorcycle so that the rear master cylinder is level.

NOTE

*The rear master cylinder is partially hidden by the exhaust system, as shown in **Figure 36**, making it very difficult to see the viewing port.*

   b. Observe the brake fluid level by looking at the sight glass on the side of the master cylinder reservoir. If the fluid level is correct, the sight glass will appear dark purple. If the level is low, the sight glass will have a lightened or clear appearance.
   c. If the fluid level can not be determined by looking at the sight glass, remove the top cover (**Figure 37**) and diaphragm as described in

32

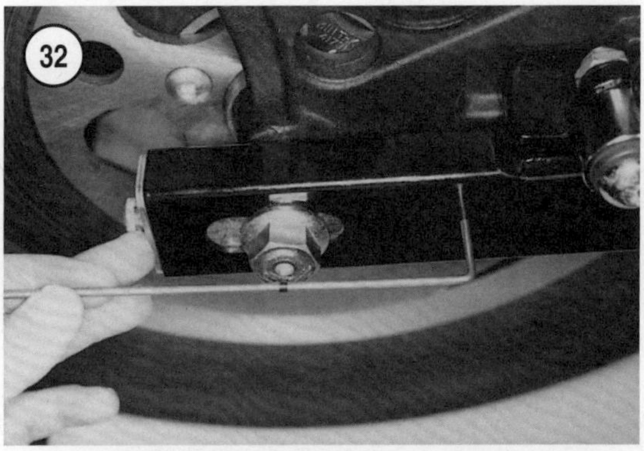

33

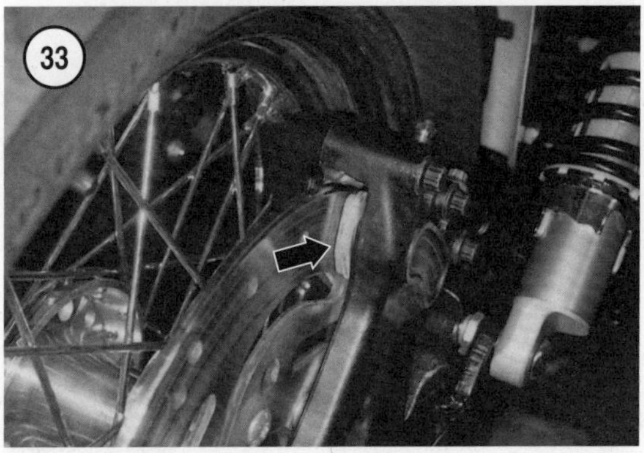

34

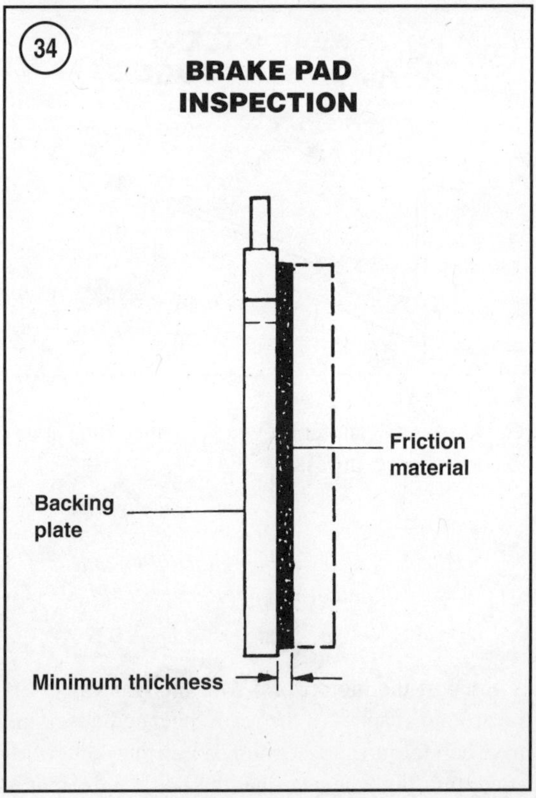

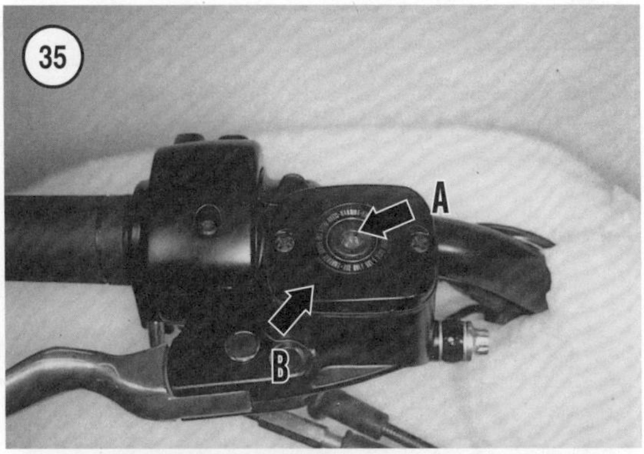

Step 3. The brake fluid must be within 1/8 in. (3.2 mm) from the top surface.

WARNING
Do not use brake fluid labeled ***DOT 5.1.*** *This is a glycol-based fluid that is* ***not compatible*** *with silicone based DOT 5. DOT 5 brake fluid is purple while DOT 5.1 is an amber/clear color. Do not intermix these two completely different types of brake fluid, as doing so will lead to brake component damage and possible brake failure.*

WARNING
Only use brake fluid clearly marked DOT 5 and specified for disc brakes. Others may vaporize, causing brake failure.

CAUTION
Do not allow the master cylinder reservoir to overflow when performing Step 3. Brake fluid will damage most surfaces it contacts.

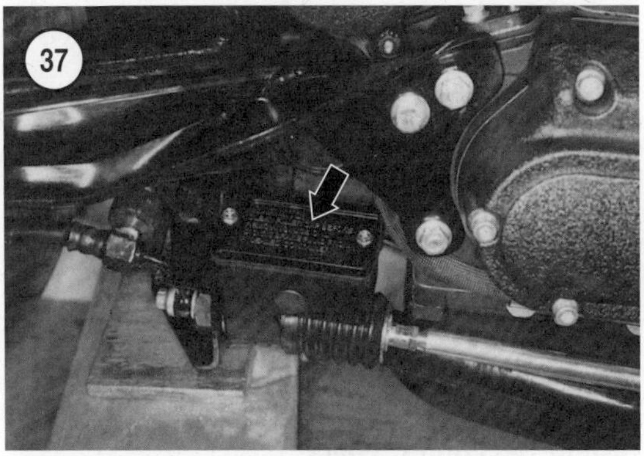

CAUTION
Cover all surrounding areas with a heavy cloth or plastic tarp to protect them from any accidental brake fluid spills. Wash brake fluid off any surfaces immediately, as it will destroy the finish. Use soapy water and rinse completely.

NOTE
To control the flow of brake fluid, punch a small hole in the seal of a new container of brake fluid next to the edge of the pour spout. This helps eliminate the fluid spillage, especially while adding fluid to the small reservoir.

3. If the brake fluid level is low, perform the following:
   a. If necessary on the rear master cylinder, remove the front cylinder's muffler as described in Chapter Seven.
   b. Clean any dirt from the master cylinder cover prior to removing it.
   c. Remove the top cover (B, **Figure 35**) and lift the diaphragm out of the reservoir.
   d. Add DOT 5 brake fluid to correct the level.
   e. Reinstall the diaphragm and top cover. Tighten the screws securely.

NOTE
If the brake fluid level is low enough to allow air in the hydraulic system, bleed the brakes as described in Chapter Twelve.

Front and Rear Brake Disc Inspection

Visually inspect the front and rear brake discs (**Figure 38**, typical) for scoring, cracks or other damage. Measure the brake disc thickness and, if necessary, service the brake discs as described in Chapter Twelve.

Disc Brake Lines and Seals

Check the brake lines between each master cylinder and each brake caliper. If there is any leakage, tighten the connections and bleed the brakes as described in Chapter Twelve.

Disc Brake Fluid Change

Every time the reservoir cover is removed, a small amount of dirt and moisture enters the brake fluid. The same thing happens if a leak occurs or if any part of the hydraulic system is loosened or disconnected. Dirt can clog the system and cause unnecessary wear. Water in the fluid vaporizes at high temperatures, impairing the hydraulic action and reducing brake performance.

To change brake fluid, follow the brake bleeding procedure in Chapter Twelve. Add new fluid to the master cylinder until the fluid leaving the caliper is clean and free of contaminants and air bubbles.

WARNING
Only use brake fluid clearly marked DOT 5. Others may vaporize and cause brake failure.

WARNING
*Do not use brake fluid labeled **DOT 5.1**. This is a glycol-based fluid that is **not compatible** with silicone-based DOT 5. DOT 5 brake fluid is purple while DOT 5.1 is an amber/clear color. Do not intermix these two completely different types of brake fluid, as doing so will lead to brake component damage and possible brake failure.*

Front Disc Brake Adjustment

The front disc brake does not require periodic adjustment.

Rear Brake Pedal Height Adjustment

The rear brake pedal on these models is not adjustable. When the rear master cylinder is properly assembled and mounted on the motorcycle, the brake pedal assembly is properly adjusted.

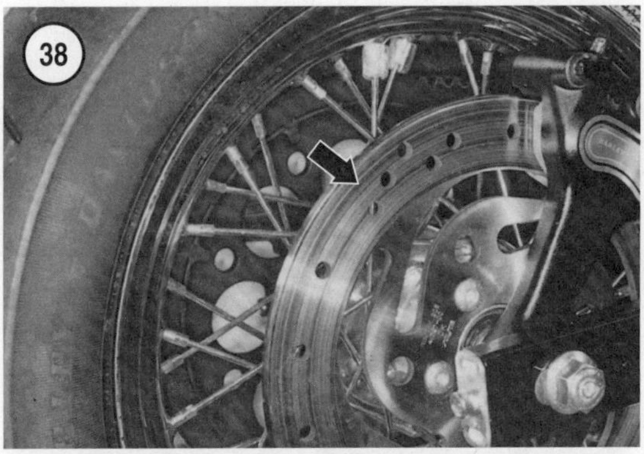

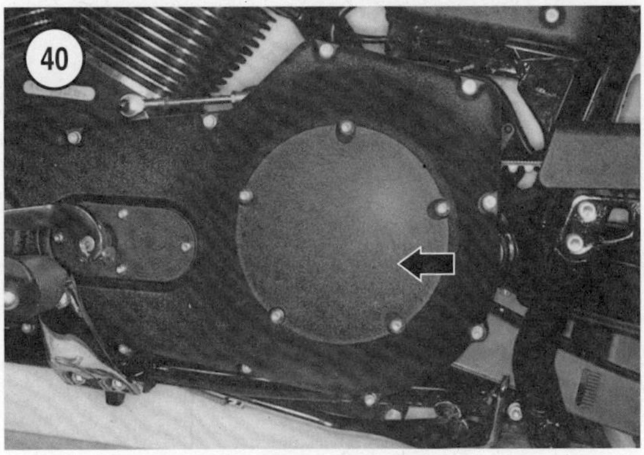

WARNING
Do not lengthen the brake rod to a point where six or more threads are visible on the brake rod. If six threads are visible past the jam nut, there is insufficient break rod thread engagement into the master cylinder push rod. This could cause the brake rod to separate from the pushrod, making the rear brake inoperative.

If minor height adjustment is required, perform the following:

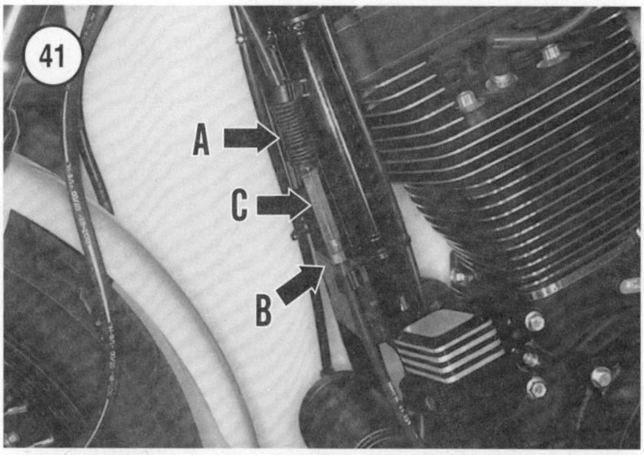

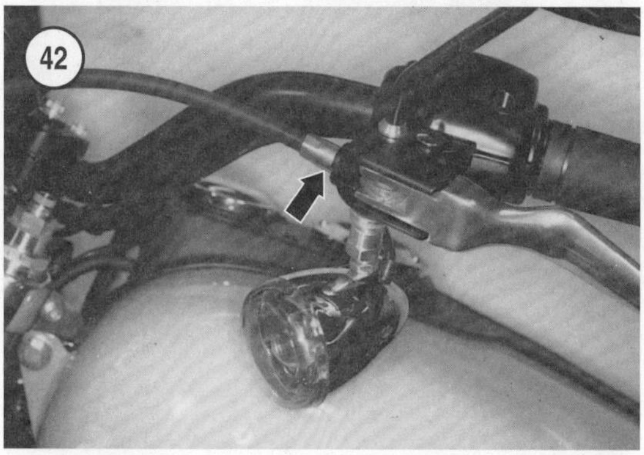

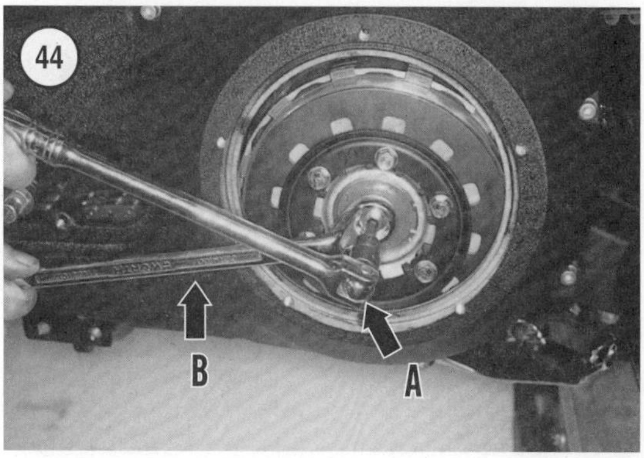

1. Loosen the brake rod jam nut (A, **Figure 39**) next to the master cylinder.
2. Rotate the brake rod (B, **Figure 39**) in either direction to gain the correct pedal height.
3. Tighten the jam nut securely.
4. If necessary, make sure the drain hole in the rubber boot is positioned to the bottom.

Clutch Adjustment

CAUTION

Because the clutch cable adjuster clearance increases with engine temperature, adjust the clutch when the engine is cold. If the clutch is adjusted when the engine is hot, insufficient pushrod clearance can cause the clutch to slip.

1. Remove the clutch inspection cover and O-ring (**Figure 40**).
2. Slide the rubber boot (A, **Figure 41**) off the clutch in-line cable adjuster.
3. Loosen the adjuster locknut (B, **Figure 41**) and turn the adjuster (C, **Figure 41**) to provide maximum cable slack.
4. Check that the clutch cable seats squarely in its perch (**Figure 42**) at the handlebar.
5. At the clutch mechanism, loosen the clutch adjusting screw locknut (A, **Figure 43**) and turn the adjusting screw (B, **Figure 43**) *clockwise* until it is lightly seated.
6. Squeeze the clutch lever three times to verify the clutch balls are seated in the ramp release mechanism located behind the transmission side cover.
7. Back out the adjusting screw (B, **Figure 43**) *counterclockwise* 1/2 to 1 turn. Then hold the adjusting screw (A, **Figure 44**) and tighten the locknut (B, **Figure 44**) to the specification in **Table 6**.
8. Once again, squeeze the clutch lever to its maximum limit three times to set the clutch ball and ramp release mechanism.
9. Check the free play as follows:
   a. At the in-line cable adjuster, turn the adjuster (C, **Figure 41**) away from the locknut until slack is eliminated at the clutch hand lever.
   b. Pull the clutch cable sheath away from the clutch lever, then turn the clutch cable adjuster (C, **Figure 41**) to obtain the free play (**Figure 45**) specified in **Table 8**.

c. When the adjustment is correct, tighten the clutch in-line cable locknut (B, **Figure 41**) and slide the rubber boot over the cable adjuster.

10. Install the clutch inspection cover O-ring (**Figure 46**) onto the primary chain case cover.

11. Install the clutch inspection cover and tighten the screws to the specification in **Table 6**.

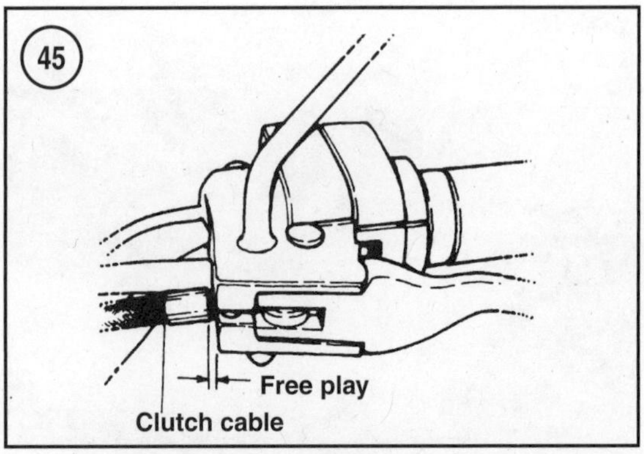

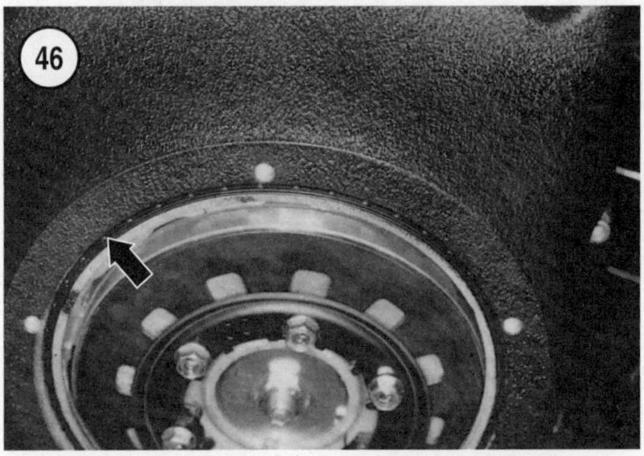

Throttle Cables Inspection

Inspect the throttle cables from grip to carburetor. Make sure they are not kinked or chafed. Replace them if necessary as described in Chapter Seven.

Make sure that the throttle grip rotates smoothly from fully closed to fully open. Check with the handlebar at center, full left and full right positions.

Throttle Cable Adjustment

There are two different throttle cables. One is the throttle control cable (A, **Figure 47** and A, **Figure 48**) and the other is the idle control cable (B, **Figure 47** and B, **Figure 48**).

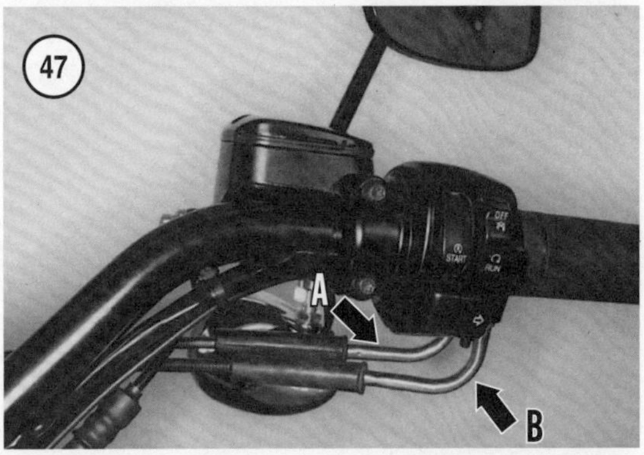

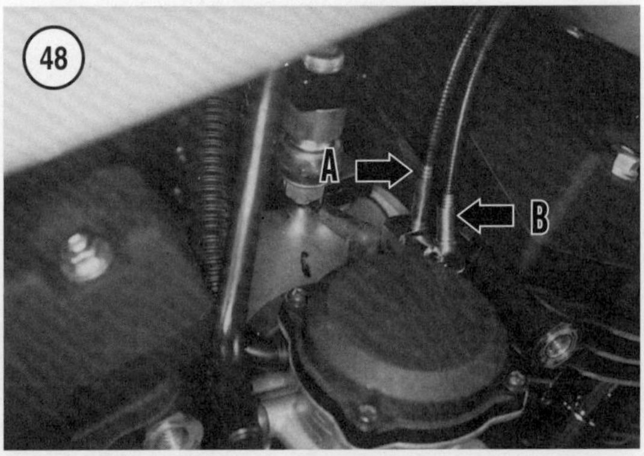

NOTE

The throttle control and idle control cables have different sizes of threads on the threaded adjusters. The throttle control cable has a 5/16×18 adjuster. The idle control cable has a 1/4×20 adjuster.

1. Remove the air filter and backing plate as described in Chapter Seven.
2. At the handlebar, perform the following:
   a. Slide the rubber boots off both cables (**Figure 49**).
   b. Loosen both control cable adjuster locknuts (A, **Figure 50**), then turn the cable adjusters (B, **Figure 50**) *clockwise* as far as possible to increase cable slack.
3. Turn the handlebars so that the front wheel points straight ahead. Then turn the throttle grip to open the throttle completely and hold it in this position.

NOTE

Figure 51 *is shown with the carburetor body removed to better illustrate the steps.*

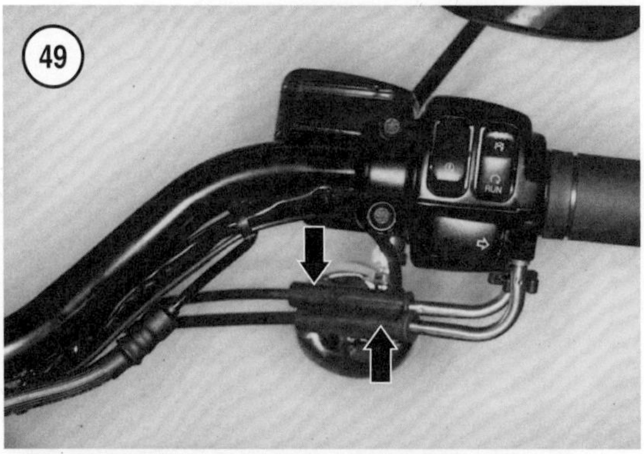

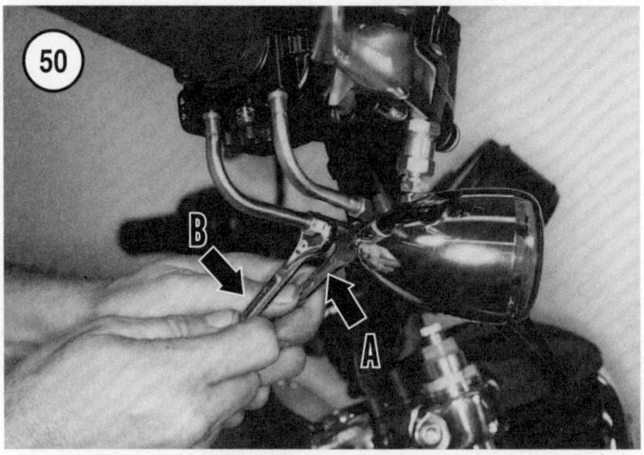

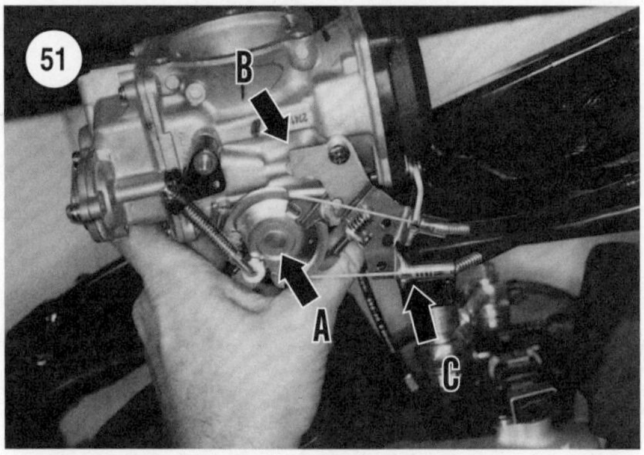

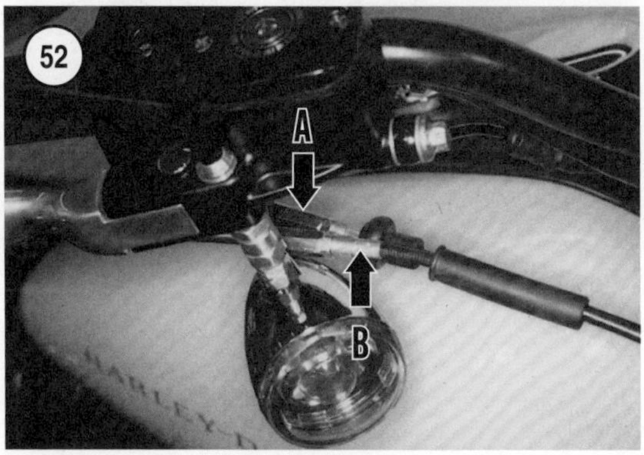

4. At the handlebar, turn the throttle control cable adjuster (A, **Figure 52**) *counterclockwise* until the throttle cam (A, **Figure 51**) stop just touches the stop boss (B, **Figure 51**) on the carburetor body. Then tighten the throttle cable adjuster locknut and release the throttle grip.

5. Turn the front wheel all the way to the full right lock position and hold it there.

6. At the handlebar, turn the idle cable adjuster (B, **Figure 52**) until the lower end of the idle control cable just contacts the spring in the carburetor cable guide (C, **Figure 51**). Tighten the idle cable locknut.

7. Shift the transmission into NEUTRAL and start the engine.

8. Increase engine speed several times. Release the throttle and make sure engine speed returns to idle. If engine speed does not return to idle, at the handlebar, loosen the idle control cable adjuster locknut and turn the cable adjuster (B, **Figure 52**) *clockwise* as required. Tighten the idle control cable adjuster locknut.

9. Allow the engine to idle in NEUTRAL. Then turn the handlebar from side to side. Do not operate the throttle. If the engine speed increases when the handlebar assembly is turned, the throttle cables are routed incorrectly or damaged. Turn off the engine. Recheck cable routing and adjustment.

WARNING

Do not ride the motorcycle until the throttle cables are properly adjusted. Likewise, the cables must not catch or pull when the handlebar is turned from side to side. Improper cable routing and adjustment can cause the throttle to stick open. This could cause loss of control and a possible crash. Recheck this adjustment before riding the motorcycle.

Starting Enrichment Valve (Choke) Cable Adjustment

The starting enrichment (choke) knob (**Figure 53**) must move from fully open to fully closed without any sign of binding. The knob must also stay in its fully closed or fully open position without creeping.

53

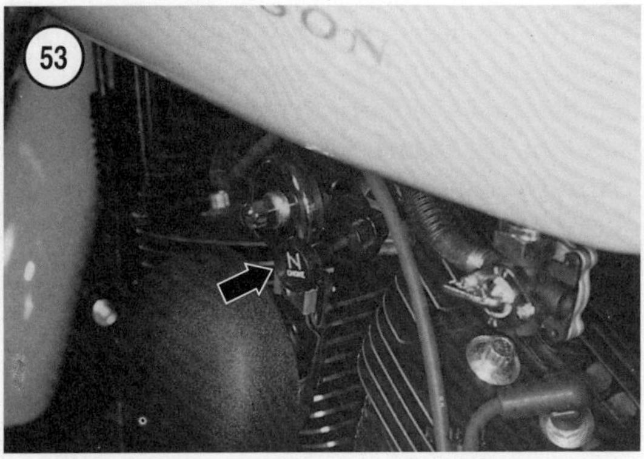

54

ENRICHENER CABLE

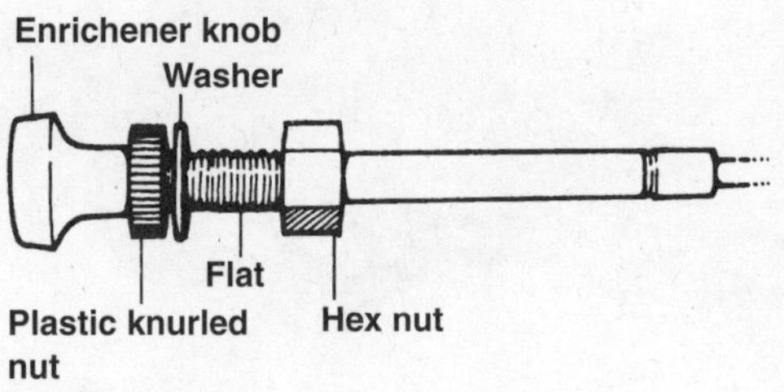

55

AIR FILTER

1. Backplate (International)
2. Grommet (California)
3. Backplate (California)
4. O-ring
5. Gasket
6. Backplate (49-state)
7. Breather hollow bolt
8. Breather hose
9. Gasket
10. Air filter
11. Mounting bracket
12. Bolts
13. Nut clip
14. Enrichment cable bracket
15. Cable strap
16. Nut
17. Grommet
18. Bolt
19. Screw
20. Trim
21. Cover
22. Gasket

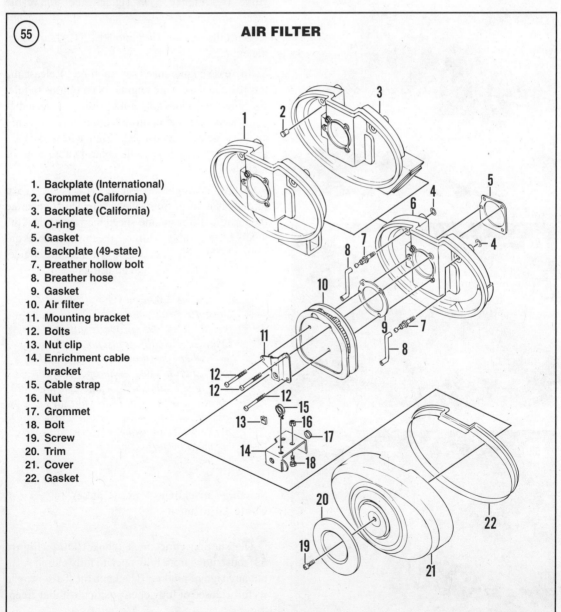

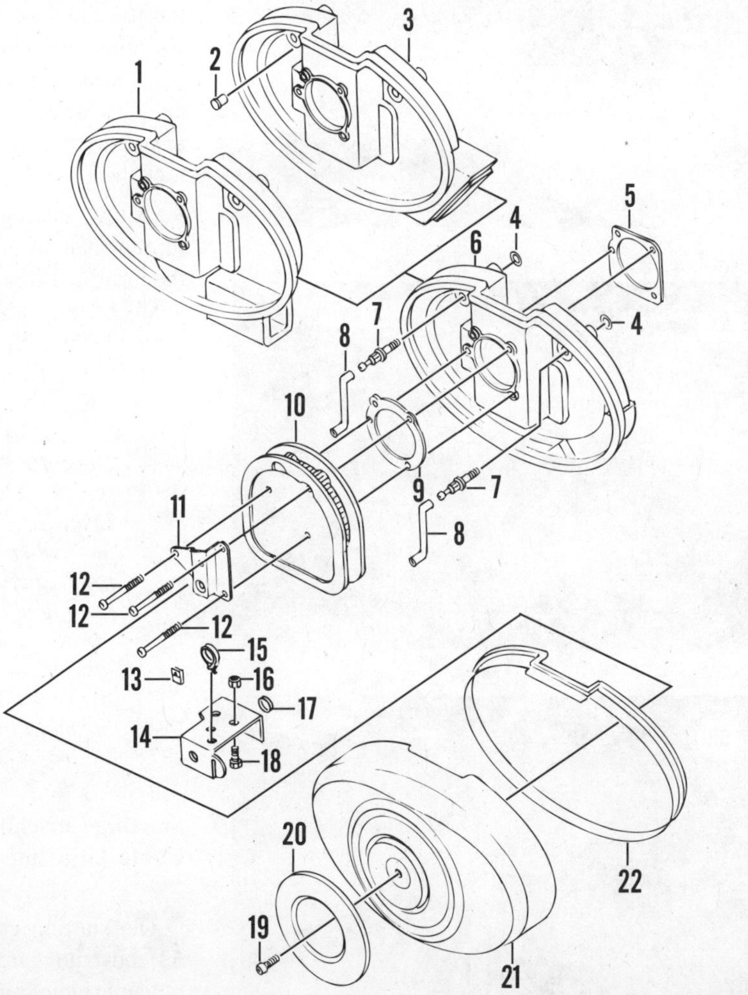

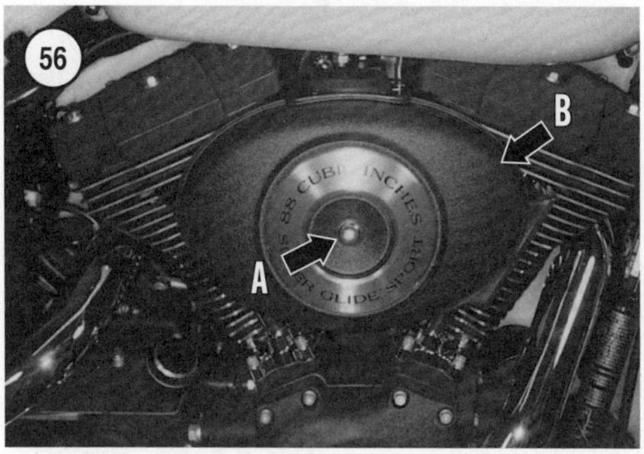

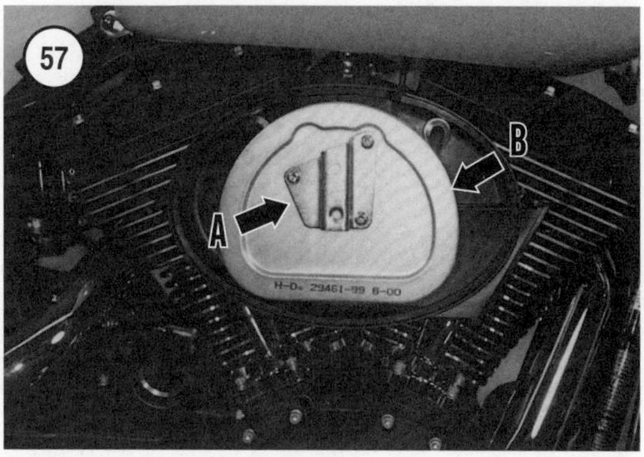

If the knob does not stay in position, adjust tension on the cable by turning the plastic knurled nut behind the knob (**Figure 54**) as follows:

CAUTION
The starting enrichment (choke) cable must have sufficient cable resistance to work properly. Do not lubricate the enrichment cable or its conduit.

1. Loosen the hex nut behind the mounting bracket. Then move the cable to free it from its mounting bracket slot.
2. Hold the cable across its flats with a wrench and turn the plastic knurled nut *counterclockwise* to reduce cable resistance. The knob must slide inward freely.
3. Turn the plastic knurled nut (**Figure 54**) *clockwise* to increase cable resistance. Continue adjustment until the knob remains stationary when pulled all the way out. The knob must move without any roughness or binding.
4. Reinstall the cable into the slot in its mounting bracket with the star washer located between the bracket and hex nut. Tighten the hex nut securely.
5. Recheck the knob movement and readjust if necessary.

Fuel Line Inspection

Inspect the fuel lines from the fuel tank to the carburetor. Replace leaking or damaged fuel lines. Make sure the hose clamps are in place and holding securely. Check the hose fittings for looseness.

WARNING
A damaged or deteriorated fuel line can cause a fire or explosion if fuel spills onto a hot engine or exhaust pipe.

Exhaust System

Check all fittings for exhaust leakage. Do not forget the crossover pipe connections. Tighten all bolts and nuts. Replace any gaskets as necessary. See Chapter Seven for removal and installation procedures.

Air Filter Element Removal/Installation

Remove and inspect the air filter at the interval in **Table 1**. If necessary, clean the element. Replace the element if it is damaged or starts to deteriorate.

The air filter removes dust and abrasive particles before the air enters the carburetor and the engine. Without the air filter, very fine particles could enter into the engine and cause rapid wear of the piston rings, cylinder bores and bearings. They also might clog small passages in the carburetor. Never run the motorcycle without the element installed.

Refer to **Figure 55** for this procedure.

1. Remove the air filter cover screw (A, **Figure 56**) and remove the cover (B, **Figure 56**).
2. Remove the Torx screws and bracket (A, **Figure 57**) from the air filter element.
3. Gently pull the air filter element away from the backplate and disconnect the two breather hoses from the breather hollow bolts on the backplate. Remove the air filter element (B, **Figure 57**).
4. Clean the air filter as described in the following procedure.

5. Inspect the gasket (**Figure 58**) for damage. Replace if necessary.
6. Inspect the breather hoses (**Figure 59**) for tears or deterioration. Replace if necessary.

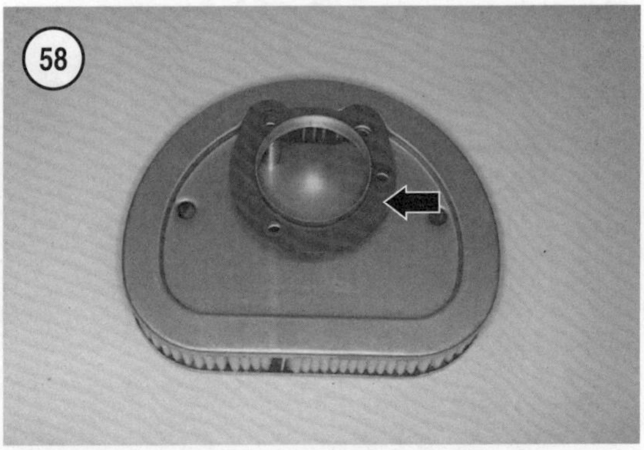
58

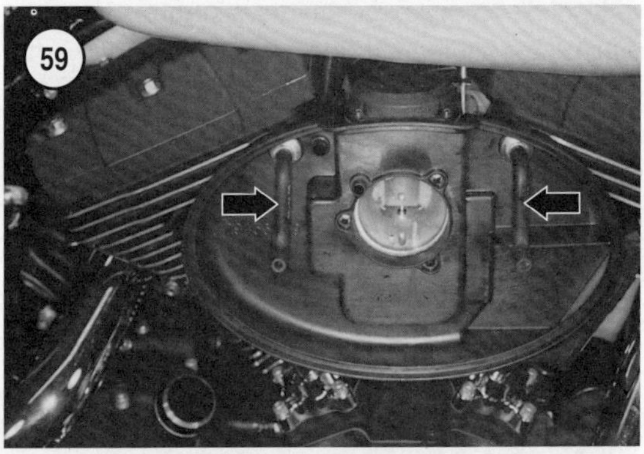
59

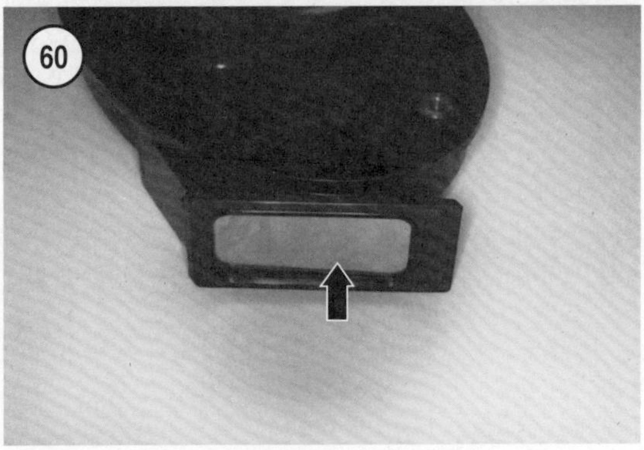
60

NOTE
Figure 60 *is shown with the air filter backplate removed to better illustrate the step.*

7. On California models, make sure the trap door swings freely (**Figure 60**).
8. If removed, install a new gasket (**Figure 58**) and breather hoses (**Figure 59**).
9. Position the element with the flat side facing down and attach the breather hoses (**Figure 61**) to the backside of the element (**Figure 62**).

NOTE
If an aftermarket air filter element is being installed, position it onto the backplate following the manufacturer's instructions.

10. Move the element into position (B, **Figure 57**) and install the mounting bracket (A, **Figure 57**) and the Torx screws. Tighten the screws to the specification in **Table 6**.
11. Apply a drop of ThreeBond TB1342 (blue), or an equivalent, threadlocking compound to the cover screw prior to installation.
12. Inspect the seal ring (**Figure 63**) on the air filter cover for hardness or deterioration. Replace if necessary.
13. Install the air filter cover (B, **Figure 56**) and the screw (A, **Figure 56**). Tighten the screw to the specification in **Table 6**.

Air Filter Element Cleaning

The air filter element is a paper/wire type (**Figure 64**). If an aftermarket element is installed, refer to the manufacturer's cleaning instructions.
1. Remove the air filter element as described in this chapter.
2. Replace the air filter if damaged.

WARNING
Do not clean the air filter in any type of solvent. Never clean the air filter element in gasoline or any type of low flash point solvent. The residual solvent or vapors left by these chemicals may cause a fire or explosion after the filter is reinstalled.

CAUTION
Do not tap or strike the air filter element on a hard surface to dislodge dirt. Doing so will damage the element.

3. Place the air filter in a pan filled with lukewarm water and mild detergent. Move the air filter element back and forth to help dislodge trapped dirt.

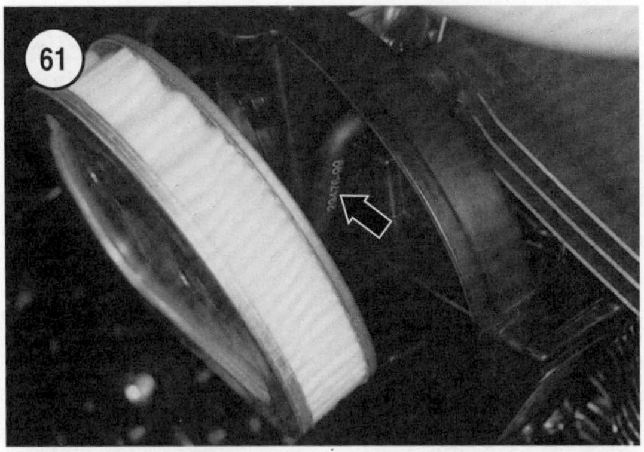

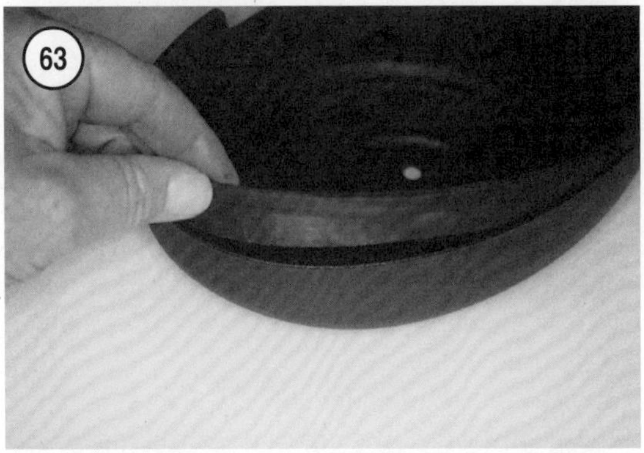

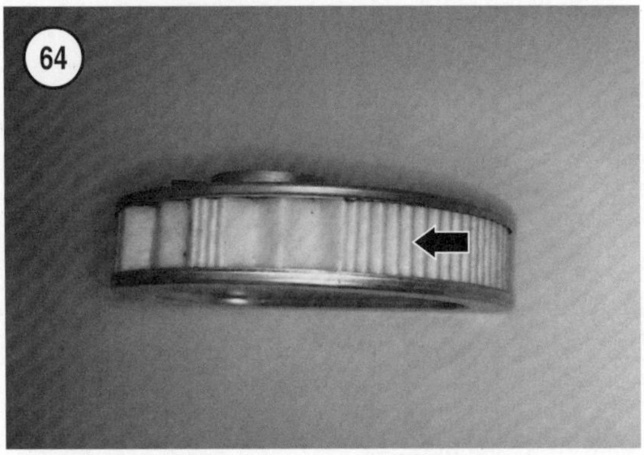

Thoroughly rinse in clean water to remove all detergent residue.

4. Remove the air filter and hold it up to a strong light. Check the filter pores for dirt and oil. Repeat Step 3 until there is no longer dirt and oil in the filter pores. If the air filter cannot be cleaned, or if the filter is saturated with oil or other chemicals, replace it.

CAUTION
Do not use high air pressure to dry the filter, as this will damage it.

CAUTION
In the next step, do not blow compressed air through the outer surface of the air filter element. Doing so can force dirt trapped on the outer filter surface deeper into the air filter element, restricting airflow and damaging the air filter element.

5. Gently apply compressed air through the inside surface of the air filter element to remove loosened dirt and dust trapped in the filter.

6. Inspect the air filter element. Replace if torn or damaged. Do not ride the motorcycle with a damaged filter element as it may allow dirt to enter the carburetor and engine.

7. Clean the breather hoses in the same lukewarm water and mild detergent. Make sure both hoses are clean and clear. Clean out with a pipe cleaner if necessary.

8. Wipe the inside of the cover and backplate with a clean damp shop rag.

CAUTION
Air will not pass through a wet or damp filter. Make sure the filter is dry before installing it.

9. Allow the filter to dry completely, then reinstall it as described in this chapter.

Steering Play

Check the steering head play (Chapter Ten) at the intervals specified in **Table 1**.

Rear Swing Arm Pivot Bolt

Check the rear swing arm pivot bolt tightness (Chapter Eleven) at the fastener interval specified in **Table 1**.

Rear Shock Absorbers

Check the rear shock absorbers for oil leakage or damaged bushings. Check the shock absorber mounting bolts and nuts for tightness. Refer to *Shock Absorbers* in Chapter Eleven for procedures.

Engine Mounts and Stabilizer

Check the stabilizer and the engine and frame mounts for loose or damaged parts. Refer to Chapter Four for procedures.

CAUTION
Special procedures must be used when tightening the cylinder head mounting bolts. To accurately check these bolts for tightness, refer to ***Cylinder Head Installation*** *in Chapter Four. Tightening these bolts incorrectly can cause an oil leak or cylinder head warpage.*

Fasteners

Constant vibration can loosen many fasteners on a motorcycle. Check the tightness of all fasteners, especially those on:

1. Engine mounting hardware.
2. Engine and primary covers.
3. Handlebar and front fork.
4. Gearshift lever.
5. Sprocket bolts and nuts.
6. Brake pedal and lever.
7. Exhaust system.
8. Lighting equipment.

Electrical Equipment and Switches

Check all of the electrical equipment and switches for proper operation.

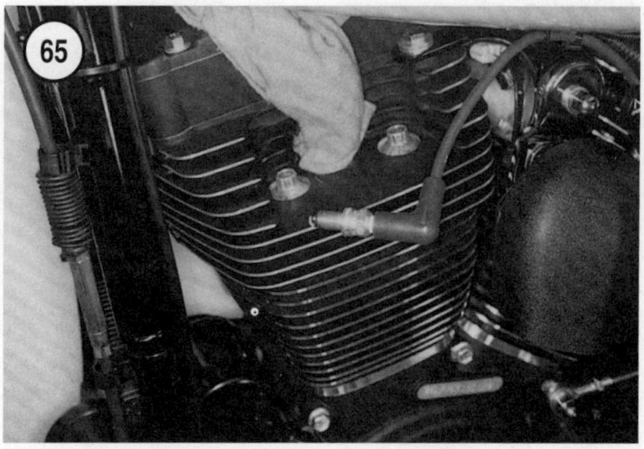

65

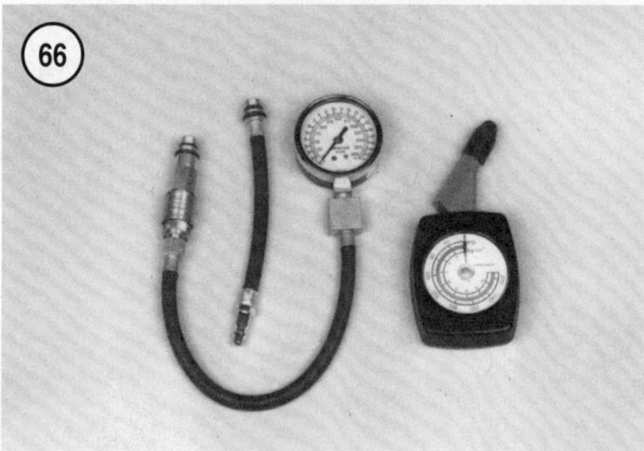

66

TUNE-UP

A complete tune-up restores performance and power lost due to normal wear and deterioration of engine parts. Because engine wear occurs over a combined period of time and mileage, perform the engine tune-up procedures at the intervals specified in **Table 1**. More frequent tune-ups may be required if the motorcycle is operated primarily in stop-and-go traffic.

Replace the spark plugs at every other tune-up or if the electrodes show signs of wear, fouling or erosion.

Perform the procedures in the following order and refer to **Table 8** for specifications.

1. Clean or replace the air filter element.
2. Check engine compression.
3. Check or replace the spark plugs.
4. Adjust carburetor idle speed.

Air Filter

Clean the air filter element before performing other tune-up procedures. Refer to *Air Filter Element* in this chapter.

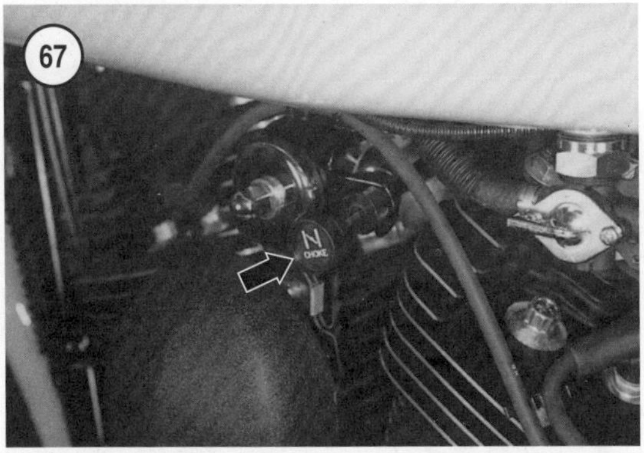

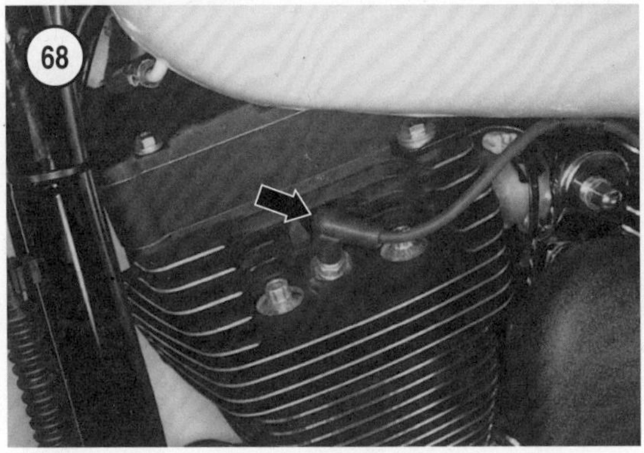

Compression Test

A compression check is one of the most effective ways to check the condition of the engine. Check the compression at each tune-up, record the readings and compare them to readings at subsequent tune-ups. This will help spot any developing problems.

1. Prior to starting the compression test, make sure the following is correct:
   a. The cylinder head bolts are tightened to the torque specification. Refer to Chapter Four.
   b. The battery is fully charged to ensure proper engine cranking speed.
2. Warm the engine to normal operating temperature. Shut off the engine.
3. Remove the spark plugs and reinstall them in their caps (**Figure 65**). Place the spark plugs against the cylinder head to ground them.
4. Connect the compression tester to one cylinder, following its manufacturer's instructions (**Figure 66**).
5. Place the throttle in the wide-open position. Make sure the starting enrichment (choke) knob (**Figure 67**) is pushed in fully to the OFF position.
6. Crank the engine over until there is no further rise in pressure.
7. Record the reading and remove the tester.
8. Repeat Steps 4-7 for the other cylinder.
9. Reinstall the spark plugs and reconnect their caps.

Results

When interpreting the results, actual readings are not as important as the difference between the readings. **Table 8** lists the standard engine compression reading. Pressure must not vary between the cylinders by more than 10 percent. Greater differences indicate worn or broken rings, leaky or sticky valves, blown head gasket or a combination of all.

If compression readings do not differ between cylinders by more than 10 percent, the rings and valves are in good condition. A low reading (10 percent or more) on one cylinder indicates valve or ring trouble. To decide which, pour about a teaspoon of engine oil into the spark plug hole. Turn the engine over once to distribute the oil, then take another compression test and record the reading. If the compression increases significantly, the valves are good but the rings are defective on that cylinder. If compression does not increase, the valves require servicing.

NOTE
An engine cannot be tuned to maximum performance with low compression.

Spark Plug Removal

CAUTION
Whenever the spark plug is removed, dirt around it can fall into the plug hole. This can cause serious engine damage.

1. Blow away any loose dirt or debris that may have accumulated around the base of the spark plug that could fall into the cylinder head.
2. Grasp the spark plug lead (**Figure 68**), and twist from side to side to break the seal loose. Then pull

the cap off the spark plug. If the cap is stuck to the plug, twist it slightly to break it loose.

NOTE
Use a special spark plug socket equipped with a rubber insert that holds the spark plug. This type of socket is necessary for both removal and installation since the spark plugs are recessed in the cylinder head.

3. Install the spark plug socket onto the spark plug. Make sure it is correctly seated and install an open-end wrench or socket handle and remove the spark plug. Mark the spark plug with which cylinder number it was removed from.
4. Repeat for the remaining spark plug.
5. Thoroughly inspect each plug. Look for broken center porcelain, excessively eroded electrodes and excessive carbon or oil fouling.

NOTE
Spark plug cleaning with a sand-blasting device is not recommended. While this type of cleaning is thorough, the plug must be completely free of all abrasive cleaning material when done. If not, it is possible for the abrasive material to fall into the cylinder during operation and cause damage.

6. Inspect the spark plug caps and secondary wires for damage, or hardness. If any portion is damaged, the cap and secondary wire must be replaced as an assembly. The front and rear cylinder assemblies have different part numbers.

Spark Plug Gapping and Installing

Carefully gap the spark plugs to ensure a reliable, consistent spark. A special spark plug gapping tool and a wire feeler gauge must be used.
1. Remove the new spark plugs from the boxes. Install the small adapter onto the end of the spark plug that may be loose in the box.
2. Insert a wire feeler gauge between the center and side electrode of the plug (**Figure 69**). The correct gap is listed in **Table 8**. If the gap is correct, a slight drag will be felt as the wire gauge is pulled through. If there is no drag, or the gauge will not pass through, bend the side electrode with a gapping tool

69

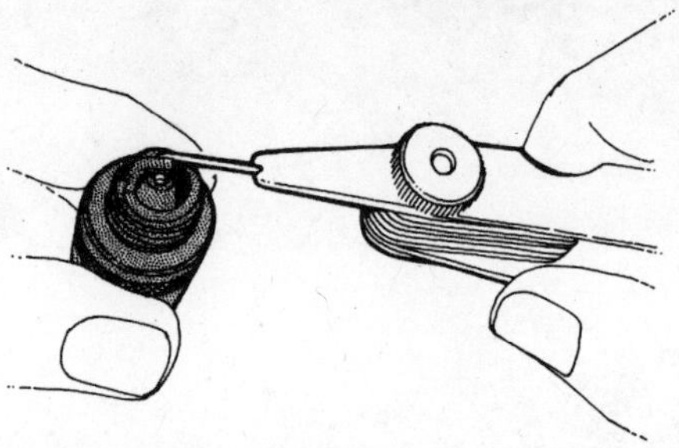

(**Figure 70**) to adjust the proper gap listed in **Table 8**.
3. Apply a *light coat* of antiseize lubricant on the threads of the spark plug before installing it. Do *not* use engine oil on the plug threads.

CAUTION
The cylinder head is aluminum and the spark plug hole can be easily damaged by cross-threading the spark plug.

4. Slowly screw the spark plug into the cylinder head by hand until it seats. Very little effort is required. If force is necessary to remove the plug , it is cross-threaded; unscrew it and try again.

NOTE
Do not overtighten. This will only squash the gasket and destroy its sealing ability.

5. Hand-tighten the plug until it seats against the cylinder head, then tighten to the specification in **Table 6**.
6. Install the spark plug cap and lead to the correct spark plug. Rotate the cap slightly in both directions and make sure it is attached to the spark plug.
7. Repeat for the other spark plug.

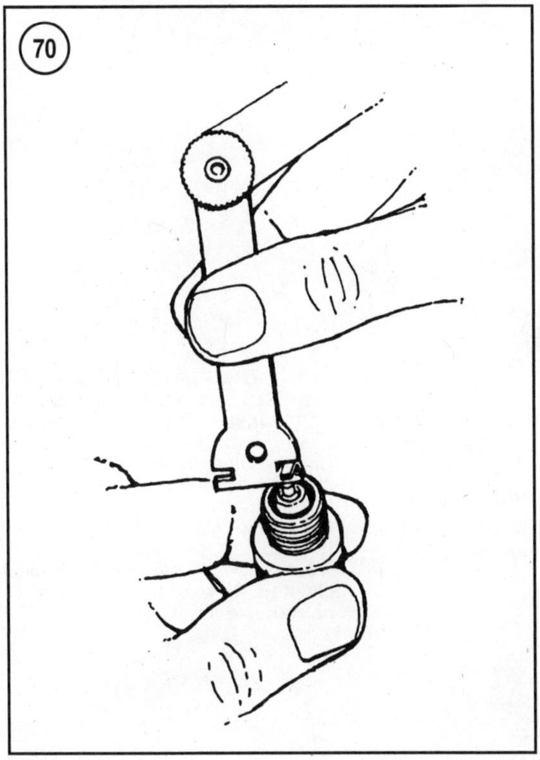

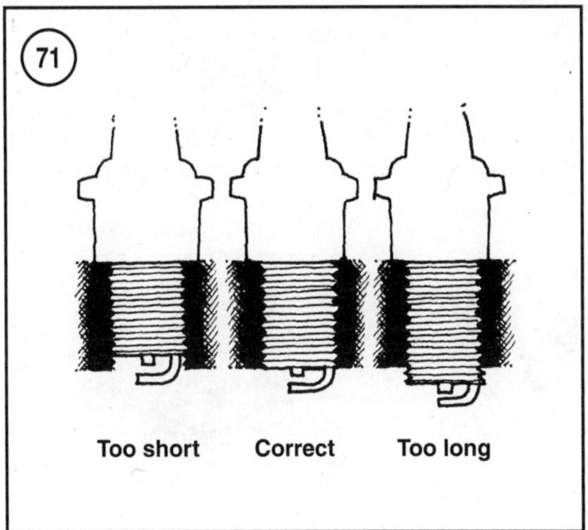

Spark Plug Heat Range

Spark plugs are available in various heat ranges, hotter or colder than the plugs originally installed by the manufacturer.

Select a plug with a heat range designed for the loads and conditions under which the motorcycle will be operated. A plug with an incorrect heat range can foul, overheat and cause piston damage.

In general, use a hot plug for low speeds and low temperatures. Use a cold plug for high speeds, high engine loads and high temperatures. The plug should operate hot enough to burn off unwanted deposits, but not so hot that it is damaged or causes preignition. To determine if plug heat range is correct, remove each spark plug and examine the insulator.

Do not change the spark plug heat range to compensate for adverse engine or carburetion conditions.

When replacing plugs, make sure the reach (**Figure 71**) is correct. A longer than standard plug could interfere with the piston, causing engine damage.

Refer to **Table 8** for recommended spark plugs.

Spark Plug Reading

Reading the spark plugs can provide a significant amount of information regarding engine performance. Reading plugs that have been in use will give an indication of spark plug operation, air/fuel mixture composition and engine conditions (such as oil consumption or pistons). Before checking the spark plugs, operate the motorcycle under a medium load for approximately 6 miles (10 km). Avoid prolonged idling before shutting off the engine. Remove the spark plugs as described in this chapter. Examine each plug and compare it to those in **Figure 72** while referring to the following sections to determine the operating conditions.

If the plugs are being read to determine if carburetor jetting is correct, start with new plugs and operate the motorcycle at the load that corresponds to the jetting information desired. For example, if the main jet is in question, operate the motorcycle at full throttle and shut the engine off and coast to a stop.

Normal condition

If the plug has a light tan- or gray-colored deposit and no abnormal gap wear or erosion, good engine, air/fuel mixture and ignition conditions are indicated. The plug in use is of the proper heat range and may be serviced and returned to use.

Carbon fouled

Soft, dry, sooty deposits covering the entire firing end of the plug are evidence of incomplete combus-

(72)

SPARK PLUG CONDITIONS

NORMAL
- Identified by light tan or gray deposits on the firing tip.
- Can be cleaned.

GAP BRIDGED
- Identified by deposit buildup closing the gap between electrodes.
- Caused by oil or carbon fouling. If deposits are not excessive, the plug can be cleaned.

OIL FOULED
- Identified by wet black deposits on the insulator shell bore and electrodes.
- Caused by excessive oil entering the combustion chamber through worn rings or pistons, excessive clearance between the valve guides and stems or worn or loose bearings. Can be cleaned. If engine is not repaired, use a hotter plug.

CARBON FOULED
- Identified by black, dry fluffy carbon deposits on insulator tips, exposed shell surfaces and electrodes.
- Caused by a too-cold plug, weak ignition, dirty air cleaner, too rich fuel mixture or excessive idling. Can be cleaned.

LEAD FOULED
- Identified by dark gray, black, yellow or tan deposits or a fused glazed coating on the insulator tip.
- Caused by highly leaded gasoline. Can be cleaned.

WORN
- Identified by severely eroded or worn electrodes.
- Caused by normal wear. It should be replaced.

FUSED SPOT DEPOSIT
- Identified by melted or spotty deposits resembling bubbles or blisters.
- Caused by sudden acceleration. Can be cleaned.

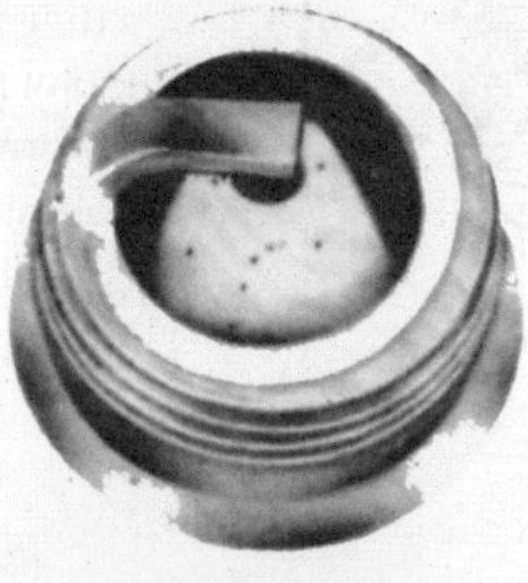

OVERHEATING
- Identified by a white or light gray insulator with small black or gray brown spots with bluish-burnt appearance of electrodes.
- Caused by engine overheating, wrong type of fuel, loose spark plugs, too hot a plug or incorrect ignition timing. Replace the plug.

PREIGNITION
- Identified by melted electrodes and possibly blistered insulator. Metallic deposits on insulator indicate engine damage.
- Caused by wrong type of fuel, incorrect ignition timing or advance, too hot a plug, burned valves or engine overheating. Replace the plug.

tion. Even though the firing end of the plug is dry, the plug's insulation decreases when in this condition. An electrical path is formed that bypasses the electrodes, resulting in a misfire condition. Carbon fouling can be caused by one or more of the following:
1. Rich fuel mixture.
2. Cold spark plug heat range.
3. Clogged air filter.
4. Improperly operating ignition component.
5. Ignition component failure.
6. Low engine compression.
7. Prolonged idling.

Oil fouled

The tip of an oil-fouled plug has a black insulator tip, a damp oily film over the firing end and a carbon layer over the entire nose. The electrodes are not worn. Oil-fouled spark plugs may be cleaned in an emergency, but it is better to replace them. It is important to correct the cause of fouling before the engine is returned to service. Common causes for this condition are:
1. Incorrect air/fuel mixture.
2. Low idle speed or prolonged idling.
3. Ignition component failure.
4. Cold spark plug heat range.
5. Engine still being broken in.
6. Valve guides worn.
7. Piston rings worn or broken.

Gap bridging

Plugs with this condition exhibit gaps shorted out by combustion deposits between the electrodes. If this condition is encountered, check for excessive carbon or oil in the combustion chamber. Be sure to locate and correct the cause of this condition.

Overheating

Badly worn electrodes and premature gap wear are signs of overheating, along with a gray or white blistered porcelain insulator surface. The most common cause for this condition is using a spark plug of the wrong heat range (too hot). If the spark plug is the correct heat range and is overheated, consider the following causes:
1. Lean air/fuel mixture.
2. Improperly operating ignition component.
3. Engine lubrication system malfunction.
4. Cooling system malfunction.
5. Engine air leak.
6. Improper spark plug installation.
7. No spark plug gasket.

Worn out

Corrosive gases formed by combustion and high voltage sparks have eroded the electrodes. A spark plug in this condition requires more voltage to fire under hard acceleration. Replace with a new spark plug.

Preignition

If the electrodes are melted, preignition is almost certainly the cause. Check for intake air leaks at the manifold and carburetor, or throttle body, and advanced ignition timing. It is also possible that a plug of the wrong heat range (too hot) is being used. Find the cause of the preignition before returning the engine into service. For additional information, refer to *Engine Performance* in Chapter Two.

Ignition Timing

The engine is equipped with a fully transistorized ignition system and is controlled by the ignition module. This solid state system uses no breaker points or other moving parts, and there are no means of adjusting ignition timing. Harley-Davidson does not provide any ignition timing procedures. Because of the solid state design, problems with the transistorized system are rare and adjusting the ignition timing is not necessary or possible. If an ignition-related problem is suspected, inspect the ignition components as described in Chapter Eight.

Incorrect ignition timing can cause a drastic loss of engine performance and efficiency. It may also cause overheating.

IDLE SPEED ADJUSTMENT

1. Start the engine and warm it to normal operating temperature. Shut off the engine.

2. Make sure the starting enrichment (choke) valve (**Figure 67**) is pushed all the way to the OFF position.
3. On models without a tachometer, connect a portable tachometer to the engine, following its manufacturer's instructions.

NOTE
***Figure 73** is shown with the air filter assembly removed to better illustrate the step.*

4. Start the engine and, with the engine idling, compare the tachometer reading to the idle speed specification in **Table 8**. If the tachometer reading is incorrect, adjust the idle speed with the carburetor throttle stop screw (**Figure 73**).

NOTE
The idle mixture is set and sealed by the manufacturer and is not adjustable.

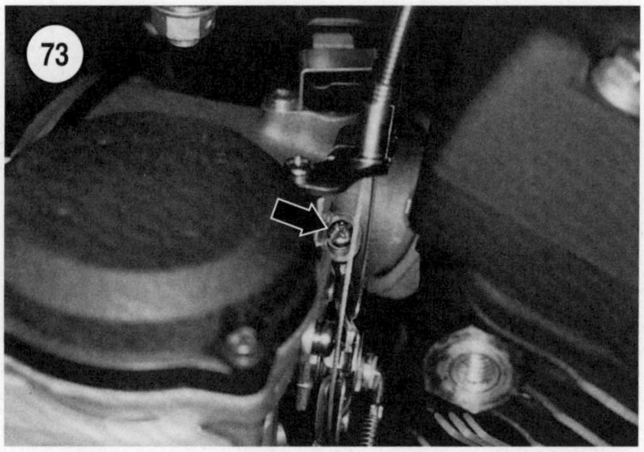

5. Accelerate the engine a couple of times and release the throttle. The idle speed must return to the speed set in Step 4. If necessary, readjust the idle speed by turning the throttle stop screw (**Figure 73**). Shut off the engine.
6. If installed, disconnect and remove the portable tachometer.

Table 1 MAINTENANCE AND LUBRICATION SCHEDULE[1]

Pre-ride check
Check tire condition and inflation pressure
Check wheel rim condition
Check engine oil level; add oil if necessary
Check brake fluid level and condition; add fluid if necessary
Check brake lever operation and travel
Check throttle and choke (enrichener) cable operation
Check fuel level in fuel tank; top off if necessary
Check drive belt tension
Initial 500 miles (800 km)
Change engine oil and filter
Check battery condition; clean cable connections if necessary
Check brake fluid level and condition; add fluid if necessary
Check front and rear brake pads and discs for wear
Check tire for correct inflation pressure and for excessive wear or damage
Check primary chain deflection; adjust if necessary
Check drive belt tension; adjust if necessary
Change primary chain case lubricant
Change transmission lubricant
Check clutch lever operation; adjust if necessary
Check drive belt and sprockets condition
Inspect spark plugs
Inspect air filter element for dirt and damage
Lubricate front brake and clutch lever pivot pin

(continued)

Table 1 MAINTENANCE AND LUBRICATION SCHEDULE (continued)

Initial 500 miles (800 km) (continued)
- Lubricate clutch cable if necessary
- Check operation of throttle and choke (enrichener)
- Check engine idle speed; adjust if necessary
- Check fuel valve, fuel lines and all fittings for leaks or damage
- Check electrical switches and equipment for proper operation
- Check oil and brake lines for leakage
- Check all fasteners for tightness[2]
- Road test the motorcycle

Every 2500 miles (4000 km)
- Check transmission lubricant level; add lubricant if necessary
- Check drive belt tension; adjust if necessary
- Inspect air filter element for dirt and damage; clean or replace as necessary
- Check operation of throttle and choke (enrichener)
- Check fuel valve, fuel lines and all fittings for leaks or damage
- Check oil and brake lines for leakage
- Check electrical switches and equipment for proper operation
- Road test the motorcycle

Every 5000 miles (8000 km)
- Change engine oil and filter
- Check battery condition; clean cable connections if necessary
- Check brake fluid level and condition; add fluid if necessary
- Check front and rear brake pads and discs for wear
- Check tire for correct inflation pressure and for excessive wear or damage
- Check wire wheel spoke nipple tightness; adjust if necessary (models so equipped)
- Check primary chain deflection; adjust if necessary
- Check drive belt tension; adjust if necessary
- Change primary chain case lubricant
- Change transmission lubricant
- Check clutch lever operation; adjust if necessary
- Check drive belt and sprockets condition
- Check steering head bearing adjustment; adjust if necessary
- Inspect spark plugs
- Inspect air filter element for dirt and damage; clean or replace as necessary
- Lubricate front brake and clutch lever pivot pin
- Lubricate clutch cable if necessary
- Check operation of throttle and choke (enrichener)
- Check engine idle speed; adjust if necessary
- Check fuel valve, fuel lines and all fittings for leaks or damage
- Check electrical switches and equipment for proper operation
- Check oil and brake lines for leakage
- Check all fasteners for tightness[2]
- Road test the motorcycle

Every 10,000 miles (16,000 km)
- Replace spark plugs
- Lubricate steering head bearings
- Repack rear swing arm bearings
- Repack wheel bearings (1999 models)
- Inspect engine mounts for wear or damage; replace if necessary

Every 20,000 miles (32,000 km)
- Change front fork oil
- Inspect fuel supply valve filter screen

1. Consider this maintenance schedule a guide to general maintenance and lubrication intervals. Harder than normal use and exposure to mud, water, high humidity indicates the need for more frequent servicing to most of the maintenance items.
2. Except cylinder head bolts. Cylinder head bolts must be tightened following the procedure listed in Chapter Four. Improper tightening of cylinder head bolts may cause cylinder gasket damage and/or cylinder head leakage.

Table 2 TIRE INFLATION PRESSURE (COLD)*

Model	kPa	psi
Front wheels		
Rider only	207	30
Rider and one passenger	207	30
Rear wheels		
Rider only	248	36
Rider and one passenger	276	40

*Tire pressure for original equipment tires. Aftermarket tires may require different inflation pressure.

Table 3 ENGINE OIL SPECIFICATIONS

Type	HD rating	Viscosity	Ambient operating temperature
HD Multi-grade	HD360	SAE 10W/40	Below 40° F
HD Multi-grade	HD360	SAE 20W/50	Above 40° F
HD Regular heavy	HD360	SAE 50	Above 60° F
HD Extra heavy	HD360	SAE 60	Above 80° F

Table 4 ENGINE AND PRIMARY DRIVE/TRANSMISSION OIL CAPACITIES

Oil tank refill capacity	
With oil filter change	2.5 U.S. qts. (2.4 L)
After engine rebuild	2.9 U.S. qts. (2.7 L)
Primary chaincase	26 U.S. oz. (768 mL)
Transmission	
Oil change	20-24 U.S. oz. (591-709 mL)
Rebuild (dry)	24 U.S. oz. (709 mL)

Table 5 RECOMMENDED LUBRICANTS AND FLUIDS

Brake fluid	DOT 5 silicone
Front fork oil	HD Type E or an equivalent
Fuel	91 pump octane or higher leaded or unleaded
Transmission	HD Transmission Lubricant or an equivalent
Primary chaincase	HD Primary Chaincase Lubricant or an equivalent

Table 6 MAINTENANCE AND TUNE-UP TORQUE SPECIFICATIONS

Item	ft.-lb.	in.-lb.	N·m
Air filter			
Backplate screws	–	20-40	2-5
Cover screw	–	36-60	4-7
Clutch adjusting screw locknut	–	72-120	8-14
Clutch inspection cover screws	–	84-108	9-12

(continued)

Table 6 MAINTENANCE AND TUNE-UP TORQUE SPECIFICATIONS (continued)

Item	ft.-lb.	in.-lb.	N•m
Crankcase oil plug	–	120-144	14-16
Engine oil drain plug	14-21	–	19-28
Front fork cap bolt	11-22	–	15-30
Primary drive chain			
Inspection cover screws	–	84-108	10-12
Chain adjuster shoe nut	21-29	–	28-39
Oil tank drain plug	14-21	–	19-28
Front axle nut	50-55	–	68-75
Rear axle nut	60-65	–	81-88
Transmission drain plug	14-21	–	19-28
Upper fork bridge pinch bolts			
FXDWG	30-35	–	41-47
All models except FXDWG	25-30	–	34-41
Spark plug	11-18	–	15-24

Table 7 FRONT FORK OIL CAPACITY AND OIL LEVEL DIMENSION

Model	Capacity oz. (ml)	Oil level dimension in. (mm)
1999 models		
FXDWG	10.2 (302)	–
All models except FXDWG	9.2 (272)	–
2000-on models		
FXD	10.6 (314)	6.69 (169.9)
FXDL	10.7 (316)	7.20 (182.0)
FXDS-CONV	11.5 (341)	6.10 (154.9)
FXDWG	12.0 (356)	7.28 (184.9)
FXDX, FXDXT	See text procedure	5.04 (128)
FXDP	NA	NA

NA = Information not available from the manufacturer.

Table 8 MAINTENANCE AND TUNE-UP SPECIFICATIONS

Item	Specification
Engine compression	90 psi (620 kPa)
Spark plugs	HD No. 6R12*
Gap	0.038-0.043 in. (0.097-1.09 mm)
Idle speed	950-1050 rpm
Ignition timing	Non-adjustable
Drive belt deflection	5/16-3/8 in. (8-10 mm)
Brake pad minimum thickness	
1999	1/16 in. (1.6 mm)
2000-on	0.04 in. (1.02 mm)
Clutch cable free play	1/16-1/8 in. (1.6-3.2 mm)

*Harley-Davidson recommends that no other type of spark plug be substituted for the recommended H-D type.

NOTE: Refer to the Supplement at the back of this manual for information unique to 2002-on models.

CHAPTER FOUR

ENGINE

All Dyna Glide models covered in this manual are equipped with the Twin Cam 88 engine, an air-cooled 4-stroke, overhead-valve V-twin engine. The engine consists of three major assemblies: engine, crankcase and gearcase. Viewed from the engine's right side, engine rotation is clockwise.

Both cylinders fire once in 720 degrees of crankshaft rotation. The rear cylinder fires 315 degrees after the front cylinder. The front cylinder fires again in another 405 degrees. Note that one cylinder is always on its exhaust stroke when the other fires on its compression stroke.

This chapter provides complete service and overhaul procedures, including information for disassembly, removal, inspection, service and engine reassembly.

Tables 1-6 at the end of the chapter provide spacer, shim and specification information.

ENGINE PRINCIPLES

Figure 1 explains basic four-stroke engine operation.

SERVICE PRECAUTIONS

Before servicing the engine, note the following:

1. Review the information in Chapter One, especially the *Basic Service Methods* and *Precision Measuring Tools* sections. Accurate measurements are critical to a successful engine rebuild.
2. Throughout the text there are references to the left and right side of the engine. This refers to the engine as it is mounted in the frame, not how it may sit on the workbench.
3. Always replace worn or damaged fasteners with those of the same size, type and torque require-

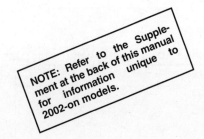

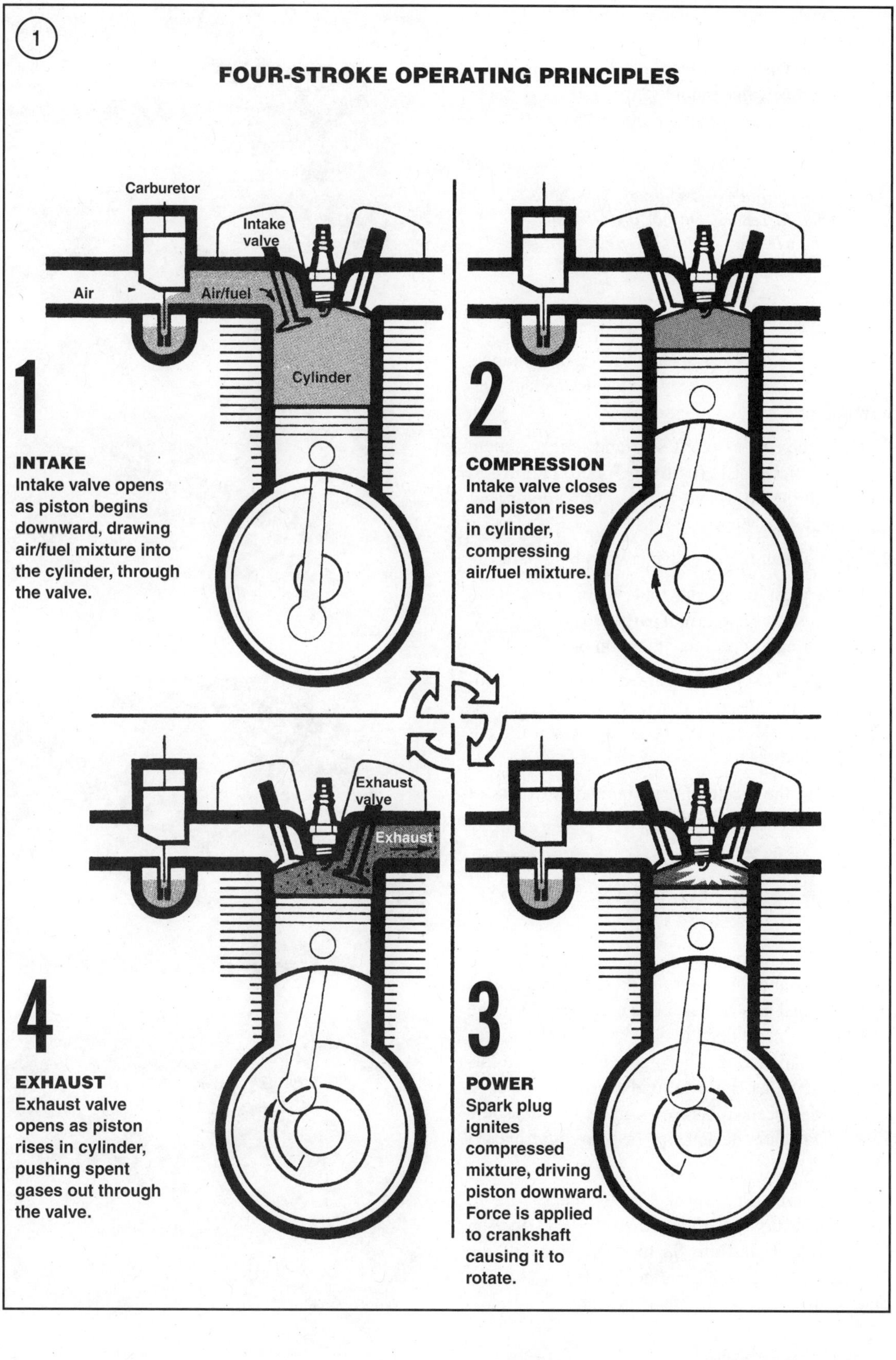
1
FOUR-STROKE OPERATING PRINCIPLES
Carburetor
Intake valve
Air
Air/fuel
Cylinder
1
INTAKE
Intake valve opens as piston begins downward, drawing air/fuel mixture into the cylinder, through the valve.
2
COMPRESSION
Intake valve closes and piston rises in cylinder, compressing air/fuel mixture.
Exhaust valve
Exhaust
4
EXHAUST
Exhaust valve opens as piston rises in cylinder, pushing spent gases out through the valve.
3
POWER
Spark plug ignites compressed mixture, driving piston downward. Force is applied to crankshaft causing it to rotate.

ments. Make sure to identify each bolt before replacing it. Lubricate bolt threads with engine oil, unless otherwise specified, before tightening. If a specific torque value is not listed in **Table 4**, refer to the general torque specifications in Chapter One.

CAUTION

The engine is assembled with hardened fasteners. Do not install fasteners with a lower strength grade classification.

4. Use special tools where noted.
5. Store parts in boxes, plastic bags and containers (**Figure 2**). Use masking tape and a permanent, waterproof marking pen to label parts.
6. Use a box of assorted size and color vacuum hose identifiers, Lisle (part No. 74600) (**Figure 3**) for identifying hoses and fittings during engine removal and disassembly.
7. Use a vise with protective jaws to hold parts.
8. Use a press or special tools when force is required to remove and install parts. Do not try to pry, hammer or otherwise force them on or off.
9. Replace all O-rings and oil seals during reassembly. Apply a small amount of grease to the inner lips of each new seal to prevent damage when the engine is first started.
10. Record the location, position and thickness of all shims as they are removed.

SPECIAL TOOLS

Engine service requires a number of special tools. These tools and their part numbers are listed with the individual procedures. For a complete list of the special tools mentioned in this manual, refer to **Table 9** in Chapter One. The engine tools used in this chapter are either Harley-Davidson or JIMS special tools. JIMS special tools are available through some Harley-Davidson dealerships or many aftermarket motorcycle suppliers.

When purchasing special tools, make sure to specify that the tools required are for the 1999-on Dyna Glide Twin-Cam 88 models. Many of the tools are specific to this engine. Tools for other engine models may be slightly different.

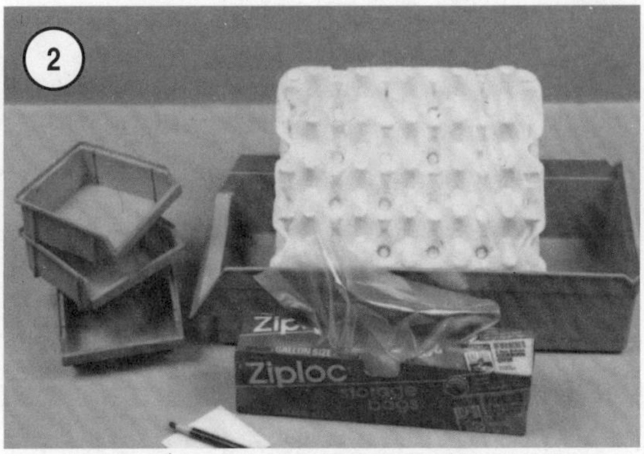

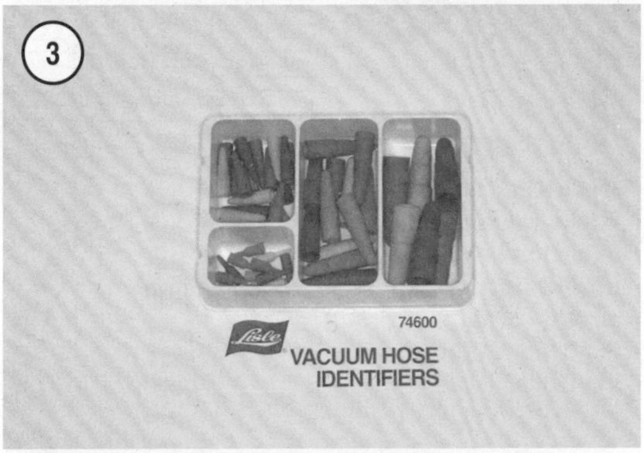

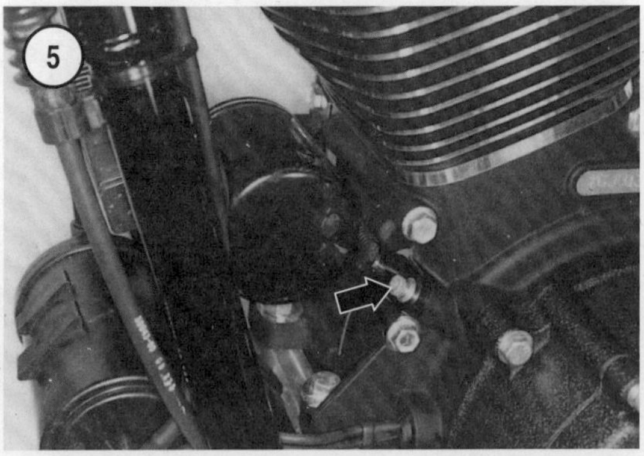

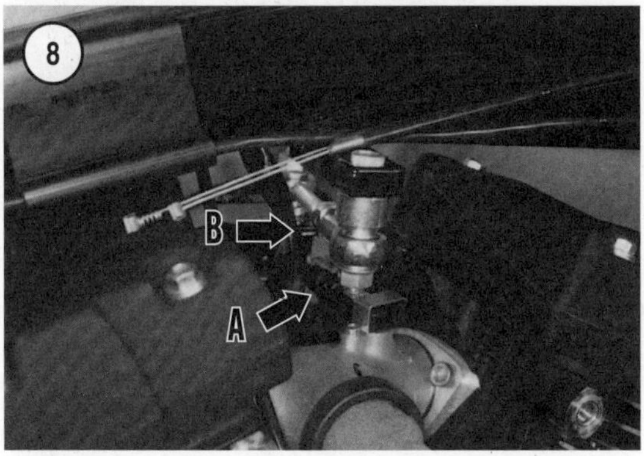

SERVICING ENGINE IN FRAME

The following components can be serviced while the engine is mounted in the frame:

1. Rocker arm cover and rocker arms.
2. Cylinder heads.
3. Cylinders and pistons.
4. Camshafts.
5. Gearshift mechanism.
6. Clutch.
7. Transmission.
8. Carburetor.
9. Starter motor and gears.
10. Alternator and electrical systems.

ENGINE

Removal

1. Thoroughly clean the engine of all dirt and debris.
2. Remove the seat as described in Chapter Thirteen.

NOTE
Always disarm the optional TSSM security system prior to disconnecting the battery or the siren will sound.

3. Disconnect the negative battery cable as described in Chapter Eight.
4. Support the motorcycle on a stand or floor jack. See *motorcycle Stands* in Chapter Nine.
5. Remove the fuel tank as described in Chapter Seven.
6. Remove the air filter and backing plate as described in Chapter Seven.
7. Remove the carburetor as described in Chapter Seven.
8. Remove the exhaust system as described in Chapter Seven.
9. Remove the rear brake pedal and right side foot peg bracket as described in Chapter Twelve.
10. Drain the engine oil as described in Chapter Three.
11. Remove the bolts securing the oil line cover and remove the cover (**Figure 4**).
12. Disconnect the three oil lines from the crankcase. Plug the oil lines to prevent dirt from entering the hoses.
13. On 1999-2000 models, remove the camshaft position sensor as described in Chapter Eight.
14. Disconnect the following electrical connectors:
    a. Crankshaft position sensor (**Figure 5**).
    b. Alternator stator and voltage regulator (**Figure 6**).
    c. Oil pressure switch (**Figure 7**).
    d. MAP sensor (A, **Figure 8**).
15. Remove the ignition coil and spark plug assembly as described in Chapter Eight.
16. Remove the primary chain case assembly, including the inner housing, as described in Chapter Five.
17. Remove the engine oil dipstick.
18. Remove the alternator rotor (A, **Figure 9**) as described in Chapter Eight.

19. On the right side of the engine stabilizer, perform the following:
   a. Remove the link nut and spacer from the frame tab (B, **Figure 8**).
   b. Remove the two bolts from the horn bracket and cylinder heads.
   c. Remove the stabilizer link and horn bracket as an assembly (**Figure 10**).
20. Remove the clutch cable from the lower portion of the crankcase as described under *Clutch Cable Replacement* in Chapter Five.
21. Wrap the frame front down tubes (A, **Figure 11**) with protective tape to prevent surface damage in the following steps.
22. Support the transmission case with a jack or wooden blocks. Apply enough jack pressure on the transmission prior to removing the engine-to-transmission mounting bolts.
23. Using a ratchet strap, secure the transmission to the frame so it will not shift after the engine is removed.
24. Remove the four bolts and washers (B, **Figure 9**) securing the engine to the transmission.
25. Support the engine with a floor jack. Apply enough jack pressure on the crankcase to support it prior to removing the engine mounting bolts.
26. Remove the two bolts and washers securing the engine to the front isolator.
27. Straighten the lockplate tabs and remove the three bolts, oil filter and oil filter mount (B, **Figure 11**).
28. Check the engine to make sure all wires, hoses, and other related components have been disconnected from the engine. Check that nothing will interfere with the removal of the engine from the right side of the frame.

NOTE

Due to the weight of the engine assembly, a minimum of two people are required to safely remove the engine from the frame.

29. Slide the engine assembly forward to clear the two locating dowels on the lower engine-to-transmission mounting bolt locations. The dowels stick out approximately 1/2 in. (12.7 mm). The engine may have to be rotated slightly to clear the dowels.
30. Remove the engine from the right side of the frame.
31. If the transmission was removed along with the engine, remove the four bolts securing the transmis-

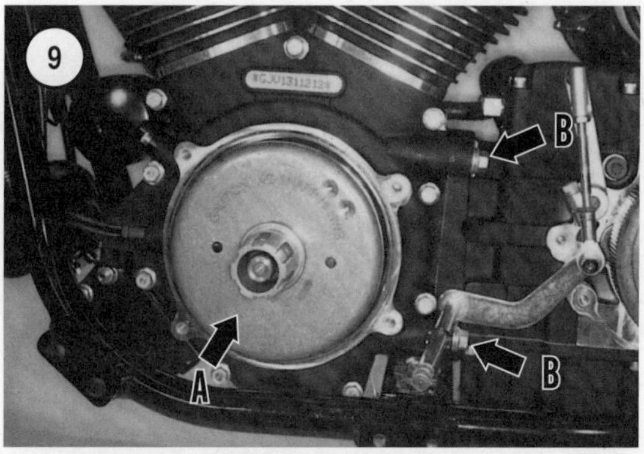

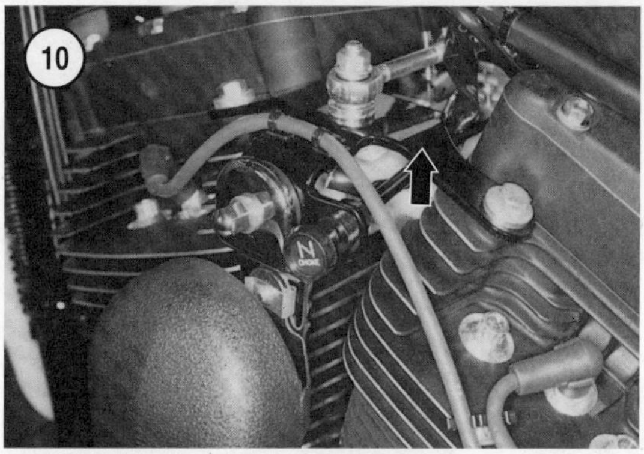

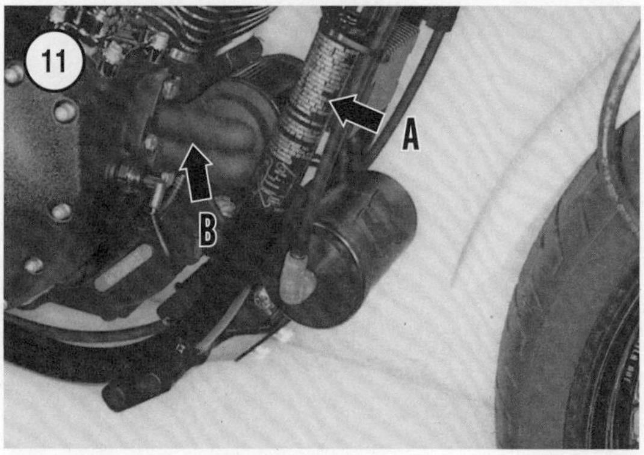

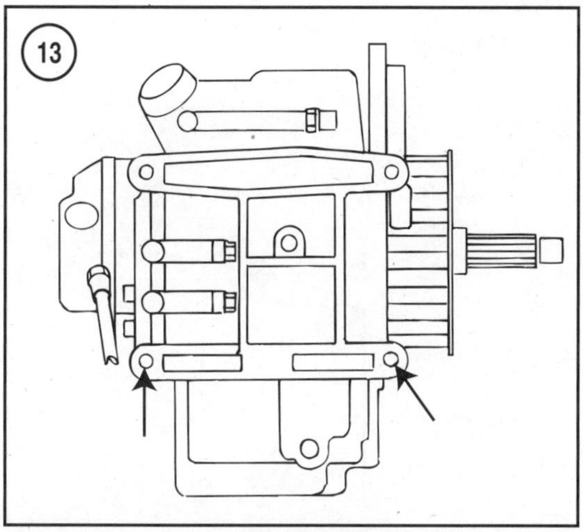

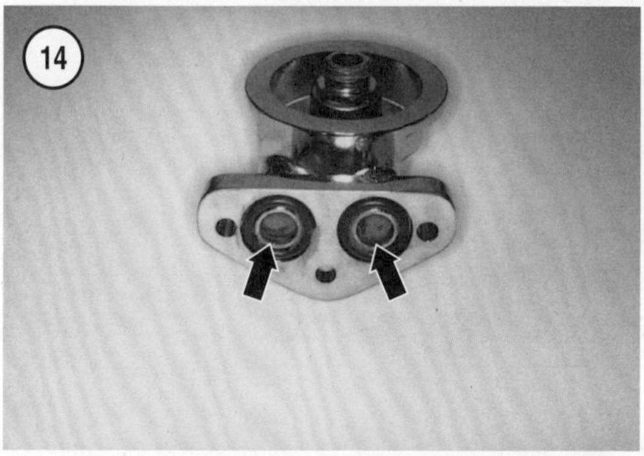

sion to the engine. Remove the transmission from the engine.

32. Mount the engine in an engine stand (**Figure 12**) (JIMS part No. 1022 or an equivalent).

33. Service the front engine mount, if necessary.

34. Clean the front and rear engine mount bolts and washers in solvent and dry thoroughly.

35. Replace leaking or damaged oil hoses.

Installation

NOTE
Due to the weight of the engine assembly, a minimum of two people is required to safely install the engine into the frame.

1. If removed, install the two lower locating dowels in the transmission case (**Figure 13**).
2. Re-check that all wiring, hoses and other related components are out of the way and will not interfere with engine installation.
3. Correctly position a floor jack and piece of wood under the frame to support the engine when it is installed into the frame.
4. Install the engine from the right side of the frame and place it on the floor jack. Apply enough jack pressure on the crankcase to support it prior to installing the engine mounting bolts.
5. Slide the engine assembly toward the rear and onto the two transmission locating dowels. The engine may have to be rotated slightly to clear the dowels.
6. Install the four engine-to-transmission bolts and washers hand-tight at this time.
7. Install the two bolts and washers securing the engine to the front isolator. Tighten finger-tight at this time.
8. Tighten the engine-to-transmission bolts in a criss-cross pattern in the following sequence:
   a. Tighten to 15 ft.-lb. (20 N•m).
   b. Tighten to 30-35 ft.-lb. (41-47 N•m).
9. Tighten the front isolator bolts to the specification in **Table 4**.
10. Remove the ratchet strap from the transmission and frame.
11. Remove the floor jack.

NOTE
Step 12 is shown with the engine removed from the frame to better illustrate the procedure.

12. Install the oil filter mount as follows:
   a. Install *new* O-ring seals (**Figure 14**) onto the mount.
   b. Apply ThreeBond TB1342, or an equivalent, to the bolt threads prior to installing them onto the *new* lockplate.
   c. Install the oil filter mount onto the crankcase and install the lockplate, three bolts and washers (**Figure 15**).

4

(16)

ROCKER ARM ASSEMBLY

1. Bolt
2. Rocker arm cover
3. Gasket
4. Bolt
5. Breather cover
6. Gasket
7. Valve
8. Breather baffle
9. Filter element
10. Gasket
11. Bushing
12. Rocker arm
    Intake–front cylinder
    Exhaust–rear cylinder
13. Rocker arm shaft
14. Washer
15. Rocker arm support
16. Rocker arm
    Intake–rear cylinder
    Exhaust–front cylinder
17. O-ring seal
18. Rocker arm housing
19. Gasket

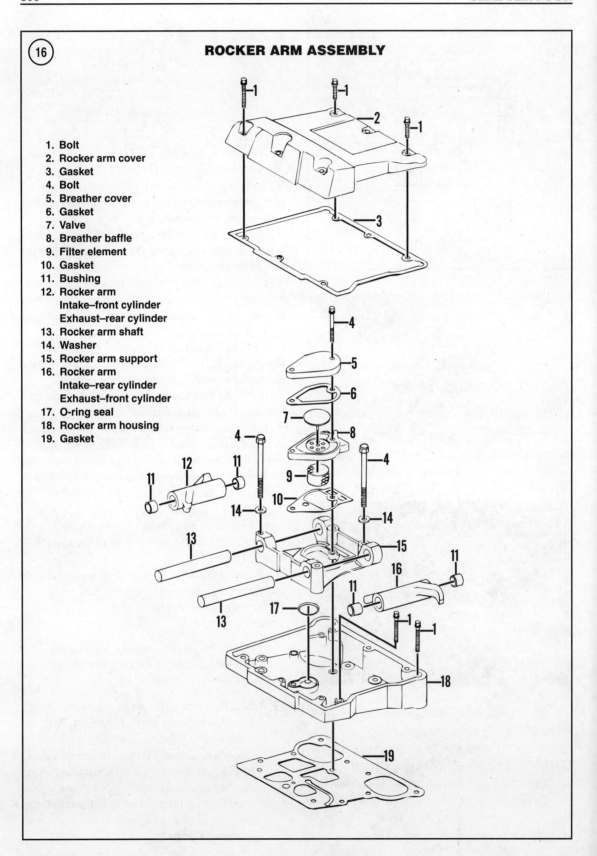

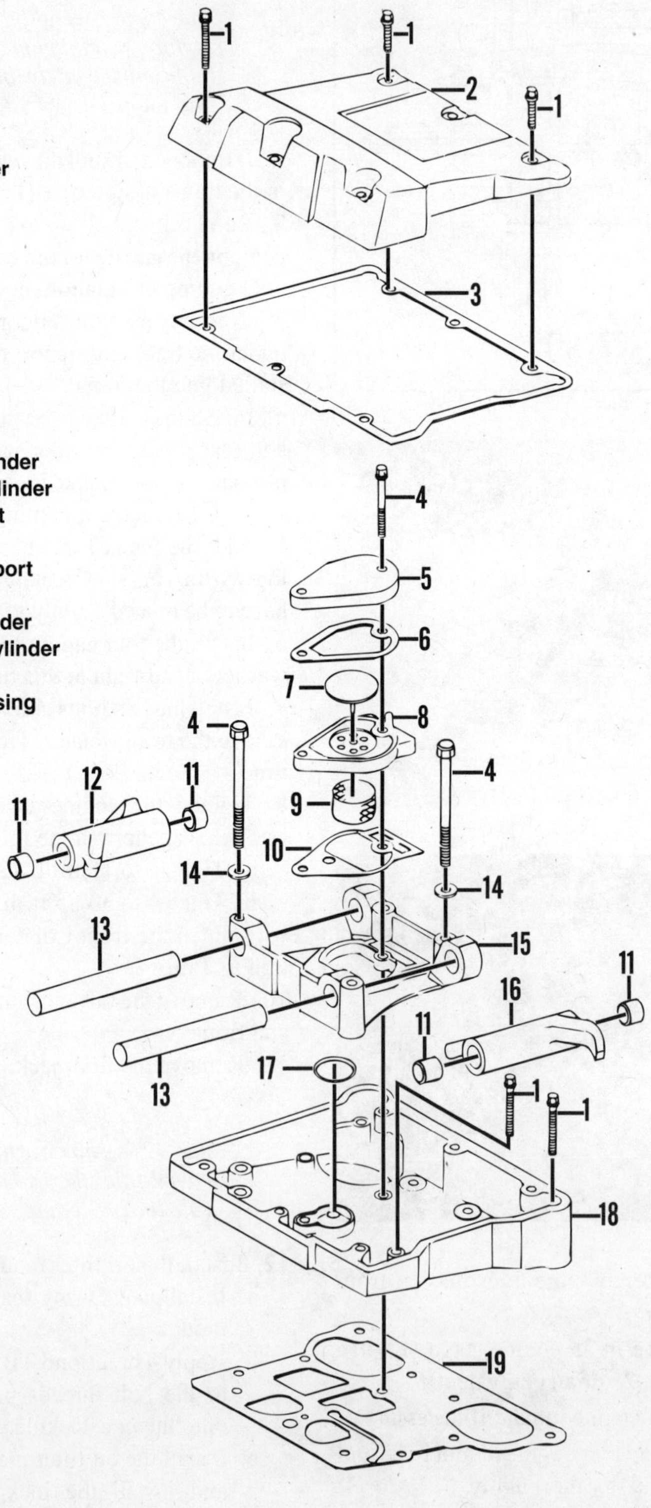

(17) PUSHROD ASSEMBLY

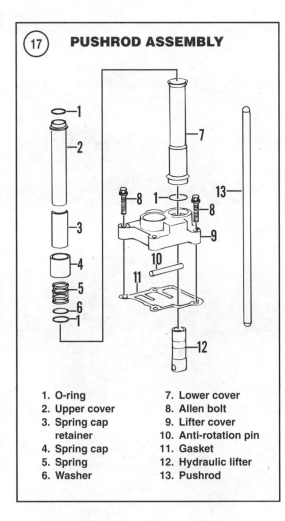

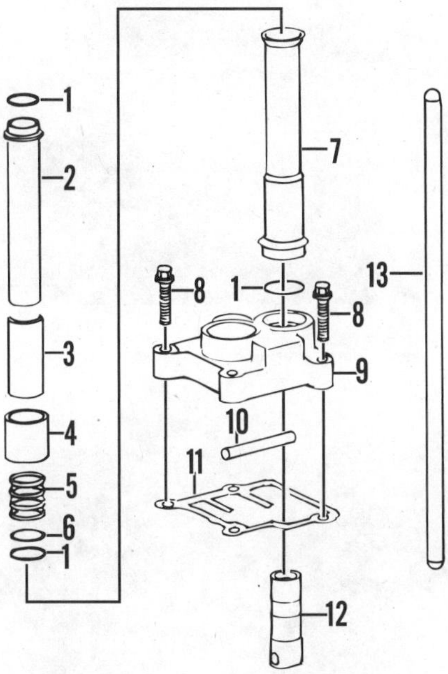

1. O-ring
2. Upper cover
3. Spring cap retainer
4. Spring cap
5. Spring
6. Washer
7. Lower cover
8. Allen bolt
9. Lifter cover
10. Anti-rotation pin
11. Gasket
12. Hydraulic lifter
13. Pushrod

d. Tighten the bolts to the specification in **Table 4**.

e. Bend down the locking tab against the top and bottom bolt heads.

f. Install the oil filter.

13. Remove the protective tape from the frame front down tubes.

14. Install the clutch cable onto the lower portion of the crankcase as described under *Clutch Cable Replacement* in Chapter Five.

15. On the right side of the engine stabilizer, perform the following:

a. Install the stabilizer link and horn bracket as an assembly (**Figure 10**).

b. Place a spacer between the frame tab and the stabilizer link.

c. Position the horn ground wire beneath the bracket and the front cylinder head.

d. Install the two bolts securing the horn bracket to the cylinder heads and tighten to the specification in **Table 4**.

e. Install the link nut and spacer onto the frame tab (B, **Figure 8**).

16. Install the alternator rotor (A, **Figure 9**) as described in Chapter Eight.

17. Install the engine oil dipstick.

18. Install the primary chain case inner housing and assembly as described in Chapter Five.

19. Adjust the clutch and primary chain as described in Chapter Three.

20. Install the ignition coil and spark plug assembly as described in Chapter Eight.

21. Connect the following electrical connectors:

a. Crankshaft position sensor (**Figure 5**).

b. Alternator stator and voltage regulator (**Figure 6**).

c. Oil pressure switch (**Figure 7**).

d. MAP sensor (A, **Figure 8**).

22. On 1999-2000 models, install the camshaft position sensor as described in Chapter Eight.

23. Connect the three oil lines onto the crankcase and install new hose clamps.

24. Install the oil line cover and bolts (**Figure 4**). Tighten the bolts to the specification in **Table 4**.

25. Install the rear brake pedal and right side foot peg bracket as described in Chapter Twelve.

26. Install the exhaust system as described in Chapter Seven.

27. Install the carburetor as described in Chapter Seven.

28. Install the air filter and backing plate as described in Chapter Seven.

29. Install the fuel tank as described in Chapter Seven.

30. Remove the stand from under the motorcycle and place the motorcycle on the jiffy stand.

31. Connect the negative battery cable as described Chapter Eight.

32. Install the seat.

33. Refill the engine oil as described in Chapter Three.

34. Check vehicle alignment as described in Chapter Nine.

ROCKER ARMS AND PUSHRODS

Refer to **Figure 16** and **Figure 17**.

The rocker arm and pushrod procedures are shown on the rear cylinder. The same procedures also relate to the front cylinder. If differences occur they are identified.

NOTE

The rocker arms and pushrod procedures are shown with the engine removed to better illustrate the steps.

Removal

1. If the engine is mounted in the frame, perform the following:
   a. Perform Steps 1-8 under *Engine Removal* in this chapter.
   b. Remove the upper cylinder head mounting bracket.
2. Using a crisscross pattern, loosen and remove the rocker arm cover bolts (**Figure 18**).
3. Remove the rocker arm cover and gasket.
4. Disassemble the breather as follows:
   a. Remove the bolts (A, **Figure 19**) and remove the cover (B) and gasket.
   b. Remove the breather baffle (A, **Figure 20**), valve (B), and gasket (**Figure 21**).
   c. Install *new* gaskets during installation.
5. Remove both spark plugs as described in Chapter Three, to make it easier to rotate the engine by hand.

CAUTION

Do not rotate the engine using the camshaft sprocket mounting bolt. Doing so may break the bolt head and damage the camshaft.

CAUTION

The piston must be at top dead center (TDC) to avoid damage to the pushrods and rocker arms in the following steps.

6A. *With the primary chain cover in place,* position the piston for the cylinder being worked on at top dead center (TDC) on the compression stroke as follows:
   a. Support the motorcycle on a stand with the rear wheel off the ground. See *motorcycle Stands* in Chapter Nine.
   b. Shift the transmission into fifth gear.

18

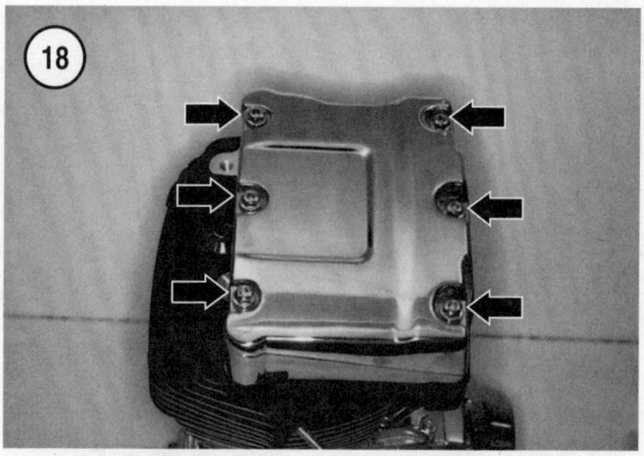

19

20

21

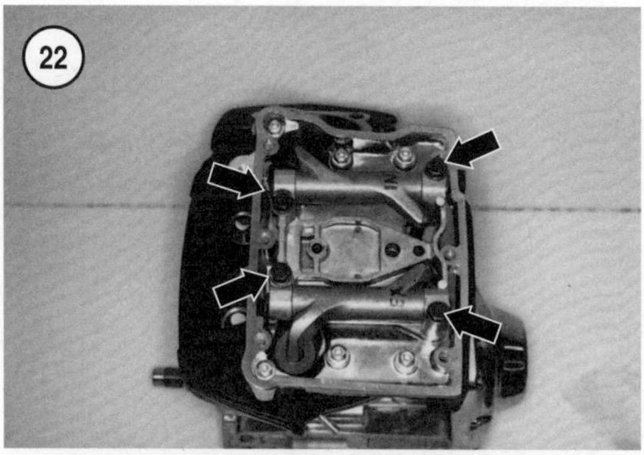

22

23

c. Rotate the rear wheel in the direction of normal rotation.
d. Stop rotating the rear wheel when both the intake and exhaust valves are closed.
e. Wiggle both rocker arms. There should be free play indicating that both valves are closed. This indicates that the piston is at top dead center (TDC) on the compression stroke and both valves are closed. Also, the push rods are in the unloaded position.
f. Look into the spark plug hole with a flashlight and verify that the piston is at TDC.

6B. *With the primary chain cover removed,* position the piston for the cylinder being worked on at top dead center (TDC) on the compression stroke as follows:

a. Shift the transmission into NEUTRAL.
b. Install the sprocket shaft nut onto the end of the left side of the crankshaft.
c. Place a socket or wrench on the compensating sprocket shaft nut.
d. Rotate the compensating sprocket shaft *counterclockwise* until both the intake and exhaust valves are closed.
e. Wiggle both rocker arms. There should be free play indicating that both valves are closed. This indicates that the piston is at top dead center (TDC) on the compression stroke and both valves are closed. Also, the push rods are in the unloaded position.
f. Look into the spark plug hole with a flashlight and verify that the piston is at TDC.

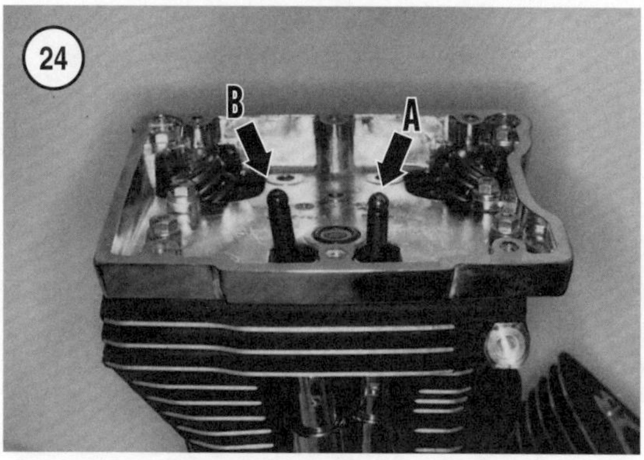

24

7. Using a crisscross pattern, loosen, then remove the four bolts and washers (**Figure 22**) securing the rocker arm support and remove the support.
8. Remove the O-ring seal (**Figure 23**) from the rocker arm housing.
9. Mark each pushrod with its top and bottom position and its operating position in the cylinder head.

NOTE
When removing the pushrods in the following steps, do not intermix the parts from each set. When reinstalling the original pushrods, install them so that each end faces its original operating position. The pushrods develop a set wear pattern and installing them upside down may cause rapid wear to the pushrod, lifter and rocker arm.

10. Remove the intake (A, **Figure 24**) and exhaust (B) pushrods up through the cylinder head.
11. Remove the pushrod covers as follows:

a. Using a screwdriver, pry the spring cap retainer (**Figure 25**) out from between the cylinder head and spring cap.
b. Slide the upper cover down (A, **Figure 26**) and remove the pushrod cover assembly (B) from the cylinder head and the lifter cover.
c. Repeat for the opposite pushrod cover.

NOTE
In order to clear the cylinder's lower cooling fins, the lifter cover's two in-

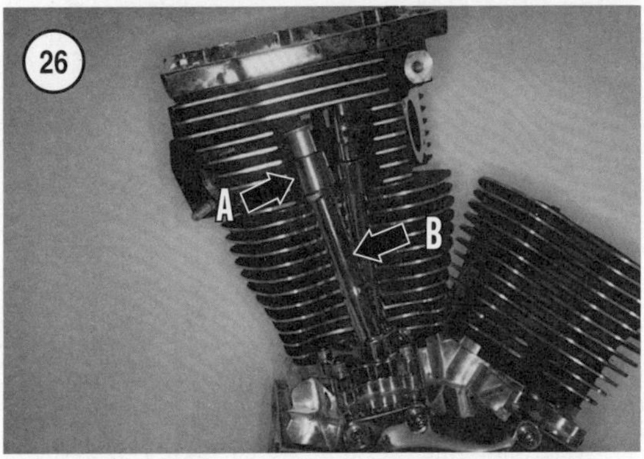

ner Allen bolts must be loosened with a short 90-degree Allen wrench (A, ***Figure 27****).*

12. Remove the lifter cover mounting bolts and remove the cover (B, **Figure 27**).
13. Remove the lifter cover gasket from the crankcase.

NOTE
Do not intermix the lifters when removing them in Step 13. Mark them so they can be installed in their original positions.

14. Remove the anti-rotation pin (A, **Figure 28**) and both hydraulic lifters (B).
15. Cover the crankcase opening with duct tape (**Figure 29**) to prevent the entry of debris.
16. Loosen the rocker housing six bolts (**Figure 30**) 1/8 turn at a time in the pattern shown in **Figure 31**.
17. Tap the rocker arm housing with a rubber mallet to free it, then lift it off the cylinder head.
18. Remove the rocker arm housing gasket.

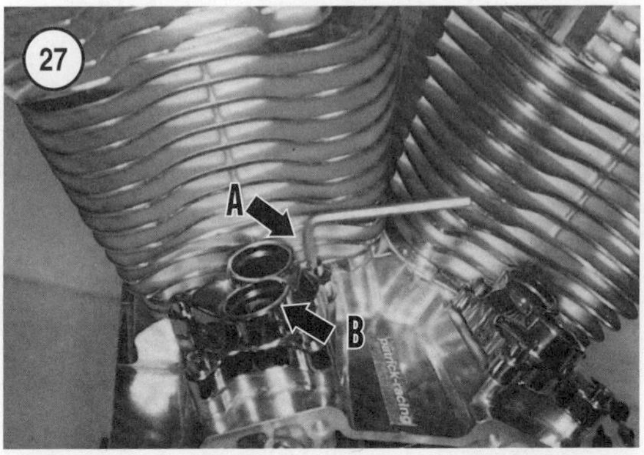

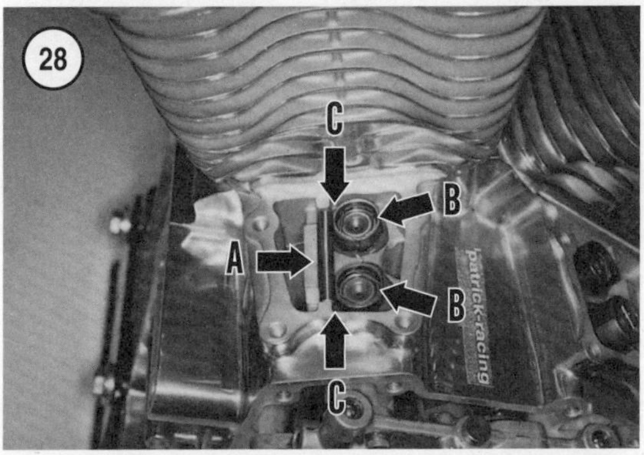

31

ROCKER ARM HOUSING TORQUE SEQUENCE

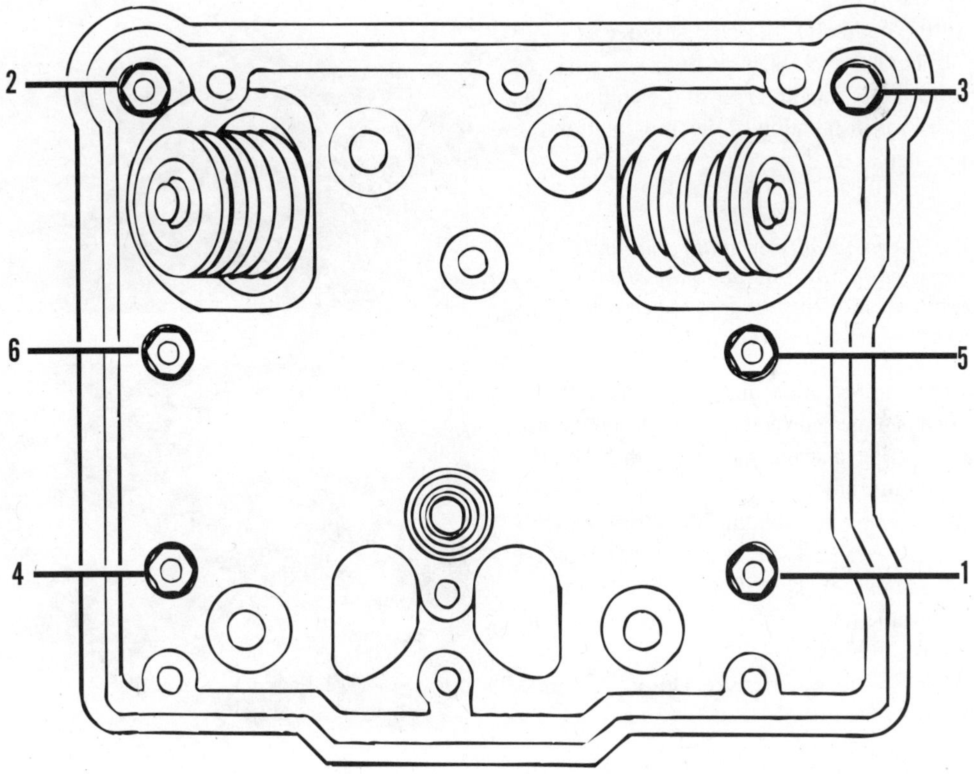

Installation

1. Position the *new* rocker arm housing gasket onto the cylinder so that the breather channel (**Figure 32**) is covered and install the gasket (**Figure 33**).
2. Install the rocker arm housing onto the cylinder head.
3. Apply ThreeBond TB1342, or an equivalent, threadlocking compound to the bolt threads. Install the rocker housing six bolts (**Figure 30**) and tighten 1/8 turn at a time in the pattern shown in **Figure 31**. Tighten to the specification in **Table 4**.
4. Install a *new* O-ring seal (**Figure 23**) onto the rocker arm housing. Apply a light coat of clean engine oil to the O-ring.
5. Install the hydraulic lifters (B, **Figure 28**) into the crankcase receptacles with both flat surfaces facing toward the front and rear of the engine. This is necessary for installation of the anti-rotation pin in the next step.

CAUTION
Failure to install the anti-rotational pin will allow the lifter to rotate off the camshaft lobe, resulting in severe internal engine damage.

6. Install the anti-rotation pin (A, **Figure 28**) and make sure it is seated correctly within the crankcase receptacle and against the flats on both hydraulic lifters (C, **Figure 28**).
7. Rotate the engine until both lifters for the cylinder head being serviced seat onto the cam's lowest position (base circle). The lifter's top surface will be flush with the top surface of the crankcase surface as shown in **Figure 34**.
8. Install a *new* lifter cover gasket (**Figure 35**) onto the crankcase.

NOTE
*In order to clear the cylinder's lower cooling fins, the lifter cover two inner Allen bolts must be tightened with a short 90-degree Allen wrench (A, **Figure 27**).*

9. Install the lifter cover and the mounting bolts (B, **Figure 27**). Tighten the bolts to the specification in **Table 4**.
10. Install *new* O-ring seals (**Figure 36**) onto each end of the pushrod covers. Apply a light coat of clean engine oil to the O-rings.

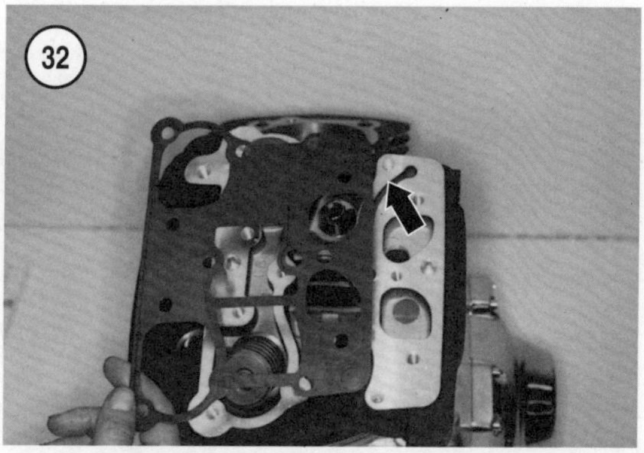

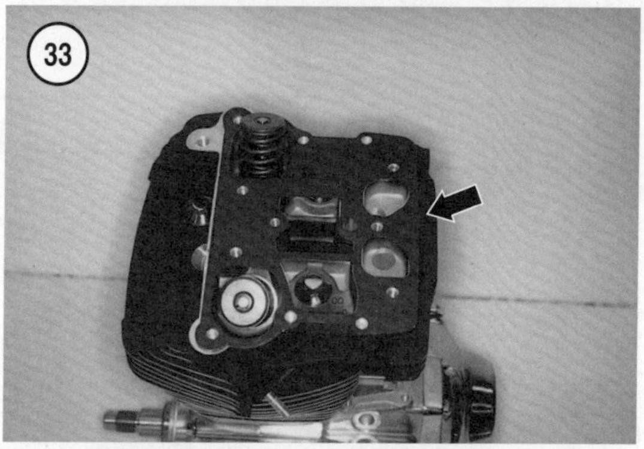

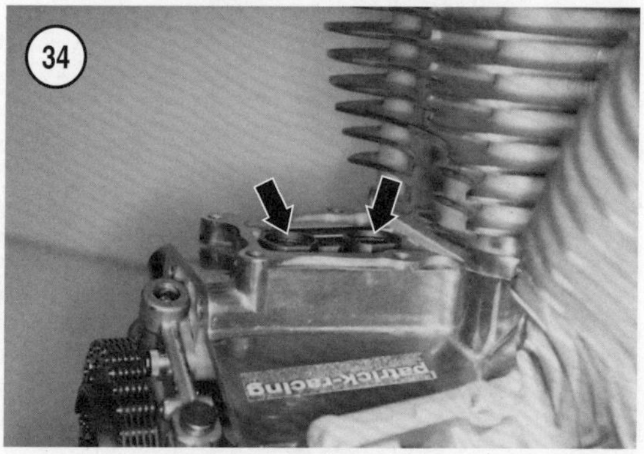

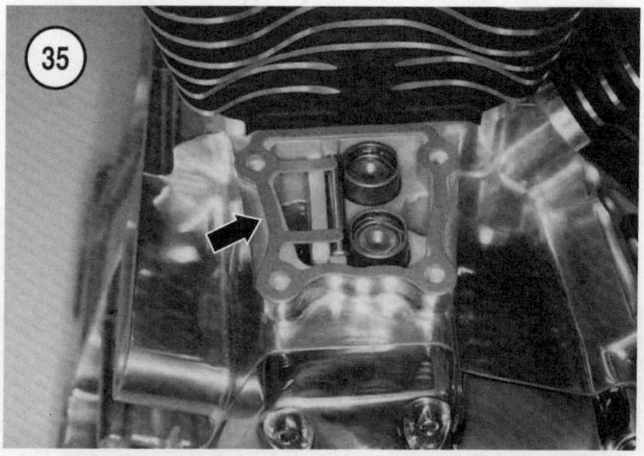

36

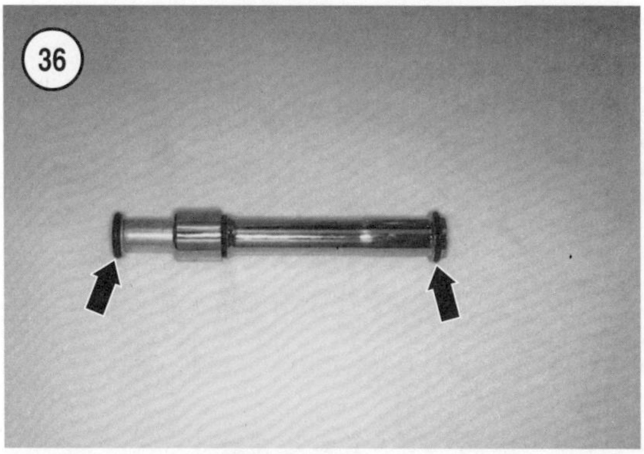

37

38

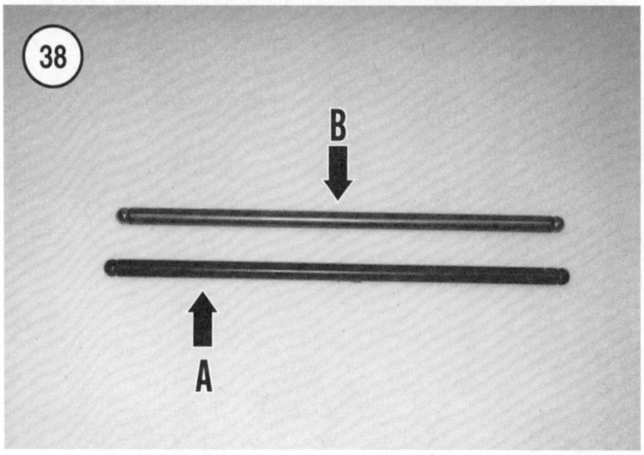

39

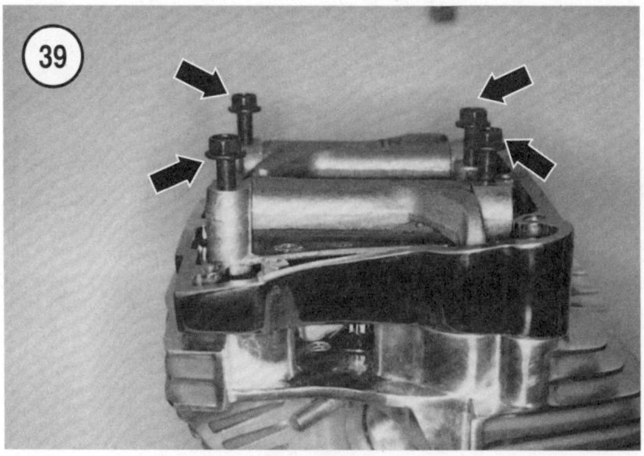

11. If the pushrod cover assembly was disassembled, reassemble it as described under *Pushrods* in this chapter.

CAUTION
The pushrod covers and the pushrods must be installed in the correct location in the cylinder head and pushrod cover as indicated in ***Table 3****.*

12. Compress the pushrod cover and install it into the correct location in the lifter cover and cylinder head (**Figure 37**). Do not install the spring cap retainer at this time.
13. Repeat Steps 11 and 12 for the other pushrod cover.
14. Install the pushrods as follows:

CAUTION
Two different length pushrods are used in the Dyna Glide's engine. The black exhaust pushrod (A, ***Figure 38****) is longer than the silver intake pushrod (B).*

a. If installing the existing pushrods, install each pushrod in its original position and in the correct orientation. Refer to (A, **Figure 24**) for intake and (B) for exhaust. The pushrods are symmetrical and can be installed with either end facing up.
b. Make sure the pushrod is centered into its respective lifter.

15. Install the rocker arm support assembly and bolts (**Figure 39**).

CAUTION
To avoid damaging a pushrod, rocker arms or valves, tighten the rocker arm support mounting bolts evenly and in a crisscross pattern. When tightening the mounting bolts, spin each pushrod by hand to ensure that the rocker arm support is being tightened evenly. If one or both pushrods cannot be rotated, loosen the mounting bolts and determine the cause.

16. Tighten the rocker arm support assembly and bolts evenly in a crisscross pattern to the torque specification in **Table 4**.
17. Ensure that the pushrod cover O-rings are correctly seated in the cylinder head and lifter cover.

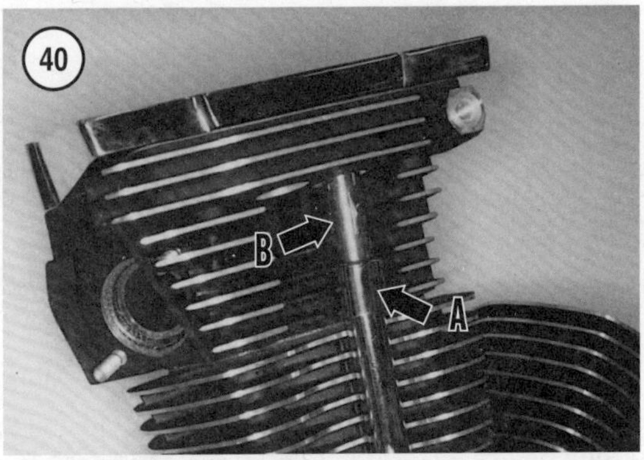

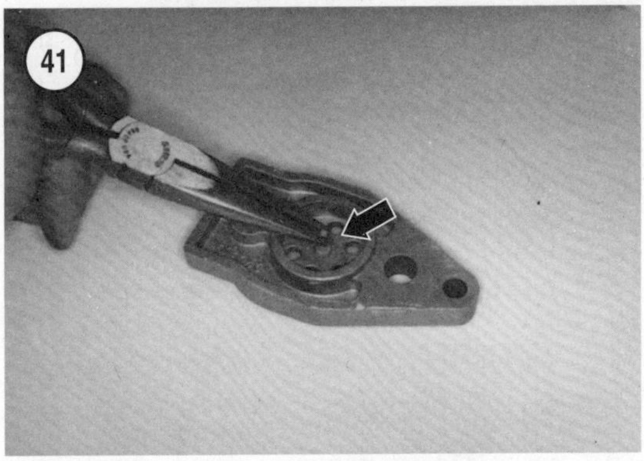

Depress the spring cap (A, **Figure 40**) and install the spring cap retainer (B). Make sure the spring cap retainer is correctly seated. Repeat for the remaining pushrod cover.

18. Assemble the breather as follows:
    a. If removed, install the valve onto the breather baffle and pull the tip through from the other side (**Figure 41**) to seat it.
    b. Install a *new* gasket (**Figure 42**).
    c. Install a *new* filter element.
    d. Hold the filter element in place and install the breather baffle (**Figure 43**).
    e. Install the cover and bolts (**Figure 44**), and tighten them securely.
19. Install a *new* rocker arm cover gasket (**Figure 45**).
20. Install the rocker arm cover.

NOTE

*There are two different length bolts (**Figure 46**) securing the rocker arm cover.*

21. Apply ThreeBond TB1342, or an equivalent, threadlocking compound to the bolt threads. Install

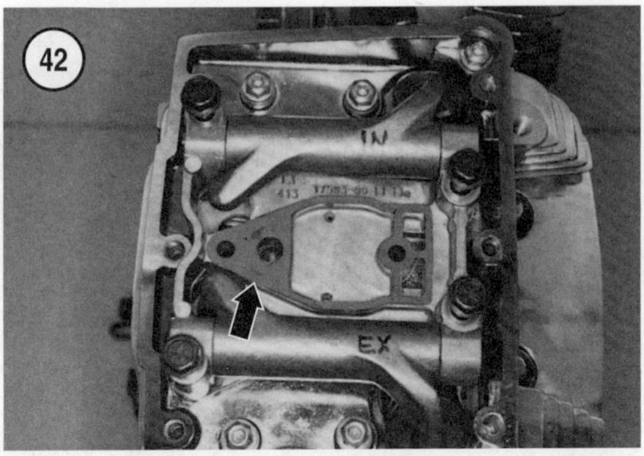

46

ROCKER ARM COVER TORQUE SEQUENCE

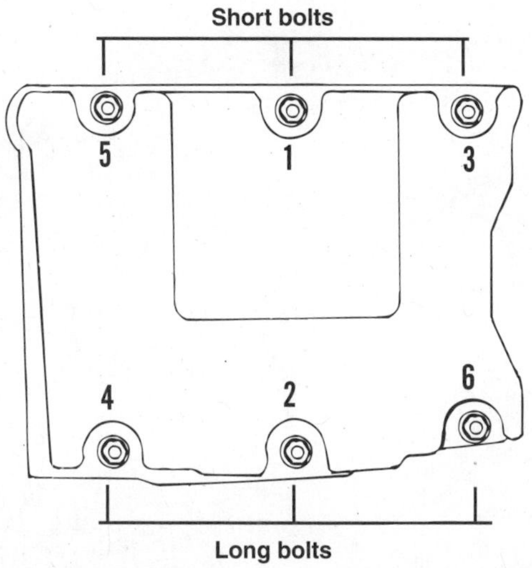

the rocker arm cover six bolts (**Figure 47**) and tighten 1/8 turn at a time in the sequence shown in **Figure 46**. Tighten to the specification in **Table 4**.

Rocker Arm Disassembly/Assembly

Refer to **Figure 48**.

1. Before removing the rocker arms, measure the rocker arm end clearance as follows:
   a. Insert a feeler gauge between the rocker arm and the inside rocker arm support boss as shown in **Figure 49**.
   b. Record the measurement.
   c. Repeat for each rocker arm.
   d. Replace the rocker arm and/or the rocker arm support if the side clearance is greater than the specification in **Table 2**.
2. Prior to disassembling the rocker arms, mark each one with an IN (intake) or EX (exhaust) (**Figure 50**) to ensure they are installed in their original positions.
3. Remove the rocker arm shafts (A, **Figure 51**) and remove the rocker arms (B).
4. Clean all parts in solvent. Blow compressed air through all oil passages.
5. Install the rocker arm shaft (A, **Figure 52**) part way into the rocker arm support (B) in its original position.
6. Install a rocker arm (C, **Figure 52**) into its original position and push the shaft part way through the rocker arm.
7. Align the notch in the rocker arm shaft (A, **Figure 53**) with the mating bolt hole (B) in the support and install the shaft all the way. Check for correct alignment (**Figure 54**).
8. Repeat Step 6 and Step 7 for the remaining rocker arm and shaft.

Rocker Arm Component Inspection

When measuring the rocker arm components, compare the actual measurements to the specifications in **Table 2**. Replace any part that is damaged or out of specification as described in this section.

48

ROCKER ARM ASSEMBLY

1. Bolt
2. Rocker arm cover
3. Gasket
4. Bolt
5. Breather cover
6. Gasket
7. Valve
8. Breather baffle
9. Filter element
10. Gasket
11. Bushing
12. Rocker arm
    Intake–front cylinder
    Exhaust–rear cylinder
13. Rocker arm shaft
14. Washer
15. Rocker arm support
16. Rocker arm
    Intake–rear cylinder
    Exhaust–front cylinder
17. O-ring seal
18. Rocker arm housing
19. Gasket

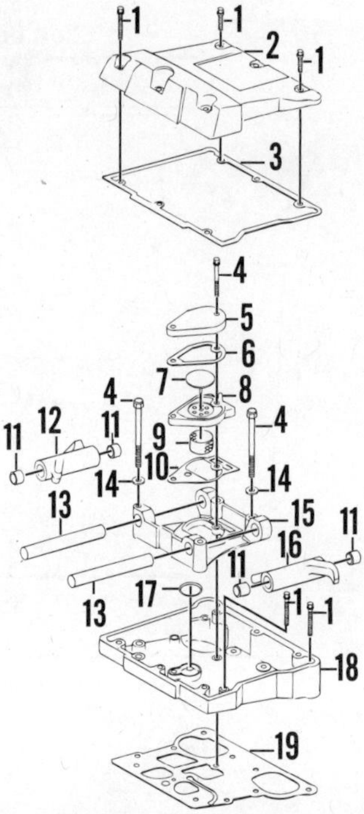

49

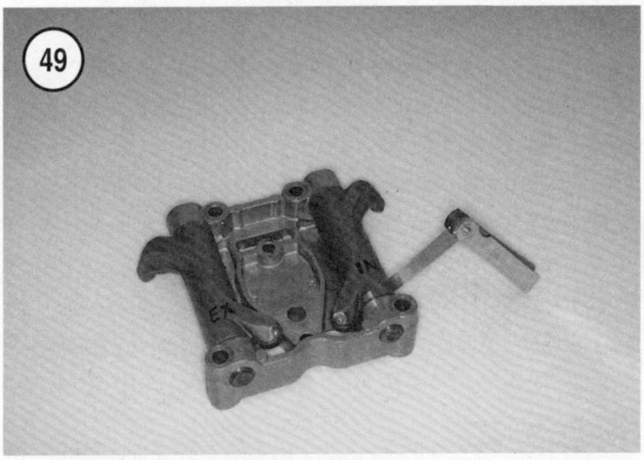

50

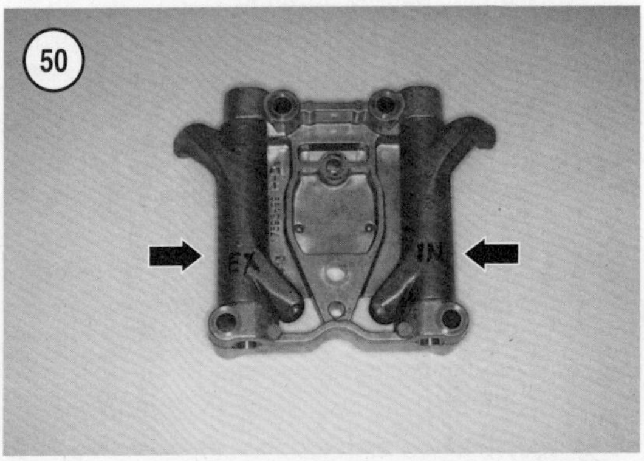

51

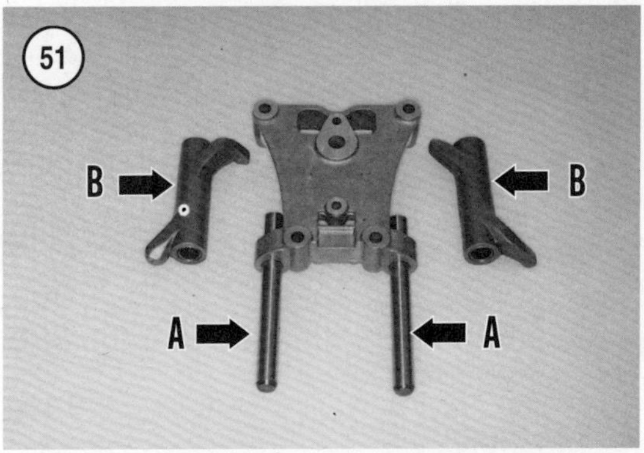

52

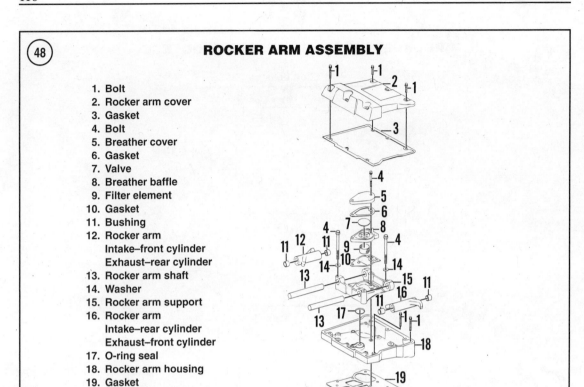

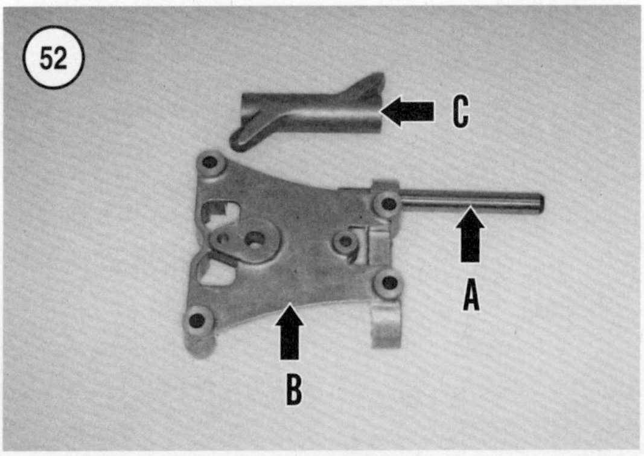

53

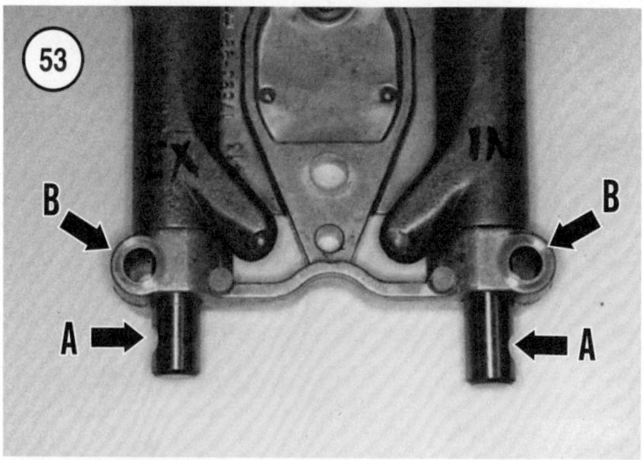

54

55

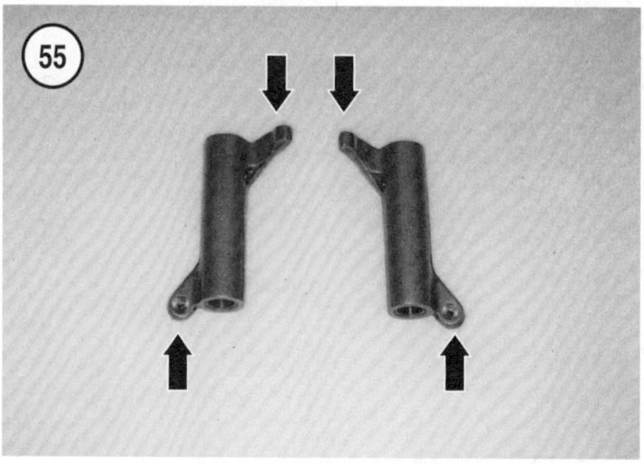

56

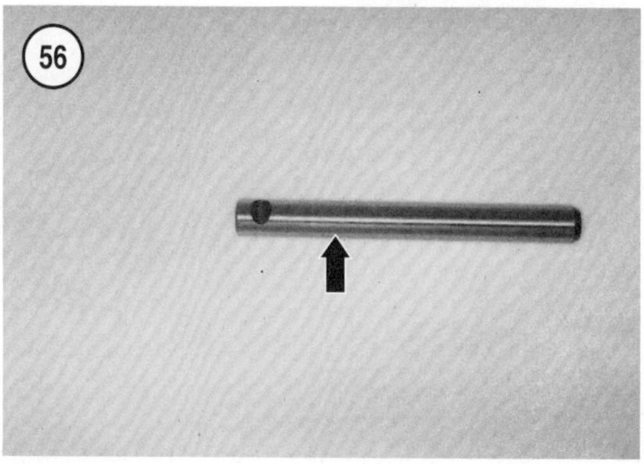

57

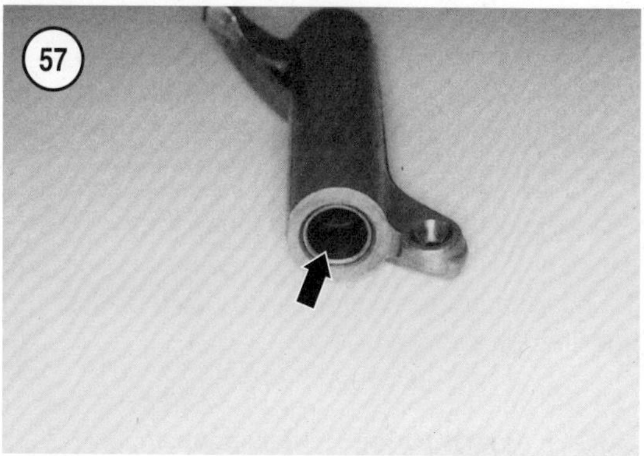

58

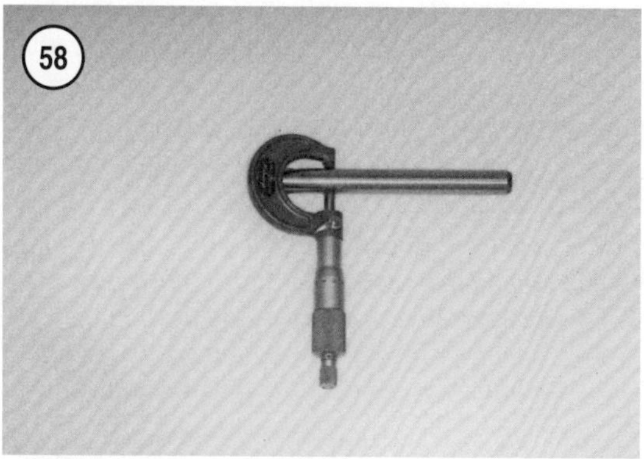

1. Inspect the rocker arm pads and ball sockets (**Figure 55**) for pitting and excessive wear.

2. Examine the rocker arm shaft (**Figure 56**) for scoring, ridge wear or other damage. If these conditions are present, replace the rocker arm shaft. If the shaft does not show any wear or damage, continue with Step 8.

3. Check the rocker arm bushing (**Figure 57**) for wear or scoring.

4. Measure the rocker arm shaft diameter (**Figure 58**) where it contacts the rocker arm bushing and rocker arm support. Measure both ends of the shaft. Record each measurement.

5. Measure the rocker arm bushing inside diameter (**Figure 59**) and the rocker arm support bore diameter. Record each measurement.

6. Subtract the measurements taken in Step 4 from those taken in Step 5 to obtain the following rocker arm shaft measurements:

   a. Shaft-to-rocker arm support.

   b. Shaft-to-rocker arm bushing.

7. Replace the rocker arm, the bushings or the rocker arm support if the clearance exceeds the specifications in **Table 2**. Rocker arm bushing replacement is described in this chapter.

8. Inspect the rocker arm shaft contact surfaces in the rocker arm support (**Figure 60**) for wear or elongation.
9. Inspect the gasket surface of the rocker arm cover for damage or warp.
10. Inspect the rocker arm support (**Figure 61**) for damage or warp.
11. Inspect both gasket surfaces of the rocker arm housing for damage or warp.

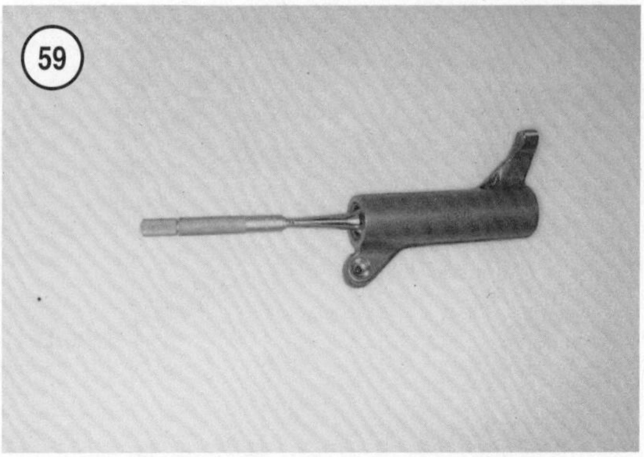

59

Rocker Arm Bushing Replacement

Each rocker arm is equipped with two bushings (**Figure 57**). Replacement bushings must be reamed after installation. Use the JIMS rocker arm bushing line reamer (part No. 94804-57). If the correct size reamer is unavailable, have the bushings replaced by a Harley-Davidson dealership.

NOTE
Since the new bushings must be reamed, remove one bushing at a time. The opposite bushing is then used as a guide when reaming the first bushing.

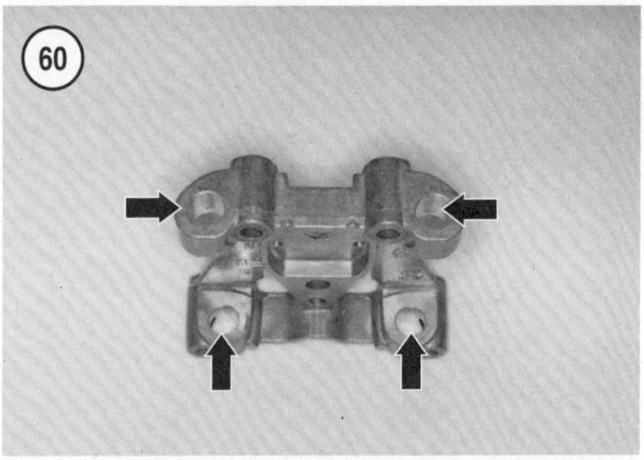

60

1. Press one bushing (**Figure 57**) out of the rocker arm. Do not remove the second bushing. If the bushing is difficult to remove, perform the following:
   a. Thread a 9/16 × 18 tap into the bushing.
   b. Support the rocker arm in a press so that the tap is at the bottom.
   c. Insert a mandrel through the top of the rocker arm and seat it on top of the tap.
   d. Press on the mandrel to force the bushing and tap out of the rocker arm.
   e. Remove the tap from the bushing and discard the bushing.
2. Position the new bushing with the split portion facing toward the top of the rocker arm.
3. Press the new bushing into the rocker arm until the bushing's outer surface is flush with the end of rocker arm bore.
4. Ream the new bushing with the bushing line reamer as follows:
   a. Mount the rocker arm in a vise with soft jaws so that the new bushing is at the bottom.

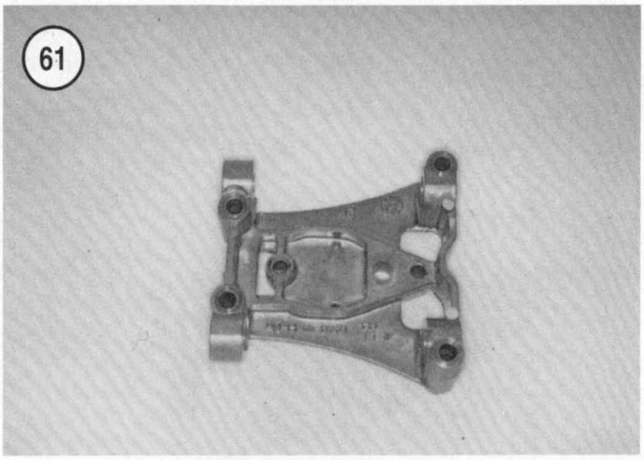

61

CAUTION
Turn the reamer clockwise only. Do not rotate the reamer counterclockwise or the reamer and bushing will be damaged.

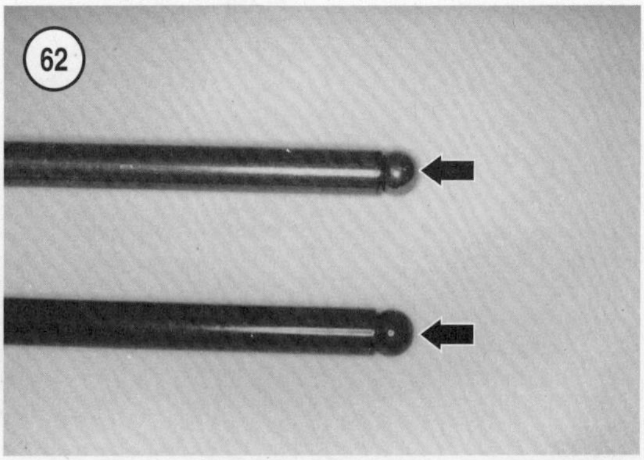

62

63

CYLINDER HEAD

1. Valve keepers
2. Upper retainer
3. Inner valve spring
4. Outer valve spring
5. Oil seal
6. Lower retainer
7. Valve guide
8. Bolt–short
9. Bolt–long
10. Cylinder head
11. Valve seat
12. Valve
13. Gasket

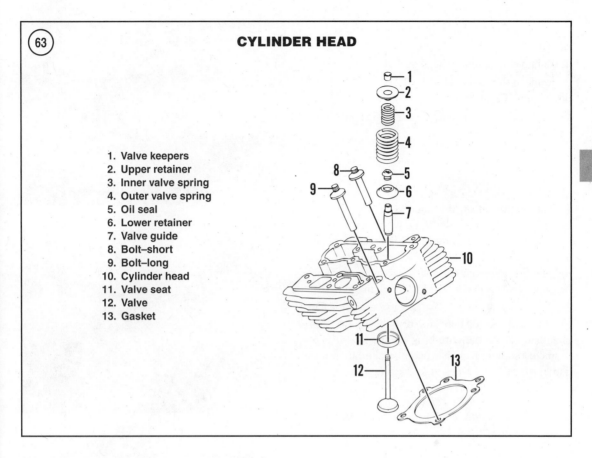

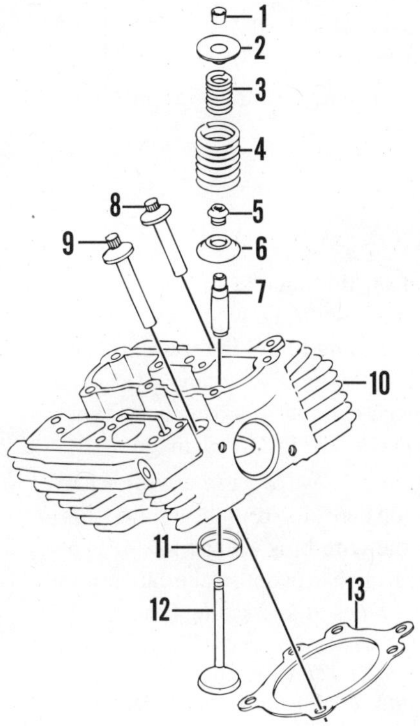

b. Mount a tap handle on top of the reamer and insert the reamer into the bushing. Turn the reamer *clockwise* until it passes through the new bushing and remove it from the bottom side.

5. Remove the rocker arm from the vise and repeat Steps 1-3 to replace the opposite bushing. The first bushing will now serve as a guide while reaming the second bushing.

6. After installing and reaming both bushings, clean the rocker arm assembly in solvent. Then clean with hot, soapy water and rinse with clear, cold water. Dry with compressed air.

7. Measure the inside diameter of each bushing. When properly reamed, the bushings must provide the shaft clearance listed in **Table 2**.

Pushrod Inspection

1. Clean the pushrods in solvent and dry with compressed air.

2. Check the pushrods for bending, cracks and worn or damaged ball heads (**Figure 62**).

3. Replace any damaged pushrod.

CYLINDER HEAD

Refer to **Figure 63**.

The cylinder head procedures are shown on the rear cylinder. The same procedures also relate to the front cylinder. If differences occur they are identified.

NOTE
The following procedures are shown with the engine removed to better illustrate the steps.

Removal

1. Remove the rocker arm assemblies and pushrods as described in this chapter.

2. Using a crisscross pattern, loosen the four cylinder head bolts (**Figure 64**) 1/8 turn at a time. Remove the four bolts and note the different lengths.

3. Tap the cylinder head with a rubber mallet to free it, then lift it off the cylinder block.
4. Remove the cylinder head gasket.
5. Remove the two O-rings and the cylinder head dowel pins (**Figure 65**).
6. Repeat these steps to remove the opposite cylinder head.

64

Inspection

1. Thoroughly clean the outside of the cylinder head. Use a stiff brush, soap and water and remove all debris from the cooling fins (**Figure 66**). If necessary, use a piece of wood and scrape away any lodged dirt. Clogged cooling fins can cause overheating, leading to possible engine damage.
2. *Without removing the valves*, use a wire brush to remove all carbon deposits from the combustion chamber. Use a fine wire brush dipped in solvent or make a scraper from hardwood. Take care not to damage the head, valves or spark plug threads.

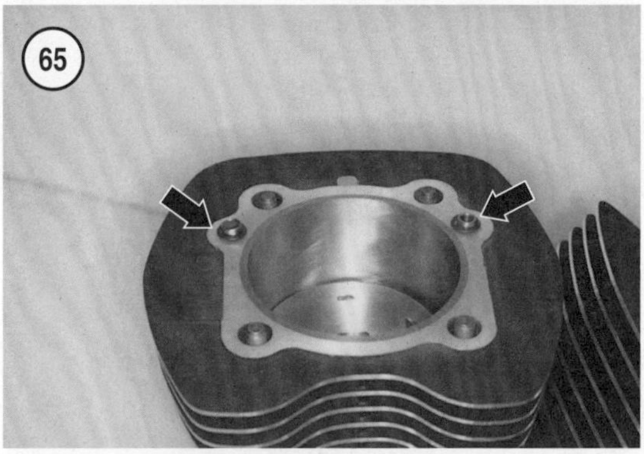
65

CAUTION
Cleaning the combustion chamber with the valves removed can damage the valve seat surfaces. A damaged or even slightly scratched valve seat will cause poor valve seating.

66

3. Examine the spark plug threads in the cylinder head for damage. If damage is minor or if the threads are dirty or clogged with carbon, use a spark plug thread tap (**Figure 67**) to clean the threads following the manufacturer's instructions. If thread damage is severe, restore the threads by installing a steel thread insert. Purchase thread insert kits at automotive supply stores or have them installed by a Harley-Davidson dealership or machine shop.

67

NOTE
When using a tap to clean spark plug threads, coat the tap with an aluminum tap-cutting fluid or kerosene.

NOTE
Aluminum spark plug threads are commonly damaged due to galling, cross-threading and over-tightening. To prevent galling, apply an antiseize compound on the plug threads before installation and do not overtighten.

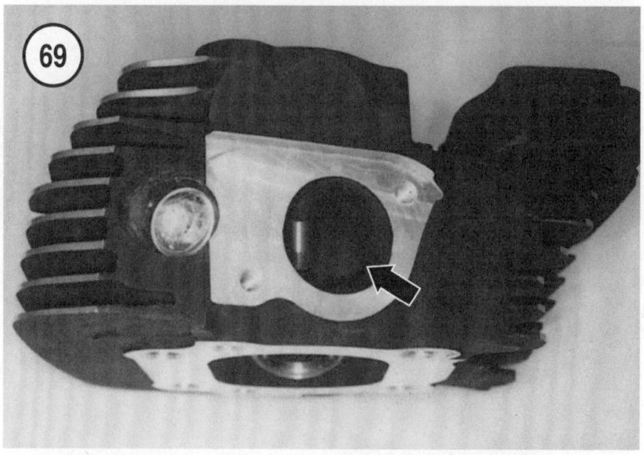

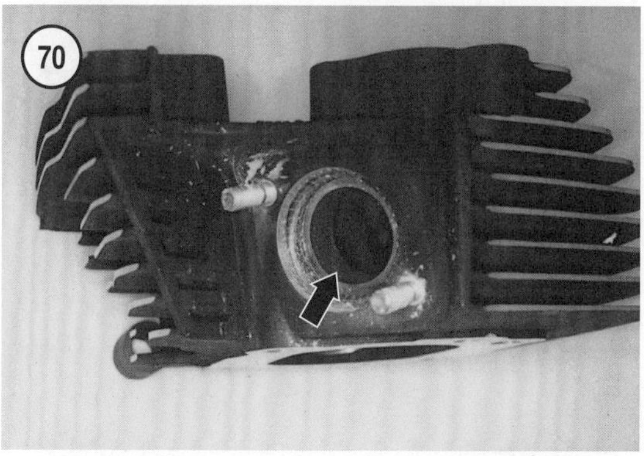

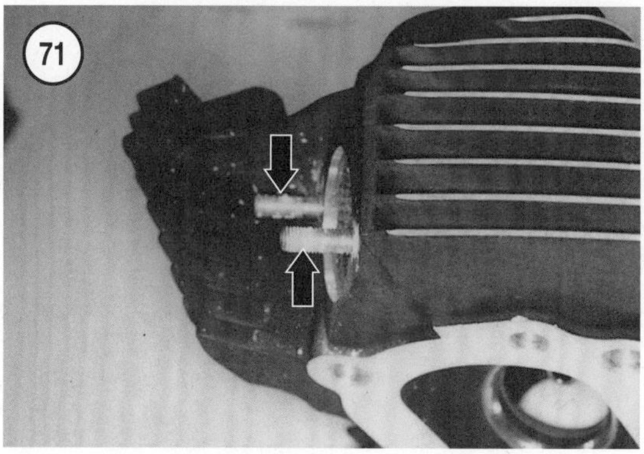

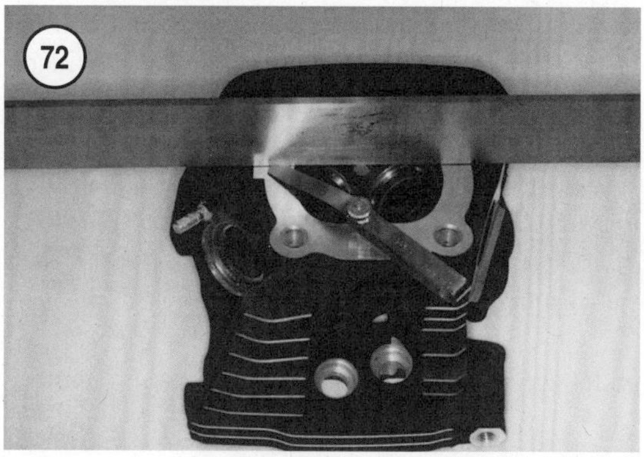

4. After all carbon is removed from combustion chambers and valve ports, and, if necessary, the spark plug thread hole is repaired, clean the entire head in solvent. Blow dry with compressed air.
5. Examine the crown on the piston (**Figure 68**). The crown should show no signs of wear or damage. If the crown appears pecked or spongy, also check the spark plug, valves and combustion chamber for aluminum deposits. If these deposits are found, the cylinder has overheated. Check for a lean fuel mixture or other conditions that could result in preignition.
6. Check for cracks in the combustion chamber, the intake port (**Figure 69**), the exhaust port (**Figure 70**). Replace a cracked head if welding can not repair it.
7. Inspect the threads (**Figure 71**) for the exhaust pipe mounting bolts for damage. Repair with a tap if damaged.

NOTE

If the cylinder head is bead-blasted, clean the head thoroughly with solvent and then with hot soapy water. Residue grit seats in small crevices and other areas and can be hard to get out. Also run a tap through each exposed thread to remove grit from the threads. Residue grit left in the engine will cause premature wear.

8. Thoroughly clean the cylinder head.
9. Place a straightedge across the gasket surface at several points and measure for warp by attempting to insert a feeler gauge between the straightedge and cylinder head at each location (**Figure 72**). Maximum allowable warp is listed in **Table 2**. Distortion or nicks in the cylinder head surface could cause an air leak and result in overheating. If warp

exceeds the limit, the cylinder head must be resurfaced or replaced. Consult a Harley-Davidson dealership or machine shop experienced in this type of work.

10. Check the rocker arm housing mating surfaces for warp (**Figure 73**) using the procedure in Step 9.

11. Make sure the breather channel is clear at each end (**Figure 74**).

12. Check the valves and valve guides as described under *Valves and Valve Components* in this chapter.

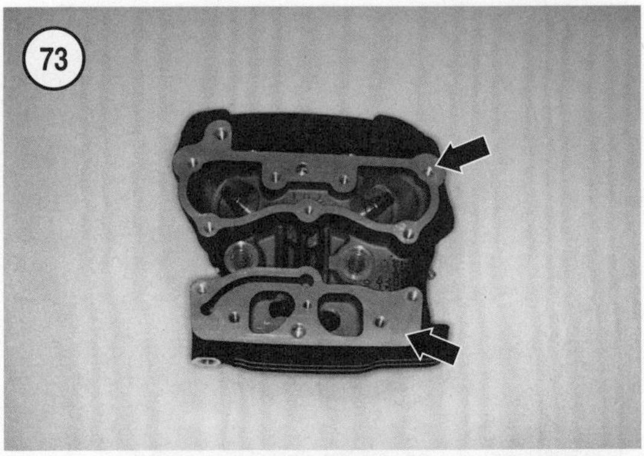

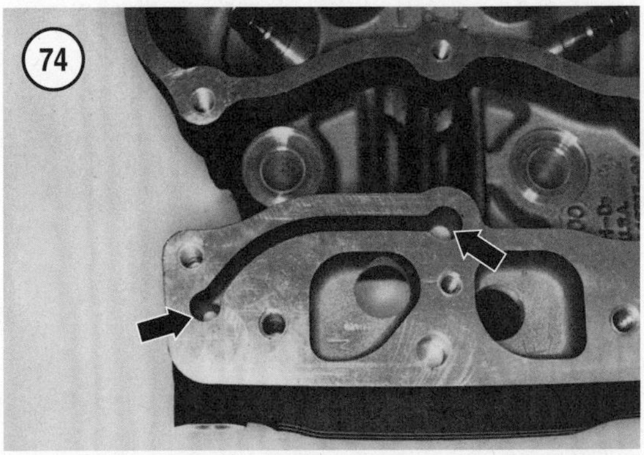

Installation

1. If removed, install the piston and cylinder as described in this chapter.

2. Lubricate the cylinder studs and cylinder head bolts as follows:
   a. Clean the cylinder head bolts in solvent and dry with compressed air.
   b. Apply clean engine oil to the cylinder head bolt threads and to the flat shoulder surface on each bolt (**Figure 75**). Wipe off any excess oil from the bolts, leave only an oil film on these surfaces.

3. Install the two dowel pins (**Figure 65**) into the top of the cylinder block.

4. Install a *new* O-ring over each dowel pin. Apply a light coat of clean engine oil to the O-rings.

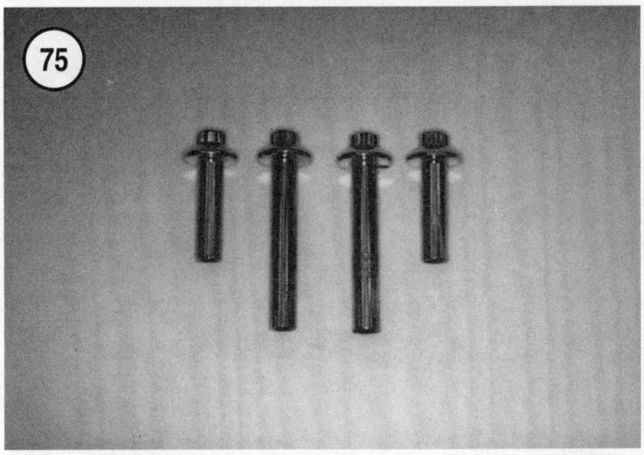

CAUTION
Because the O-rings center the head gasket on the cylinder block, install them before installing the head gasket.

5. Install a *new* cylinder head gasket (**Figure 76**) onto the cylinder block.

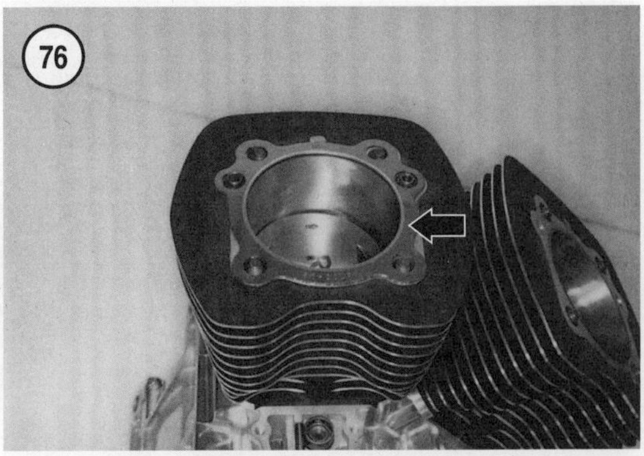

CAUTION
Do not use sealer on the cylinder head gasket. If using an aftermarket head gasket, follow the manufacturer's instructions for gasket installation.

NOTE
*The cylinder heads are not identical. Refer to the FRONT or REAR mark (**Figure** 77) cast into the top surface of the cylinder head.*

6. Install the cylinder head (**Figure 78**) onto the cylinder block and the dowel pins. Position the head

77

78

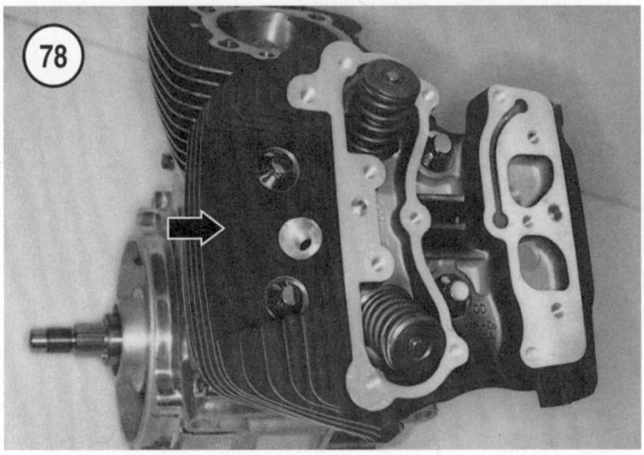

79

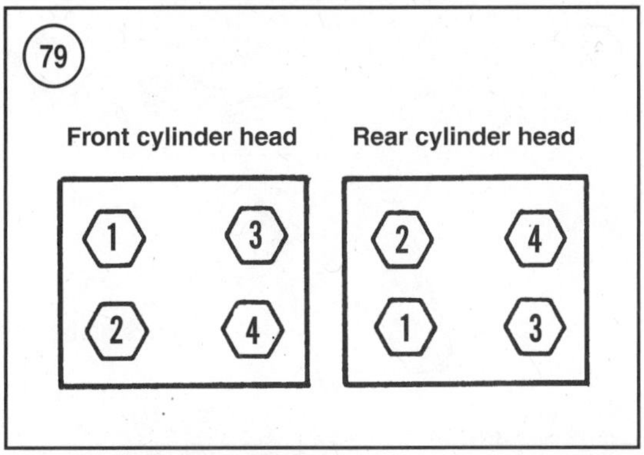

80

81

carefully to avoid moving the head gasket out of alignment.

7. Install the cylinder head long bolts in the center bolt holes; install the short bolts in the outer bolt holes next to the spark plug hole. Tighten the cylinder head bolts (**Figure 64**) only finger-tight at this time.

CAUTION
Failure to follow the torque pattern and sequence in Step 8 may cause cylinder head distortion and gasket leakage.

8. Refer to **Figure 79** for the front and rear cylinder head bolt tightening sequence. Torque the cylinder head bolts as follows:
   a. Starting with bolt No. 1, tighten each bolt in order to 84-108 in.-lb. (9-12 N•m).
   b. Starting with bolt No. 1, tighten each bolt in order to 144-168 in.-lb. (16-19 N•m).
   c. Make a vertical mark with a permanent marker on each bolt head (A, **Figure 80**). Make another mark on the cylinder head (B, **Figure 80**) at a 90-degree angle, or 1/4 turn from the mark on the bolt head.
   d. Use the marks as a guide and tighten each bolt head 90 degrees, or 1/4 turn, clockwise until the match marks are aligned (**Figure 81**).

9. Install the rocker arm assemblies and pushrods as described in this chapter.

VALVES AND VALVE COMPONENTS

Complete valve service requires a number of special tools, including a valve spring compressor, to remove and install the valves. The following procedures describe how to check for valve component wear and to determine what type of service is required.

Valve Removal

1. Remove the cylinder head as described in this chapter.
2. Install the valve spring compressor (**Figure 82**) squarely over the valve spring upper retainer (**Figure 83**) and against the valve head.

CAUTION
To avoid loss of spring tension, compress the spring only enough to remove the valve keepers.

3. Tighten the valve spring compressor until the valve keepers separate from the valve stem. Lift the valve keepers out through the valve spring compressor with a magnet or needlenose pliers.
4. Gradually loosen the valve spring compressor and remove it from the cylinder head.
5. Remove the spring retainer and the valve springs.

CAUTION
*Remove any burrs from the valve stem groove before removing the valve (**Figure 84**); otherwise the valve guide will be damaged as the valve stem passes through it.*

6. Remove the valve from the cylinder while rotating it slightly.
7. Remove the valve spring lower retainer.
8. Remove the valve guide oil seal.

CAUTION
Keep the components of each valve assembly together by placing each set in a divided carton, or into separate small boxes or small reclosable plastic bags. Identify the components as either intake or exhaust. If both cylinders are disassembled, also label the components as front and rear. Do not intermix components from the valves or excessive wear may result.

9. Repeat Steps 3-8 and remove the remaining valve.

82

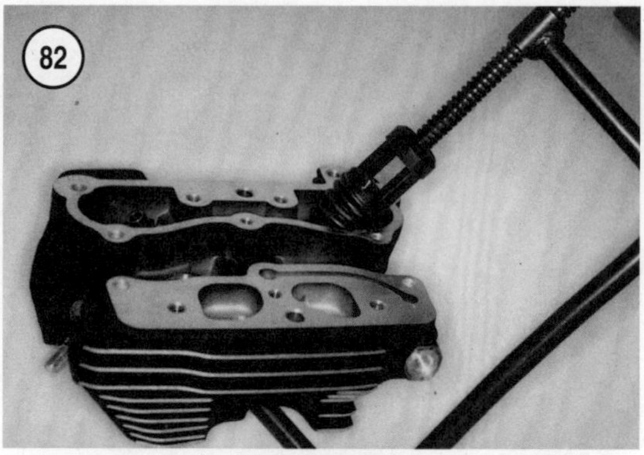

83

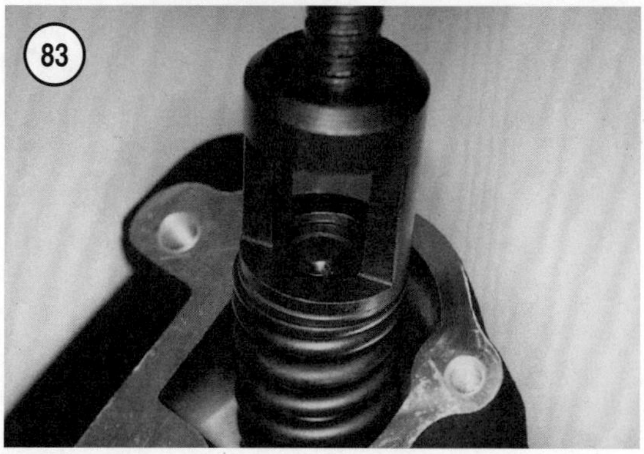

84

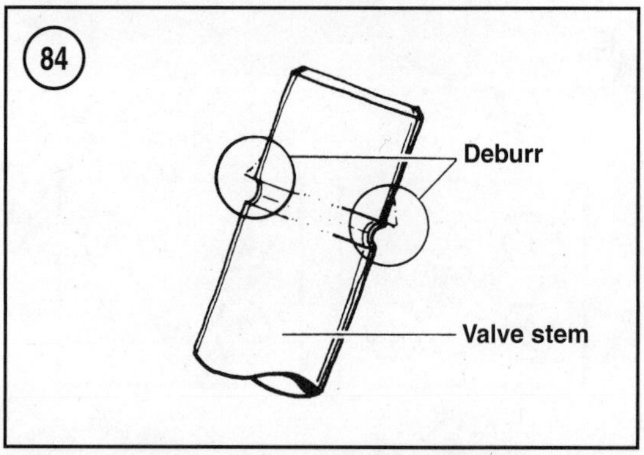

85

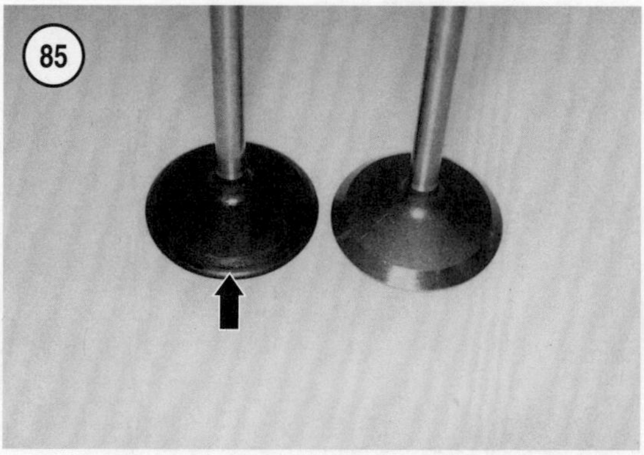

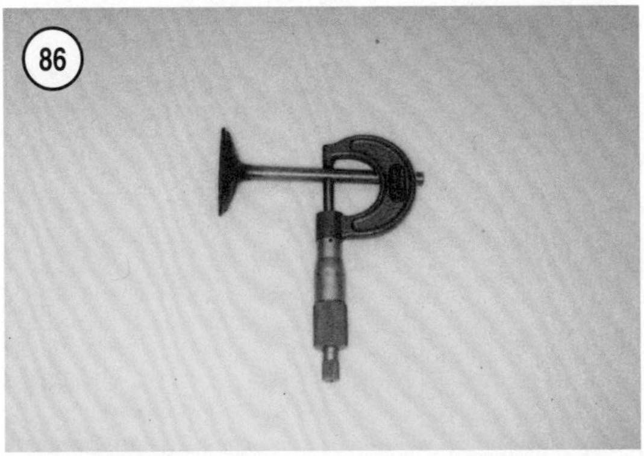

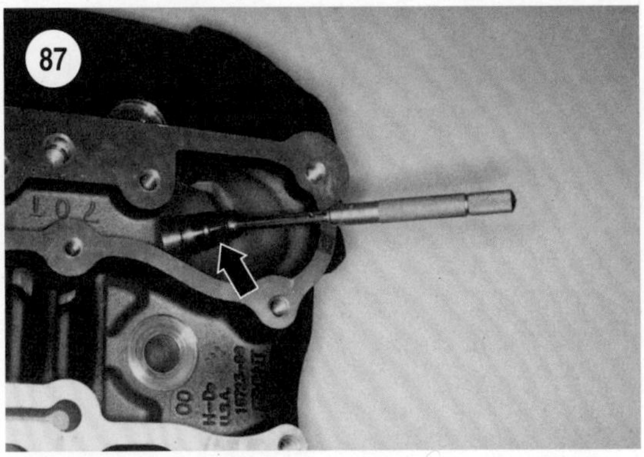

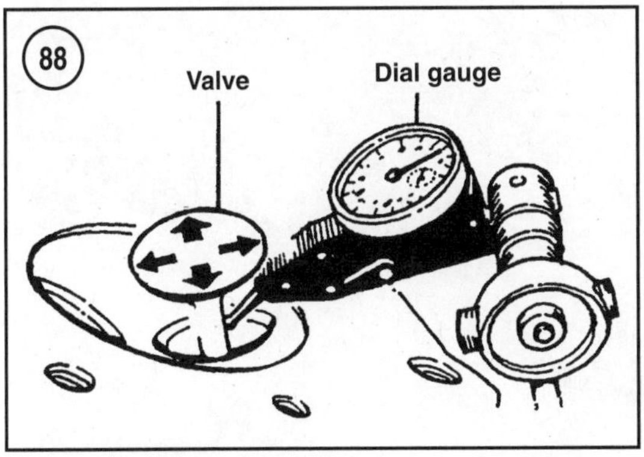

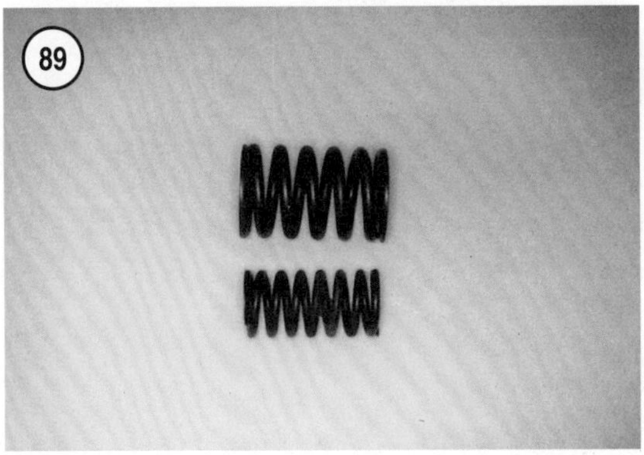

Valve Inspection

When measuring the valves and valve components in this section, compare the actual measurements to the new and wear limit specifications in **Table 2**. Replace parts that are out of specification or show damage as described in this section.

1. Clean valves in solvent. Do not gouge or damage the valve seating surface.
2. Inspect the valve face. Minor roughness and pitting (**Figure 85**) can be removed by lapping the valve as described in this chapter. Excessive unevenness to the contact surface is an indication that the valve is not serviceable.
3. Inspect the valve stem for wear and roughness. Then measure the valve stem outside diameter with a micrometer (**Figure 86**).
4. Remove all carbon and varnish from the valve guides with a stiff spiral wire brush before measuring wear.
5. Measure the valve guide inside diameter with a small hole gauge (**Figure 87**). Measure at the top, center and bottom positions. Then measure the small hole gauge.
6. Determine the valve stem-to-valve guide clearance by subtracting the valve stem outside diameter from the valve guide inner diameter. Compare this measurement to the specification listed in **Table 2**.
7. If a small hole gauge is not available, insert each valve into its guide. Attach a dial indicator to the valve stem next to the head (**Figure 88**). Hold the valve just slightly off its seat and rock it sideways in both directions 90 degrees to each other. If the valve rocks more than slightly, the guide is probably worn. However, as a final check, take the cylinder head to a Harley-Davidson dealership or machine shop and have the valve guides measured.
8. Check the inner and outer valve springs as follows:
   a. Check each of the valve springs (**Figure 89**) for visual damage.
   b. Use a square and visually check the spring for distortion or tilt (**Figure 90**).
   c. Measure the valve spring free length with a vernier caliper (**Figure 91**) and check against the dimension in **Table 2**.
   d. Repeat for each valve spring.
   e. Replace defective springs as a set (inner and outer).

4

9. Check the valve spring upper and lower retainers seats for cracks or other damage.

10. Check the valve keepers and their fit onto the valve stem end (**Figure 92**). They must index tightly into the valve stem groove.

11. Inspect the valve seats (**Figure 93**) in the cylinder head. If worn or burned, they may be reconditioned as described in this chapter. Seats and valves in near-perfect condition can be reconditioned by lapping with fine carborundum paste. Check as follows:

  a. Clean the valve seat and corresponding valve mating areas with contact cleaner.
  b. Coat the valve seat with layout fluid.
  c. Install the valve into its guide and tap it against its seat with a valve lapping tool. Do not rotate the valve.
  d. Lift the valve out of the guide and measure the seat width at various points around the seat with a vernier caliper.
  e. Compare the seat width with the specification in **Table 2**. If the seat width is less than specified or uneven, resurface the seats as described in this chapter.
  f. Remove all layout fluid residue from the seats and valves.

90

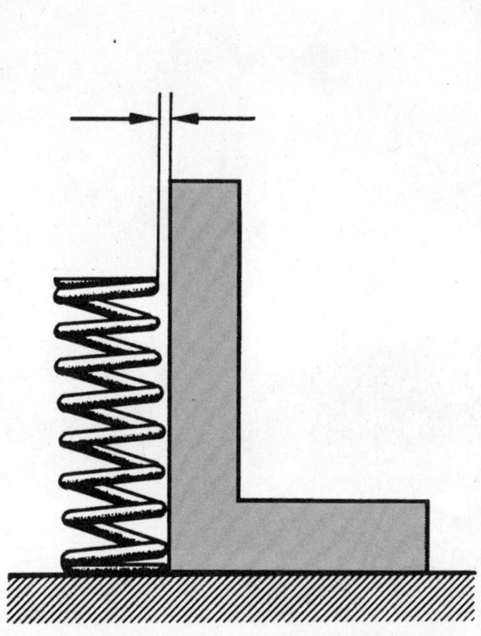

91

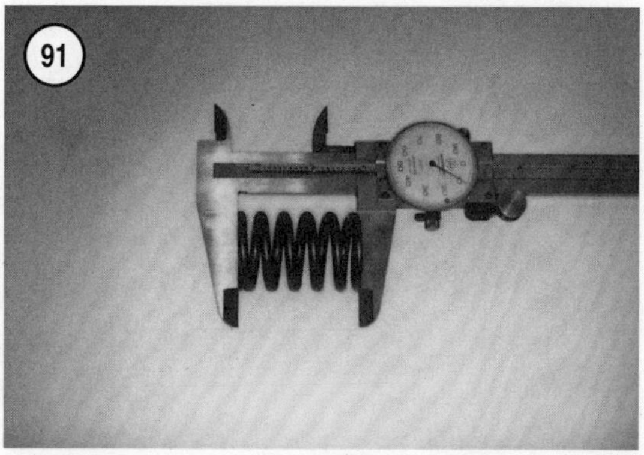

92

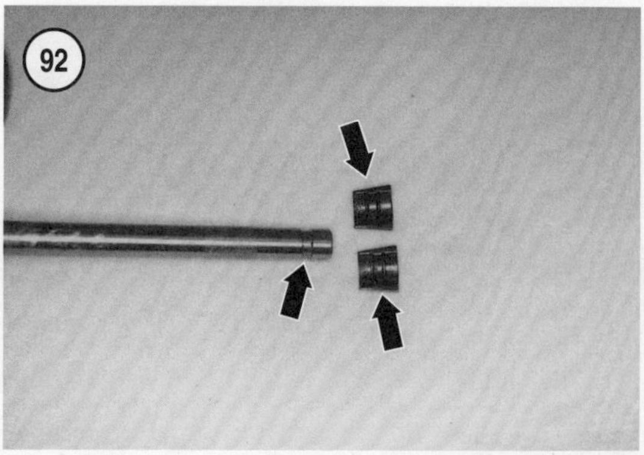

Valve Installation

1. Clean the end of the valve guide.

2. Install the spring lower retainer (**Figure 94**). Push it down until it is seated on the cylinder head surface (**Figure 95**).

3. Coat a valve stem with Torco MPZ, molybdenum disulfide paste or equivalent. Install the valve part way into the guide. Then, slowly turn the valve as it enters the oil seal and continue turning it until the valve is installed all the way.

4. Work the valve back and forth in the valve guide to ensure the lubricant is distributed evenly within the valve guide.

5. Withdraw the valve and apply an additional coat of the lubricant.

6. Reinstall the valve into the valve guide but do not push the valve past the top of the valve guide.

7. Use isopropyl alcohol and thoroughly clean all traces of lubricant from the outer surface of the valve guide.

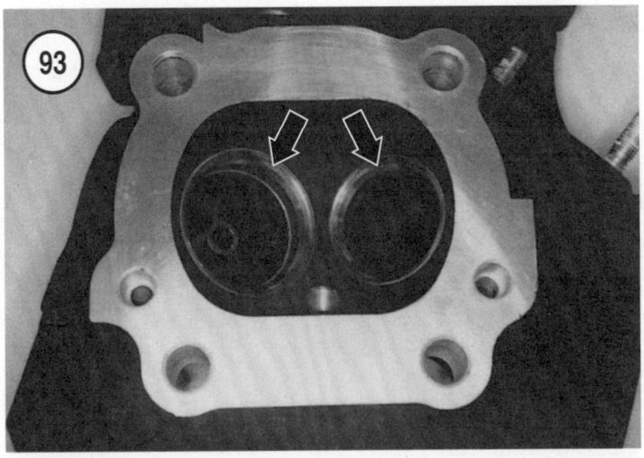
93

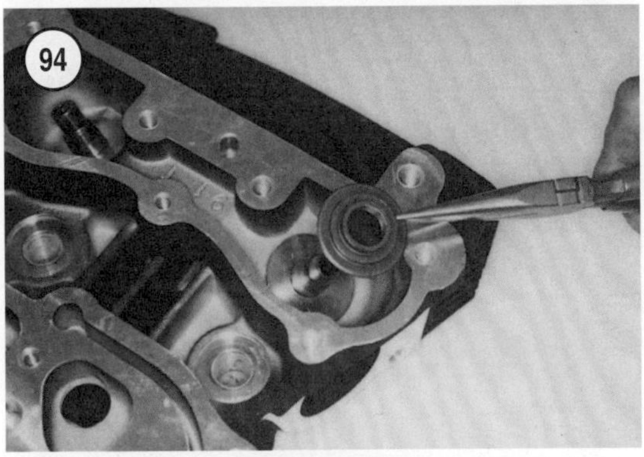
94

95

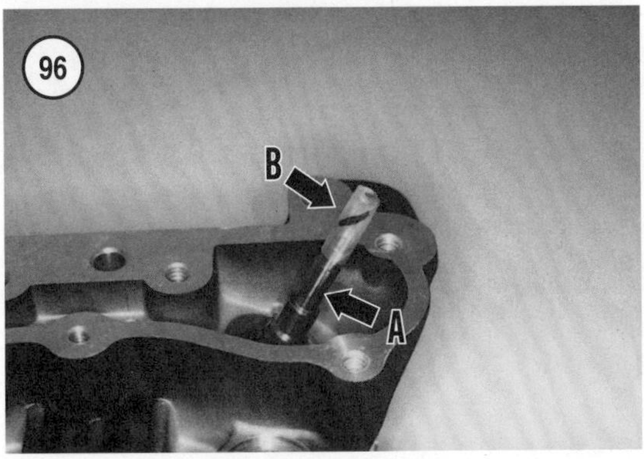

96

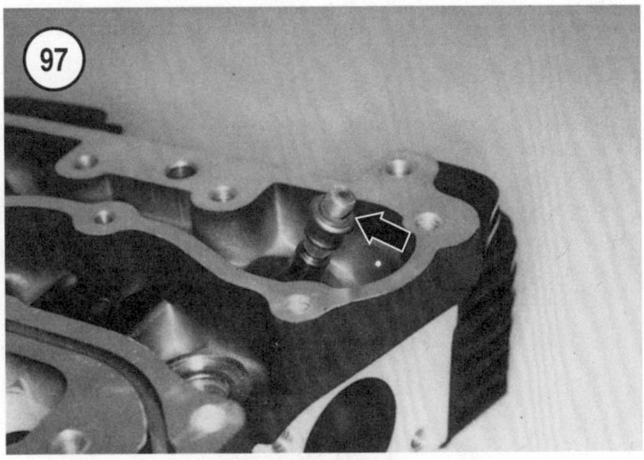
97

CAUTION
Do not allow any of the retaining compound to enter the valve guide bore.

8. Apply Loctite Retaining Compound RC/620, or an equivalent, to the oil seal seating surface and to the outer surface of the valve guide.
9. Push the valve all the way into the cylinder head until it bottoms (A, **Figure 96**).

CAUTION
The oil seal will be torn as it passes the valve stem keeper groove if the plastic capsule is not installed in Step 10. The capsule is included in the top end gasket set.

10. Hold the valve in place and install the plastic capsule (B, **Figure 96**) onto the end of the valve stem. Apply a light coat of clean engine oil to the outer surface of the capsule.
11. With the valve held in place, install the oil seal (**Figure 97**) onto the valve stem.
12A. If special tools are used, use the Harley-Davidson Valve Seal Installation tool (part No. HD-34643A) and driver handle (part No. HD-34740) (**Figure 98**) and push the oil seal down until it bottoms on the cylinder head surface.
12B. If special tools are not used, use an appropriate-size deep socket (**Figure 99**), and push the oil seal down until it bottoms on the cylinder head surface.
13. Remove the plastic capsule from the valve stem. Keep the capsule as it will be used on the remaining valves.
14. Install the inner valve spring (**Figure 100**) and make sure it is properly seated on the lower spring retainer.

98

VALVE SEAL INSTALLATION

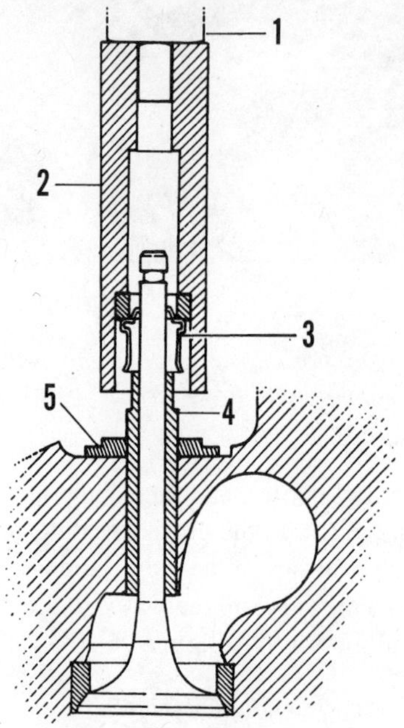

1. Driver handle
2. Valve seal installation tool
3. Valve guide seal
4. Valve guide
5. Lower spring seat

15. Install the outer valve spring (**Figure 101**) and make sure it is properly seated on the lower spring retainer.
16. Install the upper spring retainer (**Figure 102**) on top of the valve springs.

CAUTION

To avoid loss of spring tension, compress the springs only enough to install the valve keepers.

17. Compress the valve springs with a valve spring compressor (**Figure 82**) and install the valve keepers (**Figure 103**).
18. Make sure both keepers are seated around the valve stem prior to releasing the compressor.
19. Slowly release tension from the compressor and remove it. After removing the compressor, inspect the valve keepers to make sure they are prop-

99

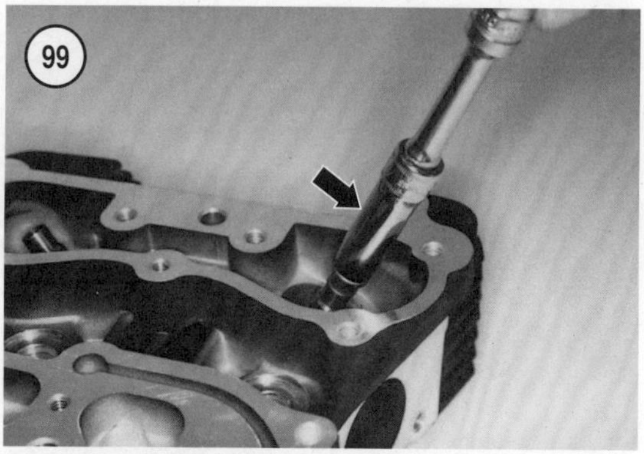

100

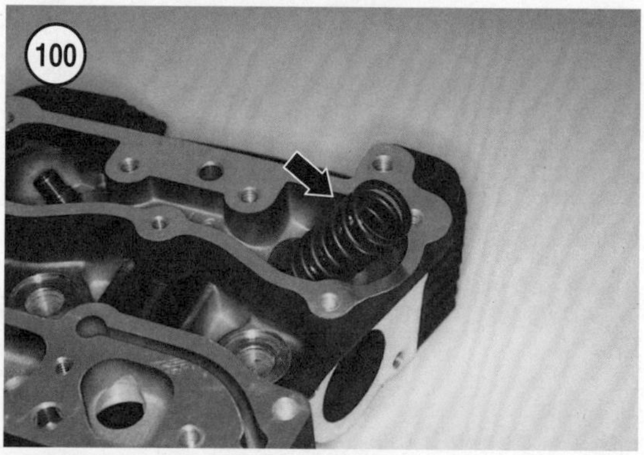

101

102

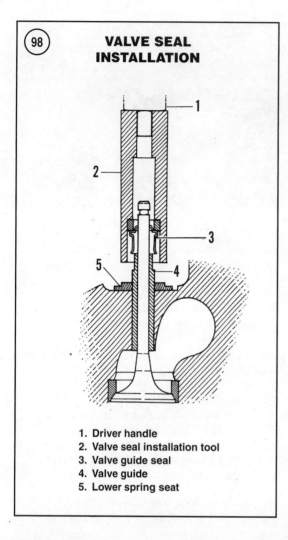

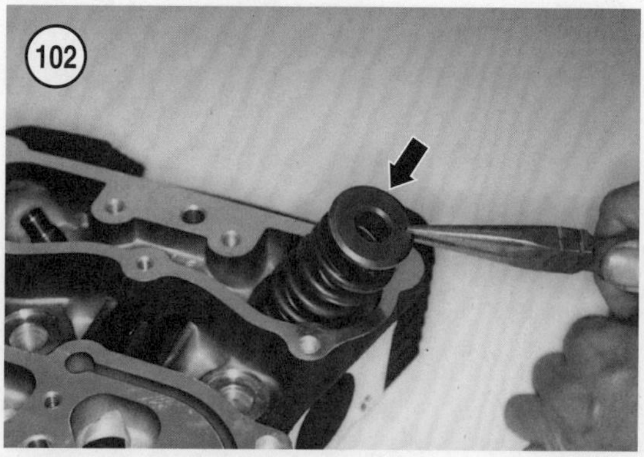

103

104

105

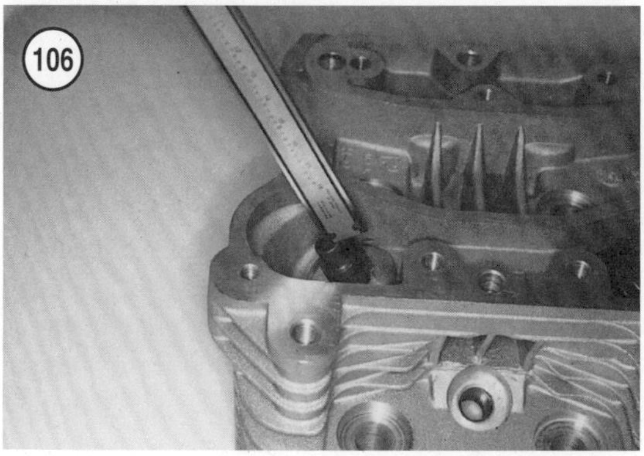
106

erly seated (**Figure 104**). Tap the end of the valve stem with a *soft-faced* hammer to ensure that the keepers are properly seated.

20. Repeat Steps 1-19 for the remaining valves.

21. Install the cylinder head as described in this chapter.

Valve Guide Replacement

Tools

The following tools or their equivalents are required to replace the valve guides.

1. Driver handle and remover (HD-34740).
2. Valve guide installation sleeve (HD-34741).
3. Valve guide, reamer (HD-39932) and T-handle (HD-39847).
4. Valve guide reamer (HD-39964) and honing lubricant.
5. Valve guide hone (HD-34723).
6. Valve guide brush (HD-34751).

Procedure

1. Place the cylinder head on a wooden surface with the combustion chamber side facing down.

2. Shoulderless valve guides (**Figure 105**) are used. Before the valve guides are removed, note and record the shape of the guide that projects into the combustion chamber. If the valve guide installation tool is *not* going to be used, measure the distance from the face of the guide to the cylinder head surface with a vernier caliper (**Figure 106**). Record the distance for each valve guide. The new valve guides must be installed to this *exact* same height dimension.

3. Remove the valve guides as follows:

CAUTION

Use the correct size valve guide removal tool when removing the valve guides; otherwise, the tool may expand the end of the guide. An expanded guide will widen and damage the guide bore in the cylinder head as it passes through it.

NOTE

The valve guides can either be pressed out or driven out. Pressing out is recommended since it lessens the chance of cylinder head damage.

a. Support the cylinder head so that the combustion chamber faces down.
b. If driving the guides out, place the cylinder on a piece of wood.
c. If pressing the guides out, support the cylinder head in the press so that the valve guide is perpendicular to the press table with a cylinder head stand (JIMS part No. 39782).
d. Insert the driver handle and remover into the top of the valve guide.
e. Press or drive the valve guide out through the combustion chamber.
f. Repeat for the remaining valve guides.

4. Clean the valve guide bores in the cylinder head.
5. Because the valve guide bores in the cylinder head may have enlarged during removal of the old guides, measure each valve guide bore prior to purchasing the new guides. Then purchase the new valve guides to match its respective bore diameter. Determine the bore diameter as follows:

a. Measure the valve guide bore diameter in the cylinder head with a bore gauge or snap gauge. Record the bore diameter.
b. The new valve guide outside diameter must be 0.0020-0.0033 in. (0.050-0.084 mm) larger than the guide bore in the cylinder head. When purchasing new valve guides, measure the new guide's outside diameter with a micrometer. If the new guide's outside diameter is not within this specification, oversize valve guide(s) must be installed. See a Harley-Davidson dealership for available sizes.

6. Apply a thin coating of molylube or white grease to the entire outer surface of the valve guide before installing it in the cylinder head.

CAUTION
When installing oversize valve guides, make sure to match each guide to its respective bore in the cylinder head.

7. Install the new guide using the driver handle and valve guide installation tools. Press or drive the guide into the cylinder head until the valve guide installation tool bottoms out on the cylinder head surface. When the tool bottoms on the cylinder head surface, the valve guide is installed to the correct height. If the driver handle tool is not used, install the valve guide to the same height recorded prior to removing the valve guide; measure the valve guide's installed height using a vernier caliper (**Figure 106**) when installing it.

107

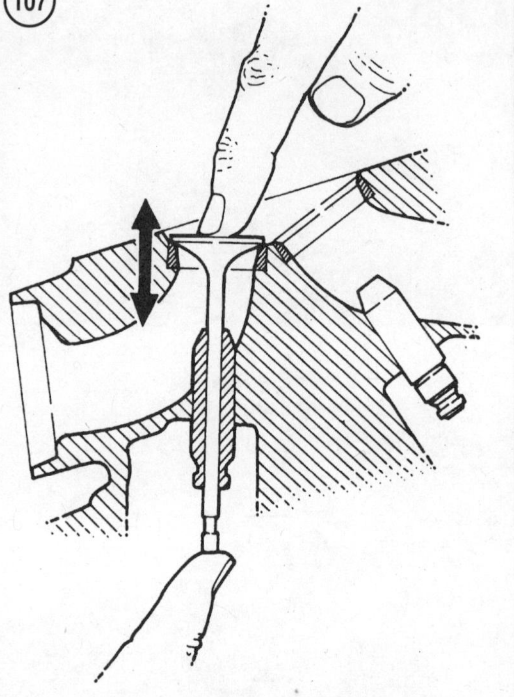

NOTE
Replacement valve guides are sold with a smaller inside diameter than the valve stem, so the guide must be reamed to fit the valve stem.

8. Ream the new valve guide as follows:

a. Apply a liberal amount of reamer lubricant to the ream bit and to the valve guide bore.
b. Start the reamer straight into the valve guide bore.

CAUTION
Apply pressure only to the end of the drive socket. If pressure is applied to the T-handle it will result in an uneven rough cut and a tapered bore.

c. Apply thumb pressure to the end of the drive socket portion of the T-handle while rotating the T-handle *clockwise*. Only *light* pressure is required. Apply additional lubricant onto the reamer and into the valve guide while rotating the reamer.

108

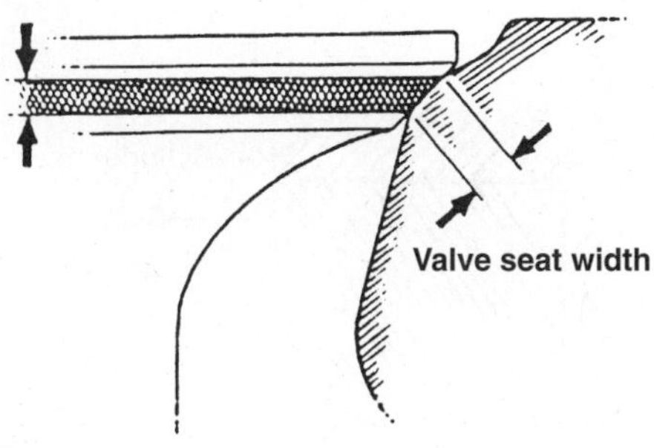

d. Continue to rotate the reamer until the entire bit has traveled through the valve guide and the shank of the reamer rotates freely.

CAUTION
Never back the reamer out through the valve guide as the guide will be damaged.

e. Remove the T-handle from the reamer. Remove the reamer out from the combustion chamber side of the cylinder head.
f. Apply low-pressure compressed air and clean out the small shavings from the valve guide bore. Then clean the valve guide bore with the small spiral brush.

9. Hone the valve guide as follows:
   a. Install the valve guide hone into a high-speed electric drill.
   b. Lubricate the valve guide bore and hone stones with the reamer lubricant—*do not use motor oil.*
   c. Carefully insert the hone stones into the valve guide bore.
   d. Start the drill and move the hone back and forth in the valve guide bore for 10 to 12 complete strokes. Work for a 60° crosshatch pattern.
10. Repeat for each valve guide.
11. Soak the cylinder head in a container filled with hot, soapy water. Then clean the valve guides with a valve guide brush or an equivalent bristle brush—*do not use a steel brush.* Do not use cleaning solvent, kerosene or gasoline as these chemicals will not remove all of the abrasive particles produced during the honing operation. Repeat this step until all of the valve guides are thoroughly cleaned. Then rinse the cylinder head and valve guides in clear, cold water and dry with compressed air.
12. After cleaning and drying the valve guides, apply clean engine oil to the guides to prevent rust.
13. Resurface the valve seats as described in *Valve Seat Reconditioning* in this chapter.

4

Valve Seat Inspection

1. Remove all carbon residue from each valve seat. Then clean the cylinder head as described under *Valve Inspection* in this chapter.

NOTE
The most accurate method of checking the valve seat width and position is with machinist's dye.

2. Check the valve seats in their original locations with machinist's dye as follows:
   a. Thoroughly clean the valve face and valve seat with contact cleaner.
   b. Spread a thin layer of Prussian blue or machinist's dye evenly on the valve face.
   c. Insert the valve into its guide.
   d. Support the valve by hand (**Figure 107**) and tap the valve up and down in the cylinder head. Do not rotate the valve or a false reading will result.
   e. Remove the valve and examine the impression left by the machinist's dye. The impressions on the valve and the seat must be even around their circumferences and the width (**Figure 108**) must be within the specifications in **Table 2**. If the width is beyond the specification or if the impression is uneven recondition the valve seats.
3. Closely examine the valve seat in the cylinder head (**Figure 93**). It must be smooth and even with a polished seating surface.
4. If the valve seat is in good condition, install the valve as described in this chapter.
5. If the valve seat is not correct, recondition the valve seat as described in this chapter.

Valve Seat Reconditioning

Valve seat reconditioning requires considerable expertise and special tools. In most cases it is more economical and practical to have these procedures performed by an experienced machinist.

The following procedure is provided for those equipped to perform the task. A valve seat cutter set (HD-35758A) or equivalent is required. Follow the manufacturer's instructions.

Refer to **Figure 109** for valve seat angles. While the valve seat angles for both the intake and exhaust valves are the same, different cutter sizes are required. Also note that a 45-degree seat angle is specified when grinding the seats, while a 46-degree seat angle is specified when cutting seats.

1. Clean the valve guides as described under *Inspection* in this chapter.
2. Carefully rotate and insert the solid pilot into the valve guide. Make sure the pilot is correctly seated.

CAUTION
Valve seat accuracy depends on a correctly sized and installed pilot.

3. Using the 45-degree grinding stone or 46-degree cutter, descale and clean the valve seat with one or two turns.

CAUTION
*Measure the valve seat contact area in the cylinder head (**Figure 108**) after each cut to make sure its size and area are correct. Over-grinding will sink the valves too far into the cylinder head, requiring replacement of the valve seat.*

4. If the seat is still pitted or burned, turn the cutter until the surface is clean. Work slowly and carefully to avoid removing too much material from the valve seat.
5. Remove the pilot from the valve guide.
6. Apply a small amount of valve lapping compound to the valve face and install the valve. Rotate the valve against the valve seat using a valve lapping tool. Remove the valve.
7. Measure the valve seat with a vernier caliper (**Figure 108** and **Figure 109**). Record the measurement to use as a reference point when performing the following.

CAUTION
The 31° cutter removes material quickly. Work carefully and check the progress often.

109

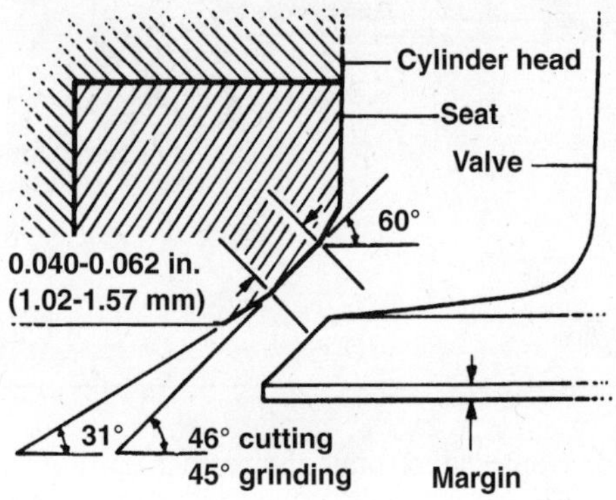

8. Reinsert the solid pilot into the valve guide. Be certain the pilot is properly seated. Install the 31° cutter onto the solid pilot and lightly cut the seat to remove 1/4 of the existing valve seat.
9. Install the 60° cutter onto the solid pilot and lightly cut the seat to remove the lower 1/4 of the existing valve seat.
10. Measure the valve seat with a vernier caliper. Then fit the 45° grinding stone or 46° cutter onto the solid pilot and cut the valve seat to the specified seat width in **Table 2**.
11. When the valve seat width is correct, check valve seating as follows.
12. Remove the solid pilot from the cylinder head.
13. Inspect the valve seat-to-valve face impression as follows:
   a. Clean the valve seat with contact cleaner.
   b. Spread a thin layer of Prussian Blue or machinist's dye evenly on the valve face.
   c. Insert the valve into its guide.
   d. Support the valve with two fingers and turn it with the valve lapping tool.
   e. Remove the valve and examine the impression left by the Prussian blue or machinist's dye.

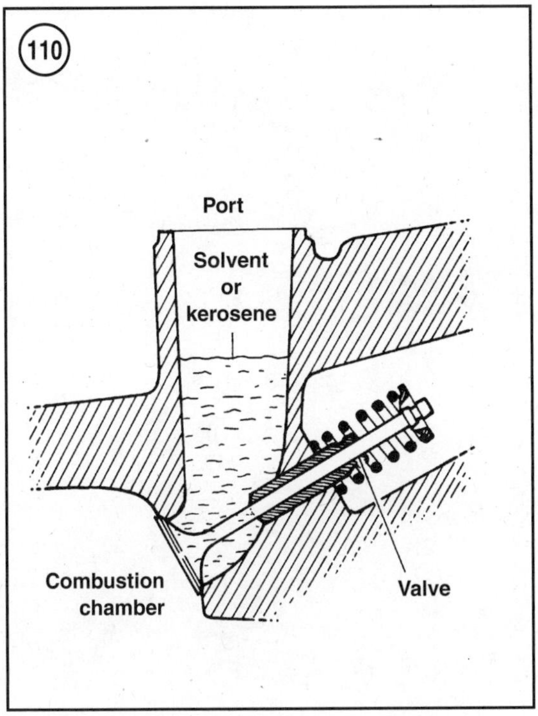

f. Measure the valve seat width (**Figure 108** and **Figure 109**). Refer to **Table 2** for the correct seat width.

g. The valve seat contact area must be in the center of the valve face area.

14. If the contact area is too high on the valve, or if it is too wide, cut the seat with the 31° cutter. This will remove part of the top valve seat area to lower or narrow the contact area.

15. If the contact area is too low on the valve, or if it is too wide, use the 60° cutter and remove part of the lower area to raise and narrow the contact area.

16. After obtaining the desired valve seat position and angle, use the 45° grinding stone or the 46° cutter and very lightly clean off any burrs caused by the previous cuts.

17. When the contact area is correct, lap the valve as described in this chapter.

18. Repeat Steps 1-17 for the remaining valve seats.

19. Thoroughly clean the cylinder head and all valve components in solvent, then clean with detergent and hot water and rinse in cold water. Dry with compressed air. Then apply a light coat of engine oil to all non-aluminum metal surfaces to prevent rust formation.

Valve Lapping

If valve wear or distortion is not excessive, attempt to restore the valve seal by lapping the valve to the seat.

After lapping the valves, install the valve assemblies and test each valve seat for a good seal by pouring solvent into the ports (**Figure 110**). If the seal is good, no solvent will leak past the seat surface. If solvent leaks past any seat the combustion chamber will appear wet. Disassemble the leaking valve and repeat the lapping procedure or recondition the valve as described in this chapter.

1. Smear a light coating of fine grade valve lapping compound on the seating surface of the valve.
2. Insert the valve into the head.
3. Wet the suction cup of the lapping tool and stick it onto the head of the valve. Lap the valve to the seat by spinning the tool between both hands while lifting and moving the valve around the seat 1/4 turn at a time.
4. Wipe off the valve and seat frequently to check the progress. Lap only enough to achieve a precise seating ring around the valve face.
5. Closely examine the valve seat in the cylinder head. The seat must be smooth and even with a polished seating ring.
6. Thoroughly clean the valves and cylinder head in solvent to remove all grinding compound residue. Compound left on the valves or the cylinder head will cause rapid engine wear.
7. After installing the valves into the cylinder head, test each valve for proper seating. Check by pouring solvent into the intake and exhaust ports. Solvent must not leak past the valve seats. If leakage occurs, the combustion chamber will appear wet. If solvent leaks past any of the seats, disassemble that valve assembly and repeat the lapping procedure until there is no leakage.

Valve Seat Replacement

Valve seat replacement requires considerable experience and equipment. Refer this work to a Harley-Davidson dealership or machine shop.

CYLINDER

Refer to **Figure 111**.

111

PISTON/CYLINDER BLOCK ASSEMBLY

1. Upper compression ring
2. Lower compression ring
3. Upper oil ring
4. Spacer
5. Lower oil ring
6. Retaining ring
7. Piston
8. Connecting rod bushing
9. Connecting rod
10. Piston pin
11. O-ring
12. Locating dowel
13. Cylinder block
14. O-ring seal

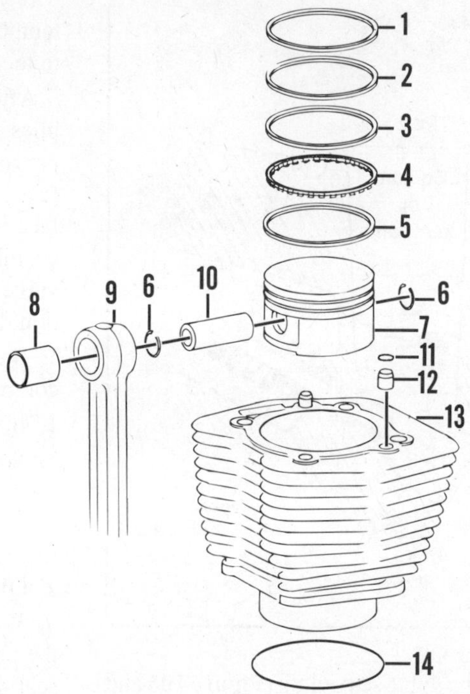

Removal

1. Remove the cylinder head as described in this chapter.
2. Remove all dirt and debris from the cylinder base.
3. If still in place, remove the two dowel pins and O-rings (**Figure 112**) from the top of the cylinder block.
4. Turn the crankshaft until the piston is at bottom dead center (BDC).

NOTE

The front and rear cylinder blocks are identical (same part number). Mark each cylinder block so they will be re-installed in their original positions.

5. Pull the cylinder straight up and off the piston and cylinder studs. If necessary, tap around the perimeter of the cylinder with a rubber or plastic mallet.
6. Place clean shop rags (A, **Figure 113**) into the crankcase opening to prevent objects from falling undetected into the crankcase.
7. Remove the O-ring seal (B, **Figure 113**) from the locating dowel. Leave the locating dowels in place unless they are loose.

112

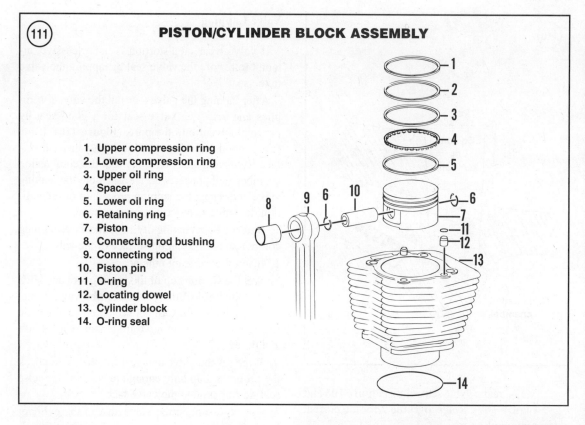

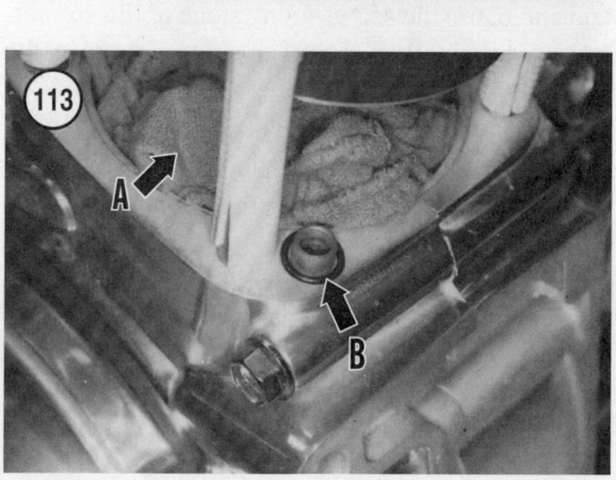

113

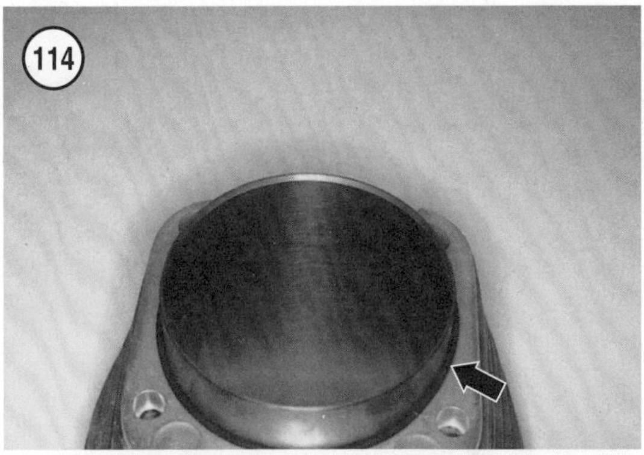

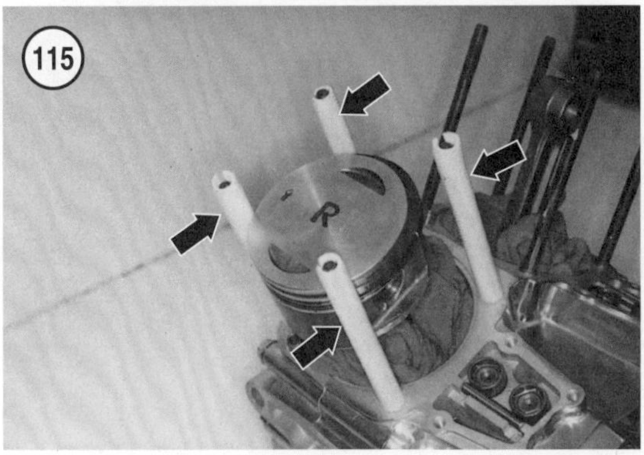

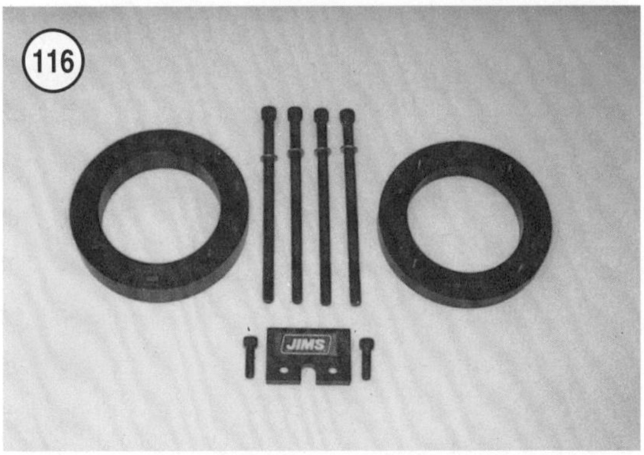

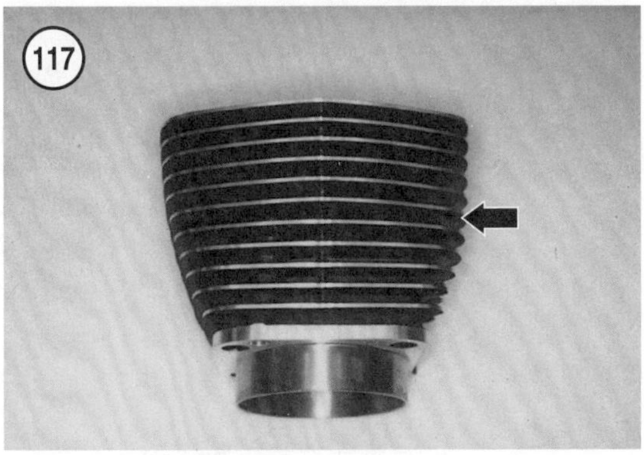

8. Remove the O-ring (**Figure 114**) from the base of the cylinder.

9. Install a vinyl or rubber hose over each stud (**Figure 115**). This will protect both the piston and the studs from damage.

CAUTION

After removing the cylinder, use care when working around the cylinder studs to prevent bending or damaging them. The slightest bend could cause the stud to fail.

10. Repeat these steps to remove the other cylinder.

Inspection

To obtain an accurate cylinder bore measurement, the cylinder must be torqued between torque plates. Measurements made without the torque plates will be inaccurate and may vary by as much as 0.001 in. (0.025 mm). Refer this procedure to a shop equipped and experienced with this procedure if the tools are not available.

The torque plates (**Figure 116**) shown in this procedure are JIMS Cylinder Torque Plates (part No. 1287).

The cylinder block bore must be thoroughly clean to obtain accurate measurements. The cylinder must be at room temperature to obtain accurate measurements. Do not measure the cylinder immediately after it has been honed, as it will still be warm. Measurements can vary by as much as 0.002 in. (0.051 mm) if the cylinder block is not at room temperature.

1. Thoroughly clean the outside of the cylinder. Use a stiff brush, soap and water and clean all debris from the cooling fins (**Figure 117**). If necessary, use a piece of wood and scrape away any lodged dirt. Clogged cooling fins can cause overheating leading to possible engine damage.

2. Carefully remove all gasket residue from the top and bottom cylinder block gasket surfaces.

3. Thoroughly clean the cylinder with solvent and dry with compressed air. Lightly oil the cylinder block bore to prevent rust.

4. Check the top and bottom cylinder gasket surfaces with a straightedge and feeler gauge (**Figure 118).** Replace the cylinder if warp exceeds the limit in **Table 2**.

5. Check the cylinder bore (**Figure 119**) for scuff marks, scratches or other damage.

6. Install the torque plate onto the cylinder (**Figure 120**) following the manufacturer's instructions.
7. Measure the cylinder bore with a bore gauge or inside micrometer (**Figure 121**) at the positions indicated in **Figure 122**. Perform the first measurement 0.500 in. (12.7 mm) below the top of the cylinder (**Figure 122**). Do not measure areas where the rings do not travel.
8. Measure in two axes-aligned with the piston pin and at 90 degrees to the pin. If the taper or out-of-round measurements exceed the service limits in **Table 2**, bore both cylinders to the next oversize and install oversize pistons and rings. Confirm the accuracy of all measurements and consult with a parts supplier on the availability of replacement parts before having the cylinder serviced.
9. Remove the torque plates.
10. If the cylinders were serviced, wash each cylinder in hot, soapy water to remove the fine grit material left from the boring or honing process. After washing, run a clean white cloth through the cylinder bore. If the cloth shows traces of grit or oil, the bore is not clean. Repeat until the cloth passes through cleanly. When the bore is clean, dry with compressed air, then lubricate with clean engine oil to prevent the bore from rusting.

CAUTION
The use of hot soapy water is the only procedure that will completely clean the cylinder bore. Solvent and kerosene cannot wash fine grit out of the cylinder crevices. Abrasive grit left in the cylinder will cause premature engine wear.

Cylinder Studs and Cylinder Head Bolts Inspection and Cleaning

The cylinder studs and cylinder head bolts must be in good condition and properly cleaned prior to installing the cylinder blocks and cylinder heads. Damaged or dirty studs may cause cylinder head distortion and gasket leakage.

CAUTION
The cylinder studs, cylinder head bolts and washers consist of hardened material. Do not substitute these items with a part made of a lower grade material. If replacement is required, purchase the parts from the manufacturer.

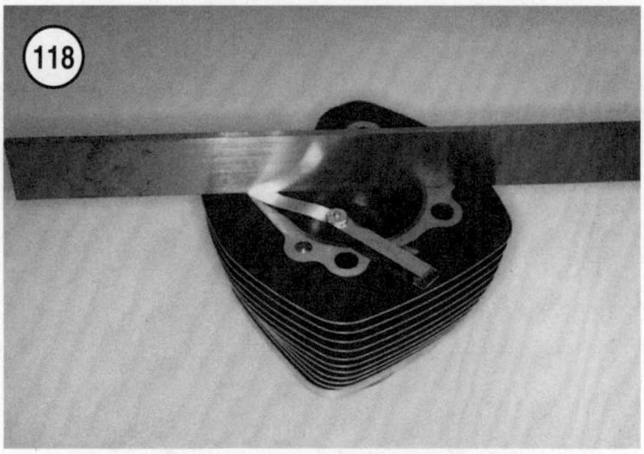
118

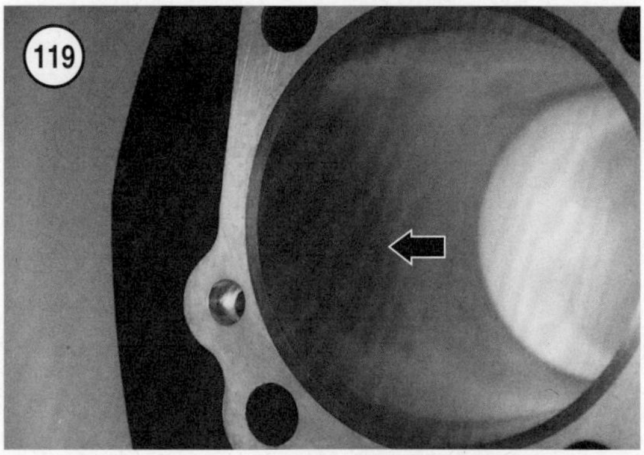
119

120

121

122

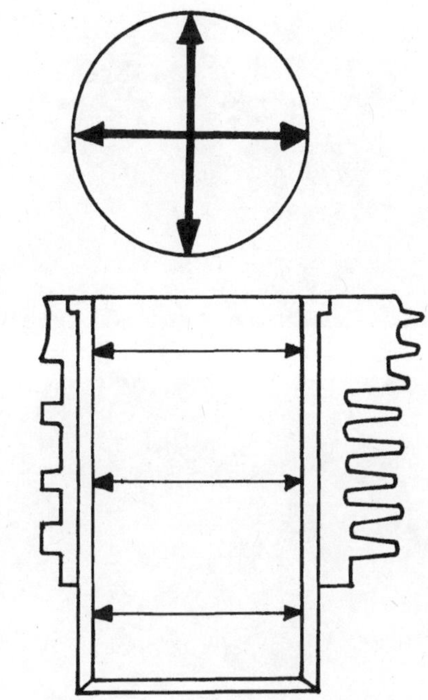

123

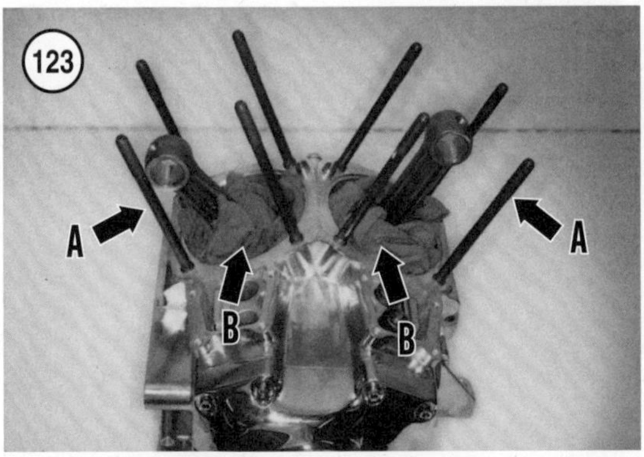

124

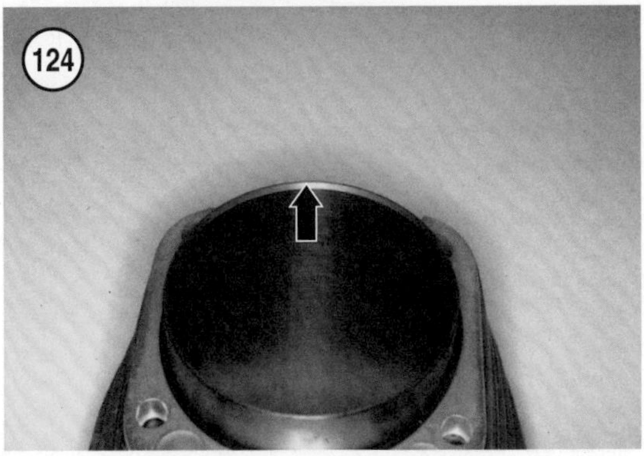

1. Inspect the cylinder head bolts. Replace any that are damaged.
2. Examine the cylinder studs (A, **Figure 123**) for bending, looseness or damage. Replace studs as described under *Cylinder Stud Replacement* in this chapter. If the studs are in good condition, perform Step 3.
3. Cover both crankcase openings with shop rags (B, **Figure 123**) to prevent debris from falling into the engine.
4. Remove all carbon residue from the cylinder studs and cylinder head bolts as follows:
   a. Apply solvent to the cylinder stud and mating cylinder head bolt threads and thread the bolt onto the stud.
   b. Turn the cylinder head bolt back and forth to loosen and remove the carbon residue from the threads. Remove the bolt from the stud. Wipe off the residue with a shop rag moistened in cleaning solvent.
   c. Repeat until both thread sets are free of all carbon residues.
   d. Spray the cylinder stud and cylinder head bolt with an aerosol parts cleaner and allow them to dry.
   e. Set the cleaned bolt aside and install it on the same stud when installing the cylinder head.
5. Repeat Step 4 for each cylinder stud and cylinder head bolt set.

Installation

NOTE

*If installing a cylinder block that has been bored oversize, the inner lead-in angle at the base of the bore skirt (**Figure 124**) has been eliminated. This lead-in angle is necessary so the piston rings can safely enter the cylinder bore. If necessary, use a chamfering cone (JIMS part No. 2078) or a hand grinder with a fine stone and grind in a new lead-in angle. The finished surface must be smooth so it will not catch and damage the piston rings during installation.*

1. If removed, install the pistons and rings as described in this chapter.
2. Remove all gasket residue and clean the cylinder block as described under *Inspection* in this chapter.

3. Remove the vinyl or rubber hose from each stud (A, **Figure 125**).
4. Install a *new* O-ring onto the base of the cylinder block. Apply a light coat of clean engine oil to the O-ring.
5. If removed, install the locating dowels (**Figure 126**) into the crankcase.
6. Install a *new* O-ring seal (B, **Figure 113**) onto the locating dowel. Apply a light coat of clean engine oil to the O-ring.
7. Turn the crankshaft until the piston is at top dead center (TDC).
8. Lubricate the cylinder bore, piston and piston rings liberally with clean engine oil.
9. Position the top compression ring gap so it is facing the intake port. Then stagger the remaining piston ring end gaps so they are 90 to 180° from the gap of the ring above it (**Figure 127**).
10. Compress the piston rings with a ring compressor (B, **Figure 125**).

NOTE
Install the cylinder in its original position as noted during removal.

11. Carefully align the cylinder (front facing forward) with the cylinder studs and slide it down (**Figure 128**) until it is over the top of the piston. Then continue sliding the cylinder down and past the rings (**Figure 129**). Remove the ring compressor once the piston rings enter the cylinder bore. Remove the shop rag from the crankcase opening.
12. Continue to slide the cylinder down until it bottoms out on the crankcase.
13. Repeat to install the other cylinder.
14. Install the cylinder heads as described in this chapter.

PISTONS AND PISTON RINGS

Refer to **Figure 111**.

Removal

1. Remove the cylinder as described in this chapter.
2. Cover the crankcase with clean shop rags.
3. Lightly mark the pistons with a F (front) or R (rear) (A, **Figure 130**).

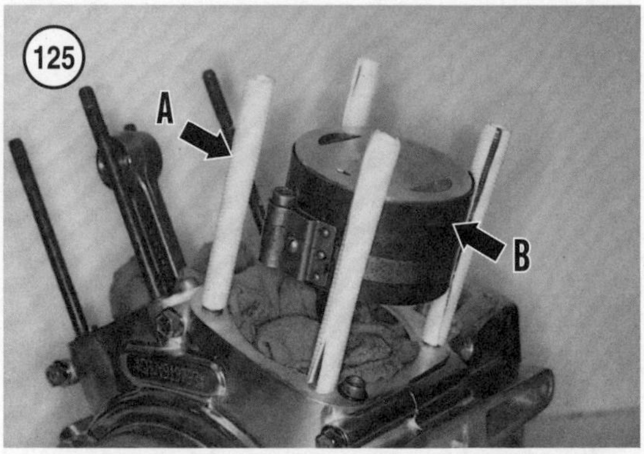

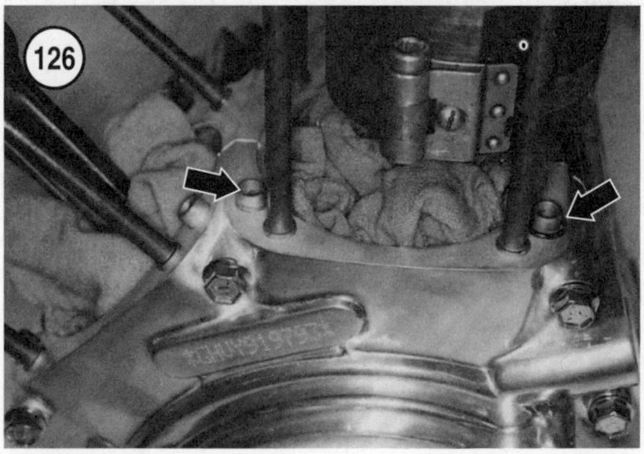

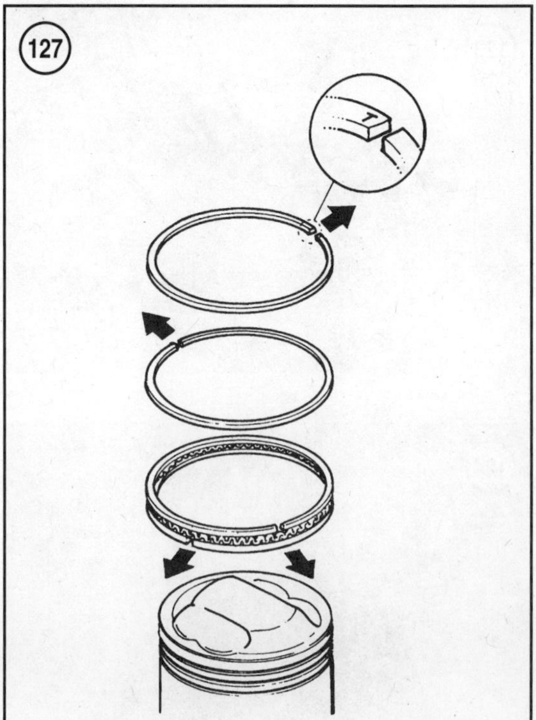

128

129

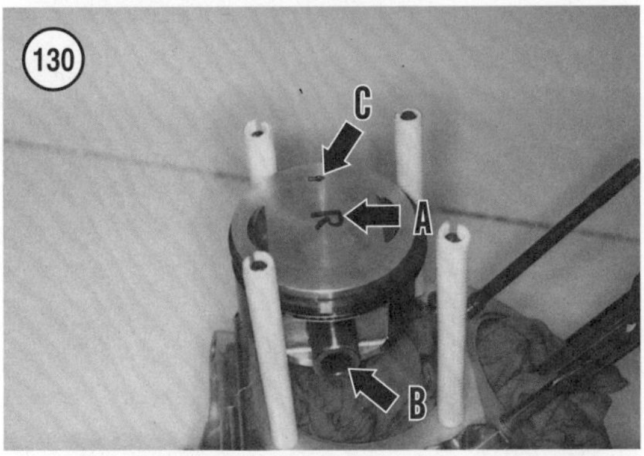

130

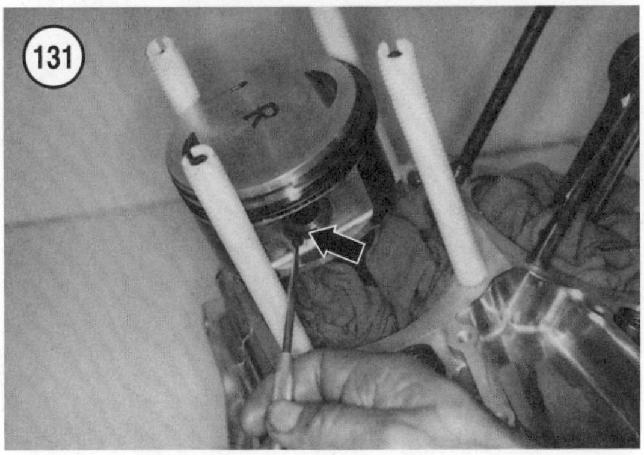
131

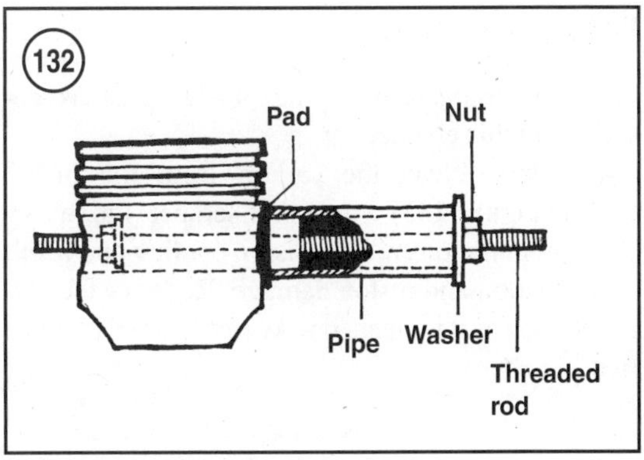

132

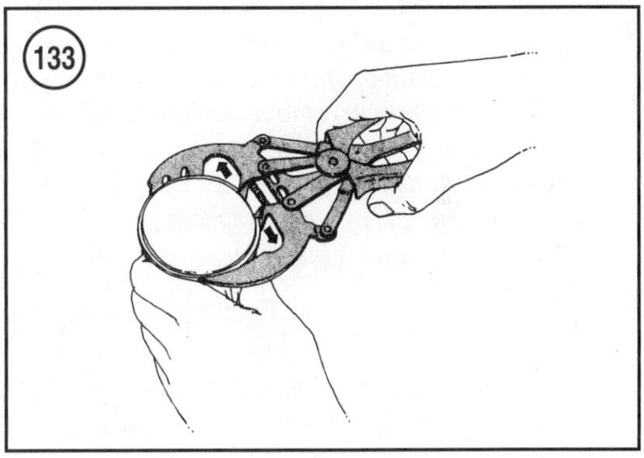
133

WARNING

The piston pin retaining rings may spring out of the piston during removal. Wear safety glasses when removing them in Step 4.

4. Using an awl, pry the piston pin retaining rings (**Figure 131**) out of the piston. Place a thumb over the hole to help prevent the rings from flying out during removal.

NOTE

Mark the piston pins so they can be reinstalled into their original pistons.

5. Support the piston and push out the piston pin (B, **Figure 130**). If the piston pin is difficult to remove, use a piston pin removal tool (**Figure 132**).
6. Remove the piston from the connecting rod.
7. Remove the piston rings using a ring expander tool (**Figure 133**) or spread them by hand (**Figure 134**) and remove them.
8. Inspect the pistons, piston pins and pistons rings as described in this chapter.

Piston Inspection

1. If necessary, remove the piston rings as described in this chapter.
2. Carefully clean the carbon from the piston crown (**Figure 135**) with a soft scraper. Large carbon accumulations reduce piston cooling and result in detonation and piston damage. Re-letter the piston as soon as it is cleaned to keep it properly identified.

CAUTION
Be very careful not to gouge or otherwise damage the piston when removing carbon. Never use a wire brush to clean the piston ring grooves. Do not attempt to remove carbon from the sides of the piston above the top ring or from the cylinder bore near the top. Removal of carbon from these two areas may cause increased oil consumption.

CAUTION
*The pistons have a special coating on the skirt (**Figure 136**). Do not scrape or use any type of abrasive on this surface as it will be damaged.*

3. After cleaning the piston, examine the crown. The crown should show no signs of wear or damage. If the crown appears pecked or spongy, check the spark plug, valves and combustion chamber for aluminum deposits. If these deposits are found, the engine is overheating.
4. Examine each ring groove for burrs, dented edges or other damage. Pay particular attention to the top compression ring groove as it usually wears more than the others. The oil rings and grooves generally wear less than compression rings and their grooves. If there is evidence of oil ring groove wear or if the oil ring assembly is tight and difficult to remove, the piston skirt may have collapsed due to excessive heat and is permanently deformed. Replace the piston.
5. Check the oil control holes (**Figure 137**) in the piston for carbon or oil sludge buildup. Clean the holes with wire and blow out with compressed air.
6. Check the piston skirt (**Figure 136**) for cracks or other damage. If a piston shows signs of partial seizure (bits of aluminum build-up on the piston skirt), the piston should be replaced to reduce the possibility of engine noise and further piston seizure.

134

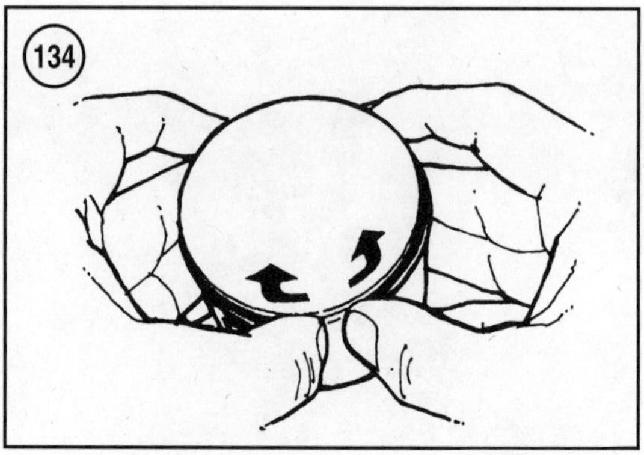

135

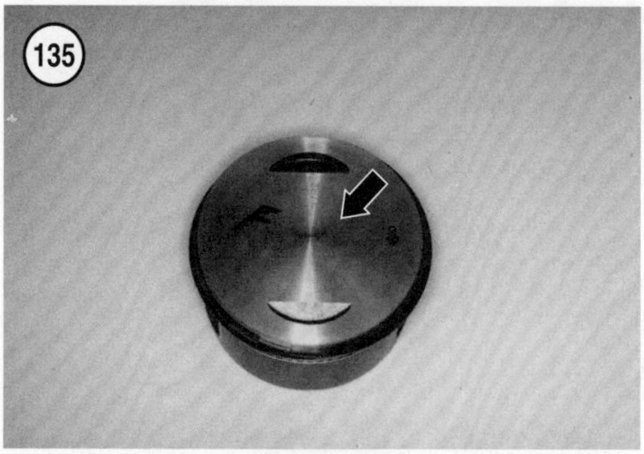

136

137

138

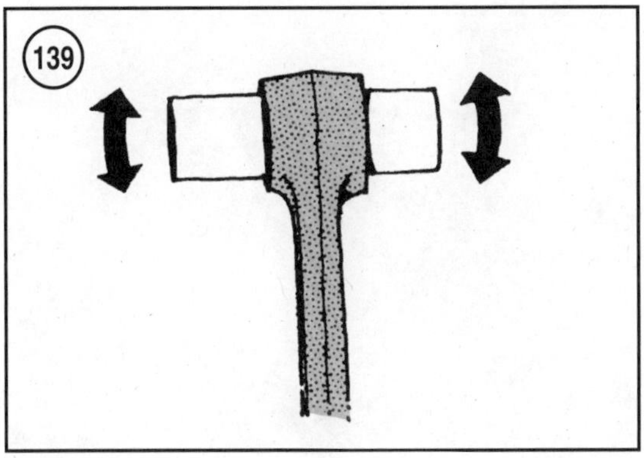
139

140

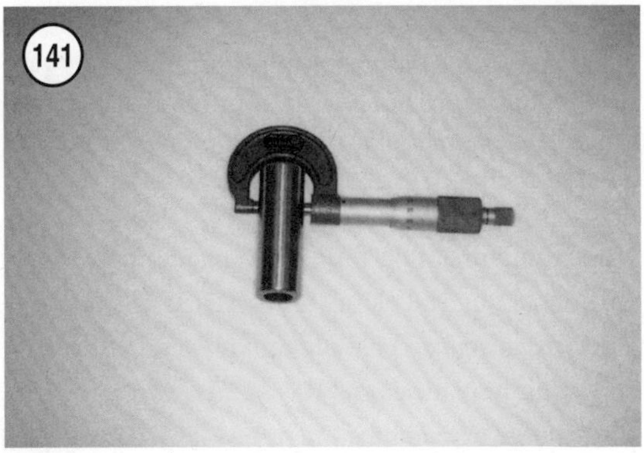
141

142

NOTE
If the piston skirt is worn or scuffed unevenly from side-to-side, the connecting rod may be bent or twisted.

7. Check the snap ring groove (**Figure 138**) on each side for wear, cracks or other damage. If the grooves are questionable, check the circlip fit by installing a new circlip into each groove and then attempt to move the circlip from side-to-side. If the circlip has any side play, the groove is worn and the piston must be replaced.
8. Measure piston-to-cylinder clearance as described under *Piston Clearance* in this chapter.
9. If damage or wear indicates piston replacement, select a new piston as described under *Piston Clearance* in this chapter. If the piston, rings and cylinder are not damaged and are dimensionally correct, they can be reused.

Piston Pin Inspection and Clearance

1. Clean the piston pin in solvent and dry thoroughly.
2. Inspect the piston pin for chrome flaking or cracks. Replace if necessary.
3. Oil the piston pin and install it in the connecting rod (**Figure 139**). Slowly rotate the piston pin and check for radial play.
4. Oil the piston pin and install it in the piston (**Figure 140**). Check the piston pin for excessive play.
5. To measure piston pin-to-piston clearance, perform the following:
   a. Measure the piston pin outer diameter with a micrometer (**Figure 141**).
   b. Measure the inside diameter of the piston pin bore (**Figure 142**) with a snap gauge. Measure the snap gauge with a micrometer.

4

c. Subtract the piston pin outer diameter from the piston pin bore to obtain the clearance dimension. Check against the specification in **Table 2**.

d. If out of specification, replace the piston and/or the piston pin.

6. Replace the piston pin and/or piston or connecting rod if necessary.

Piston Clearance

1. Make sure the piston skirt and cylinder bore is clean and dry.
2. Measure the cylinder bore with a bore gauge (**Figure 121**) as described under *Cylinder Inspection* in this chapter.
3. Measure the piston diameter with a micrometer as follows:

a. Hold the micrometer at the bottom of the piston skirt at a right angle to the piston pin bore (**Figure 143**). Adjust the micrometer so the spindle and anvil just touch the skirt.

b. Start below the bottom ring and slowly move the micrometer toward the bottom of the skirt.

c. The micrometer will be loose, then tight at about 0.5 in. (12.7 mm) from the bottom and then loose again.

d. Measure the piston skirt at the tightest point.

4. Subtract the piston diameter from the largest bore diameter; the difference is piston-to-cylinder clearance. If the clearance exceeds the specification in **Table 2**, the pistons should be replaced and the cylinders bored oversize and then honed. Purchase the new pistons first. Measure their diameter and add the specified clearance to determine the proper cylinder bore diameter.

Piston Pin Bushing in Connecting Rod Inspection and Replacement

The piston pin bushings are reamed to provide correct piston pin-to-bushing clearance. This clearance is critical in preventing pin knock and top end damage.

1. Inspect the piston pin bushings (**Figure 144**) for excessive wear or damage (pit marks, scoring or wear grooves). Then check to make sure the bushing is not loose. The bushing must be a tight fit in the connecting rods.

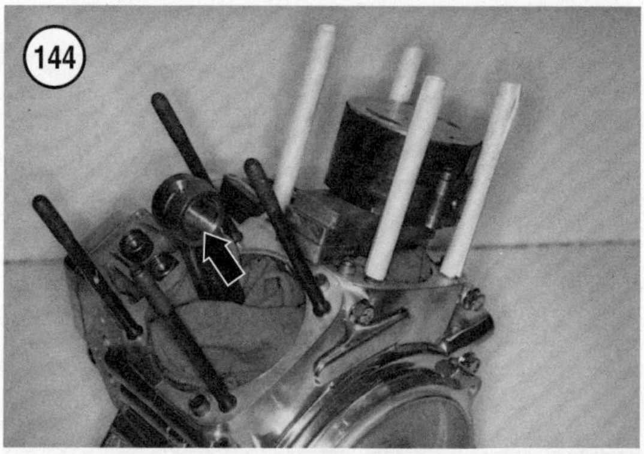

2. Measure the piston pin diameter (**Figure 141**) where it contacts the bushing.
3. Measure the piston pin bushing diameter using a snap gauge (**Figure 145**).
4. Subtract the piston pin outer diameter from bushing inner diameter to determine piston pin clearance. Replace the pin and bushing if they are worn to the service limit in **Table 2**.

Piston Pin Bushing Replacement

Tools

The following special tools are required to replace and ream the piston pin bushings. The part numbers are for Harley-Davidson or JIMS special tools. The clamp tool is required only if the bushing is being replaced with the crankcase assembled. If these tools are not available, have a shop with the proper equipment perform the procedure.

1. Connecting rod clamp tool (HD-95952-33B).
2. Connecting rod bushing tool (JIMS 1051).
3. Bushing reamer tool (JIMS 1726-3).
4. Connecting rod bushing hone (HD-422569).

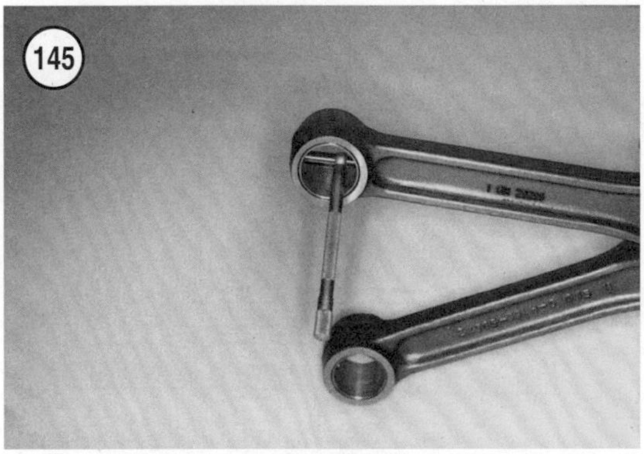
145

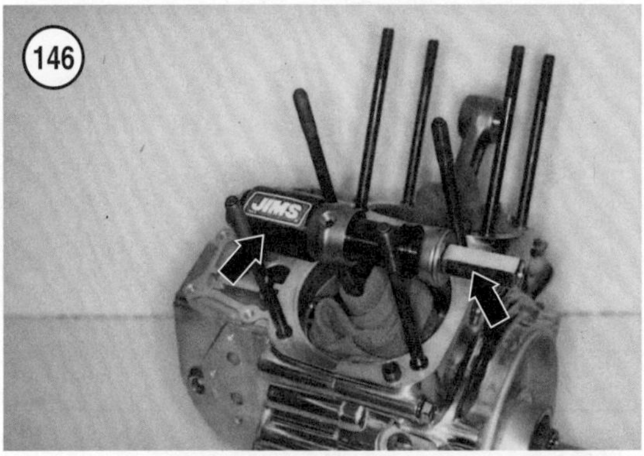

146

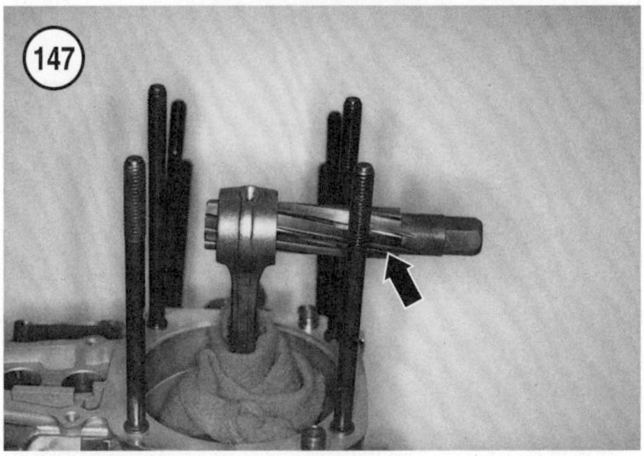
147

Procedure

1. Remove two of the plastic hoses protecting the cylinder studs.
2. Install the connecting rod clamping tool as follows:
   a. Install the clamp portion of the connecting rod clamping tool over the connecting rod so the slots engage the cylinder head studs. Do not scratch or bend the studs.
   b. Position the threaded cylinders with the knurled end facing up and install the cylinders onto the studs. Tighten securely to hold the clamp in place.
   c. Alternately tighten the thumbscrews onto the side of the connecting rod. Do not turn only one thumbscrew, as this will move the connecting rod off center and when tightening the other thumbscrew will cause the connecting rod to flex or bend.
3. Cover the crankcase opening to keep bushing particles from falling into the engine.

NOTE
When installing the new bushing, align the oil slot in the bushing with the oil hole in the connecting rod.

4. Replace the bushing using the connecting rod bushing tool (**Figure 146**), following the tool manufacturer's instructions. The new bushing must be flush with both sides of the connecting rod.
5. Ream the new bushing with the bushing reamer tool (**Figure 147**), following the manufacturer's instructions.
6. Hone the new bushing to obtain the piston pin clearance specified in **Table 2**. Use honing oil, not engine oil, when honing the bushing to size.
7. Install the piston pin through the bushing. The pin must move through the bushing smoothly. Confirm pin clearance using a micrometer and snap gauge.
8. Carefully remove all metal debris from the crankcase.

Piston Ring Inspection

1. Clean the piston ring grooves as described under *Piston Inspection*.
2. Inspect the ring grooves for burrs, nicks, or broken or cracked lands. Replace the piston if necessary.
3. Insert one piston ring into the top of its cylinder and tap it down approximately 1/2 in. (12.7 mm), using the piston to square it in the bore. Measure the ring end gap (**Figure 148**) with a feeler gauge and compare with the specification in **Table 2**. Replace the piston rings as a set if any one ring end gap measurement is excessive. Repeat for each ring.
4. Roll each compression ring around its piston groove as shown in **Figure 149**. The ring must move smoothly with no binding. If a ring binds in its

groove, check the groove for damage. Replace the piston if necessary.

Piston Ring Installation

Each piston is equipped with three piston rings: two compression rings and one oil ring assembly. The top compression ring is not marked. The lower compression is marked with a dot (**Figure 150**).

Harley-Davidson recommends that *new* piston rings be installed every time the piston is removed. Piston rings take a set after the engine has been run and must not be reused. Always lightly hone the cylinder before installing new piston rings.

1. Wash the piston in hot, soapy water. Then rinse with cold water and dry with compressed air. Make sure the oil control holes in the lower ring groove are clear.
2. Install the oil ring assembly as follows:
   a. The oil ring consists of three rings: a ribbed spacer ring (A, **Figure 151**) and two steel rings (B).
   b. Install the spacer ring into the lower ring groove. Butt the spacer ring ends together. Do not overlap the ring ends.
   c. Insert one end of the first steel ring into the lower groove so that it is below the spacer ring. Then spiral the other end over the piston crown and into the lower groove. To protect the ring end from scratching the side of the piston, place a piece of shim stock or a thin, flat feeler gauge between the ring and piston.
   d. Repeat substep c to install the other steel ring above the spacer ring.

NOTE
*When installing the compression rings, use a ring expander as shown in **Figure 133**. Do not expand the rings any more than necessary to install them.*

3. Install the lower compression ring as follows:
   a. A dot mark is located on one side of the lower compression ring (**Figure 150**).
   b. Install the lower compression ring with the dot mark facing up (**Figure 152**).
4. Install the top compression ring as follows:
   a. The top compression ring is not marked.
   b. Install the *new* top compression ring with either side facing up.

148

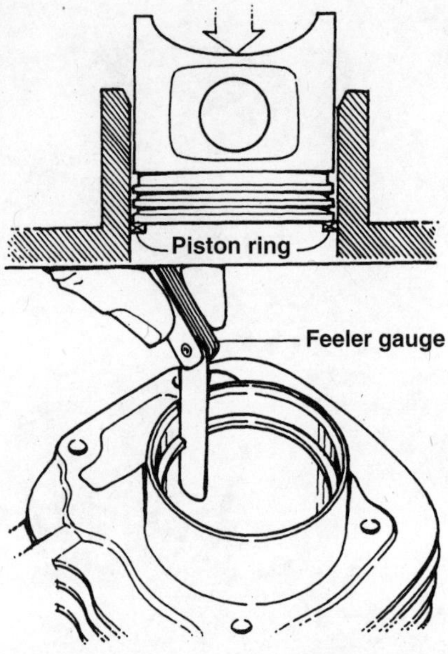

149

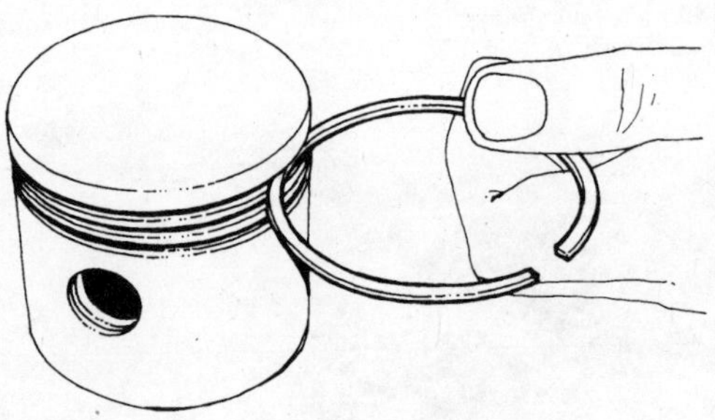

150

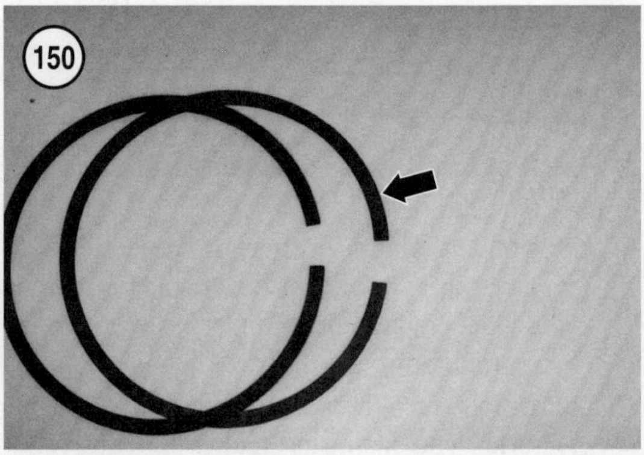

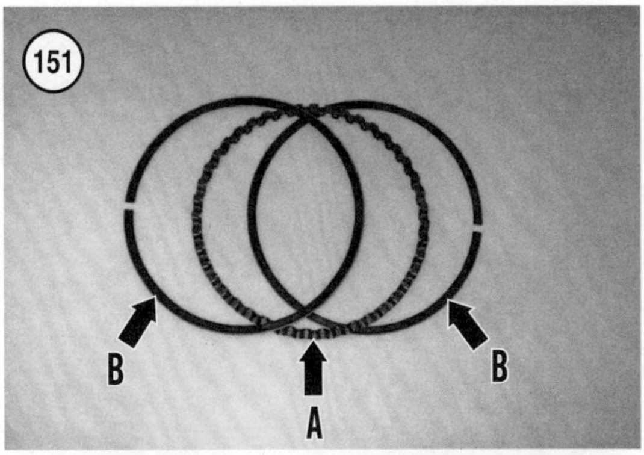

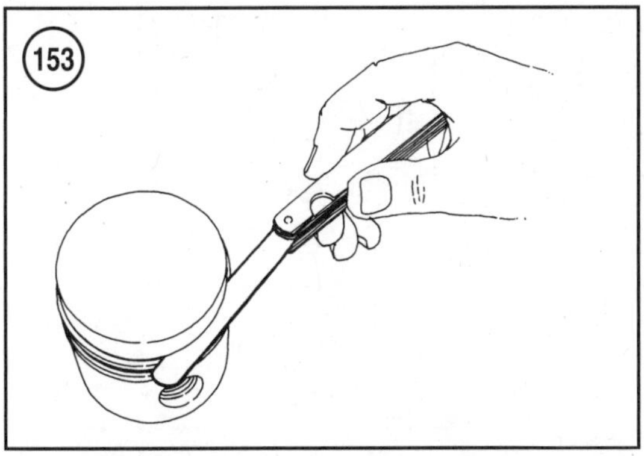

5. Check the ring side clearance with a feeler gauge as shown in **Figure 153**. Check the side clearance in several spots around the piston. If the clearance is larger than the service limit in **Table 2**, replace the piston.

6. Stagger the ring gaps around the piston as shown in **Figure 127**.

Piston Installation

1. Cover the crankcase openings to avoid dropping a retaining ring into the engine.

2. Install a *new* piston pin retaining ring into one groove in the piston. Make sure the ring seats in the groove completely.

3. Coat the connecting rod bushing and piston pin with assembly oil.

4. Slide the piston pin into the piston until its end is flush with the piston pin boss (**Figure 154**).

NOTE

The piston markings described in Step 5 are for factory Harley-Davidson pistons. If using aftermarket pistons, follow their manufacturer's directions for piston alignment and installation.

5. Place the piston over the connecting rod with its arrow mark (C, **Figure 130**) facing toward the front of the engine. Install used pistons on their original connecting rods; refer to the marks made on the piston during removal.

6. Push the piston pin (B, **Figure 130**) through the connecting rod bushing and into the other side of the piston. Push the piston pin in until it bottoms on the retaining ring.

7. Install the other *new* piston pin retaining ring (**Figure 155**) into the piston groove. Make sure it seats properly in the piston groove (**Figure 156**).

8. Repeat for the other piston.

9. Install the cylinders as described in this chapter.

PUSHRODS

Removal/Installation

Remove and install the pushrods as described under *Rocker Arm Cover and Cylinder Head Removal* in this chapter.

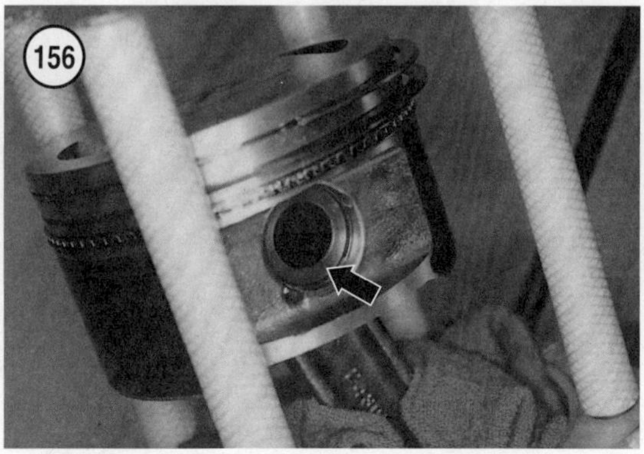

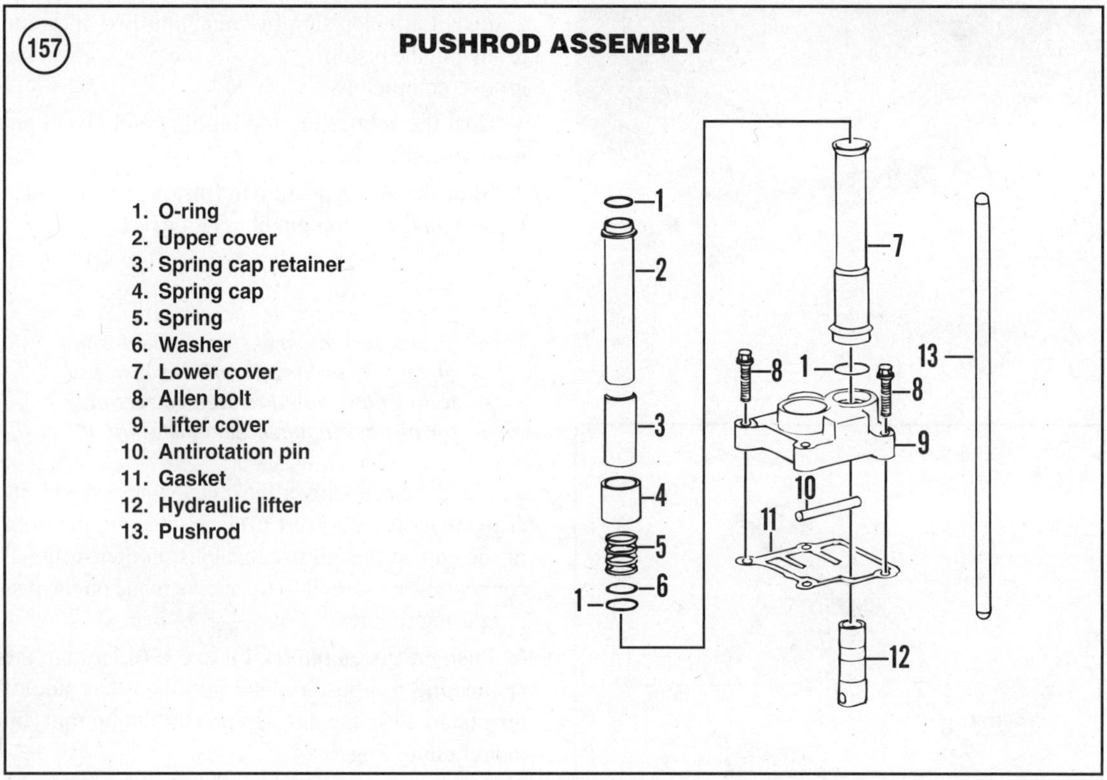

Inspection

Refer to **Figure 157**.

1. Disassemble the pushrod cover as follows:
   a. Remove the lower pushrod cover (**Figure 158**).
   b. Remove the O-ring (**Figure 159**).
   c. Remove the spacer (**Figure 160**).
   d. Remove the spring (**Figure 161**).
   e. Remove the spring cap (**Figure 162**).
2. Check the pushrod cover assembly (**Figure 163**) as follows:
   a. Check the spring for sagging or cracking.
   b. Check the spacer for deformation or damage.
   c. Check the pushrod covers for cracking or damage.
3. Check the pushrod ends (**Figure 164**) for wear.
4. Roll the pushrods on a surface plate or plate glass, and check for bending.
5. Replace all worn or damaged parts. Install *new* O-rings.
6. Reverse Step 1 to assemble the pushrod cover assembly. Push the lower pushrod cover (A, **Figure 165**) into the spring cap (B) to seat the O-ring.

158

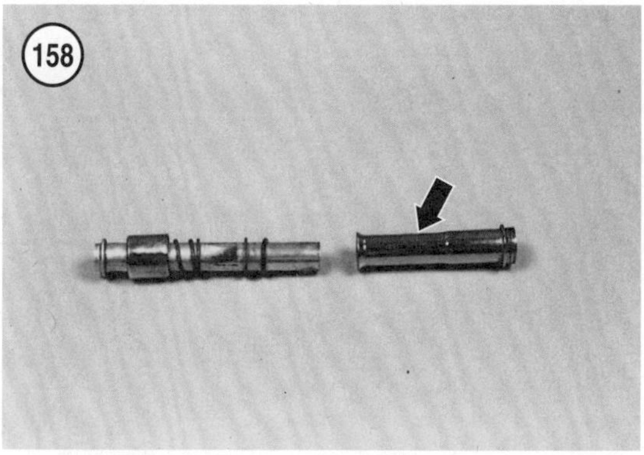

159

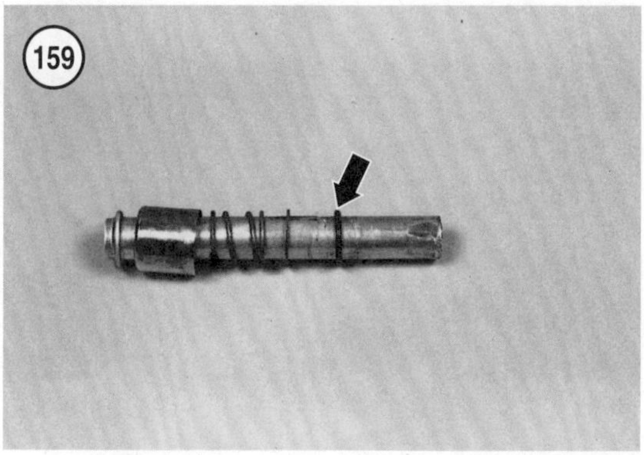

160

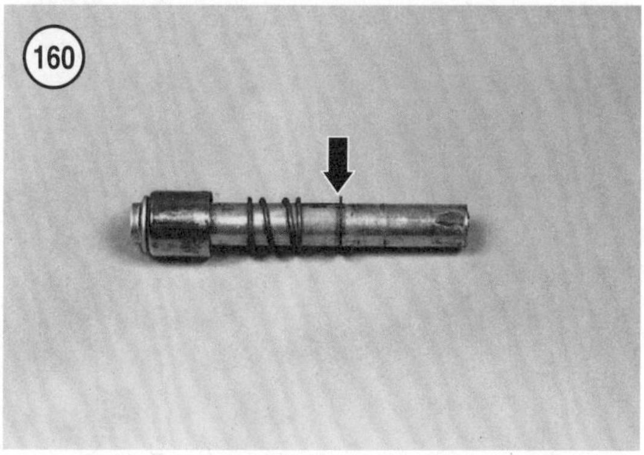

161

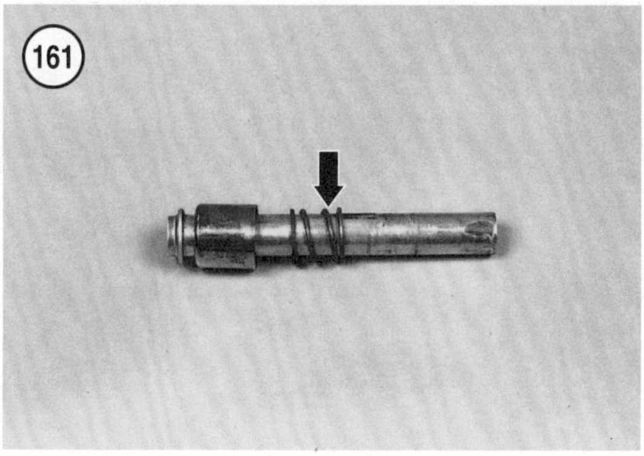

162

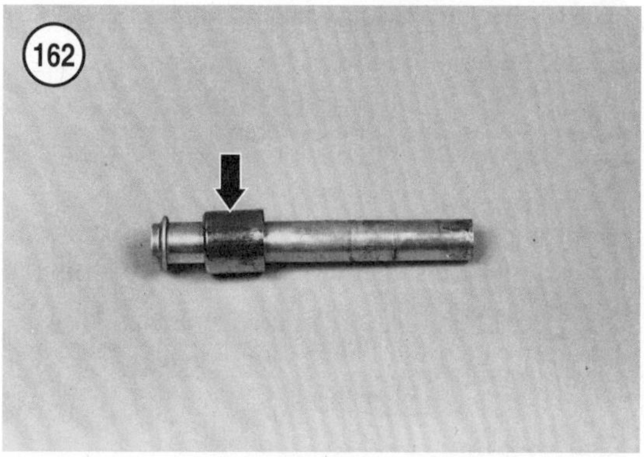

163

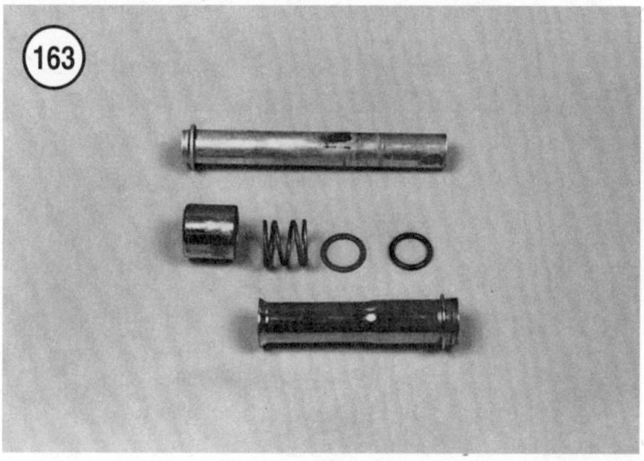

164

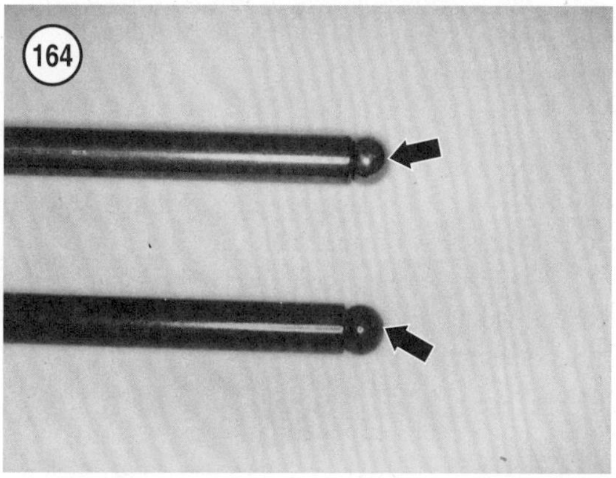

VALVE LIFTERS

Figure 157 shows a valve lifter in relation to its pushrod and valve lifter cover. The valve lifters and covers are installed on the right side of the engine. During engine operation, the lifters are pumped full with engine oil, thus taking up all play in the valve train. When the engine is turned off, the lifters will leak down after a period of time as some of the oil drains out. When the engine is started, the lifters will click until they completely refill with oil. The lifters are working properly when they stop clicking after the engine is run for a few minutes.

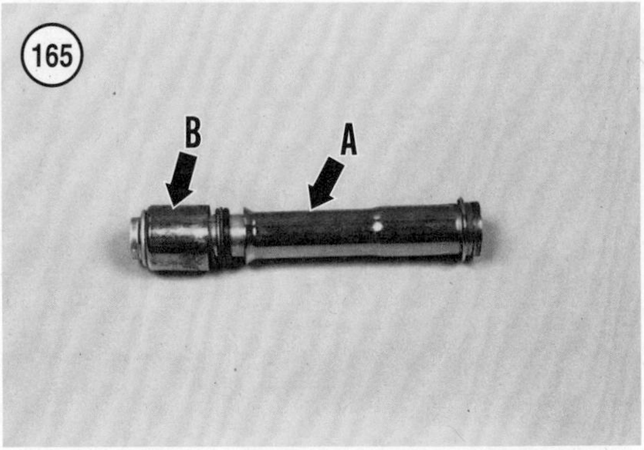

Removal

During removal, store lifters in proper sequence so they will be installed in their original position in the crankcase.

1. Remove the pushrods as described under *Rocker Arm Cover and Cylinder Head Removal* in this chapter.

NOTE
In order to clear the cylinder's lower cooling fins, the two inner lifter cover Allen bolts must be loosened with a short 90° Allen wrench as shown in A, ***Figure 166****.*

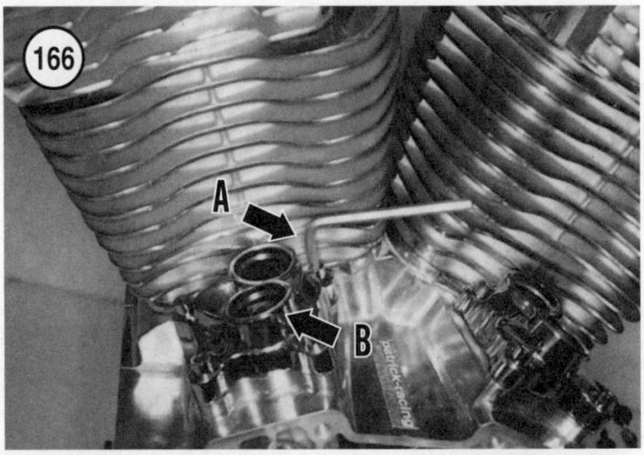

2. Remove the lifter cover mounting bolts and remove the cover (B, **Figure 166**).
3. Remove the lifter cover gasket from the crankcase.

NOTE
Do not intermix the lifters when removing them in Step 4. Mark them so they will be installed in their original position.

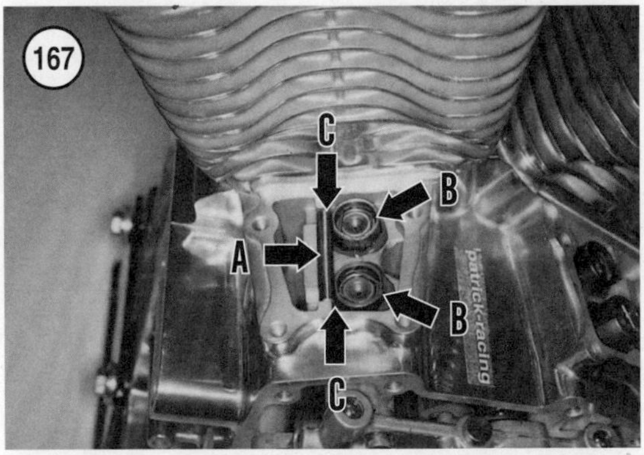

4. Remove the antirotation pin (A, **Figure 167**) and both hydraulic lifters (B).
5. Cover the crankcase opening (**Figure 168**) to prevent the entry of small parts.
6. If the lifters are not going to be inspected as described in the following section, store them upright in a container filled with clean engine oil until installation.
7. Remove the lifter cover gasket.

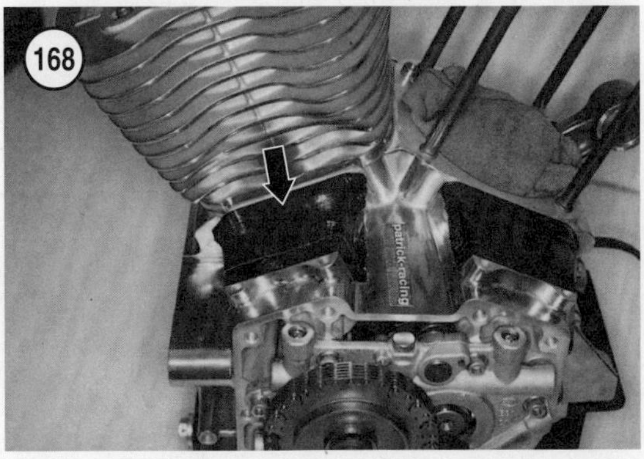

Inspection

NOTE
Place the lifters on a clean, lint-free cloth during inspection. Place inspected lifters in a container of clean engine oil.

1. Check the pushrod socket (**Figure 169**) in the top of the lifter for wear or damage.
2. Check the lifter roller (**Figure 170**) for pitting, scoring, galling or excessive wear. If the rollers are

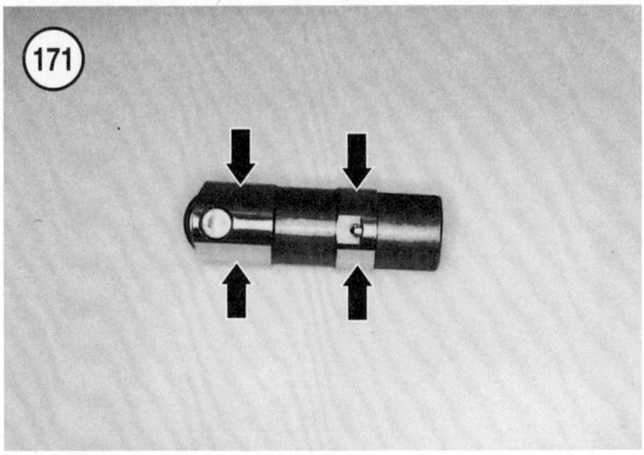

worn excessively, check the mating cam lobes for the same wear condition.

3. Clean the lifter rollers with contact cleaner. Then measure roller fit and end clearance and compare to the specification in **Table 2**. Replace the lifter assembly if either part is worn to the service limit.

4. Determine the lifter-to-guide clearance as follows:

   a. Measure the lifter bore receptacle in the crankcase and record the measurement.

   b. Measure the lifter outside diameter (**Figure 171**) and record the measurement.

   c. Subtract substep b from substep a to determine the lifter-to-crankcase bore clearance, then compare the measurement to the service limit in **Table 2**. Replace the lifter or crankcase if the clearance is worn to the limit.

5. If a lifter does not show visual damage, it may be contaminated with dirt or have internal damage. If so, replace it. The lifters are not serviceable and must be replaced as a unit.

6. After inspecting the lifters, store them in a container filled with clean engine oil until installation.

7. If most of the oil has drained out of the lifter, refill it with a pump-type oil can through the oil hole in the side of the lifter.

8. Clean all old gasket residue from the mating surfaces of the crankcase and the lifter cover.

Installation

1. Remove two of the lifters from the oil-filled container and keep them vertical.

2. Install the hydraulic lifters (B, **Figure 167**) into the crankcase receptacles with the flat surfaces facing toward the front and rear of the engine.

CAUTION

Failure to install the anti-rotation pin will allow the lifter to rotate off the camshaft lobe, resulting in severe internal engine damage.

3. Install the antirotation pin (A, **Figure 167**). Make sure it is seated correctly within the crankcase receptacle and against the flats on both hydraulic lifters (C, **Figure 167**).

4. Rotate the engine until both lifters for the cylinder head being serviced seat onto the cam's lowest position (base circle). The lifter's top surface will be flush with the top surface of the crankcase surface as shown in **Figure 172**.

5. Install a new lifter cover gasket (**Figure 173**) onto the crankcase.

NOTE

*In order to clear the cylinder's lower cooling fins, the two inner lifter cover Allen bolts must be tightened with a short 90-degree Allen wrench as shown in A, **Figure 166**.*

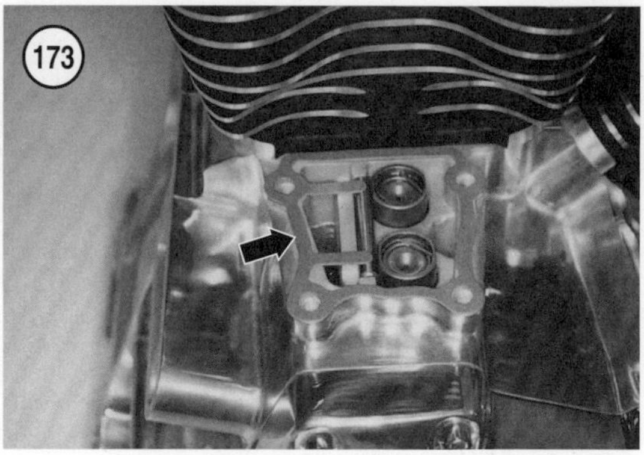

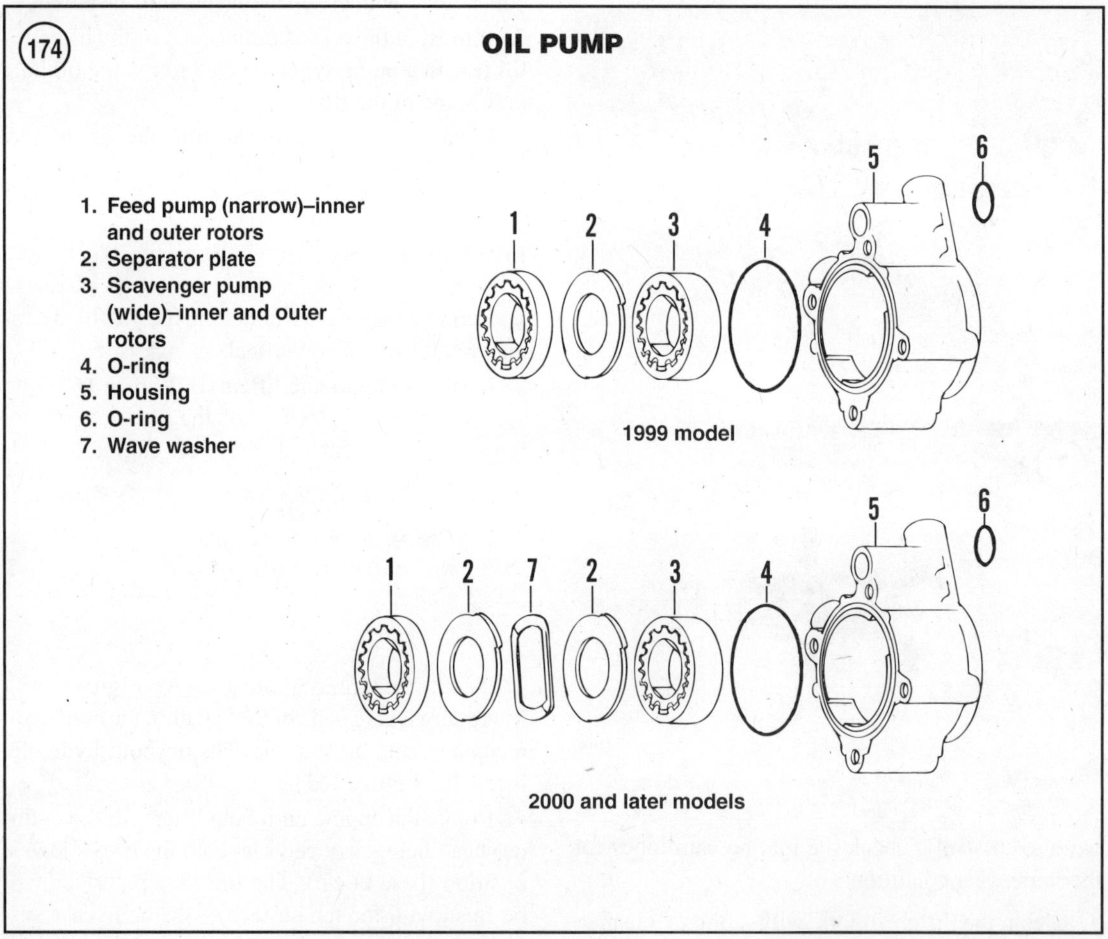

6. Install the lifter cover and the mounting bolts (B, **Figure 166**). Tighten the bolts to the specification in **Table 4**.

7. Repeat Steps 1-6 to install the other set of lifters.

8. Install the pushrods as described under *Rocker Arm Cover and Cylinder Head Installation* in this chapter.

OIL PUMP

The oil pump is mounted onto the right side of the crankcase under the camshaft support plate. The oil pump consists of two sections: a feed pump (narrow rotors) which supplies oil under pressure to the engine components, and a scavenger pump (wide ro-

tors) which returns the oil from the engine to the oil pan in the base of the transmission case. The oil travels from the engine to the oil pan through two interconnecting hoses.

Disassembly/Removal

The oil pump can be removed with the engine in the frame. This procedure is shown with the engine removed and partially disassembled to better illustrate the steps. Refer to **Figure 174**.

NOTE
The oil pump on 1999 models is slightly different from the 2000-on models. Both assemblies are covered in one procedure. Where differences occur between the different models, they are identified. Parts are not interchangeable between the two types.

1. Drain the engine oil as described in Chapter Three.
2. Remove the camshaft support plate assembly as described under *Camshaft Support Plate Removal* in this chapter.
3. Remove the feed pump inner (**Figure 175**) and outer rotors (**Figure 176**).

4A. On 1999 models, remove the separator plate (**Figure 177**).

4B. On 2000-on models, remove the outer separator plate (**Figure 178**), wave washer (**Figure 179**) and the inner separator plate (**Figure 180**).

5. Remove the scavenger pump outer and inner rotors (**Figure 181**).
6. Carefully pull the oil pump body (**Figure 182**) straight off the crankshaft.
7. Remove the O-ring (**Figure 183**) from the backside of the oil pump.

180

181

Inspection

1. Clean all parts thoroughly in solvent and place on a clean, lint-free cloth. Refer to **Figure 184** for 1999 models or **Figure 185** for 2000-on models.
2. Inspect both sets of inner and outer rotors (**Figure 186**) for scratches and abrasion.
3. Inspect the oil pump housing (**Figure 187**) for scratches caused by the rotors.
4. Inspect the interior passageways of the oil pump housing. Make sure all oil sludge and debris is removed. Blow low-pressure compressed air through all oil pump housing passages.
5. Install the inner rotor into the outer rotor. Check the clearance between the inner tip and outer rotor (**Figure 188**) with a flat feeler gauge. Replace the rotors as a set if the clearance exceeds the dimension in **Table 2**. Repeat for the other set of rotors.
6. Measure the thickness of the inner (**Figure 189**) and outer (**Figure 190**) rotors. Both rotors must be the same thickness, if not replace them as a complete set. Repeat for the other set of rotors.

182

183

Reassembly/Installation

NOTE

*Position both inner and outer rotor sets with the punch marks (**Figure 191**) facing out.*

1. Install a *new* O-ring (**Figure 183**) onto the backside of the oil pump. Apply clean engine oil to the O-ring.
2. Carefully push the oil pump body (**Figure 182**) straight onto the crankshaft. Align the O-ring and fitting onto the crankcase fitting (**Figure 192**). Push

184

185

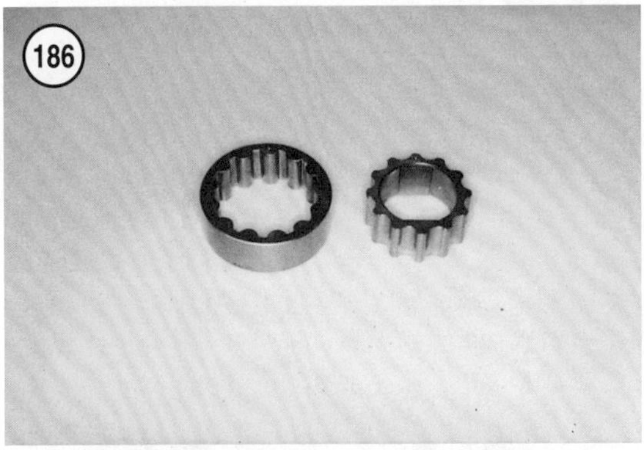

186

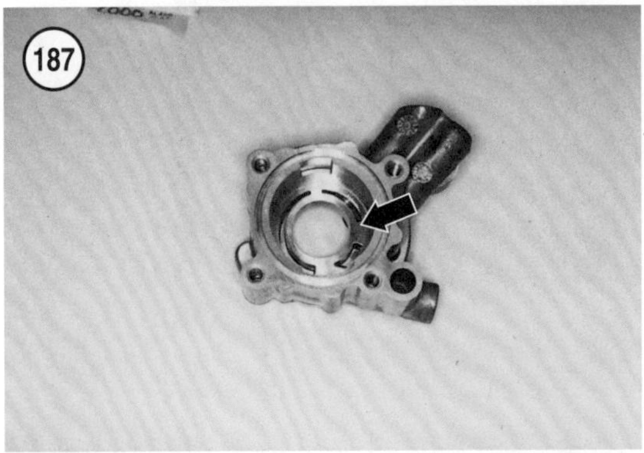

187

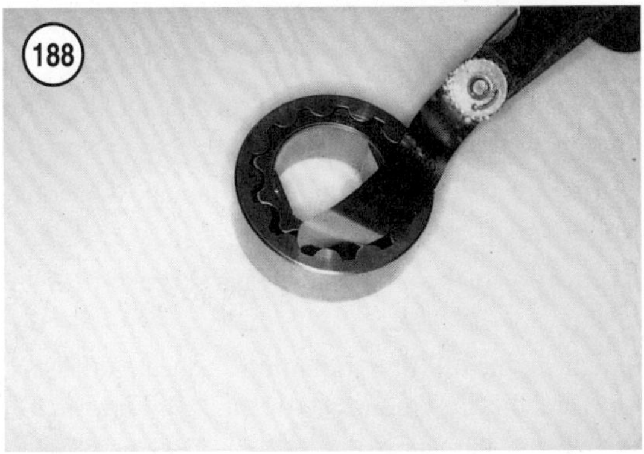

188

189

190

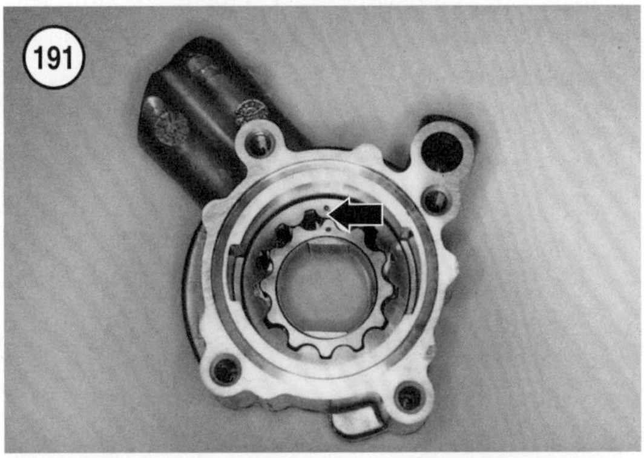

191

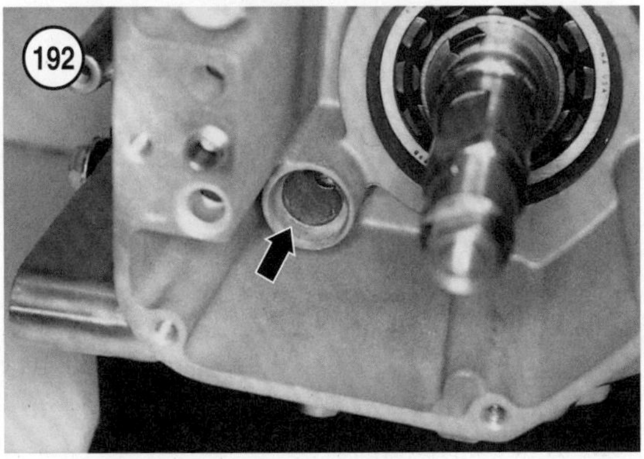

192

it on until it bottoms, making sure the O-ring seats correctly in the crankcase fitting.
3. Install the scavenge outer rotor (**Figure 193**) into the oil pump housing.
4. Align the flat on the scavenge inner rotor with the flat on the crankshaft and install the inner rotor (**Figure 194**). Push it on until it is meshed with the outer rotor.
5A. On 1999 models, align the tangs on the separator plate with the oil pump grooves and install the separator plate (**Figure 177**).
5B. On 2000-on models, perform the following:
   a. Align the tangs on the inner separator plate with the oil pump grooves and install the inner separator plate (**Figure 180**).
   b. Install the wave washer (**Figure 179**).
   c. Align the tangs on the outer separator plate with the oil pump grooves and install the outer separator plate (**Figure 178**).
6. Install the feed pump outer rotor (**Figure 176**) into the oil pump housing.
7. Align the flat on the feed pump inner rotor with the flat on the crankshaft and install the inner rotor (**Figure 175**). Push it on until it is meshed with the outer rotor.
8. Install the camshaft support plate assembly as described under *Camshaft Support Plate Installation* in this chapter.
9. Refill the engine oil as described in Chapter Three.

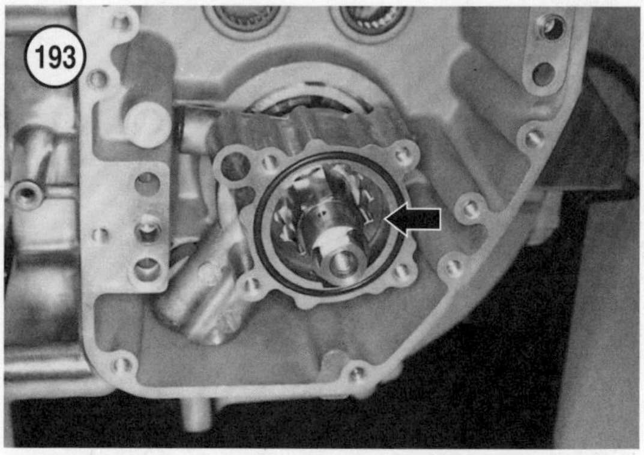

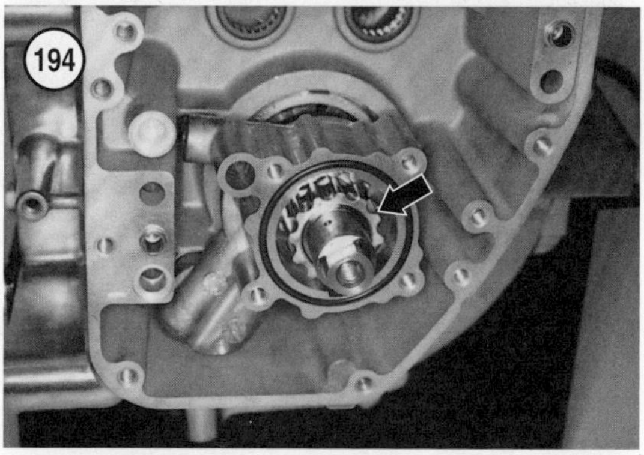

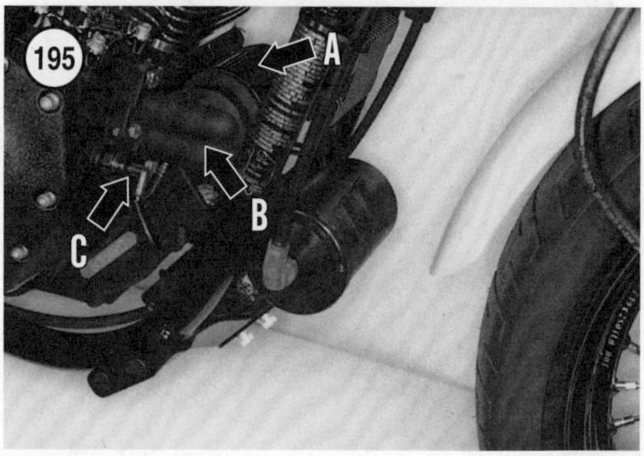

OIL FILTER MOUNT

The oil filter mount is located on the front right side of the engine and can be removed with the engine in the frame.

Removal

1. Park the motorcycle on a level surface.
2. Remove the exhaust system as described in Chapter Seven.
3. Drain the engine oil and remove the oil filter (A, **Figure 195**) as described in Chapter Three.
4. Place several shop cloths under the oil filter mount as some residual oil will drain out in the next step.
5. Straighten the lockplate tabs and remove the three bolts, oil filter and oil filter mount (B, **Figure 195**) from the crankcase.

Inspection

1. Clean the oil filter mount in solvent and dry with compressed air.
2. Inspect the oil filter mount for damage that could lead to an oil leak.
3. Make sure the oil passageways (**Figure 196**) are clear.
4. Check the oil filter mounting surface (A, **Figure 197**) and oil filter mounting threads (B, **Figure 197**) for wear or damage.

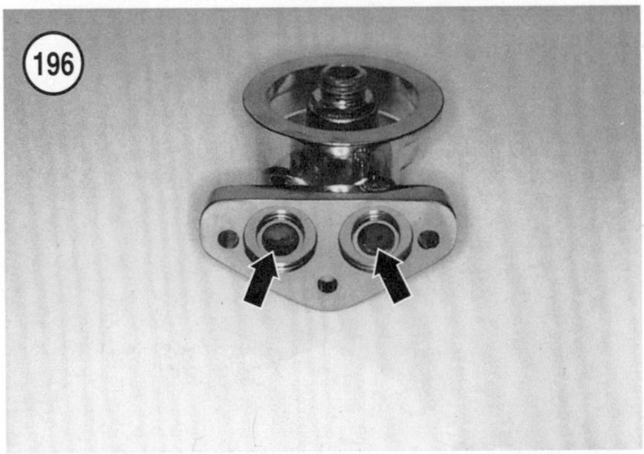

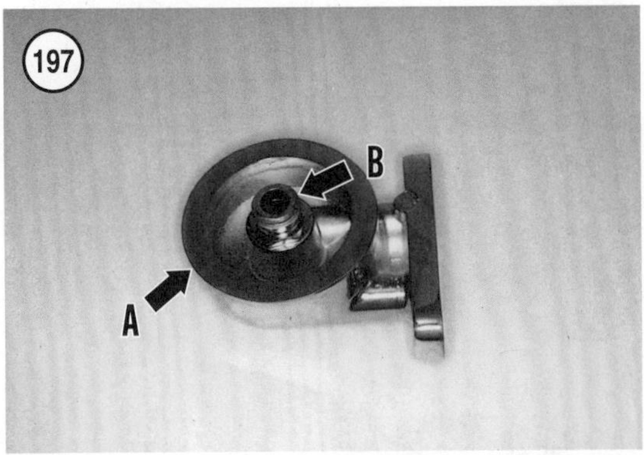

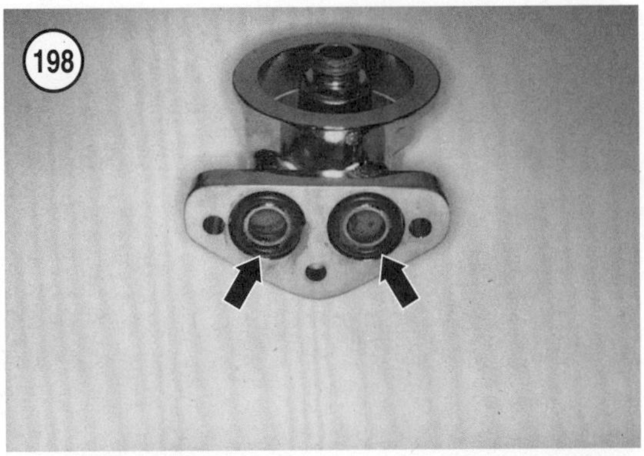

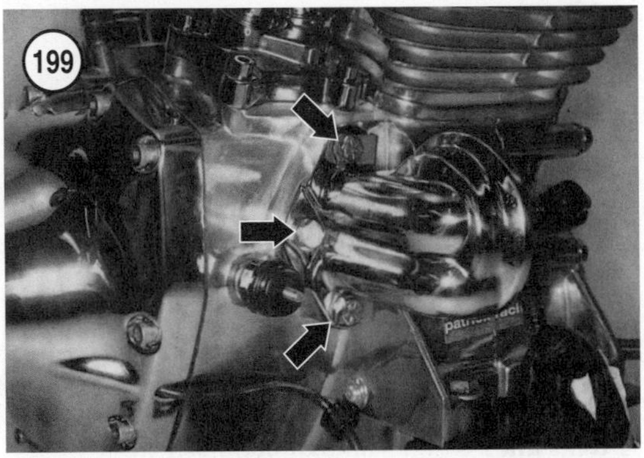

Installation

1. Thoroughly clean the crankcase mating surface.
2. Install *new* O-ring seals (**Figure 198**) onto the mount.
3. Apply ThreeBond TB1342, or an equivalent, to the three bolt threads prior to installing them onto the *new* lockplate.
4. Install the oil filter mount onto the crankcase and install the lockplate and three bolts and washers (**Figure 199**).
5. Tighten the bolts to the specification in **Table 4**.
6. Bend down the locking tab against the top and bottom bolt heads.
7. Refill the engine with oil and install a *new* oil filter (A, **Figure 195**).
8. Disconnect the electrical connector from the oil pressure switch (C, **Figure 195**). Thoroughly clean the electrical connector and the switch terminal with an aerosol parts cleaner to remove any oil that may have come in contact with these parts.
9. Install the exhaust system as described in Chapter Seven.
10. Start the engine and check for leaks.

CAMSHAFT SUPPORT PLATE

A camshaft and crankshaft sprocket lock (JIMS part No. 1285) and a camshaft chain tensioner tool (JIMS Part No. 1283) are required to remove and install the camshaft support plate.

NOTE
*During the 1999 model year, the method of securing the camshaft sprocket to the camshaft for the rear cylinder was changed. Early 1999 models use a Woodruff key as shown in **Figure 200**. This was changed to a splined attachment on later 1999-on models as shown in **Figure 201**.*

Removal

NOTE
This procedure can be accomplished with the engine mounted in the frame. This procedure is shown with the engine removed and partially disassembled to better illustrate the steps.

(200) **CAMSHAFTS AND COVER (EARLY 1999 MODELS)**

1. Screw
2. Cover
3. Camshaft cover
4. Gasket
5. Camshaft primary drive chain
6. Bolt and washer
7. Rear cylinder camshaft drive sprocket
8. Spacer
9. Oil pump relief spring
10. Oil pump relief valve
11. Primary chain tensioner
12. Snap ring
13. Crankshaft sprocket
14. Bushing
15. Roll pin
16. Chain guide
17. Plug
18. O-ring
19. Camshaft support plate
20. Bearing
21. Bearing retainer plate
22. Camshaft secondary drive chain
23. Woodruff key
24. Camshaft–rear cylinder
25. Oil pump feed rotors
26. Separator plate
27. Oil pump scavenger rotors
28. Oil pump housing
29. Camshaft–front cylinder
30. Crankcase half–right side
31. Secondary chain tensioner

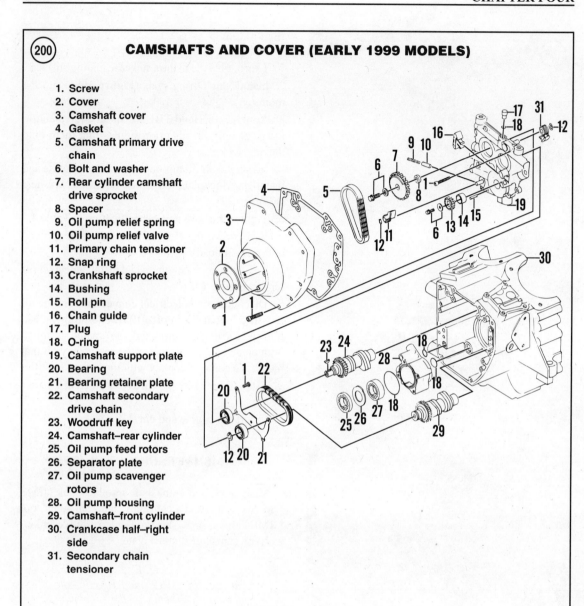

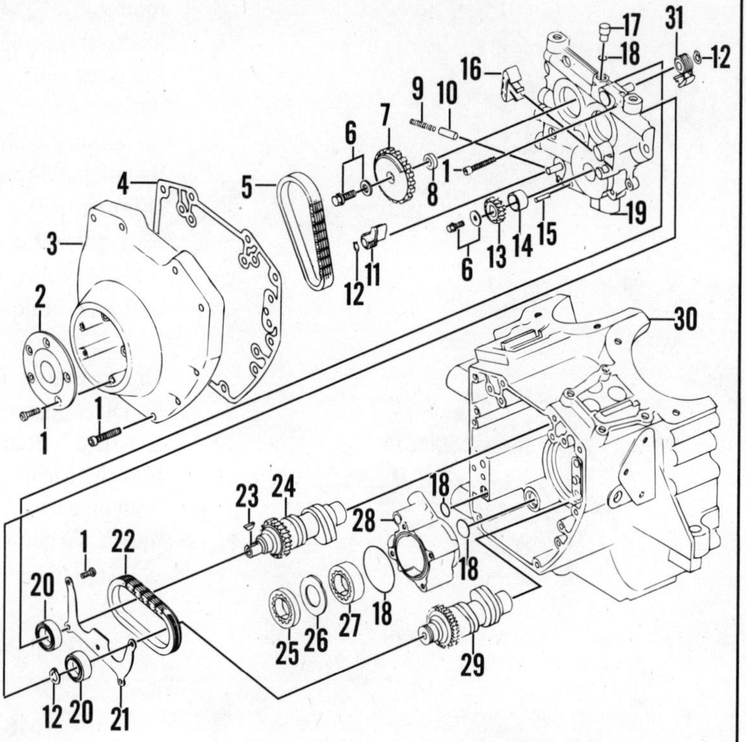

1. Remove the exhaust system as described in Chapter Seven.

2. Remove the pushrods, lifters and lifter covers as described in this chapter.

CAUTION

*On 1999-2000 models, the cam position sensor wiring (**Figure 202**) is routed through the camshaft cover. Move the cover out of the way and secure it to the frame with a piece of wire. Do not hang the cover by the wiring.*

3. Using a crisscross pattern, loosen then remove the bolts securing the camshaft cover (**Figure 203**) and remove the cover and gasket.

4. Remove the bolt securing the crankshaft position sensor (**Figure 204**) and remove the sensor from the crankcase.

5. To ensure that the camshaft primary drive chain is reinstalled in the same direction of travel, mark

(201) **CAMSHAFTS AND COVER (LATER 1999-ON MODELS)**

1. Screw
2. Cover
3. Camshaft cover
4. Gasket
5. Camshaft primary drive chain
6. Bolt and washer
7. Rear cylinder camshaft drive sprocket
8. Spacer
9. Oil pump relief spring
10. Oil pump relief valve
11. Primary chain tensioner
12. Snap ring
13. Crankshaft sprocket
14. Bushing
15. Roll pin
16. Chain guide
17. Plug
18. O-ring
19. Camshaft support plate
20. Secondary chain tensioner
21. Bearing
22. Bearing retainer plate
23. Camshaft secondary drive chain
24. Oil pump feed rotors
25. Separator plate
26. Wave washer
27. Oil pump scavenger rotors
28. O-ring
29. Camshaft–rear cylinder
30. Oil pump housing
31. Camshaft–front cylinder
32. Crankcase half–right side

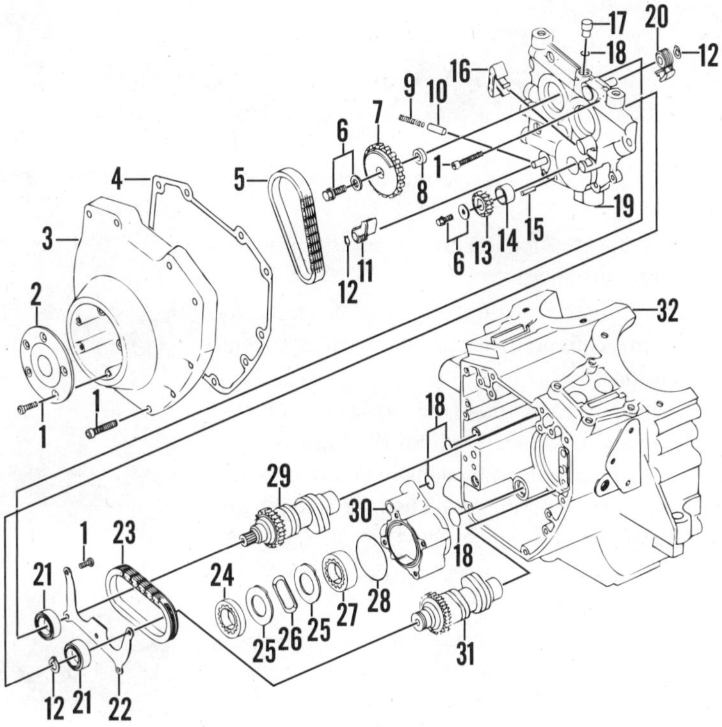

(202)

(203)

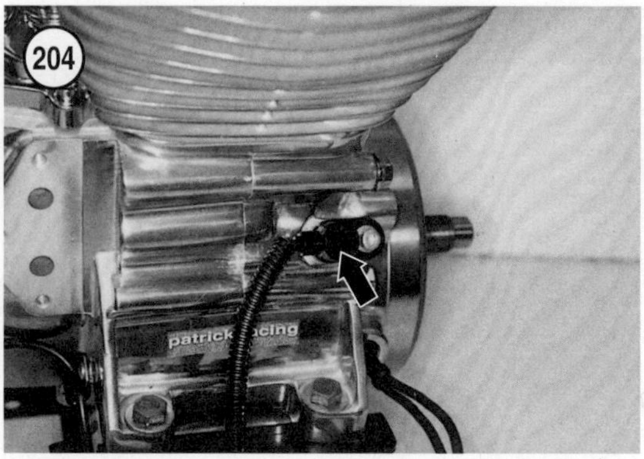

one of the link plates with a permanent marking pen or a scribe.

6. Relieve the tension on the camshaft primary drive chain as follows:
   a. Install the camshaft chain tensioner tool (A, **Figure 205**) onto the camshaft primary chain tensioner.
   b. Using a wrench, rotate the tool counterclockwise and insert the hold pin (B, **Figure 205**) through the hole in the tensioner and into the hole in the support plate. Push the hold pin all the way in until it bottoms.
   c. Remove the wrench and tensioner tool from the tensioner.

7. Install and mesh the camshaft and crankshaft sprocket lock (A, **Figure 206**) between the camshaft and crankshaft sprockets.

8. Loosen the bolt securing the crankshaft sprocket (B, **Figure 206**).

NOTE

Do not use a long pry bar to loosen the camshaft bolt as this may damage the drive chain. First, attempt to loosen the bolt with an impact driver or air impact wrench. If this fails, apply heat with a propane torch to the bolt head to loosen the thread locking compound. Heat the bolt head evenly in a circular motion. Avoid the use of excessive heat as this may damage the drive chain tensioner assembly. If the bolt cannot be loosened using these methods, have a H-D dealership perform the procedure.

9. Loosen the bolt securing the rear camshaft sprocket (C, **Figure 206**).

10. Remove the special tool installed in Step 7.

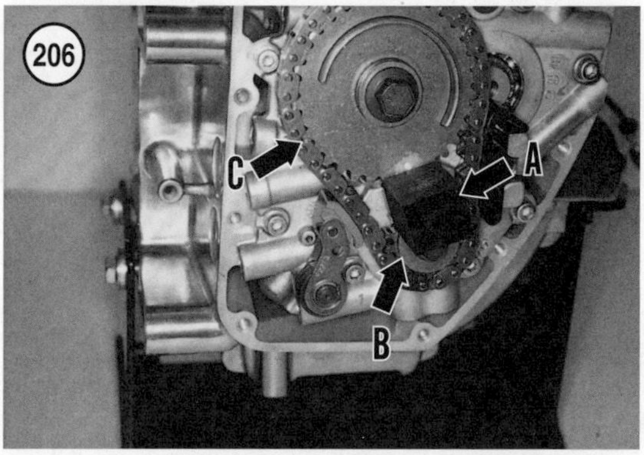

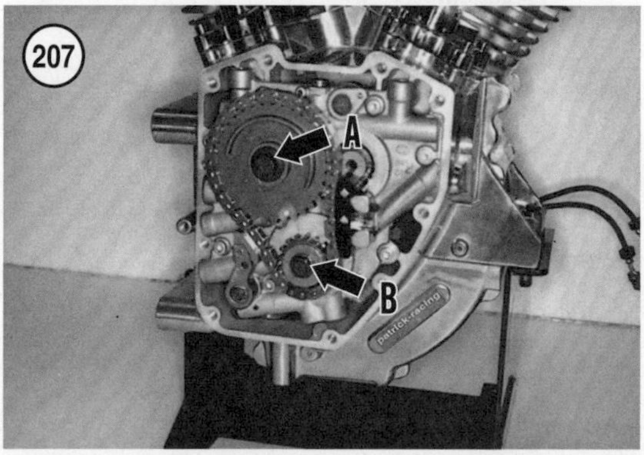

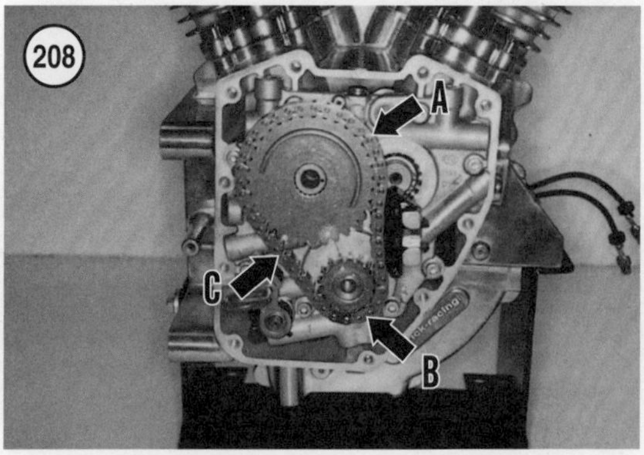

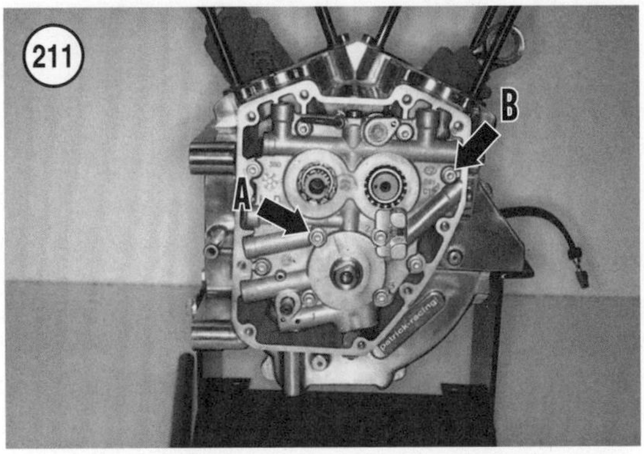

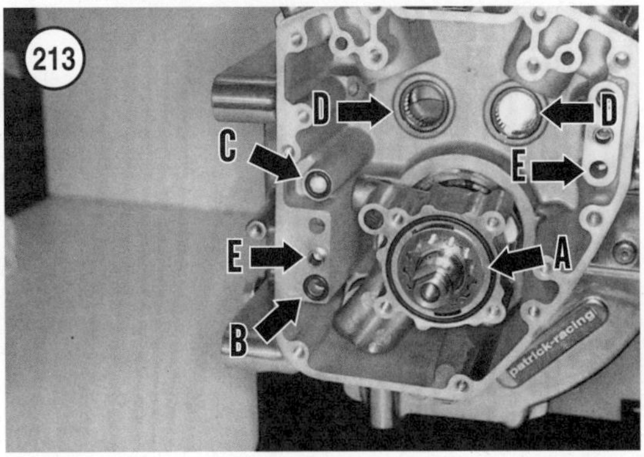

11. Remove the camshaft sprocket bolt (A, **Figure 207**) and the crankshaft sprocket bolt and washer (B, **Figure 207**).

NOTE
If it is difficult to loosen either sprocket from its respective shaft, use a small pry bar and gently loosen the sprocket(s) from the shaft.

12. Remove the rear camshaft drive sprocket (A, **Figure 208**), the crankshaft sprocket (B) and the primary camshaft drive chain (C) as an assembly. Pull the assembly straight off the shafts.
13. On models so equipped, remove the Woodruff key from the rear camshaft.
14. Remove the sprocket spacer (**Figure 209**) from the rear camshaft.
15. Squeeze the tabs and remove the camshaft chain guide (**Figure 210**).
16. Loosen the camshaft support plate Allen bolts in the following sequence:
   a. Using a crisscross pattern, loosen and remove the Allen bolts (A, **Figure 211**) securing the support plate to the oil pump assembly.
   b. Using a crisscross pattern, loosen and remove the remaining six Allen bolts (B, **Figure 211**) securing the support plate to the crankcase.
17. Withdraw the camshaft support plate assembly from the crankcase. If necessary, carefully pry the plate loose from the crankcase in the areas where the locating dowels are located (**Figure 212**).
18. Remove the O-ring (A, **Figure 213**) from the oil pump assembly and the lower O-ring (B).
19. On 2000-on models, remove the upper O-ring (C, **Figure 213**).

20. If necessary, disassemble and remove the camshafts as described in this chapter.

Installation

NOTE

It is necessary to release the secondary chain tension in order to install the camshaft inner ends into the crankcase bearings (D, ***Figure 213****). If the tension is not released, the inner ends of the camshafts are pulled together and out of alignment with the bearings, making installation difficult if not impossible.*

1. Release the tension on the camshaft secondary chain tension as follows:
   a. Install the camshaft chain tensioner tool onto the camshaft secondary chain tensioner.
   b. Using a wrench, rotate the tool counterclockwise and insert the hold pin (**Figure 214**) through the hole in the outer surface of the support plate and into the hole in the tensioner. Push the hold pin all the way in until it bottoms.
   c. Remove the wrench and tensioner tool from the tensioner.
2. Push on the oil pump assembly to make sure it is correctly seated against the crankcase.
3. Install a *new* O-ring (A, **Figure 213**) onto the oil pump assembly and a *new* O-ring (B) onto the lower location. Apply a light coat of clean engine oil to the O-rings.
4. On 2000-on models, install a new upper O-ring (C, **Figure 213**). Apply a light coat of clean engine oil to the O-ring.
5. Lubricate the camshaft needle bearing (**Figure 215**) in the crankcase and the camshaft bearing surfaces (**Figure 216**) with clean engine oil.
6. If the camshafts were removed from the support plate, check that the timing mark (**Figure 217**) on each camshaft is aligned with each other. If not, reposition the camshafts prior to installing the assembly into the crankcase.
7. If removed, install the two locating dowels (E, **Figure 213**) onto the crankcase.

CAUTION

Do not force the camshaft support plate assembly into the crankcase. During installation, the camshaft ends may not be correctly aligned with the needle bearings. If force is applied, the needle bearing(s) will be damaged.

8. Slowly install the camshaft support plate assembly into the crankcase. Guide the camshaft ends into the crankcase needle bearings. If necessary, slightly rotate and/or wiggle the end of the rear cylinder camshaft (**Figure 218**) to assist in the alignment.

214

215

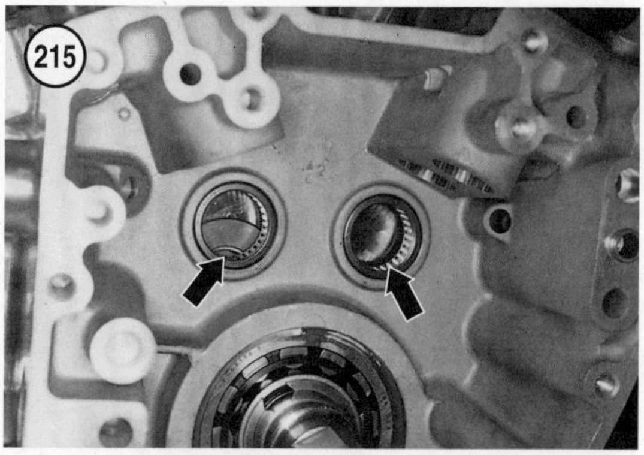

216

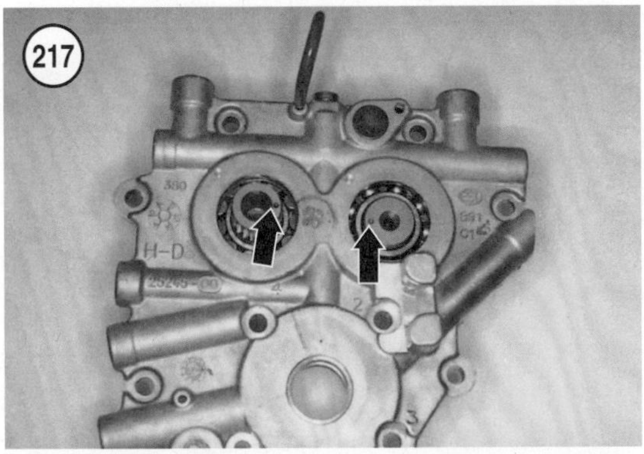
217

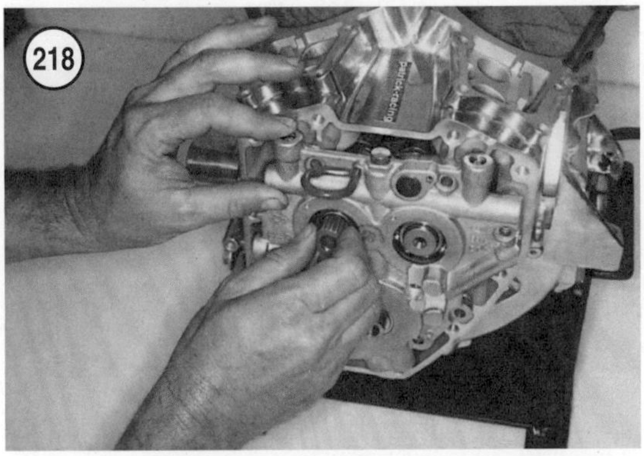
218

219

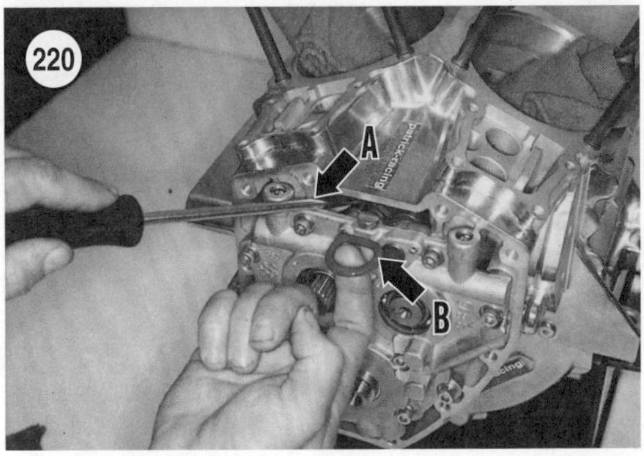

220

CAUTION
When properly aligned, the camshaft support plate assembly will fit snugly against the crankcase mating surface. If they do not meet correctly, do not attempt to pull the parts together with the mounting bolts. Separate the camshaft support plate assembly and investigate the cause of the interference.

9. Push the camshaft support plate assembly onto the crankcase until it bottoms on the two locating dowels and the crankcase mating surface.
10. Once again, check that the timing marks (**Figure 219**) on each camshaft are still aligned with each other. If not, correct the problem at this time.
11. Tighten the six camshaft support plate to crankcase Allen bolts in the following sequence:
   a. Install and loosely tighten the Allen bolts (B, **Figure 211**).
   b. Using a crisscross pattern, tighten the Allen bolts to the specification in **Table 4**.
12. Tighten the four camshaft support plate-to-oil pump Allen bolts in the following sequence:
   a. Install the Allen bolts (A, **Figure 211**). Tighten the bolts until they just contact the support plate and then back them out 1/4 turn.
   b. Rotate the engine until the oil pump is in neutral center with no load on it.
   c. Tighten the bolts until they are snug against the support plate. Then, using a crisscross pattern, tighten the Allen bolts to the specification in **Table 4**.
13. After all ten Allen bolts are tightened, check around the perimeter of the support plate to make sure it is seated against the crankcase mating surface.
14. Install an angled pick into the opening and against the secondary camshaft chain tensioner shoe (A, **Figure 220**). Slowly release the hold pin (B) and allow the tensioner shoe to gradually make contact with the chain surface. If released too fast, the shoe surface will slam against the chain and be damaged.
15. Squeeze the tabs and install the camshaft chain guide (**Figure 210**) onto the two posts.

NOTE
Step 16 is not necessary if the original camshaft support plate, both camshafts, the rear camshaft sprocket, the crankshaft drive sprocket, and the

crankshaft assembly are being reused and installed. If any one of these components have been replaced, Step 16 is necessary to ensure correct alignment between the rear camshaft sprocket and the crankshaft drive sprocket. If this alignment is incorrect, the primary drive chain and both sprockets will bind and cause premature wear.

16. If new parts have been installed, check the alignment of the rear camshaft sprocket and the crankshaft drive sprocket as described under *Rear Camshaft Sprocket and Crankshaft Drive Sprocket Alignment* in the following procedure. If all original parts have been installed, proceed to Step 17.

17. Relieve the tension on the camshaft primary drive chain as follows:

a. Install the camshaft chain tensioner tool (**Figure 221**) onto the camshaft primary chain tensioner.

b. Using a wrench (A, **Figure 222**), rotate the tool counterclockwise and insert the hold pin (B) through the hole in the tensioner and into the hole in the support plate. Push the hold pin all the way in until it bottoms.

c. Remove the wrench and tensioner tool from the tensioner.

18. Position the sprocket spacer with the manufacturer's mark side going on first, and install the sprocket spacer (**Figure 209**) onto the rear camshaft.

NOTE
Refer to the mark made prior to removal and position the camshaft primary drive chain so it will be traveling in the same direction. If installed incorrectly, the drive chain will wear prematurely.

19. Correctly assemble the rear camshaft sprocket, the crankshaft drive sprocket and the primary drive chain together as an assembly. Align the index mark on both sprockets so they face each other as shown in **Figure 223**.

20. On models so equipped, install the Woodruff key onto the rear camshaft.

21. Install the rear camshaft drive sprocket (A, **Figure 208**), the crankshaft sprocket (B), and the primary camshaft drive chain (C) as an assembly onto the crankshaft and rear camshaft. Align the flat on

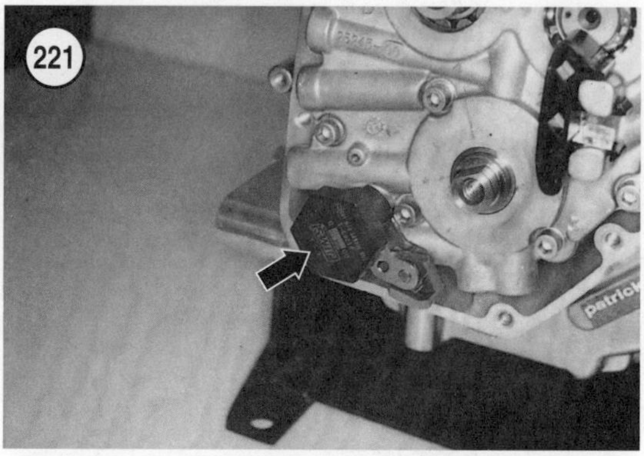

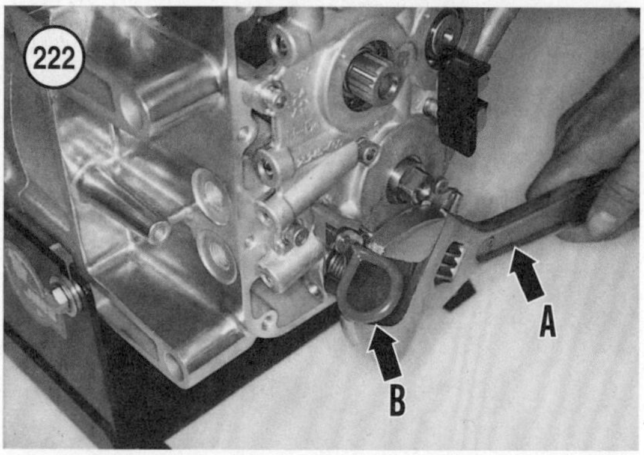

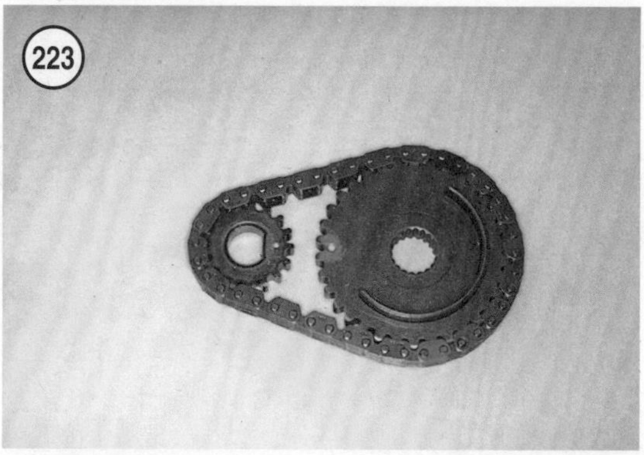

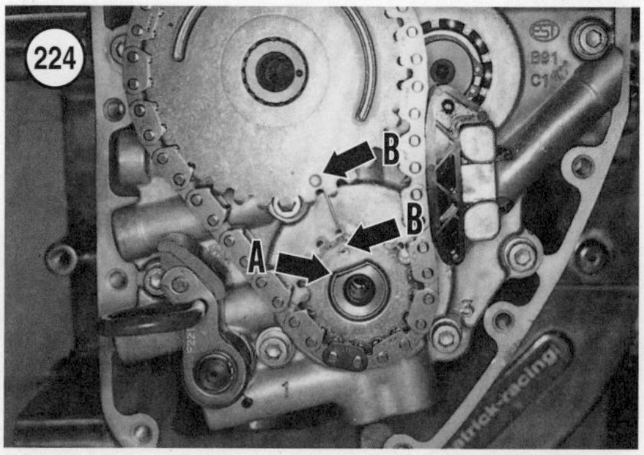

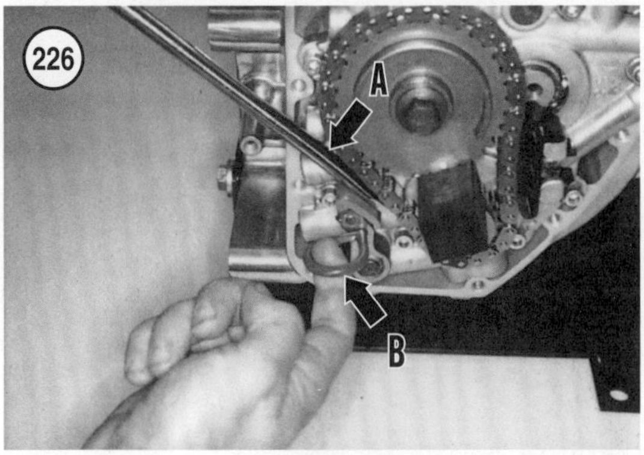

the crankshaft sprocket with the flat on the crankshaft (A, **Figure 224**). Check the alignment of the index mark on both sprockets, and make sure they face each other as shown in B, **Figure 224**. Realign the sprocket index marks if necessary.

22. Apply clean engine oil to the underside of both *new* sprocket bolts prior to installation.

23. Apply a small amount of ThreeBond TB1360, or an equivalent, threadlocking compound to the threads of the *new* rear camshaft sprocket bolt. Do not apply the locking agent to the crankshaft bolt.

24. Install a *new* camshaft sprocket bolt (A, **Figure 207**) and *new* crankshaft sprocket bolt and washer (B). Tighten the bolts finger-tight at this time.

25. Install and mesh the camshaft and crankshaft sprocket lock (**Figure 225**) between the camshaft and crankshaft sprockets.

26. Place a flat blade screwdriver (A, **Figure 226**) between the primary camshaft drive chain and the tensioner. Slowly release the hold pin (B), then slowly withdraw the screwdriver and allow the tensioner to gradually make contact with the chain surface. If released too fast, the shoe surface will slam against the chain and be damaged.

27. Tighten both bolts in the following steps:

   a. Tighten both bolts to 15 ft.-lb. (20 N•m).
   b. Loosen both bolts one complete revolution (360°).
   c. Tighten the rear camshaft bolt to 34 ft.-lb. (46 N•m).
   d. Tighten the crankshaft bolt to 24 ft.-lb. (33 N•m).

28. Remove the tool installed in Step 25.

29. Install the crankshaft position sensor (**Figure 204**) into the crankcase and tighten the bolt securely.

30. Install a new camshaft cover gasket (**Figure 227**) onto the crankcase.

NOTE

On 1999-2000 models, do not damage the cam position sensor wiring ***(Figure 202)*** *during cover installation.*

31. Install the camshaft cover onto the crankcase. Install the bolts and tighten them securely in a crisscross pattern.

32. Install the lifter covers, lifters and pushrods as described in this chapter.

33. Install the exhaust system as described in Chapter Seven.

Rear Camshaft Sprocket and Crankshaft Drive Sprocket Alignment

This procedure is required if any of the following parts have been replaced: the camshaft support plate, either or both camshafts, the rear camshaft sprocket, the crankshaft drive sprocket and the crankshaft assembly.

If any of these components have been replaced, the procedure is necessary to ensure correct alignment between the rear camshaft sprocket and the crankshaft drive sprocket. If this alignment is incorrect, the primary drive chain and both sprockets will bind and cause premature wear.

For the correct relationship between the two sprocket faces, the rear camshaft sprocket must be 0.005 in. (0.127 mm) below the surface of the crankshaft sprocket.

1. Position the sprocket spacer with the manufacturer's-mark side going on first. Install the sprocket spacer (**Figure 209**) onto the rear camshaft and push it on until it bottoms.
2. On models so equipped, install the Woodruff key onto the rear camshaft.
3. Apply clean engine oil to the camshaft splines (or Woodruff key) and rear camshaft sprocket splines.
4. Install the rear camshaft sprocket onto the camshaft. Install the *used* mounting bolt and flat washer (A, **Figure 228**). Tighten the bolt finger-tight.
5. Install the crankshaft sprocket (B, **Figure 228**) onto the crankshaft. Install the *used* mounting bolt and a *washer with a smaller outer diameter* (C). Tighten the bolt finger-tight at this time.
6. Install and mesh the camshaft and crankshaft sprocket lock (**Figure 225**) between the camshaft and crankshaft sprockets.
7. Tighten both bolts in the following steps:
   a. Tighten both bolts to 15 ft.-lb. (20 N•m).
   b. Loosen both bolts one complete revolution (360 degrees).
   c. Tighten the rear camshaft bolt to 34 ft.-lb. (46 N•m).
   d. Tighten the crankshaft bolt to 24 ft.-lb. (33 N•m).
8. Remove the special tool from the sprockets.
9. Place a straightedge (A, **Figure 229**) against the face of both sprockets. Push the straightedge against the *crankshaft sprocket* and hold it there.
10. Try to insert a 0.005 in. (0.127 mm) feeler gauge (B, **Figure 229**) between the straightedge and the camshaft sprocket face.

11A. If the 0.005 in. (0.127 mm) thickness flat feeler gauge can be inserted, the sprockets are correctly aligned to each other. Remove both sprockets and proceed with Step 17 of *Camshaft Support Plate Installation* in the previous procedure.

11B. If a different thickness feeler gauge can be inserted indicating a height difference other than 0.005 in. (0.127 mm) the rear camshaft spacer must be changed. Continue to insert the feeler gauge of a different thickness until the dimension difference is

228

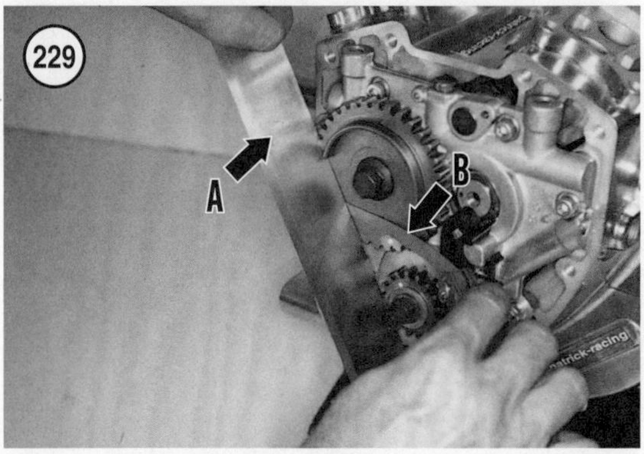

229

230

231

232

233

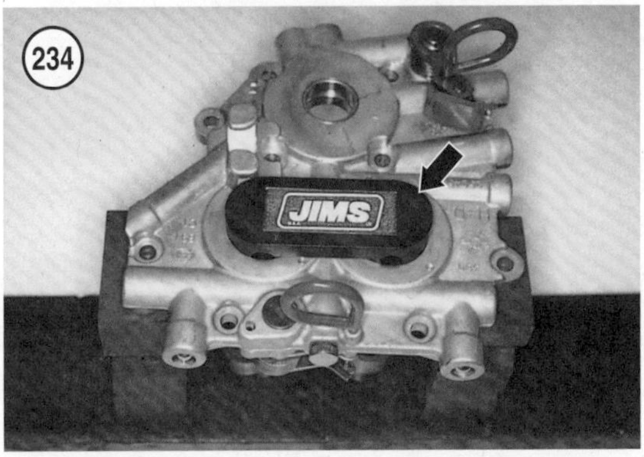

234

noted. Write down this dimension as it will be used to choose a new spacer.

12. Remove the rear camshaft sprocket bolt, washer and sprocket.

13. Remove the existing sprocket spacer (**Figure 208**) from the rear camshaft. Compare the part number stamped on the spacer with the parts numbers in **Table 5** to determine the thickness.

14A. If the crankshaft sprocket is more than 0.005 in. (0.127 mm) above the camshaft sprocket, install the next *thicker* size spacer under the camshaft sprocket.

14B. If the crankshaft sprocket is less than 0.005 in. (0.127 mm) above the camshaft sprocket, install the next *thinner* size spacer under the camshaft sprocket.

15. Install a new spacer and repeat this procedure until the correct amount of height difference of 0.005 in. (0.127mm). is obtained.

16. After the correct thickness spacer is established, proceed with Step 17 of *Camshaft Support Plate Installation* in the previous procedure.

Camshaft Support Plate and Camshafts

A hydraulic press, camshaft chain tensioner tool (JIMS part No. 1283) and camshaft remover and installer (JIMS part No. 1277) are required to perform the following procedure.

Disassembly

1. Remove the camshaft support plate as previously described.
2. Remove the snap ring (**Figure 230**) from the front cylinder camshaft.
3. Release the tension on the camshaft secondary chain tensioner as follows:
   a. Install the camshaft chain tensioner tool onto the camshaft secondary chain tensioner.
   b. Using a wrench, rotate the tool counterclockwise and insert the hold pin (**Figure 231**) through the hole in the outer surface of the support plate and into the hole in the tensioner. Push the hold pin all the way in until it bottoms.
   c. Remove the wrench and tensioner tool from the tensioner.
4. Loosen and remove the four T20 Torx screws (**Figure 232**) securing the bearing retainer plate. Remove the bearing retainer plate (**Figure 233**).
5. Press the camshafts and secondary drive chain out of the camshaft support plate as follows:
   a. Turn the camshaft support cover face up on two support blocks in a press bed. Make sure the support blocks are tall enough to allow the complete removal of the camshafts from the cover.
   b. Install the cups of the camshaft remover and installer onto the top of the camshafts (**Figure 234**) following the manufacturer's instructions.

235

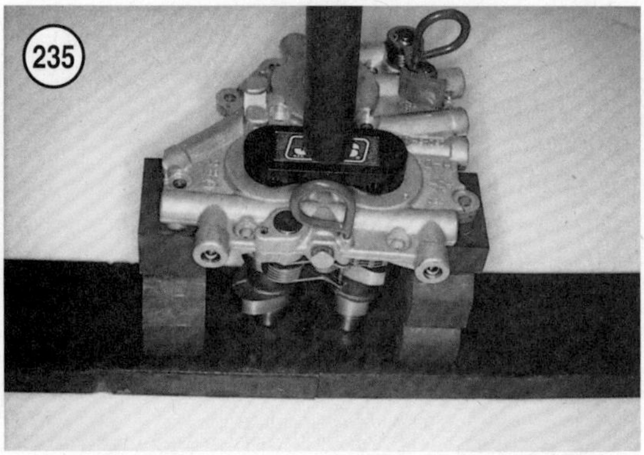

c. Center the press ram over the center of the tool (**Figure 235**).

d. Slowly apply pressure and press the assembly out of the support cover.

e. Remove the assembly, cover, and special tool from the press bed.

6. To ensure that the camshaft secondary drive chain is reinstalled in the same direction of travel, mark one of the link plates on the bearing side with a permanent marking pen (**Figure 236**) or scribe.

7. Separate the camshafts from the secondary drive chain.

Inspection

There are no manufacturer's specifications available for the camshaft. The following procedure is a visual inspection to determine if the camshafts require replacement.

1. Check the camshaft lobes (**Figure 237**) for wear. The lobes should not be scored and the edges should be square.

2. Inspect the drive chain sprocket (**Figure 238**) for broken or chipped teeth. Also check the teeth for cracking or rounding. If the sprocket is damaged or severely worn, replace the camshaft.

3. If the camshaft sprockets are worn, check the camshaft secondary drive chain (**Figure 239**) for damage.

4A. On early models, inspect the Woodruff key and key slot in the rear cylinder camshaft for wear or damage.

4B. On later models, inspect the external splines (A, **Figure 240**) on the rear cylinder camshaft and the internal splines (B, **Figure 240**) on the sprocket. Check for worn or damaged splines and replace either or both parts if necessary. The sprocket must be a tight fit on the camshaft.

236

237

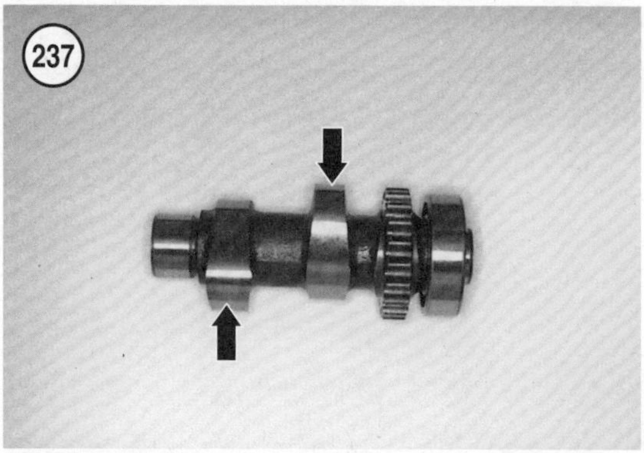

238

239

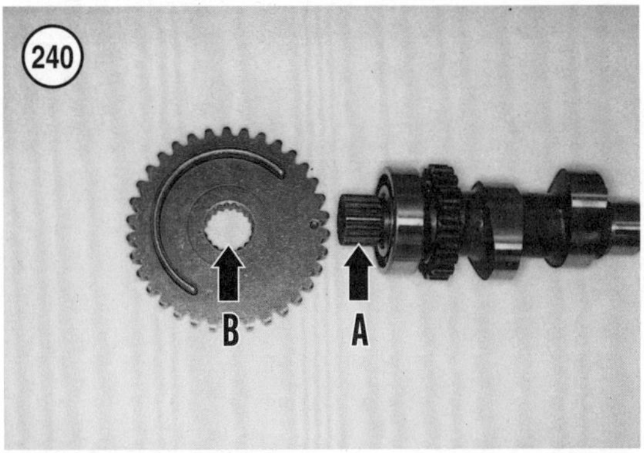

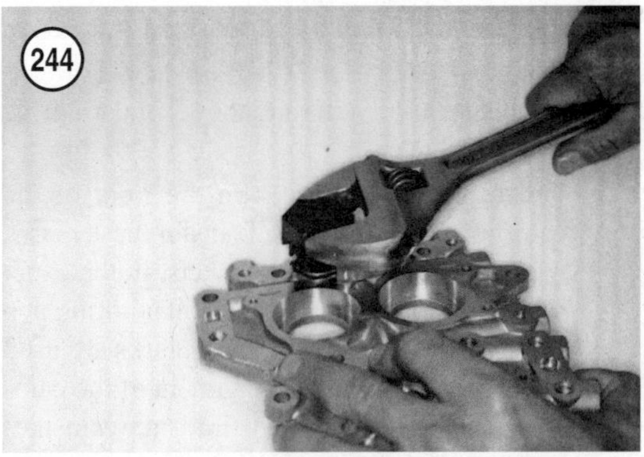

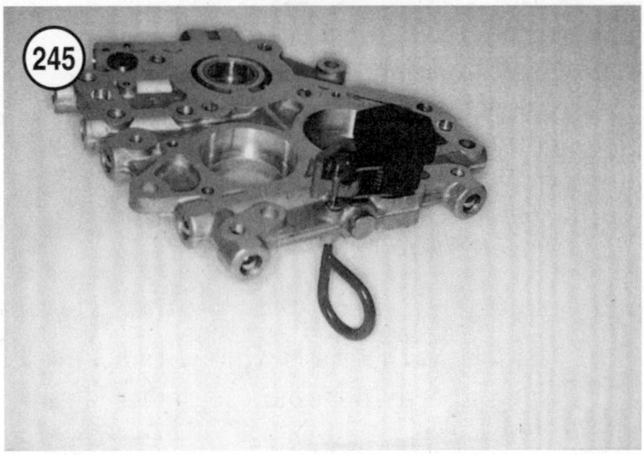

5. Check the snap ring groove (**Figure 241**) on the front cylinder camshaft for wear or damage.

6. Inspect the ball bearing (**Figure 242**) on each camshaft and rotate it. It must rotate smoothly with no roughness. If damaged, replace the ball bearing as described in this section.

Assembly

NOTE
This procedure is shown with the ball bearings in place on the camshafts since they did not require replacement.

1. Prior to installing the camshaft assembly, the tension must be relieved on the secondary cam chain tensioner. Perform the following :
   a. Install the camshaft chain tensioner tool (**Figure 243**) onto the camshaft secondary chain tensioner.
   b. Using a wrench, rotate the tool counterclockwise (**Figure 244**) and insert the hold pin through the hole in the tensioner and into the hole in the support plate. Push the hold pin all the way in until it bottoms (**Figure 245**).

   c. Remove the wrench and tensioner tool from the tensioner.

2. Assemble the camshafts and the secondary drive chain as follows:

   a. Locate the index marks on the front of the camshafts (**Figure 246**). Transfer these marks to the backside of the sprockets, in the exact same location, with a permanent marking pen or scribe (**Figure 247**). These marks are used later to observe proper alignment of the camshaft as they are pressed into the camshaft support plate.

NOTE

*Refer to the mark made on one of the link plates in **Disassembly** Step 6 and position the camshaft secondary drive chain so it will be traveling in the same direction as noted prior to removal. If installed incorrectly, the drive chain will wear prematurely.*

   b. Position the camshafts with the index marks facing directly opposite each other (**Figure 248**).
   c. Correctly position the secondary chain with the marked link plate facing up (**Figure 236**) and assemble the secondary chain onto both camshafts.
   d. Rotate the camshafts in either direction several times and recheck the alignment of the index marks. If necessary, readjust one of the camshafts to achieve correct alignment (**Figure 248**).

3. Apply a light coat of clean engine oil, or press lube, to the camshaft ends and to the bearing receptacles in the camshaft support plate.

4. Place the camshaft support plate on the press bed with the bearing receptacles facing up (**Figure 249**).

5. Correctly position the camshaft assembly onto the camshaft support plate with the rear cylinder camshaft (**Figure 250**) located toward the back of the support plate. Align the bearings with the support plate receptacles and hold the assembly in place.

NOTE

*Prior to pressing the camshaft assembly into place, check the alignment of the camshaft index marks on the backside of the sprockets (**Figure 251**). If*

246

247

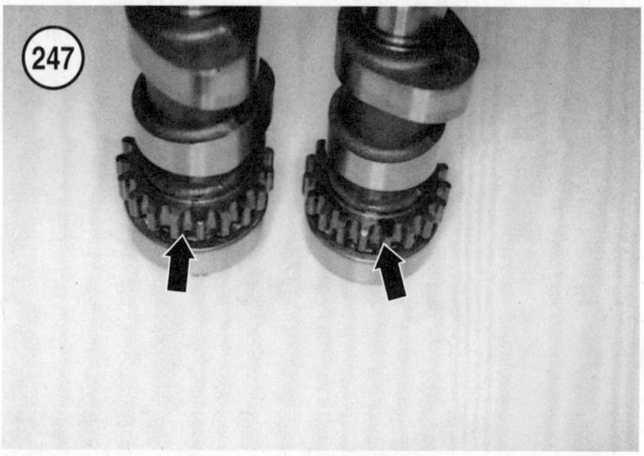

248

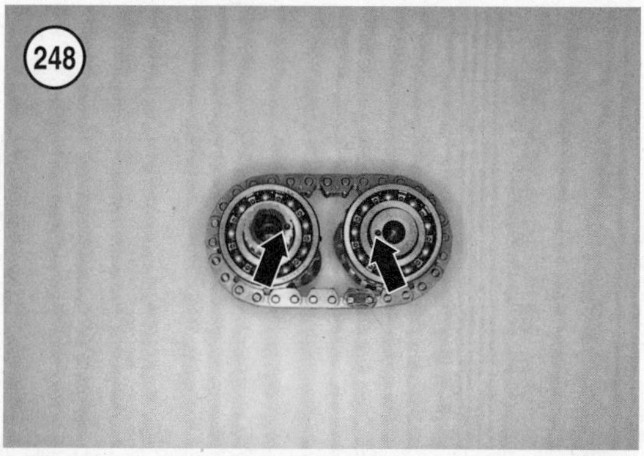

249

250

251

252

253

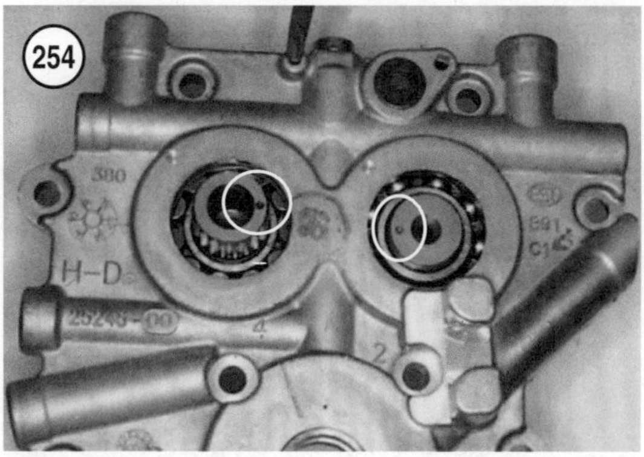

254

out of alignment, remove the assembly and correct this alignment.

6. Install the cups of the camshaft remover and installer onto the top of the camshafts (**Figure 252**), following the manufacturer's instructions.

7. Center the press ram over the center of the tool (**Figure 253**).

8. Slowly apply pressure and press the assembly into the support cover until it bottoms.

9. Remove the assembly and special tool from the press bed.

10. Turn the assembly over and double check that the camshaft index marks are still correctly aligned as shown in **Figure 254**.

11. Rotate the camshafts several complete revolutions and check for binding.

12. Install the retainer plate (**Figure 233**) into position.

13. Apply a small amount of ThreeBond TB1342 or an equivalent threadlocking compound to the Torx screw threads. Install the four T20 Torx screws (**Figure 232**) and tighten securely.

14. Place a flat blade screwdriver between the secondary camshaft drive chain and the tensioner. Slowly release the hold pin (**Figure 231**), then slowly withdraw the screwdriver and allow the tensioner to gradually make contact with the chain surface. If released too fast, the shoe surface will slam against the chain and be damaged.

15. Install the circlip (**Figure 255**) onto the front cylinder camshaft. Make sure the snap ring is correctly seated in the camshaft groove.

16. Install the camshaft support plate as previously described.

Bushing replacement

A crankshaft bushing tool (JIMS part No. 1281) is required to remove and install the crankshaft bushing.

1. Place the bushing support tool on the press bed.

NOTE
The crankshaft bushing edge is knurled on the side that faces the primary chain side.

2. Position the camshaft support plate with the primary chain side facing up. Place the camshaft support plate onto the bushing support tool and center the bushing over the tool (**Figure 256**).
3. Install the *remove side* of the driver (**Figure 257**) through the bushing and into the support tool until the shoulder of the driver contacts the edge of the bushing.
4. Apply pressure and press the bushing out of the support plate until the driver collar contacts the support plate.
5. If removed, place the bushing support tool on the press bed.
6. Position the camshaft support plate with the secondary chain side facing up. Place the camshaft support plate onto the bushing support tool.
7. Apply a light coat of clean engine oil, or press lube, to the outer surface of the bushing and to the support plate bushing receptacle.
8. Position the bushing into the receptacle with the knurled side facing up and align it.
9. Install the *install side* of the driver (**Figure 258**) through the bushing and into the support tool until the driver contacts the edge of the bushing.
10. Press the bushing into the support plate until the driver collar contacts the support plate.
11. Remove the special tools and the support plate from the press bed.

Camshaft Bearing Replacement

Ball bearings

A hydraulic press, camshaft bearing puller (JIMS part No 1280) and camshaft remover and installer (JIMS part No. 1277) are required to remove and install the camshaft ball bearings.

1. Install the camshaft bearing puller tool onto the camshaft ball bearing (**Figure 259**) and remove it following the manufacturer's instructions.

255

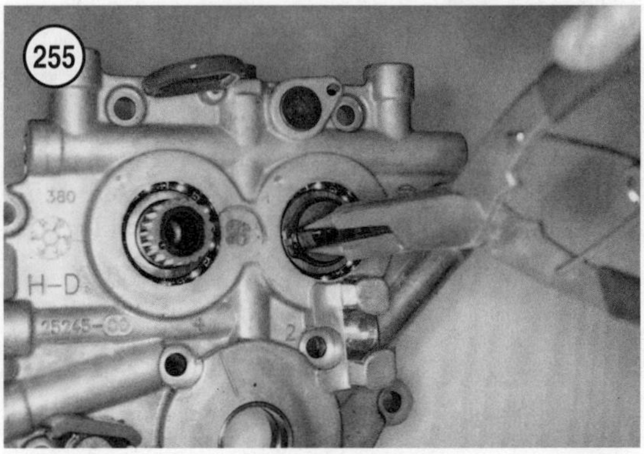

256

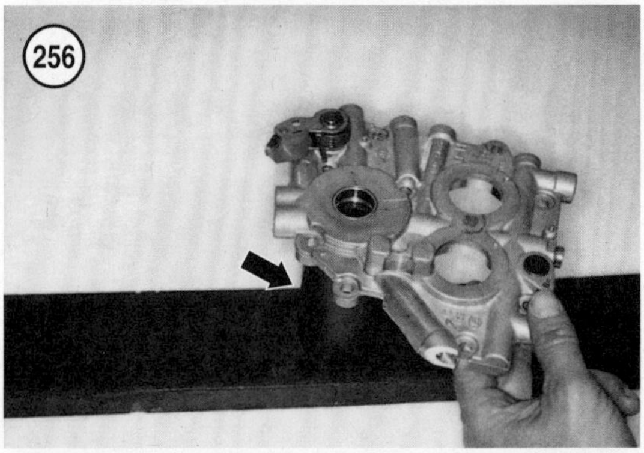

257

258

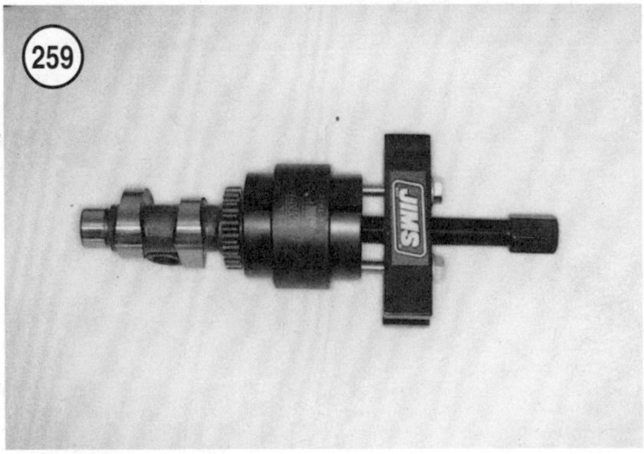

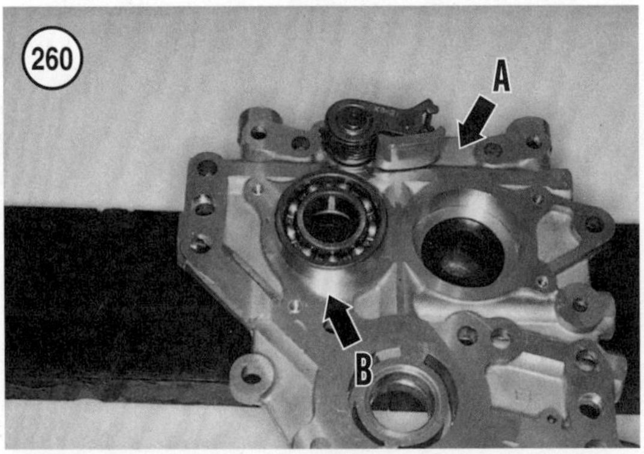

2. Repeat for the other camshaft bearing.

NOTE
The ball bearing is installed into the camshaft support plate, not onto the camshaft(s).

3. Install the ball bearing(s) into the camshaft support plate using the camshaft remover and installer as follows:

a. Place the support block on the press bed.

b. Place the camshaft support plate (A, **Figure 260**) onto a support block. Make sure the support plate is indexed correctly into the support block.

c. Apply a light coat of clean engine oil or press lube to the outer surface of the ball bearing and to the support plate bearing receptacle.

d. Place the ball bearing onto the support plate (B, **Figure 260**).

e. Install the bearing pilot (**Figure 261**) into the ball bearing.

f. Apply pressure and press the bearing straight into the support plate until it bottoms.

g. Remove the pilot from the bearing and remove the support plate from the press bed.

Needle bearings

NOTE
The camshaft needle bearings can be removed with the engine mounted in the frame and the camshaft support plate removed. This procedure is shown with the engine removed and partially disassembled to better illustrate the steps.

NOTE
Replace both needle bearings as a set even though only one requires replacement.

A twin cam 88 engine stand (JIMS part No. 1022) and flywheel press (JIMS part No. 1047-TP) were used in the following procedure.

1. Remove the camshaft support plate assembly from the engine as described in this chapter.

2. Install the puller portion of the tool set (A, **Figure 262**) part way into the needle bearing. Install a small hose clamp (B) onto the end closer to the needle bearing and tighten. This will close the end of the tool so it can pass through the needle bearing. Push the puller all the way through the needle bearing and remove the hose clamp.

3. Assemble the remainder of the tool components onto the puller portion (**Figure 263**), following the manufacturer's instructions.
4. Place a 5/8 in. wrench on the flats of the puller (A, **Figure 264**).
5. Place a 1 1/8 in. wrench, or an adjustable wrench, on the large nut (B, **Figure 264**).

CAUTION
Do not turn the 5/8 in. wrench as this will damage the special tool and the crankcase receptacle.

6. Hold onto the 5/8 in. wrench to keep the puller from rotating. Turn the 1 1/8 in. wrench *clockwise* on the large nut. Tighten the large nut and pull the needle bearing out of the crankcase receptacle.
7. Disassemble the special tool and remove the needle bearing from it.
8. Repeat Steps 2-7 for the other needle bearing.
9. Apply a light coat of clean engine oil, or press lube, to the outer surface of the ball bearings and to the crankcase needle bearing receptacles (**Figure 265**).

NOTE
The following photographs are shown with the crankcase disassembled to better illustrate the steps.

10. Apply a light coat of clean engine oil to the threads of the screw portion and to the installer plate.
11. Insert the screw portion of the special tool part way into the installer plate.
12. Install the installer onto the screw and push it on until it locks into place.
13. Position the new bearing with the manufacturer's marks facing out on the installer (**Figure 266**).
14. Install the installer plate onto the crankcase, aligning the tool to the bearing receptacle (A, **Figure 267**).
15. Install the thumb screws through the installer plate (B, **Figure 267**) and onto the crankcase threaded holes. Tighten the thumb screws securely.
16. Slowly tighten the screw until the bearing starts to enter the crankcase receptacle. Continue to tighten until the installer contacts the crankcase surface. This will correctly locate the needle bearing within the crankcase.
17. Remove the special tools.
18. Repeat Steps 10-17 for the other needle bearing.

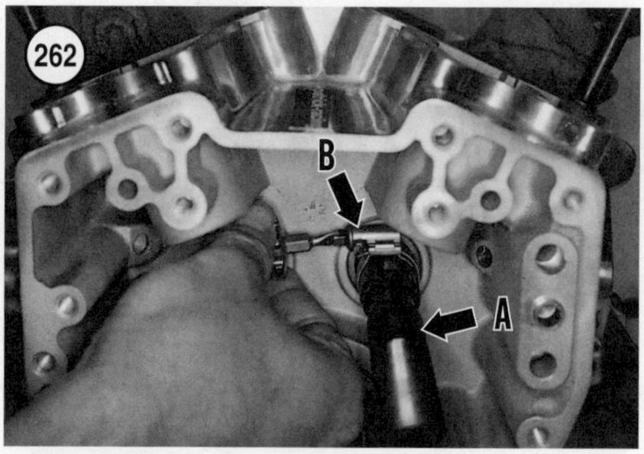

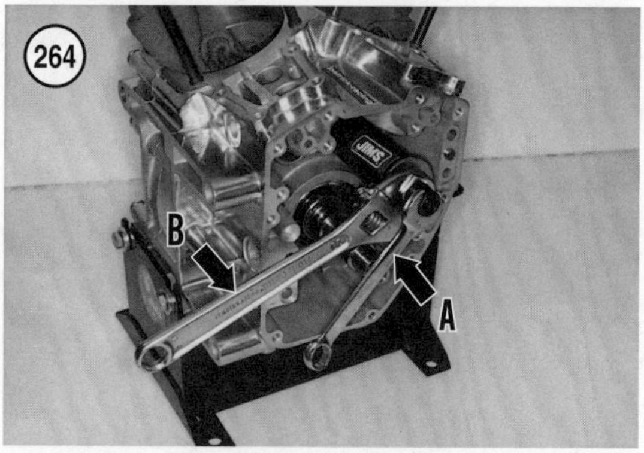

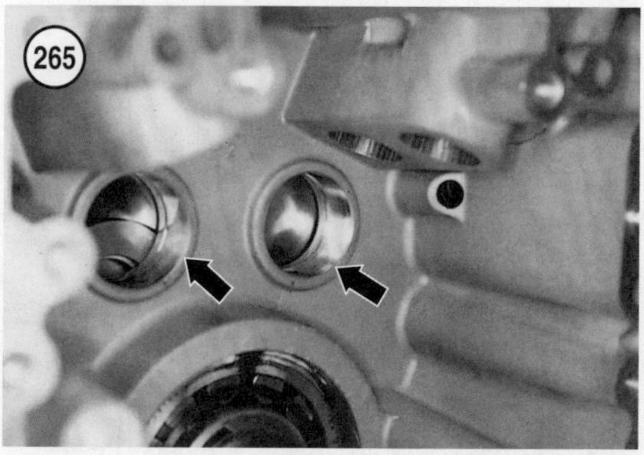

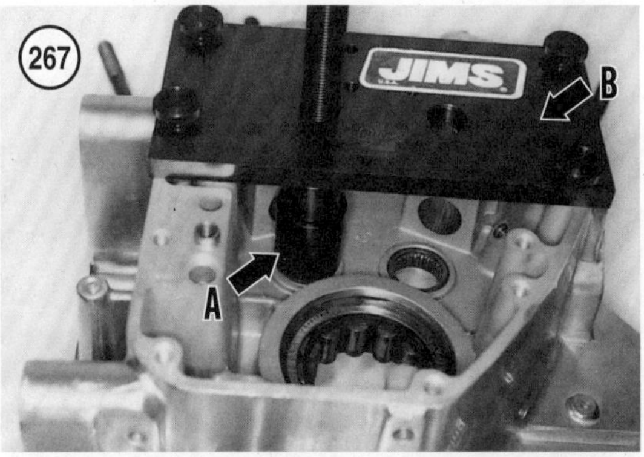

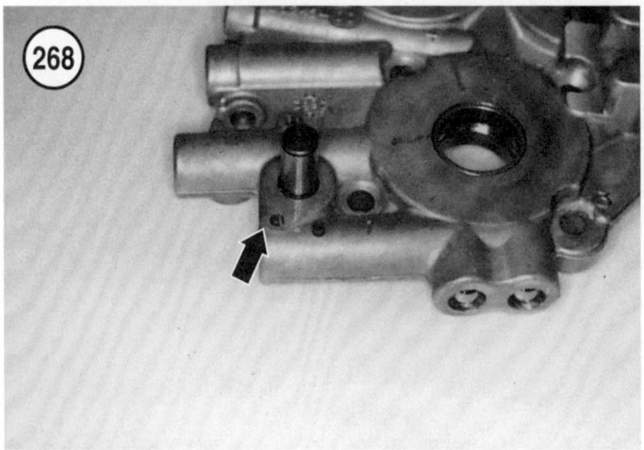

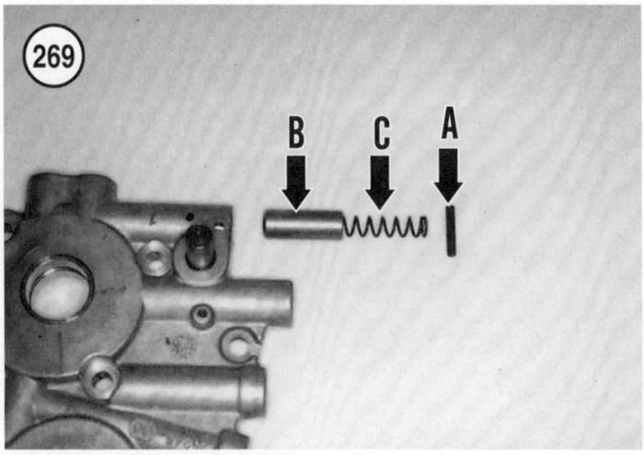

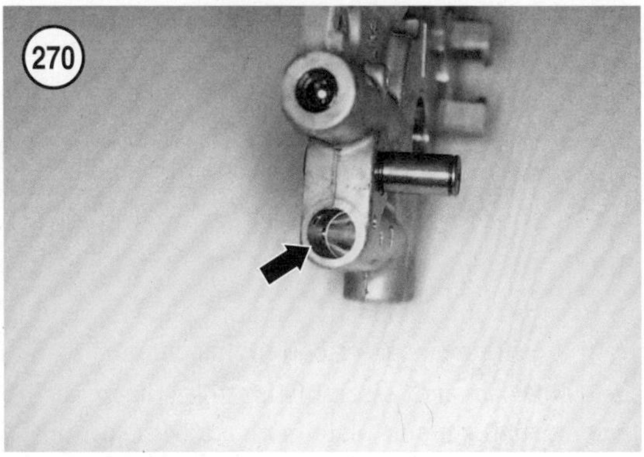

4

Oil Pressure Relief Valve Removal/Installation

NOTE
This procedure is shown with the camshaft assembly removed to better illustrate these steps.

1. Remove the camshaft support plate assembly from the engine as described in this chapter.

2A. If the camshaft assembly is still in place, secure the camshaft support plate in a vise with soft jaws.

2B. If the camshaft assembly is removed, place the camshaft support plate on a piece of soft wood.

3. Use a 1/8 in. punch and drive out the roll pin (**Figure 268**) securing the valve body and spring in place. Discard the roll pin (A, **Figure 269**).

4. Remove the valve body (B, **Figure 269**) and spring (C) from the bypass port of the camshaft support plate.

5. Inspect the valve body, spring and bypass port (**Figure 270**) for wear or damage. Replace as necessary.

6. Apply a light coat of clean engine oil to the bypass port and to the valve body.

7. Position the valve body (A, **Figure 271**) with the closed end going into the bypass port first.

8. Install the spring (B, **Figure 271**) into the valve body.

9. Push the valve body and spring into the bypass port, hold them in place and install a *new* roll pin (**Figure 272**). Tap the roll pin in until it bottoms (**Figure 268**).

Cleaning Plug Removal/Installation

NOTE
This procedure is shown with the camshaft assembly removed to better illustrate these steps.

1. Remove the camshaft support plate assembly from the engine as described in this chapter.
2A. If the camshaft assembly is still in place, secure the camshaft support plate in a vise with soft jaws.
2B. If the camshaft assembly is removed, place the camshaft support plate on piece of soft wood.
3. Use a pair of pliers and carefully remove the cleaning plug (**Figure 273**) from the camshaft support plate. Remove the O-ring.
4. Thoroughly clean the cleaning plug receptacle and support plate in solvent. Dry with compressed air.
5. Apply low-pressure compressed air to the cleaning plug receptacle (**Figure 274**) and blow out any debris. Make sure the oil hole is clear.
6. Install a *new* O-ring onto the cleaning plug and install the cleaning plug. Press it in until it bottoms.

Camshaft Primary and Secondary Chain Tensioner

Removal/Inspection/Installation

NOTE
This procedure is shown on the primary chain tensioner and also applies to the secondary chain tensioner.

1. Remove the camshaft primary and/or secondary chain as described in this chapter.
2. Remove the snap ring (**Figure 275**) securing the chain tensioner to the mounting post. Discard the snap ring.
3. Slide the chain tensioner (A, **Figure 276**) off the mounting post.
4. Inspect the chain tensioner shoe (A, **Figure 277**) for wear. If the pad surface is worn halfway through (A, **Figure 278**) or chipped (B), replace the assembly.
5. Check the spring (B, **Figure 277**) for sagging or damage. Replace the assembly if necessary.

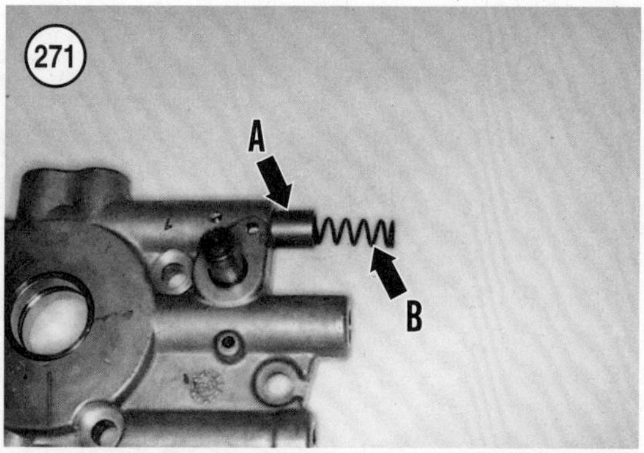

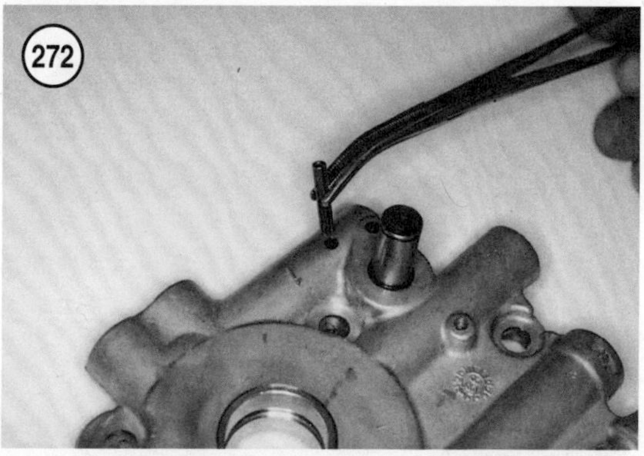

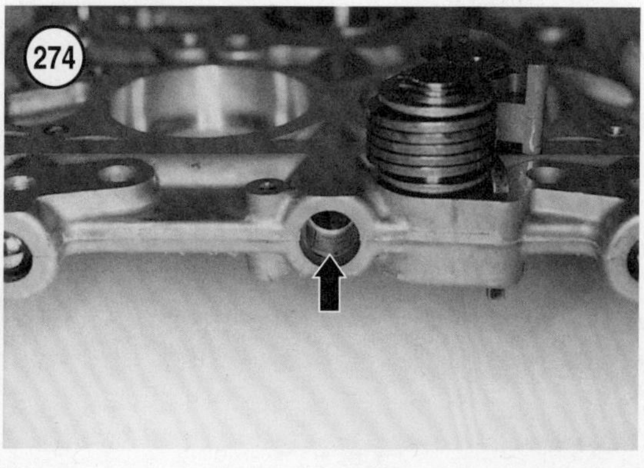

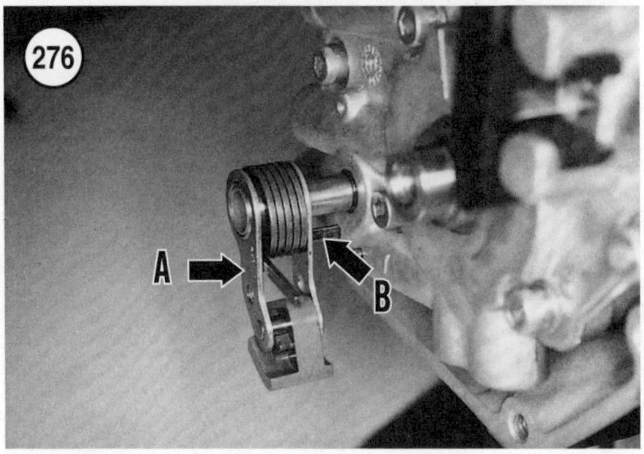

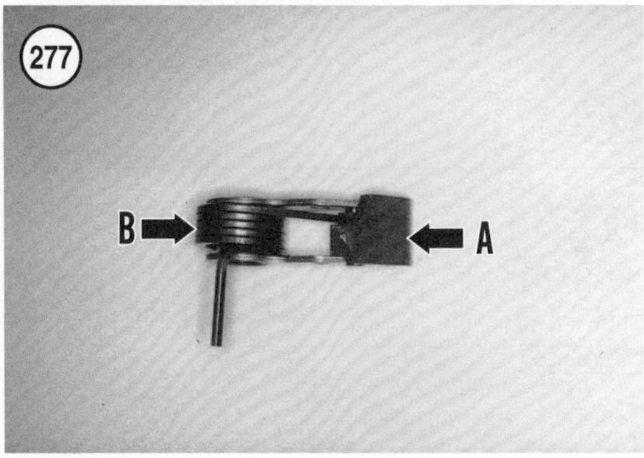

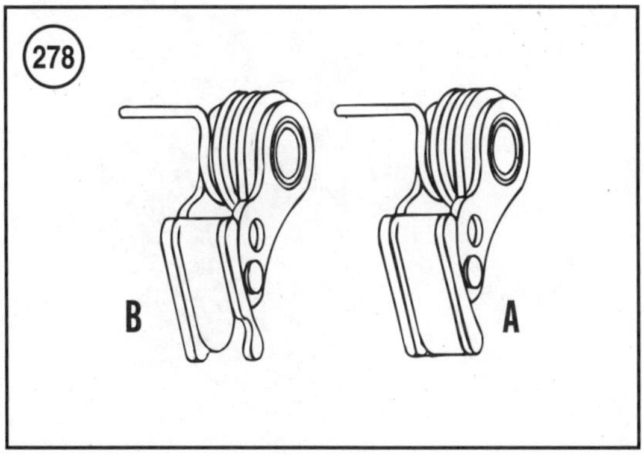

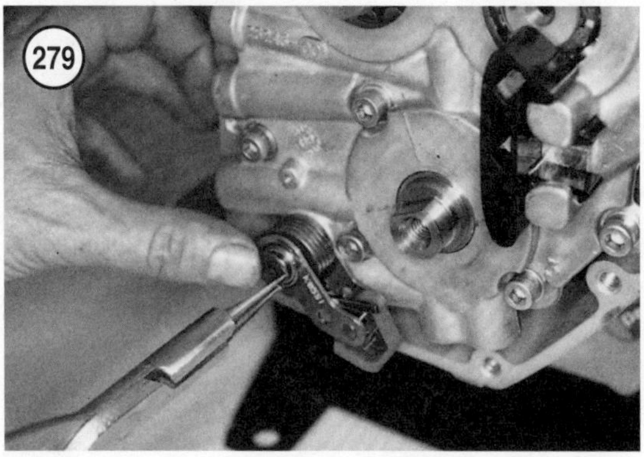

4

6. Install the chain tensioner onto the mounting post and insert the spring end into the receptacle in the cover (B, **Figure 276**). Push the chain tension on until it bottoms.
7. Install a *new* snap ring and press it into place (**Figure 279**). Make sure it is correctly seated in the mounting post groove.

CRANKCASE AND CRANKSHAFT

Disassembly

A twin cam 88 engine stand (JIMS part No. 1022) and flywheel press (JIMS part No. 1047-TP) were used in the following procedure.

CAUTION
Prior to disassembling the crankcase, measure the crankshaft end play as described in Crankcase Assembly.

Refer to **Figure 280**.
1. Remove the engine from the frame as described in this chapter.

CAUTION
Do not lift the crankcase assembly by the cylinder studs. Bent or damaged cylinder studs may cause the engine to leak oil.

2. Remove the following components as described in this chapter:
   a. Cylinder heads and cylinders.
   b. Pistons.
   c. Pushrods and valve lifters.
   d. Camshaft assembly.
   e. Oil pump.

280

CRANKCASE ASSEMBLY

1. Connecting rod bushing
2. Crankshaft assembly
3. Oil hose fitting
4. Retaining ring
5. Right side main bearing
6. Needle bearing–camshaft
7. Crankcase assembly
8. O-ring
9. Piston cooling jet
10. Screw
11. Locating dowel
12. Bolt
13. Plug
14. Bearing
15. Bearing race
16. Lock ring
17. Spacer ring
18. Oil seal
19. Sprocket shaft spacer
20. Left side main bearing (sprocket shaft) assembly
21. Locating dowel

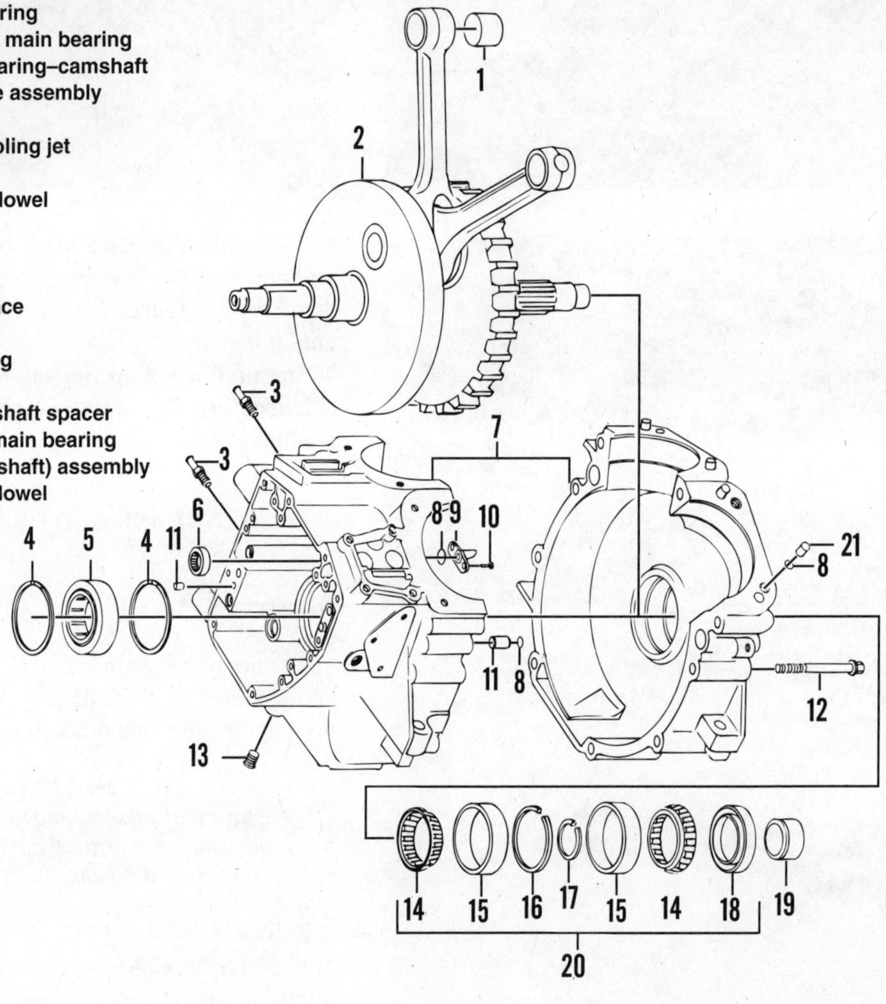

f. Alternator rotor and stator assembly (Chapter Eight).

NOTE
The bolts for the left side are to be left off so the case halves can be separated in the following steps.

3. Attach the crankcase assembly to an engine stand (**Figure 281**), following the manufacturer's instructions. Make sure that the stand is attached

281

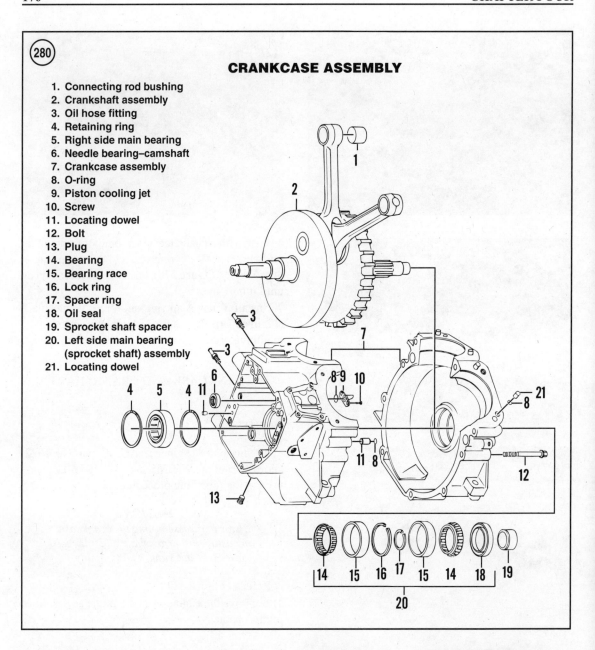

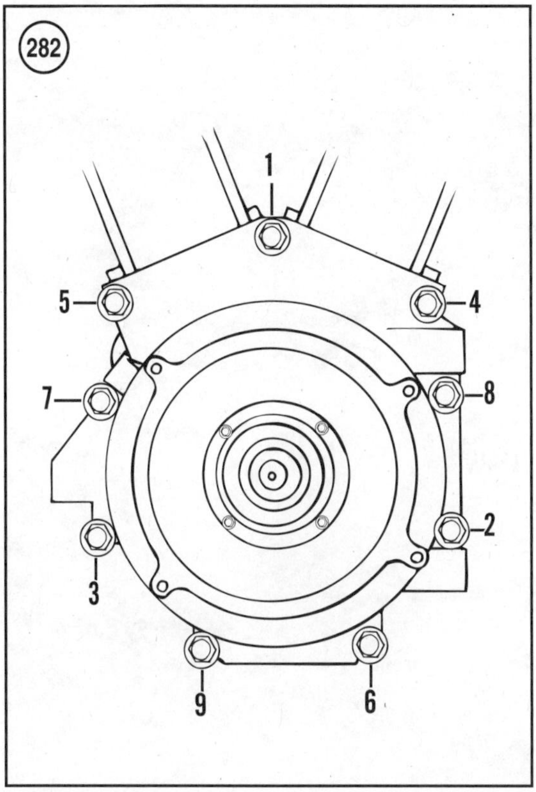

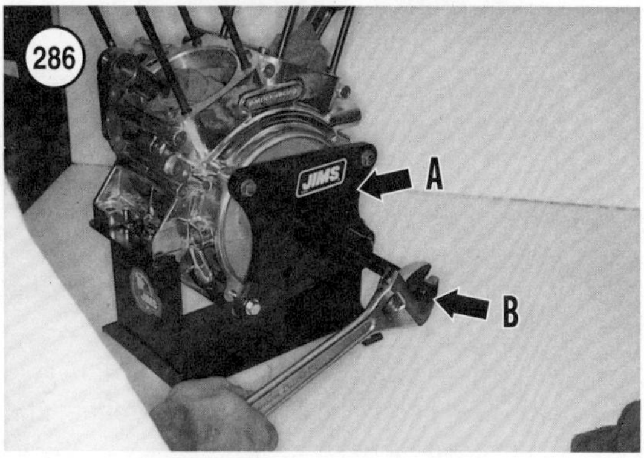

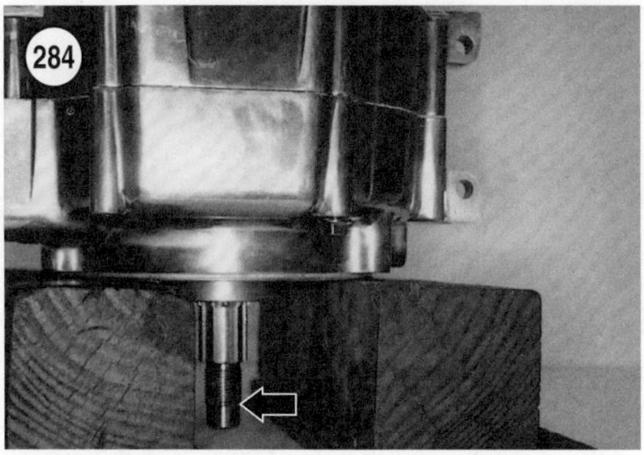

so the case can be separated in the following steps.

4. Secure the engine stand to the workbench so it cannot move.

5. Using the torque pattern shown in **Figure 282**, loosen in two to three stages, then remove the bolts from the left side of the crankcase (**Figure 283**).

6. Place the crankcase assembly on wooden blocks with the camshaft cover (left side) facing up. Use wooden blocks thick enough so the right side of the crankshaft clears the workbench surface (**Figure 284**).

7. Tap around the perimeter of the crankcase with a plastic mallet and remove the left crankcase half (**Figure 285**).

8. If the crankcase halves will not separate easily, perform the following:

   a. Install a flywheel press (A, **Figure 286**) onto the left side of the crankcase, following the manufacturer's instructions.

   b. Make sure the right side engine stand bolts (A, **Figure 287**) are not installed onto the crankcase half.

c. Apply clean engine oil, or press lube, to the end of the center screw and install it into the tool.

CAUTION
Do not use a hand impact driver or air impact wrench on the center screw, as they will damage the crankcase halves, as well as the tool.

d. Slowly turn the center screw with a wrench (B, **Figure 286**) 1/2 turn at a time. After each turn, tap on the end of the center screw with a brass mallet to relieve the stress on the center screw and the tool.
e. Repeat substep d until the center screw turns freely and the crankcase halves begin to separate (B, **Figure 287**).
f. Remove the crankcase from the engine stand.
g. Remove the right side crankcase half (**Figure 288**).
h. Remove the special tool from the left side crankcase unless the crankshaft is going to be removed in Step 10.

9. Remove the locating dowels and O-rings (**Figure 289**) from the right side crankcase.

WARNING
Wear safety glasses when pressing out the crankshaft.

CAUTION
Do not remove the crankshaft by using a hammer to drive it out of the crankcase half.

10A. If a hydraulic press is available, press the crankshaft out of the right crankcase half as follows:

a. Support the right crankcase half in a press on wooden blocks with the outer surface facing up.
b. Center the press ram onto the end of the crankshaft, then press the crankshaft out of the right crankcase half. Have an assistant support the crankshaft as it is being pressed out.
c. Remove the crankshaft.
d. Remove the right crankcase half from the press bed and take to workbench for further service.

10B. If a hydraulic press is not available, perform the following:

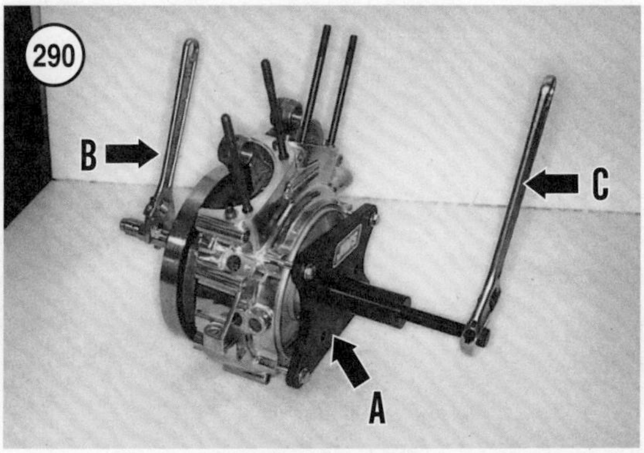

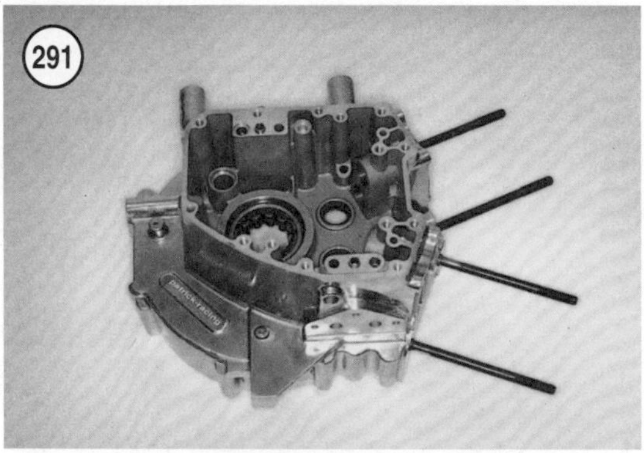
291

292

293

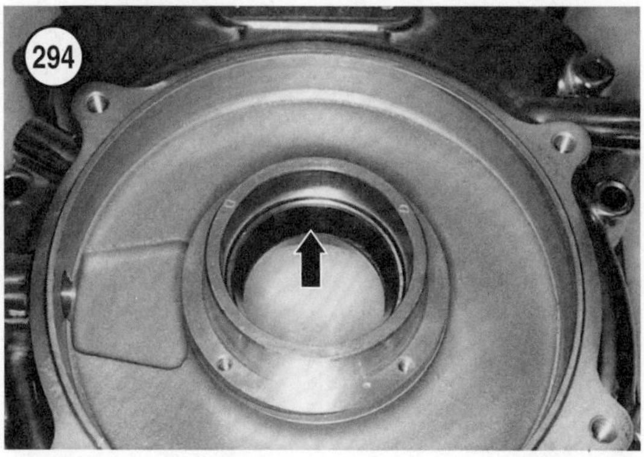
294

a. Install a flywheel press onto the left side of the crankcase, following the manufacturer's instructions (A, **Figure 290**).

b. Apply clean engine oil, or press lube, to the end of the center screw and install it into the tool.

CAUTION
Do not use a hand impact driver or air impact wrench on the center screw, as they will damage the crankcase as well as the tool.

c. Secure the right side of the crankshaft with a wrench (B, **Figure 290**) to prevent it from rotating in the following step.

d. Slowly turn the center screw with a wrench (C, **Figure 290**) 1/2 turn at a time. After each turn, tap on the end of the center screw with a brass mallet to relieve the stress on the center screw and the tool.

e. Repeat substep d until the center screw pushes the crankshaft out of the left side crankcase half.

f. Remove the special tool from the left side crankcase half.

11. To remove the left side crankshaft outer roller bearing and oil seal assembly, perform the following:

a. Place the left side crankcase on the workbench with the outer surface facing up.

b. Carefully pry the sprocket shaft spacer out of the oil seal.

c. Carefully pry the oil seal out of the crankcase using a wide-blade screwdriver. Support the screwdriver with a rag to prevent damaging the crankcase.

d. Lift the outer roller bearing from the crankcase.

Crankcase Cleaning and Inspection

1. Clean both case halves in solvent and dry with compressed air.
2. Apply a light coat of oil to the races to prevent rust.
3. Inspect the right side (**Figure 291**) and left side (**Figure 292**) case halves for cracks or other damage.
4. Inspect the case studs (**Figure 293**) for damage. If necessary, replace studs as described under *Cylinder Stud Replacement* in this chapter.
5. Inspect the left side main bearing races. Refer to **Figure 294** for the outer bearing race and **Figure**

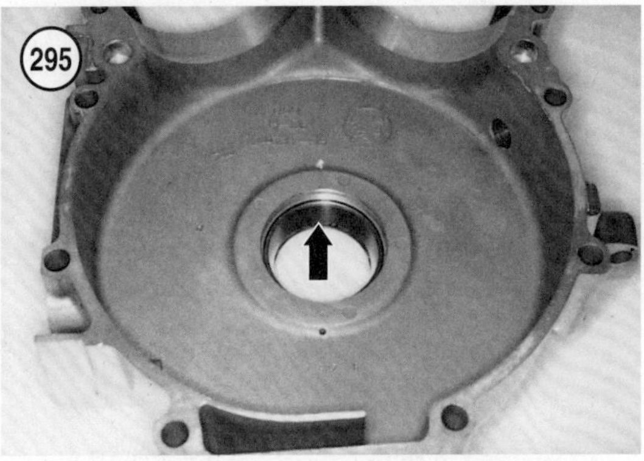

295 for the inner bearing race. Also, check the roller bearings for wear or damage. The bearings must turn smoothly with no roughness. If any of these parts are worn, replace the bearing assembly as described under *Left Side Main Bearing Assembly Replacement* in this chapter.

6. Inspect the right side main needle bearing (**Figure 296**) for wear or damage. The bearing must turn smoothly with no roughness. If damaged, replace the bearing assembly as described under *Right Side Main Bearing Replacement* in this chapter.

7. Inspect the camshaft needle bearings (**Figure 297**) in the right side crankcase for damage. To replace this bearing, refer to *Camshaft Support Plate* in this chapter.

8. Inspect the valve lifter bore receptacles (**Figure 298**) for wear or damage. Refer to *Valve Lifters* in this chapter.

NOTE

If the original piston cooling jets are being reinstalled, apply Loctite No. 222 (purple) or an equivalent threadlocking compound to the screw threads prior to installation.

9. Make sure the piston cooling jets (**Figure 299**) are clear. If necessary, remove the T20 Torx mounting screws, remove the cooling jets and O-rings. Clean the oil jets with compressed air. Install *new* O-rings and tighten the screws securely.

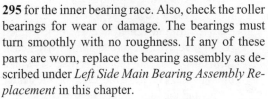

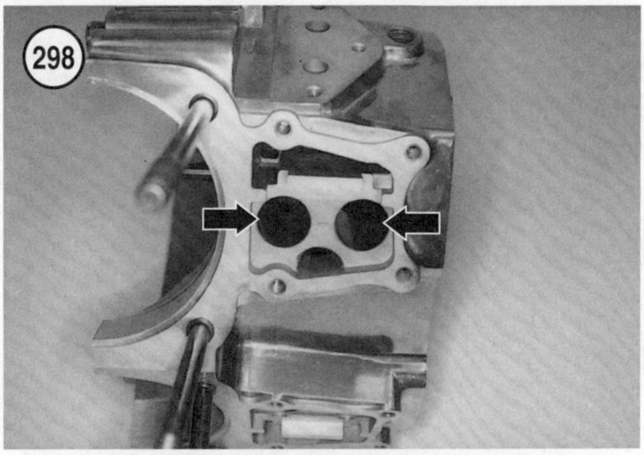

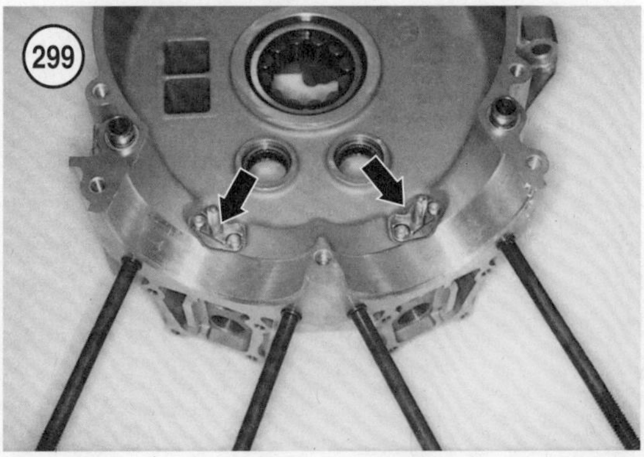

Crankshaft and Connecting Rods Cleaning and Inspection

If any portion of the crankshaft and/or connecting rods are worn or damaged, they must be replaced as

300

301

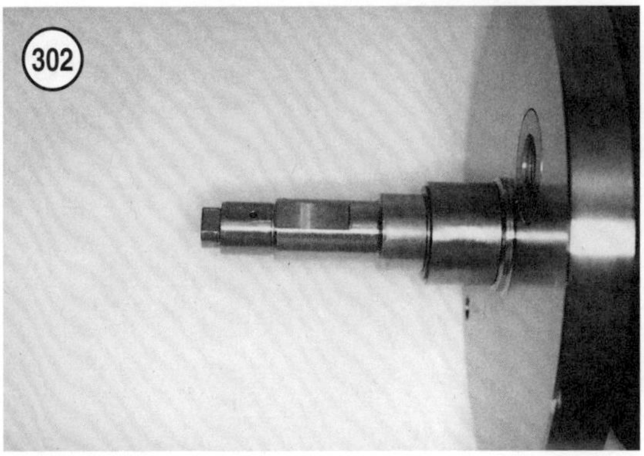
302

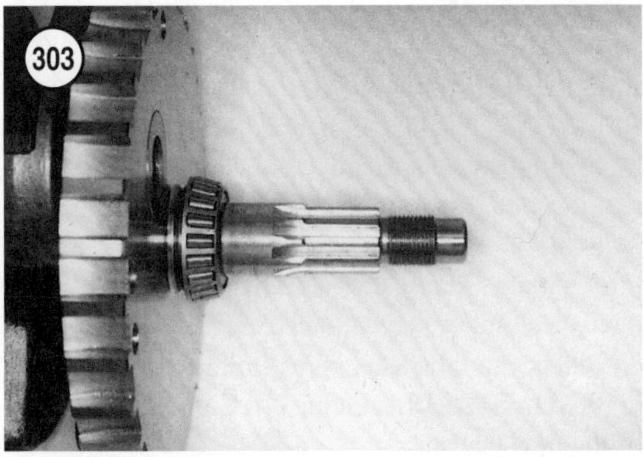
303

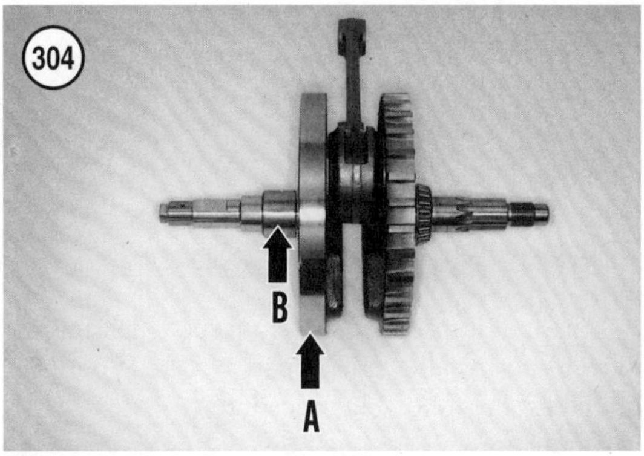

304

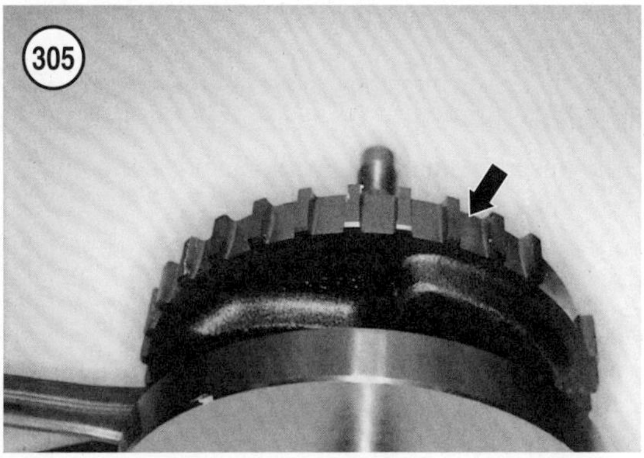
305

one assembly. If necessary, have the crankshaft overhauled by a Harley-Davidson dealership.

1. Clean the crankshaft assembly in solvent and dry thoroughly with compressed air.

2. Hold the shank portion of each connecting rod where it attaches to the crankshaft (**Figure 300**). Pull up and down on each connecting rod. Any slight amount of up and down movement indicates excessive lower bearing wear. If there is movement, the crankshaft must be overhauled.

3. Measure connecting rod sideplay with a feeler gauge (**Figure 301**) and check against the service limit in **Table 2**.

4. Inspect the right side (pinion shaft) (**Figure 302**) and the left side (sprocket shaft) (**Figure 303**) for excessive wear or damage.

5. Support the crankshaft on a truing stand or in a lathe and check runout at the flywheel outer rim (A, **Figure 304**) and at the pinion shaft (B) with a dial indicator. If the runout exceeds the service limit in **Table 2**, have the crankshaft trued or overhauled.

6. Inspect the crankshaft position sensor timing teeth (**Figure 305**) on the left side flywheel for damaged or missing teeth.

7. On 2001 models only, make sure the retaining ring (**Figure 306**) is secure on the right side of the crankshaft.

Right Side Main Bearing Replacement

A hydraulic press and a crankshaft bearing remover and installer (JIMS part No. 1275) are required for the following procedure.

Removal

1. Remove the main bearing retaining ring (**Figure 307**) from one side of the bearing as follows:
   a. Insert a small screwdriver under one end of the retaining ring.
   b. Push the end toward the bearing bore.
   c. Raise the end of the ring up and out of the crankcase groove.
   d. Work around the circumference of the ring and pull it out of the groove.
   e. Discard the retaining ring as it *cannot* be reused.
2. Turn the crankcase half over and repeat Step 1 and remove the remaining retaining ring (A, **Figure 308**). Discard the retaining ring as it *cannot* be reused.

NOTE
The JIMS support tube is marked with either REMOVER or INSTALLER side.

3. Place the support tube with the side marked REMOVER facing up on the press bed.
4. Position the right side crankcase with the outer surface facing up and position the bearing directly over the support tube on the press bed.
5. Install the pilot shaft (**Figure 309**) through the bearing and into the support tube.
6. Center the press driver over the pilot shaft.
7. Hold the crankcase half parallel to the press bed and have an assistant slowly apply press pressure on the pilot shaft until the bearing is free from the case half.
8. Remove the case half and special tools from the press bed.

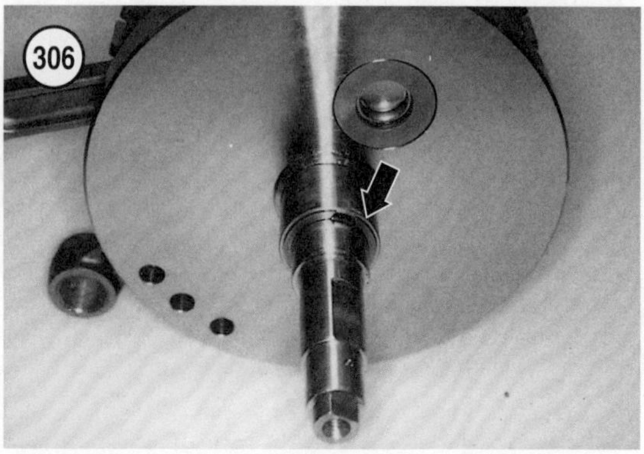
306

307

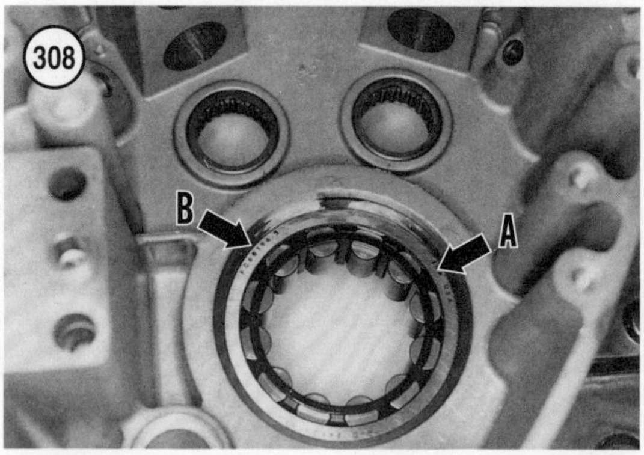

308

Installation

1. Apply a light coat of clean engine oil to the outer surface of the bearing and to the crankcase receptacle.
2. Position the right side crankcase with the outer surface facing up on the press bed.
3. Position the new bearing with the manufacturer's marks facing up (B, **Figure 308**) and place it over the crankcase receptacle.
4. Place the JIMS support tube with the side marked INSTALLER facing up (**Figure 310**) on top of the new bearing.

309

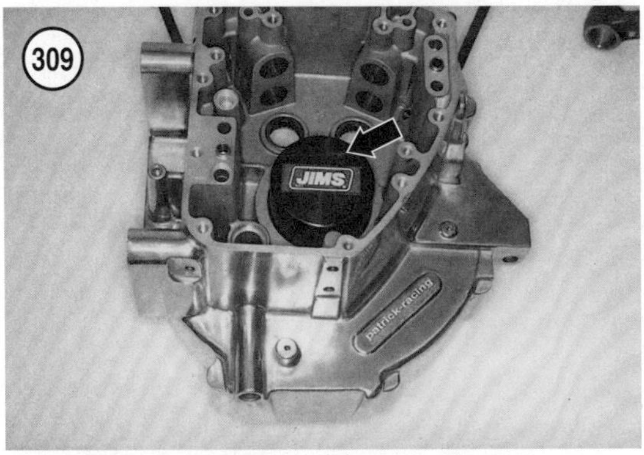

310

311

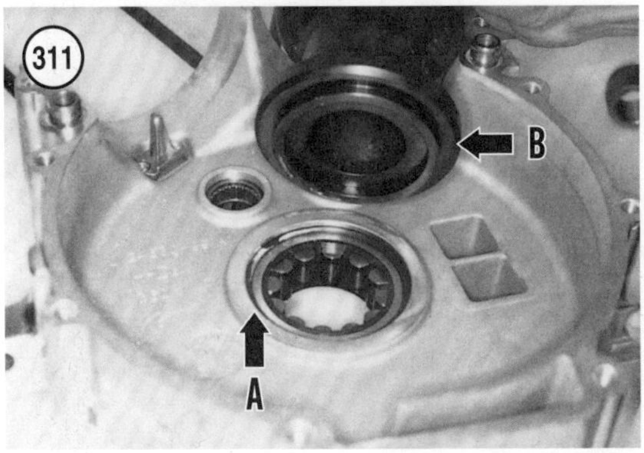

5. Center the press driver over the support tube.

6. Slowly apply press pressure on the support tube, pressing the bearing into the crankcase. Apply pressure until the support tube contacts the crankcase surface. This will correctly locate the bearing within the crankcase (A, **Figure 311**). Remove the support tube (B).

7. Remove the crankcase from the press bed.

8. Check on each side of the crankcase to make sure the bearing is centered within the receptacle. The retaining ring groove must be visible on each side of the bearing. If not, reposition the bearing until it is centered correctly.

WARNING
The edges of the new retaining rings are sharp. Wear shop gloves.

CAUTION
Both new retaining rings must be installed correctly to properly secure the bearing in the crankcase half.

9. Install a *new* retaining ring (**Figure 307**) onto each side of the new bearing as follows:
   a. Position the new retaining ring with the center of the closed end going into the ring groove.
   b. Press the center of the closed end into the groove and hold it there to keep it within the ring groove.
   c. Alternating from side-to-side, using a small screwdriver, press the retaining ring into the ring groove, working with a small section at a time.
   d. Continue to work around the circumference until the retaining ring is completely installed within the ring groove. Make sure the retaining ring is correctly seated in the ring groove.

10. Turn the crankcase half over and repeat Step 8 for the other retaining ring (A, **Figure 308**).

11. Spin the bearing to make sure it rotates smoothly with no binding.

Left Side Main Bearing Assembly Replacement

The left main bearing assembly must be replaced as a complete set even if one bearing or race is damaged.

Tools

The following tools or their equivalents are required to remove and install the left side main bearing:

1. Hydraulic press.
2. Sprocket shaft bearing race tool (JIMS part No. 94547-80A)
3. Race and bearing installation tool handle (JIMS part No. 33416-80).

4. Snap ring removal and installation tool (JIMS part No. 1710).
5. Sprocket bearing race installation tool (JIMS part No. 2246).

Inner and outer bearing race replacement

NOTE

When replacing the bearing races in the following steps, do not remove the lock ring installed between the inner and outer bearing races. This ring is under heavy tension and will damage the bearing bore as it passes through it.

1. Place the crankcase on the workbench with the inboard surface facing up.
2. Install one half of the bearing race remover tool into the crankcase and push it against the inner bearing race (A, **Figure 312**).
3. Install the other half of the bearing race remover tool into the crankcase and push it against the inner bearing race (B, **Figure 312**).
4. Hold the bearing race remover tools in place and turn the crankcase over.
5. Insert the tool handle into the center of both race remover tools. Press it into place until the ring (**Figure 313**) is locked into both bearing race remover tools (**Figure 314**).
6. Support the left crankcase half on wooden blocks on the press bed with the tool handle facing up.
7. Center the press ram directly over the tool handle and slowly press the inner bearing race out the crankcase.
8. Remove the crankcase and special tools from the press bed.
9. Place the crankcase on the workbench with the outboard surface facing up.
10. Install one half of the bearing race remover tool into the crankcase and push it against the outer bearing race (A, **Figure 315**).
11. Install the other half of the bearing race remover tool into the crankcase and push it against the outer bearing race (B, **Figure 315**).
12. Hold the bearing race remover tools in place and turn the crankcase over.
13. Insert the tool handle into the race remover tools. Press it into place until the ring (**Figure 313**) is locked into both bearing race remover tools (**Figure 316**).

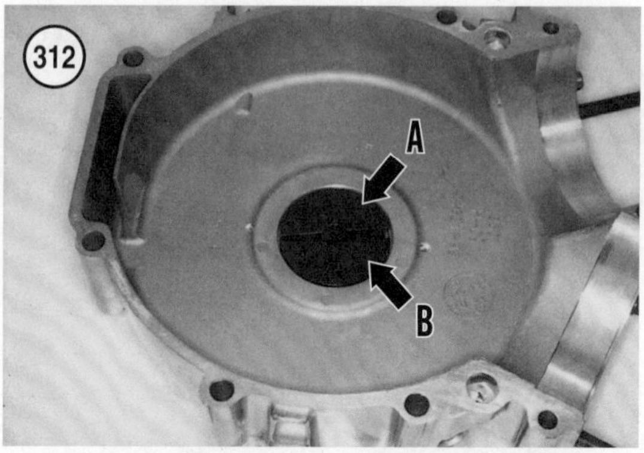

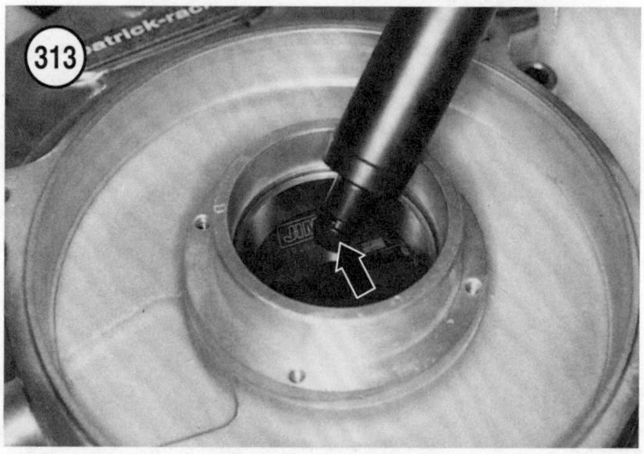

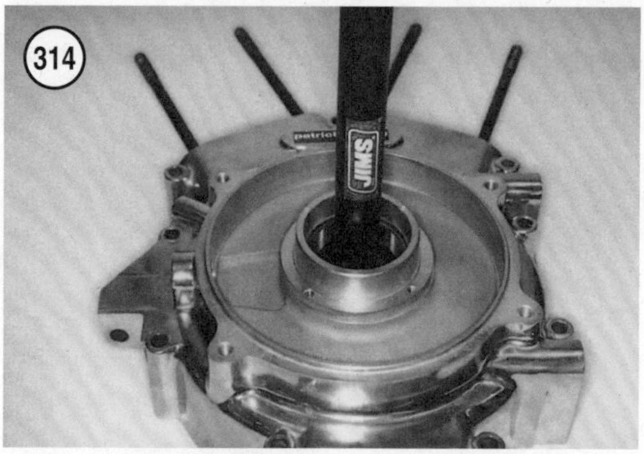

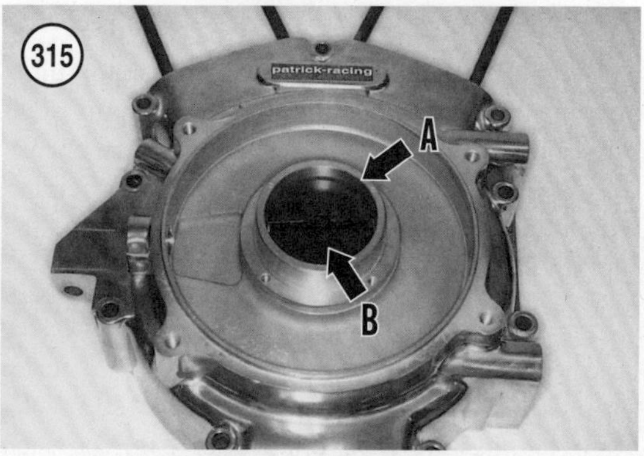

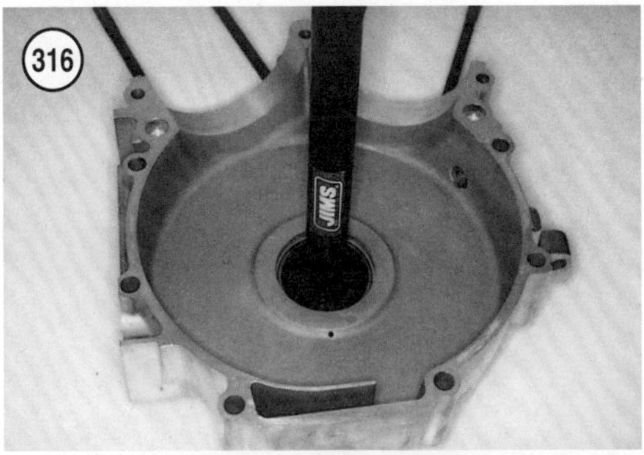

316

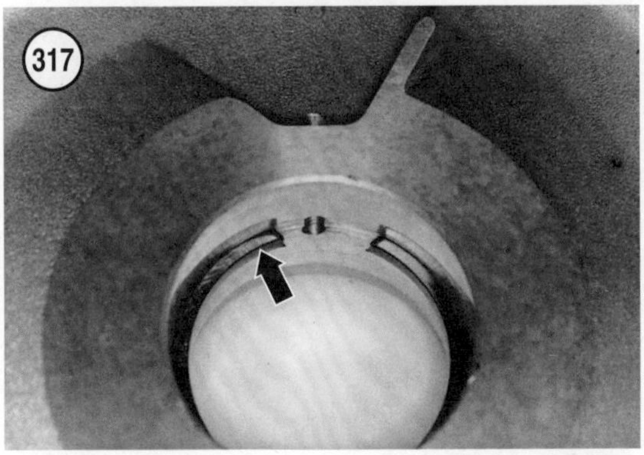

317

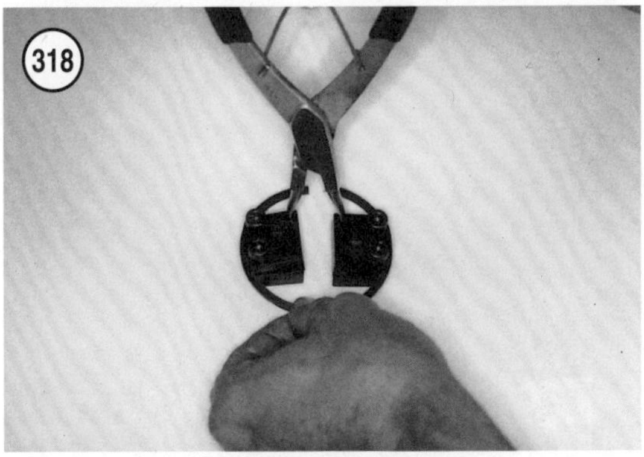

318

319

14. Support the left crankcase half on wooden blocks on the press bed with the tool handle facing up.

15. Center the press ram directly over the tool handle and slowly press the outer bearing race out of the crankcase.

16. Remove the crankcase and special tools from the press bed.

17. Clean the crankcase half in solvent and dry with compressed air.

18. Check the lock ring (**Figure 317**) for looseness or damage. If the lock ring is loose or damaged, perform the following:

   a. Place the crankcase on a workbench with the outboard side facing up.
   b. With the gap of the lock ring at the 12 o'clock position, install the special tool clamps onto each side of the lock ring at the 10 o'clock and 2 o'clock positions.
   c. Securely tighten the 9/16 in. Allen screws securing the clamps to the lock ring.
   d. Use snap ring pliers with straight tips and install them in one of the holes in each clamp.
   e. Squeeze the pliers, compress the lock ring and withdraw it from the crankcase groove.
   f. Remove the clamps from the old lock ring and install them onto the new lock ring.
   g. Squeeze the pliers (**Figure 318**) and insert the lock ring into the crankcase groove.
   h. Check that the lock ring gap is centered with the crankcase oil hole as shown in **Figure 317**.

NOTE

Install both races with their larger diameter side facing out. Install the bearing races with the same tool used to remove the old ones.

19. Apply clean engine oil, or press lube, to the bearing receptacles in the crankcase and to the outer surface of the inner bearing races.

20. Position the installer base with the large end facing up and place it on the press bed.

21. Position the crankcase with the outboard surface facing up.

22. Install the crankcase onto the installer base (**Figure 319**) until the crankcase retaining ring rests on top of the installer base.

23. Install the outboard outer race into position on the crankcase receptacle.

24. Apply clean engine oil, or press lube, to the shaft of the pressing plug and install the pressing

plug into the installer base (**Figure 320**). Push it down onto the bearing outer race.
25. Center the press ram directly over the pressing plug and slowly press the outer bearing race into the outboard surface of the crankcase until it touches the retaining ring (**Figure 321**).
26. Remove the crankcase and special tools from the press.
27. Turn the crankcase over and repeat Steps 23-26 for the inboard outer bearing race.

Crankshaft inner sprocket shaft bearing replacement

A sprocket shaft bearing cone installer (part No. HD-997225-55B) is required to install the sprocket shaft bearing (**Figure 322**).
1. Support the crankshaft with the bearing side facing up.
2. Install the bearing splitter under the bearing (**Figure 323**) and tighten securely.
3. Attach a bearing puller onto the splitter (**Figure 324**).
4. Slowly tighten the center screw and withdraw the bearing off the crankshaft shoulder.
5. Remove the bearing remover, splitter and bearing from the crankshaft.
6. Clean the sprocket shaft with contact cleaner. Check the sprocket shaft for cracks or other damage. If damaged, refer service to a Harley-Davidson dealership.
7. Slide the new bearing over the sprocket shaft.
8. Refer to **Figure 325** and press the new bearing as follows:
   a. Apply clean graphite lubricant to the installer's pilot shaft threads, flat washer and the bearing.
   b. Thread the pilot shaft (A) onto the crankshaft until it contacts the crankshaft shoulder.
   c. Slide the sleeve (B) over the pilot shaft until it contacts the bearing inner race.
   d. Install the tool's bearing (C) and washer (D) over pilot shaft and onto the top of the sleeve.
   e. Thread the handle (E) onto the pilot shaft (A).
   f. Slowly tighten the handle clockwise until the bearing bottoms on the crankshaft shoulder.
   g. Unscrew and remove all parts of the bearing installer.

320

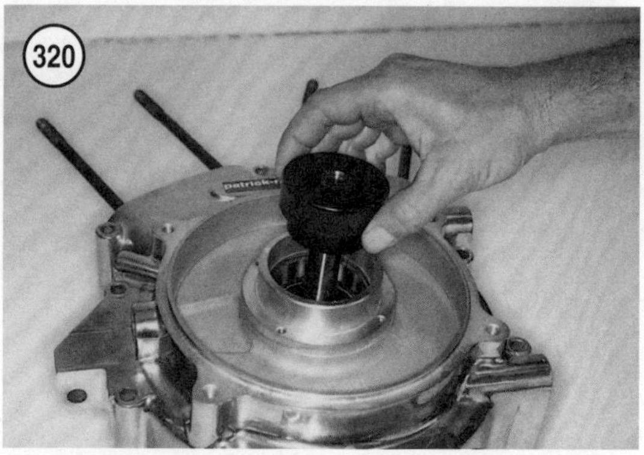

321

322

323

324

325

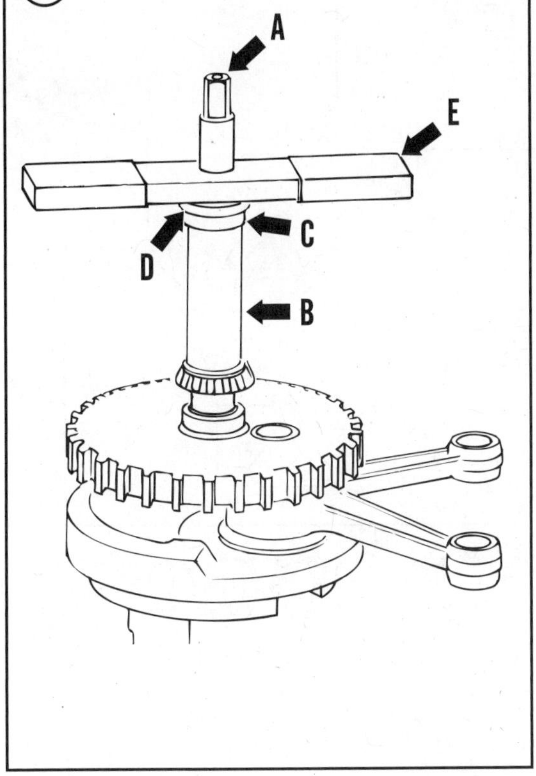

Crankshaft End Play Inspection

Correct crankshaft end play is critical. The end play must be between 0.001-0.005 in. (0.025-0.127 mm). End play is determined by the thickness of the shim between the inner and outer bearings on the left side. **Table 6** lists the shim part numbers and thickness.

If the end play was measured before disassembly and within specification, and the same components are reinstalled, then the same size shim can be reinstalled as a starting point.

Carefully measure the end play as described in Step 11. If there is any doubt about your abilities to properly set up the crankshaft end play, refer this procedure to a H-D dealership.

Tools

The following tools or their equivalents are required assemble the crankcase halves:

1. Sprocket shaft bearing installation tool (JIMS part No. 97225-55).
2. Crankshaft guide (JIMS part No. 1288).
3. Engine stand (JIMS part No. 1022).

Procedure

Refer to **Figure 326**.

1. Position the crankshaft with the left side facing up.
2. Apply clean engine oil or assembly lube to the inner bearing (**Figure 321**) and to the left side crankcase inner bearing race.
3. Install the shim of the specified thickness (see *Crankshaft End Play Inspection*) onto the inner bearing inner race.
4. Place the left crankcase half over the crankshaft sprocket and onto the inner bearing.
5. Make sure the connecting rods are correctly positioned within the crankcase openings as shown in **Figure 327**.
6. Make sure the crankcase is located correctly onto the crankshaft inner bearing.
7. Install the outer roller bearing onto the crankshaft (**Figure 328**) and push it into the outer bearing race.
8. Install the sprocket shaft bearing installation tool onto the crankshaft following the manufacturer's instructions.
9. Hold onto the handle (A, **Figure 329**) and tighten the large nut with a wrench (B). Tighten the large nut until the outer bearing is seated correctly and makes firm contact with the shim installed in Step 3.
10. Remove the special tools and make sure the outer bearing is seated correctly (**Figure 330**).

(326)

CRANKCASE ASSEMBLY

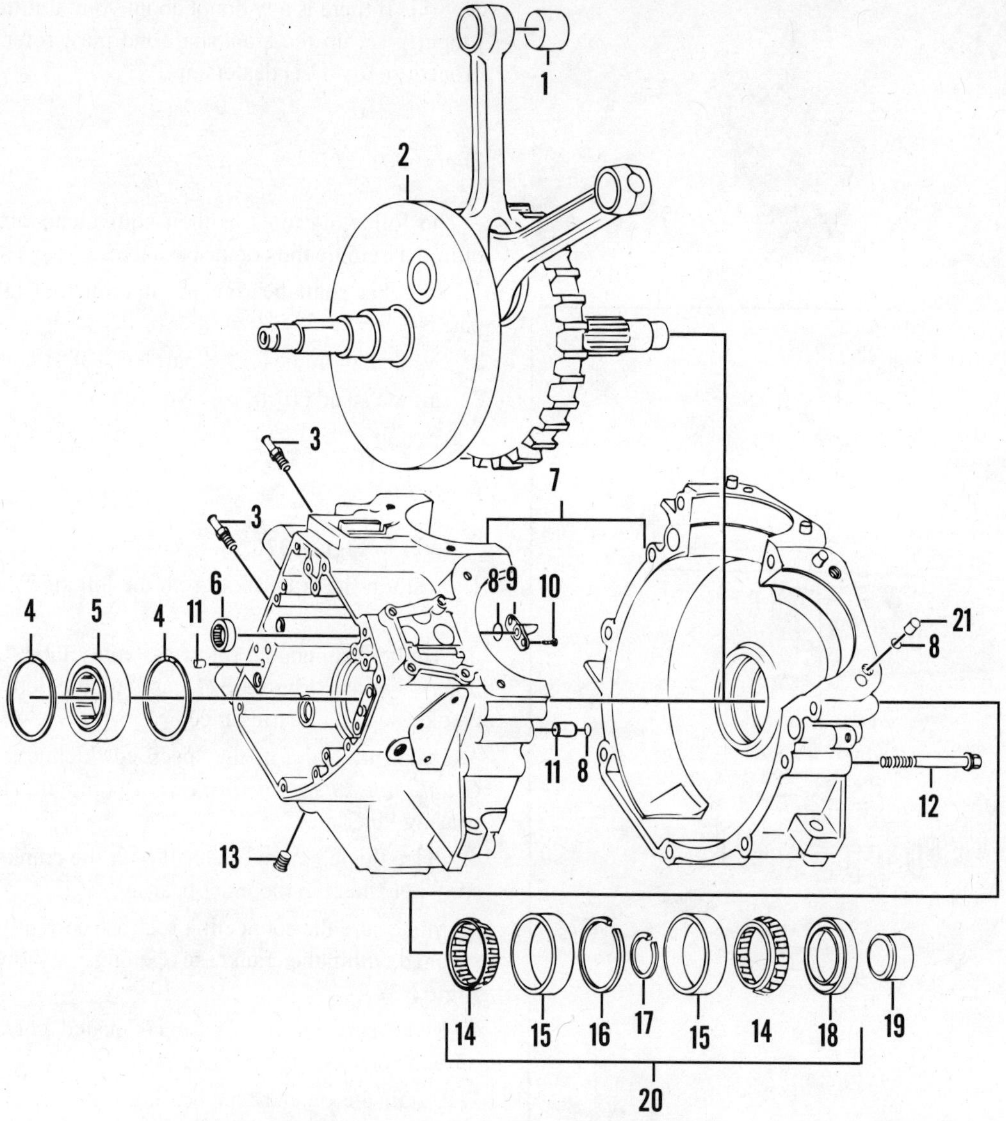

1. Connecting rod bushing
2. Crankshaft assembly
3. Oil hose fitting
4. Retaining ring
5. Right side main bearing
6. Needle bearing–camshaft
7. Crankcase assembly
8. O-ring
9. Piston cooling jet
10. Screw
11. Locating dowel
12. Bolt
13. Plug
14. Bearing
15. Bearing race
16. Lock ring
17. Spacer ring
18. Oil seal
19. Sprocket shaft spacer
20. Left side main bearing (sprocket shaft) assembly
21. Locating dowel

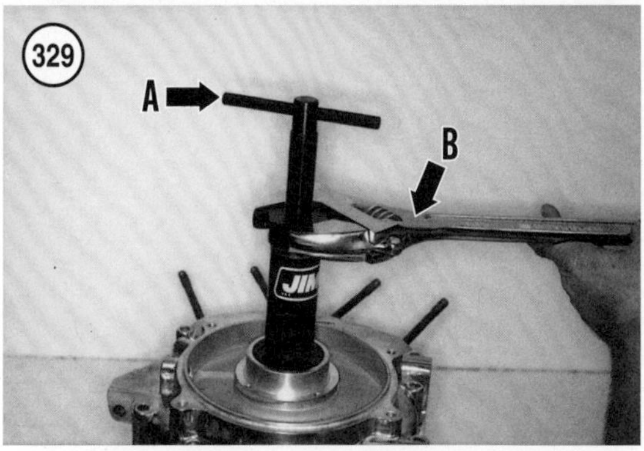

NOTE
The double check of the end play check is important to ensure correct crankshaft end play.

11. Check crankshaft end play as follows:
   a. Securely attach a dial indicator to the left crankcase half (A, **Figure 331**).
   b. Position the dial indicator contact pointer on the end of the crankshaft (B, **Figure 331**).
   c. Push down hard on the crankcase (C, **Figure 331**) while turning it back and forth.
   d. Hold the crankcase down and zero the dial gauge.
   e. Pull up on the crankcase as far as it will go while turning it back and forth. Note the dial indicator reading.
   f. Repeat this step several times and note the readings. They should all be the same.
   g. The end play must be within 0.001-0.005 in. (0.025-0.127 mm). If the end play is incorrect, the shim must be replaced using a shim of a different thickness. **Table 6** lists the various thickness shims and their part numbers.
   h. Remove the dial indicator.

12. Turn the crankcase assembly over and place it on wooden blocks (**Figure 332**) thick enough so the left side of the crankshaft clears the workbench surface.

13. Install the locating dowels and *new* O-rings (**Figure 333**) into both locations (**Figure 334**) in the right crankcase half. Apply clean engine oil to the O-rings.

14. Install the crankshaft guide (**Figure 335**) over the crankshaft.

15. Thoroughly clean and dry both crankcase gasket surfaces before applying the gasket sealer in Step 16.
16. Apply a thin coat of a non-hardening gasket sealer to the crankcase mating surfaces. Use one of the following gasket sealers:
    a. Harley-Davidson crankcase sealant (part No. HD-99650-81).
    b. 3M #800 sealant.
    c. ThreeBond Liquid Gasket 1104.
17. Align the crankcase halves and carefully lower the right crankcase half onto the crankshaft and left crankcase half (**Figure 336**). Press it down until it is seated correctly on the locating dowels. If necessary, carefully tap the perimeter of the right crankcase half until it is seated around the entire perimeter (**Figure 337**).

CAUTION
When properly aligned, the crankcase halves will fit snugly against each other around the entire perimeter. If they do not meet correctly, do not attempt to pull the case halves together with the mounting bolts. Separate the crankcase assembly and investigate the cause of the interference.

18. Place the crankcase assembly in an engine stand (A, **Figure 338**). Secure the engine stand to the workbench so it cannot move.
19. Install the nine crankcase bolts into the left crankcase half (B, **Figure 338**) and tighten as follows:
    a. Alternately tighten the nine bolts finger-tight.
    b. Using the torque pattern shown in **Figure 339**, tighten the bolts to 10 ft.-lb. (14 N•m).
    c. Using the same sequence tighten the bolts to 15-19 ft.-lb. (20-26 N•m).

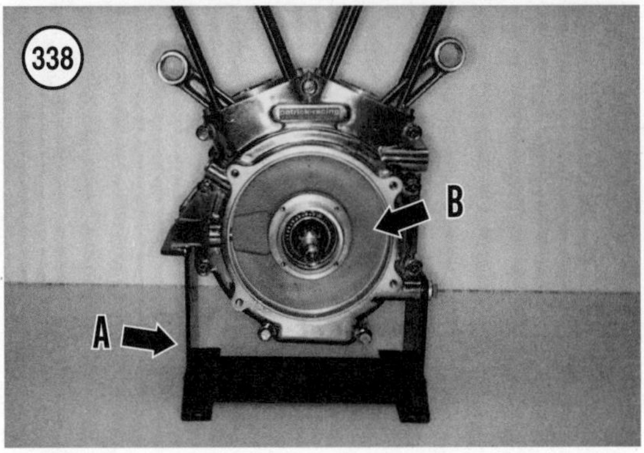

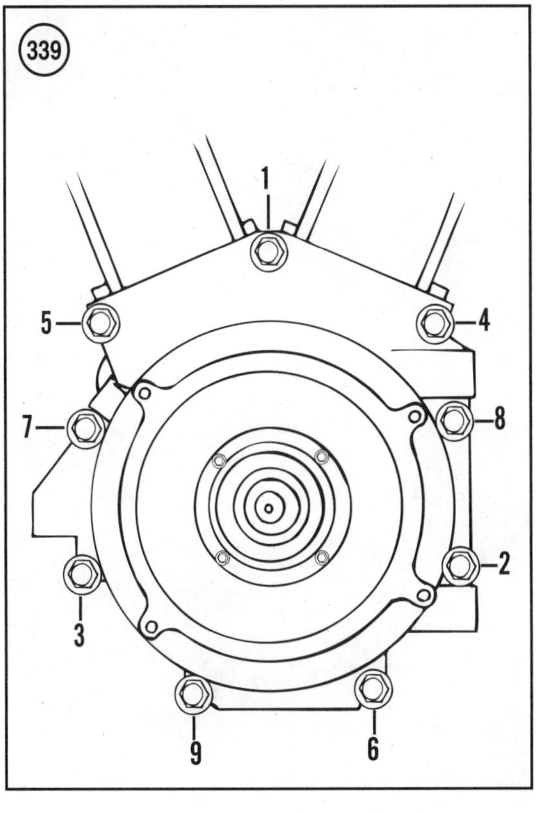

20. Install the left crankcase oil seal as described in the following procedure.
21. Apply clean engine oil to the outer surface of the sprocket shaft spacer and install it onto the crankshaft and into the oil seal (**Figure 340**).
22. Install the following components as described in this chapter:
   a. Alternator rotor and stator assembly (Chapter Eight).
   b. Oil pump.
   c. Camshaft assembly.
   d. Pushrods and valve lifters.
   e. Pistons.
   f. Cylinder heads and cylinders.
23. Install the engine into the frame as described in this chapter.

Crankcase Left Side Oil Seal Replacement

A sprocket shaft seal installer tool (JIMS part No. 39361-69 or equivalent) is required to install the oil seal.

1. Remove the sprocket shaft spacer (**Figure 340**) from the crankshaft and the oil seal.
2. Carefully pry the old oil seal (**Figure 341**) out of the bearing bore.
3. Position the *new* oil seal with the open side facing out.
4. Install the oil seal onto the crankshaft (A, **Figure 342**) and center it within the bearing bore.
5. Apply clean engine oil or press lube to the special tool threads, both washers and the radial bearing.
6. Install the main body onto the crankshaft and screw it on until it stops (B, **Figure 342**).
7. Install the shaft seal installer tool following the manufacturer's instructions.

8. Hold onto the handle (A, **Figure 343**) of the main body and tighten the large nut (B) with a wrench. Tighten the large nut slowly and check that the oil seal (**Figure 344**) is entering straight into the bearing bore.

9. Tighten the large nut slowly until the shaft seal installer tool makes contact with the crankcase surface (**Figure 345**).

10. Remove the special tools.

11. Apply clean engine oil to the outer surface of the sprocket shaft spacer and install it onto the crankshaft and into the oil seal (**Figure 340**).

Cylinder Stud Replacement

Replace bent or otherwise damaged cylinder studs (**Figure 346**) to prevent cylinder block and cylinder head leaks.

1. If the engine lower end is assembled, block off the lower crankcase opening with clean shop cloths.

2A. If the stud has broken off with the top surface of the crankcase, remove it with a stud remover. Refer to Chapter One.

2B. If the stud is still in place, perform the following:

a. Thread a 3/8 in.-16 nut onto the top of the stud.
b. Thread an additional nut onto the stud and tighten it against the first nut so that they are locked.
c. Turn the bottom nut counterclockwise and unscrew the stud.

3. Clean the stud threads in the crankcase with a spiral brush, then clean with an aerosol parts cleaner. If necessary, clean the threads with an appropriate size tap.

NOTE

New studs may have a threadlocking compound patch already applied to the lower stud threads. If so, do not apply any additional locking compound to these studs.

4. If the new stud does not have the threadlocking compound patch, apply ThreeBond TB1360 or an equivalent to the lower stud threads.

NOTE

The cylinder studs have a shoulder on one end and this end must be installed next to the crankcase surface.

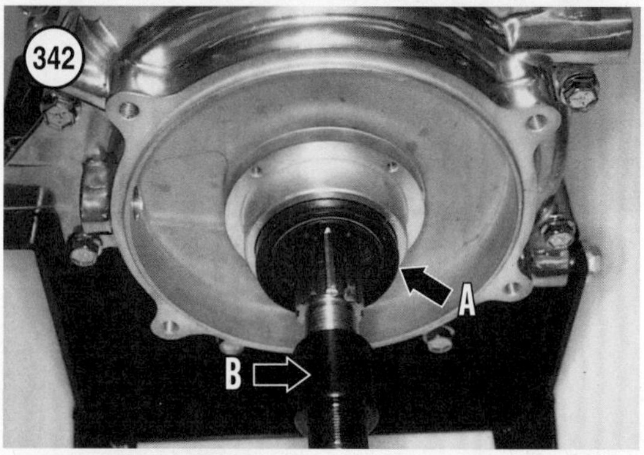

345

346

5. Place a 0.313 in. diameter steel ball (H-D part No. 8860) into a cylinder head bolt, then thread the bolt onto the end of the new stud without the collar.
6. Position the stud with the shoulder end going in first and hand-thread the new stud into the crankcase.

CAUTION
Do not use a breaker bar, ratchet or similar tool to install the studs. These tools may bend the stud and cause the engine to leak oil.

7. Hold the air impact wrench directly in-line with the stud. *Slowly* tighten the new stud with an air im-

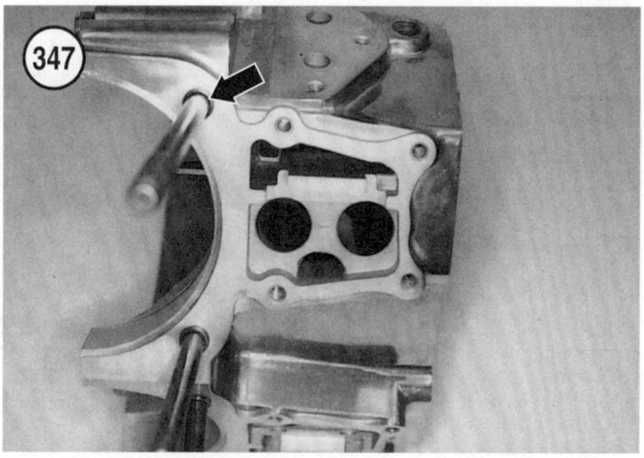
347

pact wrench until the stud shoulder (**Figure 347**) contacts the top surface of the crankcase.
8. Use a torque wrench and hand-tighten the stud to the torque specification listed in **Table 4**.
9. Remove the cylinder head bolt and steel ball from the cylinder stud.
10. Repeat for any additional studs.

ENGINE BREAK-IN

Following cylinder service (boring, honing, new rings) and major lower end work, the engine must be broken in just as though it were new. The service and performance life of the engine depends on a careful and sensible break-in.
1. For the first 50 mi. (80 km), maintain engine speed below 2500 rpm in any gear. However, do not lug the engine. Do not exceed 50 mph during this period.
2. From 50-500 mi. (80-804 km), vary the engine speed. Avoid prolonged steady running at one engine speed. During this period, increase engine speed to 3000 rpm. Do not exceed 55 mph during this period.
3. After the first 500 mi. (804 km), the engine break-in is complete.

Table 1 GENERAL ENGINE SPECIFICATIONS

Item	Specifications
Engine type	Four-stroke, 45° OHV V twin, Twin Cam 88
Bore and stroke	3.75 x 4.00 in. (95.25 x 101.6 mm)
Displacement	88 cubic inch (1450 cc)
Compression ratio	8.9 to 1
Torque	82 ft. lb. (111 N·m) @ 3500 rpm
Maximum sustained engine speed	5600 rpm

Table 1 GENERAL ENGINE SPECIFICATIONS (continued)

Item	Specifications
Engine weight	165 lbs. (74.8 kg)
Cooling system	Air cooled

Table 2 ENGINE SERVICE SPECIFICATIONS

Item	New in. (mm)	Service limit in. (mm)
Cylinder head		
Flatness limit	–	0.006 (0.15)
Valve guide fit in head	0.0020-0.0033 (0.051-0.084)	0.002 (0.051)
Valve seat fit in head	0.003-0.0045 (0.076-0.114)	0.002 (0.051)
Rocker arm		
Shaft fit in bushing	0.0005-0.0020 (0.013-0.051)	0.0035 (0.089)
Bushing fit in rocker arm	0.002-0.004 (0.051-0.102)	–
End clearance	0.003-0.013 (0.08-0.033)	0.025 (0.635)
Rocker arm shaft		
Shaft fit in rocker arm support	0.0007-0.0022 (0.018-0.056)	0.0035 (0.089)
Valves		
Valve stem-to-guide clearance		
Intake	0.0008-0.0026 (0.020-0.066)	–
Exhaust	0.0015-0.0033 (0.038-0.084)	–
Seat width	0.040-0.062 (1.02-1.58)	–
Valve stem protrusion	1.990-2.024 (50.55-51.41)	–
Valve springs		
Free length		
Outer	2.105-2.177 (53.47-55.3)	–
Inner	1.926-1.996 (48.9-50.7)	–
Piston-to-cylinder clearance	0.0006-0.0016 (0.015-0.041)	0.0016 (0.041)
Piston pin fit in piston	0.0001-0.0004 (0.003-0.010)	0.001 (0.025)
Piston rings		
Compression ring end gap		
Top ring	0.007-0.020 (0.178-0.508)	0.020 (0.508)
Second ring	0.007-0.020 (0.178-0.508)	0.024 (0.610)

(continued)

Table 2 ENGINE SERVICE SPECIFICATIONS (continued)

Item	New in. (mm)	Service limit in. (mm)
Oil control ring end gap	0.009-0.052 (0.23-1.32)	0.050 (1.27)
Compression ring side clearance		
Top ring	0.002-0.0045 (0.051-0.114)	0.0037 (0.09)
Second ring	0.0016-0.0041 (0.041-0.104)	0.0037 (0.09)
Oil control ring side clearance	0.0016-0.0076 (0.041-0.193)	0.0072 (0.18)
Cylinder		
Taper	– –	0.002 (0.05)
Cylinder		
Out of round	– –	0.003 (0.08)
Warpage		
At top (cylinder head)	–	0.006 (0.15)
At base (crankcase)	–	0.008 (0.20)
Cylinder bore		
Standard	–	3.753 (95.326)
Oversize 0.005 in.	–	3.758 (95.453)
Oversize 0.010 in.	–	3.763 (95.580)
Oversize 0.020 in.	–	3.773 (95.834)
Oversize 0.030 in.	–	3.783 (96.088)
Connecting rod		
Connecting rod-to-crankpin clearance	0.0004-0.0012 (0.0102-0.0305)	0.002 (0.05)
Piston pin clearance in connecting rod	0.0003-0.0007 (0.008-0.018)	0.002 (0.05)
Connecting rod side play	0.005-0.015 (0.13-0.38)	0.020 (0.51)
Hydraulic lifters		
Fit in guide	0.0008-0.0020 (0.02-0.05)	0.003 (0.076)
Roller fit	– –	0.0015 (0.038)
Roller end clearance	– –	0.026 (0.660)
Camshaft support plate		
Camshaft chain tensioner shoe	See text	
Camshaft support plate warpage		0.010 (0.25)
Camshaft bushing fit		0.0008-0.001 (0.0203-0.0254)

(continued)

Table 2 ENGINE SERVICE SPECIFICATIONS (continued)

Item	New in. (mm)	Service limit in. (mm)
Oil pump rotor		
tip clearance	–	0.004 (0.10)
Sprocket shaft Timken bearing		
Cup fit in crankcase	0.003-0.005 (0.08-0.13)	–
Cone fit on shaft	0.0005-0.0015 (0.013-0.038)	–
Crankshaft		
Runout (at flywheel rim)	0.000-0.010 (0.0-0.25)	0.015 (0.38)
Runout (at pinion shaft)	0.000-0.002 (0.0-0.05)	0.003 (0.08)
End play	0.001-0.005 (0.03-0.13)	0.002 (0.05)

Table 3 PUSH ROD AND LIFTER LOCATION

Cylinder	Lifter bore	Cylinder head/rocker housing bore
Front		
Intake	Inside	Rear
Exhaust	Outside	Front
Rear		
Intake	Inside	Front
Exhaust	Outside	Rear

Table 4 ENGINE TORQUE SPECIFICATIONS

Item	ft.-lb.	in.-lb.	N·m
Bearing retainer			
plate screws	–	20-30	2-3
Breather cover bolts	–	90-120	10-14
Camshaft cover screws	–	90-120	10-14
Camshaft support plate			
Allen bolt	–	90-120	10-14
Crankshaft position			
sensor screw	–	90-120	10-14
Crankshaft sprocket			
bolt	Refer to text		
Crankcase bolts	15-19	–	20-26
Cylinder head bolts	Refer to text		
Cylinder head			
bracket bolts	28-35	–	38-47
Cylinder stud	10-20	–	14-27
Engine oil drain plug	14-21	–	19-28
Front isolator			
mounting bolts	21-27	–	28-37
Left side footpeg			
bracket screws	25-30	–	34-41
Lifter cover bolts	–	90-120	10-14
Oil filter mount bolts	–	90-120	10-14

(continued)

Table 4 ENGINE TORQUE SPECIFICATIONS (continued)

Item	ft.-lb.	in.-lb.	N•m
Oil fitting	–	120-144	14-16
Oil line cover bolts	–	84-108	9-12
Oil pump screws	–	90-120	10-14
Pipe plug	–	120-144	14-16
Piston oil jet screw	–	20-30	2-3
Rear camshaft sprocket bolt	Refer to procedure in text		
Rear footpeg bracket screws	25-30	–	34-41
Rocker arm			
Support bolts	15-18	–	20-24
Housing bolts	–	124-168	14-19
Arm cover bolts	15-18	–	20-24
Shift lever pinch bolt	18-22	–	24-30
Sprocket shaft nut	150-165	–	203-224
Stabilizer link bolt	18-22	–	24-30
Horn bracket-to-cylinder head bolt	28-35	–	38-48
Transmission			
Mounting bolts			
Preliminary	15	–	20
Final	30-35	–	41-47
Drain plug	14-21	–	19-29

4

Table 5 REAR CAMSHAFT SPROCKET SPACERS

Part No.	in.	mm
25722-99	0.230	5.84
25723-99	0.240	6.10
25721-99	0.250	6.35
25719-99	0.260	6.60
25717-99	0.270	6.86

Table 6 CRANKSHAFT LEFT SIDE BEARING SPACER SHIM

Shim Part No.	in.	mm
9110	0.0905-0.0895	2.299-2.273
9120	0.0925-0.0915	2.350-2.324
9121	0.0945-0.0935	2.400-2.375
9122	0.0965-0.0955	2.451-2.426
9123	0.0985-0.0975	2.502-2.476
9124	0.1005-0.0995	2.553-2.527
9125	0.1025-0.1015	2.602-2.578
9126	0.1045-0.1035	2.654-2.629
9127	0.1065-0.1055	2.705-2.680
9128	0.1085-0.1075	2.756-2.731
9129	0.1105-0.1095	2.807-2.781
9130	0.1125-0.1115	2.858-2.932
9131	0.1145-0.1135	2.908-2.883

(continued)

Table 6 CRANKSHAFT LEFT SIDE BEARING SPACER SHIM (continued)

Shim Part No.	in.	mm
9132	0.1165-0.1155	2.959-2.934
9133	0.1185-0.1175	3.010-2.985
9134	0.1205-0.1195	3.061-3.035

NOTE: Refer to the Supplement at the back of this manual for information unique to 2002-on models.

CHAPTER FIVE

CLUTCH AND PRIMARY DRIVE

5

This chapter describes service procedures for the clutch and primary drive assemblies.

Tables 1-3 are at the end of the chapter.

Table 1 lists the clutch general specifications and sprocket sizes

Table 2 lists clutch torque specifications.

Table 3 lists sprocket alignment spacers.

PRIMARY CHAINCASE OUTER COVER

Removal

Refer to **Figure 1**.

NOTE

On models so equipped, always disarm the optional TSSM security system prior to disconnecting the battery or the siren will sound.

1. Disconnect the negative battery cable as described in Chapter Eight.

WARNING

Disconnect the negative battery cable before working on the clutch or any primary drive component to avoid accidentally activating the starter motor.

2. Remove the bolts securing the left side footpeg assembly (**Figure 2**) and remove the assembly.
3. Drain the primary chain oil as described in Chapter Three.

NOTE

Note the location of the inspection cover bolts. There are two different length bolts and they must be reinstalled in the correct location.

4A. On all models except FXDWG, perform the following:

a. Make an alignment mark (A, **Figure 3**) on the outer shift lever and the end of the inner shift lever shaft.

1

PRIMARY CHAINCASE

1. Oil seal
2. Chaincase inner housing
3. Snap ring
4. O-ring
5. Pin
6. Gasket
7. Bushing
8. Locking tab
9. Bolt
10. Washer
11. Chaincase cover
12. Clutch cover
13. Drain plug
14. Gasket
15. Inspection cover
16. Bearing

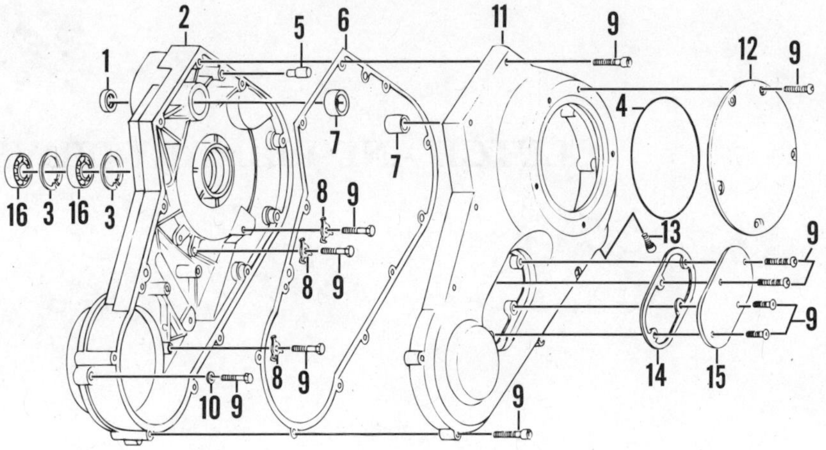

2

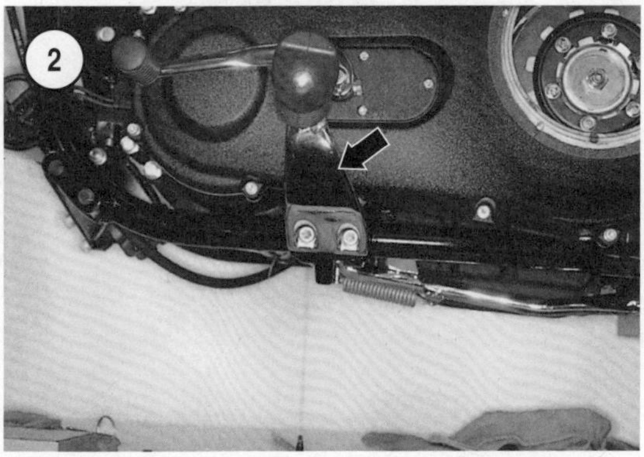

3

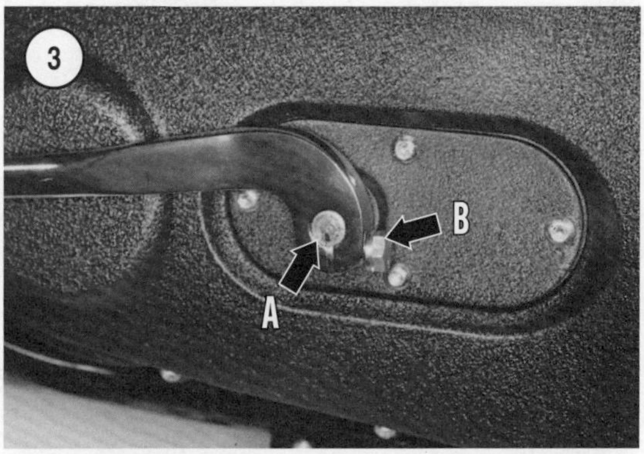

b. Remove the clamping bolt (B, **Figure 3**) and remove the outer shift lever.

c. Remove the screws and the inspection cover and gasket (**Figure 4**) from the primary chaincase cover.

4

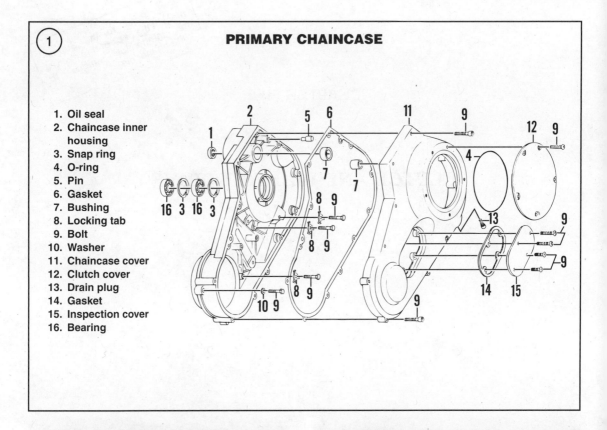

4B. On FXDWG models, remove the primary chain inspection cover and gasket.

5. Remove the bolts and washers securing the chaincase outer cover (**Figure 5**) and remove the chaincase outer cover. Note the location of the two different length bolts.

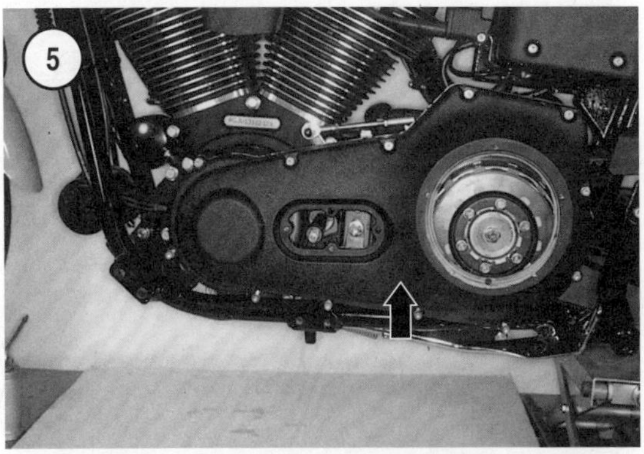

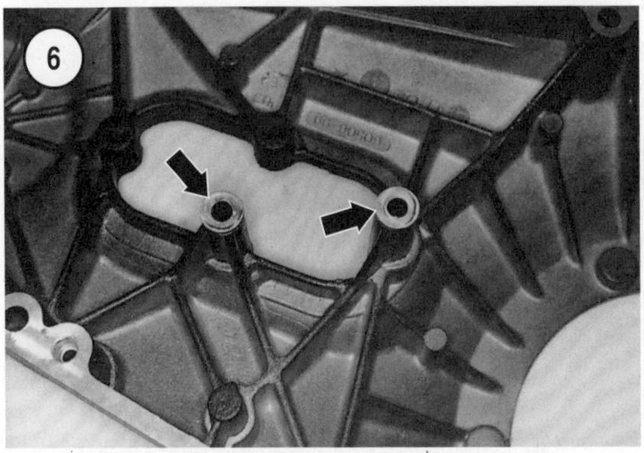

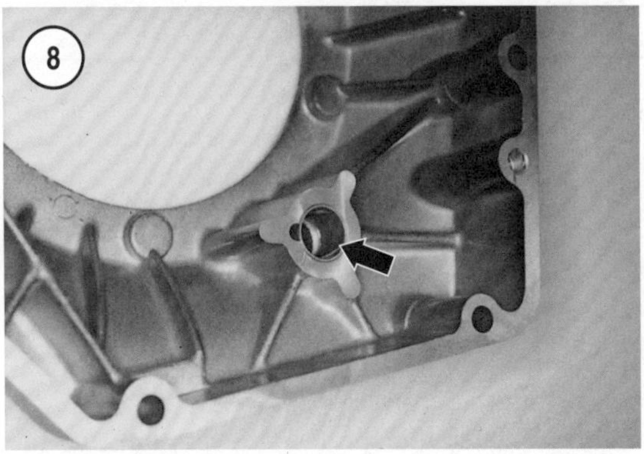

6. Remove the two round gaskets (**Figure 6**) installed between the chaincase outer cover and chaincase inner housing. The gaskets may stick to either part.
7. Remove the chaincase outer cover gasket.
8. Remove the dowel pins, if necessary.

Inspection

1. Remove all gasket residue from the chaincase outer cover (**Figure 7**) and chaincase inner housing gasket surfaces.
2. Clean the primary cover in solvent and dry with compressed air.
3. Inspect the chaincase outer primary cover for cracks or damage.
4. Inspect the starter jackshaft bushing (**Figure 8**) for excessive wear or damage. To replace the bushing, perform the following:
   a. Remove the bushing with a blind bearing removal tool.
   b. Clean the bushing bore in the housing.
   c. Press in the new bushing until its outer surface is flush with the edge of the bushing bore.

Installation

1. Install two *new* round gaskets (**Figure 6**) on the chaincase outer cover studs.
2. If removed, install the dowel pins (A, **Figure 9**) onto the chaincase inner housing.

CAUTION
Harley-Davidson specifies that a new Print-O-Seal gasket must be installed every time the chaincase outer cover is removed.

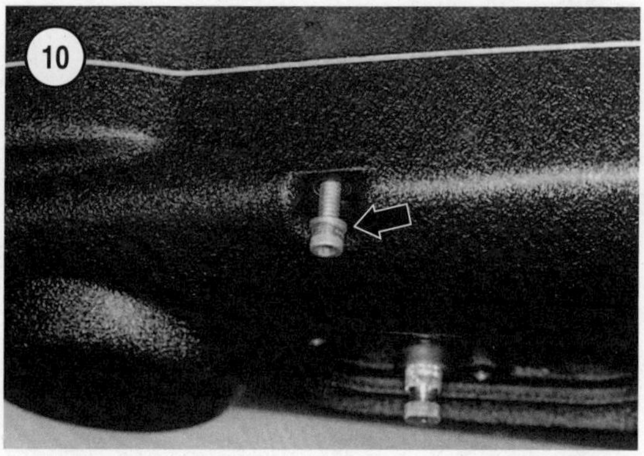

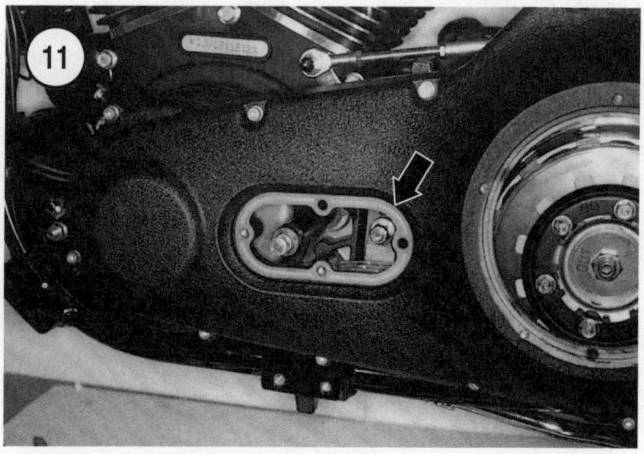

12

CLUTCH ASSEMBLY

1. Snap ring
2. Clutch shell and sprocket
3. Bearing
4. Snap ring
5. Clutch hub
6. Clutch nut
7. Diaphragm spring seat
8. Diaphragm spring
9. Friction disc B
10. Clutch plates
11. Friction disc A
12. Pressure plate
13. Damper spring
14. Damper spring retainer
15. Bolt
16. Release plate
17. Snap ring
18. Snap ring
19. Thrust washer
20. Radial bearing
21. Oil slinger
22. Pushrod (right side)
23. Pushrod (right side
24. Pushrod (left side)
25. Locknut

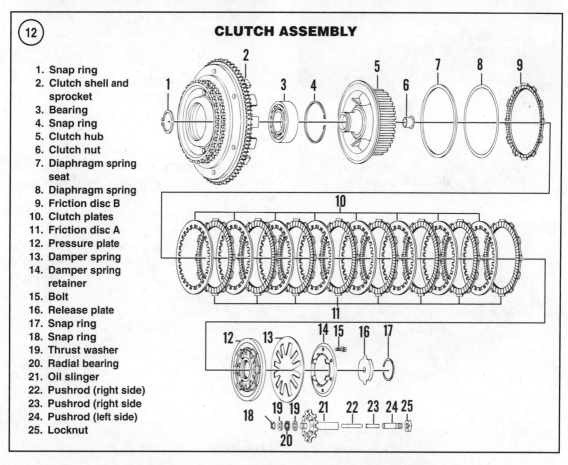

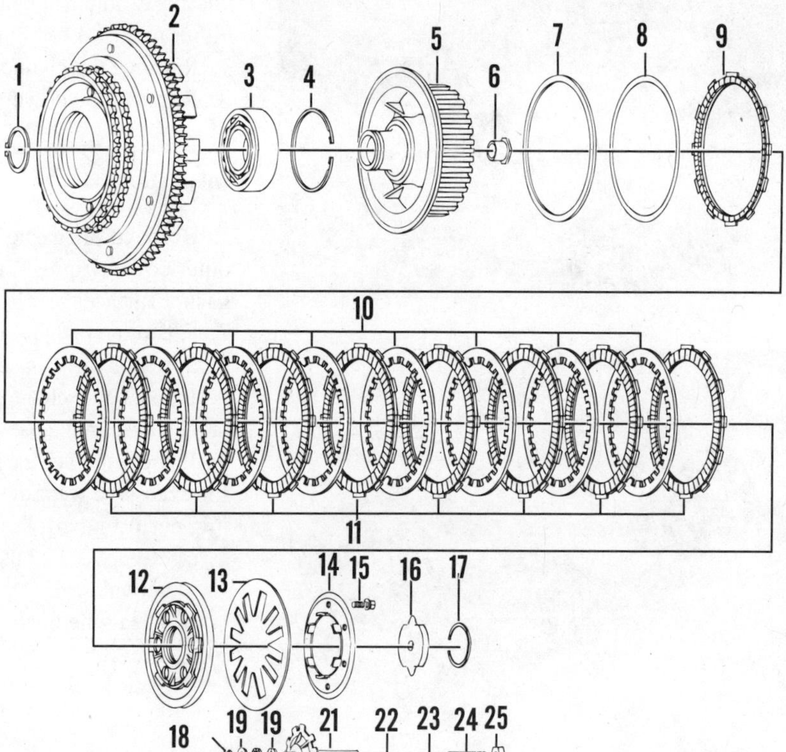

3. Install a *new* gasket (B, **Figure 9**) over the locating pins and seat it against the gasket surface of the chaincase inner housing.

4. Slide the primary cover (**Figure 5**) over the locating dowels and seat it flush against the gaskets.

NOTE

The gasket sealing surface is very thin and the overall size of the gasket is very large. The gasket may shift prior to installing the cover bolts, so make sure the gasket is positioned correctly while installing the cover bolts in Step 5.

5. Install the primary cover bolts and washers (**Figure 10**) into the correct locations noted during removal. Tighten the primary cover bolts to the

specification in **Table 2**. Check that the gasket seats flush around the cover.

6A. On all models except FXDWG, perform the following:

a. Install a *new* gasket (**Figure 11**) and the inspection cover (**Figure 4**) onto the primary chaincase cover. Install the screws and tighten to the specification in **Table 2**.

b. Align the mark made in Step 4 *Removal* and install the outer shift lever (A, **Figure 3**) onto inner shift lever shaft.

c. Install the clamping bolt (B, **Figure 3**) and tighten securely.

6B. On FXDWG models, install a *new* gasket and the inspection cover onto the primary chaincase cover. Install the screws and tighten to the specification in **Table 2**.

7. Install the left side footpeg assembly (**Figure 2**) and tighten the bolts securely.

8. Refill the primary chaincase with the type and quantity of oil specified under *Primary Chain Lubrication* in Chapter Three.

9. Connect the negative battery cable as described in Chapter Eight.

CLUTCH PLATES AND FRICTION DISCS

This section describes removal, inspection and installation of the clutch plates. If the clutch requires additional service, refer to *Clutch Shell* in this chapter.

Refer to **Figure 12**.

Removal

NOTE
On models so equipped, always disarm the optional TSSM security system prior to disconnecting the battery or the siren will sound.

1. Disconnect the battery negative lead as described in Chapter Eight.

2. Remove the clutch mechanism inspection cover and O-ring (**Figure 13**).

3. At the clutch mechanism, loosen the clutch adjusting screw locknut (A, **Figure 14**) and turn the adjusting screw (B) *counterclockwise* to allow slack against the diaphragm spring.

4. Remove the primary chaincase outer cover as described in this chapter.

5. Loosen the bolts securing the diaphragm spring retainer (A, **Figure 15**) in a crisscross pattern. Remove the bolts, retainer and diaphragm spring (B, **Figure 15**).

6. Remove the pressure plate (**Figure 16**).

7. Remove the clutch plates and friction discs from the clutch shell. After the first six clutch plates and friction discs are removed, carefully remove the remaining ones with a pick tool.

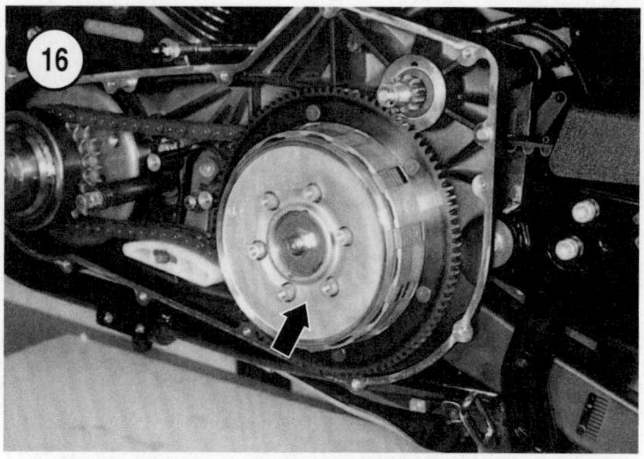

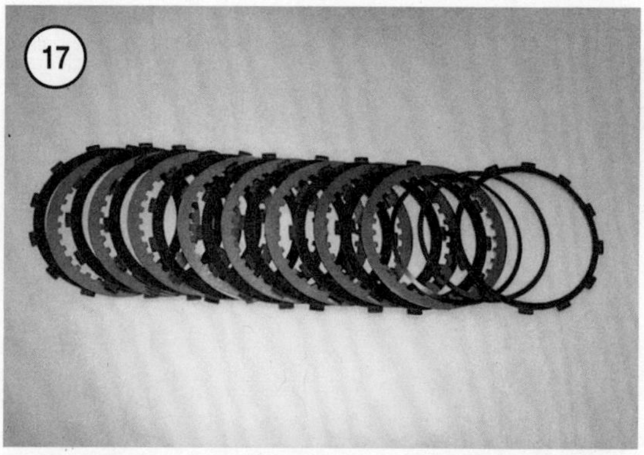

8. Remove the damper spring and damper spring seat from the clutch shell. Keep all parts in order as shown in **Figure 17**.

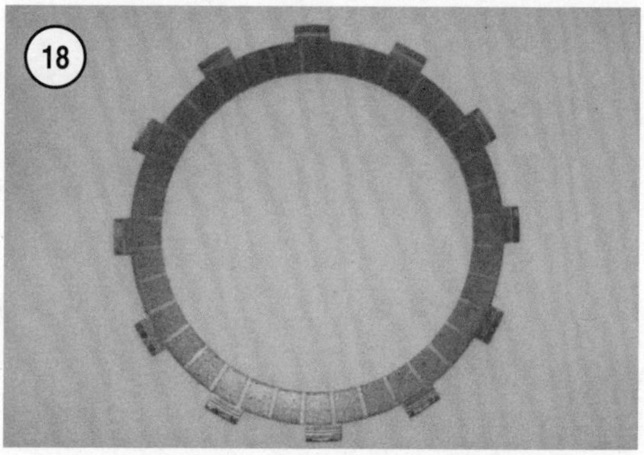

Inspection

When measuring the clutch components, compare the actual measurements to the specifications in **Table 1**. Replace parts that are out of specification or show damage as described in this section.

1. Clean all parts in solvent and thoroughly dry with compressed air.

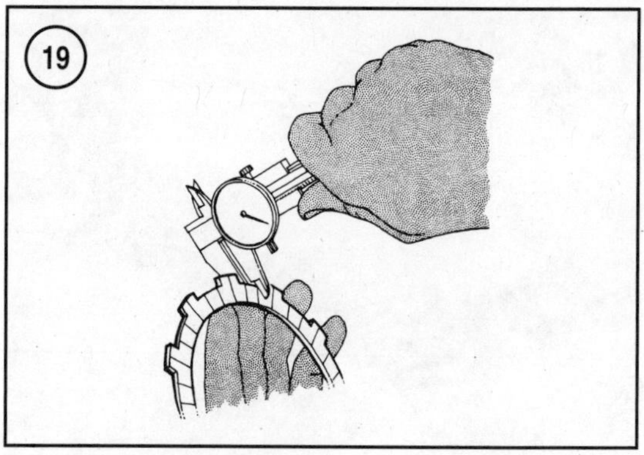

2. Inspect the friction discs as follows:

NOTE
If any friction disc is damaged or out of specification as described in the following steps, replace all of the friction discs as a set. Never replace only one or two discs.

a. The friction material used on the friction discs (**Figure 18**) is bonded onto an aluminum plate for warp resistance and durability. Inspect the friction material for excessive or uneven wear, cracks and other damage. Check the disc tangs for surface damage. The sides of the disc tangs must be smooth where they contact the clutch shell fingers; otherwise, the discs cannot engage and disengage correctly.

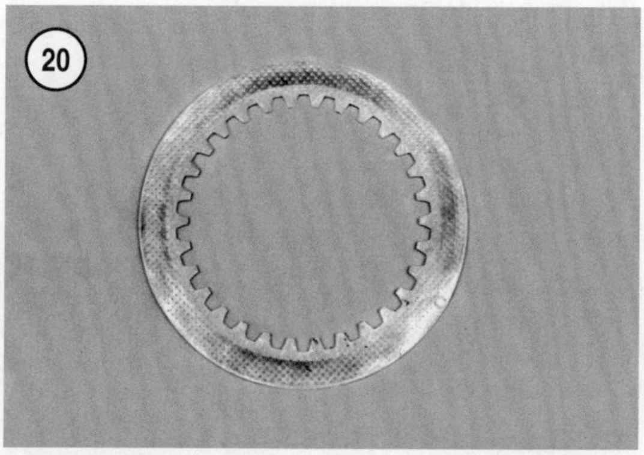

NOTE
If the disc tangs are damaged, inspect the clutch shell fingers carefully as described later in this section.

21

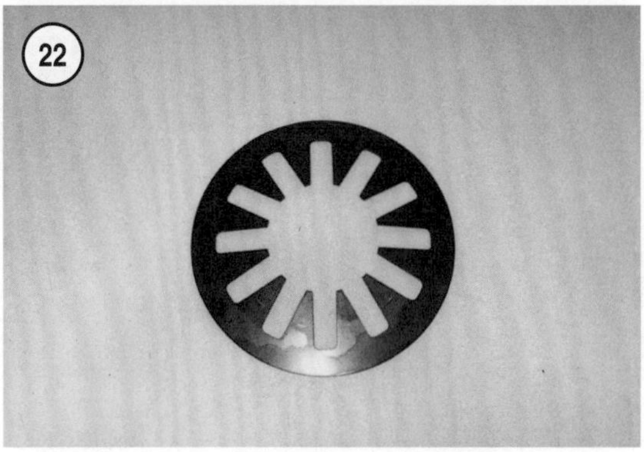
22

23

24

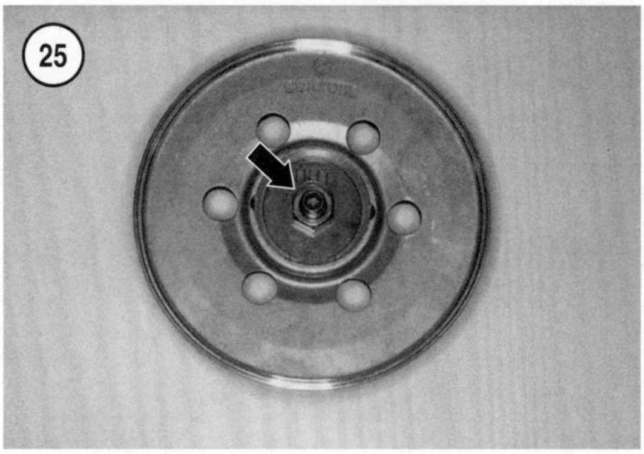
25

b. Measure the thickness of each friction disc with a vernier caliper (**Figure 19**). Measure at several places around the disc.

3. Inspect the clutch plates (**Figure 20**) as follows:
   a. Inspect the clutch plates for cracks, damage or color change. Overheated clutch plates will have a blue discoloration.
   b. Check the clutch plates for an oil glaze buildup. Remove by lightly sanding both sides of each plate with 400 grit sandpaper placed on a surface plate or piece of glass.
   c. Place each clutch plate on a flat surface and check for warp with a feeler gauge (**Figure 21**).
   d. The clutch plate inner teeth mesh with the clutch hub splines. Check the clutch plate teeth for any roughness or damage. The teeth contact surfaces must be smooth; otherwise, the plates cannot engage and disengage correctly.

NOTE
If the clutch plate teeth are damaged, inspect the clutch hub splines carefully as described later in this section.

4. Inspect the diaphragm spring (**Figure 22**) for cracks or damage.
5. Inspect the diaphragm spring retainer for cracks or damage. Also check for bent or damaged tabs (**Figure 23**).
6. Inspect the pressure plate contact surface (**Figure 24**) for cracks or other damage.
7. If necessary, disassemble the pressure plate as follows:
   a. Remove the snap ring and remove the release plate, left side pushrod and locknut (**Figure 25**) from the pressure plate.

5

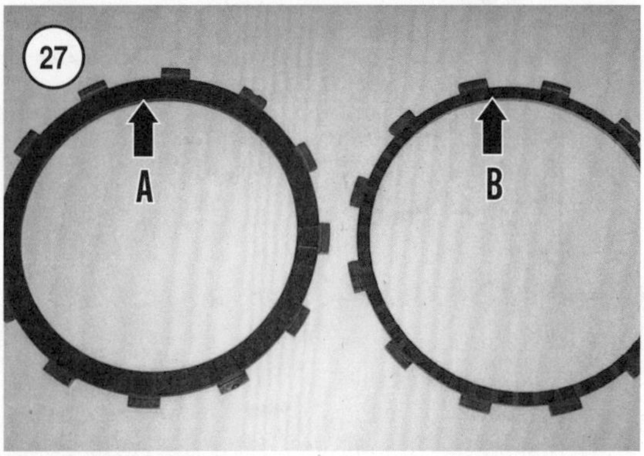

b. Inspect the release plate, left side pushrod and locknut for wear or damage.
c. Inspect its snap ring groove for damage.
d. Position the release plate with the OUT mark facing out (**Figure 26**) and install the assembly into the pressure plate.
e. Install the snap ring and make sure it is correctly seated in the pressure plate groove.

Installation

NOTE
*The clutch assembly (**Figure 17**) has nine friction plates, eight steel plates, one damper spring and one damper spring seat. Make sure each is installed. If installing an aftermarket clutch plate assembly, follow the manufacturer's instructions for plate quantity, alignment and installation sequence.*

1. Soak the clutch friction disc and clutch plates in new primary drive oil for approximately 5 minutes before installing them.

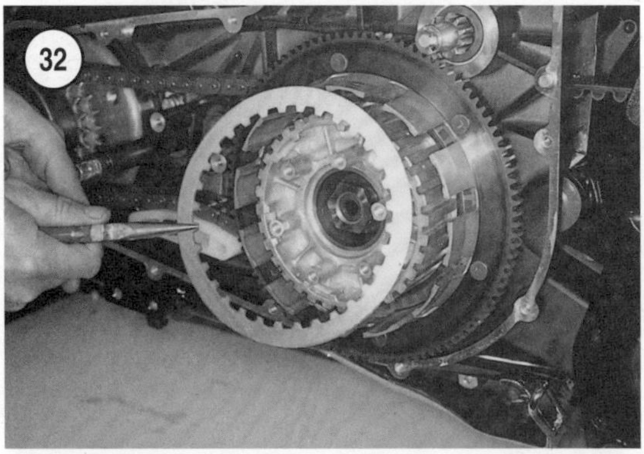
32

33

34

35

36

NOTE

*There are two different types of clutch friction discs (**Figure 27**). The wider friction disc A is the normal width disc, while the narrow width friction disc B is installed first, as it works in conjunction with the damper spring and damper spring seat.*

2. Install the clutch friction disc B (**Figure 28**) onto the clutch shell and clutch hub. Push it on all the way until it bottoms within the clutch hub.

3. Install the damper spring seat (**Figure 29**) onto the clutch hub and push it in until it seats within the clutch friction disc B.

4. Position the damper spring with the dome side facing out (**Figure 30**) and install it onto the clutch hub against the damper spring seat (**Figure 31**).

5. Install a clutch plate (**Figure 32**), then a friction disc A (**Figure 33**). Continue to alternately install the clutch plates and friction discs. The last part installed is a friction disc A (**Figure 34**).

6. Make sure the oil slinger assembly (**Figure 35**) is in place in the pressure plate. Install the pressure plate onto the clutch hub (**Figure 16**).

7. Position the diaphragm spring with the dished side facing out (**Figure 36**) and install it onto the pressure plate (**Figure 37**). Hold the pressure plate in place.

8. Position the diaphragm spring retainer with the finger side (**Figure 38**) facing in toward the diaphragm spring (B, **Figure 15**). Install the diaphragm spring retainer (A, **Figure 15**) and bolts.

9. Tighten the bolts in a crisscross pattern to the specification in **Table 2**.

10. Install the primary chaincase outer cover as described in this chapter.

37

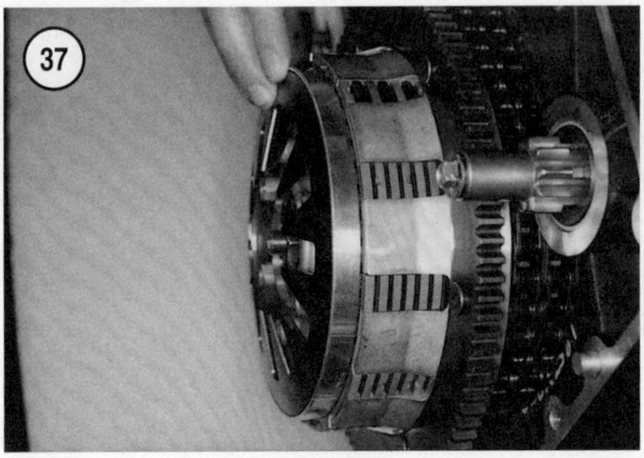

38

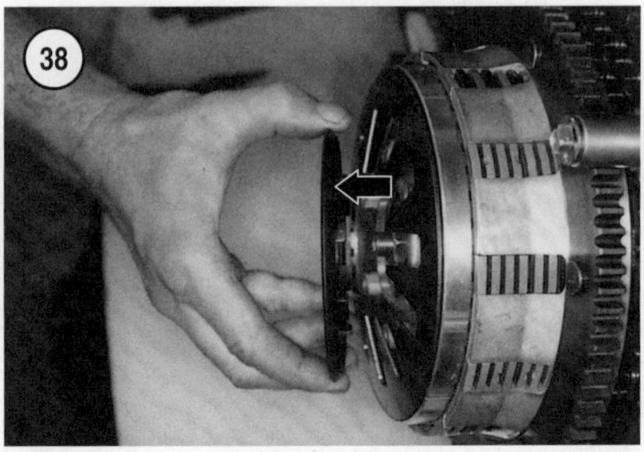

39

COMPENSATING SPROCKET (1999-2000)

1. Bolt
2. Anchor plate
3. Screw
4. Chain tensioner
5. Plate
6. Washer
7. Nut
8. Tensioner pad
9. Washer
10. Lockwasher
11. Bolt
12. Primary chain
13. Spacer
14. Shaft extension
15. Compensating sprocket
16. Sliding cam
17. Cover assembly with springs*
18. Nut*

*Spacer between No. 17 and No. 18 for 1999 models not shown

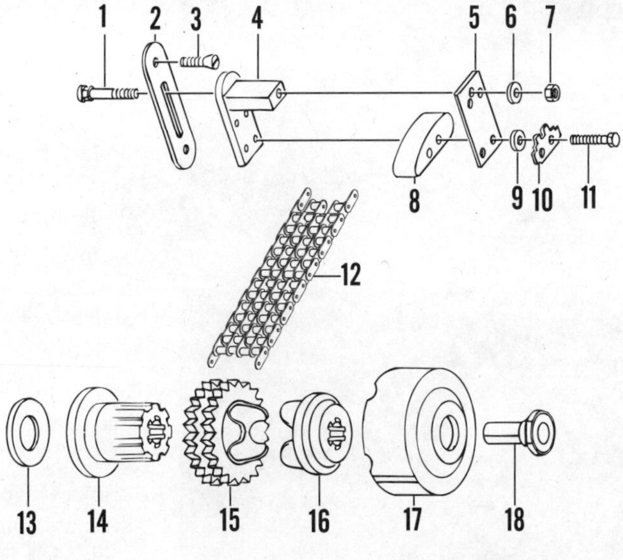

11. Install the clutch mechanism inspection cover and O-ring (**Figure 13**).
12. Connect the negative battery cable as described in Chapter Eight.

CLUTCH SHELL, COMPENSATING SPROCKET AND PRIMARY DRIVE CHAIN

Removal

This procedure describes clutch shell, primary chain and engine sprocket removal. These components must be removed as an assembly.

Refer to **Figure 12** (clutch assembly), **Figure 39** (1999-2000 models) and **Figure 40** (2001 models).

NOTE

On models so equipped, always disarm the optional TSSM security system prior to disconnecting the battery or the siren will sound.

1. Disconnect the negative battery cable from the battery as described in Chapter Eight
2. Remove the primary chaincase outer cover as described in this chapter.

40

COMPENSATING SPROCKET (2001)

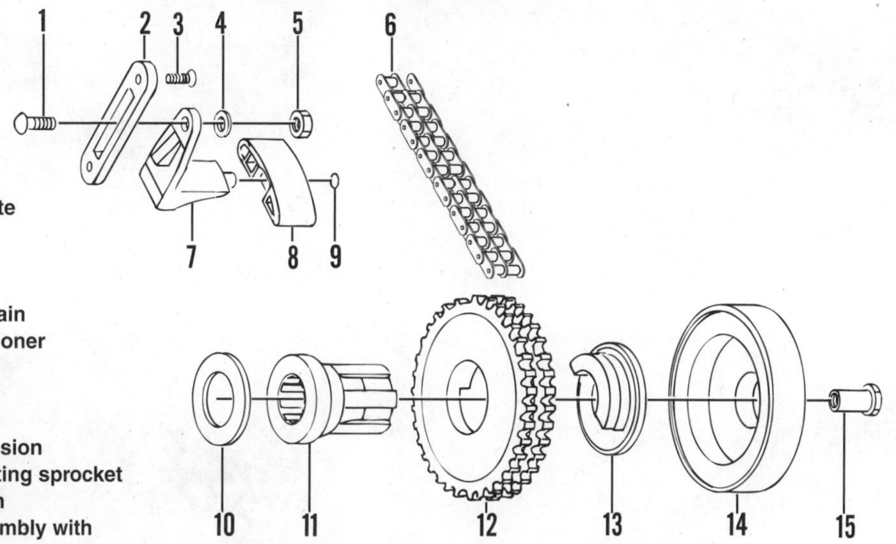

1. Bolt
2. Anchor plate
3. Screw
4. Washer
5. Nut
6. Primary chain
7. Chain tensioner
8. Pad
9. Snap ring
10. Spacer
11. Shaft extension
12. Compensating sprocket
13. Sliding cam
14. Cover assembly with springs*
15. Nut*

*Spacer between No. 14 and No. 15 not shown

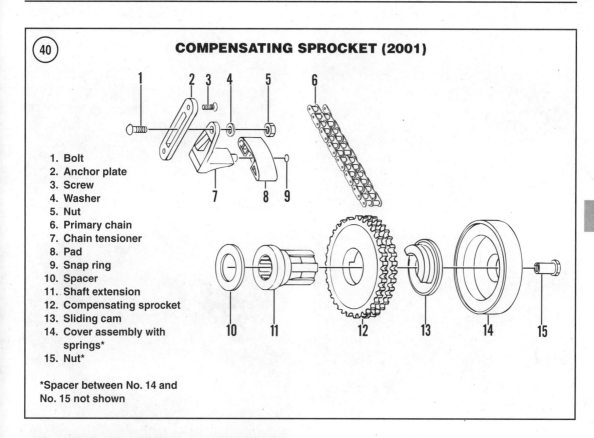

3. Remove the diaphragm spring, pressure plate, clutch plates and friction discs as described in this chapter.

CAUTION

Do not clamp the special tool too tight as it may damage the grooves in the clutch hub.

4A. If the special tool is available, such as the Grabbit (**Figure 41**), attach it to the clutch hub to keep it from turning.

4B. If the special tool is not available, shift the transmission into fifth gear. Have an assistant apply the rear brake.

CAUTION

*The clutch nut has **left-hand threads**. Turn the clutch nut **clockwise** to loosen it.*

5. Loosen the clutch nut (**Figure 42**) with an impact wrench. Remove the clutch nut.

6. Loosen the compensating sprocket nut (**Figure 43**) with an impact wrench.

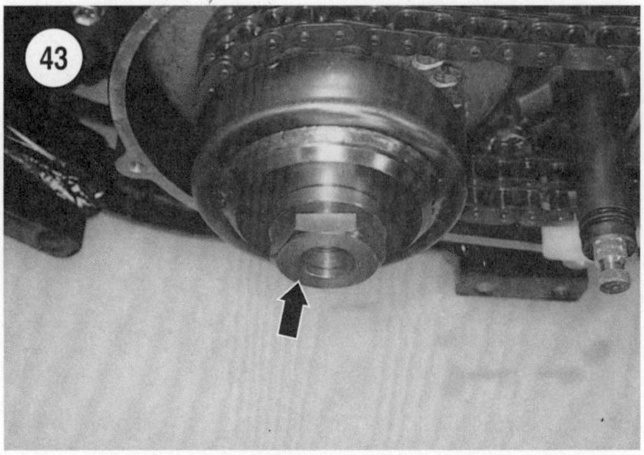

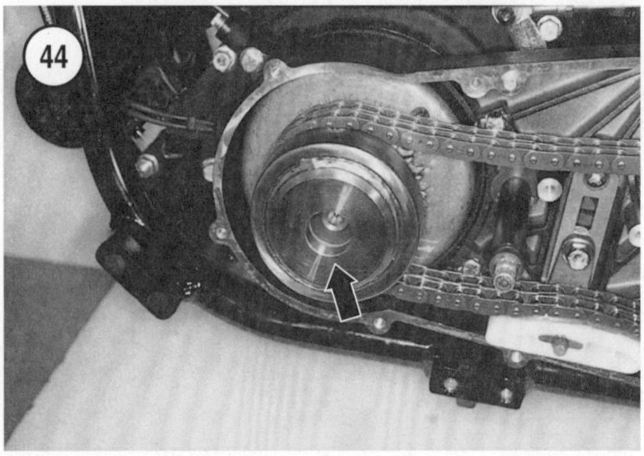

7. Remove the compensating sprocket nut (**Figure 43**), washer (1999 models), cover (**Figure 44**) and sliding cam (**Figure 45**).

8A. On 1999-2000 models, perform the following:

a. Remove the primary chain shoe adjuster locknut (**Figure 46**).
b. Remove the compensating sprocket, primary chain, chain adjuster and clutch assembly (**Figure 47**) at the same time. See **Figure 48**.

8B. On 2001 models, perform the following:

a. Loosen the primary chain shoe adjuster locknut (A, **Figure 49**) and push the tensioner assembly down to relieve tension on the primary chain.
b. Remove the compensating sprocket, primary chain and clutch assembly (B, **Figure 49**) at the same time. See **Figure 50**.

9. Remove the shaft extension (**Figure 51**) and the spacer (**Figure 52**).

10. Inspect the various components as described in this chapter.

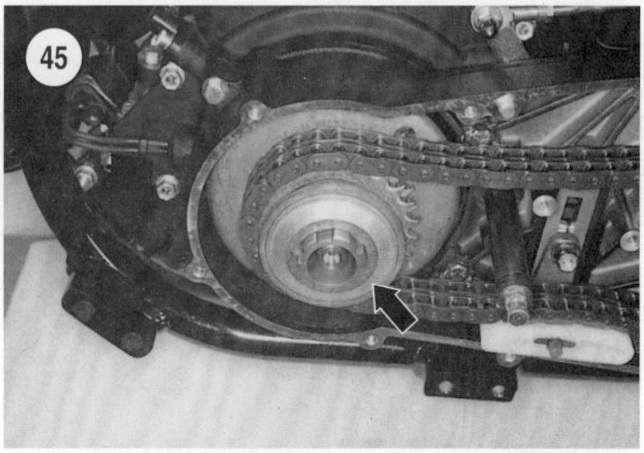

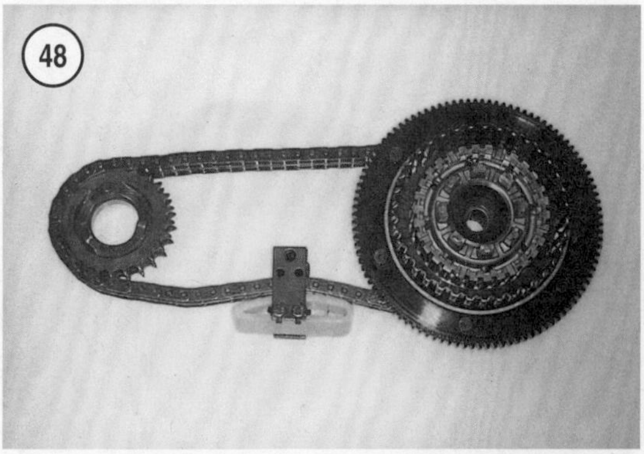

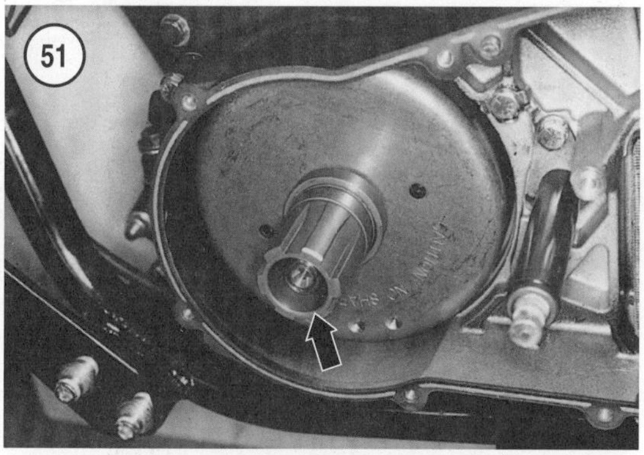

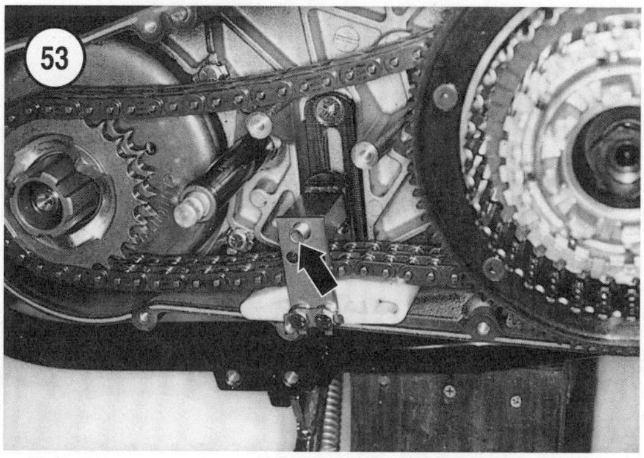

5

Installation

1. Remove all threadlocking compound residue from the crankshaft and mainshaft threads and from the compensating sprocket nut and the clutch nut.
2. Remove all gasket residue from the inner primary housing gasket surfaces.
3. Install the spacer (**Figure 52**) and the shaft extension (**Figure 51**) onto the crankshaft.
4A. On 1999-2000 models, perform the following:
   a. Assemble the compensating sprocket, primary chain, chain adjuster and clutch as shown in **Figure 48**.
   b. Install the compensating sprocket, primary chain, chain adjuster and clutch as shown in **Figure 47**. Insert the chain adjuster bolt through the chain adjuster hole as shown in **Figure 53**.
   c. Install the primary chain shoe adjuster locknut (**Figure 46**) and tighten finger-tight at this time.
4B. On 2001 models, perform the following:
   a. Assemble the compensating sprocket, primary chain and clutch as shown in **Figure 50**.
   b. Install the compensating sprocket, primary chain and clutch as shown in B, **Figure 49**.
5. Install the compensating sprocket (**Figure 45**) and the cover (**Figure 44**).
6. On 1999 models, install the washer.
7. Install the same tool setup (A, **Figure 54**) used during removal or shift the transmission into fifth gear to prevent the compensating sprocket and clutch shell from rotating during the following steps.
8. Apply two drops of ThreeBond TB1360 or an equivalent to the compensating sprocket nut

threads. Install the nut (**Figure 43**) **and tighten (Figure 55**) to the specification in **Table 2**.

NOTE
*The clutch nut has **left-hand threads**. Turn the nut **counterclockwise** to tighten it.*

9. Apply two drops of ThreeBond TB1360 or an equivalent to the clutch nut threads. Install the nut (**Figure 42**) and tighten (B, **Figure 54**) to the specification in **Table 2**.
10. If used, remove the special tool from the clutch shell.
11. Adjust the primary chain as described in Chapter Three.
12. Install the clutch plates and friction discs, pressure plate and diaphragm spring as described in this chapter.
13. Install the primary chaincase outer cover as described in this chapter.
14. Adjust the clutch as described in Chapter Three.
15. Connect the negative battery cable to the battery as described in Chapter Eight.

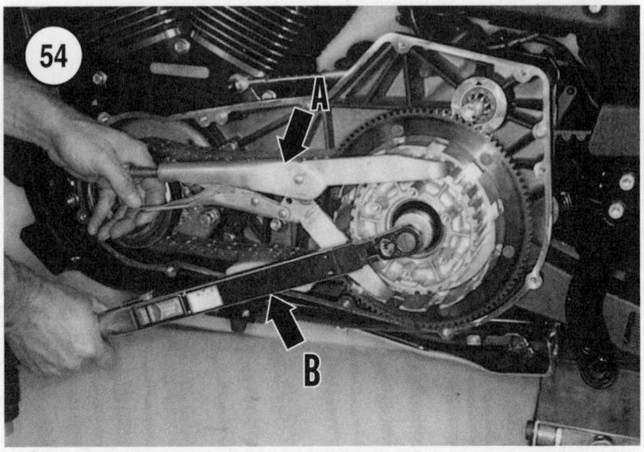

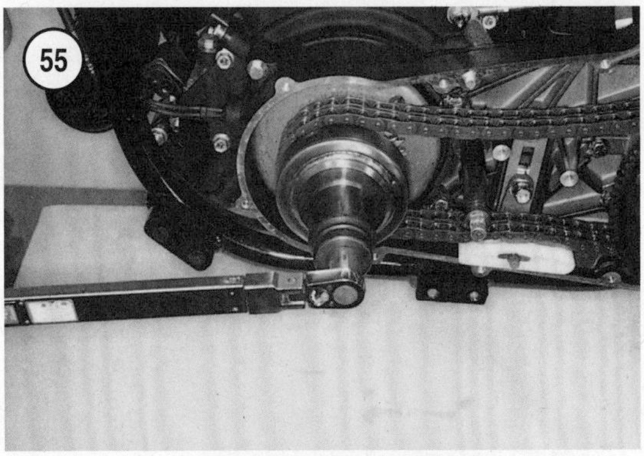

CLUTCH SHELL, CLUTCH HUB AND SPROCKET

Inspection

The clutch shell is a subassembly consisting of the clutch shell, the clutch hub, the bearing and two snap rings.

1. Remove the clutch shell as described in this chapter.
2. Hold the clutch shell and rotate the clutch hub by hand. The bearing is damaged if the clutch hub binds or turns roughly.
3. Check the sprocket (A, **Figure 56**) and the starter ring gear (B, **Figure 56**) on the clutch shell for cracks, deep scoring, excessive wear or heat discoloration.
4. If the sprocket or the ring gear are worn or damaged, replace the clutch shell. If the primary chain sprocket is worn, also check the primary chain and the compensating sprocket as described in this chapter.
5. Inspect the clutch hub for the following conditions:

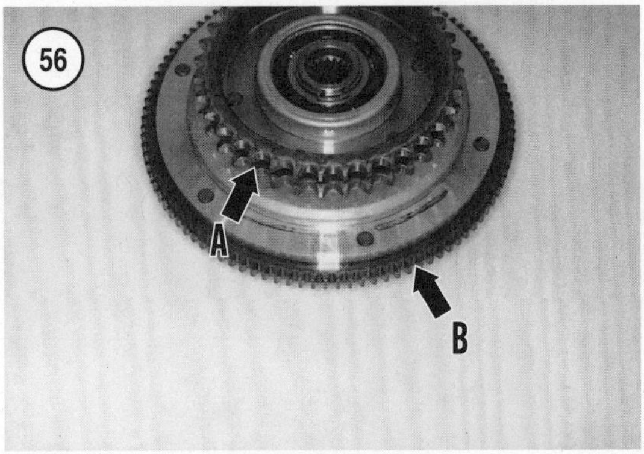

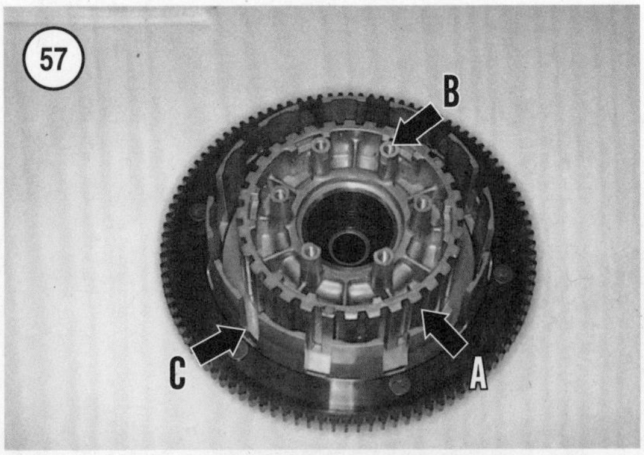

58

59

60

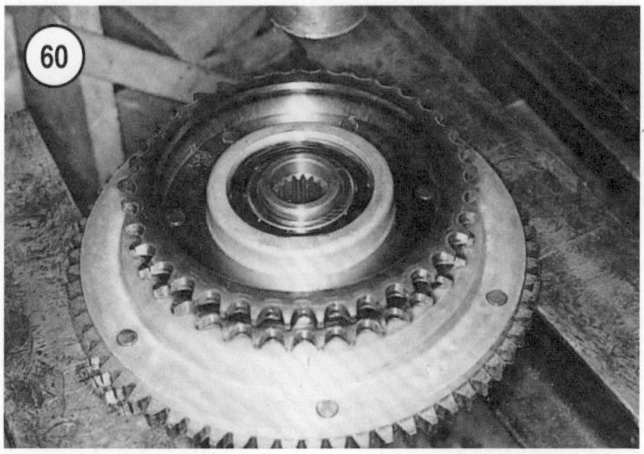

61

a. The clutch plate teeth slide in the clutch hub splines (A, **Figure 57**). Inspect the splines for rough spots, grooves or other damage. Repair minor damage with a file or oil stone. If the damage is severe, replace the clutch hub.

b. Inspect the clutch hub inner splines (**Figure 58**) for galling, severe wear or other damage. Repair minor damage with a fine cut file. If damage is severe, replace the clutch hub.

c. Inspect the bolt towers and threads (B, **Figure 57**) for thread damage or cracks at the base of the tower. Repair thread damage with correct size metric tap. If the tower(s) is cracked or damaged, replace the clutch hub.

6. Check the clutch shell. The friction disc tangs slide in the clutch housing grooves (C, **Figure 57**). Inspect the grooves for cracks or galling. Repair minor damage with a file. If the damage is severe, replace the clutch housing.

7. If the clutch hub, the clutch shell or bearings are damaged, replace them as described in the following procedure.

5

Disassembly/Assembly

Do not separate the clutch hub and shell unless the bearing or either part is going to be replaced. If the two parts are separated the bearing will be damaged.

Removal and installation of the bearing requires the use of a hydraulic press.

Refer to **Figure 12**.

1. Remove the clutch as described in this chapter. Remove the clutch shell assembly from the primary drive chain.

2. Remove the snap ring (**Figure 59**) from the clutch hub groove.

3. Position the clutch hub and shell with the primary chain sprocket side facing up.

4. Support the clutch hub and clutch shell in a press (**Figure 60**).

5. Place a suitable size arbor in the clutch hub surface and press the clutch hub (A, **Figure 61**) out of the bearing.

6. Remove the clutch shell from the press (B, **Figure 61**).

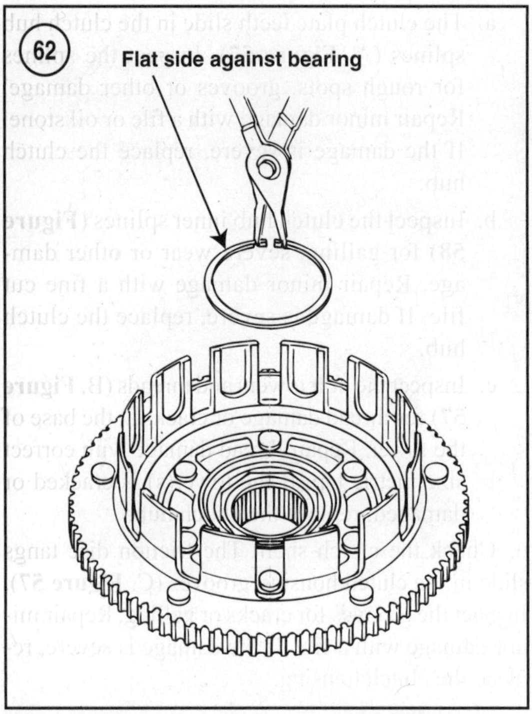

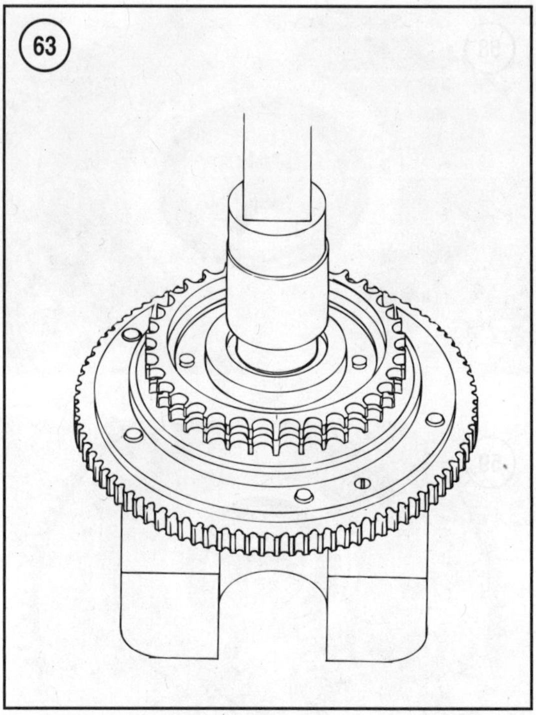

7. On the inner surface of the clutch shell, remove the bearing retaining snap ring (**Figure 62**) from the groove in the middle of the clutch shell.

CAUTION

Press the bearing out from the primary chain sprocket side of the clutch shell. The bearing bore has a shoulder on the primary chain side.

8. Support the clutch shell in the press with the primary chain sprocket side *facing up*.
9. Place a suitable size arbor on the bearing inner race and press the bearing out of the clutch shell (**Figure 63**).
10. Thoroughly clean the clutch hub and shell in solvent and dry with compressed air.
11. Inspect the bearing bore in the clutch shell for damage or burrs. Clean off any burrs that would interfere with new bearing installation.
12. Support the clutch shell in the press with the primary chain sprocket side *facing down*.
13. Apply chaincase lubricant to the clutch shell bearing receptacle and the outer surface of the bearing.
14. Align the bearing with the clutch shell receptacle.
15. Place a suitable size arbor on the bearing outer race and slowly press the bearing into the clutch

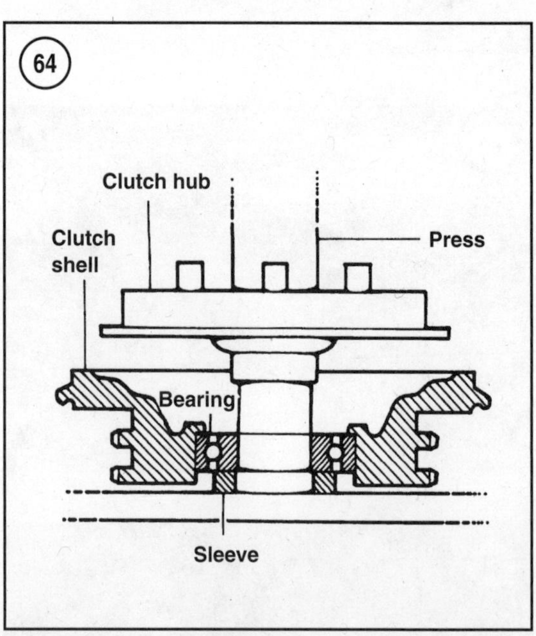

shell until it bottoms on the lower shoulder. Press only on the outer bearing race. Applying force to the bearing's inner race will damage the bearing. Refer to *Basic Service Methods* in Chapter One for additional information.

16. Position the new snap ring with the flat side against the bearing and install the snap ring into the

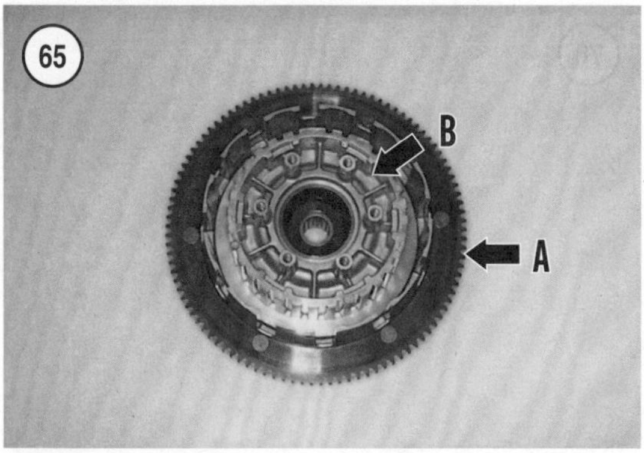

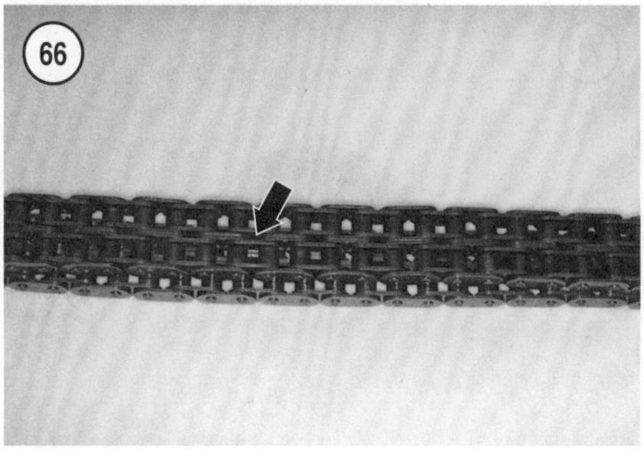

clutch shell groove (**Figure 62**). Make sure the snap ring is seated correctly in the clutch shell groove.

17. Press the clutch hub into the clutch shell as follows:

CAUTION
Failure to support the inner bearing race properly will cause bearing and clutch shell damage.

a. Place the clutch shell in a press. Support the inner bearing race with a sleeve as shown in **Figure 64**.
b. Align the clutch hub with the bearing and slowly press the clutch hub into the bearing until the clutch hub shoulder seats against the bearing inner race.
c. Install a *new* snap ring (**Figure 59**) into the clutch hub. Make sure the snap ring is seated correctly in the clutch hub groove.

18. After completing assembly, hold the clutch shell (A, **Figure 65**) and rotate the clutch hub (B) by hand. The shell must turn smoothly with no roughness or binding. If the clutch shell binds or turns

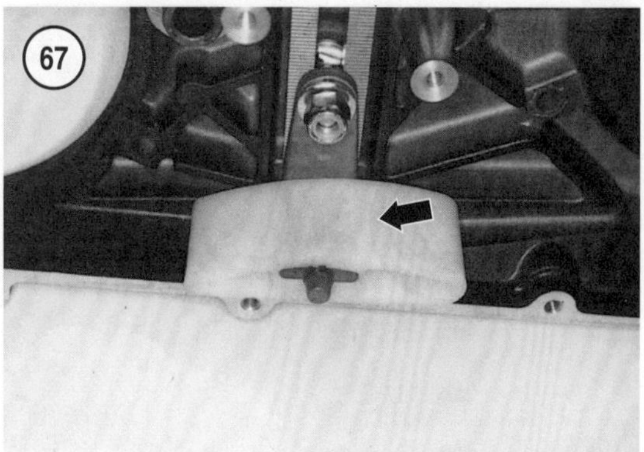

roughly, the bearing was installed incorrectly. Repeat this procedure until this problem is corrected.

PRIMARY CHAIN AND GUIDE INSPECTION

1. Remove the primary chain as described under the *Clutch Shell, Compensating Sprocket and Primary Drive Chain* in this chapter.
2. Clean the primary chain in solvent and dry thoroughly.
3. Inspect the primary chain (**Figure 66**) for excessive wear, cracks or other damage. If the chain is worn or damaged, check both sprockets for wear and damage.

NOTE
*If the primary chain is near the end of its adjustment level or if no more adjustment is available, and the adjusting guide (**Figure 67**) is not worn or damaged, the primary chain is excessively worn. Service specifications for chain wear are not available.*

4. Inspect the adjusting guide (**Figure 67**) for cracks, severe wear or other damage. Replace the adjusting shoe if necessary.

PRIMARY CHAIN ALIGNMENT

A spacer, installed behind the compensating sprocket, aligns the compensating and clutch sprockets. Install the original spacer when reinstalling the compensating sprocket, primary chain and clutch assembly. However, if the primary chain is showing wear on one side, or if new components

have been installed that could affect alignment, perform the following check.

1. Remove the outer primary cover as described in this chapter.
2. Adjust the primary chain tension so the chain is snug against both the compensating sprocket and clutch shell sprocket.
3. Push the primary chain toward the engine and transmission (at both sprockets) as far as it will go.
4. Place a straightedge on the primary chain side plates, close to the compensating sprocket.
5. Measure the distance from the chain link side plates to the primary chaincase housing gasket surface. Record the measurement.
6. Repeat Steps 4 and 5 with the end of the straightedge as close to the clutch sprocket as possible. Record the measurement.
7. The difference between the 2 measurements must be within 0.030 in. (0.76 mm) of each other. If the difference exceeds this amount, replace the spacer (**Figure 52**) with a suitable size spacer. Refer to **Table 3** for spacer thickness and part number.
8. To replace the spacer, perform the *Clutch Shell, Compensating Sprocket and Primary Drive Chain* in this chapter.

(74) **PRIMARY CHAINCASE**

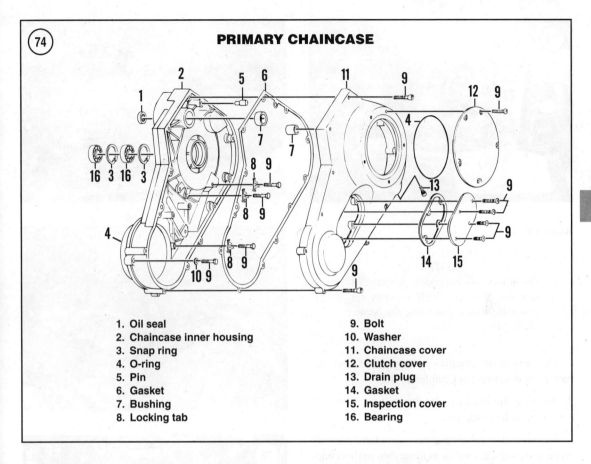

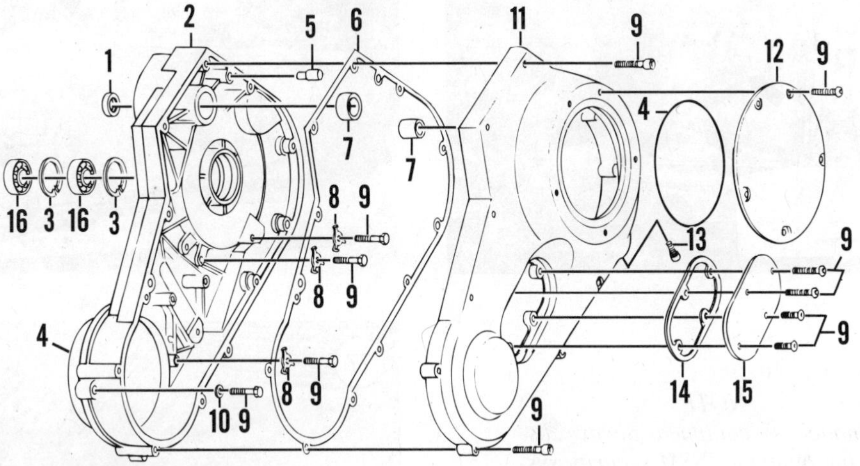

1. Oil seal
2. Chaincase inner housing
3. Snap ring
4. O-ring
5. Pin
6. Gasket
7. Bushing
8. Locking tab
9. Bolt
10. Washer
11. Chaincase cover
12. Clutch cover
13. Drain plug
14. Gasket
15. Inspection cover
16. Bearing

9. Install the outer primary cover as described in this chapter.
10. Check and adjust the primary chain tension as described in Chapter Three.

COMPENSATING SPROCKET INSPECTION

Refer to **Figure 39** (1999-2000 models) and **Figure 40** (2001 models).

1. Remove the compensating sprocket assembly as described in this chapter.
2. Clean all parts in solvent and dry with compressed air.
3. Check the cam surfaces (**Figure 68**) for cracks, deep scoring or wear.
4. Check the compensating sprocket gear teeth (**Figure 69**) for cracks or wear.

NOTE
If the compensating sprocket teeth are worn, check the primary chain and the clutch shell gear teeth for wear.

5. Check the compensating sprocket inner bushing (**Figure 70**) for wear.
6. Check the sliding cam inner splines (**Figure 71**) for wear.
7. Check the shaft extension splines for wear or galling.
8. Check the cover (**Figure 72**) for damage.
9. Inspect the inner threads (**Figure 73**) of the nut for damage.
10. If any of these components were replaced, check the primary chain alignment as described in this chapter.

PRIMARY CHAINCASE INNER HOUSING

The primary chaincase inner housing is bolted to the engine and transmission. It houses the primary drive assembly, flywheel, starter jackshaft and the mainshaft oil seal and bearing assembly.

Refer to **Figure 74**.

Removal

NOTE

On models so equipped, always disarm the optional TSSM security system prior to disconnecting the battery or the siren will sound.

1. Disconnect the negative battery cable from the battery as described in Chapter Eight.

2. Remove the primary chaincase outer cover as described in this chapter.

3. Remove the compensating sprocket, primary chain and clutch assembly as described in this chapter.

4. Remove the starter motor as described in Chapter Eight.

5. Pry the lockwasher tabs away from the inner primary housing bolts (**Figure 75**, typical).

6. Loosen and then remove the five bolts (**Figure 76**) securing the inner housing to the engine and the transmission. Discard the lockwashers, as new ones must be installed.

7. Remove the starter jackshaft assembly from the inner housing.

8. Tap the inner primary housing loose.

9A. On all models except the FXDWG, carefully pull the inner housing (A, **Figure 77**) away from the engine and transmission. Guide the inner shift shaft (B, **Figure 77**) out from the inner housing.

9B. On FXDWG models, remove the inner housing from the engine and transmission.

10. Remove the O-ring (**Figure 78**) from the engine crankcase shoulder.

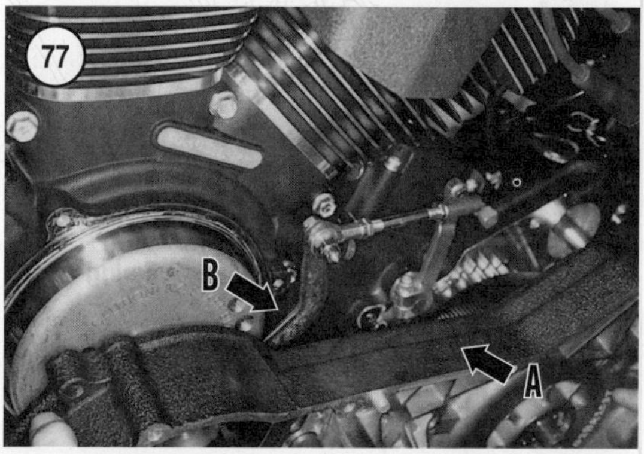

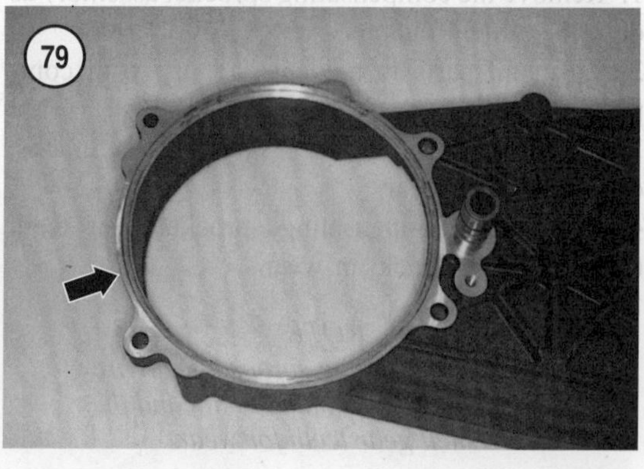

80

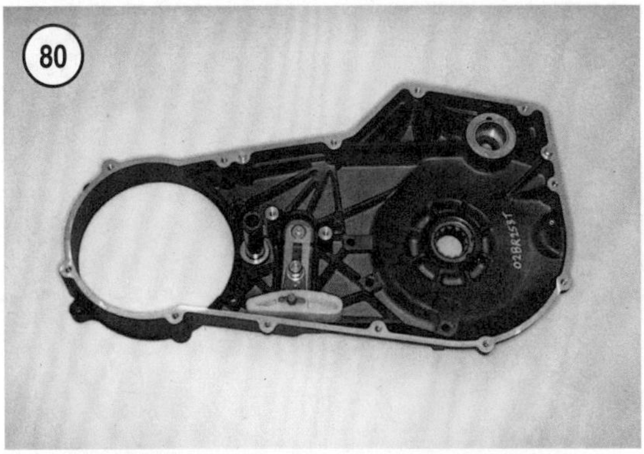

81

82

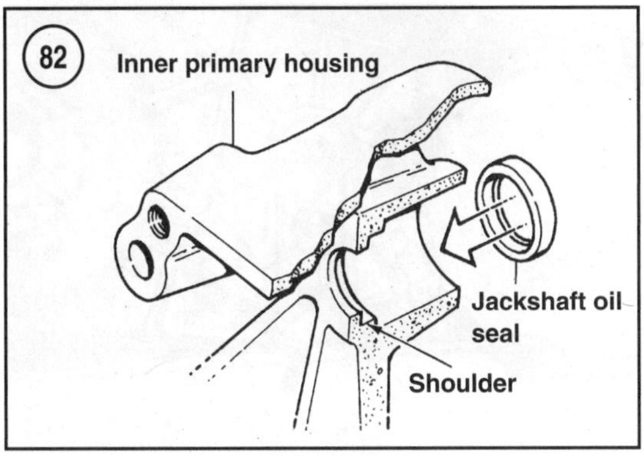

83

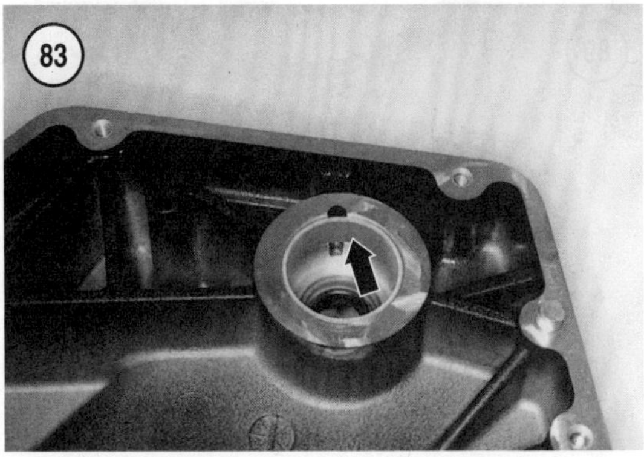

84

5

Inspection

1. Remove all gasket residue from the inner housing gasket surfaces (**Figure 79**).
2. Clean the inner housing in solvent and dry thoroughly.
3. Check the inner housing (**Figure 80**) for cracks or other damage.
4. Check the starter jackshaft oil seal (**Figure 81**) for excessive wear or damage. To replace the oil seal, perform the following:
   a. Note the direction the oil seal lip faces in the housing.
   b. Pack the new oil seal lips with grease.
   c. Pry the oil seal out of the inner primary housing.
   d. Carefully drive the *new* oil seal into the housing until it seats against the housing shoulder (**Figure 82**).
5. Inspect the starter jackshaft bushing (**Figure 83**) for excessive wear, cracks or other damage. To replace the bushing, perform the following:
   a. Remove the bushing with a blind bearing removal tool.
   b. Clean the bushing bore in the housing.
   c. Press in the new bushing until its outer surface is flush with the edge of the bushing bore.
6. Turn the inner bearing race (**Figure 84**) by hand. Replace the bearing as follows:
   a. Remove the oil seal (**Figure 85**) as described in Step 7.
   b. Remove the inner and outer bearing snap rings (**Figure 86**).
   c. Support the inner primary housing and press the bearing out.

d. Install the outer snap ring (clutch side). Make sure the snap ring is correctly seated in the groove.

CAUTION
When pressing the bearing into the housing, support the outer snap ring. The force required to press the bearing into the inner primary housing may force the snap ring out of its groove, damaging the housing.

e. Support the inner housing and outer snap ring.
f. Press the bearing into the inner housing until it seats against the snap ring.
g. Install the inner snap ring (**Figure 86**). Make sure the snap ring is seated correctly in the groove.
h. Install a *new* oil seal as described in Step 7.

7. Inspect the inner primary cover oil seal (**Figure 85**) for excessive wear, tearing or other damage. To replace the oil seal, perform the following:
a. Remove the oil seal with a wide-blade screwdriver.
b. Clean the oil seal bore.
c. Pack the oil seal lip with a waterproof bearing grease.
d. Position the oil seal with its closed side facing out. Press in the *new* oil seal until its outer surface is flush with the edge of the bearing bore (**Figure 87**).

8A. On 1999-2000 models, check the primary chain adjuster rack screws (**Figure 88**) for looseness. Tighten the screws, if necessary.

8B. On 2001 models, check the primary chain adjuster rack screws (**Figure 89**) for looseness. Tighten the screws, if necessary.

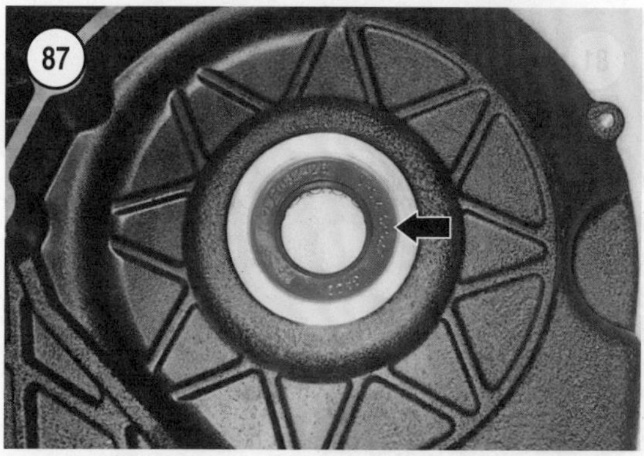

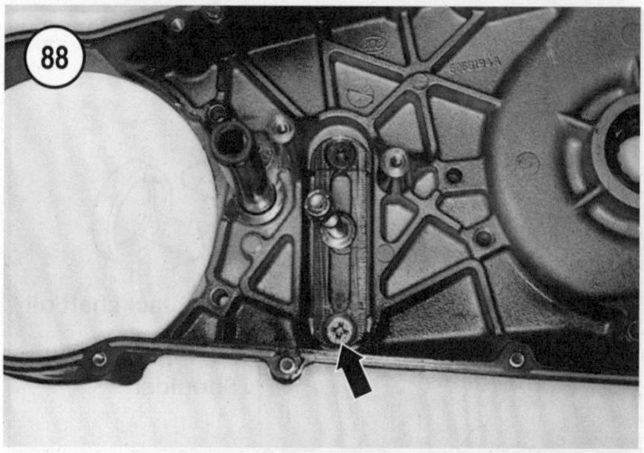

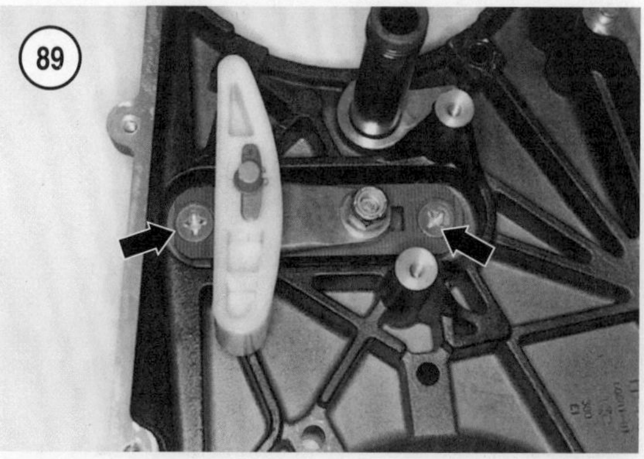

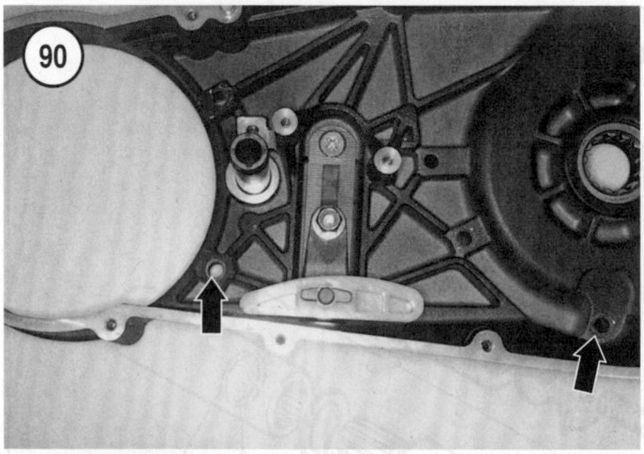

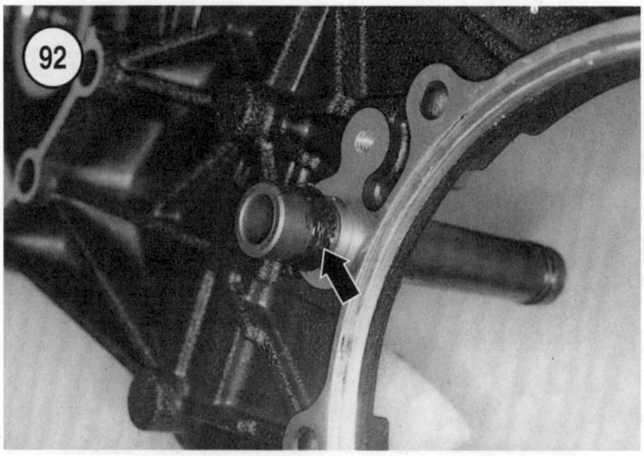

Installation

NOTE

In Step 1, apply the RTV sealant to the inner surface of the two bolt holes. ***Figure 90*** *shows only the bolt hole location and is pointing to the outer surface.*

1. Thoroughly clean the *inner surface* of the two lower bolt holes (**Figure 90**) of the inner cover. Apply a light coat of RTV to these inner surfaces.
2. On all models except FXDWG, if the shift lever sleeve was removed, perform the following:
   a. Install a *new* O-ring (**Figure 91**) onto the outer groove.
   b. Apply a light coat of RTV to the sleeve (**Figure 92**).
   c. Pull the sleeve into the inner cover until the grooves are visible on the outer side of the inner cover.
   d. Install the clip into the second groove and tighten the bolt.
3. Install the O-ring (**Figure 78**) onto the engine crankcase shoulder.
4. To prevent the mainshaft splines (**Figure 93**) from damaging the inner cover oil seal as it passes over, wrap the mainshaft splines with tape.
5. If removed, install the drive belt prior to installing the inner housing.
6. On all models except the FXDWG, insert the inner shift shaft (**Figure 94**) through the collar and install the inner housing.
7. Align the inner housing with the engine and transmission and install it.
8. Apply a bead of RTV sealant around the *outer surface* of the two bottom bolt holes (**Figure 90**).

95

STARTER JACKSHAFT

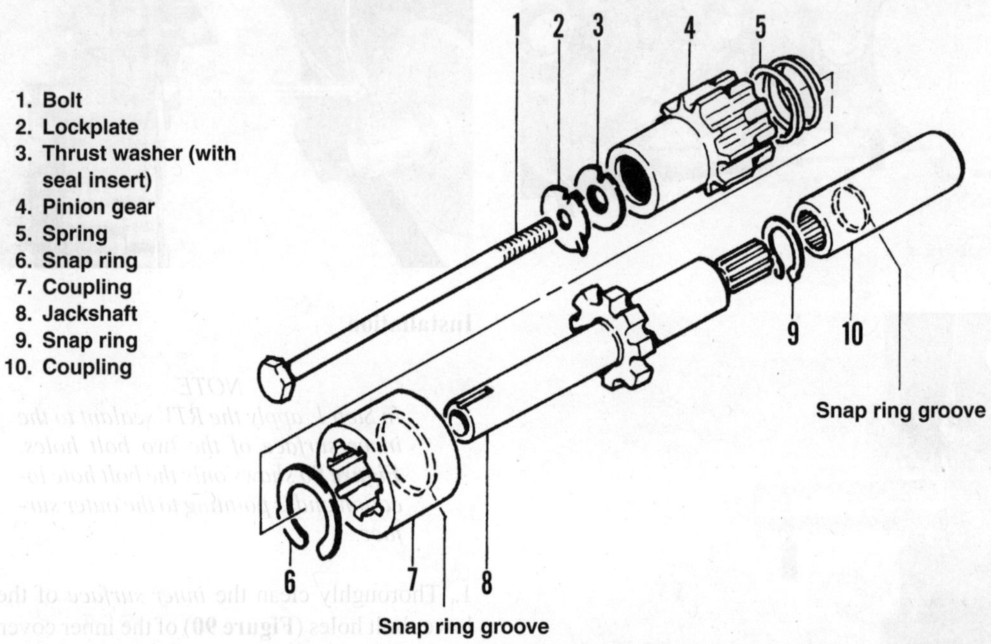

9. Install the inner housing bolts (**Figure 76**) and *new* lockwashers (**Figure 75**).

NOTE
Tighten the inner housing bolts in the following order.

10. Tighten the inner housing-to-engine mounting bolts to the specification in **Table 2**. Bend the lockwasher tabs against the bolt heads.

11. Tighten the inner housing-to-transmission mounting bolts to the specification in **Table 2**. Bend the lockwasher tabs against the bolt heads.

12. Install the starter jackshaft as described in this chapter.

13. Install the starter motor as described in Chapter Eight.

14. Install the compensating sprocket, primary chain and clutch assembly as described in this chapter.

15. Install the primary chaincase outer cover as described in this chapter.

16. Connect the negative battery cable as described in Chapter Eight.

96

97

98

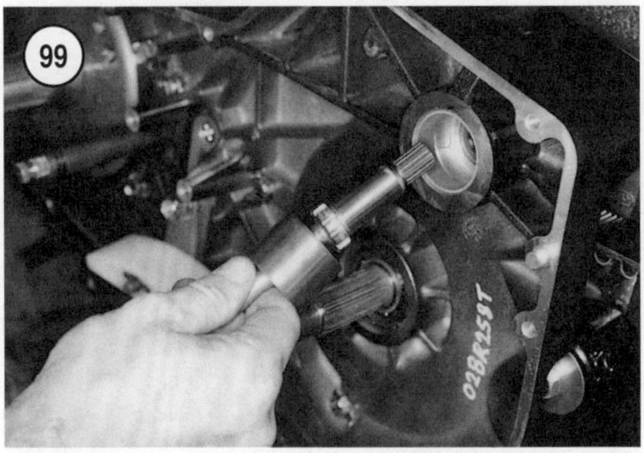

99

100

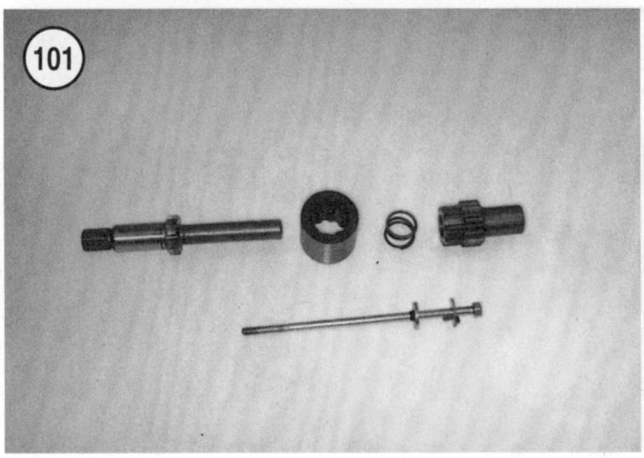

101

STARTER JACKSHAFT

Refer to **Figure 95**.

Removal

NOTE

On models so equipped, always disarm the optional TSSM security system prior to disconnecting the battery or the siren will sound.

1. Disconnect the negative battery cable as described in Chapter Eight.
2. Remove the primary chaincase outer cover as described in this chapter.

NOTE

If only removing parts 1-5 listed in ***Figure 95****, do not perform Step 3.*

3. Remove the compensating sprocket, primary chain and clutch assembly as described in this chapter.
4. Straighten the tab on the lockplate (**Figure 96**).
5. Wrap the pinion gear with a cloth to protect the finish, then secure it with locking pliers (A, **Figure 97**).
6. Loosen and remove the bolt (B, **Figure 97**), lockplate and thrust washer from the starter jackshaft assembly and the end of the starter motor.
7. Remove the pinion gear (**Figure 98**) from the jackshaft.
8. Remove the jackshaft assembly (**Figure 99**) from the inner housing.

CAUTION

Do not remove the coupling ***(Figure 100)*** *through the oil seal in the inner cover. If removed, the oil seal will be damaged.*

9. To remove the coupling (**Figure 100**), remove the starter motor as described in Chapter Eight, then remove the coupling.

Inspection

1. Clean the jackshaft assembly (**Figure 101**) in solvent and dry with compressed air.

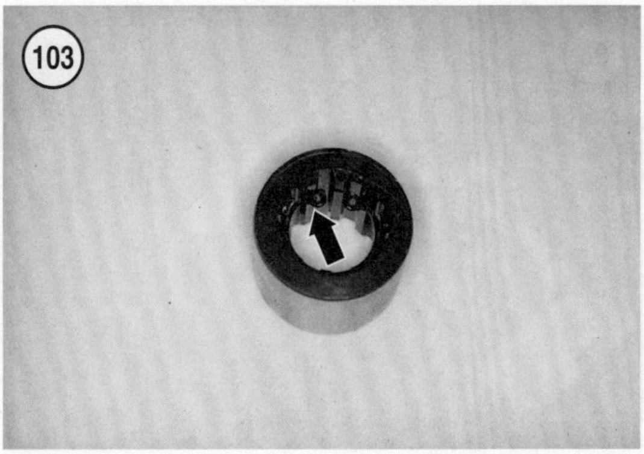

2. Check the snap ring installed in each coupling (**Figure 102** and **Figure 103**). Replace any loose or damaged snap rings.
3. Replace all worn or damaged parts.

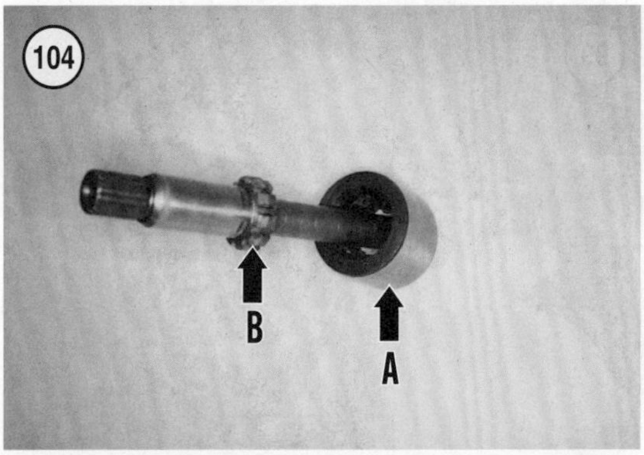

Installation

NOTE
*Before installing the coupling in Step 4, note the snap ring (**Figure 102**) installed inside the coupling. The coupling side with the snap ring closest to its end slides over the jackshaft.*

1. If removed install the coupling (**Figure 100**) and then the starter motor as described in Chapter Eight.
2. Install the coupling (A, **Figure 104**) onto the jackshaft (B, **Figure 104**) with the coupling's counterbore facing toward the jackshaft (**Figure 105**).
3. Install the jackshaft into the inner housing (**Figure 99**) and push it in until it bottoms (A, **Figure 106**).
4. Install the spring (B, **Figure 106**) onto the jackshaft.
5. Install the bolt (A, **Figure 107**), lockplate (B), thrust washer (C) and pinion gear (D) onto the jackshaft.
6. Push the assembly on until it bottoms.
7. Align the lockplate tab with the thrust washer, then insert the tab into the notch in the end of the jackshaft.
8. Screw the bolt into the starter motor shaft by hand.
9. Wrap the pinion gear with a cloth to protect the finish, then secure it with locking pliers (A, **Figure 97**).

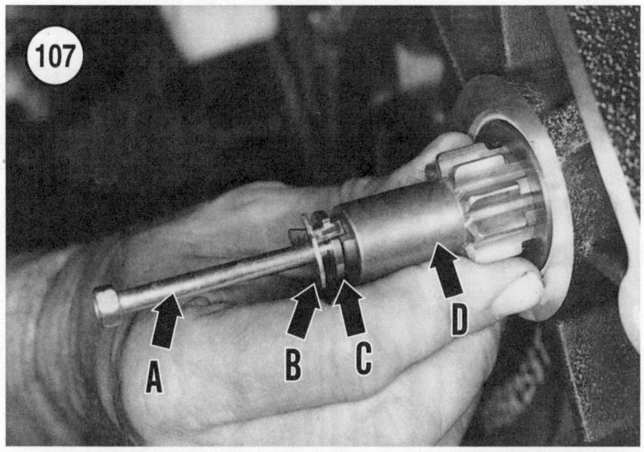

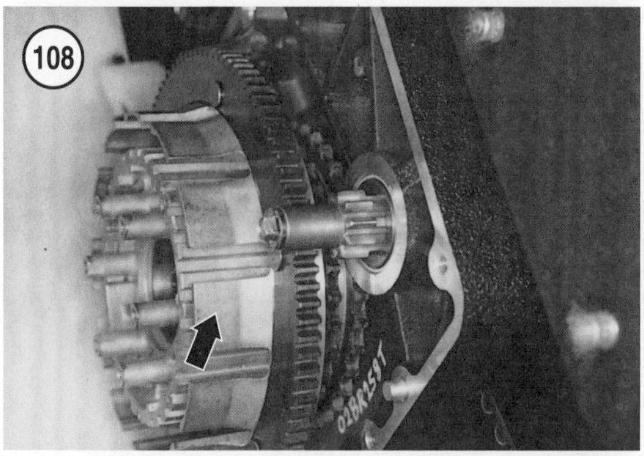

10. Tighten the bolt (B, **Figure 97**) onto the starter motor to the specification in **Table 2**. Bend the outer lockplate tab against the bolt head (**Figure 96**).

11. To ensure that all components have been installed correctly, perform the following:

a. Install the clutch shell (**Figure 108**) onto the transmission mainshaft.

b. With the starter motor not engaged, the pinion gear (A, **Figure 109**) must not engage the clutch shell gear (B, **Figure 109**).

c. To check for proper engagement, pull out on the pinion gear (A, **Figure 109**) and engage it with the clutch shell gear (B, **Figure 109**). Then rotate the clutch shell in either direction (**Figure 110**) and make sure the pinion gear rotates with it.

d. If engagement is incorrect, remove the clutch shell and correct the problem.

e. Remove the clutch shell.

12. Install the compensating sprocket, primary chain and clutch assembly as described in this chapter.

13. Install the primary chaincase outer cover as described in this chapter.

14. Connect the negative battery cable as described in Chapter Eight.

CLUTCH CABLE REPLACEMENT

1. Before removing the clutch cable, make a drawing of its routing path from the handlebar to the transmission side door.

2. Disconnect the clutch cable from the clutch release mechanism (**Figure 111**) as described under *Transmission Side Cover* in Chapter Six.

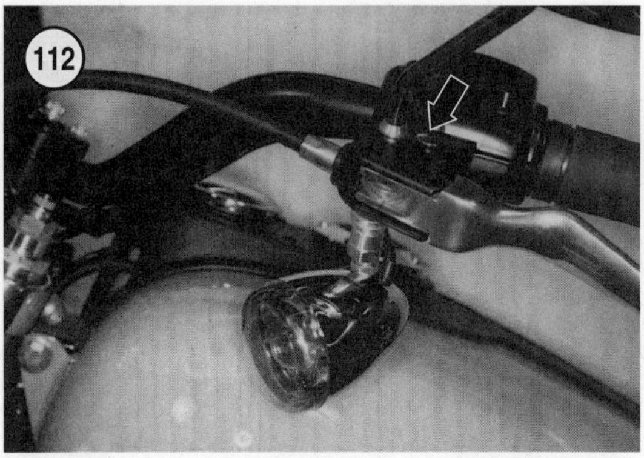

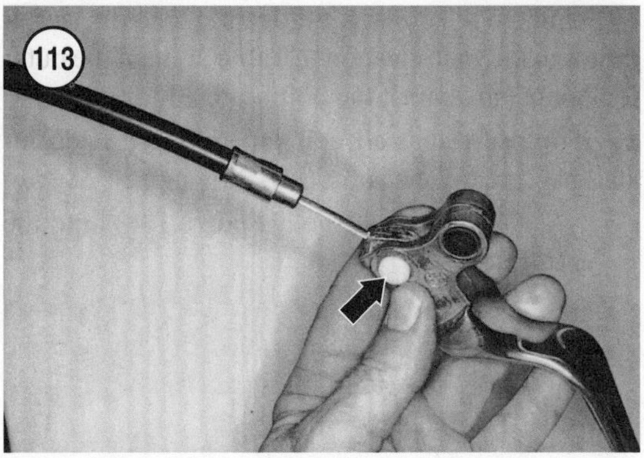

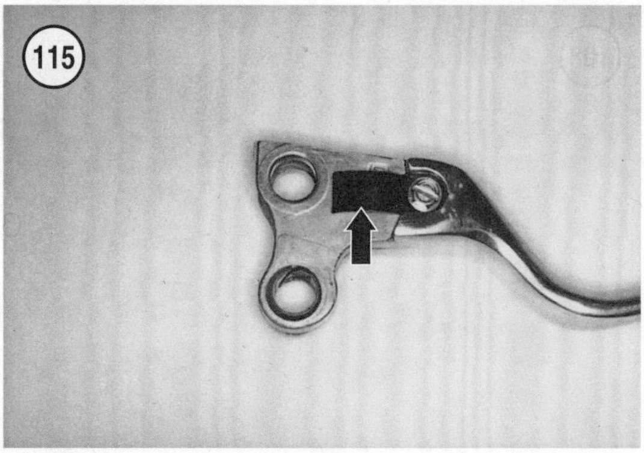

3. Remove the snap ring from the base of the clutch lever pivot pin.

4. Remove the pivot pin (**Figure 112**) and slide the clutch lever out its perch.

5. Remove the plastic anchor pin (**Figure 113**) and disconnect the clutch cable from the lever.

6. Check the clutch lever components (**Figure 114**) for worn or damaged parts.

7. Check that the anti-slack spring screw (**Figure 115**) on the bottom of the clutch lever is tight.

8. Route the new clutch cable from the handlebar to the transmission side cover, following the drawing made in Step 1.

9. Fit the clutch cable into its lever and secure with the plastic anchor pin (**Figure 113**).

10. Slide the clutch lever into the perch and install the pivot pin (**Figure 112**).

11. Secure the pivot pin with the snap ring.

12. Reconnect the clutch cable to the clutch release mechanism as described under *Transmission Side Cover* in Chapter Six.

13. Adjust the clutch as described in Chapter Three.

Table 1 CLUTCH SPECIFICATIONS AND SPROCKET SIZES

Item	Specification
Clutch type	Wet, multiplate disc
Clutch lever free play	1/16-1/8 in. (1.6-3.2 mm)
Clutch friction plate thickness	
Service limit	0.143 in. (3.62 mm)
Clutch plate warpage	
Service limit	0.006 in. (0.15 mm)
Compensating sprocket	25 teeth
Clutch sprocket	36 teeth
Transmission sprocket	32 teeth

Table 2 CLUTCH AND PRIMARY CHAINCASE TORQUE SPECIFICATIONS

Item	ft.-lb.	in.-lb.	N•m
Diaphragm spring bolts	–	90-110	10-12
Clutch hub bolt*	70-80	–	95-108
Compensating sprocket nut	150-165	–	203-224
Inner primary-to-engine bolt	17-21	–	23-29
Primary chaincase cover bolts	–	108-120	12-14
Primary chaincase inspection cover			
Long and short bolts	–	84-108	9-12
Primary chain case (inner)			
Bolts to engine and transmission	17-21	–	23-29
Starter jackshaft bolt	–	84-108	9-12

Table 3 SPROCKET ALIGNMENT SPACERS

Spacer Part No.	in.	mm
35850-84	0.010	0.25
35851-84	0.020	0.51
35852-84	0.030	0.76
24032-70	0.060	1.52
24033-70	0.090	2.29
24034-70	0.120	3.05
24035-70	0.150	3.81
24036-70	0.180	4.57
24037-70	0.210	5.33

5

NOTE: Refer to the Supplement at the back of this manual for information unique to 2002-on models.

CHAPTER SIX

TRANSMISSION

All Dyna Glide models are equipped with a 5-speed transmission. The transmission and shifter assemblies are housed in a separate case behind the engine. The transmission shaft assemblies and the shifter assemblies can be serviced with the transmission case mounted in the frame. The oil pan mounts to the bottom of the transmission case and procedures for it are described in this chapter.

Transmission service requires a number of special tools. These tools and their part numbers are listed at the start of the individual procedures. For a complete list of the special tools mentioned in this manual, refer to **Table 9** in Chapter One. The transmission tools used in this chapter are either H-D or JIMS special tools. JIMS special tools are available through some H-D dealerships or many aftermarket motorcycle suppliers.

Specifications are in **Tables 1-3** at the end of this chapter.

SHIFTER ADJUSTMENT

The shifter assembly mounts on top of the transmission case, underneath the transmission top cover. The shifter cam can be serviced with the transmission mounted in the frame.

The first step in troubleshooting a shift problem is to determine whether the problem is caused by the clutch, shifter, or transmission. Adjusting the clutch

(1)

SHIFTER ASSEMBLY (1999-2000)

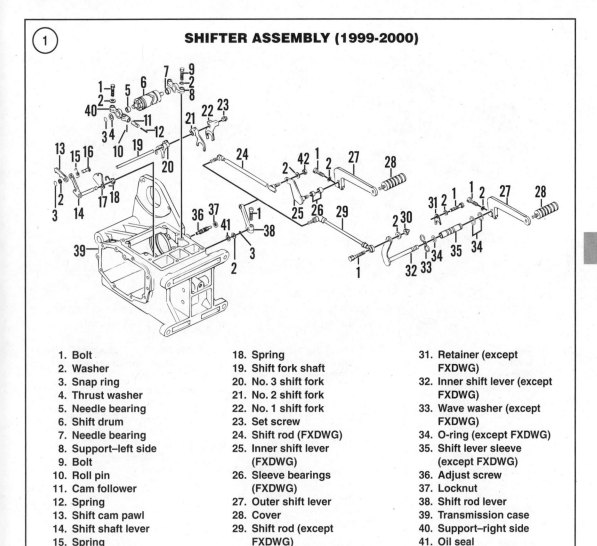

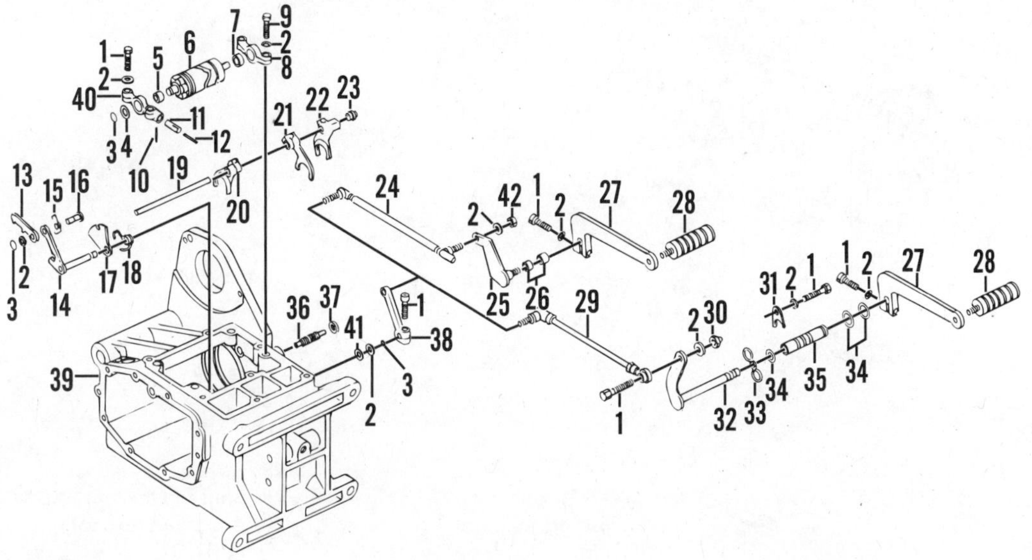

1. Bolt
2. Washer
3. Snap ring
4. Thrust washer
5. Needle bearing
6. Shift drum
7. Needle bearing
8. Support–left side
9. Bolt
10. Roll pin
11. Cam follower
12. Spring
13. Shift cam pawl
14. Shift shaft lever
15. Spring
16. Pin
17. Centering plate
18. Spring
19. Shift fork shaft
20. No. 3 shift fork
21. No. 2 shift fork
22. No. 1 shift fork
23. Set screw
24. Shift rod (FXDWG)
25. Inner shift lever (FXDWG)
26. Sleeve bearings (FXDWG)
27. Outer shift lever
28. Cover
29. Shift rod (except FXDWG)
30. Acorn nut (except FXDWG)
31. Retainer (except FXDWG)
32. Inner shift lever (except FXDWG)
33. Wave washer (except FXDWG)
34. O-ring (except FXDWG)
35. Shift lever sleeve (except FXDWG)
36. Adjust screw
37. Locknut
38. Shift rod lever
39. Transmission case
40. Support–right side
41. Oil seal
42. Nut

(Chapter Three) can generally fix minor clutch problems. If the shifter linkage or adjuster is out of adjustment, perform the following procedure. Make sure to eliminate all clutch or shifter mechanism problems *before* assuming a problem is in the transmission.

Refer to **Figure 1** (1999-2000 models), **Figure 2** (2001 models except FXDP) and **Figure 3** (FXDP models).

Shift Linkage Adjustment

The shift linkage assembly consists of the shift linkage rod and two ball joints. The shift linkage assembly connects the transmission shifter rod lever to the foot-operated shift lever. The shift linkage adjustment does not require adjustment unless the shift linkage is replaced or the transmission gears do not engage properly.

NOTE

On models so equipped, always disarm the optional TSSM security system prior to disconnecting the battery or the siren will sound.

1. Disconnect the negative battery cable as described in Chapter Eight.

(2)

SHIFTER ASSEMBLY (2001 EXCEPT FXDP)

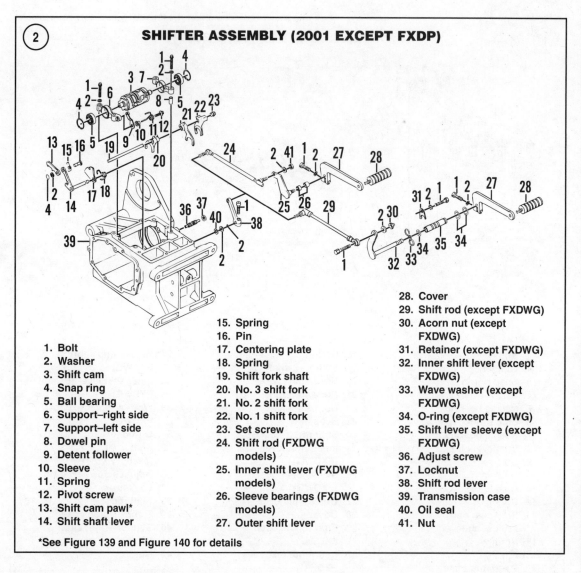

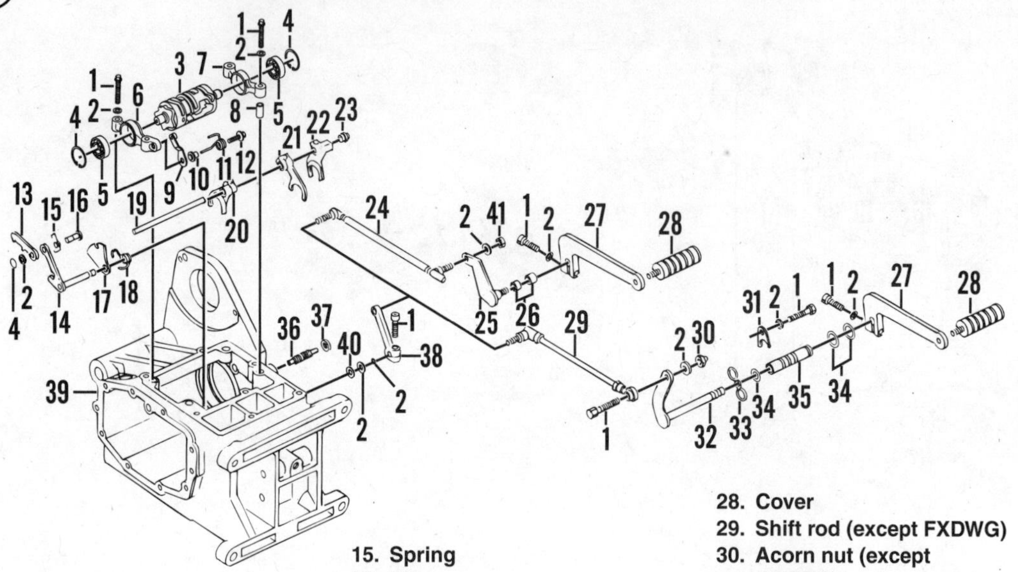

1. Bolt
2. Washer
3. Shift cam
4. Snap ring
5. Ball bearing
6. Support–right side
7. Support–left side
8. Dowel pin
9. Detent follower
10. Sleeve
11. Spring
12. Pivot screw
13. Shift cam pawl*
14. Shift shaft lever
15. Spring
16. Pin
17. Centering plate
18. Spring
19. Shift fork shaft
20. No. 3 shift fork
21. No. 2 shift fork
22. No. 1 shift fork
23. Set screw
24. Shift rod (FXDWG models)
25. Inner shift lever (FXDWG models)
26. Sleeve bearings (FXDWG models)
27. Outer shift lever
28. Cover
29. Shift rod (except FXDWG)
30. Acorn nut (except FXDWG)
31. Retainer (except FXDWG)
32. Inner shift lever (except FXDWG)
33. Wave washer (except FXDWG)
34. O-ring (except FXDWG)
35. Shift lever sleeve (except FXDWG)
36. Adjust screw
37. Locknut
38. Shift rod lever
39. Transmission case
40. Oil seal
41. Nut

***See Figure 139 and Figure 140 for details**

2. Loosen the two shift linkage rod locknuts (A, **Figure 4**).

3. Remove the acorn nut, washers and bolt (B, **Figure 4**) securing the shift linkage rod to the inner shift lever.

4. Turn the shift linkage rod (C, **Figure 4**) as necessary to change the linkage adjustment.

5. Tighten the locknuts and reconnect the shift linkage rod to the shift lever.

6. Recheck the shifting. Readjust if necessary.

7. If proper shifting cannot be obtained by performing this adjustment, check the shift linkage for any interference problems. Then check the shift linkage assembly for worn or damaged parts. Perform the *Gear Engagement Check/Adjustment* procedure if there are no visible interference problems or damage.

Gear Engagement Check/Adjustment (1999-2000 Models Only)

If the transmission gears do not engage properly, check and adjust gear engagement as follows:

NOTE
The 2001 models do not require this check and adjustment procedure.

1. Make sure the clutch is working properly. Refer to clutch adjustment in Chapter Three. If the clutch is working properly, continue with Step 2.

3

SHIFTER ASSEMBLY (2001 FXDP)

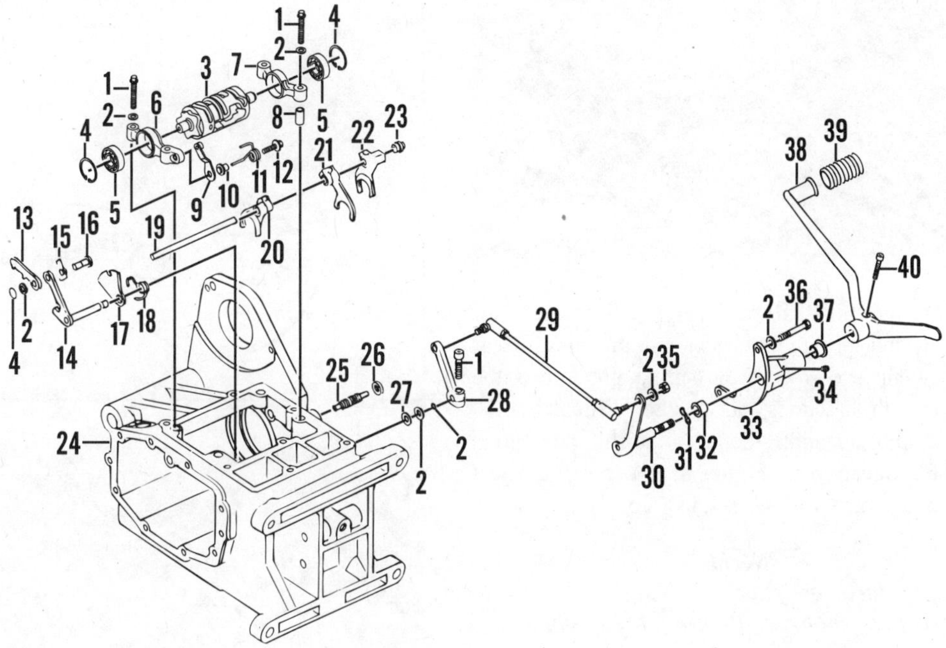

1. Bolt
2. Washer
3. Shift cam
4. Snap ring
5. Ball bearing
6. Support–right side
7. Support–left side
8. Dowel pin
9. Detent follower
10. Sleeve
11. Spring
12. Pivot screw
13. Shift cam pawl*
14. Shift shaft lever
15. Spring
16. Pin
17. Centering plate
18. Spring
19. Shift fork shaft
20. No. 3 shift fork
21. No. 2 shift fork
22. No. 1 shift fork
23. Set screw
24. Transmission case
25. Adjust screw
26. Locknut
27. Oil seal
28. Shift lever
29. Shift rod
30. Inner shift lever
31. Wave washer
32. Bushing
33. Shift lever plate
34. Grease fitting
35. Acorn nut
36. Bolt
37. Bushing
38. Outer shift lever
39. Cover
40. Set screw

*See Figure 139 and Figure 140 for details

4

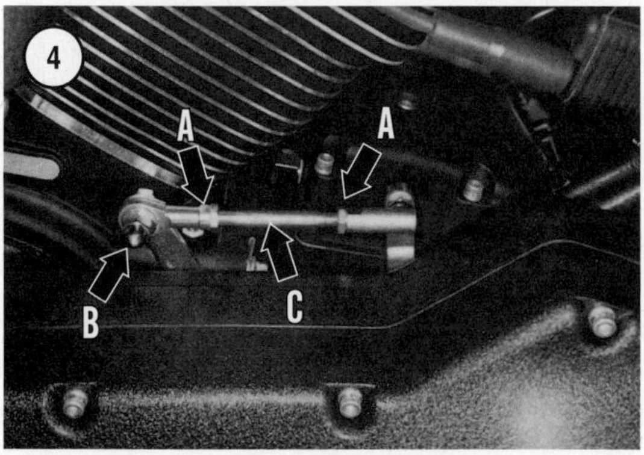

NOTE

On models so equipped, always disarm the optional TSSM security system prior to disconnecting the battery or the siren will sound.

2. Disconnect the negative battery cable as described in Chapter Eight.

3. Shift the transmission into third gear. Make sure third gear is fully engaged.

4. Remove the transmission top cover as described in this chapter.

5. Move the shift shaft pawl (**Figure 5**) to check for free play and spring pressure in both directions. Gear engagement is correct if the spring pressure is the same in both directions and with approximately 0.10 in. (0.25 mm) clearance between the shift pawl arms and the shift cam pins (**Figure 6**). If necessary, adjust gear engagement as described in Step 6.

NOTE

An incorrectly adjusted shift pawl causes many shifting-related problems.

6. To adjust the gear engagement, follow these steps:
   a. The shifter pawl adjuster is mounted on the left-hand side of the transmission case (**Figure 7**). It is between the transmission case and primary chain housing. **Figure 8** shows the shifter pawl adjusting screw and locknut with the inner primary housing removed for clarity.
   b. Use the transmission pawl adjuster (part No. HD-39618) to adjust the shifter pawl adjuster.
   c. Loosen the adjuster screw locknut (**Figure 8**) and turn the shifter pawl adjuster in 1/4 turn (or less) increments (either clockwise or counterclockwise). Turn the screw until the shifter lever travel spring pressure is equal on both sides while maintaining a clearance of 0.010 in. (0.25 mm). Tighten the locknut and recheck the adjustment.
7. Reinstall the transmission top cover as described in this chapter.
8. Reconnect the negative battery cable.

TRANSMISSION TOP COVER

The transmission top cover assembly can be serviced with the transmission installed in the frame.

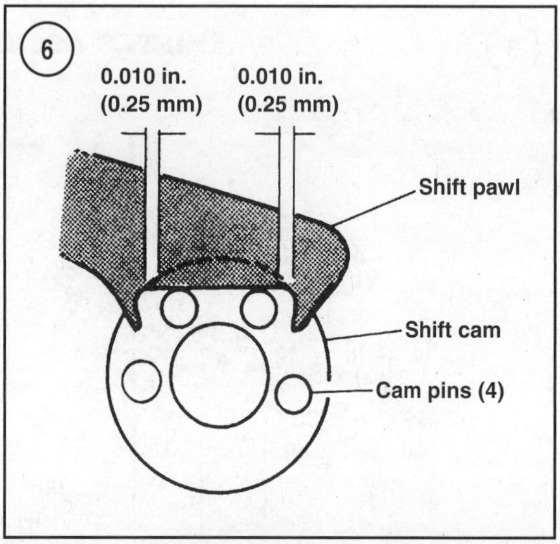

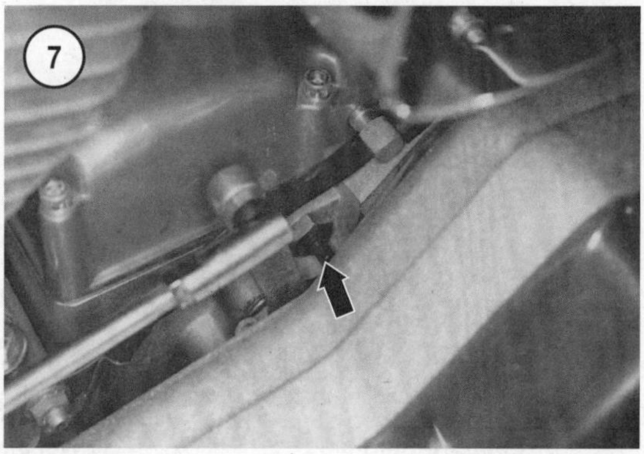

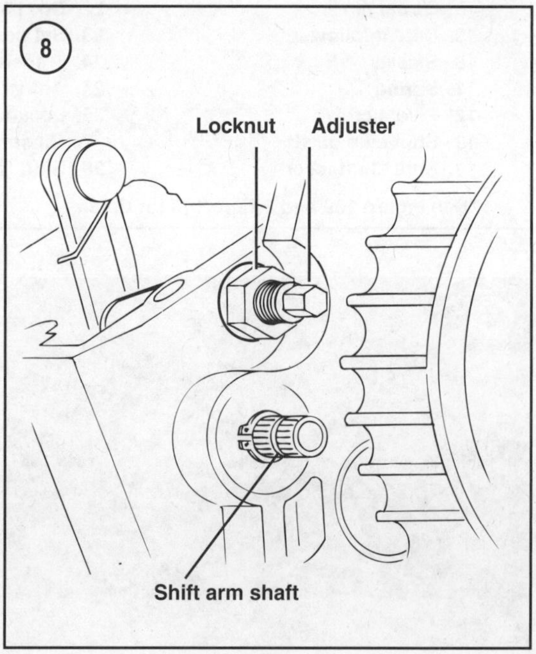

9

10

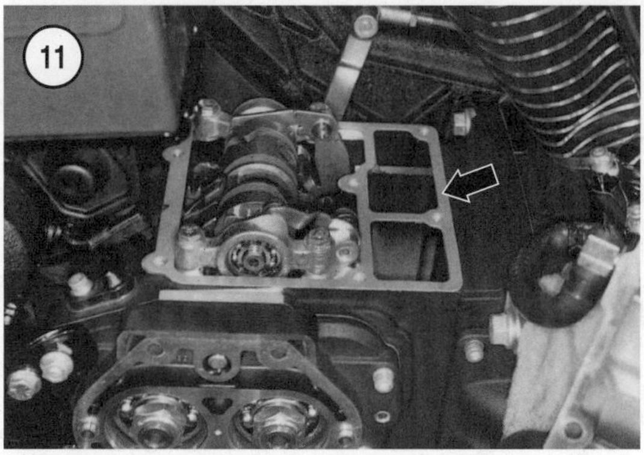
11

Removal/Installation

1. Remove the rear exhaust pipe or entire exhaust system as described in Chapter Seven.
2. Disconnect the wire from the neutral indicator switch (**Figure 9**).
3. Remove the transmission oil dipstick.
4. Disconnect the hoses (A, **Figure 10**) from the top cover or their fittings.
5. Remove the bolts and washers securing the transmission cover to the transmission case. Remove the top cover (B, **Figure 10**) and the gasket.
6. Remove the gasket residue from the transmission cover and transmission case gasket surfaces.
7. Install a *new* gasket (**Figure 11**) onto the transmission case.
8. Install the transmission top cover, bolts and washers. Tighten the bolts in a crisscross pattern to the specification in **Table 3**.
9. Reconnect the hoses to the fittings and install new hose clamps.
10. Install the transmission oil dipstick.
11. Connect the wire to the neutral indicator switch (**Figure 9**).
12. Install the rear exhaust pipe or entire exhaust system as described in Chapter Seven.

SHIFTER CAM (1999-2000)

The shifter cam mounts on top of the transmission case, underneath the transmission top cover. The shifter cam assembly can be serviced with the transmission installed in the frame.

Refer to **Figure 12**.

Removal

1. Remove the transmission top cover as described in this chapter.
2. Remove the shifter cam support block mounting bolts and lockwashers.
3. Carefully lift the shifter cam assembly up and out of the transmission case.
4. Remove the four dowel pins from the transmission case.

Installation

1. Install the four dowel pins into the transmission case.
2. Measure shifter cam end play as follows:
   a. Position the left support block with the numbers facing down toward the transmission case.
   b. Install the shifter cam/support block assembly onto the transmission case. Align the shift fork pins with the shifter cam slots.
   c. Use a flat feeler gauge (A, **Figure 13**) and measure the clearance between the outer thrust washer and the shifter cam (B, **Figure 13**). This clearance is shifter cam end play.

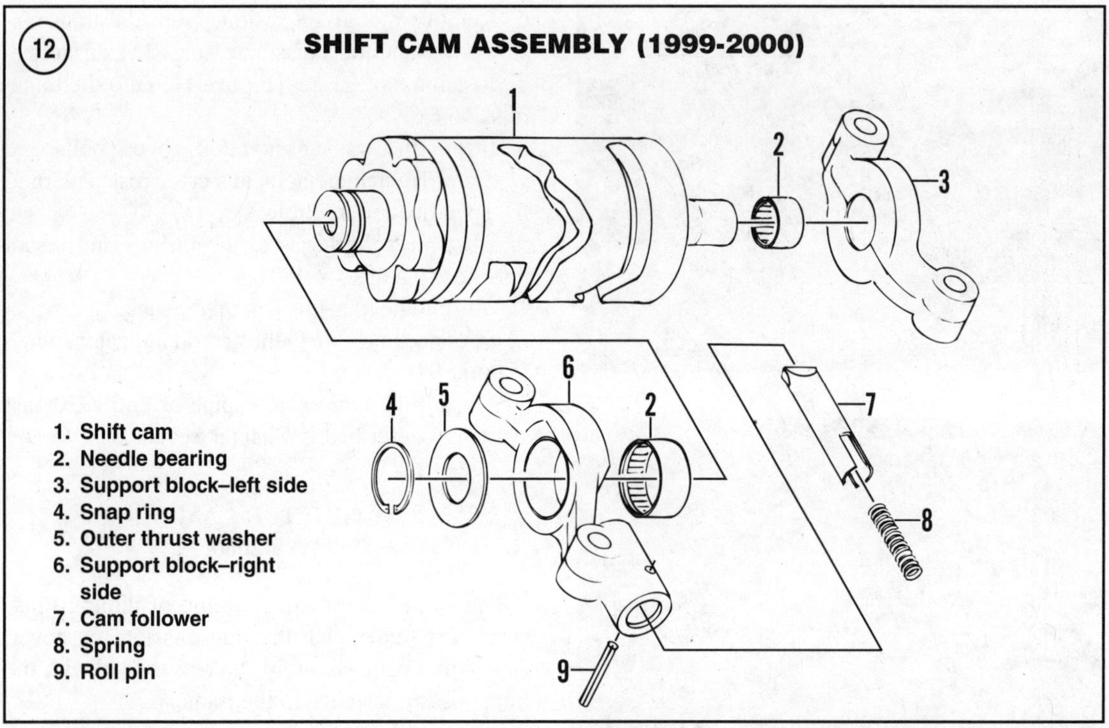

Refer to **Table 2** for the end play measurement.

d. To correct end play, replace the outer thrust washer (**Figure 12**) with a suitable thickness thrust washer.

NOTE

Inner and outer thrust washers are available from Harley-Davidson dealers in the following thicknesses: 0.017, 0.020, 0.022, 0.025, 0.028, 0.031, 0.035 and 0.039 in. (0.43, 0.51, 0.56, 0.63, 0.71, 0.79, 0.89 and 0.99 mm).

e. If necessary, remove the shifter cam assembly from the transmission case and install a new outer thrust washer.

3. Apply engine oil to the shifter cam bearing surfaces.
4. Align the shift fork pins with the shifter cam slots and install the shifter cam into position (**Figure 14**).
5. Engage the shifter pawl with the shifter cam (**Figure 15**).

CAUTION

Do not overtighten the shifter cam mounting bolts as this can distort the

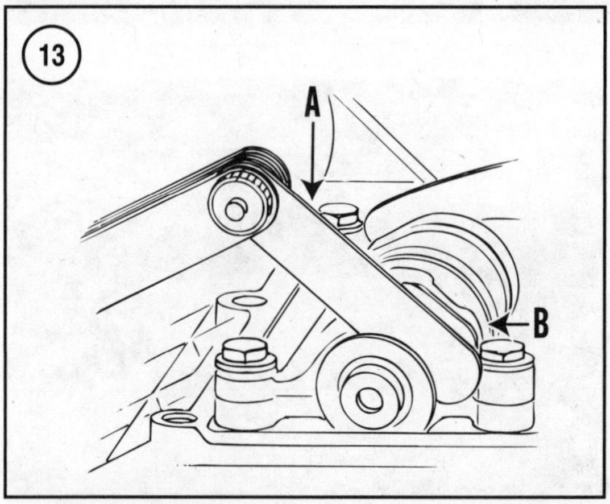

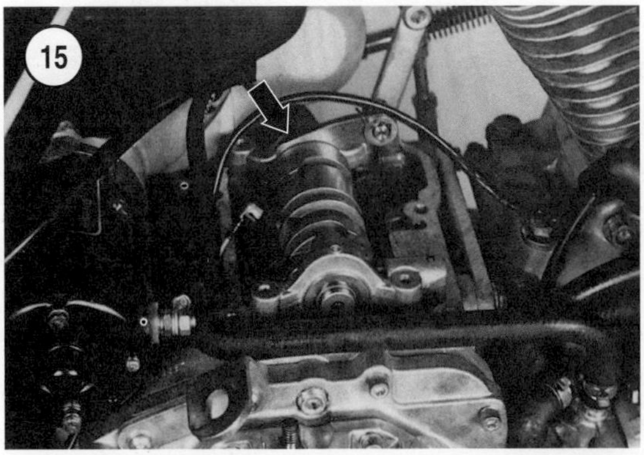

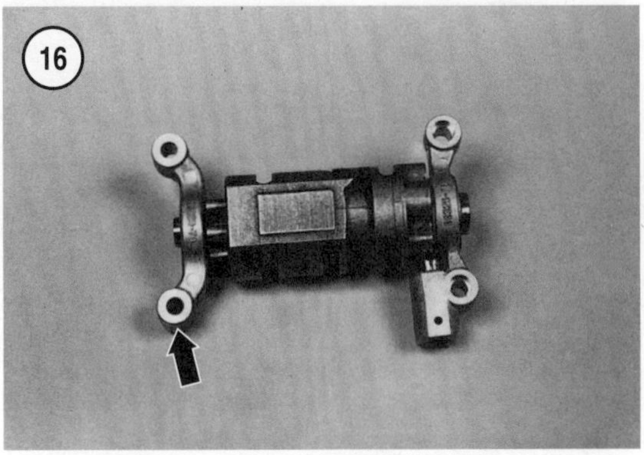

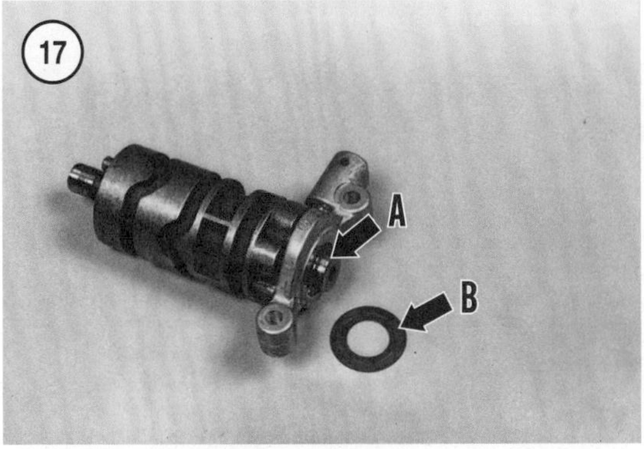

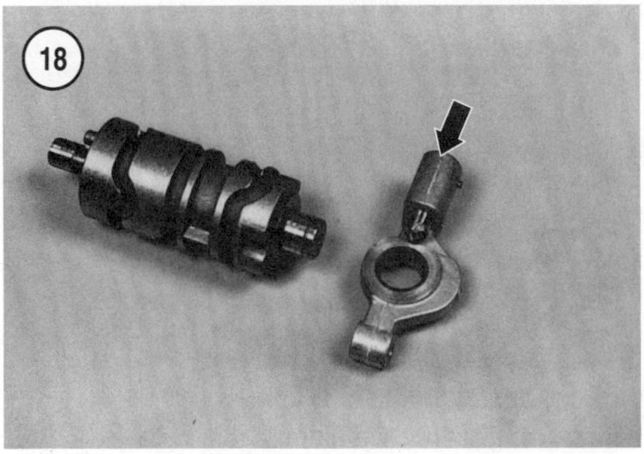

cam follower and cause shifting problems. Do not exceed the torque specification in Step 6.

6. Install the shifter cam support block mounting bolts and lockwashers. Tighten in a crisscross pattern to the specification in **Table 3**.
7. Perform the *Gear Engagement Check/Adjustment* in this chapter.
8. Install the transmission top cover as described in this chapter.

Disassembly

1. Slide the left side support block (**Figure 16**) off the shifter cam.
2. Remove the shifter cam snap ring (A, **Figure 17**) and the outer thrust washer (B, **Figure 17**).
3. Remove the right side support block (**Figure 18**).

Inspection

1. Clean all parts except the support block bearings in solvent and thoroughly dry.
2. Check the shifter cam grooves (**Figure 19**) for wear or roughness. Replace the shifter cam if the groove profiles show excessive wear or damage.
3. Check the shifter cam ends where the cam contacts the bearings. If the ends show wear or damage, replace the shifter cam and both support block bearings. Refer to *Support Block Bearing Replacement* in this chapter.
4. Check the support block bearings for excessive wear, cracks, or other damage. See **Figure 20** and **Figure 21**. If necessary, refer to *Support Block Bearing Replacement* in this chapter to replace the bearings.

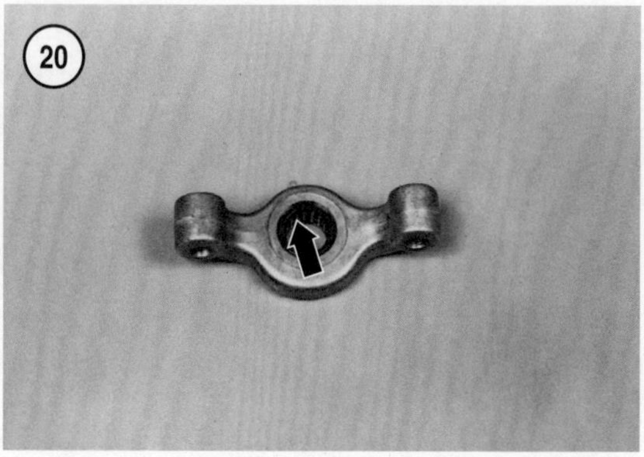

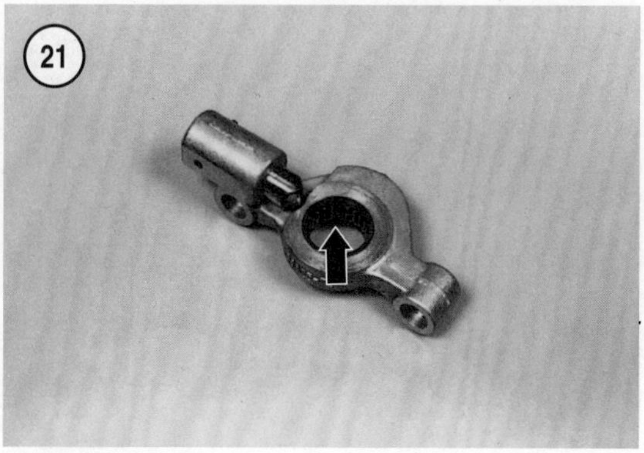

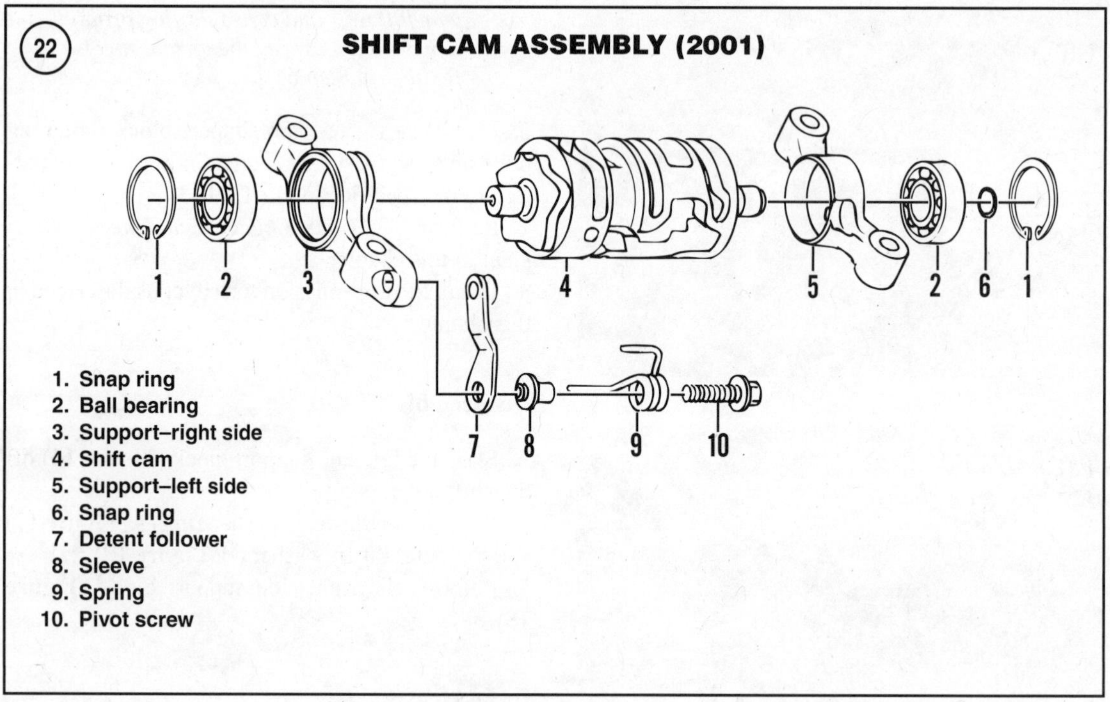

5. Check the support blocks for wear, cracks or other damage. Replace the support blocks if necessary.

Assembly

1. Coat all bearing and sliding surfaces with assembly oil.

2. Install the right support block (**Figure 18**) on the shifter cam.

3. Install the outer thrust washer (B, **Figure 17**) and a new snap ring (A, **Figure 17**). Make sure the snap ring seats in the shifter cam groove.

NOTE
After installing the snap ring, make sure the outer thrust washer can be rotated by hand.

4. Install the left support block (**Figure 16**) onto the shifter cam.
5. Rotate the support blocks so their numbered side is facing down.

Support Block Bearing Replacement

Each support block is equipped with a single needle bearing. See **Figure 20** and **Figure 21**. Replace both bearings at the same time. The removal and in-

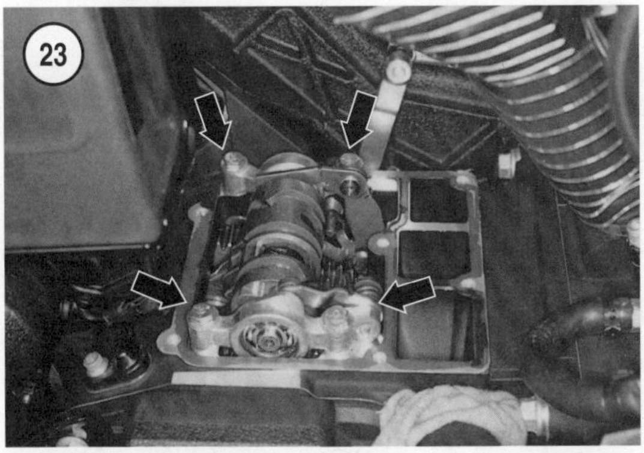

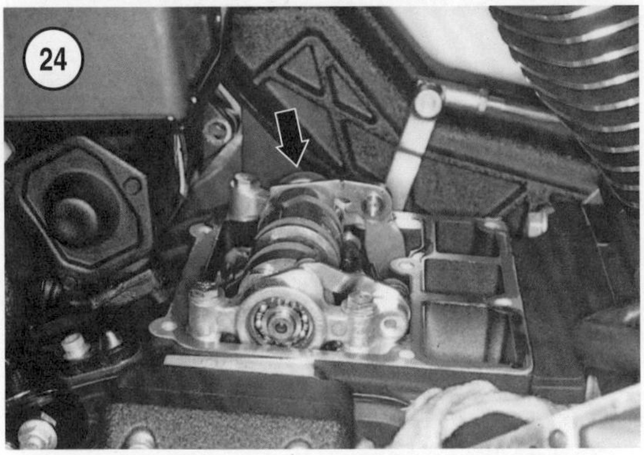

stallation of the bearings requires a press. Refer to *Bearing Replacement* in Chapter One. Before removing the bearings, record the direction in which the bearing manufacturer's marks face for proper installation.

SHIFTER CAM (2001)

The shifter cam mounts on top of the transmission case, underneath the transmission top cover. The shifter cam assembly can be serviced with the transmission installed in the frame.

Refer to **Figure 22**.

Removal

1. Remove the transmission top cover as described in this chapter.
2. Remove the shifter cam support block mounting bolts and lockwashers (**Figure 23**).
3. Lift the shifter cam pawl off the cam pins to free the assembly.
4. Carefully lift the shifter cam assembly up and out of the transmission case.

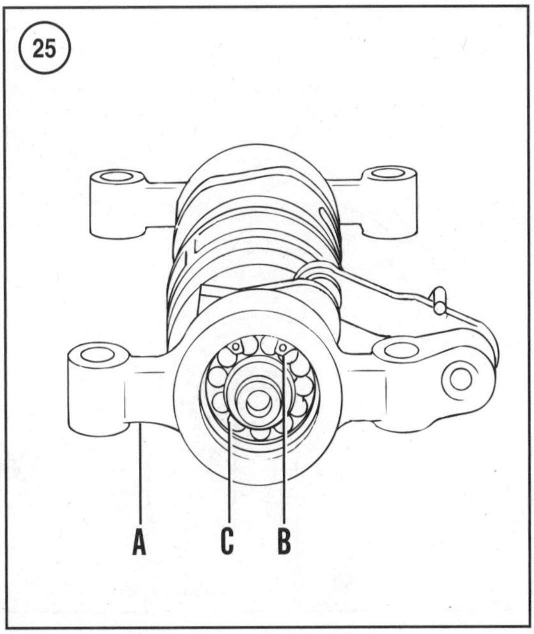

5. Remove the four dowel pins from the transmission case.

Installation

1. Install the four dowel pins into the transmission case.
2. Lift the shifter cam pawl up out of the way.
3. Carefully install the shifter cam assembly into the transmission case. Align the shifter fork pins with the shifter cam slots (**Figure 24**).
4. Lower the shifter cam pawl and engage it with the cam pins.
5. Install the shifter cam support block mounting bolts and lockwashers (**Figure 23**). Tighten in a crisscross pattern to the specification in **Table 3**.
6. Install the transmission top cover as described in this chapter.

Disassembly

1. On the right side, perform the following:
   a. Slide the right side support block (A, **Figure 25**) off the shifter cam.
   b. Remove the retaining ring (B, **Figure 25**) and withdraw the bearing (C, **Figure 25**) from the support block.
2. On the left side, perform the following:

6

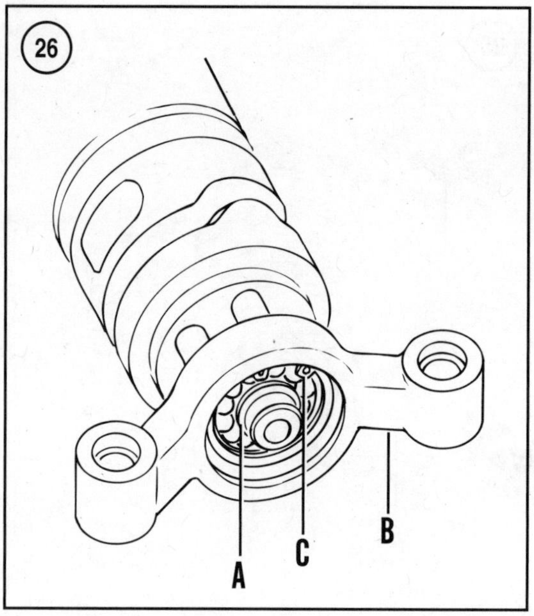

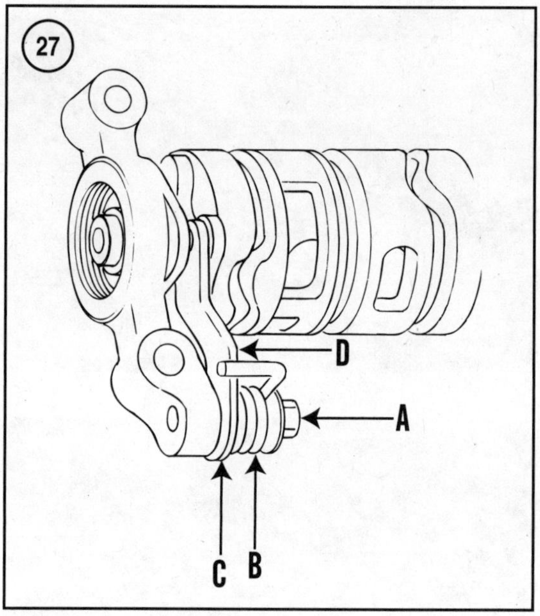

a. Remove the small retaining ring (A, **Figure 26**) from the shifter cam.
b. Slide the left side support block (B, **Figure 26**) off the shifter cam.
c. Remove the large retaining ring (C, **Figure 26**) and withdraw the bearing from the support block.

3. To remove the detent follower, unscrew the pivot bolt (A, **Figure 27**). Remove the spring (B), spring sleeve (C) and the detent follower (D).

Inspection

1. Clean all parts except the support block bearings in solvent and dry thoroughly.
2. Check the shifter cam grooves (**Figure 19**) for wear or roughness. Replace the shifter cam if the groove profiles show excessive wear or damage.
3. Check the shifter cam ends where the cam contacts the bearings. If the ends show wear or damage, replace the shifter cam and both support block bearings; see *Support Block Bearing Replacement* in this chapter.
4. Check the support block bearings for excessive wear, cracks, or other damage. See **Figures 20** and **21**. If necessary, refer to *Support Block Bearing Replacement* in this chapter to replace the bearings.
5. Check the support blocks for wear, cracks or other damage. Replace the support blocks if necessary.

Assembly

1. Coat all bearing and sliding surfaces with assembly oil.
2. To install the detent follower, perform the following:
   a. Slide the spring sleeve (C, **Figure 27**) into the spring (B).
   b. Insert the pivot bolt (A) through the spring and sleeve.
   c. Correctly position the detent follower onto the bolt and place the spring end over the detent follower.
   d. Install the assembly onto the right side support and insert the spring's other end into the receptacle in the right side support. Screw the bolt into place and tighten to the specification in **Table 3**.
3. On the left side, perform the following:
   a. Position the bearing with the manufacturer's numbers facing out. Install the bearing into the support block.
   b. Position the new large retaining ring (C, **Figure 26**) so the larger tab will be on the right side when looking at the end of the support block. Install the large retaining ring.
   c. Make sure the retaining ring is correctly seated in the groove.
   d. Slide the left side support block (B, **Figure 26**) onto the shifter cam.

28

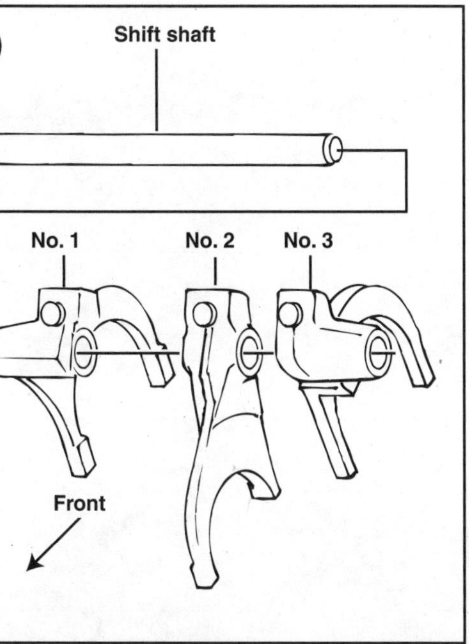

30

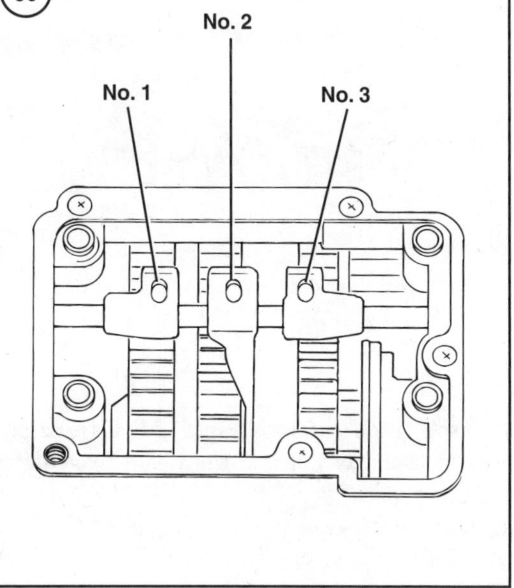

29

e. Install a *new* small retaining ring (A, **Figure 26**) onto the shifter cam.

f. Make sure the small retaining ring is correctly seated in the groove.

4. On the right side, perform the following:

a. Position the bearing with the manufacturer's numbers facing out. Install the bearing into the support block.

b. Position the *new* retaining ring (B, **Figure 25**) with the beveled side facing out when looking at the end of the support block. Install the large retaining ring.

c. Make sure the retaining ring is correctly seated in the groove.

d. Slide the right side support block (A, **Figure 25**) onto the shifter cam.

SHIFT FORKS

The shift forks are installed at the top of the transmission case, underneath the shifter cam. The shift forks can be serviced with the transmission installed in the frame.

Refer to **Figure 1** (1999-2000 models), **Figure 2** (2001 models except FXDP) and **Figure 3** (FXDP models).

Removal

1. Remove the shifter cam as described in this chapter.

2. Remove the transmission side cover as described in this chapter.

NOTE

*Use a waterproof felt-tip pen or scribe to mark the installed position of each shift fork as it sits in the transmission (**Figure 28**). All three shift forks are unique and must be reinstalled in the correct position.*

3. Slide the shift shaft (A, **Figure 29**) out of the transmission case and remove the shift forks (**Figure 30**) from the transmission case.

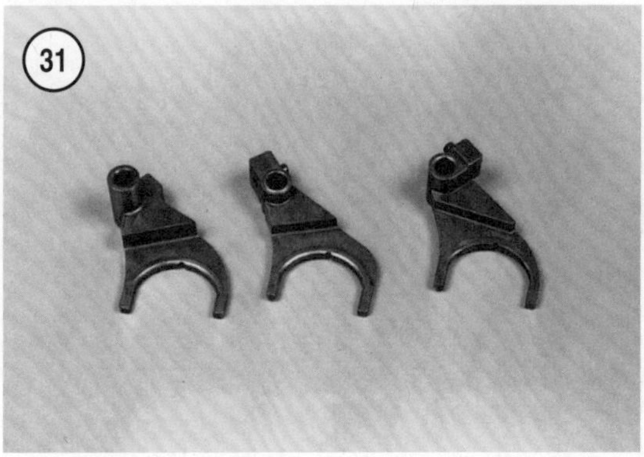

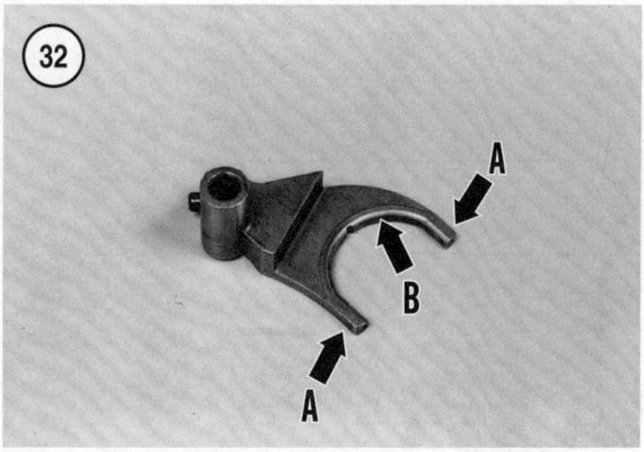

Inspection

1. Inspect each shift fork (**Figure 31**) for excessive wear or damage. Replace worn or damaged shift forks as required.
2. Measure the thickness of each shift fork finger (A, **Figure 32**) where it contacts the sliding gear groove (**Figure 33**). Replace any shift fork with a finger thickness worn to the specification in **Table 2**.
3. Check the shift forks for arc-shaped wear or burn marks (B, **Figure 32**). Replace damaged shift forks.
4. Roll the shift fork shaft on a flat surface and check for bending. Replace the shaft if bent.
5. Install each shift fork on the shift shaft. The shift fingers must slide smoothly with no binding or roughness.

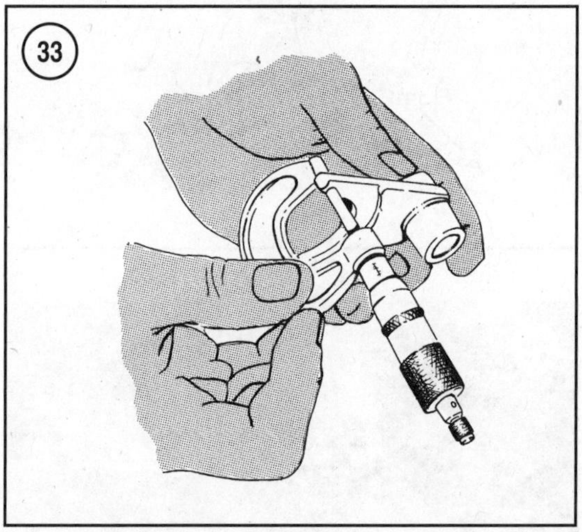

Assembly

Refer to **Figure 34** to identify the transmission gears.

1. Coat all bearing and sliding surfaces with assembly oil.
2. To install the shift forks and shaft (**Figure 28**), perform the following:
   a. Insert the No. 1 shift fork into the mainshaft first gear groove.
   b. Install the No. 2 shift fork into the countershaft third gear groove.
   c. Install the No. 3 shift fork into the mainshaft second gear groove.
3. Insert the shift shaft through the transmission case (A, **Figure 29**), through each of the three shift forks and into the transmission case.
4. Install the transmission side door as described in this chapter.
5. Check that the shift forks move smoothly when shifting the gears by hand.

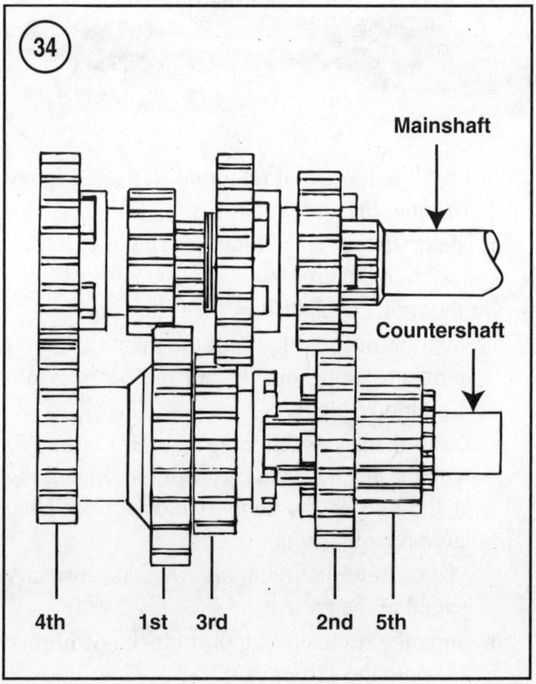

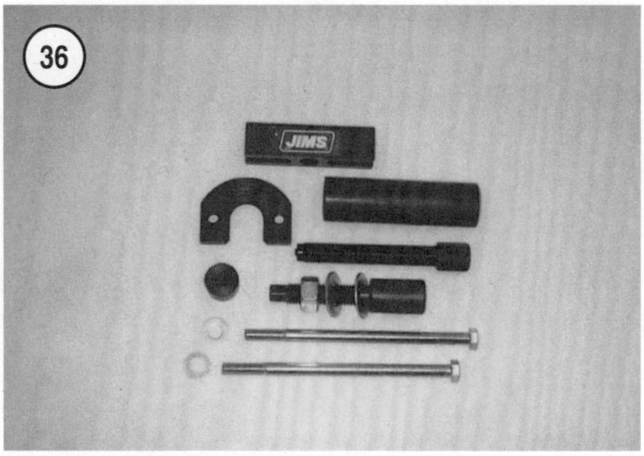

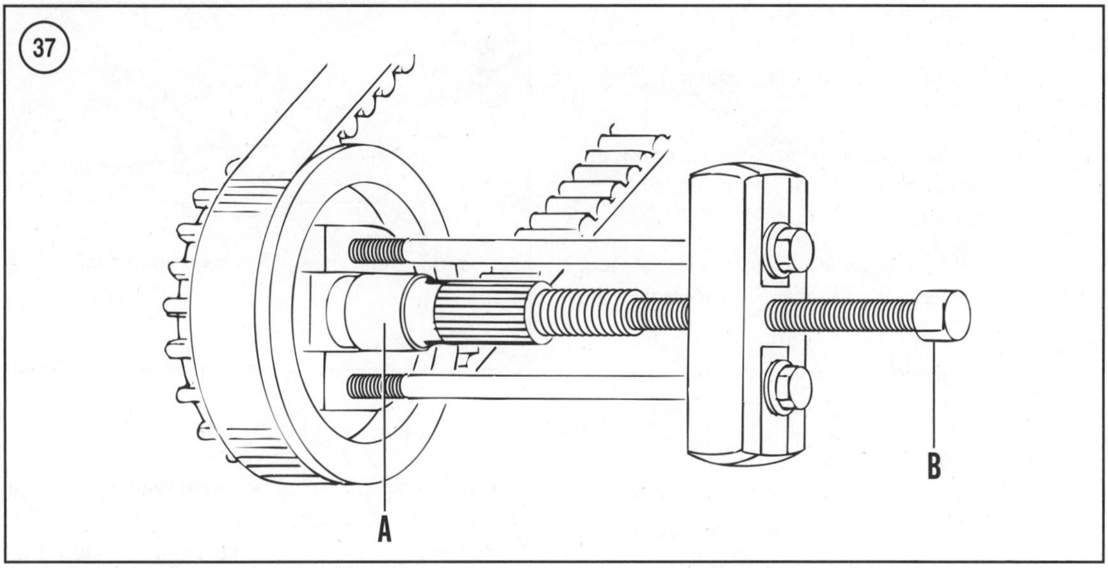

6

6. Install the shifter cam as described in this chapter.

TRANSMISSION SIDE DOOR AND TRANSMISSION SHAFT ASSEMBLIES

The transmission side door and transmission shaft assemblies can be serviced with the transmission installed in the frame.

Removal

This section describes removal of the transmission and side door assembly.

1. Remove the exhaust system as described in Chapter Seven.
2. Drain the transmission oil as described in Chapter Three.
3. Remove the primary chaincase cover as described in Chapter Five.
4. Remove the clutch release cover and clutch assembly as described in Chapter Five.
5. Remove the primary chaincase housing as described in Chapter Five.
6. Remove the shift forks as described in this chapter.
7. Remove the bearing inner race (**Figure 35**) from the mainshaft, and perform the following:
   a. Attach the mainshaft bearing race puller and installation tool (**Figure 36**) against the inner bearing race (A, **Figure 37**), following the manufacturer's instructions.
   b. Tighten the puller bolt (B, **Figure 37**) and withdraw the inner race from the mainshaft.
8. Remove the pushrod assembly (B, **Figure 29**).
9. Turn the transmission by hand and shift the transmission into two different gears to lock the transmission in place.

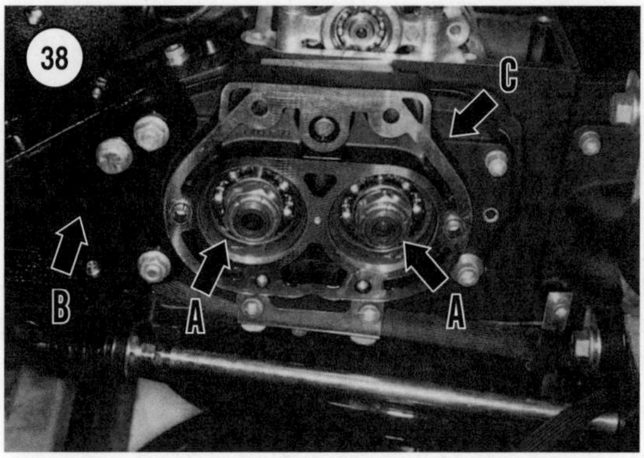

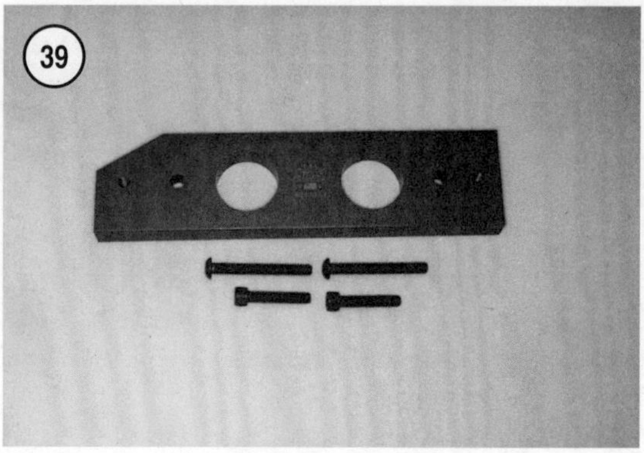

10. If the transmission gear assemblies are going to be removed from the side door, loosen, but do not remove, the countershaft and mainshaft locknuts (A, **Figure 38**).

11. If the main drive gear is going to be removed, remove the drive sprocket as described under *Drive Sprocket* in Chapter Nine.

12. Remove the bolts securing the exhaust system mounting bracket (B, **Figure 38**). Remove the bracket.

13. Remove the bolts securing the transmission side door (C, **Figure 38**) to the transmission case.

CAUTION
When removing the transmission side door in Step 14, do not tap against the transmission shafts from the opposite side. Doing so will damage the side door bearings.

14. Tap against the transmission side door to loosen its seal against the transmission case.

15. Install the transmission door bearing puller (**Figure 39**) onto the door, following the manufacturer's instructions. Tighten the outside screws 1/2 turn at a time, alternating from side-to-side until the door releases from the transmission case. Remove the special tool.

16. Slowly withdraw the transmission side door and the transmission gear assemblies from the transmission case.

17. Remove the transmission side door gasket. Do not lose the locating pins.

18. If necessary, service the side door and transmission assembly as described in this chapter.

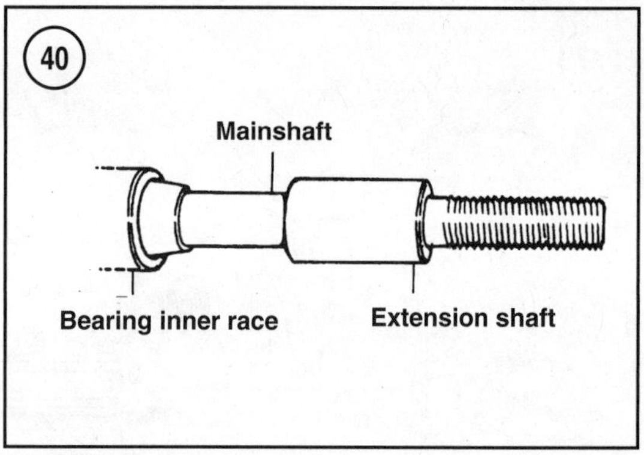

Installation

1. If the main drive gear was removed, install it as described in this chapter.
2. Remove all gasket residue from the side door and transmission case mating surfaces.
3. Install a *new* gasket onto the transmission case. If removed, install the locating pins.
4. Install the side door and transmission assembly into the transmission case. Check that the side door fits flush against the transmission case.
5. Install the transmission side door 5/16 in. and 1/4 in. bolts finger-tight. Tighten the 5/16 in. bolts to the specifications in **Table 3**. Then do the same for the 1/4 in. bolts.
6. Turn the transmission by hand and shift the transmission into two different gear speeds to lock the transmission from rotation.
7. To install the bearing inner race (**Figure 35**) onto the mainshaft, perform the following:
   a. The bearing inner race is 0.950-1.000 in. (24.13-25.40 mm) long. When installing a new race, measure it to confirm its length. Race length determines its final installation position.

(41)

TRANSMISSION

1. Mainshaft first gear
2. Mainshaft
3. Snap ring
4. Thrust washer
5. Mainshaft third gear
6. Mainshaft second gear
7. Split bearings
8. Oil slinger assembly
9. Clutch pushrod
10. Locknut
11. Washer
12. Side door
13. Gasket
14. Spacer
15. Mainshaft fourth gear
16. Spacer
17. Countershaft fourth gear
18. Countershaft first gear
19. Countershaft
20. Countershaft third gear
21. Countershaft second gear
22. Countershaft fifth gear

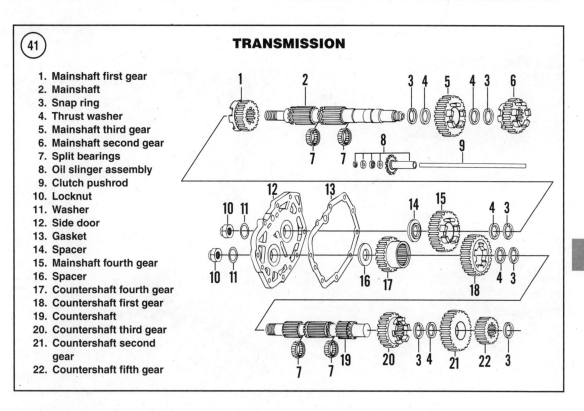

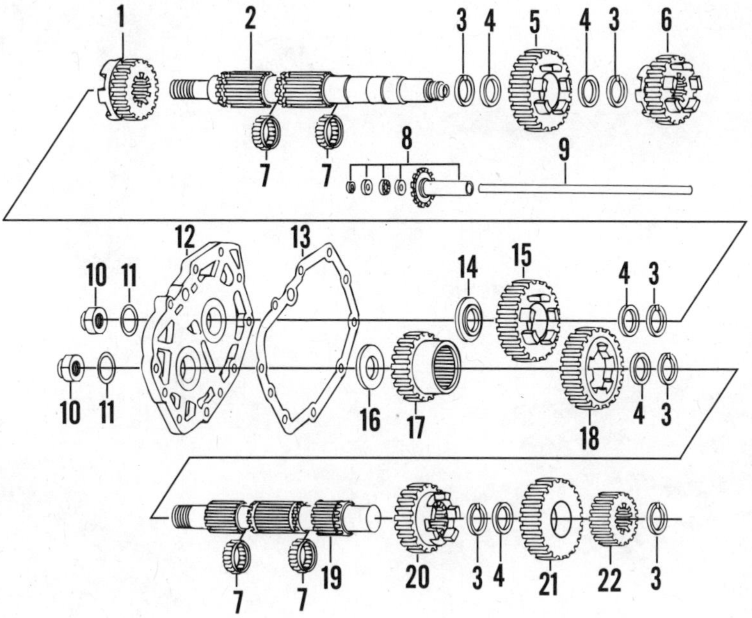

b. Use the same tool setup used for bearing inner race removal.
c. Apply clean oil to the transmission shaft bearing surface, shaft threads and to the inner surface of the inner race.
d. Position the bearing inner race with the chamfered end going on first and slide it onto the mainshaft (**Figure 40**).
e. Install the extension shaft onto the mainshaft.
f. Place the pusher tube over the extension shaft, along with the two flat washers and nut.

CAUTION
Install the inner bearing race to the dimension listed in substep g. This will align the race with the bearing outer race installed in the primary chaincase. Installing the wrong race or installing it incorrectly will damage the bearing and race assembly.

g. Hold the extension shaft and tighten the nut to press the bearing inner race onto the mainshaft. The mainshaft and countershaft nuts have left-hand threads. Turn the mainshaft nut counterclockwise to tighten it. Install the race so that its inside edge is 0.100-0.150 in. (2.540-3.810 mm.) away from the main drive gear.
h. Remove the special tools.

8. Install the pushrod assembly (B, **Figure 29**).
9. Install the shift forks as described in this chapter.
10. Install the primary chaincase housing as described in Chapter Five.
11. Install the clutch assembly and clutch release cover as described in Chapter Five.
12. Install the primary chaincase cover as described in Chapter Five.
13. Install the drain plug and refill the transmission oil as described in Chapter Three.
14. Install the bolts securing the exhaust system mounting bracket (B, **Figure 38**) and tighten securely.
15. Install the exhaust system as described in Chapter Seven.
16. Test ride the motorcycle slowly and check for proper transmission operation.

TRANSMISSION SHAFTS

This section describes service to the side door and both transmission shaft assemblies.

Refer to **Figure 41**.

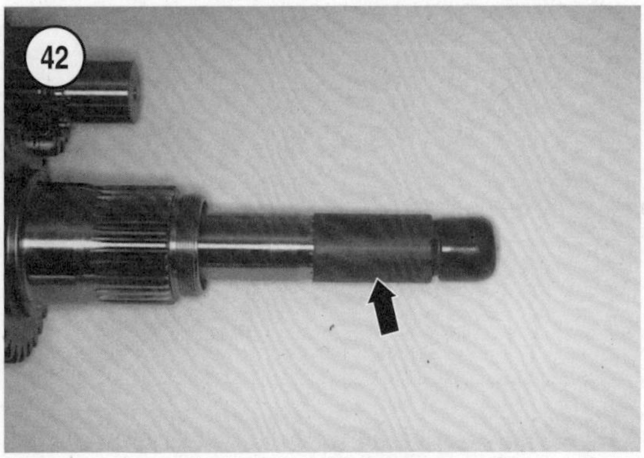

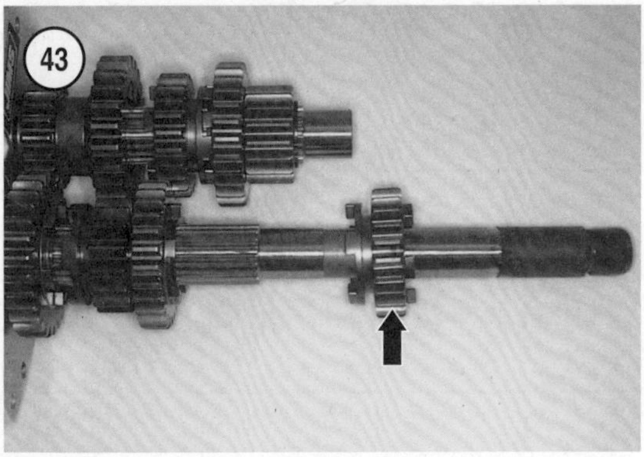

Transmission Disassembly

The transmission shaft assemblies must be partially disassembled prior to removing both shafts from the side door. Do not try to remove the shafts with all of the gears in place.

Store all of the transmission gears, snap rings, washers and split bearings in their order of removal.

The snap rings are very difficult to loosen and remove, even with high-quality snap ring pliers. A heavy-duty type retaining ring pliers (H-D part No. J-5586), or an equivalent, are recommended for this procedure.

1. Remove the transmission side door and transmission shaft assemblies as described in this chapter.
2. Protect the splines and threads on the mainshaft with tape or a plastic sleeve (**Figure 42**).
3. Remove the mainshaft second gear (**Figure 43**).
4. Remove the snap ring (**Figure 44**) from the countershaft.
5. Remove the countershaft fifth gear (**Figure 45**).
6. Remove the countershaft second gear (**Figure 46**).

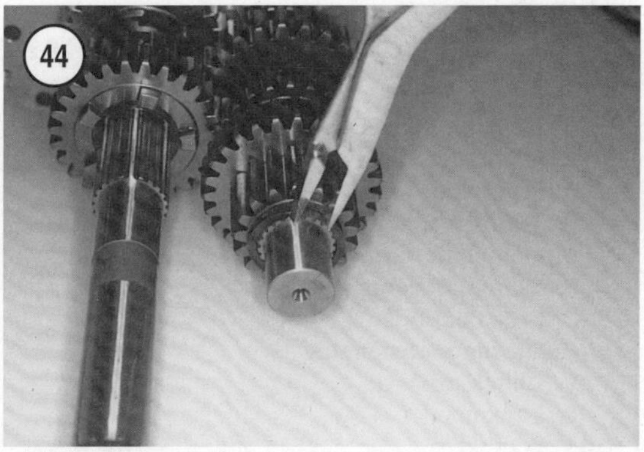

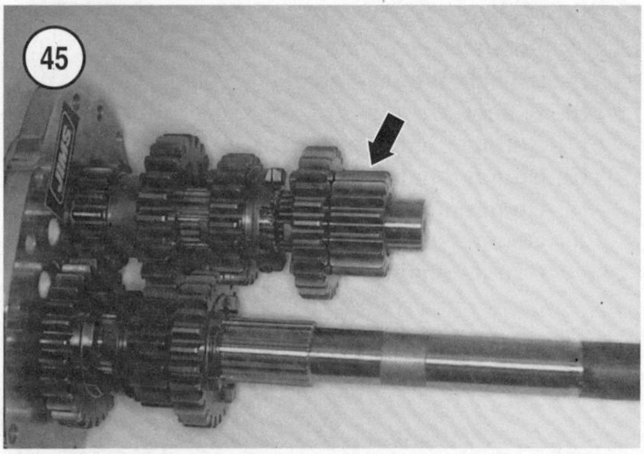

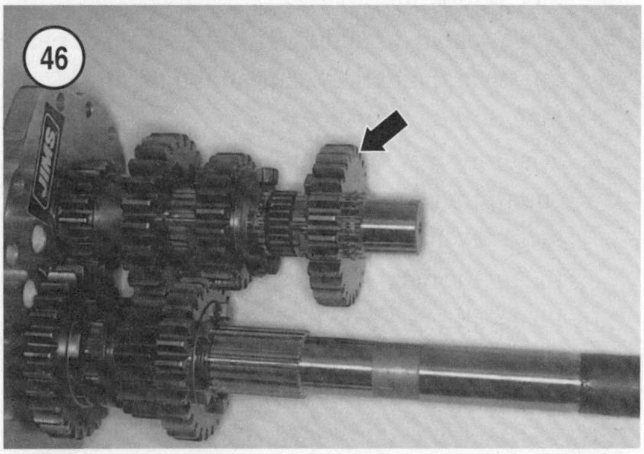

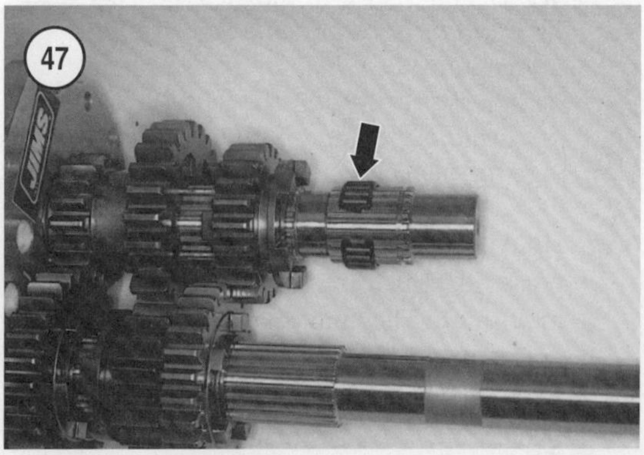

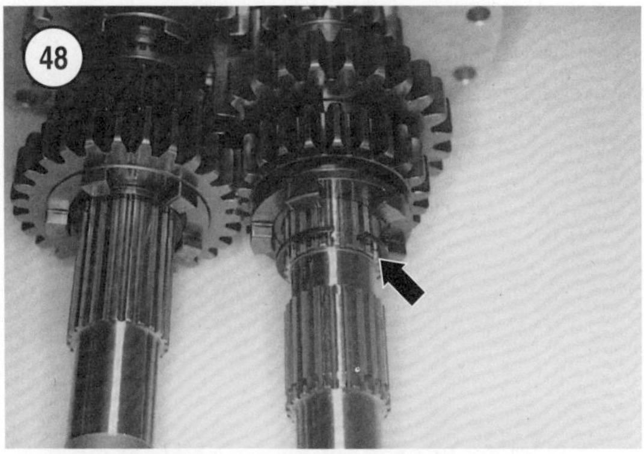

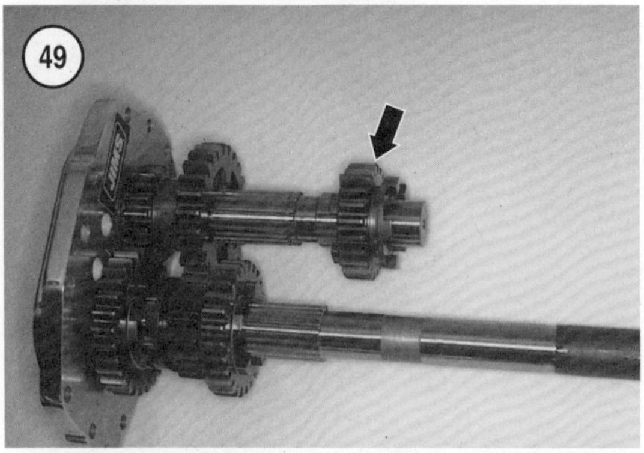

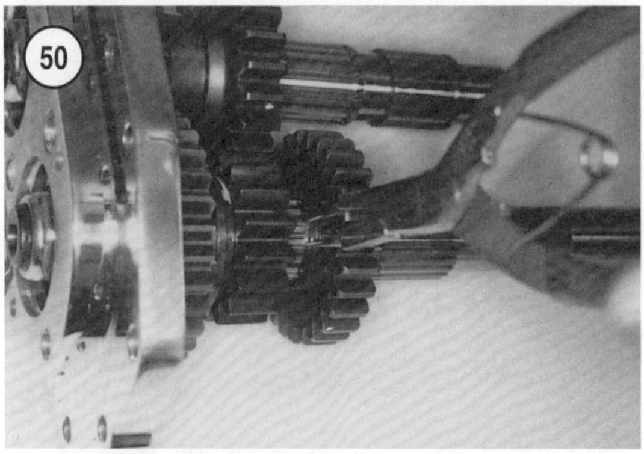

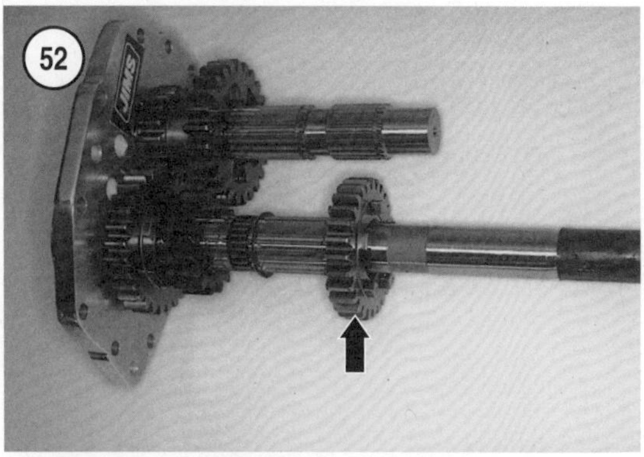

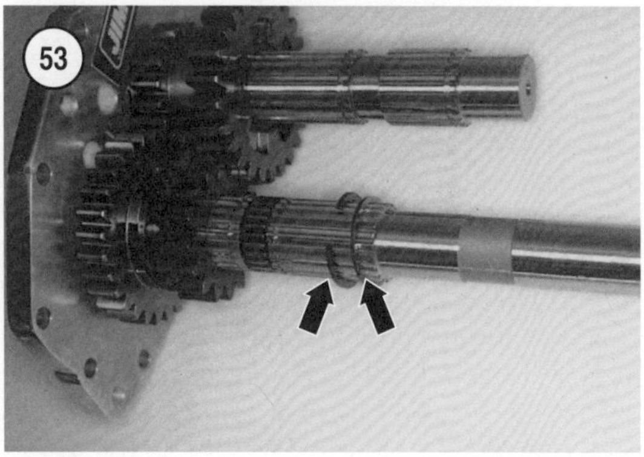

CAUTION
Do not expand the split bearings any more than necessary to slide them off the shaft. The bearing carriers are plastic and will fracture if expanded too far.

7. Remove the split bearing (**Figure 47**) from the countershaft.
8. Slide off the washer and remove the snap ring (**Figure 48**) from the countershaft.
9. Remove the countershaft third gear (**Figure 49**).

NOTE
The snap ring in Step 10 must be released and moved in order to gain access to the snap ring on the other side of the third gear.

10. Using snap ring pliers, release the snap ring (**Figure 50**) behind the mainshaft third gear. Slide the snap ring away from the third gear.
11. Slide the third gear toward the side door and remove the snap ring (**Figure 51**) and washer.
12. Remove the mainshaft third gear (**Figure 52**).
13. Remove the washer and snap ring (**Figure 53**).

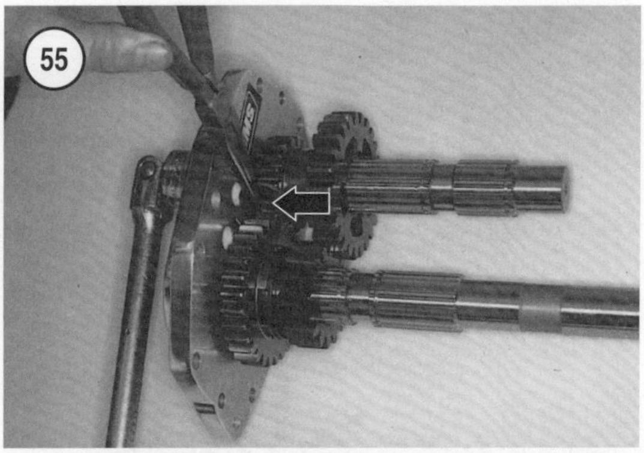

14. Remove the split bearing (**Figure 54**) from the mainshaft.

15. Place a brass or aluminum washer (**Figure 55**) between the countershaft fourth gear and the mainshaft fourth gear. This will lock both transmission shafts from rotation.

16. Loosen and remove the locknuts and washers (**Figure 56**) securing the shaft assemblies to the side door. Remove the brass or aluminum washer. New locknuts must be installed during assembly.

17. Press the countershaft out of its side door bearing as follows:

a. Support the countershaft first gear on a tube (A, **Figure 57**) in a press so that the countershaft can be pressed out without any interference. Center the countershaft under the press ram.

b. Place a mandrel (B, **Figure 57**) on top of the countershaft and press the countershaft out of the side door.

18. Remove the spacer (A, **Figure 58**), fourth gear (B), first gear (C) and washer (D) from the countershaft.

19. Remove the split bearing (A, **Figure 59**) from the countershaft.

20. If necessary, remove the snap ring (B, **Figure 59**) from the countershaft.

21. Remove the first gear (**Figure 60**) from the mainshaft.

22. Remove the snap ring and washer (A, **Figure 61**) from the mainshaft.

23. Press the mainshaft out of its side door bearing as follows:

a. Support the mainshaft fourth gear on a tube (A, **Figure 62**) in a press so that the mainshaft can be pressed out without any interference. Center the mainshaft under the press ram.

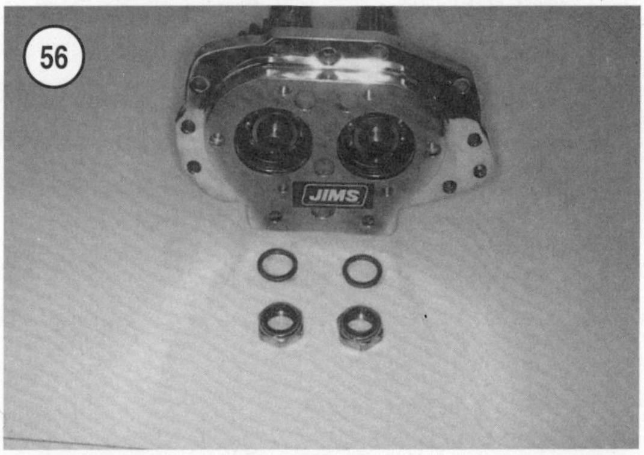

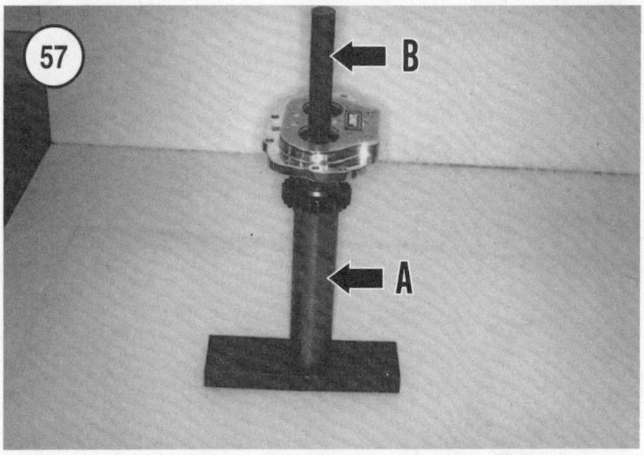

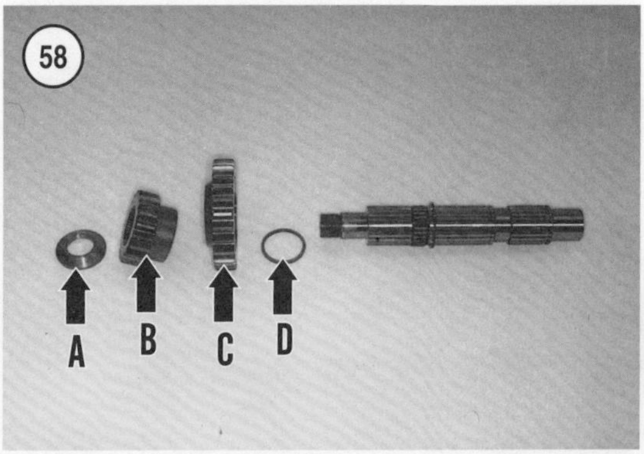

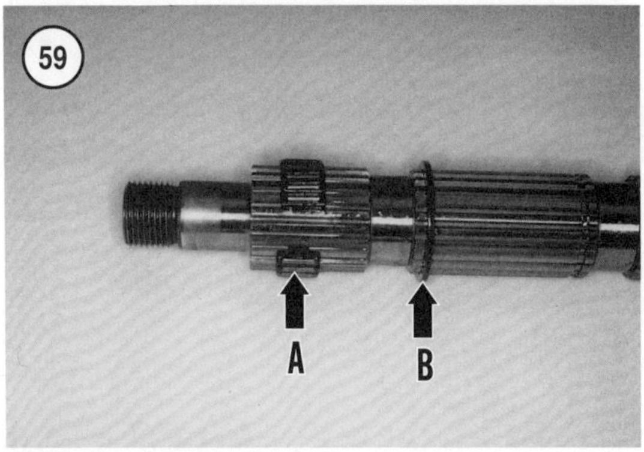

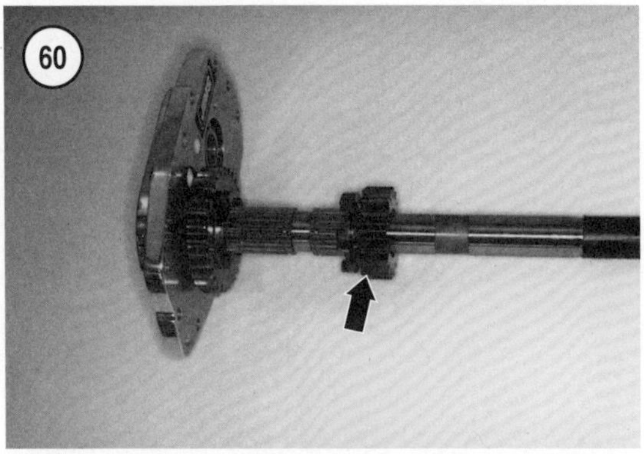

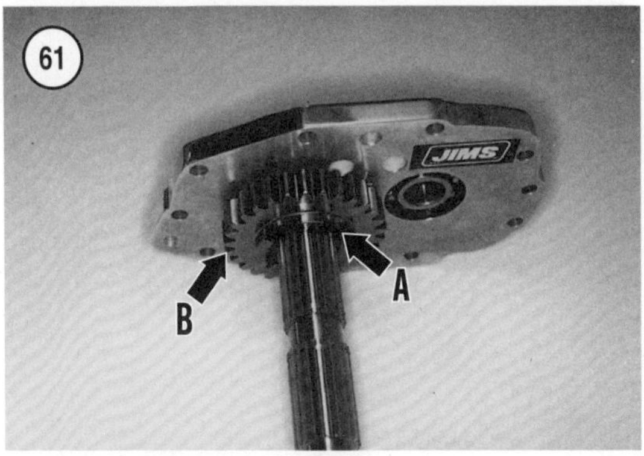

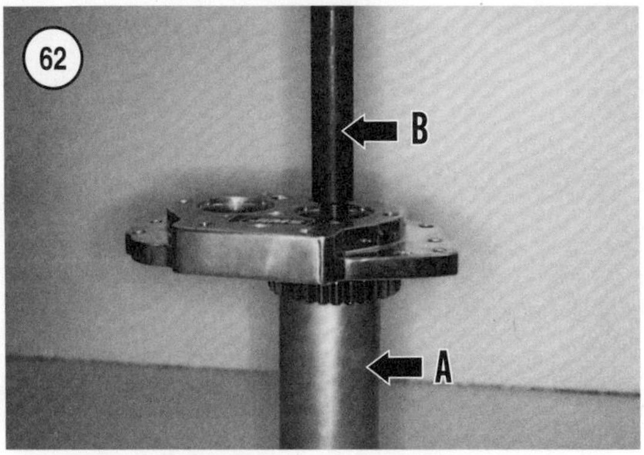

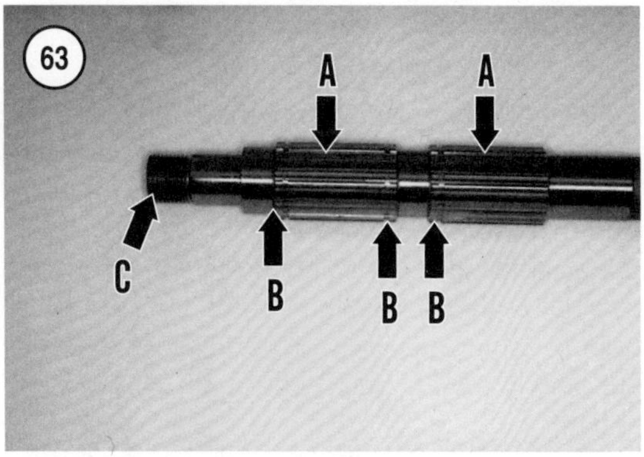

b. Place a mandrel (B, **Figure 62**) on top of the mainshaft and press the mainshaft out of the side door.

24. From the mainshaft, remove the fourth gear and spacer (B, **Figure 61**).

25. Inspect all parts as described in this section.

6

Transmission Inspection

Maintain the alignment of the transmission components when cleaning and inspecting the individual parts in the following section. To prevent intermixing parts, work on only one shaft at a time.

Refer to **Table 2** and inspect the service clearance and end play of the indicated gears and shafts. Replace parts that show excessive wear or damage as described in this section.

CAUTION

Do not clean the split bearings in solvent. It is difficult to remove all traces of solvent from the bearing plastic retainers. Flush the bearings clean with new transmission oil.

1. Clean and dry the shaft assembly.
2. Inspect the mainshaft and countershaft for:
   a. Worn or damages splines (A, **Figure 63**).
   b. Excessively worn or damaged bearing surfaces.
   c. Cracked or rounded-off snap ring grooves (B, **Figure 63**).
   d. Worn or damaged threads (C, **Figure 63**).
3. Check each gear for excessive wear, burrs, pitting, and chipped or missing teeth. Check the inner splines (**Figure 64**) on sliding gears and the bore on stationary gears for excessive wear or damage.

4. Check the gear bushings (**Figure 65**) for wear, cracks or other damage.

5. To check stationary gears for wear, install them on their correct shaft and in the original operating position. If necessary, use the old snap rings to secure them in place. Then spin the gear by hand. The gear should turn smoothly. A rough turning gear indicates heat damage—check for a dark blue color or galling on the operating surfaces. Rocking indicates excessive wear, either to the gear or shaft or both.

6. To check the sliding gears, install them on their correct shaft and in their original operating position. The gear should slide back and forth without any binding or excessive play.

7. Check the shift fork slot (**Figure 66**) for wear or damage.

8. Check the dogs on the gears for excessive wear, rounding, cracks or other damage. Refer to **Figure 67**. When wear is noticeable, make sure it is consistent on each gear dog. If one dog is worn more than the others, the others will be overstressed during operation and will eventually crack and fail. Check engaging gears as described in Step 9.

9. Check each gear dog slot for cracks, rounding and other damage. Check engaging gears as described in Step 6.

10. Check engaging gears by installing the two gears on their respective shafts and in their original operating position. Mesh the gears together. Twist one gear against the other and then check the dog engagement. Then reverse the thrust load to check in the other operating position. Make sure the engagement in both directions is positive and without any slippage. Check that there is equal engagement across all of the engagement dogs.

NOTE
*When there is excessive or uneven wear to the gear engagement dogs, check the shift forks carefully for bending and other damage. Refer to **Shifter Adjustment** in this chapter.*

NOTE
Replace defective gears along with their mating gears, though they may not show as much wear or damage.

64

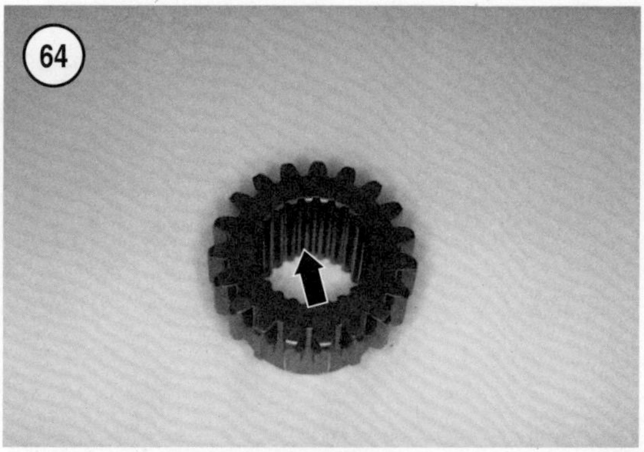

65

66

67

68

69

11. Check the spacers (**Figure 68**) for wear or damage.

12. Check the split bearings (**Figure 69**) for excessive wear or damage.

13. Replace all of the snap rings during reassembly. In addition, check the washers for burn marks, scoring or cracks. Replace as necessary.

Side Door Bearings Inspection and Replacement

The side door bearings are pressed into place and secured with a snap ring. They can be removed and installed using a special transmission door bearing remover and installer tool set (JIMS part No. 1078) (**Figure 70**). If the special tool set is not available, a press is required.

Refer to **Figure 71**.

1. Clean the side door and bearings in solvent and dry with compressed air.

2. Turn each bearing inner race (**Figure 72**) by hand. The bearings must turn smoothly.

If replacement is necessary, continue to Step 3.

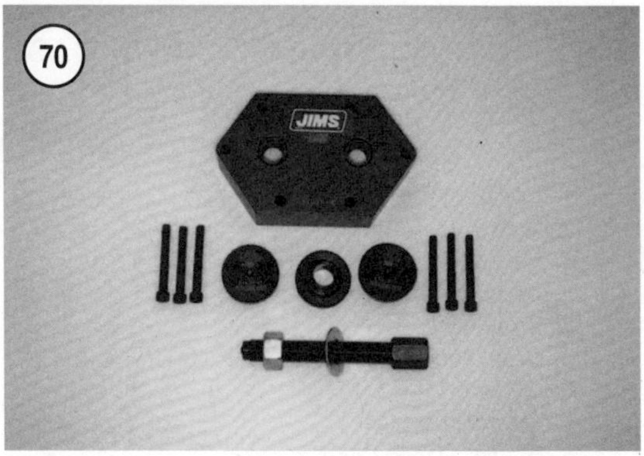

70

3. Remove both snap rings (**Figure 73**) from the outer surface of the side door.

4A. If the special tool set is used, follow the manufacturer's instructions and remove the bearings.

4B. If a press is used, perform the following:

  a. Support the side door on the press bed with the outer surface facing up.
  b. Use a driver or socket and press the bearing out of the backside of the side door.
  c. Repeat for the opposite bearing.

5. Clean the side door again in solvent and dry thoroughly.

6. Inspect the bearing bores in the side cover for cracks or other damage. Replace the side door if damaged.

NOTE
Both side door bearings have the same part number.

7A. If the special tool set is used, follow the manufacturer's instructions and install the bearings.

7B. If a press is used, perform the following:

  a. Support the side door in a press with the backside facing up.
  b. Install bearings with their manufacturer's marks facing out.
  c. Use a driver that matches the bearing outer race. Press the bearing into the side door until it bottoms.
  d. Repeat for the opposite bearing.

8. Position the beveled snap ring with the sharp side facing toward the bearing outer race and install the snap ring. Make sure the snap ring is correctly seated in the side door groove (**Figure 73**).

(71)

TRANSMISSION CASE BEARINGS AND COVERS

1. Locating pin
2. Transmission case
3. Mainshaft bearing–left side
4. Snap ring
5. Quad seal
6. Oil seal
7. Sprocket spacer
8. Spacer (1999-2000)
9. Bearing
10. Transmission side door
11. Gasket
12. Bolt
13. Bolt
14. Locknut
15. Washer
16. Bolt
17. Bolt
18. Washer
19. Bolt
20. Washer
21. Harness retainer
22. Gasket
23. Coupling
24. Ball (3)
25. Inner ramp
26. Filler plug/dipstick
27. O-ring
28. Clutch release cover
29. Bolt
30. Clutch cable
31. Plug
32. Outer ramp

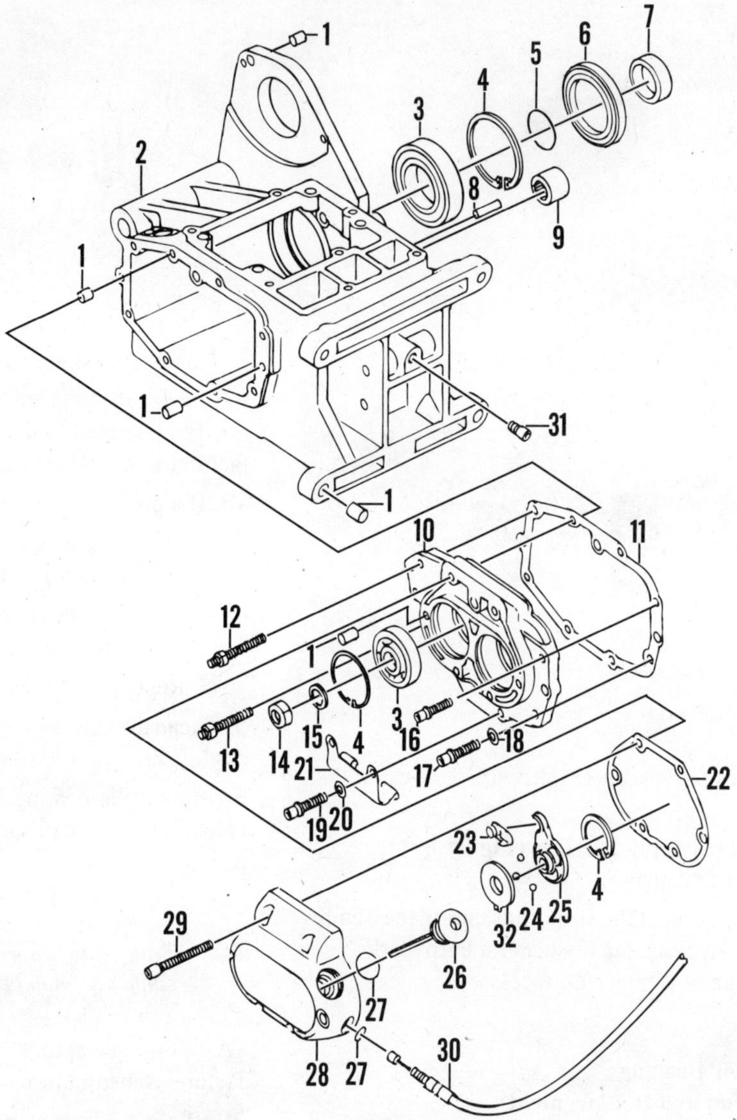

(72)

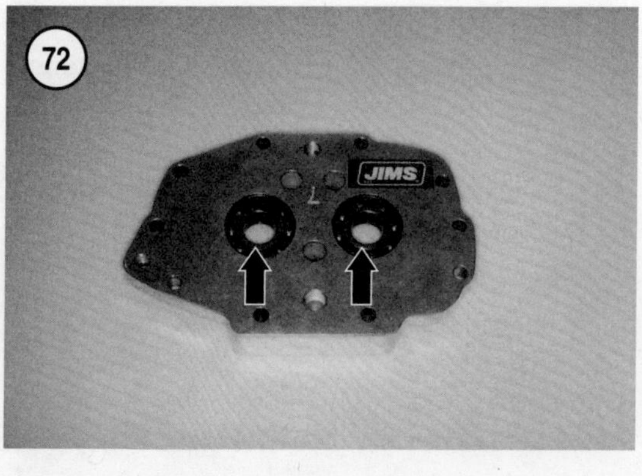

(73)

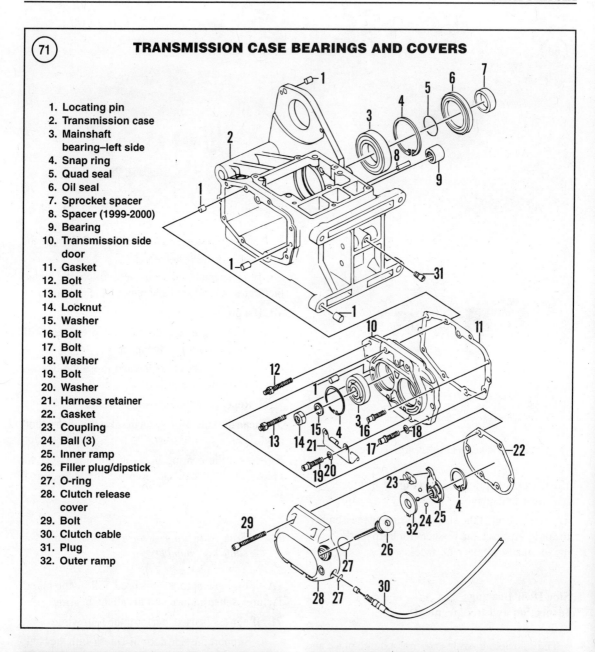

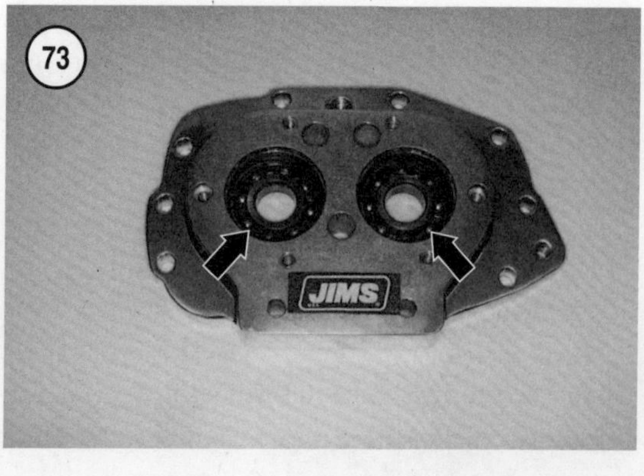

74

TRANSMISSION

1. Mainshaft first gear
2. Mainshaft
3. Snap ring
4. Thrust washer
5. Mainshaft third gear
6. Mainshaft second gear
7. Bearings
8. Oil slinger assembly
9. Clutch pushrod
10. Locknut
11. Washer
12. Side door
13. Gasket
14. Spacer
15. Mainshaft fourth gear
16. Spacer
17. Countershaft fourth gear
18. Countershaft first gear
19. Countershaft
20. Countershaft third gear
21. Countershaft second gear
22. Countershaft fifth gear

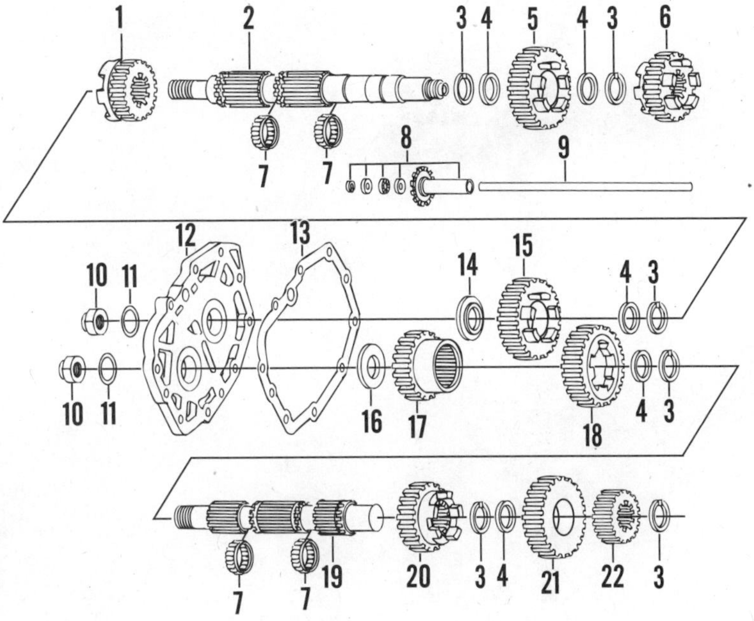

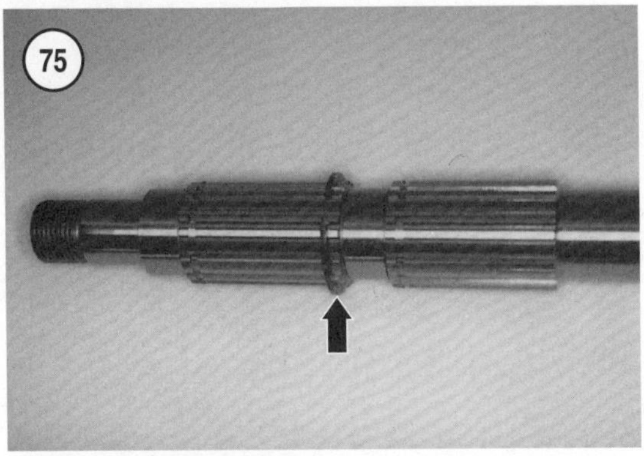
75

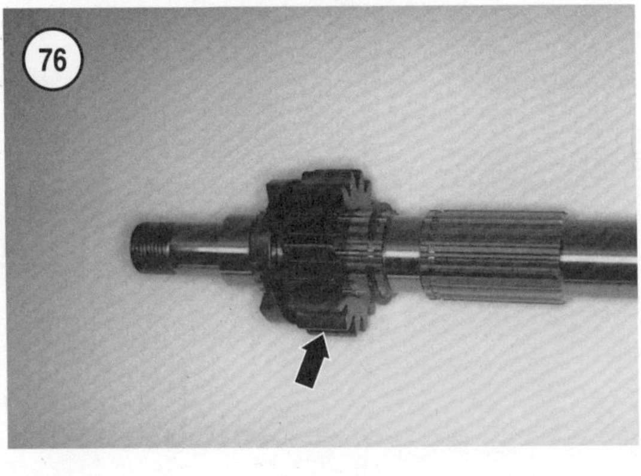
76

Transmission Assembly

Refer to **Figure 74**.

CAUTION
*Install a **new** snap ring at every location to ensure proper gear alignment and engagement. Never reinstall a snap ring that has been removed, since it has become distorted and weakened and may fail. Make sure each **new** snap ring is correctly seated in its respective shaft groove.*

1. Apply a light coat of clean transmission oil to all mating gear surfaces and to all split bearing halves before assembly.
2. If removed, install the side door bearings as described in this chapter.
3. Onto the mainshaft, install the following:
   a. If removed, install the *new* snap ring (**Figure 75**).
   b. Position the first gear with the shift dog side going on last and install the first gear (**Figure 76**).

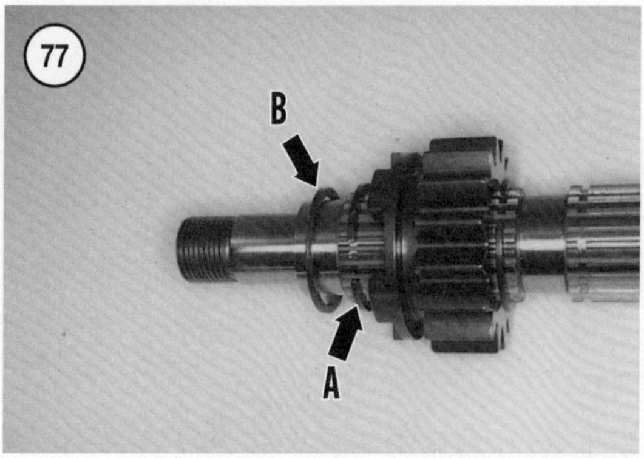

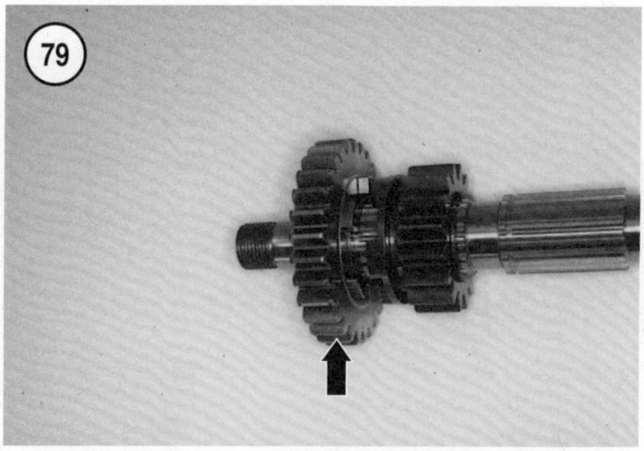

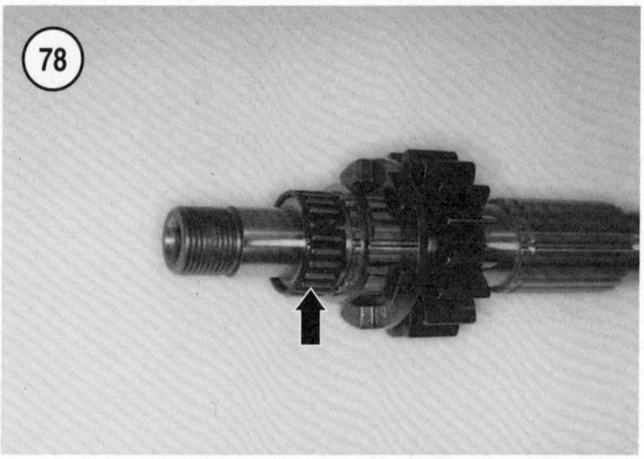

c. Install the snap ring (A, **Figure 77**) and washer (B).
d. Install the split bearing (**Figure 78**).
e. Position the fourth gear with the shift dog side going on first and install the fourth gear (**Figure 79**).
f. Position the spacer with the beveled side facing out (**Figure 80**) and install the spacer.

4. Onto the countershaft, install the following:
a. If removed, install the *new* snap ring (A, **Figure 81**).
b. Install the washer (B, **Figure 81**) and push it against the snap ring.
c. Install the split bearing (**Figure 82**).
d. Position the first gear with the shoulder side (**Figure 83**) going on last and install the first gear onto the split bearing (**Figure 84**).
e. Position the fourth gear with the wide shoulder (**Figure 85**) going on first and install the fourth gear.
f. Position the spacer with the beveled side facing out (**Figure 86**) and install the spacer.

5. Apply transmission oil to the inner race of both bearings and onto the shoulder of both shaft assem-

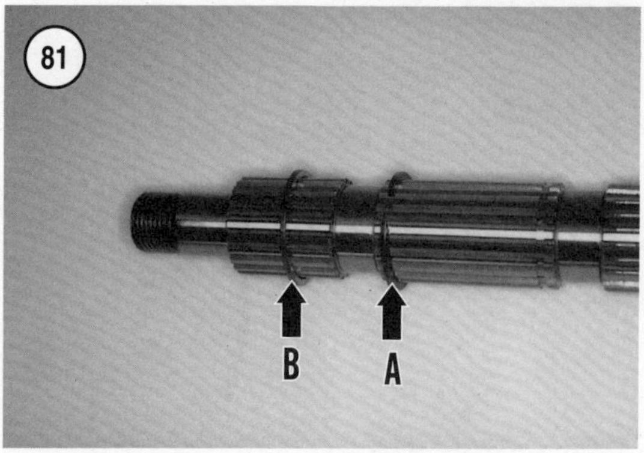

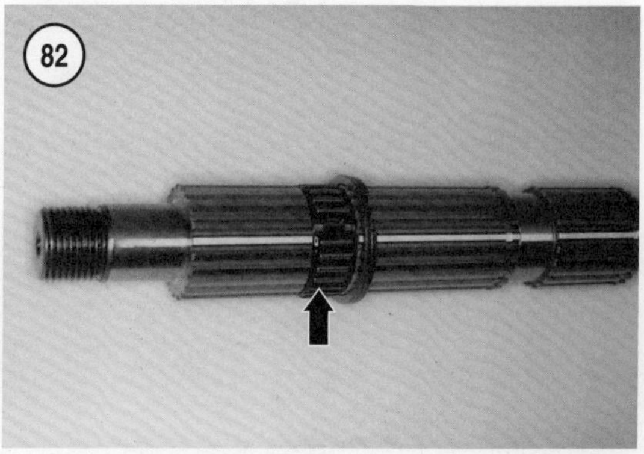

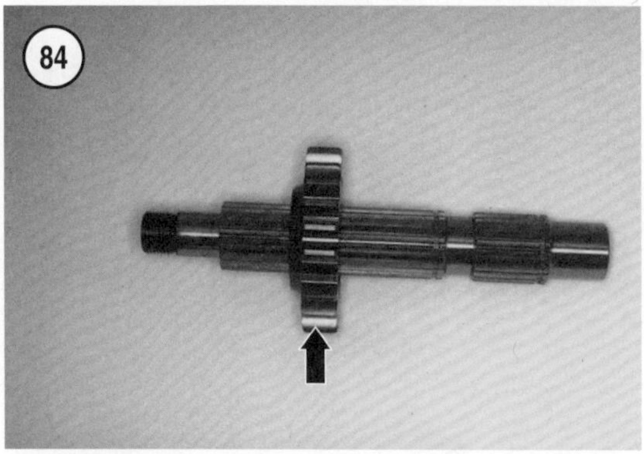

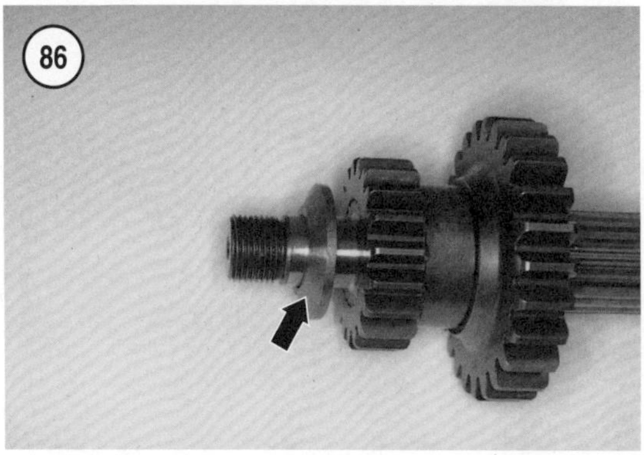

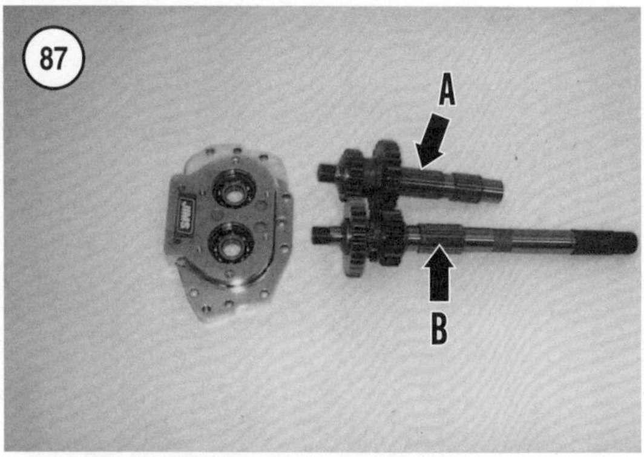

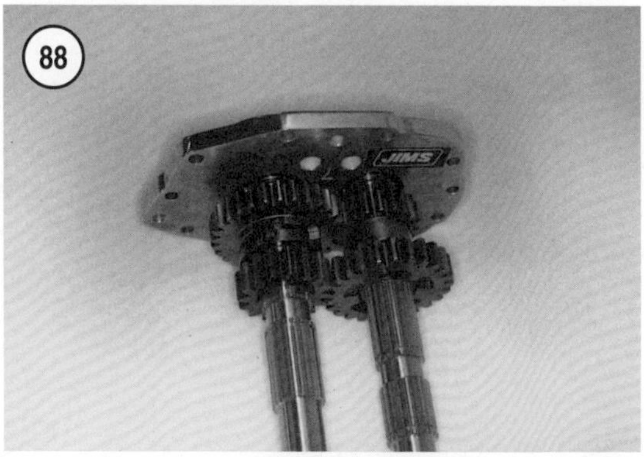

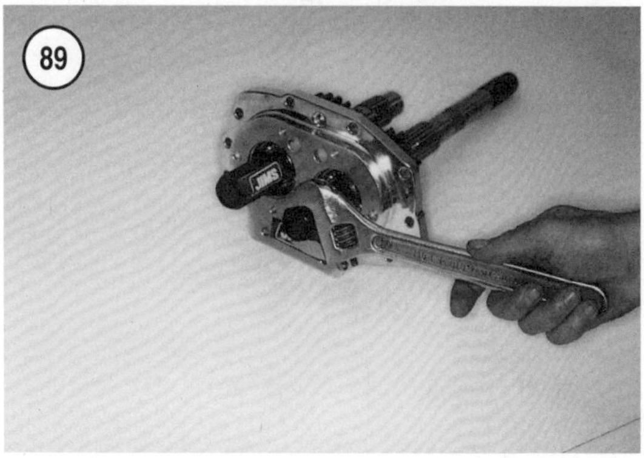

blies. Also apply transmission oil to the inner threads and ends of the special tools used in Step 8.

6. Position the countershaft (A, **Figure 87**) on the left side of the side door. Position the mainshaft (B, **Figure 87**) on the right side of the side door.

7. Mesh the two shaft assemblies together and start them into the side door bearings (**Figure 88**).

8. Attach the shaft installers (JIMS part No. 2189) onto the ends of both shafts.

9. Tighten the special tools (**Figure 89**), alternating between both shafts, until both shaft shoulders bot-

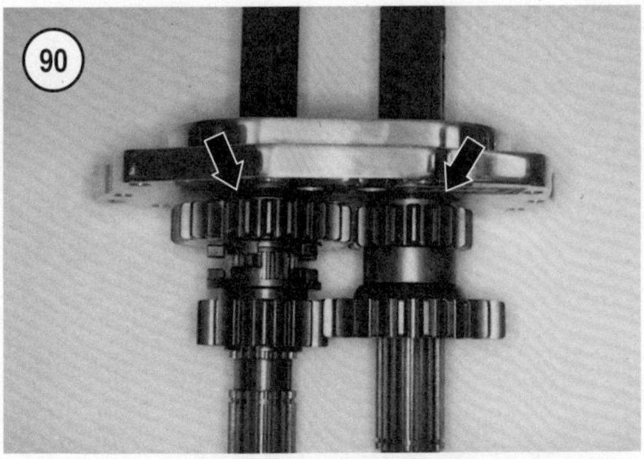

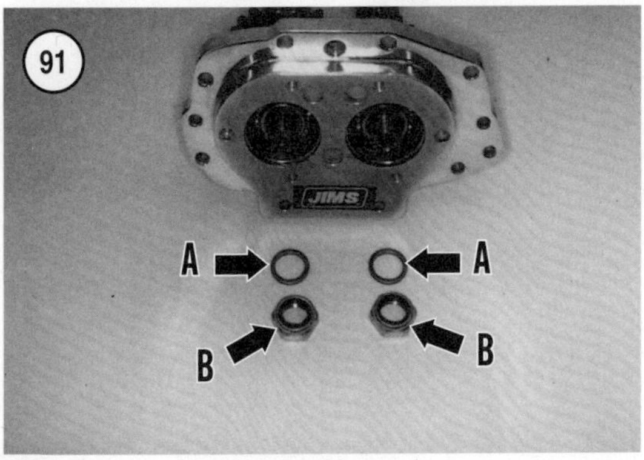

tom on the inner race of the side door bearings (**Figure 90**).

10. Unscrew and remove the special tools.

CAUTION

*Always install **new** locknuts. If an old locknut is reinstalled, it may work loose, resulting in costly transmission damage.*

11. Install the spacers (A, **Figure 91**) and *new* locknuts (B).

12. Start the new locknuts by hand until the locking portion of the nut touches the end of the transmission shaft.

13. Place a brass or aluminum washer (**Figure 55**) between the countershaft fourth gear and the mainshaft fourth gear. This will lock both transmission shafts.

14. Tighten the locknuts (**Figure 92**) to the specification in **Table 3**.

15. Onto the mainshaft, install the following:

a. Install the split bearing (**Figure 93**).

b. Move the snap ring (A, **Figure 94**) installed in Step 3 out of the groove and toward the first gear.

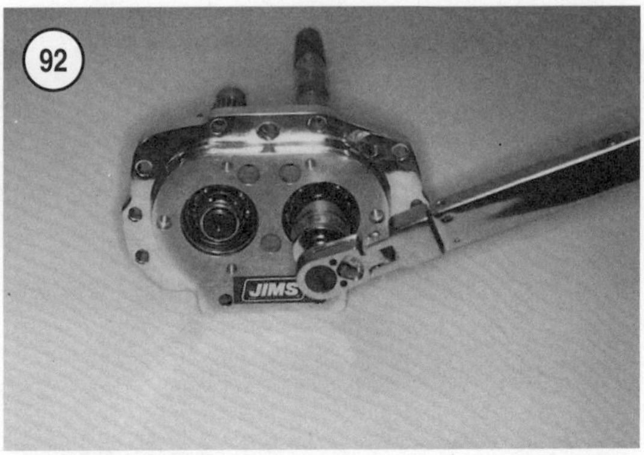

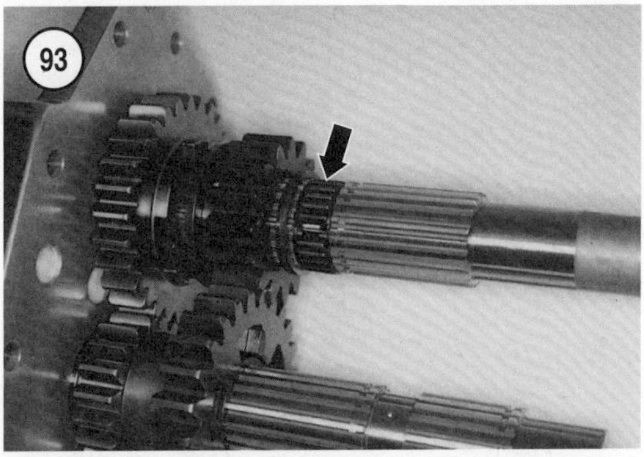

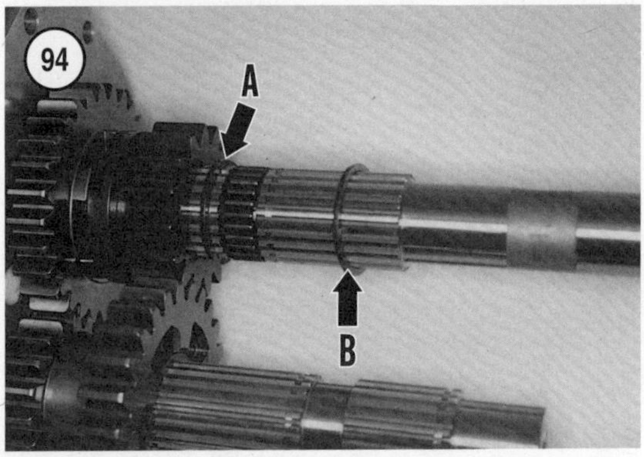

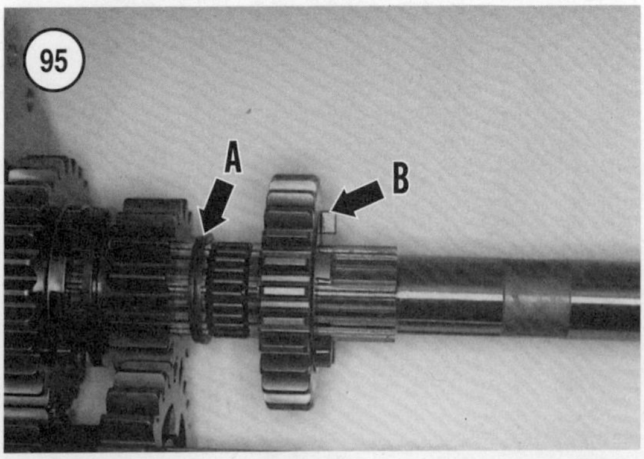

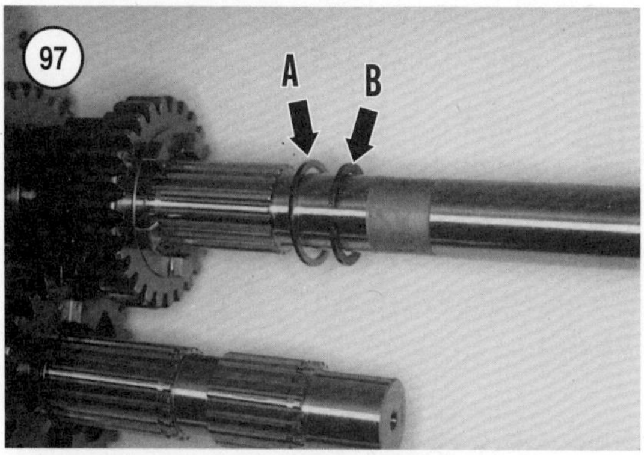

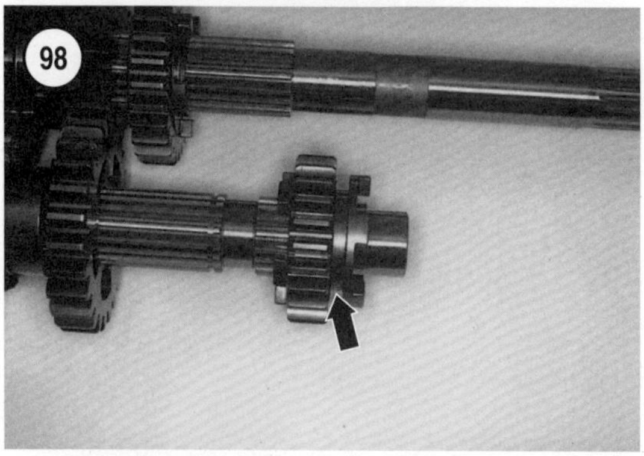

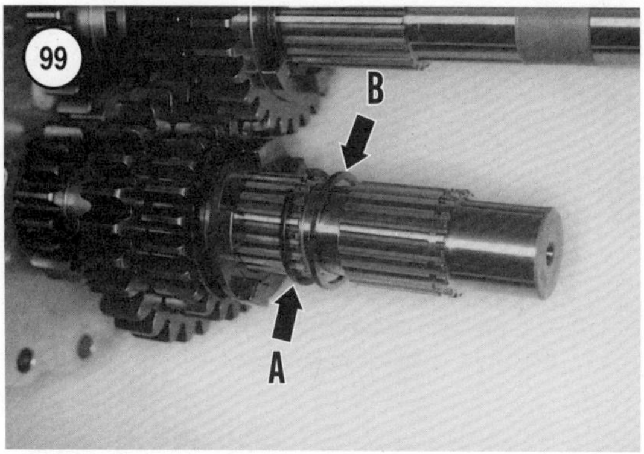

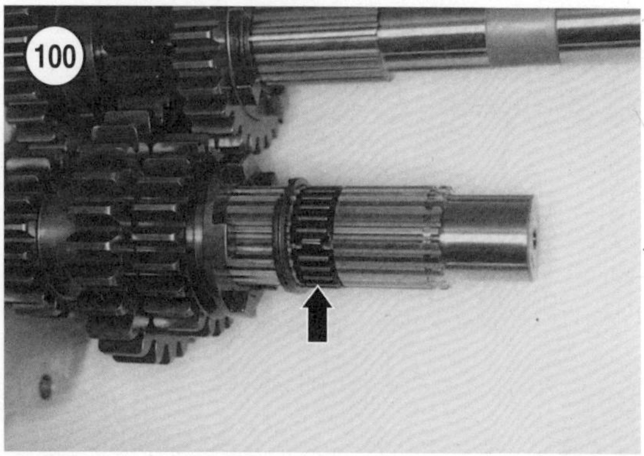

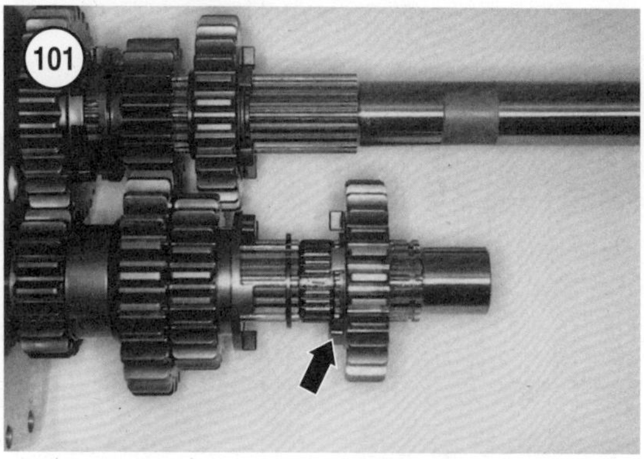

   c. Install the washer (B, **Figure 94**) and slide it against the snap ring (A, **Figure 95**).
   d. Position the third gear with the shift dogs side (B, **Figure 95**) going on last. Install the third gear onto the split bearing (**Figure 96**).
   e. Install the washer (A, **Figure 97**) and snap ring (B). Make sure the snap ring is correctly seated in the mainshaft groove.
   f. Move the third gear away from the first gear and up against the washer and snap ring installed in sub-step e.
   g. Reposition the washer and snap ring (A, **Figure 95**) behind the third gear into the mainshaft groove. Make sure the snap ring is correctly seated in the mainshaft groove.

16. Onto the countershaft, install the following:
   a. Position the third gear with the shift fork groove (**Figure 98**) side going on last and install the third gear.
   b. Install the circlip (A, **Figure 99**) and washer (B).
   c. Install the split bearing (**Figure 100**).
   d. Position the second gear with the shift dog side (**Figure 101**) going on first. Install the

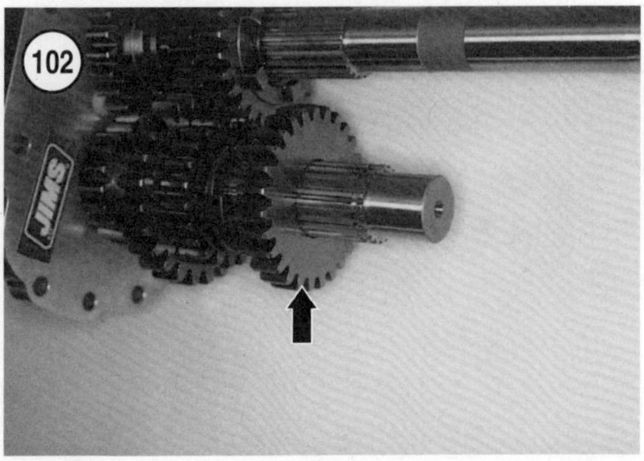

102

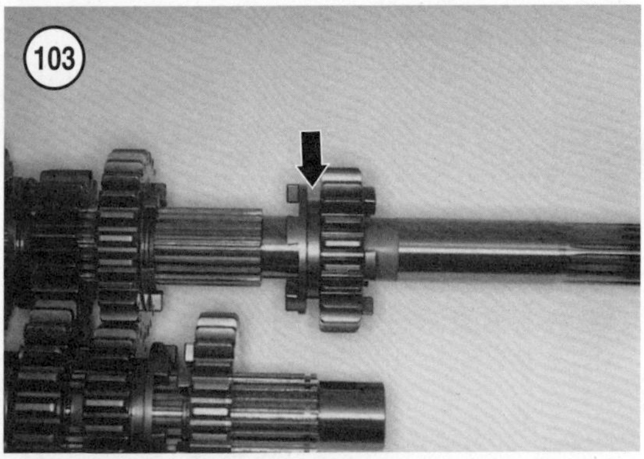
103

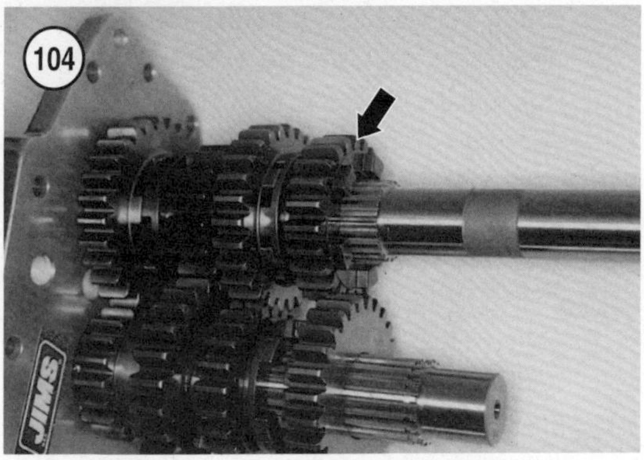

104

second gear onto the split bearing (**Figure 102**).

17. Onto the mainshaft, position the second gear with the shift fork groove (**Figure 103**) side going on first and install the second gear (**Figure 104**).

18. Onto the countershaft, install the fifth gear (**Figure 105**), then install the snap ring (**Figure 106**). Make sure the snap ring is correctly seated in the countershaft groove.

19. Refer to **Figure 107** for correct placement of all gears. Also check that the gears mesh properly to

105

106

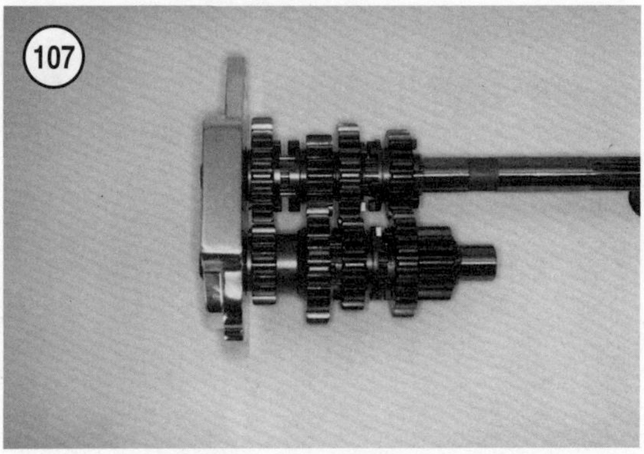
107

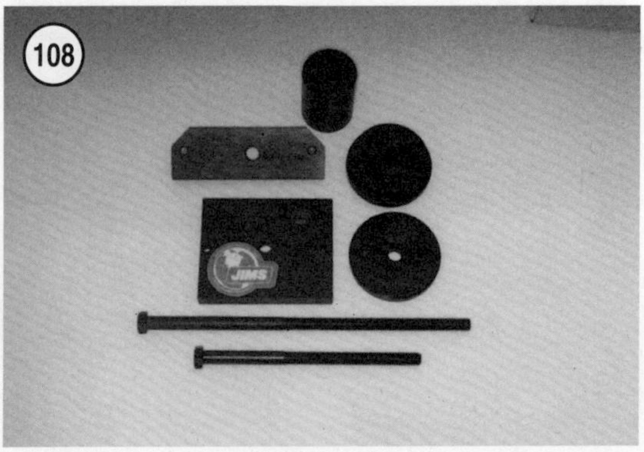

108

(109) **MAIN DRIVE GEAR**

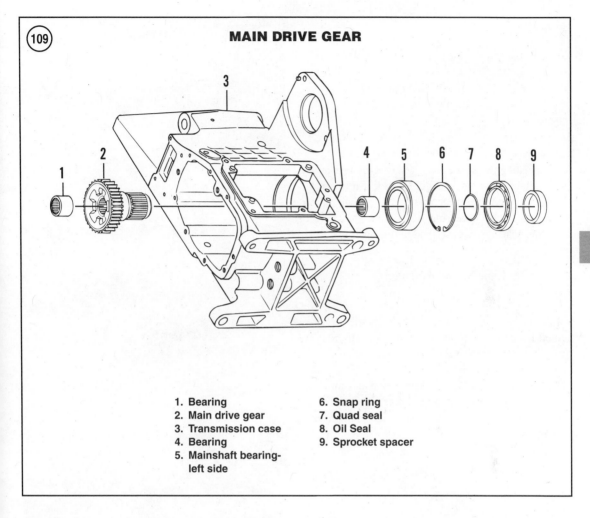

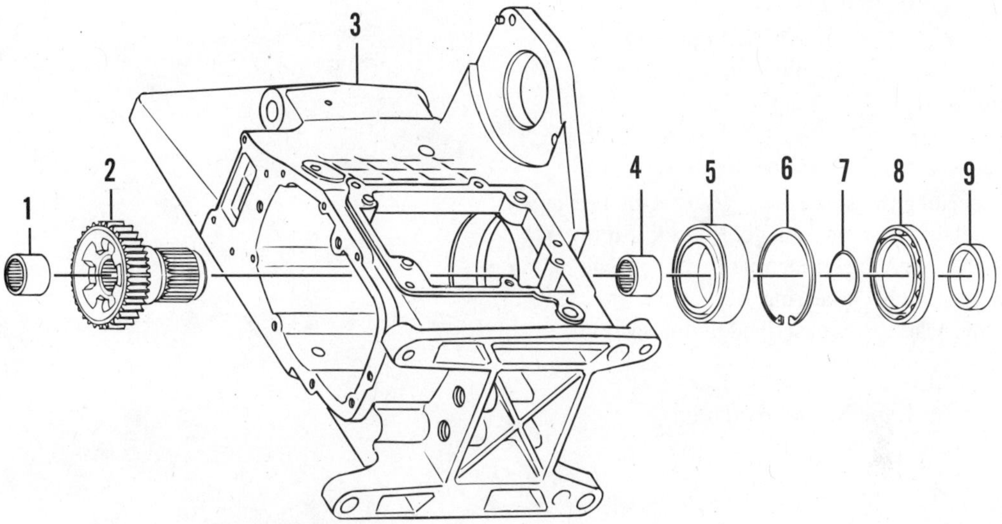

1. Bearing
2. Main drive gear
3. Transmission case
4. Bearing
5. Mainshaft bearing-left side
6. Snap ring
7. Quad seal
8. Oil Seal
9. Sprocket spacer

the adjoining gear where applicable. This is the last chance prior to installing the shaft assemblies into the transmission case. Make sure they are correctly assembled.

MAIN DRIVE GEAR

The main drive gear and bearing assembly are pressed into the transmission case. If the transmission case is installed in the frame, a special transmission main drive gear tool set (JIMS part No. 35316-80) is required to remove the main drive gear (**Figure 108**). If the transmission has been removed, use a press to remove and install the main drive gear.

Whenever the main drive gear is removed, the main drive gear bearing must be replaced at the same time.

Refer to **Figure 109**.

Removal

1. Remove the transmission shaft assemblies from the transmission case as described in this chapter.
2. Remove the spacer from the main drive gear oil seal.
3. Remove the snap ring behind the bearing.

NOTE
If the main drive gear will not loosen from the bearing in Step 4 due to corrosion, remove the special tools and heat the bearing with a heat gun.

4. Assemble the special tool set onto the main drive gear following the manufacturer's instructions. Then tighten the puller nut slowly to pull the main drive gear from the bearing in the transmission case.
5. Remove the main drive gear bearing from the transmission case as described in this section.

Inspection

1. Clean the main drive gear in solvent and dry with compressed air, if available.
2. Check each gear tooth (A, **Figure 110**) for excessive wear, burrs, galling and pitting. Check for missing teeth.
3. Check the gear splines (B, **Figure 110**) for excessive wear, galling or other damage.
4. Inspect the two main drive gear needle bearings for excessive wear or damage. Refer to **Figure 111** and **Figure 112**. Insert the mainshaft into the main drive gear to check bearing wear. If necessary, replace the bearings as described in this section.

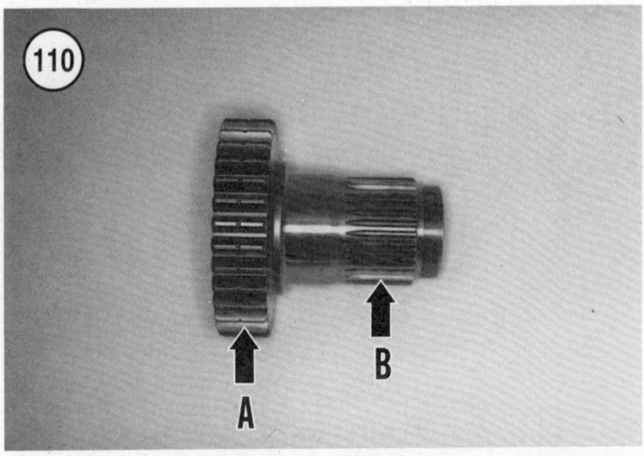

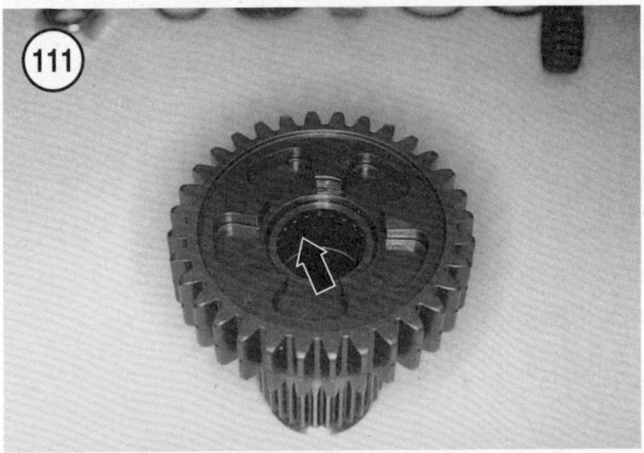

Main Drive Gear Needle Bearing Replacement

Both main drive gear needle bearings must be installed to the correct depth within the main drive gear. The correct depth is obtained with the use of a main drive gear bearing tool (JIMS part No. 37842-91). This tool is also used to install the oil seal. If this tool is not available, a press is required.

If this tool is not available, measure the depth of both bearings before removing them.

Replace both main drive gear needle bearings as a set.

CAUTION
Never re-install a main drive gear needle bearing, as it was distorted during removal.

1. Remove the oil seal (**Figure 113**) from the clutch side of the main drive gear.
2. If the special tool is not used, measure and record the depth of both bearings.
3. Support the main drive gear in a press and press out one needle bearing. Then turn the gear over and press out the opposite bearing.
4. Clean the gear and its bearing bore in solvent and dry thoroughly.
5. Apply transmission oil to the bearing bore in the main drive gear and to the outer surface of both bearings.

NOTE
Install both needle bearings with their manufacturer's name and size code facing out.

114

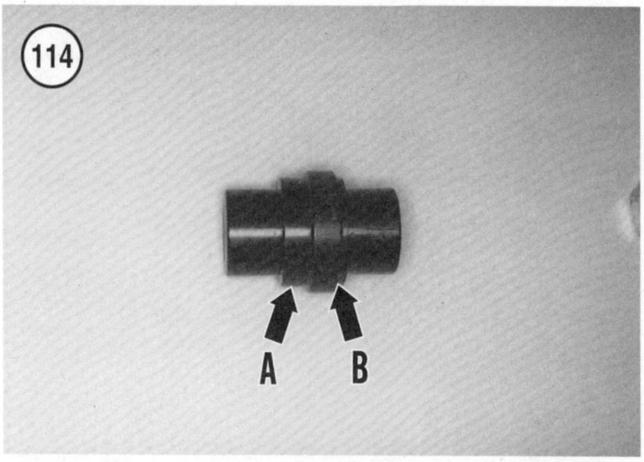

115

116

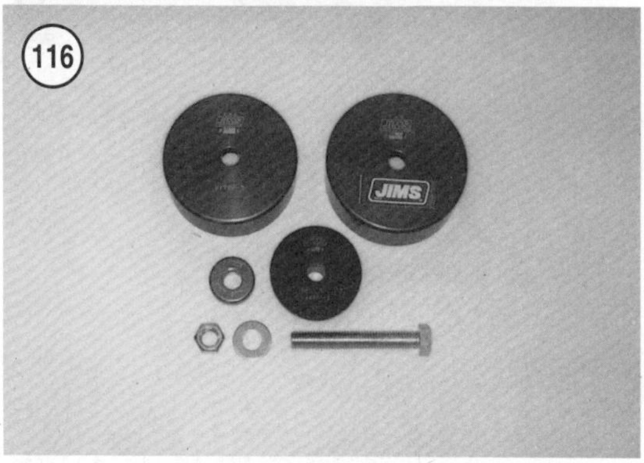

6A. To install the bearings with the special tool, perform the following steps:

a. The special tool has two different length ends. The tool's long side (A, **Figure 114**) is for the clutch side of the main drive gear (**Figure 112**). The tool's short side (B, **Figure 114**) is for the transmission side of the main drive gear (**Figure 111**).

b. Install the main drive gear in a press with the transmission end facing up. Align the new bearing with the main drive gear and place the installation tool, with the *short side facing down* (**Figure 115**), inserted into the bearing. Operate the press until the tool's shoulder bottoms against the gear.

c. Turn the main drive gear over so that the inner end faces up. Align the new bearing with the main drive gear and place the installation tool, with the *long side facing down*, inserted into the bearing. Operate the press until the tool's shoulder bottoms against the gear.

6B. If the bearings are being installed without the installation tool, use a suitable mandrel and press in the bearing to the depth recorded in Step 2.

7. Install a *new* oil seal (**Figure 113**) into the clutch side of the main drive gear.

Main Drive Gear Bearing Replacement

The main drive gear bearing (**Figure 109**) is pressed into the transmission case. If the transmission case is installed in the frame, a transmission main bearing remover set (JIMS part No. 1720) (**Figure 116**), or equivalent, is required to remove the main drive gear bearing.. If the transmission has been removed, use a press to remove the main drive gear bearing.

Whenever the main drive gear is removed, the main drive gear bearing is damaged and must be replaced at the same time.

CAUTION
Failure to use the correct tools to install the bearing will cause premature failure of the bearing and related parts.

1. Remove the main drive gear from the transmission case as described in this chapter.
2. Assemble the special tool set onto the main drive gear bearing following the manufacturer's instructions. Then tighten the bolt and nut slowly to pull the main drive gear bearing from the transmission case.
3. Clean the bearing bore and dry with compressed air. Check the bore for nicks or burrs. Check the snap ring groove for damage.

NOTE
Install the bearing into the transmission case with the bearing manufacturer's name and size code facing out.

4. Apply transmission oil to the bearing bore in the transmission case and to the outer surface of the

bearing. Also apply oil to the nut and threaded shaft of the installer tool.

5. Install the bearing onto the installation tool and assemble the installation tool following the manufacturer's instructions.

6. Slowly tighten the puller nut to pull the bearing into the transmission case. Continue until the bearing bottoms in the case.

7. Disassemble and remove the installation tool.

Main Drive Gear Installation

1. Replace the main drive gear bearing and oil seal as described in the previous section.

2. Install a *new* snap ring. Position it with the flat side facing the bearing.

3. Install the snap ring and position the open end within 45° of horizontal at the rear of the transmission case (**Figure 117**). Make sure it is fully seated in the snap ring groove.

4. Install the *new* oil seal into the case so its closed side faces out.

5. Apply transmission oil to the bearing bore and to the outer surface of the main drive gear. Also apply oil to the nut and threaded shaft of the installer tool.

6. Insert the main drive gear into the main drive gear bearing as far as it will go. Then hold it in place and assemble the special tool onto the main drive gear and transmission case following the manufacturer's instructions.

7. Slowly tighten the puller nut to pull the main drive gear into the bearing in the transmission case. Continue until the gear bottoms in the bearings inner race.

8. Disassemble and remove the installation tool.

9. Install the spacer into the main drive gear oil seal.

10. Install the transmission shaft assemblies from the transmission case as described in this chapter.

EXTERNAL SHIFT MECHANISM

Removal/Installation (FXD, FXDL, FXDS-CON, FXDX, FXDXT Models)

1. Make an alignment mark (A, **Figure 118**) on the outer shift lever and the end of the inner shift lever shaft.

2. Remove the clamping bolt (B, **Figure 118**) and remove the outer shift lever.

117

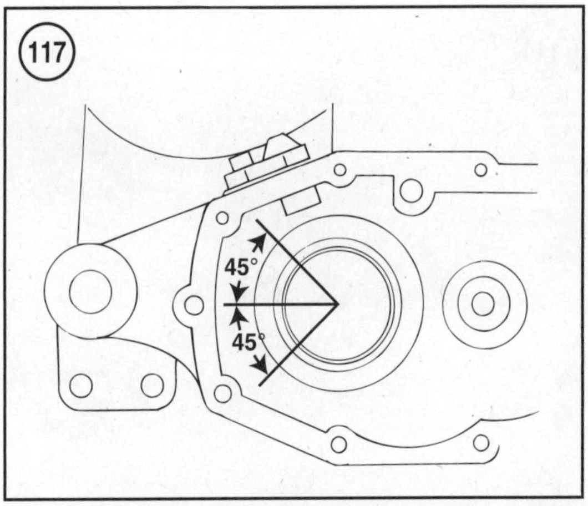

118

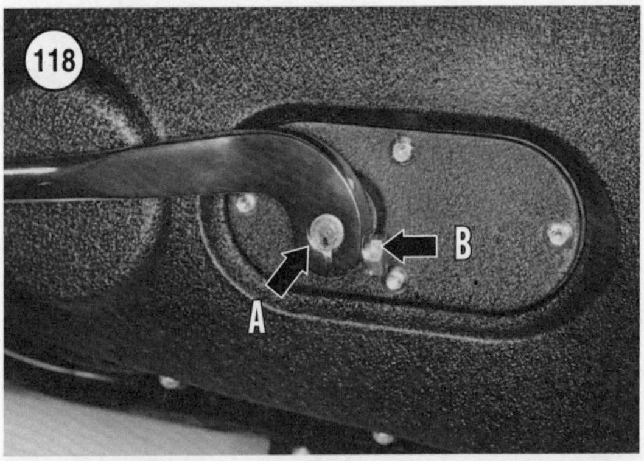

119

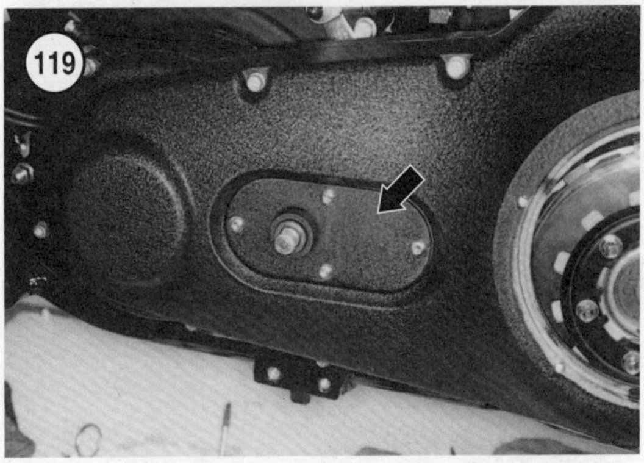

3. Remove the screws and the inspection cover and gasket (**Figure 119**) from the primary chaincase cover.

4. Remove the primary chaincase cover and inner housing as described in Chapter Five.

5. Disconnect the shift rod (A, **Figure 120**) from the shift rod lever (B, **Figure 120**) on the transmission case.

6. Remove the shift linkage assembly.

7. Install by reversing these removal steps.

Removal/Installation (FXDWG Models)

1. Make an alignment mark on the outer shift lever and the end of the inner shift lever shaft.
2. Remove the clamping bolt and remove the outer shift lever.
3. Remove the inner shift lever from the right side foot peg assembly. Do not lose the two bushing sleeves within the foot peg assembly.
4. Disconnect the shift rod from the shift rod lever on the transmission case.
5. Remove the shift linkage assembly.
6. Install by reversing these removal steps.

Removal/Installation (FXDP Models)

1. Make an alignment mark on the outer shift lever and the end of the inner shift lever shaft.
2. Remove the clamping bolt and remove the outer shift lever.
3. Remove the acorn nut and washer securing the shift rod to the inner shift lever and disconnect the shift rod.
4. Remove the inner shift lever from the shift lever plate. Do not lose the wave washer on the shaft.
5. Disconnect the shift rod from the shift rod lever on the transmission case.
6. Remove the shift rod.
7. Install by reversing these removal steps.

6

TRANSMISSION SIDE COVER AND CLUTCH RELEASE MECHANISM

Removal

1. Remove the exhaust system.
2. Drain the transmission oil as described in Chapter Three.

NOTE
If the cover is difficult to remove from the gasket and transmission case, apply the clutch lever after the mounting bolts are removed. This will usually break the cover loose.

3. Remove the side cover mounting bolts and remove the side cover (**Figure 121**). Remove the gasket. Do not lose the locating dowels.
4. At the clutch cable in-line adjuster, perform the following:
   a. Slide the rubber boot (A, **Figure 122**).
   b. Loosen the adjuster locknut (B, **Figure 122**) and turn the adjuster (C) to provide as much slack in the cable as possible.

Disassembly

Refer to **Figure 123**.

NOTE
Before removing the snap ring in Step 1, note the position of the snap ring opening. The snap ring must be reinstalled with its opening in the same position.

1. Remove the snap ring (A, **Figure 124**) from the groove in the side cover.
2. Lift the inner ramp (A, **Figure 125**) out of the cover and disconnect it from the clutch cable coupling (B, **Figure 125**).
3. Remove the clutch cable coupling (A, **Figure 126**).
4. Remove the inner ramp and balls (B, **Figure 126**).
5. If necessary, remove the clutch cable (B, **Figure 124**) from the side cover.

Inspection

1. Clean the side cover and all components thoroughly in solvent and dry with compressed air.
2. Check the release mechanism balls and ramp ball sockets for cracks, deep scoring or excessive wear (**Figure 127**).
3. Check the side cover (**Figure 128**) for cracks or damage. Check the clutch cable threads and the coupling snap ring groove for damage. Check the ramp bore in the side cover for excessive wear or lips or grooves that could catch the ramps and bind them sideways, causing improper clutch adjustment.
4. Replace the clutch cable O-ring if damaged.
5. Replace all worn or damaged parts.

Assembly

1. If removed, screw the clutch cable into the side cover. Do not tighten the cable fitting at this time.
2. Install the inner ramp and balls (B, **Figure 126**). Center a ball into each socket.
3. Install the clutch cable coupling onto the clutch cable as shown in A, **Figure 126**.
4. Connect the inner ramp onto the clutch cable coupling (B, **Figure 125**).
5. Align the inner ramp socket with the balls and install the inner ramp as shown in **Figure 129**.
6. Install the snap ring into the side cover groove. Position the snap ring so that its opening faces to the right

123

CLUTCH RELEASE MECHANISM

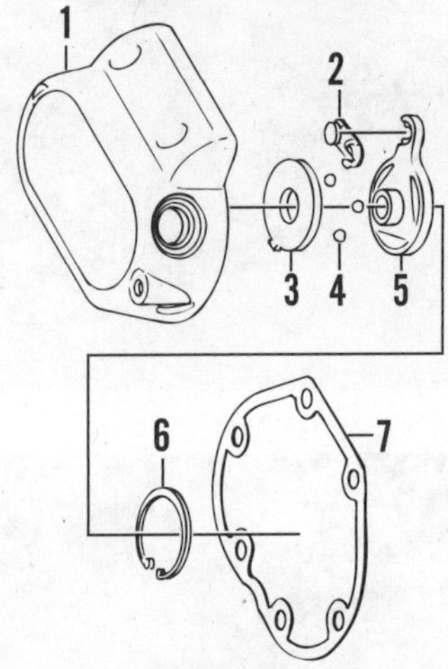

1. Clutch release cover
2. Ramp coupling
3. Outer ramp
4. Balls (3)
5. Inner ramp
6. Snap ring
7. Gasket

124

125

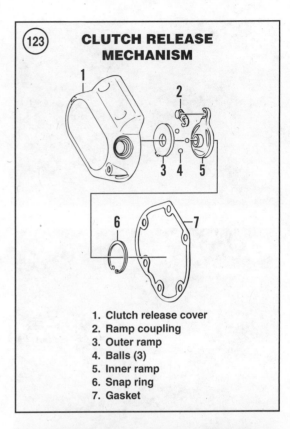

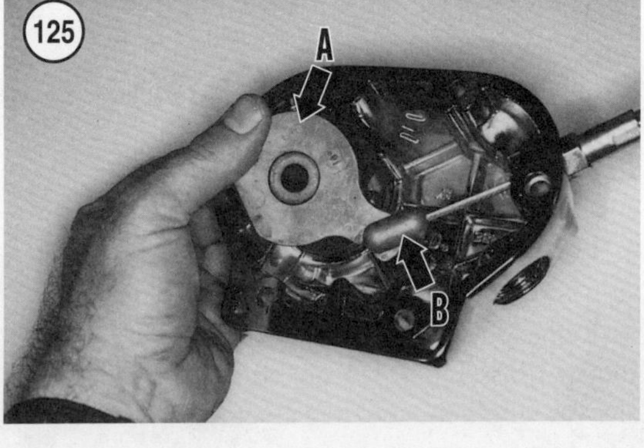

(126)

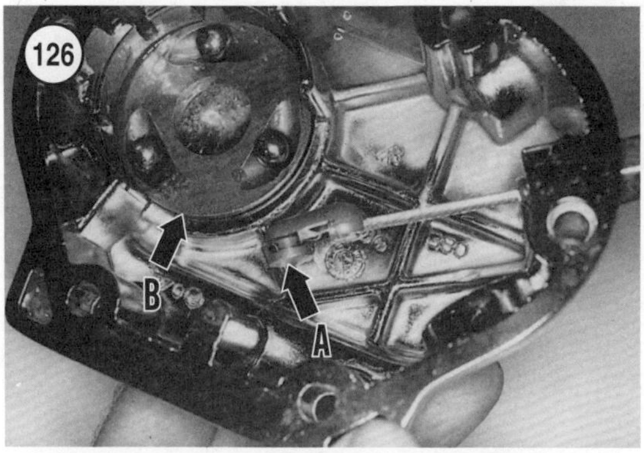

(127)

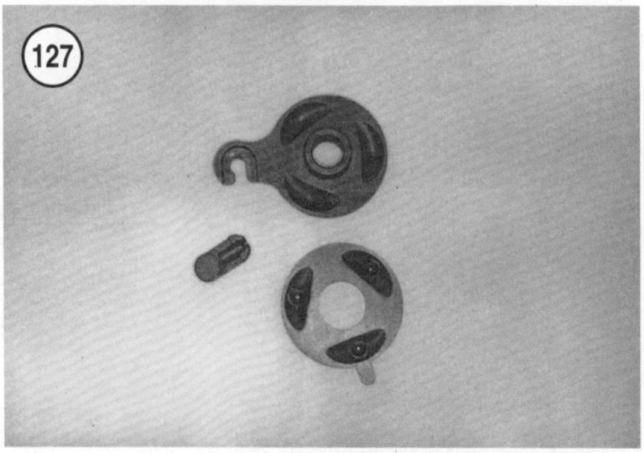

(128)

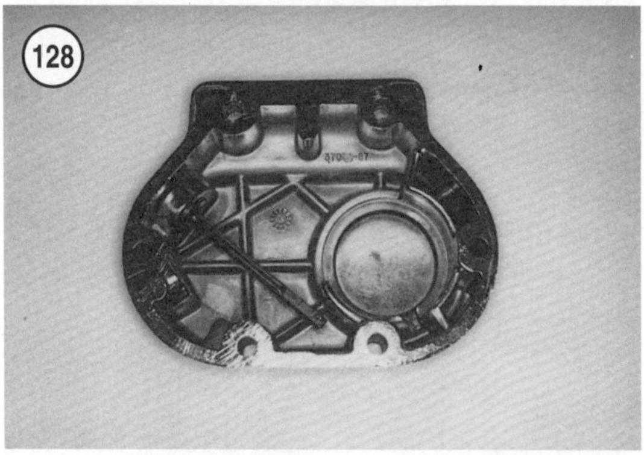

(129)

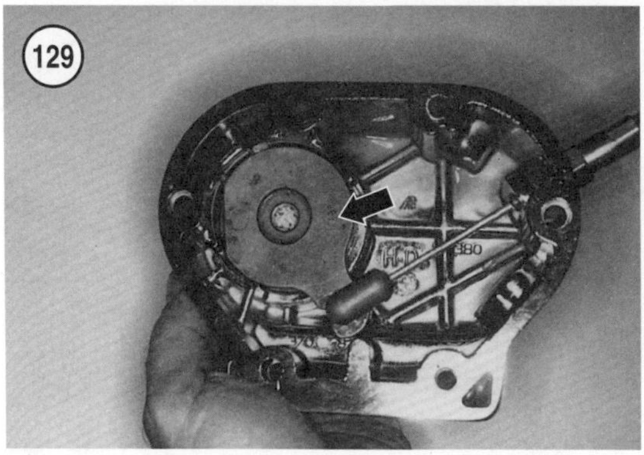

(130)

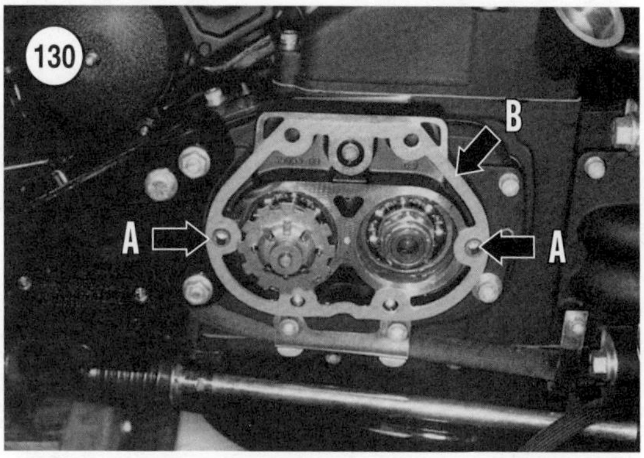

of the outer ramp tang slot as shown in A, **Figure 124**. Make sure the snap ring is seated correctly in the groove.

6

Installation

1. If removed, install the locating dowels (A, **Figure 130**).
2. Install a *new* gasket (B, **Figure 130**).
3. Install the side cover (**Figure 121**) and bolts. Tighten the bolts in a crisscross patter to the specification in **Table 3**.
4. Refill the transmission with oil as described in Chapter Three.
5. Install the exhaust system as described in Chapter Seven.
6. Adjust the clutch as described in Chapter Three.

TRANSMISSION DRIVE SPROCKET

Removal/Installation

NOTE
It is not necessary to remove the mainshaft bearing race to remove the transmission drive sprocket.

1. Remove the primary chain case assembly as described in Chapter Five.
2. Remove the two Allen bolts (A, **Figure 131**) and the lock plate (B).
3. If the drive belt has been removed, install a sprocket locker tool (JIMS part No. 2260) (**Figure 132**) onto the transmission drive sprocket, following the manufacturer's instructions.
4A. Shift the transmission into gear.
4B. If the drive belt is still in place, have an assistant apply the rear brake.

5. Using a countershaft sprocket nut wrench (JIMS part No. 946600-37A), install the inner collar (A, **Figure 133**) onto the mainshaft.

CAUTION
*The sprocket nut has left-hand threads. Turn the tool **clockwise** to loosen it in Step 6.*

6. Install the wrench onto the nut (**Figure 134**), turn it *clockwise* and loosen the nut.
7. Remove the special tools and the nut (B, **Figure 133**) from the mainshaft.
8. Carefully remove the transmission drive sprocket from the mainshaft, being careful to not damage the bearing race.
9. Install by reversing these removal steps while noting the following:
   a. Use the same tool setup used during removal.
   b. Apply Loctite TB1360 or an equivalent to the nut and Allen bolts prior to installation.
   c. Locate the nut with the flanged side facing the drive sprocket.

CAUTION
In substep d, do not tighten the nut past an additional 45° to align the lock plate bolt holes or the nut will be damaged.

   d. Tighten the nut *counterclockwise* to the specification in **Table 3**. Then tighten an additional 30° until the lock plate holes are aligned.

TRANSMISSION CASE

Transmission case removal is only necessary if it requires replacement or when performing extensive frame repair or replacing the frame. All internal components can be removed with the case in the frame.

Refer to **Figure 135**.

Removal/Installation

1. Drain the transmission oil and primary chain case lubricant as described in Chapter Three.
2. Remove the primary chaincase cover as described in Chapter Five.
3. Remove the clutch assembly as described in Chapter Five.

131

132

133
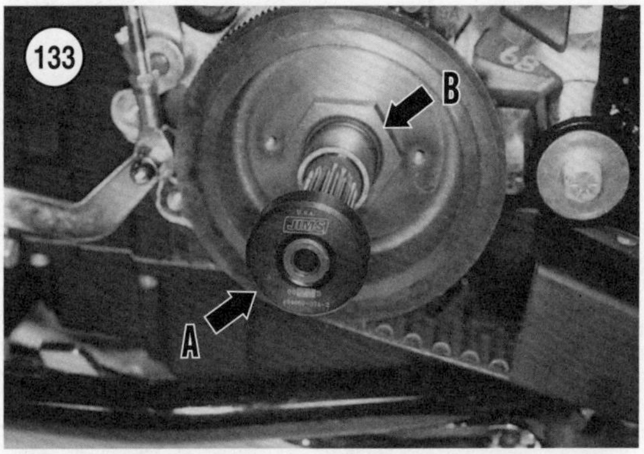

134
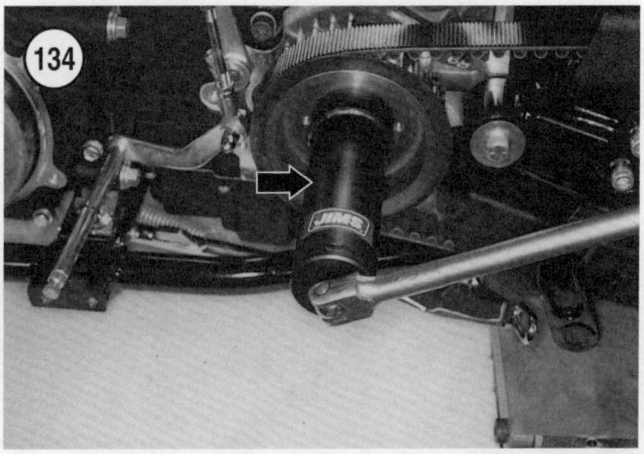

(135) **TRANSMISSION CASE**

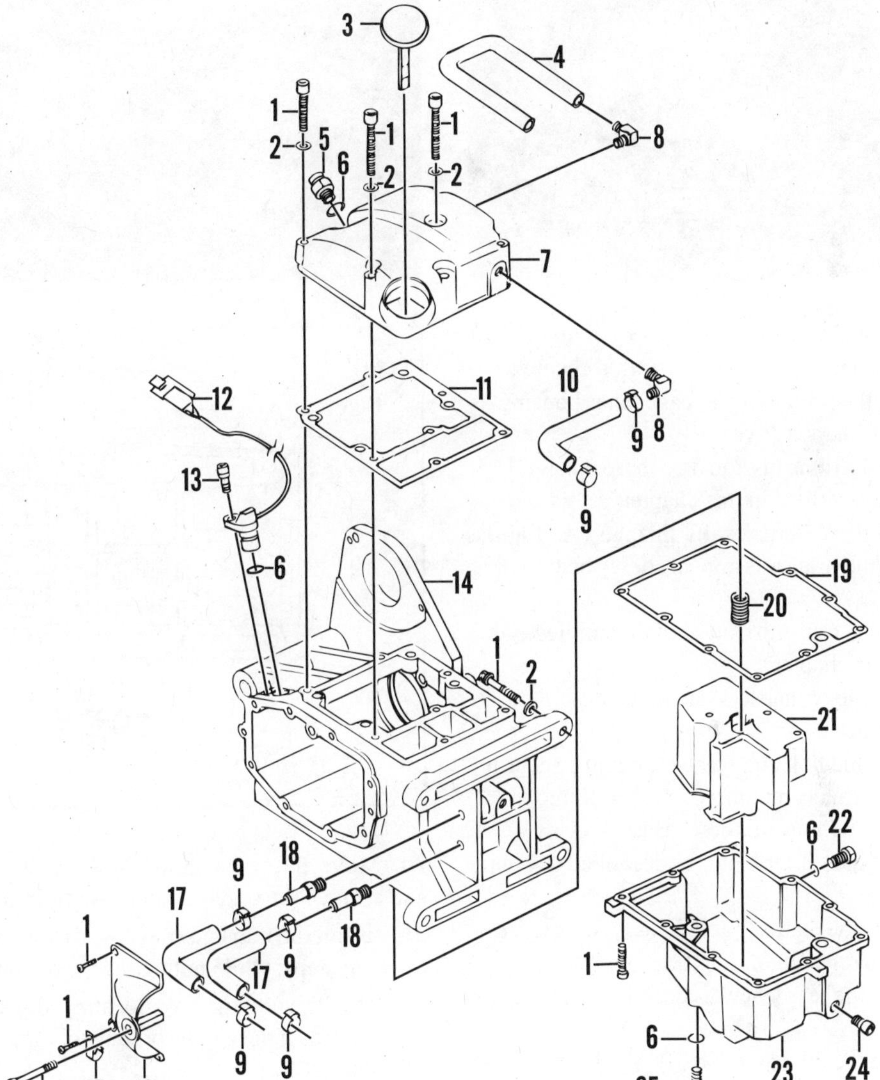

1. Bolt
2. Washer
3. Dipstick
4. Vent hose
5. Neutral indicator switch
6. O-ring
7. Top cover
8. Elbow fitting
9. Hose clamp
10. Hose
11. Gasket
12. Speed sensor indicator
13. Screw
14. Transmission case
15. Clip
16. Oil hose cover
17. Oil hose
18. Fittings
19. Gasket
20. Baffle spring
21. Baffle
22. Engine oil drain plug
23. Oil pan
24. Plug
25. Transmission oil drain bolt

4. Remove the transmission side cover and clutch release mechanism as described in this chapter.
5. Remove the primary chaincase inner housing as described in Chapter Five.
6. Remove the transmission drive sprocket (A, **Figure 136**) as described in this chapter.
7. Remove the external shift linkage (A, **Figure 137**) from the transmission as described in this chapter.
8. Remove the transmission shaft assemblies as described in this chapter.
9. Remove the exhaust system as described in Chapter Seven.
10. Remove the bolt and washer and nuts securing the left side exhaust mounting bracket. Remove the bracket from the transmission case.
11. Remove the starter motor as described in Chapter Eight.
12. Remove the battery and battery case as described in Chapter Eight.
13. Remove the rear wheel as described in Chapter Nine.
14. Remove the oil pan and baffle (B, **Figure 136**) from the bottom of the transmission case as described in this chapter.
15. Remove the external components of the shift arm assembly as described in the following procedure.
16. Support the swing arm, then remove the swing arm pivot bolt as described in Chapter Eleven.
17. Disconnect the two oil hoses (B, **Figure 137**) connecting the transmission to the crankcase.
18. Remove the four transmission case-to-engine mounting bolts (C, **Figure 136**). There are two bolts on each side.
19. Move the transmission case to the rear to clear the two lower locating dowels.

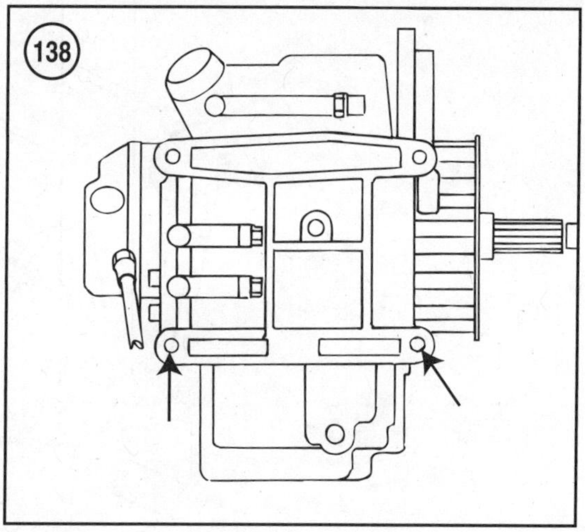

20. Move the transmission toward the right side and remove the transmission case from the frame.
21. Install the transmission case by reversing these removal steps, while noting the following:
   a. Make sure the two locating dowels are in place on the engine or transmission case (**Figure 138**).
   b. Tighten the transmission mounting bolts in a crisscross pattern to the specification in **Table 3**.

Shift Arm Assembly

Removal/disassembly

Refer to **Figure 139** and **Figure 140**.

1. Remove the transmission side door assembly as described in this chapter.
2. Make an alignment mark on the shift rod lever and on the shift arm shaft

(139)

SHIFT ARM ASSEMBLY (1999-2000)

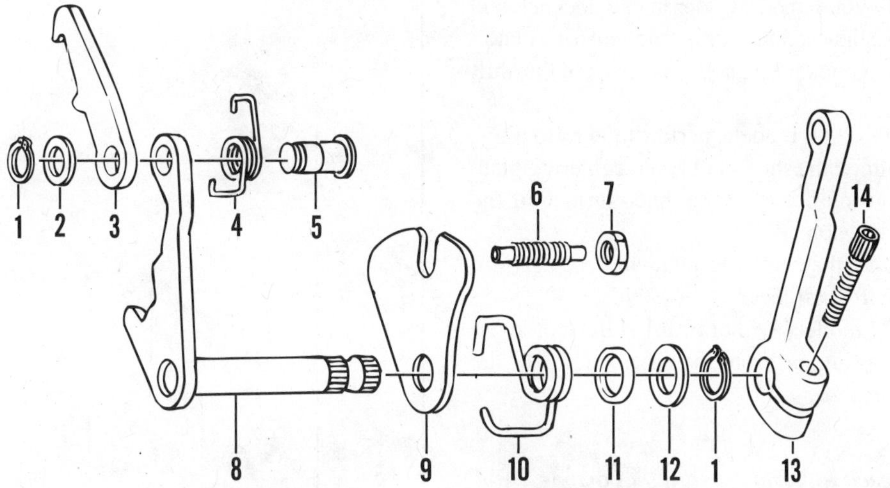

1. Snap ring
2. Washer
3. Shift arm pawl
4. Spring
5. Pivot pin
6. Adjuster
7. Locknut
8. Shift shaft lever
9. Centering plate
10. Spring
11. Oil seal
12. Washer
13. Shift rod lever
14. Clamp bolt

(140)

SHIFT ARM ASSEMBLY (2001)

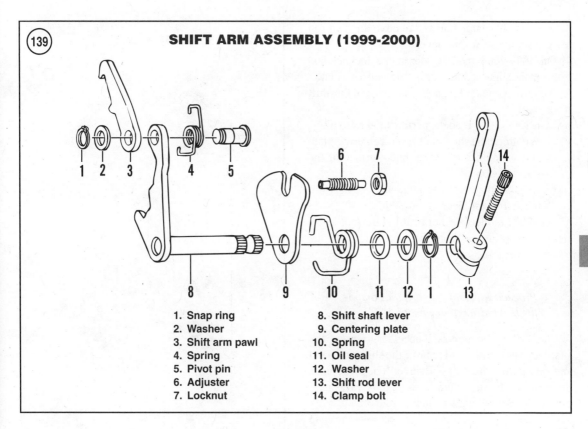

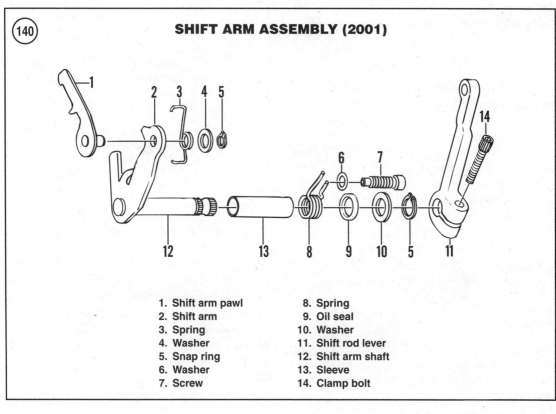

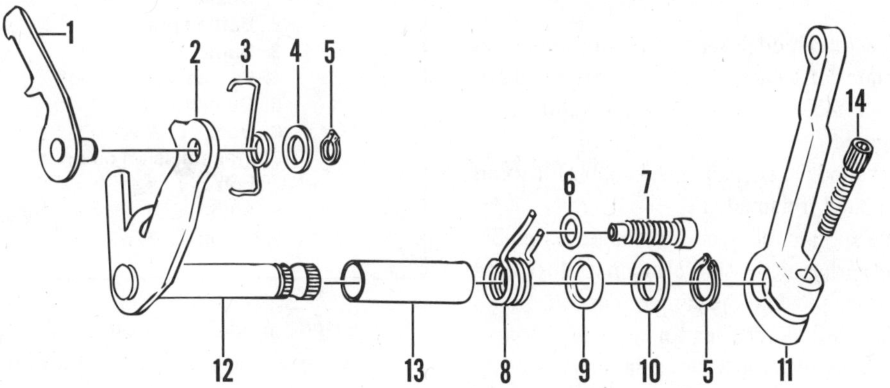

1. Shift arm pawl
2. Shift arm
3. Spring
4. Washer
5. Snap ring
6. Washer
7. Screw
8. Spring
9. Oil seal
10. Washer
11. Shift rod lever
12. Shift arm shaft
13. Sleeve
14. Clamp bolt

3. Remove the clamp bolt and remove the shift rod lever from the shift shaft lever.
4. On 1999-2000 models, loosen the locknut and back out the adjuster until it clears the centering plate.
5. Remove the snap ring and washer from the shift lever shaft.
6A. On 1999-2000 models, perform the following:
   a. Withdraw the shift shaft lever, centering plate and spring out from the inner surface of the transmission case.
   b. Remove the centering plate and spring from the shift shaft lever.
6B. On 2001 models, withdraw the shift shaft lever, sleeve and spring out from the inner surface of the transmission case

NOTE
Proceed with Step 6 only if the components require replacement.

7A. On 1999-2000 models, if necessary, remove the snap ring and washer and remove the shift cam pawl and spring from the shift shaft lever. The pivot pin is pressed into the shift shaft lever. If removal is necessary, drive it out with a suitable size punch.
7B. On 2001 models, if necessary, remove the snap ring and washer and remove the shift cam pawl and spring from the shift shaft lever.

Inspection

1A. On 1999-2000 models, check the shift pawl and centering plate for wear. Replace the pawl if damaged. Replace the centering plate if its adjustment slot is elongated.
1B. On 2001 models, check the shift pawl for wear. Replace the pawl if damaged.
2. Check the springs for wear or damage. Assemble the pawl and spring on the shift arm pin. If the spring will not hold the pawl on the cam, replace it.
3. Check the shift shaft lever for wear or damage. Check the end splines for wear or damage.
4. Check the shift rod lever for wear or damage. Check the internal splines for wear or damage.

Assembly/installation

1A. On 1999-2000 models, if disassembled, install the shift cam pawl and spring onto the shift shaft lever pivot pin. Secure it with the washer and *new* snap ring.

(141) OIL PAN

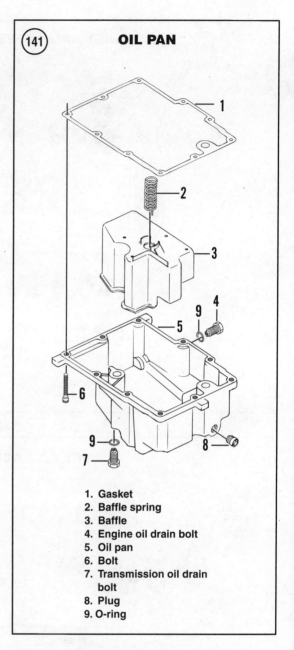

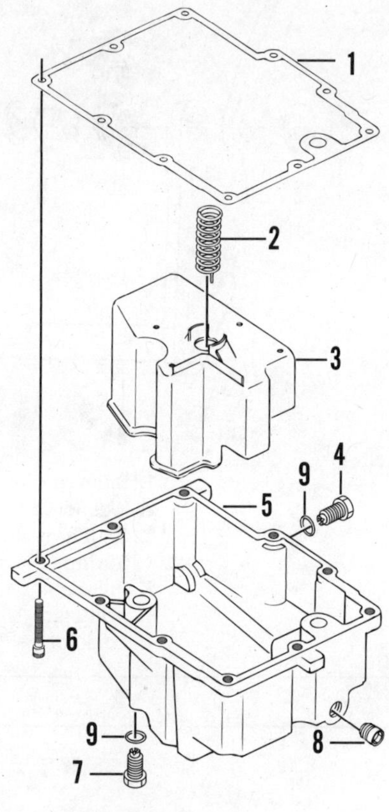

1. Gasket
2. Baffle spring
3. Baffle
4. Engine oil drain bolt
5. Oil pan
6. Bolt
7. Transmission oil drain bolt
8. Plug
9. O-ring

1B. On 2001 models, if disassembled, install the shift cam pawl and spring onto the shift shaft. Secure it with the washer and *new* snap ring.
2. On 1999-2000 models, install the centering plate on the shift shaft lever and spring.
3. Install the shift shaft lever assembly into the transmission case.
4A. On 1999-2000 models, align the slot in the centering plate with the adjuster.
4B. On 2001 models, align the spring with the screw.

5. Refer to the alignment marks made in Step 1 *Removal/Disassembly* and install the shift rod lever onto the shift shaft lever. Push it on until the bolt hole aligns with the shaft lever groove.
6. Install the clamp bolt and tighten to the specification in **Table 3**.
7. Install the transmission side door assembly as described in this chapter.

OIL PAN

The oil pan mounts onto the bottom of the transmission case. It can be removed with the transmission mounted in the frame.

Refer to **Figure 141**.

Removal

1. Drain the engine oil as described in Chapter Three.
2. Drain the transmission oil as described in Chapter Three.
3. Remove the ten bolts securing the oil pan to the transmission case.
4. Lower and remove the oil pan baffle and baffle spring from the transmission case.
5. Remove the gasket.

Inspection

1. Clean the oil tank, baffle and spring in solvent and dry thoroughly.
2. Remove all old gasket residue from the oil tank and transmission case gasket surfaces.
3. Inspect the oil pan for cracks or damage. Replace if necessary.

Installation

1. Install a new oil tank gasket on the oil pan.
2. Install the baffle and baffle spring into the oil pan.
3. Install the oil pan onto the bottom of the transmission case, and secure with the ten bolts.
4. Tighten the oil pan mounting bolts securely in a crisscross pattern.
5. If necessary, replace the engine oil filter as described in Chapter Three.
6. Refill the oil pan with new engine oil as described in Chapter Three.
7. Refill the transmission with new oil as described in Chapter Three.
8. Start the engine and check for leaks.

Table 1 TRANSMISSION SPECIFICATIONS

Transmission type	Five-speed, constant mesh
Gear ratios	
First	3.21
Second	2.21
Third	1.57
Fourth	1.23
Fifth	1.00
Transmission fluid capacity	
Oil change	20-24 U.S. oz. (591-709 ml)
Rebuild (dry)	24 U.S. oz. (709 ml)

Table 2 TRANSMISSION SERVICE SPECIFICATIONS

Item	In.	mm
Countershaft		
Runout	0.000-0.003	0.00-0.08
Endplay	None	

(continued)

Table 2 TRANSMISSION SERVICE SPECIFICATIONS (continued)

Item	In.	mm
Countershaft (continued)		
First gear		
Clearance	0.0003-0.0019	0.008-0.048
End play	0.005-0.0039	0.127-0.099
Second gear		
Clearance	0.0003-0.0019	0.008-0.048
End play	0.005-0.0440	0.127-1.118
Third gear		
Clearance	0.000-0.0080	0.000-0.203
Fourth gear		
Clearance	0.000-0.0080	0.000-0.203
End play	0.005-0.0390	0.127-0.991
Fifth gear		
Clearance	0.000-0.0080	0.000-0.203
End play	0.005-0.0040	0.127-0.102
Mainshaft		
Runout	0.000-0.003	0.00-0.08
Endplay	None	–
First gear		
Clearance	0.000-0.0080	0.000-0.203
Second gear		
Clearance	0.000-0.0800	0.000-2.032
Third gear		
Clearance	0.0003-0.0019	0.008-0.048
End play	0.0050-0.0420	0.127-1.067
Fourth gear		
Clearance	0.0003-0.0019	0.008-0.048
End play	0.0050-0.0310	0.127-0.787
Main drive gear (fifth)		
Bearing fit in transmission case	0.0003-0.0017	0.0076-0.043
Fit in bearing		
Tight fit	0.0009	0.023
Loose fit	0.0001	0.0025
Fit on mainshaft	0.0001-0.0009	0.0025-0.023
End play	None	–
Shifter cam assembly		
Right edge of middle cam groove to right support block distance	1.992-2.002	50.60-50.85
Shifter cam end play	0.0001-0.004	0.0025-0.10
Shifter forks		
Shifter fork-to-cam groove end play	0.0017-0.0019	0.043-0.048
Shifter fork-to-gear groove end play	0.0010-0.0011	0.025-0.0279
Shift fork finger thickness	0.165	4.19
Side door bearing		
Fit in side door	0.0014-0.0001	0.036-0.0025
Fit on countershaft		
Tight fit	0.0007	0.018
Loose fit	0.0001	0.0025
Fit on mainshaft		
Tight fit	0.0007	0.018
Loose fit	0.0001	0.0025

Table 3 TRANSMISSION TORQUE SPECIFICATIONS

Item	ft.-lb.	in.-lb.	N·m
Clutch cable fitting	–	30-60	3-7
Clutch release			
cover screws	–	84-108	9-12
Mainshaft and			
countershaft nuts	45-55	–	61-75
Shift rod			
Locknuts	20-24	–	27-32
Clamp bolts	18-22	–	24-30
Shift cam support blocks	–	84-108	9-12
Top cover screws	–	84-108	9-12
Transmission main and			
countershaft locknuts			
at side door	27-33	–	37-45
Transmission case door			
1/4 in. fasteners	–	84-108	9-12
5/16 in. fasteners	13-16	–	18-22
Transmission drain plug	14-21	–	19-28
Transmission mounting			
bolts	30-35	–	41-47
Detent follower bolt (2001)	–	84-108	9-12
Transmission drive			
sprocket			
Mounting nut*	50	–	68
Lockplate bolts	–	84-108	9-12

* Tighten an additional 30°—not to exceed 45°.

NOTE: Refer to the Supplement at the back of this manual for information unique to 2002-on models.

CHAPTER SEVEN

FUEL, EXHAUST AND EMISSION CONTROL SYSTEMS

The fuel system consists of the fuel tank, fuel shutoff valve, single side-draft carburetor and air filter housing.

The emission control consists of the Evaporative Emission Control System on all California models.

This chapter includes service procedures for all parts of the fuel system and the air filter backplate. Air filter service is covered in Chapter Three.

Specifications and jet sizes are in **Tables 1-3** at the end of the chapter.

Table 1 lists carburetor jet sizes.

Table 2 lists fuel system torque specifications.

Table 3 lists exhaust system torque specifications.

WARNING

Gasoline is a known carcinogenic, as well as an extremely flammable liquid, and must be handled carefully. Wear latex gloves to avoid contact. If gasoline does contact skin, immediately and thoroughly wash the area with soap and warm water.

CARBURETOR OPERATION

An understanding of the function of each of the carburetor components and their relation to one an-

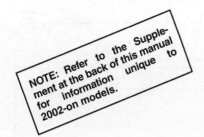

(1)

AIR FILTER

1. Backplate (international)
2. Grommet (California)
3. Backplate (California)
4. O-ring
5. Gasket
6. Backplate (49-state)
7. Breather hollow bolt
8. Breather hose
9. Gasket
10. Air filter
11. Mounting bracket
12. Torx screws
13. Nut clip
14. Enrichment cable bracket
15. Cable strap
16. Nut
17. Grommet
18. Bolt
19. Screw
20. Trim
21. Cover
22. Seal

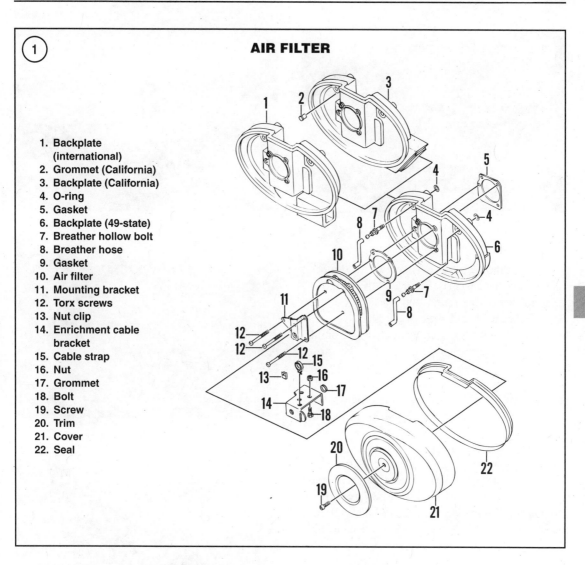

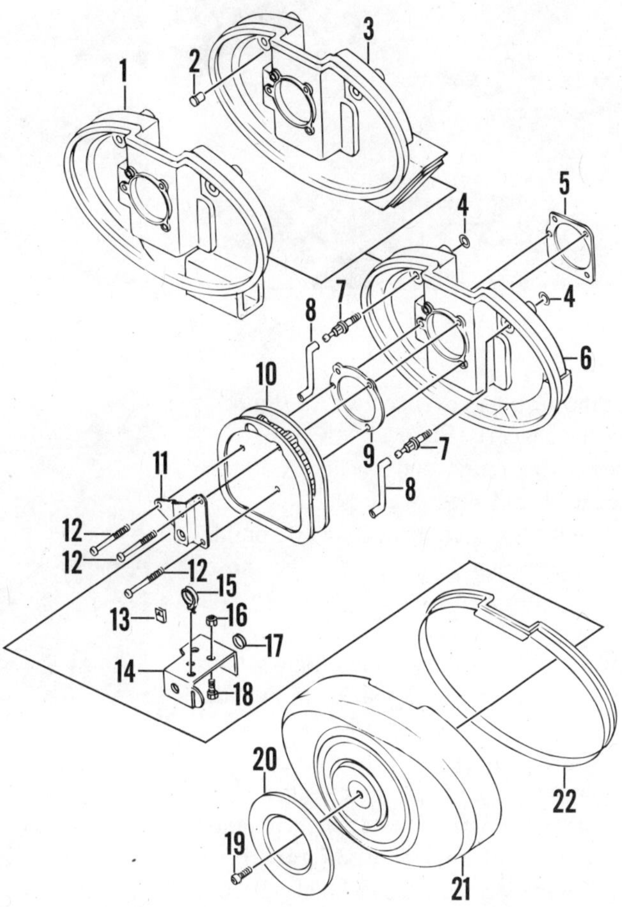

other is a valuable aid for pinpointing a source of carburetor trouble.

The carburetor's purpose is to supply and atomize fuel and mix it in correct proportions with air that is drawn in through the air intake. At the primary throttle opening (idle), a small amount of fuel is siphoned through the pilot jet by the incoming air. As the throttle is opened further, the air stream begins to siphon fuel through the main jet and needle jet. The tapered needle increases the effective flow capacity of the needle jet as it is lifted, in that it occupies progressively less of the area of the jet. At full throttle the carburetor venturi is fully open and the needle is lifted far enough to permit the main jet to flow at full capacity.

The choke circuit is a starting enrichment valve system in which the choke knob on the left side of the engine next to the horn opens an enrichment valve, rather than closing a butterfly in the venturi area as on some carburetors. In the open position, the slow jet discharges a stream of fuel into the carburetor venturi to enrich the mixture when the engine is cold.

The accelerator pump circuit reduces engine hesitation by injecting a fine spray of fuel into the carburetor intake passage during sudden acceleration.

AIR FILTER BACKPLATE

Routine air filter maintenance is described in Chapter Three.

Refer to **Figure 1**.

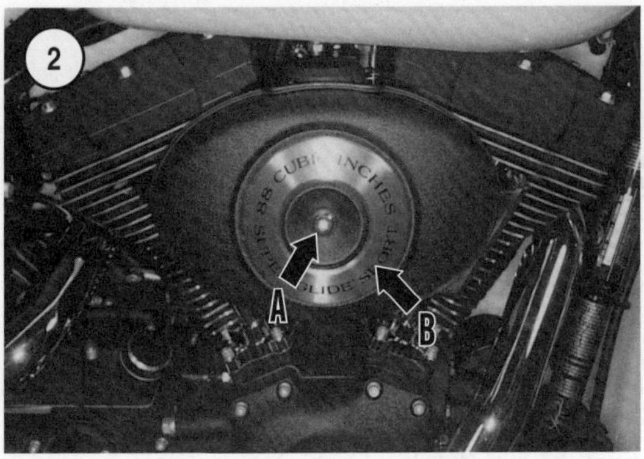

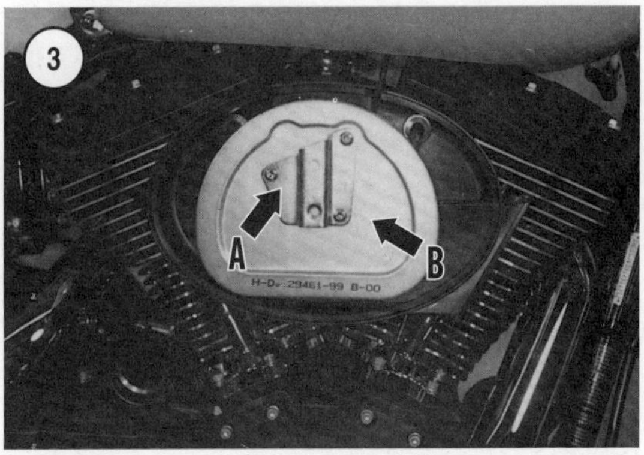

Removal

1. Remove the air filter cover screw (A, **Figure 2**) and remove the cover (B, **Figure 2**).
2. Remove the Torx screws and bracket (A, **Figure 3**) from the air filter element.
3. Gently pull the air filter element away from the backplate and disconnect the two breather hoses from the hollow bolts on the backplate. Remove the air filter element (B, **Figure 3**).
4. Unscrew and remove the breather hollow bolts (A, **Figure 4**) securing the backplate to the cylinder heads.

5A. On California models, pull the backplate (B, **Figure 4**) partially away from the cylinder heads and the carburetor, then disconnect the evaporation emission control clean air inlet hose (**Figure 5**).

5B. On all other models, pull the backplate (B, **Figure 4**) away from the cylinder heads and remove it.

6. Remove the carburetor gasket.

Inspection

1. Inspect the backplate (**Figure 6**) for damage.
2. On California models, make sure the trap door swings freely (**Figure 7**).
3. Make sure the breather hollow bolts and breather hoses (**Figure 8**) are clear. Clean out if necessary.

Installation

1. Apply a couple dabs of gasket sealer to the new carburetor gasket and attach it to the backside of the backplate.
2. Move the backplate into position.
3. On California models, move the backplate part way into position. Connect the evaporation emis-

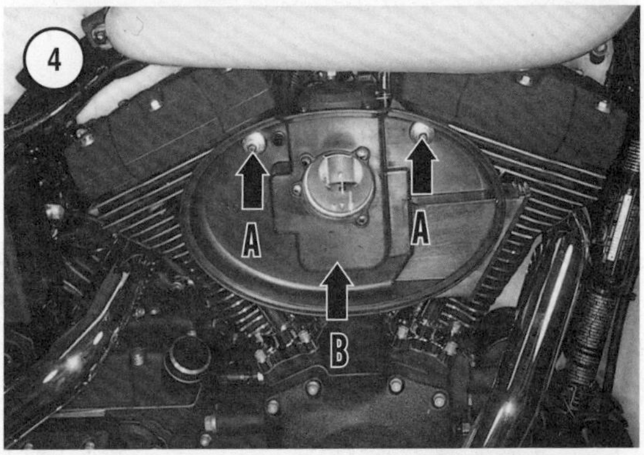

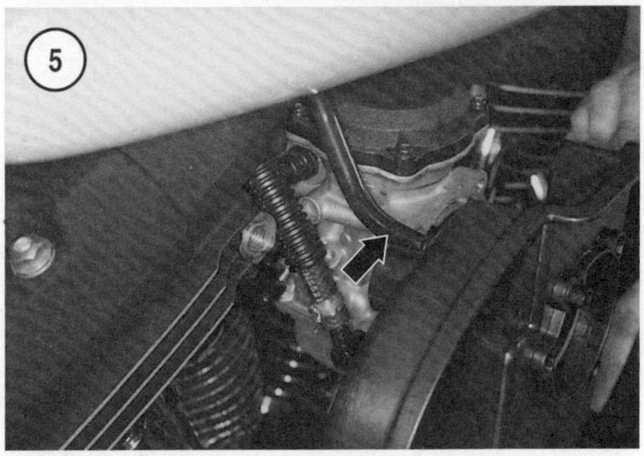

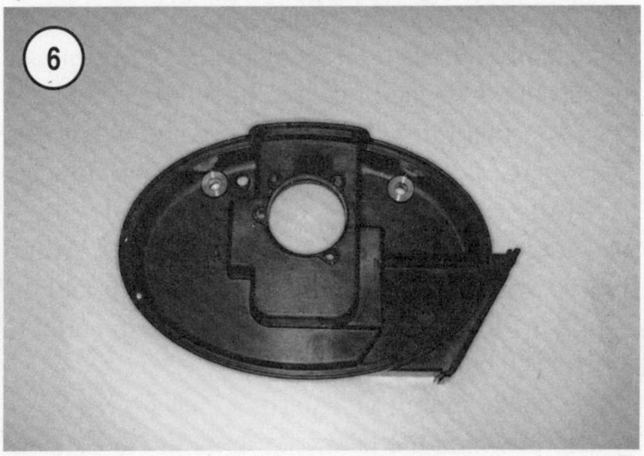

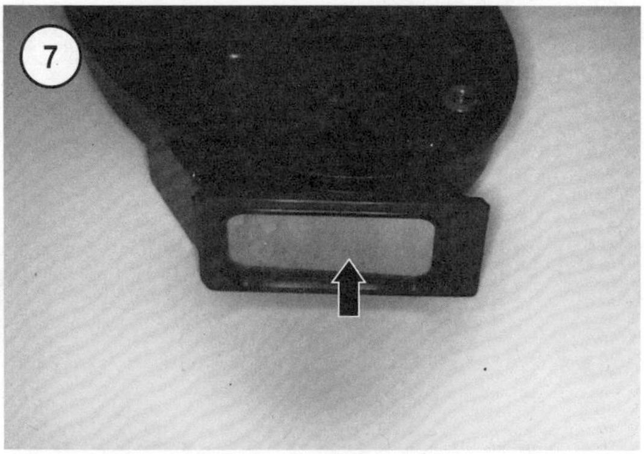
7

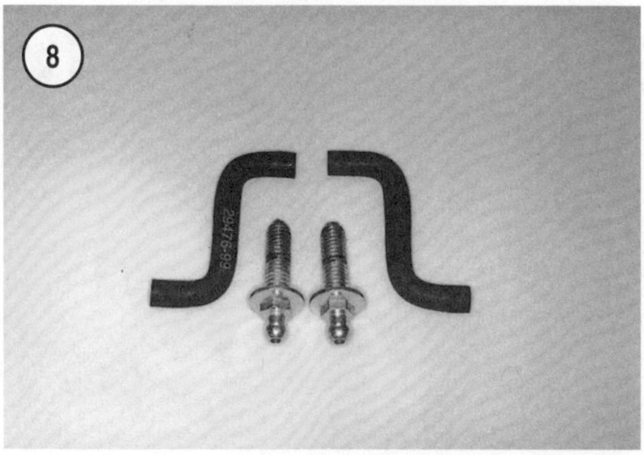
8

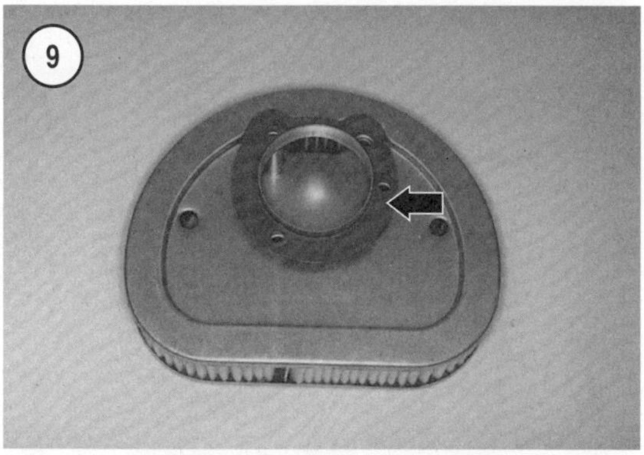
9

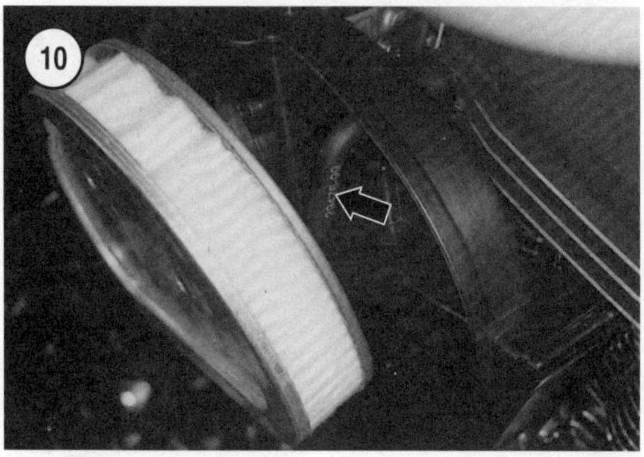
10

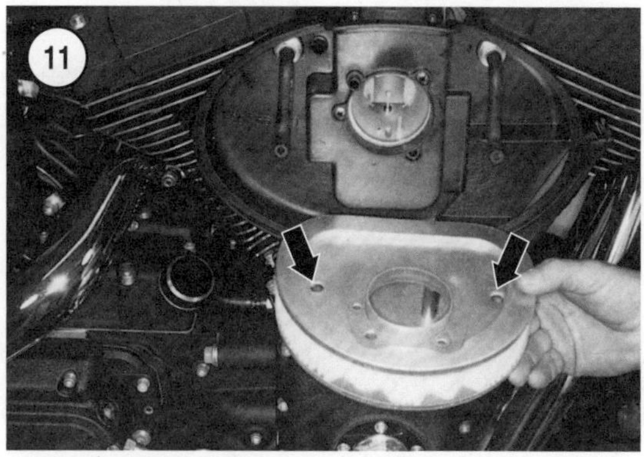
11

sion control clean air inlet hose (**Figure 5**) to the fitting on the backside of the backplate.

4. Position the backplate (B, **Figure 4**) against the carburetor and cylinder heads. Make sure the Torx bolt holes of the gasket and backplate are aligned with the carburetor. Reposition the gasket if necessary.

5. Install the breather hollow bolts (A, **Figure 4**) securing the backplate to the cylinder heads. Tighten to the specification in **Table 2**.

6. If removed, install a *new* gasket (**Figure 9**) onto the air filter element.

7. Position the element with the flat side facing down and attach the breather hoses (**Figure 10**) to the backside of the element (**Figure 11**). If an aftermarket air filter element is being installed, position it onto the backplate following the manufacturer's instructions.

8. Move the element into position (B, **Figure 3**) and install the mounting bracket (A, **Figure 3**) and the Torx screws. Tighten the Torx screws to the specification in **Table 2**.

9. Apply a drop of ThreeBond TB1342 (blue) or an equivalent threadlocking compound to the cover screw prior to installation.

10. Inspect the seal ring (**Figure 12**) on the air filter cover for hardness or deterioration. Replace if necessary.

11. Install the air filter cover (B, **Figure 2**) and the screw (A, **Figure 2**). Tighten the screw to the specification in **Table 2**

CARBURETOR

Removal

1. Remove the air filter and backplate as described in this chapter.

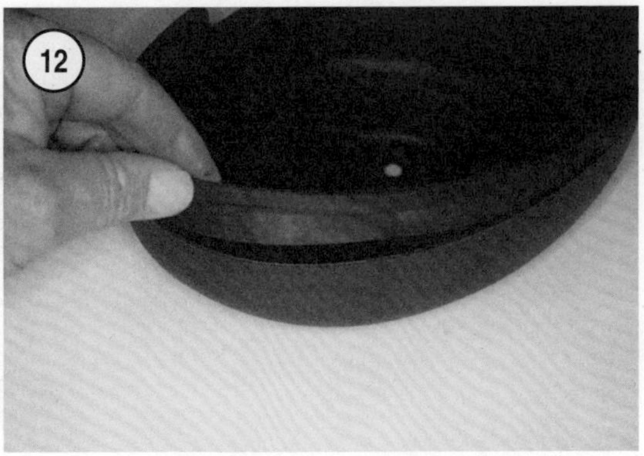

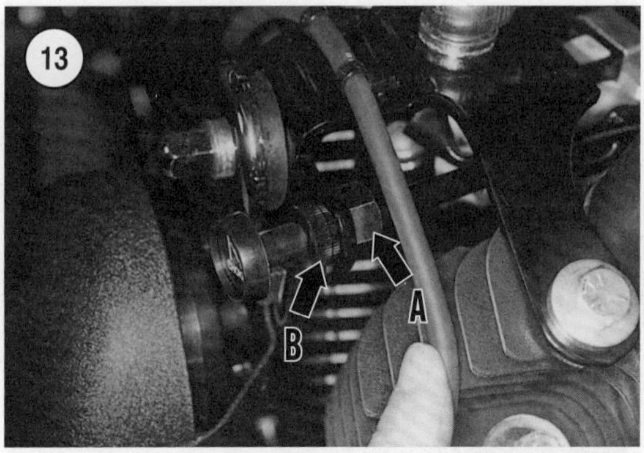

2. Remove the fuel tank as described in this chapter.

3. Loosen the locknut (A, **Figure 13**) and disconnect the starting enrichment valve cable to the mounting bracket (B, **Figure 13**). Move the end of the cable out of the mounting bracket.

4. There are two different throttle cables. Label the two cables at the carburetor before disconnecting them. One is the throttle control cable and the other is the idle control cable. They are identified as follows:

   a. Throttle control cable: A, **Figure 14**.

   b. Idle control cable: B, **Figure 14**.

5. At the handlebar, perform the following:

   a. Slide the rubber boot off both cables.

   b. Loosen both control cable adjuster locknuts (A, **Figure 15**), then turn the cable adjusters (B) *clockwise* as far as possible to increase slack.

6. Disconnect the fuel supply hose (**Figure 16**) from the carburetor fitting.

7. Twist and then pull the carburetor off the seal ring and intake manifold.

8. Disconnect the vacuum hose (**Figure 17**) from the carburetor fitting.

9. Disconnect the throttle control cable (A, **Figure 18**) and the idle control cable (B) from the carburetor cable guide and the throttle wheel.

10. Drain the gasoline from the carburetor assembly.

11. Inspect the carburetor seal ring (**Figure 19**) on the intake manifold for wear, hardness, cracks or other damage. Replace if necessary.

12. If necessary, service the intake manifold as described under *Intake Manifold* in this chapter.

13. Insert a clean lint-free shop cloth into the intake manifold opening.

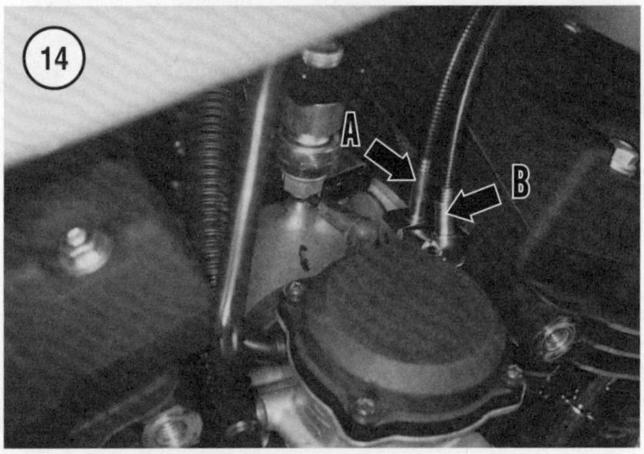

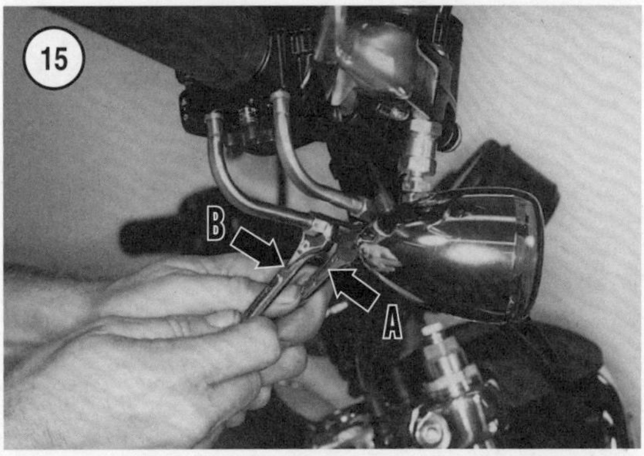

17

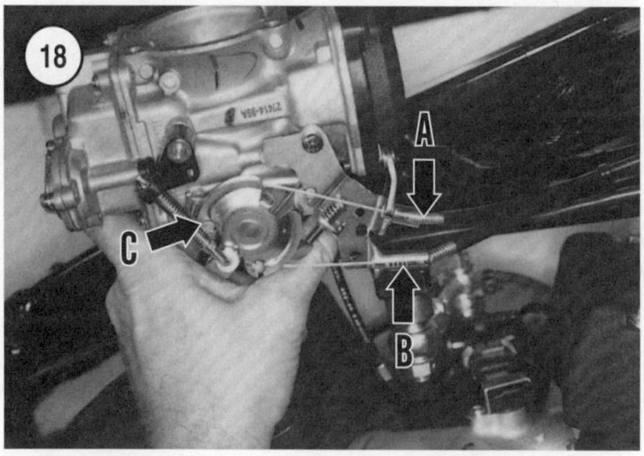

18

19

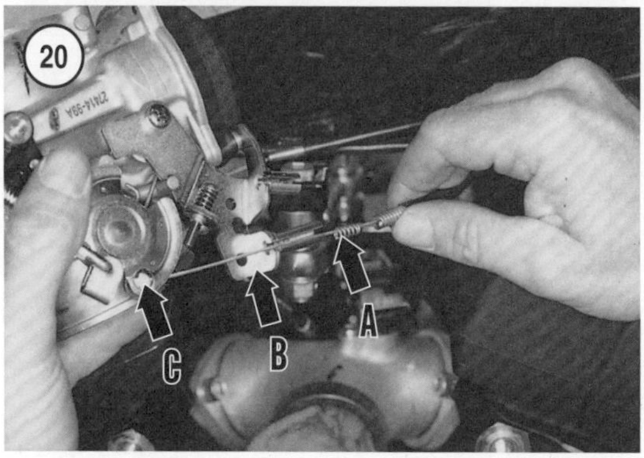

20

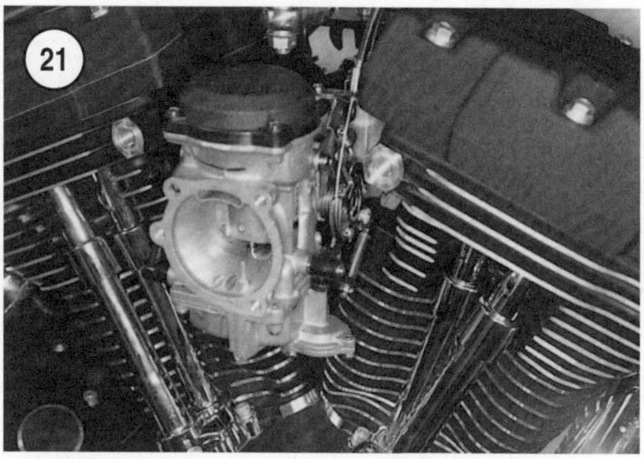
21

Installation

1. If removed, seat the seal ring (**Figure 19**) onto the intake manifold. Make sure it is correctly seated to avoid a vacuum leak.
2. Route the starting enrichment valve cable between the cylinders and toward its mounting bracket on the left side.
3. Connect the idle cable (B, **Figure 14**) to the carburetor as follows:
   a. The idle cable has the small spring (A, **Figure 20**) on the end of the cable.
   b. Insert the idle cable sheath into the rear cable bracket guide on the carburetor (B, **Figure 20**).
   c. Attach the end of the idle cable into the throttle wheel (C, **Figure 20**).
4. Connect the throttle cable (A, **Figure 14**) to the carburetor as follows:
   a. Insert the throttle cable sheath (A, **Figure 18**) into the carburetor front cable bracket guide.
   b. Attach the end of the throttle cable into the throttle wheel (C, **Figure 18**).
5. Operate the hand throttle a few times, making sure the throttle wheel operates smoothly. Also check that both cable ends are seated squarely in their cable bracket guides and in the throttle wheel.

CAUTION

The carburetor must fit squarely onto the intake manifold. If misaligned, it may damage the intake manifold seal ring, resulting in a vacuum leak.

6. Align the carburetor squarely with the intake manifold (**Figure 21**), then push it into the manifold until it bottoms. Position the carburetor so that it sits square and vertical with the manifold.
7. Connect the vacuum hose (**Figure 17**) onto the carburetor fitting. Make sure it is seated correctly.

(22) **CARBURETOR**

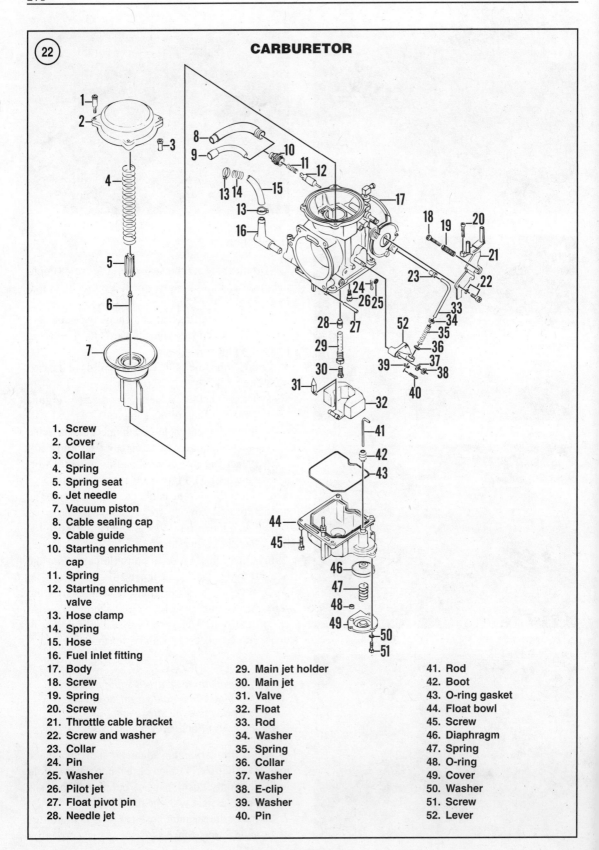

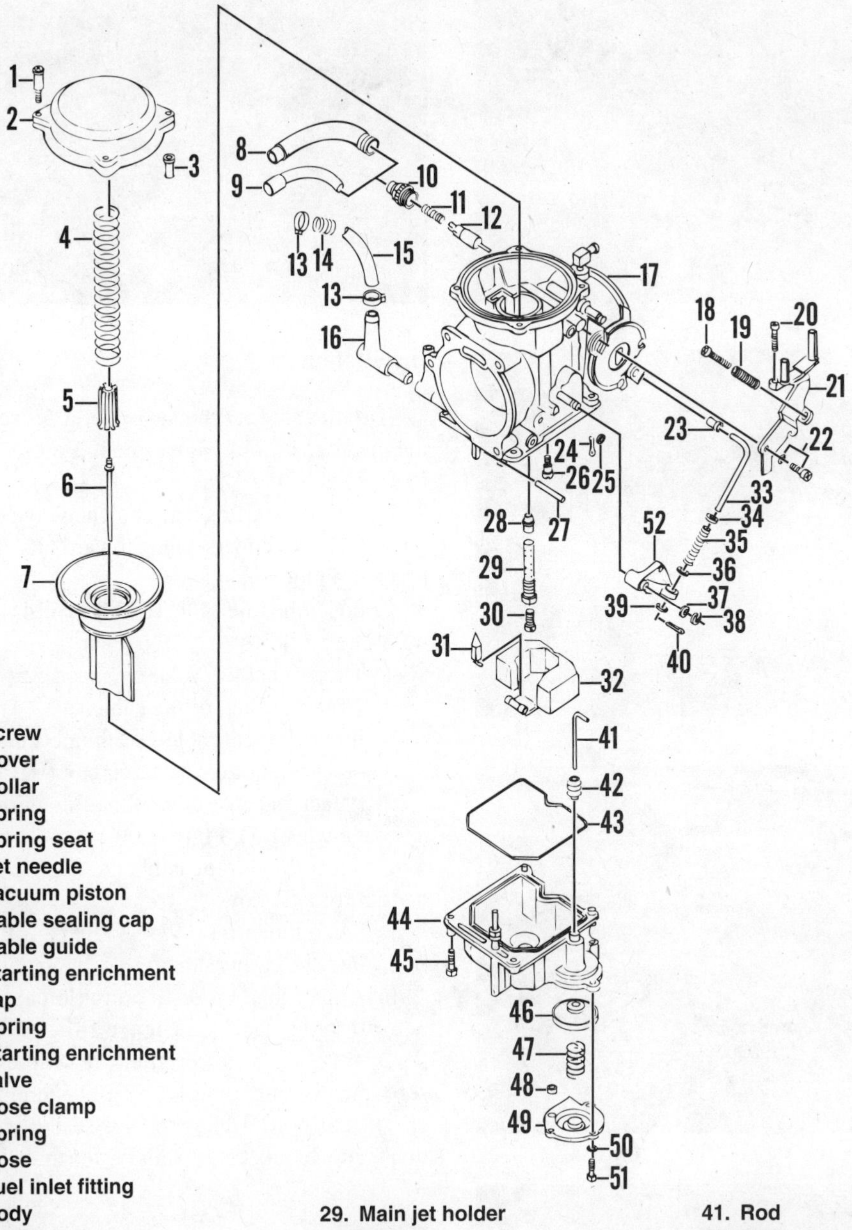

1. Screw
2. Cover
3. Collar
4. Spring
5. Spring seat
6. Jet needle
7. Vacuum piston
8. Cable sealing cap
9. Cable guide
10. Starting enrichment cap
11. Spring
12. Starting enrichment valve
13. Hose clamp
14. Spring
15. Hose
16. Fuel inlet fitting
17. Body
18. Screw
19. Spring
20. Screw
21. Throttle cable bracket
22. Screw and washer
23. Collar
24. Pin
25. Washer
26. Pilot jet
27. Float pivot pin
28. Needle jet
29. Main jet holder
30. Main jet
31. Valve
32. Float
33. Rod
34. Washer
35. Spring
36. Collar
37. Washer
38. E-clip
39. Washer
40. Pin
41. Rod
42. Boot
43. O-ring gasket
44. Float bowl
45. Screw
46. Diaphragm
47. Spring
48. O-ring
49. Cover
50. Washer
51. Screw
52. Lever

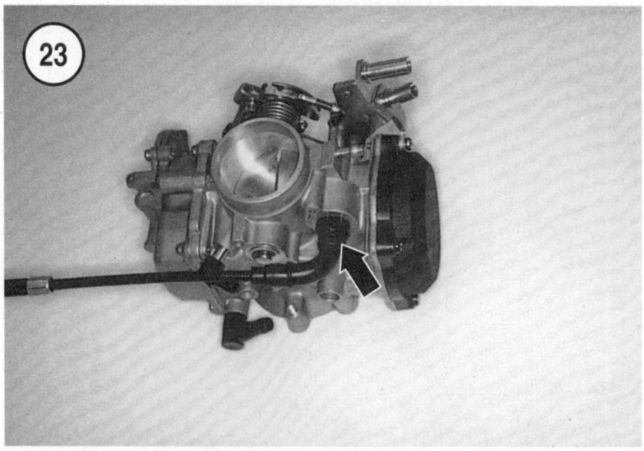
23

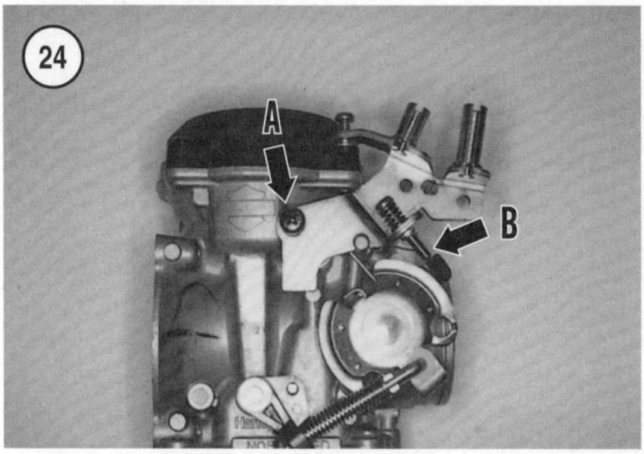

24

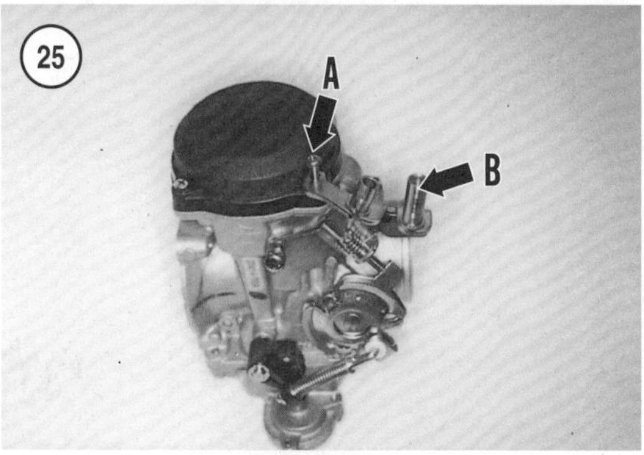

25

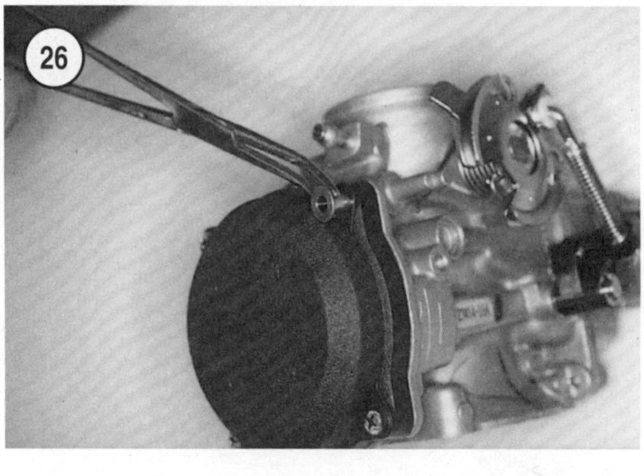
26

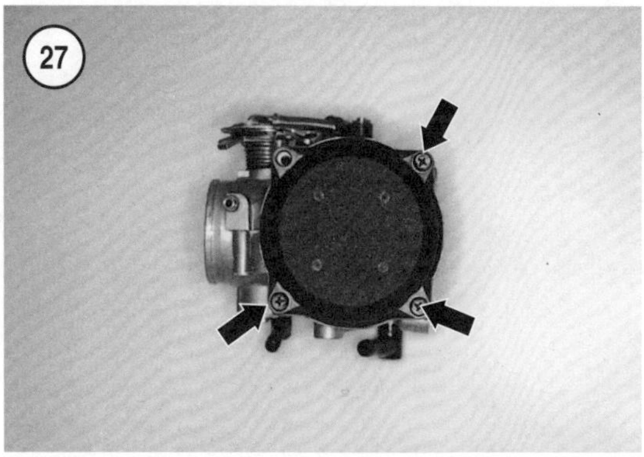
27

8. Slide a new hose clamp over the fuel supply hose, then connect the fuel hose to the hose fitting on the carburetor (**Figure 16**).

9. Position the starting enrichment valve cable into the mounting bracket (B, **Figure 13**), then tighten the locknut (A, **Figure 13**) securely.

10. Before installing the fuel tank, recheck the idle and throttle cable operation. Open and release the hand throttle. Make sure the carburetor throttle valve opens and closes smoothly. Check that both cables are routed properly. If necessary, adjust the throttle cables as described in Chapter Three.

11. Install the air filter backplate and air filter as described in this chapter.

12. Install the fuel tank as described in this chapter.

13. Start the engine. Allow it to idle and check for fuel leaks.

14. With the engine idling in NEUTRAL, turn the handlebar side-to-side. The idle speed must remain the same. If the idle speed increases while turning the handlebars, the cables are installed incorrectly or damaged. Remove the fuel tank and inspect the cables.

Disassembly

Refer to **Figure 22**.

1. Unscrew and remove the starting enrichment valve and cable (**Figure 23**).

2. Remove the screw and washer (A, **Figure 24**) on the side and the top screw (A, **Figure 25**) securing the throttle cable bracket to the carburetor. Remove the bracket (B, **Figure 25**).

3. Remove the collar (**Figure 26**) from the cover.

4. Remove the remaining cover screws (**Figure 27**). Remove the cover and spring (A, **Figure 28**).

5. Remove the vacuum piston (B, **Figure 28**) from the carburetor housing. Do not damage the jet nee-

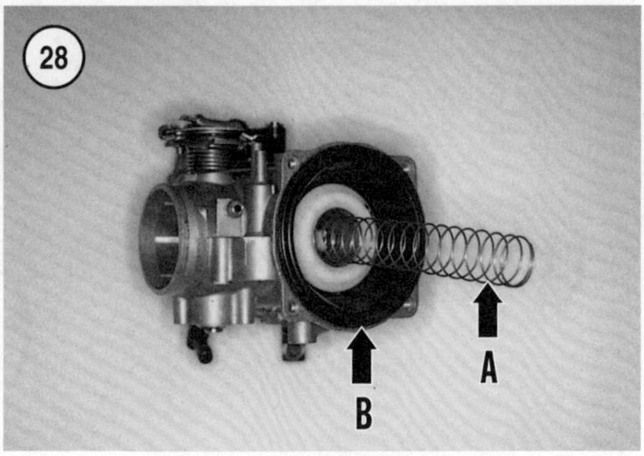

dle extending out of the bottom of the vacuum piston.

6. Remove the float bowl as follows:
   a. Remove the screws (**Figure 29**) securing the float bowl to the carburetor.
   b. Slowly remove the float bowl body and withdraw the pump rod (**Figure 30**) from the boot on the bowl.
   c. Disconnect the pump rod from the lever assembly on the carburetor (**Figure 31**).

NOTE
*One of the float pin pedestals has an interference fit that holds the float pin in place. An arrow, (**Figure 32**) cast into the carburetor, points to this pedestal. To remove this float pin, tap it out from the interference side in the direction of the arrow.*

CAUTION
If the float pin is removed in the direction opposite of the arrow, the opposite pedestal may crack or break off. If this occurs the carburetor must be replaced.

7. Carefully tap the float pin (**Figure 33**) out of the pedestals and remove it.
8. Remove the float and needle valve assembly (**Figure 34**).
9. Unscrew and remove the pilot jet (**Figure 35**).
10. Unscrew and remove the main jet (**Figure 36**).
11. Unscrew and remove the needle jet holder (**Figure 37**).
12. Remove the needle jet (A, **Figure 38**) from the needle jet bore in the carburetor.

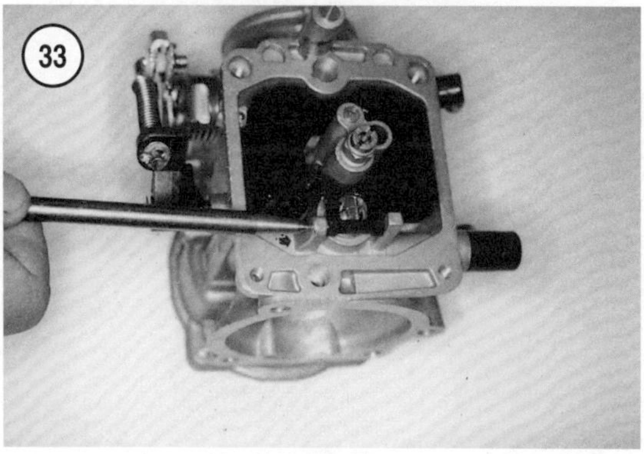

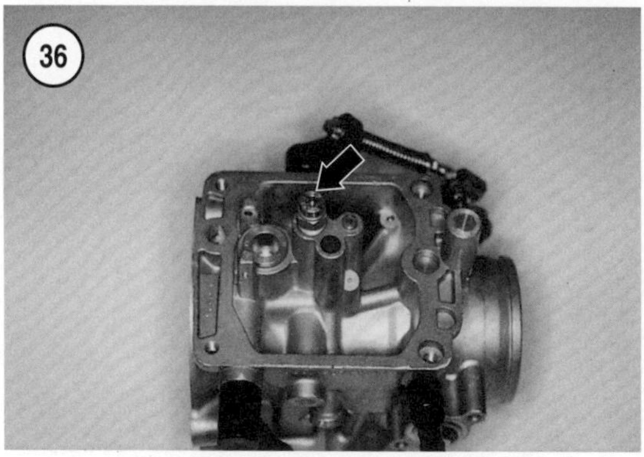

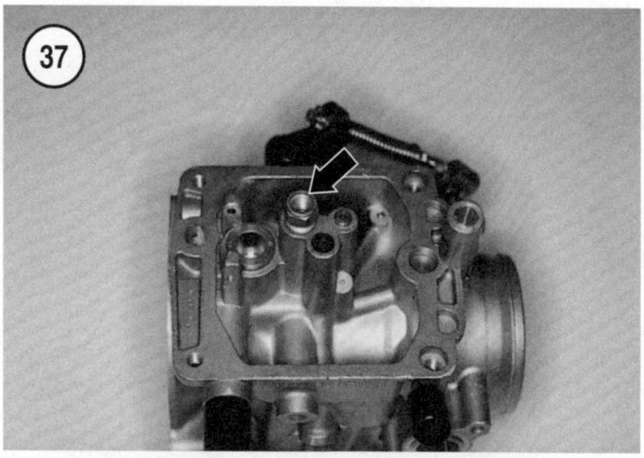

Cleaning and Inspection

Replace worn or damaged parts as described in this section.

CAUTION

The carburetor body is equipped with plastic parts that cannot be removed. Do not dip the carburetor body, O-rings, float assembly, needle valve or vacuum piston in a carburetor cleaner or other harsh solution that can damage these parts. The use of a caustic carburetor cleaning solvent is not recommended. Instead, clean the carburetor and related parts in a petroleum-based solvent, or Simple Green. Then rinse in clean water.

1. Initially clean all parts in a mild petroleum based cleaning solution. Then clean in hot soap and water and rinse with cold water. Blow dry with compressed air.

CAUTION

If compressed air is not available, allow the parts to air dry or use a clean

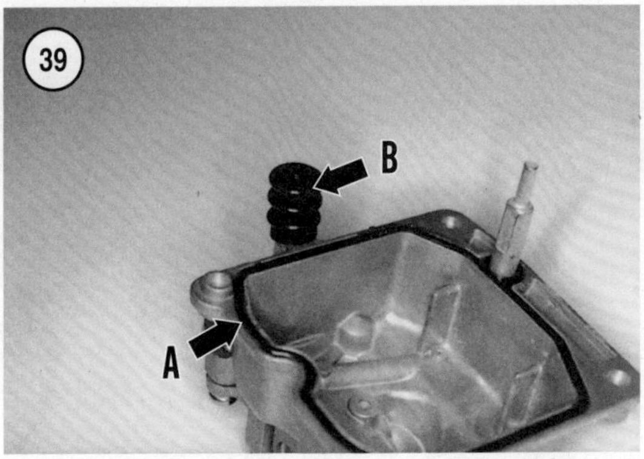

*lint-free cloth. Do **not** use a paper towel to dry carburetor parts, as small paper particles may plug openings in the carburetor housing or jets.*

2. Allow the carburetor to dry thoroughly before assembly and blow dry with compressed air. Blow out the jets and the needle jet holder with compressed air.

CAUTION

*Do **not** use wire or drill bits to clean jets as minor gouges in the jet can alter flow rate and upset the air/fuel mixture.*

3. Inspect the float bowl O-ring gasket (A, **Figure 39**) for hardness or deterioration.
4. Inspect the accelerator pump boot (B, **Figure 39**) for hardness or deterioration.
5. Make sure the accelerator pump cover (**Figure 40**) screws are tight.
6. Inspect the vacuum piston diaphragm (**Figure 41**) for cracks, deterioration or other damage. Check the vacuum piston sides (**Figure 42**) for excessive wear. Install the vacuum piston into the carburetor body and move it up and down in the bore. The vacuum piston should move smoothly with no binding or excessive play. If there is excessive play, the vacuum piston slide and/or carburetor body must be replaced.
7. Inspect the needle valve tapered end for steps, uneven wear or other damage (**Figure 43**).
8. Inspect the needle valve seat (B, **Figure 38**) for steps, uneven wear or other damage. Insert the needle valve and slowly move it back and forth and check for smooth operation. If either part is worn or damaged, replace both parts as a pair for maximum performance.

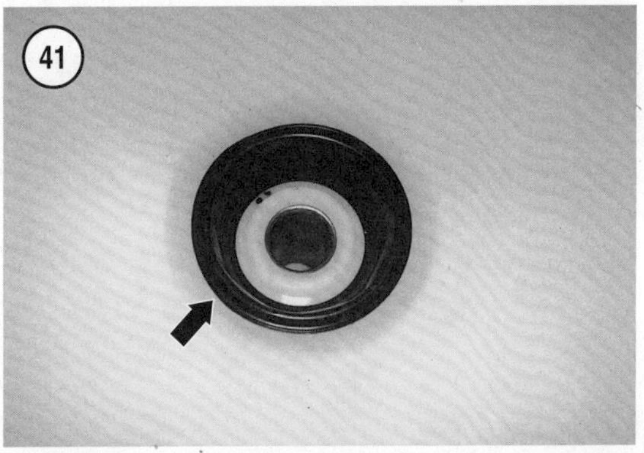

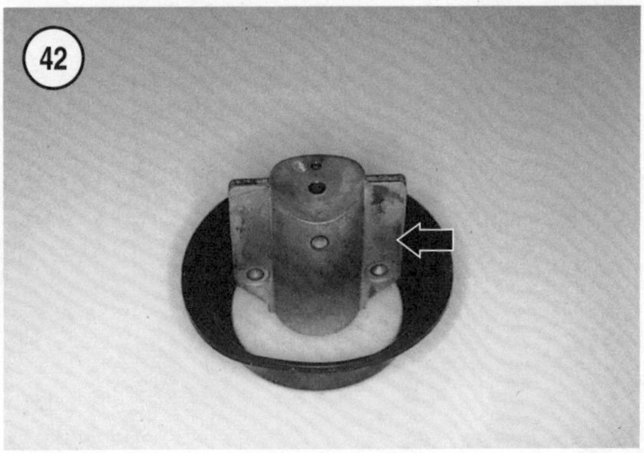

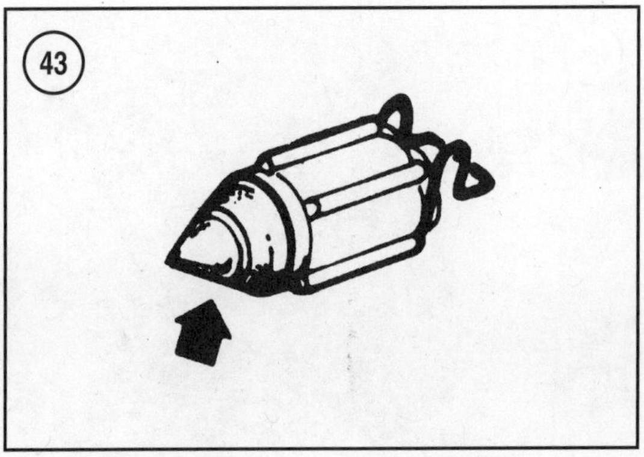

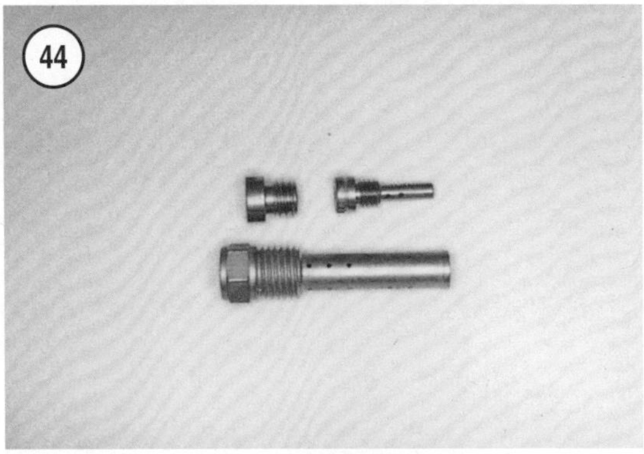
44

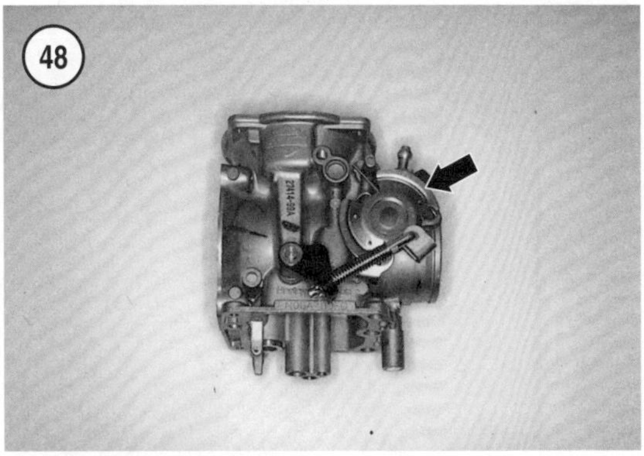
48

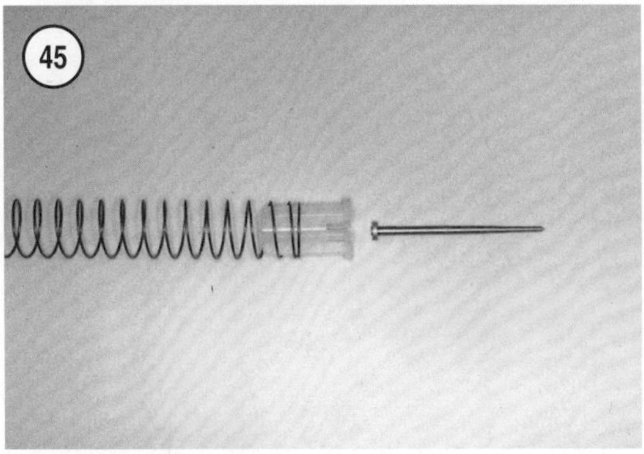
45

49

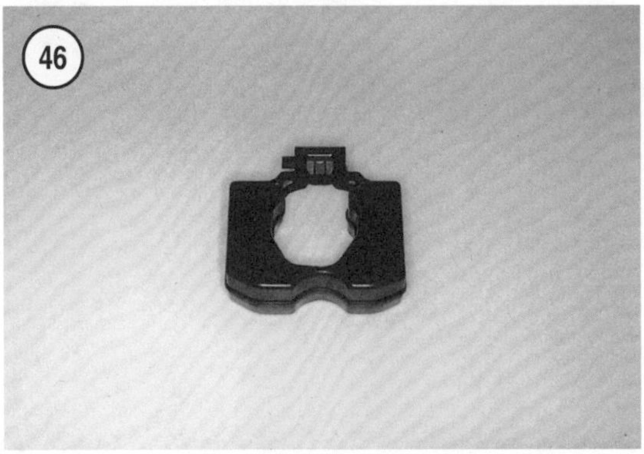
46

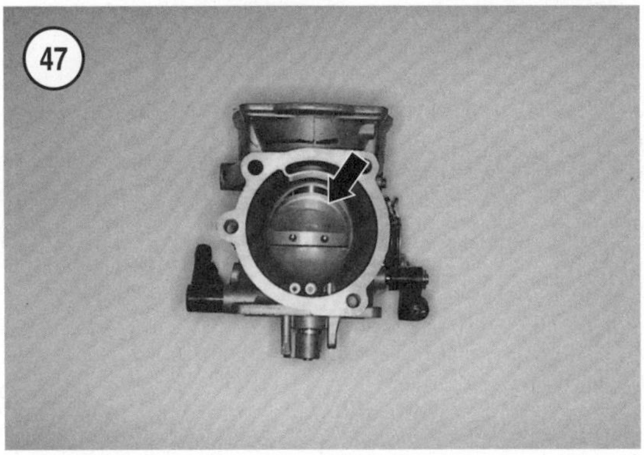
47

9. Inspect the needle jet holder, pilot jet and main jet (**Figure 44**). Make sure all holes are open and none of the parts are either worn or damaged.
10. Inspect the jet needle, spring and spring seat (**Figure 45**) for deterioration or damage.
11. Inspect the jet needle tapered end for steps, uneven wear or other damage.
12. Inspect the float (**Figure 46**) for deterioration or damage. If the float is suspected of leakage, place it in a container of water and push it down. If the float sinks or if bubbles appear (indicating a leak), the float must be replaced.
13. Make sure the throttle plate (**Figure 47**) screws are tight. Tighten if necessary.
14. Move the throttle wheel (**Figure 48**) back and forth from stop to stop and check for free movement. The throttle lever should move smoothly and return under spring tension.
15. Check the throttle wheel return spring (**Figure 49**) for free movement. Make sure it rotates the throttle wheel back to the stop position with no hesitation.
16. Make sure all openings in the carburetor housing are clear. Clean out if they are plugged in any way, then apply compressed air to all openings.

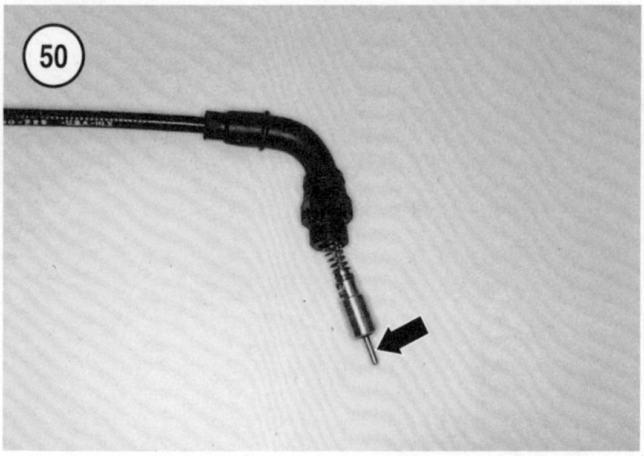
50

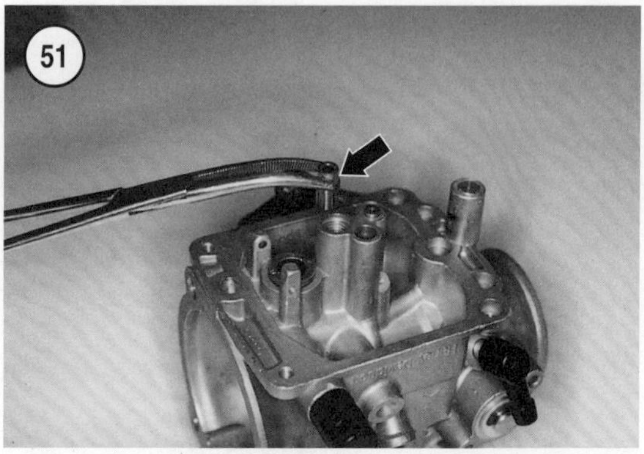
51

17. Inspect the carburetor body for internal or external damage. If damaged, replace the carburetor assembly, as the body cannot be replaced separately.

18. Check the top cover for cracks or damage.

19. Check the starting enrichment valve and cable as follows:

a. Check the end of the valve (**Figure 50**) for damage.

b. Check the entire length of the cable for bends, chafing or other damage.

c. Check the knob, nut and lock washer for damage. Move the knob and check for ease of movement.

Assembly

NOTE
The needle jet has two different sides and must be installed correctly as described in Step 1.

1. Position the needle jet with the long end going in first (**Figure 51**) and install it (A, **Figure 38**).

2. Install the needle jet holder (**Figure 37**) into the main jet passage. Make sure it passes through the opening in the venturi (**Figure 52**), then tighten securely.

3. Install the main jet and tighten securely (**Figure 36**).

4. Install the pilot jet and tighten securely (**Figure 35**).

5. Install the fuel valve onto the float (**Figure 53**) and position the float onto the carburetor so that the valve drops into its seat.

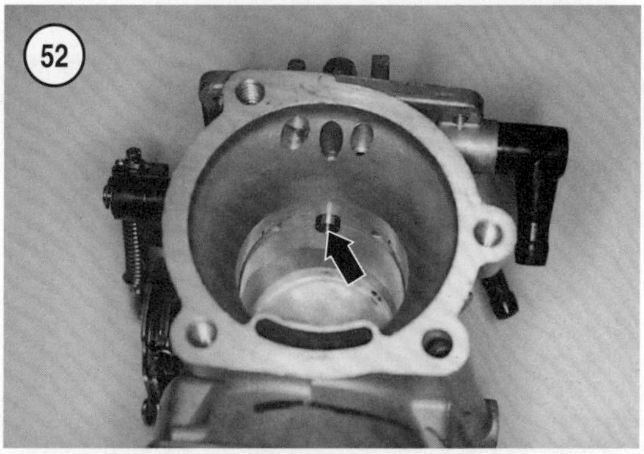
52

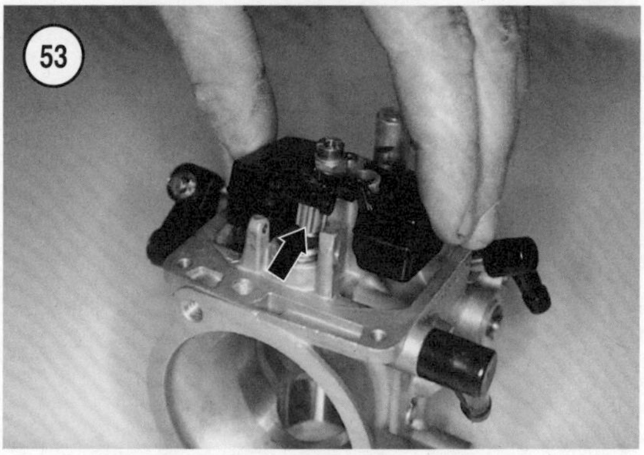
53

54

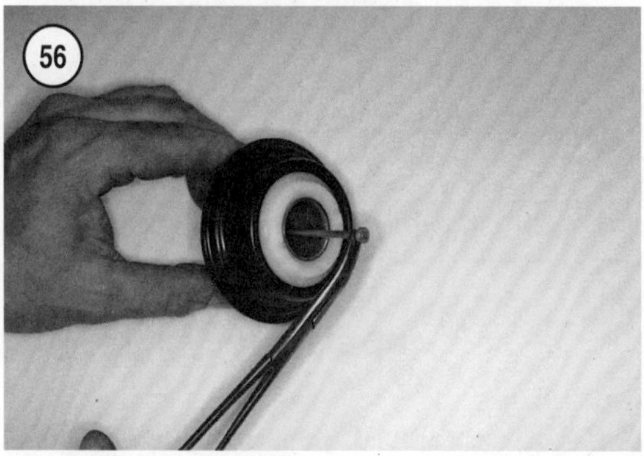

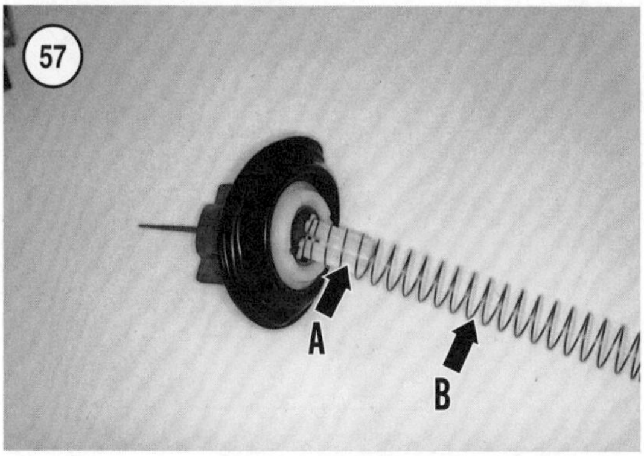

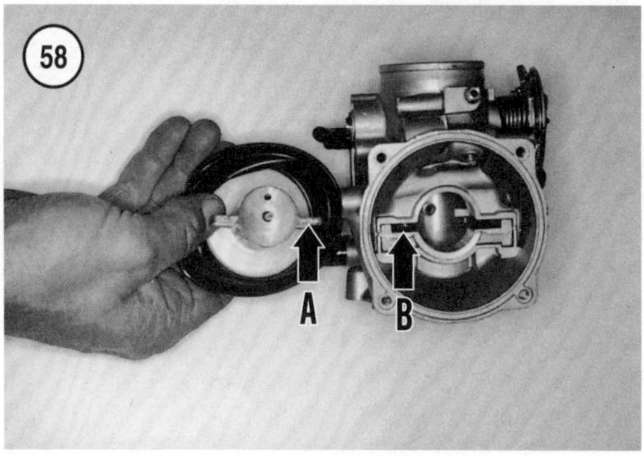

CAUTION
The pedestals that support the float pin are fragile. In the next step, support the pedestal on the arrow side while tapping the float pin into place.

6. Align the float pin with the two pedestals.
7. Install the float pin (A, **Figure 54**) from the side opposite the arrow (B, **Figure 54**). Support the pedestal and tap the float pin into place in the pedestal.
8. Check the float level as described in this chapter.
9. Install the float bowl as follows:
   a. Make sure the float bowl O-ring seal (A, **Figure 39**) and accelerator rod boot (B) are in place.
   b. Connect the pump rod onto the lever assembly on the carburetor (**Figure 55**).
   c. Slowly install the float bowl body and insert the accelerator pump rod through the boot (**Figure 30**) on the float bowl. Engage the rod with the diaphragm while installing the float bowl.
   d. Install the float bowl and screws (**Figure 29**) and tighten the screws securely in a crisscross pattern.
10. Insert the jet needle (**Figure 56**) through the center hole in the vacuum piston.
11. Install the spring seat (A, **Figure 57**) and spring (B) over the top of the needle to secure it in place.
12. Align the slides (A, **Figure 58**) on the vacuum piston with the grooves (B) in the carburetor bore and install the vacuum piston (B, **Figure 28**). The slides on the piston are offset, so the piston can only be installed one way. When installing the vacuum piston, make sure the jet needle drops through the needle jet.
13. Seat the outer edge of the vacuum piston diaphragm into the piston chamber groove (**Figure 59**).

14. Align the free end of the spring with the carburetor top and install the top onto the carburetor.
15. Hold the carburetor top in place and lift the vacuum piston with a finger (**Figure 60**). The piston must move smoothly. If the piston movement is rough or sluggish, the spring is installed incorrectly. Remove the carburetor top and reinstall the spring.
16. Install the carburetor top three screws (**Figure 27**) finger-tight.
17. Install the collar (**Figure 26**) into the cover.
18. Install the throttle cable bracket (B, **Figure 25**) onto the carburetor so that the end of the idle speed screw engages the top of the throttle cam stop (B, **Figure 24**). Hold the bracket in place and install the bracket's side mounting screw and washer (A, **Figure 24**). Tighten the screw securely.
19. Install the top screw (A, **Figure 25**) and tighten securely.
20. Install the starting enrichment cable and valve into the carburetor body and tighten the nut securely (**Figure 23**).

Float Adjustment

The carburetor must be removed and partially disassembled for this adjustment.
1. Remove the carburetor as described in this chapter.
2. Remove the float bowl as described in this chapter.
3. Place the engine manifold side of the carburetor on a clean flat surface as shown in **Figure 61**. This is the base position.
4. Tilt the carburetor upward 15-20° as shown in **Figure 62**. At this position, the float will come to rest without compressing the pin return spring.

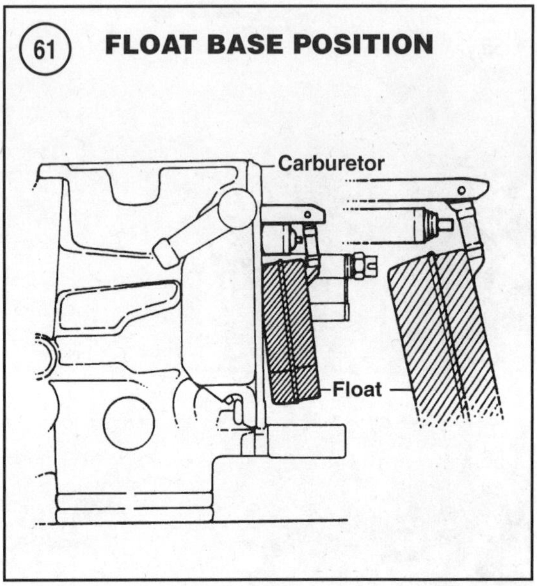

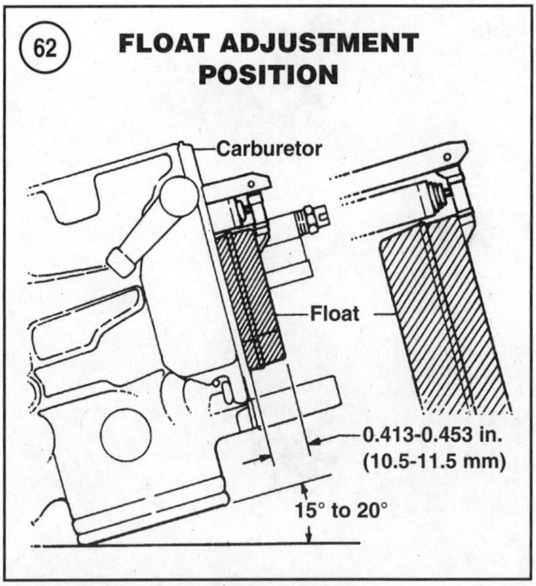

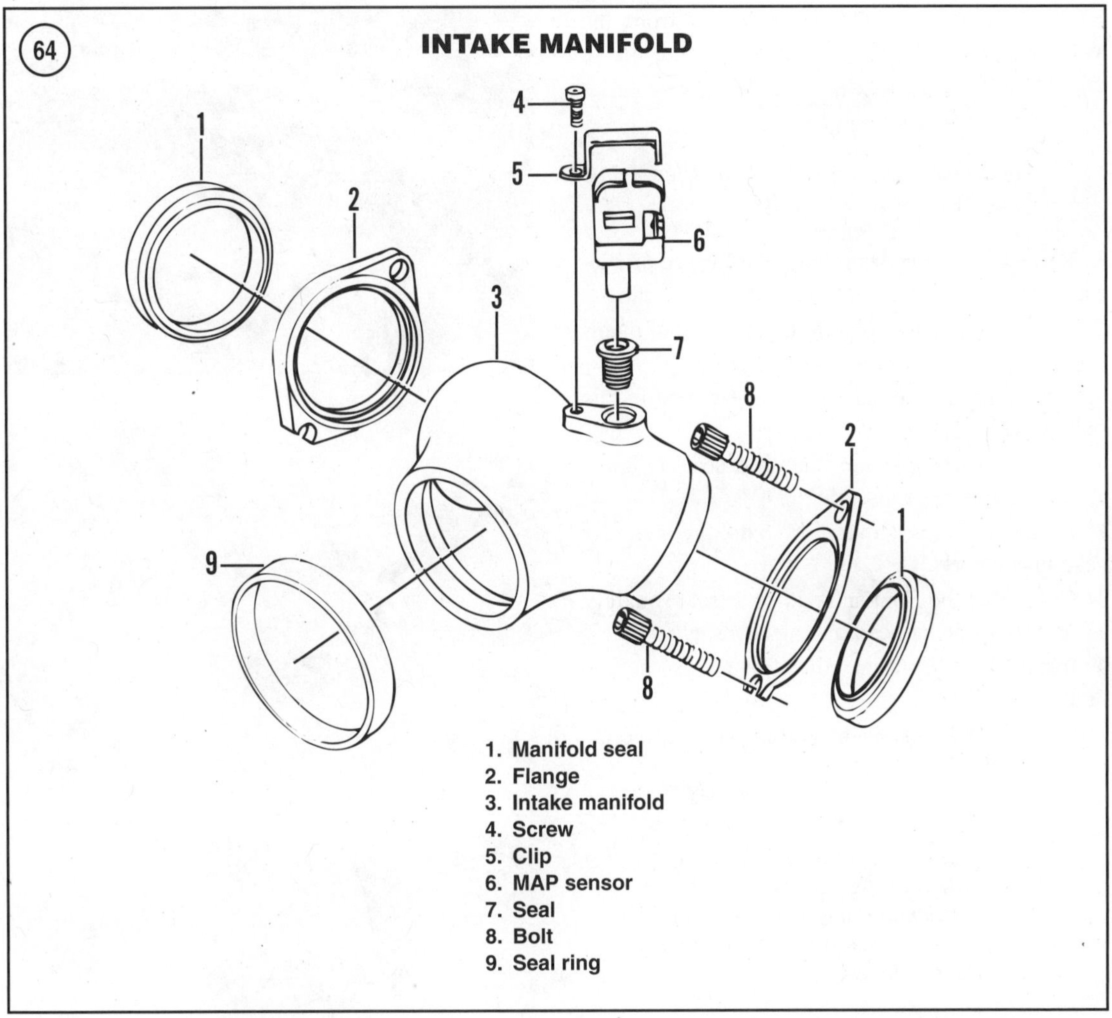

NOTE
If the carburetor is tilted less than 15° or more than 20°, the float measurement will be incorrect.

5. Measure from the carburetor flange surface to the top of the float as shown in **Figure 62**. When measuring float level, do not compress the float. The correct float level measurement is 0.413-0.453 in. (10.5-11.5 mm).

6. If the float level is incorrect, remove the float pin and float as described under *Carburetor Disassembly* in this chapter.

7. Slowly bend the float tang (**Figure 63**) with a screwdriver and adjust to the correct position.

8. Reinstall the float and the float pin as described under *Carburetor Assembly* in this chapter. Recheck the float level.

9. Repeat these steps until the float level is correct.

10. Install the float bowl and carburetor as described in this chapter.

INTAKE MANIFOLD

Removal/Installation

Refer to **Figure 64**.

1. Remove the carburetor as described in this chapter.

NOTE
The front and rear intake manifold flanges are different. If the flanges are not marked, label them with an F and R so they will be reinstalled in the correct location.

2. Disconnect the electrical connector from the MAP sensor (A, **Figure 65**) on top of the intake manifold.

NOTE
***Figure 65** shows only two of the Allen bolts. Remove all four bolts.*

3. Remove the four Allen bolts (B, **Figure 65**) securing the intake manifold to the cylinder heads.
4. Remove the intake manifold, flanges and manifold seals.
5. Inspect the intake manifold as described in this section.
6. Install the flanges and manifold seals (**Figure 66**) onto the intake manifold.
7. Install the intake manifold onto the cylinder head intake ports.
8. Check that the front and rear seals seat squarely against the cylinder head mating surfaces.
9. Install all four Allen bolts finger-tight at this time.
10. Temporarily install the carburetor into the intake manifold.

CAUTION
Do not attempt to align the intake manifold after tightening the bolts. This will damage the manifold seals. If necessary, loosen the bolts, then align the manifold.

11. Check that the intake manifold seats squarely against the cylinder heads. Then check that the carburetor seats squarely in the intake manifold. Remove the carburetor.

NOTE
It is very difficult to get an Allen wrench and torque wrench onto the two inboard Allen bolts to tighten them to a specific torque value. Tighten the outboard Allen bolts to the specified torque value, then tighten the inboard Allen bolts to the same approximate tightness.

12. Tighten the intake manifold Allen bolts to the specification in **Table 2**.
13. If the MAP sensor was removed, install a *new* seal in the manifold receptacle, then install the MAP sensor.

65

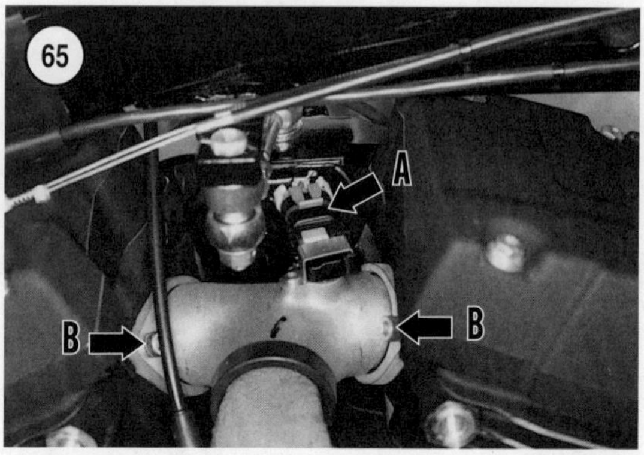

66

67

14. Connect the electrical connector onto the MAP sensor (A, **Figure 65**).
15. Install the carburetor as described in this chapter.

Inspection

1. Check the intake manifold seals (**Figure 66**) for wear, deterioration or other damage. Replace the seals as a set if necessary.

68

THROTTLE CABLES

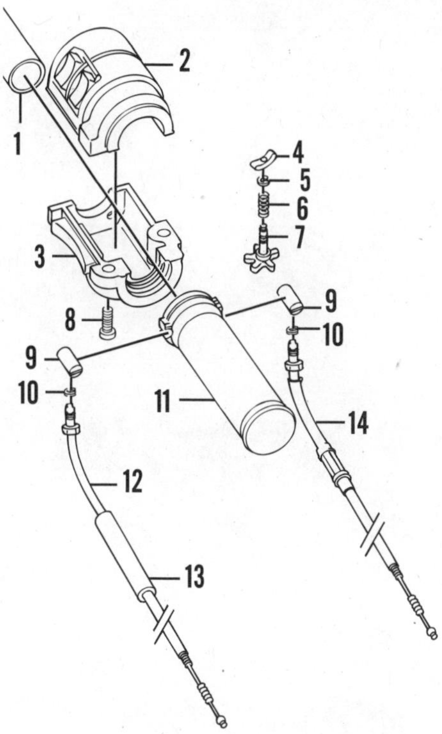

1. Handlebar
2. Upper housing
3. Lower housing
4. Friction shoe
5. Snap ring
6. Spring
7. Adjusting screw
8. Screw
9. Ferrule
10. Clip
11. Throttle grip
12. Throttle control cable
13. Boot
14. Idle control cable

69

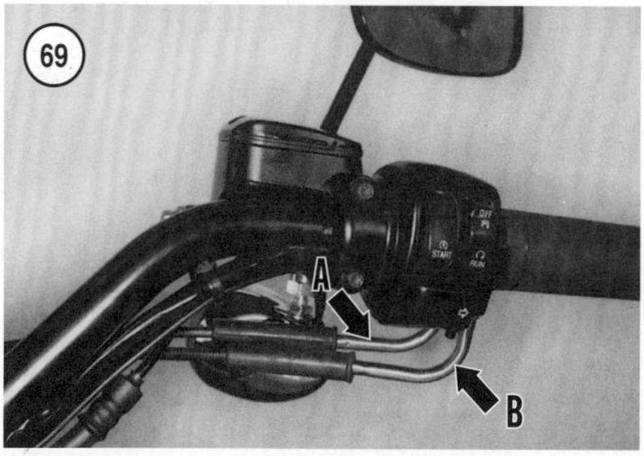

70

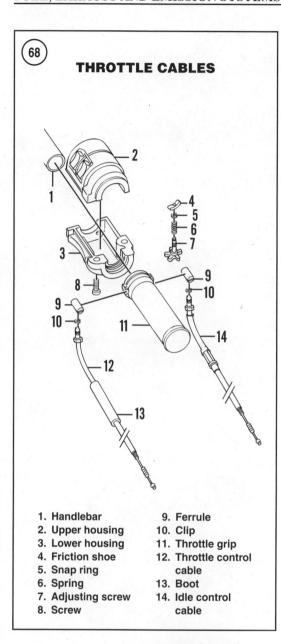

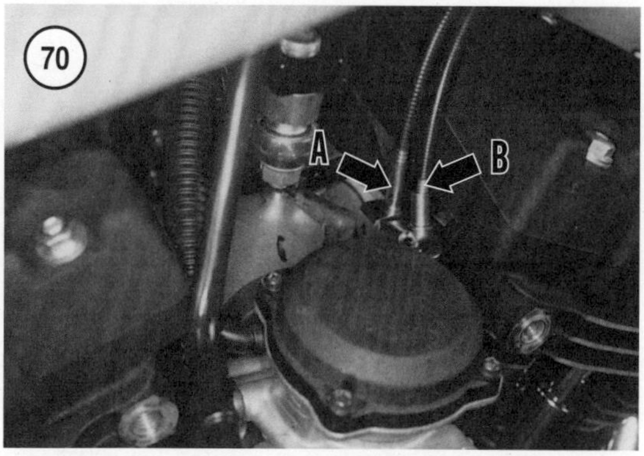

2. Check the intake manifold seal ring (**Figure 67**) for cracks, flat spots or other damage. Replace if necessary.
3. If necessary, remove the self-tapping screw and clamp and remove the MAP sensor.

THROTTLE AND IDLE CABLE REPLACEMENT

There are two different throttle cables (**Figure 68**). One is the throttle control cable (A, **Figure 69** and A, **Figure 70**) and the other is the idle control cable (B, **Figure 69** and B, **Figure 70**). **Figure 68** shows the throttle housing and cable assembly. The cables are identified as follows:

a. Throttle control cable.
b. Idle cable.

NOTE
The throttle control and idle control cables have differently sized threads on the cable's threaded adjusters. The throttle control cable has a 5/16-18 threaded adjuster. The idle control cable has a 1/4-20 threaded adjuster.

1. Remove the fuel tank as described in this chapter.
2. Remove the air filter and backing plate as described in this chapter.
3. Make a drawing or take a picture of the cable routing from the carburetor through the frame to the right side handlebar.
4. At the right side handlebar, perform the following:
   a. Slide the rubber boot off both cables.

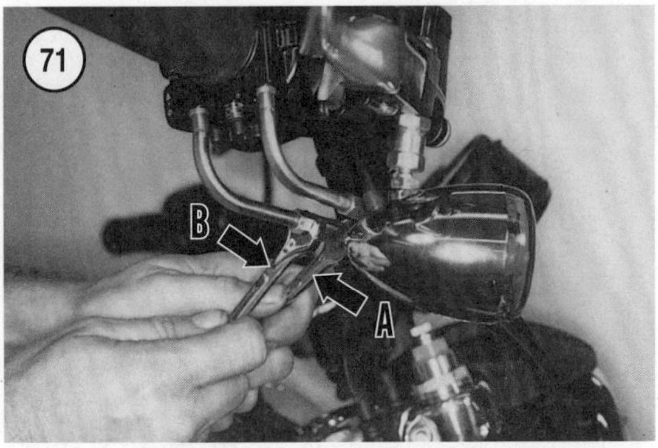

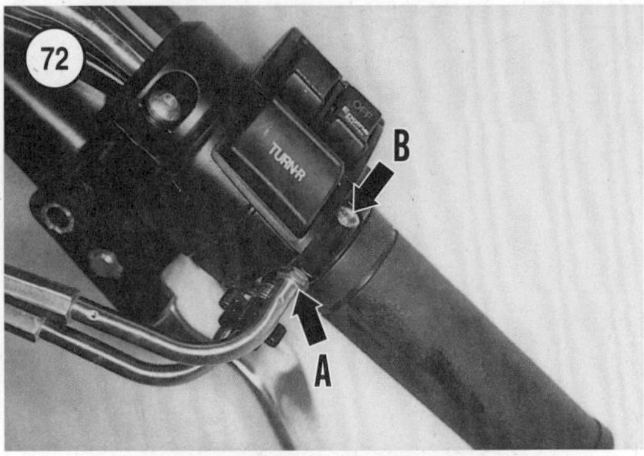

b. Loosen both control cable adjuster locknuts (A, **Figure 71**), then turn the cable adjusters (B, **Figure 71**) *clockwise* as far as possible to increase cable slack.

5. Loosen the cable jam nuts (A, **Figure 72**) at the throttle housing.

6. Remove the screws (B, **Figure 72**) securing the upper and lower housings to the handlebar, then separate the housings.

7. Remove the friction pad (**Figure 73**) from the lower throttle housing.

8. Unhook the cables (**Figure 74**) from the throttle grip and remove the ferrule from the end of each cable (**Figure 75**).

9. Pull the crimped inserts at the end of the throttle and idle control cable housings from the switch lower housing.

10. Partially remove the carburetor, as described in this chapter, until the throttle cables can be disconnected from the throttle wheel.

11. Disconnect the throttle control cable (A, **Figure 76**) and the idle control cable (B) from the carburetor cable guide and the throttle wheel (C).

12. Remove the cables from the frame.

13. Clean the throttle grip assembly and dry thoroughly. Check the throttle slots for cracks or other damage. Replace the throttle if necessary.

14. The friction adjust screw is secured to the lower switch housing with a snap ring. If necessary, remove the friction spring, snap ring, spring and friction adjust screw. Check these parts for wear or damage. Replace damaged parts and reverse to install. Make sure the snap ring seats in the friction screw groove completely.

15. Clean the throttle area on the handlebar with solvent.

16. Apply a light coat of graphite to the housing inside surfaces and to the handlebar.

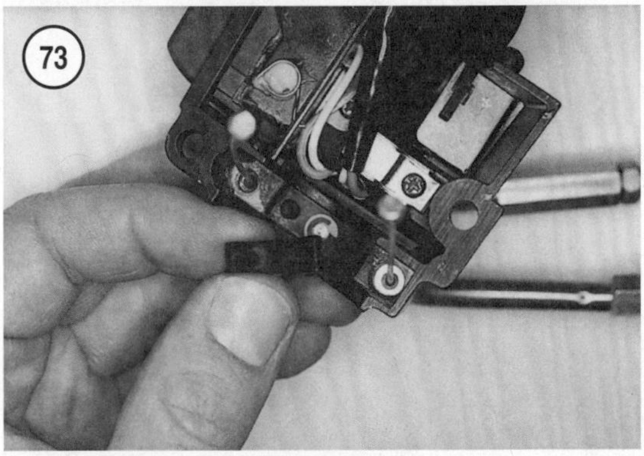

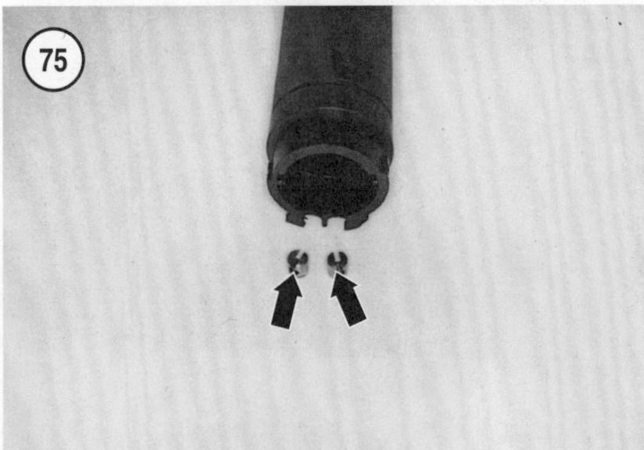

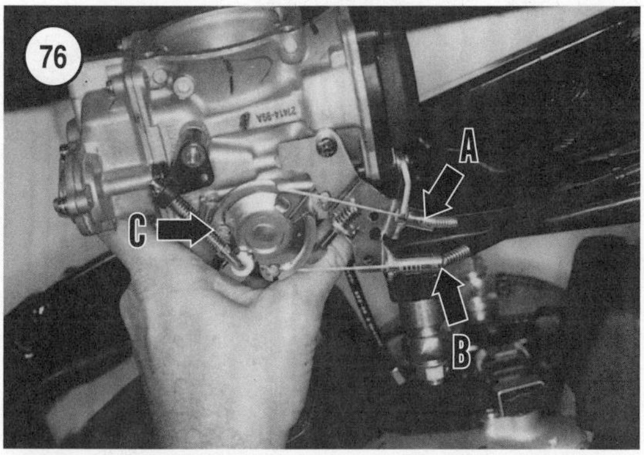

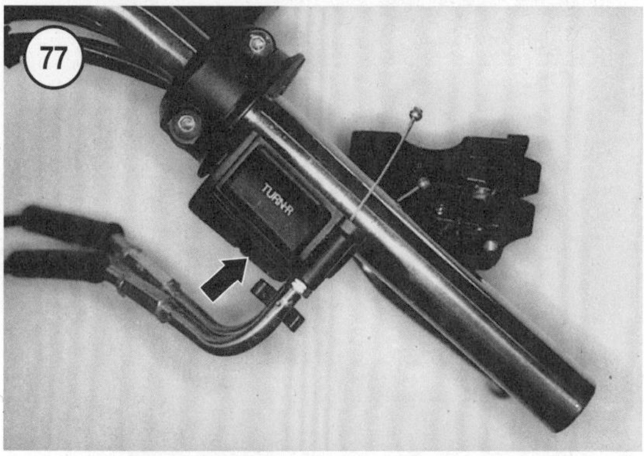

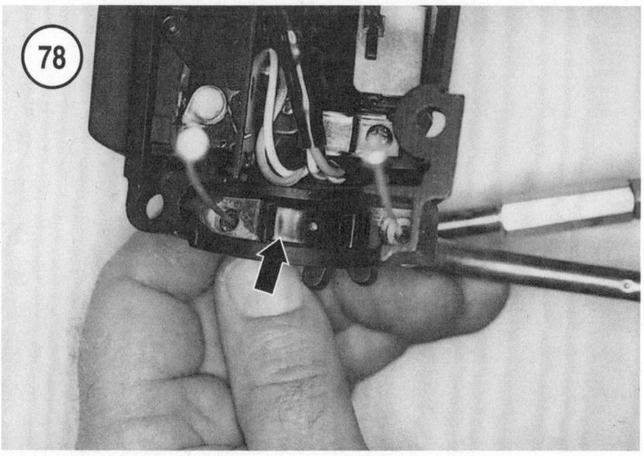

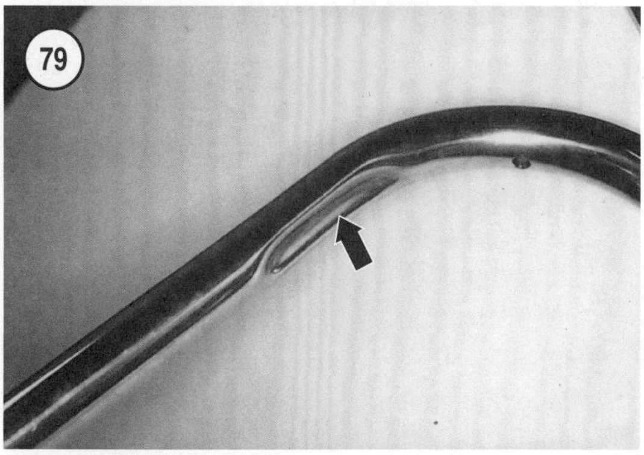

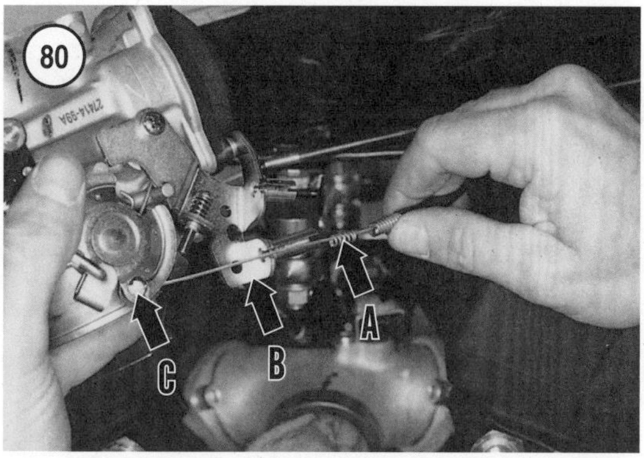

17. On the lower switch housing, push the larger diameter silver throttle cable insert into the larger hole in front of the tension adjust screw. Push it in until it snaps into place.

18. Push the smaller diameter gold throttle cable insert into the smaller hole in the rear of the tension adjust screw. Push it in until it snaps into place.

19. Install the friction pad (**Figure 73**) into the lower housing (**Figure 78**). Match the curvature on the friction pad with the handlebar.

20. Install a ferrule (**Figure 75**) onto the end of each cable, then insert the ferrules into the throttle grip slots (**Figure 74**).

NOTE

*If the master cylinder is not mounted on the handlebar, fit the throttle housing wiring harness into the depression (**Figure 79**) in the bottom of the handlebar.*

21. Assemble the upper and lower switch housings and the throttle grip. Install the lower switch housing screws (B, **Figure 72**) and tighten securely. Operate the throttle and make sure both cables move in and out properly.

22. Route the cables from the handlebar to the carburetor.

23. Connect the idle cable (B, **Figure 70**) to the carburetor as follows:

   a. The idle cable has the small spring (A, **Figure 80**) on the end of the cable.

   b. Insert the idle cable sheath into the rear cable bracket guide on the carburetor (B, **Figure 80**).

   c. Attach the end of the idle cable into the throttle wheel (C, **Figure 80**).

24. Connect the throttle cable (A, **Figure 70**) to the carburetor as follows:

7

a. Insert the throttle cable sheath (A, **Figure 76**) into the front cable bracket guide on the carburetor.
b. Attach the end of the throttle cable into the throttle wheel (C, **Figure 76**).

25. Operate the hand throttle a few times, making sure the throttle wheel operates smoothly with no binding. Also check that both cable ends are seated squarely in their cable bracket guides and in the throttle wheel.

26. Adjust the throttle and idle cables as described in Chapter Three.

27. Reinstall the carburetor as described in this chapter.

28. Install the air filter backplate and air filter as described in this chapter.

29. Install the fuel tank as described in this chapter.

30. Start the engine and allow it to idle in NEUTRAL. Then turn the handlebar from side to side. Do not operate the throttle. If the engine speed increases when turning the handlebar assembly, the throttle cables are routed incorrectly or damaged. Recheck cable routing and adjustment.

WARNING

Do not ride the motorcycle until the throttle cables are properly adjusted. Improper cable routing and adjustment can cause the throttle to stick open. This could cause loss of control. Recheck the work before riding the motorcycle.

STARTING ENRICHMENT VALVE (CHOKE) CABLE REPLACEMENT

1. Remove the air filter and backplate as described in Chapter Three.

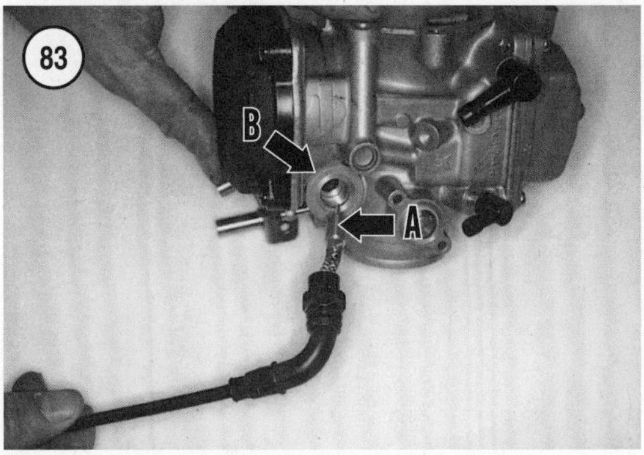

2. Note the routing of the enrichener cable from its mounting bracket to the carburetor.

3. Loosen the locknut (A, **Figure 81**) and disconnect the starting enrichment valve cable to the mounting bracket (B). Move the end of the cable out of the mounting bracket.

4. Partially remove the carburetor, as described in this chapter, until the starting enrichment valve cable can be disconnected from the backside of the carburetor.

5. Unscrew and remove the starting enrichment valve and cable (**Figure 82**) from the carburetor and remove the cable from the frame.

6. Install by reversing these removal steps while noting the following:

a. Align the starting enrichment valve needle (A, **Figure 83**) with the needle passage in the carburetor (B) and install the starting enrichment valve. Tighten the valve nut securely.
b. Position the starting enrichment valve cable into the mounting bracket (B, **Figure 81**), then tighten the locknut (A) securely.

84

FUEL TANK (FXDP)

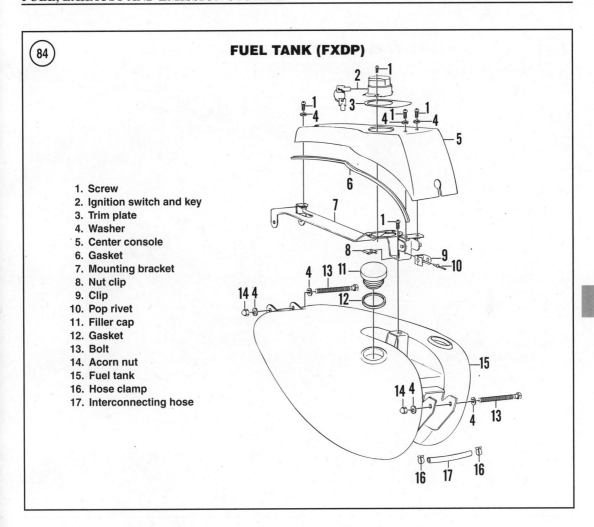

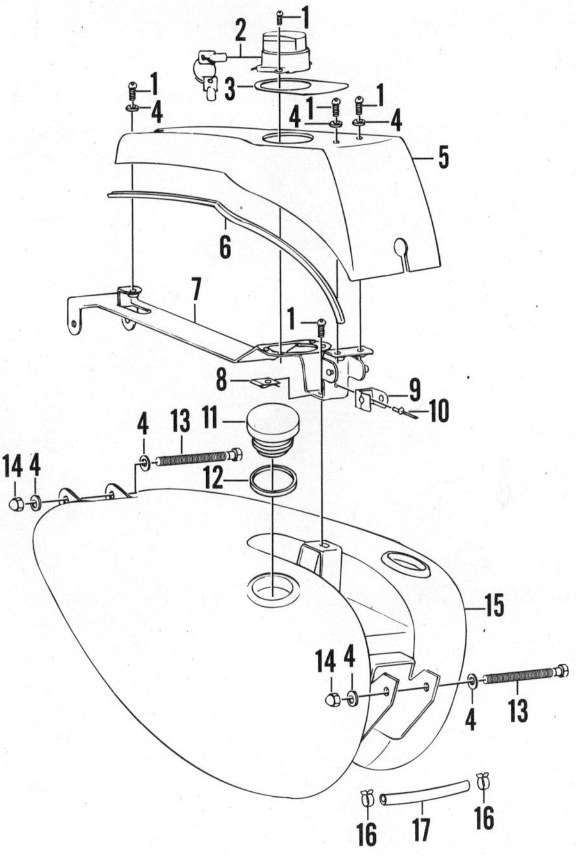

1. Screw
2. Ignition switch and key
3. Trim plate
4. Washer
5. Center console
6. Gasket
7. Mounting bracket
8. Nut clip
9. Clip
10. Pop rivet
11. Filler cap
12. Gasket
13. Bolt
14. Acorn nut
15. Fuel tank
16. Hose clamp
17. Interconnecting hose

FUEL TANK

WARNING
Some fuel may spill from the fuel tank hose when performing this procedure. Because gasoline is extremely flammable and explosive, perform this procedure away from all open flames (including appliance pilot lights) and sparks. Do not smoke or allow someone who is smoking in the work area, as an explosion and fire may occur. Always work in a well-ventilated area. Wipe up any spills immediately.

WARNING
Make sure to route the fuel tank vapor hoses so that they cannot contact any hot engine or exhaust component. These hoses contain flammable vapors. If a hose melts from contacting a hot part, leaking vapors may ignite, causing a fire.

Removal/Installation

The fuel hose is secured to the fuel tank with a non-reusable clamp. If the same type of clamp is going to be reinstalled, purchase one before servicing the fuel tank.

Refer to **Figure 84**, **Figure 85** and **Figure 86** for fuel tank components and lines.

NOTE
On models so equipped, always disarm the optional TSSM security system prior to disconnecting the battery or the siren will sound.

1. Disconnect the negative battery cable from the battery.

85 **FUEL TANK (ALL MODELS EXCEPT FXDP)**

1. Hose clamp
2. Interconnecting hose
3. Filler cap
4. Gasket
5. Bolt
6. Washer
7. Acorn nut
8. Fuel tank (FXDWG, FXDL)
9. Boot
10. Fuel tank (FXDS-CON, FXD, FXDX, FXDXT)

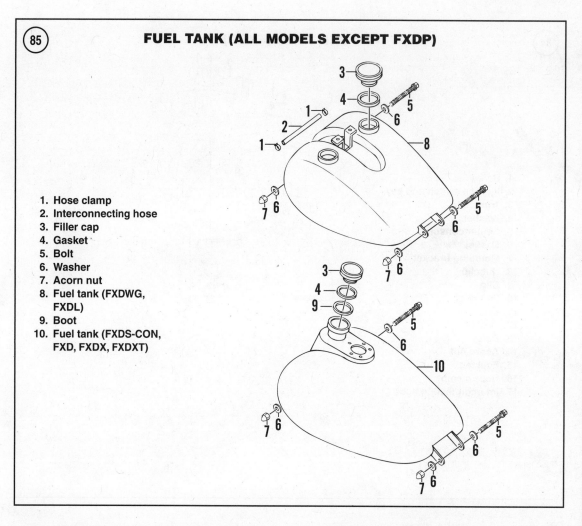

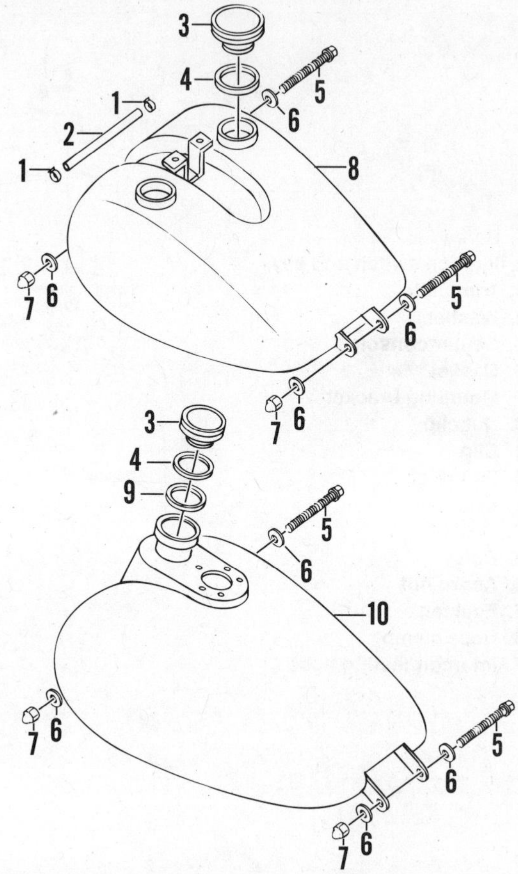

2. Remove the seat as described in Chapter Thirteen.

3. Turn the fuel valve to the OFF position (A, **Figure 87**).

4. Remove the factory hose clamp and disconnect the fuel hose (B, **Figure 87**) from the valve.

NOTE

On some models, a crossover tube connects the two fuel tanks. Drain the tanks before removing them in the following steps.

5. Drain the fuel tank as follows:

NOTE

All models have a vacuum-operated fuel valve installed. A hand-operated vacuum pump is required to drain the fuel tank.

a. Connect the drain hose to the fuel valve and secure it with a hose clamp. Insert the end of the drain hose into a gas can.
b. Disconnect the vacuum hose (**Figure 88**) from the fuel valve.
c. Connect a hand-operated vacuum pump (**Figure 89**) to the fuel valve vacuum hose fitting.
d. Turn the fuel valve to the RES position.

CAUTION

In the following step, do not apply more vacuum than 25 in. (635 mm) Hg or the fuel valve diaphragm will be damaged.

e. Gently operate the vacuum pump handle and apply up to a *maximum* of 25 in. (635 mm) Hg of vacuum. Once the vacuum is applied the fuel will start to flow into the gas can.

86 FUEL TANK LINES AND FITTINGS (ALL MODELS)

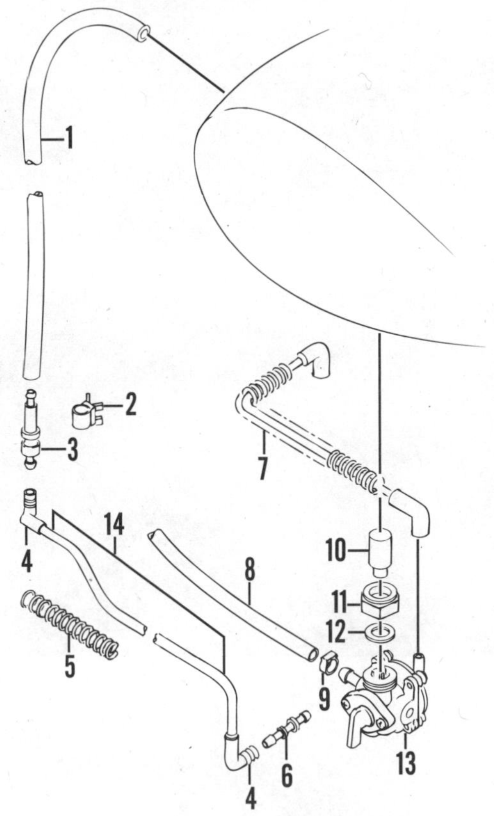

1. Hose
2. Hose clamp
3. Vapor valve
4. Vent tube
5. Hose insulator
6. Connector
7. Vacuum hose
8. Fuel hose (to carburetor)
9. Hose clamp
10. Filter
11. Hex fitting
12. Gasket
13. Shutoff valve
14. Hose

87

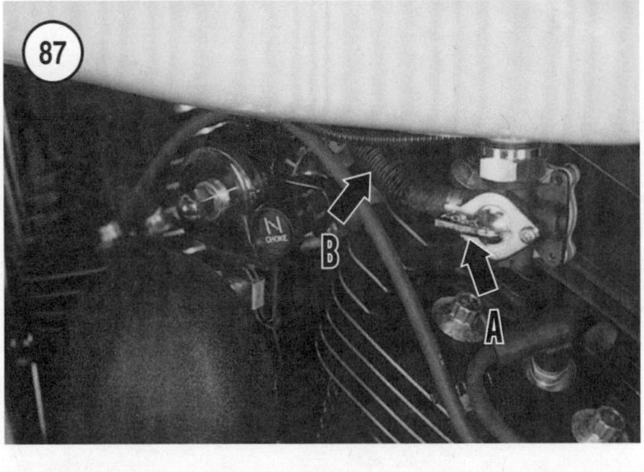

88

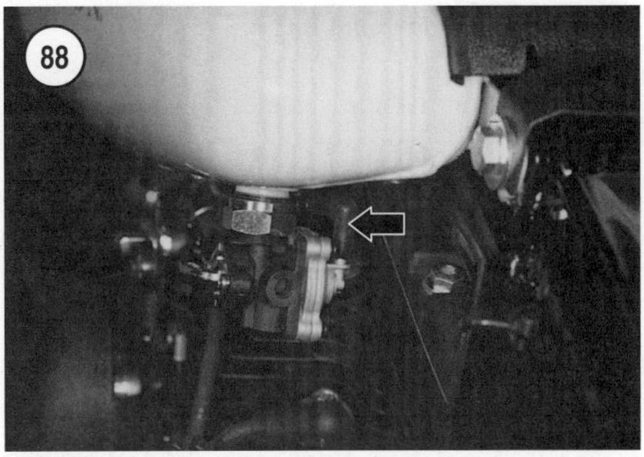

89

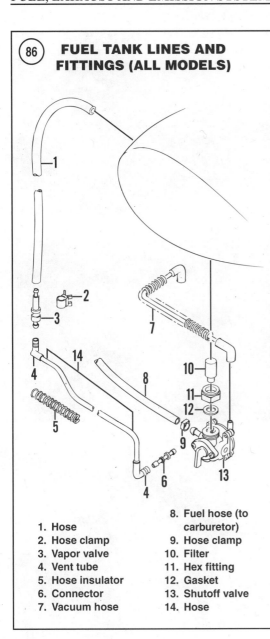

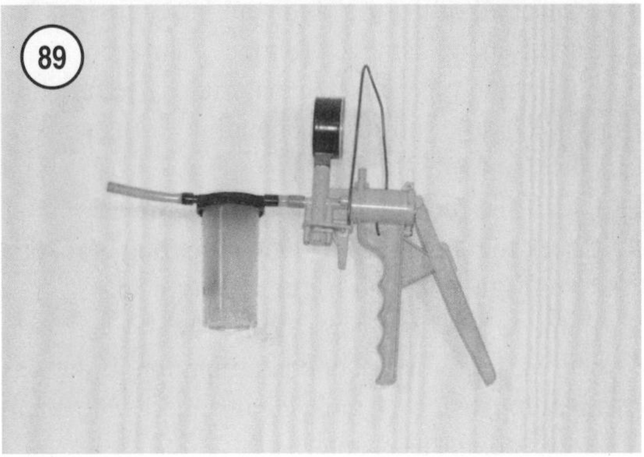

f. When fuel stops flowing through the hose, turn the fuel valve off and release the vacuum. Disconnect the vacuum pump and drain hose.

6. Disconnect the vent hose from the fuel tank.
7. On FXDP models, perform the following:
   a. Remove screws and washers securing the center console and remove the console.
   b. Disconnect all remaining electrical connectors. Move the connectors and harness wires out of the way.
   c. Remove the screw and washer securing the center console at the rear of the tank.
8. Disconnect the electrical connectors leading from the gauges mounted on the fuel tank.
9. Disconnect the crossover hose from one side of the fuel tank. Plug the tank opening and apply a hemostat to the crossover hose (**Figure 90**).
10. Remove the nuts, washers and bolts (**Figure 91**) securing the fuel tank to the frame.
11. Lift off and remove the fuel tank.

NOTE

Store the fuel tank in a safe place—away from open flames or where it could be damaged.

7

12. Drain any remaining fuel left in the tank into a gas can.
13. Installation is the reverse of these steps while noting the following:
   a. Tighten the front and rear bolts and nuts to the specification in **Table 2**.
   b. Reconnect the fuel hose to the fuel valve and secure it with a *new* hose clamp.
   c. Refill the tank and check for leaks.

Inspection

1. Inspect all of the fuel and vent hoses for cracks, deterioration or damage. Replace damaged hoses with the same type and size materials. The fuel line must be flexible and strong enough to withstand engine heat and vibration.
2. Check the fuel line insulator for damage.
3. Check for damaged fuel tank mounting brackets. Refer to **Figure 92** and **Figure 93**, typical.
4. Remove the filler cap (**Figure 94**, typical) and inspect the tank for rust or contamination. If there is rust buildup inside the tank, clean and flush the tank as described in this chapter.
5. Inspect the fuel tank for leaks.

FUEL SHUTOFF VALVE

A three-way vacuum-operated fuel shutoff valve is mounted to the left side of the fuel tank. A replaceable fuel filter is mounted to the top of the fuel shutoff valve (**Figure 95**).

To troubleshoot this valve, refer to *Vacuum Operated Fuel Shutoff Valve Testing* in Chapter Two.

Removal

WARNING
Gasoline is very volatile and presents an extreme fire hazard. Be sure to work in a well-ventilated area away from any open flames (including pilot lights on household appliances). Do not allow anyone to smoke in the area and have a fire extinguisher rated for gasoline fires nearby.

1. Disconnect the negative battery cable from the battery.
2. Turn the fuel shutoff valve to the OFF position.

90

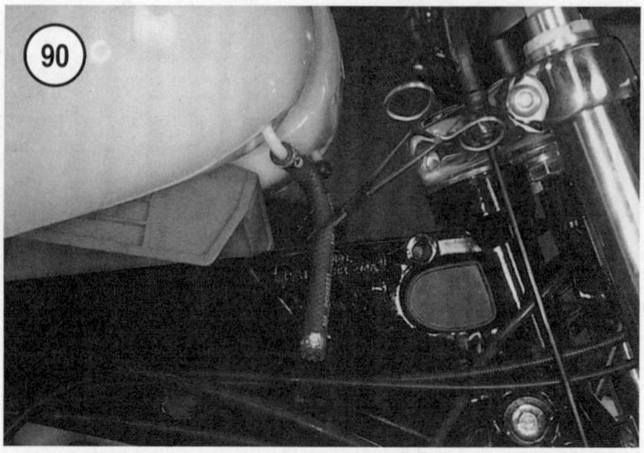

91

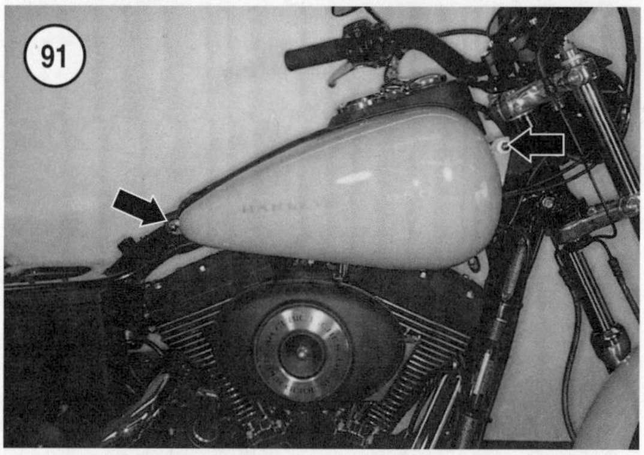

92

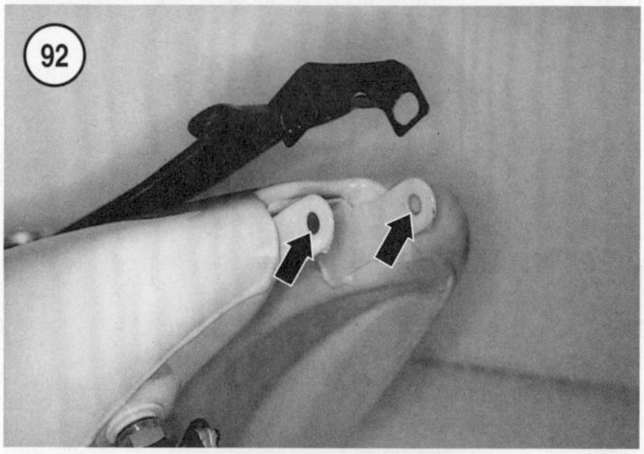

93

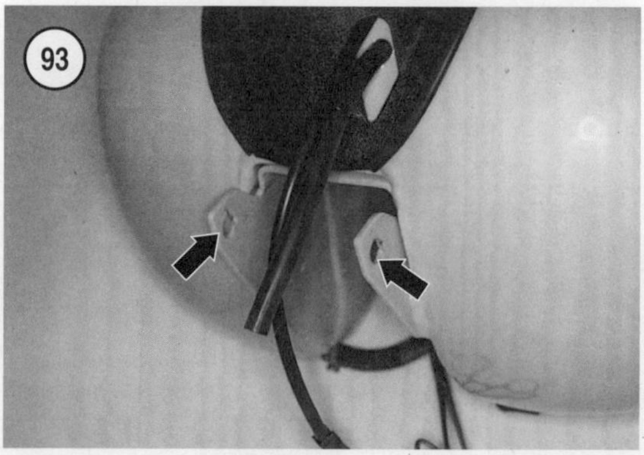

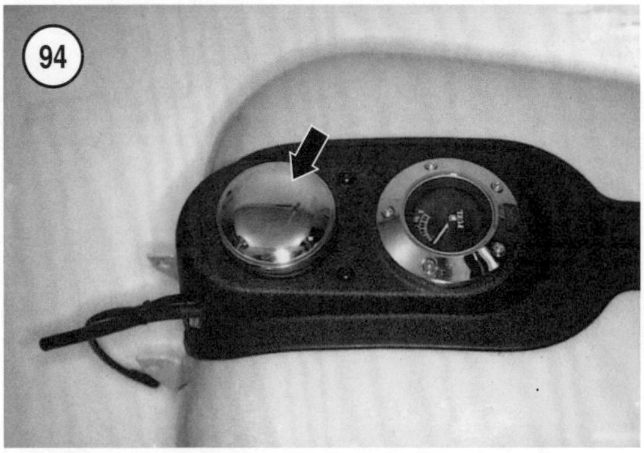

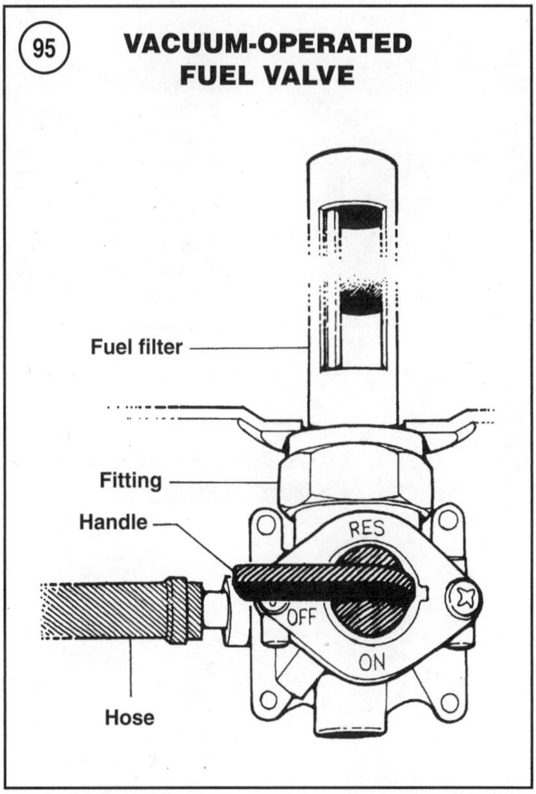

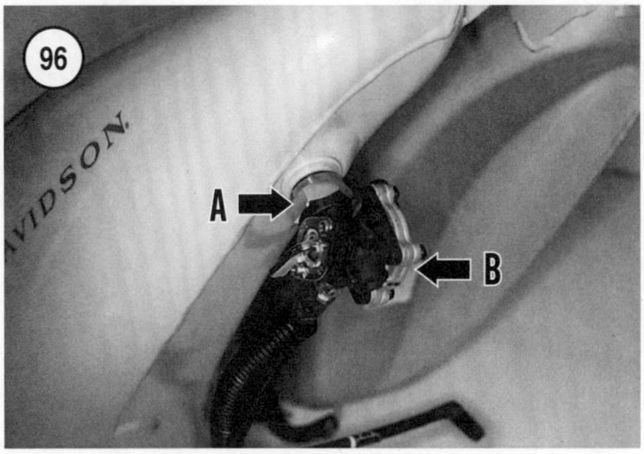

3. Drain the fuel tank as described under *Fuel Tank Removal/Installation* in this chapter.

NOTE
The fuel shutoff valve can be removed with the fuel tank in place. ***Figure 96*** *is shown with the fuel tank removed to better illustrate the step.*

4. Loosen the fuel valve fitting (A, **Figure 96**) and remove the fuel shutoff valve (B) from the fuel tank. Drain any residual gasoline that may still be in the tank after the valve is removed.

Cleaning and Inspection

1. Inspect the filter mounted on top of the fuel valve. Remove and clean the filter of all contamination. Replace the filter if damaged.
2. Install a *new* filter gasket before installing the filter onto the fuel valve.
3. Remove all sealant residue from the fuel tank and fuel valve threads.

Installation

1. Install a *new* filter gasket onto the fuel shutoff valve, then install the filter.
2. Coat the fuel valve threads with Loctite pipe sealant.
3. Insert the fuel valve into the tank, then tighten the hex fitting onto the fuel tank two turns.
4. Hold the hex fitting and tighten the fuel valve (left-hand threads) two turns into the hex fitting.
5. Hold the fuel valve and tighten the hex fitting to the specification in **Table 2**.

WARNING
If the hex fitting is turned more than two turns on the valve, it may bottom out on the valve and cause a fuel leak. This could result in a dangerous fire.

6. Install the insulator tube over the fuel hose.
7. Reconnect the fuel hose to the fuel shutoff valve and secure it with a hose clamp.
8. Refill the fuel tank and check for leaks.

FUEL TANK GAUGE

WARNING

Because gasoline is extremely flammable and explosive, perform this procedure away from all open flames (including appliance pilot lights) and sparks. Do not smoke or allow someone who is smoking in the work area, as an explosion and fire may occur. Always work in a well-ventilated area. Wipe up any spills immediately.

Removal/Installation (FXD, FXDS-CONV, FXDX [1999-2000])

Refer to **Figure 97**.

1. Remove the fuel tank as described in this chapter.
2. Remove the gas filler cap.
3. Remove the five screws securing the fuel gauge retainer. Remove the retainer.
4. Use a flat-blade screwdriver and carefully pry the fuel gauge loose from the sending unit.
5. Withdraw the fuel gauge from the sending unit.
6. Remove the five screws and washers securing the sending unit to the fuel tank.

CAUTION

Do not bend the float arm during removal of the sending unit. If bent, the gauge will give inaccurate readings.

7. Carefully withdraw the sending unit while moving it back and forth, lifting and turning it in either direction.
8. Remove the gasket from the fuel tank.
9. Install by reversing these removal steps while noting the following:
   a. Install a *new* gasket between the sending unit and fuel tank.
   b. Carefully install the sending unit to avoid damage to the float arm.
   c. Tighten all screws securely.

Removal/Installation (FXDL, FXDWG [1999-2000])

Refer to **Figure 98**.

1. Remove the fuel tank as described in this chapter.

(97) **FUEL GAUGE ASSEMBLY (FXD, FXDS-CONV, FXDX 1999-2000)**

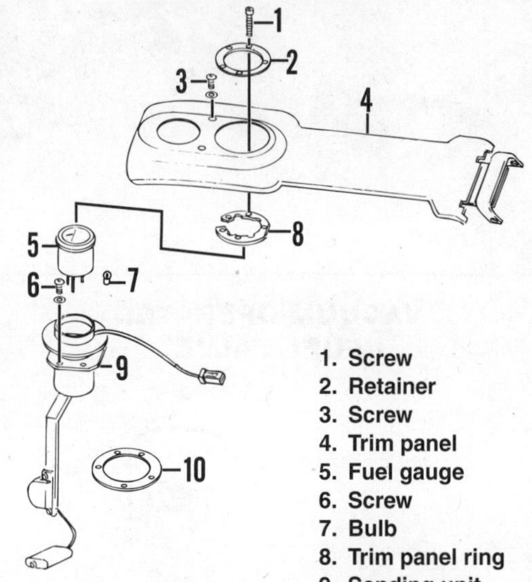

1. Screw
2. Retainer
3. Screw
4. Trim panel
5. Fuel gauge
6. Screw
7. Bulb
8. Trim panel ring
9. Sending unit
10. Gasket

(98) **FUEL GAUGE ASSEMBLY (FXDL, FXDWG 1999-2000)**

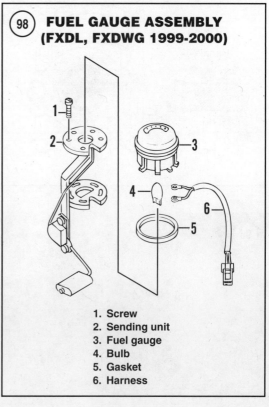

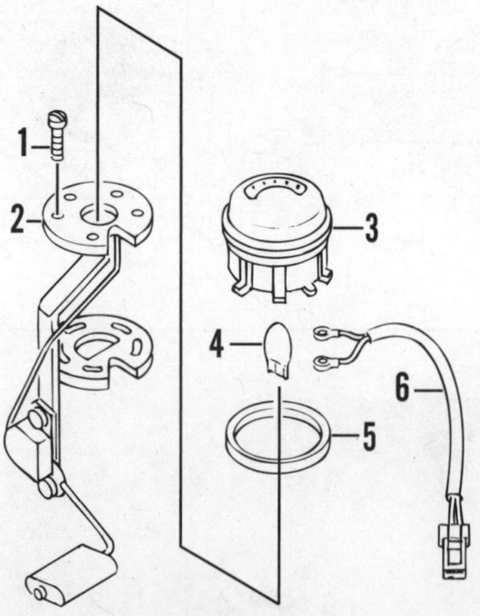

1. Screw
2. Sending unit
3. Fuel gauge
4. Bulb
5. Gasket
6. Harness

(99) **FUEL GAUGE ASSEMBLY (FXD, FXDX, FXDXT 2001)**

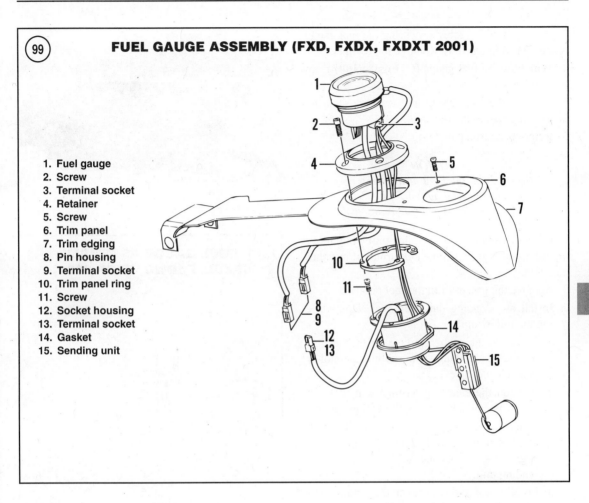

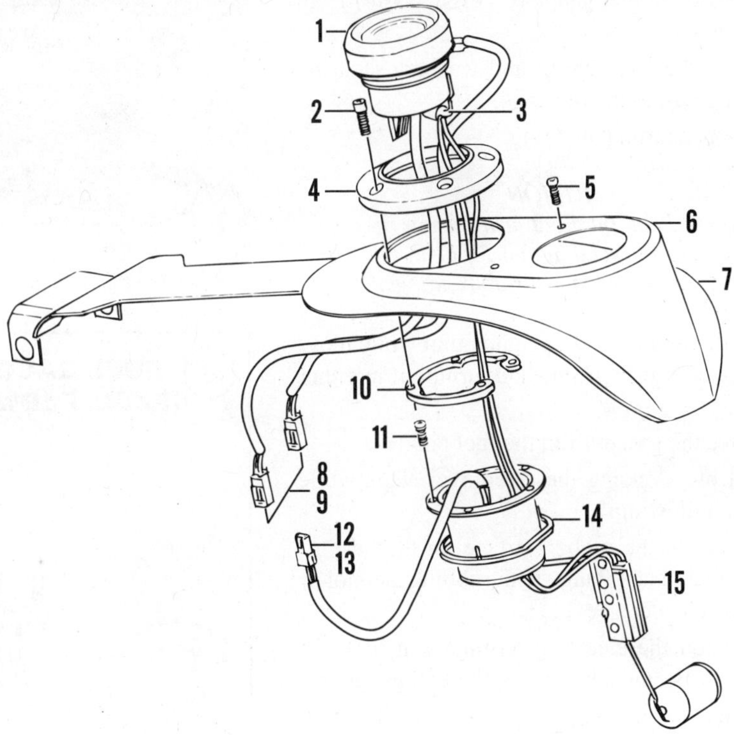

1. Fuel gauge
2. Screw
3. Terminal socket
4. Retainer
5. Screw
6. Trim panel
7. Trim edging
8. Pin housing
9. Terminal socket
10. Trim panel ring
11. Screw
12. Socket housing
13. Terminal socket
14. Gasket
15. Sending unit

NOTE

The fuel gauge electrical wires are routed through a tube in the fuel tank and are secured with a clamp at the bottom of the fuel tank. Loosen the clamp and make sure there is enough slack in the wires to allow the gauge to be pulled up and out of the fuel tank.

2. Pull straight up on the gauge and partially remove it from the tank.

3. Disconnect the electrical connector from the wires within the fuel tank. Do not disconnect the electrical wires from the fuel gauge.

4. Remove the fuel gauge and the gasket.

5. Remove the five screws securing the sending unit to the fuel tank.

CAUTION

Do not bend the float arm during removal of the sending unit. If bent, the gauge will give inaccurate readings.

6. Carefully withdraw the sending unit while moving it back and forth, lifting and turning it in either direction.

7. Remove the gasket from the fuel tank.

8. Install by reversing these removal steps while noting the following:

   a. Install a *new* gasket between the fuel gauge and fuel tank.

   b. Carefully install the sending unit to avoid damage to the float arm.

   c. Tighten all screws securely.

Removal/Installation (FXD, FXDX, FXDXT [2001])

Refer to **Figure 99**.

1. Remove the fuel tank as described in this chapter.

2. Remove the gas filler cap (A, **Figure 100**).

3. Remove the five screws securing the fuel gauge retainer (B, **Figure 100**). Remove the retainer.
4. Withdraw the fuel gauge (C, **Figure 100**) from the sending unit,
5. Remove the five screws and washers securing the sending unit to the fuel tank.
6. Remove the trim panel ring.

CAUTION
Do not bend the float arm during removal of the sending unit. If bent, the gauge will give inaccurate readings.

7. Carefully withdraw the sending unit while moving it back and forth, lifting and turning it in either direction.
8. Remove the gasket from the fuel tank.
9. Install by reversing these removal steps while noting the following:
   a. Lubricate the rubber surface on the base of the fuel gauge flange with rubbing alcohol or glass cleaner.
   b. Position the electrical terminals in between the posts on the bottom of the fuel gauge.
   c. Align the fuel gauge with the first scribe mark on the sending unit, then turn it clockwise to align with the second scribe mark on the sending unit.
   d. Install a *new* gasket between the sending unit and fuel tank.
   e. Carefully install the sending unit to avoid damage to the float arm.
   f. Tighten all screws securely.

Removal/Installation (FXDX, FXDWG, FXDP [2001])

Refer to **Figure 101**.

1. Remove the fuel tank as described in this chapter.

NOTE
The fuel gauge electrical wires are routed through a tube in the fuel tank and are secured with a clamp at the bottom of the fuel tank. Loosen the clamp and make sure there is enough slack in the wires to allow the gauge to be pulled up and out of the fuel tank.

100

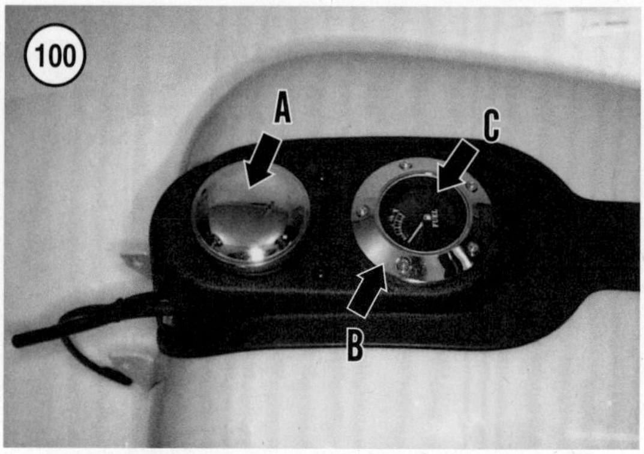

101 **FUEL GAUGE ASSEMBLY (FXDL, FXDWG, FXDP 2001)**

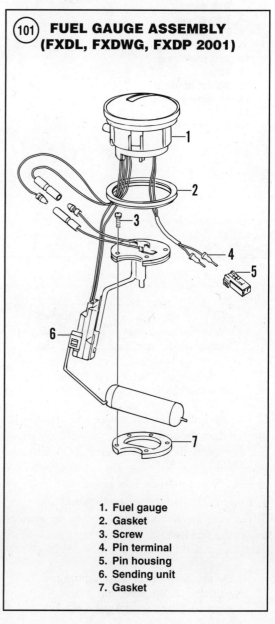

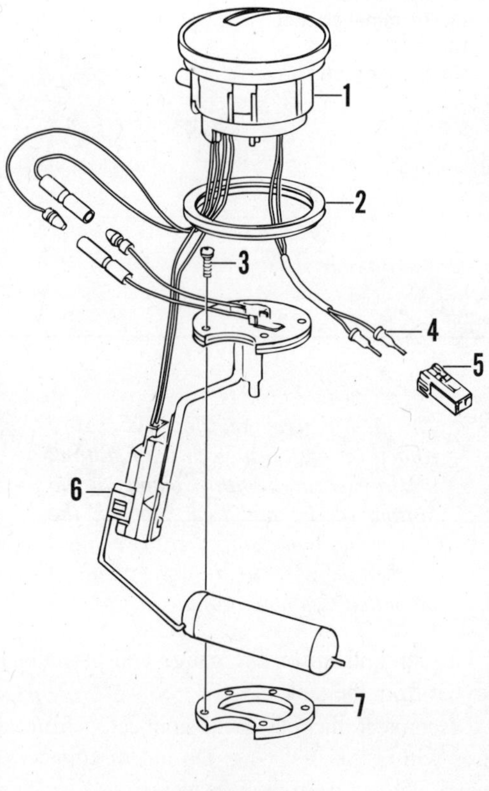

1. Fuel gauge
2. Gasket
3. Screw
4. Pin terminal
5. Pin housing
6. Sending unit
7. Gasket

102

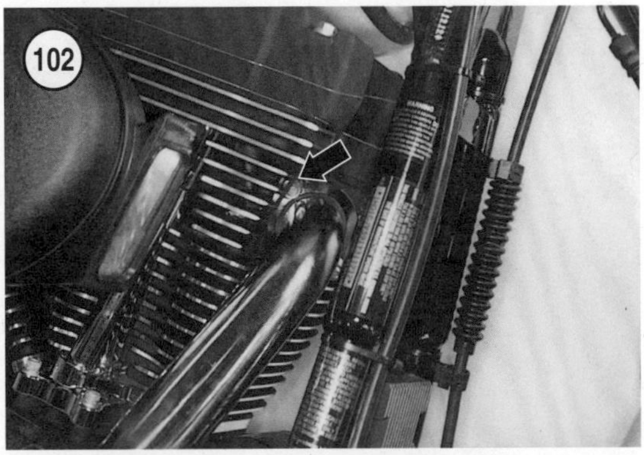

103

104

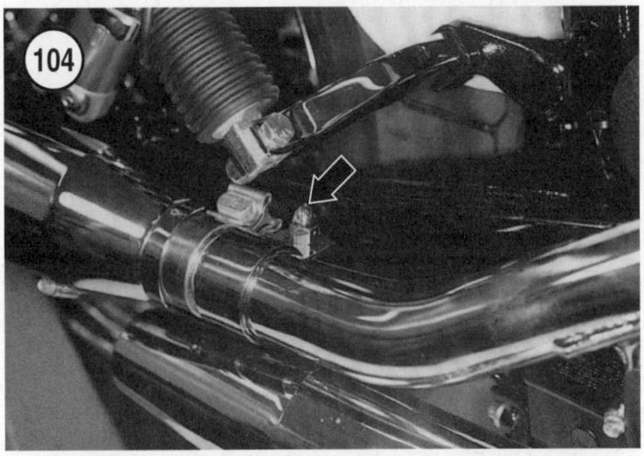

105

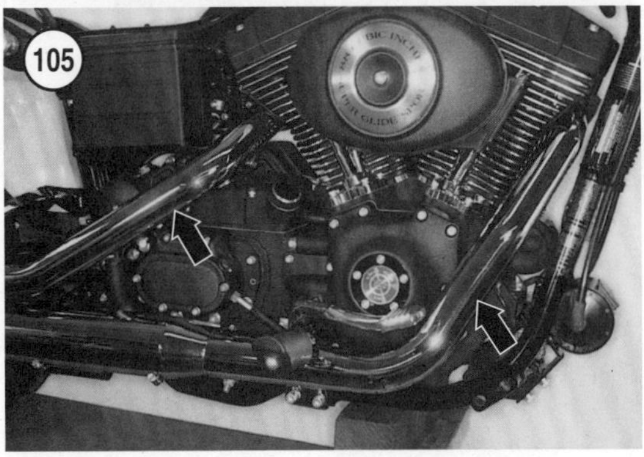

2. Pull straight up on the gauge and partially remove it from the tank.

3. Disconnect the electrical connector from the wires within the fuel tank. Do not disconnect the electrical wires from the fuel gauge.

4. Remove the fuel gauge and the gasket.

5. Remove the five screws securing the sending unit to the fuel tank.

CAUTION

Do not bend the float arm during removal of the sending unit. If bent, the gauge will give inaccurate readings.

6. Carefully withdraw the sending unit while moving it back and forth and lifting and turning it in either direction.

7. Remove the gasket from the fuel tank.

8. Install by reversing these removal steps while noting the following:

  a. Install a *new* gasket between the fuel gauge and fuel tank.

  b. Carefully install the sending unit to avoid damage to the float arm.

  c. Tighten all screws securely.

EXHAUST SYSTEM

Removal

1. Support the motorcycle on a work stand. See *motorcycle Stands* in Chapter Nine.

2. At each cylinder head, loosen and remove the two flange nuts (**Figure 102**) securing both the front and rear exhaust pipes to the cylinder heads.

3. Slide the exhaust flange and retaining ring off the cylinder head studs.

4. Remove the nut and bolt (**Figure 103**) securing the front exhaust pipe to the frame bracket.

5. Remove the nut and bolt (**Figure 104**) securing the rear exhaust pipe to the frame bracket.

6. Carefully pull the exhaust assembly (**Figure 105**) away from the motorcycle and remove it as an assembly.

7. Remove the exhaust port gaskets (**Figure 106**).

8. Inspect the exhaust system as described in this chapter.

9. Store the exhaust system in a safe place until it is reinstalled.

106

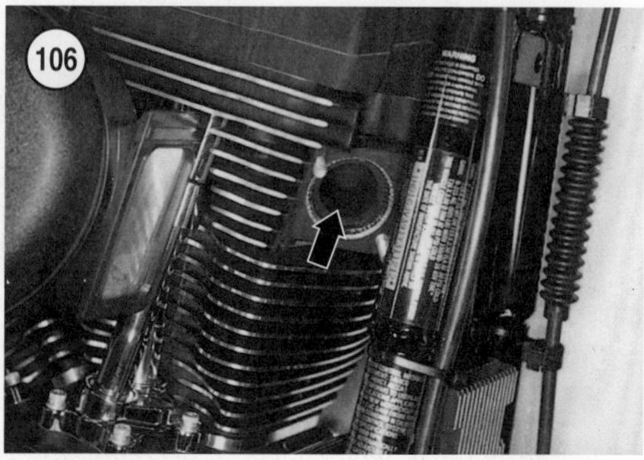

107

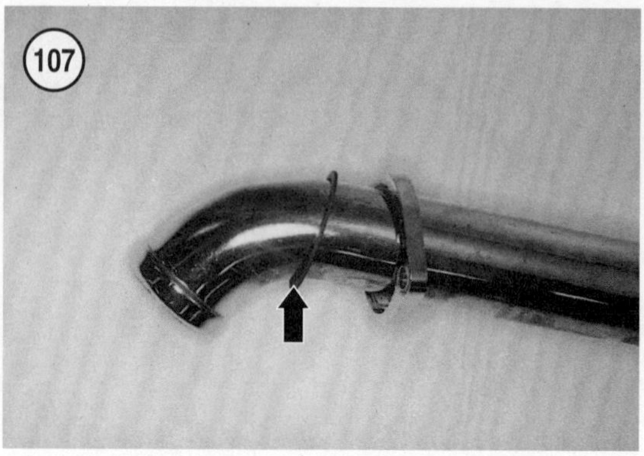

108

EXHAUST SYSTEM

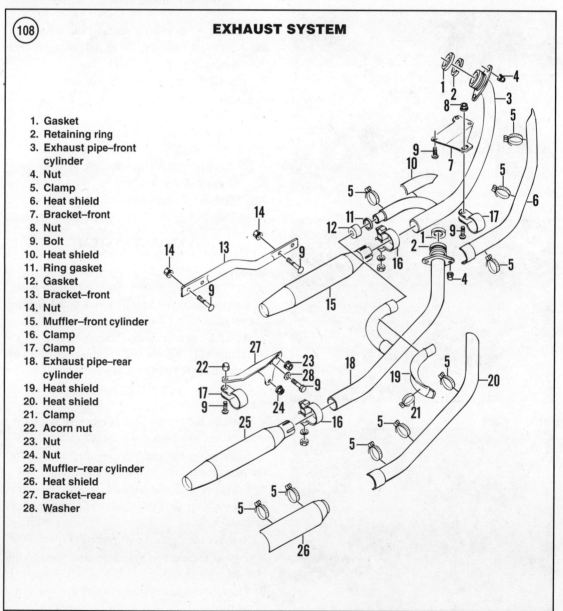

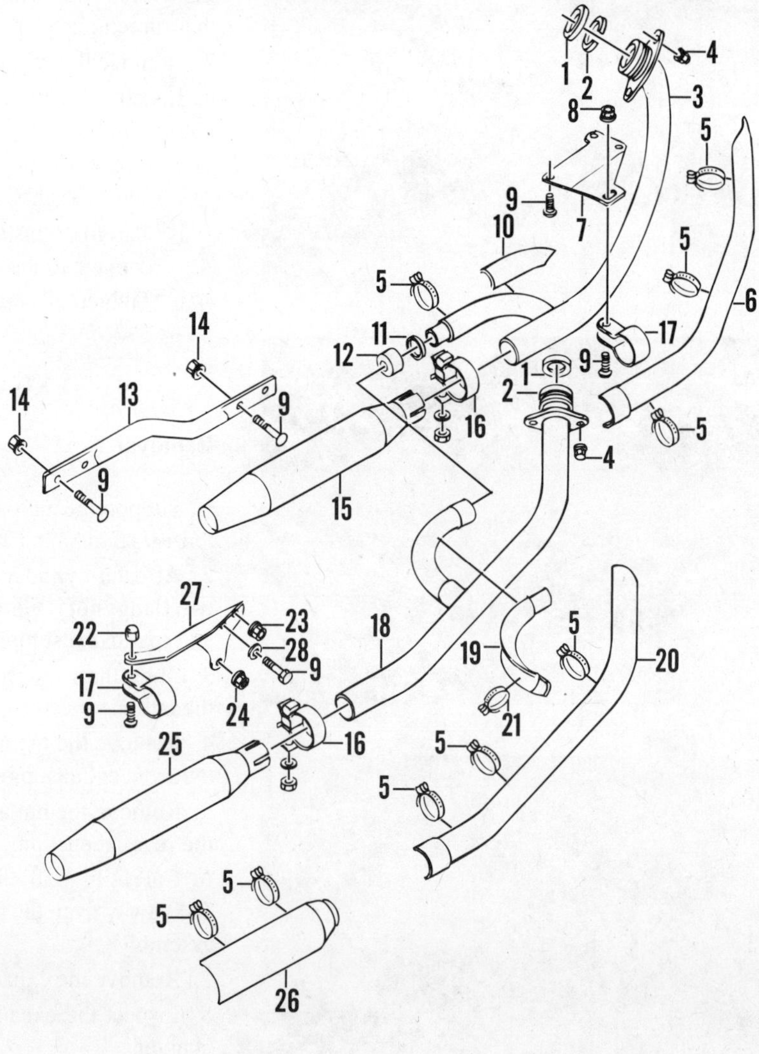

1. Gasket
2. Retaining ring
3. Exhaust pipe–front cylinder
4. Nut
5. Clamp
6. Heat shield
7. Bracket–front
8. Nut
9. Bolt
10. Heat shield
11. Ring gasket
12. Gasket
13. Bracket–front
14. Nut
15. Muffler–front cylinder
16. Clamp
17. Clamp
18. Exhaust pipe–rear cylinder
19. Heat shield
20. Heat shield
21. Clamp
22. Acorn nut
23. Nut
24. Nut
25. Muffler–rear cylinder
26. Heat shield
27. Bracket–rear
28. Washer

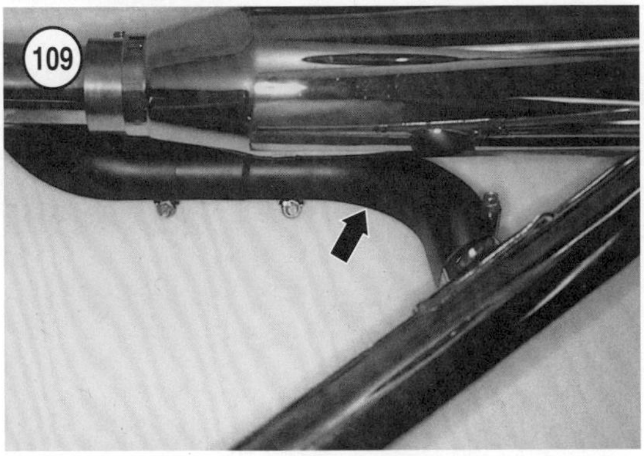

Installation

NOTE
If the mufflers were removed from the exhaust pipes, new clamps must be installed to ensure correct sealing integrity. The new clamps eliminate the need for graphite or silicone tape during installation of the mufflers.

1. Before installing the *new* exhaust port gaskets, scrape the exhaust port surfaces to remove all carbon residue—removing the carbon will ensure a good gasket fit. Then wipe the port with a rag.
2. Position the *new* gasket with the wider diameter end facing out toward exhaust pipe.
3. Before installing the exhaust pipes, check that the retaining rings (**Figure 107**) fit tightly against the pipe flanges.
4. Position the exhaust pipe assembly so that the front and rear exhaust pipes fit into the front and rear cylinder head ports. Slide the retaining ring and exhaust flange over the mounting studs and install the lock nuts. Tighten the nuts finger-tight only.
5. Position the rear exhaust pipe clamp onto the frame bracket and install the nut and bolt (**Figure 104**).
6. Position the front exhaust pipe clamp onto the frame bracket and install the nut and bolt (**Figure 103**).
7. Check the exhaust assembly alignment, then tighten the cylinder head stud nuts as follows:
   a. Tighten the upper nut finger-tight.
   b. Tighten the lower nut to 10 in-lbs. (1 N•m).
   c. Tighten the upper nut to 60-80 in-lbs. (7-9 N•m).
   d. Tighten the lower nut to 60-80 in-lbs. (7-9 N•m).
8. Tighten the front and then the rear exhaust pipe clamp bolts and nuts to the specification in **Table 3**.
9. If removed, install the heat shields and tighten the clamps securely.
10. Start the engine and check for leaks.

Inspection

Refer to **Figure 108**.

1. Replace rusted or damaged exhaust system components.
2. Inspect the crossover pipe (**Figure 109**) for rust or corrosion.
3. Remove all rust from exhaust pipe and muffler mating surfaces.
4. The muffler clamps are not reusable. Replace the muffler clamps if they are removed.
5. Replace damaged exhaust pipe retaining rings (**Figure 107**).
6. Replace all worn or damaged heat shield clamps as required.
7. Check the mounting bracket bolts and nuts for tightness.

EVAPORATIVE EMISSION CONTROL SYSTEM (CALIFORNIA MODELS)

An evaporative emission control system prevents gasoline vapor from escaping into the atmosphere.

When the engine is not running, the system directs the fuel vapor from the fuel tank through the vapor valve and into the charcoal canister. Also when the engine is not running, the gravity-operated trap door in the air filter backplate blocks the inlet port of the air filter. This prevents hydrocarbon vapors emanating from the carburetor venturi from escaping into the atmosphere.

When the engine is running, these vapors are drawn through a purge hose and into the carburetor where they burn in the combustion chambers. The vapor valve also prevents gasoline vapor from escaping from the carbon canister if the motorcycle falls on its side.

Also when the engine is running, the engine vacuum pulls the air filter backplate trap door open, allowing air to enter.

Inspection/Replacement

Refer to **Figure 110** for component and hose routing. Before removing the hoses from any of the parts, mark the hose and the fitting with a piece of masking tape to identify where the hose goes.

110

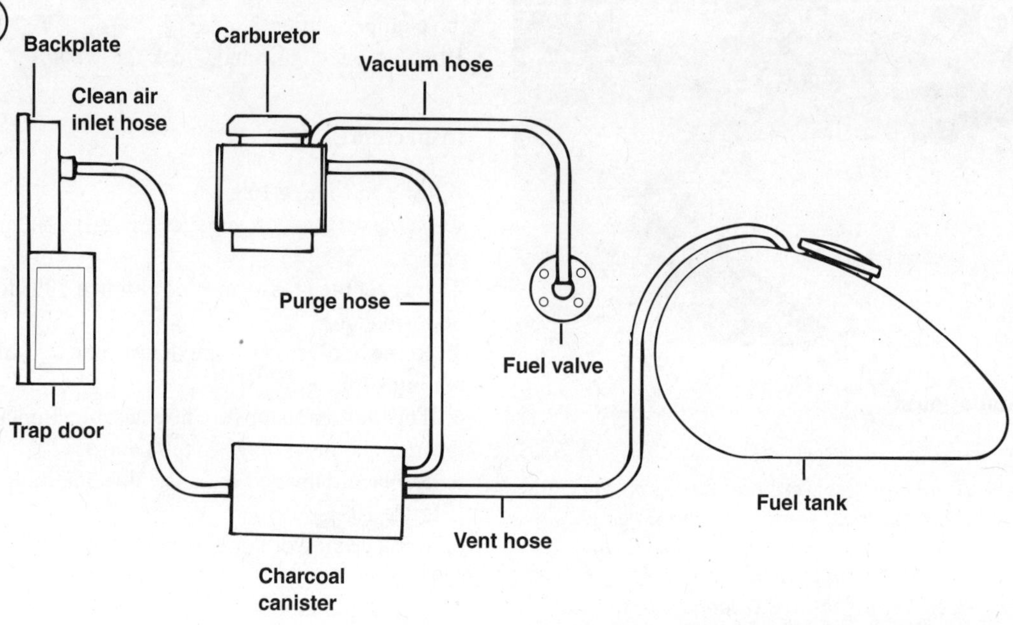

1. Check all emission control lines and hoses to make sure that they are correctly routed and connected.

WARNING
Make sure the fuel tank vapor hoses are routed so they cannot contact any hot engine or exhaust component. These hoses contain flammable vapor. If a hose melts from contacting a hot part, leaking vapor may ignite, causing severe motorcycle damage and rider injury.

2. Make sure there are no kinks in the lines or hoses. Also inspect the hose and lines for excessive wear or burning on lines that are routed near engine hot spots.

3. Check the physical condition of all lines and hoses in the system. Check for cuts, tears or loose connections. These lines and hoses are subjected to various temperature and operating conditions and eventually become brittle and crack. Replace damaged lines and hoses.

4. Check all components in the emission control system for damage, such as broken fittings or broken nipples on the component.

111

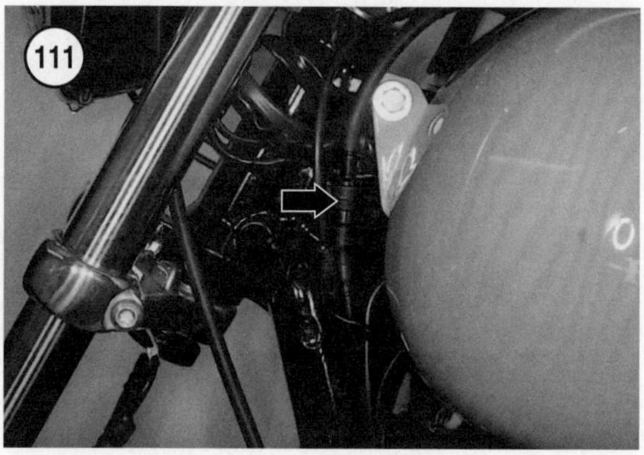

5. When replacing one or more lines or hoses, refer to the diagram for the specific model being worked on.

Vapor Valve Replacement

The vapor valve (**Figure 111**) is connected in the vent hose between the fuel tank and carbon canister.

1. Label the hoses at the vapor valve, then disconnect them.
2. Remove the vapor valve.

CAUTION
The vapor valve must be installed in the vent hose in a vertical position

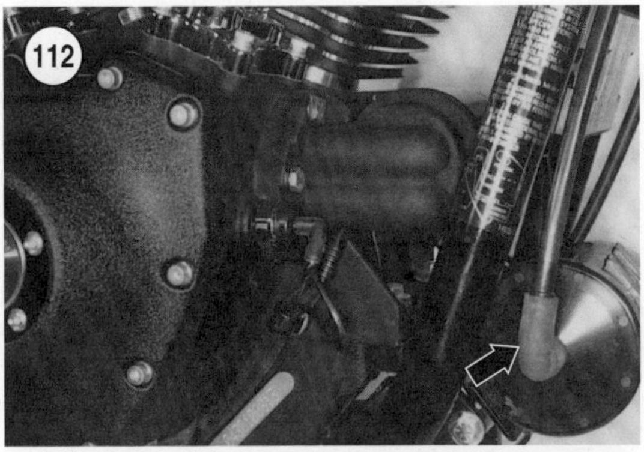

with the longer end facing up toward the fuel tank.

3. Install the vapor valve and secure both hoses.

Carbon Canister Replacement

1. Prior to disconnecting any of the hoses, label the hoses and the canister fittings. Plug the open end of each hose to prevent contamination.
2. Disconnect the clean air hose (**Figure 112**) from the right side of the canister.
3. Disconnect the purge hose and the vent hose (A, **Figure 113**) from the left side of the canister.
4. Using a flat-blade screwdriver, lift up the tang on the base of the canister, slide the canister toward the left side and remove the canister (B, **Figure 113**) from the mounting bracket.
5. Install the carbon canister by reversing these steps while noting the following:
   a. Slide the canister into the mounting bracket until it clicks.
   b. Attach the hoses to the correct fittings as noted during removal.

7

Table 1 CARBURETOR JET SIZES

Year and model	Main jet	Pilot jet
All years and models	190	45

Table 2 FUEL SYSTEM TORQUE SPECIFICATIONS

Item	ft.-lb.	in.-lb.	N•m
Air filter cover screw	–	36-60	4-7
Air filter backplate screws	–	20-40	2-5
Breather hollow bolts	–	124-142	14-16
Fuel shutoff valve			
Mounting hex fitting	15-20	–	20-27
Diaphragm screws	–	18.5	2.1
Fuel tank mounting bolts	10-18	–	14-24
Intake manifold Allen bolts	15-17	–	20-23

Table 3 EXHAUST SYSTEM TORQUE SPECIFICATIONS

Item	ft.-lb.	in.-lb.	N•m
Exhaust flange nuts	Refer to text procedure		
Muffler clamp nuts	45-60	–	61-81

NOTE: Refer to the Supplement at the back of this manual for information unique to 2002-on models.

CHAPTER EIGHT

ELECTRICAL SYSTEM

This chapter contains service and test procedures for electrical and ignition system components. Spark plugs are covered in Chapter Three.

The chapter is divided into the following sections:

1. Basic information.
2. Battery.
3. Charging.
4. Starting.
5. Lighting.
6. Switches and other electrical components.

Refer to **Tables 1-8** at the end of the chapter for specifications.

BASIC INFORMATION

Wiring and Connectors

Many electrical troubles can be traced to damaged wiring or to contaminated or loose connectors.

The location of the connectors varies by model. The photographs in this chapter may not show the location of the model being serviced. Also, if the motorcycle has been serviced previously, the connector may be in a different location.

Always check the wire colors listed in the procedure or wiring diagrams to verify that the correct component has been identified.

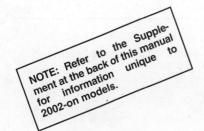

Perform the following steps first if an electrical system fault is encountered.

1. Inspect all wiring for fraying, burning and any other visual damage.
2. Check the main fuse and make sure it is not blown. Replace it if necessary.
3. Check the individual fuse(s) for each circuit. Make sure it is not blown. Replace it if necessary.
4. Inspect the battery as described in this chapter. Make sure it is fully charged and that the battery cables are clean and securely attached to the battery terminals.
5. Clean connectors with an aerosol electrical contact cleaner. After a thorough cleaning, pack multi-pin electrical connectors with dielectric grease to seal out moisture.
6. Disconnect electrical connectors in the suspect circuits and check for bent metal pins on the male side of the electrical connector. A bent pin will not connect to the female end of the connector, causing an open circuit.
7. Check each female end of the connector. Make sure that the metal connector on the end of each wire is pushed all the way into the plastic connector. If not, carefully push them in with a narrow-blade screwdriver.
8. After everything is checked, push the connectors together and make sure they are fully engaged and locked together.
9. Never pull on the electrical wires when disconnecting an electrical connector; pull only on the connector plastic housing.

NOTE
Step 10 checks the continuity of individual circuits.

10. Check wiring continuity as follows:
    a. Disconnect the negative battery cable as described in this chapter.

    NOTE
    When making a continuity test, it is best not to disconnect the electrical connector. Instead, insert the test leads into the back of the connectors and check both sides. Because corrosion between the connector contacts may be causing an open circuit, the trouble may be in the connector instead of with the wiring.

    b. If using an analog ohmmeter, always touch the test leads, then zero adjust the needle according to manufacturer's instructions to assure correct readings.
    c. Attach the test leads to the circuit to be tested.
    d. There should be continuity. If there is no continuity (infinite resistance), there is an open in the circuit.

Wiring Diagrams

Wiring diagrams are located at the end of this book.

Electrical Component Resistance Testing

Because the resistance of a component varies with temperature, perform the resistance tests with the component at room temperature (68° F [20° C]). The specifications provided in this manual are based on tests performed at this temperature.

NOTE
When using an analog ohmmeter, always touch the test leads, then zero adjust the needle to ensure correct readings.

Electrical Component Replacement

Most motorcycle dealerships and parts suppliers will not accept returns of electrical parts. Avoid purchasing parts unless the cause of the malfunction has been determined. If a thorough diagnosis has not located the exact cause of the electrical system malfunction, have a Harley-Davidson dealership determine the possible cause.

BATTERY

The battery is an important component in the motorcycle's electrical system, yet most electrical system troubles can be traced to battery neglect. Clean and inspect the battery at periodic intervals. All models are equipped with a maintenance-free sealed battery and the electrolyte level cannot be checked.

On all models covered in this manual, the negative side is the ground. When removing the battery, disconnect the negative (–) cable first, then the positive (+) cable. This minimizes the chance of a tool shorting to ground when disconnecting the battery positive cable.

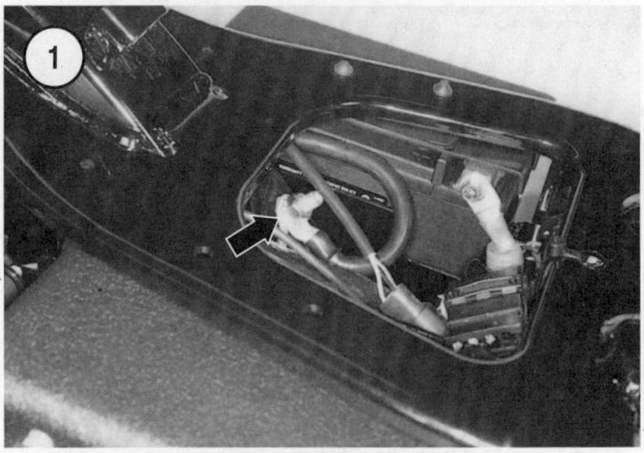

Negative Cable

Some of the component replacement procedures and some of the test procedures in this chapter require disconnecting the negative battery cable as a safety precaution.

NOTE
Always disarm the optional TSSM security system prior to disconnecting the battery or the siren will sound.

1. Remove the seat as described in Chapter Thirteen.
2. Remove the nut (**Figure 1**) securing the negative cable to the frame. Move the cable away from the battery to avoid making accidental contact with the battery post.
3. Connect the negative cable onto the frame post, reinstall the nut (**Figure 1**) and tighten securely.
4. Install the seat.

Battery Cable Service

To ensure good electrical contact between the battery and the electrical cables, the cables must be clean and free of corrosion.

1. If the electrical cable terminals are badly corroded, disconnect them from the motorcycle's electrical system.
2. Thoroughly clean each connector with a wire brush and then with a baking soda solution. Rinse thoroughly with clean water and wipe dry with a clean cloth.
3. After cleaning, apply a thin layer of dielectric grease to the battery terminals before reattaching the cables.
4. If disconnected, attach the electrical cables to the motorcycle's electrical system.
5. After connecting the electrical cables, apply a light coat of dielectric grease to the terminals to retard corrosion and decomposition of the terminals.

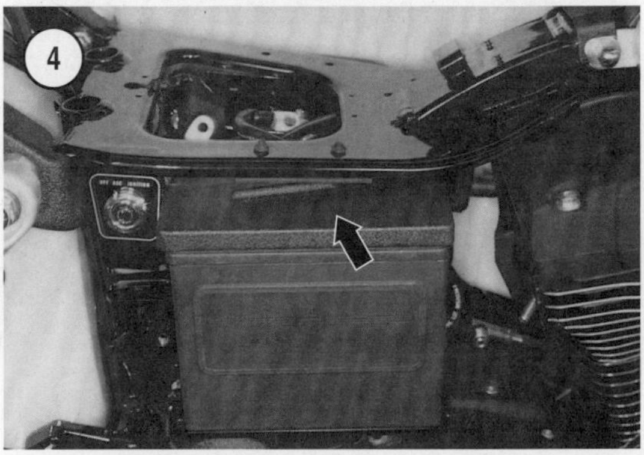

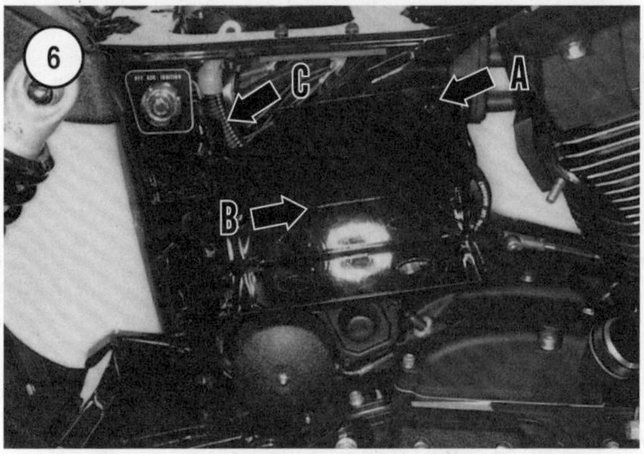

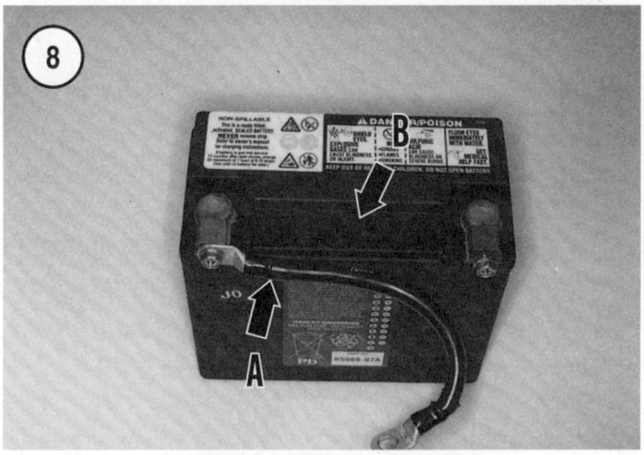

Battery and Tray Removal/Installation

NOTE
Always disarm the optional TSSM security system prior to disconnecting the battery or the siren will sound.

1. Remove the seat as described in Chapter Thirteen.
2. Remove the nut (**Figure 1**) securing the negative cable to the frame.
3. Disconnect the negative cable from the frame post and reinstall the nut to avoid misplacing it.
4. Remove the bolt (**Figure 2**) securing the positive cable to the battery. Disconnect the cable.
5. Remove the bolt (**Figure 3**), at the rear of the battery case, securing the battery tray to the chassis.
6. Carefully tilt the battery and tray down and remove the top cover (**Figure 4**).
7. Remove the battery (**Figure 5**) from the tray and frame.
8. If necessary, unhook the tab on the backside of the battery tray (A, **Figure 6**) from the frame mount and remove the battery tray (B) from the frame.
9. Inspect the battery tray for corrosion or damage. Replace if necessary.
10. If removed, hook the front of the battery tray onto the frame mount (**Figure 7**) and install the battery tray (B, **Figure 6**) onto the frame. Correctly locate the battery positive cable (C, **Figure 6**) behind the battery tray.
11. If removed, install the negative battery cable as shown in A, **Figure 8**. Do not wait until the battery is installed, since there is limited working room after the battery is installed.
12. Position the battery with the cable terminal side going in first.
13. Reinstall the battery onto the battery tray in the frame (**Figure 5**). Direct the negative cable through the frame and into position on the frame mount.
14. Install the battery top cover (**Figure 4**).
15. Install the bolt (**Figure 3**) securing the battery tray to the chassis and tighten securely.
16. Connect the positive cable (**Figure 2**) to the battery. Tighten the bolt securely.
17. Connect the negative cable onto the frame post, reinstall the nut (**Figure 1**) and tighten securely.
18. After connecting the electrical cables, apply a light coat of dielectric grease to the battery termi-

nals to prevent corrosion and deterioration of the terminals.

19. Install the seat.

Inspection and Testing

The battery electrolyte level cannot be serviced. *Never* attempt to remove the sealing bar cap (B, **Figure 8**) from the top of the battery. This bar cap was removed for the initial filling of electrolyte prior to delivery of the motorcycle, or the installation of a new battery, and is not to be removed thereafter. The battery does not require periodic electrolyte inspection or water refilling. Refer to the label (**Figure 9**) on top of the battery.

Even though the battery is a sealed type, protect eyes, skin and clothing; electrolyte, which is very corrosive, may have spilled out and can cause severe chemical skin burns and permanent injury. The battery case may be cracked and leaking electrolyte. If any electrolyte is spilled or splashed on clothing or skin, immediately neutralize with a solution of baking soda and water, then flush with an abundance of clean water.

WARNING
Electrolyte splashed into the eyes is extremely harmful. Always wear safety glasses while working with a battery. If electrolyte gets into the eyes, call a physician immediately and force the eyes open and flood them with cool, clean water for approximately 15 minutes.

1. Remove the battery as described in this chapter. Do not clean the battery while it is mounted in the frame.
2. Set the battery on a stack of newspapers or shop cloths to protect the surface of the workbench.
3. Check the entire battery case (A, **Figure 10**) for cracks or other damage. If the battery case is warped, discolored or has a raised top, the battery has been overcharged and overheated.
4. Check the battery terminal bolts, spacers and nuts (B, **Figure 10**) for corrosion or damage. Clean parts thoroughly with a solution of baking soda and water. Replace corroded or damaged parts.
5. If corroded, clean the top of the battery with a stiff bristle brush using the baking soda and water solution.

9

6. Check the battery cable ends (C, **Figure 10**) for corrosion and damage. If corrosion is minor, clean the battery cable ends with a stiff wire brush. Replace worn or damaged cables.
7. Connect a digital voltmeter between the battery negative and positive leads. Note the following:
   a. If the battery voltage is 12.6 volts (at 20° C [68° F]), or greater, the battery is fully charged.
   b. If the battery voltage is 12.0 to 12.5 volts (at 20° C [68° F]), or lower, the battery is undercharged and requires charging.
8. If the battery is undercharged, recharge it as described in this chapter. Then test the charging system as described in Chapter Two.
9. Inspect the battery case for contamination or damage. Clean with a solution of baking soda and water.

Charging

Refer to *Battery Initialization* in this chapter if the battery is new.

If recharging is required on a maintenance-free battery, a digital voltmeter and a charger with an adjustable amperage output are required. If this equipment is not available, it is recommended that battery charging be entrusted to a shop with the proper equipment. Excessive voltage and amperage from an unregulated charger can damage the battery and shorten service life.

The battery should only self-discharge approximately one percent each day. If a battery not in use, with no loads connected, loses its charge within a week after charging, the battery is defective.

If the motorcycle is not used for long periods of time, an automatic battery charger with variable

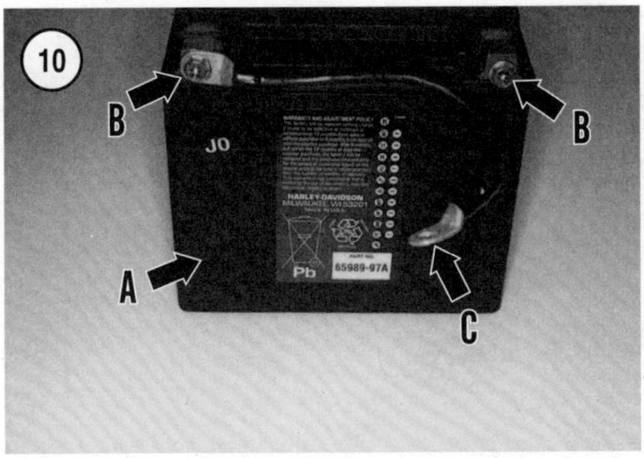

voltage and amperage outputs is recommended for optimum battery service life.

WARNING
During charging, highly explosive hydrogen gas is released from the battery. The battery should be charged only in a well-ventilated area away from open flames (including pilot lights on some gas home appliances). Do not allow any smoking in the area. Never check the charge of the battery by arcing across the terminals; the resulting spark can ignite the hydrogen gas.

CAUTION
Always disconnect the battery cables from the battery. If the cables are left connected during the charging procedure, the charger may destroy the diodes in the voltage regulator/rectifier.

1. Remove the battery from the motorcycle as described in this chapter.
2. Set the battery on a stack of newspapers or shop cloths to protect the surface of the workbench.
3. Make sure the battery charger is turned to the OFF position, prior to attaching the charger leads to the battery.
4. Connect the positive charger lead to the positive (+) battery terminal and the negative charger lead to the negative (–) battery terminal.
5. Set the charger at 12 volts. If the output of the charger is variable, select the low setting.
6. The charging time depends on the discharged condition of the battery. Refer to **Table 3** for the suggested charging time. Normally, a battery should be charged at 1/10th its given capacity.

CAUTION
If the battery emits an excessive amount of gas during the charging cycle, decrease the charge rate. If the battery becomes hotter than 110° F (43° C) during the charging cycle, turn the charger to the OFF position and allow the battery to cool. After cooling down, continue with a reduced charging rate and continue to monitor the battery temperature.

7. Turn the charger to the ON position.
8. After the battery has been charged for the pre-determined time, turn the charger to the OFF position, disconnect the leads and measure the battery voltage. Refer to the following:
   a. If the battery voltage is 12.6 volts (at 20° C [68° F]), or greater, the battery is fully charged
   b. If the battery voltage is 12.5 volts (at 20° C [68° F]), or lower, the battery is undercharged and requires additional charging time.
9. If the battery remains stable for one hour, the battery is charged.
10. Install the battery into the motorcycle as described in this chapter.

Battery Initialization

A new battery must be *fully* charged to a specific gravity of 1.260-1.280 before installation. To bring the battery to a full charge, give it an initial charge. Using a new battery without an initial charge will cause permanent battery damage. That is, the battery will never be able to hold more than an 80% charge. Charging a new battery after it has been used will not bring its charge to 100%. When purchasing a new battery, verify its charge status.

NOTE
***Recycle the old battery**. When a new battery is purchased, turn in the old one for recycling. Most motorcycle dealerships will accept the old battery in trade when purchasing a new one. Never place an old battery in the household trash since it is illegal, in most states, to place any acid or lead (heavy metal) contents in landfills.*

Load Testing

A load test checks the battery's performance under full current load and is the best indication of battery condition.

A battery load tester is required for this procedure. When using a load tester, follow the manufacturer's instructions. **Figure 11** shows a typical load tester and battery arrangement.

1. Remove the battery from the motorcycle as described in this chapter.

NOTE
If the battery required charging, let the battery stand for at least one hour prior to performing this test.

2. The battery must be fully charged before beginning this test. If necessary, charge the battery if necessary as described in this section.

WARNING
The battery load tester must be turned to the OFF position prior to connecting or disconnecting the test cables to the battery. Otherwise, a spark could cause the battery to explode.

CAUTION
To prevent battery damage during load testing, observe these two requirements: Do not load test a discharged battery and do not load test the battery for more than 20 seconds. Performing a load test on a discharged battery can result in permanent battery damage.

3. Load test the battery as follows:
   a. Connect the load tester cables to the battery following its manufacturer's instructions.
   b. Load the battery at 50% of the cold cranking amperage (CCA), or 135 amperes.
   c. After 15 seconds, the voltage reading (with the load still applied) must be 9.6 volts or higher at 70° F (21° C). Now quickly remove the load and turn the tester OFF.
4. If the voltage reading is 9.6 volts or higher, the battery output capacity is good. If the reading is below 9.6 volts, the battery is defective.
5. With the tester in the OFF position, disconnect the cables from the battery.
6. Install the battery as described in this chapter.

11 **LOAD TEST**

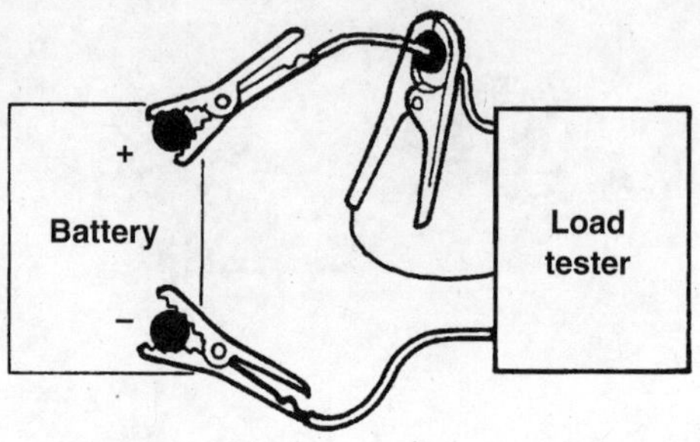

CHARGING SYSTEM

An electrical diagram of the charging system is shown in **Figure 12** for 1999-2001 models. Refer to the wiring diagrams at the end of the manual for 2002-on models. The charging system consists of the battery, alternator and voltage regulator/rectifier (**Figure 13** and **Figure 14**). Alternating current generated by the alternator is rectified to direct current. The voltage regulator maintains a constant voltage to the battery and additional electrical loads, such as the lights and ignition system, at a constant voltage regardless of variations in engine speed and load.

A malfunction in the charging system generally causes the battery to remain undercharged. To prevent damage to the alternator and the regulator/rectifier when testing and repairing the charging system, note the following precautions:

1. Disarm the optional TSSM security system prior to disconnecting the battery or the siren will sound.
2. Always disconnect the negative battery cable, as described in this chapter, before removing a component from the charging system.
3. When it is necessary to charge the battery, remove the battery from the motorcycle and recharge it as described in this chapter.
4. Inspect the battery case. Look for bulges or cracks in the case, leaking electrolyte or corrosion build-up.
5. Check the charging system wiring for signs of chafing, deterioration or other damage.
6. Check the wiring for corroded or loose connections. Clean, tighten or reconnect as required.

Battery Drain

Perform this test prior to performing the output test.

(12)

CHARGING SYSTEM (1999-2001 MODELS)

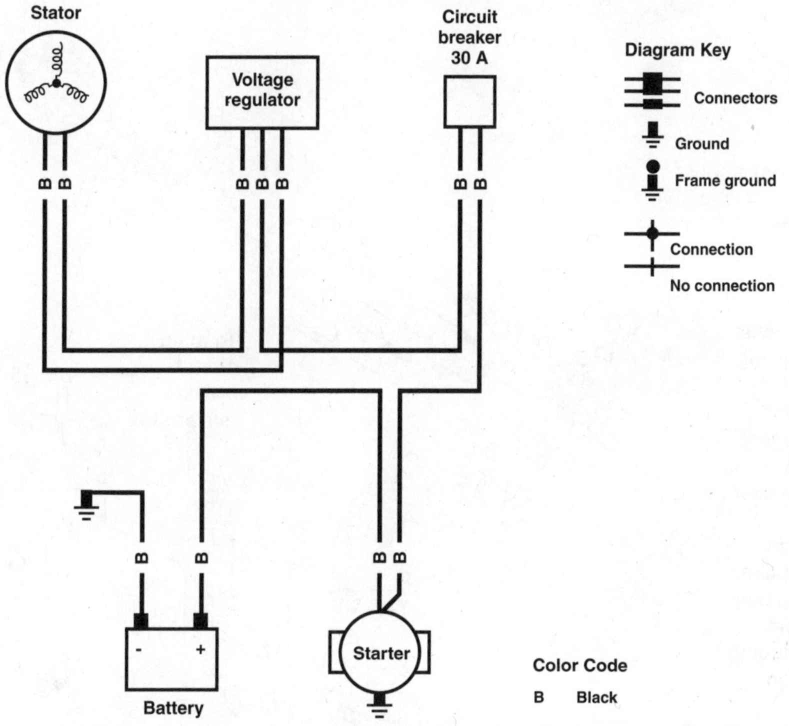

*Refer to the wiring diagrams at the end of this manual for 2002-on models

(13)

CHARGING SYSTEM COMPONENTS (FXDP)

1. Stator coil assembly
2. Allen bolt
3. Rotor
4. Washer
5. Cable seal
6. Terminal socket
7. Socket housing
8. Primary lock
9. Rubber boot
10. Secondary lock
11. Connector
12. Terminal pin
13. Heat sink tubing
14. Bolt
15. Voltage regulator
16. Nut
17. Mounting bracket
18. Washer
19. Lockwasher
20. Allen bolt

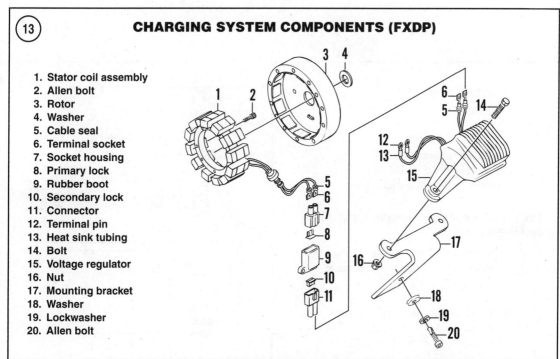

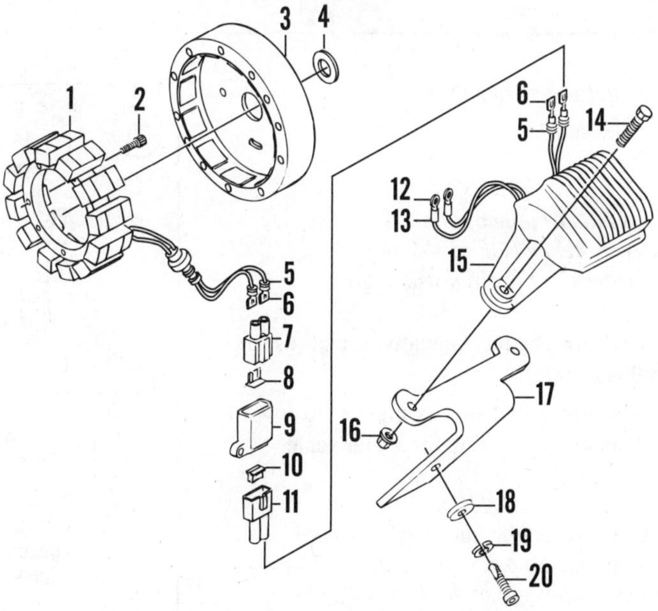

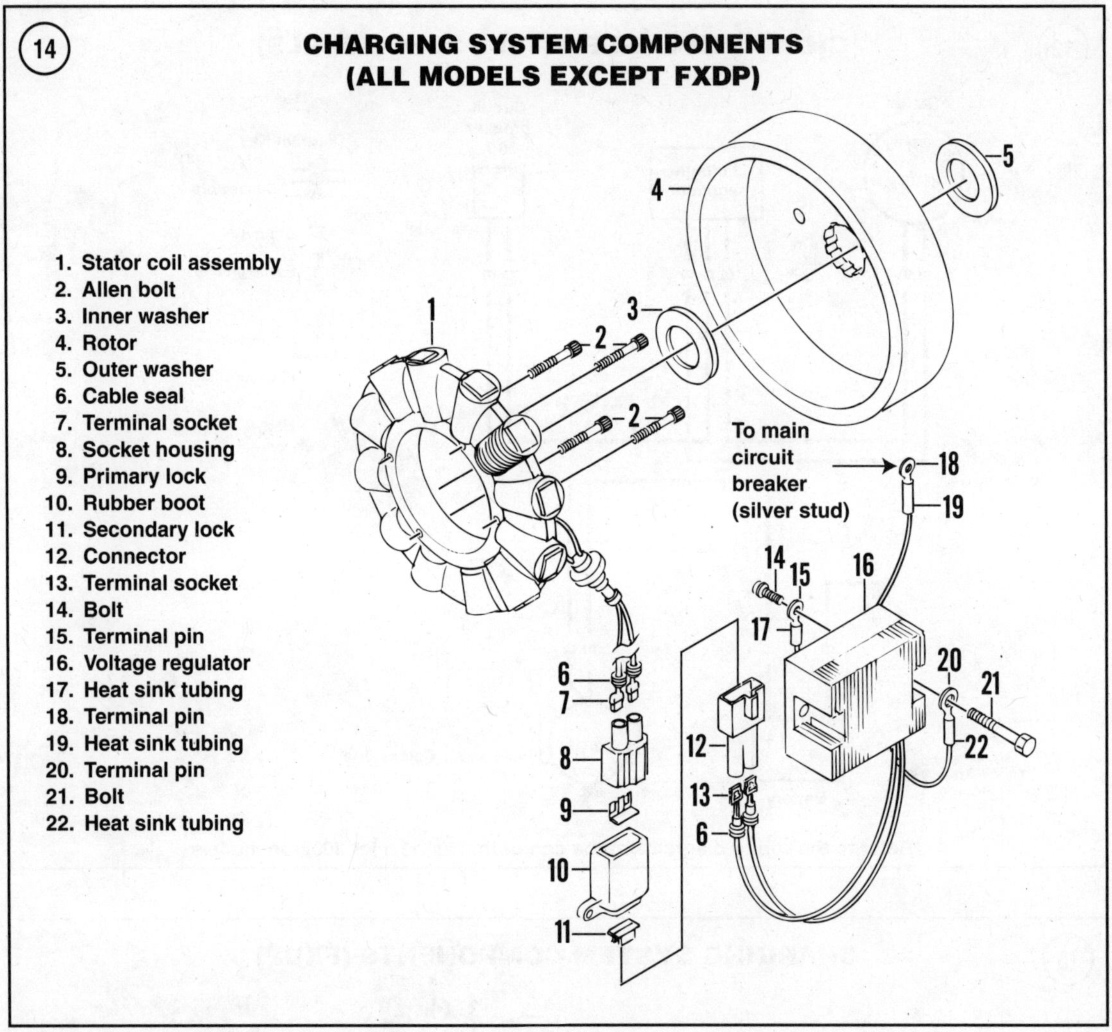

1. Turn the ignition switch OFF.
2. Remove the seat.

NOTE
Always disarm the optional TSSM security system prior to disconnecting the battery or the siren will sound.

3. Disconnect the battery negative lead as described in this chapter.
4. Switch the ammeter from its highest to lowest amperage scale while reading the meter scale.

CAUTION
Before connecting the ammeter into the circuit in Step 4, set the meter to its highest amperage scale. This will prevent a possible large current flow

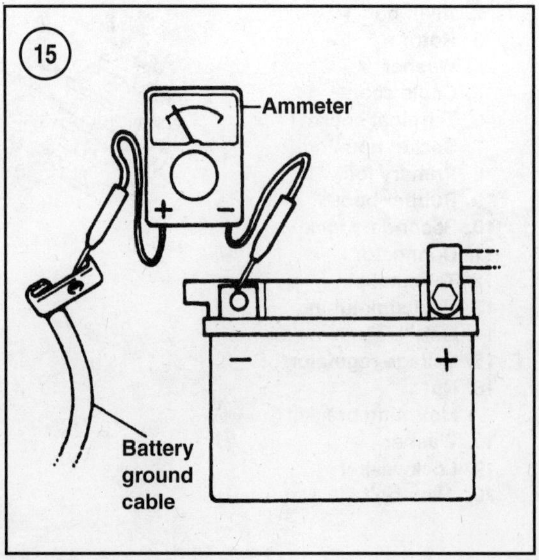

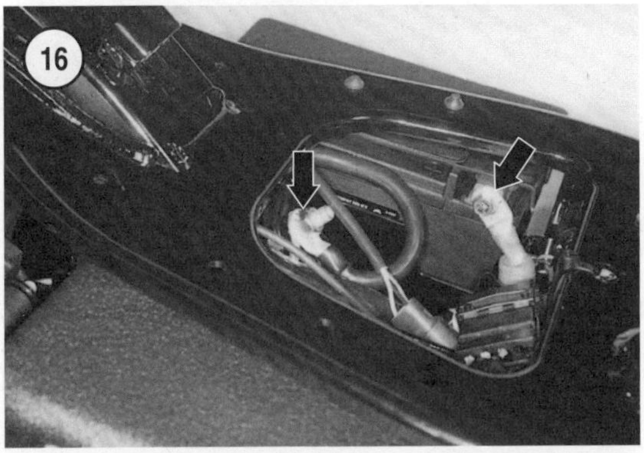

from damaging the meter or blowing the meter's fuse, if so equipped.

5. Connect the ammeter between the negative battery cable and the negative terminal of the battery (**Figure 15**). If the needle swings even the slightest amount when the meter is connected, there is a current draw in the system that will discharge the battery.
6. If the current draw is excessive, the probable causes are:
   a. Damaged battery.
   b. Short circuit in the system.
   c. Loose, dirty or faulty electrical system connectors in the charging system wiring harness.
7. Disconnect the ammeter test leads and reconnect the battery negative lead.

Testing

A malfunction in the charging system generally causes the battery to remain undercharged. Perform the following visual inspection to determine the cause of the problem. If the visual inspection proves satisfactory, test the charging system as described under *Charging System* in Chapter Two.

1. Make sure the battery cables (**Figure 16**) are connected properly. If polarity is reversed, check for a damaged rectifier.
2. Inspect the terminals for loose or corroded connections. Tighten or clean as required.
3. Inspect the battery case. Look for bulges or cracks in the case, leaking electrolyte or corrosion buildup.
4. Carefully check all connections at the alternator to make sure they are clean and tight.
5. Check the circuit wiring for corroded or loose connections. Clean, tighten or connect as required.

ALTERNATOR

Rotor Removal/Installation

NOTE
Always disarm the optional TSSM security system prior to disconnecting the battery or the siren will sound.

1. Disconnect the negative battery cable as described in this chapter.
2. Remove the primary chain case cover and inner housing as described in Chapter Five.
3. If still in place, remove the shaft extension (A, **Figure 17**) and outer spacer (B) from the crankshaft.
4. Slide the rotor (A, **Figure 18**) off the crankshaft. If necessary, insert two wire hooks into the holes in the face of the rotor. Slide the rotor off.
5. On 1999 models, remove the inner spacer (**Figure 19**) from the crankshaft.

6. Inspect the rotor magnets (**Figure 20**) for small bolts, washers or other metal debris that may have been picked up by the magnets. These small metal bits can cause severe damage to the alternator stator assembly.
7. Check the inner splines (**Figure 21**) for wear or damage. Replace the rotor if necessary.
8. Install by reversing these removal steps.

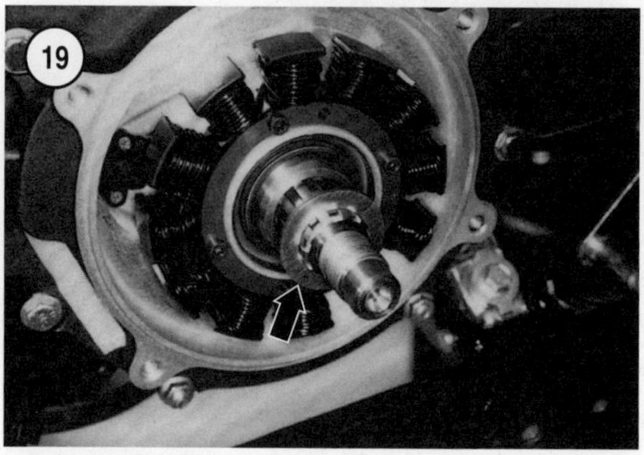

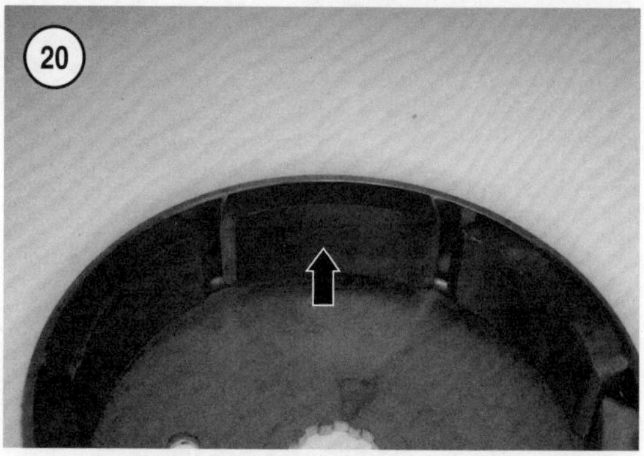

Stator Removal

1. Remove the rotor as described in this chapter.
2. Disconnect the stator electrical connector (B, **Figure 18**) from the wiring harness.

NOTE
The following photographs are shown with the engine removed to better illustrate the steps.

3. Remove the four T27 Torx screws securing the stator assembly (**Figure 22**). New Torx screws must be used on installation.

NOTE
If necessary, spray electrical contact cleaner or glass cleaner around the wiring harness grommet to help ease it out of the crankcase boss receptacle.

4. Carefully pull the stator wiring harness and grommet out of the crankcase boss receptacle (A, **Figure 23**) and remove the stator assembly (B).
5. Inspect the stator mounting surface on the crankcase (**Figure 24**) for any oil residue that may have passed by a damaged oil seal. Clean off if necessary.
6. Inspect the stator wires (A, **Figure 25**) for fraying or damage.
7. Inspect the rubber grommet (B, **Figure 25**) for deterioration or hardness.
8. Check the stator connector pins (**Figure 26**) for looseness or damage.

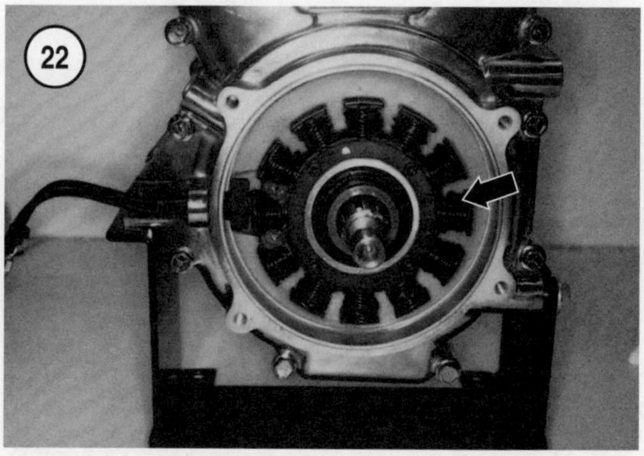

Stator Installation

1. Apply a light coat of electrical contact cleaner or glass cleaner to the wiring harness grommet to help ease it into the crankcase boss receptacle.
2. Insert the electrical harness and grommet into the crankcase boss receptacle and carefully pull it

23

24

25

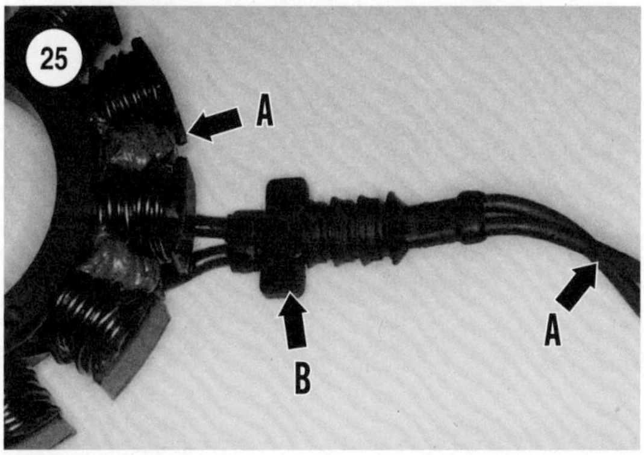

26

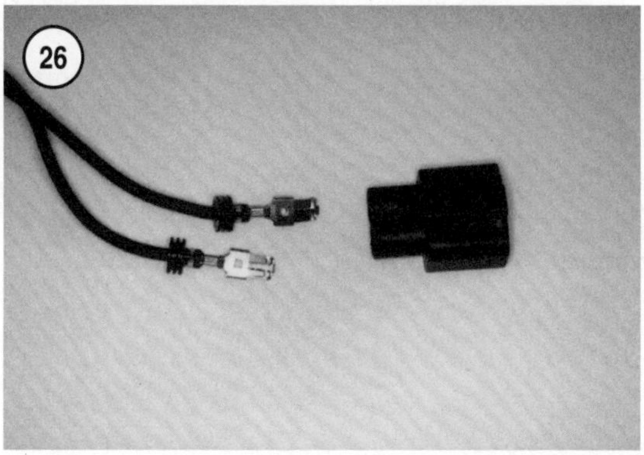

27

through until the grommet is correctly seated (**Figure 27**).

CAUTION
New T27 Torx screws must be installed. The threadlocking compound originally applied to the Torx screws is sufficient for one time use only. If a used Torx screw is installed, it can work loose and cause engine damage.

3. Move the stator into position on the crankcase and install four *new* T27 Torx screws. Tighten the screws to the specifications in **Table 6**.
4. Connect the stator electrical connector (B, **Figure 18**) onto the wiring harness.
5. Install the rotor as described in this chapter.

VOLTAGE REGULATOR

Removal/Installation

NOTE
Always disarm the optional TSSM security system prior to disconnecting the battery or the siren will sound.

1. Disconnect the negative battery cable from the battery as described in this chapter.
2. Remove the fuel tank as described in Chapter Seven.
3. Refer to *Electrical Panel* in this chapter. Remove the cover and outer panel to gain access to the circuit breaker.
4. Disconnect the voltage regulator black wire (**Figure 28**) from the main circuit breaker.
5. Disconnect and remove any cable straps and clips securing the voltage regulator black wire to the frame.

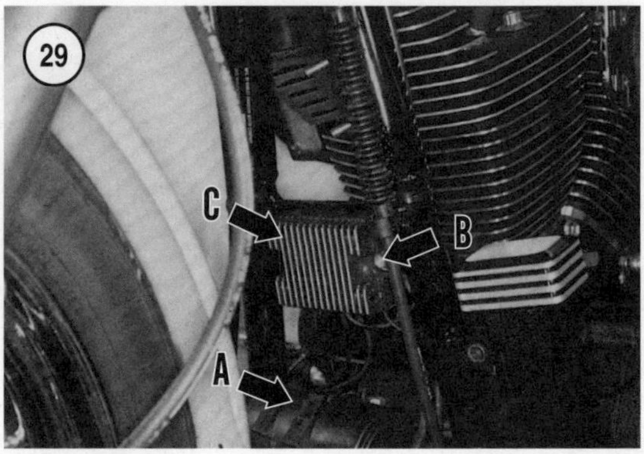

30

ENGINE SENSORS AND SWITCHES

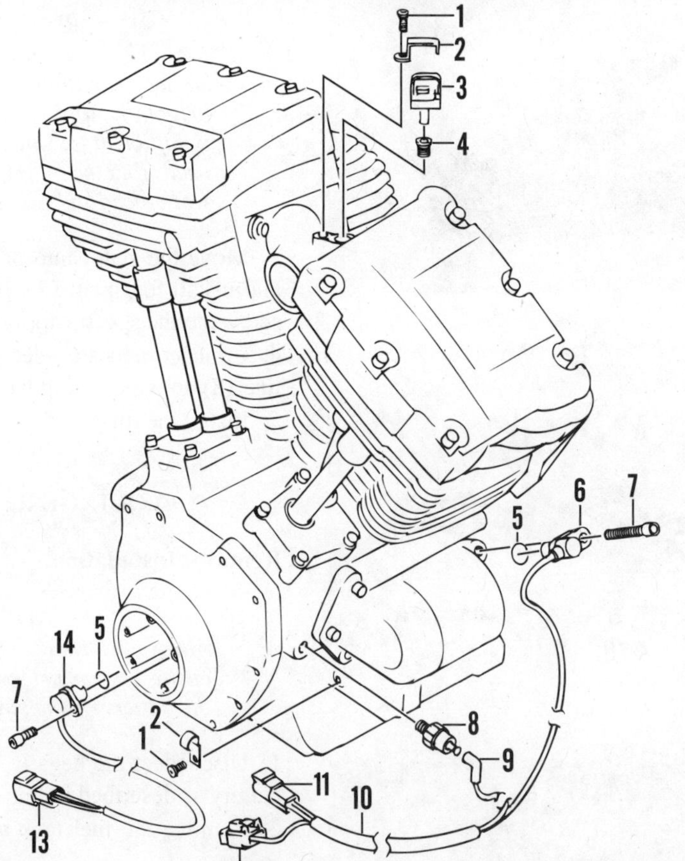

1. Screw
2. Clip
3. MAP sensor
4. Seal
5. O-ring seal
6. Crankshaft position sensor
7. Allen bolt
8. Oil pressure switch
9. Oil pressure switch harness connector
10. Harness sleeve
11. Connector–crankshaft position sensor
12. Connector–oil pressure switch
13. Connector–camshaft position sensor (1999-2000)
14. Camshaft position sensor (1999-2000)

31

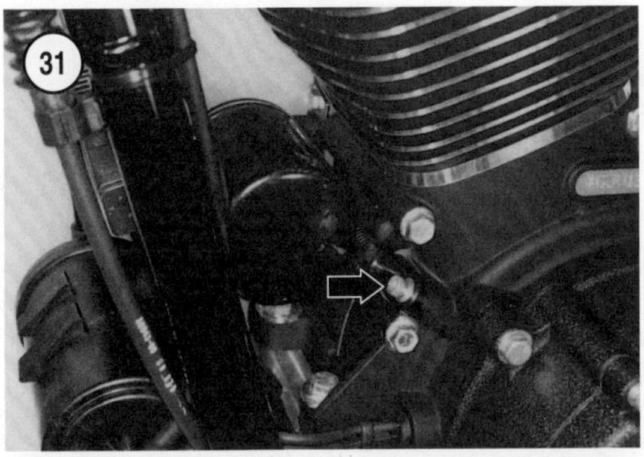

32

6. Tie a piece of string to the voltage regulator wire at the electrical panel. Tie the other end of the string to the frame next to the electrical panel. If necessary, make a drawing of the wire routing through the frame. It is easy to forget the routing path after removing the wire.
7. Carefully pull the black wire and string toward the front of the motorcycle and through the frame. If the wire becomes tight or stuck, do not force it.

NOTE
*On California models, the connector is located behind the evaporation emission charcoal canister (A, **Figure 29**).*

8. Disconnect the voltage regulator electrical connector from the wiring harness as follows:
   a. Remove the screw securing the rubber boot and electrical connector from the front engine mount.
   b. Slide the rubber boot off the connector.
   c. Remove the secondary lock off the electrical wire connectors.
   d. Remove the electrical wires from the connector.
9. Remove the bolts securing the voltage regulator to the frame. Note the location of the ground strap on the left side mounting bolt (B, **Figure 29**).
10. Remove the voltage regulator (C, **Figure 29**). Untie the string from the black wire.
11. Install by reversing these removal steps while noting the following:
   a. Tie the string to the voltage regulator black wire.
   b. Carefully pull the string and black wire back through the frame to the electrical panel. Untie and remove the string.
   c. Be sure to install the ground wire under the left side mounting screw (B, **Figure 29**).

IGNITION SYSTEM

The ignition system consists of an ignition coil, two spark plugs, the ignition module, crankshaft position sensor (CKP), manifold absolute pressure sensor (MAP) and the bank angle sensor (BAS). The 1999-2000 models are also equipped with the camshaft position sensor (CMP) that was eliminated on 2001-on models. Refer to **Figure 30** for the location of all sensors.

The ignition module is located behind the electrical panel. It determines the spark advance for correct ignition timing based on signals from the CKP, MAP and BAS (and CMP on 1999-2000 models). The ignition system fires the spark plugs near top dead center for starting, then varies the spark advance from 0 to 50° depending on engine speed, crankshaft position, and intake manifold pressure. It also regulates the low-voltage circuits between the battery and the ignition coil. The ignition module is a non-repairable item and, if defective, must be replaced.

The crankshaft position sensor (CKP) (**Figure 31**) is mounted on the front left side of the crankcase next to the oil filter. The CKP provides engine speed and position data to the ignition module. The sensor is an induction-type pulse generator that generates an alternating current (AC) signal as the 30 teeth of the flywheel (speed) and the two-tooth gap (reference position TDC) pass by the sensor.

The MAP sensor (**Figure 32**) is located on top of the intake manifold. This sensor monitors the intake manifold vacuum and sends this information to the ignition module where the module adjusts the ignition timing advance curve for maximum performance.

On 1999-2000 models, the camshaft position sensor (CMP) (**Figure 33**) is located in the camshaft cover on the right side of the crankcase. The raised ridge on the rotor operates at one-half crankshaft speed and it breaks the magnetic field of the Hall-effects device on the camshaft position sensor. The logic-type signal of the Hall-effect device gives accurate timing information to the ignition module.

The bank angle sensor mounts on a frame-mounted panel behind the electric panel, on the left side of the motorcycle on 1999-2000 models. On 2001-on models, the bank angle sensor is an integral part of the turn signal/turn signal security module (TSM/TSSM) that is mounted onto the electrical panel. The sensor consists of a small magnetic disc that rides within a V-shaped channel. If the motorcycle is tilted over at an angle of 55° on 1999-2000 models or 45° on 2001 models, for more than one second, the ignition system is shut off. Once the sensor is activated, the motorcycle must be placed upright and the ignition turned OFF and then ON again. Once this is done, the ignition system is operational and the engine can be restarted.

Electrical diagrams of the ignition systems are shown in **Figures 34-38** for 1999-2001 models. Refer to the wiring diagrams at the end of the manual for 2002-on models.

Ignition Coil

Performance test

1. Disconnect the plug wire and remove one of the spark plugs as described in Chapter Three.

NOTE

A spark tester is a useful tool for testing the ignition system's spark output. ***Figure 39*** *shows the Motion Pro Ignition System Tester (part No. 08-0122). This tool is inserted in the spark plug cap and its base is grounded against the cylinder head. The tool's air gap is adjustable, and it allows the visual inspection of the spark while testing the intensity of the spark.*

33

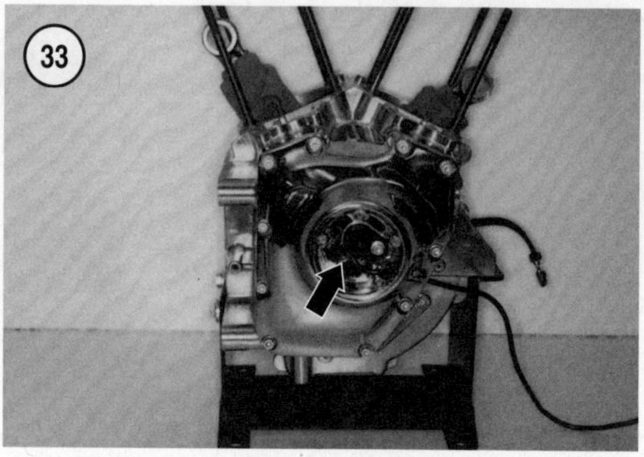

2. Insert a clean shop cloth into the spark plug hole in the cylinder head to lessen the chance of gasoline vapors being emitted from the hole.

3. Insert the spark plug (**Figure 40**), or spark tester (**Figure 41**), into its cap and touch the spark plug base against the cylinder head to ground it. Position the spark plug so the electrode is visible.

NOTE

If not using a spark tester, always use a new spark plug for this test procedure.

WARNING

Mount the spark plug, or tester, away from the spark plug hole in the cylinder so that the spark or tester cannot ignite the gasoline vapors in the cylinder. If the engine is flooded, do not perform this test. The firing of the spark plug can ignite fuel that is ejected through the spark plug hole.

4. Turn the engine over with the electric starter. A fat blue spark should be evident across the spark plug electrode. If there is strong sunlight on the plug, shade the plug so the spark is more visible. Repeat for the other cylinder.

WARNING

If necessary, hold onto the spark plug wire with a pair of insulated pliers. Do ***not*** *hold the spark plug, wire or connector or a serious electrical shock may result.*

5. If a fat blue spark occurs, the ignition coil is good. If not, perform the following resistance test.

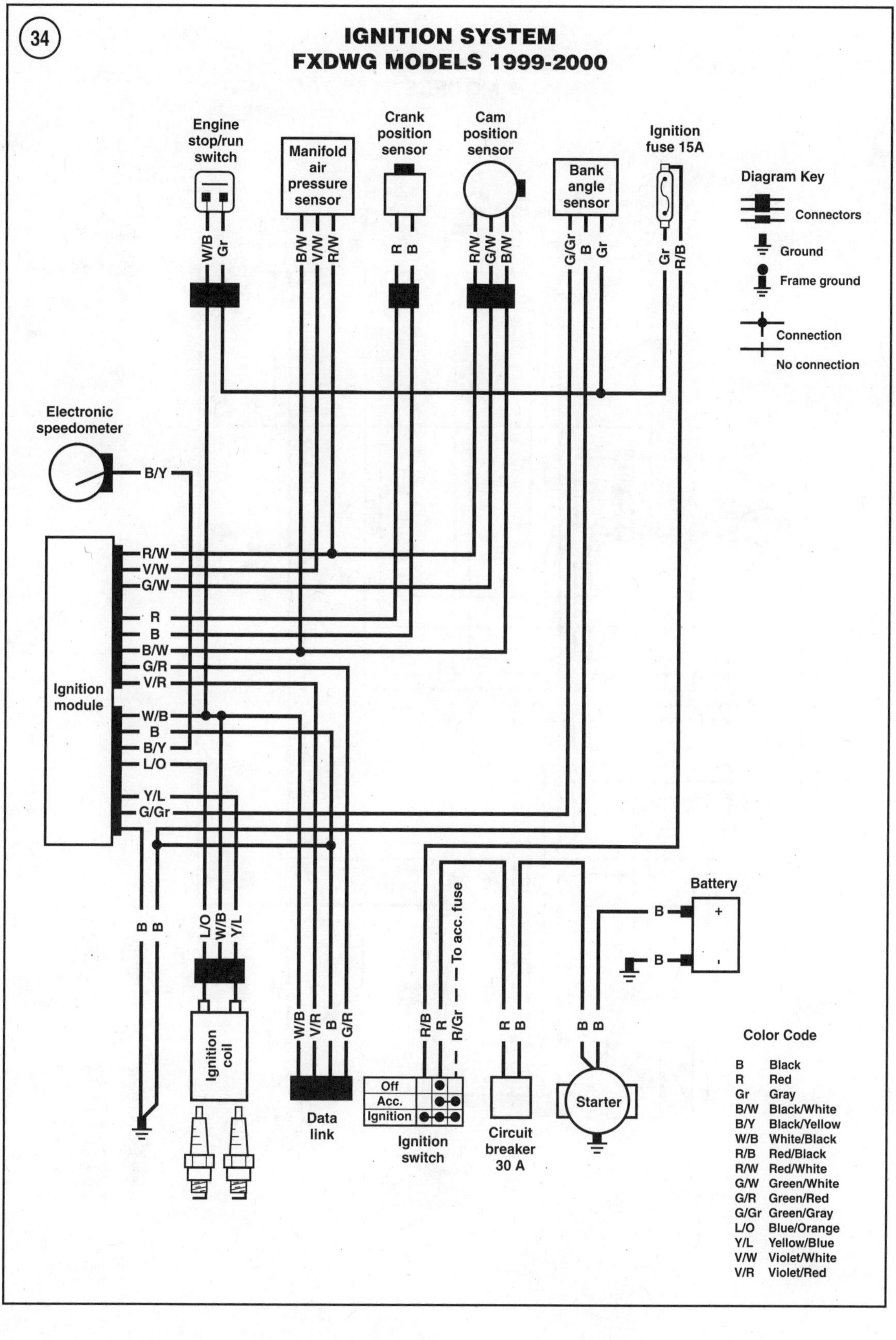
34
IGNITION SYSTEM
FXDWG MODELS 1999-2000
Engine stop/run switch
W/B
Gr
Manifold air pressure sensor
B/W
V/W
R/W
Crank position sensor
R
B
Cam position sensor
R/W
G/W
B/W
Bank angle sensor
G/Gr
B
Gr
Ignition fuse 15A
Gr
R/B
Diagram Key
Connectors
Ground
Frame ground
Connection
No connection
Electronic speedometer
B/Y
Ignition module
R/W
V/W
G/W
R
B
B/W
G/R
V/R
W/B
B
B/Y
L/O
Y/L
G/Gr
B
B
L/O
W/B
Y/L
Ignition coil
W/B
V/R
B
G/R
Data link
R/B
R
R/Gr
To acc. fuse
Off
Acc.
Ignition
Ignition switch
R
B
Circuit breaker 30 A
B
B
Starter
Battery
B
+
B
-
Color Code
B Black
R Red
Gr Gray
B/W Black/White
B/Y Black/Yellow
W/B White/Black
R/B Red/Black
R/W Red/White
G/W Green/White
G/R Green/Red
G/Gr Green/Gray
L/O Blue/Orange
Y/L Yellow/Blue
V/W Violet/White
V/R Violet/Red

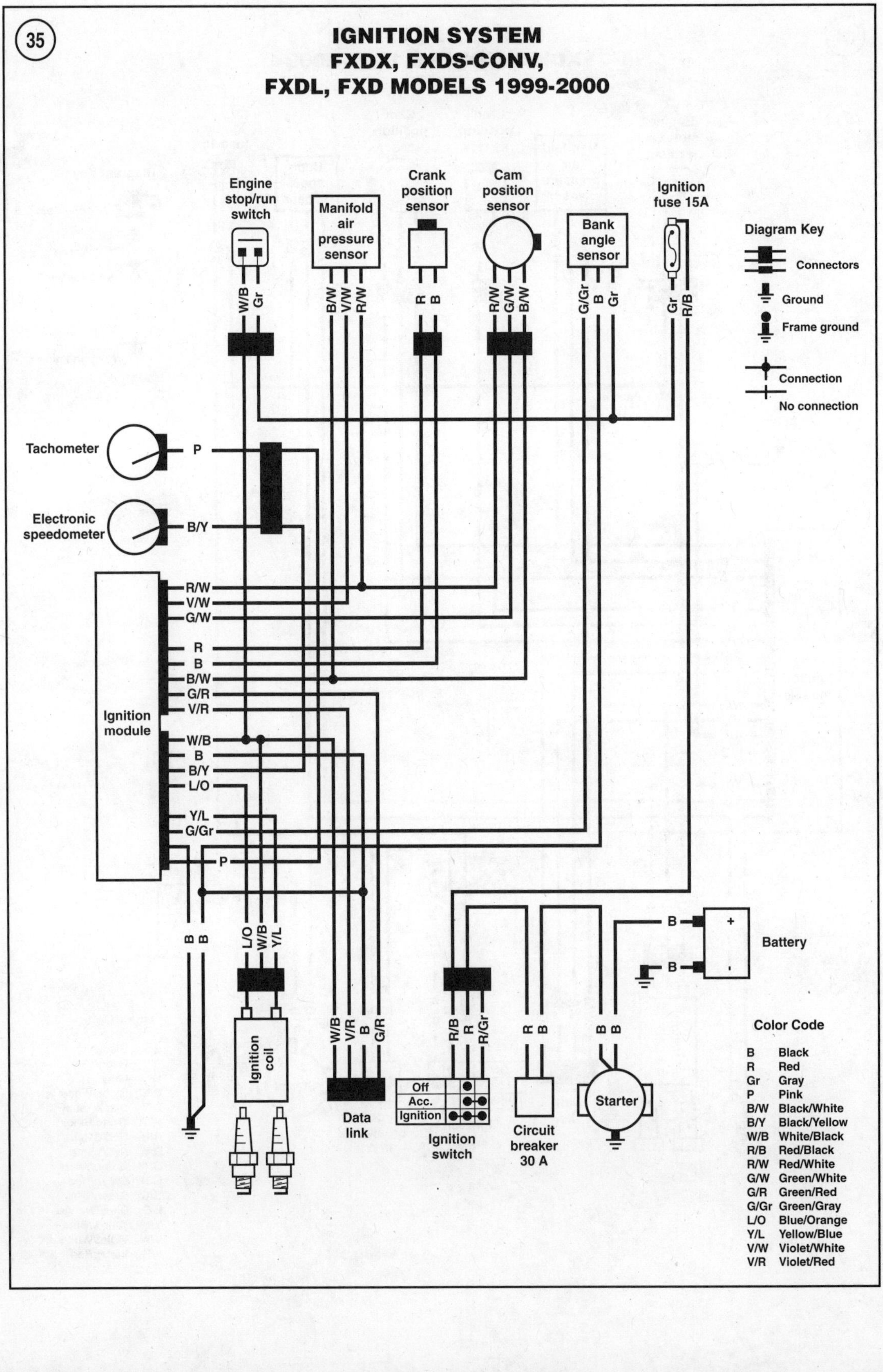
35
IGNITION SYSTEM
FXDX, FXDS-CONV,
FXDL, FXD MODELS 1999-2000
Engine stop/run switch
Manifold air pressure sensor
Crank position sensor
Cam position sensor
Bank angle sensor
Ignition fuse 15A
Diagram Key
Connectors
Ground
Frame ground
Connection
No connection
Tachometer
Electronic speedometer
Ignition module
Ignition coil
Data link
Off
Acc.
Ignition
Ignition switch
Circuit breaker 30 A
Starter
Battery
Color Code
B Black
R Red
Gr Gray
P Pink
B/W Black/White
B/Y Black/Yellow
W/B White/Black
R/B Red/Black
R/W Red/White
G/W Green/White
G/R Green/Red
G/Gr Green/Gray
L/O Blue/Orange
Y/L Yellow/Blue
V/W Violet/White
V/R Violet/Red

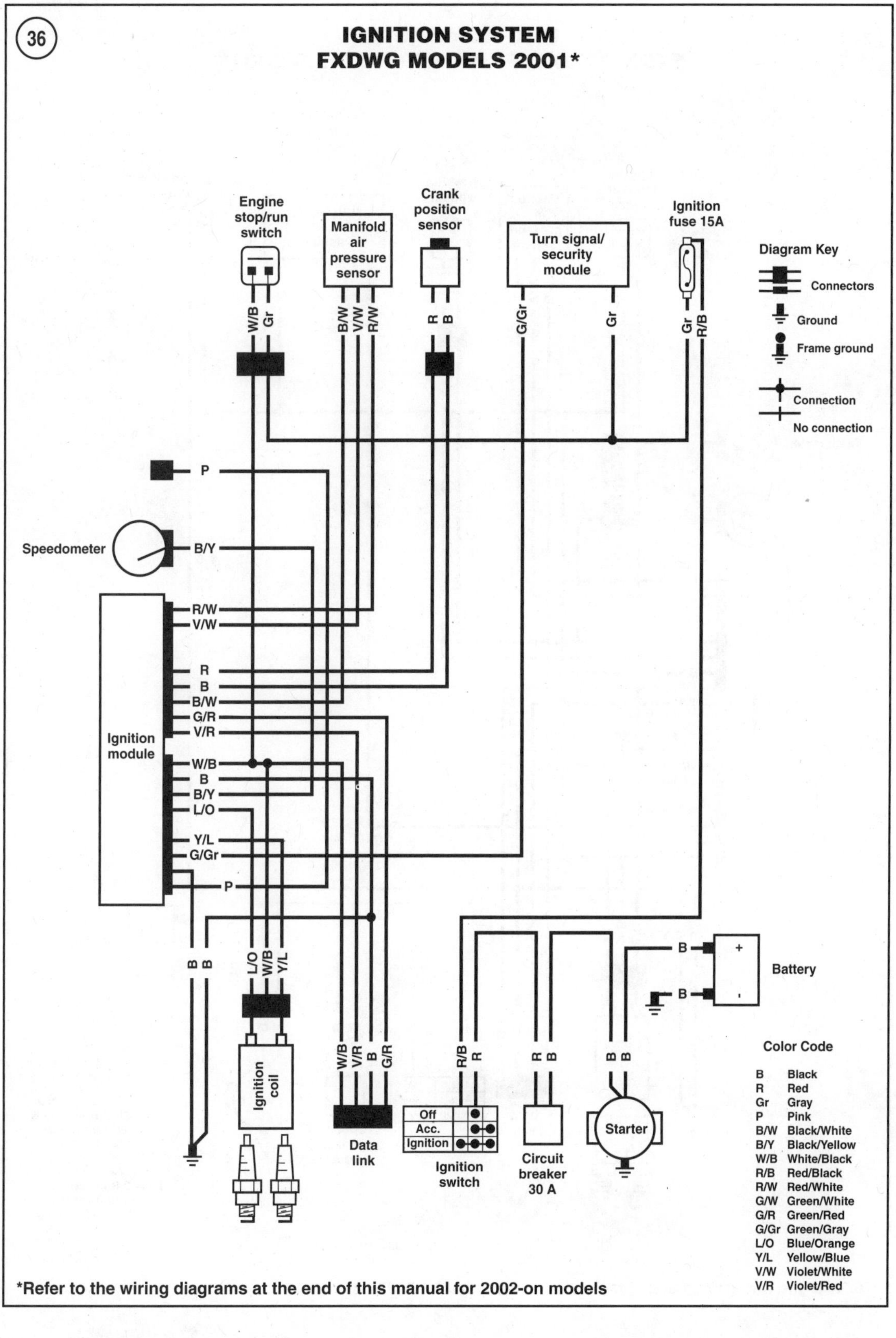
36
IGNITION SYSTEM
FXDWG MODELS 2001*
Engine stop/run switch
Manifold air pressure sensor
Crank position sensor
Turn signal/ security module
Ignition fuse 15A
Diagram Key
Connectors
Ground
Frame ground
Connection
No connection
W/B Gr
B/W V/W R/W
R B
G/Gr
Gr
Gr R/B
P
Speedometer
B/Y
Ignition module
R/W
V/W
R
B
B/W
G/R
V/R
W/B
B
B/Y
L/O
Y/L
G/Gr
P
B B
L/O W/B Y/L
Ignition coil
W/B V/R B G/R
Data link
Off
Acc.
Ignition
Ignition switch
R/B R
R B
Circuit breaker 30 A
B B
Starter
B
B
Battery
Color Code
B Black
R Red
Gr Gray
P Pink
B/W Black/White
B/Y Black/Yellow
W/B White/Black
R/B Red/Black
R/W Red/White
G/W Green/White
G/R Green/Red
G/Gr Green/Gray
L/O Blue/Orange
Y/L Yellow/Blue
V/W Violet/White
V/R Violet/Red
*Refer to the wiring diagrams at the end of this manual for 2002-on models

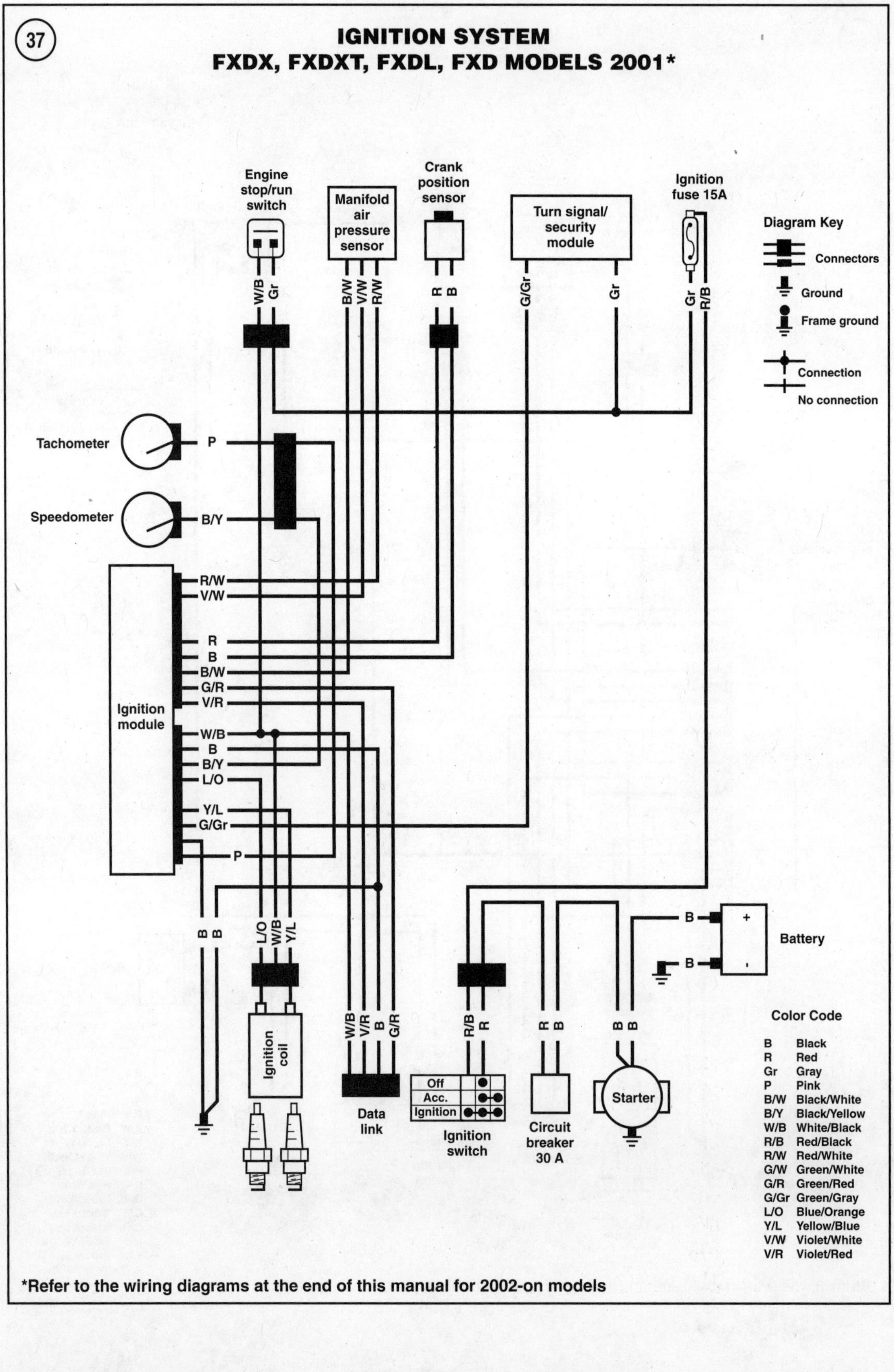
37
IGNITION SYSTEM
FXDX, FXDXT, FXDL, FXD MODELS 2001*
Engine stop/run switch
Manifold air pressure sensor
Crank position sensor
Turn signal/ security module
Ignition fuse 15A
Diagram Key
Connectors
Ground
Frame ground
Connection
No connection
W/B
Gr
B/W
V/W
R/W
R
B
G/Gr
Gr
Gr
R/B
Tachometer
P
Speedometer
B/Y
Ignition module
R/W
V/W
R
B
B/W
G/R
V/R
W/B
B
B/Y
L/O
Y/L
G/Gr
P
B
B
L/O
W/B
Y/L
Ignition coil
W/B
V/R
B
G/R
Data link
R/B
R
Off
Acc.
Ignition
Ignition switch
R
B
Circuit breaker 30 A
B
B
Starter
B
B
Battery
+
-
Color Code
B Black
R Red
Gr Gray
P Pink
B/W Black/White
B/Y Black/Yellow
W/B White/Black
R/B Red/Black
R/W Red/White
G/W Green/White
G/R Green/Red
G/Gr Green/Gray
L/O Blue/Orange
Y/L Yellow/Blue
V/W Violet/White
V/R Violet/Red
*Refer to the wiring diagrams at the end of this manual for 2002-on models

38

IGNITION SYSTEM
FXDP MODELS 2001-2004

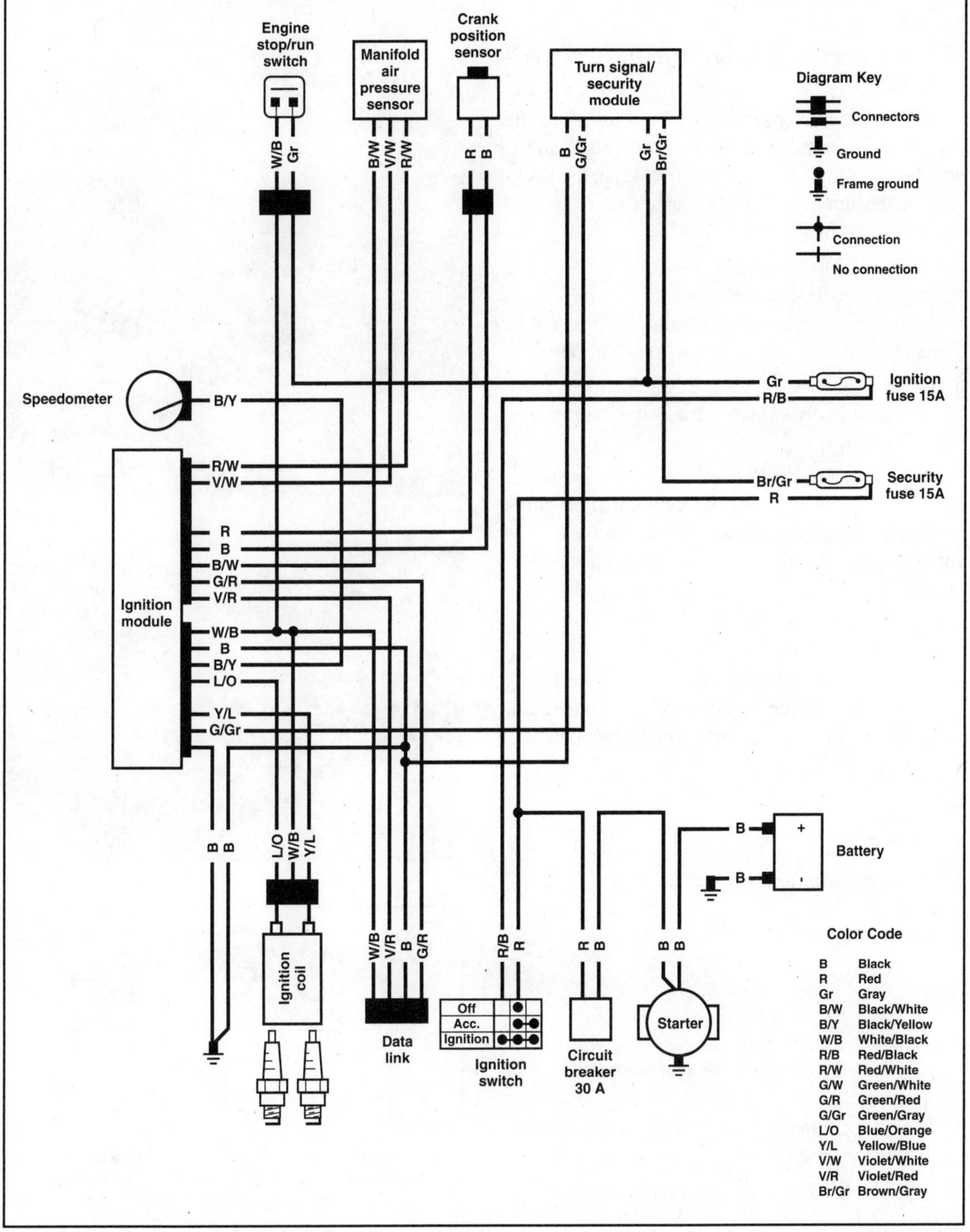

Resistance test

NOTE
Refer to the ***Basic Information*** *section at the beginning of this chapter.*

1. Remove the ignition coil as previously described.
2. Disconnect the secondary wires from the ignition coil.
3. Use an ohmmeter set at R × 1 and measure the primary coil resistance between terminals A and B and then terminals B and C (**Figure 42**) at the backside of the ignition coil. The specified resistance value is listed in **Table 1**.
4. Using an ohmmeter set at R × 1000, measure the secondary coil resistance between the spark plug leads of the secondary coil terminals (**Figure 42**). The specified resistance value is listed in **Table 1**.
5. If the resistance values are less than specified, there is most likely a short in the coil windings. Replace the coil.
6. If the resistance values are more than specified, this may indicate corrosion or oxidation of the coil's terminals. Thoroughly clean the terminals, then spray with an aerosol electrical contact cleaner. Repeat Step 3 and Step 4 and if the resistance value is still high, replace the coil.
7. If the coil resistance does not meet (or come close to) either of these specifications, the coil must be replaced. If the coil exhibits visible damage, it should be replaced as described in this chapter.
8. Install the ignition coil as described in this chapter.

Removal/installation

Refer to **Figure 43**.

NOTE
Always disarm the optional TSSM security system prior to disconnecting the battery or the siren will sound.

1. Disconnect the negative battery cable as described in this chapter.
2. Remove the fuel tank as described in Chapter Seven.

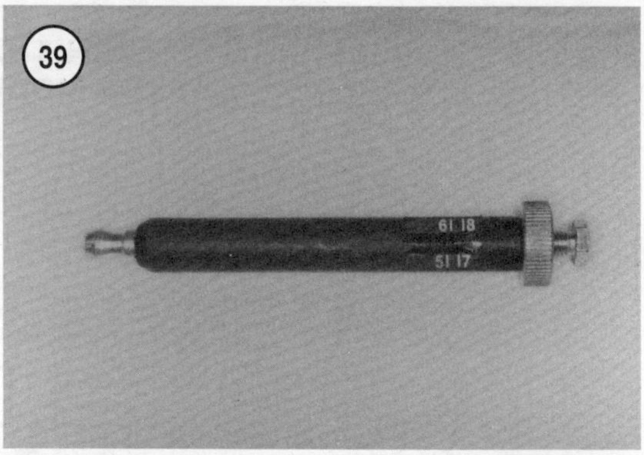

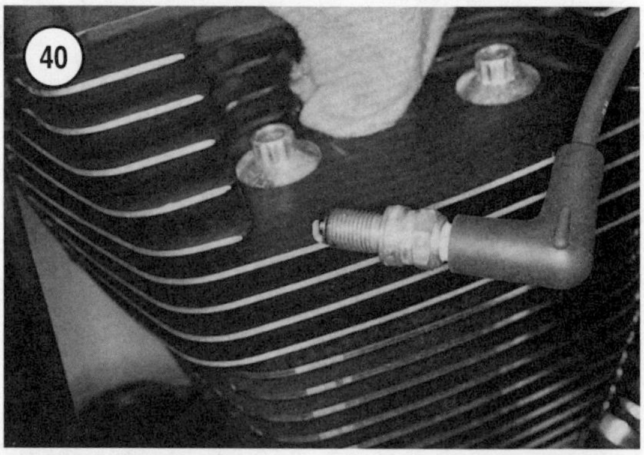

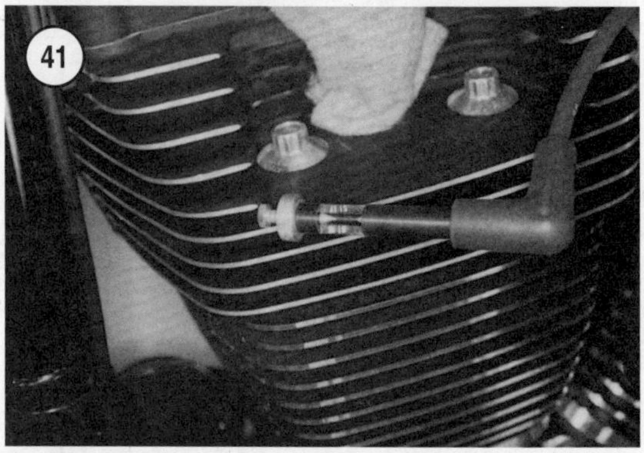

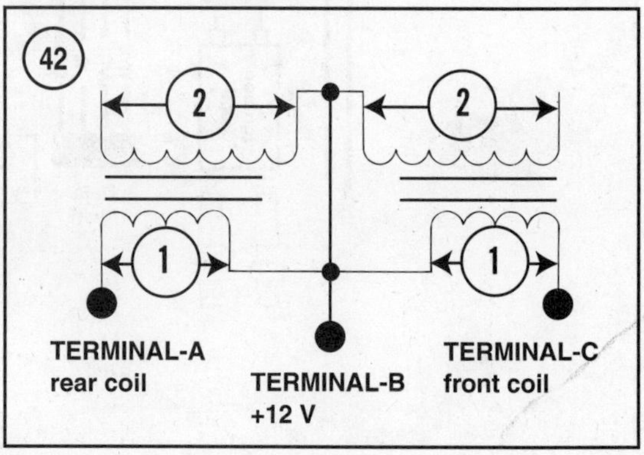

(43) **IGNITION SYSTEM COMPONENTS**

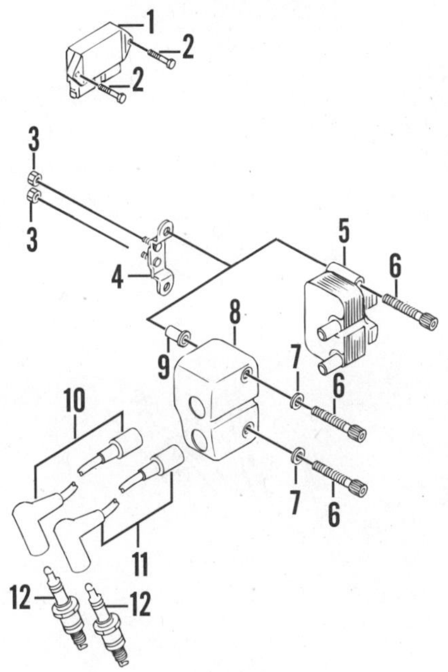

1. Ignition module
2. Screw
3. Nut
4. Bracket
5. Ignition coil
6. Allen bolt
7. Washer
8. Cover (on models so equipped)
9. Collar
10. Spark plug cable–rear cylinder
11. Spark plug cable–front cylinder
12. Spark plugs

(44)

(45)

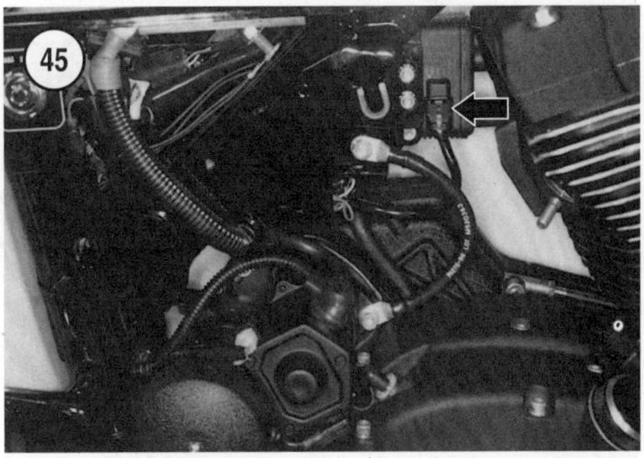

NOTE
Label all wiring connectors prior to disconnecting them in the following steps.

3. Disconnect the secondary lead (A, **Figure 44**) from each spark plug.
4. Disconnect the front cylinder's secondary lead from the clip on the frame.
5. Disconnect the primary wire connector (**Figure 45**) from the backside of the ignition coil.
6A. On models with a chrome cover, remove the Allen bolts and washers securing the ignition coil and cover to the frame.
6B. On all other models, remove the Allen bolts (B, **Figure 44**) securing the ignition coil to the frame.
7. Remove the ignition coil (C, **Figure 44**).
8. Install the ignition coil by reversing these steps.

Ignition Module Removal/Installation

The ignition module mounts behind the electric panel cover, on the left side of the motorcycle.

NOTE
Always disarm the optional TSSM security system prior to disconnecting the battery or the siren will sound.

1. Disconnect the negative battery cable as described in this chapter.
2. Refer to *Electrical Panel* in this chapter and remove the outer and inner panel to gain access to the ignition module.
3. Remove the two screws securing the ignition module to the backside of the inner panel.
4. Disconnect the 12-pin black and 12-pin gray electrical connectors from the ignition module.

46

INTAKE MANIFOLD

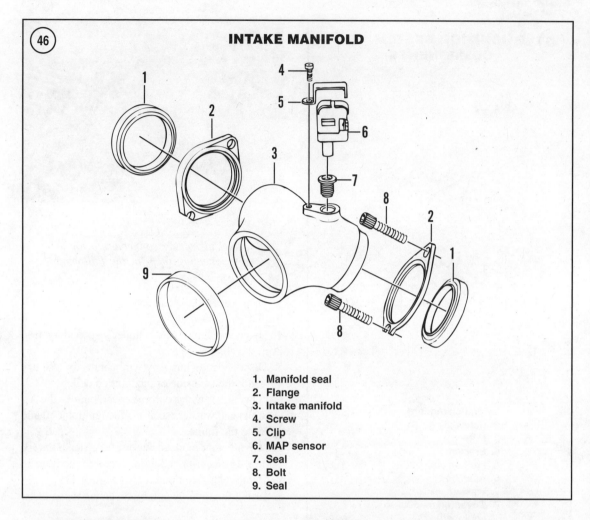

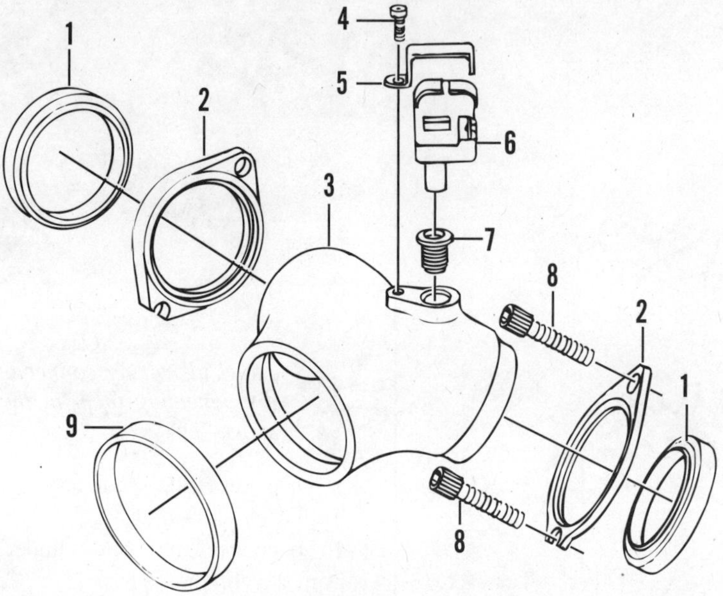

1. Manifold seal
2. Flange
3. Intake manifold
4. Screw
5. Clip
6. MAP sensor
7. Seal
8. Bolt
9. Seal

5. Remove the ignition module.

6. Install the ignition module by reversing these steps while noting the following:

   a. Apply a light coat of dielectric compound to the electrical connectors prior to installing them.

   b. Make sure the electrical connectors are pushed tightly onto the ignition module.

Manifold Absolute Pressure (MAP) Sensor Removal/Installation

The MAP sensor (**Figure 32**) is located on top of the intake manifold. Refer to **Figure 46**.

NOTE
Always disarm the optional TSSM security system prior to disconnecting the battery or the siren will sound.

1. Disconnect the negative battery cable as described in this chapter.

2. Remove the fuel tank as described in Chapter Seven.

3. Remove the carburetor as described in Chapter Seven. Place a lint-free shop cloth into the intake manifold opening (A, **Figure 47**) to prevent the entry of debris.

4. Remove the screw and clip (B, **Figure 47**) securing the MAP sensor to the top of the intake manifold.

5. Pull the MAP sensor (C, **Figure 47**) straight up out of the seal in the intake manifold.

6. Disconnect the electrical connector from the MAP sensor and remove the sensor.

7. Install the MAP sensor by reversing these steps while noting the following:

   a. Apply a light coat of dielectric compound to the electrical connector prior to installing it.

47

48

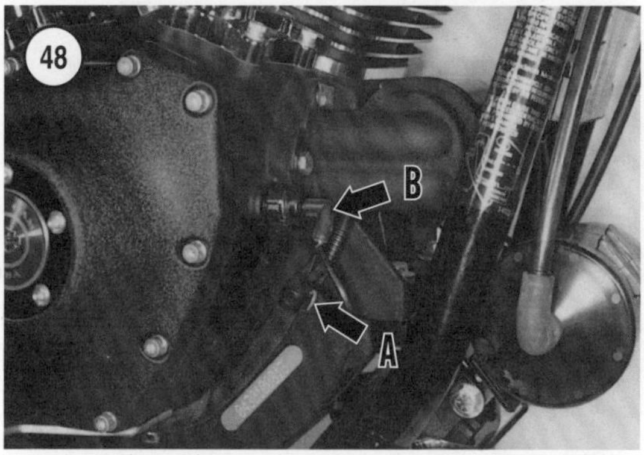

49

50

b. Make sure the electrical connector is pushed tightly onto the MAP sensor.
c. If necessary, replace the seal in the intake manifold.

Crankshaft Position Sensor (CKP)

Sensor Removal/installation

The crankshaft position sensor (CKP) (**Figure 31**) is mounted on the front left side of the crankcase next to the oil filter.

The CKP and the oil pressure switch are included in one wiring harness. If one of the components is defective, both must be replaced.

1. Remove the seat as described in Chapter Thirteen.

NOTE
Always disarm the optional TSSM security system prior to disconnecting the battery or the siren will sound.

2. Disconnect the negative battery cable as described in this chapter.
3. Remove the fuel tank as described in Chapter Seven.
4. Remove the exhaust system as described in Chapter Seven.
5. Remove the T20 Torx screw, then open the clamp (A, **Figure 48**) securing the electrical harness to the engine.
6. Disconnect the single green/yellow wire from the oil pressure switch (B, **Figure 48**).
7. Remove the Allen screw and withdraw the CKP sensor (**Figure 49**) and O-ring from the crankcase.
8. Move the CKP sensor and wiring over the right side of the engine.

NOTE
*The following electrical connector(s) are not visible in **Figure 50** as they are located under the frame cross-member.*

9A. On 1999 models, the following Mini-Deutsch connector, located under the seat, must be disconnected. The single connector has three wires with one red, one black and one green/yellow wire.

9B. On 2000-on models, the following Mini-Deutsch connectors, located under the seat, must be disconnected:

8

a. CKP connector has two wires with one red and one black wire.
b. Oil pressure connector has a single green/yellow wire.

10. Carefully pull the electrical connector(s), noted in Step 9, out from under the frame cross-member. Disconnect the secondary locks on the Mini-Deutsch connector(s) (**Figure 50**) and disconnect the connector(s).
11. Tie a piece of string to the electrical connector(s). Tie the other end of the string to the frame cross-member. If necessary, make a drawing of the wire routing through the frame. It is easy to forget the routing path after removing the wire.
12. Carefully pull the wiring harness, connector(s) and string out of the frame on the right side. If the wire becomes tight or stuck, do not force it.
13. Untie the string from the wiring harness.
14. Install by reversing these removal steps while noting the following:

a. Tie the string to the wiring harness and connector(s).
b. Carefully pull the string and the wiring harness and connector(s) through the right side of the frame and into position under the seat. Untie and remove the string.
c. Apply a light coat of dielectric compound to the electrical connector(s) prior to installing them.
d. Apply clean engine oil to the *new* O-ring on the CKP sensor prior to installation. Install the sensor and tighten the Allen screw to the specification in **Table 6**.

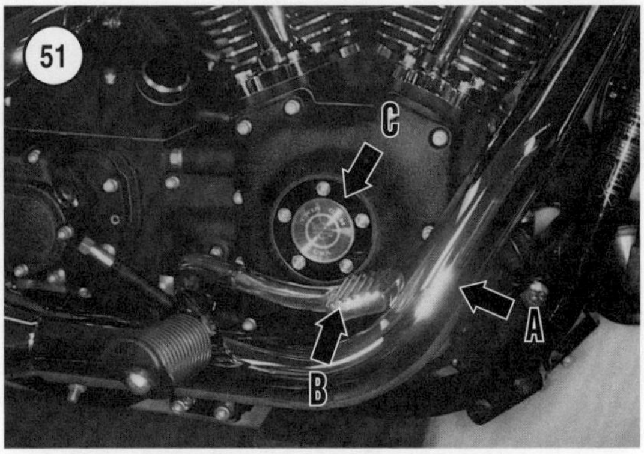

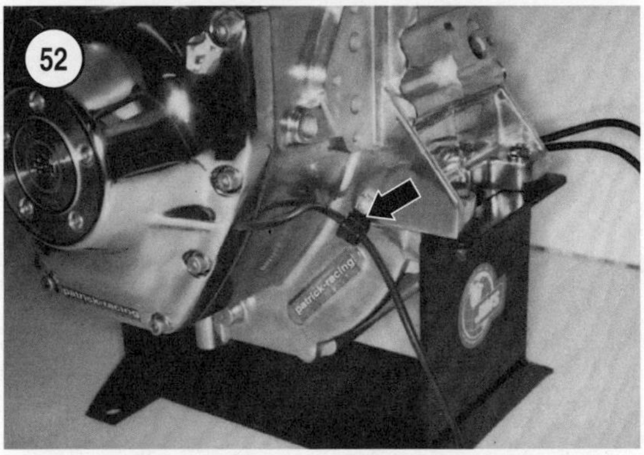

Camshaft Position Sensor (CMP) (1999-2000) Removal/installation

The camshaft position sensor (CMP) (**Figure 33**) is located in the camshaft cover on the right side of the crankcase.

1. Remove the seat as described in Chapter Thirteen.

NOTE
Always disarm the optional TSSM security system prior to disconnecting the battery or the siren will sound.

2. Disconnect the negative battery cable as described in this chapter.
3. The following Mini-Deutsch connector, located under the seat, must be disconnected. The single connector has three wires with one red/white, one black/white and one green/white wire.

NOTE
*The electrical Mini-Deutsch connector is not visible in **Figure 50**. It is located under the frame cross-member.*

4. Carefully pull the electrical connector out from under the frame cross-member. Disconnect the secondary locks on the Mini-Deutsch connector (**Figure 50**).

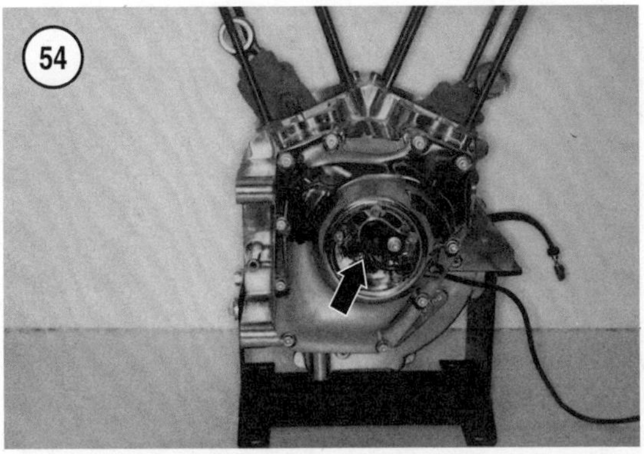

5. Note the location of each of the three individual wires within the Mini-Deutsch connector, then disconnect the three wires.

6. Tape a piece of string to the three individual electrical wires in the harness. Tie the other end of the string to the frame cross-member. If necessary, make a drawing of the wire routing through the frame. It is easy to forget the routing path after removing the wire.

7. Carefully pull the wiring harness out of the frame on the right side. If the wire becomes tight or stuck, do not force it.

8. Untie the string from the wiring harness, but leave it within the frame.

9. Remove the exhaust system (A, **Figure 51**) as described in Chapter Seven.

10. Tie the rear brake pedal (B, **Figure 51**) down to gain access to the inspection cover (C, **Figure 51**) on the camshaft cover.

NOTE

The following photographs are shown with the engine removed and partially disassembled to better illustrate the steps.

11. Remove the screw and clamp (**Figure 52**) securing the wiring harness to the crankcase.

12. Remove the T20 Torx screws securing the inspection cover (**Figure 53**) and remove the cover.

13. Tie a different piece of string onto the end of the wiring harness.

14. Remove the screw and washer securing the CMP sensor (**Figure 54**) to the camshaft cover. Remove the sensor and O-ring from the cover.

NOTE

***Figure 55** is shown with the camshaft cover removed to better illustrate the step.*

15. Carefully pull the electrical harness, along with the piece of string, out through both openings in the camshaft cover (**Figure 55**).

16. Untie the string and retie it to the new CMP sensor wiring harness.

17. Carefully pull the new wiring harness back through the two openings in the camshaft cover (**Figure 55**). Untie and remove the string.

18. Apply a light coat of new engine oil to the CMP sensor O-ring.

19. Carefully push the new sensor into place in the camshaft cover and install the screw and washer. Tighten the screw to the specification in **Table 6**.

20. Tie the piece of string onto the end of the new CMP sensor wire harness.

21. Carefully pull the string and the wiring harness and connectors through the right side of the frame and into position under the seat. Untie and remove the string.

22. Apply a light coat of dielectric compound to the electrical connectors prior to connecting them.

23. Refer to the notes made in Step 5 and connect the three individual wires into the correct location within the Mini-Deutsch connector. Lock the secondary lock on the Mini-Deutsch connector.

24. Install the inspection cover and the T20 Torx screws. Tighten the screw to the specification in **Table 6**.

25. Install the exhaust system as described in Chapter Seven.

26. Unhook the rear brake pedal.

27. Install the seat

Bank Angle (BAS) Sensor (1999-2000) Removal/installation

The bank angle sensor mounts onto a frame-mounted panel behind the electric panel, on the left side of the motorcycle.

NOTE
*The bank angle sensor is an integral part of the turn signal module/turn signal security module (TSM/TSSM) on the 20001 models. This sensor is covered under **Turn Signal Module** in this chapter.*

1. Remove the seat as described in Chapter Thirteen.

NOTE
Always disarm the optional TSSM security system prior to disconnecting the battery or the siren will sound.

2. Disconnect the negative battery cable as described in this chapter.
3. Remove the screw securing the bank angle sensor to the backside of the frame panel.
4. Carefully disconnect the 3-pin electrical connector (**Figure 56**) containing one black wire, one gray wire and one light green/gray wire.
5. Remove the bank angle sensor.
6. Install the bank angle sensor by reversing these steps while noting the following:
   a. Apply a light coat of dielectric compound to the electrical connector prior to installing it.
   b. Make sure the electrical connector is pushed tightly onto the bank angle sensor.

STARTING SYSTEM

Electrical diagrams of the starting systems are shown in **Figures 57-61** for 1999-2001 models. Refer to the wiring diagrams at the end of the manual for 2002-on models.

CAUTION
Do not operate the starter for more than five seconds at a time. Let it cool approximately 10 seconds before operating it again.

56

Troubleshooting

Refer to Chapter Two.

Starter Removal

1. Remove the seat as described in Chapter Thirteen.

NOTE
Always disarm the optional TSSM security system prior to disconnecting the battery or the siren will sound.

2. Disconnect the negative battery cable as described in this chapter.
3. Remove the primary cover as described in Chapter Five.

NOTE
The following photographs are shown with the clutch assembly removed to better illustrate the steps.

4. Straighten the tab on the lockplate (**Figure 62**).
5. Wrap the pinion gear with a cloth to protect the finish, then secure it with locking pliers (A, **Figure 63**).
6. Loosen and remove the bolt (B, **Figure 63**), lockplate and thrust washer from the starter jackshaft assembly at the end of the starter motor.
7. Remove the rear exhaust pipe as described in Chapter Seven.
8. Remove the bolt and the cover (A, **Figure 64**) from the end of the starter motor.
9. Disconnect the solenoid electrical connector (B, **Figure 64**) from the starter motor.

57

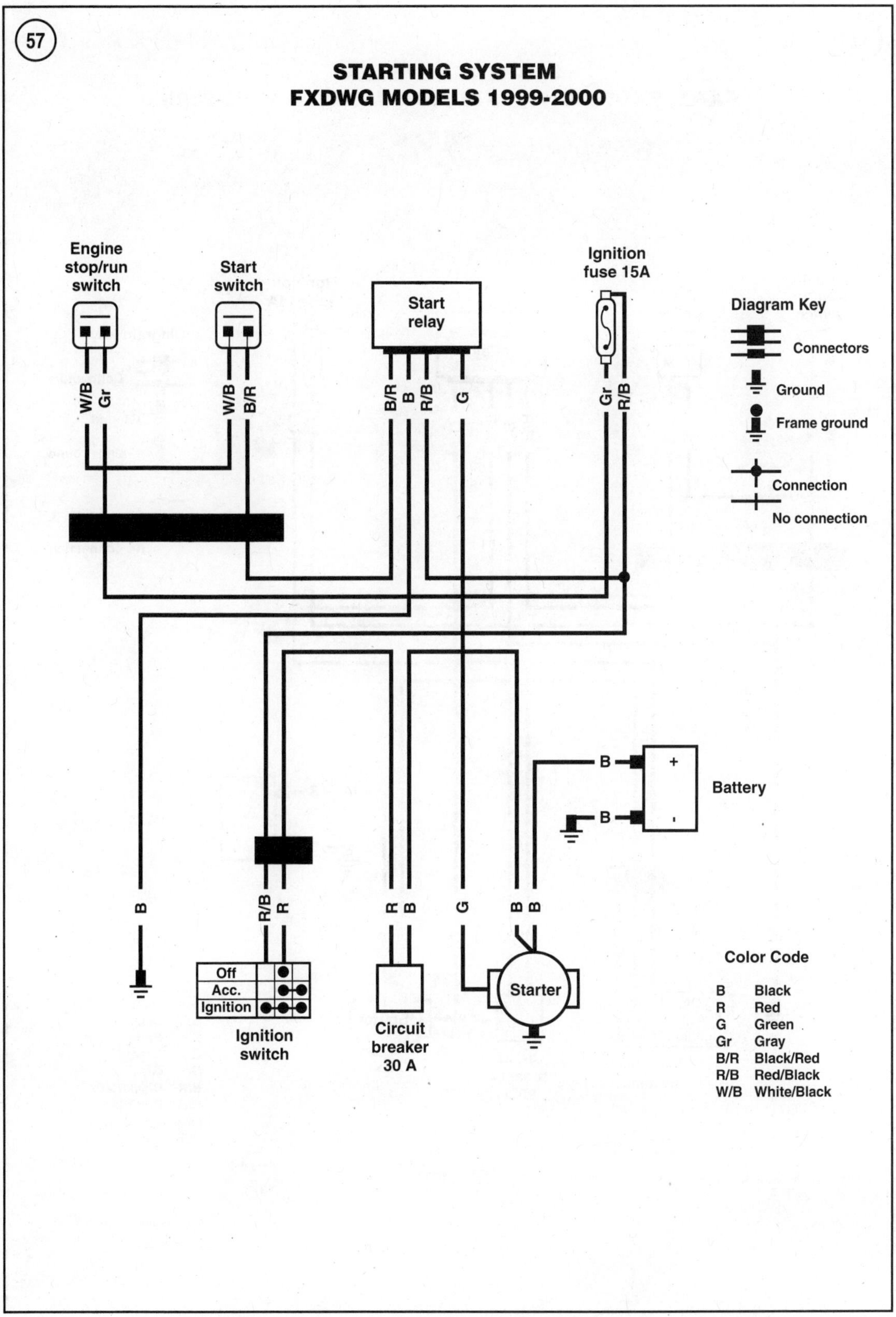

STARTING SYSTEM
FXDWG MODELS 1999-2000
Engine stop/run switch
Start switch
Start relay
Ignition fuse 15A
Diagram Key
Connectors
Ground
Frame ground
Connection
No connection
W/B
Gr
W/B
B/R
B/R
B
R/B
G
Gr
R/B
B
B
Battery
B
R/B
R
R
B
G
B
B
Off
Acc.
Ignition
Ignition switch
Circuit breaker 30 A
Starter
Color Code
B Black
R Red
G Green
Gr Gray
B/R Black/Red
R/B Red/Black
W/B White/Black

58

STARTING SYSTEM
FXDX, FXDS-CONV, FXDL, FXD MODELS 1999-2000

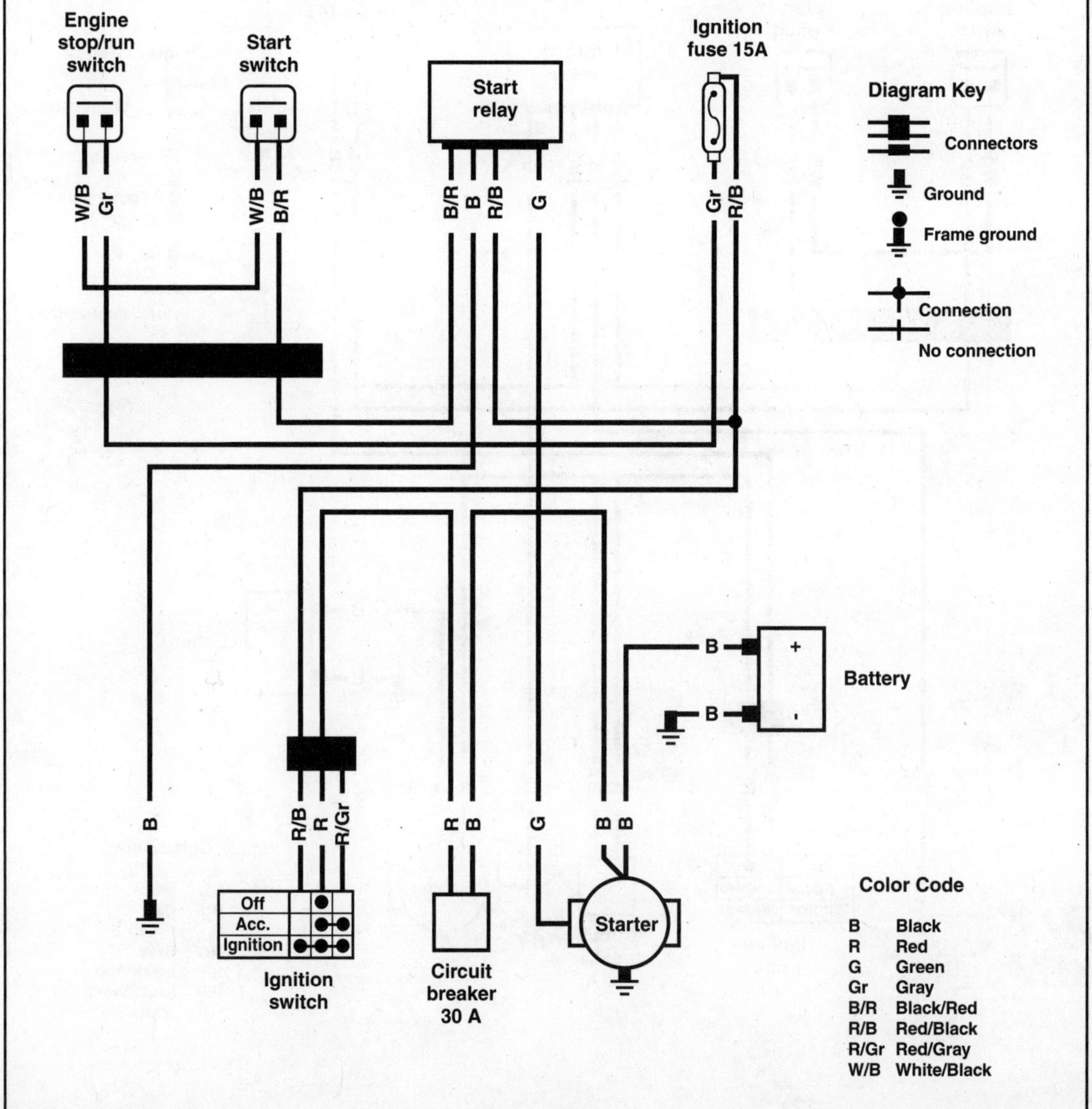

59

STARTING SYSTEM
FXDWG MODELS 2001*

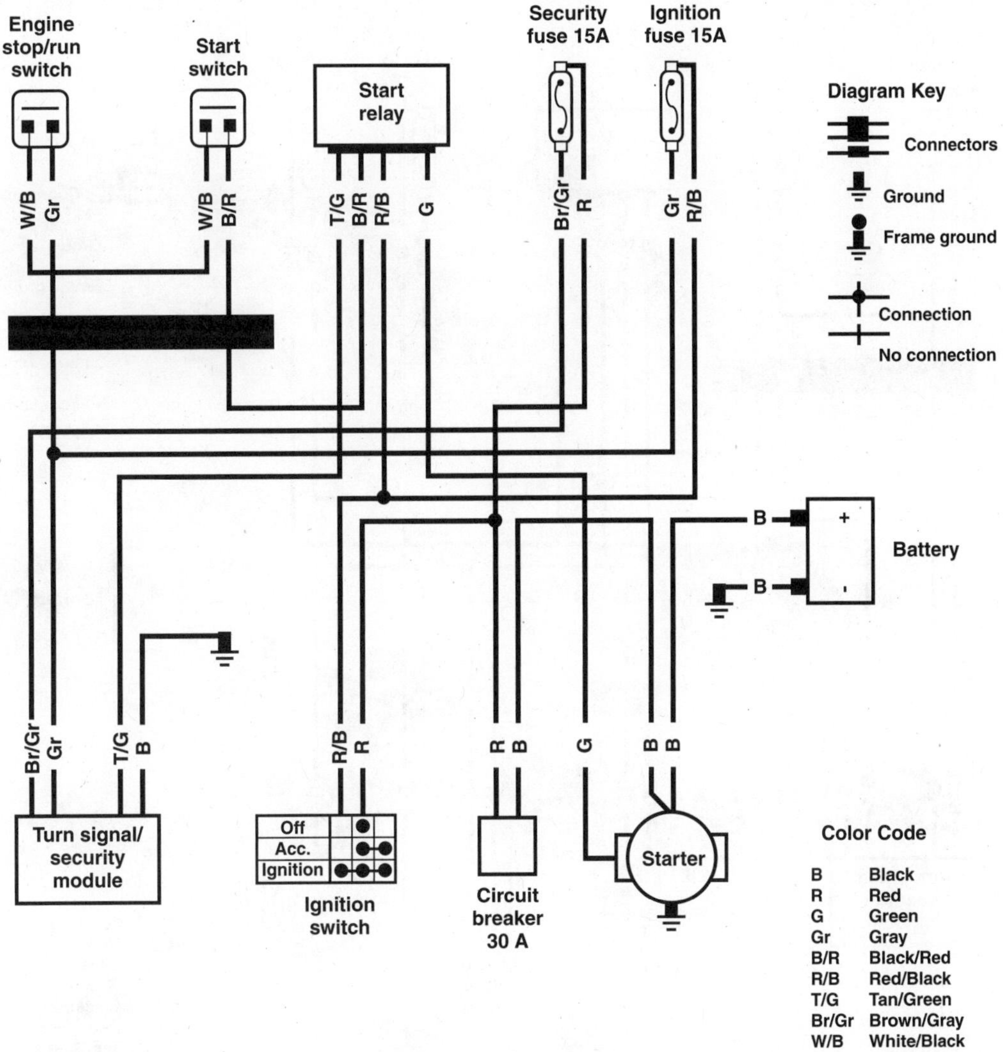

*Refer to the wiring diagrams at the end of this manual for 2002-on models

STARTING SYSTEM
FXDX, FXDL, FXDXT, FXD MODELS 2001*

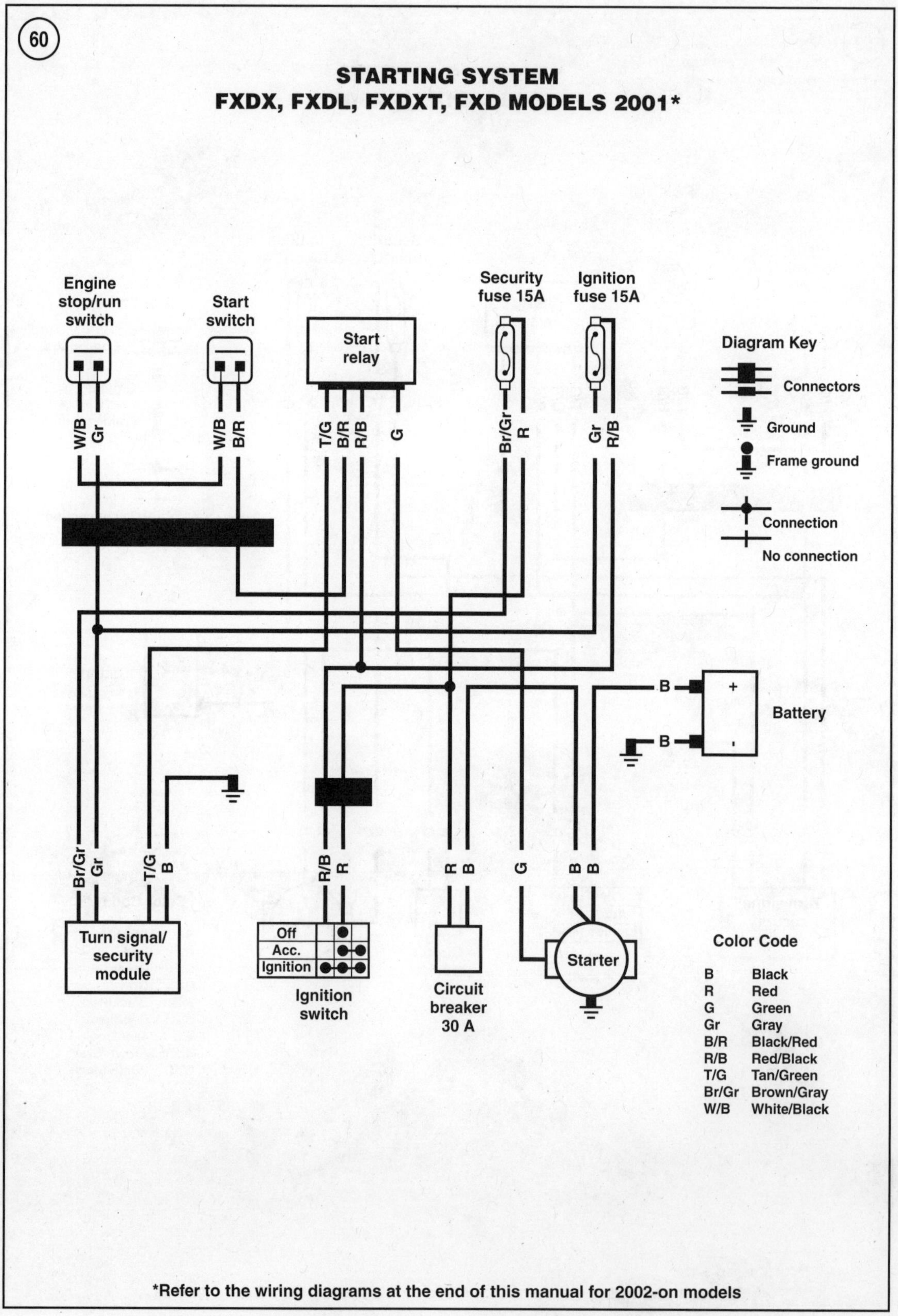

*Refer to the wiring diagrams at the end of this manual for 2002-on models

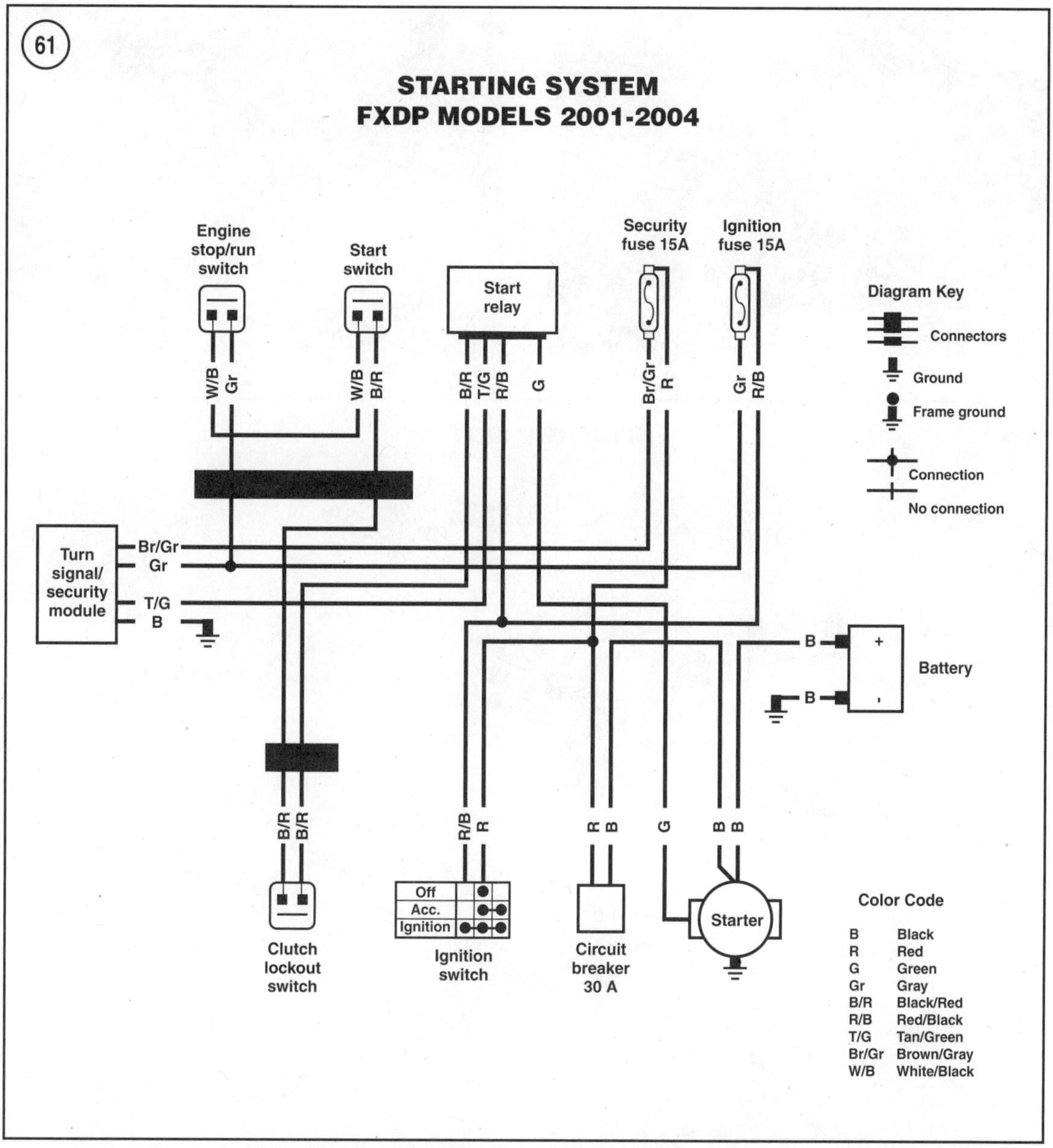

61

STARTING SYSTEM
FXDP MODELS 2001-2004

Engine stop/run switch

Start switch

Start relay

Security fuse 15A

Ignition fuse 15A

Diagram Key

Connectors

Ground

Frame ground

Connection

No connection

W/B Gr

W/B B/R

B/R T/G R/B G

Br/Gr R

Gr R/B

Turn signal/ security module

Br/Gr
Gr
T/G
B

B

B

Battery

+

-

B/R B/R

R/B R

R B

G

B B

Clutch lockout switch

Off		●	
Acc.		●	●
Ignition	●	●	●

Ignition switch

Circuit breaker 30 A

Starter

Color Code

B	Black
R	Red
G	Green
Gr	Gray
B/R	Black/Red
R/B	Red/Black
T/G	Tan/Green
Br/Gr	Brown/Gray
W/B	White/Black

8

62

63

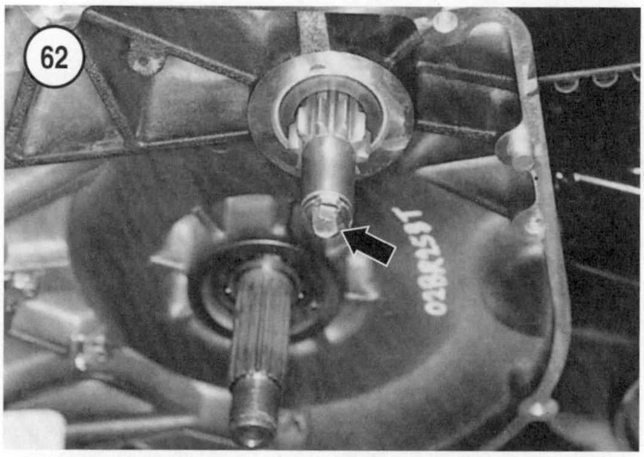

64

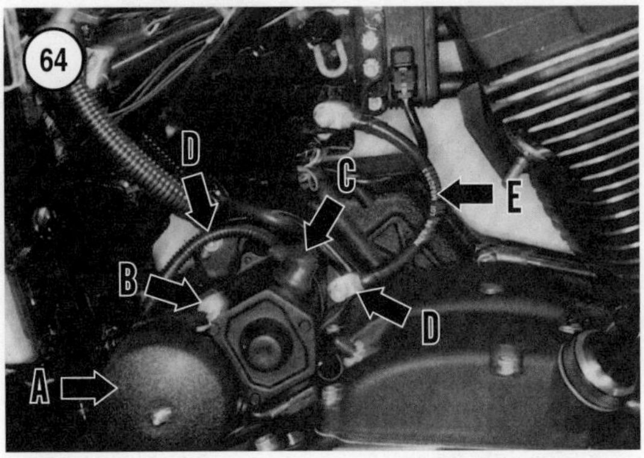

65

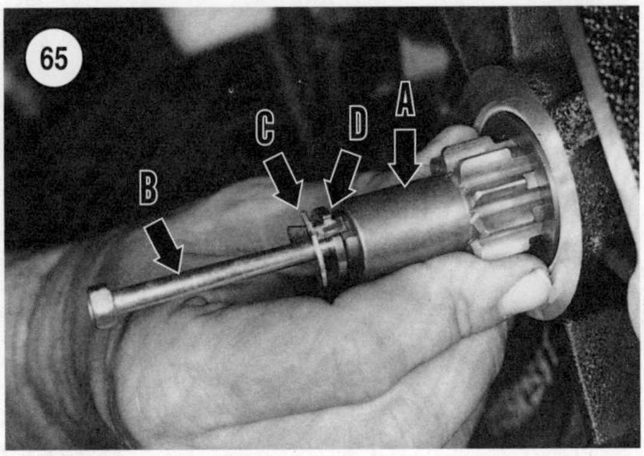

66

STARTER MOTOR

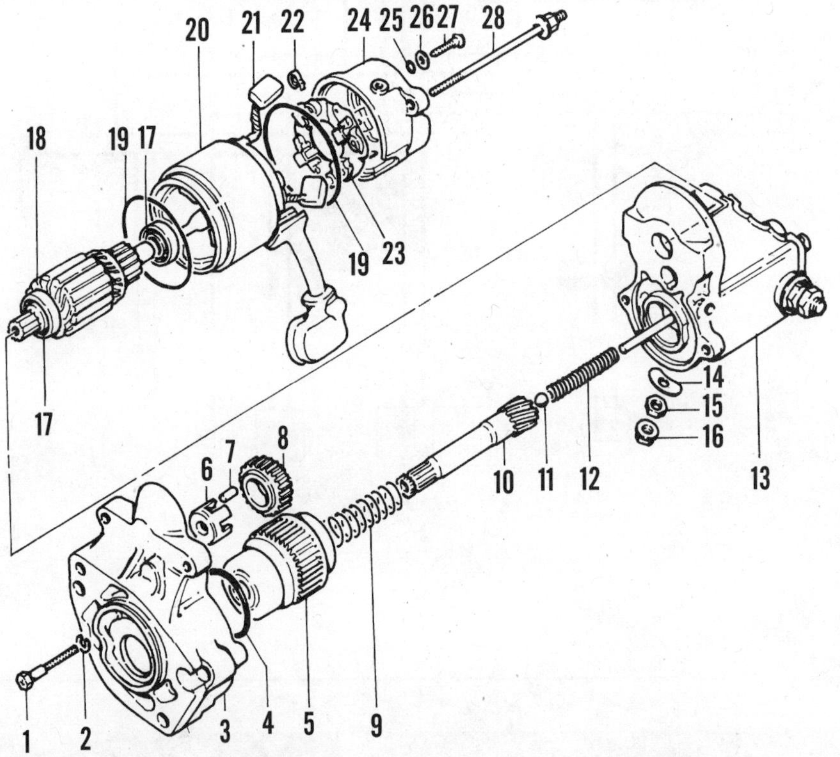

1. Screw
2. Lockwasher
3. Drive housing
4. O-ring
5. Drive assembly
6. Idler gear bearing
7. Bearing rollers (5)
8. Idler gear
9. Drive spring
10. Clutch shaft
11. Ball
12. Return spring
13. Solenoid housing
14. Tab
15. Nut
16. Nut
17. Bearing
18. Armature
19. O-ring
20. Field coil assembly
21. Brushes
22. Brush springs
23. Brush holder
24. End cap
25. O-ring
26. Washer
27. Screw
28. Through bolt

67

68

10. Slide back the rubber boot, remove the nut and disconnect the positive cable (C, **Figure 64**) from the starter motor terminal.

11. Remove the starter motor mounting bolts and washers (D, **Figure 64**). Note the location of the negative ground cable (E) under the front bolt and washer.

12. Pull the starter motor straight out of the crankcase and remove it.

13. If necessary, service the starter motor as described in this chapter.

Installation

1. If the jackshaft coupling was removed or if it was removed after the starter motor was removed, install the coupling (A, **Figure 65**) onto the jackshaft before installing the starter motor.

2. Install the starter motor straight into the crankcase from the right side. Carefully engage the starter motor shaft with the jackshaft coupling.

3. Install the starter motor mounting bolts and washers (D, **Figure 64**). Be sure to install the negative ground cable (E) under the front bolt and washer. Tighten the bolts to the specification in **Table 6**.

4. Connect the solenoid electrical connector (B, **Figure 64**) onto the starter motor.

5. Connect the positive cable (C, **Figure 64**) onto the starter motor terminal and tighten the nut to the specification in **Table 6**. Slide the rubber boot back over the connection.

6. Install the cover and the bolt (A, **Figure 64**) onto the end of the starter motor. Tighten the bolt securely.

7. Install the bolt (B, **Figure 65**), lockplate (C), and thrust washer (D) through the pinion gear (A) and onto the jackshaft.

8. Align the lockplate tab with the thrust washer, then insert the tab into the notch in the end of the jackshaft.

9. Screw the bolt into the starter motor shaft by hand.

10. Wrap the pinion gear with a cloth to protect the finish, then secure it with locking pliers (A, **Figure 63**).

11. Tighten the bolt (B, **Figure 63**) onto the starter motor to the specification in **Table 6**. Bend the outer lockplate tab against the bolt head (**Figure 62**).

12. Install the primary cover as described in Chapter Five.

13. Install the rear exhaust pipe as described in Chapter Seven.

14. Connect the negative battery cable.

15. Install the seat.

Disassembly

Refer to **Figure 66**.

NOTE
*If only the solenoid assembly requires service, refer to **Solenoid Housing** in this chapter.*

1. Clean all grease, dirt and carbon from the exterior of the starter assembly.

2. Remove the two through bolts (**Figure 67**).

3. Remove the two drive housing Phillips screws (**Figure 68**) and lockwashers.

4. Tap the drive housing and remove it from the starter assembly (**Figure 69**).

5. Disconnect the C terminal field wire (A, **Figure 70**) from the solenoid housing.

8

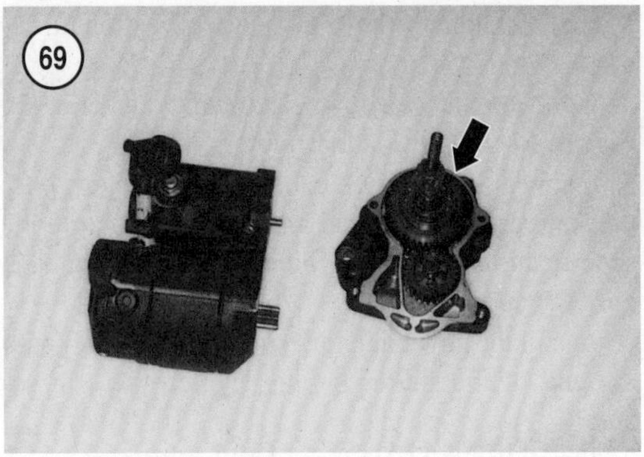

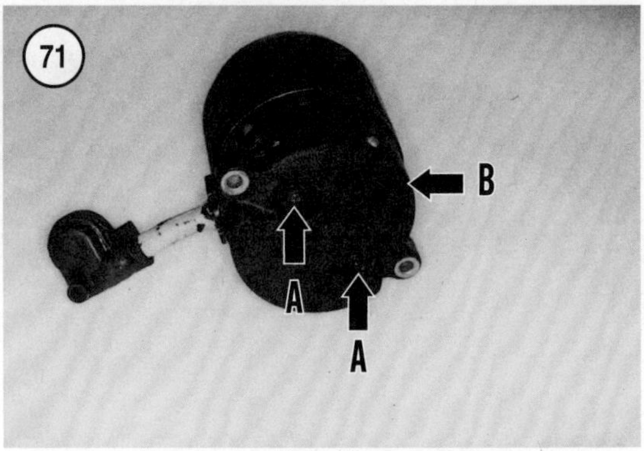

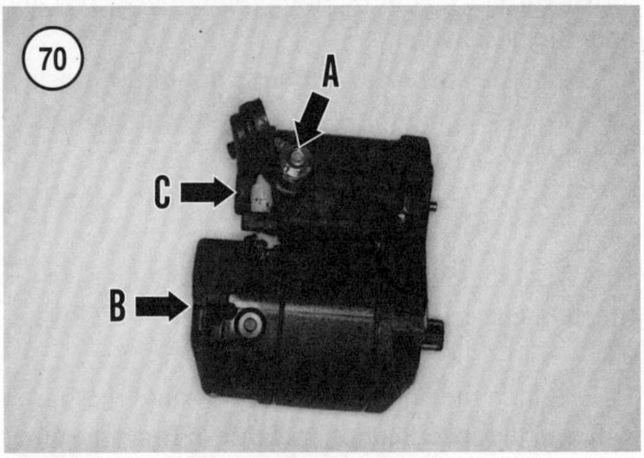

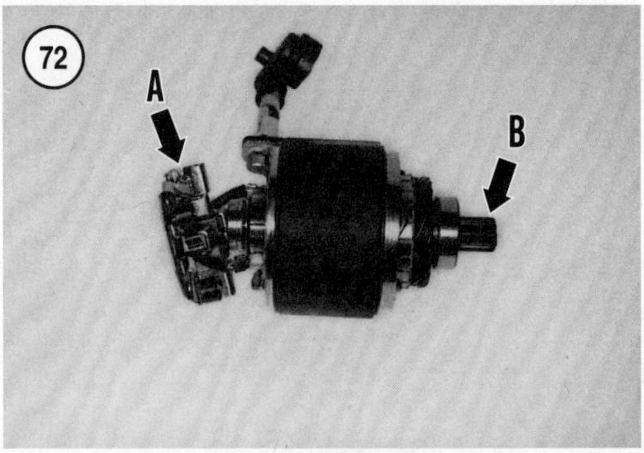

6. Separate the field coil (B, **Figure 70**) from the solenoid housing (C).

7. Remove the end cap screws, washers and O-rings (A, **Figure 71**). Then remove the end cap (B).

8. Pull the brush holder (A, **Figure 72**) away from the commutator and remove the armature (B) from the field coil assembly.

9. Remove the two field coil brushes from the brush holder (**Figure 73**).

10. Clean all grease, dirt and carbon from the armature, field coil assembly and end covers.

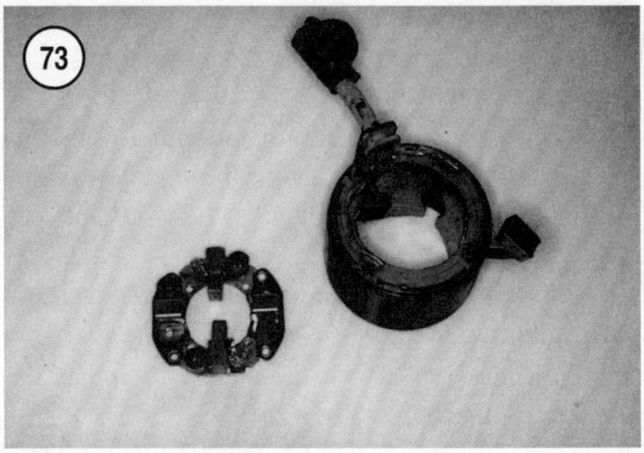

CAUTION

Be extremely careful when selecting a solvent to clean the electrical components. Do not immerse any of the wire windings in solvent, because the insulation may be damaged. Wipe the windings with a cloth lightly moistened with solvent, then allow the solution to dry thoroughly.

11. To service the drive housing assembly, refer to *Drive Housing Disassembly/Inspection/Assembly* in this chapter.

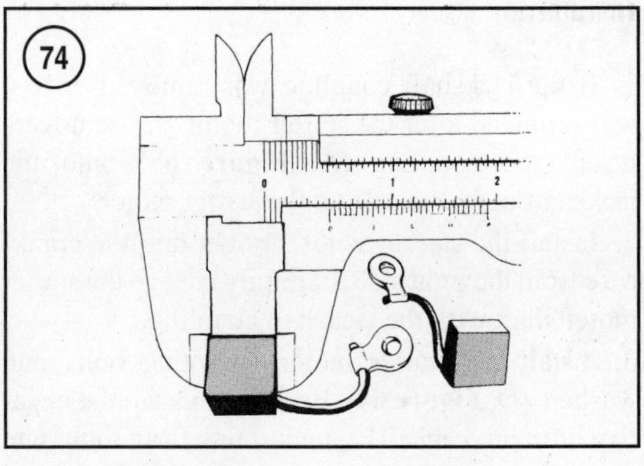

75

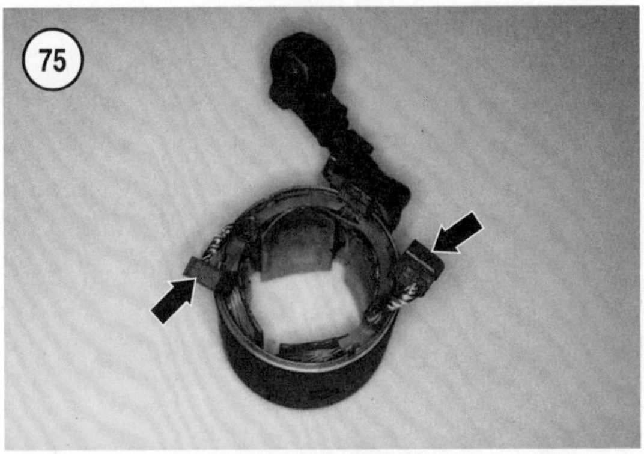

76

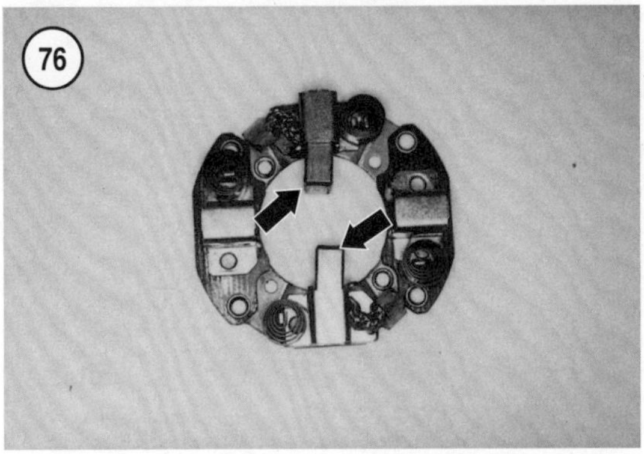

77

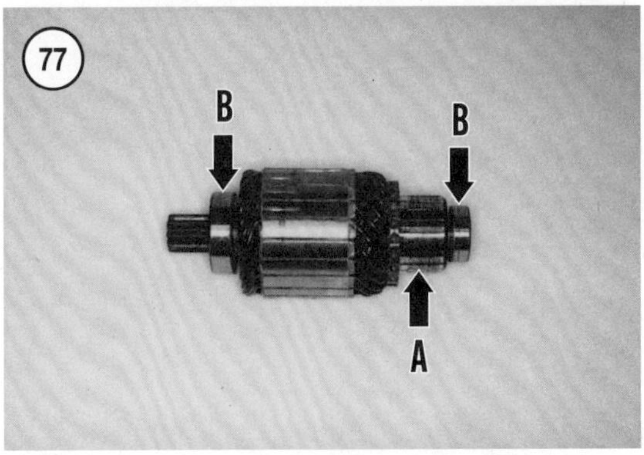

78

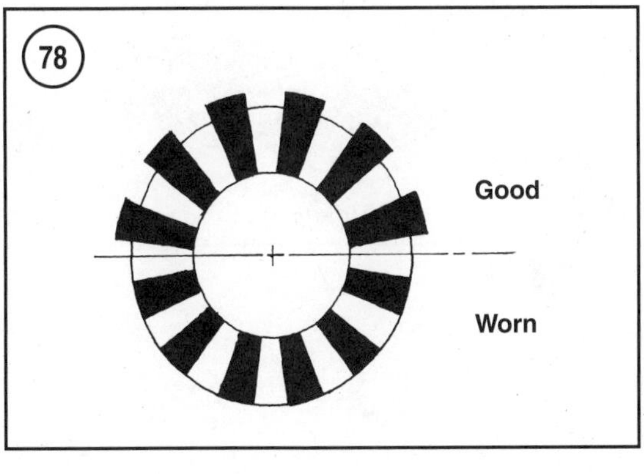

79

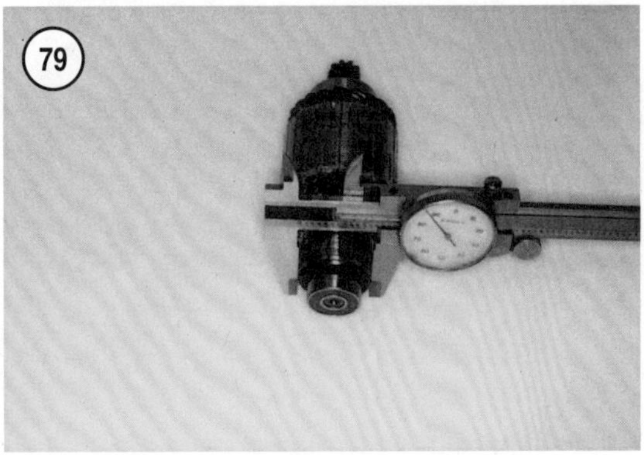

12. To service the solenoid housing, refer to *Solenoid Housing Disassembly/Inspection/Assembly* in this chapter.

Inspection

1. Measure the length of each brush with a vernier caliper (**Figure 74**). If the length is less than the minimum specified in **Table 4**, replace all of the brushes as a set. See **Figure 75** for the field coil and **Figure 76** for the brush holder.

NOTE

*The field coil brushes (**Figure** 75) are soldered in position. To replace, unsolder the brushes by heating their joints with a soldering gun, then pull them out with a pair of pliers. Position the new brushes and solder in place with rosin core solder—do not use acid core solder.*

2. Inspect the commutator (A, **Figure 77**). The mica should be below the surface of the copper commutator segments (**Figure 78**). If the commutator bars are worn to the same level as the mica insulation, have the commutator serviced by a dealership or electrical repair shop.

3. Inspect the commutator copper segments for discoloration. If the commutator segments are rough, discolored or worn, have the commutator serviced by a dealership or electrical repair shop.

4. Measure the outer diameter of the commutator with a vernier caliper (**Figure 79**). Replace the armature if worn to the service limit listed in **Table 4**.

5. Use an ohmmeter to perform the following:

80

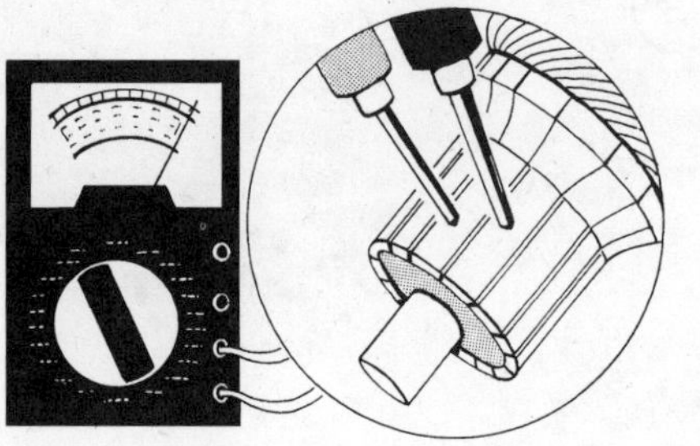

81

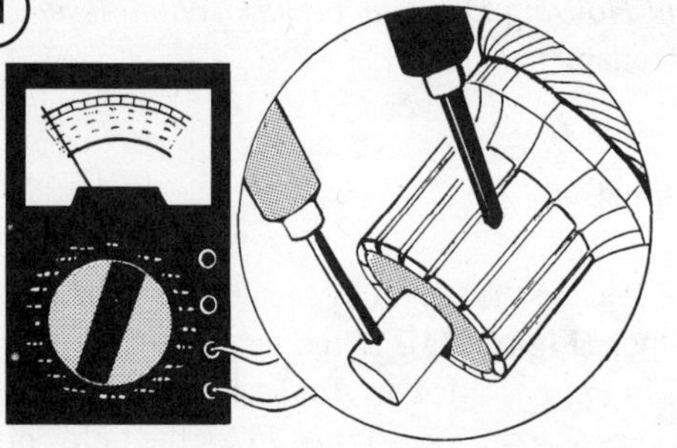

82

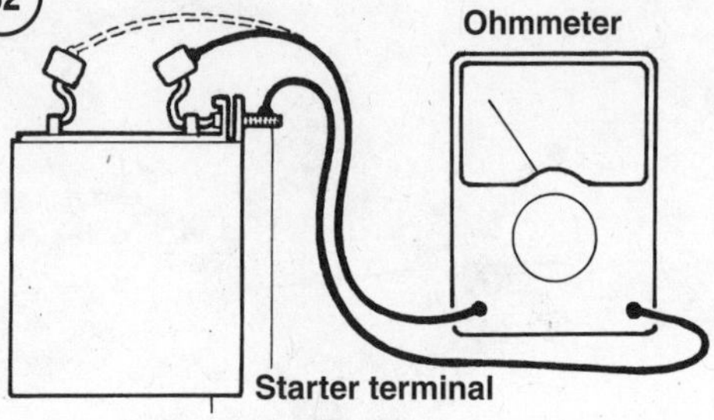

83

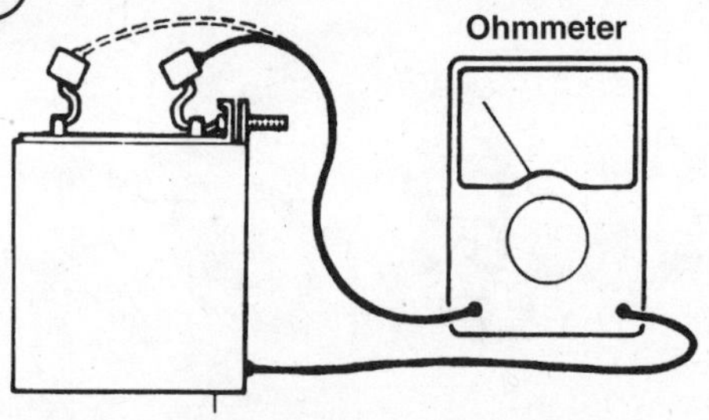

a. Check for continuity between the commutator bars (**Figure 80**); there must be continuity between pairs of bars.

b. Check for continuity between any commutator bar and the shaft (**Figure 81**). There must be no continuity.

c. If the unit fails either of these tests, replace the armature.

6. Use an ohmmeter to perform the following:

a. Check for continuity between the starter cable terminal and each field frame brush (**Figure 82**); there must be continuity.

b. Check for continuity between the field frame housing and each field frame brush (**Figure 83**); there must be no continuity.

c. If the unit fails either of these tests, replace the field frame assembly.

7. Use an ohmmeter and check for continuity between the brush holder plate and each brush holder (**Figure 84**); there must be no continuity. If the unit fails this test, replace the brush holder plate.

8. Service the armature bearings as follows:

a. Check the bearings (B, **Figure 77**) on the armature shaft. Replace worn or damaged bearings.

84

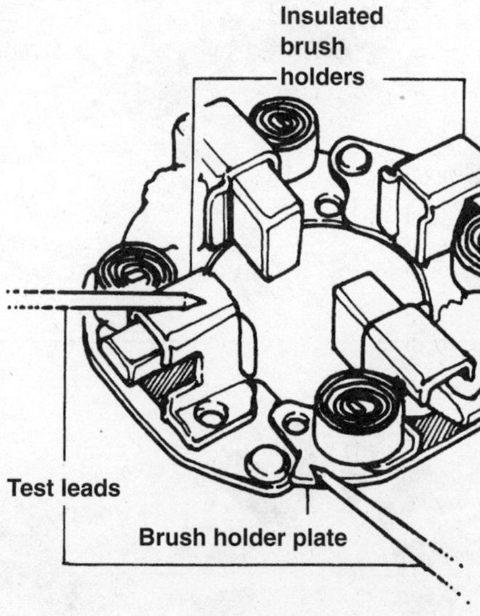

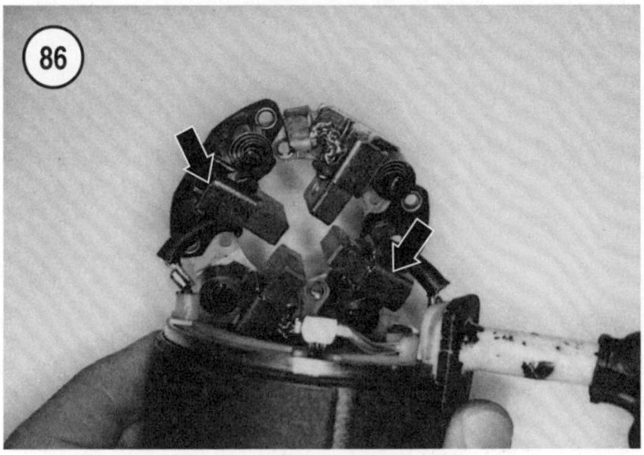

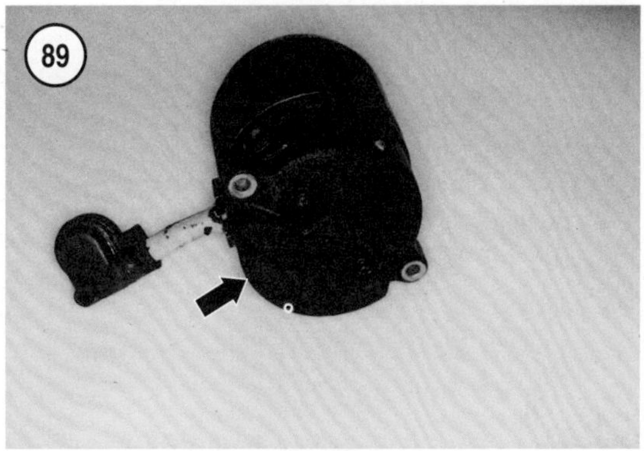

NOTE
The armature shaft bearings have different part numbers. Identify the old bearings before removing them.

b. Check the bearing bores in the end cover and solenoid housing. Replace the cover or housing if the area is worn or cracked.

Assembly

Refer to **Figure 66**.

1. If serviced, assemble the drive housing as described in this chapter.
2. If serviced, assemble the solenoid housing as described in this chapter.
3. Lubricate the armature bearings (B, **Figure 77**) with high-temperature grease.
4. Install two *new* O-rings onto the field coil shoulders (**Figure 85**).
5. Install the two field coil brushes into the brush plate holders (**Figure 86**).
6. Install the armature partially through the field coil as shown in **Figure 72**. Then pull the brushes back and push the armature forward so that when released, all of the brushes contact the commutator as shown in **Figure 87** and **Figure 88**.
7. Install the end cap (**Figure 89**) and the two screws, washers and O-rings. Tighten the screws securely.
8. Align the field coil (A, **Figure 90**) with the solenoid housing (B) and assemble both housings. Hold the assembly together while installing the drive housing in Step 9.
9. Align the drive housing (**Figure 91**) with the field coil and solenoid housing assembly and install it. Install the two drive housing screws and lockwashers (**Figure 68**) and tighten securely.

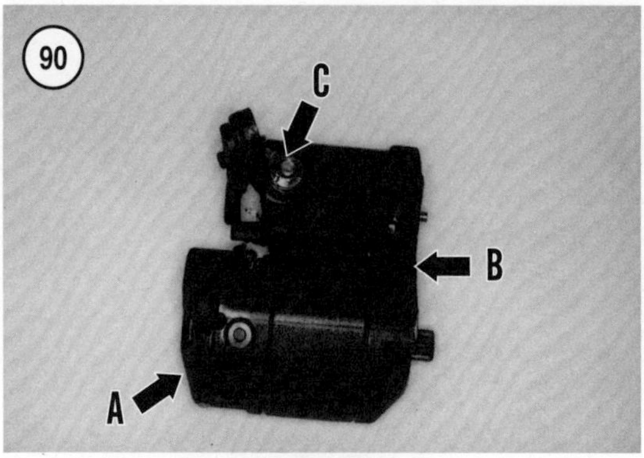

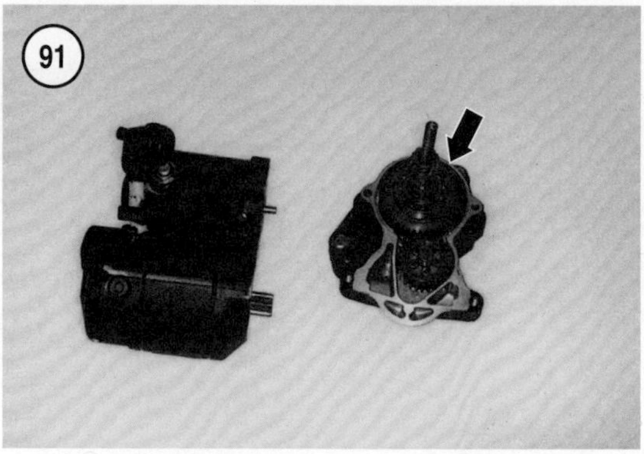

10. Install the two through bolts, washers and O-rings (**Figure 67**) and tighten securely.
11. Reconnect the C terminal field wire (C, **Figure 90**) at the solenoid housing.

Drive Housing Disassembly/Inspection/Assembly

The drive housing was removed during starter disassembly.

1. Remove the return spring (A, **Figure 92**), ball, clutch shaft (B), and drive spring (**Figure 93**) from the drive assembly.
2. Remove the idler gear (**Figure 94**) from the drive housing.
3. Remove the idler gear bearing and cage assembly (A, **Figure 95**). There are five individual bearing rollers (**Figure 96**).
4. Remove the drive assembly (B, **Figure 95**).
5. Replace the drive housing O-ring (**Figure 97**) if worn or damaged. Lubricate the O-ring with high temperature grease.
6. Inspect the idler gear bearing and cage assembly (**Figure 96**) for worn or damaged parts.

CAUTION
*The drive assembly (**Figure 98**) is a sealed unit. Do not clean or soak it in any type of solvent.*

7. Inspect the drive assembly and its bearings (**Figure 98**) for worn or damaged parts. If the bearings are worn or damaged, replace the drive assembly and bearings as a set.
8. Assemble the drive housing by reversing these steps, while noting the following.
9. Lubricate the following components with high temperature grease:

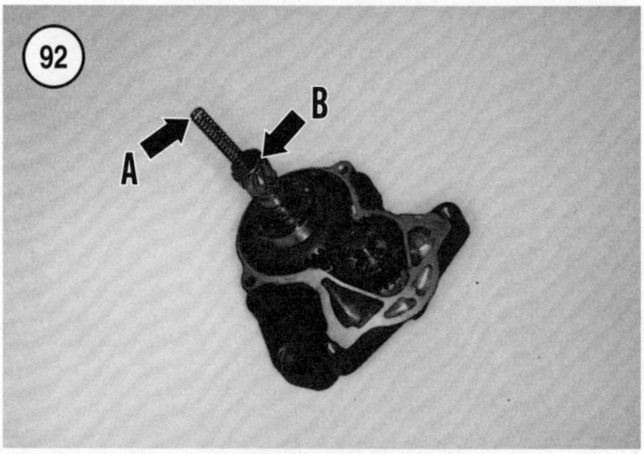

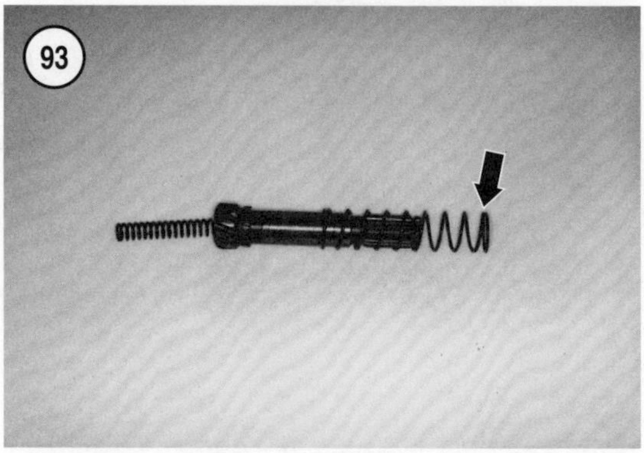

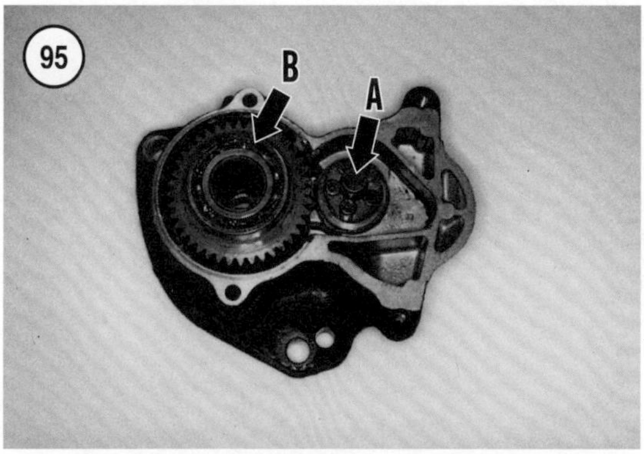

99 STARTER SOLENOID

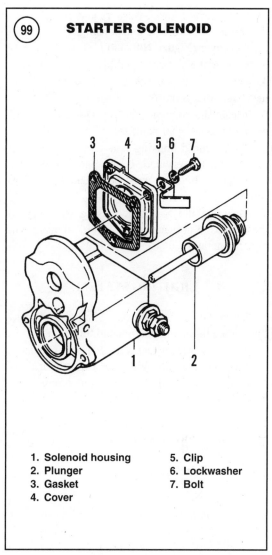

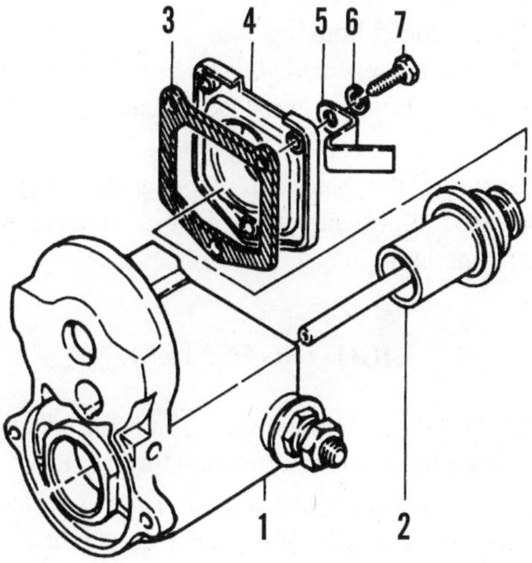

1. Solenoid housing
2. Plunger
3. Gasket
4. Cover
5. Clip
6. Lockwasher
7. Bolt

a. Idler gear bearing and cage assembly (**Figure 96**).
b. Drive housing O-ring and shaft (**Figure 97**).
c. Drive assembly (**Figure 98**).
d. Clutch shaft, drive spring, return spring, and ball.

10. Install the idler gear bearing and cage assembly so that the open side of the cage (A, **Figure 95**) faces toward the solenoid housing.

Solenoid Housing Disassembly/Inspection/Assembly

1. Remove the solenoid housing (**Figure 99**) as described during starter disassembly.

2. Remove the screws, washers and clip securing the end cover to the solenoid housing. Then remove the end cover (**Figure 100**) and gasket.
3. Remove the plunger assembly (**Figure 101**).
4. Inspect the plunger (**Figure 102**) for scoring, deep wear marks or other damage.
5. Inspect the solenoid housing (**Figure 103**) for wear, cracks or other damage.
6. The solenoid housing is a separate assembly and cannot be serviced. If any part is defective, the solenoid housing must be replaced as an assembly.
7. Assemble the solenoid housing by reversing these steps. Lubricate the solenoid plunger with high temperature grease.

LIGHTING SYSTEM

The lighting system consists of a headlight, taillight/brake light combination and turn signals.

Always use the correct wattage bulb. The use of a larger wattage bulb will give a dim light and a smaller wattage bulb will burn out prematurely. **Table 5** lists replacement bulbs.

Headlight Bulb Replacement

Refer to **Figure 104**.

CAUTION
All models are equipped with a quartz-halogen bulb. Do not touch the bulb glass. Traces of oil on the bulb will drastically reduce the life of the bulb. Clean all traces of oil from the bulb glass with a cloth moistened in alcohol or lacquer thinner.

WARNING
If the headlight has just burned out or been turned off it will be hot. To avoid burned fingers, do not touch the bulb. Allow the bulb to cool prior to removal.

1. Loosen the pinch screw (A, **Figure 105**) and remove the trim bezel (B).
2. Pull *straight out* and disconnect the electrical connector from the bulb (**Figure 106**) and remove the headlight assembly.

100

101

102

103

104

HEADLIGHT

1. Plug (all models except FXDWG)
2. Nut (all models except FXDWG)
3. Lockwasher (all models except FXDWG)
4. Washer (all models except FXDWG)
5. Bracket (all models except FXDWG)
6. Trim (all models except FXDWG)
7. Bolt
8. Housing (all models except FXDWG)
9. Housing (FXDWG models)
10. Washer (FXDWG models)
11. Mounting block (FXDWG models)
12. Washer (FXDWG models)
13. Lockwasher (FXDWG models)
14. Nut (FXDWG models)
15. Mounting bracket (FXDWG models)
16. Mounting ring
17. Rubber cover
18. Bulb
19. Lens
20. Trim bezel
21. Nut
22. Connector

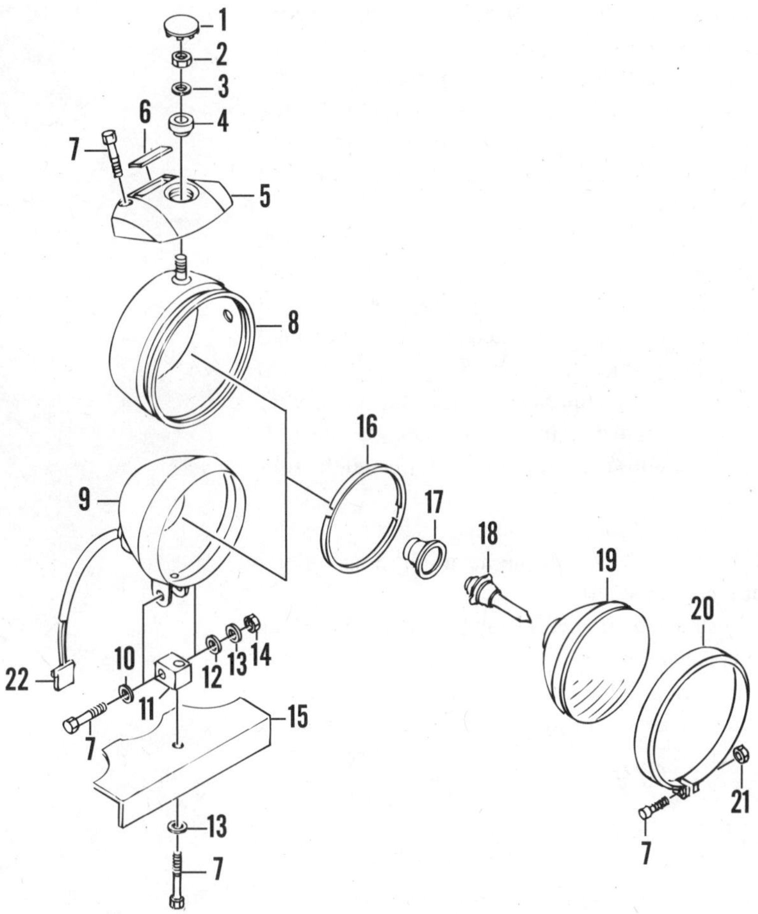

3. Remove the rubber cover (**Figure 107**) from the back of the headlight lens. Check the rubber boot for tears or deterioration; replace if necessary.
4. Unhook the light bulb retaining clip (**Figure 108**) and pivot it out of the way.
5. Remove the blown bulb (**Figure 109**).
6. Align the tangs on the new bulb with the notches in the headlight lens and install the bulb.
7. Securely hook the retaining clip onto the bulb (**Figure 108**).
8. Position the rubber cover so that the TOP mark on the boot is positioned at the top of the headlight lens. Install the rubber cover (**Figure 107**) and make sure it is correctly seated against the bulb and the headlight lens.
9. Correctly align the electrical plug terminals with the bulb (**Figure 106**) and connect it. Push it *straight on* until it bottoms on the bulb and the rubber cover.
10. Check headlight operation.
11. Insert the lens into the headlight housing and seat it correctly.
12. Install the trim bezel onto the headlight lens and housing.
13. Securely tighten the pinch screw.
14. Check headlight adjustment as described in this chapter.

107

108

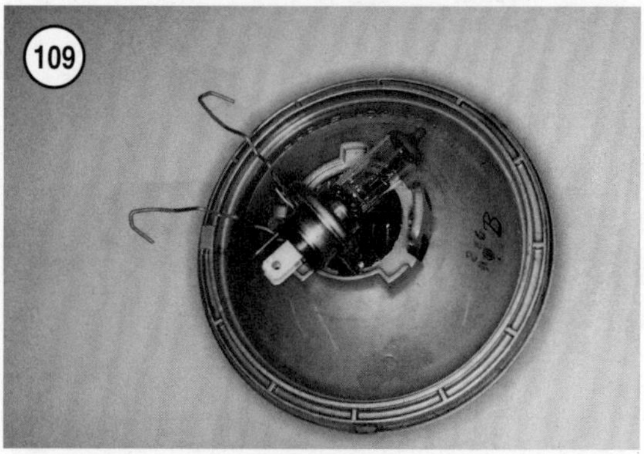
109

Headlight Adjustment

1. Park the motorcycle on a level surface approximately 25 ft. (7.6 m) from the wall (**Figure 110**).
2. Check tire inflation pressure, and adjust if necessary as described in Chapter Three.
3. Draw a horizontal line on the wall that is 35 in. (0.9 m) above the floor.
4. Have a rider sit on the seat.
5. Aim the headlight at the wall and turn on the headlight. Switch the headlight to the high beam. The front wheel must be pointing straight ahead.
6. Check the headlight beam alignment. The broad, flat pattern of light (main beam of light) must be centered on the horizontal line (equal area of light above and below line).
7. Now check the headlight beam lateral alignment. With the headlight beam pointed straight ahead (centered), there must be an equal area of light to the left and right of center.
8A. On models except FXDWG, if the beam is incorrect as described in Step 6 or Step 7, adjust as follows.

a. Remove the plug (**Figure 111**) from the top of the headlight housing.
b. Loosen the headlight clamp nut (**Figure 112**).
c. Tilt the headlight assembly up or down to adjust the beam vertically.
d. Turn the assembly to the left or right sides to adjust the beam horizontally.
e. When the beam is properly adjusted, tighten the headlight adjust nut securely.
f. Push the plug into the headlight housing.

8B. On FXDWG models, if the beam is incorrect as described in Step 6 or Step 7, adjust as follows.

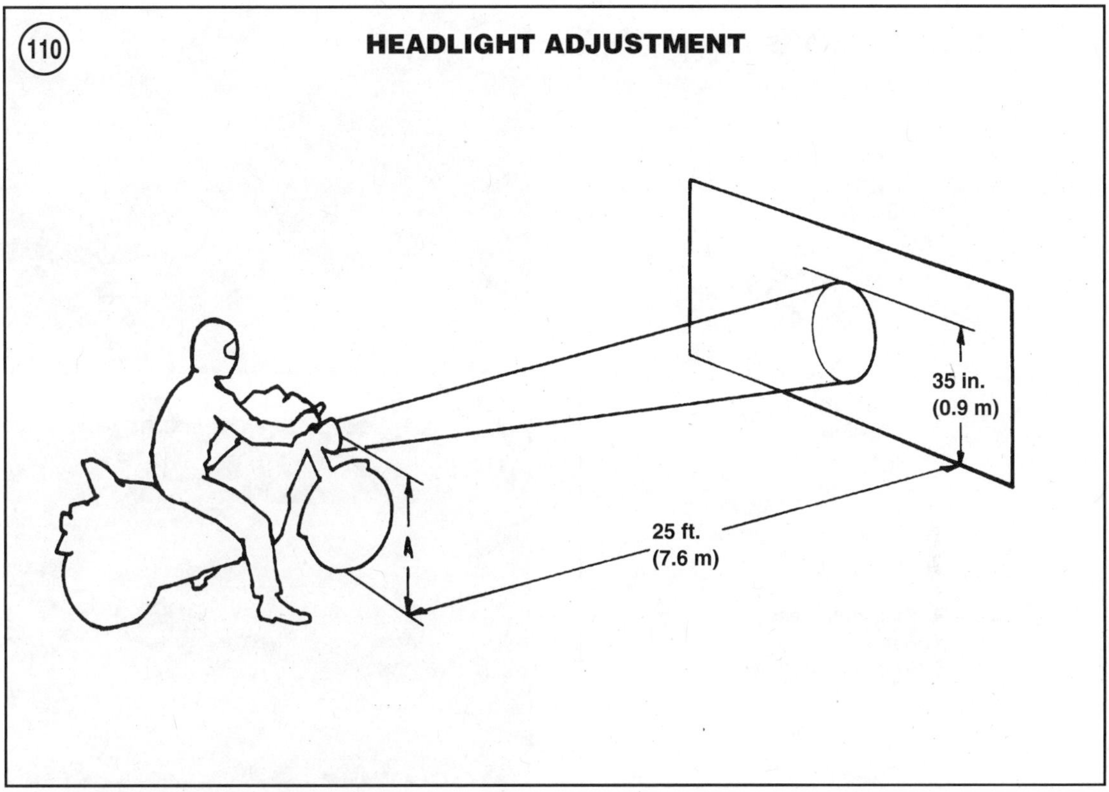

a. Loosen the vertical adjust bolt at the base of the headlight unit.
b. Tilt the headlight assembly up or down to adjust the beam vertically. Tighten the bolt securely.
c. Loosen the horizontal adjust bolt at the base of the steering stem lower bracket.
d. Turn the assembly left or right to adjust the beam horizontally. Tighten the bolt securely.

Taillight/Brake Light Replacement

Refer to **Figure 113**.

1. Remove the screws securing the lens (**Figure 114**).
2. Pull the lens off the base and disconnect the electrical connector (**Figure 115**).
3. Pull the bulb/socket assembly (**Figure 116**) out from the backside of the lens.
4. Rotate the bulb and remove it from the socket assembly (**Figure 117**).
5. Install a new bulb, then install the socket assembly into the lens.
6. Connect the electrical connector (**Figure 115**) and install the lens onto the base.

113 **TAILLIGHT/BRAKE LIGHT**

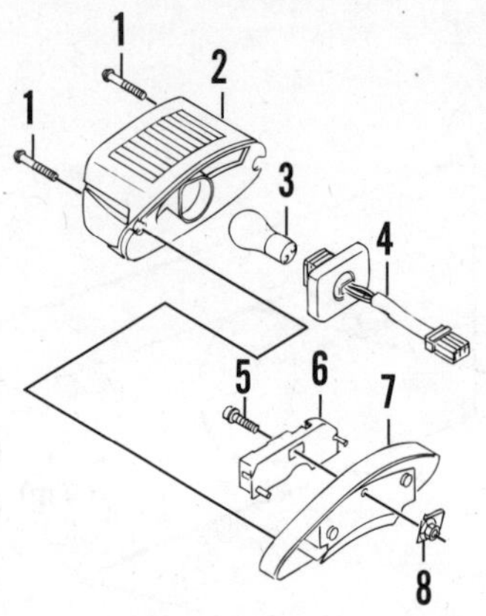

1. Screw
2. Lens
3. Bulb
4. Socket/harness
5. Screw
6. Circuit board/cover assembly
7. Base
8. Cage nut

114

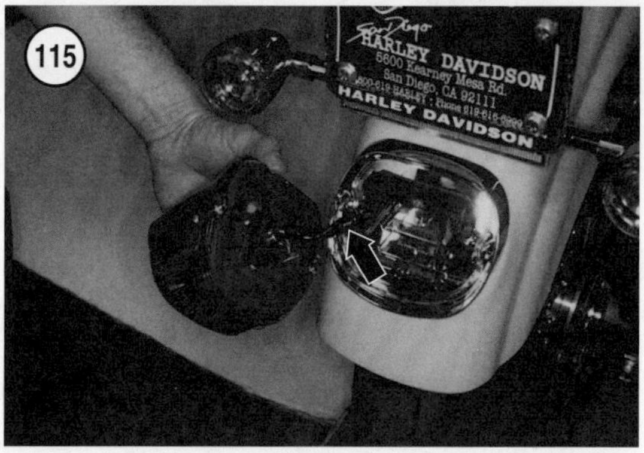

115

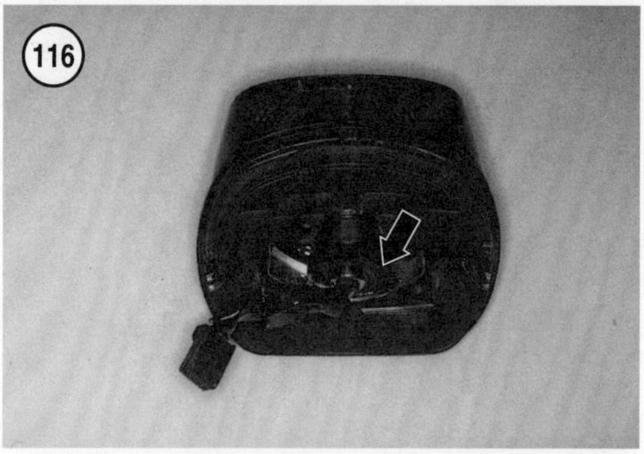
116

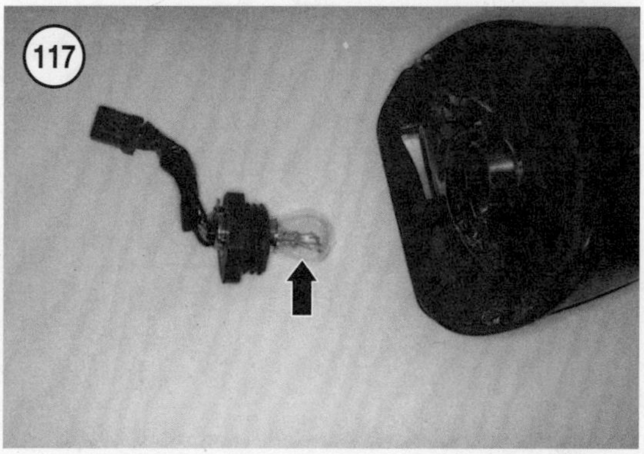
117

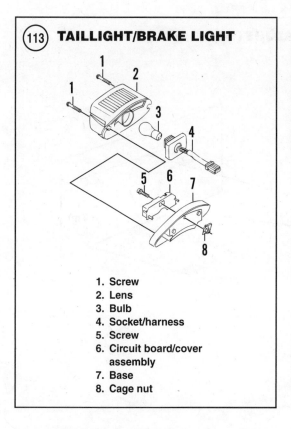

7. Install the screws and tighten securely. Do not overtighten the screws as the lens may crack.
8. To replace the base, perform the following:
   a. From underneath the rear fender, disconnect the wiring harness from the backside of the base.
   b. Remove the screw securing the printed circuit board and base (**Figure 118**) to the rear fender.
   c. Remove the base.

Turn Signal Light Replacement

1A. On 1999-2000 models, remove the screws securing the lens and remove the lens.

1B. On 2001-on models, carefully pry the lens (**Figure 119**) from the base.

2. Push in on the bulb, rotate it and remove it.

3. Install a new bulb and lens.

4. On 1999-2000 models, install the screws and tighten securely. Do not overtighten the screws as the lens may crack.

118

119

120

Position \ Switch	Red/Black	Red	Red/Gray
Off		●	
Acc.		●——	——●
Ignition	●——	——●——	——●

SWITCHES

Testing

Test switches for continuity by using an ohmmeter (see Chapter One) or a self-powered test light at the switch connector plug and operating the switch in each of its operating positions. Compare these results with the switch operating diagrams included in the wiring diagrams at the end of the manual. For example, **Figure 120** shows a continuity diagram for the ignition switch. It shows which terminals should show continuity when the switch is in a given position.

When the ignition switch is in the IGNITION position, there should be continuity between the red/black, the red and red/gray terminals. The line on the continuity diagram indicates this. An ohmmeter connected between these three terminals should indicate little or no resistance, or a test light should light. When the starter switch is OFF, there should be no continuity between the same terminals.

When testing the switches, note the following:

1. Check the battery as described under *Battery* in this chapter; if necessary, charge or replace the battery.
2. Disconnect the negative battery cable (see this chapter) before checking the continuity of any switch.
3. Detach all connectors located between the switch and the electrical circuit.

CAUTION
Do not attempt to start the engine with the battery disconnected.

4. When separating two connectors, pull on the connector housings and not the wires.
5. After locating a defective circuit, check the connectors to make sure they are clean and properly connected. Check all wires going into a connector housing to make sure each wire is positioned properly and that the wire end is not loose.
6. To reconnect connectors properly, push them together until they click or snap into place.

If the switch or button does not perform properly, replace it.

121

122

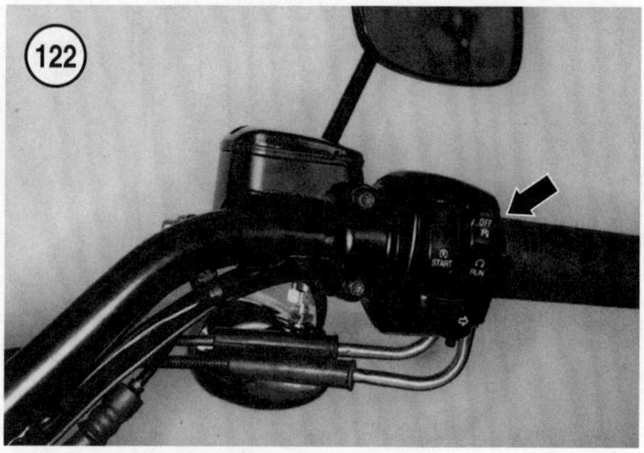

123

LEFT SIDE HANDLEBAR SWITCH

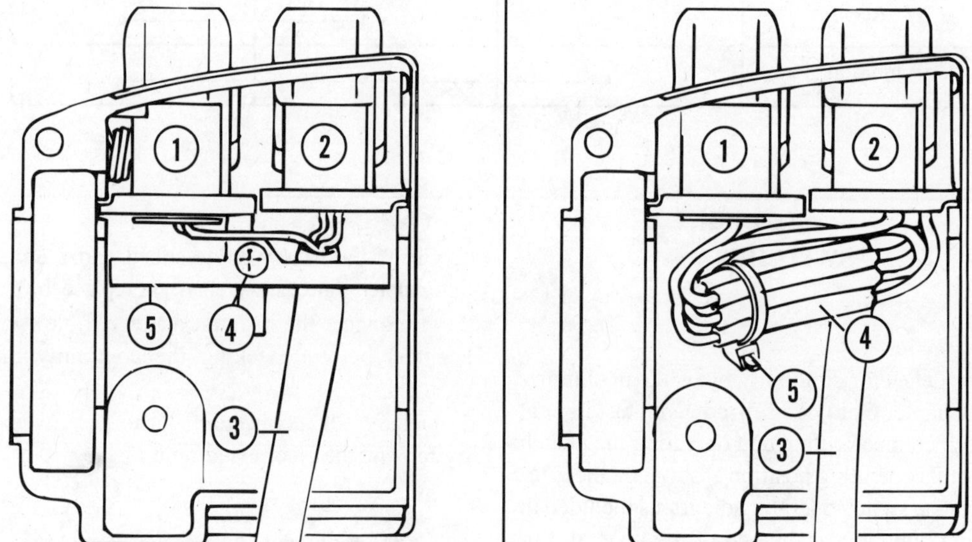

Upper housing without splices

1. Horn switch
2. Headlight high/low beam switch
3. Conduit
4. Phillips screw and washer
5. Bracket

Upper housing with splices

1. Horn switch
2. Headlight high/low beam switch
3. Conduit or splices
4. Splices
5. Cable strap

124

RIGHT SIDE HANDLEBAR SWITCH

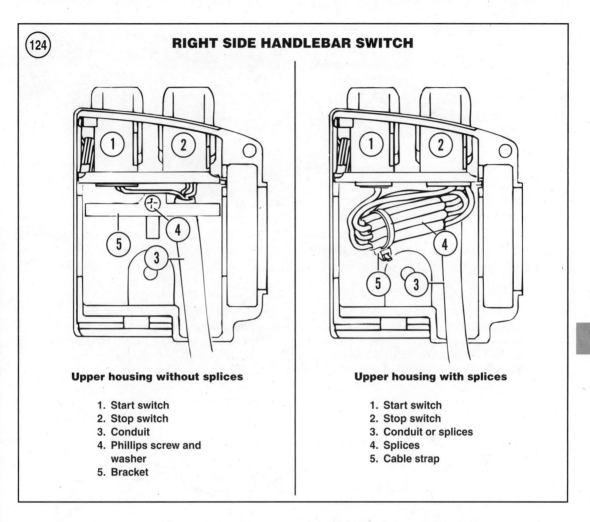

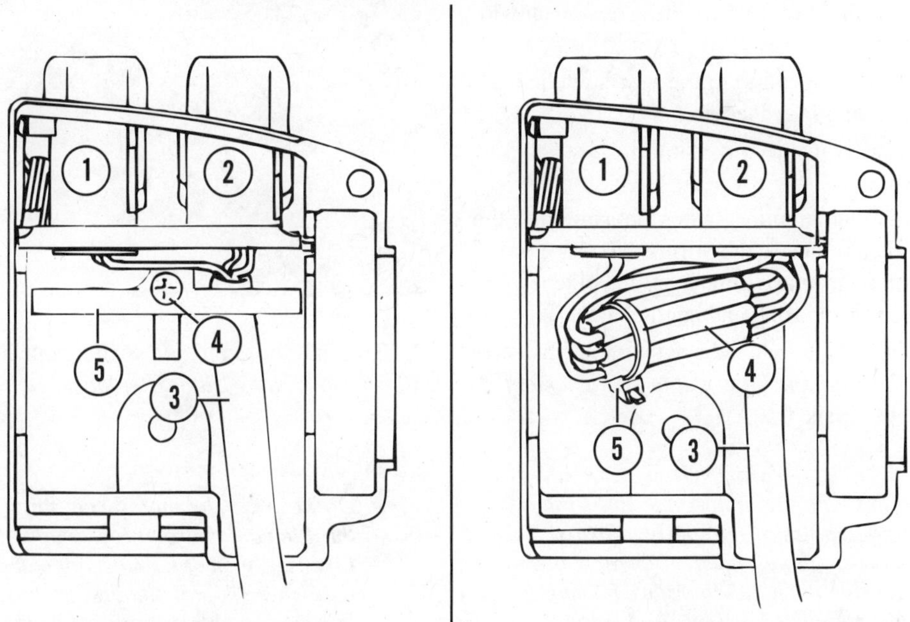

Upper housing without splices

1. Start switch
2. Stop switch
3. Conduit
4. Phillips screw and washer
5. Bracket

Upper housing with splices

1. Start switch
2. Stop switch
3. Conduit or splices
4. Splices
5. Cable strap

Left handlebar switch description

The left side handlebar switch housing (**Figure 121**) is equipped with the following switches:

1. Headlight HI-LO beam.
2. Horn.
3. Left side turn signal.
4. Siren on/off (FXDP models).
5. Clutch lockout (FXDP models).

Right handlebar switch description

The right side handlebar switch housing (**Figure 122**) is equipped with the following switches:

1. Engine stop/run.
2. Starter.
3. Right side turn signal.
4. Front brake light.
5. Pursuit (FXDP models).

Handlebar Switch Replacement

1. Remove the screws securing the left side switch housing (**Figure 121**) to the handlebar. Then carefully separate the switch housing to access the defective switch (**Figure 123**).
2. Remove the screws securing the right side switch housing (**Figure 122**) to the handlebar. Then carefully separate the switch housing to see the defective switch (**Figure 124**).

NOTE

*To service the front brake light switch, refer to **Front Brake Light Switch Replacement** in this chapter.*

3A. On models without splices, remove the screw and bracket.

3B. On models with splices, remove the cable strap.

4. Pull the switch(es) out of the housing.

5. Cut the switch wire(s) from the defective switch(s).
6. Slip a piece of heat shrink tubing over each wire cut in Step 2.
7. Solder the wire end(s) to the new switch. Then shrink the tubing over the wire(s).
8. Install the switch by reversing these steps, plus the following:
   a. When clamping the switch housing onto the handlebar, check the wiring harness routing position to make sure it is not pinched between the housing and handlebar.
   b. To install the right side switch housing, refer to *Throttle and Idle Cable Replacement* in Chapter Seven.

WARNING
Do not ride the motorcycle until the throttle cables are properly adjusted. Also, the cables must not catch or pull when the handlebars are turned. Improper cable routing and adjustment can cause the throttle to stick open. This could cause loss of control. Recheck all work before riding the motorcycle.

Front Brake Light Switch Replacement

The front brake light switch (**Figure 125**) is mounted in the right side switch lower housing.

1. Separate the right side switch housing as described under *Handlebar Switch Replacement* in this chapter.
2. If still in place, remove the wedge between the switch and the switch housing.
3. While depressing the switch plunger, slowly rotate the switch upward, rocking it slightly, and remove it from the switch housing.
4. Cut the switch wires from the defective switch.
5. Slip a piece of heat shrink tubing over each wire cut in Step 4.
6. Solder the wire ends to the new switch. Then shrink the tubing over the wires.
7. Install the switch by reversing these steps, plus the following.
8. When clamping the switch housing onto the handlebar, check the wiring harness routing position to make sure it is not pinched between the housing and handlebar.

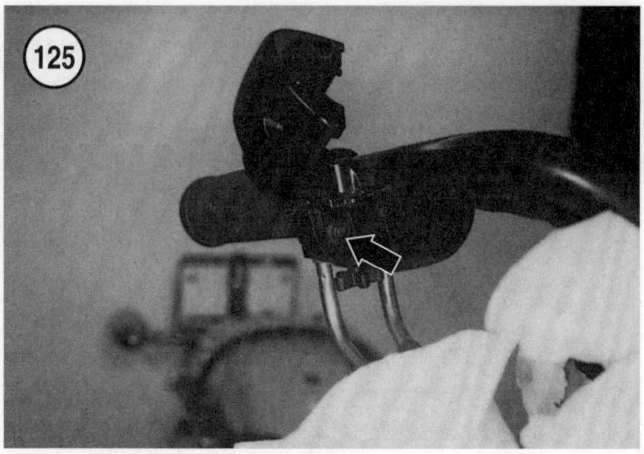

9. To install the right side switch housing, refer to *Throttle and Idle Cable Replacement* in Chapter Seven.

WARNING
Do not ride the motorcycle until the throttle cables are properly adjusted. Likewise, the cables must not catch or pull when the handlebars are turned. Improper cable routing and adjustment can cause the throttle to stick open. This could cause loss of control. Recheck the work before riding the motorcycle.

Ignition/Light Switch Removal/Installation

FXDWG and FXDP models

1. Disconnect the negative battery cable as described in this chapter.
2. Turn the ignition switch OFF and remove the ignition key.

3A. On FXDWG models (**Figure 126**), remove the acorn nut from the instrument panel on the fuel tank.

3B. On FXDP models (**Figure 127**), remove the four screws and washers from the center console on the fuel tank.

4. Lift the instrument panel, or center console, up and then turn it over. Place a heavy cloth under the instrument panel to avoid scratching the fuel tank.

NOTE
Before disconnecting the wires in Step 5, confirm the wire color connections at the ignition switch with the wiring

(126)

INSTRUMENTS (FXDWG)

1. Speedometer
2. Gasket
3. Trim plate
4. Indicator light bezel
5. Acorn nut
6. Console
7. Boot
8. Reset switch
9. Set screw
10. Clip
11. Trim piece
12. Ignition switch and key
13. Cage nut
14. Clamp
15. Cable strap
16. Screw
17. Indicator light panel

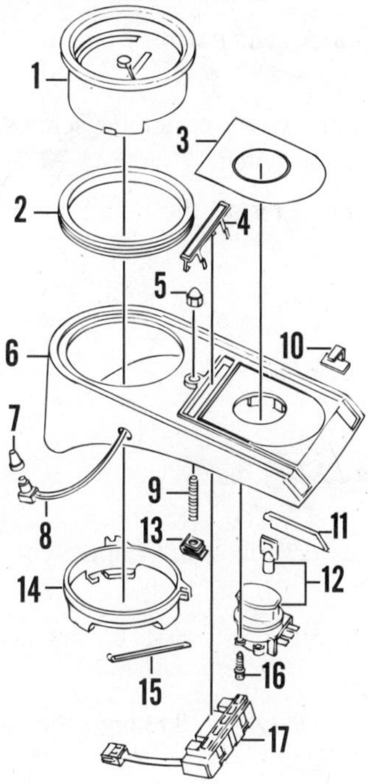

(127)

IGNITION SWITCH (FXDP)

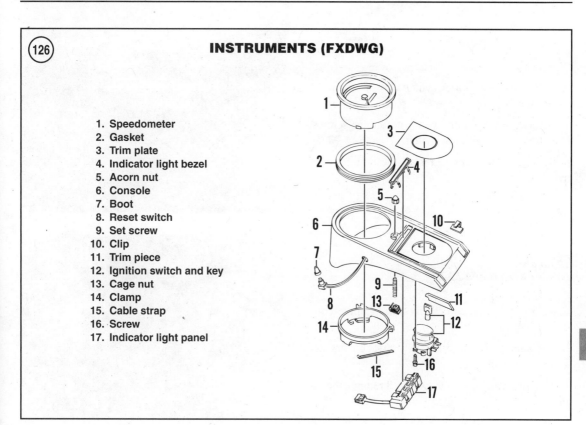

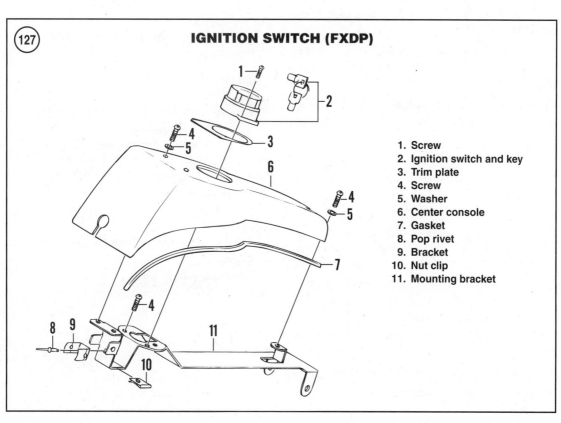

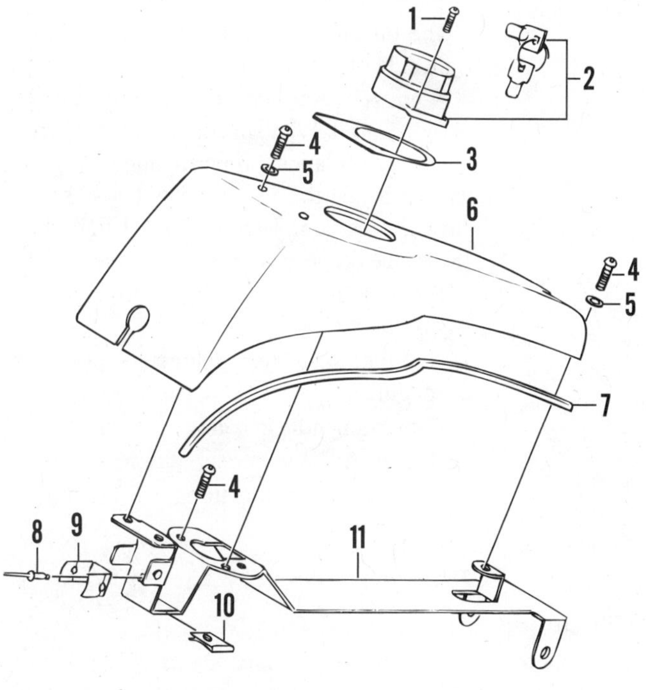

1. Screw
2. Ignition switch and key
3. Trim plate
4. Screw
5. Washer
6. Center console
7. Gasket
8. Pop rivet
9. Bracket
10. Nut clip
11. Mounting bracket

diagram for the model being worked on.

5. Disconnect the ignition switch wires from the ignition switch.
6. Remove the ignition switch mounting screws. Then remove the ignition switch.
7. Reverse these steps to install the new ignition switch.
8. Check the switch in each of its operating positions.

All models except FXDWG and FXDP

1. Remove the seat as described in Chapter Thirteen.
2. Disconnect the negative battery cable as described in this chapter.
3. Turn the ignition switch OFF and remove the ignition key.
4. Loosen and remove the outer chrome nut securing the ignition switch to the mounting plate (**Figure 128**).
5. Push the ignition switch through the cover (toward inside) and remove it from the mounting plate (**Figure 129**).
6. Remove the ignition switch harness cover and cut the switch wires 3 in. (76.2 mm) from the switch.
7. To reconnect the new ignition switch:
   a. Slide the replacement conduit onto the wire harness.
   b. Match the ignition switch and wire harness color codes, and then install new butt connectors to the wire harness and ignition switch wires. Seal the butt splice connectors as shown in **Figure 130**.
8. Install the ignition switch into the hole in the switch cover so that the TOP mark stamped on the switch body faces up (toward the switch position decal).
9. Tighten the ignition switch locknut securely.
10. Check the switch operation in each of its operating positions.

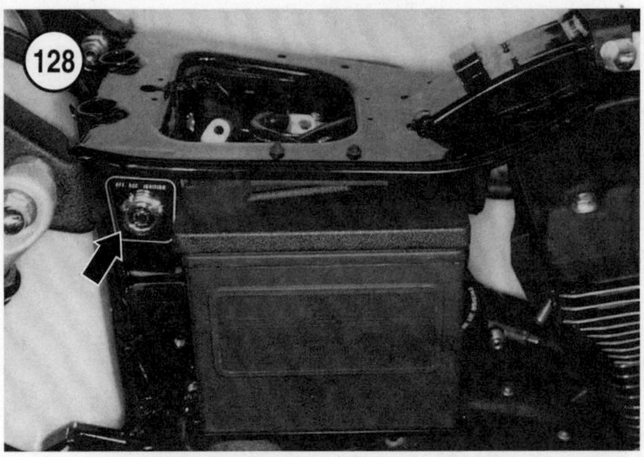

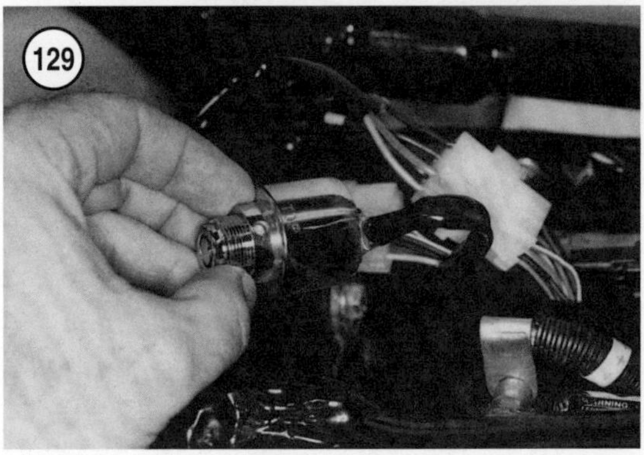

Oil Pressure Switch

Operation

The oil pressure switch is located on the front right side of the crankcase.

A pressure-actuated diaphragm-type oil pressure switch is used. When the oil pressure is low or when oil is not circulating through a running engine, spring tension inside the switch holds the switch contacts closed. This completes the signal light circuit and causes the oil pressure indicator lamp to light.

The oil pressure signal light should turn on when any of the following occurs:

1. The ignition switch is turned on prior to starting the engine.
2. The engine idle is below 1000 rpm.
3. The engine is operating with low oil pressure.
4. Oil is not circulating through the running engine.

Testing/replacement

NOTE
The oil pressure signal light may not come on when the ignition switch is

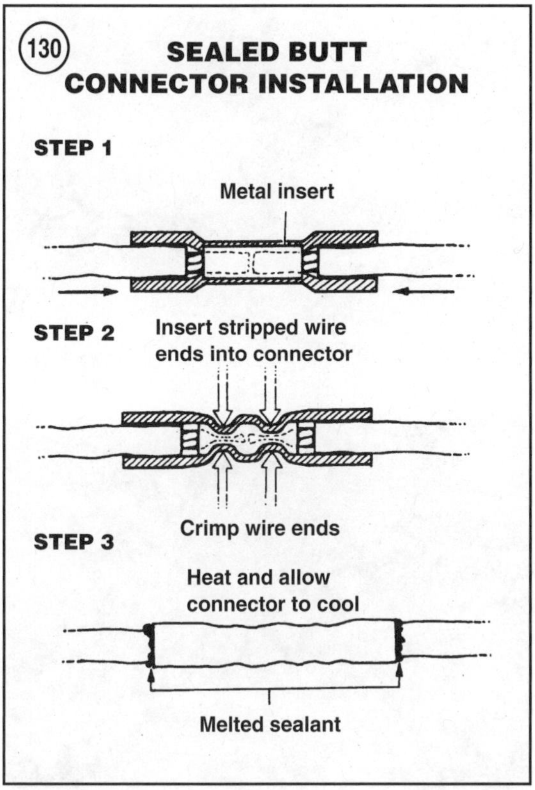

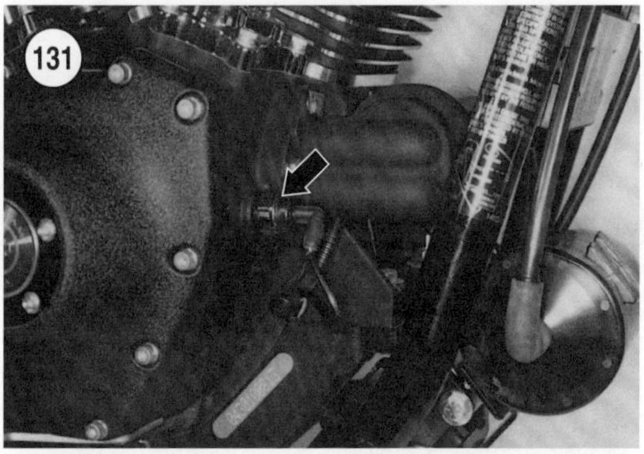

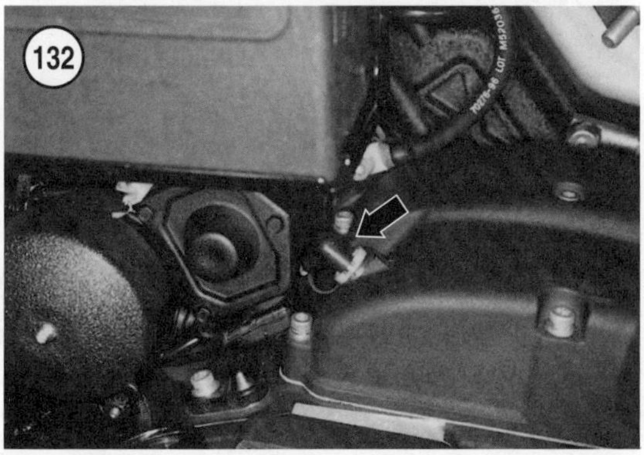

turned off and then back on immediately. This is due to the oil pressure retained in the oil filter housing.

The following steps test the electrical part of the oil pressure switch. If the oil pressure switch, indicator lamp and related wiring are in good condition, inspect the lubrication system as described in Chapter Two.

1. Remove the rubber boot and disconnect the electrical connector from the switch (**Figure 131**).
2. Turn the ignition switch ON.
3. Ground the switch wire to the engine.
4. The oil pressure indicator lamp on the instrument panel must light.
5. If the signal indicator lamp does not light, check for a defective indicator lamp and inspect all wiring between the switch and the indicator lamp.

6A. If the oil pressure warning light operates properly, attach the electrical connector to the pressure switch. Make sure the connection is tight and free from oil. Slide the rubber boot back into position.

6B. If the warning light remains ON when the engine is running, shut the engine off. Check the engine lubrication system as described in Chapter Two.

7. To replace the switch, perform the following:
   a. Unscrew it from the engine.
   b. Apply Loctite pipe sealant with Teflon to the switch threads prior to installation.
   c. Install the switch and tighten to the specification in **Table 6**.
   d. Test the new switch as described in Steps 1-4.

Neutral Indicator Switch Replacement

The neutral indicator switch is located on the transmission top cover. The neutral indicator light on the instrument panel must light when the ignition is turned ON and the transmission is in NEUTRAL.

1. Disconnect the electrical connector from the neutral indicator switch (**Figure 132**).
2. Turn the ignition switch on.
3. Ground the neutral indicator switch wire to the transmission.
4. If the neutral indicator lamp lights, the neutral switch is defective. Replace the neutral indicator switch and retest.

5. If the neutral indicator lamp does not light, check for a defective indicator lamp, faulty wiring or a loose or corroded connection.

NOTE
The electrical connector can be attached to either stud on the switch.

6A. If the neutral switch operates correctly, attach the electrical connector to the neutral switch. Make sure the connection is tight and free from oil.
6B. If the neutral switch is defective, replace the neutral indicator switch.
7. To replace the old switch, perform the following:
   a. Shift the transmission into NEUTRAL.
   b. Unscrew and remove the old switch and O-ring from the transmission top cover.
   c. Apply clean transmission oil to the *new* O-ring seal.
   d. Install the new switch and tighten to the specification in **Table 6**.

Rear Brake Light Switch Testing/Replacement

A hydraulic, normally-open rear brake light switch is used on all models. The rear brake light is attached to the rear brake caliper brake hose (**Figure 133**). When the rear brake pedal is applied, hydraulic pressure closes the switch contacts, providing a ground path so the rear brake lamp comes on. If the rear brake lamp does not come on, perform the following.

NOTE
Removal of the exhaust system is not necessary, but it does provide additional work room for this test and replacement if necessary.

1. If necessary, remove the exhaust system as described in Chapter Seven.
2. Turn the ignition switch OFF.
3. Disconnect the electrical connector from the switch (**Figure 134**).
4. Connect an ohmmeter between the switch terminals and check the following:
   a. Apply the rear brake pedal. There must be continuity.
   b. Release the rear brake pedal. There must be no continuity.

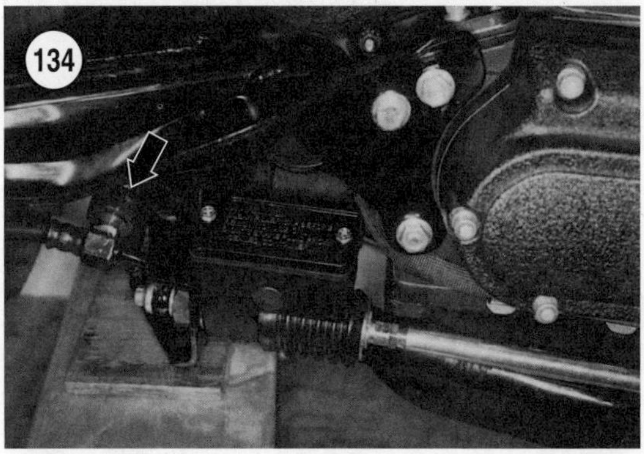

   c. If the switch fails either of these tests, replace the switch.
5. Place a drip pan under the switch, as some brake fluid will drain out when the switch is removed.
6. Loosen and remove the switch from the fitting on the rear brake line.
7. Thread the new switch into the fitting and tighten securely.
8. Reconnect the switch electrical connectors.
9. Bleed the rear brake as described in Chapter Twelve.
10. Check the rear brake light with the ignition switch turned ON and the rear brake applied.

HORN

The horn is mounted on the frame boss on the left side of the frame.

Testing

1. Remove the seat.

2. Disconnect the negative battery cable as described in this chapter.
3. Disconnect the electrical connectors from the backside of the horn.
4. Connect a 12-volt battery to the horn as follows:
   a. Connect the negative lead to the top (silver) horn terminal.
   b. Connect the positive lead to the bottom (gold) horn terminal.
5. If the horn is good, it will sound. If not, replace the horn.
6. Reconnect the electrical connectors to the horn as follows:
   a. Connect the black wire connector to the top (silver) horn terminal.
   b. Connect the yellow/black wire connector to the bottom (gold) horn terminal.
7. Connect the negative battery cable as described in this chapter.

Replacement

1. Remove the seat as described in Chapter Thirteen.
2. Disconnect the negative battery cable as described in this chapter.
3. Remove the long acorn nut (A, **Figure 135**) securing the horn assembly bracket to the frame post.
4. Move the horn assembly (B, **Figure 135**) to the frame and engine and disconnect the electrical connectors from the horn terminals.
5. Remove the screw and nut securing the horn to the mounting bracket and remove the horn.
6. Install the horn by reversing these removal steps. Note the following:
   a. Make sure the electrical connectors and horn spade terminals are free of corrosion.
   b. Connect the black wire connector to the top (silver) horn terminal.
   c. Connect the yellow/black wire connector to the bottom (gold) horn terminal.
   d. Check that the horn operates correctly.

ELECTRIC PANEL

The electric panel assembly mounts on the left side of the motorcycle. The panel assembly houses the circuit breaker, fuses, ignition module, starter relay, turn signal canceller, security module (models so equipped) and the main wiring harness connector.

Refer to **Figure 136** (1999-2000 models) and **Figure 137** (2001-on models).

1. Disconnect the negative battery cable as described in this chapter.
2. Carefully pull out and remove the electric panel cover (**Figure 138**).
3. Remove the nuts securing the outer panel (**Figure 139**) and remove the outer panel.
4. Install the outer panel (**Figure 139**) and tighten the nuts.
5. Correctly position the electrical panel cover with the *this side down* label facing down (**Figure 140**).
6. Carefully push the electric panel cover (**Figure 138**) back into position. Push it on until it bottoms.

TURN SIGNAL MODULE (1999-2000 MODELS)

The turn signal module (TSM) is an electronic microprocessor that controls the turn signals and the four-way hazard flasher. The turn signal module receives its information from the speedometer and turn signal switches.

The turn signal module is located in the electrical panel on the left side of the frame.

If the following tests do not solve or confirm the problem with the TSM, have a Harley-Davidson dealership test the unit by using the Speedometer Tester along with the specific diagnostic code retrieval.

Operation

For example, when the rider signals for left turn, the following occurs. Refer to **Figure 141**.

(136) **ELECTRICAL PANEL (1999-2000)**

1. Cover
2. Grommet
3. Outer plate
4. Bolt
5. Washer
6. Label
7. Nut
8. Starter relay (diode)
9. Mounting bracket
10. Bolt
11. Turn signal canceller module (TSM)
12. Electrical panel
13. Nut
14. Circuit breaker–30 amp
15. Pop rivet
16. Screw
17. Nut
18. Nut
19. Bolt
20. Bank angle sensor
21. Nut
22. Bracket
23. Stand off stud
24. Decal
25. Ignition key
26. Face nut
27. Ignition switch
28. Electrical connector

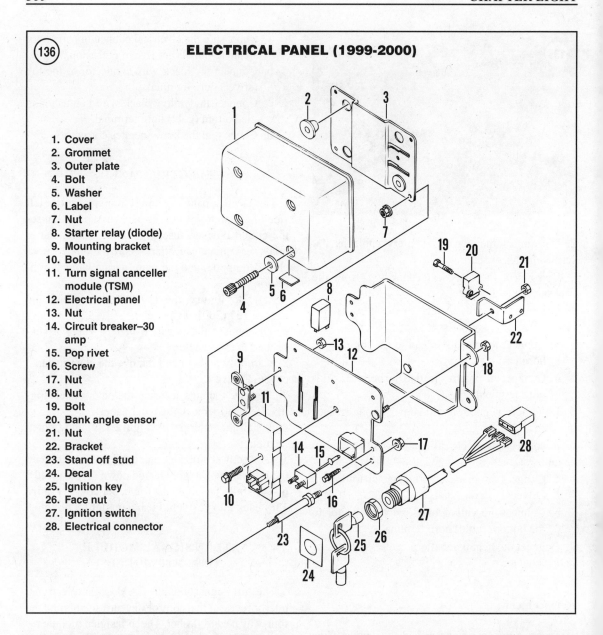

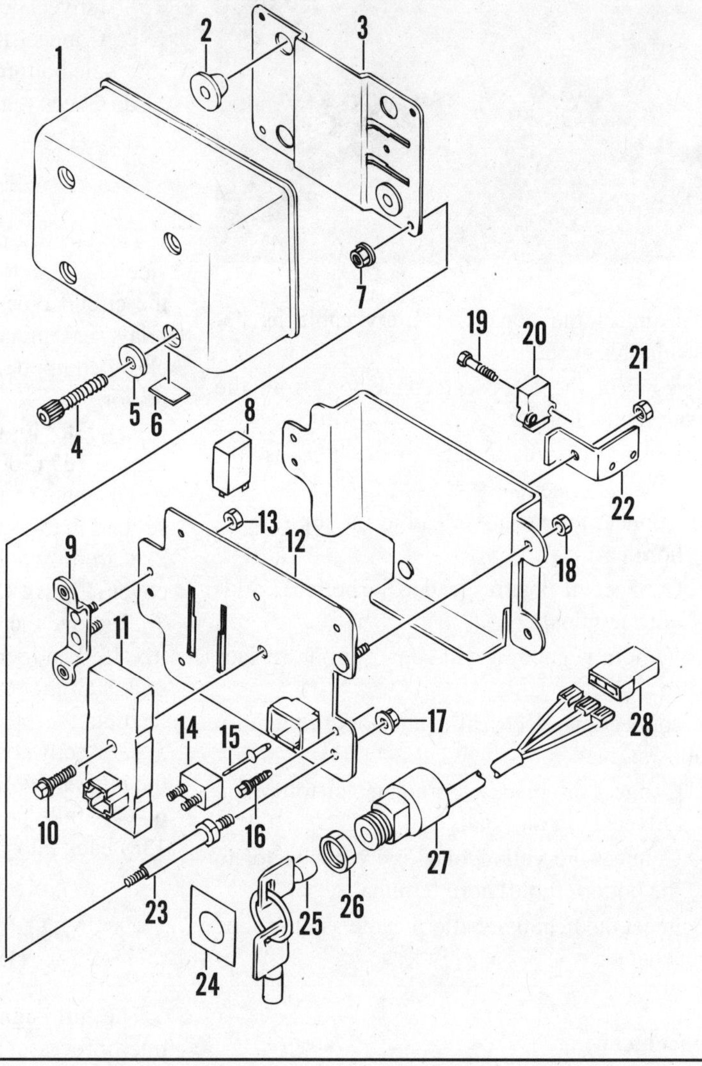

1. When the left turn signal switch is pressed, a momentary 12 VDC pulse is sent to Pin No. 8 (input) on the TSM module. The module responds to this signal by sending a series of 12 VDC pulses to Pin No. 4 (output) to flash the left front and rear turn signal lamps.
2. The TSM module then monitors the number of vehicle speed sensor pulses sent from the speedometer sending unit to Pin No. 3. These pulses indicate the distance the motorcycle has traveled. When the number of speedometer pulses is equal to the quantity preset in the module program, the turn signal is cancelled.
3. When the right turn signal switch is pressed, a momentary 12 VDC pulse is sent to Pin No. 7 (input) on the TSM module and an output signal at Pin No. 3 (output). The remaining signal process is identical to the left turn signal operation.

Preliminary Troubleshooting

If one or all of the turn signals do not flash, perform the following:

1. Remove the lens and check for a defective bulb(s). Replace the bulb(s) if necessary.

137

ELECTRICAL PANEL (2001-ON)

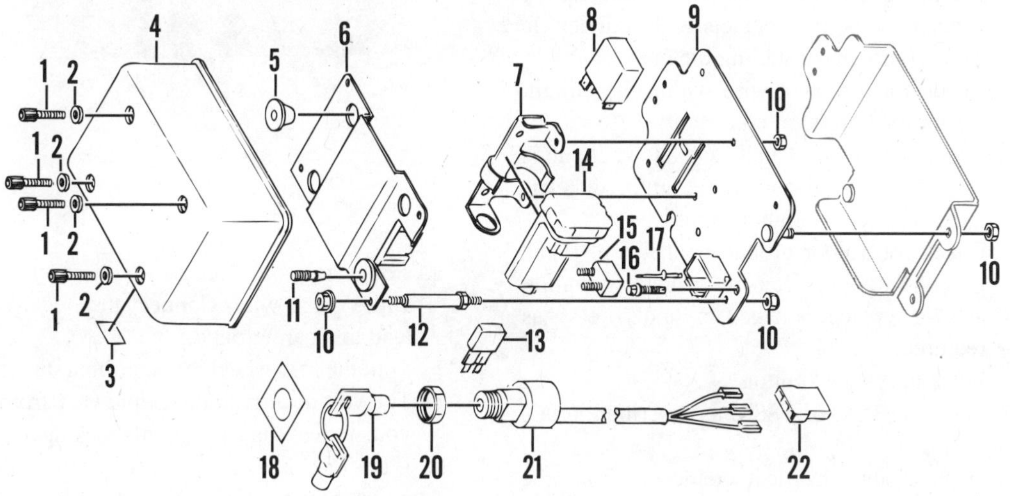

1. Screw
2. Washer
3. Label
4. Cover
5. Grommet
6. Outer plate
7. Module bracket
8. Starter relay
9. Electrical panel
10. Nut
11. Pin
12. Stand off stud
13. Fuses
14. Turn signal canceller module or Turn signal canceller/security system module (optional)
15. Circuit breaker–30 or 40 amp
16. Screw
17. Pop rivet
18. Decal
19. Ignition key
20. Face nut
21. Ignition switch
22. Electrical connector

138

139

2. If the bulb(s) is good, check for one of the following problems:
   a. Check the bulb socket contacts for corrosion. Clean the contacts and then recheck. If there is a problem with corrosion building on the contacts, wipe the contacts with a dielectric grease before re-installing the bulb.
   b. Check for a broken wire within the circuit. Repair the wire(s) or connector(s).
   c. Check for a loose bulb socket where it is staked to the housing. If the bulb socket is loose, replace the light assembly.
   d. Check for a poor ground connection. If the ground is poor, clean the ground mounting area or replace damaged ground wire(s), as required.
   e. Stuck turn signal button.
3. Remove the TSM or TSSM as described in this chapter.
4. Disconnect the electrical connector from the TSM or TSSM.
5. Check the electrical connectors in the TSM or TSSM and in the wiring harness for corrosion. Clean off if necessary.

Distance Test

The turn signal module (TSM) recognizes four different speed ranges and uses these distances to activate the cancellation action. Refer to the speed and distance ranges listed in **Table 7**.

1. Ride the motorcycle at the mid-point of speed range No. 1.
2. Press and release the right turn button and closely check the vehicle speed and the odometer at the time the button is released and the time the turn signal is cancelled.
3. Repeat Step 1 and Step 2 for right and left turns at the midpoint of speed ranges No. 2 through No. 4.
4. If the distances observed in Steps 1-3 are not correct, check the following steps:
   a. Check the TSM ground connection and module pin connections for corrosion.
   b. Check all lamps and lamp connections.
   c. Check the vehicle speed sensor (**Figure 142**) connections and ground for corrosion.
5. Raise the motorcycle with the rear wheel off the ground.
6. At the speedometer electrical connector, perform the following:

140

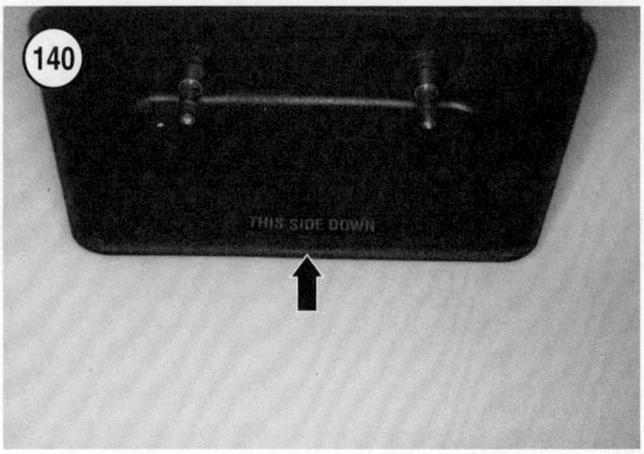

   a. Connect a voltmeter positive test lead to the white/green wire. Connect the negative test lead to a bare ground.
   b. Spin the rear wheel in the normal direction.
   c. The voltmeter reading should vary from 6-12 volts to less than 1 volt and back again.
   d. If the TSM fails this test, replace the TSM and repeat Steps 1-3 with a good module.

Time Test

This is an alternate test to the Distance Test, previously described, to check if the TSM module is operating correctly. Measure the turn signal ON time at the four indicated constant speed and time ranges listed in **Table 8**.

If the TSM fails this test, replace the TSM and repeat with a good module.

Rider Preference Setting

If the rider desires the turn signals to flash for a longer or shorter distance that the pre-set time, perform the following:

1. Longer distance cycle: hold the turn signal longer and release it closer to the turning point.
2. Shorter distance cycle: press the button a second time to cancel the turn signals.

Turn Signal Module (TSM) Removal/Installation

1. Remove the seat as described in Chapter Thirteen.
2. Turn the ignition switch OFF.
3. Remove the electrical panel cover and outer plate as described in this chapter.

141

TURN SIGNAL MODULE (TSM) (1999-2000)

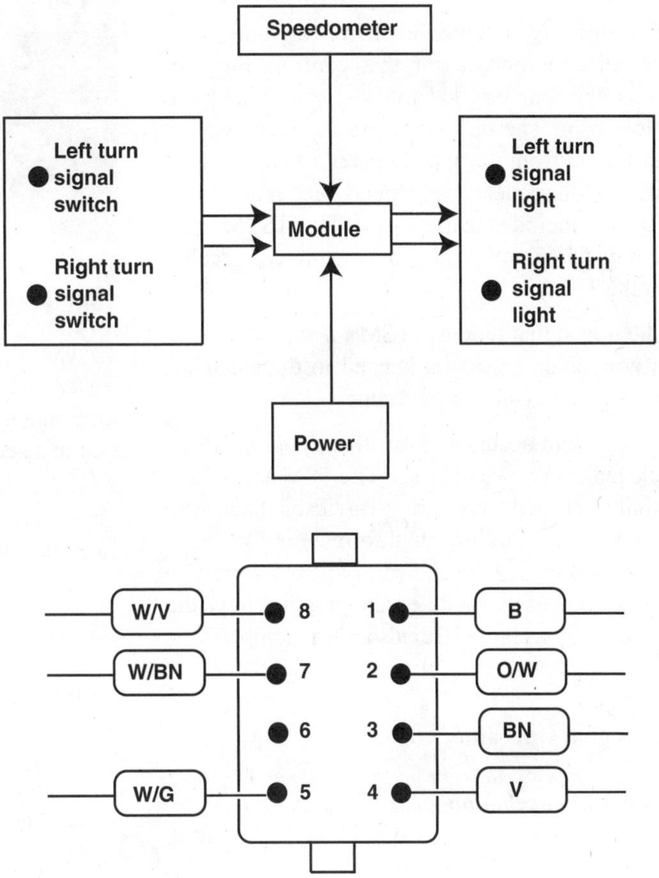

1. Module ground to motorcycle
2. 12 VDC input from accessory circuit breaker
3. Pulsed 12 VDC for flashing right signal lights
4. Pulsed 12 VDC for flashing left signal lights
5. Vehicle speed sensor input (from speedometer)
6. Not used
7. 12 VDC input from right side handlebar switch
8. 12 VDC input from left side handlebar switch

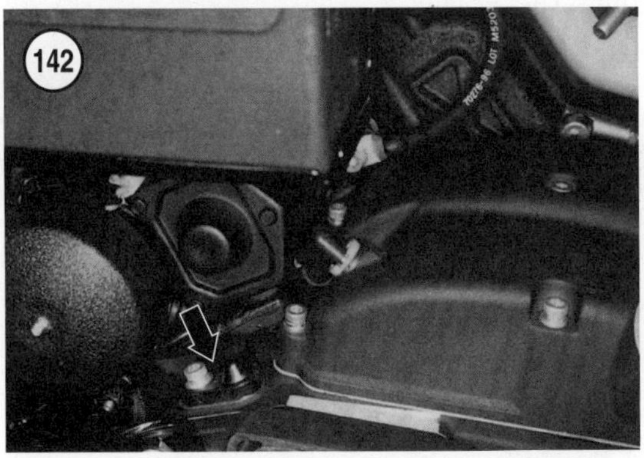

4. Disconnect the harness connector from the module.

5. Remove the screw securing the module to the inner panel and remove the module.

6. Install the module by reversing these removal steps while noting the following:

   a. Make sure the electrical connectors are free of corrosion.

   b. Tighten the screw securely.

   c. Check that the turn signal and flasher systems work properly.

TURN SIGNAL MODULE AND TURN SIGNAL/SECURITY MODULE (2001-ON MODELS)

The turn signal module (TSM) module is an electronic microprocessor that controls the turn signals, the four-way hazard flasher and the bank angle sensor. The turn signal module receives its information from the speedometer and turn signal switches. On models so equipped, the security system is also included in the TSSM. This TSSM has a different part number and is not interchangeable with the TSM.

The turn signal module (TSM) or turn signal security module (TSSM) is located in the electrical panel on the left side of the frame.

If a problem occurs within either system, a diagnostic fault code(s) will be set. The TSM and TSSM can only be tested with Harley-Davidson diagnostic equipment. The following information illustrates how the systems are designed to operate correctly. If any portion of the module is inoperative, have the unit tested by a Harley-Davidson dealership.

Turn Signal Operation

Automatic cancellation

NOTE
The TSM/TSSM will not cancel the signal before the turn is actually completed.

1. When the turn signal button is depressed, then released, the system begins a 20 count. As long as the motorcycle is moving above 7 MPH (11 KPH) the turn signals will always cancel after the 20 bulb flashes, providing the TSM does not receive any additional input.

2. If the motorcycle's speed drops to 7 MPH (11 KPH) or less, including stopping, the turn signals will continue to flash. The counting will continue when the motorcycle reaches 8 MPH (13 KPH) and will automatically cancel when the count total equals 20 bulb flashes.

3. The turn signals will cancel within two seconds after the turn of 45 degrees or more is completed

143

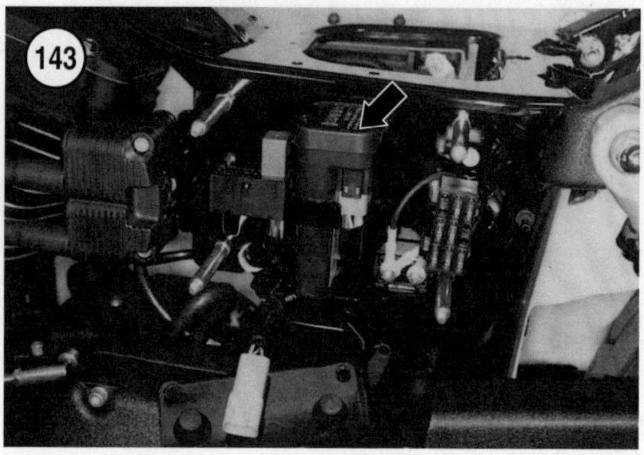

Manual cancellation

1. After the turn signal button is depressed, then released, the system begins a 20 count. To cancel the turn signal from flashing, depress the turn signal button a second time.
2. If the turn direction is to be changed, depress the opposite turn signal button. The primary signal is cancelled and the opposite turn signal will flash.

Four-way flashing

1. Turn the ignition key to the ON position. On models so equipped, disarm the security system. Press both the right and left turn signal buttons at the same time. All four turn signals will flash at the same time.
2. On models with the security system, turn the ignition key to the OFF position and arm the security system. Press both the right and left turn signal buttons at the same time. All four turn signals will now flash at the same time for up to two hours.
3. To cancel the four-way flashing, disarm the security system (models so equipped), and press both the right and left turn signal buttons at the same time. The flashing will stop.

Bank angle sensor

The bank angle sensor will automatically shut off the engine if the motorcycle tilts to more than 45 degrees from vertical for longer than one second. The shutoff will occur even at a very slow speed if the tilt reaches this angle.

To restart the motorcycle, return it to a vertical position. Turn the ignition key from OFF to ON, then restart the engine.

Security System (TSSM) Functions

If a theft attempt is detected and the TSSM is in operation, it will immobilize the starting and ignition systems. It will also alternately flash the right and left turn signals and sound the siren, if so equipped. The following conditions will activate the armed security system.

1. Detecting small motorcycle movement: The turn signals will flash three times and the optional siren will chirp once, then turn off. If the motorcycle is not returned to its original position, the warnings will reactivate after four seconds. This cycle will repeat a maximum of 255 times.
2. Detecting large motorcycle movement: The previous system will activate for 30 seconds and then turn off. If the motorcycle is not returned to its original position, the warnings will reactivate after ten seconds. This cycle may repeat a maximum of ten times.
3. Detects tampering of security lamp circuit: System activates for 30 seconds. The cycle will repeat for each tampering incident.
4. Detecting that a battery ground or ground disconnect has occurred while the system is armed: The siren will sound, if so equipped, but the turn signals will not flash.

NOTE

Always disarm the optional TSSM prior to disconnecting the battery or the siren will sound. If the TSSM is in auto-alarming mode, disarm the system with two clicks of the key fob and disconnect the battery or remove the TSSM fuse before the 30-second arming period expires.

Turn Signal Security Module (TSSM) Removal/Installation

1. Remove the seat as described in Chapter Thirteen.
2. Turn the ignition switch off.
3. Remove the electrical panel cover and outer plate as described in this chapter.
4. Remove the TSSM (**Figure 143**) from the clip on the inner plate.
5. Disconnect the harness connector from the module.
6. Install the module by reversing these removal steps while noting the following:
   a. Make sure the electrical connectors are free of moisture.
   b. Make sure the module is secure in its clip.
   c. Check that the turn signal and flasher systems work properly.

SPEEDOMETER SPEED SENSOR

All models are equipped with an electronic speedometer assembly that consists of the speedometer, speed sensor and function switch.

The speed sensor mounts inside the transmission housing, directly over fourth gear.

Performance Check

The Harley-Davidson Speedometer Tester must be used to check the performance of the speedometer.

NOTE

This test cannot be used to verify the calibration of the speedometer and will not verify the speedometer's function to support legal proceedings. The test will verify speedometer function when performing service diagnosis or repair and to verify if the speedometer requires replacement.

Speedometer Speed Sensor Removal/Installation

The speedometer speed sensor mounts on top of the transmission case.

1. Remove the seat.
2. Disconnect the negative battery cable as described in this chapter.

3. Remove the Allen screw and remove the speed sensor (**Figure 142**) from the transmission case.
4. Disconnect the three-pin Mini-Deutsch connector containing one red, one black, and one white wire.

NOTE
*The electrical connector is not shown in **Figure 144** since it is located under the frame cross-member.*

5. Carefully pull the electrical connector out from under the frame cross-member (**Figure 144**). Disconnect the secondary locks on the Mini-Deutsch connector and disconnect the connector.
6. Tie a piece of string to the electrical connector. Tie the other end of the string to the frame cross-member.
7. Carefully pull the wiring harness and connector out of the frame on the right side. If the wire becomes tight or stuck, do not force it. If necessary, make a drawing of the wire routing through the frame. It is easy to forget the routing path after removing the wire.
8. Untie the string from the wiring harness.
9. Install by reversing these removal steps while noting the following:
   a. Tie the string to the wiring harness and connector.
   b. Carefully pull the string, wiring harness and connector through the right side of the frame and into position under the seat. Untie and remove the string.
   c. Apply a light coat of dielectric compound to the electrical connector(s) prior to installing them.
   d. Apply clean engine oil to the *new* O-ring on the speedometer sensor prior to installation. Install the sensor and tighten the Allen screw to the specification in **Table 6**.

STARTER RELAY SWITCH REPLACEMENT

The starter relay switch is mounted inside the electrical panel.
1. Remove the seat as described in Chapter Thirteen.
2. Disconnect the negative battery cable as described in this chapter.

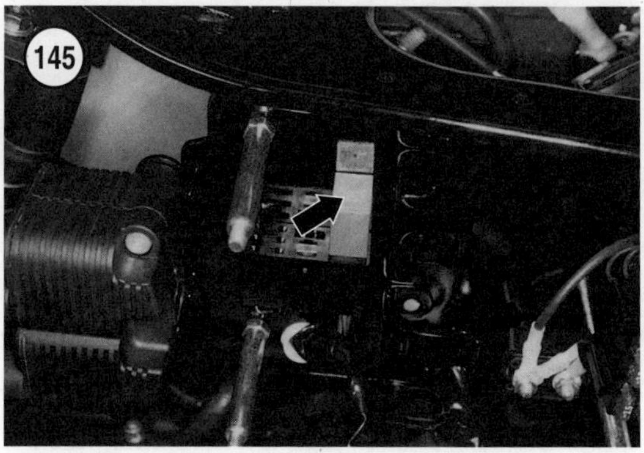

3. Remove the electrical panel cover and outer plate as described in this chapter.
4. Unplug the starter relay switch (**Figure 145**) and remove it from the relay block.
5. To test the switch, refer to *Starter Relay Testing* under *Electric Starting System* in Chapter Two.
6. Install by reversing these steps.

INSTRUMENTS

Removal/Installation (FXD, FXDS-CONV, FXDX, FXDXT, FXDP)

Refer to **Figure 146**.
1. Remove the seat.

NOTE
Always disarm the optional TSSM security system prior to disconnecting the battery or the siren will sound.

2. Disconnect the negative battery cable as described in this chapter.
3. On models so equipped, remove the windshield or front fairing.
4. To remove the speedometer, perform the following:
   a. Remove the two screws securing the backplate (A, **Figure 147**) and take it off.
   b. Depress the tab and disconnect the 12-pin electrical connector from the back of the speedometer.
   c. Carefully push the speedometer and front gasket (A, **Figure 148**) out through the front of the meter housing.
   d. Remove the front gasket from the speedometer.

146

INSTRUMENTS (FXD, FXDS-CON, FXDX, FXDXT, FXDP)

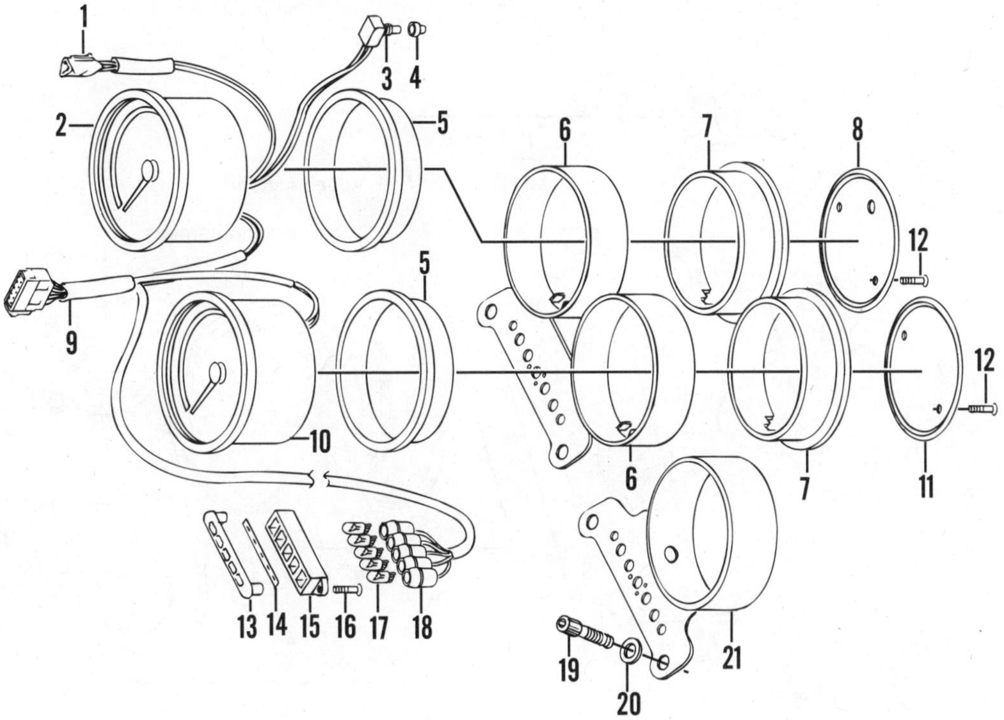

1. Socket lock
2. Speedometer
3. Reset switch
4. Boot
5. Front gasket
6. Meter housing (except FXD)
7. Rear gasket
8. Backplate
9. Wiring harness to main harness
10. Tachometer (except FXD)
11. Backplate
12. Screw
13. Indicator light bezel
14. Indicator light lens
15. Indicator light housing
16. Screw
17. Bulbs
18. Sockets
19. Allen bolt
20. Washer
21. Meter housing (FXD)

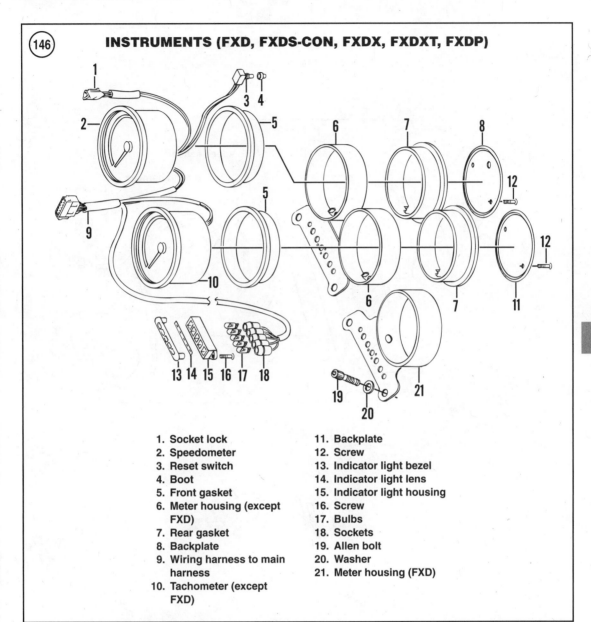

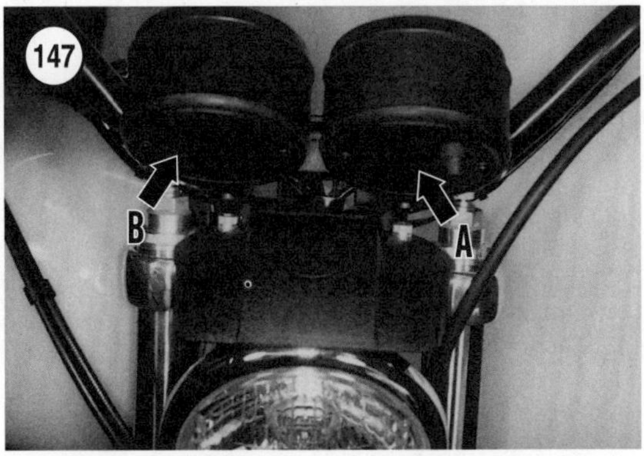

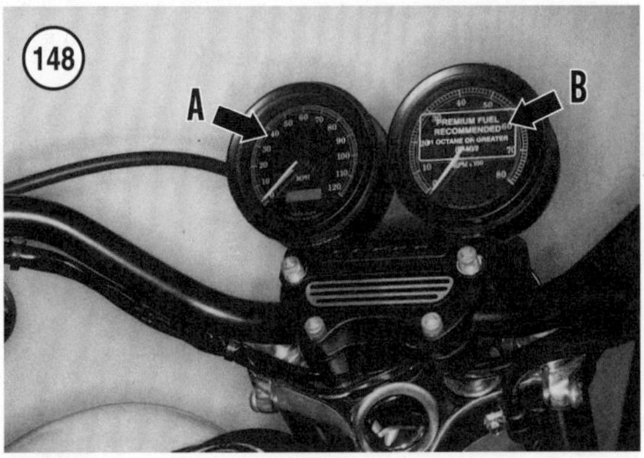

(149)

INSTRUMENTS (FXDL)

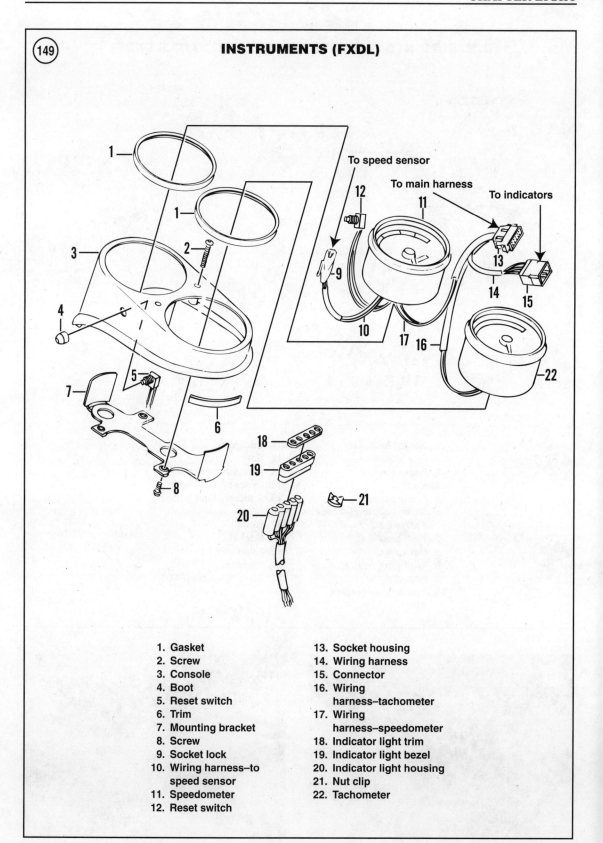

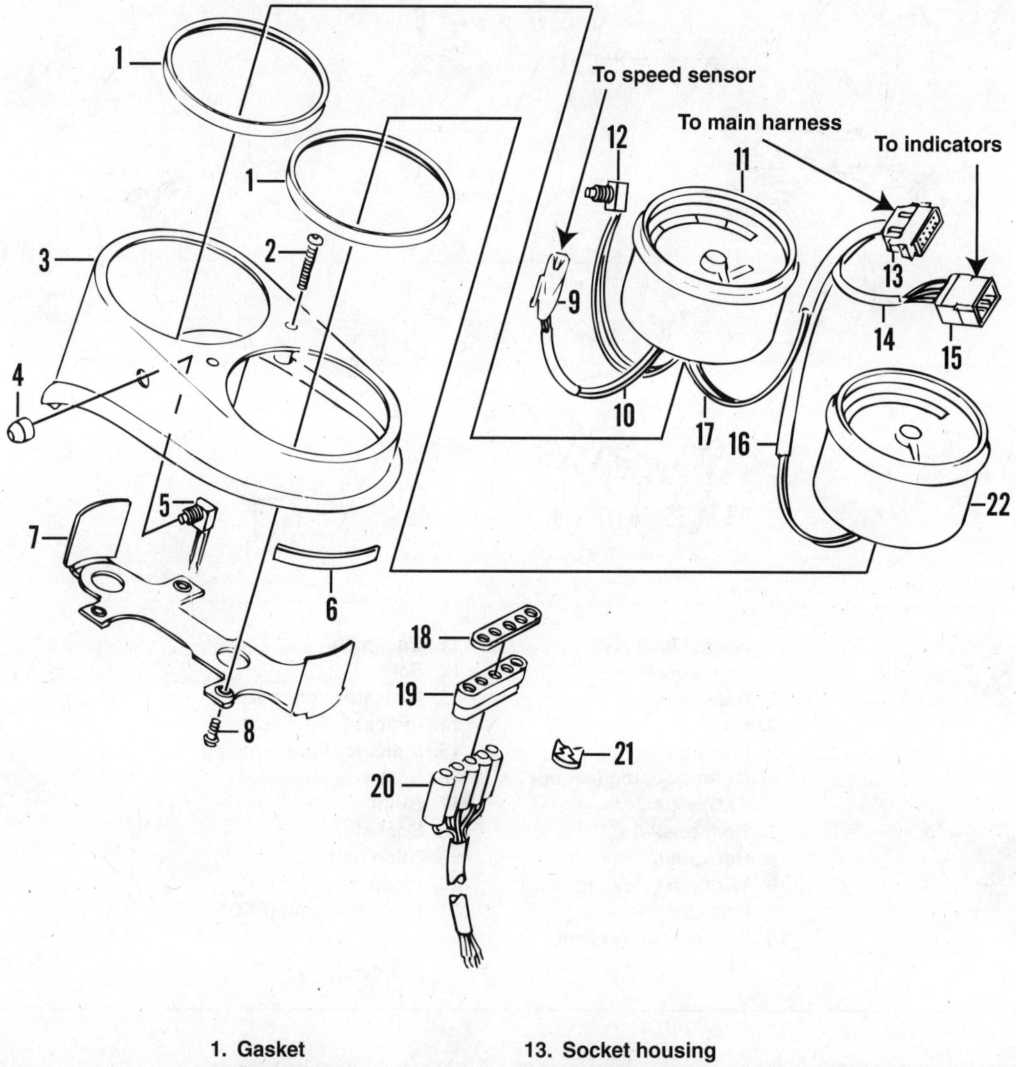

1. Gasket
2. Screw
3. Console
4. Boot
5. Reset switch
6. Trim
7. Mounting bracket
8. Screw
9. Socket lock
10. Wiring harness–to speed sensor
11. Speedometer
12. Reset switch
13. Socket housing
14. Wiring harness
15. Connector
16. Wiring harness–tachometer
17. Wiring harness–speedometer
18. Indicator light trim
19. Indicator light bezel
20. Indicator light housing
21. Nut clip
22. Tachometer

5. To remove the tachometer, perform the following:
   a. Remove the two screws securing the backplate (B, **Figure 147**) and take it off.
   b. Depress the tab and disconnect the 6-pin electrical connector from the back of the tachometer.
   c. Carefully push the tachometer and front gasket (B, **Figure 148**) out through the front of the meter housing.
   d. Remove the front gasket from the tachometer.
6. Store the meters in a safe place.
7. Remove the rear gasket(s) from the meter housing. They are identical with the same part number.

NOTE

If necessary, apply alcohol or glass cleaner to the gasket surfaces to ease installation of the meters.

8. If removed, install the front gasket onto the meter and install it into the meter housing. Press firmly until the meter is correctly seated.
9. Connect the electrical connector to the backside of the meter. Route the electrical wiring through the slot in the backside of the meter housing.
10. Install the rear gasket onto the meter and housing.
11. Install the backplate and tighten the screws securely.
12. On models so equipped, install the windshield or front fairing.

Removal/Installation (FXDL)

Refer to **Figure 149**.

1. Remove the seat as described in Chapter Thirteen.
2. Disconnect the negative battery cable as described in this chapter.
3. Cover the fuel tank surrounding the instrument assembly with towels to protect the finish.
4. To remove the speedometer, perform the following:
   a. Remove the two Allen screws securing the console assembly to the fuel tank.
   b. Lift the console assembly up, turn it over and place it on the fuel tank towels.
   c. Remove the four Allen screws and remove the mounting bracket securing the speedometer and tachometer to the underside of the console.
   d. Depress the tab and disconnect the 12-pin electrical connector from the back of the speedometer.
   e. Carefully remove the speedometer and gasket out through the front of the console.
   f. Remove the gasket from the speedometer.
5. To remove the tachometer, perform the following:
   a. Perform Steps 4a-4c of speedometer removal.
   b. Remove the T15 Torx screw securing the wiring harness clip to the backside of the tachometer.
   c. Gently pry on each end of the 6-pin electrical connector and disconnect it from the backside of the tachometer.
   d. Carefully remove the tachometer and gasket out through the front of the console.
   e. Remove the gasket from the tachometer.
6. If removed, install the gasket onto the perimeter of the console where it mounts onto the fuel tank.
7. To install the speedometer, perform the following:
   a. Install the gasket onto the console.
   b. Install the speedometer onto the console and gasket. Make sure the speedometer is seated correctly onto the gasket.
   c. Connect the 12-pin electrical connector onto the back of the speedometer.
8. To install the tachometer, perform the following:
   a. Install the gasket onto the console.
   b. Install the tachometer onto the console and gasket. Make sure the tachometer is seated correctly onto the gasket.
   c. Install and push down and install the 6-pin electrical connector onto the back of the tachometer.
   d. Install the wire harness and clip to the backside of the tachometer. Install the T15 Torx screw securing the wiring harness clip and tighten securely.
9. Install the mounting bracket to the underside of the console. Align the bolt holes in the mounting bracket and the speedometer and tachometer.
10. Install the four Allen screws securing the mounting bracket to the backside of the speedometer and tachometer.

11. Check that there will be no binding with the wiring harness and the bracket after the console is installed onto the fuel tank.
12. Carefully turn the console assembly over and position it on the fuel tank aligning the screw holes.
13. Install the two Allen screws securing the console assembly to the fuel tank and tighten securely.
14. Connect the negative battery cable as described in this chapter.
15. Install the seat.

Removal/Installation (FXDWG)

Refer to **Figure 150**.

1. Remove the seat as described in Chapter Thirteen.
2. Disconnect the negative battery cable as described in this chapter.
3. Cover the fuel tank surrounding the instrument assembly with towels to protect the finish.
4. Remove the acorn nut securing the console assembly to the set screw on the fuel tank.
5. Lift the console assembly up, turn it over and place it on the fuel tank towels.
6. Depress the tab and disconnect the 12-pin electrical connector from the back of the speedometer.
7. Unscrew the rubber boot from the reset switch on the left side of the console.
8. Remove the reset switch from the side of the console.
9. Carefully pry and raise the three tabs and the speedometer to release the back clamp from the speedometer.
10. Remove the speedometer and gasket out through the front of the console.
11. Remove the gasket from the speedometer.
12. Install the gasket onto the speedometer.
13. Install the speedometer into the console.
14. Press on the three tabs and push onto the backside of the speedometer until they are engaged.
15. Insert the reset switch through the side in the console and install the rubber boot.
16. Connect the 12-pin electrical connector onto the back of the speedometer.
17. Carefully turn the console assembly over and position it on the fuel tank aligning the set screw with the console hole.

(150) **INSTRUMENTS (FXDWG)**

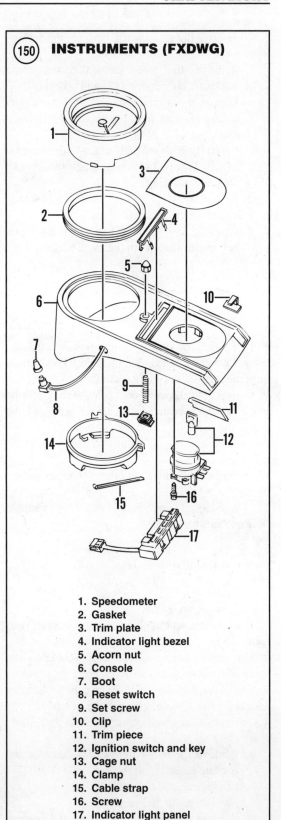

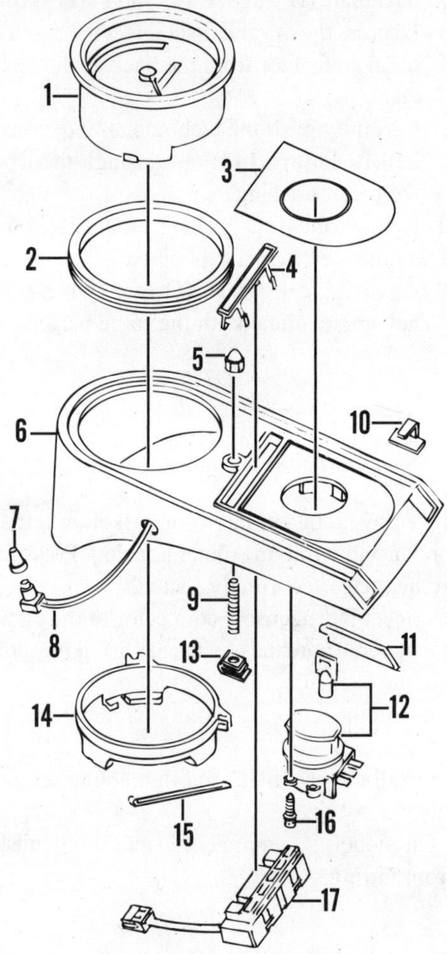

1. Speedometer
2. Gasket
3. Trim plate
4. Indicator light bezel
5. Acorn nut
6. Console
7. Boot
8. Reset switch
9. Set screw
10. Clip
11. Trim piece
12. Ignition switch and key
13. Cage nut
14. Clamp
15. Cable strap
16. Screw
17. Indicator light panel

151

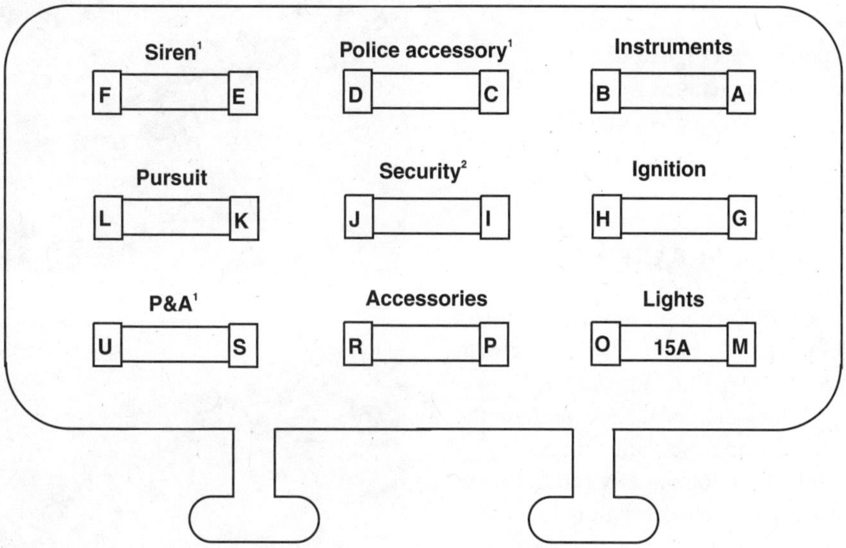

1. FXDP Dyna Police models only.
2. FXDP turn signal use only. Security not available on FXDP models.

152

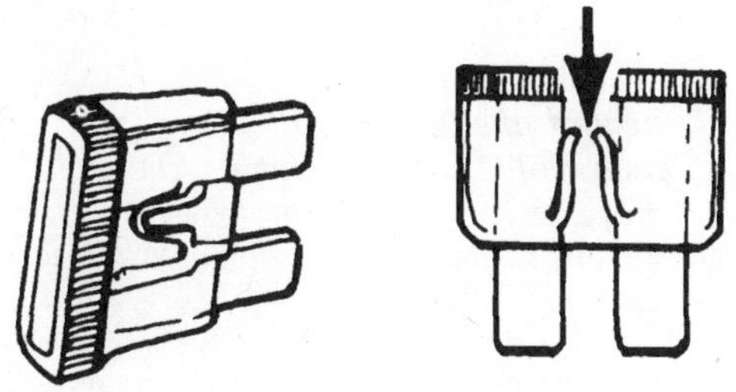

18. Install the acorn nut securing the console assembly to the fuel tank and tighten securely.
19. Connect the negative battery cable as described in this chapter.
20. Install the seat.

FUSES

All models are equipped with a series of fuses to protect the electrical system. The number of fuses varies, depending on the model. The fuse ratings are listed in **Table 1**. Refer to **Figure 151** for fuse location on the panel.

All fuses are located on a single panel within the electrical panel. If there is an electrical failure, first check for a blown fuse. A blown fuse will have a break in the element (**Figure 152**).

Whenever the fuse blows, find out the reason for the failure before replacing the fuse. Usually, the trouble is a short circuit in the wiring. This may be caused by worn-through insulation or a disconnected wire shorted to ground. Check the circuit the fuse protects.

Fuse Replacement

1. Remove the seat as described in Chapter Thirteen.

NOTE
Always disarm the optional TSSM security system prior to disconnecting the battery or the siren will sound.

2. Disconnect the negative battery cable as described in this chapter.
3. Remove the electrical panel cover as described in this chapter.
4. Locate the blown fuse (**Figure 153**) and install a new one of the *same* amperage.

NOTE
Always carry spare fuses.

CIRCUIT BREAKER

All models use a single circuit breaker to protect the electrical circuits. **Table 1** lists the circuit breaker rating for the different models.

Whenever a failure occurs in any part of the electrical system, the circuit breaker is self-resetting and will automatically return power to the circuit when the electrical fault is found and corrected.

CAUTION
If the electrical fault is not found and corrected, the circuit breaker will cycle on and off continuously. This will cause the motorcycle to run erratically.

Usually the trouble to a short circuit is found in the wiring connected to the circuit breaker.

The circuits protected by the circuit breaker can be determined by following the wiring diagrams at the end of the book.

Do not consider a tripped circuit breaker as just a minor annoyance; it indicates that something is wrong in the electrical system that must be corrected immediately.

Replacement

The circuit breaker is located inside the electrical panel.
1. Remove the seat as described in Chapter Thirteen.

NOTE
Always disarm the optional TSSM security system prior to disconnecting the battery or the siren will sound.

153

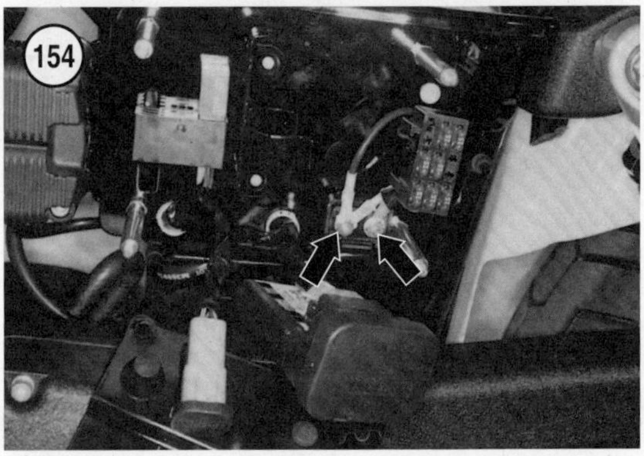
154

2. Disconnect the negative battery cable as described in this chapter.
3. Remove the electric panel cover and inner panel as described in this chapter.

NOTE
Record the number of wires and their color and to which terminal they are connected. The wires must be reinstalled onto the correct terminal.

4. Remove the nuts and wire connections at the circuit breaker (**Figure 154**).
5. Remove the circuit breaker from the mounting bracket on the inner panel.
6. Install the circuit breaker by reversing these steps.

DIAGNOSTIC TROUBLE CODES

Refer to *Ignition System* in Chapter Two to retrieve the diagnostic trouble codes.

Table 1 ELECTRICAL SPECIFICATIONS

Battery	12 volts, 19 amp hour
Alternator	
AC voltage output	16-20 VAC per 1000 rpm
Stator coil resistance	0.1-0.2 ohm
Regulator	
Voltage output @ 3600 rpm	14.3-14.7 @ 75° F (24° C)
Amperes at 3600 rpm	32 amp
Ignition coil	
Primary resistance	0.5-0.7 ohm
Secondary resistance	5500-7500 ohms
Spark plug cable resistance	
Front cylinder cable	4700-11230 ohms
Rear cylinder cable	1812-4375 ohms
Circuit breaker	
FXDP	40 amp
All models except FXDP	30 amp
Fuses	
Ignition fuse	15 amp
Lighting fuse	15 amp
Accessory fuse	15 amp
Instrument fuse	15 amp
Security system*	15 amp

*Models so equipped.

Table 2 MAINTENANCE FREE BATTERY VOLTAGE READINGS

State of Charge	Voltage reading
100%	13.0-13.2
75%	12.8
50%	12.5
25%	12.2
0%	12.0 volts or less

Table 3 BATTERY CHARGING RATES/TIMES (APPROXIMATE)

Voltage	% of Charge	3 amp Charger	6 amp Charger	10 amp Charger	20 amp Charger
12.8	100%	–	–	–	–
12.6	75%	1.75 hours	50 minutes	30 minutes	15 minutes
12.3	50%	3.5 hours	1.75 hours	1 hour	30 minutes
12.0	25%	5 hours	2.5 hours	1.5 hours	45 minutes
11.8	0%	6 hours and 40 minutes	3 hours and 20 minutes	2 hours	1 hour

Table 4 STARTER MOTOR SPECIFICATIONS

Minimum free speed	3000 rpm @ 11.5 volts
Maximum free current	90 amp @ 11.5 volts
Cranking current	200 amp maximum @ 68° F (20° C)
Brush length (minimum)	0.433 in. (11.0 mm)
Commutator diameter (minimum)	1.141 in. (28.98 mm)

Table 5 REPLACEMENT BULBS

Item	Size (all 12 volt) × quantity
Headlamp	55/60
Position lamp*	3.9
Indicator lamps	
FXDL	1.1 x 4
FXDP	2.1 x 4
All models except FXDL and FXDP	2.2 x 3
Fuel gauge	
FXDL, FXDWG	2.7
FXD, FXDX, FXDX-CONV, FXDXT	3.7
FXDP	NA
Front turn signal/running light	27/7 x 2
Front turn signal*	21 x 2
Rear turn signal	27 x 2
Rear turn signal*	21 x 2
Tail/brake lamp	7/27
Tail/brake lamp*	5/21

*Indicates bulb specification for HD International models.

Table 6 ELECTRICAL SYSTEM TORQUE SPECIFICATIONS

Item	ft.-lb.	in.-lb.	N•m
Alternator stator			
Torx screws	–	30-40	3-5
Camshaft position sensor (1999-2000)			
Inspection cover screws	–	20-30	2-3
Sensor screw	–	20-30	2-3
Crankshaft position sensor (CKP)			
Allen screw	–	90-120	10-14
Fuel gauge sending unit plate screws	–	17	2
Fuel tank			
Console nut	–	80-100	9-11
Mounting bolt	10-18	–	14-24
Handlebar switch housing screw	–	35-45	4-5
Headlight			
Mounting block bolt	25-30	–	34-41
Mounting nut	–	120-180	14-20
Mounting screw	25-30	–	34-41
Shade bolt	–	120-144	14-16
Horn mounting nut	–	110	12
Ignition coil bolts	–	24-72	3-8
Ignition module screw	–	15-21	2-3
Instrument cluster bolt	12-18	–	16-24
Jackshaft lockplate bolt	–	84-108	9-12
MAP sensor screw	–	20-30	2-3
Speedometer sensor mounting bolt	–	84-108	9-12
Starter			
Mounting bolts	13-20	–	18-27
Positive terminal nut	–	65-80	7-9

(continued)

Table 6 ELECTRICAL SYSTEM TORQUE SPECIFICATIONS (continued)

Item	ft.-lb.	in.-lb.	N·m
Starter jackshaft bolt	–	84-108	9-12
Switches			
Neutral	–	120-180	14-20
Oil pressure	–	96-120	11-14
Rear stop light	–	96-120	11-14
Tail/brake light			
Base screws	–	40-48	4-5
Lens screws	–	20-24	2-3
Voltage regulator screws	–	60-80	7-9

Table 7 TURN SIGNAL SPEED AND DISTANCE TEST

Range	1	2	3	4
MPH	0-34	35-44	45-60	61+
KMH	0-56	56-71	72-97	98+
Feet	221	339	680	1051
Miles	0.04	0.06	0.13	0.20
Meters	67	103	207	320

Table 8 TURN SIGNAL SPEED AND TIME TEST

Constant speed MPH	KMH	Signal ON time in seconds
25	40	5-7
38	61	5-7
52	84	8-10
65	105	10-12

8

CHAPTER NINE

WHEELS, HUBS AND TIRES

This chapter describes disassembly and repair of the front and rear wheels, hubs and tire service. For routine maintenance, see Chapter Three.

Tables 1-3 are at the end of the chapter.

MOTORCYCLE STANDS

Many procedures in this chapter require that the front or rear wheel be lifted off the ground. To do this, a quality motorcycle front end stand (**Figure 1**), swing arm stand, or suitable size jack is required. Before purchasing or using a stand, check the manufacturer's instructions to make sure the stand will work with the Dyna Glide model being worked on. If any adjustments or accessories are required for the motorcycle and/or stand, perform the necessary adjustments or install the correct parts before lifting

1

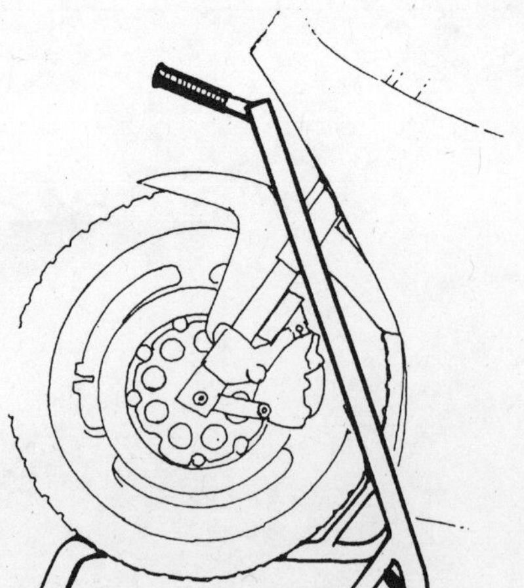

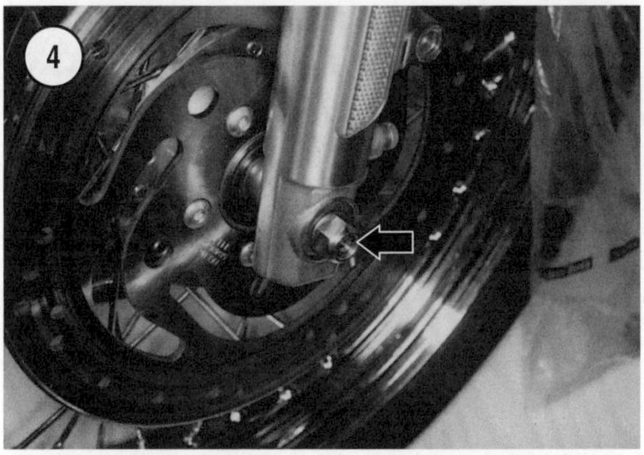

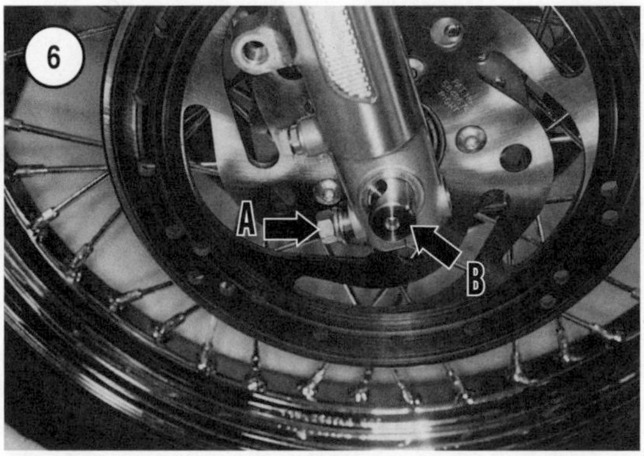

the motorcycle. When using the motorcycle stand, have an assistant standing by to help. Some means to tie down one end of the motorcycle may also be required. After lifting the motorcycle on a stand, make sure the motorcycle is properly supported before walking away from it.

FRONT WHEEL

Removal

1. Support the motorcycle with the front wheel off the ground. See *Motorcycle Stands* in this chapter.

NOTE
On models with dual front calipers, both calipers must be removed to remove the front wheel.

2A. On 1999 models, remove the caliper mounting bolts (**Figure 2**) and remove the caliper(s) as described in Chapter Twelve.
2B. On 2000-on models, remove the caliper mounting bolts (**Figure 3**) and remove the caliper(s) as described in Chapter Twelve.

NOTE
Place a plastic or wooden spacer between the brake pads in place of the disc. Then, if the brake pedal is inadvertently depressed, the pistons will not be forced out of the caliper. If this occurs, disassemble the caliper to reseat the pistons.

3. On the left side, remove the axle nut (**Figure 4**), lockwasher and flat washer (**Figure 5**).
4A. On all models except FXDWG, loosen the front axle pinch bolt (A, **Figure 6**).

4B. On FXDWG models, loosen the nuts on the fork slider cap.

NOTE
On some models, the wheel spacers are different. Identify the spacers before removing them.

5. Prior to removing the front axle, note the location of the right side spacer (**Figure 7**) and left side spacer (**Figure 8**). The spacer must be reinstalled on the correct side during installation.
6. Insert a drift or screwdriver into the hole (**Figure 9**) in the end of the front axle (B, **Figure 6**). Withdraw the front axle from the fork sliders and front wheel. Remove the tool from the axle.
7. Pull the wheel away from the fork sliders and remove it.

CAUTION
Do not set the wheel down on the brake disc surface, as it may be damaged.

8. Inspect the front wheel assembly as described in this chapter.

Installation

1. Clean the axle in solvent and dry thoroughly. Make sure the axle bearing surfaces on both fork sliders and the axle are free of burrs and nicks.
2. Apply an antiseize lubricant to the axle shaft prior to installation.
3. If the oil seals or bearings were replaced, confirm front axle spacer alignment as described under *Front Hub* in this chapter.
4. Install the left side and right side axle spacers in the wheel. The left side axle spacer is longer than the right side spacer.
5. Install the wheel between the fork sliders and install the axle from the right side (**Figure 9**).
6. Check that axle spacers are installed correctly. Refer to **Figure 7** for the right side and to **Figure 8** for the left side.
7. Install the flat washer, lockwasher (**Figure 5**) and axle nut (**Figure 4**) finger-tight. Check that axle spacers are installed correctly.
8A. On all models except FXDWG, tighten the front axle pinch bolt (A, **Figure 6**) to the specification in **Table 2**.

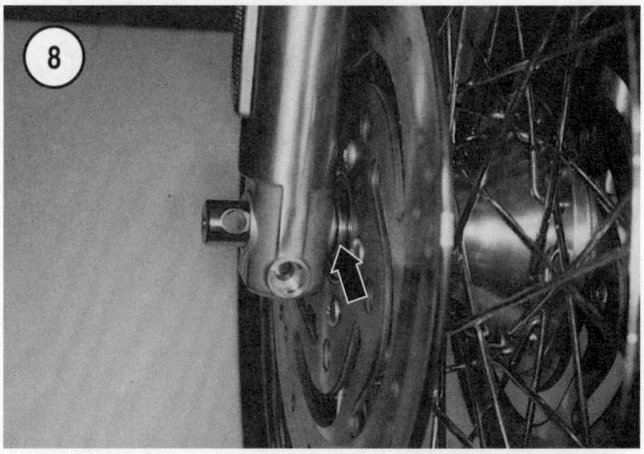

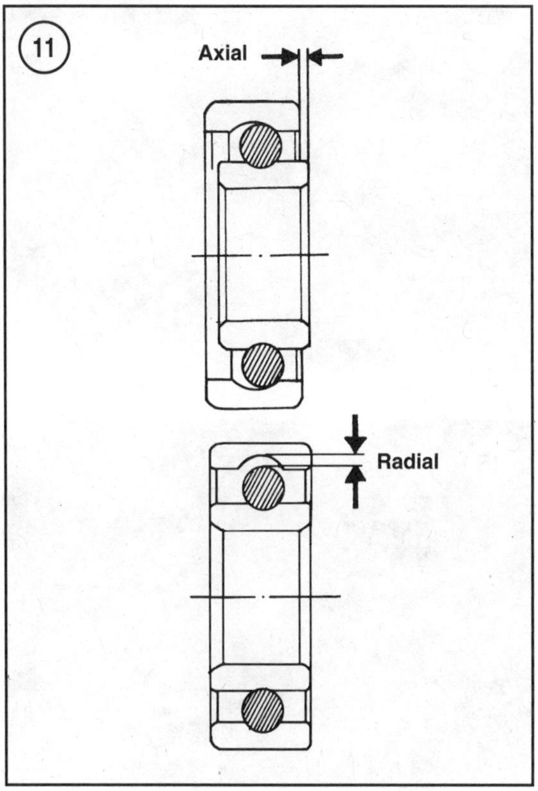

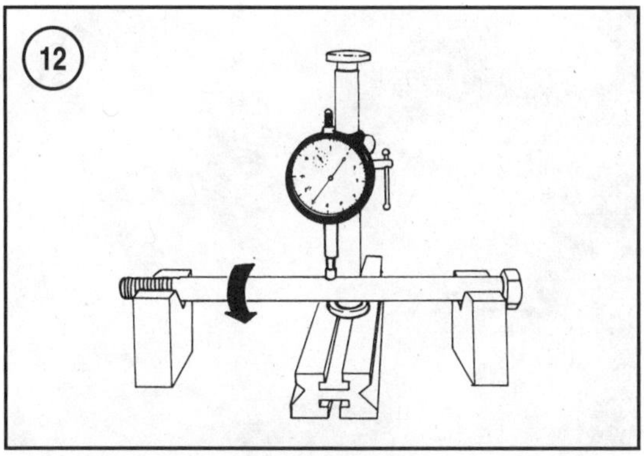

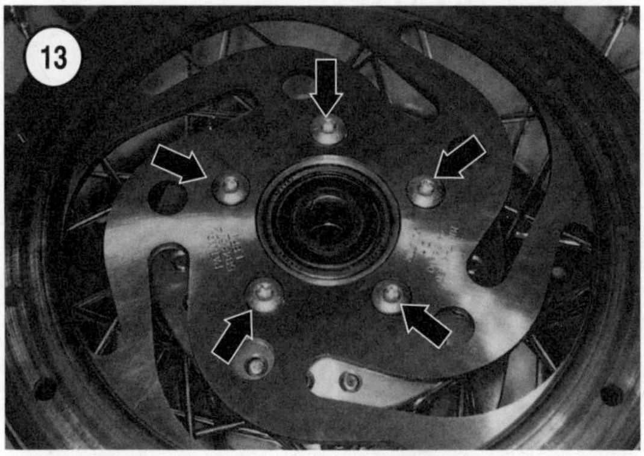

8B. On FXDWG models, tighten the nuts on the fork slider cap to the specification in **Table 2**.

9. Insert a drift or screwdriver into the hole (**Figure 9**) in the end of the front axle (B, **Figure 6**) to keep it from rotating.

10. Tighten the front axle nut (**Figure 4**) to the specification in **Table 2**.

11. Remove the tool used in Step 8 from the front axle.

12. Check that the front wheel is centered between the fork sliders. If not, check the position of the left and right axle spacers.

13. On 1999 models, perform the *Front Wheel Bearing End Play Check* in this chapter.

14. Install the front brake caliper(s) as described in Chapter Twelve.

15. With the front wheel off the ground, rotate it several times and apply the front brake to seat the brake pads against the disc(s).

16. Remove the stand and lower the front wheel onto the ground.

9

Inspection

Replace any worn or damaged parts as described in this section.

1. On 1999 models, inspect the oil seals (**Figure 10**) for excessive wear, hardness, cracks or other damage. If necessary, replace the seals as described under *Front and Rear Hubs* in this chapter.

2. Turn each bearing inner race by hand. The bearing must turn smoothly. Some axial play (end play) is normal, but radial play (side play) must be negligible. See **Figure 11**. If one bearing is damaged, replace both bearings as a set. Refer to *Front and Rear Hubs* in this chapter.

3. Clean the axle and axle spacers in solvent to remove all grease and dirt. Make sure the axle contact surfaces are clean and free of dirt and old grease.

4. Check the axle runout with a set of V-blocks and dial indicator (**Figure 12**).

5. Check the spacers for wear, burrs and damage. Replace as necessary.

6. Check the brake disc bolts (**Figure 13**) for tightness. To service the brake disc, refer to Chapter Twelve.

7. Check wheel runout and spoke tension as described in this chapter.

REAR WHEEL

Removal

1. Support the motorcycle with the rear wheel off the ground with an appropriate size jack (A, **Figure 14**).

NOTE
This procedure is shown with the complete exhaust system removed to better illustrate the steps.

2. Remove the rear cylinder's muffler as described in Chapter Seven.
3. Remove the bolts and nuts securing the drive belt guard (A, **Figure 15**) and remove the guard.
4. On models with a low cut rear fender, it may be necessary to remove the screws securing the drive belt lower deflector (B, **Figure 15**) and remove it.

NOTE
The rear wheel is heavy and can be difficult to remove. Check the tire-to-ground clearance before removing the rear axle. If necessary, have an assistant help in the removal.

5. On international models, remove the cover from the rear axle nut.
6. Remove the spring clip (A, **Figure 16**) from the rear axle nut and axle.
7. Loosen and remove the axle nut (B, **Figure 16**) and washer.
8. From the right side, withdraw the rear axle (B, **Figure 14**) while holding onto the rear wheel. Lower the rear wheel to the ground.
9. On 2000-on models, remove the rear brake caliper (**Figure 17**) from the swing arm and tie it up to the frame with a bungee cord or wire.
10. Remove the right side (**Figure 18**) and left side (**Figure 19**) spacers from the wheel hub.
11. Lift the drive belt off the driven sprocket (A, **Figure 20**) and remove the rear wheel (B).
12. On 1999 models, slide the rear brake caliper off the locating post on the swing arm and tie it up to the frame with a bungee cord or wire.

NOTE
Place a plastic or wooden spacer between the brake pads in place of the disc. Then, if the brake pedal is inad-

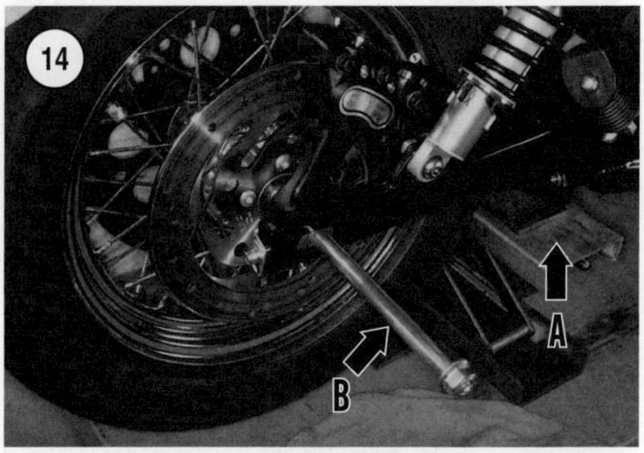

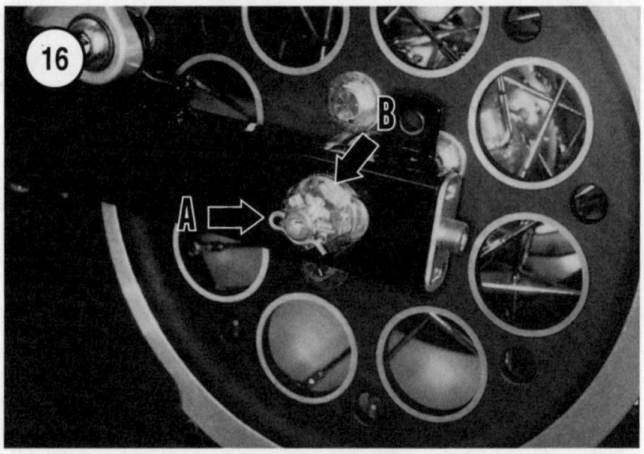

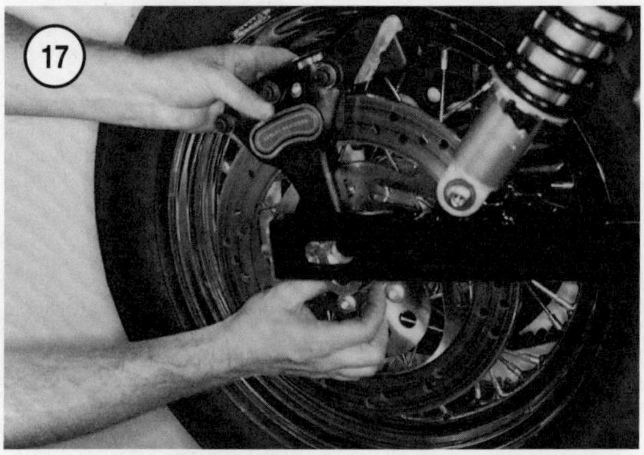

18

19

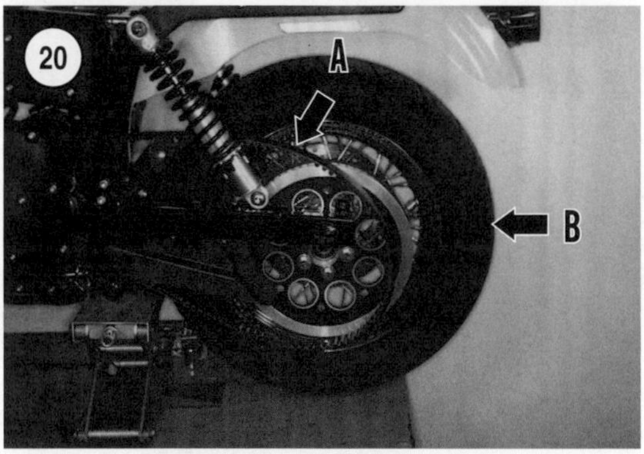

20

21

vertently depressed, the pistons will not be forced out of the caliper. If this occurs, disassemble the caliper to reseat the pistons.

CAUTION
Do not set the wheel down on the brake disc surface, as it may be damaged.

13. Inspect the rear wheel as described in this chapter.

Installation

1. Clean the axle in solvent and dry thoroughly. Make sure the bearing surfaces on the axle are free from burrs and nicks.
2. Apply an antiseize lubricant to the axle shaft prior to installation.
3. On 1999 models, slide the rear brake caliper onto the locating post on the swing arm.
4. Position the rear wheel between the swing arm sides and place the drive belt on the sprocket.
5. Install the right side (**Figure 18**) and left side (**Figure 19**) spacers into the rear wheel oil seals.
6. Remove the spacer block from between the brake pads.

CAUTION
When installing the rear wheel in the following steps, carefully insert the brake disc between the brake pads in the caliper assembly. Do not force the brake disc as it can damage the leading edge of both brake pads.

7. On 2000-on models, move the rear brake caliper (**Figure 17**) into position on the swing arm.
8. Lift the rear wheel and install the rear axle from the right side (B, **Figure 14**). Install the axle through the swing arm, the rear brake caliper mounting bracket and the other side of the swing arm.
9. After the rear axle is installed, check to make sure both axle spacers are still in place.
10. Install the washer and axle nut (**Figure 21**). Tighten the axle nut to the specification in **Table 2**.
11. On 1999 models, perform the *Front and Rear Axle End Play Check* in this chapter. When the rear axle end play is correct, continue with Step 12.

24

FRONT LACED WHEEL (1999)

1. Front axle
2. Right side axle spacer
3. Brake disc
4. Oil seal
5. Bearing
6. Spacer sleeve
7. Wheel rim
8. Hub
9. Shim pack
10. Spacer washer
11. Left side axle spacer
12. Washer
13. Lockwasher
14. Axle nut
15. Bolt
16. Valve stem cap
17. Nut
18. Spoke
19. Balance weight
20. Spoke nipple

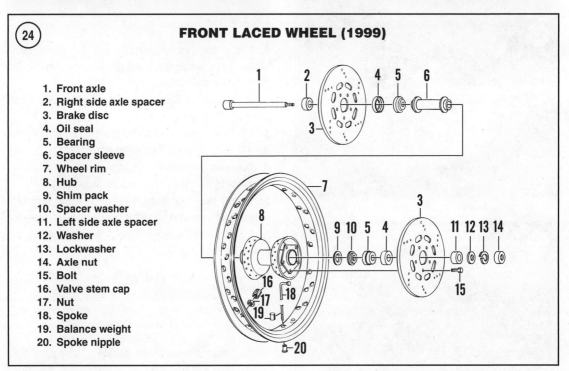

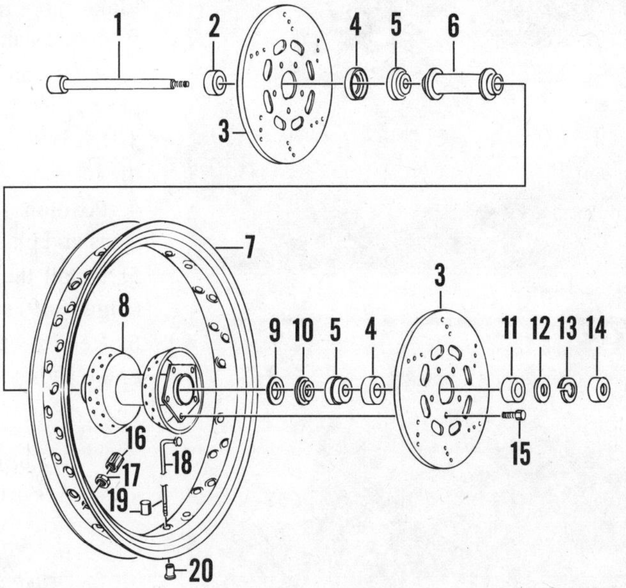

12. Check drive belt tension and alignment as described in Chapter Three.

13. If necessary, tighten the axle nut to align the spring pin hole with the nut slot. Then install a spring pin (A, **Figure 16**) and snap it into place.

14. Install the belt guard (A, **Figure 15**) and tighten the bolts and nuts securely.

15. If removed install the debris deflector (B, **Figure 15**) and tighten the screws securely.

16. Install the rear cylinder's muffler, or exhaust system, as described in Chapter Seven.

17. Rotate the wheel several times to make sure it rotates freely. Then apply the rear brake pedal several times to seat the pads against the disc.

18. Remove the stand and lower the rear wheel to the ground.

Inspection

Replace any worn or damaged parts as described in this section.

1. On 1999 models, inspect the oil seals for excessive wear, hardness, cracks or other damage. If necessary, replace the seals as described under *Front and Rear Hubs* in this chapter.

2. Turn each bearing inner race by hand. The bearing must turn smoothly. Some axial play (end play) is normal, but radial play (side play) must be negli-

25

FRONT CAST WHEEL (1999)

1. Front axle
2. Right side axle spacer
3. Brake disc
4. Oil seal
5. Bearing
6. Cast wheel
7. Spacer sleeve
8. Shim pack
9. Spacer washer
10. Left side axle spacer
11. Washer
12. Lockwasher
13. Axle nut
14. Bolt

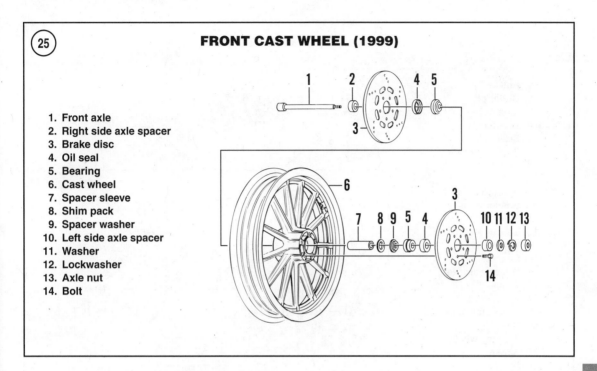

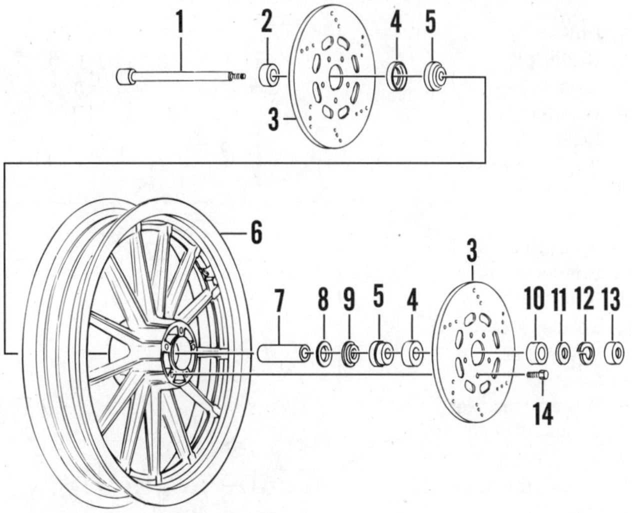

gible. See **Figure 11**. If one bearing is damaged, replace both bearings as a set. Refer to *Front and Rear Hubs* in this chapter.

3. Clean the axle and axle spacers in solvent to remove all grease and dirt. Make sure the axle contact surfaces are free of dirt and old grease.
4. Check the axle runout with a set of V-blocks and a dial indicator (**Figure 12**).
5. Check the spacers for wear, burrs and damage. Replace as necessary.
6. Check the brake disc bolts (**Figure 22**) for tightness. To service the brake disc, refer to Chapter Twelve.
7. Check the final drive sprocket bolts (**Figure 23**) for tightness. Service for the final drive sprocket is covered in this chapter.
8. Check wheel runout and spoke tension as described in this chapter.

FRONT AND REAR HUBS (1999)

Non-sealed tapered roller bearings are installed on each side of the hub. Oil seals are installed on the outside of each bearing to protect them from dirt and other contaminants.

The bearing outer races are pressed into the hub. Do not remove the bearing races unless they require replacement.

Preliminary Inspection

Inspect each wheel bearing prior to removing it from the wheel hub.

CAUTION

Do not remove the wheel bearing outer races for inspection purposes as they will be damaged during the removal process. Remove wheel bearings only if they are to be replaced.

1. Perform Steps 1-4 of the *Disassembly* procedure.
2. Turn each bearing by hand. The bearings must turn smoothly with no roughness.
3. Inspect the play of the inner race of each wheel bearing. Check for excessive axial play and radial play. Replace the bearing if it has an excess amount of free play.
4. Check the balls for evidence of wear, pitting or excessive heat (bluish tint). Replace the bearings if necessary; always replace as a complete set. When replacing the bearings, make sure the replacement bearings match.

Disassembly

Refer to **Figures 24-27**.

(26)

REAR LACED WHEEL (1999)

1. Bolt
2. Cotter pin
3. Axle nut
4. Washer
5. Brake disc
6. Right side axle spacer
7. Oil seal
8. Bearing
9. Bearing outer race
10. Spacer washer
11. Shim pack
12. Spacer sleeve
13. Wheel rim
14. Spacer
15. Driven sprocket
16. Washer
17. Bolt
18. Valve stem cap
19. Nut
20. Balance weight
21. Spoke
22. Spoke nipple
23. Left side axle spacer
24. Rear axle

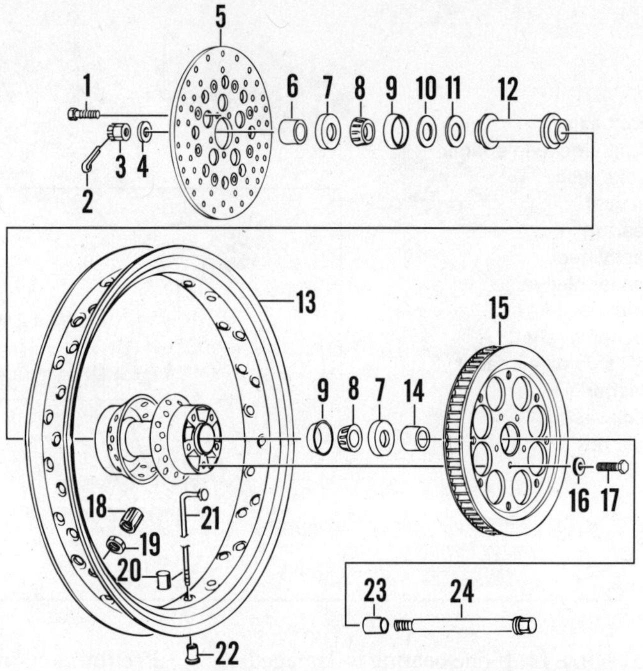

(27)

REAR CAST WHEEL (1999)

1. Bolt
2. Cotter pin
3. Axle nut
4. Washer
5. Brake disc
6. Right side axle spacer
7. Oil seal
8. Bearing
9. Bearing outer race
10. Spacer washer
11. Shim pack
12. Spacer sleeve
13. Cast wheel
14. Valve stem cap
15. Nut
16. Valve stem
17. Spacer
18. Driven sprocket
19. Washer
20. Bolt
21. Left side axle spacer
22. Rear axle

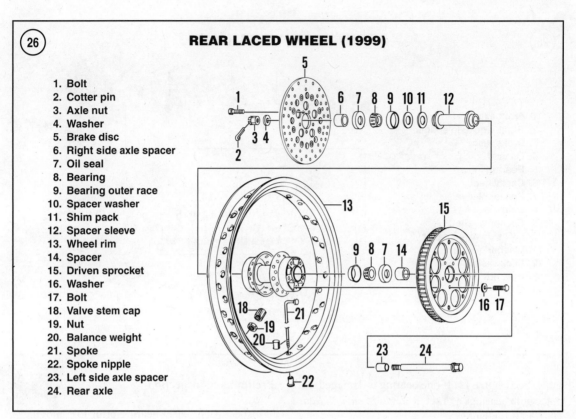

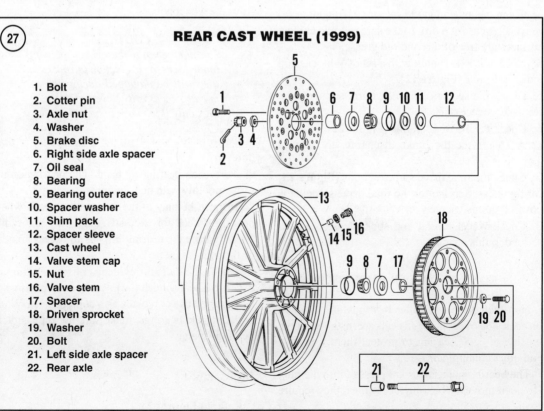

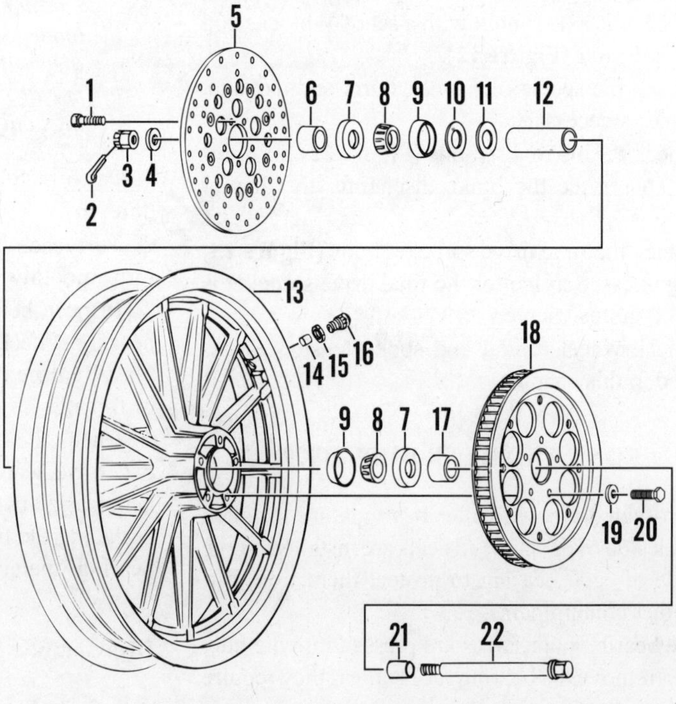

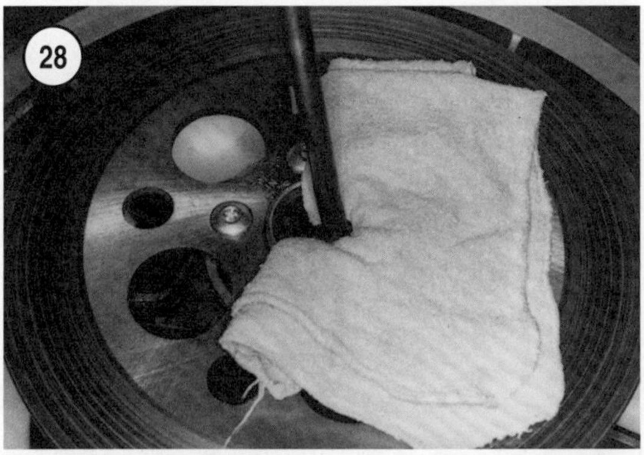
28

29

30

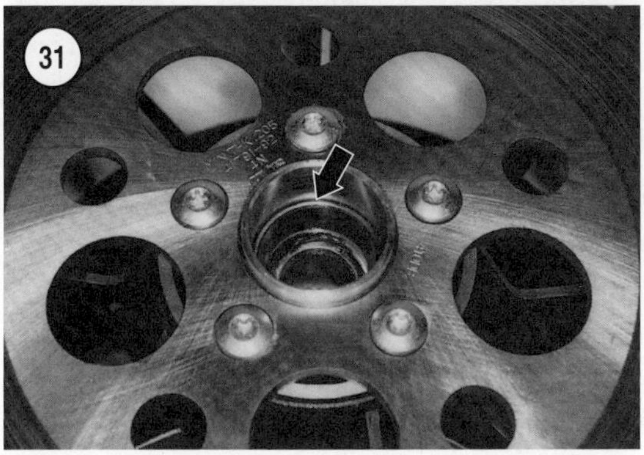
31

This procedure applies to both the front and rear wheel and hub assemblies. Where differences occur between the different hubs they are identified.

NOTE
The bearings and races are matched pairs. Label all parts so that they will be returned to their original positions.

1A. Remove the front wheel as described in this chapter.

1B. Remove the rear wheel as described in this chapter.

2. If necessary, remove the brake disc as described in Chapter Twelve.

3. If still in place, remove the axle spacers from the hub.

4. Pry one of the oil seals out of the hub (**Figure 28**) and remove the bearing (**Figure 29**) and spacer sleeve (**Figure 30**). Turn the wheel over and remove the opposite oil seal and bearing. Remove the washer and spacer shimpack.

5. Wash the bearings in clean solvent and dry with compressed air. Wipe the bearing races off with a clean rag dipped in solvent.

6. Check the roller bearings and races (**Figure 31**) for wear, pitting or excessive bluish tint. Replace the bearings and races as a complete set on each side of the wheel. Perform Step 7 to replace the bearing races. If the bearings and races do not require replacement, go to Step 8. If original bearings are to be reused, pack the bearings with grease and then wrap in a clean lint-free cloth until assembly. Apply a film of grease across the bearing race (**Figure 31**).

NOTE
*A wheel bearing race remover and installer tool (JIMS part No. 33461-80) (**Figure 32**) is available.*

7A. To remove the right and left side wheel bearing outer races (**Figure 31**) using special tools, perform the following:

a. Install the special tool into the hub against the bearing race following the manufacturer's instructions.
b. Tap the bearing race out of one side of the hub.
c. Reposition the special tool and tap the other bearing race out of other side of the hub.
d. Remove the special tool.

7B. To remove the right and left side wheel bearing outer races (**Figure 31**) without using special tools, perform the following:

a. Insert a drift punch through the hub and drive the bearing outer race out of the hub. Tap on alternate sides of the race to drive it squarely out of the hub. If the race binds in the hub bore, level it by tapping it from its opposite side.
b. Repeat substep a for the outer race on the other side of the hub.

8. Clean the hub with solvent. Dry with compressed air.

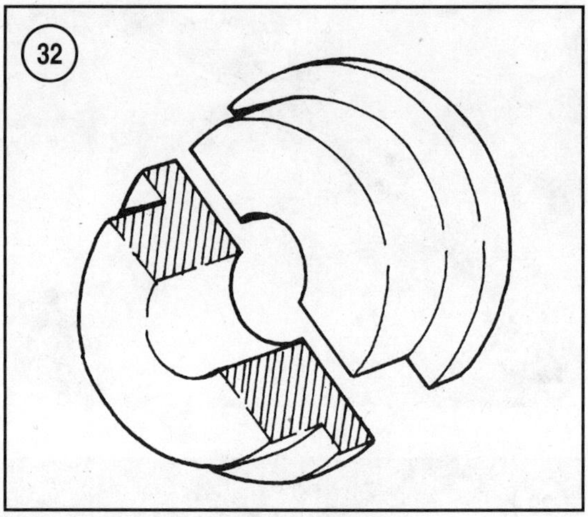

Installation

1. Wipe the outside of the new race and the hub receptacle with oil and align it with its bore in the hub.

NOTE
When installing the race, stop and check the work often, making sure the race is square with the hub bore. Do not allow the race to bind during installation or the bore in the hub will be damaged.

2A. To install the right and left side wheel bearing outer races (**Figure 31**) using special tools, perform the following:

a. Install the special tool into the bearing outer race and the hub following the manufacturer's instructions.
b. Tap the bearing race straight into one side of the hub until it bottoms on the hub shoulder.
c. Reposition the special tool and tap the other bearing race into the other side of the hub.
d. Remove the special tool.

2B. To install the right and left side wheel bearing outer races (**Figure 31**) without using special tools, perform the following:

a. Select a driver with the outside diameter slightly smaller than the bearing race's outside diameter.
b. Drive the bearing outer race squarely into the hub bore until it bottoms on the hub shoulder.
c. Repeat substep b for the outer race on the other side of the hub.

3. Pack the bearings with grease and install them in their original position as noted during removal.

4. Pack each seal lip with grease and install it with a bearing driver or socket with an outer diameter smaller than the oil seal.

5A. On cast wheels, assemble the front hub in the order shown in **Figure 25** or **Figure 27**, while noting the following:

a. Apply grease to both ends of the spacer sleeve.
b. Install the spacer washer with its shoulder (smaller diameter) facing toward its adjacent bearing.

CAUTION
If the spacer washer is installed with its larger diameter side toward the bearing, the spacer washer could contact the bearing cage and damage it.

c. After installing the bearings, pack the area between the bearings and oil seals with grease.
d. Install the oil seals until they are flush with the hub or recessed 0.04 in. (1.0 mm) below the hub surface (**Figure 10**).
e. Install the spacer so that its large chamfered end faces toward the bearing on the valve stem hole side of the wheel.

5B. On laced wheels, assemble the front hub in the order shown in **Figure 24** or **Figure 26**, while noting the following:

a. Apply grease to both ends of the spacer sleeve.
b. Install the spacer washer with its shoulder (smaller diameter) facing toward its adjacent bearing.

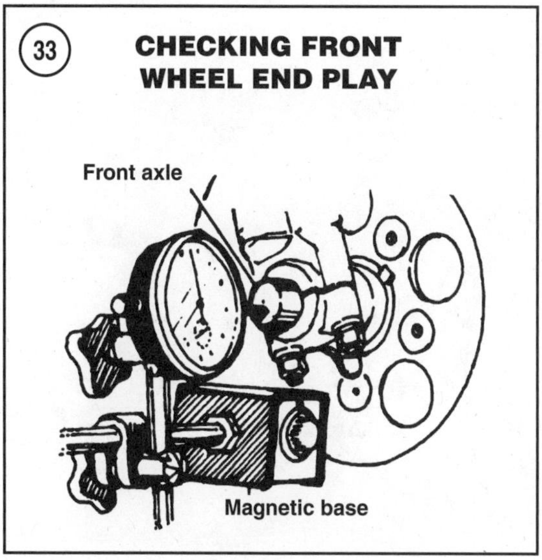

CAUTION
If the spacer washer is installed with its larger diameter side toward the bearing, the spacer washer could contact the bearing cage and damage it.

c. After installing the bearings, pack the area between the bearings and oil seals with grease.
d. Install the oil seals until they are flush with the hub or recessed 0.020 in. (0.51 mm) below the hub surface (**Figure 10**).
e. Install the spacer so that its large chamfered end faces toward the bearing on the valve stem hole side of the wheel.

6. If removed, install the brake disc as described in Chapter Twelve.
7. After the wheel is installed and the axle nut tightened, check bearing end play as described in this chapter.

FRONT AND REAR WHEEL BEARING END PLAY CHECK (1999 MODELS)

Front and rear wheel bearing end play establishes the amount of axial (lengthwise) movement between the left and right bearings. **Table 1** lists the correct end play specifications. Excessive end play can cause bearing side loading. If the end play is too tight, bearing seizure could result. Check end play each time the rear wheel is installed.

The thickness of the spacer shim (**Table 3**) controls end play between the spacer sleeve and spacer washer.

1. Support the motorcycle on a stand with the front or rear wheel off the ground.
2. On the rear wheel, remove the spring pin from the rear axle nut.
3. Tighten the front or rear axle to the specification in **Table 2**.
4. Mount a dial indicator securely on the brake disc and center its stem against the end of the axle (**Figure 33**). Then zero the dial gauge. Grasp the tire and move it (with the axle) in and out along the axle center line and note the indicator reading. The total indicator reading is axle end play.
5. If there is not enough end play, install a thinner spacer shim.
6. If the end play is excessive, install a thicker spacer shim.
7. To replace a spacer shim, disassemble the front or rear hub as described in this chapter.

9

FRONT AND REAR HUBS (2000-ON)

Sealed ball bearings are installed on each side of the hub. Do not remove the bearing assemblies unless they require replacement.

Preliminary Inspection

Inspect each wheel bearing prior to removing it from the wheel hub.

CAUTION
Do not remove the wheel bearings for inspection purposes as they will be damaged during the removal process. Remove wheel bearings only if they are to be replaced.

1. Perform Steps 1-3 of *Disassembly* in the following procedure.
2. Turn each bearing by hand. The bearings must turn smoothly with no roughness.
3. Inspect the play of the inner race of each wheel bearing. Check for excessive axial play and radial play (**Figure 11**). Replace the bearing if it has an excess amount of free play.

(34)

FRONT LACED WHEEL (2000-ON)

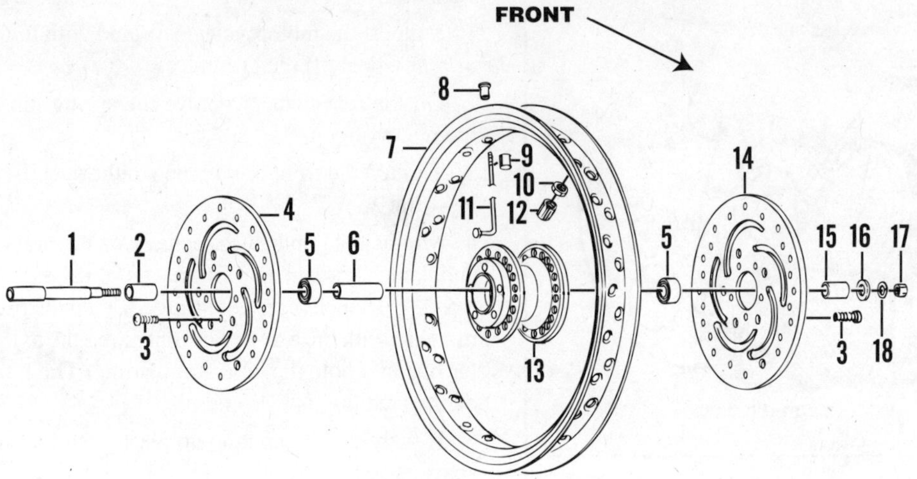

1. Front axle
2. Right side axle spacer
3. Bolt
4. Brake disc
5. Bearing
6. Spacer sleeve
7. Wheel rim
8. Spoke nipple
9. Balance weight
10. Nut
11. Spoke
12. Valve stem cap
13. Wheel hub
14. Brake disc
15. Left side axle spacer
16. Washer
17. Axle nut
18. Lockwasher

(35)

FRONT CAST WHEEL (2000-ON)

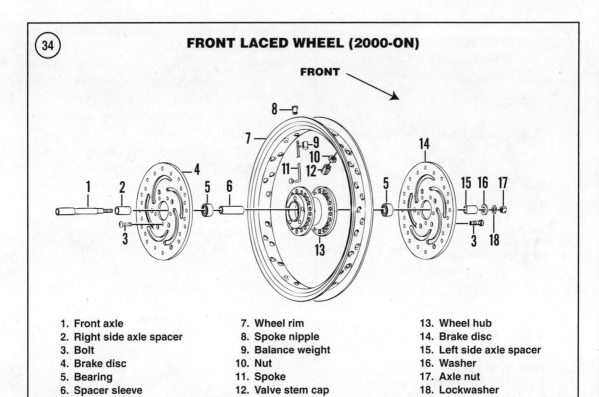

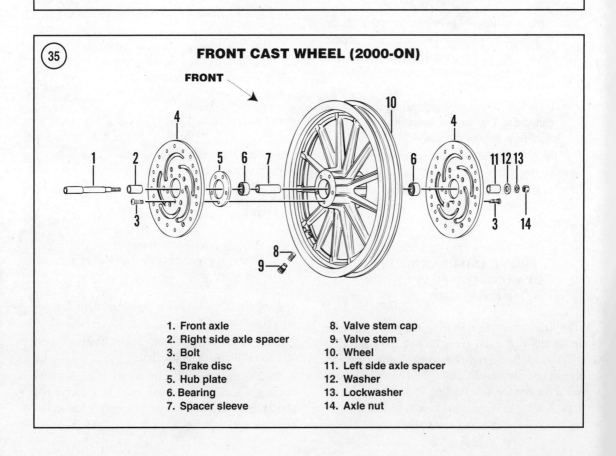

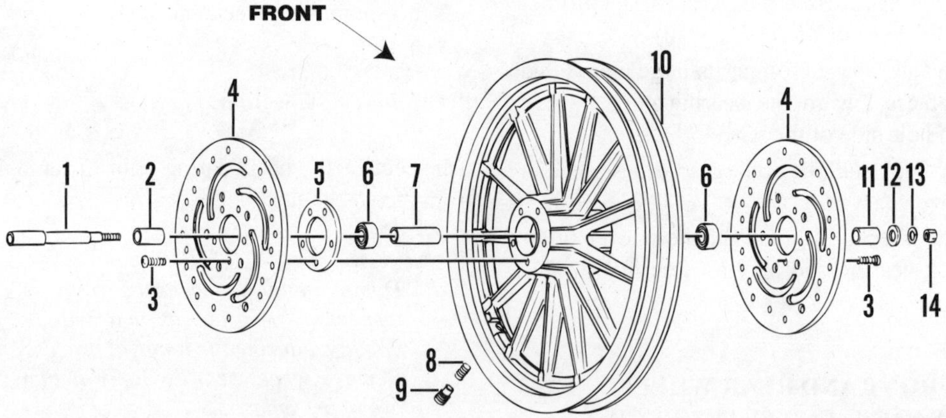

1. Front axle
2. Right side axle spacer
3. Bolt
4. Brake disc
5. Hub plate
6. Bearing
7. Spacer sleeve
8. Valve stem cap
9. Valve stem
10. Wheel
11. Left side axle spacer
12. Washer
13. Lockwasher
14. Axle nut

(36) **REAR LACED WHEEL (2000-ON)**

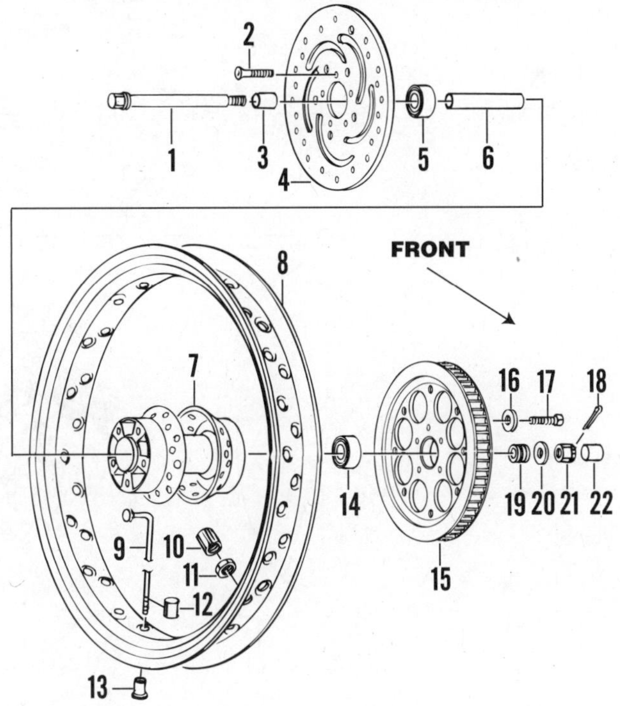

1. Rear axle
2. Bolt
3. Right side axle spacer
4. Brake disc
5. Bearing
6. Spacer sleeve
7. Wheel hub
8. Wheel rim
9. Spoke
10. Valve stem cup
11. Nut
12. Balance weight
13. Spoke nipple
14. Bearing
15. Driven sprocket
16. Washer
17. Bolt
18. Cotter pin
19. Left side axle spacer
20. Washer
21. Axle nut
22. Cover (international models only)

Disassembly

This procedure applies to both the front and rear wheel and hub assemblies. Where differences occur between the different hubs they are identified. Refer to **Figures 34-37**.

1A. Remove the front wheel as described in this chapter.

1B. Remove the rear wheel as described in this chapter.

2. If still in place, remove the axle spacers from each side of the hub.

3. If necessary, remove the bolts securing the brake disc and remove the disc.

4. Before proceeding further, inspect the wheel bearings as described in this chapter. If they must be replaced, proceed as follows.

5A. If the special tools are not used, perform the following:

   a. To remove the right- and left-hand bearings and spacer collar, insert a soft aluminum or brass drift into one side of the hub.
   b. Push the spacer collar over to one side and place the drift on the inner race of the lower bearing.

37

REAR CAST WHEEL (2000-ON)

1. Rear axle
2. Bolt
3. Right side axle spacer
4. Brake disc
5. Bearing
6. Spacer sleeve
7. Valve stem cap
8. Nut
9. Valve stem
10. Wheel
11. Driven sprocket
12. Washer
13. Cotter pin
14. Left side axle spacer
15. Washer
16. Axle nut
17. Cover (international models only)

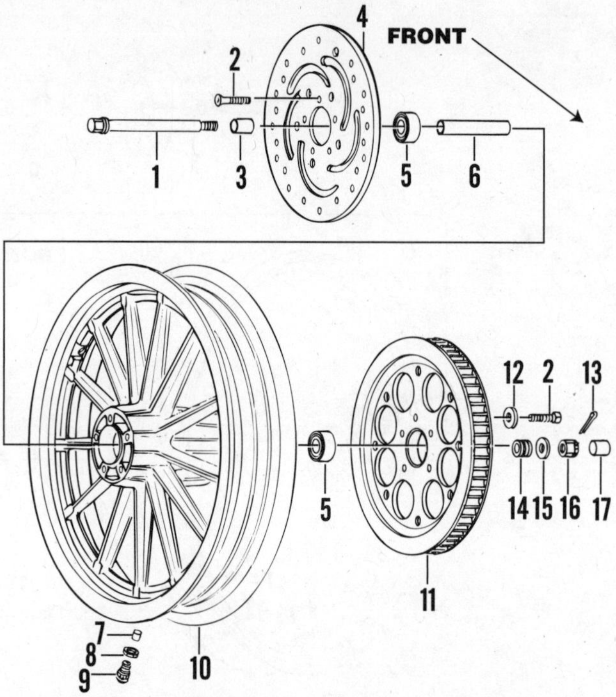

c. Tap the bearing out of the hub with a hammer, working around the perimeter of the inner race (**Figure 38**). Remove the bearing and distance collar.

d. Repeat for the bearing on the other side.

NOTE
The Kowa Seiki Wheel Bearing Remover set can be ordered through a K & L Supply dealer.

WARNING
Be sure to wear safety glasses while using the wheel bearing remover set.

5B. To remove the bearings with the Kowa Seiki Wheel Bearing Remover set, perform the following:

a. Select the correct size remover head tool and insert it into the bearing.

b. Turn the wheel over and insert the remover shaft into the backside of the adapter. Tap the wedge and force it into the slit in the adapter (**Figure 39**). This will force the adapter against the bearing inner race.

38

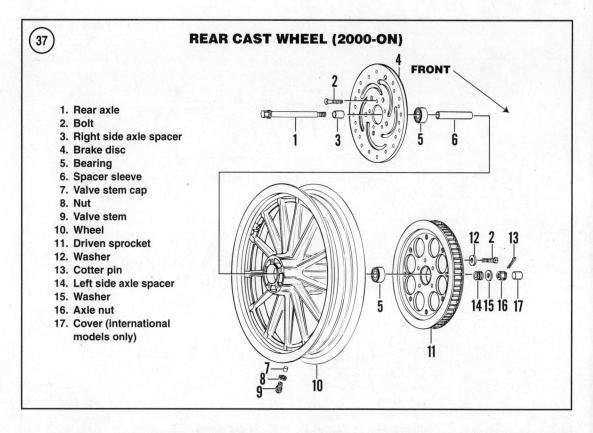

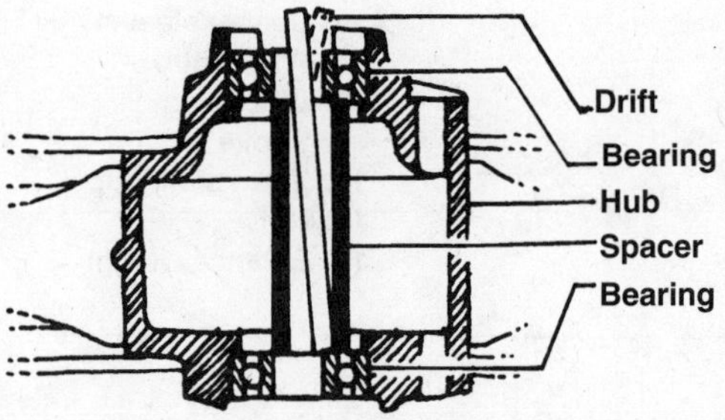

c. Tap on the end of the wedge bar with a hammer and drive the bearing out of the hub. Remove the bearing and the distance collar.

d. Repeat for the bearing on the other side.

6. Clean the inside and the outside of the hub with solvent. Dry with compressed air.

39

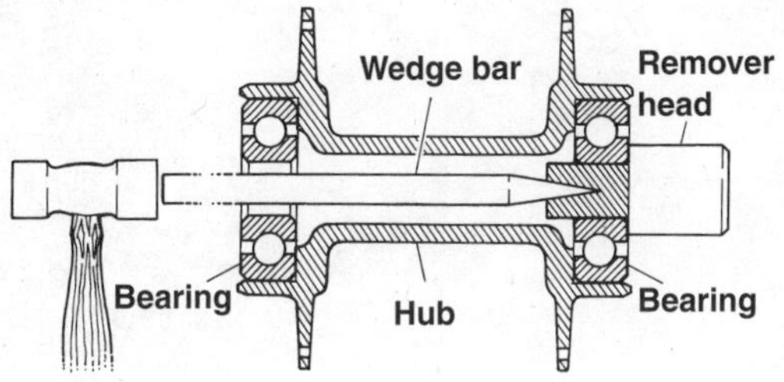

40

41

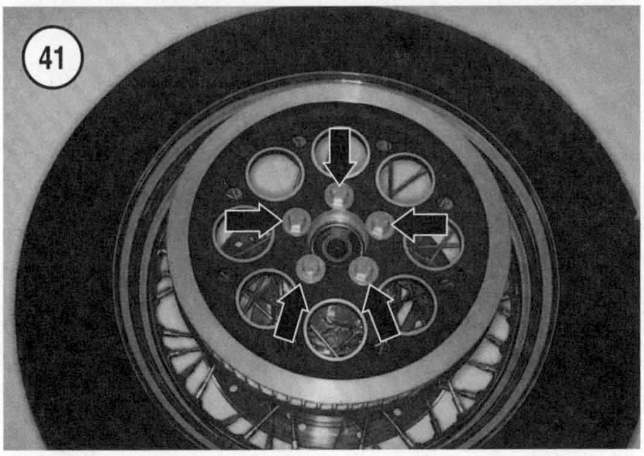

Assembly

CAUTION
The removal process will generally damage bearings. ***Never*** *reinstall them after they are removed. Always install* ***new*** *bearings. Replace the bearings in pairs.*

1. Blow any debris out of the hub prior to installing the new bearings.
2. Apply a light coat of wheel bearing grease to the bearing seating areas of the hub. This will make bearing installation easier.

CAUTION
Install non-sealed bearings with the single sealed side facing outward. Tap the bearings squarely into place and tap on the outer race only. Do not tap on the inner race or the bearing might be damaged. Be sure that the bearings are completely seated.

3. Select a driver with an outside diameter slightly smaller than the bearing's outside diameter.
4. Tap the right side bearing squarely into place and tap on the outer race only. Tap the bearing into the hub bore until it bottoms. Be sure that the bearing is completely seated.
5. Turn the wheel over (right side up) on the workbench and install the spacer collar.
6. Use the same tool set-up and drive in the left side bearing.
7. If the brake disc was removed, install it as described in Chapter Twelve.

8A. Install the front wheel as described in this chapter.

8B. Install the rear wheel as described in this chapter.

DRIVEN SPROCKET ASSEMBLY

Inspection

Inspect the sprocket teeth (**Figure 40**). If the teeth are visibly worn, replace the drive belt and both sprockets.

Removal/Installation

1. Remove the rear wheel as described in this chapter.
2. Remove the bolts, washers (**Figure 41**) and nuts (if so equipped) securing the driven sprocket to the hub and remove the sprocket.
3. Position the driven sprocket onto the rear hub.
4. Apply a light coat of ThreeBond TB1360 or an equivalent to the bolts prior to installation.

9

5. Install the bolts and washers and nuts (if so equipped) and tighten to specifications in **Table 2**.

DRIVE SPROCKET

The drive sprocket is covered in Chapter Six under *Transmission Drive Sprocket*.

DRIVE BELT

CAUTION

When handling a new or used drive belt, never wrap the belt in a loop that is smaller than 5 in. (130 mm) or bend it sharply in any direction. This will weaken or break the belt fibers and cause premature belt failure.

Removal/Installation

1. Remove the compensating sprocket and clutch as described in Chapter Five.
2. Remove the primary chain housing as described in Chapter Five.

WARNING

Make sure the motorcycle is securely supported before removing the rear wheel.

3. Support the motorcycle with the rear wheel off the ground.
4. Remove the rear wheel as described in this chapter.

NOTE

If the existing drive belt is going to be reinstalled, it must be installed so it travels in the original direction. Before removing the belt, draw an arrow on the top surface of the belt facing forward.

5. Refer to *Rear Swing Arm* in Chapter Eleven and perform the following:
   a. Leave both shock absorbers in place on the frame and rear swing arm.
   b. If still in place, remove the screws securing the drive belt lower deflector (A, **Figure 42**) and remove it.
   c. Remove the rear swing arm pivot bolt (B, **Figure 42**) nut (1999) or bolt (2000-on).

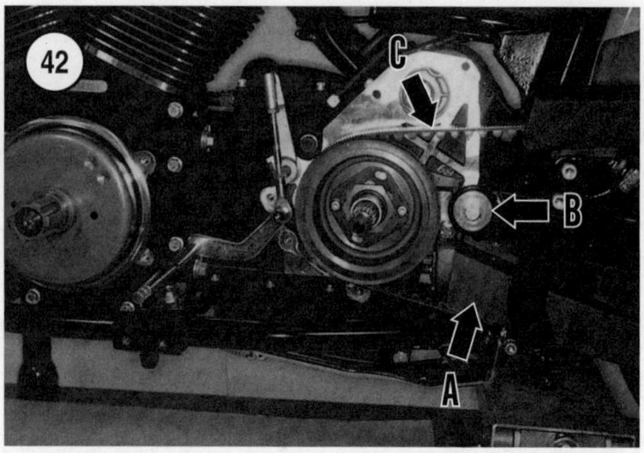

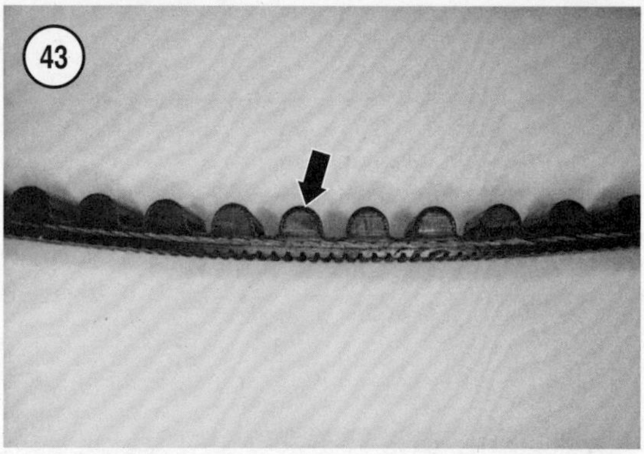

   d. Withdraw the pivot bolt from the frame and transmission case.
   e. Pivot the front of the rear swing arm down sufficiently to slip the drive belt past the pivot area of the frame.
   f. If the drive belt is going to remain off for a period of time, move the swing arm up into position and reinstall the pivot bolt and nut, or bolt.
6. Remove the drive belt (C, **Figure 42**) from the drive sprocket.
7. Installation is the reverse of these steps while noting the following:
   a. Tighten the swing arm pivot bolt nut or bolt as described in Chapter Eleven.
   b. Adjust the drive belt tension as described in Chapter Three.

Inspection

Do not apply any type of lubricant to the drive belt. Inspect the drive belt and teeth (**Figure 43**) for severe wear, damage or oil contamination.

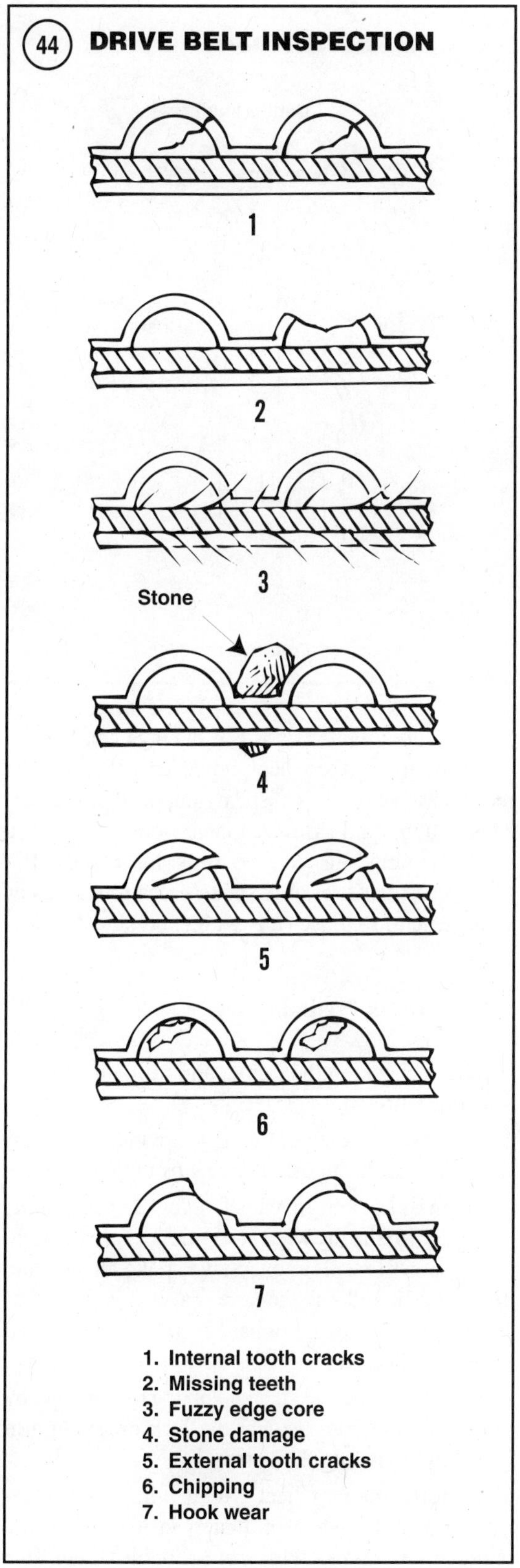

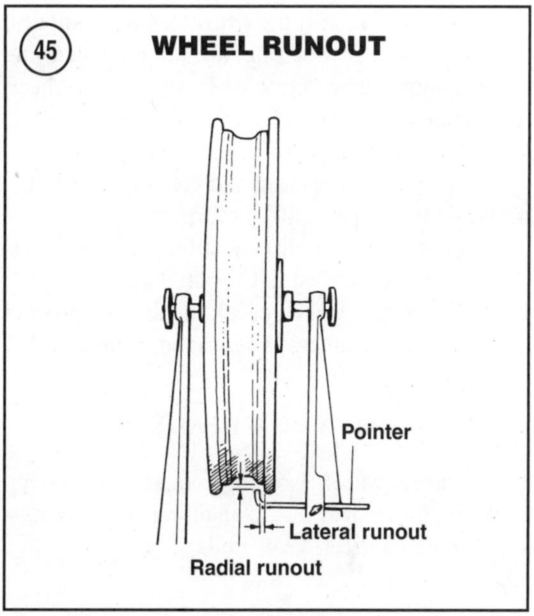

Refer to **Figure 44** for various types of drive belt wear or damage. Replace the drive belt if worn or damaged.

WHEEL RUNOUT

1. Remove the front or rear wheel as described in this chapter.
2. Install the wheel in a wheel truing stand and check the wheel for excessive wobble or runout.
3. If the wheel is not running true, remove the tire from the rim as described in this chapter. Then remount the wheel into the truing stand and measure axial and lateral runout (**Figure 45**) with a pointer or dial indicator. Compare actual runout readings with the service limit specification in **Table 1**. Note the following:
   a. Cast wheels: If the runout meets or exceeds the service limit (**Table 1**), check the wheel bearings as described under *Front and Rear Hub* in this chapter. If the wheel bearings are acceptable, the cast wheel must be replaced as it cannot be serviced. Inspect the wheel for cracks, fractures, dents or bends. Replace a damaged wheel.

WARNING
Do not try to repair any damage to a cast wheel as it will result in an unsafe riding condition.

b. Laced wheels: If the wheel bearings, spokes, hub and rim assembly are not damaged, the runout can be corrected by truing the wheel. Refer to *Spoke Adjustment* in this chapter. If the rim is dented or damaged in any way, the rim must be replaced and the wheel rebuilt.

4. While the wheel is off, perform the following:
   a. Check the brake disc mounting bolts for tightness as described in Chapter Twelve.
   b. On the rear wheel, check the driven sprocket bolts for tightness as described in this chapter.

RIM AND LACED WHEEL SERVICE

The laced wheel assembly consists of a rim, spokes, nipples and hub containing the bearings, spacer collar and, on 1999 models, oil seals.

Component Condition

Riding subjects the wheels to a significant amount of punishment. It is important that the wheel is inspected regularly for lateral (side-to-side) and radial (up-and-down) runout, even spoke tension and visible rim damage. When a wheel has a noticeable wobble, it is out of true. This is usually cause by loose spokes, but it can be caused by an impact-damaged rim.

Truing a wheel corrects the lateral and radial runout to bring the wheel back into specification.

The condition of the individual wheel components will affect the ability to successfully true the wheel. Note the following:

1. *Spoke condition*—Do not attempt to true a wheel with bent or damaged spokes. Doing so places an excessive amount of tension on the spoke and rim. The spoke may break and/or pull through the spoke nipple hole in the rim. Inspect the spokes carefully and replace any that are damaged.
2. *Nipple condition*—When truing the wheels the nipples must turn freely on the spoke, however, it is quite common for the spoke threads to become corroded and make it difficult to turn the nipple. Spray a penetrating liquid onto the nipple and allow sufficient time for it to penetrate before trying to force the nipple loose. Work the spoke wrench in both directions and continue to apply penetrating liquid. If the spoke wrench rounds off the nipple, it will be necessary to remove the tire from the rim and cut the spoke(s) out of the wheel.

(46) LATERAL ADJUSTMENT

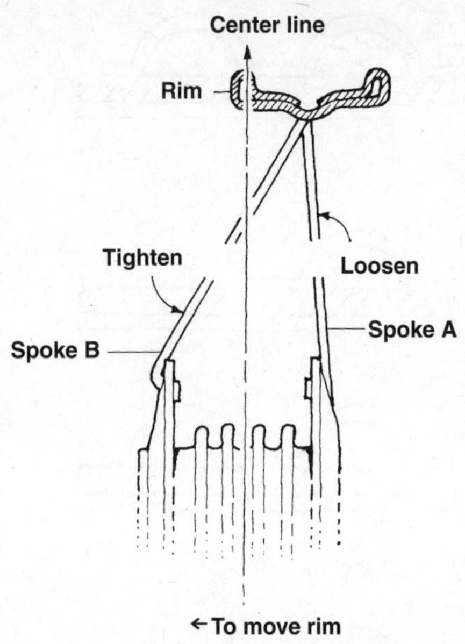

3. *Rim condition*—Minor rim damage can be corrected by truing the wheel, however, trying to correct excessive runout caused by impact damage will cause hub and rim damage due to spoke overtightening. Inspect the rims for cracks, flat spots or dents. Check the spoke holes for cracks or enlargement. Replace rims with excessive damage.

Wheel Truing Preliminaries

Before checking the runout and truing the wheel, note the following:

1. Make sure the wheel bearings are in good condition. Refer to *Front and Rear Hubs* in this chapter.
2. A small amount of wheel runout is acceptable, do not try to true the wheel to a perfect zero reading. Doing so will result in excessive spoke tension and possible rim and hub damage. **Table 1** lists the lateral (side-to-side) and radial (up-and-down) runout limit specifications.
3. The runout can be checked on the motorcycle by mounting a pointer against the fork or swing arm and slowly rotating the wheel.
4. Perform major wheel truing with the tire removed and the wheel mounted in a truing stand (**Figure 45**). If a stand is not available, mount the

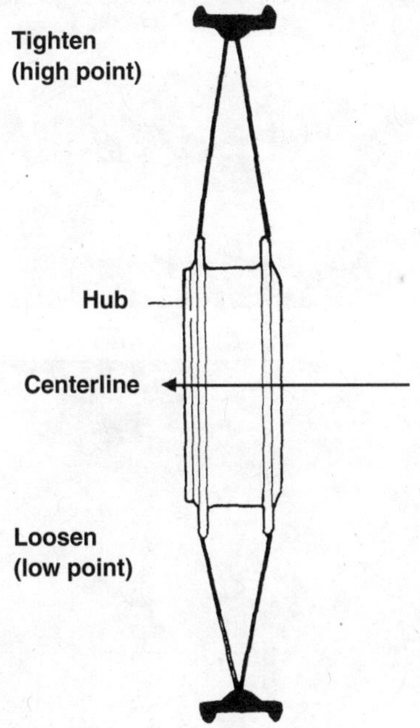

47 **RADIAL ADJUSTMENT**

wheel on the motorcycle with spacers on each side of the wheel to prevent it from sliding on the axle.
5. Use a spoke nipple wrench of the correct size. Using the wrong type of tool or one that is the incorrect size will round off the spoke nipples, making adjustment difficult. Quality spoke wrenches have openings that grip the nipple on four corners to prevent nipple damage.
6. Refer to the spoke nipple torque specifications in **Table 2** when using a torque wrench.

Wheel Truing Procedure

1. Position a pointer facing toward the rim (**Figure 45**). Then spin the wheel slowly and check the lateral and radial runout. If the rim is out of adjustment, continue with Step 2.

NOTE
If there is a large number of loose spokes, check the hub to make sure it is centered in the rim. This must be done visually as there are no hub and rim centering specifications for these models.

NOTE
The number of spokes to loosen and tighten in Steps 2 and 3 will depend on how far the runout is out of adjustment. As a minimum, always loosen two or three spokes, then tighten the opposite two or three spokes. If the runout is excessive and affects a greater area along the rim, a greater number of spokes will require adjustment.

2. If the lateral (side-to-side) runout is out of specification, adjust the wheel by using **Figure 46** as an example. To move the rim to the left in **Figure 46**, loosen spoke A and tighten spoke B. Always loosen and tighten the spokes an equal number of turns.
3. If the radial (up and down) runout is out of specification, the hub is not centered in the rim. Draw the high point of the rim toward the centerline of the wheel by tightening the spokes in the area of the high point and loosening the spokes on the side opposite the high point (**Figure 47**). Tighten spokes in equal amounts to prevent distortion.
4. After truing the wheel, seat each spoke in the hub by tapping it with a flat nose punch and hammer. Then recheck the spoke tension and wheel runout. Readjust if necessary.
5. Check the ends of the spokes where they are threaded in the nipples. Grind off any ends that protrude through the nipples.

CAST WHEELS

Cast wheels consist of a single assembly equipped with bearings, a spacer sleeve and, on 1999 models, oil seals.

While these wheels are virtually maintenance free, they must be checked for damage at the maintenance intervals listed in Chapter Three. Wheel bearing service is described in this chapter.

To check these wheels, refer to Inspection under *Wheel Runout* in this chapter.

WARNING
Do not try to repair any damage to a cast wheel as it will result in an unsafe riding condition.

WHEEL BALANCE

An unbalanced wheel is unsafe. Depending on the degree of unbalance and the speed of the motorcycle, the rider may experience anything from a mild vibration to a violent shimmy that may result in loss of control.

On alloy wheels, weights are attached to the flat surface on the rim (**Figure 48**). On laced wheels, the weights are attached to the spoke nipples (**Figure 49**).

Before attempting to balance the wheel, make sure the wheel bearings are in good condition and properly lubricated. The wheel must rotate freely.

1A. Remove the front wheel as described in this chapter.

1B. Remove the rear wheel as described in this chapter.

2. Mount the wheel on a fixture (**Figure 50**) so it can rotate freely.

3. Spin the wheel and let it coast to a stop. Mark the tire at the lowest point.

4. Spin the wheel several more times. If the wheel keeps coming to rest at the same point, it is out of balance.

5A. On alloy wheels, tape a test weight to the upper (or light) side of the wheel (**Figure 48**).

5B. On laced wheels, attach a weight to the upper or light side of the wheel on the spoke (**Figure 49**).

6. Experiment with different weights until the wheel comes to a stop at a different position each time it is spun.

7. On cast wheels, remove the test weight and install the correct size weight.

   a. Attach the weights to the flat surface on the rim (**Figure 48**). Clean the rim of all road residue before installing the weights; otherwise, the weights may fall off.

   b. Add weights in 1/4 oz. (7g) increments. If 1 oz. (28 g) or more must be added to one location, apply half the amount to each side of the rim.

   c. To apply Harley-Davidson wheel weights, remove the paper backing from the weight and apply 3 drops of Loctite 420 Superbonder to the bottom of the weight. Position the weight on the rim, press it down, and hold in position for 10 seconds. To allow the adhesive to cure properly, do not use the wheel for 8 hours.

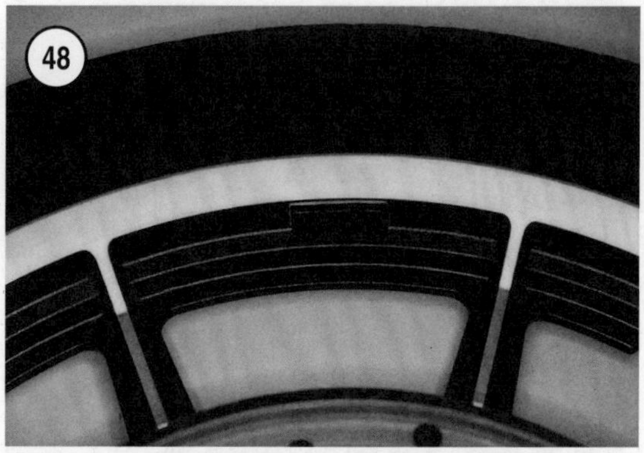

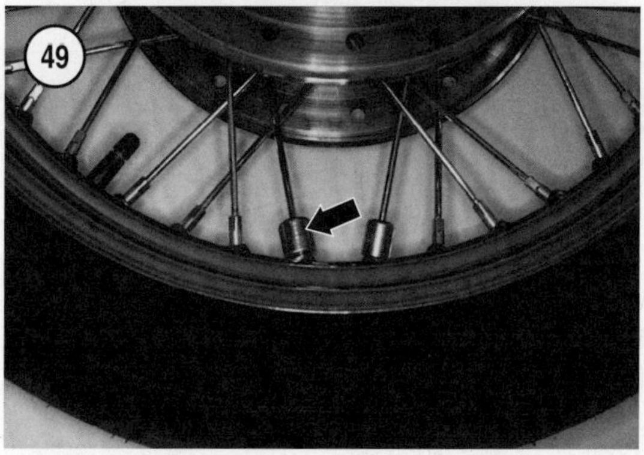

8. When fitting weights on laced wheels for the final time, crimp the weights onto the spoke with slip-joint pliers.

TIRES

Tire Safety

After installing new tires on the motorcycle, break them in correctly. Remember that a new tire has relatively poor adhesion to the road surface until it is broken in properly. Do *not* subject a new tire to any high speed riding for at least the first 60 miles (100 km).

Even after the tires are broken in properly, always warm them up prior to the first ride of the day, especially in cold weather. This will lessen the possibility of loss of control of the motorcycle. If using a new tire brand other than those originally installed by the Harley-Davidson factory, maintain the tire inflation pressure recommended by that tire manufacturer and not those listed in **Table 4**, located at the end of this chapter. **Table 4** is for original equipment tires only.

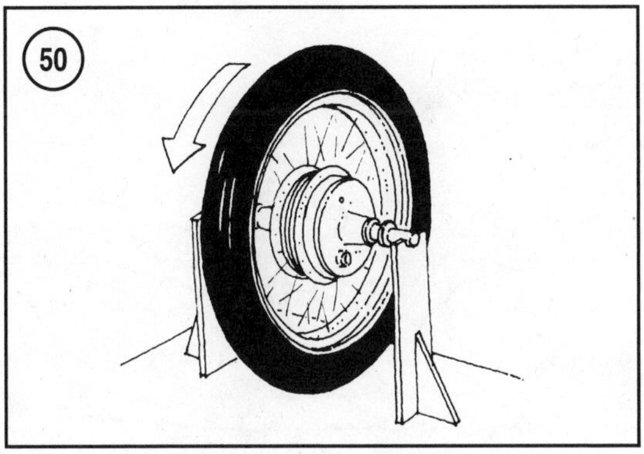

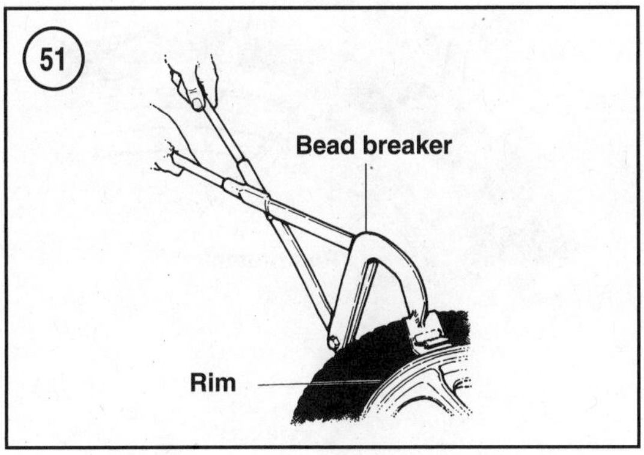

TUBELESS TIRE CHANGING

The cast alloy wheels can easily be damaged during tire removal. Special care must be taken with tire irons when changing a tire to avoid scratches and gouges to the outer rim surface. Insert scraps of leather between the tire iron and the rim to protect the rim from damage. All original equipment laced and cast wheels are designed for use with tubeless tires only.

When removing a tubeless tire, take care not to damage the tire beads, inner liner of the tire or the wheel rim flange. Use tire levers, flat handles or tire irons with rounded heads

Tire Removal

CAUTION

To avoid damage when removing the tire, support the wheel on two wooden blocks, so the brake discs or the driven sprocket does not contact the floor.

NOTE

To make tire removal easier, warming the tire will make it softer and more pliable. Place the wheel and tire assembly in the sun. If possible, place the wheel assembly in a completely closed vehicle. At the same time, place the new tire in the same location.

1A. Remove the front wheel as described in this chapter.

1B. Remove the rear wheel as described in this chapter.

2. If not already marked by the tire manufacturer, mark the valve stem location on the tire, so the tire can be installed in the same location for easier balancing.

3. Remove the valve core from the valve stem and deflate the tire.

NOTE

*The removal of tubeless tires from their rims can be very difficult because of the exceptionally tight tire bead-to-rim seal. Breaking the bead seal may require the use of a special tool (**Figure 51**). If unable to break the seal loose, take the wheel to a motorcycle dealership or tire repair shop and have them break it loose on a tire changing machine.*

CAUTION

The inner rim and tire bead area are the sealing surfaces on the tubeless tire. Do not scratch the inside of the rim or damage the tire bead.

4. Press the entire bead on both sides of the tire away from the rim and into the center of the rim.

5. Lubricate both beads with soapy water.

CAUTION

*Use rim protectors (**Figure 52**) or insert scraps of leather between the tire iron and the rim to protect the rim from damage.*

NOTE

Use only quality tire irons without sharp edges. If necessary, file the ends of the tire irons to remove rough edges.

6. Insert a tire iron under the top bead next to the valve stem (**Figure 53**). Force the bead on the opposite side of the tire into the center of the rim and pry the bead over the rim with the tire iron.
7. Insert a second tire iron next to the first iron to hold the bead over the rim. Then work around the tire with the first tire iron, prying the bead over the rim (**Figure 54**).
8. Stand the wheel upright. Insert a tire iron between the back bead and the side of the rim that the top bead was pried over (**Figure 55**). Force the bead on the opposite side from the tire iron into the center of the rim. Pry the back bead off the rim working a round as with the first.
9. Inspect the valve stem seal. Because rubber deteriorates with age, it is advisable to replace the valve stem when replacing the tire.
10. Remove the old valve stem and discard it. Inspect the valve stem hole (**Figure 56**) in the rim. Remove any dirt or corrosion from the hole and wipe dry with a clean cloth. Install a new valve stem and make sure it is properly seated in the rim.
11. Carefully inspect the tire and wheel rim for any damage as described in the following.

Tire and Wheel Rim Inspection

1. Wipe off the inner surfaces of the wheel rim. Clean off any rubber residue or any oxidation.

WARNING

Carefully consider whether a tire should be replaced. If there is any doubt about the quality of the existing tire, replace it with a new one. Do not take a chance on a tire failure at any speed.

2. If any one of the following are observed; replace it with a new one:
   a. A puncture or split whose total length or diameter exceeds 0.24 in. (6 mm).
   b. A scratch or split on the side wall.
   c. Any type of ply separation.
   d. Tread separation or excessive abnormal wear pattern.
   e. Tread depth of less than 1/16 in. (1.6 mm) on original equipment tires. Tread depth minimum may vary on aftermarket tires.
   f. Scratches on either sealing bead.
   g. The cord is cut in any place.
   h. Flat spots in the tread from skidding.

52

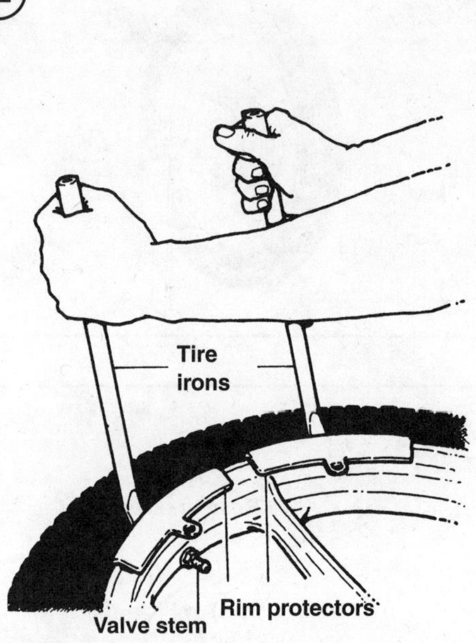

53

54

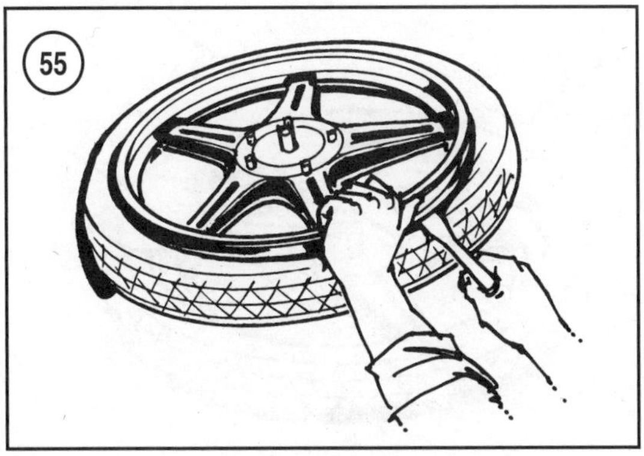

55

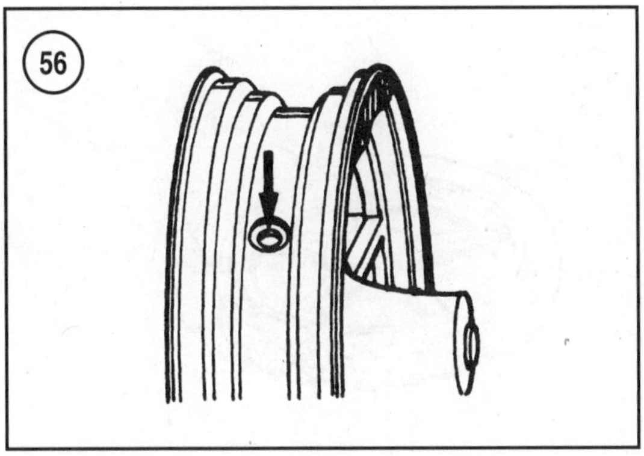

56

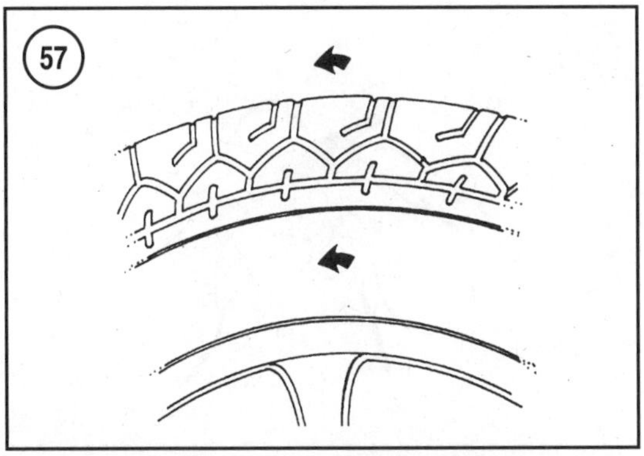

57

58

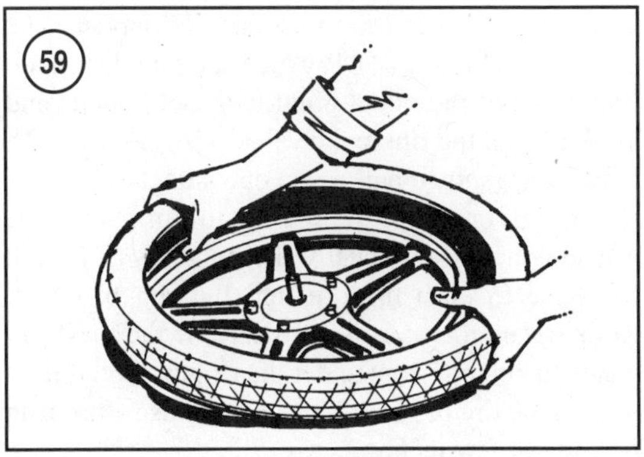

59

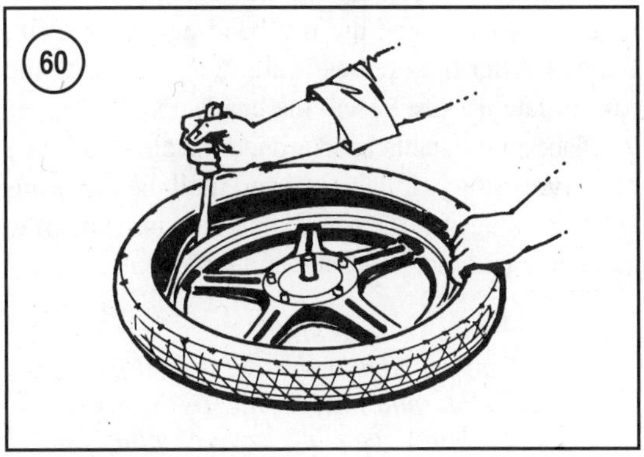

60

i. Any abnormality in the inner liner.

Tire Installation

1. Inspect the valve stem core rubber seal for hardness or deterioration. Replace if necessary.
2. A new tire may have balancing rubbers inside. These are not patches. Do not remove them.
3. Lubricate both beads of the tire with soapy water.
4. When installing the tire on the rim, make sure the correct tire (either front or rear) is installed on the correct wheel and also that the direction arrow faces the direction of wheel rotation (**Figure 57**).
5. If remounting the old tire, align the mark made in Step 2, *Removal*, with the valve stem (**Figure 58**). If a new tire is being installed, align the colored spot near the bead (indicating the lightest point of the tire) with the valve stem.
6. Align the tire with the rim, then place the backside of the tire into the center of the rim. The lower bead should go into the center of the rim and the upper bead inside. Work around the tire in both directions (**Figure 59**), using a tire iron for the last few inches of bead (**Figure 60**).

7. Press the upper bead into the rim opposite the valve stem (**Figure 61**). Pry the bead into the rim on both sides of the initial point with both hands and work around the rim to the valve stem (**Figure 62**). If the tire wants to pull up on one side, either use a tire iron or one knee to hold the tire in place. The last few inches are usually the toughest to install. Continue to push the tire into the rim by hand. Re-lubricate the bead if necessary. If the tire bead wants to pull out from under the rim use both knees to hold the tire in place. If necessary, use a tire iron for the last few inches.

8. Bounce the wheel several times, rotating it each time. This will force the tire bead against the rim flanges. After the tire beads are in contact with the rim, inflate the tire to seat the beads.

9. Place an inflatable band around the circumference of the tire. Slowly inflate the band until the tire beads are pressed against the rim. Inflate the tire enough to make it seat, deflate the band and remove it.

WARNING
In the next step, never exceed 40 psi (276 kPa) inflation pressure as the tire could burst, causing severe injury. Never stand directly over a tire while inflating it.

10. After inflating the tire, check to see that the beads are fully seated and that the rim lines are the same distance from the rim all the way around the tire. If the beads will not seat, deflate the tire and lubricate the rim and beads with soapy water.

11. Re-inflate the tire to the pressure listed in **Table 4**. Install the valve stem cap.

12. Balance the wheel as described in this chapter.

13A. Install the front wheel as described in this chapter.

13B. Install the rear wheel as described in this chapter.

61

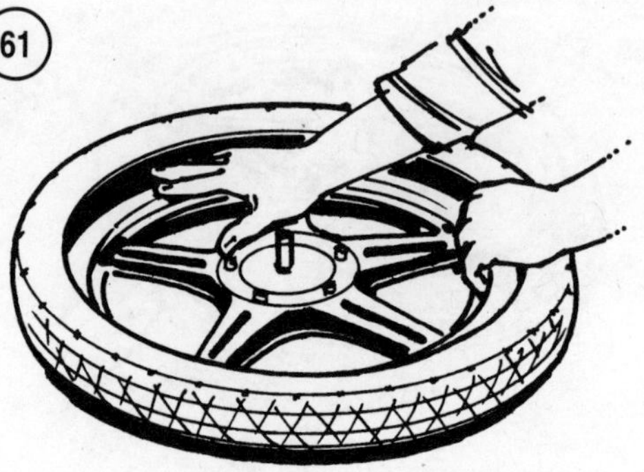

62

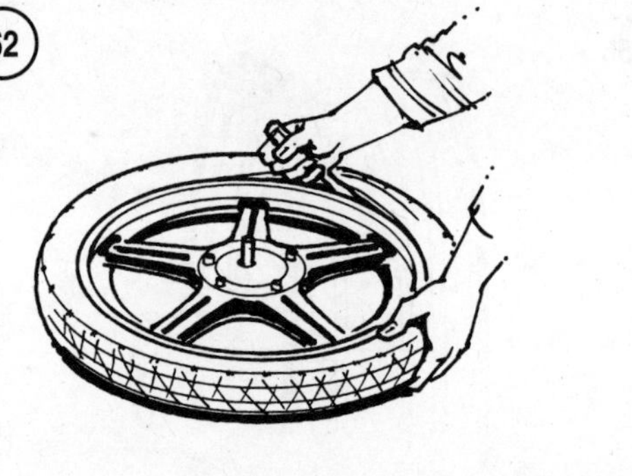

63

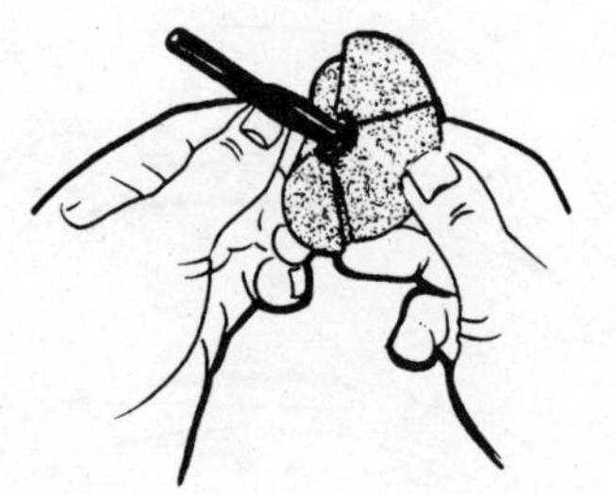

TIRE REPAIRS

NOTE
Changing or patching on the road is very difficult. A can of pressurized tire inflator and sealer may inflate the tire and seal the hole, although this is only a temporary fix.

WARNING
Do not install an inner tube inside a tubeless tire. The tube will cause an abnormal heat buildup in the tire.

Tubeless tires have TUBELESS molded into the sidewall and the rims have SUITABLE FOR TUBELESS TIRES or equivalent stamped or cast on them.

If the tire is punctured, it must be removed from the rim to inspect the inside of the tire and to apply a combination plug/patch from inside the tire (**Figure 63**). Never attempt to repair a tubeless motorcycle tire using a plug or cord patch applied from outside the tire.

After repairing a tubeless tire, don't exceed 50 mph (80 km/h) for the first 24 hours.

64

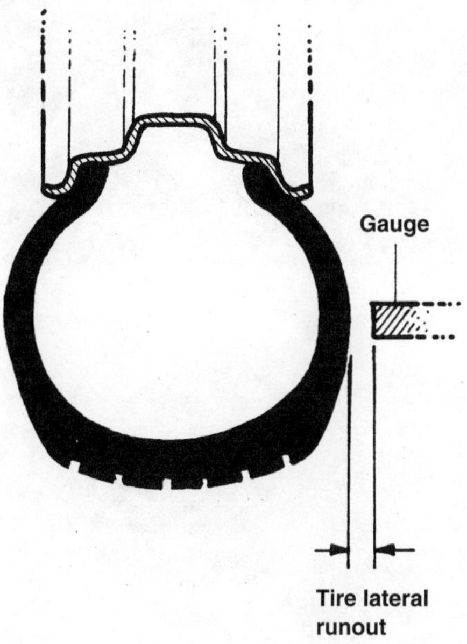

65

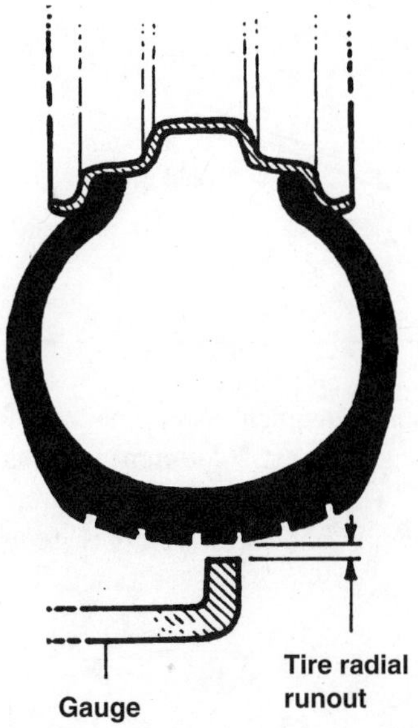

Repair

Do not rely on a plug or cord patch applied from outside the tire. Use a combination plug/patch applied from inside the tire (**Figure 63**).

1. Remove the tire from the wheel rim as described in this chapter.
2. Inspect the rim inner flange. Smooth any scratches on the sealing surface with emery cloth. If a scratch is deeper than 0.5 mm (0.020 in.), the wheel should be replaced.
3. Inspect the tire inside and out. Replace a tire if any of the following is found:
   a. A puncture larger than 3 mm (1/8 in) diameter.
   b. A punctured or damaged side wall.
   c. More than 2 punctures in the tire.
4. Apply the plug/patch following the manufacturer's instructions with the patch kit.

Tire Runout

Check the tires for excessive lateral and radial runout after a wheel has been mounted or if the motorcycle developed a wobble that cannot be traced to another component. Mount the wheels on their axles when making the following checks.

1. *Lateral runout*: This procedure will check the tire for excessive side-to-side play. Perform the following:
   a. Position a fixed pointer next to the tire sidewall as shown in **Figure 64**. Position the pointer tip so that it is not directly in line with the molded tire logo or any other raised surface.
   b. Rotate the tire and measure lateral runout.
   c. The lateral runout must not exceed 0.080 in. (2.03 mm). If runout is excessive, remove the tire from the wheel and recheck the wheel's lateral runout as described in this chapter. If the runout is excessive, the wheel must be trued (laced wheels) or replaced (alloy wheels). If wheel runout is correct, the tire runout is excessive and the tire must be replaced.
2. *Radial runout*: This procedure will check the tire for excessive up-and-down play. Perform the following:
   a. Position a fixed pointer at the center bottom of the tire tread as shown in **Figure 65**.
   b. Rotate the tire and measure the amount of radial runout.
   c. The radial runout must not exceed 0.090 in. (2.29 mm). If runout is excessive, remove the

tire from the wheel and recheck the wheel's radial runout as described in this chapter. If the runout is excessive, true or replace the wheel. If wheel runout is correct, the tire runout is excessive and the tire must be replaced.

VEHICLE ALIGNMENT

This procedure checks the alignment of the rear axle with the swing arm pivot shaft. It also checks the engine stabilizer adjustment that aligns the engine in the frame. These checks determine the condition and alignment of the components that hold the motorcycle together: steering stem, front axle, engine, swing arm pivot shaft and rear axle. If any of these items are out of alignment, the motorcycle will not handle properly. Bad handling will increase the motorcycle's vibration level while reducing its overall performance and driveability.

Preliminary Inspection

Before checking vehicle alignment, make the following checks to spot problems caused from normal wear. Adjust, repair or replace any component as required.

1. The engine stabilizer (**Figure 66**), mounted between the cylinder heads and upper frame tube, aligns the engine in the frame. Check the engine stabilizer every 10,000 miles (16,000 km) for loose or damaged parts. To service or replace the engine stabilizer, refer to Chapter Four. To adjust the engine stabilizer, perform the *Alignment* procedure in this section.
2. Check the steering head bearing adjustment as described under *Steering Play Adjustment* in Chapter Ten.
3. Check the runout of each wheel as described in this chapter.

Special Tools

The following tools are required to check vehicle alignment:

1. An inclinometer (**Figure 67**) checks the vertical position (angle) of the brake discs when checking engine alignment. This tool, which has a magnetic base and a 360-degree dial, can be purchased from most tool and hardware stores.

66

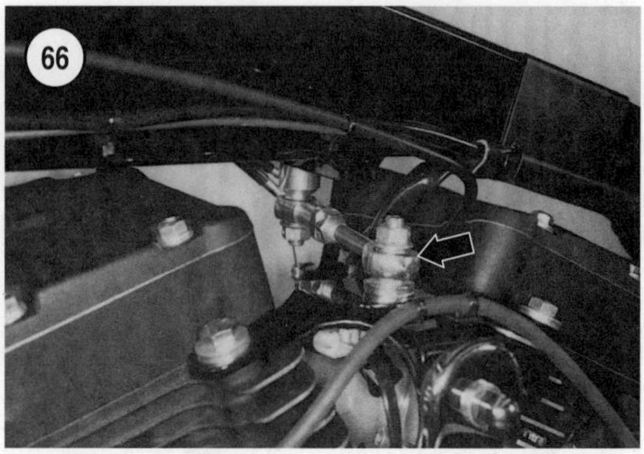

67

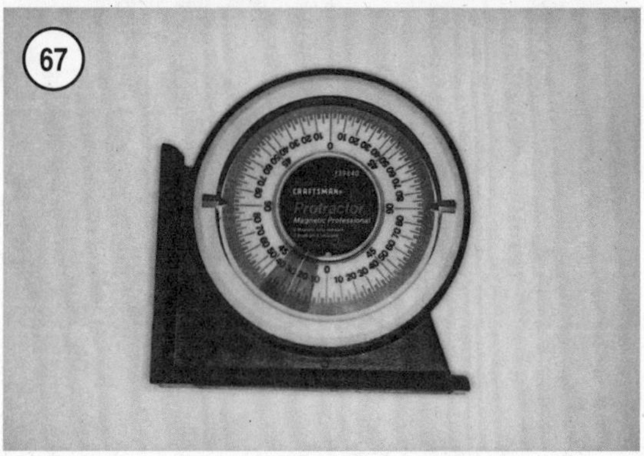

68

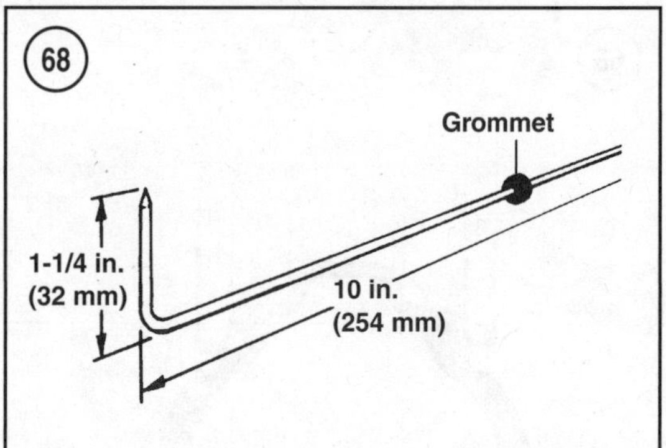

2. A rear axle alignment tool is made of 1/8 in. (3.2 mm) welding rod 11 in. (280 mm) long, as shown in **Figure 68**. The grommets can be purchased from electronic supply and hardware stores. To use this tool accurately, the grommet must be a snug fit on the tool.

Alignment

Each alignment step (check and adjustment) affects the next one. Work carefully and accurately when performing the following steps.

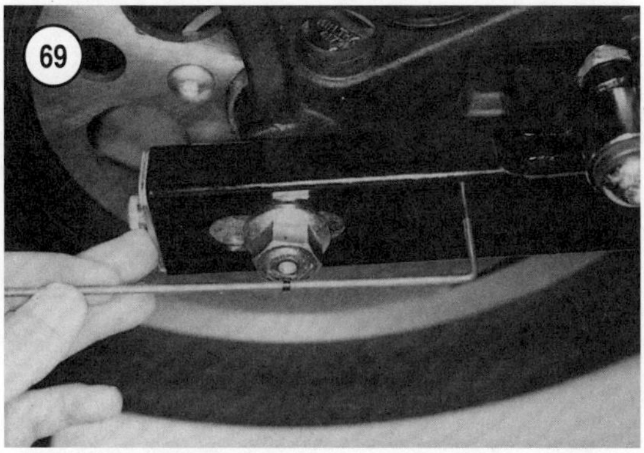

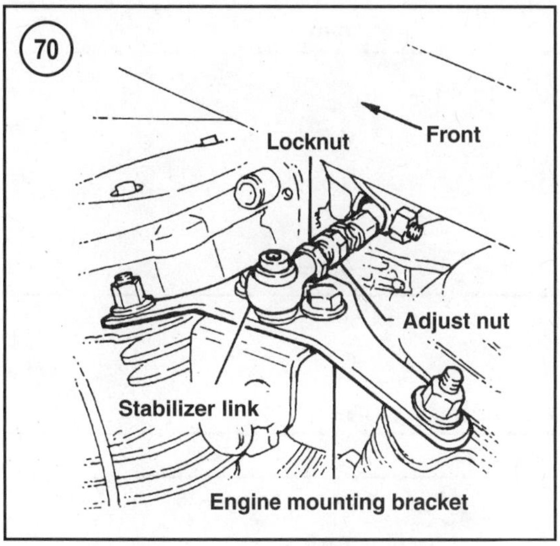

1. Perform all of the checks listed under *Preliminary Inspection* in this section. When all of the checks are within the specifications, continue with Step 2. If the motorcycle has been involved in a crash, refer frame alignment to a Harley-Davidson dealership or motorcycle frame alignment specialist.

2. The exhaust system must be installed on the motorcycle when performing the following steps.

3. Support the motorcycle with the rear wheel off the ground.

4. Insert the alignment tool (**Figure 68**) into one of the swing arm index holes. Then hold it parallel with the rear axle and slide the grommet along the tool until it is centered with the axle (**Figure 69**).

5. Remove the alignment tool without disturbing the position of the grommet and insert the tool into the opposite side of the swing arm. Compare the axle center point with the position of the grommet. Axle alignment is correct if the two measurements are within 0.032 in. (0.8 mm) of each other.

6. If the alignment is incorrect, perform the *Final Drive Belt Adjustment* procedure in Chapter Three. When the drive belt adjustment is correct, continue with Step 7.

NOTE

The following steps must be performed with the rear wheel off the ground.

7. Remove the bolt (**Figure 70**) securing the stabilizer link to the engine mounting bracket. Do not remove the bolt securing the stabilizer link to the frame.

8. Place the inclinometer on the front brake disc. Position the front wheel so that the brake disc is vertical (90°). This position must be maintained when performing Steps 9 and 10.

9. Align the stabilizer link hole with the engine mounting bracket and install the stabilizer link bolt (**Figure 70**). Do not force the bolt into position. Note the following:

   a. If the holes do not align, adjust the stabilizer, starting with Step 10.
   b. If the holes align, go to Step 14.

10. Loosen the stabilizer locknut. Then adjust the stabilizer link until the bolt can be installed without moving the engine. Tighten the locknut when the adjustment is correct.

11. Now put the inclinometer on the rear brake disc and compare its position with the front brake disc. If the readings are not within 1° of each other, continue with Step 12.

12. Readjust the stabilizer link (Step 10) until the rear brake disc is within 1° of the front brake disc. Note the following:

   a. If the adjustment cannot bring the brake discs within 1° of each other, inspect the swing arm, frame, steering head and front forks for damage. If necessary, take the motorcycle to a Harley-Davidson dealership for further inspection.
   b. If the adjustment can bring the brake disc angle to within 1°, but it takes more than five turns of the stabilizer link to do so, perform the chassis inspections described in substep a. If a problem can not be found with a chassis component, go to Step 13.
   c. If the adjustment cannot bring the brake discs within 1° and it takes less than five turns of

the stabilizer link, tighten the stabilizer locknut and go to Step 14.

13. These steps center the frame and engine mounts. Perform this procedure if it takes more than five turns to align the brake discs. Read through the substeps and then follow these steps:

a. Loosen, but do not remove, the front and rear engine isolator mounting bolts.

b. Lower the motorcycle so that both wheels are on the ground.

c. With the transmission in NEUTRAL, start the motorcycle and let it idle for approximately 5 seconds. Then shut the engine off.

d. Tighten all of the isolator mounting bolts to 25 ft.-lb. (34 N•m).

14. Tighten the stabilizer link-to-engine mounting bracket bolt securely.

Table 1 WHEEL SPECIFICATIONS

	In.	mm
Wheel runout (maximum)		
Laced wheels		
Lateral and radial	0.31	0.79
Cast wheels		
Lateral	0.040	1.02
Radial	0.030	0.76
End play (1999)		
Front and rear	0.002-0.006	0.05-0.15

Table 2 WHEEL TORQUE SPECIFICATIONS

Item	ft.-lb.	in.-lb.	N•m
Front axle nut	50-55	–	68-75
Front axle pinch bolt nut except FXDWG	25-30	–	34-41
Front fork slider cap nuts	–	60-132	7-15
Front brake caliper mounting bolt	28-38	–	38-52
Front fender nuts			
FXDWG	15-21	–	20-28
All models except FXDWG	–	120-168	14-19
Driven sprocket bolts			
Laced wheel	45-55	–	61-75
Cast wheel	55-65	–	75-88
Rear axle nut	60-65	–	81-88
Rear wheel belt sprocket screws			
Laced wheel	45-55	–	61-75
Cast wheel	55-65	–	75-88
Brake disc bolts			
Front wheel	16-24	–	22-33
Rear wheel	30-45	–	41-61
Spoke nipples	–	40-50	4-6
Valve stem nut	–	12-15	1-2

Table 3 FRONT AND REAR WHEEL BEARING SPACER SHIMS (1999)

Part No.	Thickness In. (mm)
43290-82	0.030-0.033 (0.76-0.84)
43291-82	0.015-0.017 (0.38-0.43)
43292-82	0.0075-0.0085 (0.190-0.216)
43293-82	0.0035-0.0045 (0.089-0.114)
43294-82	0.0015-0.0025 (0.038-0.064)

Table 4 TIRE INFLATION PRESSURE (COLD)*

Model	kPa	PSI
Front wheels		
Rider only	207	30
Rider and one passenger	207	30
Rear wheels		
Rider only	248	36
Rider and one passenger	276	40

*Tire pressure for factory equipped tires. After market tires may require different inflation pressure.

NOTE: Refer to the Supplement at the back of this manual for information unique to 2002-on models.

CHAPTER TEN

FRONT SUSPENSION AND STEERING

This chapter covers the handlebar, steering head and front fork assemblies.

Tables 1-3 are at the end of the chapter.

HANDLEBAR

Removal/Installation

Refer to **Figure 1**.

1. Support the motorcycle with the front wheel off the ground. See *Motorcycle Stands* in Chapter Nine.

NOTE

Cover the fuel tank with a heavy cloth or plastic tarp to protect it from accidental scratches or dents when removing the handlebar.

NOTE

Before removing the handlebar, make a drawing of the clutch and throttle cable routing from the handlebar and through the frame. This information will prove helpful when reinstalling the handlebar and connecting the cables.

2. On the right side of the handlebar, perform the following:
   a. Remove the front turn signal (A, **Figure 2**) from the master cylinder.

1

HANDLEBAR

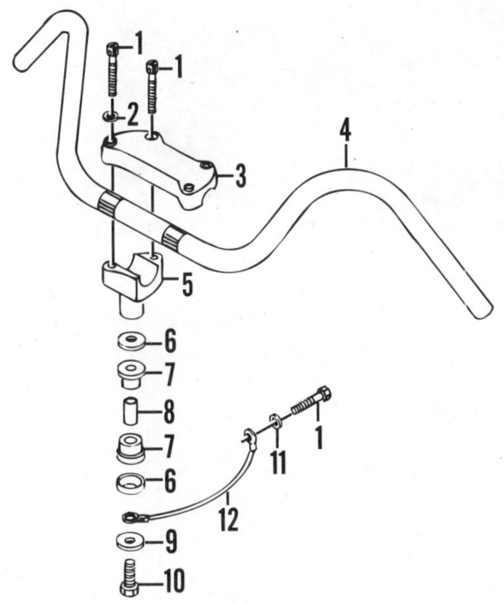

1. Allen bolt
2. Washer
3. Holder
4. Handlebar
5. Lower clamp
6. Cup washer
7. Rubber bushing
8. Collar
9. Washer
10. Bolt
11. Washer
12. Ground cable

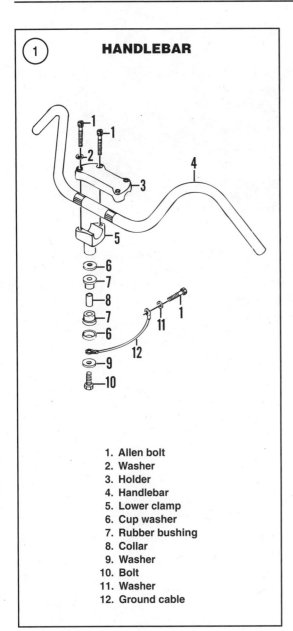

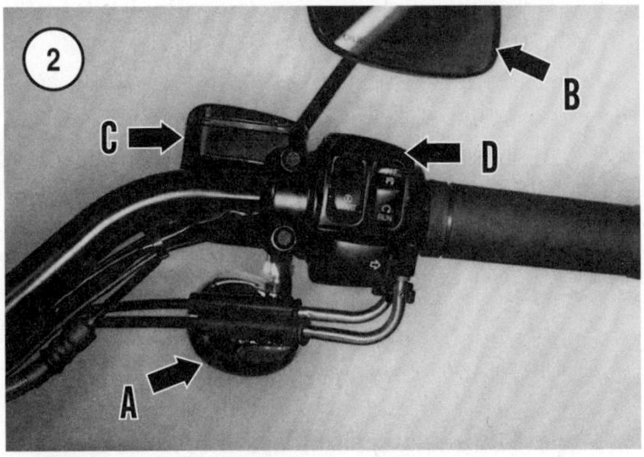

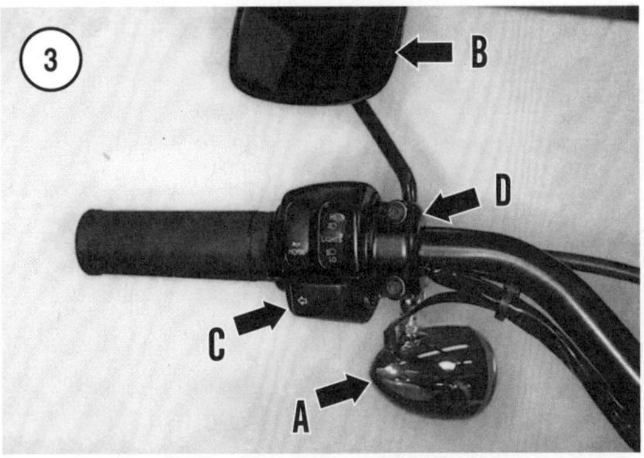

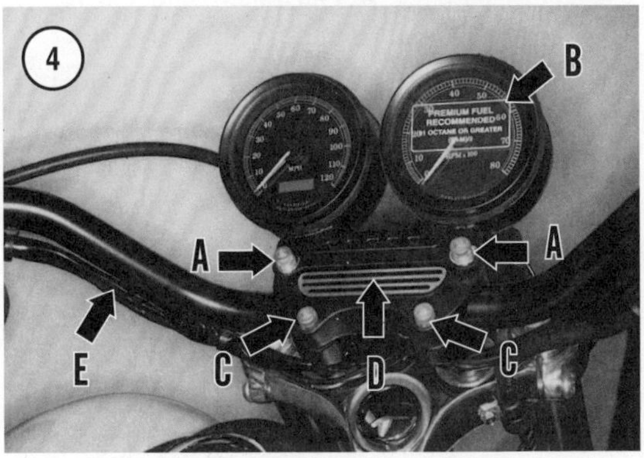

b. Unscrew and remove the mirror (B, **Figure 2**).

c. Remove the screws securing the master cylinder (C, **Figure 2**). Do not disconnect the hydraulic brake line.

d. Loosen the throttle housing (D, **Figure 2**) screws and slide the assembly off the handlebar.

3. On the left side of the handlebar, perform the following:

a. Remove the front turn signal (A, **Figure 3**) from the master cylinder.

b. Unscrew and remove the mirror (B, **Figure 3**).

c. Remove the screws securing the left side switch assembly together (C, **Figure 3**) and separate the housing halves.

d. Remove the clutch lever clamp (D, **Figure 3**) mounting screws and separate the clamp halves.

4. Disconnect or remove any wiring harness clamps at the handlebar.

5A. On FXD, FXDS-CON, FXDX and FXDXT models, remove the two front handlebar clamp bolts (A, **Figure 4**) and washers. Then set the instrument housing forward (B) so it does not scratch the handlebar clamp.

5B. On all other models, remove the two front handlebar clamp bolts (A, **Figure 4**) and washers.

6. Remove the two rear clamp bolts (C, **Figure 4**), then remove the holder (D) and handlebar (E).

7. Install the handlebar by reversing these steps while noting the following:

   a. Check the knurled rings on the handlebar for galling and bits of aluminum. Clean the knurled section with a wire brush.
   b. Check the handlebar for cracks, bends or other damage. Replace the handlebar if necessary. Do not attempt to repair it.
   c. Thoroughly clean the clamp halves of all residue.
   d. After installing the handlebar, reposition the handlebar while sitting on the motorcycle.
   e. Tighten the handlebar clamp bolts securely.
   f. Adjust the mirrors.

FRONT FORK (FXD, FXDL, FXDS-CON, FXDWG, FXDP AND 1999 FXDX)

Front Fork Service

Before assuming that a fork is internally malfunctioning, drain the front fork oil and refill with the proper type and quantity of fork oil as described in Chapter Three. If there is still a problem, such as poor damping or a tendency to bottom or top out, follow the service procedures in this section.

To simplify fork service and to prevent the mixing of parts, remove, service and install the fork legs individually.

Removal

1. Support the motorcycle with the front wheel off the ground. See *Motorcycle Stands* in Chapter Nine.
2. Remove the front fender and front wheel as described in Chapter Nine.
3. If both fork tube assemblies are going to be removed, mark them with an R (right side) and L (left side) so the assemblies will be reinstalled on the correct side.
4. On FXDX-CON models, remove the windshield and its mounting clamps as described in Chapter Thirteen.

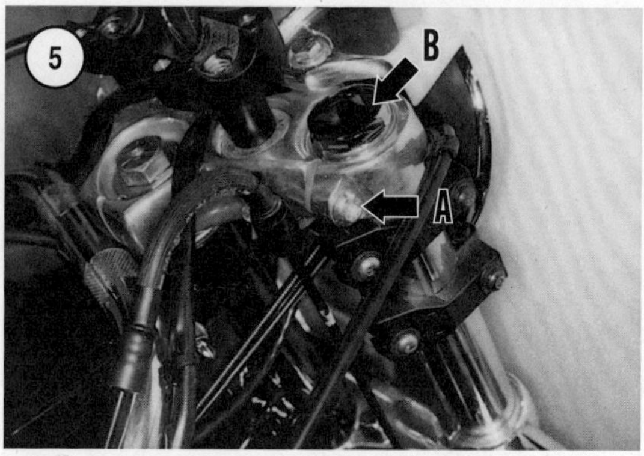

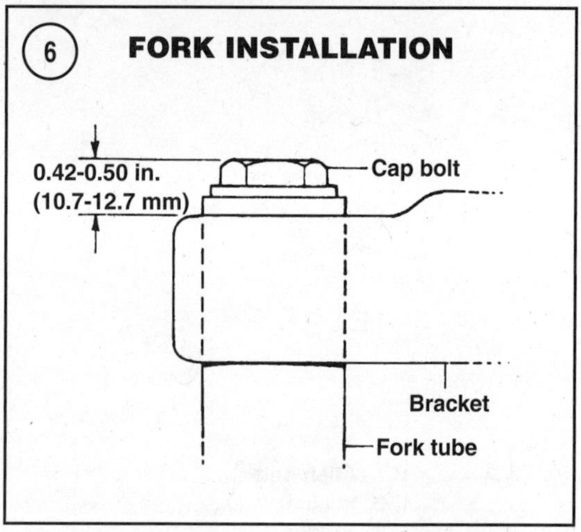

5. On FXDWG models, remove the fork tube cap, spacer and oil seal from the top of one fork tube.
6. Loosen the upper fork bracket pinch bolt (A, **Figure 5**).

7A. On FXDWG models, if the forks are going to be disassembled, loosen the fork tube plug.

7B. On all models other than FXDWG models, if the forks are going to be disassembled, loosen the fork cap (B, **Figure 5**).

8. Loosen the lower fork bracket pinch bolt and slide the fork tube out of the fork brackets. It may be necessary to rotate the fork tube slightly while pulling it down and out. Remove the fork assembly and take it to the workbench for service. If the fork is not going to be serviced, wrap it in a bath towel or blanket to protect the surface from damage.

NOTE
Identify the fork tubes so they will be installed on the correct side.

9. Repeat for the other fork assembly.

(7) **FRONT FORK (FXD, FXDL, FXDS-CON, FXDP, 1999 FXDX)**

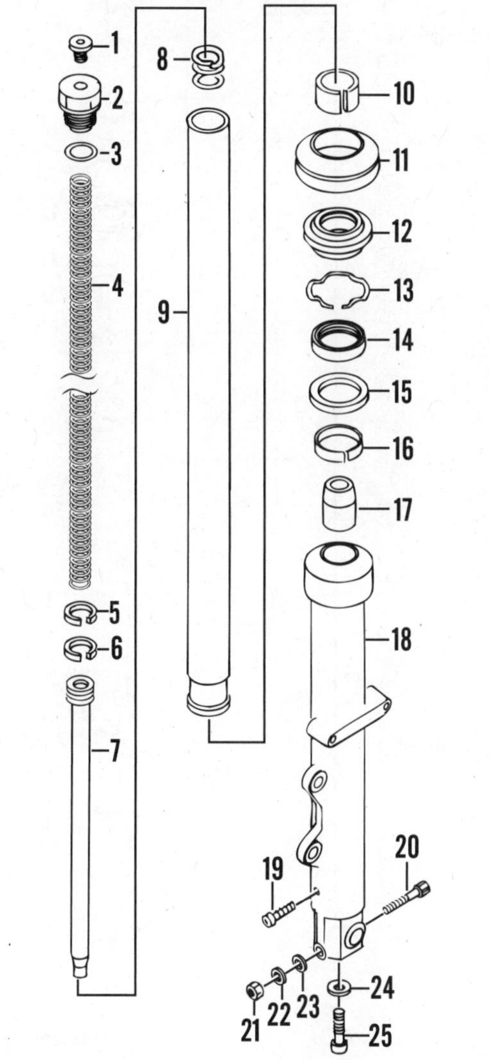

1. Center plug
2. Top cap
3. O-ring
4. Spring
5. Piston ring
6. Piston ring
7. Damper rod
8. Rebound spring
9. Fork tube
10. Fork tube bushing
11. Dust seal cover
12. Dust seal
13. Retainer ring
14. Oil seal
15. Oil seal spacer
16. Slider bushing
17. Oil lock piece
18. Slider
19. Drain screw
20. Clap bolt
21. Nut
22. Lockwasher
23. Washer
24. Washer
25. Allen bolt

Installation

1. Clean off any corrosion or dirt on the upper and lower fork bracket receptacles.

2A. On FXD, FXDL, FXDS-CON and 1999 FXDX models, install each fork tube so that the tube extends 0.42-0.50 in. (10.7-12.7 mm) above the upper fork bracket as shown in **Figure 6**.

2B. On FXDWG models, perform the following:

a. Install a fork tube through the fork brackets and tighten the lower pinch bolt.

b. Position the fork tube so that one flat on the fork tube plug faces toward the steering stem. Hold the fork in this position and install the *new* oil seal, washer and the fork tube top cap. Repeat for the other fork tube.

c. Position the fork tube so it is flush with the top surface of the upper fork bracket.

3. Tighten the lower fork bracket pinch bolt to the specification in **Table 1**.

4. If loose, tighten the fork cap (B, **Figure 5**) securely.

5. Tighten the upper fork bracket pinch bolt (A, **Figure 5**) to the specification in **Table 1**.

6. On FXDWG models, tighten the fork tube cap securely.

7. Install the front fender and front wheel as described in Chapter Nine.

8. Apply the front brake and pump the front fork several times to seat the fork and front wheel.

Disassembly

Refer to **Figure 7** or **Figure 8**.

1. Clamp the fork slider's front axle boss in a vise with soft jaws. Do not clamp the slider at any point above the fork axle boss in a vise.

NOTE

Loosen the bottom Allen bolt before removing the fork cap and spring. Leaving the cap on provides spring tension against the damper rod. This prevents the damper rod from turning when loosening the Allen bolt.

2. Loosen the Allen bolt from the bottom of the slider. Do not remove it at this time, as fork oil will drain out.

3A. On all models except FXDWG, if the fork top cap was not loosened during removal, hold the fork tube in a vise with soft jaws and loosen the fork top cap.

3B. On FXDWG models, if the fork top plug was not loosened during removal, hold the fork tube in a vise with soft jaws and loosen the fork top plug.

WARNING

Be careful when removing the top cap, or top plug, as the spring is under pressure. Protect eyes and face accordingly.

4. With the fork assembly vertical, remove the fork top cap, or top plug, from the top of the fork tube.

5. Remove the spring from the fork tube.

6. Remove the fork tube from the vise and pour the oil into a drain pan. Pump the fork several times by hand to expel most of the remaining oil.

7A. On all models except FXDWG, remove the dust seal cover from the slider. Insert a small flat-tipped screwdriver under the dust seal (**Figure 9**) and carefully pry the dust seal out of the slider and remove it.

7B. On FXDWG models, insert a small flat-tipped screwdriver under the dust cover and carefully pry the dust cover out of the slider and remove it.

8. Pry the retaining ring (**Figure 10**) out of the groove in the slider and remove it.

9. Remove the Allen bolt and washer (**Figure 11**) at the bottom of the slider.

10. There is an interference fit between the bushing in the fork slider and the bushing on the fork tube. In order to remove the fork tube from the slider, pull hard on the fork tube using quick in-and-out strokes (**Figure 12**). Doing so will withdraw the bushing and the oil seal from the slider.

NOTE

It may be necessary to slightly heat the area on the slider around the oil seal prior to removal. Use a rag soaked in hot water; do not apply a flame directly to the fork slider.

11. Withdraw the fork tube from the slider.

NOTE

Do not remove the fork tube bushing unless it is going to be replaced. Inspect it as described in this chapter.

12. Remove the oil lock piece (**Figure 13**) from the damper rod.

8

FRONT FORK (FXDWG)

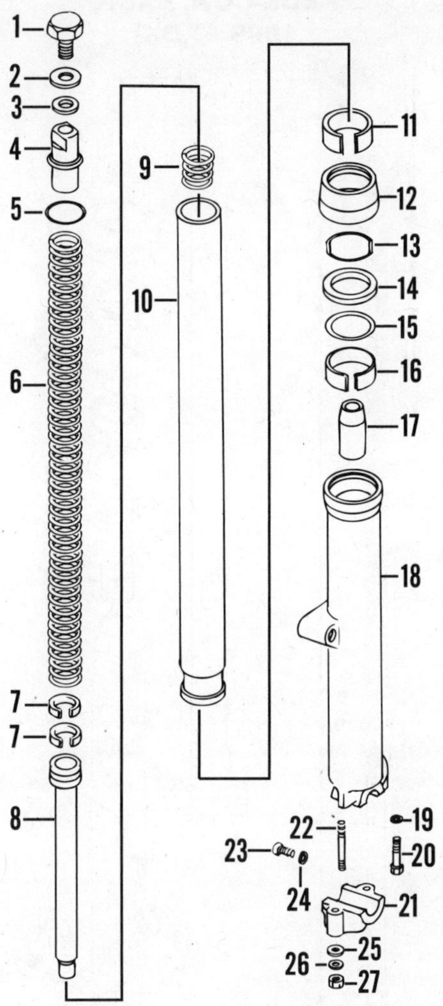

1. Top cap
2. Spacer
3. Oil seal
4. Fork tube plug
5. O-ring
6. Spring
7. Piston ring
8. Damper rod
9. Rebound spring
10. Fork tube
11. Fork tube bushing
12. Dust seal cover
13. Retainer ring
14. Oil seal
15. Oil seal spacer
16. Slider bushing
17. Oil lock piece
18. Slider
19. Washer (damper rod)
20. Allen bolt (damper rod)
21. Axle cap
22. Stud
23. Drain screw
24. Washer
25. Washer
26. Lockwasher
27. Nut

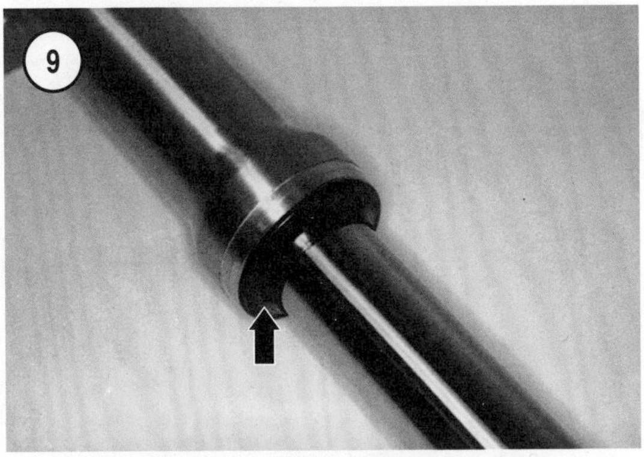

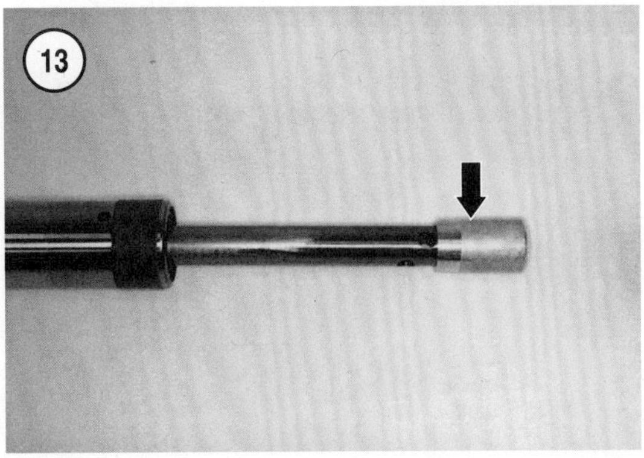

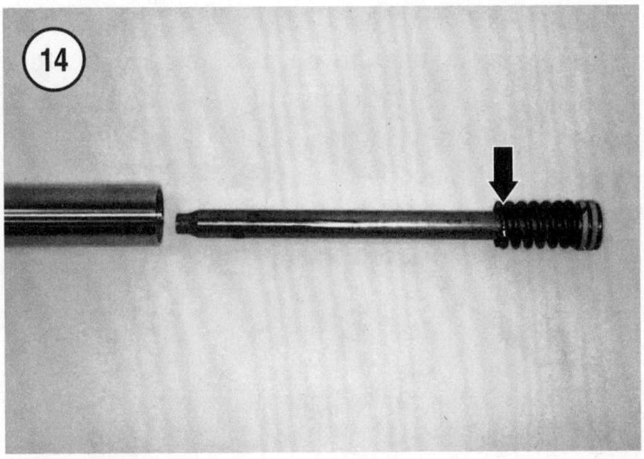

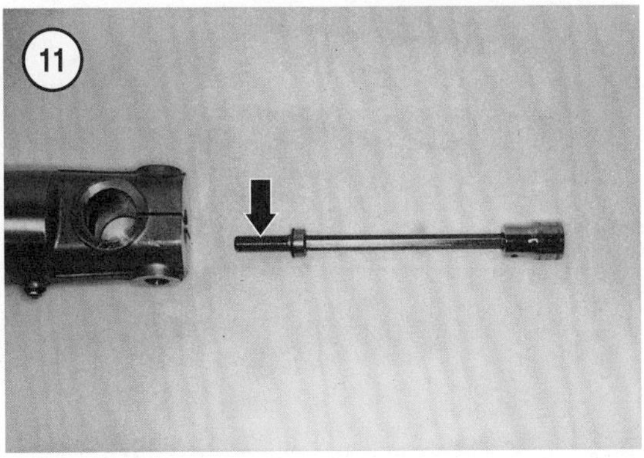

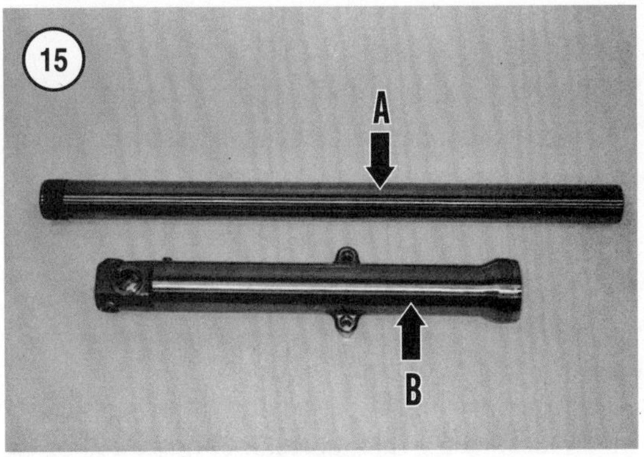

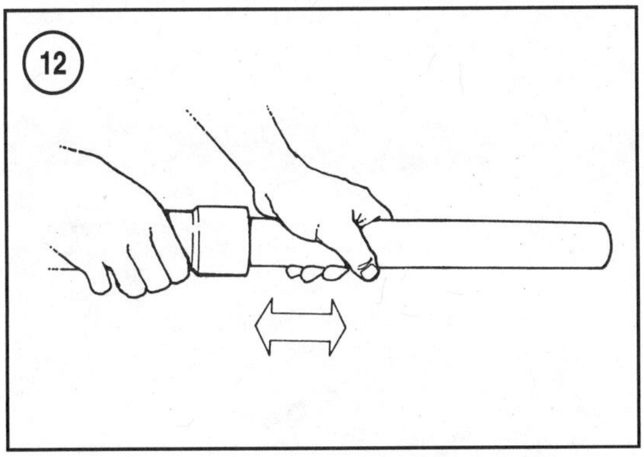

13. Remove the damper rod and rebound spring (**Figure 14**) from the fork tube.

Inspection

Replace any worn or damaged parts.

1. Thoroughly clean all parts in solvent and dry them. Check the fork tube for signs of wear or scratches.
2. Check the fork tube (A, **Figure 15**) for bending, nicks, rust or other damage. Place the fork tube on a

16

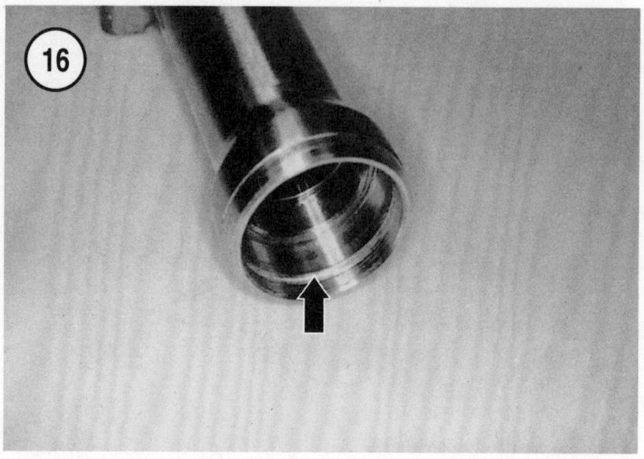

17

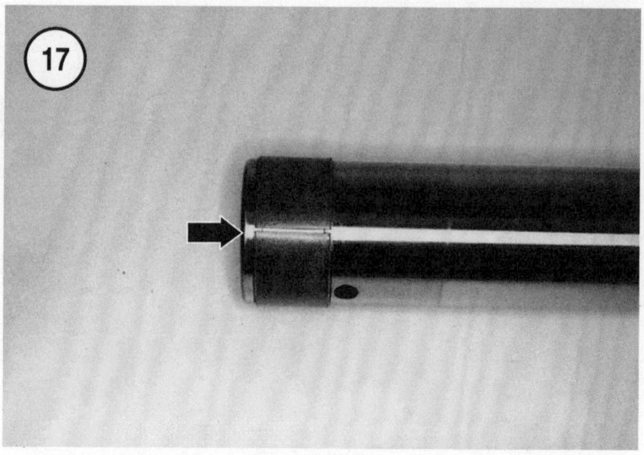

set of V-blocks and check runout with a dial indicator. If the special tools are not available, roll the fork tube on a large plate glass or other flat surface. Specifications for runout are not available.

3. Check the slider (B, **Figure 15**) for dents or other exterior damage. Check the retaining ring groove (**Figure 16**) in the top of the slider for cracks or other damage.
4. Check the slider and fork tube bushings for excessive wear, cracks or damage.
5. To remove the fork tube bushing, perform the following:
   a. Expand the bushing slit (**Figure 17**) with a screwdriver and then slide the bushing off the fork tube.
   b. Coat the new bushing with new fork oil.
   c. Install the new bushing by expanding the slit with a screwdriver.
   d. Seat the new bushing into the fork tube groove.
6. Check the damper rod piston rings (**Figure 18**) for excessive wear, cracks or other damage. If necessary, replace both rings as a set.
7. Check the damper rod for straightness with a set of V-blocks and a dial indicator (**Figure 19**) or by rolling it on a piece of plate glass. Service limit specifications for runout are not available. If the damper rod is not straight, replace it.
8. Make sure the oil passage holes in the damper rod (**Figure 20**) are open. If clogged, flush with solvent and dry with compressed air.
9. Check the threads in the bottom of the damper rod for stripping, cross-threading or sealer residue. Use a tap to true up the threads and to remove sealer deposits.
10. Check the damper rod rebound spring and the fork spring for wear or damage. Service limit specifications for spring free length are not available.

18

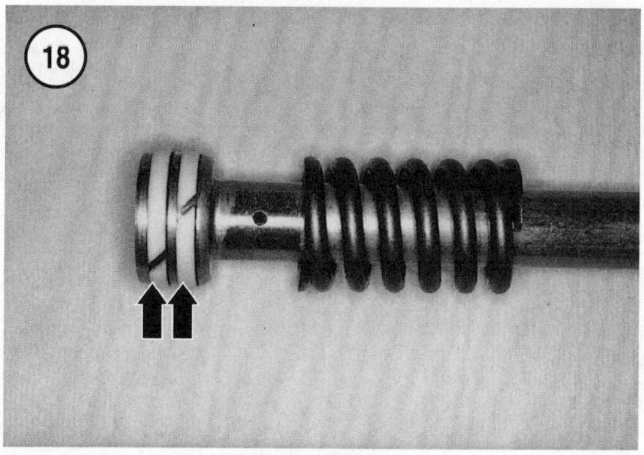

19

20

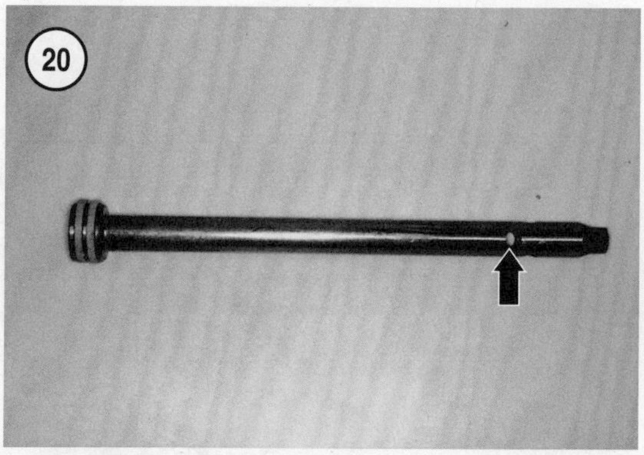

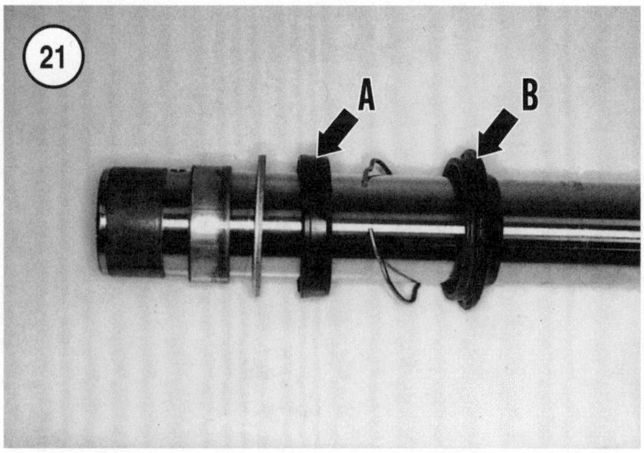

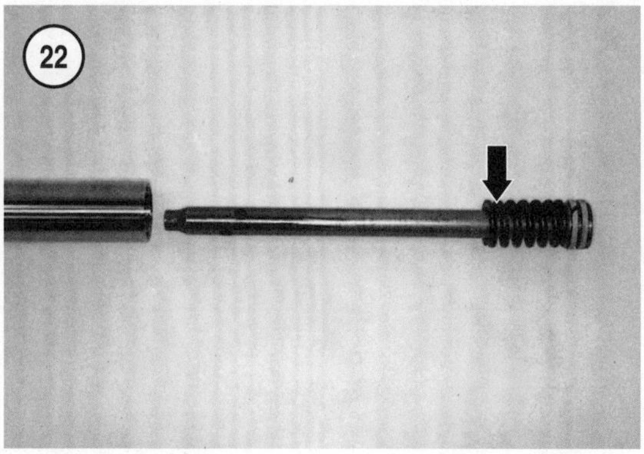

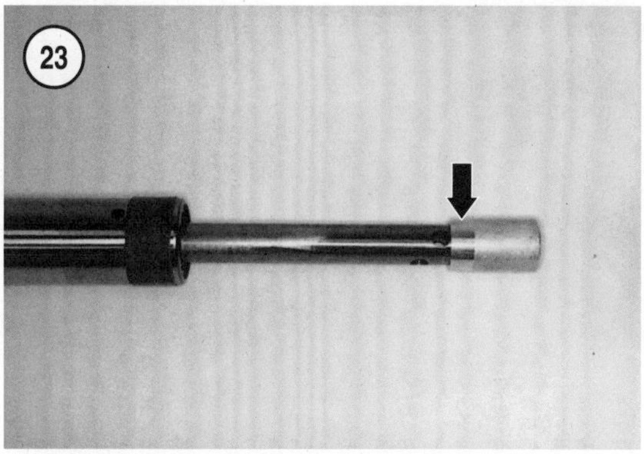

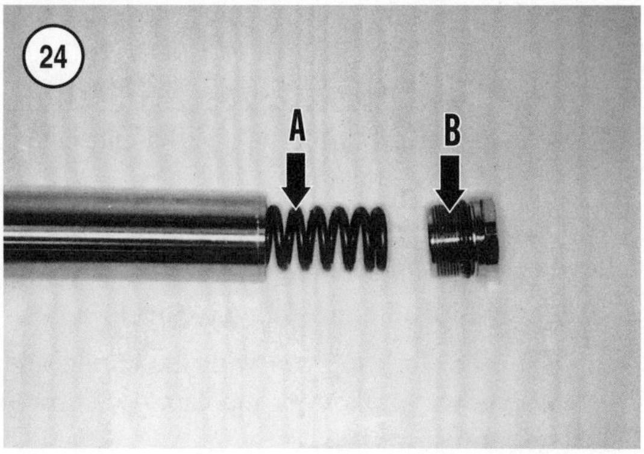

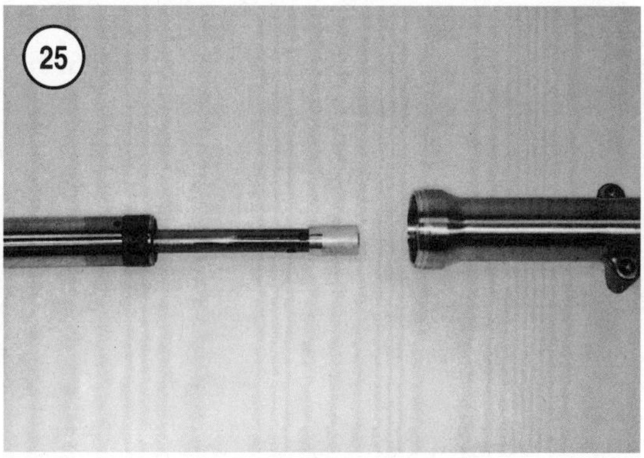

11. Replace the oil seals (A, **Figure 21**) whenever they are removed. Always replace both oil seals as a set.

12. Inspect the dust seals (B, **Figure 21**) or dust covers, for cracks, deterioration or other damage. A damaged dust seal, or dust cover, will allow dirt to pass through and damage the oil seal.

13. Replace the fork top cap, fork tube plug, or O-ring if leaking or if wear or damage is apparent.

Assembly

1. Coat all parts with Harley-Davidson Type E Fork Oil, or an equivalent, fork oil before assembly.

2. Install the rebound spring onto the damper rod (**Figure 22**) and slide the damper rod into the fork tube until it extends out the end of the fork tube.

3. Install the oil lock piece (**Figure 23**) onto the end of the damper rod.

4. Temporarily install the fork spring (A, **Figure 24**) into the fork tube so that the tapered side of the spring faces down toward the damper rod.

5A. On all models except FXDWG, install the fork top cap (B, **Figure 24**), screw it into place to hold the damper rod in place.

5B. On FXDWG models, install the fork top plug and screw it into place to hold the damper rod in place.

6. Push the fork slider and damper rod through the opening in the bottom of the fork tube.

7. Make sure the oil lock piece is mounted on the end of the damper rod. Install the fork tube into the slider (**Figure 25**) until it bottoms.

8. Install a new washer onto the damper rod Allen bolt.

9. Apply a non-permanent threadlocking compound to the damper rod Allen bolt threads prior to

installation. Insert the Allen bolt (**Figure 11**) through the lower end of the slider and thread it into the damper rod. Tighten the bolt securely.

NOTE
To protect the oil and dust seal lips, place a thin plastic bag on top of the fork tube. Before installing the seals in the following steps, lightly coat the bag and the seal lips with fork oil.

10. Slide the fork slider bushing (A, **Figure 26**), oil seal spacer (B) and oil seal (C) (with the letters facing up) down into the fork tube receptacle.

NOTE
A 39 mm fork seal driver is required to install the fork tube bushing and seal into the fork tube. A number of different aftermarket fork seal drivers are available that can be used for this purpose. Another method is to use a piece of pipe or metal collar with correct dimensions to slide over the fork tube and seat against the seal. When selecting or fabricating a driver tool, it must have sufficient weight to drive the bushing and oil seal into the fork tube. A fork seal and cap installer (JIMS part No. 2046) is used in this procedure.

11. Slide the fork seal driver down the fork tube and seat it against the seal (**Figure 27**).
12. Operate the driver and drive the fork slider bushing and new seal into the fork tube. Continue until the stopper ring groove in the tube is visible above the fork seal. Remove the fork seal driver tool.
13. Install the retaining ring (**Figure 28**) into the slider groove. Make sure the retaining ring seats in the groove.
14A. On all models except FXDWG, install the dust seal (**Figure 29**) and seat it into the slider, then install the dust seal cover.
14B. On FXDWG models, install the dust cover and seat it into the slider.
15A. On all models except FXDWG, unscrew and remove the fork top cap.
15B. On FXDWG models, unscrew and remove the fork top plug.
16. Remove the fork spring.

26

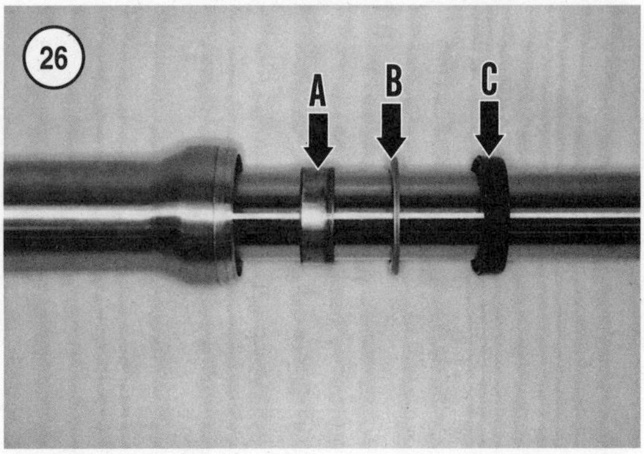

27

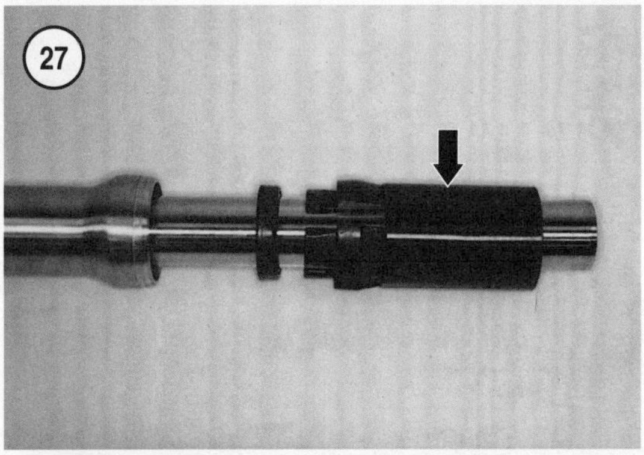

28

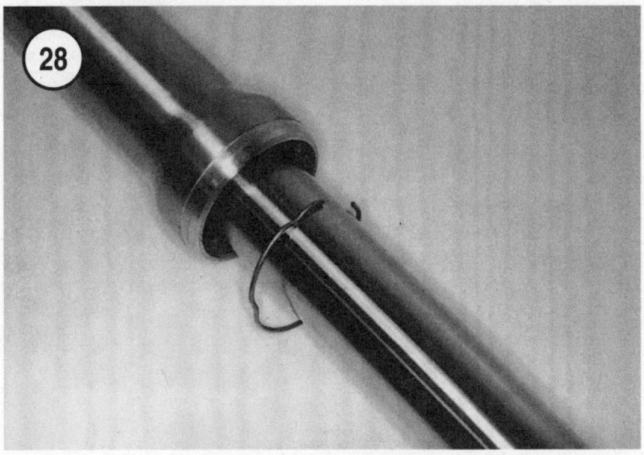

17. Fill the fork tube with the correct quantity of Harley-Davidson Type E Fork Oil listed in **Table 2**.
18. The fork spring is tapered at one end. Install the spring (A, **Figure 24**) with the tapered end facing down toward the damper rod.
19A. On all models except FXDWG, perform the following:

a. Apply fork oil to the fork top cap O-ring.
b. Align the fork top cap with the spring and push down on the fork top cap to compress the spring.

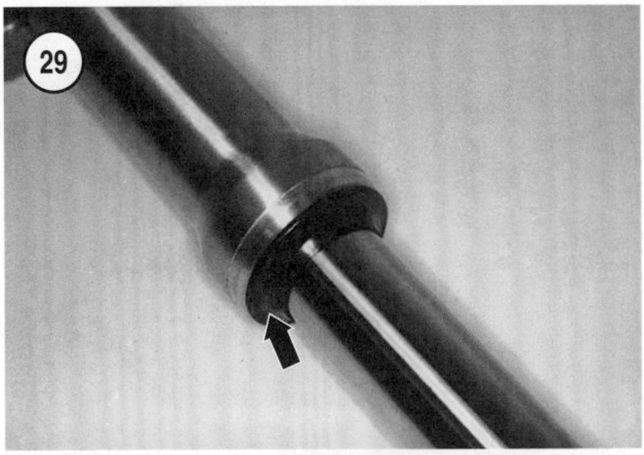

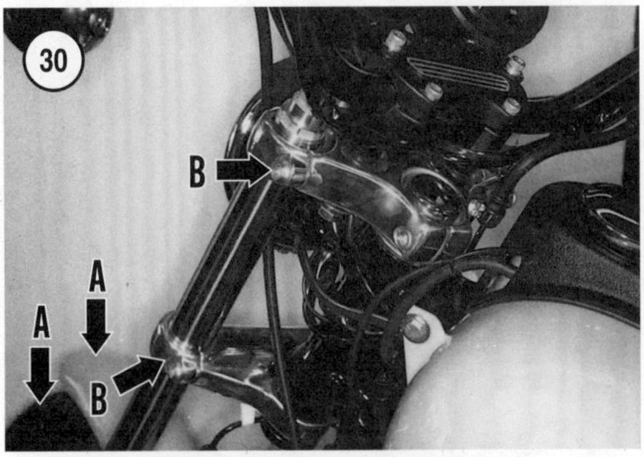

c. Start the cap slowly, making sure it is not cross-threaded. Tighten it finger-tight.

19B. On FXDWG models, perform the following:

a. Apply fork oil to the fork top plug O-ring.
b. Align the fork top plug with the spring and push down on the fork top plug to compress the spring.
c. Start the plug slowly, making sure it is not cross-threaded. Tighten it finger-tight.

20. Place the slider in a vise with soft jaws and tighten the fork top cap, or fork top plug, securely.
21. Install the fork tube as described in this chapter.

FRONT FORK (FXDXT, 2000-ON FXDX)

Front Fork Service

Before assuming that a fork is internally malfunctioning, drain the front fork oil and refill with the proper type and quantity of fork oil as described in this chapter. If there is still a problem, such as poor damping, or a tendency to bottom or top out, follow the service procedures in this section.

To simplify fork service and to prevent the mixing of parts, remove, service and install fork legs individually.

Removal/Installation (Fork Not To Be Serviced)

1. Remove the front fender and front wheel (A, **Figure 30**) as described in Chapter Eleven.
2. Loosen the upper and lower bracket pinch bolts (B, **Figure 30**).
3. If both fork tube assemblies are going to be removed, mark them with an R (right side) and L (left side) so the assemblies will be reinstalled on the correct side.
4. Carefully lower the fork assembly out of the upper and lower fork brackets. It may be necessary to rotate the fork tube slightly while pulling it down and out. Remove the fork assembly and take it to a workbench for service. If the fork is not going to be serviced, wrap it in a bath towel or blanket to protect the surface from damage.
5. Slowly install the fork tube into the lower fork bracket then the upper fork bracket.

NOTE
*There is no specification for the location of the top of the fork tube. However, as a guideline, set the fork tube approximately 0.08 in (2.0 mm) above the top surface of the upper fork bracket (**Figure 31**).*

6. With the fork assembly in position, tighten the upper and lower bracket pinch bolts to the torque specification listed in **Table 2**.
7. Install the front wheel and front fender as described in Chapter Nine.

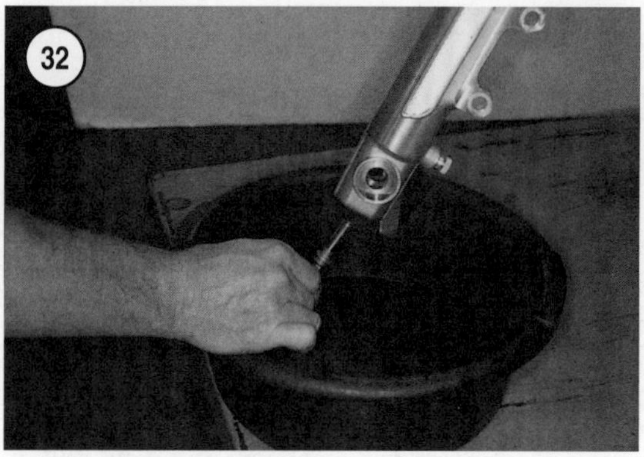

Removal/Installation (Fork To Be Serviced)

1. Remove the front fender and front wheel as described in Chapter Eleven.
2. If both fork tube assemblies are going to be removed, mark them with an R (right side) and L (left side) so the assemblies will be reinstalled on the correct side.
3. Place a drain pan under the fork slider.
4. Use an 8 mm Allen wrench and impact driver and loosen the damper rod cartridge 8 mm Allen bolt at the base of the slider.
5. Remove the Allen bolt (**Figure 32**) and drain the fork oil. Pump the slider several times to expel most of the fork oil. Reinstall the Allen bolt to keep residual oil in the fork.
6. Carefully pry the cover (A, **Figure 33**) from the fork slider.
7. Remove the dust seal and stopper ring (B, **Figure 33**) from the fork slider.
8. Lower the fork slider on the fork tube.

NOTE

It may be necessary to slightly heat the area on the slider around the oil seal prior to removal. Use a rag soaked in hot water; do not apply a flame directly to the fork slider.

9. There is an interference fit between the bushing in the fork slider and the bushing on the fork tube. In order to remove the fork tube from the slider, pull hard on the fork tube using quick in-and-out strokes (**Figure 34**). Doing so will withdraw the bushing and the oil seal from the slider.
10. Loosen the upper and lower bracket pinch bolts (**Figure 35**).

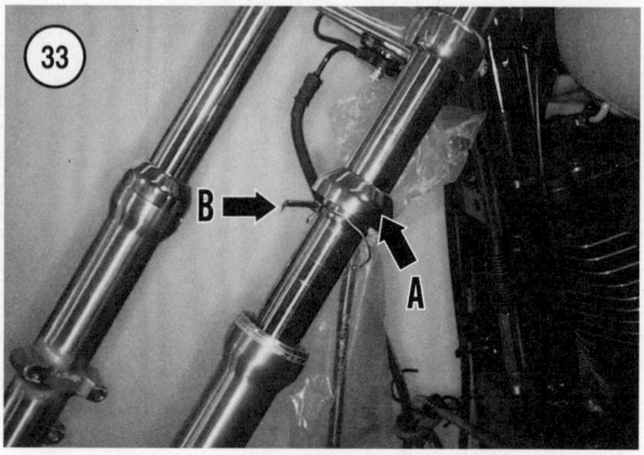

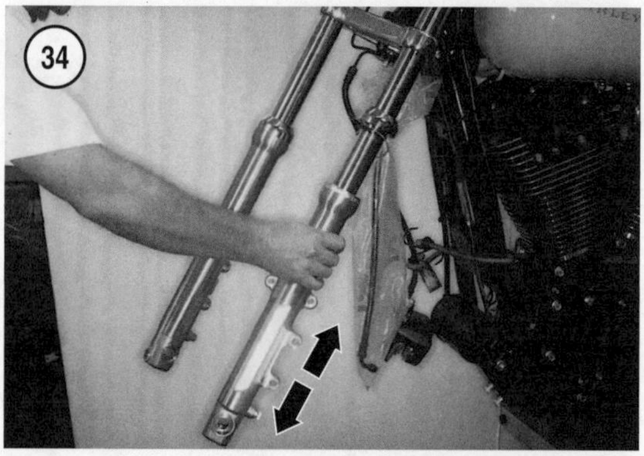

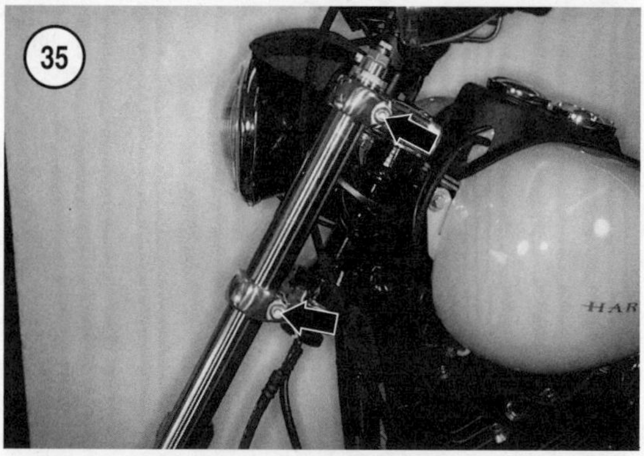

(37) **FRONT FORK (FXDX 2000-ON, FXDXT)**

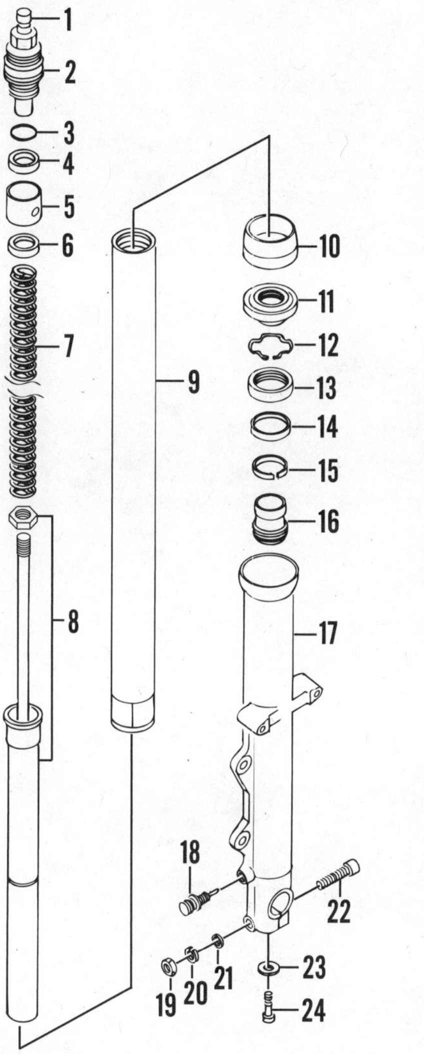

1. Rebound adjuster
2. Fork cap bolt assembly
3. O-ring
4. Upper spacer
5. Spring collar
6. Lower spacer
7. Fork spring
8. Damper rod/cartridge assembly
9. Fork tube and bushing
10. Dust seal cover
11. Dust seal
12. Stopper ring
13. Oil seal
14. Oil seal spacer
15. Slider bushing
16. Lower stop
17. Slider
18. Compression damper adjuster
19. Nut
20. Lockwasher
21. Washer
22. Clamping bolt
23. Washer
24. Allen bolt

11. Carefully lower the fork assembly out of the upper bracket. It may be necessary to rotate the fork tube slightly while pulling it down.
12. Lower the fork tube between the upper and the lower brackets and tighten the lower bracket pinch bolt.
13. Loosen the fork cap bolt (**Figure 36**).
14. Loosen the lower bracket pinch bolt and remove the fork from the lower bracket.
15. Service the fork assembly as described in this chapter.
16. Slowly install the fork tube into the lower fork bracket, then the upper fork bracket.

NOTE
*There is no specification to the location of the top of the fork tube. However, as a guideline, set the fork tube approximately 0.08 in (2.0 mm) above the top surface of the upper fork bracket (**Figure 31**).*

17. With the fork assembly in the correct location, tighten the upper and lower bracket pinch bolts to the specification in **Table 2**.
18. Install the front wheel and front fender as described in Chapter Nine.

Disassembly

Refer to **Figure 37**.

NOTE
A special fork holding tool is required to disassemble and assemble this fork assembly. The fork spring is so strong that it cannot be compressed sufficiently by hand to gain access to the nut on top of the damper rod. This special tool is available from motorcycle dealerships or motorcycle parts suppliers.

1. Hold the fork in a vertical position and completely unscrew the fork cap bolt from the fork tube. The cap bolt cannot be removed at this time as it is still attached to the damper rod cartridge.
2. Turn the fork assembly upside down and drain the residual fork oil into a suitable container. Pump the fork several times by hand to expel most of the oil. Dispose of the fork oil properly.

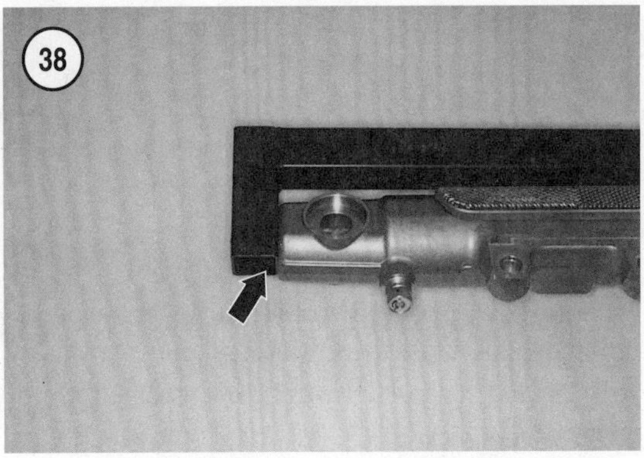

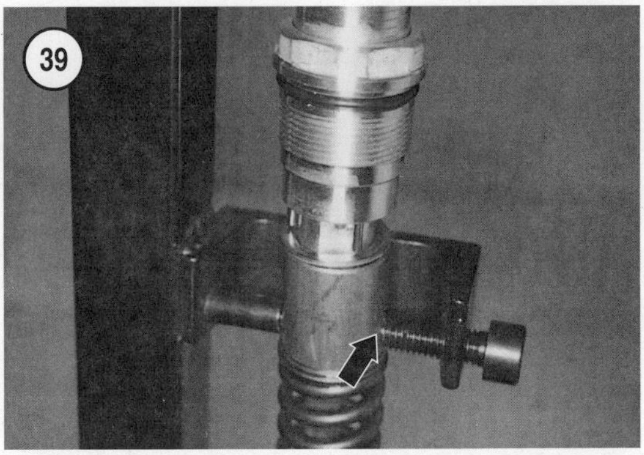

3. Install the lower end of the fork assembly in the fork holding tool, following the manufacturer's instructions. Make sure the tool is indexed properly in the lower hole in the slider (**Figure 38**).
4. Slide the fork tube down into the fork slider to expose the spring collar.
5. Install the special tool's upper bolt into the hole in the spring collar (**Figure 39**) following the manufacturer's instructions. Make sure the tool is indexed properly in the hole in the spring spacer.
6. Slowly tighten the special tool and compress the fork assembly until the upper portion of the damper rod cartridge and nut are exposed (**Figure 40**).
7. Install an open end wrench on the damper rod cartridge nut (A, **Figure 41**) and another one on the flats on the fork cap bolt (B, **Figure 41**).
8. Hold onto the cap bolt and loosen the damper rod cartridge nut.
9. Completely unscrew the cap bolt from the damper rod cartridge.
10. Measure the distance between the top of the damper rod nut and the top of the damper rod cartridge (**Figure 42**). Note the dimension as it will be used during assembly.
11. Withdraw the fork cap bolt (A, **Figure 43**) and inner rod (B) from the damper rod cartridge.
12. Slowly loosen the special tool and release the spring pressure within the fork assembly.
13. Remove the fork assembly from the special tool.
14. Remove the upper spacer, spring collar and lower spacer from above the fork spring.
15. Withdraw the fork spring and damper rod cartridge.
16. Slide the slider bushing, spacer, oil seal, retaining ring, dust seal and cover from the fork tube. Keep them in the order of removal (**Figure 44**).

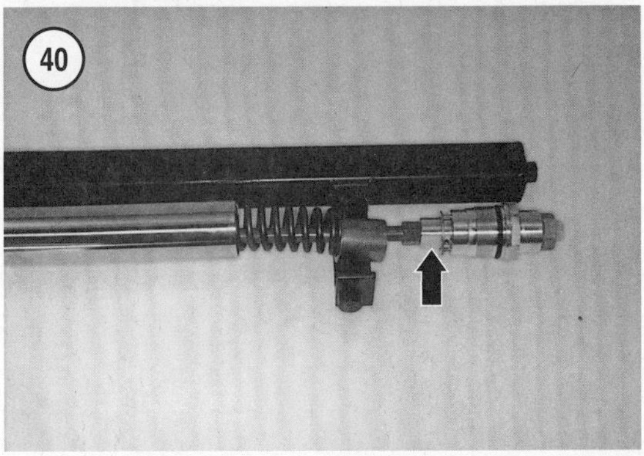

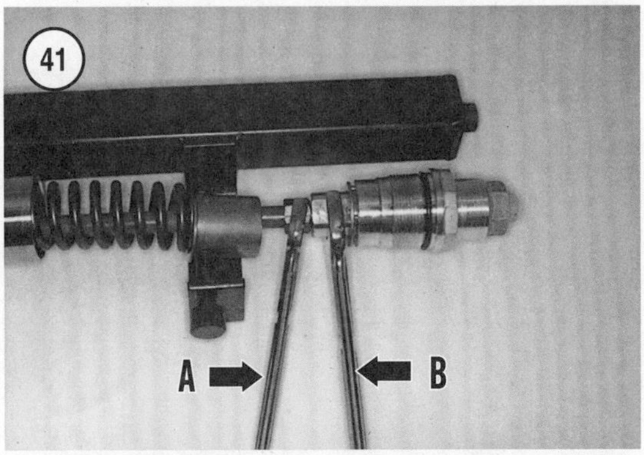

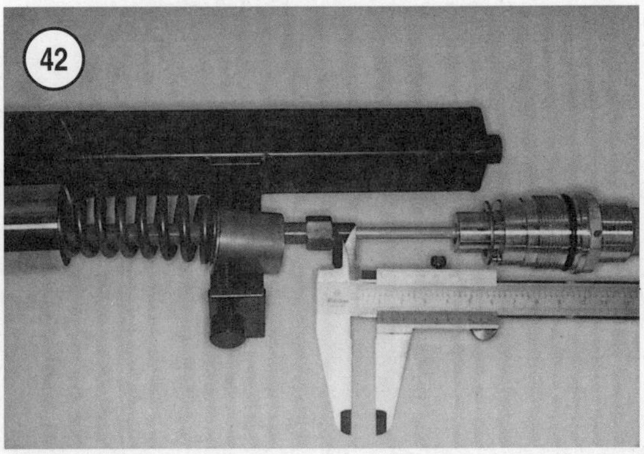

43

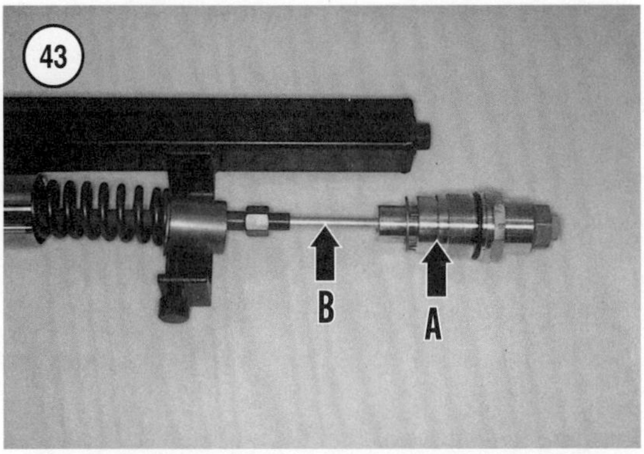

44

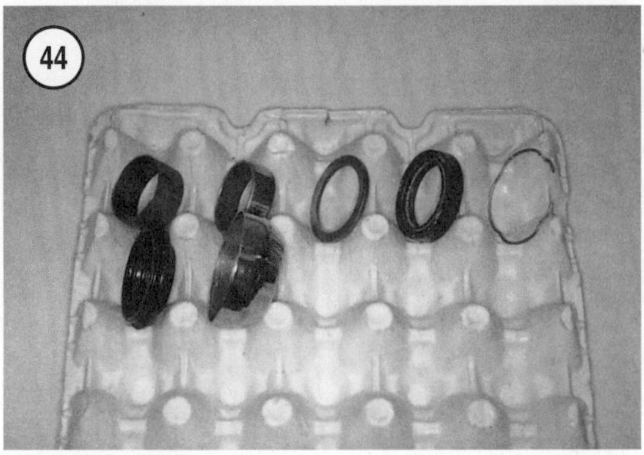

45

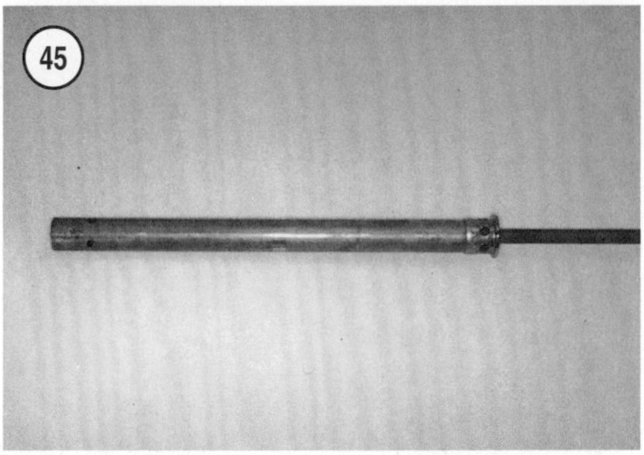

46

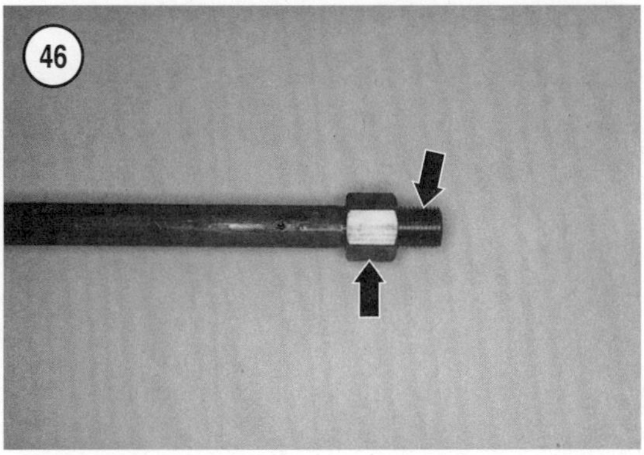

47

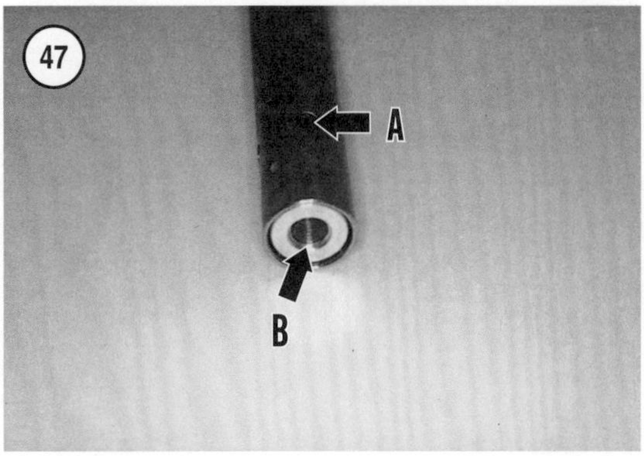

NOTE

Do not remove the fork tube bushing unless it is going to be replaced. Inspect it as described in this chapter.

17. Do not try to remove the lower stop in the base of the slider. It is pressed into place. If necessary, have a Harley-Davidson dealership remove it and install a new one.

18. Inspect the components as described in this chapter.

10

Inspection

Replace any damaged or excessively worn components. Repair damaged threads with an appropriately sized metric tap or die. Simply cleaning and reinstalling unserviceable components will not improve performance of the front suspension.

1. Thoroughly clean all parts in solvent and dry them. Check the fork tube for signs of wear or scratches.
2. Check the damper rod cartridge for straightness and damage (**Figure 45**).
3. Check the threads and nut (**Figure 46**) at the top of the damper rod cartridge for damage.
4. Make sure the oil hole (A, **Figure 47**) in the damper rod cartridge is clear. Clean out if necessary.
5. Inspect the damper rod cartridge threads for the Allen bolt (B, **Figure 47**) for wear or damage.

NOTE

*Do not disassemble the fork cap bolt and rebound adjuster (**Figure 48**). Replacement parts are not available. If this component is defective, replace the unit as an assembly.*

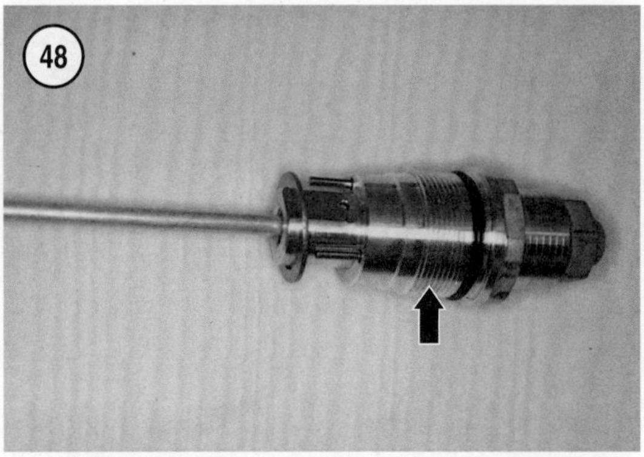

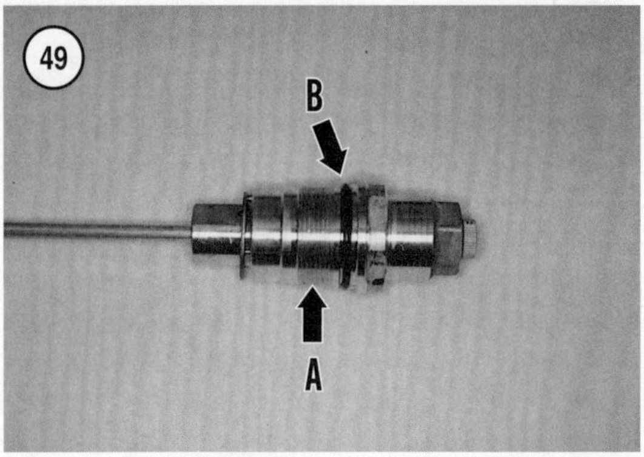

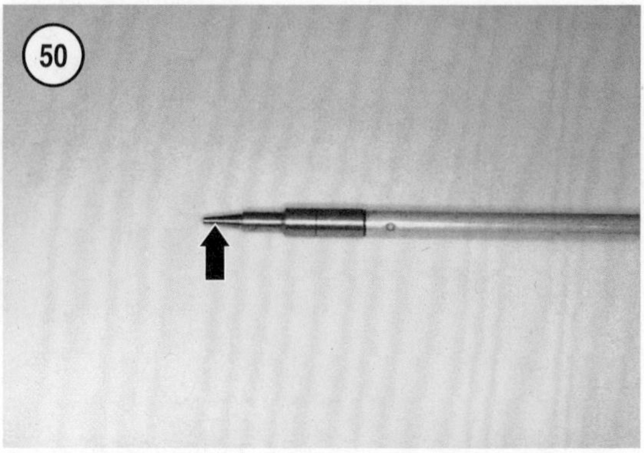

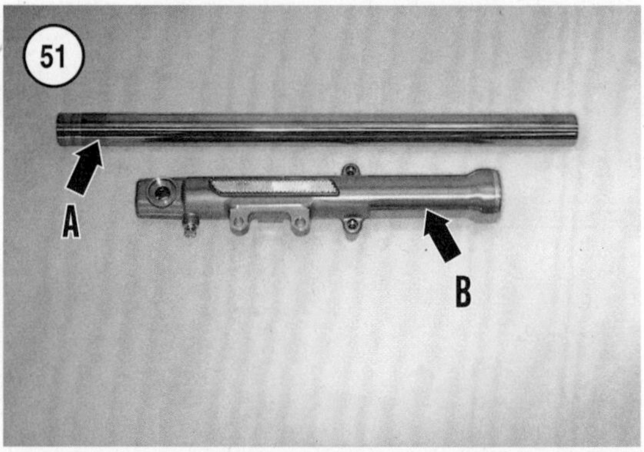

6. Inspect the fork cap bolt threads (A, **Figure 49**) for wear or damage.

7. Install a *new* O-ring (B, **Figure 49**) on the fork cap bolt.

8. Inspect the needle tip (**Figure 50**) on the end of the fork cap bolt and inner rod for damage.

9. Check the fork tube (A, **Figure 51**) for straightness. Refer to **Table 3** for maximum runout.

10. Inspect the fork cap bolt threads in the fork tube (**Figure 52**) for wear or damage.

11. Make sure the oil hole (**Figure 53**) in the fork tube is clear. Clean out if necessary.

12. Check the slider (B, **Figure 51**) for dents or exterior damage that may cause the upper fork tube to stick.

13. Inspect the brake caliper mounting bosses (**Figure 54**) on the slider for cracks or other damage.

14. Check the front axle bore (**Figure 55**) in the slider for burrs or damage.

15. Check the compression damping adjuster (**Figure 56**). Make sure it can be turned from one stop to the other.

16. Inspect the oil seal seating area (**Figure 57**) in the slider for damage or burrs.

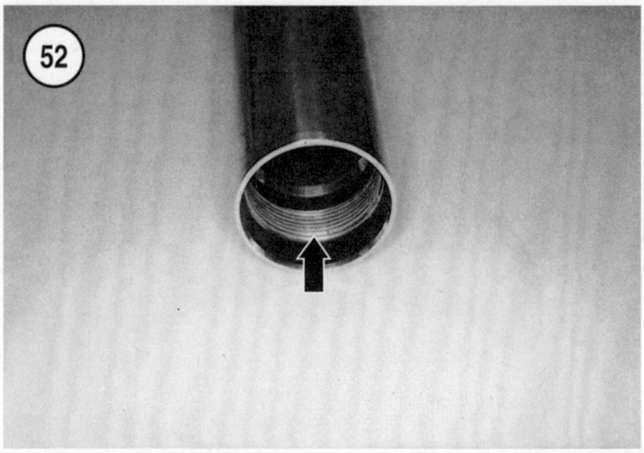

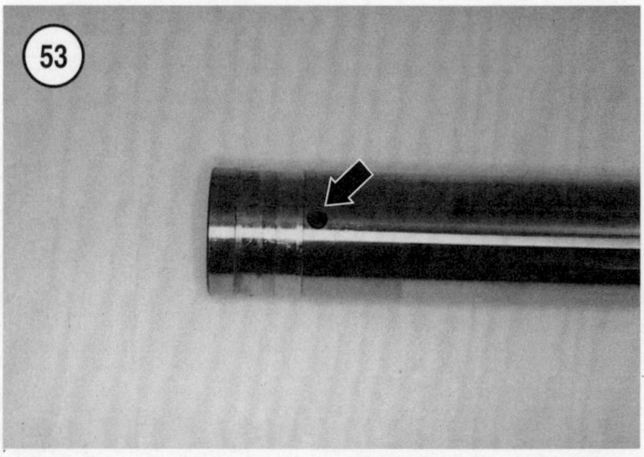

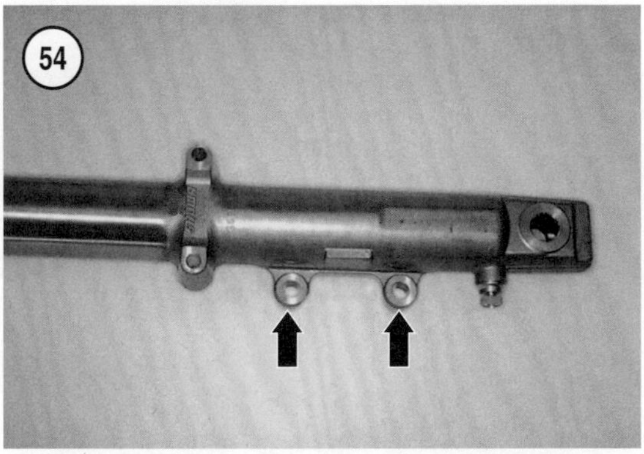

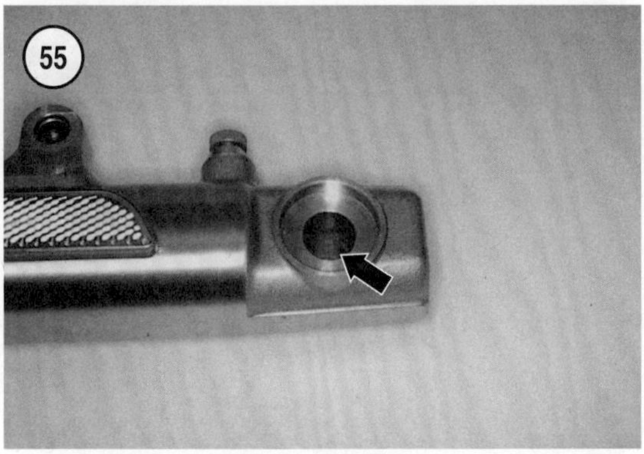

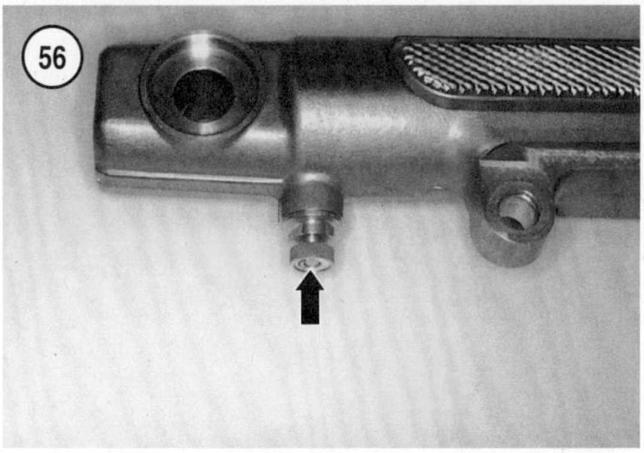

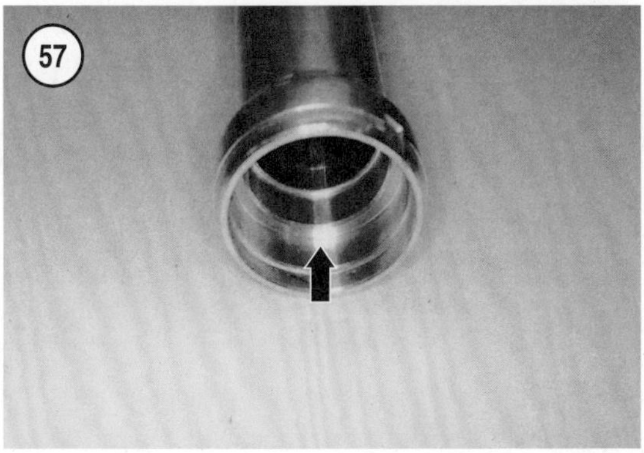

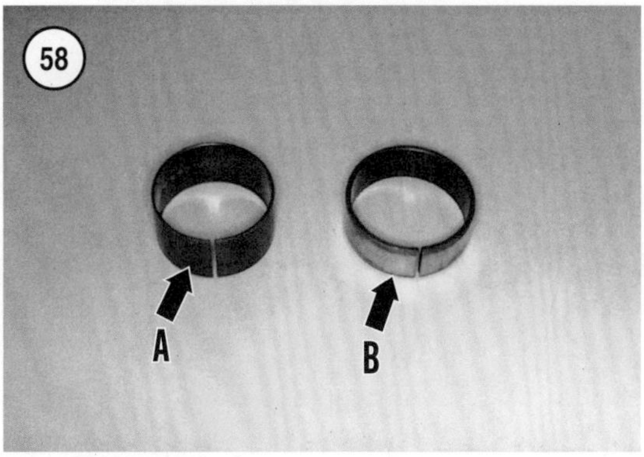

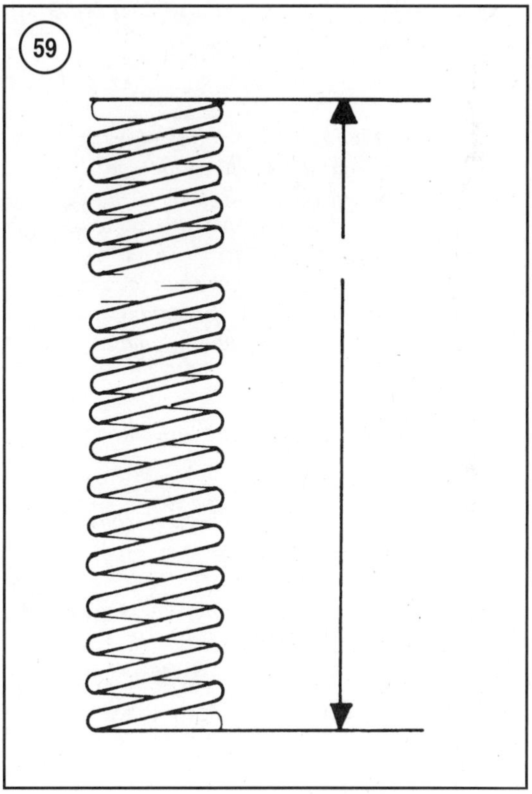

17. Inspect the slider bushing (A, **Figure 58**) and fork tube bushing (B). If either is scratched or scored, they must be replaced.

18. Measure the uncompressed length of the fork spring as shown in **Figure 59**. Replace the spring if it has sagged to the service limit listed in **Table 3**.

Assembly

1. Coat all parts with clean H-D Type E fork oil prior to installation.

10

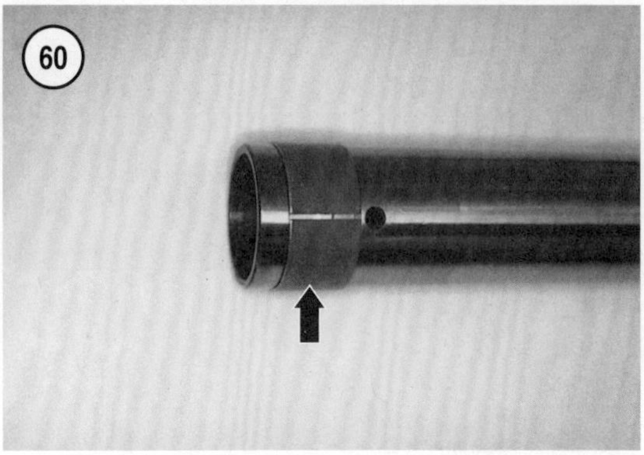

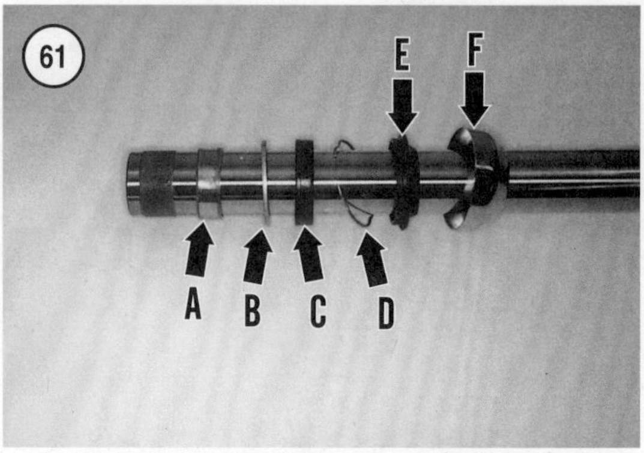

2. If removed, install a new bushing (**Figure 60**) onto the fork tube.

NOTE
Place a clinging-type plastic wrap over the end of the slider and coat it with fork oil. This will prevent damage to the dust seal and the oil seal lips when installing them over the top of the fork tube. The parts can then be carefully slid over the fork tube and the plastic wrap without damaging the seal.

3. Coat the *new* seal with clean fork oil.

NOTE
Position the new oil seal with the open groove facing upward.

4. Slide the fork slider bushing (A, **Figure 61**), spacer (B), oil seal (C), stopper ring (D), dust seal (E) and cover (F) down into the fork tube.
5. Insert the damper rod cartridge into the fork tube (**Figure 62**).

NOTE
The slider bushing opening must be positioned to either side of the slider after the fork tube has been installed. Orientate the opening in relation to the front fender mounting bosses. If the opening is positioned toward either the front or rear of the slider, it will wear prematurely.

6. Position the slider bushing with the opening (**Figure 63**) toward either side of the slider.
7. Insert the fork tube into the slider until the slider bushing reaches the slider.

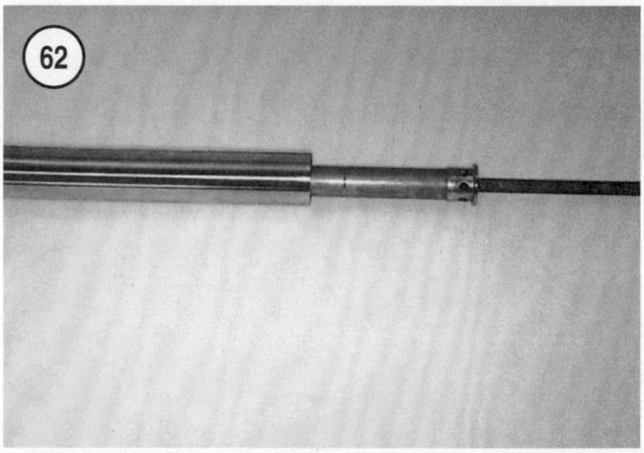

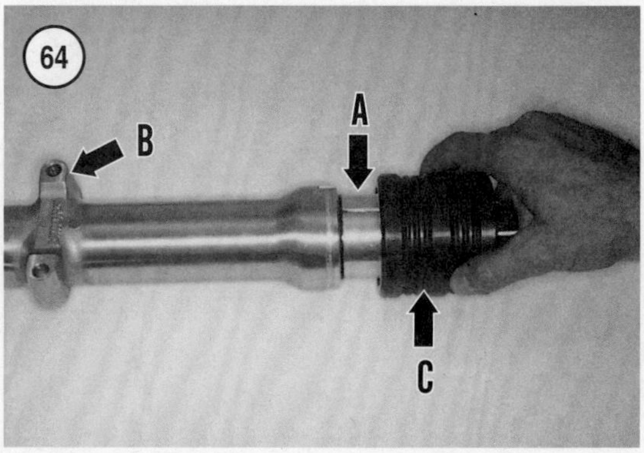

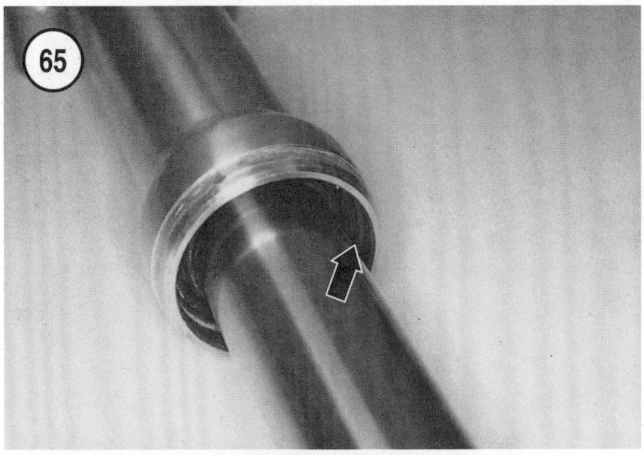

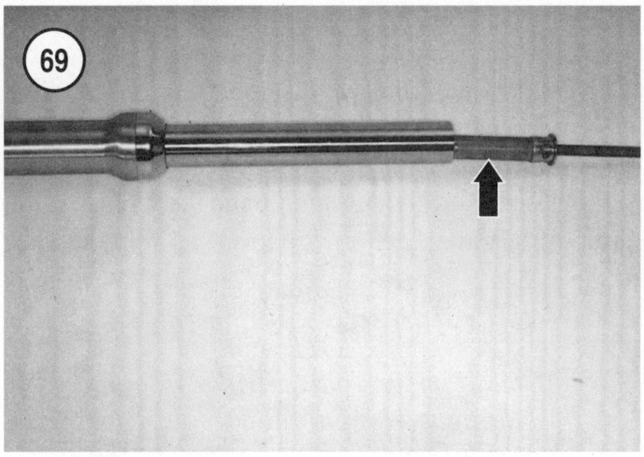

8. Once again make sure the slider bushing opening (A, **Figure 64**) is correctly located in relation to the fender bosses (B). Readjust if necessary.

NOTE
A fork seal driver like is required to install the fork tube bushing and seal into the fork tube. A number of different aftermarket fork seal drivers are available that can be used for this purpose. Another method is to use a piece of pipe or metal collar with correct dimensions to slide over the fork tube and seat against the seal. When selecting or fabricating a driver tool, it must have sufficient weight to drive the bushing and oil seal into the fork tube. A fork seal and cap installer (JIMS part No. 2046) is used in this procedure.

9. Slide the fork seal driver down the fork tube and seat it against the seal (C, **Figure 64**).
10. Operate the driver and drive the fork slider bushing, spacer and new seal into the fork tube. Continue until the fork tube stopper ring groove is visible above the fork seal (**Figure 65**).
11. Slide the stopper ring down the fork tube.
12. Install the stopper ring and make sure it is completely seated in the groove in the fork slider (**Figure 66**).
13. Install the dust seal into the slider. Index it into the groove in the slider (**Figure 67**).
14. Install the cover and carefully tap it into place (**Figure 68**).
15. Insert the damper rod cartridge into the fork tube (**Figure 69**).

NOTE
The lower end of the damper rod cartridge must be guided into the lower

10

stop in the base of the slider. If not aligned correctly, the Allen bolt can not be installed in Step 16.

16. Insert a scribe or thin screwdriver into the hole in the base of the slider to guide the lower end of the damper rod cartridge into the lower stop in the base of the slider.

NOTE
If the damper rod cartridge rotates while tightening the Allen bolt, temporarily install the fork spring and the cap bolt to hold it stationary.

17. Install a *new* washer on the Allen bolt (**Figure 70**). Install it in the fork slider and tighten to the specification in **Table 1**. If installed, remove the cap bolt and fork spring.

NOTE
The following special tool is usually part of the fork holding tool. If not so equipped, one can be fabricated that is approximately 2 inches long with an inner metric thread of 12 × 1.0. This tool is to extend the length of the damper rod for fork bleeding process.

18. Install the special tool extension (**Figure 71**) onto the damper rod cartridge.
19. Secure the fork assembly in a vertical position.

NOTE
To measure the correct amount of fluid, use a plastic baby bottle. These bottles have measurements in milliliters (ml) on the side.

20. Completely compress the fork tube into the slider.
21. Add one-half of the recommended amount (**Table 2**) of H-D Type E fork oil to the fork assembly (**Figure 72**).

NOTE
During the bleeding procedure, maintain the fork oil level above the sliding portion of the damper rod cartridge. If the oil level drops below this level, air may enter the cartridge, nullifying the bleeding procedure.

22. Bleed air from the damper rod cartridge as follows:

70

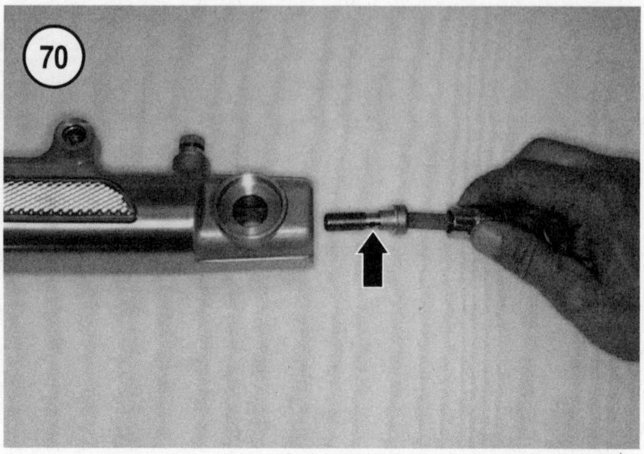

71

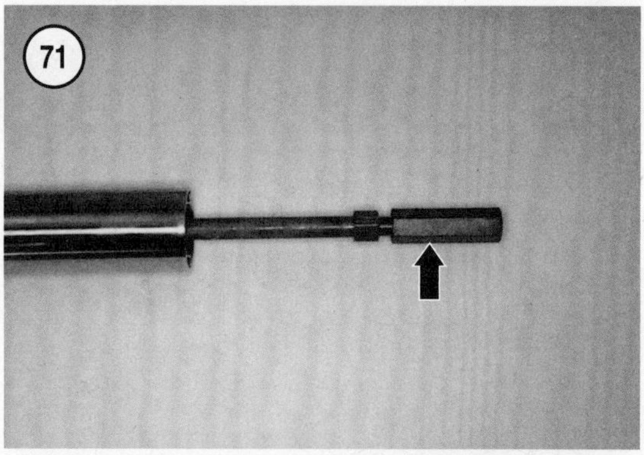

72

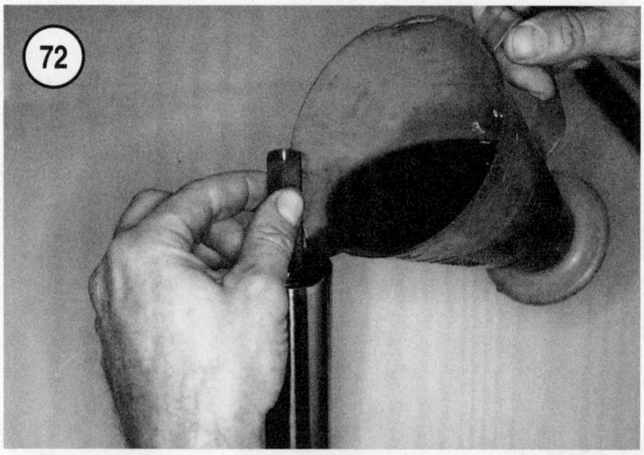

73

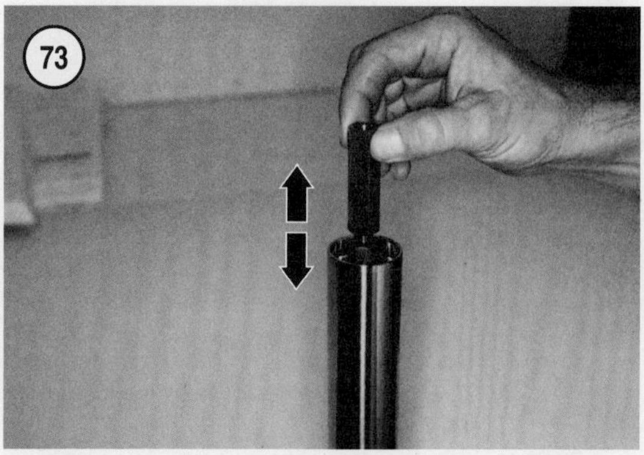

74

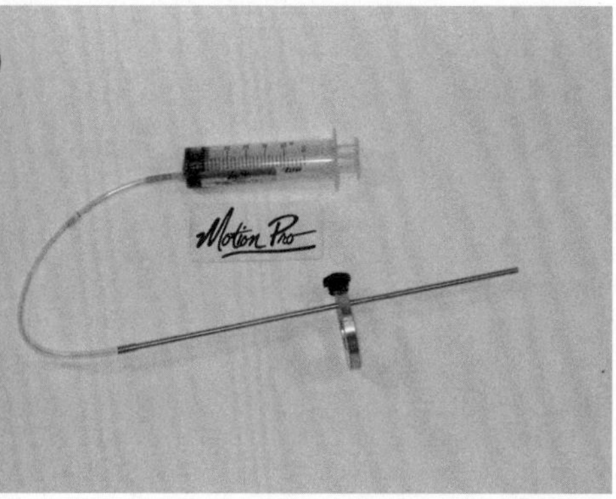

75

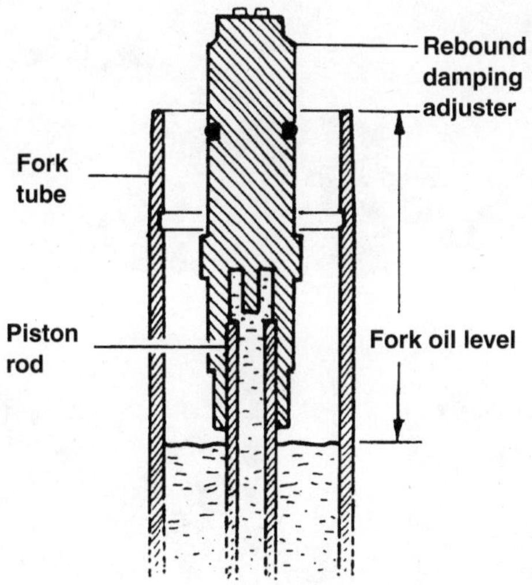

76

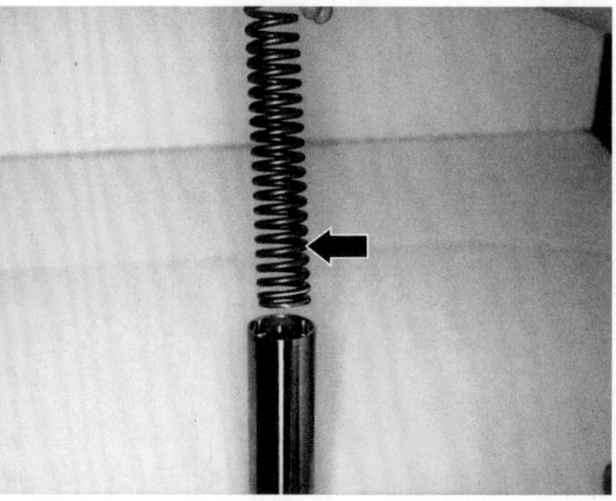

a. Hold the fork assembly in a vertical position and hold it this way during this step.
b. Hold on to the special tool extension installed in Step 18 and *slowly* move the damper rod cartridge up and down (**Figure 73**) using full travel strokes.
c. Repeat this at least ten times, or until the fork oil is free of bubbles.
d. If necessary, add additional fork oil until the oil is almost level with the top of the compressed fork tube.
e. Slowly move the fork tube up and down several strokes or until bubbles do not come from the oil.
f. Secure the fork assembly in this vertical position for 5-10 minutes to allow any additional trapped air to escape. Tap on the side of the fork assembly to break away any bubbles adhering to the side of the fork.
g. Add the remaining amount of the fork oil.

NOTE
Harley-Davidson recommends that the fork oil level be measured, if possible, to ensure a more accurate filling.

23. Adjust the fork oil as follows:
    a. Hold the fork assembly vertically, and fully compress the fork tube.
    b. Use an accurate ruler or the Motion Pro oil gauge (part No. 08-0121) (**Figure 74**), or an equivalent, to achieve the oil level listed in **Table 3**.
    c. Allow the oil to settle completely and recheck the oil level measurement (**Figure 75**). Adjust the oil level if necessary.
    d. Remove the special tools.
24. Fully extend the fork tube.
25. Position the fork spring with the closer wound coils (**Figure 76**) going in first and install the fork spring.
26. Keeping the fork assembly upright so the fork oil will not drain out, slightly compress the fork so the top of the damper rod is extended up through the top of the spring.
27. Position the lower spacer with the sharp side facing UP and install it (**Figure 77**).
28. Install the spring collar (**Figure 78**) with the hole toward the spring.
29. Install the lower end of the fork assembly in the fork holding tool (**Figure 38**), following the manu-

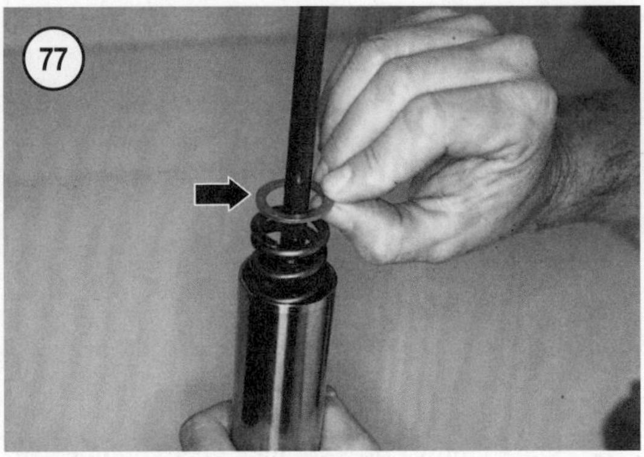

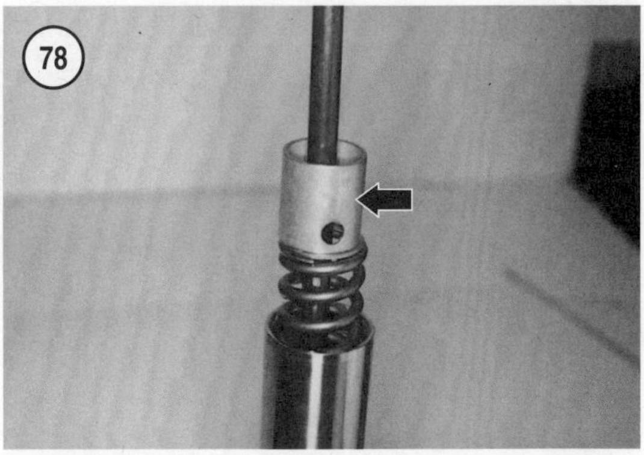

facturer's instructions. Make sure the tool is indexed properly in the lower hole in the slider.

30. Install the special tool upper bolt into the hole in the spring spacer (A, **Figure 79**), following the manufacturer's instructions. Make sure the tool is indexed properly in the hole in the spring spacer.

31. Slowly tighten the special tool and compress the fork assembly until the damper rod cartridge nut is slightly above the spring spacer (B, **Figure 79**).

32. Unscrew and remove the special tool extension (C, **Figure 79**) from the damper rod cartridge.

33. Correctly position the nut down from the top of the damper rod cartridge (**Figure 80**) to the dimension noted in *Disassembly* Step 10.

34. Position the upper spacer with the sharp side facing DOWN and install it (A, **Figure 81**).

35. Install the inner rod (**Figure 82**) into the damper rod cartridge.

36. Screw the fork cap bolt assembly (B, **Figure 81**) onto the damper rod cartridge until the rebound damping force adjuster, within the fork cap bolt, seats on the inner rod.

37. Install an open end wrench on the flats on the cap bolt (A, **Figure 83**) and another onto the damper rod nut (B, **Figure 83**).

38. Hold onto the fork cap bolt and tighten the damper rod nut against it securely. Remove the wrenches.

39. Slowly loosen the special tool and disconnect the upper portion of the tool from the spring spacer.

40. Remove the fork assembly from the special tool.

41. Pull the fork tube (A, **Figure 84**) up against the fork cap bolt (B) and screw the cap bolt into the fork tube and tighten securely. Do not try to tighten to the final torque at this time.

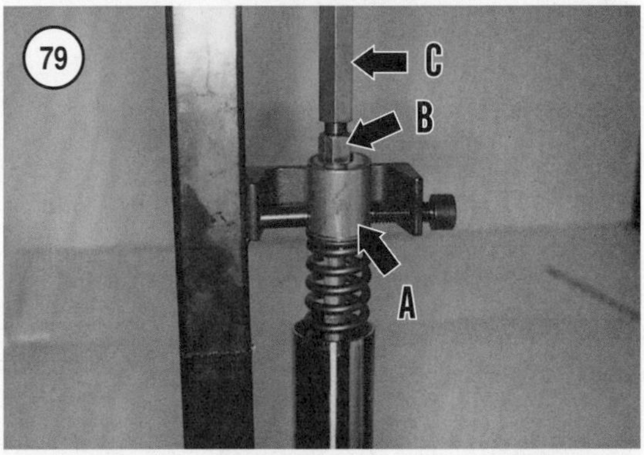

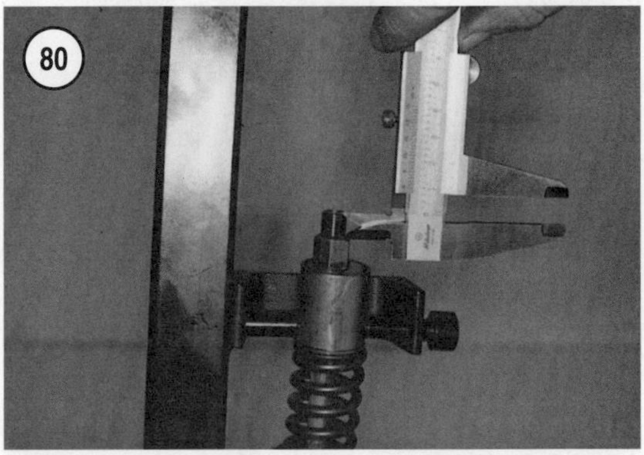

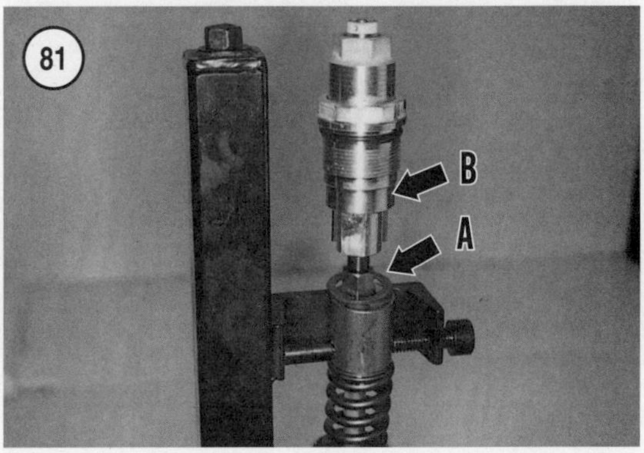

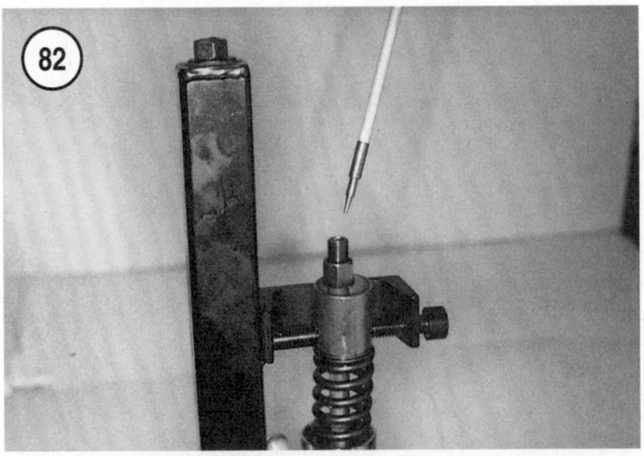

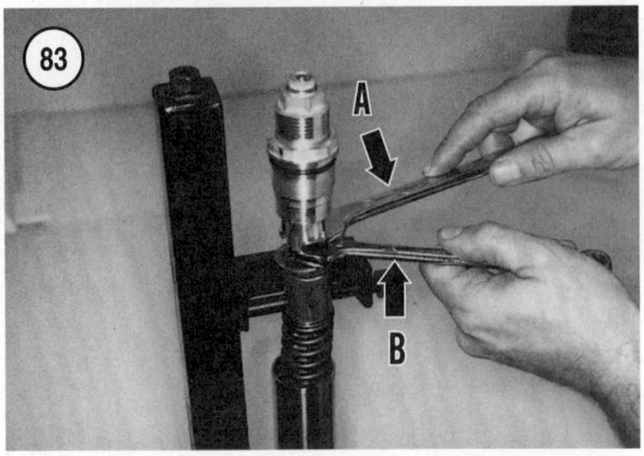

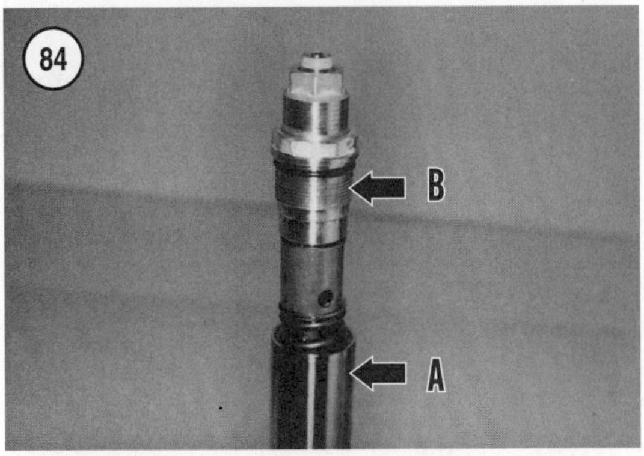

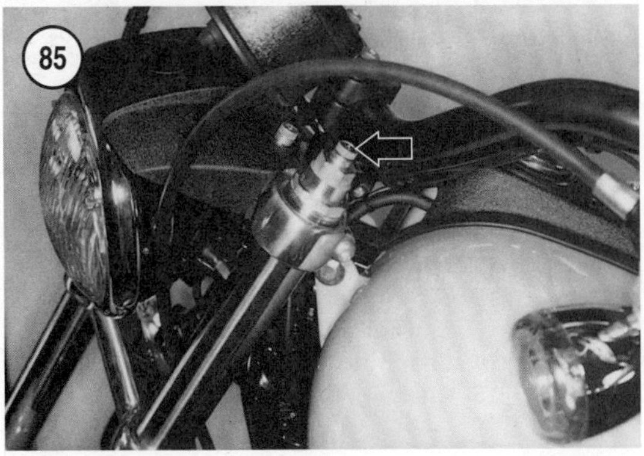

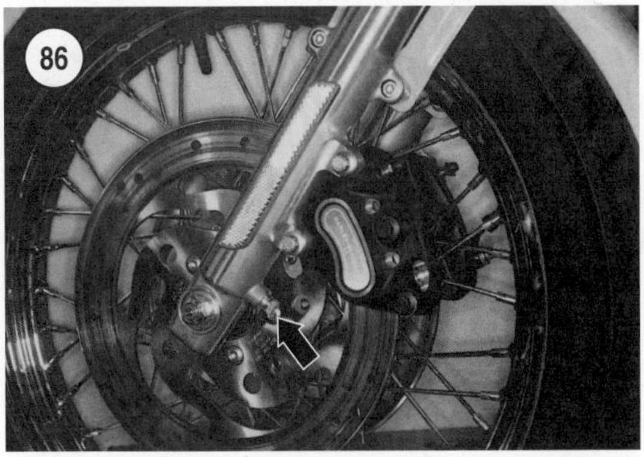

42. Install the fork assemblies as described in this chapter and tighten the cap bolt to the specification in **Table 1**.

FRONT SUSPENSION ADJUSTMENT (FXDXT, 2000-ON FXDX)

Rebound Damping Force Adjustment

The rebound damping can be adjusted by turning the knob adjuster on top of the fork cap bolt. The knob adjuster has 17 positions.

The standard adjuster setting is eight turns out from the base position. Turning the adjuster all the way clockwise results in the stiffer setting, while turning the adjuster counterclockwise results in the softer setting.

1. Turn the knob adjuster (**Figure 85**) in either direction to achieve the desired rebound damping.
2. Turning the adjuster clockwise will increase rebound damping.
3. Turning the adjuster counterclockwise will decrease rebound damping.
4. Repeat for the other fork assembly. Ensure both fork legs are adjusted to the same setting.

Compression Damping Force Adjustment

The compression damping force can be adjusted by turning the screw adjuster on the base of the fork slider. The knob adjuster has 14 positions.

The standard adjuster setting is ten turns out from the base position.

1. Turn the adjuster (**Figure 86**) and rotate it in either direction to achieve the desired compression damping force adjustment.

2. Turning the adjuster clockwise will increase compression damping force.
3. Turning the adjuster counterclockwise will decrease compression damping force.
4. Repeat for the other fork assembly. Ensure both fork legs are adjusted to the same setting.

STEERING HEAD AND STEM

Removal (All Models Except FXDWG)

Refer to **Figure 87**.

1. Remove the front fender and front wheel as described in Chapter Nine.
2. Remove the fuel tank (A, **Figure 88**) as described in Chapter Seven.
3. Remove the brake hose union from the bottom of the lower fork bracket (B, **Figure 88**). Do not disconnect any brake hose connections.
4. Remove the headlight mounting bracket bolt and remove the bracket (**Figure 89**) from the upper fork bracket.
5. Remove the two front handlebar clamp bolts and washers or collars. Then set the instrument housing forward (A, **Figure 90**) so that it does not scratch the handlebar clamp.
6. Remove the two rear clamp bolts, then remove the holder (B, **Figure 90**) and handlebars.
7. Unscrew and remove the cap (C, **Figure 90**) from the steering stem bolt.
8. Remove the front fork legs (A, **Figure 91**) as described in this chapter.
9. Loosen the steering stem pinch bolt (B, **Figure 91**).

NOTE
Hold or secure the steering stem to keep it from falling after removing the steering stem bolt in Step 10.

10. Remove the steering stem bolt (C, **Figure 91**) and washer. Then lift the upper fork bracket off the steering stem and lower the steering stem out of the frame and remove it.
11. Remove the upper dust shield and bearing.
12. Inspect the steering stem and bearing assembly as described under *Inspection (All Models)* in this section.

87 **STEERING STEM (ALL MODELS EXCEPT FXDWG)**

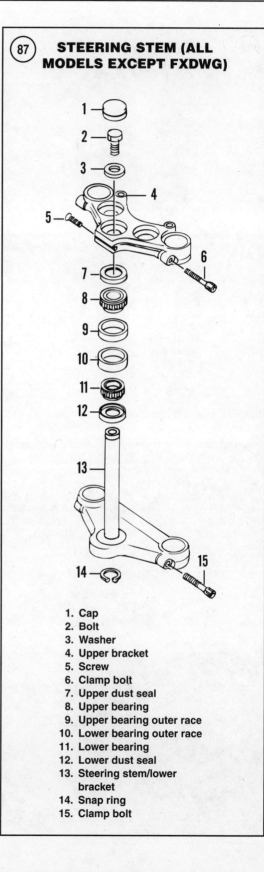

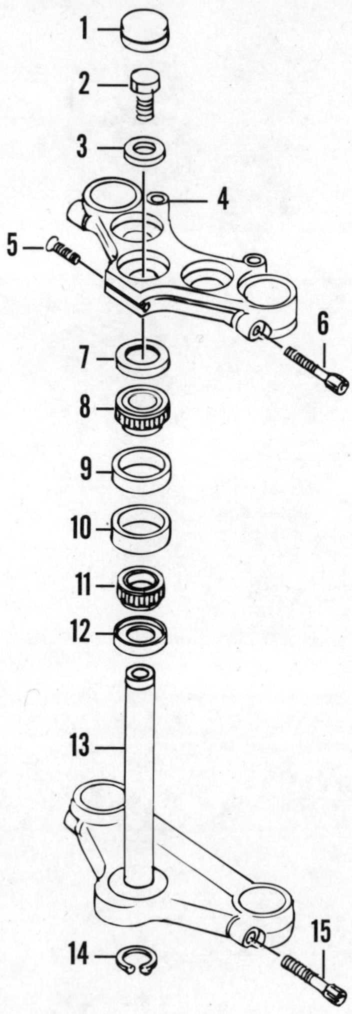

1. Cap
2. Bolt
3. Washer
4. Upper bracket
5. Screw
6. Clamp bolt
7. Upper dust seal
8. Upper bearing
9. Upper bearing outer race
10. Lower bearing outer race
11. Lower bearing
12. Lower dust seal
13. Steering stem/lower bracket
14. Snap ring
15. Clamp bolt

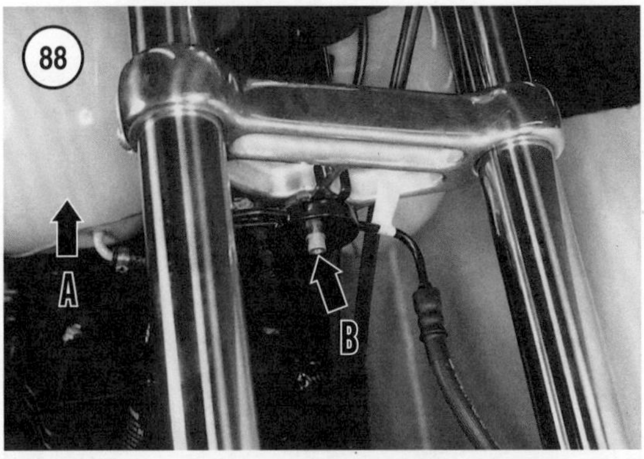

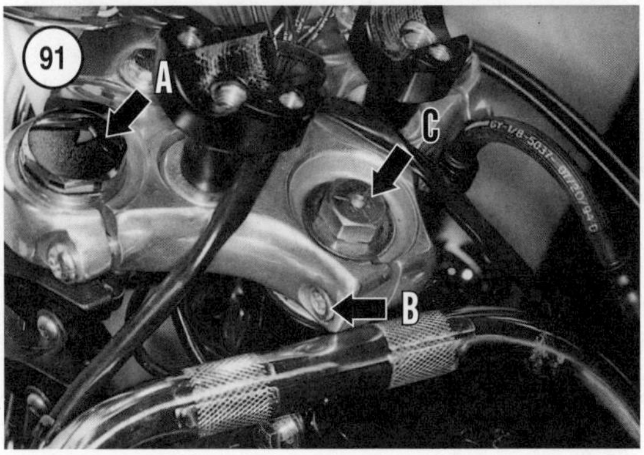

Installation
(All Models Except FXDWG)

1. Make sure to seat the steering head bearing races in the frame.
2. Wipe the bearing races with a clean lint-free cloth. Then lubricate each race with bearing grease.
3. Pack the upper and lower bearings with bearing grease. Install the lower bearing and lower dust shield on the steering stem before installing the steering stem in the frame. If necessary, install the lower bearing as described in this chapter.
4. Insert the steering stem into the frame steering head and hold it firmly in place.
5. Install the upper bearing over the fork stem and seat it into to the upper race. Install the upper dust shield.
6. Install the upper fork bracket over the steering stem.
7. Install the washer and the steering stem bolt (C, **Figure 91**). Tighten the bolt hand-tight only.
8. Install the front fork legs (A, **Figure 91**) as described in this chapter.

CAUTION
Do not overtighten the steering stem bolt in Step 9 or damage will occur to the bearings and races. Final adjustment of the fork stem will take place after the front wheel is installed.

9. Tighten the steering stem bolt (C, **Figure 91**) until the steering stem can be turned from side to side with no noticeable axial or lateral play. When the play feels correct, tighten the steering stem pinch bolt (B, **Figure 91**) to the specification in **Table 1**.
10. Install the handlebar and tighten the clamp bolts as described in this chapter.
11. Install the headlight mounting bracket (**Figure 89**) onto the upper fork bracket. Tighten the mounting bolts securely.
12. Install the brake hose union onto the bottom of the lower fork bracket (B, **Figure 88**). Tighten the bolt securely.
13. Install the front wheel as described in Chapter Nine.
14. Install the fuel tank (A, **Figure 88**) as described in Chapter Seven.
15. Adjust the steering play as described under *Steering Play Adjustment* in this chapter.

Removal (FXDWG)

Refer to **Figure 92**.

1. Remove the front wheel as described in Chapter Nine.
2. Remove the fuel tank as described in Chapter Seven.
3. Remove the brake hose union from the bottom of the lower fork bracket. Do not disconnect any brake hose connections.
4. Remove the headlight mounting bracket bolt and remove the bracket from the fork bracket.
5. Remove the two front handlebar clamp bolts and washers or collars. Then set the instrument housing forward so that it does not scratch the handlebar clamp.
6. Remove the two rear clamp bolts, then remove the holder and handlebar.
7. Unscrew and remove the cap from the steering stem nut.
8. Remove the front fork legs as described in this chapter.
9. Bend the lockwasher tab away from the steering stem nut, then remove the nut and lockwasher.
10. Lift the upper fork bracket off the steering stem and remove it.

NOTE

Make sure to hold or secure the steering stem/lower fork bracket. This will prevent it from falling after removing the steering stem adjust nut in Step 11.

11. Loosen and remove the adjust nut. Then lower the steering stem assembly out of the frame and remove it.
12. Remove the upper dust shield and upper bearing.
13. Inspect the steering stem and bearing assembly as described under *Inspection (All Models)* in this section.

Installation (FXDWG)

1. Make sure the steering head bearing races are seated in the frame.
2. Wipe the bearing races with a clean lint-free cloth. Then lubricate each race with bearing grease.
3. Pack the upper and lower bearings with bearing grease. Install the lower bearing and the lower dust

(92) **STEERING STEM (FXDWG)**

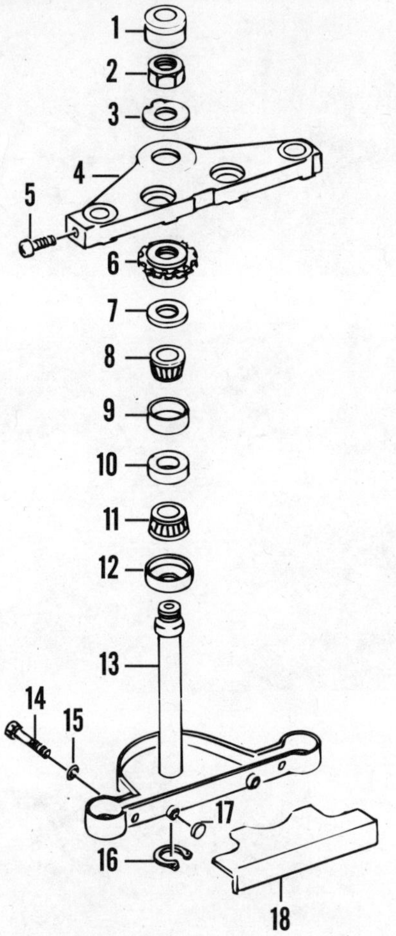

1. Cap
2. Nut
3. Lockwasher
4. Upper bracket
5. Clamp bolt
6. Adjust nut
7. Upper dust seal
8. Upper bearing
9. Upper bearing outer race
10. Lower bearing outer race
11. Lower bearing
12. Lower dust seal
13. Steering stem/lower bracket
14. Bolt
15. Washer
16. Circlip
17. Pad
18. Headlight mounting bracket

shield onto the steering stem before installing the steering stem in the frame. If necessary, install the lower bearing as described in this chapter.
4. Insert the steering stem into the frame and hold it firmly in place.
5. Install the upper bearing over the fork stem and seat it into to the upper race. Install the upper dust shield.

CAUTION
Do not overtighten the adjust nut in Step 6 or the bearings and races will be damaged. Final adjustment of the fork stem will take place after the front wheel is installed on the motorcycle.

6. Thread the adjust nut onto the steering stem. Tighten the adjust nut until the steering stem can be turned from side to side with no noticeable axial or lateral play. The steering stem must turn with no binding or roughness.
7. Install the upper fork bracket over the steering stem.
8. Install a *new* lockwasher over the steering stem. Engage the lockwasher pin into the hole in the upper fork bracket. Then install the steering stem nut. Tighten the steering stem nut securely.
9. Install the front fork legs as described in this chapter.
10. Install the handlebar and tighten the clamp bolts as described under *Handlebar Removal/Installation* in this chapter.
11. Install the headlight mounting bracket onto the fork bracket. Tighten the mounting bolts securely.
12. Install the brake hose bracket onto the bottom of the lower fork bracket. Tighten the brake hose bracket bolt to the specification in **Table 1**.
13. Install the front wheel as described in Chapter Nine.
14. Adjust the steering play as described under *Steering Play Adjustment* in this chapter.
15. Tighten the steering stem nut to the specification in **Table 1**. Bend the lockwasher tab against one nut flat.
16. Install the cap onto the steering stem nut.

Inspection (All Models)

The bearing outer races are pressed into the steering head.

1. Wipe the bearing races with a solvent-soaked rag and then dry with compressed air or a lint-free cloth. Check the races in the steering head for pitting, scratches, galling or excessive wear. If any of these conditions exist, replace the races as described in this chapter. If the races are good, wipe each race with grease.
2. Clean the bearings in solvent to remove all of the old grease. Blow the bearing dry with compressed air, making sure not to allow the air jet to spin the bearing. Do not remove the lower bearing from the fork stem unless it is to be replaced. Clean the bearing while installed in the steering stem.
3. After the bearings are dry, hold the inner race with one hand and turn the outer race with the other hand. Turn the bearing slowly, the bearing must turn smoothly with no roughness. Visually check the bearing for pitting, scratches or visible damage. If the bearings are worn, check the dust covers for wear or damage or for improper bearing lubrication. Replace the bearing if necessary. If a bearing is going to be reused, pack it with grease and wrap it with wax paper or some other type of lint-free material until it is reinstalled. Do not store the bearings for any length of time without lubricating them or they will rust.
4. Check the steering stem for cracks or damage. Check the threads at the top of the stem for damage. Check the steering stem bolt or nut for damage. Thread it into the steering stem; make sure the bolt threads easily with no roughness.
5. Replace all worn or damaged parts. Replace bearing races as described in this chapter.
6. Replace the lower steering stem bearing and the dust shield as described in this chapter.
7. Check for broken welds on the frame around the steering head. If any are found, have them repaired by a competent frame shop or welding service familiar with motorcycle frame repair.

STEERING HEAD BEARING RACE REPLACEMENT

The upper and lower bearing outer races are pressed into the frame. Do not remove the bearing races unless replacement is necessary. If removed, replace both the outer race along with the bearing at the same time. Never reinstall an outer race that has been removed as it is no longer true and will damage the bearing if reused.

1. Remove the steering stem as described in this chapter.
2. To remove a race, insert an aluminum or brass rod into the steering head and carefully tap the race out from the inside (**Figure 93**). Tap all around the race so that neither the race nor the steering head is bent.
3. Clean the steering head with solvent and dry thoroughly.
4A. Install the bearing races with a steering head bearing race installer tool (JIMS part No. 1725), following the manufacturer's instructions.
4B. If the special tools are not available, install the bearing races as follows:
   a. Clean the race thoroughly before installing it.
   b. Align the upper race with the frame steering head and tap it slowly and squarely in place. Make sure not to contact the bearing race surfaces. See **Figure 94**. Drive the race into the steering head until it bottoms out on the bore shoulder.
   c. Repeat to install the lower race into the steering head.
5. Apply bearing grease to the face of each race.

Fork Stem Lower Bearing Replacement

Do not remove the steering stem lower bearing and lower seal unless it is going to be replaced. The lower bearing can be difficult to remove. If the lower bearing cannot be removed as described in this procedure, take the steering stem to a Harley-Davidson dealership and have them remove it and reinstall a new part.

Never reinstall a lower bearing that has been removed as it is no longer true and will damage the rest of the bearing assembly if reused.

1. Install the steering stem bolt onto the top of the steering stem to protect the threads.
2. Loosen the lower bearing from the shoulder at the base of the steering stem with a chisel as shown in **Figure 95**. Slide the lower bearing and grease seal off the steering stem.
3. Clean the steering stem with solvent and dry thoroughly.
4. Position the new lower dust seal with the flange side facing up.

93

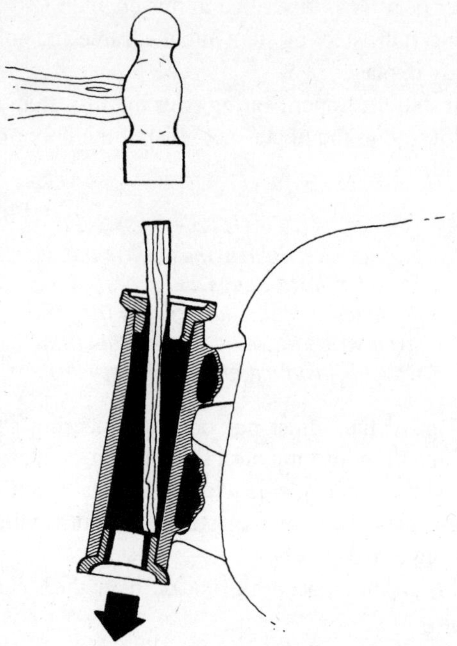

94

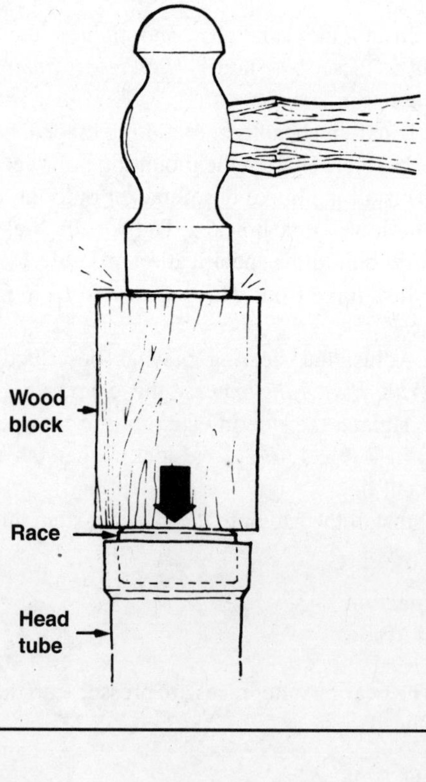

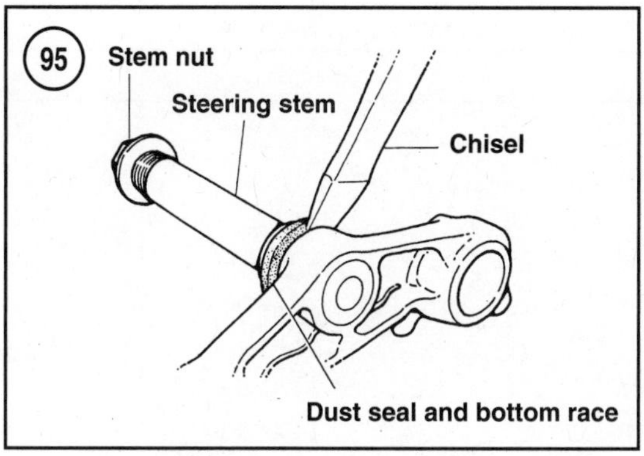

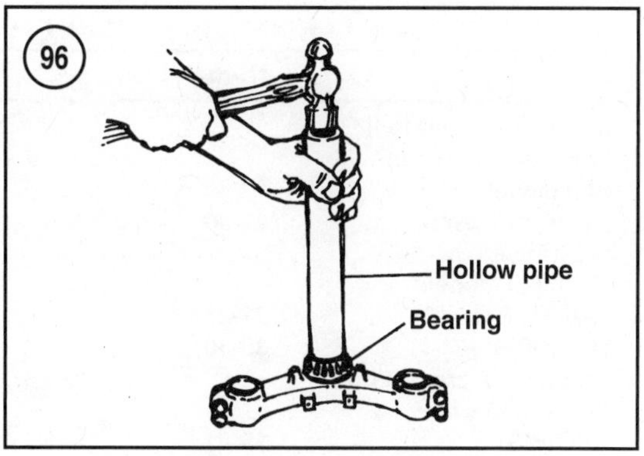

5. Slide a new grease seal and the lower bearing onto the steering stem until it stops on the raised shoulder.

6. Align the lower bearing with the machined shoulder on the steering stem. Press or drive the lower bearing onto the steering stem until it bottoms (**Figure 96**).

STEERING PLAY ADJUSTMENT

1. Support the motorcycle with the front wheel off the ground. See *Motorcycle Stands* in Chapter Nine.

2. On models so equipped, remove the windshield, as described in Chapter Thirteen, and all other accessory weight from the handlebar and front fork that could affect this adjustment.

NOTE
If a control cable affects handlebar movement, disconnect it.

3. Apply a strip of masking tape across the front end of the front fender. Draw a vertical line across the tape at the center of the fender.
4. Turn the handlebar so that the front wheel faces straight ahead.
5. Install a pointer so the base is stationary on the floor and the pointer indicates the center of the fender tape mark when the wheel is facing straight ahead.
6. Loosen the lower bracket pinch bolt on both fork tubes.
7. Lightly push the fender toward the right side until the front end starts to turn by itself. Mark this point on the tape.
8. Repeat Step 6 for the left side.
9. Measure the distance between the 2 marks on the tape. The correct distance is 1-2 in. (25-50 mm). If the distance is incorrect, perform Step 10.
10. Loosen or tighten the steering stem nut or bolt until the measurement is within the limits.
11. Tighten the lower fork bracket pinch bolts to the torque specification in **Table 1**.
12. Reinstall all parts previously removed.

10

Table 1 FRONT SUSPENSION TORQUE SPECIFICATIONS

Item	ft.-lb.	in.-lb.	N•m
Fork cap FXDX, FXDXT	22-29	–	30-39
Fork cap screw FXDX, FXDXT	22-29	–	30-39
Fork slider tube cap			
FXDWG	11-22	–	15-30
All models except FXDWG	11-22	–	15-30
Upper fork bridge pinch bolt			
FXDWG	21-27	–	29-37

(continued)

Table 1 FRONT SUSPENSION TORQUE SPECIFICATIONS (continued)

Item	ft.-lb.	in.-lb.	N•m
Upper and lower fork bracket pinch bolts			
All models except FXDWG	25-30	–	34-41
Steering stem			
Bolt (all models except FXDWG)	21-27	–	29-37
Nut (FXDWG)	35-40	–	47-54
Brake hose bracket bolt	–	132	15
Front fender nuts			
FXDWG	15-21	–	20-28
All models except FXDWG	–	120-168	14-19

Table 2 FRONT FORK OIL CAPACITY AND OIL LEVEL DIMENSIONS

Model	Capacity oz. (ml)	Oil level dimension in. (mm)
1999 models		
FXDWG	10.2 (302)	–
All models except FXDWG	9.2 (272)	–
2000-on models		
FXD	10.6 (314)	6.69 (169.9)
FXDS-CONV	11.5 (341)	6.10 (154.9)
FXDWG	12.0 (356)	7.28 (184.9)
FXDX, FXDXT	Use oil level	5.04 (128.0)
FXDP	NA	
2000-2001		
FXDL	10.7 (316)	7.20 (182.0)

NA = Information not available from the manufacturer.
Refer to page 561 for 2002-on models

Table 3 FRONT FORK SPECIFICATIONS (FXDXT AND 2000-ON FXDX)*

Fork spring minimum length	17.0 in. (431.8 mm)
Fork tube maximum runout	0.008 in. (0.2 mm)

*Service specifications for all other fork assemblies are not available from the manufacturer.

NOTE: Refer to the Supplement at the back of this manual for information unique to 2002-on models.

CHAPTER ELEVEN

REAR SUSPENSION

This chapter describes repair and replacement procedures for the rear suspension components. Refer to **Table 1** at the end of this chapter for torque specifications.

WARNING
All nuts and bolts used on the rear suspension must be replaced with parts of the same type. Do not use a replacement part of lesser quality or substitute design, as it may affect the performance of the rear suspension or fail, leading to loss of control of the motorcycle. The torque specifications listed in ***Table 1*** *must be used during installation to ensure proper retention of these components.*

SHOCK ABSORBERS

The shock absorbers are spring controlled and hydraulically damped. Spring preload is adjustable on all models and the rebound compression is also adjustable on FXDX and FXDXT models. Refer to *Shock Absorber Adjustment* in this chapter.

Removal/Installation

When servicing the rear shocks, remove one shock at a time. If it is necessary to remove both shocks, support the motorcycle with the rear wheel off the ground.

1. Support the motorcycle with the rear wheel off the ground. See *Motorcycle Stands* in Chapter Nine.

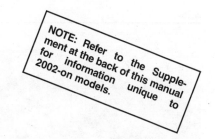

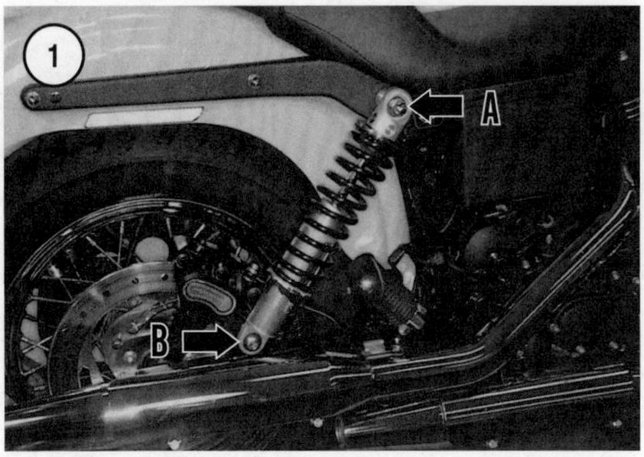

2. Place wooden blocks under the rear wheel to place the rear wheel in a neutral position with no strain on the shock absorber mounting hardware.

3A. On FXDX and FXDXT models, perform the following:

   a. Remove the upper acorn nut and washer (A, **Figure 1**) securing the shock absorber to the frame shock stud.
   b. Remove the lower acorn nut and washer (B, **Figure 1**) securing the shock absorber to the swing arm mounting bracket.
   c. Pull the shock absorber straight off the frame upper stud and remove the shock absorber.

3B. On all models except FXDX and FXDXT, perform the following:

   a. Remove the upper acorn nut and washer (A, **Figure 2**) securing the shock absorber to the frame shock stud.
   b. Remove the lower acorn nut and washer (**Figure 3**) securing the shock absorber to the swing arm mounting bracket.
   c. On models so equipped, remove the chrome cover (B, **Figure 2**).
   d. Pull the shock absorber straight off the frame upper stud and remove the shock absorber.

4. Check the upper shock stud (**Figure 4**) for looseness. Securely tighten if necessary.

5. Repeat for the other shock absorber if necessary.

6. Inspect the shock absorber as described in this chapter.

7. Install the shocks by reversing these removal steps while noting the following:

   a. Apply a few drops of ThreeBond TB1342 or an equivalent to the shock stud and bolt threads.
   b. Install the washers and nuts and tighten to the specification in **Table 1**.

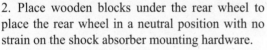

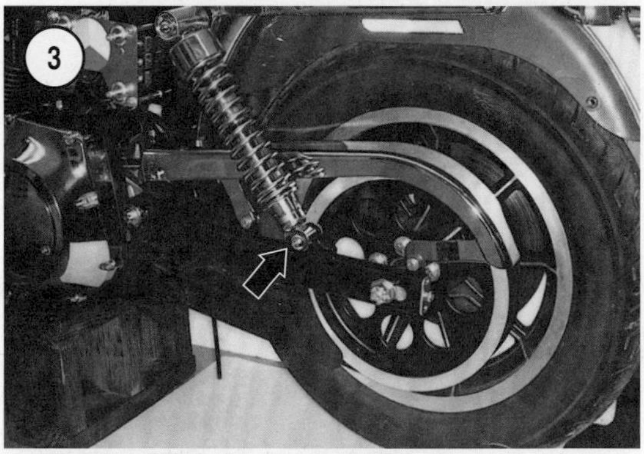

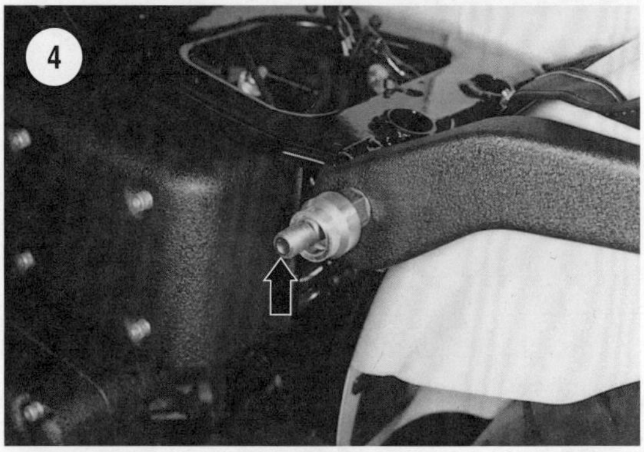

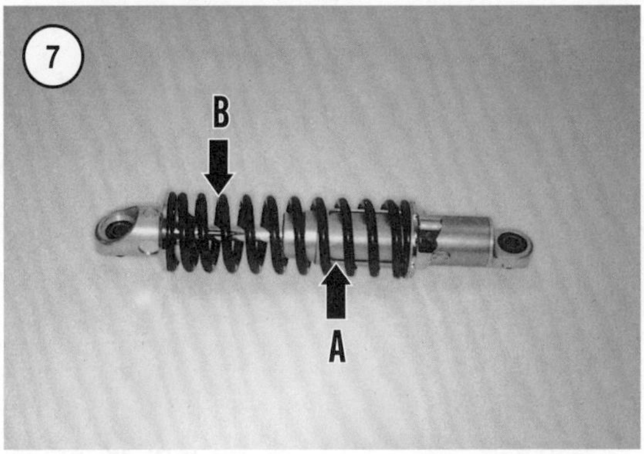

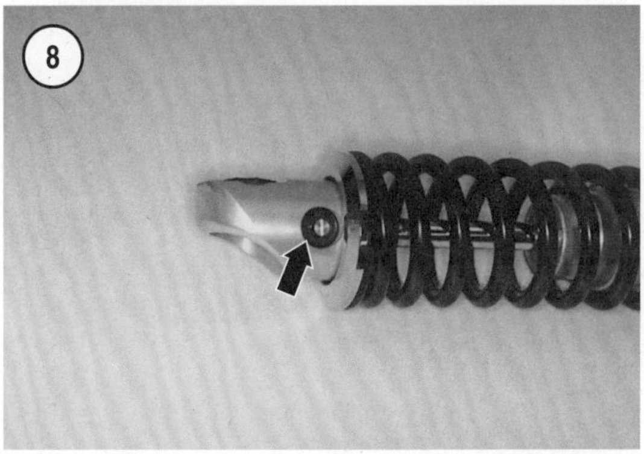

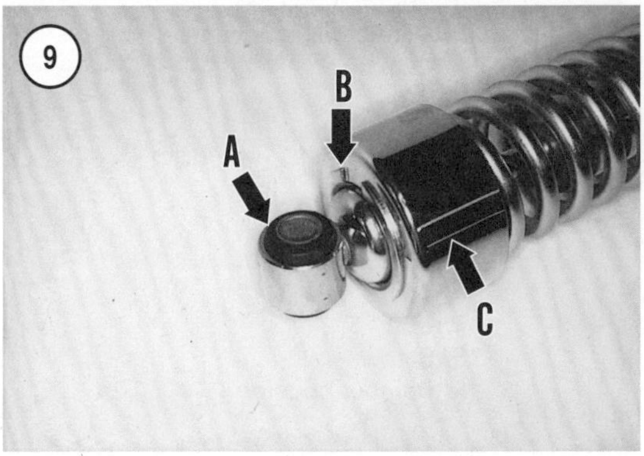

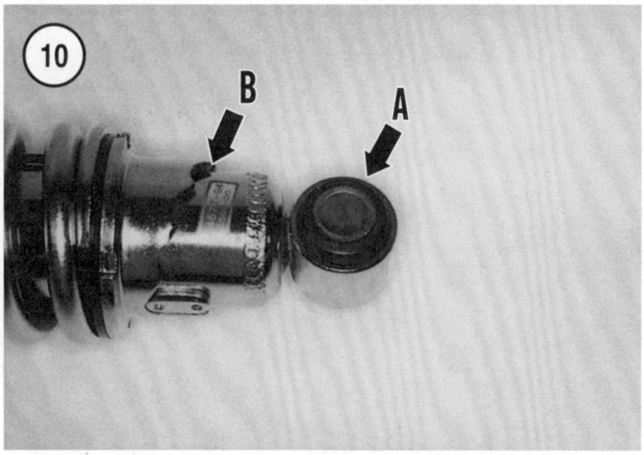

c. Adjust the shock absorbers as described in this chapter.
d. Lower the motorcycle and test ride it to make sure the rear suspension is working properly.

Inspection (FXDX and FXDXT Models)

There are no shock replacement parts available for these models. If any part other than the mounting hardware is damaged, replace the shock assembly.

1. Remove the shock absorber as described in this chapter.
2. Inspect the upper shock bushing (**Figure 5**) and lower shock bushing (**Figure 6**) for wear and deterioration.
3. Inspect the shock absorber. If the damper housing (A, **Figure 7**) is leaking, bent, or in any way damaged, replace the shock absorber.
4. Inspect the shock spring (B, **Figure 7**), spring retainer, cover and spring adjust cam for cracks or damage.
5. Note the existing setting of the rebound adjuster.
6. Rotate the rebound adjuster (**Figure 8**) through all of its ten settings. Make sure the adjuster rotates freely and engages the detent in each position. Return the adjuster to the setting noted in Step 5.

Inspection (All Models Except FXDX and FXDXT)

1. Remove the shock absorber as described in this chapter.
2. Inspect the upper shock bushing (A, **Figure 9**) and lower shock bushing (A, **Figure 10**) for wear and deterioration. Replace worn or damaged bushings.

11

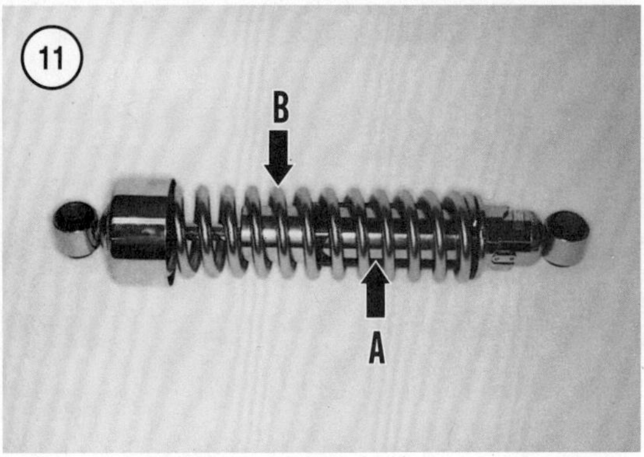

3. Inspect the shock absorber. If the damper housing (A, **Figure 11**) is leaking, bent, or in any way damaged, replace the shock absorber.
4. Inspect the shock spring (B, **Figure 11**), spring retainer, cover and cam for cracks or damage. If necessary, replace the shock spring as described in this section.

Shock Bushing Inspection and Replacement (All Models Except FXDX and FXDXT)

Refer to **Figure 12**.

Replace both bushings at the same time.

1. Remove the shock absorber as described in this chapter.

CAUTION
When supporting the shock absorbers in a press in Step 2, position the press blocks or other equipment so that they do not dent or otherwise damage the damper body.

2. Support the shock absorber in a press and press out the bushing.
3. Repeat for the bushing on the other end.
4. Clean the shock eyelets of all rust and rubber residue. Then check the eyelets for cracks, burrs, dents and other problems. Replace the shock absorber if damaged.

NOTE
The upper and lower shock bushings are identical.

5. Align the new bushing with the shock eyelet and start it into place. Then support the shock absorber in a press and press the bushing into place, centering

12 **REAR SHOCK ABSORBER**

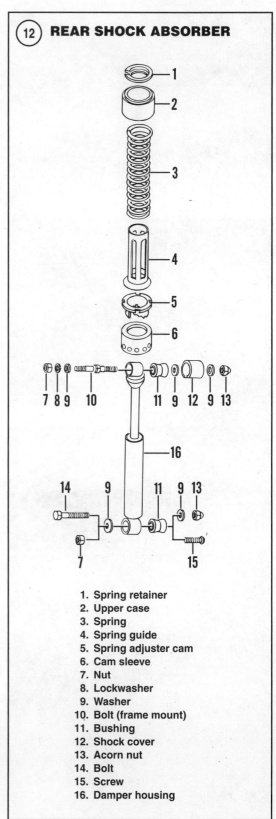

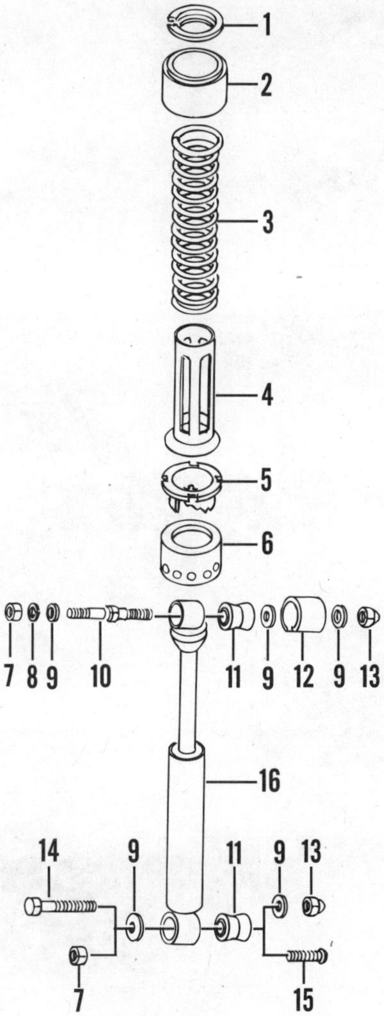

1. Spring retainer
2. Upper case
3. Spring
4. Spring guide
5. Spring adjuster cam
6. Cam sleeve
7. Nut
8. Lockwasher
9. Washer
10. Bolt (frame mount)
11. Bushing
12. Shock cover
13. Acorn nut
14. Bolt
15. Screw
16. Damper housing

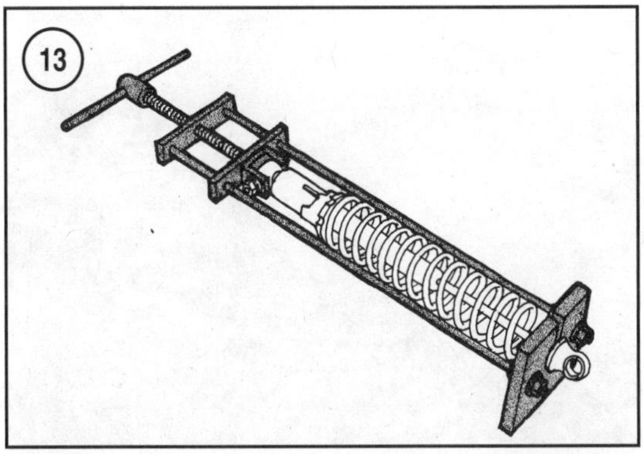

it in the shock eyelet. Repeat for the bushing in the other end.

Spring Removal/Installation (All Models Except FXDX and FXDXT)

A spring compressor is required to remove and install the shock spring. When servicing aftermarket shocks, follow the manufacturer's instructions.

Refer to **Figure 12**.

1. Remove the shock absorber as described in this chapter.
2. Rotate the spring adjuster cam to the lowest setting to reduce the amount of spring pressure on the shock absorber.
3. Mount the shock absorber in a spring compressor tool (**Figure 13**).

WARNING

Do not attempt to remove the spring from the shock absorber without a spring compressor. Because the spring is under considerable pressure, using makeshift tools or incorrect procedures may allow the spring retainer to fly off, causing severe personal injury.

4. Compress the spring and remove the spring retainer (B, **Figure 9**). Then release spring tension and remove the shock absorber from the tool. Complete the disassembly by removing the parts in the order shown in **Figure 12**.
5. Spring free length specifications are not available. If the spring has sagged, remove the other shock spring and compare the length of both springs. Replace both springs if one is shorter than the other one.
6. Inspect the spring adjuster for cracks, excessive wear or other damage.
7. Assemble by reversing these disassembly steps, while noting the following:
   a. Make sure the spring retainer (B, **Figure 9**) is seated correctly in the cover (C, **Figure 9**) before releasing the pressure of the spring compressor tool.
   b. Adjust the spring pre-load as described in this chapter.

SHOCK ABSORBER ADJUSTMENT

11

Spring Preload Adjustment

The ride height (height of a motorcycle at rest with no rider or passenger) can be adjusted with the cam preload adjuster at the base of each shock spring (B, **Figure 10**). Turning the cam adjuster to the five different steps moves the cam ramps up or down, either compressing or extending the spring. Increasing the cam angle increases the spring load and raises the ride height. Spring preload also controls how far the shock absorber compresses under the weight of the motorcycle and rider.

Select the position that best suits the vehicle load requirements. The cam positions range from the No. 1 for a rider with no luggage to the No. 5 consisting of the maximum allowable GVWR loads listed in the owner's manual. The standard factory setting is the third cam step position.

Rotate the cam (**Figure 14**) with a spanner wrench to compress the spring (heavy loads) or extend the spring (light loads). Set the cam on both shock absorbers to the same preload position.

Compression Rebound Adjustment (FXDX, FXDXT)

The compression rebound adjuster (**Figure 15**) has ten stop positions. The No. 1 position which is all the way clockwise, is the hardest, while the No. 10 position, all the way counterclockwise, is the softest. The standard factory setting is No. 3.

To adjust the compression damping, turn the compression damping adjuster with a small blade screwdriver located at the top of the shock absorber.

NOTE

When turning the adjuster, make sure it clicks into one of the detent positions. Otherwise, the adjuster will automatically be set at the stiffest position.

REAR SWING ARM

Refer to **Figure 16** and **Figure 17**.

Rear Swing Arm Bearing Check

The swing arm pivots on a combination bushing and bearing assembly. Service limit specifications for the bushing and bearing assemblies are not available; therefore, check for wear or damage with the swing arm mounted on the frame.

1. Remove the rear wheel (A, **Figure 18**) as described in this chapter.
2. Remove the lower acorn nut and washer (B, **Figure 18**) securing both shock absorbers to the swing arm. Move them up away from the swing arm.
3. Check that the swing arm pivot shaft nut or bolt is tight.
4. Have an assistant hold the motorcycle securely.
5. Grasp the back of the swing arm and try to move it from side to side. Any play (movement) between the swing arm and the frame and transmission may suggest worn or damaged swing arm bearings and/or bushings. If there is any play, remove the swing arm and inspect the bushing and bearing assemblies.
6. Install all components removed.

Rear Swing Arm Removal

1. Remove the exhaust system as described in Chapter Seven.

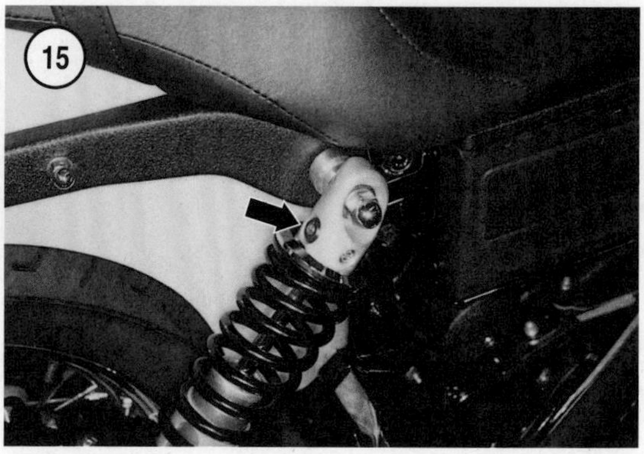

2. Remove the bolts and nuts securing the drive belt upper guard (A, **Figure 19**) and remove the guard.
3. Remove the rear wheel (B, **Figure 19**) as described in Chapter Nine.
4. On 1999 models, slide the rear brake caliper off the swing arm as described in Chapter Twelve.
5. Remove the mounting bolts securing the left side rear footpeg and mounting bracket assembly (A, **Figure 20**). Remove the assembly.
6. Remove the acorn nut and washer (A, **Figure 21**) securing each shock absorber to the swing arm. Pivot both shock absorbers up and tie it to the frame.
7. On the right side, remove the bolts securing the muffler support bracket (A, **Figure 22**) to the frame and remove it.
8. Remove the clamps securing the rear brake hose to the swing arm.
9. On the right side, pry the pivot shaft chrome cap (B, **Figure 22**) from the swing arm.

10A. On 1999 models, perform the following:
   a. On the left side, remove the cotter pin from the end of the pivot shaft (**Figure 23**). Install a new cotter pin during installation.
   b. Hold the nut and loosen the pivot shaft (**Figure 24**) on the right side. Remove the nut and washer.
   c. Support the swing arm and remove the pivot shaft (**Figure 24**) from the right side.
   d. Remove the swing arm (**Figure 25**).

10B. On 2000-on models, perform the following:
   a. On the right side, hold onto the hex fitting on the end of the pivot shaft to keep the shaft from rotating.
   b. On the left side, remove the bolt and lockwasher (B, **Figure 20**) from the pivot shaft.

16

REAR SWING ARM (1999 MODELS)

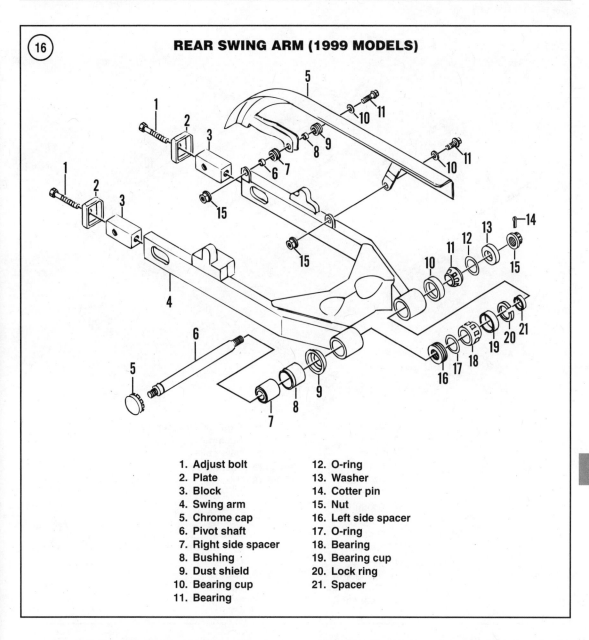

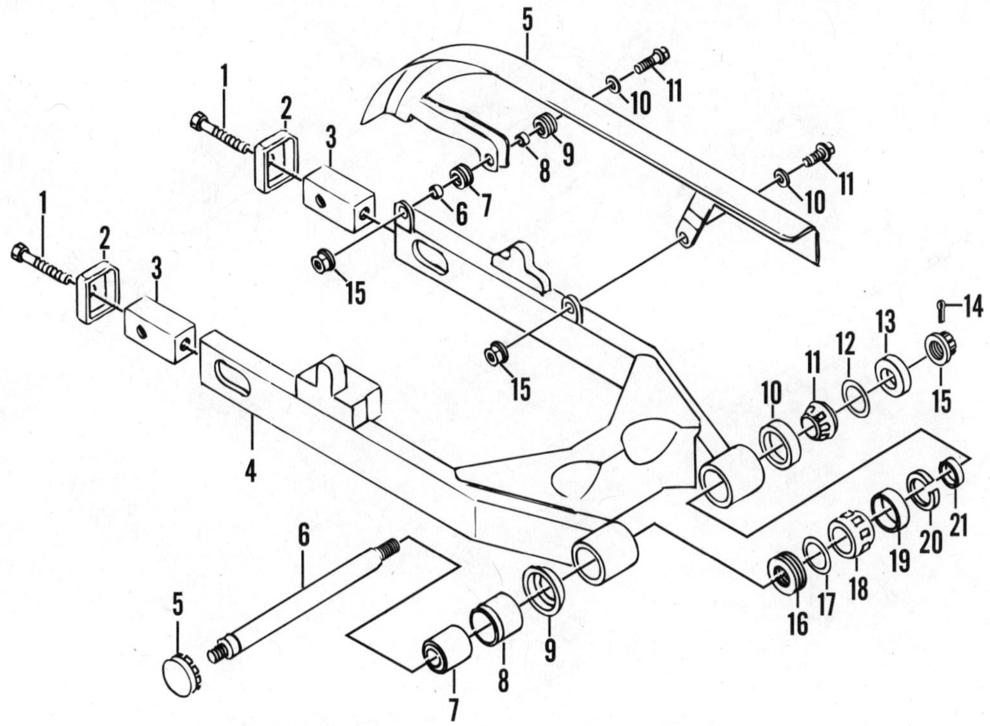

1. Adjust bolt
2. Plate
3. Block
4. Swing arm
5. Chrome cap
6. Pivot shaft
7. Right side spacer
8. Bushing
9. Dust shield
10. Bearing cup
11. Bearing
12. O-ring
13. Washer
14. Cotter pin
15. Nut
16. Left side spacer
17. O-ring
18. Bearing
19. Bearing cup
20. Lock ring
21. Spacer

c. Support the swing arm and remove the pivot shaft (B, **Figure 22**) from the right side.
d. Remove the swing arm (B, **Figure 21**).

11. Clean and lubricate the swing arm assembly as described in the following procedure.

Rear Swing Arm Bushing and Bearing Lubrication

To prevent premature wear of the bushings and bearings lubricate them at the interval in Chapter Three.

The left side of the swing arm is equipped with the two roller bearings and the right side is equipped with the pivot bushing.

NOTE

If reusing the roller bearings, install them in their original operating positions. Wear patterns have developed on the individual bearing and cup assemblies and rapid wear could occur if the bearings are intermixed. Also, the two washers installed on

17

REAR SWING ARM (2000-2005 MODELS)

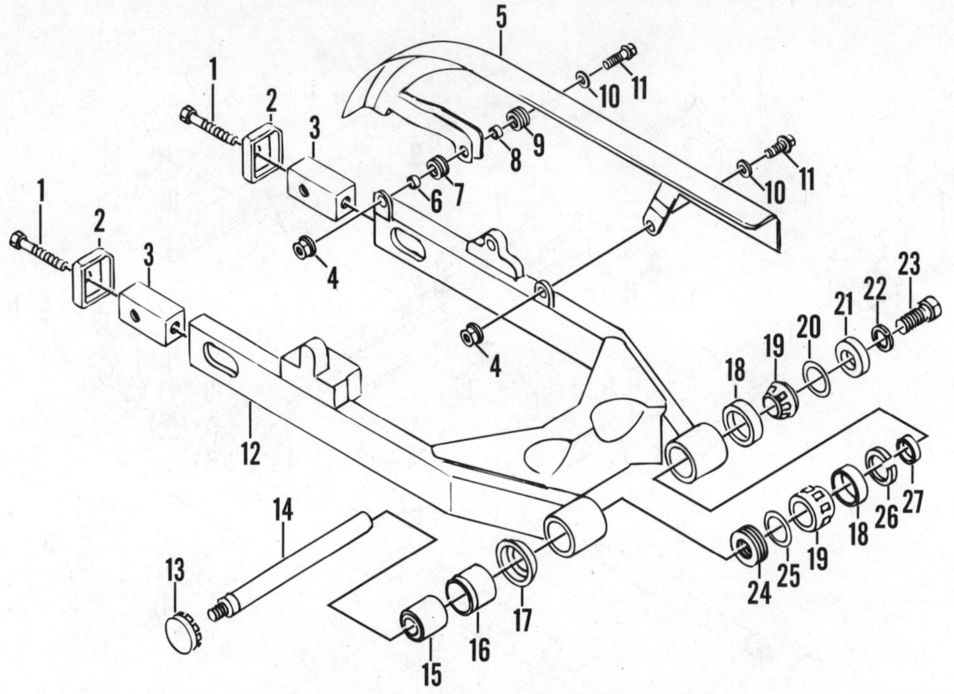

1. Adjust bolt
2. Plate
3. Block
4. Nut
5. Belt guard
6. Collar
7. Grommet
8. Collar
9. Grommet
10. Washer
11. Bolt
12. Swing arm
13. Chrome cap
14. Pivot shaft
15. Right side spacer
16. Bushing
17. Dust shield
18. Bearing cup
19. Bearing
20. O-ring
21. Washer
22. Washer
23. Bolt
24. Left side spacer
25. O-ring
26. Lock ring
27. Spacer

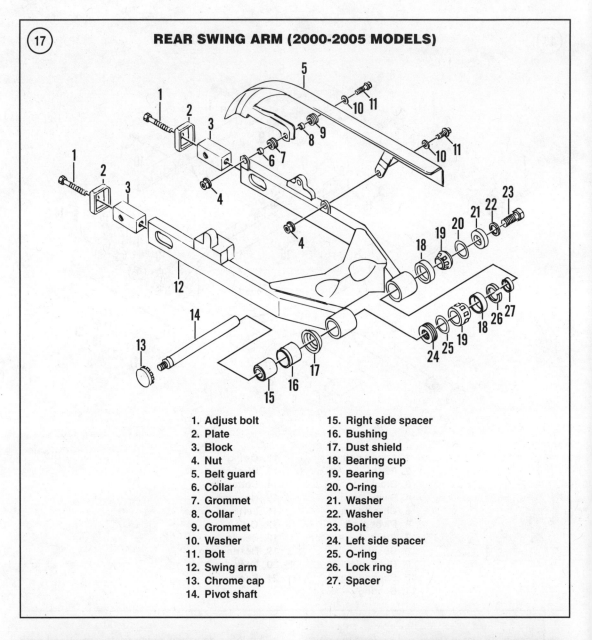

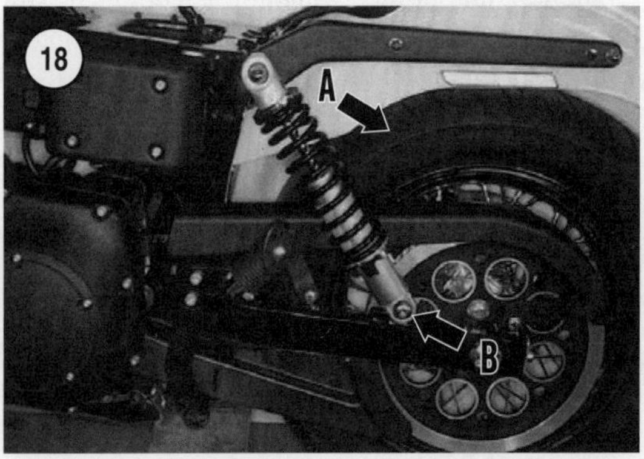

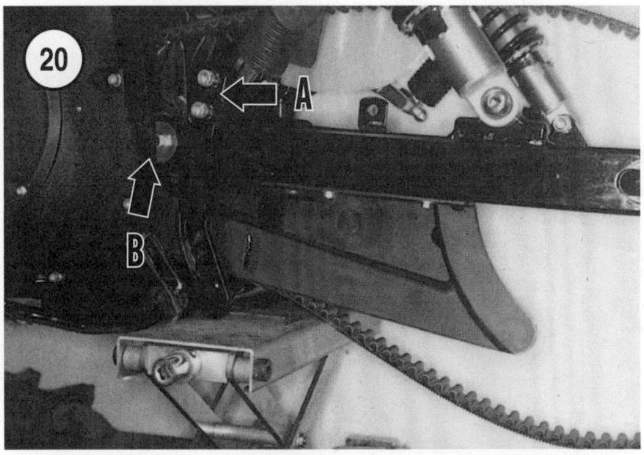

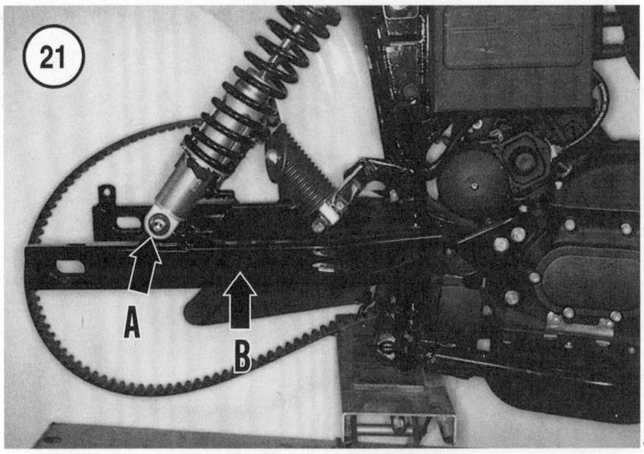

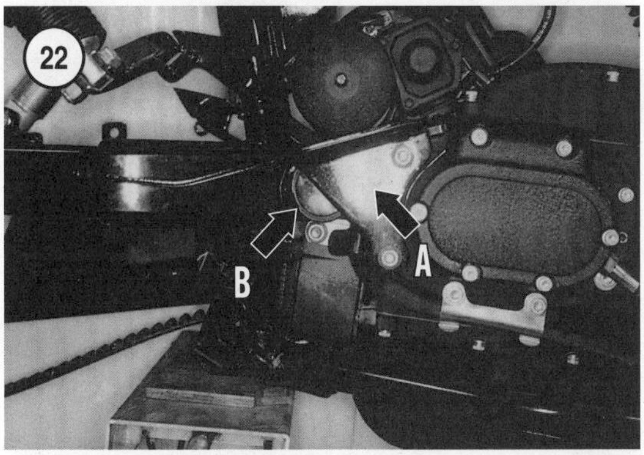

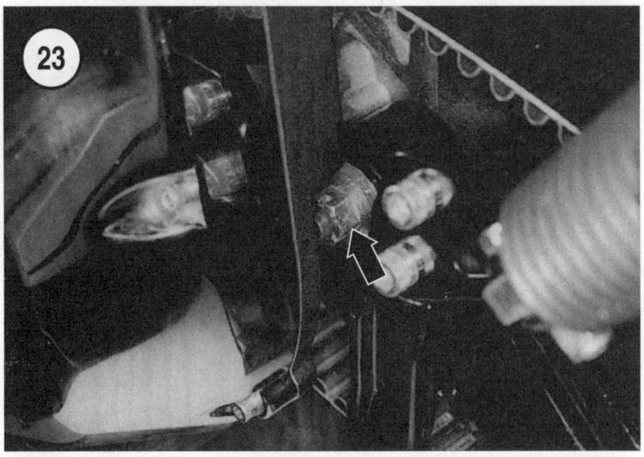

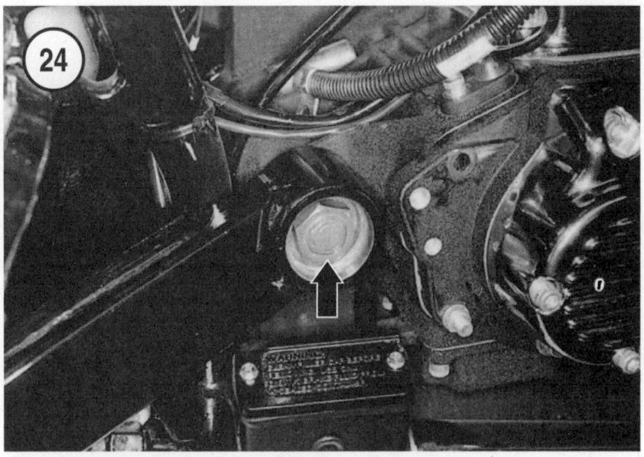

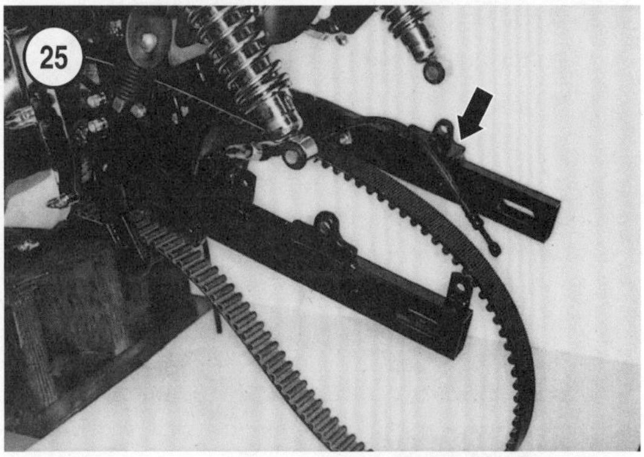

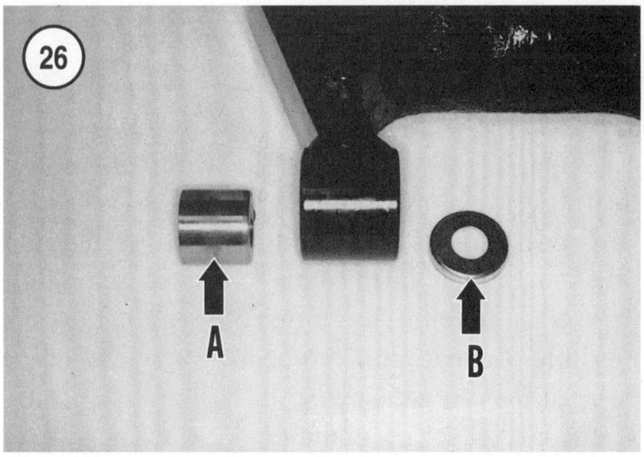

the outside of each bearing are different. The outer washer is thicker.

1. From the right side, remove the right side spacer (A, **Figure 26**) and dust cover (B, **Figure 26**).

2. From the left side of the swing arm, remove the following:

   a. Remove the outer washer (A, **Figure 27**) and the roller bearing (B).

   b. Remove the bearing spacer (**Figure 28**).

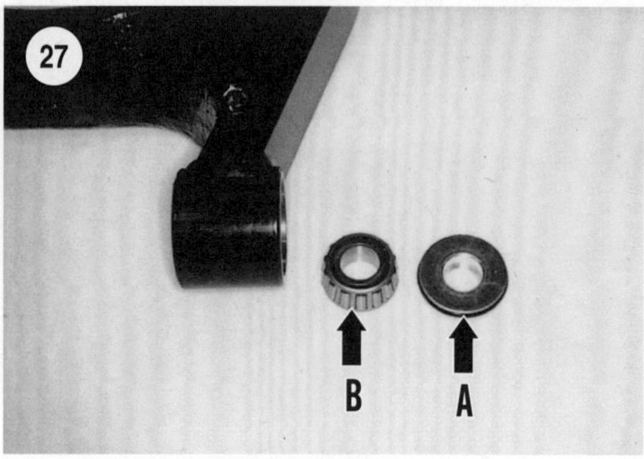

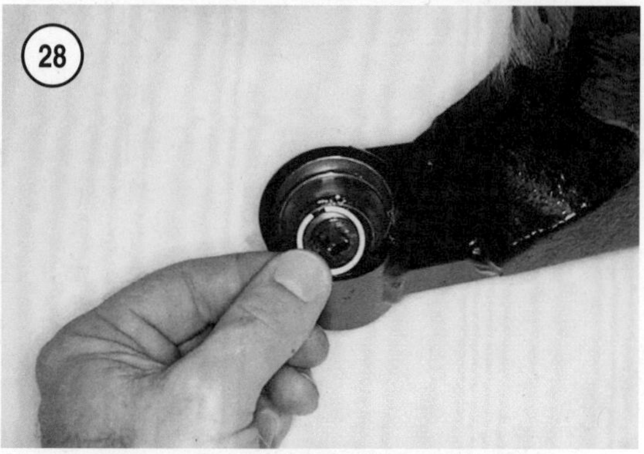

c. Remove the inner washer (A, **Figure 29**) and roller bearing (B).

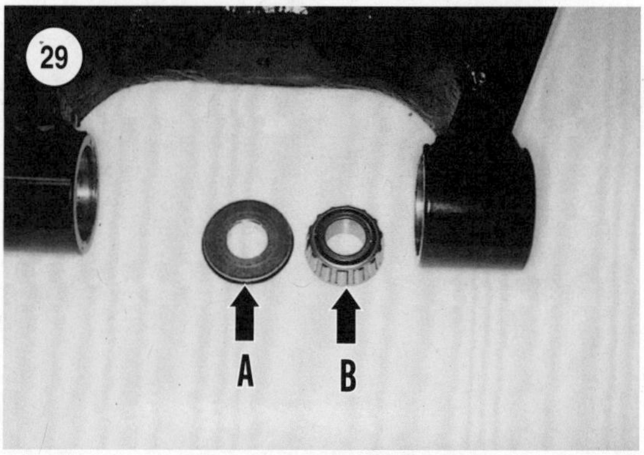

NOTE
*Do not remove the swing arm bushing and bearing cups unless they are going to be replaced. Refer to **Swing Arm Overhaul** in this section.*

3. Clean the pivot shaft, spacer, bushing, bearing cups, and washers in solvent and dry with compressed air, if available.

4. Inspect the O-rings installed in the outer edge of each washer (**Figure 30**). Replace worn or damaged O-rings.

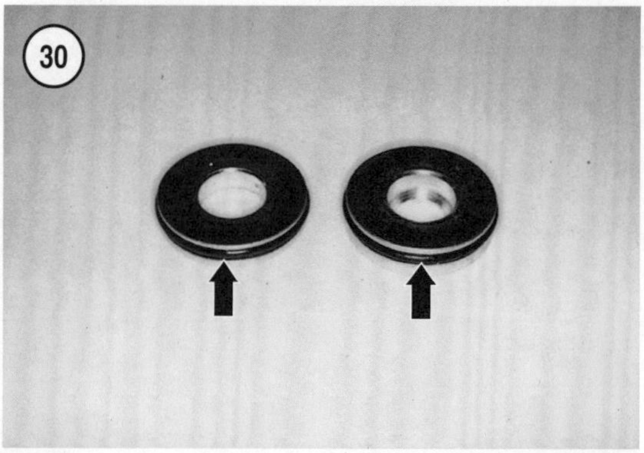

5. Wipe off all excess grease from one roller bearing and then soak it in a container filled with kerosene. Brush the bearing with a soft nylon brush and then blow with low pressure compressed air to remove as much of the old grease as possible. Repeat until the bearing is clean, with none of the old grease visible. When the bearing is clean, dip it in a container of new kerosene, then remove and blow it off. Repeat for the opposite bearing.

6. To assemble the roller bearing into the left side of the swing arm, perform the following:

a. Apply wheel bearing grease to each cup (**Figure 31**) installed in the swing arm.

b. Pack the bearing with wheel bearing grease. If a bearing packer is not available, thoroughly work the grease into the bearing by hand until it is fully packed.

c. Repeat to lubricate the opposite bearing.

(32)

(33)
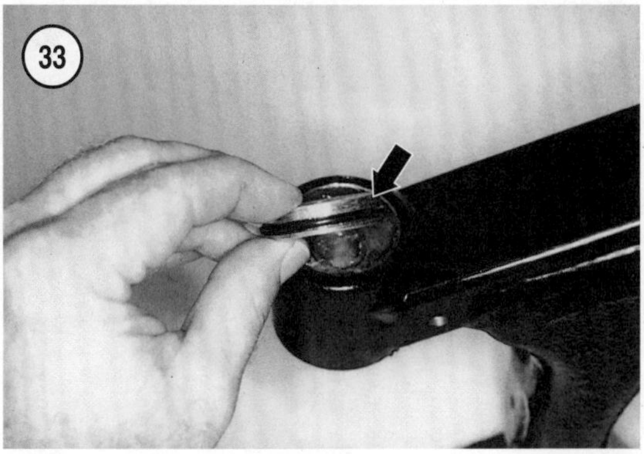

(34)

(35)
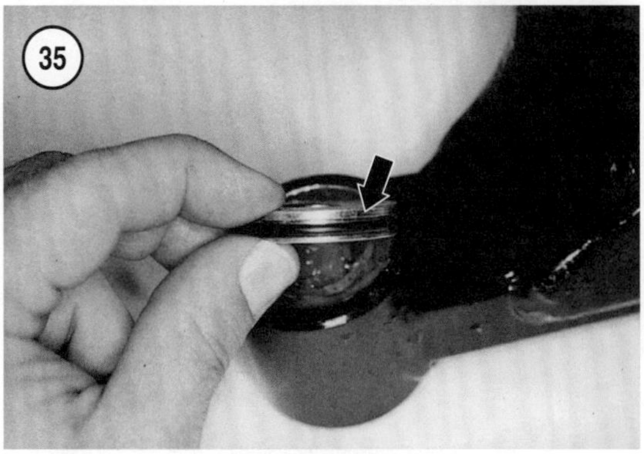

(36)

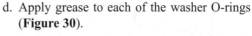

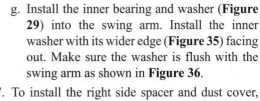

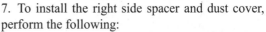

NOTE
*When installing the washers (**Figure 30**) in the following steps, note that the washers are different. Install the washer with the smaller inside diameter hole into the outside of the swing arm. The pivot shaft will not pass through this washer if it is installed on the inside of the swing arm. **Figure 32** shows the pivot shaft and outer washer.*

d. Apply grease to each of the washer O-rings (**Figure 30**).

e. Install the outer bearing and washer (**Figure 27**) into the swing arm. Install the outer washer with its wider edge (**Figure 33**) facing out. Make sure the washer is flush with the swing arm as shown in **Figure 34**.

f. Grease the bearing spacer (**Figure 28**) and install it against the outer bearing.

CAUTION
Install the bearing spacer between the bearing races; otherwise, the bearings may fail during operation.

g. Install the inner bearing and washer (**Figure 29**) into the swing arm. Install the inner washer with its wider edge (**Figure 35**) facing out. Make sure the washer is flush with the swing arm as shown in **Figure 36**.

7. To install the right side spacer and dust cover, perform the following:

a. Lubricate the spacer and bushing (**Figure 37**) with wheel bearing grease.

b. Install the dust cover (**Figure 38**) into the swing arm and seat it against the bushing. The dust cover must seat flush with or be recessed

11

0.06 in. (1.5 mm) from the edge of the swing arm. See **Figure 39**.

c. Install the spacer (**Figure 26**) through the bushing and seat it against the dust cover.

8. Install the rear swing arm as described in this chapter.

Rear Swing Arm Overhaul

This procedure describes the replacement of the swing arm bushing and bearing cup assemblies.

1. Remove the spacer and roller bearing assemblies as described under *Swing Arm Bushing and Bearing Lubrication* in this chapter.
2. To replace the bushing (**Figure 37**) on the left side, perform the following:
   a. Before removing the bushing (**Figure 37**), measure its installed position from the inside edge of the swing arm to the bushing edge.
   b. Using an expandable puller or a press, remove the bushing (**Figure 37**) from the swing arm.
   c. Clean the swing arm bushing bore with solvent and dry with compressed air, if available.
   d. Align the new bushing with the swing arm and press it into the swing arm. Press it into the recorded dimension.
3. To remove the bearing cups (**Figure 31**) on the right side, perform the following:
   a. **Figure 40** shows a complete roller bearing assembly. Do not intermix the bearing assemblies.
   b. Remove the inner and outer bearing cups (**Figure 41**) from the swing arm with a puller.

NOTE

*The lock ring (**Figure 42**) is seated in a groove inside the swing arm bore. Do not try to pry the lock ring out of the groove as it is under considerable tension. Perform the following procedure to safely remove the lock ring.*

4. To replace the lock ring (**Figure 42**), perform the following:

NOTE

In the following steps the hacksaw will only cut through the exposed portion of the lock ring. Cut down only to the swing arm bore surface. These cuts are not meant to cut completely

37

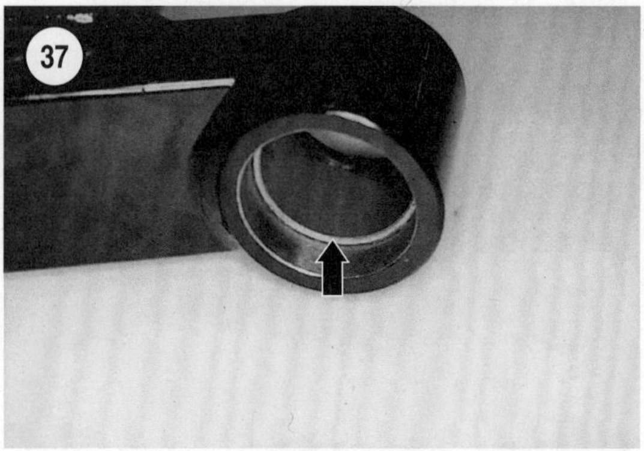

38

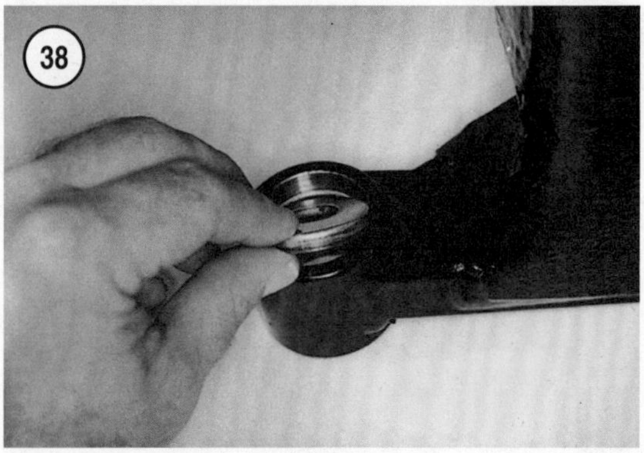

39

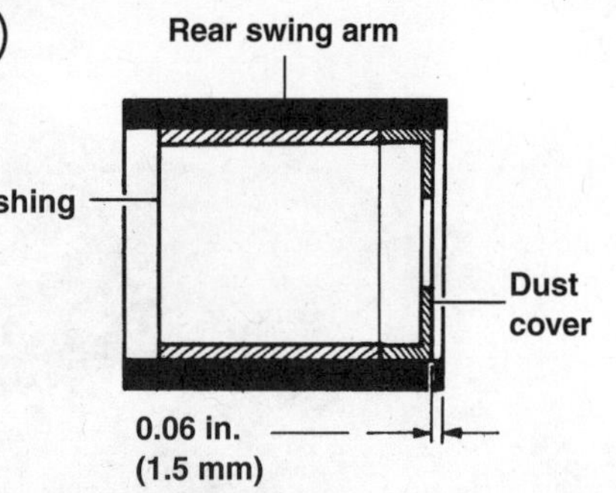

40

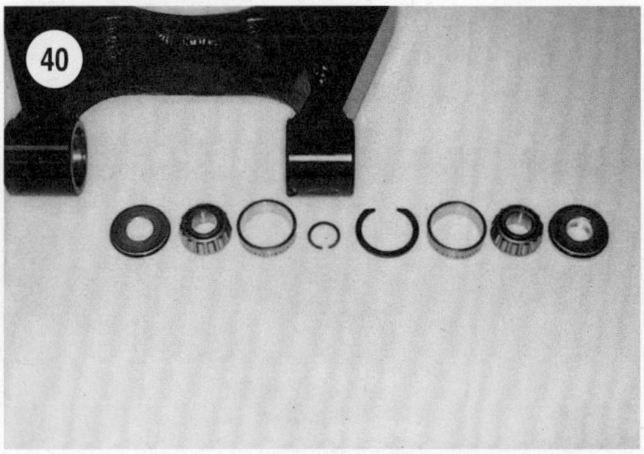

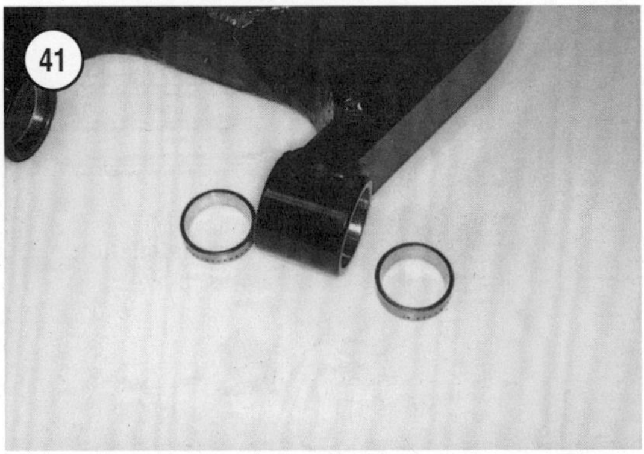

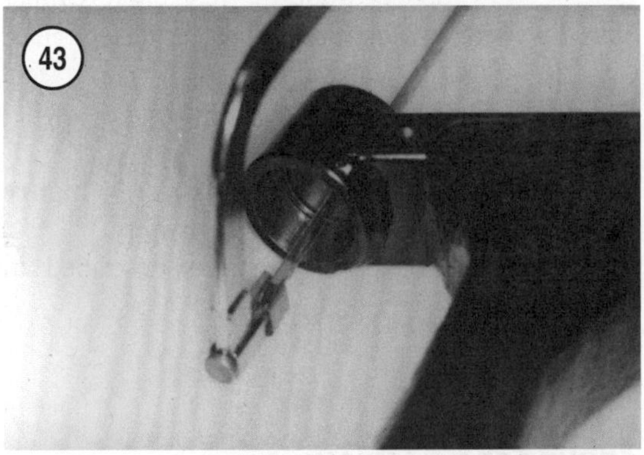

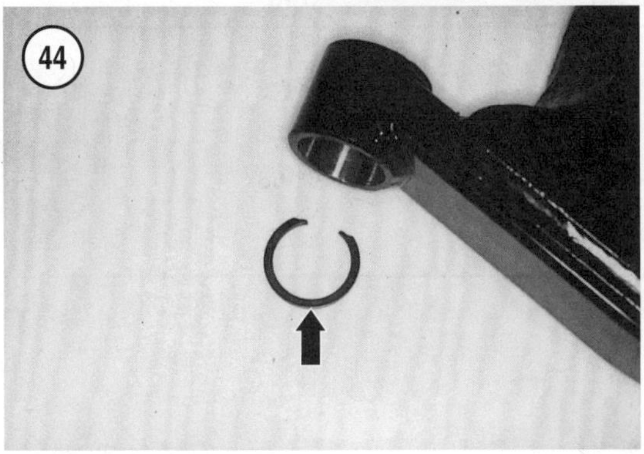

through the lock ring, only weaken it so it can be removed safely from the swing arm bore groove.

a. Insert a fine tooth hacksaw blade (24 or 32 teeth per inch) through the swing arm bearing bore and mount it onto a hacksaw (**Figure 43**).

b. With the lock ring opening positioned at 12 o'clock, make a cut at the 4 o'clock and the 8 o'clock positions. Cut the lock ring down to the swing arm bore surface. Do not cut into the swing arm bore.

WARNING
Wear safety glasses when removing and installing the lock ring.

c. Using a screwdriver at one end of the lock ring, carefully pry it up and out of the swing arm groove. If the lock ring is still under sufficient tension, try to remove it at the other end. Remove and discard the lock ring.

d. Clean the swing arm bore and the lock ring groove of all metal particles with solvent and dry.

WARNING
Wear safety glasses when installing the lock ring.

e. To install the *new* lock ring (**Figure 44**), lubricate the swing arm bore and the lock ring with oil. Start one end of the lock ring in the bore, then tap the other end into place with a hammer. Tap it in until both ends are in the bore and parallel with the groove. Then drive or press it into the groove with a suitable bearing driver. Check that the lock ring (**Figure 42**) is correctly seated in the groove.

5. Press the inner and outer bearing cups (**Figure 41**) into the swing arm (**Figure 31**). Seat both bearings against the lock ring.

6. Install the spacer and roller bearing assemblies as described under *Swing Arm Bushing and Bearing Lubrication* in this chapter.

Rear Swing Arm Installation

1. Lubricate the pivot shaft with wheel bearing grease.

11

2. If removed, install the spacer, roller bearings and washers as described under *Swing Arm Bushing and Bearing Lubrication* in this chapter.

3. Slide the swing arm onto the transmission housing mounting boss. Be sure to install and position the drive belt over the front of the swing arm.

4A. On 1999 models, perform the following:

  a. Install the pivot shaft (**Figure 24**) from the right side through the swing arm and the transmission. Install the washer and nut on the left side.

  b. Hold the pivot shaft (**Figure 24**) on the right side and tighten the nut to the specification in **Table 1**.

  c. Install a *new* cotter pin (**Figure 23**) and bend the ends over completely (**Figure 45**).

4B. On 2000-on models, perform the following:

  a. Install the pivot shaft (B, **Figure 22**) from the right side. Install the bolt and lockwasher (B, **Figure 20**) on the left side.

  b. Hold onto the hex fitting on the end of the pivot shaft on the right side and tighten the bolt to the specification in **Table 1**.

5. Grasp the swing arm by hand and swing it up and down. The swing arm must move without binding or excessive bearing play.

6. Install the rear brake hose and clamps securing it to the swing arm.

7. On the right side, install the pivot shaft chrome cap (B, **Figure 22**) onto the swing arm.

45

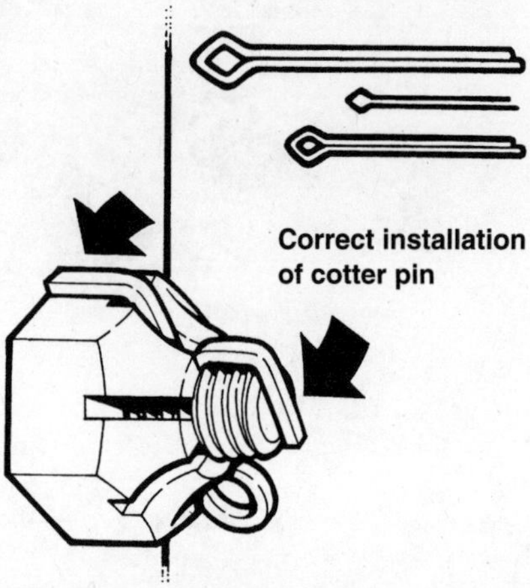

8. On the right side, install the muffler support bracket (A, **Figure 22**) and bolts. Tighten the bolts securely.

9. Move both shock absorbers down into position and install the acorn nut and washer (A, **Figure 21**). Tighten the nuts to the specification in **Table 1**.

10. Install the left side rear footpeg and mounting bracket assembly (A, **Figure 20**) and bolts. Tighten the bolts securely.

11. On 1999 models, slide the rear brake caliper onto the swing arm mounting boss as described in Chapter Twelve.

12. Install the rear wheel (B, **Figure 19**) as described in Chapter Nine.

13. Install the drive belt upper guard (A, **Figure 19**) and tighten the bolts and nuts securely.

14. Install the exhaust system as described in Chapter Seven.

Table 1 REAR SUSPENSION TORQUE SPECIFICATIONS

Item	ft.-lb.	in.-lb.	N•m
Shock absorber upper and lower nuts	25-40	–	34-54
Swing arm pivot bolt			
Nut 1999 models	70	–	95
Bolt 2000 and later	45-50	–	61-68
Swing arm debris deflector screws	–	40-60	4-7

NOTE: Refer to the Supplement at the back of this manual for information unique to 2002-on models.

CHAPTER TWELVE

BRAKES

This chapter describes repair and replacement procedures for all brake components.

Table 1 contains brake system specifications and **Table 2** contains the brake system torque specifications. **Table 1** and **Table 2** are located at the end of this chapter.

BRAKE SERVICE

WARNING

*Do not use brake fluid labeled **DOT 5.1**. This is a glycol-based fluid that is **not compatible** with silicone based DOT 5. DOT 5 brake fluid is purple while DOT 5.1 is an amber/clear color. Do not intermix these two completely different types of brake fluid, doing so will lead to brake component damage and possible brake failure.*

WARNING

Do not intermix DOT 3, DOT 4, or DOT 5.1 brake fluids, as they are not silicone-based. Use of non-silicone brake fluid in the Dyna Glide can cause brake failure.

WARNING

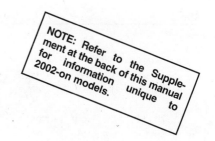

*When working on the brake system, do **not** inhale brake dust. It may contain asbestos, which is a known carcinogen. Do **not** use compressed air to blow off brake dust. Use an aerosol*

brake cleaner. Wear a facemask and wash thoroughly after completing the work.

The disc brake system transmits hydraulic pressure from the master cylinders to the brake calipers. This pressure is transmitted from the caliper(s) to the brake pads, which grip both sides of the brake disc(s) and slow the motorcycle. As the pads wear, the pistons move out of the caliper bores to automatically compensate for wear. As this occurs, the fluid level in the reservoir goes down. This must be compensated for by occasionally adding fluid.

The proper operation of this system depends on a supply of clean brake fluid (DOT 5) and a clean work environment when any service is being performed. Any tiny particle of debris that enters the system can damage the components and cause poor brake performance.

Brake fluid is hygroscopic (easily absorbs moisture) and moisture in the system will reduce brake performance. It is a good idea to purchase brake fluid in small containers and discard any small quantities that remain. Small quantities of fluid will quickly absorb the moisture in the container. Use only fluid clearly marked DOT 5. If possible, use the same brand of fluid. Do not replace the fluid with a non-silicone fluid. It is not possible to remove all of the old fluid. Other types are not compatible with DOT 5. Do not reuse drained fluid and discard old fluid properly. Do not combine brake fluid with fluids for recycling.

Proper service also includes carefully performed procedures. Do not use any sharp tools inside the master cylinders or calipers or on the pistons. Any damage to these components could cause a loss in the system's ability to maintain hydraulic pressure. If there is any doubt about having the ability to correctly and safely service the brake system, have a professional technician perform the task.

Consider the following when servicing the brake system:

1. The hydraulic components rarely require disassembly. Make sure it is necessary.
2. Keep the reservoir covers in place to prevent the entry of moisture and debris.
3. Clean parts with an aerosol brake part cleaner or isopropyl alcohol. Never use petroleum-based solvents on internal brake system components. They will cause seals to swell and distort.

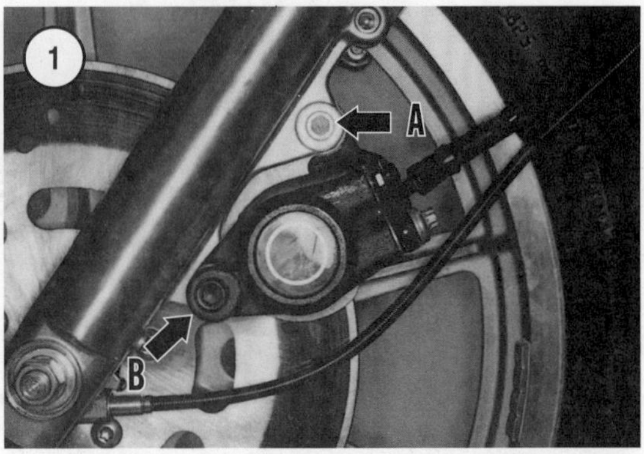

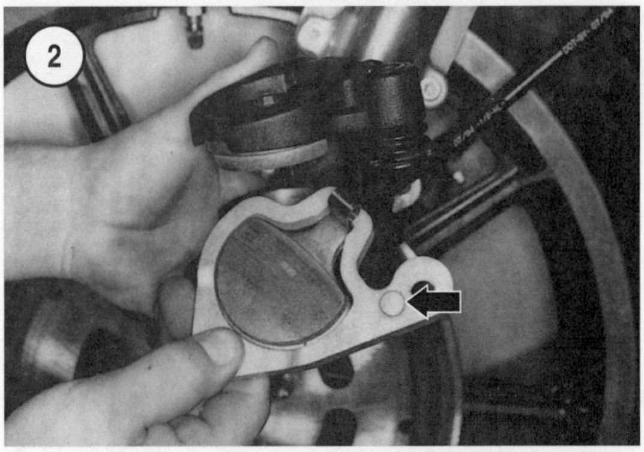

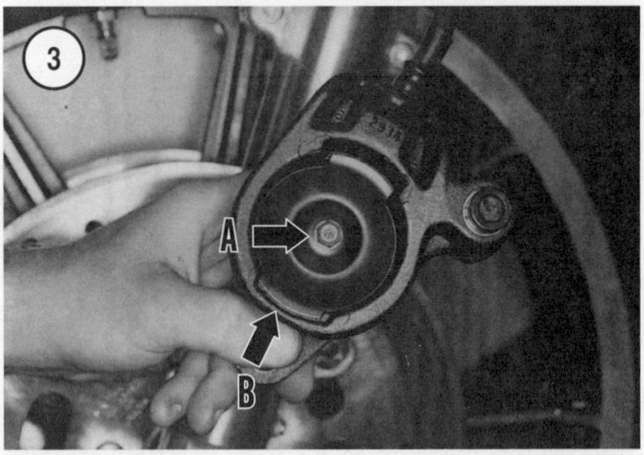

4. Do not allow brake fluid to contact plastic, painted or plated parts. It will damage the surface.
5. Dispose of brake fluid properly.
6. If the hydraulic system has been opened (not including the reservoir cover) the system must be bled to remove air from the system. Refer to *Bleeding the System* in this chapter.
7. The manufacturer does not provide wear limit specifications for the caliper and master cylinder assemblies. Use good judgment when inspecting these components or consult a professional technician for advice.

4

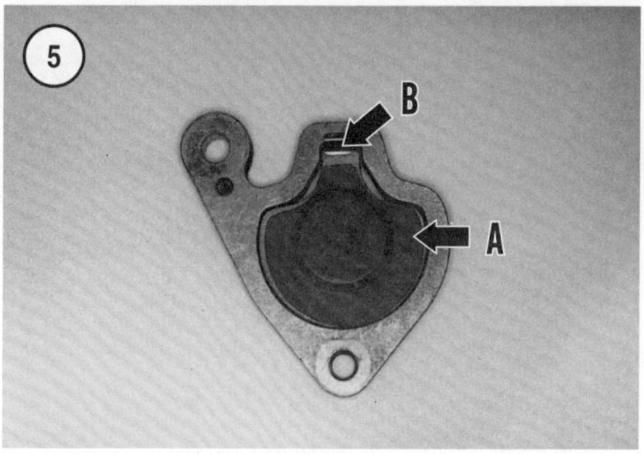

5

FRONT BRAKE PAD REPLACEMENT (1999 MODELS)

There is no recommended mileage interval for changing the brake pads. Pad wear depends greatly on riding habits and conditions. Frequently check the pads for wear. After removal, measure the thickness of each brake pad with a vernier caliper or ruler and compare to the dimensions in **Table 1**.

To maintain even brake pressure on the disc, always replace both pads in the caliper at the same time. Also, on dual-disc models, replace both brake pads in *both calipers* at the same time. Do not disconnect the hydraulic brake hose from the brake caliper for brake pad replacement. Disconnect the hose only if the caliper assembly is going to be removed.

CAUTION
Check the pads more frequently when the lining approaches the pad metal backing plate. If pad wear happens to be uneven for some reason, the backing plate may come in contact with the disc and cause damage.

1. Read the information under *Brake Service* in this chapter.
2. Park the motorcycle on a level surface.
3. To prevent the front brake lever from being applied, place a spacer between the brake lever and the throttle grip and secure it in place. If the brake lever is inadvertently squeezed, this will prevent the piston from being forced out of the cylinder.
4. Loosen the brake caliper upper mounting bolt (A, **Figure 1**) and the lower mounting pin (B, **Figure 1**). Remove the upper mounting bolt, washer and the lower mounting pin.
5. Slide the brake caliper off the brake disc.

NOTE
If the brake pads are going to be reused, mark them so they can be reinstalled in their original locations.

6. Remove the outboard pad, pad holder and spring clip as an assembly (**Figure 2**).
7. Remove the screw (A, **Figure 3**) and the pad retainer (B) securing the inner pad to the caliper.
8. Remove the inboard pad (**Figure 4**).
9. Push the outboard pad (A, **Figure 5**) free of the spring clip (B, **Figure 5**) and remove it.
10. Check the brake pads for wear or damage. Measure the thickness of the brake pad friction material. Replace the brake pads if they are worn to the service limit listed in **Table 1**. On dual-disc models, replace both pad sets at the same time.
11. Check the friction surface of the new pads for any debris or manufacturing residue. If necessary, clean off with an aerosol brake cleaner.

NOTE
When purchasing new pads, check with the dealer to make sure the friction compound of the new pad is compatible with the disc material. Remove any roughness from the backs of the new pads with a fine-cut file, then thoroughly clean them off.

12. Inspect the upper mounting bolt and the lower mounting pin. Replace if damaged or badly corroded.
13. Replace the pad retainer if damaged.
14. Check the piston dust boot (**Figure 6**) in the caliper. Remove and overhaul the caliper if the boot is swollen or damaged, or if brake fluid is leaking

from the caliper. Refer to *Front Brake Caliper (1999 Models)* in this chapter.

15. Remove all corrosion from the pad holder.

16. Replace the spring clip if damaged or badly corroded.

17. Check the brake disc for wear as described under *Brake Disc* in this chapter. Service the brake disc if necessary.

18. Assemble the pad holder, spring clip and outboard brake pad as follows:

   a. Lay the pad holder on a workbench so that the upper mounting screw hole is positioned at the upper right as shown in A, **Figure 7**.
   b. Install the spring clip (B, **Figure** 7) at the top of the pad holder so that the spring loop faces in the direction shown in **Figure 8**.
   c. The outboard brake pad has an insulator pad mounted on its backside (A, **Figure 5**).
   d. Center the outboard brake pad into the pad holder so that the lower end of the pad rests inside the pad holder. Push firmly on the upper end of the brake pad, past the spring clip and into the holder (**Figure 7**).

19. After installing new brake pads, the caliper piston must be relocated into the caliper before installing the caliper over the brake disc. Doing so will force brake fluid back up into the reservoir. To prevent the reservoir from overflowing, perform the following:

   a. Remove the screws (A, **Figure 9**) securing the cover and remove the cover and diaphragm (B).
   b. Use a large shop syringe and remove about 50 percent of the brake fluid from the reservoir. This will prevent the master cylinder from overflowing when the piston is pushed back into the caliper bore. Do *not* drain more than 50 percent of the brake fluid or air will enter the system. Discard the brake fluid.

CAUTION

Do not allow the master cylinder to overflow when performing this step. Wash brake fluid off any painted, plated or plastic surfaces or plastic parts immediately, as it will damage most surfaces it contacts. Use soapy water and rinse completely.

   c. Install the old outer brake pad into the caliper and against the piston.
   d. Slowly push the outer brake pad and piston back into the caliper and watch the brake fluid level in the master cylinder reservoir. If necessary, siphon off fluid prior to it overflowing.
   e. Remove the old brake pad.
   f. Temporarily install the diaphragm and cover. Install the screws finger-tight at this time.

6

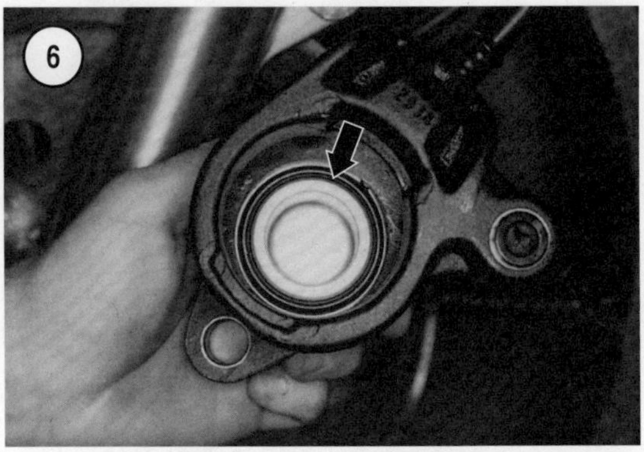

7

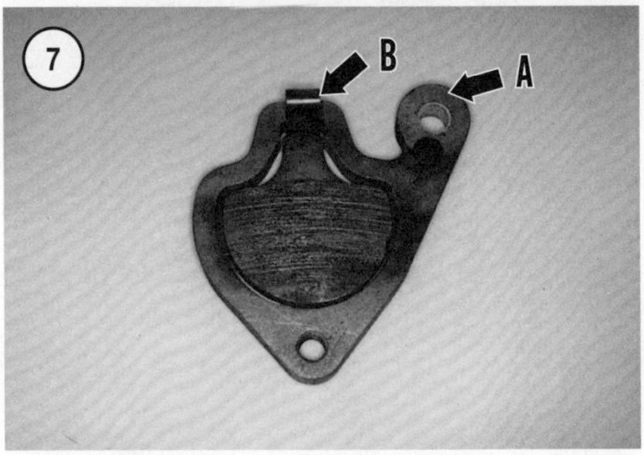

8

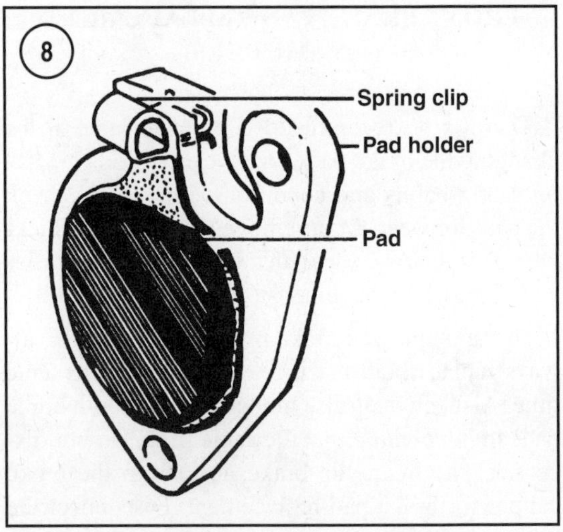

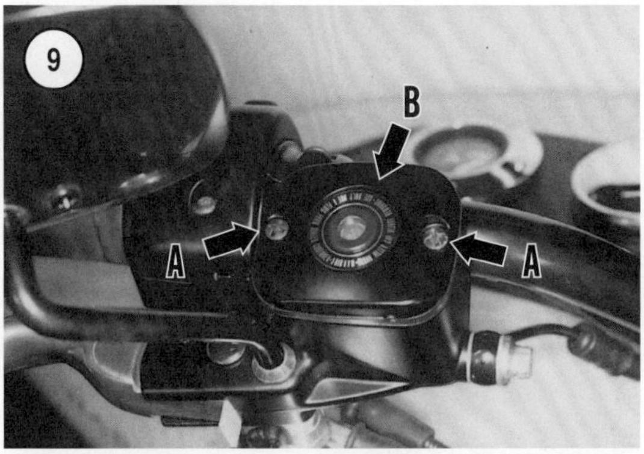

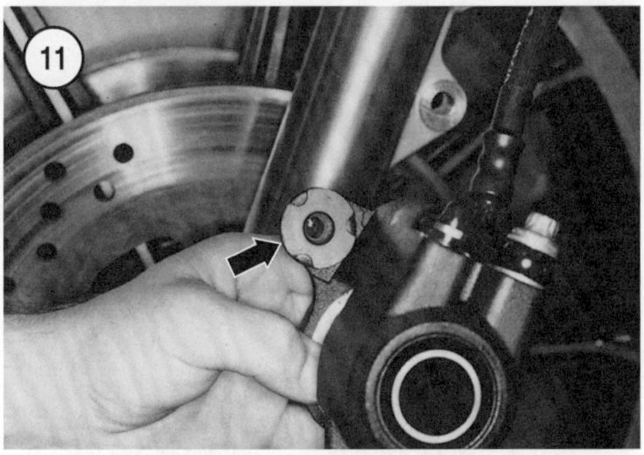

20. Install the inner brake pad into the caliper (**Figure 4**) from the inside surface. Push the pad into place.

21. Install the pad retainer (B, **Figure 3**), onto the backside of the caliper, indexing the tabs into the caliper recesses.

22. Install the screw through the pad retainer and into the backside of the inner brake pad. Tighten the screw to the specification in **Table 2**.

WARNING
*The bushings on the fork slider (**Figure 10**) locate the brake caliper on the fork slider in relation to the brake disc. The bushings must be in place as noted in Step 23. If not installed, the brake may lock up when applied and cause a loss of motorcycle control.*

23. If removed, install the caliper bushings into the fork slider lugs (**Figure 10**).

24. Install the outer brake pad/pad holder assembly (**Figure 2**) as follows:

WARNING
*The spring clip loop and the brake pad friction material (**Figure 8**) must face away from the piston when the pad holder is installed in the caliper. Brake failure will occur if this assembly is installed incorrectly.*

a. Insert the outer brake pad/pad holder assembly into the caliper so that the brake pad insulator backing faces against the piston.

CAUTION
*The brake caliper threaded bushing shoulder (**Figure 11**) must be positioned as described in this step. Otherwise, the pad holder rivet and bushing will be damaged when the caliper mounting screw and pin are tightened.*

b. Position the threaded bushing flange (**Figure 11**) with its shoulder between the pad holder and the rivet head. Position the bushing so that one notch engages the rivet (**Figure 12**).

25. Carefully install the caliper over the brake disc, making sure the friction surface on each pad faces against the disc.

12

26. Coat the lower mounting pin shoulder (**Figure 13**) and O-ring with Dow Corning Moly 44 grease or an equivalent prior to installation.

27. Align the caliper mounting holes with the fork slider mounting lugs.

28. Install the brake caliper upper mounting bolt and washer (A, **Figure 1**) through the fork slider mounting lug and thread it into the caliper bushing. Tighten the bolt finger-tight at this time.

29. Insert the lower mounting pin (B, **Figure 1**) through the caliper and thread it into the slider mounting lug. Tighten the mounting pin finger-tight at this time.

30. First tighten the lower mounting pin, then the upper mounting bolt, to the specification in **Table 2**.

31. On dual-disc models, repeat this procedure for the other caliper assembly.

32. Refill the master cylinder reservoir with DOT 5 silicone-based brake fluid, if necessary, to maintain the correct fluid level. Install the diaphragm, top cover and tighten the screws to the specification in **Table 2**.

33. Apply the front brake lever several times to seat the pads against the disc.

WARNING

Do not ride the motorcycle until the front brakes operate correctly with full hydraulic advantage. If necessary, bleed the brake as described in this chapter.

FRONT BRAKE PAD REPLACEMENT (2000-2001 MODELS)

There is no recommended mileage interval for changing the brake pads. Pad wear depends greatly on riding habits and conditions. Frequently check the pads for wear. After removal, measure the thickness of each brake pad with a vernier caliper or ruler and compare to the dimensions in **Table 1**.

To maintain an even brake pressure on the disc, always replace both pads in the caliper at the same time. Also, on dual-disc models, replace both brake pads in *both calipers* at the same time. Do not disconnect the hydraulic brake hose from the brake caliper for brake pad replacement. Disconnect the hose only if the caliper assembly is going to be removed.

13

14

CAUTION

Check the pads more frequently when the lining approaches the pad metal backing plate. If pad wear happens to be uneven for some reason, the backing plate may come in contact with the disc and cause damage.

1. Read the information under *Brake Service* in this chapter.

2. Park the motorcycle on level ground.

3. Place a spacer between the brake lever and the throttle grip and secure it in place. If the brake lever is inadvertently squeezed, this will prevent the pistons from being forced out of the cylinders.

4. Clean the top of the master cylinder of all debris.

5. Remove the screws (A, **Figure 9**) securing the cover. Remove the cover and diaphragm (B).

6. Use a shop syringe and remove about 50 percent of the brake fluid from the reservoir. This will prevent the master cylinder from overflowing when the pistons are compressed for reinstallation. Do *not* drain more than 50 percent of the brake fluid or air will enter the system. Discard the brake fluid.

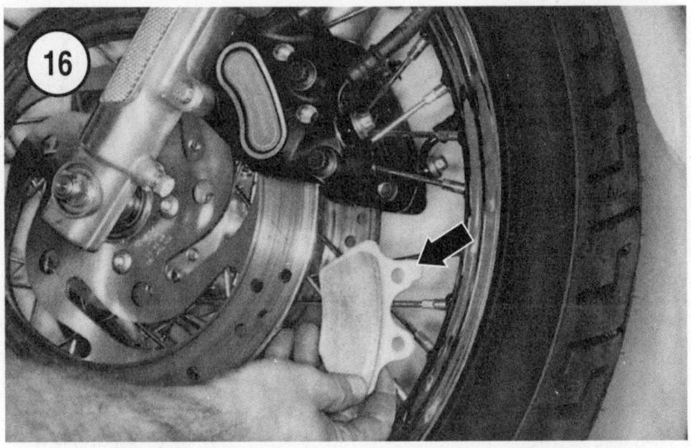

CAUTION
Do not allow the master cylinder to overflow when performing Step 7. Wash brake fluid off any painted, plated or plastic surfaces immediately, as it will damage most surfaces it contacts. Use soapy water and rinse completely.

7. Loosen the pad pin bolts (**Figure 14**).

CAUTION
The brake disc is thin in order to dissipate heat and therefore may bend easily. When pushing against the disc in the following step, support the disc adjacent to the caliper to prevent damage to the disc.

8. Hold the caliper body from the outside and push it toward the brake disc. This will push the outer pistons into the caliper bores to make room for the new brake pads. Constantly check the reservoir to make sure brake fluid does not overflow. Remove fluid, if necessary, prior to it overflowing. Install the diaphragm and cover. Tighten the screws finger-tight.
9. Remove the pad pin bolts.
10. Remove the inboard and outboard brake pads from the caliper.
11. Check the brake pads for wear or damage. Measure the thickness of the brake pad friction material. Replace the brake pads if they are worn to the service limit listed in **Table 1**.
12. Carefully remove any rust or corrosion from the disc.
13. Thoroughly clean the pad pin bolts of any corrosion or road dirt.
14. Check the friction surface of the new pads for any debris or manufacturing residue. If necessary, clean off with an aerosol brake cleaner.

NOTE
When purchasing new pads, check with the dealer to make sure the friction compound of the new pad is compatible with the disc material. Remove any roughness from the backs of the new pads with a fine-cut file; then thoroughly clean off.

NOTE
*The brake pads are not symmetrical. The pad with two tabs (**Figure 15**) must be installed on the outboard side of the left side caliper and on the inboard side of the right side caliper. The pad with one tab (**Figure 16**) must be installed on the inboard side of the left side caliper and on the outboard side of the right side caliper*

15. Install the inboard pad (**Figure 16**) and the outboard pad (**Figure 15**) into the caliper.
16. Hold the pads in place and install the pad pin bolts through the caliper and both brake pads (**Figure 14**).
17. Tighten the pad pins to the specification in **Table 2**.
18. On dual-disc models, repeat Steps 7-17 and replace the brake pads in the other caliper assembly.
19. Remove the spacer from the front brake lever.
20. Check to make sure there is sufficient brake fluid in the master cylinder reservoir. Top off if necessary.
21. Pump the front brake lever to reposition the brake pads against the brake disc. Roll the motorcycle back and forth and continue to pump the brake lever as many times as it takes to refill the cylinders in the calipers and correctly locate the brake pads against the disc.

NOTE
To control the flow of fluid, punch a small hole into the seal of a new con-

17

FRONT BRAKE CALIPER (1999)

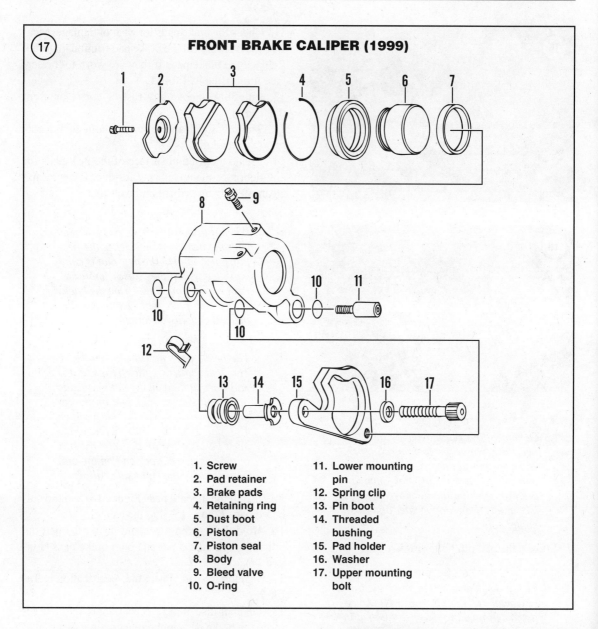

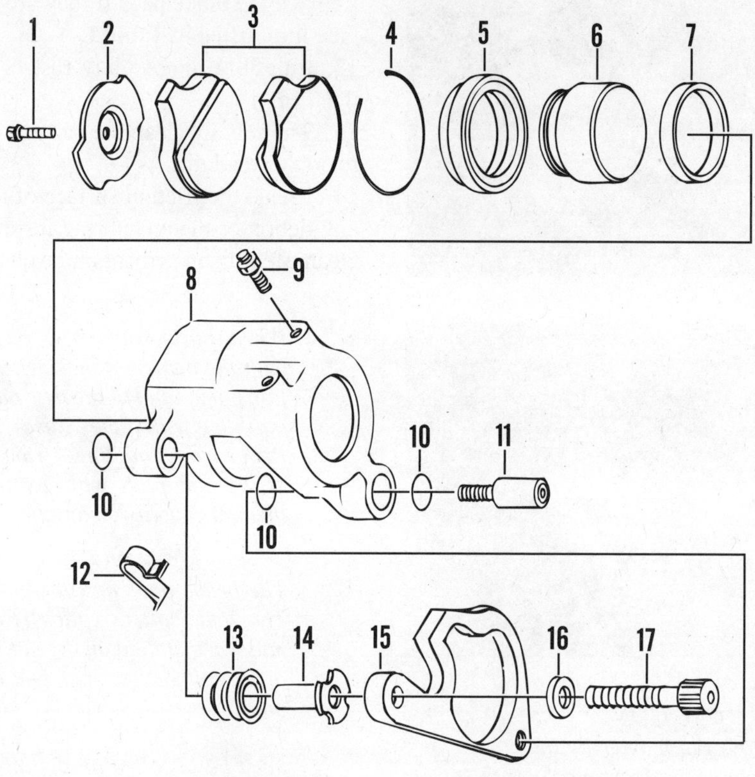

1. Screw
2. Pad retainer
3. Brake pads
4. Retaining ring
5. Dust boot
6. Piston
7. Piston seal
8. Body
9. Bleed valve
10. O-ring
11. Lower mounting pin
12. Spring clip
13. Pin boot
14. Threaded bushing
15. Pad holder
16. Washer
17. Upper mounting bolt

tainer of brake fluid next to the edge of the pour spout. This will help eliminate fluid spillage, especially while adding fluid to the very small reservoir.

WARNING

Use brake fluid clearly marked DOT 5 from a sealed container. Other types may vaporize and cause brake failure. Always use the same brand name; do not intermix, as many brands are not compatible. Do not intermix DOT 3, DOT 4 or DOT 5.1 brake fluid, as it can cause brake component damage leading to brake system failure.

22. Refill the master cylinder reservoir, if necessary, to maintain the correct fluid level as indicated on the side of the reservoir. Install the diaphragm and the top cover. Tighten the screws to the specification in **Table 2**.

WARNING

Do not ride the motorcycle until the front brakes operate correctly with full hydraulic advantage. If neces-

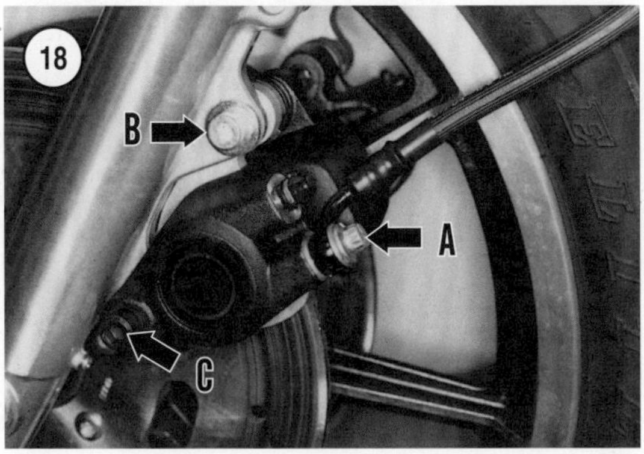

sary, bleed the brake as described in this chapter.

FRONT BRAKE CALIPER (1999 MODELS)

Removal (Caliper Will Not Be Disassembled)

Refer to **Figure 17**.

To remove the brake caliper without disassembling it, perform this procedure. To disassemble the brake caliper, refer to *Caliper Removal/Piston Removal* in this chapter.

1A. To remove the brake caliper from the motorcycle, perform the following:

a. Loosen and remove the banjo bolt at the caliper (A, **Figure 18**). Remove the bolt and the 2 washers.
b. Remove the upper mounting bolt and washer (B, **Figure 18**) and the lower mounting pin (C).
c. Lift the brake caliper off the brake disc and remove it.

1B. To remove the brake caliper partially from the motorcycle (brake hose will not be disconnected), perform the following:

a. Remove the upper mounting screw and washer (B, **Figure 18**) and the lower mounting pin (C).
b. Lift the brake caliper off the brake disc.
c. Insert a wooden or plastic spacer block between the brake pads in the caliper.

NOTE

Squeezing the brake lever with the caliper removed from the brake disc will force the piston out of its bore. Using the spacer block as mentioned in the previous step can prevent this from happening.

d. Support the caliper to the frame with a bungee cord or piece of heavy wire.

Installation (Caliper Was Not Disassembled)

WARNING

*The bushings on the fork slider (**Figure 10**) locate the brake caliper on the fork slider in relation to the brake disc. The bushings must be in place as noted in Step 1. If not installed, the brake may lock up when applied and cause loss of control.*

1. If removed, install the caliper bushings into the fork slider lugs (**Figure 10**).
2. If removed, install the brake pads as described in this chapter.
3. Carefully install the caliper over the brake disc, making sure the friction surface on each pad faces against the disc.
4. Coat the lower mounting pin shoulder (**Figure 13**) and O-ring with Dow Corning Moly 44 grease or an equivalent prior to installation.
5. Align the caliper's two mounting holes with the fork slider mounting lugs.
6. Install the brake caliper upper mounting bolt and washer (A, **Figure 1**) through the fork slider mounting lug and thread it into the caliper bushing. Tighten the bolt finger-tight at this time.
7. Insert the lower mounting pin (B, **Figure 1**) through the caliper and thread it into the slider mounting lug. Tighten the mounting pin finger-tight at this time.
8. First tighten the lower mounting pin, then the upper mounting bolt, to the specification in **Table 2**.

NOTE

Install new steel/rubber banjo bolt washers in Step 9.

9. If removed, assemble the brake line onto the caliper with a new washer on both sides of the brake line fitting, then secure the fitting to the caliper with the banjo bolt (A, **Figure 18**). Tighten the banjo bolt to the specification in **Table 2**. Make sure the fitting seats against the caliper as shown in A, **Figure 18**.

12

10. On dual-disc models, if necessary, repeat this procedure for the other caliper assembly.

11. Refill the master cylinder reservoir with DOT 5 silicone-based brake fluid, if necessary, to maintain the correct fluid level. Install the diaphragm, top cover and tighten the screws to the specification in **Table 2**.

12. Apply the front brake lever several times to seat the pads against the disc.

WARNING

Do not ride the motorcycle until the front brakes operate correctly with full hydraulic advantage. If necessary, bleed the brake as described in this chapter.

Caliper Removal/Piston Removal (Caliper Will Be Disassembled)

Force is required to remove the piston from the caliper. This procedure describes how to remove the piston with the caliper connected to the brake hose.

1. Remove the brake pads as described in this chapter.

2. Insert a small screwdriver into the notched groove machined in the bottom of the piston bore (**Figure 19**). Then pry the retaining ring (**Figure 20**) out of the caliper body.

3. Wrap a large cloth around the brake caliper.

4. Hold the caliper by hand away from the piston/brake pad area.

5. Operate the front brake lever to force the piston part way out of the caliper. Do not completely remove the piston until after it is removed for disassembly. Leaving the piston partially in the bore prevents brake fluid from spilling out.

NOTE

*If the piston did not come out, remove it as described under **Disassembly** in this section.*

6. Remove the caliper banjo bolt (A, **Figure 18**) and washers. Seal the brake hose to prevent brake fluid from dripping out.

7. Place the caliper on a workbench for disassembly.

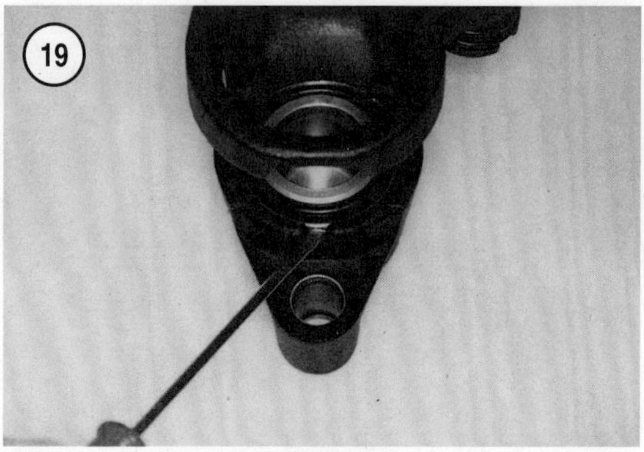

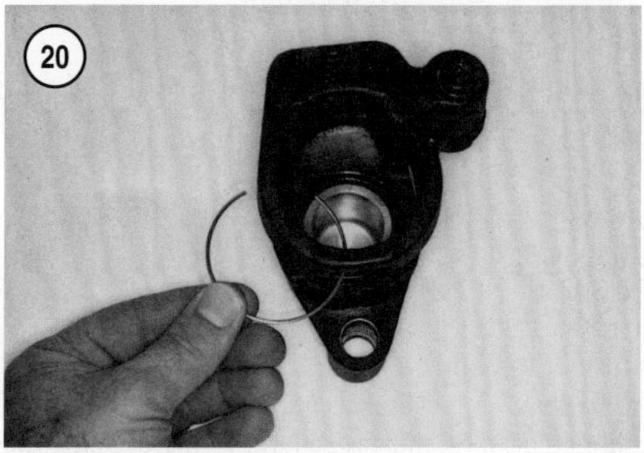

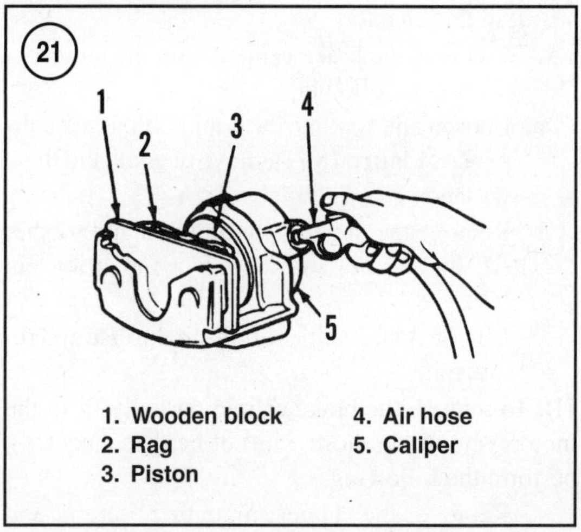

Disassembly

Service specifications for the caliper components are not available. Replace any worn, damaged or questionable part.

Refer to **Figure 17**.

1. Partially remove the piston from the caliper as described under *Caliper Removal/Piston Removal*

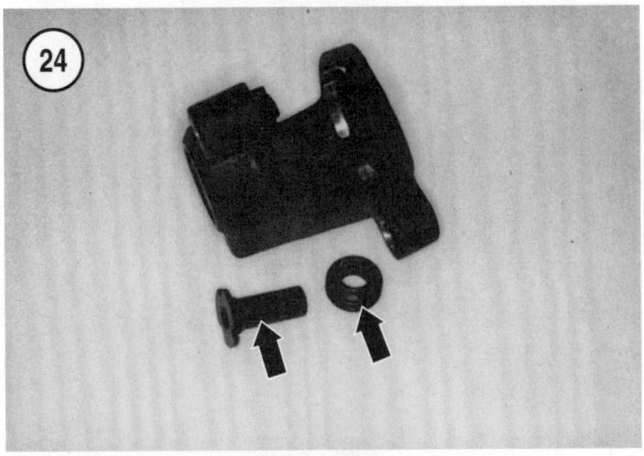

(Caliper Will Be Disassembled) in the previous procedure.

WARNING
Compressed air will force the piston out of the caliper under considerable force. Do not block the piston by hand, as injury will result.

2. If the piston did not come partially out of the caliper bore, perform the following:
   a. Place a rag and a piece of wood in the caliper (**Figure 21**). Keep fingers out of the way of the piston.
   b. Apply compressed air through the brake hose port and force the piston out of the caliper.
3. Remove the piston and dust boot assembly (**Figure 22**).
4. Remove the piston seal (**Figure 23**) from the groove in the caliper body.
5. Pull the threaded bushing out of the caliper, then remove the pin boot (**Figure 24**).
6. Remove the three O-rings from the caliper body (**Figure 25**).

Inspection

1. Clean the caliper body and piston in clean DOT 5 brake fluid or isopropyl alcohol and dry with compressed air.
2. Make sure the fluid passageway in the base of the piston bore is clear. Apply compressed air to the opening to make sure it is clear. Clean out, if necessary, with clean brake fluid.
3. Inspect the piston seal groove in the caliper body for damage. If damaged or corroded, replace the caliper assembly.
4. Inspect the banjo bolt threaded hole in the caliper body. If worn or damaged, clean out with a metric thread tap or replace the caliper assembly.
5. Inspect the bleed screw threaded hole in the caliper body. If worn or damaged, clean out with a metric thread tap or replace the caliper assembly.
6. Inspect the bleed screw. Apply compressed air to the opening and make sure it is clear. Clean out if necessary with clean brake fluid. Install the bleed screw and tighten to the specification in **Table 2**.
7. Inspect the caliper body for damage.

8. Inspect the cylinder wall and piston (**Figure 26**) for scratches, scoring or other damage.

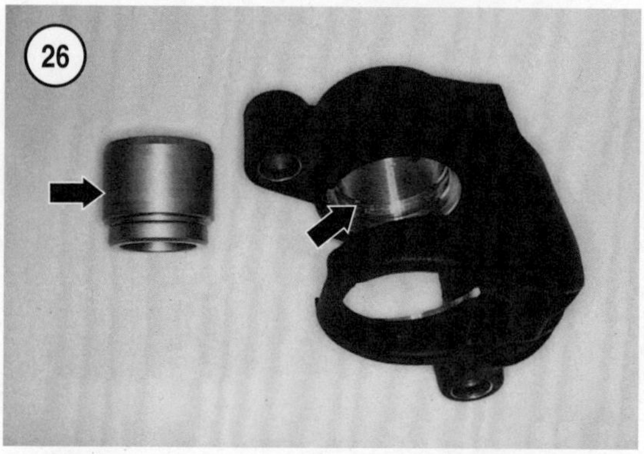

Assembly

1. The following parts are included in a H-D rebuild kit (part No. 44020-83): piston seal (A, **Figure 27**), piston (B), dust boot (C) and retaining ring (D).

NOTE
Never reuse an old dust boot or piston seal. Very minor damage or age deterioration can make the boot and seal useless.

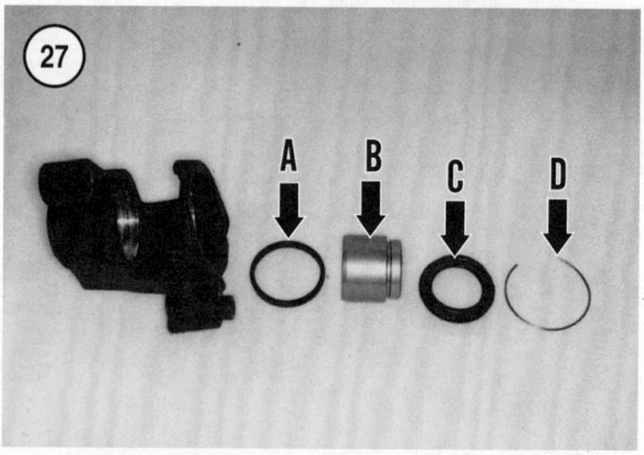

2. Soak the new dust and piston seal in clean DOT5 brake fluid.
3. Carefully install the *new* piston seal into the groove. Make sure the seal is properly seated in its groove.
4. Install *new* O-rings into the caliper grooves.
5. Wipe the inside of the pin boot with Dow Corning MOLY 44 grease. Then insert the boot into the bushing bore with the boots flange end seating in the bore groove (**Figure 28**).
6. Insert the threaded bushing into the boot (**Figure 29**).

7. Install the piston dust boot on the piston before the piston is installed in the caliper bore. Perform the following:
   a. Place the piston on the workbench with its open side facing up.
   b. Align the piston dust boot with the piston so that the shoulder on the dust boot faces up.
   c. Slide the piston dust boot onto the piston until the inner lip on the dust boot seats in the piston groove (**Figure 22**).
8. Coat the piston and the caliper bore with DOT 5 brake fluid.
9. Align the piston with the caliper bore so that its open end faces out (**Figure 22**). Then push the piston in until it bottoms.

10. Seat the piston dust boot (**Figure 30**) into the caliper bore.
11. Locate the retaining ring groove in the top end of the caliper bore. Align the retaining ring so that its gap (**Figure 31**) is at the top of the caliper bore and install the ring into the ring groove. Make sure the retaining ring is correctly seated in the groove.

30

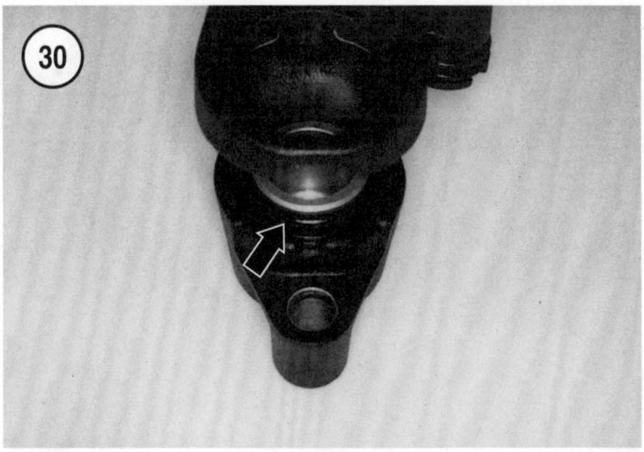

31

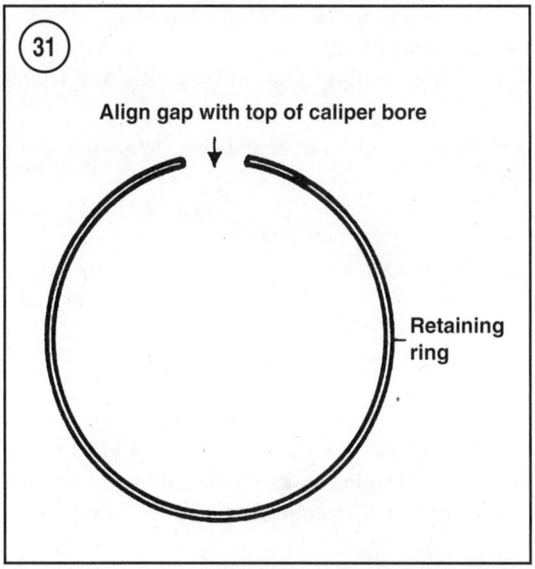

32

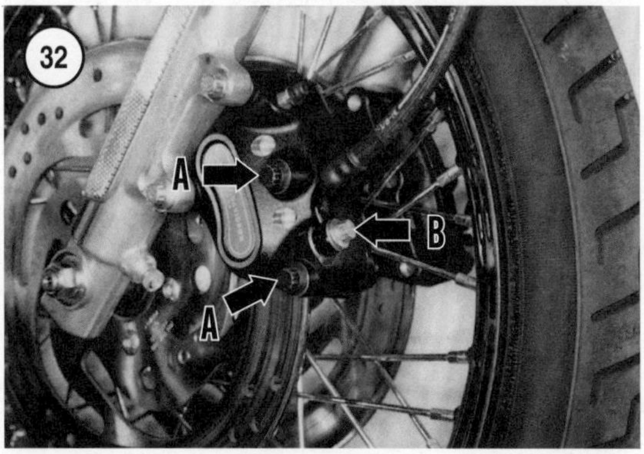

12. Apply a light coat of Dow Corning MOLY 44 grease to the caliper mounting lug bores.
13. If removed, install the bleed screw assembly and tighten to the specification in **Table 2**.
14. Install the caliper and brake pads as described in this chapter.
15. Bleed the brake as described under *Bleeding the System* in this chapter.

FRONT BRAKE CALIPER (2000-ON MODELS)

Removal/Installation

CAUTION
Do not spill any brake fluid on the front fork or front wheel. Wash brake fluid off any painted, plated or plastic surfaces or plastic parts immediately, as it will destroy most surfaces it contacts. Use soapy water and rinse completely.

1. If the caliper assembly is going to be disassembled for service, perform the following:

NOTE
By performing Steps 1a and 1b, compressed air may not be necessary for piston removal during caliper disassembly.

a. Remove the brake pads as described in this chapter.

CAUTION
Do not allow the pistons to travel out far enough to come in contact with the brake disc. If this happens, the pistons may scratch or gouge the disc during caliper removal.

b. Slowly apply the brake lever to push the pistons part way out of the caliper assembly for ease of removal during caliper service.
c. Loosen the two body mounting bolts (A, **Figure 32**).
d. Loosen the brake hose banjo bolt (B, **Figure 32**).

2. Remove the banjo bolt and sealing washers (B, **Figure 32**) attaching the brake hose to the caliper assembly. Do not lose the sealing washer on each side of the hose fitting(s).
3. Place the loose end of the brake hose in a reclosable plastic bag to prevent the entry of foreign matter and prevent any residual brake fluid from leaking out.

4. Remove the bolts (**Figure 33**) securing the brake caliper assembly to the front fork and remove the caliper.
5. If necessary, disassemble and service the caliper assembly as described in this chapter.
6. Install by reversing these removal steps while noting the following:
   a. Carefully install the caliper assembly onto the disc, being careful not to damage the leading edge of the brake pads.
   b. Install the bolts (**Figure 33**) securing the brake caliper assembly to the front fork and tighten to the specifications in **Table 2**.
   c. Apply clean DOT 5 brake fluid to the rubber portions of the new sealing washers prior to installation.
   d. Install a new sealing washer on each side of the brake hose fitting and install the banjo bolt (B, **Figure 32**). Tighten the banjo bolt to the specification in **Table 2**.
   e. Bleed the brake as described under *Bleeding the System* in this chapter.

WARNING
Do not ride the motorcycle until the front brakes operate correctly with full hydraulic advantage. If necessary, bleed the brake as described in this chapter.

Disassembly

Refer to **Figure 34**.
1. Remove the caliper and brake pads as described in this chapter.
2. Remove the two caliper body bolts (**Figure 35**) loosened during the removal procedure.
3. Separate the caliper body halves. Remove the O-ring seals (**Figure 36**). New O-ring seals must be installed every time the caliper is disassembled.

NOTE
If the pistons were partially forced out of the caliper body during removal, steps 4-6 may not be necessary. If the pistons or caliper bores are corroded or very dirty, a small amount of compressed air may be necessary to completely remove the pistons from the body bores.

33

4. Place a piece of soft wood or folded shop cloth over the end of the pistons and the caliper body. Turn this assembly over with the pistons facing down.
5. Perform this step over and close to a workbench top.

WARNING
Compressed air will force the pistons out of the caliper bodies under considerable force. Do not block the piston by hand, as injury will result.

6. Apply the air pressure in short spurts to the hydraulic fluid passageway and force out the pistons. Repeat for the other caliper body half. Use a service station air hose if compressed air is not available.

CAUTION
In the following step, do not use a sharp tool to remove the dust and piston seals from the caliper cylinders. Do not damage the cylinder surface.

7. Use a piece of wood or plastic scraper and carefully push the dust seal and the piston seal (**Figure 37**) in toward the caliper cylinder and out of their grooves. Remove the dust and piston seals.
8. If necessary, unscrew and remove the bleed valve (A, **Figure 38**).
9. Inspect the caliper assembly as described in this section.

Inspection

1. Clean both caliper body halves and pistons in clean DOT 5 brake fluid or isopropyl alcohol and dry with compressed air.

FRONT BRAKE CALIPER (2000-ON)

34

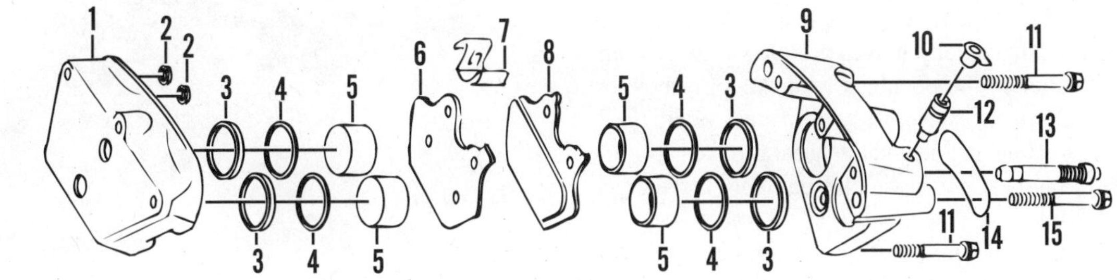

1. Inboard caliper body
2. O-rings
3. Piston seal
4. Dust seal
5. Piston
6. Inboard brake pad
7. Anti-rattle spring
8. Outboard brake pad
9. Outboard caliper body
10. Cap
11. Mounting bolt
12. Bleed valve
13. Pad pin bolt
14. Trim plate
15. Mounting bolt

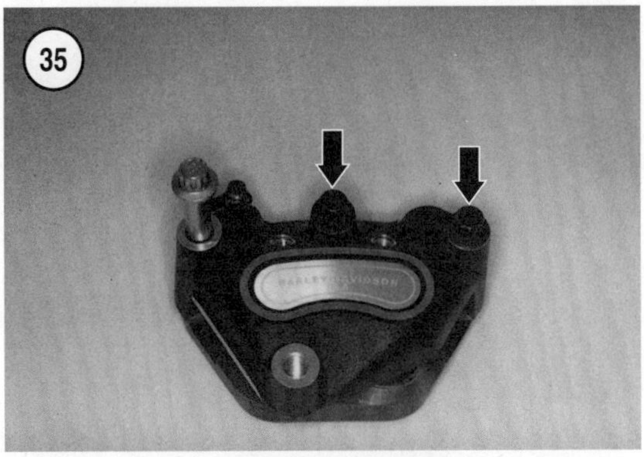

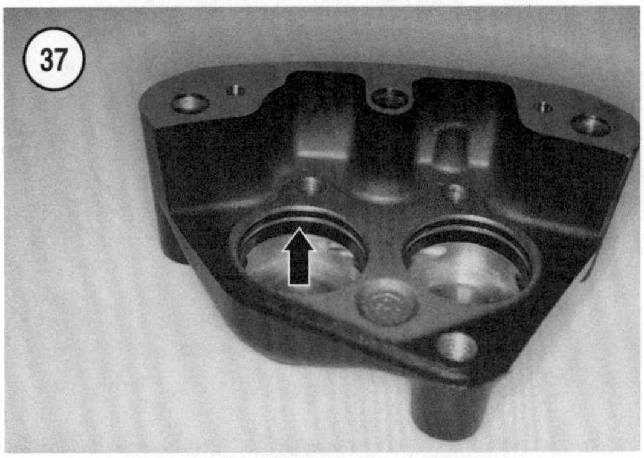

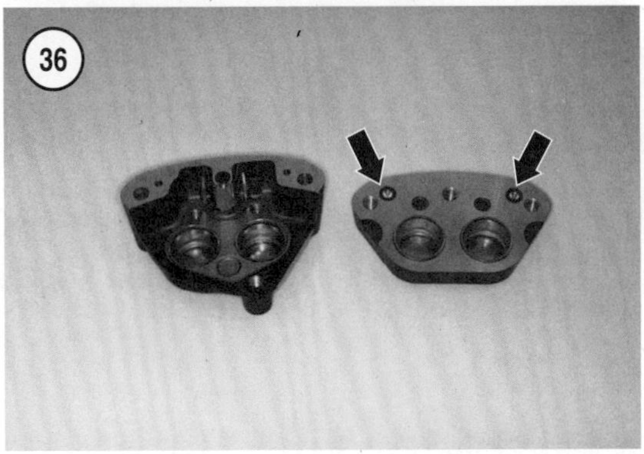

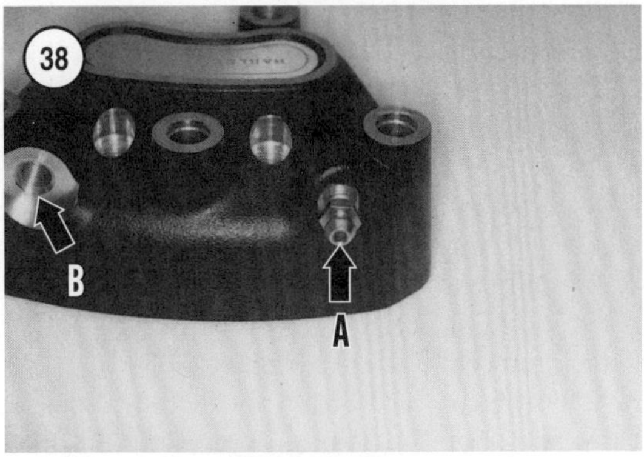

2. Make sure the fluid passageways (**Figure 39**) in the piston bores are clear. Apply compressed air to the openings to make sure they are clear. Clean out, if necessary, with clean brake fluid.
3. Make sure the fluid passageways (A, **Figure 40**) in both caliper body halves are clear. Apply compressed air to the openings to make sure they are clear. Clean out, if necessary, with clean brake fluid.
4. Inspect the piston and dust seal grooves (**Figure 41**) in both caliper bodies for damage. If damaged or corroded, replace the caliper assembly.
5. Inspect the banjo bolt threaded hole (B, **Figure 38**) in the outboard caliper body. If worn or damaged, clean out with a metric thread tap or replace the caliper assembly.
6. Inspect the bleed valve threaded hole in the caliper body. If worn or damaged, clean out with a metric thread tap or replace the caliper assembly.
7. Inspect the bleed valve. Apply compressed air to the opening and make sure it is clear. Clean out, if necessary, with clean brake fluid. Install the bleed screw and tighten to the specification in **Table 2**.
8. Inspect both caliper bodies for damage. Check the inboard caliper mounting bolt hole threads (B, **Figure 40**) for wear or damage. Clean up with an appropriately sized metric tap or replace the caliper assembly.
9. Inspect the cylinder walls and pistons for scratches, scoring or other damage.
10. Check the anti-rattle spring (**Figure 42**) for wear or damage.

Assembly

NOTE
Never reuse old dust seals or piston seals. Very minor damage or age deterioration can make the seals useless.

1. Soak the new dust and piston seals in clean DOT5 brake fluid.
2. Coat the piston bores and pistons with clean DOT5 brake fluid.
3. Carefully install the new piston seals into the lower grooves. Make sure the seals are properly seated in their respective grooves.
4. Carefully install the new dust seals into the upper grooves. Make sure all seals are properly seated in their respective grooves (**Figure 43**).
5. Repeat Step 3 and Step 4 for the other caliper body half.

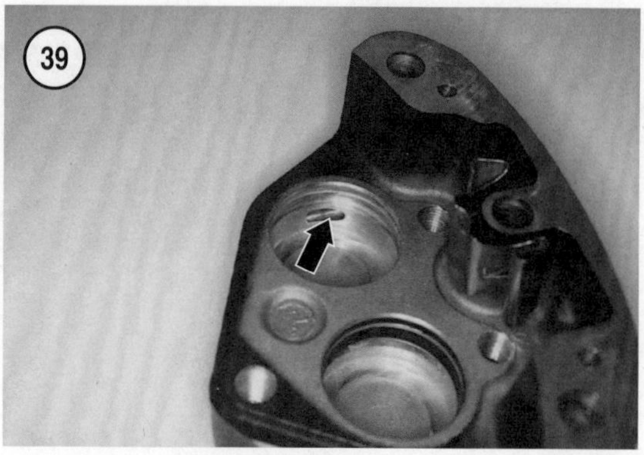

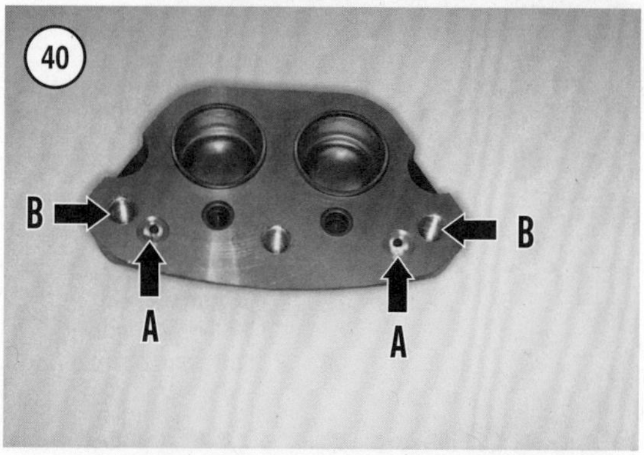

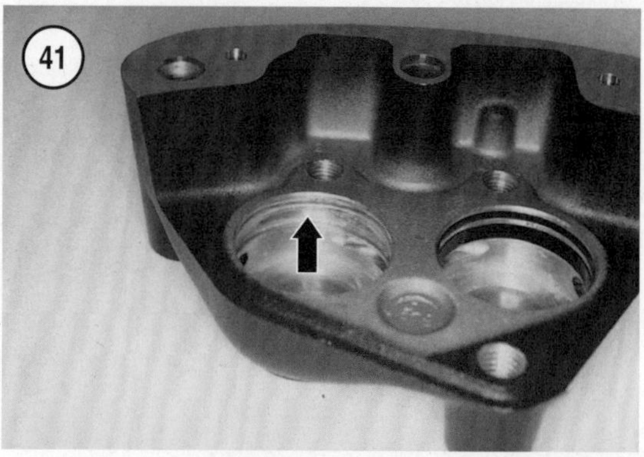

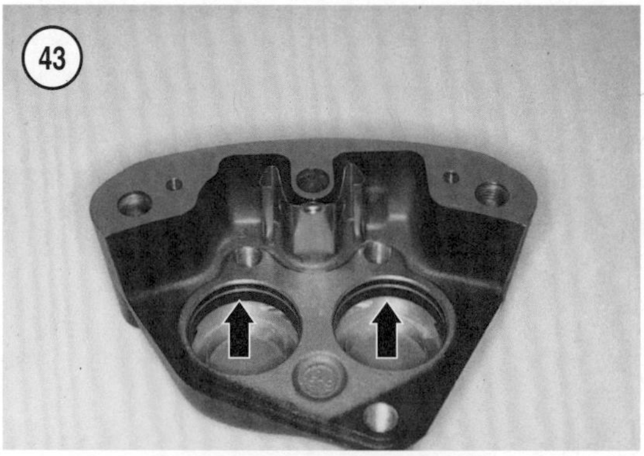

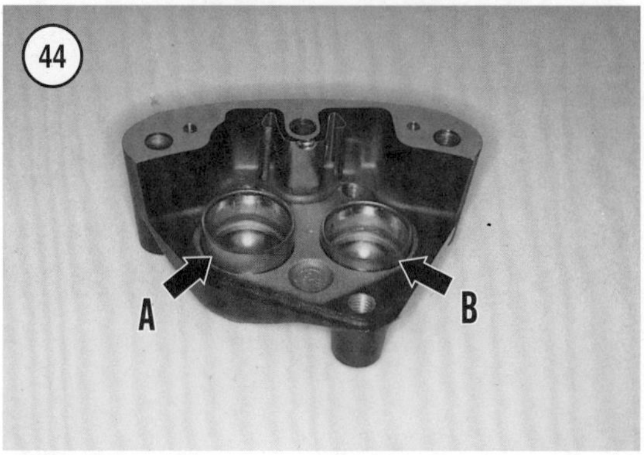

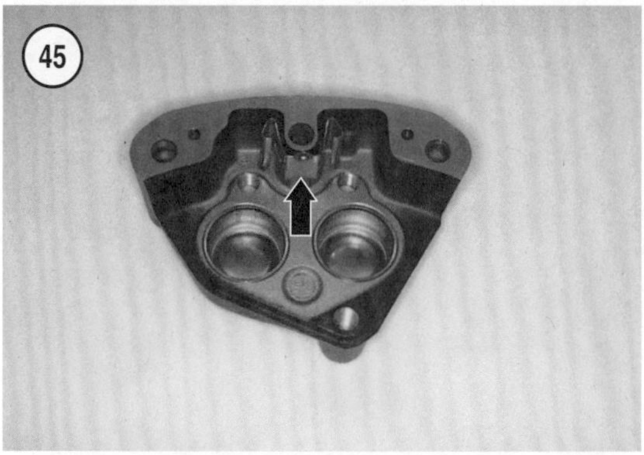

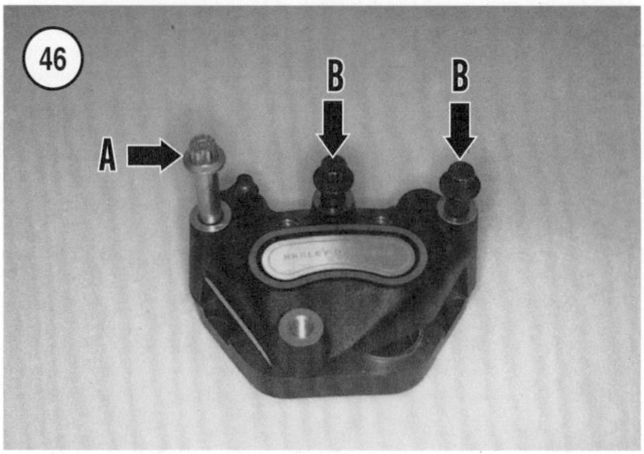

6. Position the pistons with the open end facing out and install the pistons into the caliper cylinders (A, **Figure 44**). Push the pistons in until they bottom (B, **Figure 44**).

7. Repeat Step 6 for the other caliper body half. Make sure all pistons are installed correctly.

8. Coat the *new* O-ring seals in DOT5 brake fluid and install the O-rings (**Figure 36**) into the inboard caliper half.

9. Install the anti-rattle spring (**Figure 45**) onto the boss on the outboard caliper half.

10. Make sure the O-rings are still in place and assemble the caliper body halves.

11. Install one of the caliper mounting bolts through the upper hole (A, **Figure 46**) to correctly align the caliper halves.

12. Install the two caliper body bolts (B, **Figure 46**) and tighten securely. They will be tightened to the specification after the caliper is installed on the front fork.

13. If removed, install the bleed valve assembly and tighten to the specification in **Table 2**.

14. Install the caliper and brake pads as described in this chapter.

15. Tighten the two caliper body mounting bolts (A, **Figure 32**) to the specification in **Table 2**.

16. Bleed the brake as described under *Bleeding the System* in this chapter.

FRONT MASTER CYLINDER

Removal

CAUTION

Cover the fuel tank and front fairing with a heavy cloth or plastic tarp to protect them from accidental brake fluid spills. Wash brake fluid off any painted, plated or plastic surfaces immediately, as it will damage most surfaces it contacts. Use soapy water and rinse completely.

1. Clean the top of the master cylinder of all debris.

2. Remove the screws (A, **Figure 47**) securing the top cover.

3. Remove the top cover (B, **Figure 47**) and diaphragm from the master cylinder reservoir.

4. Use a shop syringe and draw all of the brake fluid out of the master cylinder reservoir. Tempo-

rarily reinstall the diaphragm and the cover. Tighten the screws finger-tight.

5. On models so equipped, remove the windshield or front fairing.

6. Loosen and remove the mirror (A, **Figure 48**) from the master cylinder.

7. On models so equipped, remove the front turn signal assembly (B, **Figure 48**) from the master cylinder.

CAUTION

Failure to install the spacer in Step 8 will result in damage to the rubber boot and plunger on the front brake switch.

8. Insert a 5/32 in. (4 mm) thick spacer (A, **Figure 49**) between the brake lever and lever bracket. Make sure the spacer stays in place during the following steps.

9. Remove the banjo bolt and sealing washers (B, **Figure 49**) securing the brake hose to the master cylinder.

10. Place the loose end of the brake hose in a reclosable plastic bag to prevent the entry of moisture and debris. Tie the loose end of the hose up to the handlebar.

11. Remove the screw securing the right side switch together and separate the switch (A, **Figure 50**).

12. Remove the T27 Torx bolts and washers (B, **Figure 50**) securing the clamp and master cylinder to the handlebar.

13. Remove the master cylinder assembly (C, **Figure 49**) from the handlebar.

14. Drain any residual brake fluid from the master cylinder and dispose of properly.

15. If the master cylinder assembly is not going to be serviced, reinstall the clamp and Torx bolts to the master cylinder. Place the assembly in a reclosable plastic bag to protect it from foreign matter.

Installation

1. If not in place, insert the 5/32 in. (4 mm) thick spacer (A, **Figure 49**) between the brake lever and lever bracket. Make sure the spacer stays in place during the following steps.

2. Position the front master cylinder onto the handlebar. Align the master cylinder notch (A, **Figure**

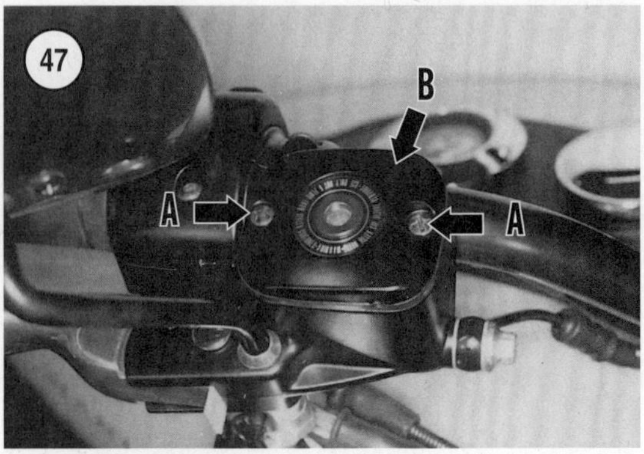

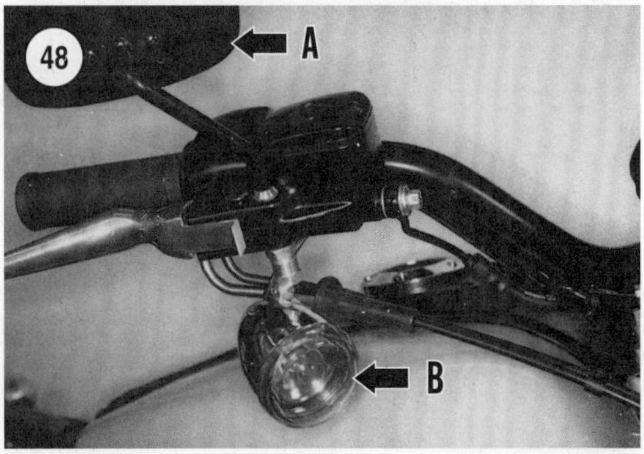

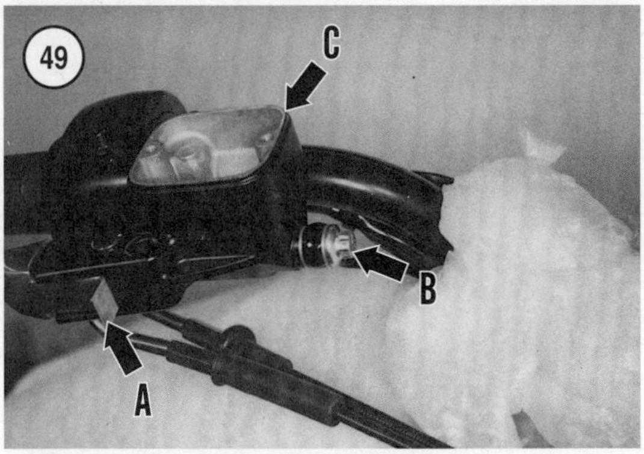

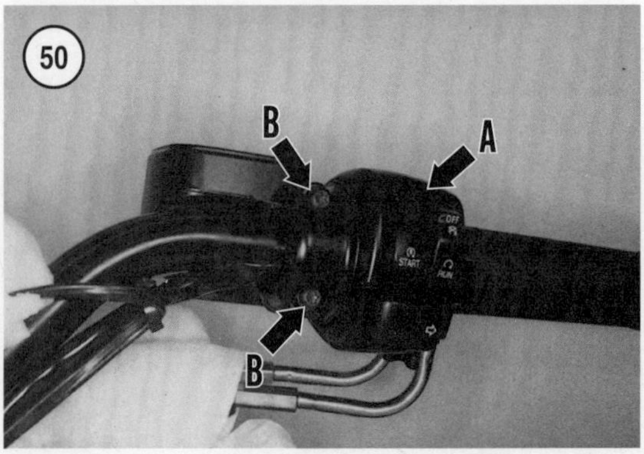

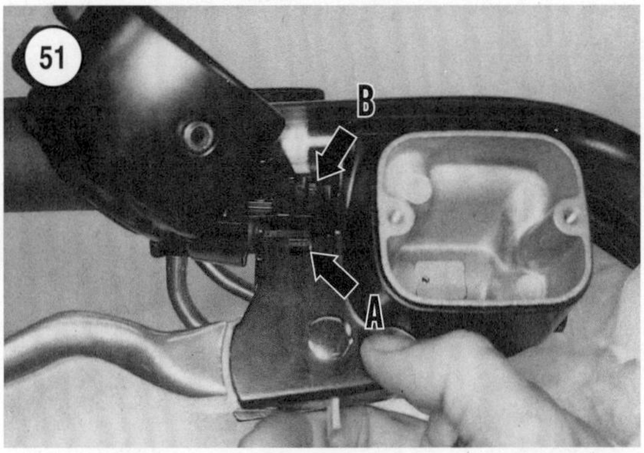

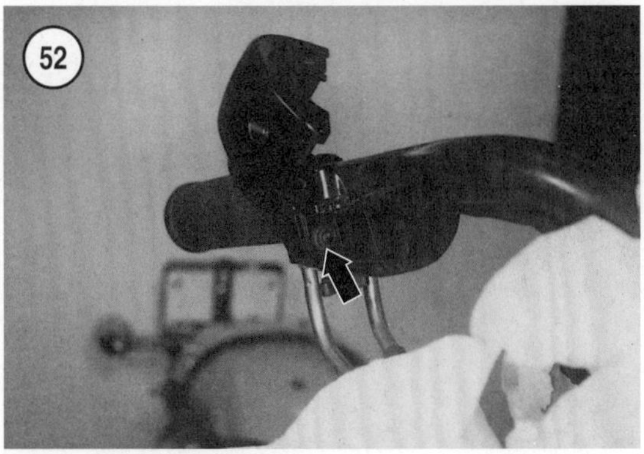

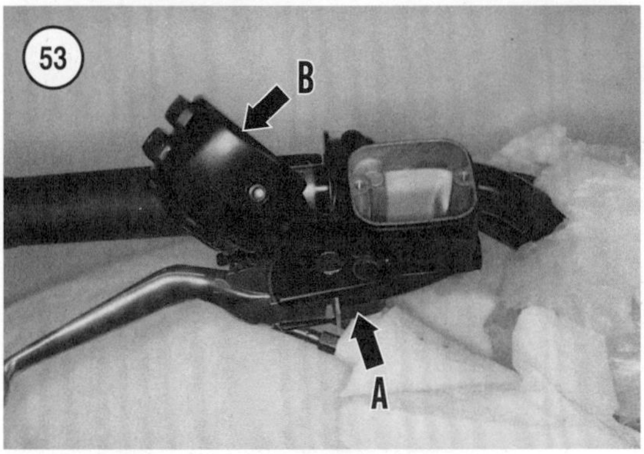

51) with the locating tab (B, **Figure 51**) on the lower portion of the right side switch.

CAUTION

*Do not damage the front brake light switch and rubber boot (**Figure 52**) when installing the master cylinder in Step 3.*

3. Push the master cylinder all the way onto the handlebar (A, **Figure 53**), hold it in this position and install the upper portion of the right side switch (B, **Figure 53**) into place. Install the switch's clamping screw and tighten securely.
4. Position the clamp and install the clamping Torx bolts and washers (B, **Figure 50**). Tighten the upper mounting bolt first, then the lower bolt. Tighten the bolts to the specification in **Table 2**.
5. Apply clean DOT 5 brake fluid to the rubber portions of the new sealing washers prior to installation.
6. Install new sealing washers and the banjo bolt (B, **Figure 49**) securing the brake hose to the master cylinder. Tighten the banjo bolt to the specification in **Table 2**.
7. Remove the spacer (A, **Figure 49**) from the brake lever.
8. On models so equipped, install the front turn signal assembly (B, **Figure 48**) onto the master cylinder. Aim the lens in the same direction as the one on the left side.
9. Install the mirror (A, **Figure 48**) onto the master cylinder. Correctly adjust the mirror.
10. On models so equipped, install the windshield or front fairing.
11. Temporarily install the diaphragm and top cover (B, **Figure 47**) onto the reservoir. Tighten the screws finger-tight at this time.
12. Refill the master cylinder reservoir and bleed the brake system as described under *Bleeding the System* in this chapter.

12

Disassembly

Refer to **Figure 54**.

1. Store the master cylinder components in a divided container, such as a restaurant-size egg carton, to help maintain their correct alignment position.
2. If still in place, remove the screws securing the top cover. Remove the top cover and the diaphragm from the master cylinder.
3. Remove the master cylinder assembly as described in this chapter.
4. Remove the snap ring (A, **Figure 55**) and pivot pin securing the hand lever to the master cylinder. Remove the hand lever (B, **Figure 55**).
5. Remove the retainer (A, **Figure 56**) and the rubber boot (B, **Figure 56**) from the area where the hand lever actuates the piston assembly.
6. Remove the piston assembly (**Figure 57**) and the spring.

54

FRONT MASTER CYLINDER

1. Screw
2. Sight glass
3. Top cover
4. Diaphragm
5. Pivot pin
6. T27 Torx screw
7. Washer
8. Clamp
9. Body
10. Piston assembly
11. Bushing
12. Hand lever
13. Snap ring
14. Washer
15. Acorn nut

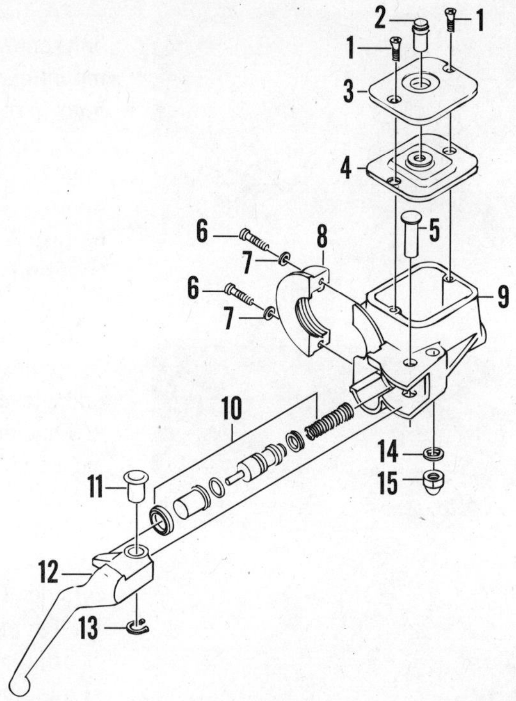

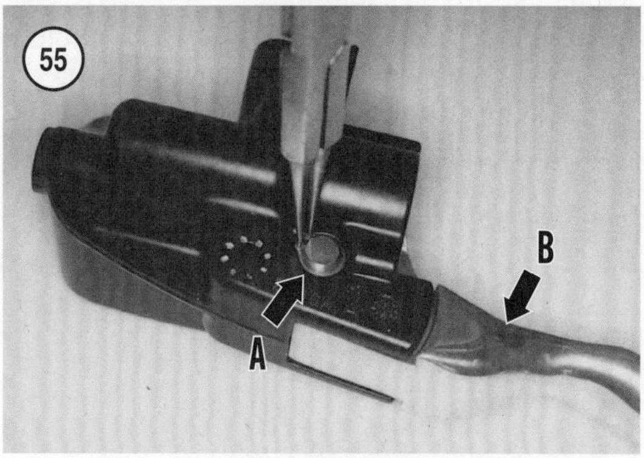

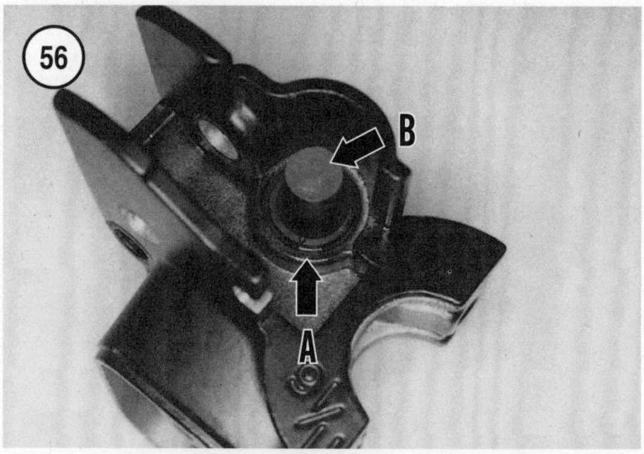

7. Inspect all parts as described in this section.

Inspection

Replace worn or damage parts as described in this section. It is recommended that a new piston kit assembly be installed every time the master cylinder is disassembled.

1. Clean all parts in isopropyl alcohol or clean DOT5 brake fluid. Inspect the body cylinder bore surface for signs of wear and damage. If less than

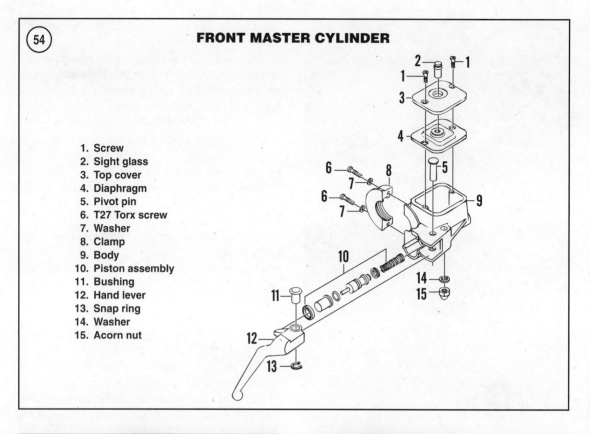

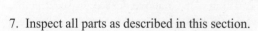

58

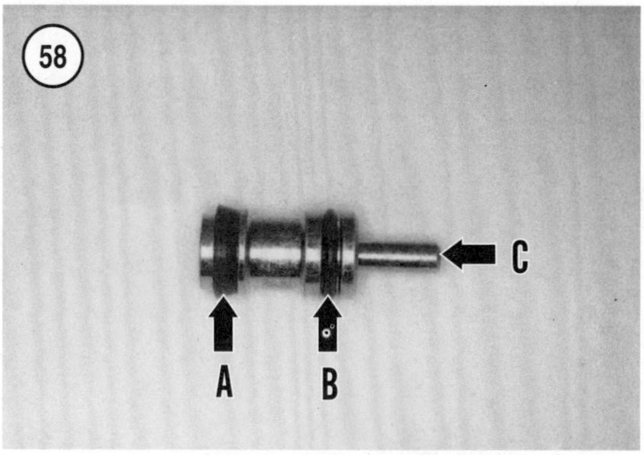

59

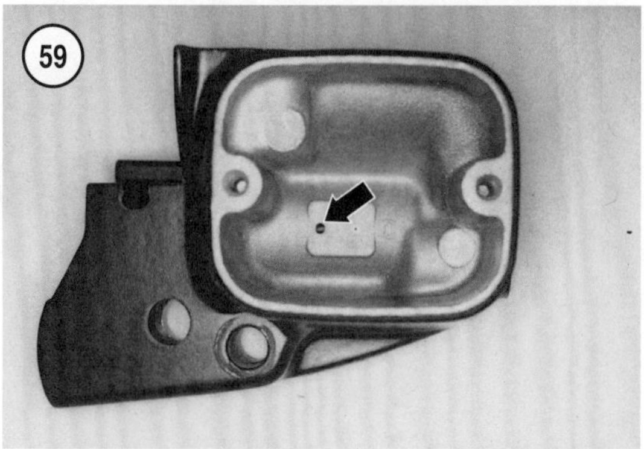

60

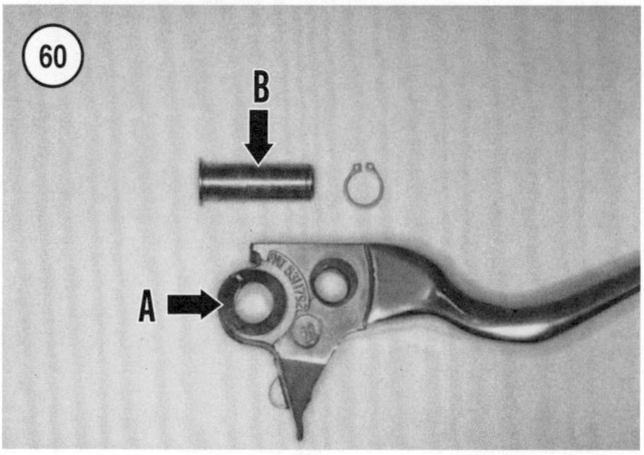

61

62

perfect, replace the master cylinder assembly. The body cannot be replaced separately.

2. Inspect the piston cup (A, **Figure 58**) and O-ring (B) for signs of wear and damage.

3. Make sure the fluid passage (**Figure 59**) in the bottom of the master cylinder reservoir is clear. Clean out if necessary.

4. Inspect the piston contact surface for signs of wear and damage.

5. Check the end of the piston (C, **Figure 58**) for wear caused by the hand lever.

6. Check the hand lever pivot lugs in the master cylinder body for cracks or elongation.

7. Inspect the hand lever pivot hole and bushing (A, **Figure 60**) and the pivot pin (B) for wear, cracks or elongation.

8. Inspect the piston cap and retainer (**Figure 61**) for wear or damage.

9. Inspect the threads in the bore for the banjo bolt. If worn or damaged, clean out with a thread tap or replace the master cylinder assembly.

10. Check the top cover and diaphragm for damage and deterioration.

11. If necessary, separate the cover from the diaphragm as follows:

   a. Pull straight up on the sight glass (**Figure 62**) and remove it from the cover and diaphragm.
   b. Separate the diaphragm from the cover.
   c. The trim plate may separate from the cover.

Assembly

NOTE

If installing a new piston assembly, coat all parts with the lubricant provided in the new H-D parts kit instead of using DOT5 brake fluid. If install-

12

ing existing parts, coat them with DOT5 brake fluid.

NOTE
Be sure to purchase the correct new piston parts kit for the specific motorcycle being worked on. The piston bore diameter is larger on models equipped with dual front discs. The parts for the two different master cylinders are not interchangeable.

NOTE
The cover and diaphragm must be assembled as follows. If the sight glass is not installed correctly through the cover and diaphragm neck, brake fluid will leak past these components.

1. If disassembled, assemble the cover and the diaphragm as follows:
   a. If removed, install the trim plate (**Figure 63**) onto the cover.
   b. Insert the neck of the diaphragm into the cover. Press it in until it seats correctly and the outer edges are aligned with the cover.
   c. Push the sight glass (**Figure 62**) straight down through the cover and the neck of the diaphragm (**Figure 64**) until it snaps into place. The sight glass must lock these two parts together to avoid a brake fluid leak.
2. Soak the *new* cup and O-ring and piston assembly in clean DOT5 brake fluid for at least 15 minutes to make them pliable. Coat the inside of the cylinder bore with clean brake fluid prior to the assembly of parts.

CAUTION
When installing the piston assembly, do not allow the cup to turn inside out as it will be damaged and allow brake fluid leakage within the cylinder bore.

3A. On 1999 and 2000 models, position the flared end of the spring so it enters the master cylinder first.
3B. On 2001 models, position the metal tab end of the spring (**Figure 65**) so it enters the master cylinder first.
4. Install the spring and piston assembly into the cylinder (**Figure 66**). Push them in until they bottom in the cylinder (**Figure 57**).
5. Position the retainer with the flat side going on first and install the piston cap and retainer onto the piston end.

63

64

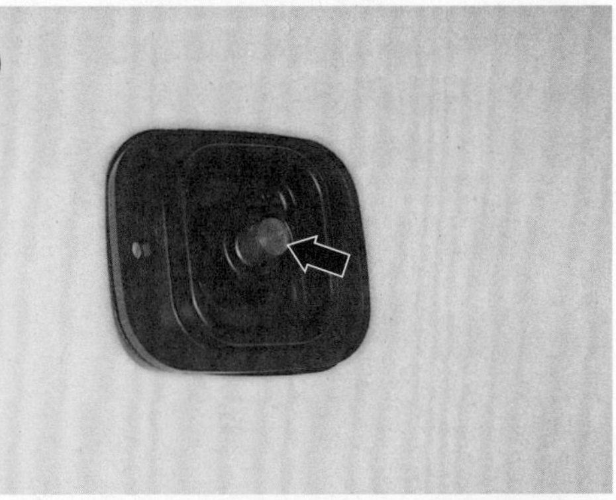

65

66

67

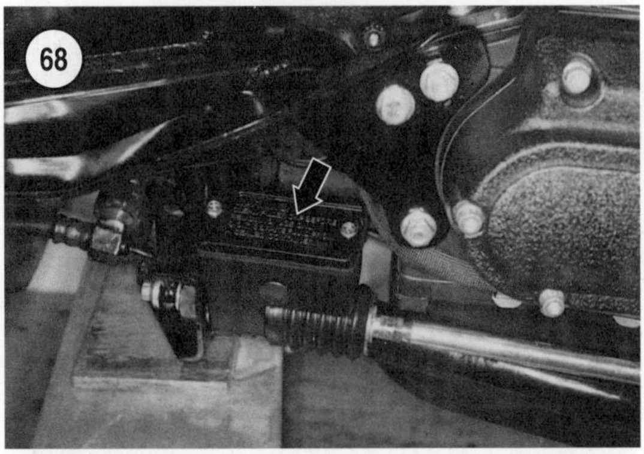
68

69

6. Push down on the piston cap (**Figure 67**), hold it there and press the retainer down until it correctly seats in the cylinder groove (A, **Figure 56**).
7. Make sure the bushing is in place in the hand lever pivot area.
8. Install the hand lever (B, **Figure 55**) into the master cylinder, install the pivot pin and secure it with the snap ring. Make sure the snap ring is correctly seated in the pivot pin groove (A, **Figure 55**).
9. Slowly apply the lever to make sure it pivots freely.
10. Install the master cylinder as described in this chapter.

REAR BRAKE PAD REPLACEMENT (1999 MODELS)

There is no recommended mileage interval for changing the brake pads. Pad wear depends greatly on riding habits and conditions. Frequently check the pads for wear. After removal, measure the thickness of each brake pad with a vernier caliper or ruler and compare to the dimensions in **Table 1**.

To maintain an even brake pressure on the disc, always replace both pads in the caliper at the same time.

CAUTION
Check the pads more frequently when the lining approaches the pad metal backing plate. If pad wear happens to be uneven for some reason, the backing plate may come in contact with the disc and cause damage.

1. Read the *Brake Service* information in this chapter.
2. Park the motorcycle on level ground.
3. Tie the end of the brake pedal up to the frame. If the brake pedal is inadvertently applied, this will prevent the piston from being forced out of the cylinder.
4. On models so equipped, remove the right side saddlebag.
5. Clean the top of the master cylinder of all debris.
6. Remove the screws securing the cover (**Figure 68**) and remove the cover and diaphragm.
7. Use a shop syringe and remove about 50 percent of the brake fluid from the reservoir. This will prevent the master cylinder from overflowing when the pistons are compressed for reinstallation. Do *not* drain more than 50 percent of the brake fluid or air will enter the system. Discard the brake fluid.

CAUTION
Do not allow the master cylinder to overflow when performing Step 7. Wash brake fluid off any painted, plated or plastic surfaces immediately, as it will damage most surfaces it contacts. Use soapy water and rinse completely.

8. Loosen both pad pin bolts (A, **Figure 69**).

CAUTION
The brake disc is thin and easily damaged. When pushing against the disc in the following step, support the disc

adjacent to the caliper to prevent damage.

9. Hold the caliper body from the outside and push it toward the brake disc. This will push the piston into the caliper bore to make room for the new brake pads. Constantly check the reservoir to make sure brake fluid does not overflow. Remove fluid, if necessary, prior to it overflowing. Install the diaphragm and cover. Tighten the screws finger-tight.
10. Remove the two caliper pin bolts (A, **Figure 69**) and lift the caliper (B, **Figure 69**) off the mounting bracket. Do not disconnect the brake hose from the caliper. Support the caliper with a piece of heavy wire.
11. Lift and then pull the retainer clip (**Figure 70**) over the mounting bracket and remove it.

NOTE
If the pads are to be reused, mark them so they will be reinstalled in their original locations.

12. Slide the outboard brake pad (A, **Figure 71**) off the mounting bracket.
13. Slide the inboard brake pad (B, **Figure 71**) toward the wheel and off the mounting bracket.
14. Remove both pad shims (**Figure 72**) from the mounting bracket.
15. Check the brake pads for wear or damage. Measure the thickness of the brake pad friction material. Replace the brake pads if they are worn to the service limit listed in **Table 1**. Replace both pads as a set.
16. Clean the pad shims and check for cracks or damage.
17. Clean the pad shim mounting areas on the mounting bracket.
18. Check the retainer clip for rust, cracks or other damage.
19. Inspect the caliper pin bolts for cracks, corrosion or other damage. Replace if necessary.
20. Check the piston dust boot (**Figure 73**) for damage. Remove and overhaul the caliper if the boot is swollen or damaged or if brake fluid is leaking from the caliper. Refer to *Rear Brake Caliper (1999 Models)* in this chapter.
21. Check the brake disc for wear.
22. Install the pad shims so that their retaining loops face against the outer caliper mounting bracket rails, as shown in **Figure 72**.

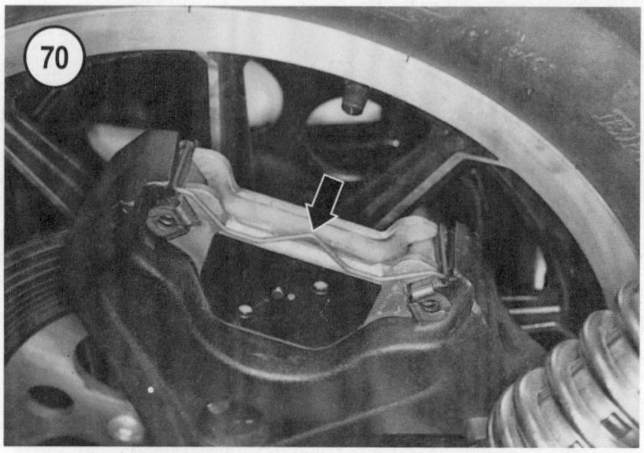
70

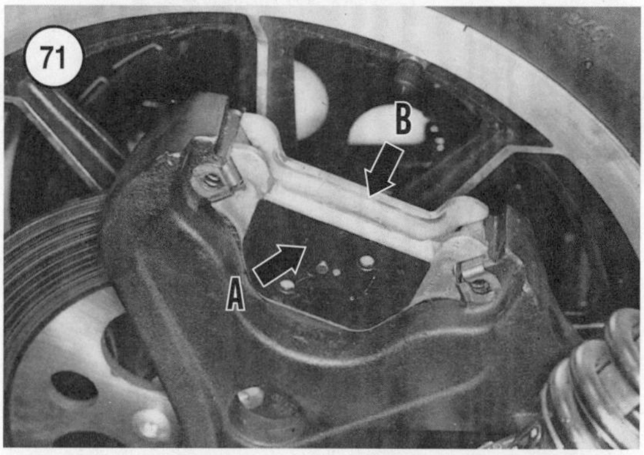

71

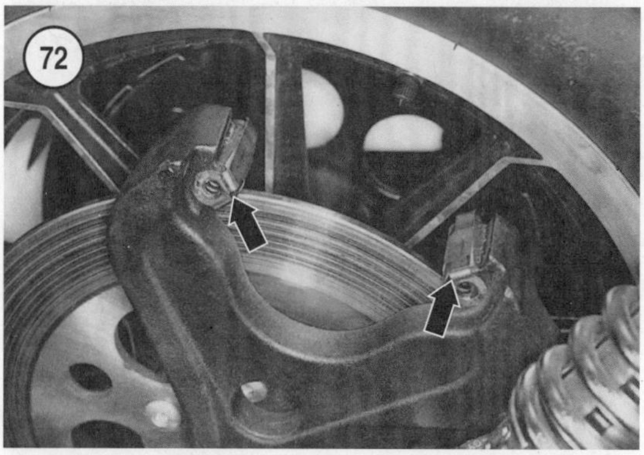
72

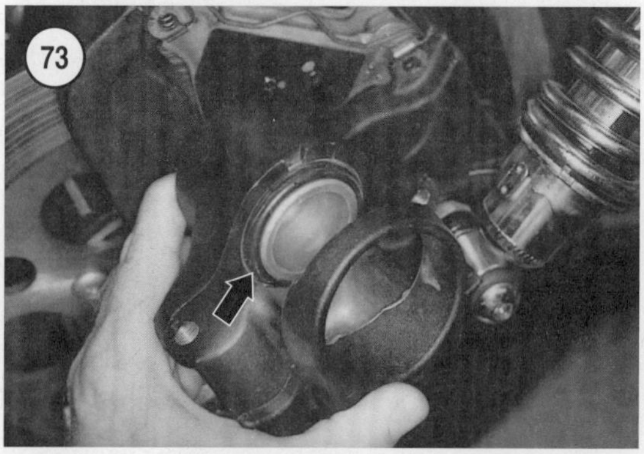
73

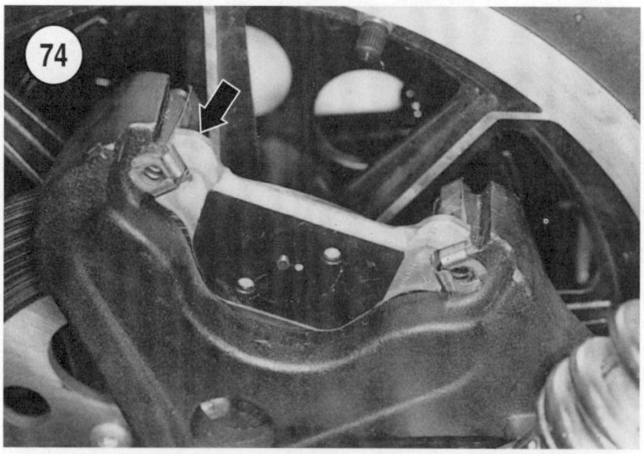

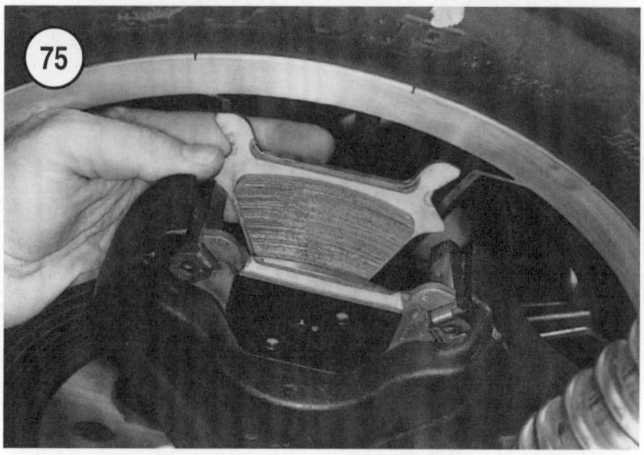

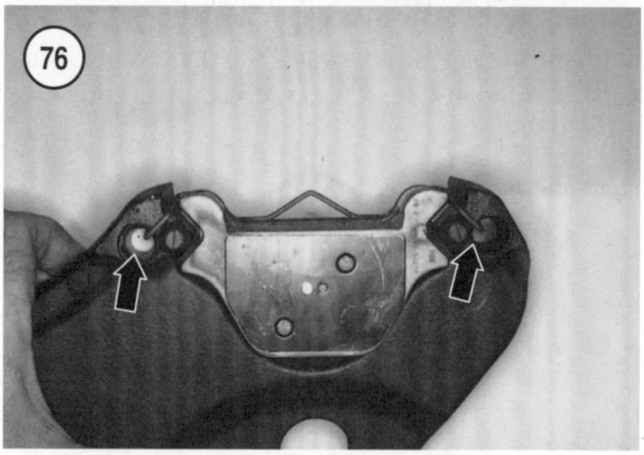

23. Slide the outboard brake pad (**Figure 74**) over the pad shims and against the outer brake disc surface.

24. Slide the inboard brake pad (**Figure 75**) over the pad shims and against the inner brake disc surface.

25. Check that the pad shims did not move out of position.

NOTE

***Figure 76** shows the caliper mounting bracket removed to better illustrate the step.*

26. Insert the retainer clip into the two large holes (**Figure 76**) in the back of the caliper mounting bracket. Then swing the retainer clip over the top of the brake pads and snap it in place against the outer brake pad (**Figure 70**).

CAUTION

*The brake pads must seat against both pad shims evenly (**Figure 70**). If not, the rear brake will drag, causing uneven pad wear and caliper bracket damage.*

NOTE

When installing the caliper over the brake pads, do not dislodge the brake pads and pad shims.

27. Slide the caliper (B, **Figure 69**) over the brake pads. Install the two pad pin bolts (A, **Figure 69**) and tighten to the specificationin **Table 2**.

28. Check to make sure there is sufficient brake fluid in the master cylinder reservoir. Top off if necessary.

29. Untie the brake pedal from the frame and pump the rear brake pedal to reposition the brake pads against the brake disc. Roll the motorcycle back and forth and continue to pump the brake pedal as many times as it takes to refill the cylinder in the caliper and correctly locate the brake pads against the disc.

NOTE

To control the flow of hydraulic fluid, punch a small hole into the seal of a new container of hydraulic (brake) fluid next to the edge of the pour spout. This will help eliminate fluid spillage, especially while adding fluid to the very small reservoir.

WARNING

Use brake fluid clearly marked DOT 5 from a sealed container. Other types may vaporize and cause brake failure. Always use the same brand name; do not intermix, as many brands are not compatible. Do not intermix DOT 3, DOT4 or DOT5.1 brake fluid, as it can cause brake component damage, leading to brake system failure.

30. Refill the master cylinder reservoir, if necessary, to maintain the correct fluid level as indicated on the side of the reservoir. Install the diaphragm

12

and the top cover. Tighten the screws to the specification in **Table 2**.

WARNING
Do not ride the motorcycle until the rear brake is operating correctly with full hydraulic advantage. If necessary, bleed the brake as described in this chapter.

31. On models so equipped, install the right side saddlebag.

REAR BRAKE PAD REPLACEMENT (2000-2001 MODELS)

There is no recommended mileage interval for changing the brake pads. Pad wear depends greatly on riding habits and conditions. Frequently check the pads for wear. Increase the inspection interval when the wear indicator reaches the edge of the brake disc. After removal, measure the thickness of each brake pad with a vernier caliper or ruler and compare to the dimensions listed in **Table 1**.

To maintain an even brake pressure on the disc, always replace both pads in the caliper at the same time. Do not disconnect the hydraulic brake hose from the brake caliper for brake pad replacement, disconnect the hose only if the caliper assembly is going to be removed.

CAUTION
Check the pads more frequently when the lining approaches the pad metal backing plate. If pad wear happens to be uneven for some reason, the backing plate may come in contact with the disc and cause damage.

1. Read the *Brake Service* section in this chapter.
2. Park the motorcycle on level ground.
3. Tie the end of the brake pedal to the frame. If the brake pedal is inadvertently applied, this will prevent the pistons from being forced out of the cylinders.
4. On models so equipped, remove the right side saddlebag.
5. Clean the top of the master cylinder of all debris.
6. Remove the screws securing the cover and remove the cover (**Figure 68**) and diaphragm.
7. Use a shop syringe and remove about 50 percent of the brake fluid from the reservoir. This will prevent the master cylinder from overflowing when the pistons are compressed for reinstallation. Do *not* drain more than 50 percent of the brake fluid or air will enter the system. Discard the brake fluid.

77

78

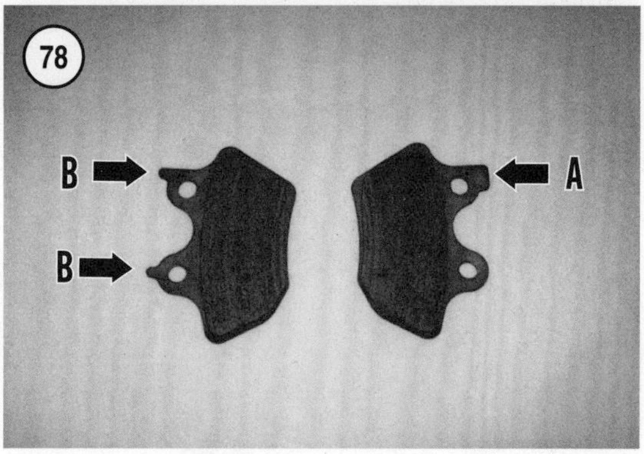

CAUTION
Do not allow the master cylinder to overflow when performing Step 7. Wash brake fluid off any painted, plated or plastic surfaces immediately, as it will damage most surfaces it contacts. Use soapy water and rinse completely.

8. Loosen the pad pin bolts (**Figure 77**).

CAUTION
The brake disc is thin and easily damaged. When pushing against the disc in the following step, support the disc adjacent to the caliper to prevent damage.

9. Hold the caliper body from the outside and push it toward the brake disc. This will push the outer pistons into the caliper bores to make room for the new brake pads. Constantly check the reservoir to make sure brake fluid does not overflow. Remove fluid, if

necessary, prior to it overflowing. Install the diaphragm and cover. Tighten the screws finger-tight.

10. Remove the pad pin bolts (**Figure 77**).

11. Remove the inboard and outboard brake pads from the caliper.

12. Check the brake pads for wear or damage. Measure the thickness of the brake pad friction material. Replace the brake pads if they are worn to the service limit listed in **Table 1**.

13. Carefully remove any rust or corrosion from the disc.

14. Thoroughly clean the pad pins of any corrosion or debris.

15. Check the friction surface of the new pads for any debris or manufacturing residue. If necessary, clean off with an aerosol brake cleaner.

NOTE
When purchasing new pads, check with the dealer to make sure the friction compound of the new pad is compatible with the disc material. Remove any roughness from the backs of the new pads with a fine-cut file, then thoroughly clean off.

NOTE
*The brake pads are not symmetrical. The pad with one tab (A, **Figure 78**) must be installed on the outboard side. The pad with two tabs (B, **Figure 78**) must be installed on the inboard side of the caliper.*

16. Install the outboard pad (**Figure 79**) into the caliper.

17. Hold the pad in place and install the pad pin bolts (**Figure 80**) part way in to hold the outboard pad in place.

18. Install the inboard pad (**Figure 81**) into the caliper.

19. Push the pad pin bolts through the inboard pad (**Figure 77**) and tighten to the specification in **Table 2**.

20. Check to make sure there is sufficient brake fluid in the master cylinder reservoir. Top off if necessary.

21. Untie the brake pedal from the frame and pump the rear brake pedal to reposition the brake pads against the brake disc. Roll the motorcycle back and forth and continue to pump the brake pedal as many times as it takes to refill the cylinders in the calipers and correctly locate the brake pads against the disc.

NOTE
To control the flow of hydraulic fluid, punch a small hole into the seal of a new container of hydraulic (brake) fluid next to the edge of the pour spout. This will help eliminate fluid spillage, especially while adding fluid to the very small reservoir.

WARNING
Use brake fluid clearly marked DOT 5 from a sealed container. Other types

may vaporize and cause brake failure. Always use the same brand name; do not intermix, as many brands are not compatible. Do not intermix DOT 3, DOT 4 or DOT 5.1 brake fluid, as it can cause brake component damage leading to brake system failure.

22. Refill the master cylinder reservoir, if necessary, to maintain the correct fluid level as indicated on the side of the reservoir. Install the diaphragm and the top cover. Tighten the screws to the specification in **Table 2**.

WARNING
Do not ride the motorcycle until the rear brake is operating correctly with full hydraulic advantage. If necessary, bleed the brake as described in this chapter.

REAR BRAKE CALIPER (1999 MODELS)

Removal/Installation

1. If the caliper assembly is going to be disassembled for service, perform the following:

NOTE
By performing Steps 1a-1e, compressed air may not be necessary for piston removal during caliper disassembly.

a. Remove the caliper pad pin bolts (A, **Figure 82**) and remove the caliper from the caliper mounting bracket and the brake pads.
b. Insert a small screwdriver into the notched groove machined in the bottom of the piston bore (A, **Figure 83**). Then pry the retaining ring (A, **Figure 83**) out of the caliper body.
c. Wrap a large cloth around the brake caliper.
d. Hold the caliper away from the piston/brake pad area.
e. Operate the rear brake pedal to force the piston part way out of the caliper. Do not completely remove the piston until after it is removed for disassembly. Leaving the piston partially in the bore helps prevent brake fluid from spilling out.

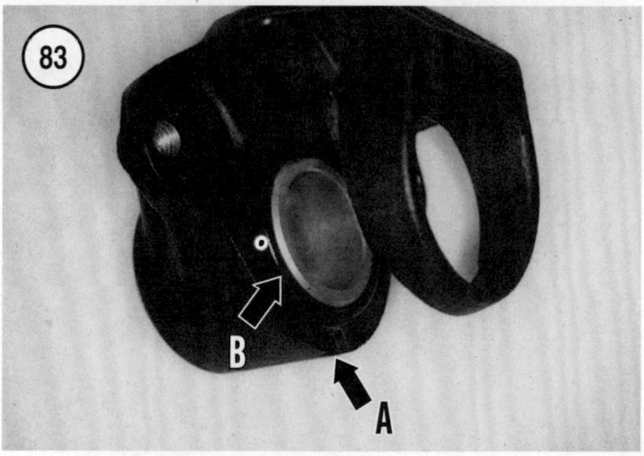

NOTE
*If the piston did not come out, remove it as described under **Disassembly** in this section.*

2. Remove the banjo bolt (B, **Figure 82**) and sealing washers attaching the brake hose to the caliper assembly.
3. To remove the rear caliper mounting bracket, refer to *Rear Wheel Removal* in Chapter Eleven.
4. Install by reversing these removal steps while noting the following:
   a. If removed, install the piston assembly as described in this chapter.
   b. If removed, install the brake pads as described in this chapter.
   c. Carefully install the caliper assembly onto the brake pads.
   d. Install the bolts (A, **Figure 82**) securing the brake caliper assembly and tighten to the torque specifications listed in **Table 2**.
   e. Apply clean DOT 5 brake fluid to the rubber portions of the new sealing washers prior to installation.

84 **REAR BRAKE CALIPER (1999)**

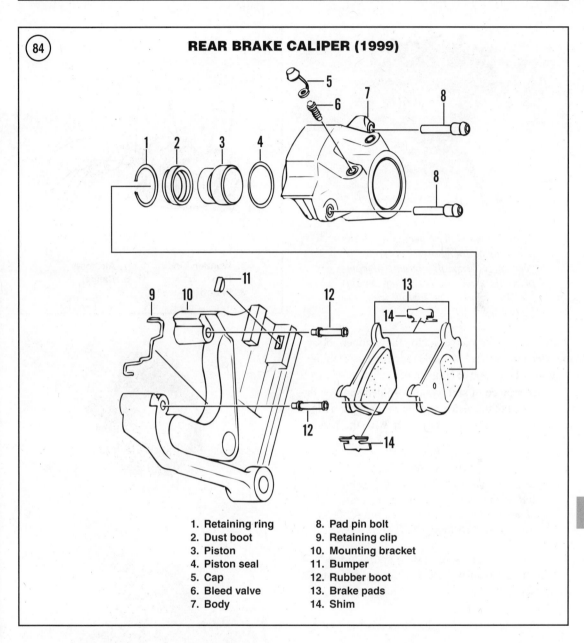

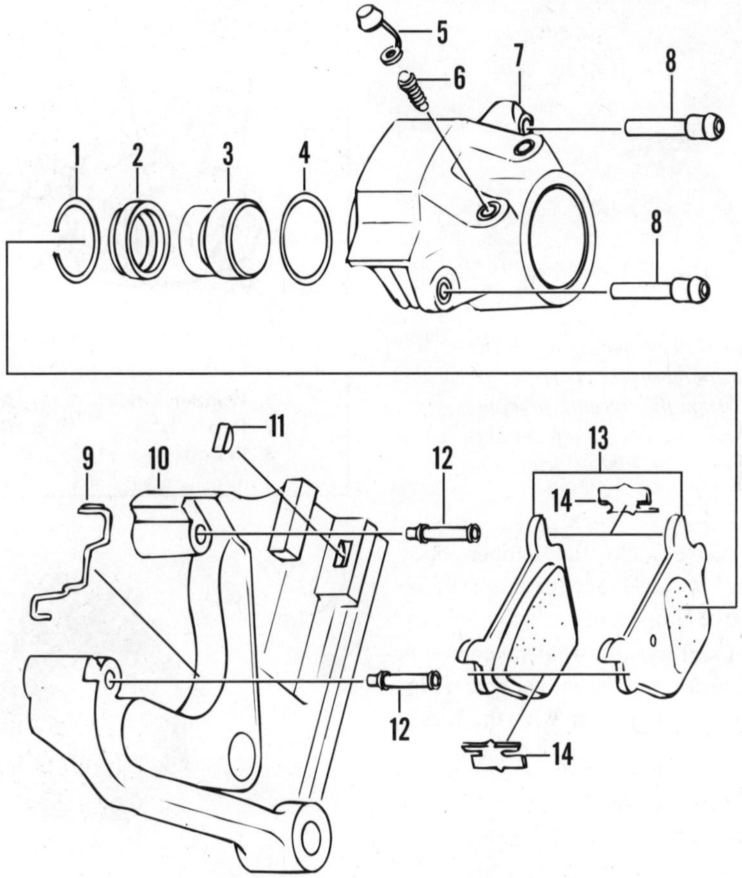

1. Retaining ring
2. Dust boot
3. Piston
4. Piston seal
5. Cap
6. Bleed valve
7. Body
8. Pad pin bolt
9. Retaining clip
10. Mounting bracket
11. Bumper
12. Rubber boot
13. Brake pads
14. Shim

f. Install a new sealing washer on each side of the brake hose fitting and install the banjo bolt (B, **Figure 82**). Tighten the banjo bolt to the specification in **Table 2**.

g. Bleed the brake as described under *Bleeding the System* in this chapter.

WARNING
Do not ride the motorcycle until the rear brake is operating correctly with full hydraulic advantage. If necessary, bleed the brake as described in this chapter.

Disassembly

Refer to **Figure 84**.

1. Remove the brake caliper as described in this chapter.

NOTE
If the piston was partially forced out of the caliper body during removal,

85

Steps 2-4 may not be necessary. If the piston or caliper bore is corroded or very dirty, a small amount of compressed air may be necessary to completely remove the piston from the body bore.

2. Insert a screwdriver into the caliper body notched groove (A, **Figure 83**) and pry the retaining ring out of the groove (**Figure 85**).
3. Place a piece of soft wood or folded shop cloth over the end of the piston and the caliper body (**Figure 86**). Turn this assembly over with the piston facing down.

WARNING
Compressed air will force the piston out of the caliper bodies under considerable force. Do not block the piston by hand, as injury will result.

4. Apply the air pressure in short spurts to the hydraulic fluid passageway and force out the piston. Use a service station air hose if compressed air is not available.
5. Remove the piston and dust boot assembly (**Figure 87**).
6. Remove the piston seal (**Figure 88**) from the groove in the caliper body.

Inspection

Service specifications for the caliper components are not available (except brake pads). Replace any worn, damaged or questionable part.

1. Clean the caliper body and piston in clean DOT 5 brake fluid or isopropyl alcohol and dry with compressed air.

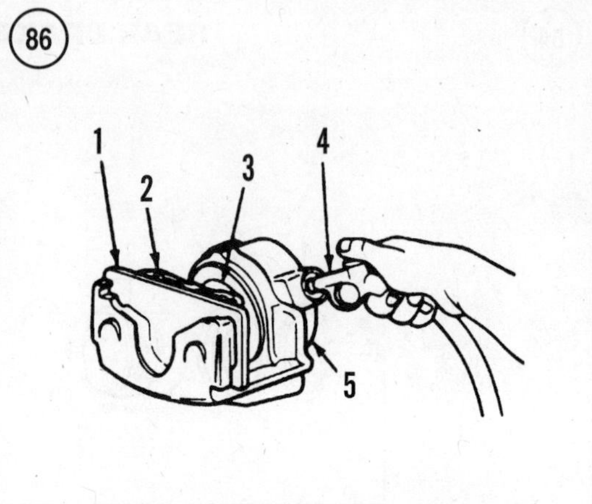

1. Wooden block
2. Rag
3. Piston
4. Air hose
5. Caliper

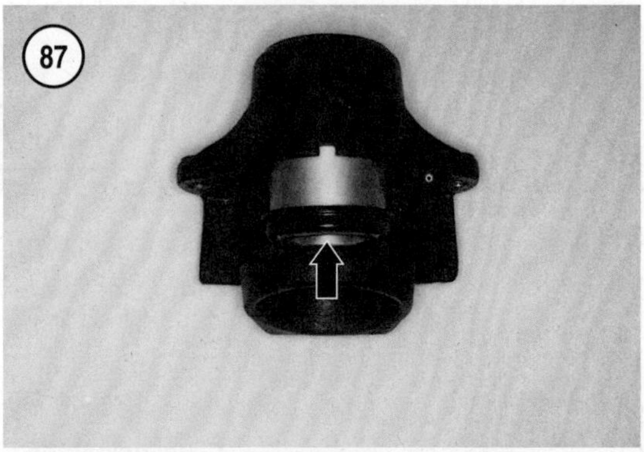

87

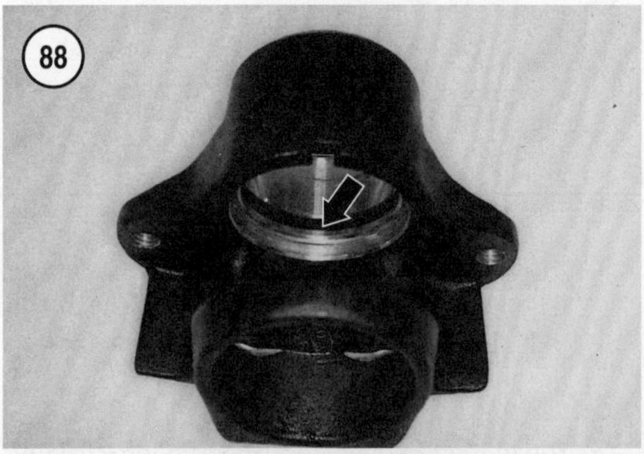

88

2. Inspect the hydraulic fluid passageway in the cylinder bore. Make sure it is clean and open. Clean with compressed air.
3. Inspect the piston and cylinder bore wall for scratches, scoring or other damage.

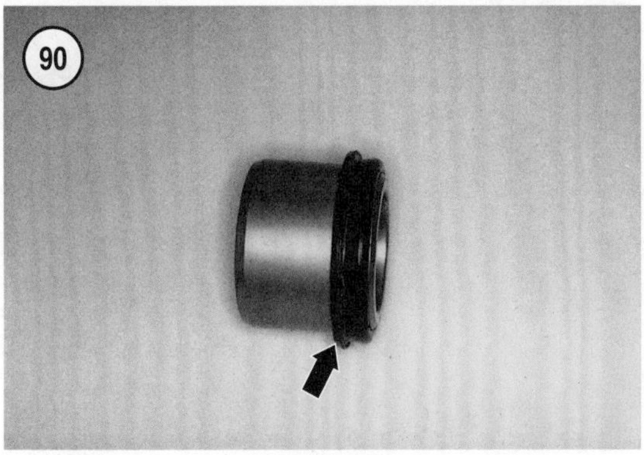

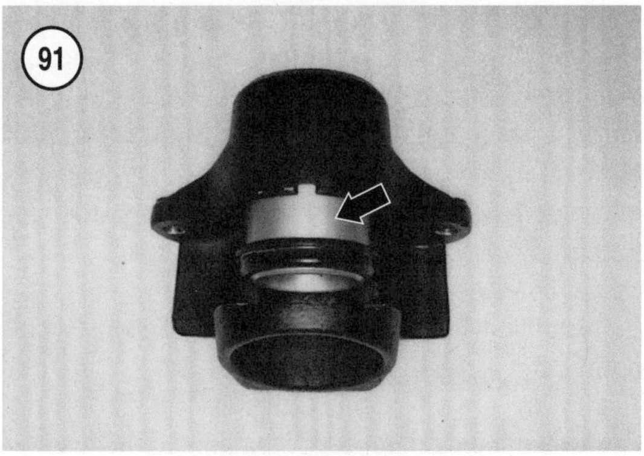

4. Make sure the hole in the bleed valve screw is clean and open. Clean with compressed air.

5. Check the pin bolts for wear or damage.

6. Replace the pad shims if corroded or damaged.

7. Check the brake pads for excessive wear or damage. Measure the thickness of the brake pad friction material. Replace the brake pads if they are worn to the service limit dimension listed in **Table 1**.

8. Check all of the rubber parts for cracks, wear or deterioration.

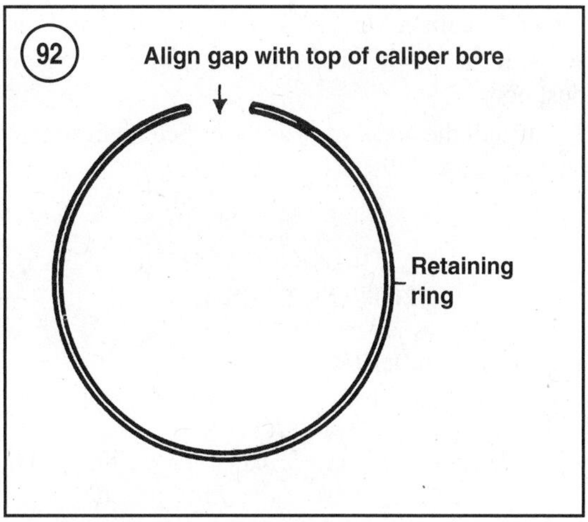

Assembly

1. The following parts are included in a H-D rebuild kit (part No. 43946-86): piston seal (A, **Figure 89**), piston (B), dust boot (C) and retaining ring (D).

NOTE
Never reuse an old dust boot or piston seal. Minor damage or age deterioration can make the boot and seal useless.

2. Soak the new dust and piston seal in clean DOT5 brake fluid.
3. Make sure the retaining ring, piston and caliper bore are thoroughly clean.
4. Install the piston seal (**Figure 88**) into the caliper body groove.
5. Before installing the piston in the caliper bore, iInstall the piston dust boot on the piston as follows:
   a. Place the piston on the workbench with its open side facing up.
   b. Align the piston dust boot with the piston so that the shoulder on the dust boot faces up.
   c. Slide the dust boot over the piston until the inner lip on the dust boot seats in the piston groove (**Figure 90**).
6. Coat the piston and caliper bore with DOT 5 brake fluid.
7. Align the piston with the caliper bore so that its open end faces out (**Figure 91**), then push the piston in until it bottoms out.
8. Seat the piston dust boot (B, **Figure 83**) into the caliper bore.
9. Find the retaining ring groove in the end of the caliper bore. Then install the retaining ring (**Figure 85**) so that the gap in the ring (**Figure 92**) is at the

12

top of the caliper bore. Make sure the retaining ring seats in the groove and pushes against the piston dust boot.

10. Install the brake pads as described in this chapter.

REAR BRAKE CALIPER (2000-ON MODELS)

Removal/Installation

CAUTION
Do not spill any brake fluid on the rear wheel. Wash brake fluid off any painted, plated or plastic surfaces immediately, as it will damage most surfaces it contacts. Use soapy water and rinse completely.

1. If the caliper assembly is going to be disassembled for service, perform the following:

NOTE
By performing Steps 1b and 1c, compressed air may not be necessary for piston removal during caliper disassembly.

a. Remove the brake pads as described in this chapter.

CAUTION
Do not allow the pistons to travel out far enough to come in contact with the brake disc. If this happens the pistons may scratch or gouge the disc during caliper removal.

b. Slowly apply the brake lever to push the pistons part way out of caliper assembly for ease of removal during caliper service.
c. Loosen the three body mounting bolts (A, **Figure 93**).
d. Loosen the brake hose banjo bolt (B, **Figure 93**).

2. Remove the banjo bolt and sealing washers (B, **Figure 93**) attaching the brake hose to the caliper assembly.
3. Place the loose end of the brake hose in a reclosable plastic bag to prevent the entry of debris and prevent any residual brake fluid from leaking out.

93

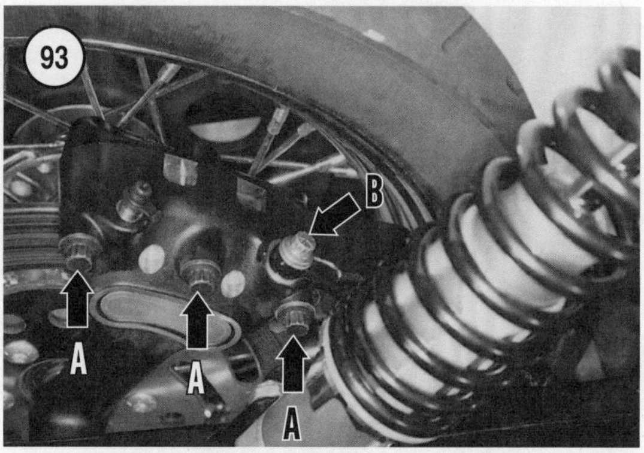

94

4. Refer to *Rear Wheel Removal/Installation* in Chapter Nine and follow the procedure until the rear axle is removed sufficiently to allow removal of the rear caliper assembly as shown in **Figure 94**. After removal of the caliper assembly, push the rear axle back into place and install the nut on the other side.
5. If necessary, disassemble and service the caliper assembly as described in this chapter.
6. Install by reversing these removal steps while noting the following:
   a. Carefully install the caliper assembly onto the disc, being careful not to damage the leading edge of the brake pads.
   b. Refer to Chapter Nine and complete the installation of the rear axle.
   c. Apply clean DOT5 brake fluid to the rubber portions of the *new* sealing washers prior to installation.
   d. Install a *new* sealing washer on each side of the brake hose fitting and install the banjo bolt (B, **Figure 93**). Tighten the banjo bolt to the specification in **Table 2**.
   e. If disassembled, tighten the three caliper body bolts (A, **Figure 93**) to the specification in **Table 2**.

(95) **REAR BRAKE CALIPER (2000-ON)**

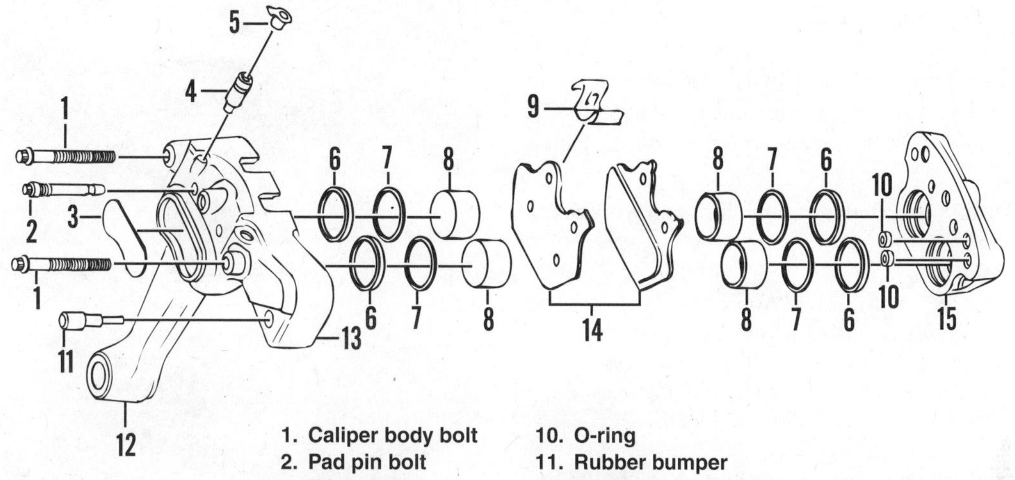

1. Caliper body bolt
2. Pad pin bolt
3. Trim plate
4. Bleed valve
5. Cap
6. Piston seal
7. Dust seal
8. Piston
9. Anti-rattle spring
10. O-ring
11. Rubber bumper
12. Bushing
13. Outboard caliper body
14. Brake pads
15. Inboard caliper body

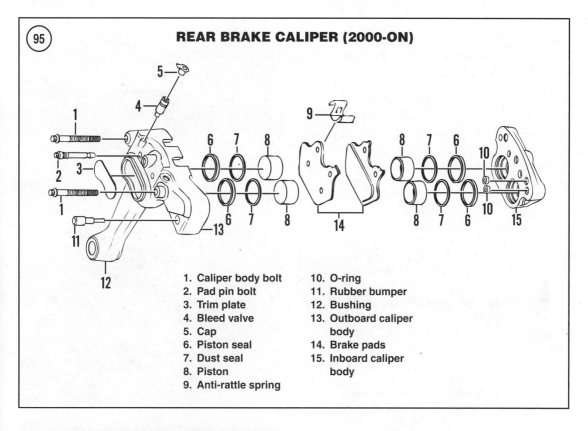

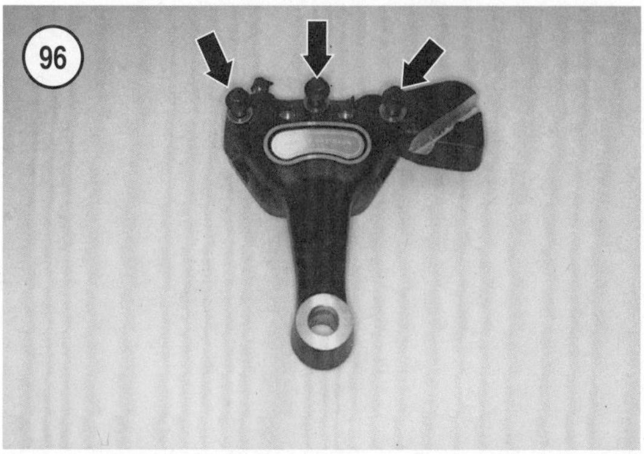

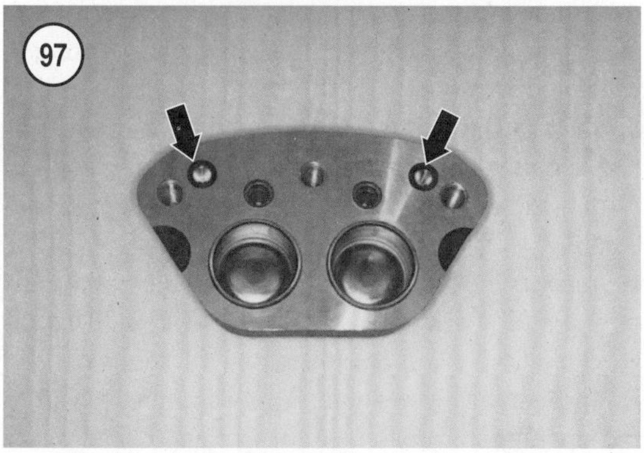

f. Bleed the brake as described under *Bleeding the System* in this chapter.

WARNING
Do not ride the motorcycle until the rear brake is operating correctly with full hydraulic advantage. If necessary, bleed the brake as described in this chapter.

Disassembly

Refer to **Figure 95**.

1. Remove the caliper and brake pads as described in this chapter.
2. Remove the three caliper body bolts (**Figure 96**) loosened during the removal procedure.
3. Separate the caliper body halves. Remove the O-ring seals (**Figure 97**). New O-ring seals must be installed every time the caliper is disassembled.

NOTE
If the pistons were partially forced out of the caliper body during removal, steps 4-6 may not be necessary. If the pistons or caliper bores are corroded

or very dirty, a small amount of compressed air may be necessary to completely remove the pistons from the body bores.

4. Place a piece of soft wood or folded shop cloth over the end of the pistons and the caliper body. Turn this assembly over with the pistons facing down.
5. Perform this step over and close to a workbench top.

WARNING
Compressed air will force the pistons out of the caliper bodies under considerable force. Do not block the piston by hand, as injury will result.

6. Apply the air pressure in short spurts to the hydraulic fluid passageway and force out the pistons. Repeat for the other caliper body half. Use a service station air hose if compressed air is not available.

CAUTION
In the following step, do not use a sharp tool to remove the dust and piston seals from the caliper cylinders. Do not damage the cylinder surface.

7. Use a piece of wood or plastic scraper and carefully push the dust seal and the piston seal in toward the caliper cylinder and out of their grooves. Remove the dust and piston seals.
8. If necessary, unscrew and remove the bleed screw (**Figure 98**).
9. Inspect the caliper assembly as described in this section.

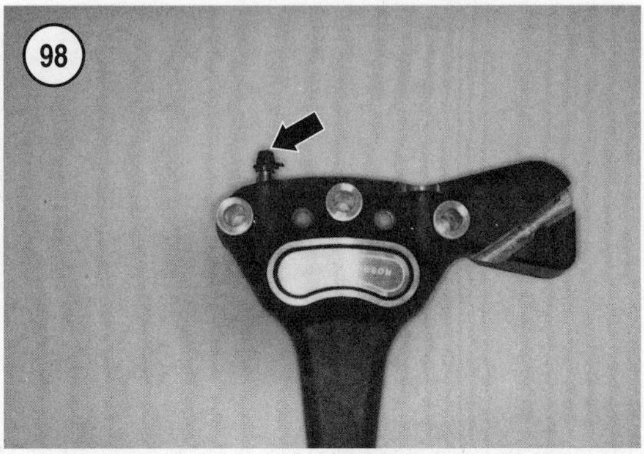

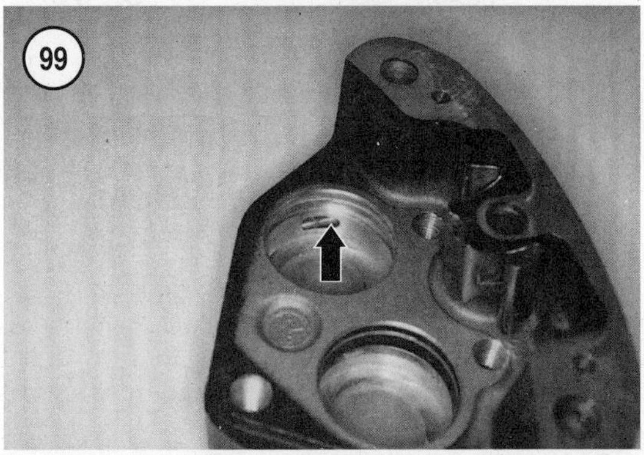

Inspection

1. Clean both caliper body halves and pistons in clean DOT5 brake fluid or isopropyl alcohol and dry with compressed air.
2. Make sure the fluid passageways (**Figure 99**) in the piston bores are clear. Apply compressed air to the openings to make sure they are clear. Clean out if necessary with clean brake fluid.
3. Make sure the fluid passageways (**Figure 100**) in both caliper body halves are clear. Apply compressed air to the openings to make sure they are clear. Clean out if necessary with clean brake fluid.
4. Inspect the piston and dust seal grooves in both caliper bodies for damage. If damaged or corroded, replace the caliper assembly.
5. Inspect the banjo bolt threaded hole in the outboard caliper body. If worn or damaged, clean out with a metric thread tap or replace the caliper assembly.
6. Inspect the bleed valve threaded hole in the caliper body. If worn or damaged, clean out with a metric thread tap or replace the caliper assembly.
7. Inspect the bleed valve. Apply compressed air to the opening and make sure it is clear. Clean out if

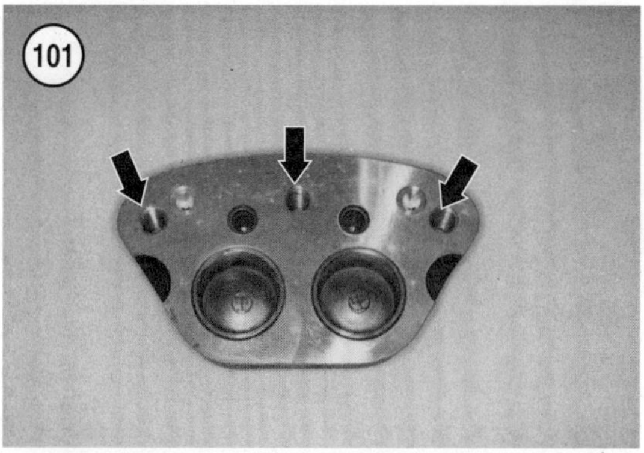

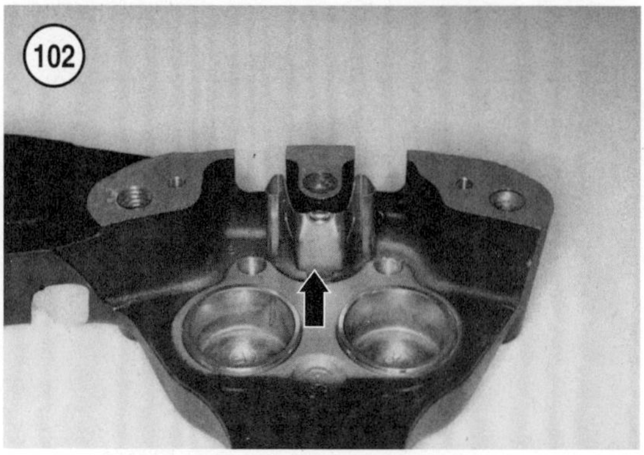

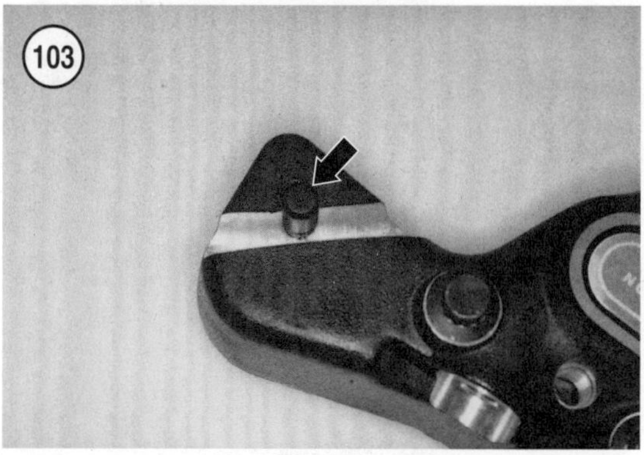

necessary with clean brake fluid. Install the bleed valve and tighten to the specification in **Table 2**.

8. Inspect both caliper bodies for damage. Check the inboard caliper mounting bolt hole threads (**Figure 101**) for wear or damage. Clean up with an appropriate size metric tap or replace the caliper assembly.

9. Inspect the cylinder walls and pistons for scratches, scoring or other damage.

10. Check the anti-rattle spring for wear or damage.

Assembly

NOTE
Never reuse old dust seals or piston seals. Very minor damage or age deterioration can make the seals useless.

1. Soak the new dust and piston seals in clean DOT5 brake fluid.

2. Coat the piston bores and pistons with clean DOT5 brake fluid.

3. Carefully install the new piston seals into the lower grooves. Make sure the seals are properly seated in their respective grooves.

4. Carefully install the new dust seals into the upper grooves. Make sure all seals are properly seated in their respective grooves.

5. Repeat Step 3 and Step 4 for the other caliper body half.

6. Position the pistons with the open end facing out and install the pistons into the caliper cylinders. Push the pistons in until they bottom.

7. Repeat Step 6 for the other caliper body half. Make sure all pistons are installed correctly.

8. Coat the *new* O-ring seals in DOT5 brake fluid and install the O-rings (**Figure 97**) into the inboard caliper half.

9. Install the anti-rattle spring (**Figure 102**) onto the boss on the outboard caliper half.

10. Make sure the O-rings are still in place and assemble the caliper body halves.

11. Install the three caliper body bolts (**Figure 96**) and tighten securely. They will be tightened to the specification after the caliper is installed on the rear swing arm.

12. If removed, install the rubber bumper (**Figure 103**).

13. If removed, install the bleed screw assembly (**Figure 98**) and tighten to the specification in **Table 2**.

14. Install the caliper and brake pads as described in this chapter.

15. Tighten the three caliper body mounting bolts to the specification in **Table 2**.

16. Bleed the brake as described under *Bleeding the System* in this chapter.

12

REAR MASTER CYLINDER

Removal

1. Remove the exhaust system as described in Chapter Seven.
2. On models so equipped, remove the right side saddlebag.
3. At the rear brake caliper, perform the following:
   a. Insert a hose onto the end of the bleed valve. Insert the open end of the hose into a container.
   b. Open the bleeder valve and operate the rear brake pedal to drain the brake fluid. Remove the hose and close the bleeder valve after draining the assembly. Discard the brake fluid properly.
4. Remove the screws securing the cover and remove the cover (**Figure 104**) and diaphragm.
5. Remove the banjo bolt and sealing washers (**Figure 105**) securing the brake hose to the rear of the master cylinder cartridge body.
6. Place the loose end of the brake hose in a reclosable plastic bag to prevent the entry of debris and prevent any residual brake fluid from leaking out.
7. Remove the cotter pin and pivot pin securing the pushrod to the brake pedal. Disconnect the pushrod from the brake pedal.
8. Loosen and remove the nut (**Figure 106**) from the cartridge body securing the rear portion of the master cylinder to the mounting bracket on the frame.
9. Pull the master cylinder and pushrod (**Figure 107**) forward out of the mounting bracket and remove it.
10. If necessary, service the master cylinder as described in this chapter.

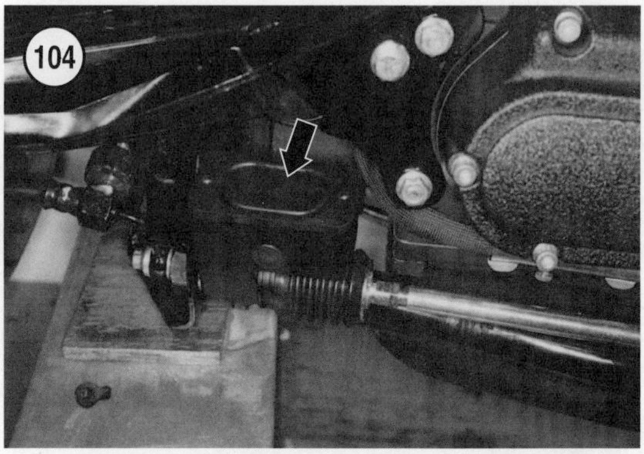

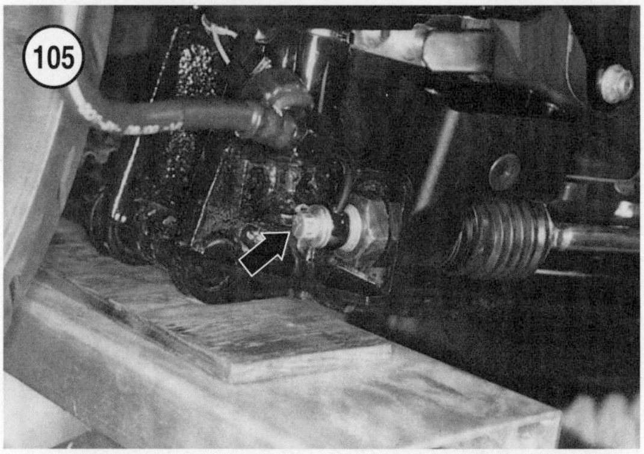

Installation

1. Insert the master cylinder cartridge body threads through the square hole in the frame mounting bracket (**Figure 107**). Index the square portion of the cartridge body into the square hole in the mounting bracket.
2. Install the nut (**Figure 106**) onto the cartridge body. Ensure that the cartridge body is engaged properly with the mounting bracket prior to tightening the nut. Tighten the nut to the specification in **Table 2**.

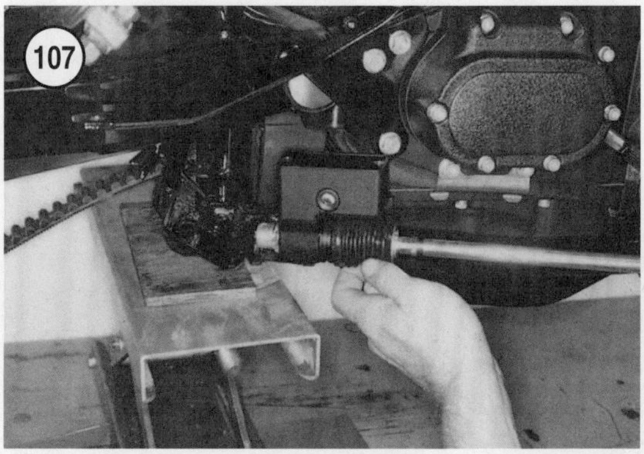

(108) **REAR MASTER CYLINDER**

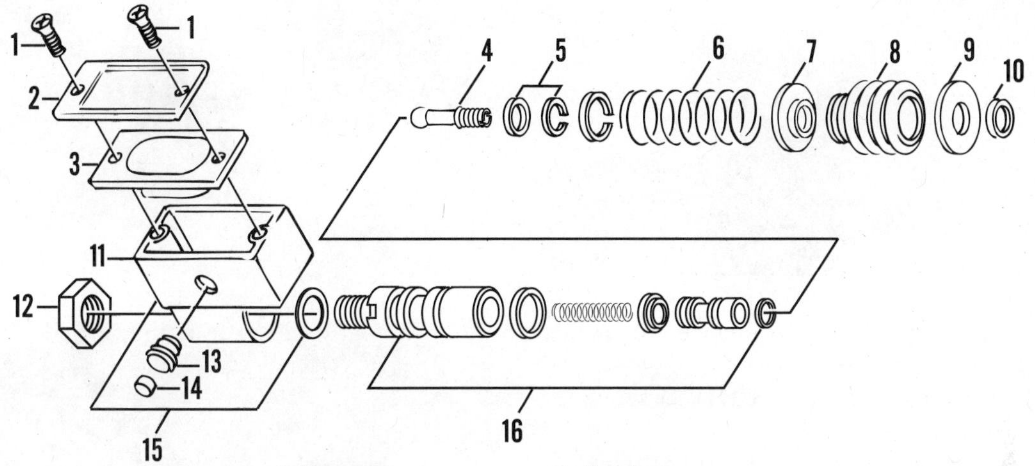

1. Screw
2. Top cover
3. Diaphragm
4. Pushrod
5. Seal and snap ring
6. Spring
7. Retainer
8. Rubber boot
9. Retainer
10. Snap ring
11. Body
12. Nut
13. Retainer
14. Sight glass
15. Body rebuild kit
16. Piston assembly

(109)

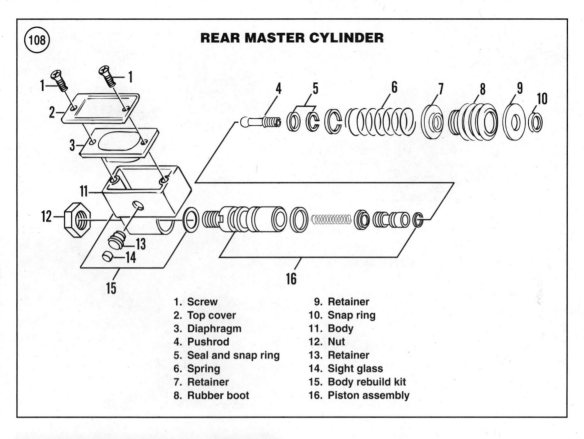

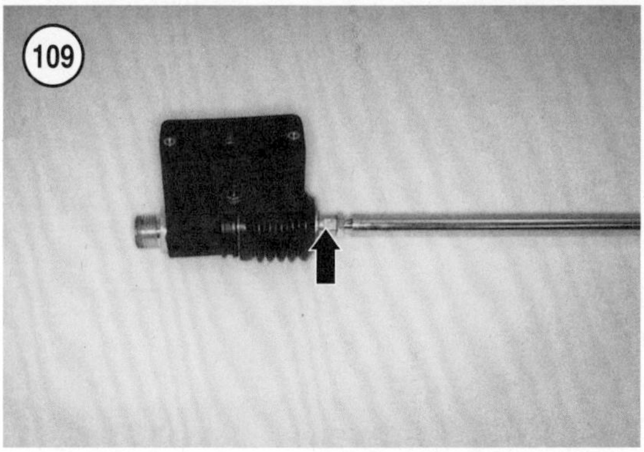

3. Connect the pushrod onto the brake pedal and install the pivot pin. Install a *new* cotter pin and bend the ends over completely.

4. Apply clean DOT 5 brake fluid to the rubber portions of the new sealing washers prior to installation.

5. Install a new steel/rubber washer on each side of the brake hose banjo fitting. Insert the banjo bolt through the washers and banjo fitting and thread into the cartridge body (**Figure 105**). Then tighten the banjo bolt to the specification in **Table 2**.

6. Bleed the brake as described under *Bleeding the System* in this chapter.

WARNING
Do not ride the motorcycle until the rear brake is operating correctly with full hydraulic advantage. If necessary, bleed the brake as described in this chapter.

Disassembly

Refer to **Figure 108**.

1. Clean the exterior master cylinder housing with clean DOT 5 brake fluid or isopropyl alcohol and dry.

2. Store the master cylinder components in a divided container, such as a restaurant-size egg carton, to help maintain their correct alignment position.

3. If still installed, remove the master cylinder cover and diaphragm.

4. Unscrew and disconnect the brake rod (**Figure 109**) from the master cylinder.

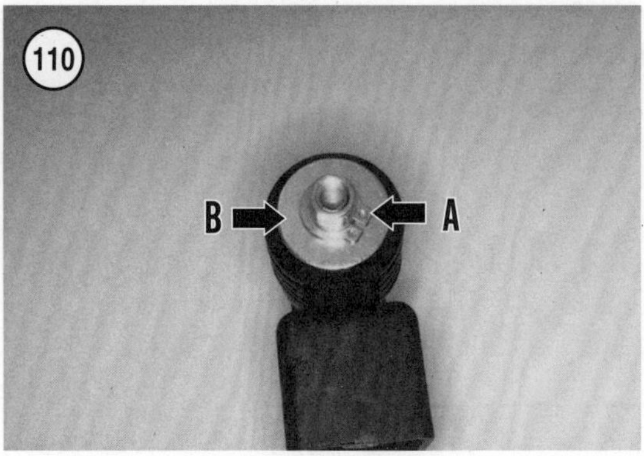

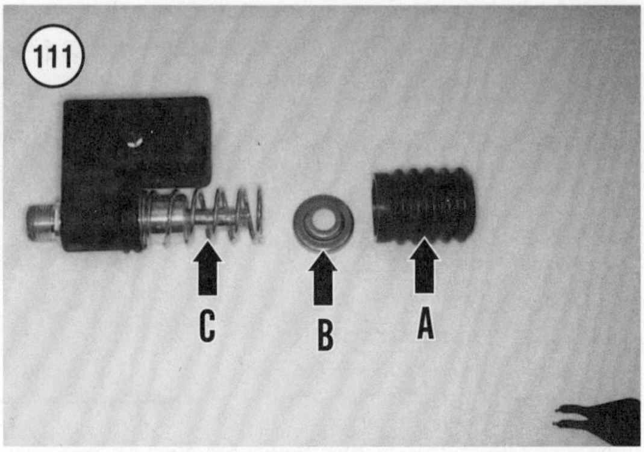

5. Remove the snap ring (A, **Figure 110**) and the washer (B, **Figure 110**).
6. Remove the boot (A, **Figure 111**), the spring seat (B) and the spring (C).
7. Depress the pushrod (A, **Figure 112**) and remove the snap ring (B).
8. Remove the pushrod (**Figure 113**).
9. Remove the piston assembly (A, **Figure 114**) and spring from the cartridge.

NOTE
*On some models and years, the cartridge (B, **Figure 114**) within the master cylinder reservoir is not available as a replacement part. Prior to removing the cartridge, check with a Harley-Davidson dealership to make sure the cartridge is available.*

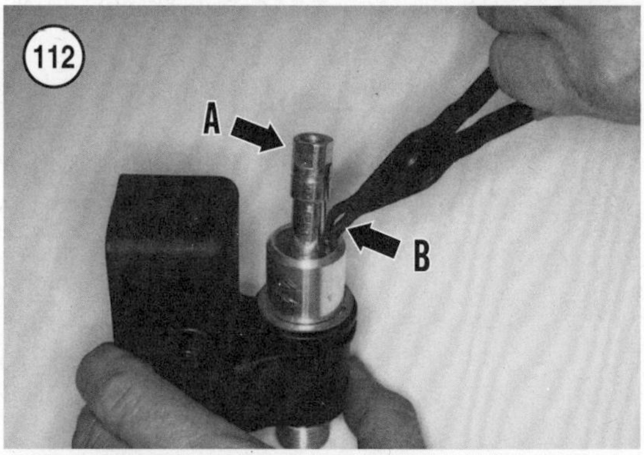

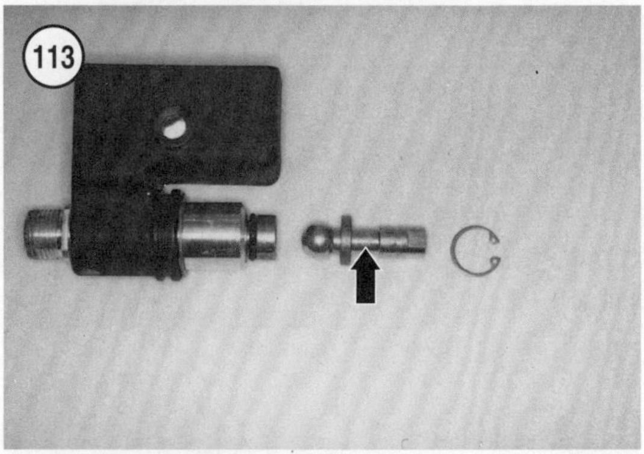

Inspection

1. Clean all parts in clean DOT5 brake fluid or isopropyl alcohol and dry with compressed air.
2. Replace worn or damage parts as described in this section. It is recommended that a new piston kit assembly be installed every time the master cylinder is disassembled.
3. Inspect the cartridge body cylinder bore surface for signs of wear and damage. Do not hone the cartridge bore to clean or repair it. If less than perfect, replace the cartridge and/or the master cylinder reservoir.
4. Check the piston primary cup (A, **Figure 115**) and the O-ring (B) for deterioration or damage.
5. Check the spring for bending, unequally spaced coils or corrosion.
6. Check the pushrod and washer (**Figure 116**) for bending, wear or damage.

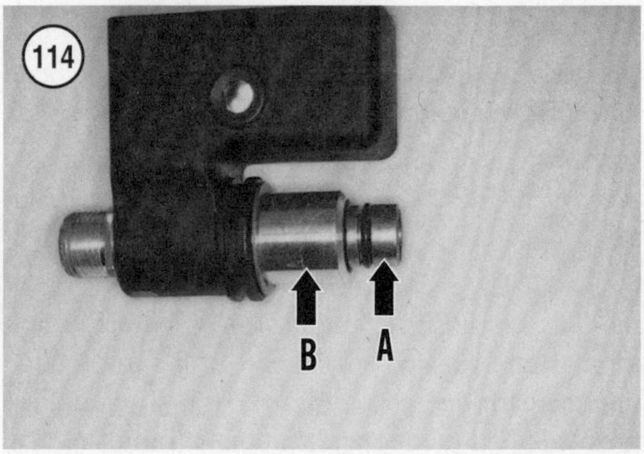

115
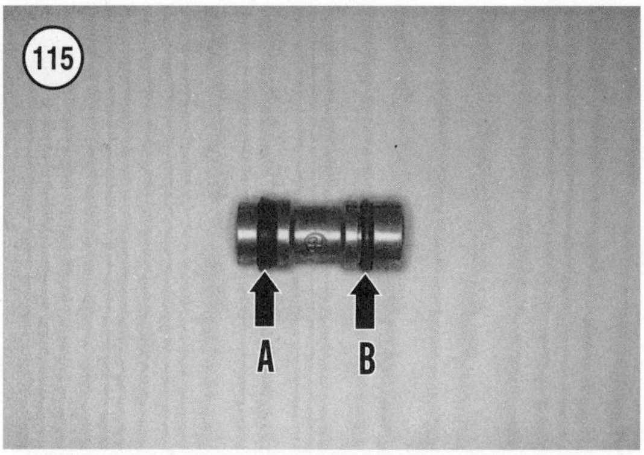

116
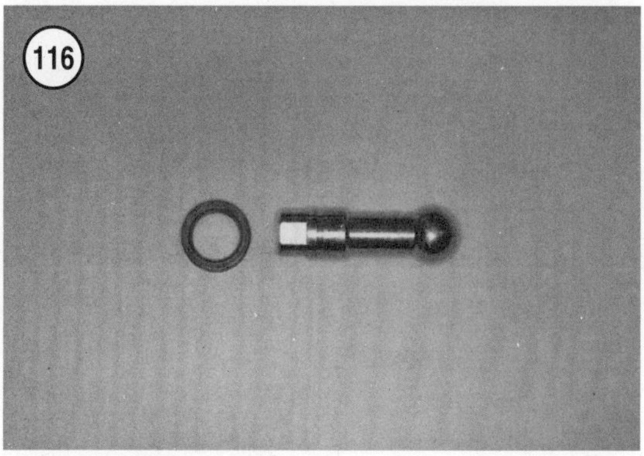

117
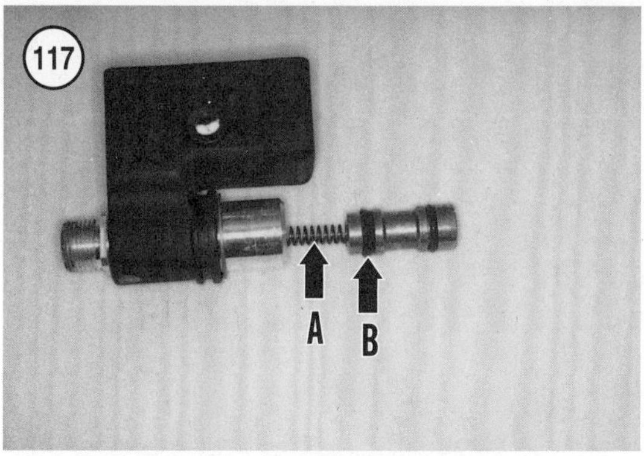

118
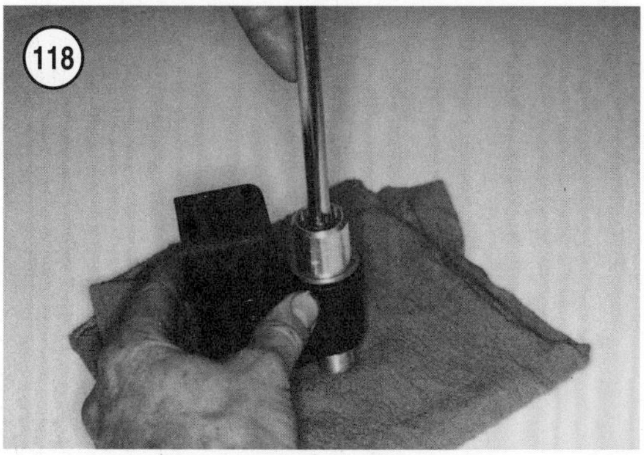

119
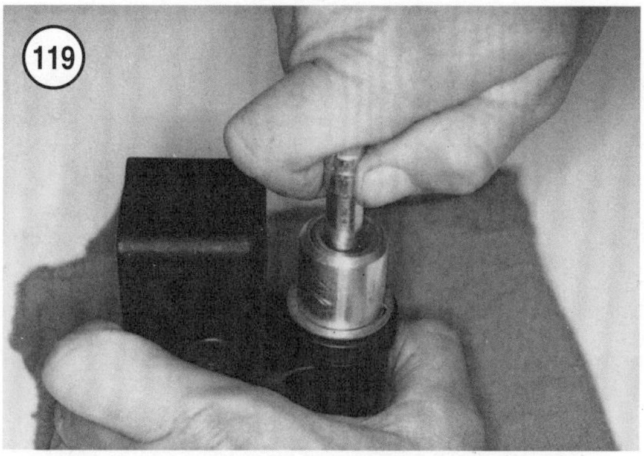

7. Inspect the boot for tears or deterioration.
8. Check the reservoir body for corrosion or other damage.
9. Check the reservoir cap and diaphragm for damage.
10. Check the brake rod and nut for thread damage. Repair if necessary.

Assembly

1. Coat all parts with clean DOT5 brake fluid.
2. Soak the primary cup, O-ring and piston assembly in clean DOT5 brake fluid for at least 15 minutes to make them pliable. Coat the inside of the cartridge bore with clean brake fluid prior to the assembly of parts.

CAUTION
When installing the piston assembly, do not allow the primary cup to turn inside out as it will be damaged and allow brake fluid leakage within the cartridge cylinder bore.

3. Install the spring (A, **Figure 117**) into the cartridge.
4. Position the piston assembly with the primary cup (B, **Figure 117**) end going in first. Make sure the piston cup does not tear as it passes through the bore entrance.
5. Turn the reservoir on end on a shop cloth. Carefully push the piston assembly into the cartridge with a Phillips screwdriver (**Figure 118**). Push the piston assembly in and then let it move out several times and check for ease of movement.
6. Position the pushrod onto the end of the piston and push the piston into the cartridge (**Figure 119**). Hold the pushrod (A, **Figure 112**) and install the

12

120

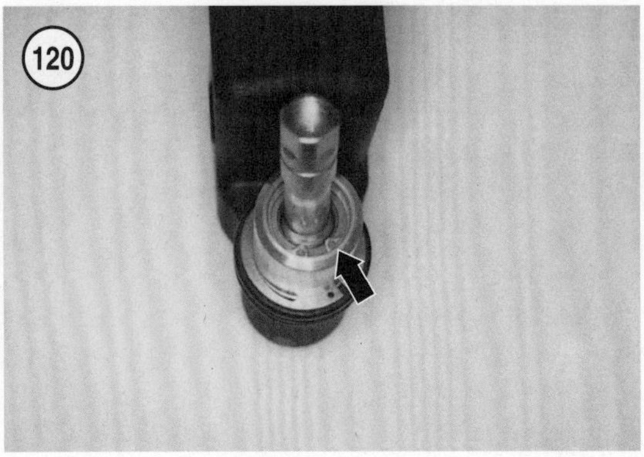

121

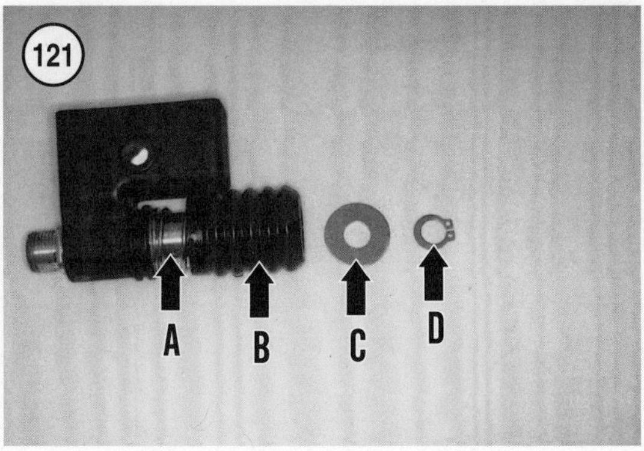

122

FRONT BRAKE LINES

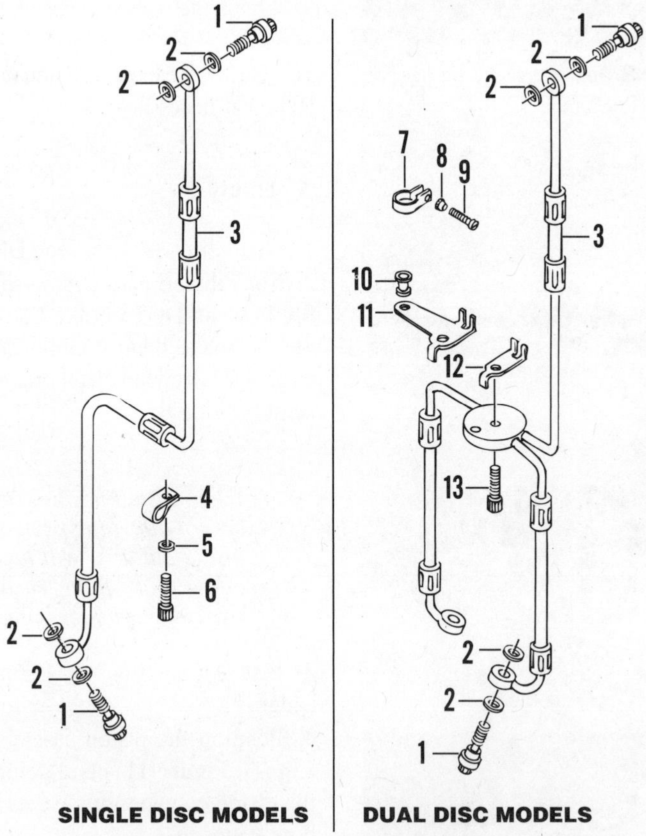

1. Banjo bolt
2. Sealing washer
3. Brake hose assembly
4. Clip
5. Washer
6. Allen bolt
7. Clamp
8. Collar
9. Screw
10. Grommet
11. Guide–turn signal harness
12. Guide–brake line
13. Allen bolt

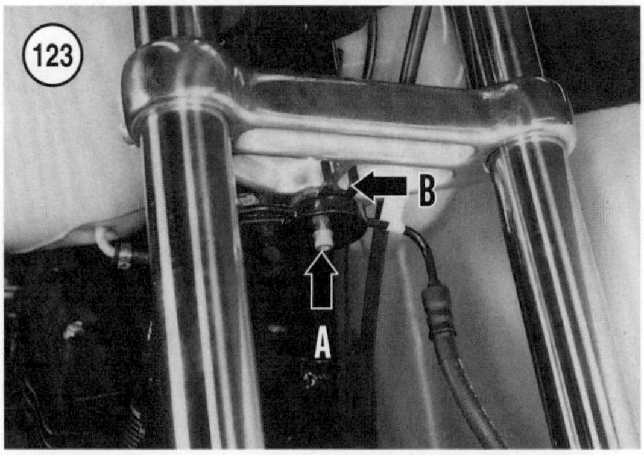

snap ring (B). Make sure the snap ring is correctly seated in the cartridge groove (**Figure 120**).

7. Install the spring and spring seat (A, **Figure 121**) onto the pushrod.
8. Install the boot (B, **Figure 121**), washer (C) and snap ring (D). Make sure the snap ring (A, **Figure 110**) is correctly seated in the push rod groove.
9. Connect the brake rod (**Figure 109**) onto the master cylinder and tighten the locknut securely.
10. Install the diaphragm and reservoir cover.
11. Install the master cylinder as described in this chapter.

WARNING
Do not ride the motorcycle until the rear brake is operating correctly with full hydraulic advantage. If necessary, bleed the brake as described in this chapter.

BRAKE HOSE AND LINE REPLACEMENT

A combination of steel and flexible brake lines connect the master cylinder to its brake calipers. Banjo fittings and bolts connect brake hoses to the master cylinder and brake calipers. Steel/rubber washers seal the banjo fittings.

Replace a hose if the flexible portion shows swelling, cracking or other damage. Likewise, replace the brake hose if the metal portion leaks or if there are dents or cracks.

Front Brake Hose Removal/Installation

A combination steel/flexible brake hose (**Figure 122**) connects the front master cylinder to the front brake caliper(s). When purchasing a new hose, compare it to the old hose to make sure that the length and angle of the steel hose portion are correct. Install new banjo bolt washers at both ends.

CAUTION
Do not spill any brake fluid on the front fork or front wheel. Wash brake fluid off any painted, plated or plastic surfaces immediately, as it will damage most surfaces it contacts. Use soapy water and rinse completely.

1. Drain the front brake system as follows:
   a. Connect a hose over the bleed valve.
   b. Insert the loose end of the hose in a container to catch the brake fluid.
   c. Open the bleed valve and apply the front brake lever to pump the fluid out of the master cylinder and brake line. Continue until the fluid is removed.
   d. Close the bleed valve and disconnect the hose.
   e. On models with dual front brakes, repeat for the opposite side.
   f. Dispose of this brake fluid—never reuse brake fluid. Contaminated brake fluid will cause brake failure.
2. Before removing the brake line(s), note the brake line routing from the master cylinder to the caliper(s). In addition, note the number and position of the metal hose clamps and plastic ties used to hold the brake line(s) in place. Install the brake hose along its original path. The metal clamps can be reused.
3. Cut any plastic ties and discard them.
4. On dual disc models, remove the bolt (A, **Figure 123**) securing the brake hose mounting plate to the lower steering stem. Do not lose the guide plate (B, **Figure 123**) between the hose mounting plate and the steering stem.
5. Remove the screw or nut securing the metal clamps around the brake line. Spread the clamp and remove it from the brake line.
6. Remove the banjo bolt and washers (A, **Figure 124**) securing the hose to the brake caliper(s).
7. Remove the banjo bolt and washers securing the hose to the master cylinder (**Figure 125**).
8. Cover the ends of the brake hose(s) to prevent brake fluid from leaking out.

9. Remove the brake hose(s) (B, **Figure 124**) from the motorcycle.

10. If the existing brake hose assembly is going to be reinstalled, inspect it as follows:

   a. Check the metal pipe where it enters and exits at the flexible hose. Check the crimped clamp for looseness or damage.

   b. Check the flexible hose portion for swelling, cracks or other damage.

   c. If any wear or damage is found, replace the brake hose assembly.

11. Install the brake hose, washers (**Figure 122**) and banjo bolts in the reverse order of removal while noting the following:

   a. Install *new* sealing washers against the side of each hose fitting.

   b. Carefully install the clips and guides to hold the brake hose in place.

   c. Tighten the banjo bolts to the specification in **Table 2**.

   d. Refill the master cylinder with clean brake fluid clearly marked DOT 5. Bleed the front brake system as described in this chapter.

WARNING

Do not ride the motorcycle until the front brakes operate correctly with full hydraulic advantage. If necessary, bleed the brake as described in this chapter.

Rear Brake Hose Removal/Installation

A single combination steel and rubber brake hose (**Figure 126**) connects the rear master cylinder to the rear brake caliper. The rear brake switch is installed in the rear brake hose. When buying a new hose, compare it to the old hose. Make sure the length and angle of the steel hose portion is correct. Install new banjo bolt washers at both hose ends.

CAUTION

Do not spill any brake fluid on the swing arm, frame or rear wheel. Wash brake fluid off any painted, plated or plastic surfaces immediately, as it will damage most surfaces it contacts. Use soapy water and rinse completely.

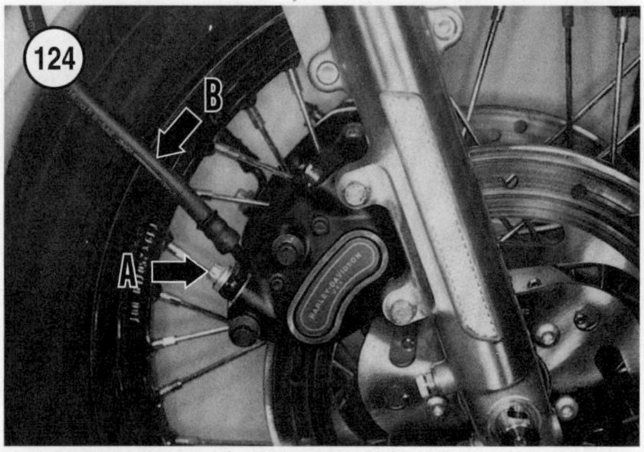

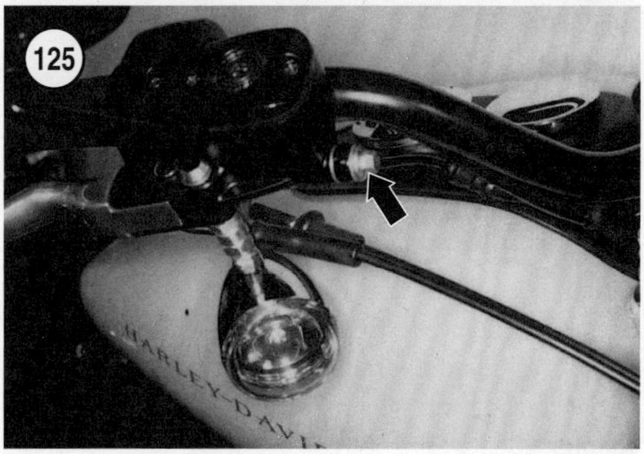

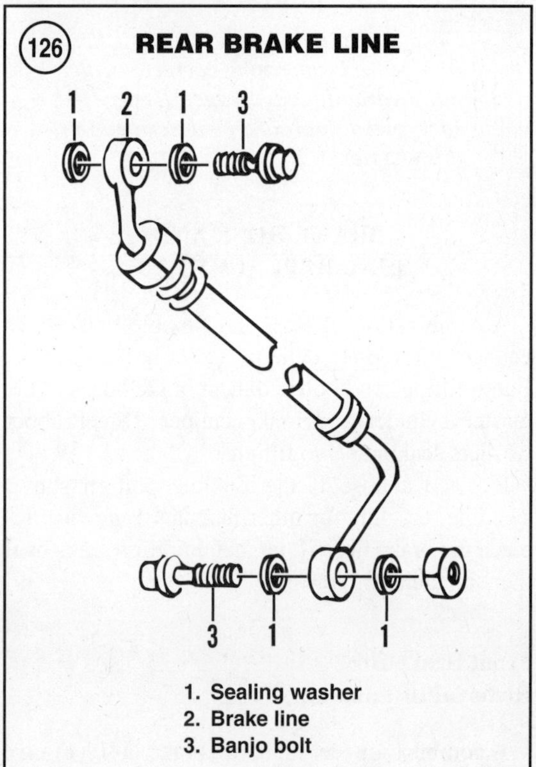

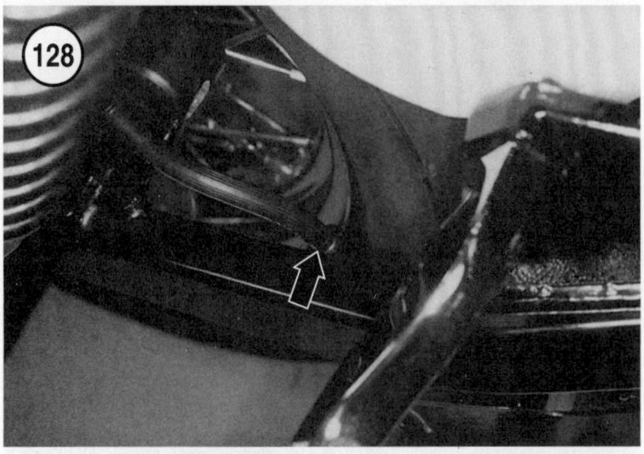

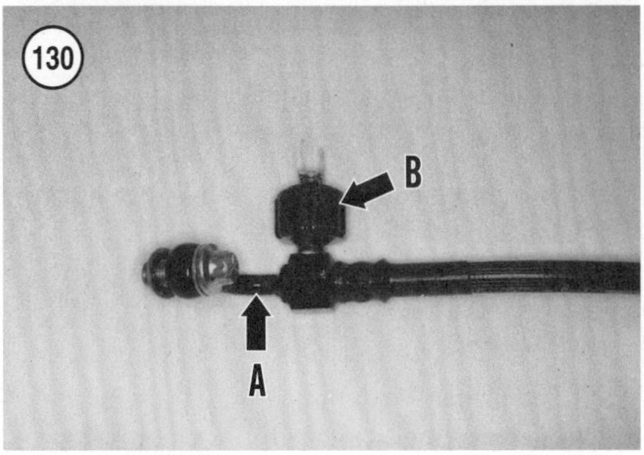

1. Remove the exhaust system as described in Chapter Seven.
2. On models so equipped, remove the right side saddlebag.
3. Drain the hydraulic brake fluid from the rear brake system as follows:
   a. Connect a hose to the bleed valve. Refer to A, **Figure 127**, typical.
   b. Insert the loose end of the hose in a container to catch the brake fluid.
   c. Open the caliper bleed valve and operate the rear brake pedal to pump the fluid out of the master cylinder and brake line. Continue until all of the fluid is removed.
   d. Close the bleed valve and disconnect the hose.
   e. Dispose of this brake fluid—never reuse brake fluid. Contaminated brake fluid will cause brake failure.
4. Before removing the brake line, note the brake line routing from the master cylinder to the caliper. In addition, note the number and position of the metal hose clamps and plastic ties used to hold the brake line in place. Install the brake hose along its original path. The metal clamp can be reused. However, new plastic ties will have to be installed.
5. Cut the plastic ties and discard them.
6. Remove the bolt and clamp securing the brake hose to the rear swing arm (**Figure 128**).
7. Disconnect the electrical connector (A, **Figure 129**) from the rear brake switch.
8. Remove the banjo bolt and washers securing the hose to the brake caliper. Refer to B, **Figure 127**, typical.
9. Remove the banjo bolt and washers (B, **Figure 129**) securing the hose to the master cylinder.
10. Remove the brake hose from the motorcycle.
11. If the existing brake hose assembly is going to be reinstalled , inspect it as follows:
    a. Check the metal pipe (A, **Figure 130**) where it enters and exits the flexible hose. Check the crimped clamp for looseness or damage.
    b. Check the flexible hose portion for swelling, cracks or other damage.
    c. If any wear or damage is found, replace the brake hose.
12. If necessary, remove the stoplight switch (B, **Figure 130**) from the rear brake hose fitting. Reverse to install the switch. Tighten the switch securely.

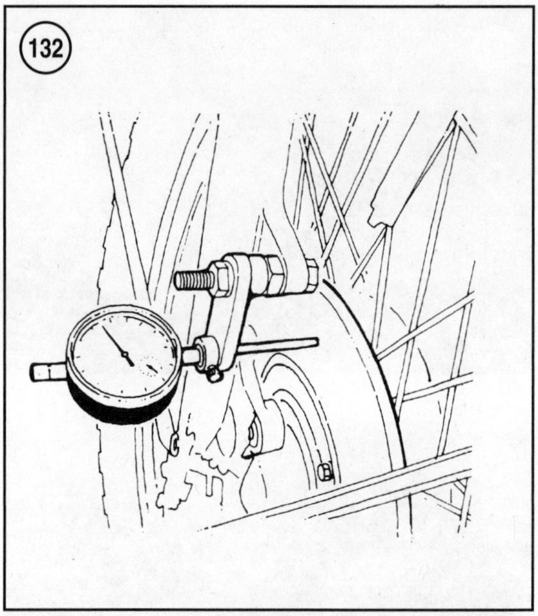

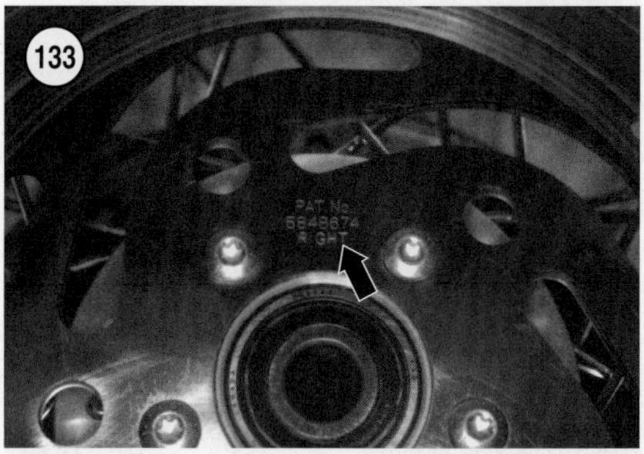

13. Install the brake hose in the reverse order of removal while noting the following:
    a. Install *new* sealing washers against the side of each hose fitting.
    b. Carefully install the clips and guides to hold the brake hose in place.
    c. Tighten the banjo bolts to the specification in **Table 2**.
    d. Refill the master cylinder with clean brake fluid clearly marked DOT 5. Bleed the rear brake system as described in this chapter.

WARNING

Do not ride the motorcycle until the rear brake is operating correctly with full hydraulic advantage. If necessary, bleed the brake as described in this chapter.

BRAKE DISC

The brake discs are separate from the wheel hubs and can be removed once the wheel is removed from the motorcycle.

Inspection

It is not necessary to remove the disc from the wheel to inspect it. Small nicks and marks on the disc are not important, but radial scratches deep enough to snag a fingernail reduce braking effectiveness and increase brake pad wear. If these grooves are evident, and the brake pads are wearing rapidly, the disc should be replaced.

The minimum (MIN) disc thickness is stamped on the disc.

When servicing the brake discs, do not have the discs surfaced to compensate for any warp. The discs are thin, and grinding will only reduce their thickness, causing them to warp quite rapidly. If the disc is warped, the brake pads may be dragging on the disc due to a faulty caliper and causing the disc to overheat. Overheating can also be caused when there is unequal pad pressure on both sides of the disc.

Three main causes of unequal brake pad pressure are:

a. The brake caliper piston seals are worn or damaged.

b. The small master cylinder relief port is plugged.

c. The primary cup on the master cylinder piston is worn or damaged.

134

135

NOTE
It is not necessary to remove the wheel to measure the disc thickness. The measurement can be performed with the wheel installed or removed.

1. Measure the thickness of the disc at several locations around the disc with a vernier caliper or a micrometer (**Figure 131**). The disc must be replaced if the thickness in any area is less than the marked MIN dimension on the disc.

2. Make sure the disc mounting bolts are tight prior to running this check. Check the disc runout with a dial indicator as shown in **Figure 132**.

NOTE
When checking the front disc, turn the handlebar all the way to one side, then to the other side.

3. Slowly rotate the wheel and watch the dial indicator. If the runout exceeds that listed in **Table 1**, replace the disc(s).

4. Clean the disc of any rust or corrosion and wipe clean with lacquer thinner. Never use an oil-based solvent that may leave an oil residue on the disc.

Removal/Installation

1. Remove the front or rear wheel as described in Chapter Nine.

NOTE
*On dual disc models, the disc is marked with a LEFT or RIGHT (**Figure 133**). The disc must be reinstalled on the correct side of the wheel.*

2. Remove the Torx bolts (**Figure 134**) securing the brake disc to the hub and remove the disc.
3. Check the brake disc bolts for thread damage. Replace worn or damaged fasteners.
4. Check the brake disc threaded bolt holes in the wheel hub for thread damage. Clean out with a tap if necessary.
5. Clean the disc and the disc mounting surface thoroughly with brake cleaner or contact cleaner. Allow the surfaces to dry before installation.
6A. On 1999 models, to install the front brake disc(s) perform the following:
   a. Install the disc onto the correct side of the wheel hub, aligning the notch in the brake disc with the 1/4 in. (6.3 mm) blind hole in the hub (**Figure 135**).
   b. Apply a drop of ThreeBond TB1342 or an equivalent to each bolt thread prior to installation.
   c. Install new Torx bolts and tighten to the specification in **Table 2**.
6B. On 2000-on models, to install the front brake disc(s) perform the following:
   a. Install the disc onto the correct side of the wheel hub.
   b. Apply a drop of ThreeBond TB1342 or an equivalent to each bolt thread prior to installation.
   c. Install new Torx bolts and tighten to the specification in **Table 2**.
7. To install the rear brake disc, perform the following:
   a. Apply a drop of ThreeBond TB1342 or an equivalent to each bolt thread prior to installation.

b. Install new Torx bolts and tighten to the specification in **Table 2**.

BLEEDING THE SYSTEM

If air enters the brake system, the brake will feel soft or spongy, greatly reducing braking pressure. If this happens, the system must be bled to remove the air. Air can enter the system if there is a leak in the system, the brake fluid level in a master cylinder runs low, a brake line is opened, or the brake fluid is replaced.

When bleeding the brakes, two different methods can be used—with a brake bleeder or manually. This section describes both procedures separately.

Before bleeding the brake system, observe the following conditions:

1. Check the brake lines to make sure that all fittings are tight.
2. Check that the caliper piston does not stick or bind in its bore.
3. Check piston movement in each master cylinder. Operate the lever or brake pedal, making sure there is no binding or other abnormal conditions present.

Brake Bleeder Process

This procedure uses the Mityvac hydraulic brake bleeding kit (**Figure 136**) that is available from automotive or motorcycle supply stores or from mail order outlets.

NOTE
This procedure is shown on the rear wheel and relates to the front wheel as well.

1. Remove the dust cap from the caliper bleed valve.
2. Place a clean shop cloth (A, **Figure 137**) over the caliper to protect it from accidental brake fluid spills.
3. Open the bleed screw approximately 1/2 turn (B, **Figure 137**).
4. Assemble the brake bleeder according to its manufacturer's instructions. Secure it to the caliper bleed valve (**Figure 138**).
5. Clean the top of the master cylinder of all debris.
6. Remove the screws securing the master cylinder top cover and remove the cover and rubber diaphragm.
7. Fill the reservoir almost to the top with DOT5 brake fluid and reinstall the diaphragm and cover.

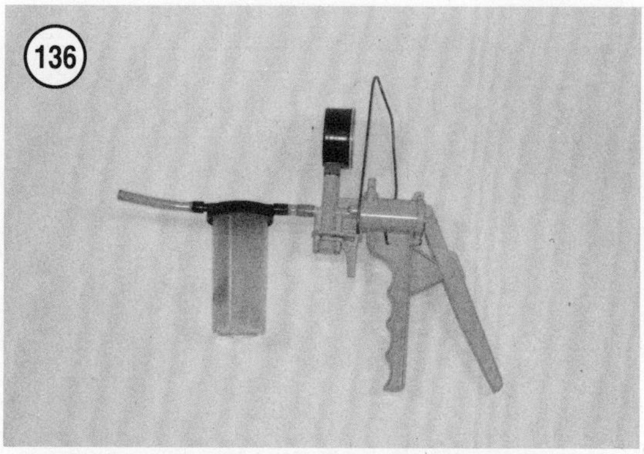

Leave the cover in place during this procedure to prevent the entry of dirt.

WARNING
Use brake fluid clearly marked DOT 5 from a sealed container. Other types may vaporize and cause brake failure. Always use the same brand name; do not intermix, as many brands are not compatible. Do not intermix DOT 3, DOT 4 or DOT 5.1 brake fluid, as it can cause brake component damage leading to brake system failure.

8. Operate the pump several times to create a vacuum in the line. Brake fluid will quickly flow from the caliper into the pump's reservoir. Tighten the caliper bleed valve before the fluid stops flowing through the hose. To prevent air from being drawn through the master cylinder, add fluid to maintain its level at the top of the reservoir.

NOTE
Do not allow the master cylinder reservoir to empty during the bleeding operation or more air will enter the

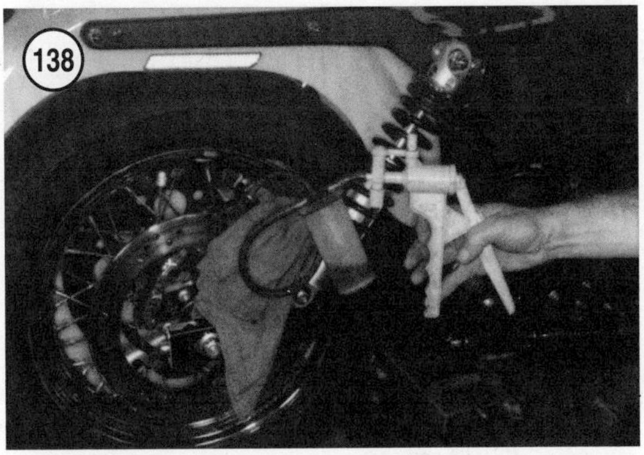

system. If this occurs, the procedure must be repeated.

9. Continue the bleeding process until the fluid drawn from the caliper is bubble free. If bubbles are withdrawn with the brake fluid, more air is trapped in the line. Repeat Step 8, making sure to refill the master cylinder to prevent air from being drawn into the system.
10. When the brake fluid is free of bubbles, tighten the bleed valve and remove the brake bleeder assembly. Reinstall the bleed valve dust cap.

NOTE
Dispose of the brake fluid expelled during the bleeding process. Do not reuse the brake fluid.

11. If necessary, add fluid to correct the level in the master cylinder reservoir. When topping off the front master cylinder, turn the handlebar until the reservoir is level; add fluid until it is level with the reservoir gasket surface. The fluid level in the rear master cylinder must be slightly below the upper gasket surface.
12. On front dual-disc models, repeat steps 1-9 for the other caliper.
13. Reinstall the reservoir diaphragm and cover. Install the screws and tighten securely.
14. Test the feel of the brake lever or pedal. It must be firm and offer the same resistance each time it is operated. If it feels spongy, it is likely that there is still air in the system and it must be bled again. After bleeding the system, check for leaks and tighten all fittings and connections as necessary.

WARNING
Do not ride the motorcycle until the front and/or rear brake are operating correctly with full hydraulic advantage.

15. Test ride the motorcycle slowly at first to make sure that the brakes are operating properly.

Without a Brake Bleeder

NOTE
Before bleeding the brake, check that all brake hoses and lines are tight.

1. Connect a length of clear tubing to the bleed valve on the caliper. Place the other end of the tube into a clean container. Fill the container with enough clean DOT 5 brake fluid to keep the end of the tube submerged. The tube must be long enough so that a loop can be made higher than the bleeder valve to prevent air from being drawn into the caliper during bleeding.
2. Clean the top of the master cylinder of all debris.
3. Remove the screws securing the master cylinder top cover. Remove the cover and diaphragm.
4. Fill the reservoir almost to the top with DOT5 brake fluid and reinstall the diaphragm and cover. Leave the cover in place during this procedure to prevent the entry of dirt.

WARNING
Use brake fluid clearly marked DOT 5 from a sealed container. Other types may vaporize and cause brake failure. Always use the same brand name; do not intermix, as many brands are not compatible. Do not intermix DOT 3, DOT 4 or DOT 5.1 brake fluid, as it can cause brake component damage leading to brake system failure.

NOTE
During this procedure, it is important to check the fluid level in the master cylinder reservoir often. If the reservoir runs dry, air will enter the system.

5. Slowly apply the brake lever several times. Hold the lever in the applied position and open the bleed valve about 1/2 turn. Allow the lever to travel to its limit. When the limit is reached, tighten the bleed valve, then release the brake lever. As the brake

(139) REAR BRAKE PEDAL

1. Nut
2. Pushrod
3. Clevis pin
4. Acorn nut
5. Washer
6. Brake pedal
7. Washer
8. Footrest and brake pedal bracket
9. Bolt
10. Washer
11. Cotter pin
12. Bolt
13. Pad

1. Nut
2. Pushrod
3. Spring washer
4. Brake pedal
5. Snap ring
6. Cotter pin
7. Pivot pin

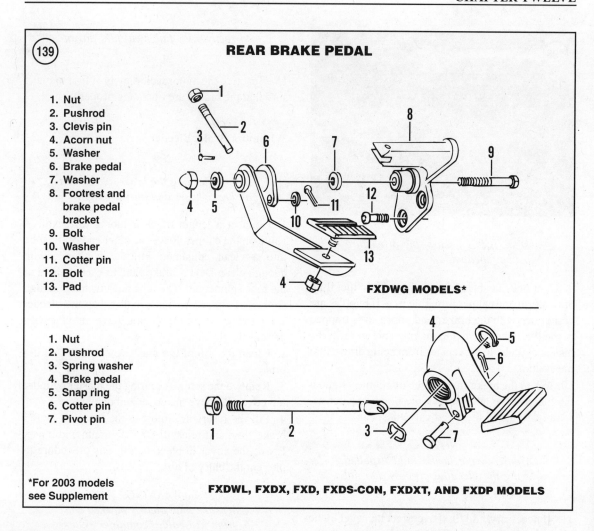

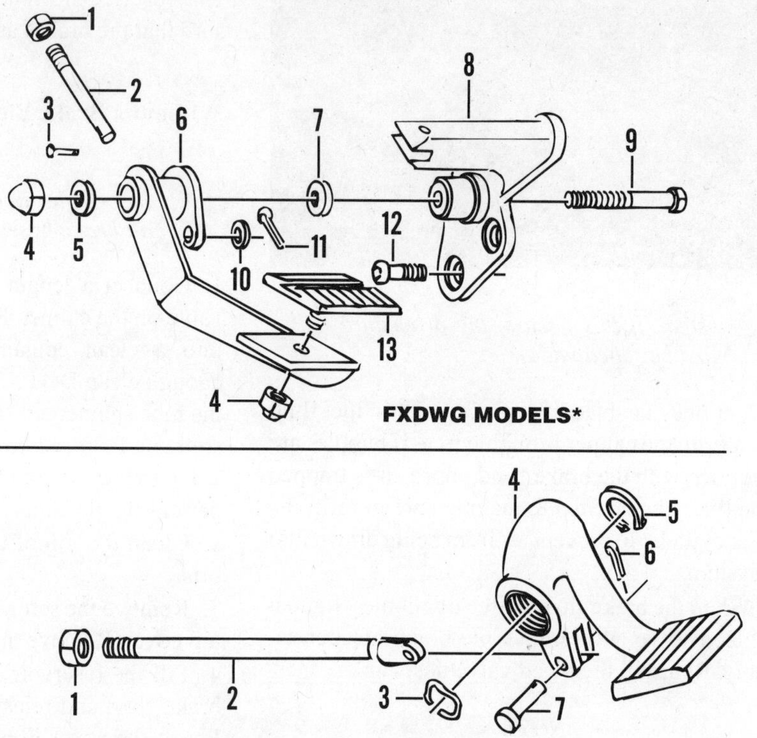

*For 2003 models see Supplement

FXDWL, FXDX, FXD, FXDS-CON, FXDXT, AND FXDP MODELS

fluid enters the system, the level will drop in the master cylinder reservoir. Maintain the level at the top of the reservoir to prevent air from being drawn into the system.

6. Continue the bleeding process until the fluid emerging from the hose is completely free of air bubbles. If the fluid is being replaced, continue until the fluid emerging from the hose is clean.

NOTE
If bleeding is difficult, allow the fluid to stabilize for a few hours. Repeat the bleeding procedure when the tiny bubbles in the system settle out.

7. Hold the lever in the applied position and tighten the bleed valve. Remove the bleed tube and install the bleed valve dust cap.

NOTE
Dispose of the brake fluid expelled during the bleeding process. Do not reuse the brake fluid.

8. If necessary, add fluid to correct the level in the master cylinder reservoir. When topping off the front master cylinder, turn the handlebar until the reservoir is level; add fluid until it is level with the reservoir gasket surface. The fluid level in the rear master cylinder must be slightly below the upper gasket surface.
9. On front dual-disc models, repeat steps 1-9 for the other caliper.
10. Install the diaphragm and top cover and tighten the screws securely.
11. Test the feel of the brake lever or pedal. It must be firm and offer the same resistance each time it is operated. If it feels spongy, it is likely that there is still air in the system and it must be bled again. After

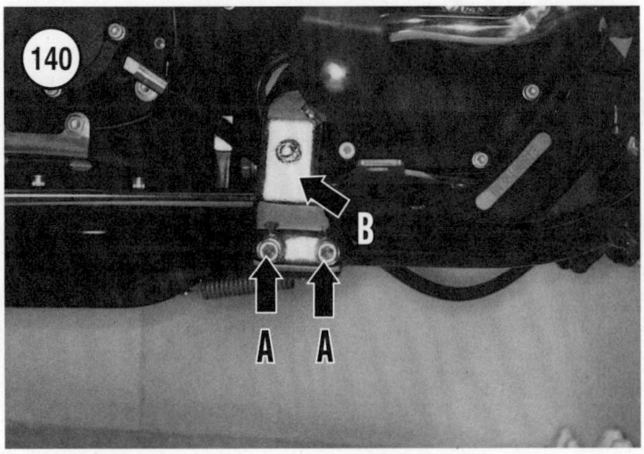

bleeding the system, check for leaks and tighten all fittings and connections as necessary.

WARNING
Do not ride the motorcycle until the front and/or rear brake are operating correctly with full hydraulic advantage.

12. Test ride the motorcycle slowly at first to make sure that the brakes are operating properly.

REAR BRAKE PEDAL

Removal/Lubrication/Installation

Refer to **Figure 139**.

1. Remove the exhaust system as described in Chapter Seven.
2. Remove the bolts (A, **Figure 140**) securing the brake pedal bracket to the frame.
3. Remove the bracket (B, **Figure 140**) and pedal assembly.
4. Disconnect the push rod from the pedal assembly.
5A. On FXDWG models, remove the bolt, washers and acorn nut securing the pedal to the mounting bracket. Remove the pedal.
5B. On all models except FXDWG models, remove the snap ring securing the pedal to the mounting bracket. Remove the pedal.
6. Inspect the brake pedal for fractures or damage and replace if necessary.
7. On FXDWG models, perform the following:
   a. Inspect the bushing within the pedal for wear. Replace if necessary.
   b. Inspect the shoulder on the bracket where the pedal rides for wear.
   c. Lubricate the bushing and bracket shoulder with waterproof grease.
8. Install the pedal by reversing these removal steps while noting the following:
   a. Tighten the special bolt securely.
   b. Install a new cotter pin and bend the ends over completely.
   c. Adjust the rear brake pedal height as described in Chapter Three.

Table 1 BRAKE SYSTEM SPECIFICATIONS

Brake fluid	DOT 5 silicone base
Brake pad minimum thickness	
1999 models	1/16 in. (1.6 mm)
2000 and later	0.04 in. (1.02 mm)
Brake disc	
Thickness	Stamped on disc
Runout	0.008 in. (0.20 mm)

Table 2 BRAKE SYSTEM TORQUE SPECIFICATIONS

Item	ft.-lb.	in.-lb.	N•m
Bleed valves	–	80-100	9-11
Caliper bridge bolts			
(front and rear)	28-38	–	38-51
Brake disc bolts			
Front wheel	16-24	–	22-32
Rear wheel	30-45	–	41-61
Brake pad pins (2000-on)			
Front and rear calipers	–	180-200	20-23

(continued)

Table 2 BRAKE SYSTEM TORQUE SPECIFICATIONS (continued)

Item	ft.-lb.	in.-lb.	N•m
Front brake caliper (1999)			
Inner brake pad retainer screw	–	40-50	5-6
Upper mounting bolt	25-30	–	34-41
Lower mounting pin	25-30	–	34-41
Front master cylinder			
Clamp screw	–	70-80	8-9
Cover screws	–	6-8	1
Rear brake caliper (1999)			
Brake pad pins	15-20	–	20-27
Rear master cylinder			
Mounting nut	40-50	–	54-68
Cover screws	–	6-8	1
Brake line banjo bolts	17-22	–	23-30

CHAPTER THIRTEEN

BODY

SEAT

Removal/Installation

1. Remove the bolt (A, **Figure 1**) securing the rear of the seat to the fender bracket. Do not lose the nylon retaining clip between the bracket and the rear fender.

2. Pull the seat toward the rear to release the seat front hook from the frame bracket.

3. Carefully slide the seat forward and out of the seat strap (B, **Figure 1**). Remove the seat.

4. Install the strap under the seat.

5. Slide the seat forward and insert the front hook under the frame bracket (**Figure 2**).

6. Make sure the nylon retaining clip is in place, then install the bolt securing the rear of the seat to the fender bracket. Tighten the bolt securely.

7. Pull up on the front of the seat to ensure the seat front hook is secured in place on the frame bracket.

WINDSHIELD

Removal/Installation (FXDS-CONV)

1. Place the motorcycle on level ground on the jiffy stand.

2. Loosen, but do not remove, the two screws on each side securing the windshield and bracket to the mounting brackets on the forks.

3. Carefully slide the windshield forward and off the fork brackets. Remove the windshield.
4. Install by reversing these removal steps. Do not overtighten the two screws on each side to avoid cracking the windshield.

Removal/Installation (FXDXT)

1. Place the motorcycle on level ground on the jiffy stand.
2. Remove the headlamp as described under *Headlight Bulb Replacement* in Chapter Eight.
3. Loosen, but do not remove, the upper screw on each side securing the windshield and front fairing to the support brackets on the fork.
4. Remove the lower screw on each side securing the windshield and front fairing to the support brackets on the fork.
5. Carefully pull the windshield and front fairing slightly away from the support bracket on each side.
6. Move the windshield and front fairing up and away toward the front of the motorcycle.
7. Slide the front fairing support brackets off the upper screws loosened in Step 3.
8. Remove the windshield and front fairing.
9. Install by reversing these removal steps. Tighten the screws securely.

SADDLEBAGS

1. Place the motorcycle on level ground on the jiffy stand.
2. On FXDS-CONV models, perform the following:
   a. Hold onto the saddlebag handle.
   b. Working under the saddlebag, unscrew the two large knobs securing the saddlebag frame to the mounting studs on the fender brace.

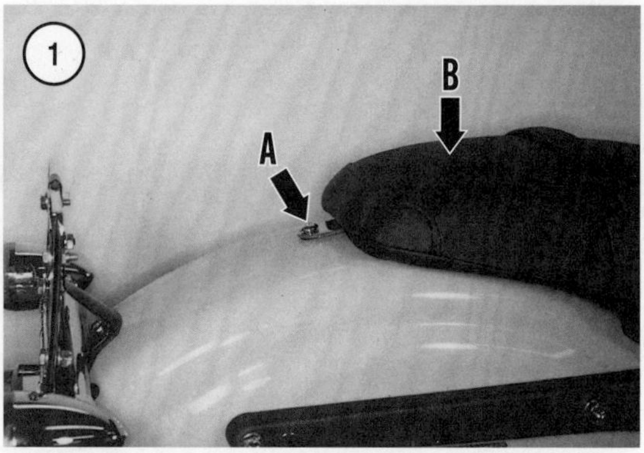

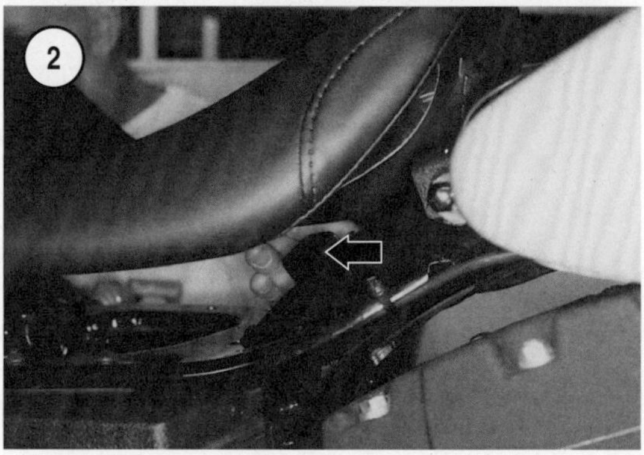

   c. Lift the saddlebag assembly slightly up and forward and pull it off the mounting studs.
   d. Remove the saddlebag assembly.
3. On FXDXT models, perform the following:
   a. Hold onto the saddlebag handle.
   b. Press the release pin at the rear of the saddlebag frame.
   c. Pull the bottom of the saddlebag slightly away from the frame.
   d. Slide the saddlebag up and toward the front of the motorcycle and pull it off the mounting bushings and acorn nuts.
   e. Remove the saddlebag assembly.
4. Install by reversing these removal steps. Make sure the saddlebag is locked into place.

SUPPLEMENT

2002-2005 MODEL SERVICE INFORMATION

This Supplement contains all procedures and specifications unique to the 2002-2005 models. If a specific procedure is not included, refer to the procedure in the prior chapter in the main body of this manual. This Supplement is divided into sections that correspond to the chapters in the main body of this manual **Tables 1-12** are located at the end of the appropriate sections.

CHAPTER ONE

GENERAL INFORMATION

Table 1 MODEL DESIGNATION

2005
FXDC, FXDCI Dyna Super Glide Custom

Table 2 MOTORCYCLE DIMENSIONS

Wheel base	
FXDWG, FXDWGI	66.10 in. (1678.95 mm)
FXDL, FXDLI	65.60 in. (1666.24 mm)
FXD (2003)	62.80 in. (1595.12 mm)
FXD, FXDI (2004-on)	62.50 in. (1587.50 mm)
FXDX, FXDXI	63.88 in. (1622.55 mm)
FXDX T-Sport	63.90 in. (1623.06 mm)
FXDC, FXDCI	62.50 in. (1587.50 mm)
Overall length	
FXDWG (2003)	94.50 in. (2400.30 mm)
FXDWG, FXDWGI (2004-on)	93.60 in. (2377.40 mm)
FXDL, FXDLI	94.00 in. (2387.60 mm)
FXD, FXDI	91.00 in. (2311.40 mm)
FXDX (2003)	92.88 in. (2359.15 mm)
FXDX, FXDXI (2004-on)	91.40 in. (2321.56 mm)
FXDX T-Sport	92.60 in. (2352.04 mm)
FXDC, FXDCI	91.00 in. (2311.40 mm)
Overall width	
FXDWG (2003)	33.50 in. (850.90 mm)
FXDWG, FXDWGI (2004-on)	35.00 in. (889.00 mm)
FXDL (2003)	28.50 in. (723.90 mm)
FXDL, FXDLI (2004-on)	36.80 in. (934.72 mm)
FXD (2003)	28.50 in. (723.90 mm)
FXD, FXDI (2004-on)	36.80 in. (934.72 mm)
FXDX (2003)	33.00 in. (838.20 mm)
FXDX, FXDXI (2004-on)	36.80 in. (934.72 mm)
FXDX T-Sport	33.00 in. (838.20 mm)
FXDC, FXDCI	36.80 in. (934.72 mm)
Road clearance	
FXDWG, FXDWGI	5.40 in. (137.16 mm)
FXDL, FXDLI	4.60 in. (116.84 mm)
FXD, FXDI	5.40 in. (137.16 mm)
FXDX, FXDXI	5.40 in. (137.16 mm)
FXDX T-Sport	5.90 in. (149.86 mm)
FXDC, FXDCI	5.40 in. (137.16 mm)
Overall height	
FXDWG (2003)	47.50 in. (1206.50 mm)
FXDWG, FXDWGI (2004-on)	47.80 in. (1214.12 mm)
FXDL (2003)	47.50 in. (1206.50 mm)
FXDL, FXDLI (2004-on)	44.80 in. (1137.92 mm)
FXD (2003)	47.50 in. (1206.50 mm)

(continued)

Table 2 MOTORCYCLE DIMENSIONS (continued)

Overall height (continued)	
FXD, FXDI (2004-on)	47.80 in. (1214.12 mm)
FXDX (2003)	51.25 in. (1301.75 mm)
FXDX, FXDXI (2004-on)	47.40 in. (1204.00 mm)
FXDX T-Sport	51.25 in. (1301.75 mm)
FXDC, FXDCI	44.80 in. (1137.92 mm)
Saddle height	
FXDWG (2003)	26.75 in. (679.45 mm)
FXDWG, FXDWGI (2004-on)	26.80 in. (680.72 mm)
FXDL, FXDLI	25.20 in. (640.08 mm)
FXD, FXDI	26.50 in. (673.10 mm)
FXDX (2003)	27.25 in. (692.15 mm)
FXDX, FXDXI (2004-on)	27.30 in. (693.42 mm)
FXDX T-Sport	27.88 in. (708.15 mm)
FXDC, FXDCI	26.50 in. (673.10 mm)

Table 3 MOTORCYCLE WEIGHT (DRY)

Model	lbs.	kg
FXDWG (2003)	612	277.6
FXDWG, FXDWGI (2004-on)	639	290
FXDL (2003)	614	278.5
FXDL, FXDLI (2004-on)	623	282.6
FXD (2003)	612	277.6
FXD, FXDI (2004-on)	622	282
FXDX (2003)	612	277.6
FXDX, FXDXI (2004-on)	622	282
FXDX T-Sport	642	291.2
FXDC, FXDCI	622	282

Table 4 SPECIAL TOOLS

Description	Manufacturer	Part No.
Cylinder head support stand	H-D	HD-39782-A
Intake valve seat adapter	H-D	HD-39782A-3
Exhaust valve seat adapter	H-D	HD-39782A-4
Valve guide driver	H-D	B-45524-1
Valve guide installer sleeve	H-D	B-45524-2A
Valve guide brush	H-D	HD-34751-A
Valve guide reamer	H-D	B-45523
T-handle	H-D	HD-39847
Valve guide reamer honing lubricant	H-D	HD-39964
Valve guide hone	H-D	B-45525
Crankshaft bearing support tube	H-D	HD-42720-5
Pilot/driver	H-D	B-45655
Crankshaft support fixture	H-D	HD-44358
Sprocket shaft bearing cone installer	H-D	HD-997225-55B

CHAPTER THREE

LUBRICATION, MAINTENANCE AND TUNE-UP

1

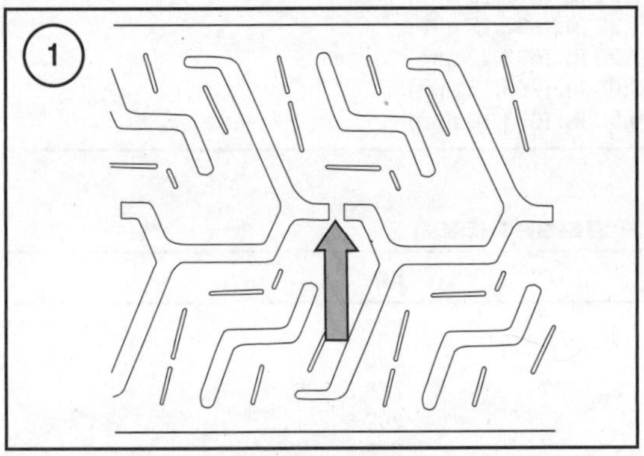

2

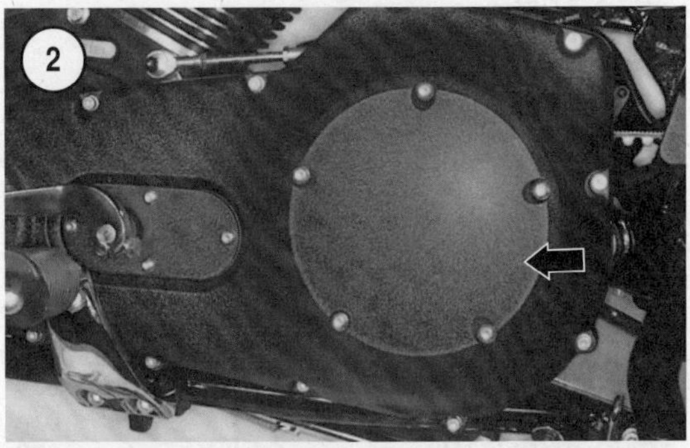

3

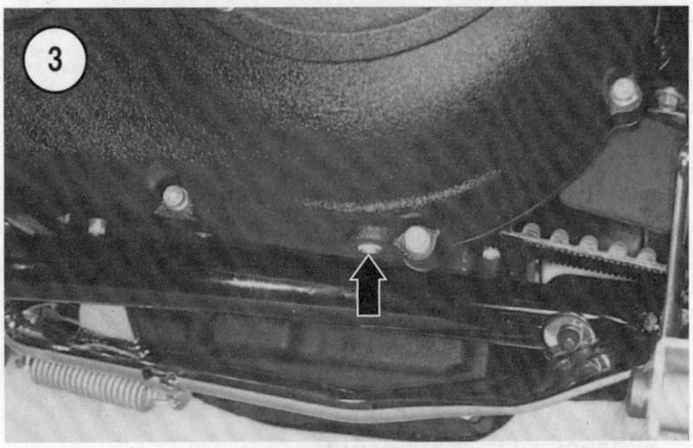

4

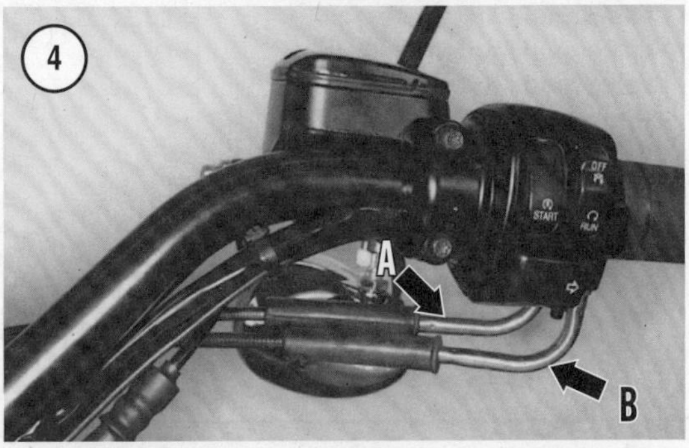

TIRES AND WHEELS

Tire Inspection

Tire inspection is the same as on previous models with the addition of tread wear indicator bars on original equipment Dunlop tires.

When the tire tread is worn to 1/32 in. (0.8 mm) or less, the tread wear indicator bars will appear on the tread surface as shown in **Figure 1**. The location of the bars is noted with a raised triangle on the tire sidewall. The tire must be replaced at this time.

PERIODIC LUBRICATION

Primary Chaincase Oil Level Check (All 2005 Models)

The primary chaincase oil level check is identical to prior to years with the exception of the seal on the clutch inspection cover. The O-ring has been replaced with a large gasket. Install the *new* large gasket as follows:

1. Position the *new* gasket with the rubber molding and the words *Toward Engine* facing away from the clutch inspection cover.
2. Align the triangular shaped hole in the *new* gasket with the top hole in the clutch inspection cover.

CAUTION
Do not push the screw through the triangular shaped hole in the new gasket as the sealing qualities of the gasket will be damaged.

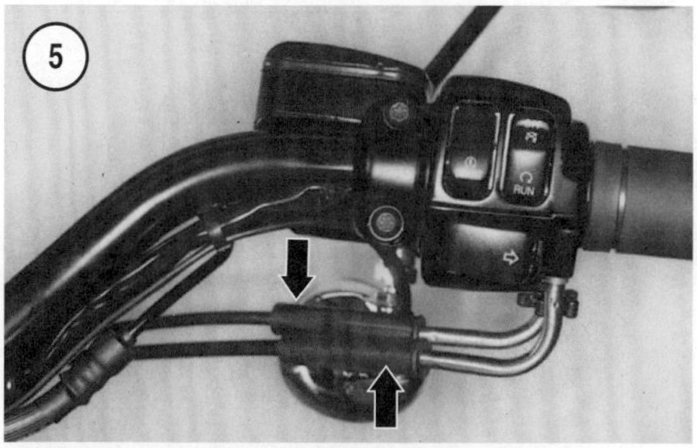

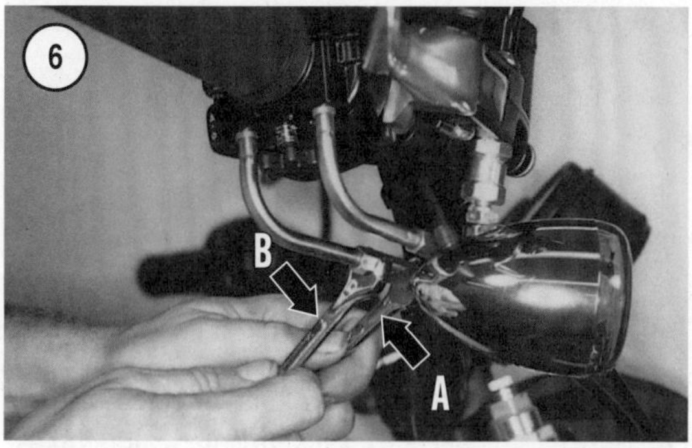

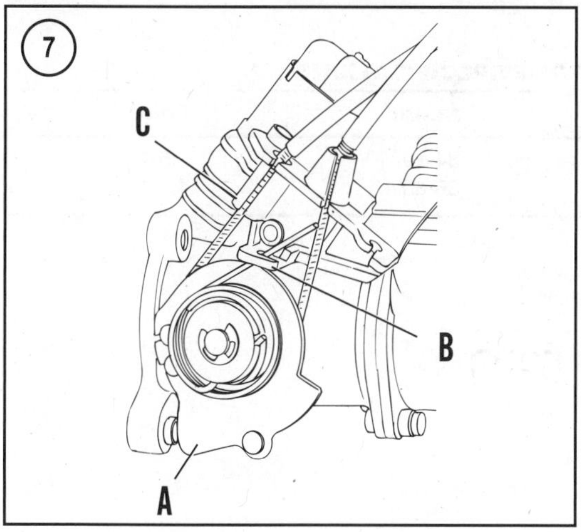

3. Insert the screw, with the captive washer, though the clutch inspection cover and carefully *thread it* it all the way through the triangular shaped hole in the new gasket.
4. Install the clutch inspection cover and new gasket onto the chaincase cover and thread the top screw part way in.
5. Make sure the clutch inspection cover (**Figure 2**) is correctly aligned with the chaincase cover and install the remaining four screws with captive washers.
6. Use a T27 Torx driver and tighten the screws in a crisscross pattern to 84-108 in.-lb. (9.5-12.2 N•m).

Primary Chaincase Oil Change (2004-On Models)

The primary chaincase oil change is the same as on previous models with the exception of the additional O-ring seal on the drain plug (**Figure 3**). The drain plug is now equipped with an O-ring seal that must be replaced every time the drain plug is removed. Install a *new* O-ring onto the drain plug, install it and tighten to 36-60 in.-lb (4.1-6.8 N•m).

Refer to the preceding procedure regarding the installation of the new clutch cover gasket.

PERIODIC MAINTENANCE

Throttle Cable Adjustment (Fuel Injected Models)

There are two different throttle cables. At the throttle grip, the front cable is the throttle control cable (A, **Figure 4**) and the rear cable is the idle control cable (B). At the fuel induction module, the throttle control cable is located at the bottom receptacle in the throttle wheel and the idle control cable is located at the top.

1. Remove the air filter and backing plate as described in Chapter Seven.
2. At the handlebar, perform the following:
   a. Roll the rubber boots (**Figure 5**) off the adjusters.
   b. Loosen both control cable adjuster locknuts (A, **Figure 6**), then turn the cable adjusters (B) *clockwise* as far as possible to increase cable slack.
3. Turn the handlebars so the front wheel points straight ahead. Then turn the throttle grip to open the throttle completely and hold it in this position.
4. At the handlebar, turn the throttle control cable adjuster (B, **Figure 6**) *counterclockwise* until the throttle cam (A, **Figure 7**) stops just touches the cam stop (B) on the throttle body. Then tighten the throttle cable adjuster and release the throttle grip.
5. Turn the front wheel all the way to the full right lock position and hold it there.
6. At the handlebar, turn the idle cable adjuster until the lower end of the idle control cable housing just contacts the spring in the cable support sleeve (C, **Figure 7**). Tighten the idle control cable locknut.

7. Check the adjustment as follows:
   a. Operate the throttle grip to make sure the cables return to the idle position when released.
   b. If the cable does not return to idle, turn the idle adjuster shortening the sleeve until correct adjustment is reached. Tighten the locknut.
8. Install the backing plate and the air filter as described in Chapter Seven.
9. Shift the transmission into neutral and start the engine.
10. Increase engine speed several times. Release the throttle and make sure the engine speed returns to idle. If the engine speed does not return to idle, at the handlebar, loosen the idle control cable adjuster locknut and turn the cable adjuster *clockwise* as required. Tighten the idle control cable adjuster locknut.
11. Allow the engine to idle. Then turn the handlebar from side to side. Do not operate the throttle. If the engine speed increases when the handlebar assembly is turned, the throttle cables are routed incorrectly or damaged. Turn off the engine. Recheck cable routing and adjustment.
12. Roll the rubber boots (**Figure 5**) back onto the adjusters.

WARNING

Do not ride the motorcycle until the throttle cables are properly adjusted. Also, the cables must not catch or pull when the handlebar is turned from side to side. Improper cable routing and adjustment can cause the throttle to stick open. This could cause loss of control and a possible crash. Recheck this adjustment before riding the motorcycle.

Air Filter Element Removal/Installation (Fuel Injected Models)

Air filter service is identical to carbureted models.

IDLE SPEED ADJUSTMENT

Fuel Injected Models

Idle speed adjustment on fuel injected models *can only* be set by a Harley-Davidson dealership using the Digital Technician diagnostic unit.

Table 5 MAINTENANCE TORQUE SPECIFICATIONS

Item	ft.-lb.	in.-lb.	N•m
Clutch inspection cover screws	–	84-108	9.5-12
Primary chaincase drain plug	–	36-60	4.1-6.8

CHAPTER FOUR

ENGINE

Refer to **Table 6** and **Table 7** for revised engine specifications for 2003-2005 models.

ENGINE

Removal/Installation

The removal procedure is the same as on prior years. On fuel injected models, remove the fuel injection module as described in the Chapter Seven section of this Supplement.

ROCKER ARMS AND PUSHRODS

Removal/Installation

The removal procedure is the same as on prior years.

The installation procedure is the same as on prior years with the exception of the breather assembly components. The 1999-2002 models were equipped with a breather assembly consisting of four parts, the cover, filter element, breather baffle and gaskets. On the 2003 models the breather assembly was combined

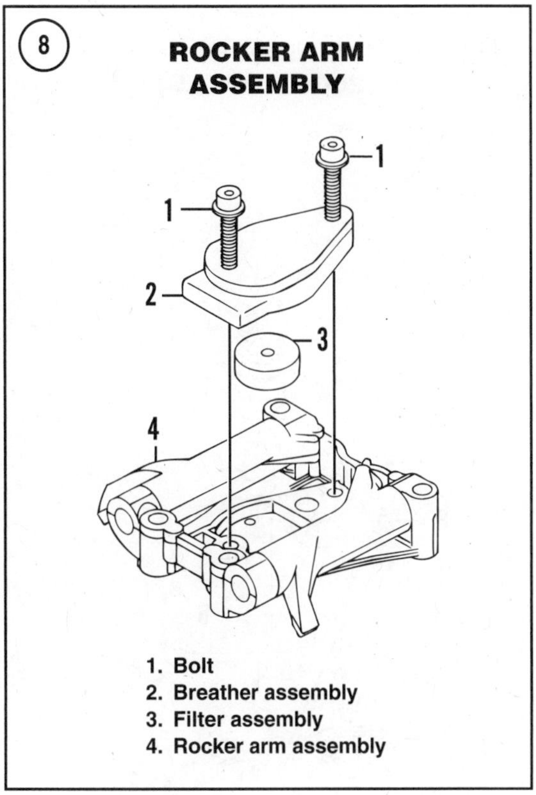

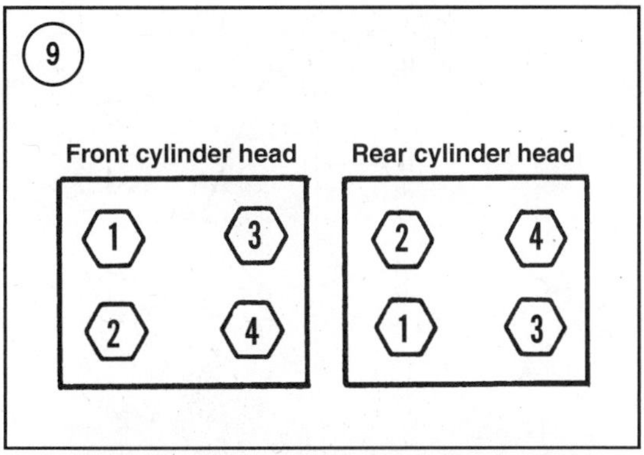

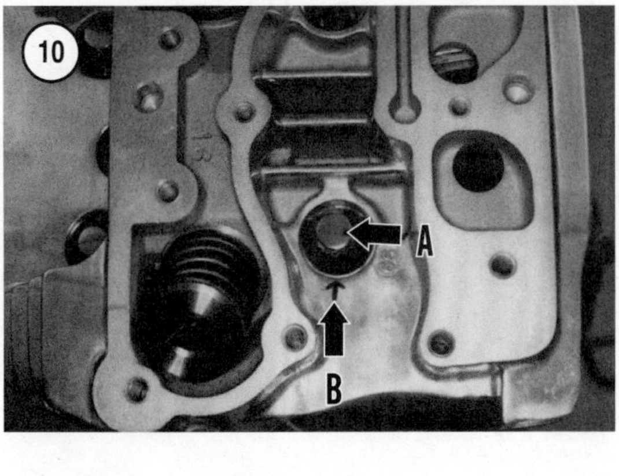

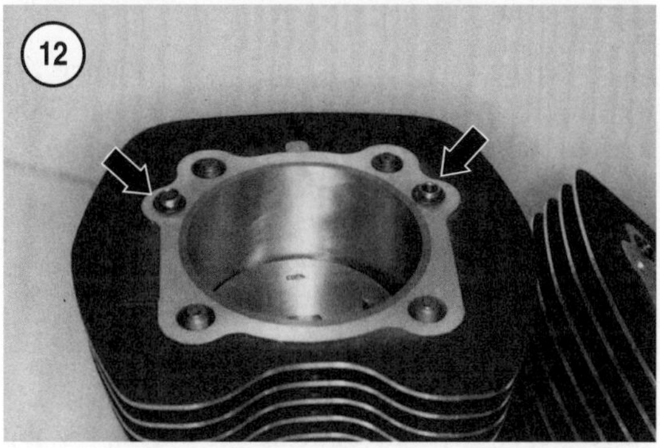

into a one-piece unit along with the filter element and gasket (**Figure 8**). The 2004-on models use the components equipped on the 1999-2002 models.

CYLINDER HEAD

Removal/Installation

On 2004-on models, refer to **Figure 9** for the front and rear cylinder head bolt tightening sequence. Tighten the cylinder head bolts as follows:

1. Starting with bolt No. 1, tighten each bolt in order to 120-144 in.-lb. (13.6-16.3 N•m).
2. Starting with bolt No. 1, tighten each bolt in order to 15-17 ft.-lb. (20.3-23.1 N•m).
3. Make a vertical mark with a permanent marker on each bolt head (A, **Figure 10**). Make another mark on the cylinder head (B, **Figure 10**) at a 90° angle, or 1/4 turn from the mark on the head bolt.
4. Use the marks as a guide and tighten each bolt head 90°, or 1/4 turn, clockwise until the marks are aligned (**Figure 11**).

On 2004-on models, the two O-rings (**Figure 12**) are no longer used in junction with the cylinder head dowel pins.

VALVE AND VALVE COMPONENTS (2005 MODELS)

Complete valve service requires a number of special tools, including a valve spring compressor, to remove and install the valves. The following procedures describe how to check for valve component wear and to determine what type of service is required.

Refer to **Figure 13**.

Valve Removal

1. Remove the cylinder head as described in Chapter Four.
2. Install the valve spring compressor (**Figure 14**) squarely over the valve spring upper retainer (**Figure 15**) and against the valve head.

CAUTION
To avoid loss of spring tension, compress the spring only enough to remove the valve keepers.

3. Tighten the valve spring compressor until the valve keepers separate from the valve stem. Lift the valve keepers out through the valve spring compressor with a magnet or needlenose pliers.
4. Gradually loosen the valve spring compressor and remove it from the cylinder head.
5. Remove the spring upper retainer and the valve spring.

CAUTION
*Remove any burrs from the valve stem groove before removing the valve (**Figure 16**); otherwise the valve guide will be damaged as the valve stem passes through it.*

6. Remove the valve from the cylinder head while rotating it slightly.
7. Using needlenose pliers, carefully twist and remove the valve stem seal/spring seat assembly from the valve guide. Discard the valve stem seal/spring seat assembly.

CAUTION
Keep the components of each valve assembly together by placing each set in a divided carton, or into separate small boxes or small reclosable plastic bags. Identify the components as either intake or exhaust. If both cylin-

13

CYLINDER HEAD (2005 MODELS)

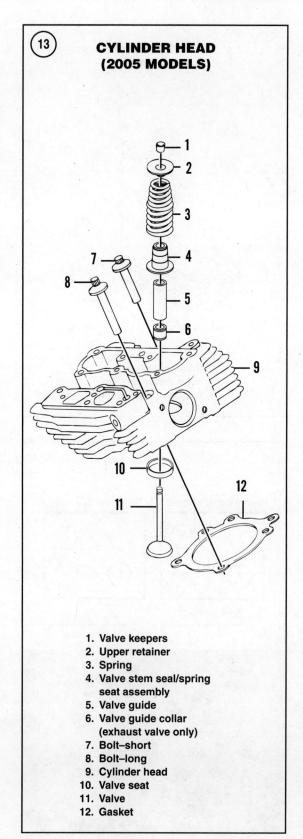

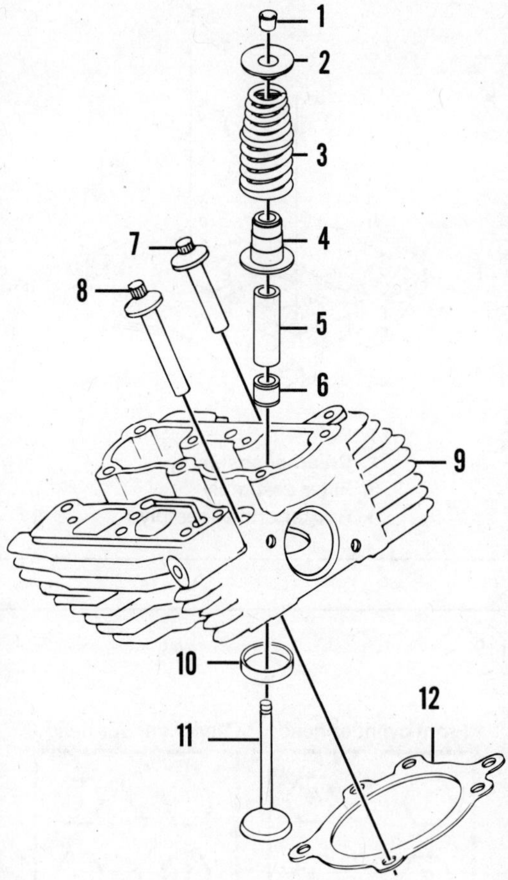

1. Valve keepers
2. Upper retainer
3. Spring
4. Valve stem seal/spring seat assembly
5. Valve guide
6. Valve guide collar (exhaust valve only)
7. Bolt–short
8. Bolt–long
9. Cylinder head
10. Valve seat
11. Valve
12. Gasket

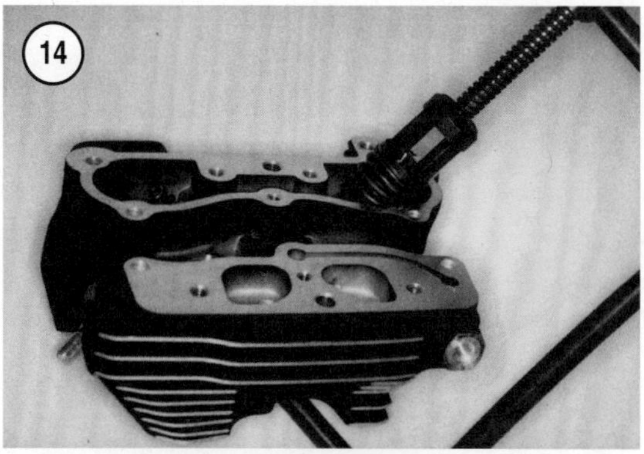
14

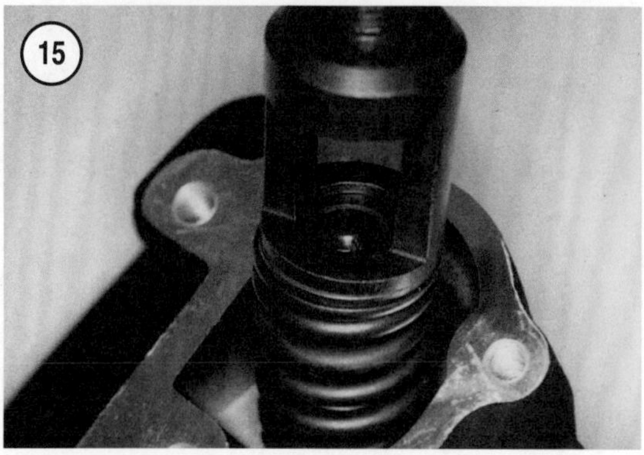
15

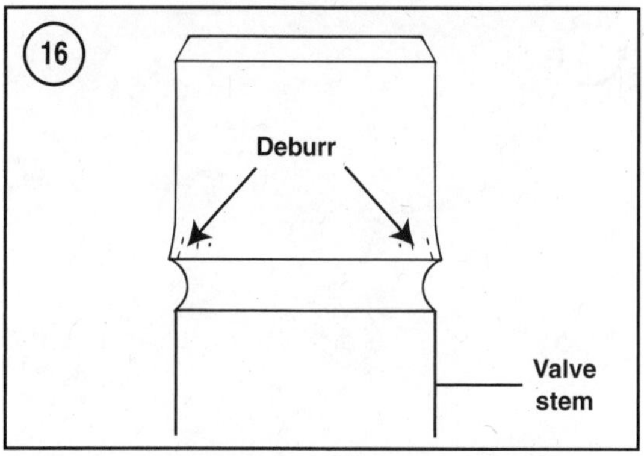

16

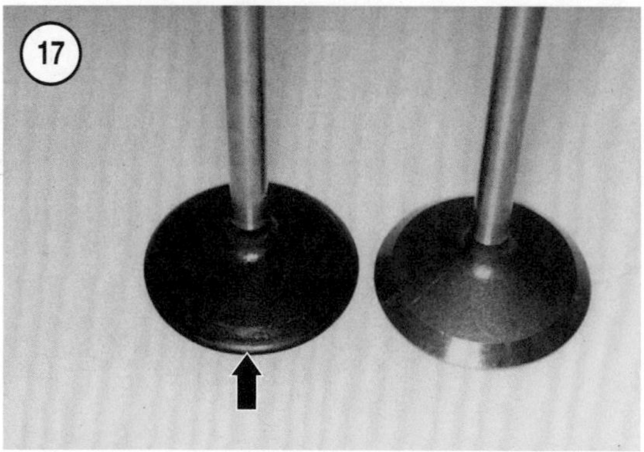
17

18

ders are disassembled, also label the components as front and rear. Do not intermix components from the valves or excessive wear may result.

8. Repeat Steps 3-7 to remove the remaining valve.

Valve Inspection

When measuring the valves and valve components in this section, compare the actual measurements to the new and wear limit specifications in **Table 6**. Replace parts that are out of specification or are damaged as described in this section.

1. Clean valves in solvent. Do not gouge or damage the valve seating surface.
2. Inspect the valve face. Minor roughness and pitting (**Figure 17**) can be removed by lapping the valve as described in this chapter. Excessive unevenness to the contact surface indicates the valve is not serviceable.
3. Inspect the valve stem for wear and roughness. Then measure the valve stem outside diameter with a micrometer (**Figure 18**).
4. Remove all carbon and varnish from the valve guides with a stiff spiral wire brush before measuring wear.
5. Measure the valve guide inside diameter with a small hole gauge (**Figure 19**) at the top, center and bottom locations. Then measure the small hole gauge.
6. Determine the valve stem-to-valve guide clearance by subtracting the valve stem outside diameter from the valve guide inner diameter.
7. If a small hole gauge is not available, insert each valve into its guide. Attach a dial indicator to the valve stem next to the head (**Figure 20**). Hold the valve slightly off its seat and rock it sideways in both directions 90° to each other. If the valve rocks

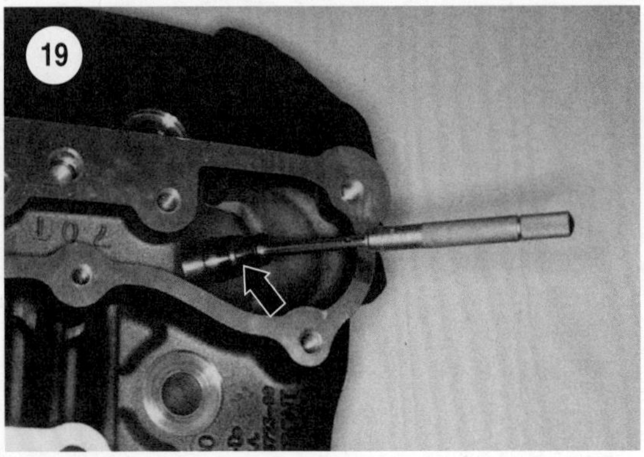

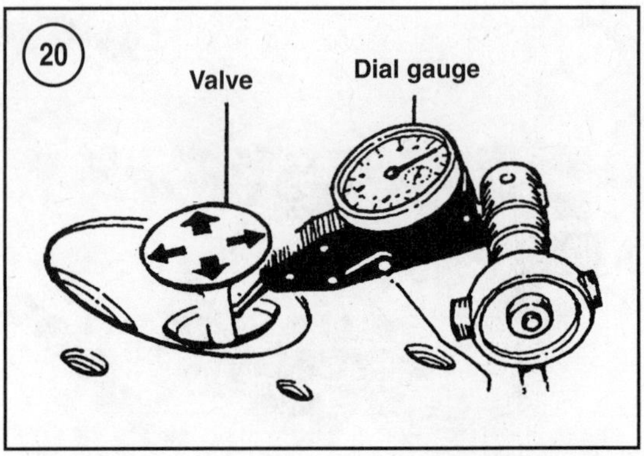

more than slightly, the guide is probably worn. Take the cylinder head to a Harley-Davidson dealership or machine shop and have the valve guides measured.

8. Check the valve spring as follows:
   a. Inspect the valve spring for visual damage.
   b. Use a square to visually check the spring for distortion or tilt (**Figure 21**).
   c. Measure the valve spring free length with a vernier caliper (**Figure 22**) and compare it to the specifications.
   d. Repeat sub-steps a-c for each valve spring.
   e. Replace the defective spring(s).

9. Check the valve spring upper retainer seats for cracks or other damage.

10. Check the valve keepers fit on the valve stem end (**Figure 23**). They should index tightly into the valve stem groove.

11. Inspect the valve seats (**Figure 24**) in the cylinder head. If they are worn or burned, they can be reconditioned as described in Chapter Four. Seats and valves in near-perfect condition can be reconditioned by lapping with fine Carborundum paste.
   a. Clean the valve seat and corresponding valve mating areas with contact cleaner.
   b. Coat the valve seat with layout fluid.
   c. Install the valve into its guide and tap it against its seat. Do not rotate the valve.
   d. Lift the valve out of the guide and measure the seat width at various points around the seat with a vernier caliper.
   e. Compare the seat width with the specifications. If the seat width is less than specified or uneven, resurface the seats as described in Chapter Four.
   f. Remove all layout fluid residue from the seats and valves.

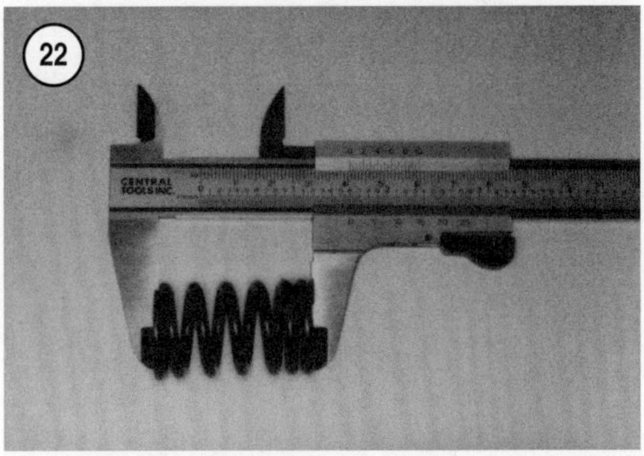

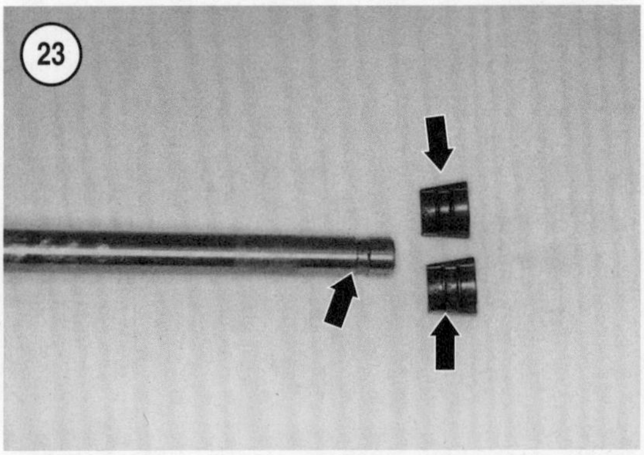

24

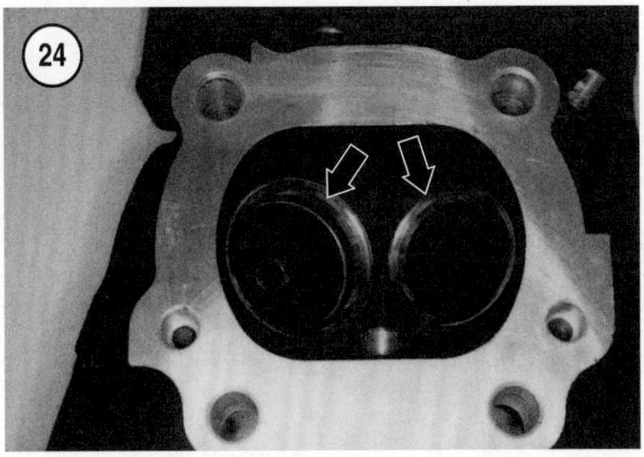

25

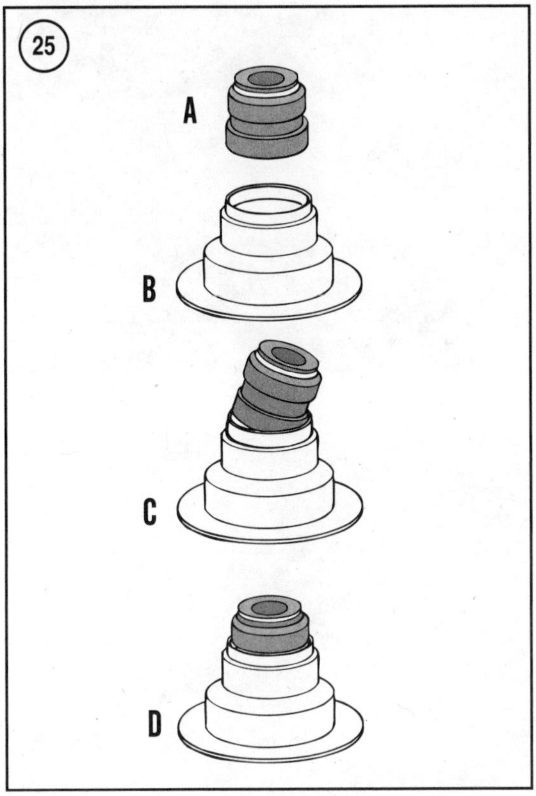

26

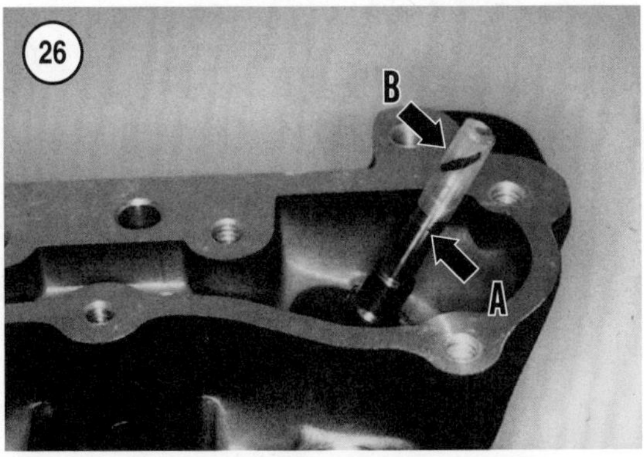

Valve Installation

1. Clean the end of the valve guide.
2. Assemble the valve stem seal/spring seat assembly as follows:
   a. Apply engine oil to the oil seal (A, **Figure 25**) and the spring seat (B).
   b. Position the oil seal with the spring end going in last (C, **Figure 25**) and insert it into the spring seat.
   c. Press the oil seal down until it seats completely within the spring seat (D, **Figure 25**).
3. Coat a valve stem with Torco MPZ, molybdenum disulfide paste or equivalent. Install the valve part way into the guide. Then slowly turn the valve as it enters the oil seal and continue turning it until the valve is installed all the way.
4. Work the valve back and forth in the valve guide to ensure the lubricant is distributed evenly within the valve guide.
5. Withdraw the valve and apply an additional coat of the lubricant.
6. Reinstall the valve into the valve guide but do not push the valve past the top of the valve guide.
7. Push the valve all the way into the cylinder head until it bottoms (A, **Figure 26**).

CAUTION
The oil seal will be torn as it passes the valve stem keeper groove if the plastic capsule is not installed in Step 8. The capsule is included in the top end gasket set.

8. Hold the valve in place and install the plastic capsule (B, **Figure 26**) onto the end of the valve stem. Apply a light coat of clean engine oil to the outer surface of the capsule.
9. With the valve held in place, slowly slide the valve stem seal/spring seat assembly onto the valve stem. Push the assembly down until it bottoms on the machined surface of the cylinder head.
10. Remove the plastic capsule from the valve stem. Keep the capsule as it will be used on the remaining valves.
11. Position the valve spring with tapered end going on last and install the valve spring (A, **Figure 27**). Make sure it is properly seated on the spring seat.
12. Install the upper spring retainer (B, **Figure 27**) on top of the valve spring.

CAUTION

To avoid loss of spring tension, only compress the springs enough to install the valve keepers.

13. Compress the valve spring with a valve spring compressor (**Figure 14**) and install the valve keepers (**Figure 28**).
14. Make sure both keepers are seated around the valve stem prior to releasing the compressor.
15. Slowly release tension from the compressor and remove it. After removing the compressor, inspect the valve keepers to make sure they are properly seated (**Figure 29**). Tap the end of the valve stem with a *soft-faced* hammer to ensure the keepers are properly seated.
16. Repeat Steps 1-15 for the remaining valve.
17. Install the cylinder head as described in this Supplement.

Valve Guide Replacement

Tools

The following tools or their equivalents are required to replace the valve guides.

1. Cylinder head support stand (HD-39782-A).
2. Intake valve seat adapter (HD-39782A-3).
3. Exhaust valve seat adapter (HD-39782A-4).
4. Valve guide driver (B-45524-1).
5. Valve guide installer sleeve (B-45524-2A).
6. Valve guide brush (HD-34751-A).
7. Valve guide reamer (B-45523) and T-handle (HD-39847).
8. Valve guide reamer honing lubricant (HD- 39964).
9. Valve guide hone (B-45525).
10. Hydraulic press.

Procedure

CAUTION

The valve guides must be removed and installed using the following special tools to avoid damage to the cylinder head. Use the correct size valve guide removal tool to remove the valve guides or the tool may expand the end of the guide. An expanded guide will widen and damage the guide bore in the cylinder head as it passes through it.

1. Remove the old valve guide as follows:

27

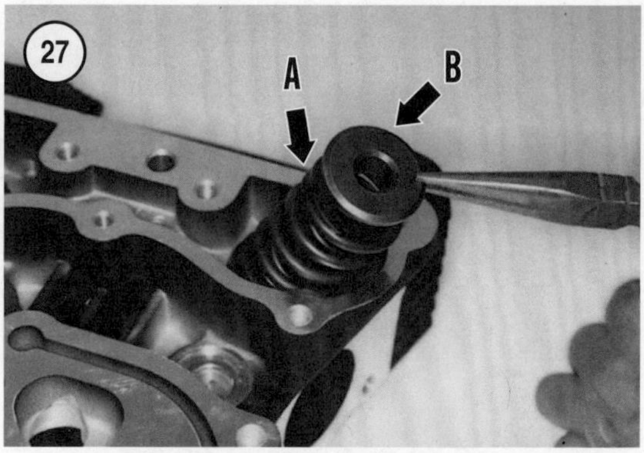

28

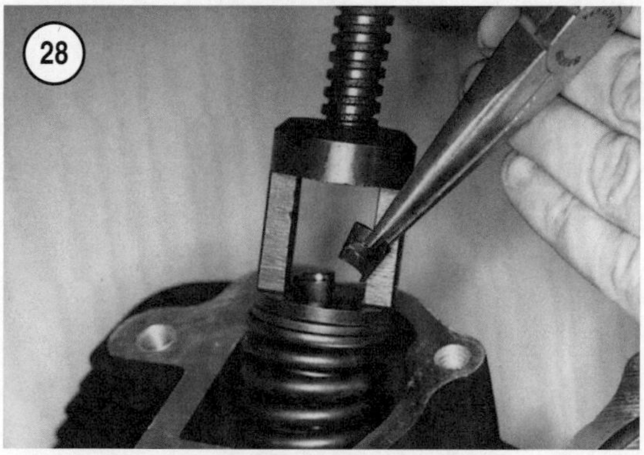

29

a. Install the intake (A, **Figure 30**) or exhaust (B) valve seat adapter into the tube at the top of the support stand (C).

b. Install the support stand on the hydraulic press table.

c. Install the cylinder head (A, **Figure 31**) onto the support stand (B) *centering* the cylinder head valve seat onto the seat adapter.

d. Insert the valve guide driver (C, **Figure 31**) into the valve guide bore until it stops on the valve guide shoulder.

30

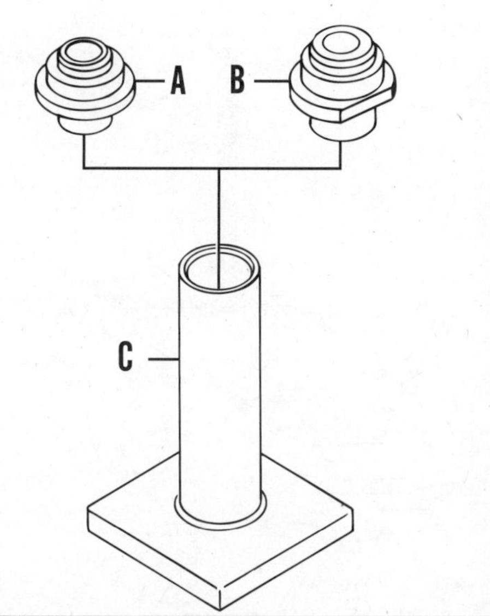

32

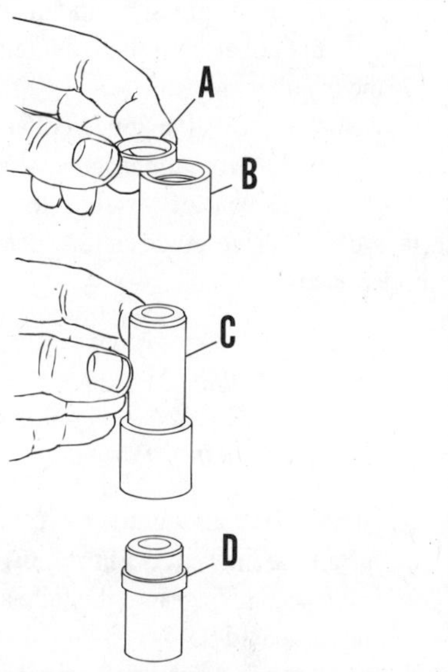

31

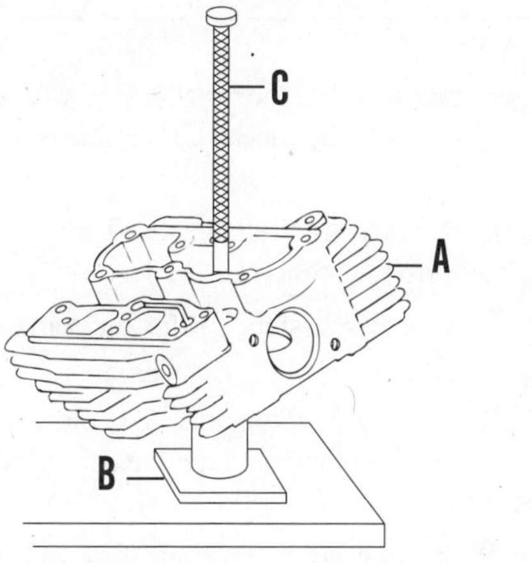

e. Center the valve guide driver under the press ram and make sure the driver is perpendicular to the press table.

f. Support the cylinder head, slowly apply pressure and drive valve guide out through the combustion chamber side. Discard the valve guide.

g. Remove the cylinder head and special tools from the press bed.

h. Repeat sub-steps a-g for the remaining valve guide.

2. Clean the valve guide bores in the cylinder head.

3. Because the valve guide bores in the cylinder head may have enlarged during removal of the old guides, measure each valve guide bore prior to purchasing the new guides. Then purchase the new valve guides to match their respective bore diameters. Determine the bore diameter as follows:

a. Measure the valve guide bore diameter in the cylinder head with a bore gauge or snap gauge. Record the bore diameter.

b. The *new* valve guide outside diameter must be 0.0020-0.0033 in. (0.050-0.083 mm) larger than the guide bore in the cylinder head. When purchasing new valve guides, measure the new guide's outside diameter with a micrometer. If the new guide's outside diameter is not within this specification, install oversize valve guide(s). See a Harley-Davidson dealership for available sizes and part numbers.

NOTE

The intake valves are not equipped with the valve guide collar. On exhaust valves, the collar must be installed onto the valve guide, see Step 4.

4. On *exhaust valve guides*, install the collar onto the valve guide as follows:

a. Insert the valve guide collar (A, **Figure 32**) onto the installer sleeve (B) and center it squarely onto the counter bore of the installer sleeve.

b. Install the *new* valve guide (C, **Figure 32**) into the installer sleeve (B) until it contacts the valve guide collar.

c. Install the installer sleeve and valve guide onto the press table and center it.

d. Slowly apply pressure and drive valve guide onto the collar until the valve guide bottoms in the installer sleeve.
e. Remove the valve guide/collar assembly (D, **Figure 32**) from the installer sleeve.

5. Apply a thin coat of Vaseline to the entire outer surface of the valve guide before installing it in the cylinder head.

CAUTION

When installing oversize valve guides, make sure to match each guide to its respective bore in the cylinder head.

6. Install the *new* valve guide as follows:
a. Install the intake (A, **Figure 30**) or exhaust (B) valve seat adapter into the tube at the top of the support stand (C).
b. Install the support stand on the hydraulic press table.
c. Install the cylinder head (A, **Figure 33**) onto the support stand (B) *centering* the cylinder head valve seat onto the seat adapter.
d. On exhaust valves, position the valve guide with the collar end going in last. The intake valve guides are non-directional, either end can go in first.
e. Install the valve guide onto the cylinder head receptacle.
f. Install the valve guide installer sleeve (C, **Figure 33**) over the valve guide, and insert the tapered end of the valve guide driver (D) into the installer sleeve.
g. Center the valve guide driver under the press ram and make sure the driver is perpendicular to the press table.
h. Support the cylinder head, slowly apply pressure and slowly start to drive the valve guide into the cylinder head receptacle. Stop and back off the press ram to allow the valve guide to center itself.
i. Verify that the support stand (A, **Figure 33**) and valve guide driver (D) are square with the press table.
j. Once again apply press pressure and continue to drive the valve guide part way into the cylinder head receptacle. Once again, stop and back off the press ram to allow the valve guide to center itself.
k. Again apply press pressure and continue to drive the valve guide into the cylinder head receptacle until the installer sleeve (C, **Figure 33**) contacts the machined surface of the cylinder head.

33

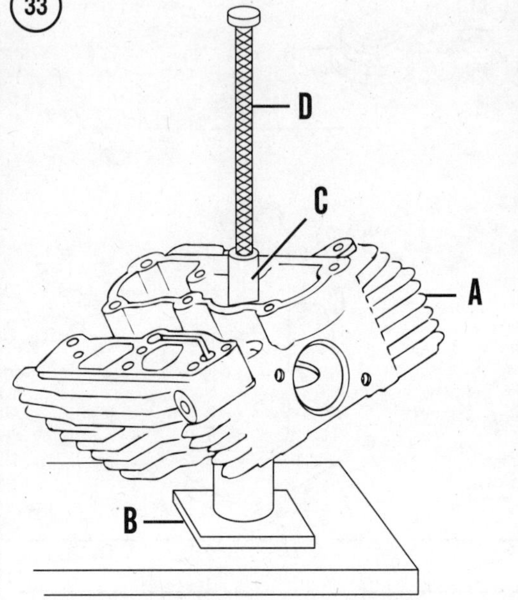

l. Remove the cylinder head and special tools from the press bed.
m. Repeat sub-steps a-l for the remaining valve guides.

7. Replacement valve guides are sold with a smaller inside diameter than the valve stem. Ream the guide to fit the valve stem as follows:
a. Apply a liberal amount of reamer lubricant to the ream bit and to the valve guide bore.
b. Start the reamer straight into the valve guide bore.

CAUTION

Only apply pressure to the end of the drive socket. If pressure is applied to the T-handle, the bore will be uneven, rough cut and tapered.

c. Apply thumb pressure to the end of the drive socket portion of the T-handle while rotating the T-handle *clockwise*. Only *light* pressure is required. Apply additional lubricant to the reamer and into the valve guide while rotating the reamer.

d. Continue to rotate the reamer until the entire bit has traveled through the valve guide and the shank of the reamer rotates freely.

CAUTION
Never back the reamer out through the valve guide as the guide will be damaged.

e. Remove the T-handle from the reamer. Remove the reamer from the combustion chamber side of the cylinder head.

f. Apply low-pressure compressed air to remove the small shavings from the valve guide bore. Then clean the valve guide bore with the small spiral brush.

8. Hone the valve guide as follows:

a. Install the valve guide hone into a high-speed electric drill.

b. Lubricate the valve guide bore and hone stones with the reamer lubricant—*do not use motor oil.*

c. Carefully insert the hone stones into the valve guide bore.

d. Start the drill and move the hone back and forth in the valve guide bore for 10 to 12 complete strokes to obtain a 60° crosshatch pattern.

9. Repeat Steps 7 and 8 for each valve guide.

10. Soak the cylinder head in a container filled with hot, soapy water. Then clean the valve guides with a valve guide brush or an equivalent bristle brush. *Do not use a steel brush.* Do not use cleaning solvent, kerosene or gasoline as these chemicals will not remove all of the abrasive particles produced during the honing operation. Repeat this step until all of the valve guides are thoroughly cleaned. Then rinse the cylinder head and valve guides in clear, cold water and dry them with compressed air.

11. After cleaning and drying the valve guides, apply clean engine oil to the guides to prevent rust.

12. Resurface the valve seats as described in *Valve Seat Reconditioning* in this chapter.

PISTONS AND PISTON RINGS

Piston Clearance

Later model 2003 and the 2004-on models have a small oval-shaped opening on the piston skirt coating. This opening is used to locate the micrometer for an accurate outer diameter measurement. This small oval-shaped opening is too small for the standard flat anvil micrometer to obtain an accurate measurement. Use a 3-4 in. blade or ball anvil style micrometer, or a 4-5 in. micrometer with spherical ball adapters to achieve a correct measurement.

1. Make sure the piston skirt and cylinder bore is clean and dry.

2. Measure the cylinder bore with a bore gauge (**Figure 34**) as described under *Cylinder Block Inspection* in Chapter Four.

NOTE
Some early 2003 models were not equipped with the bare aluminum spots on the piston skirt coating.

3A. On early 2003 models, measure the piston diameter with a micrometer as follows:

a. Hold the micrometer at the bottom of the piston skirt at a right angle to the piston pin bore (**Figure 35**). Adjust the micrometer so the spindle and anvil just touch the skirt.

14

b. Start below the bottom ring and slowly move the micrometer toward the bottom of the skirt.
c. The micrometer will be loose, then tight at about 0.5 in. (12.7 mm) from the bottom and then loose again.
d. Measure the piston skirt at the tightest point.

3B. On late 2003 and 2004-on models, measure the piston diameter with a micrometer as follows:

a. Use the previously described special micrometer and correctly position it on the bare aluminum spot on each side of the piston as shown in **Figure 36**.
b. Measure the piston at this location only.

4. Subtract the piston diameter from the largest bore diameter; the difference is piston-to-cylinder clearance. If the clearance exceeds the specification in **Table 6**, the pistons should be replaced and the cylinders bored oversize and then honed. Purchase the new pistons first. Measure their diameter and add the specified clearance to determine the proper cylinder bore diameter.

CAMSHAFT SUPPORT PLATE

Rear Camshaft Sprocket and Crankshaft Drive Sprocket Alignment

The procedure is identical to previous models. Refer to **Table 7** for sprocket spacer thickness and part numbers.

CRANKCASE AND CRANKSHAFT

Right Side Main Bearing Replacement

Refer to **Figure 37**.

The following tools or their equivalents are required to remove and install the right side main bearing:

1. Hydraulic press.
2. Crankshaft bearing support tube: (HD-42720-5).
3. Pilot/driver: (B-45655).

Removal

NOTE
The Harley-Davidson support tube is marked with an A on one end and a B on the other.

36

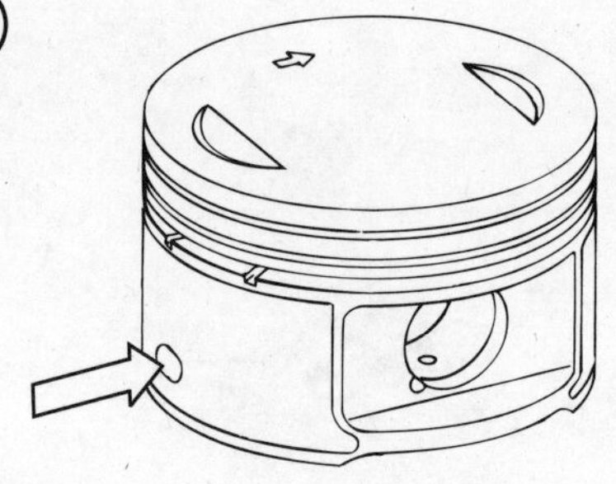

1. Place the support tube with the A side facing up on the press bed.
2. Position the right side crankcase with the outer surface facing up and position the bearing directly over the support tube on the press bed.
3. Install the pilot shaft through the bearing and into the support tube.
4. Center the press driver over the pilot shaft.
5. Hold the crankcase half parallel to the press bed and have an assistant slowly apply press pressure on the pilot shaft until the bearing is free from the case half.
6. Remove the case half and special tools from the press bed.

Installation

1. Apply a light coat of clean engine oil to the outer surface of the bearing and to the crankcase receptacle.
2. Place the support tube with the *B* side facing up on the press bed.
3. Position the right side crankcase with the outer surface facing up on the press bed.
4. Position the new bearing with the manufacturer's marks facing up and place it over the crankcase receptacle.
5. Install the pilot/driver through the bearing and into the support tube.
6. Center the press driver over the pilot driver.
7. Slowly apply press pressure on the pilot driver, pressing the bearing into the crankcase. Apply pressure until resistance is felt and the bearing bottoms in the support tube. This will correctly locate the bearing within the crankcase. Remove the pilot driver.
8. Remove the crankcase and the support tube from the press bed.

37

CRANKCASE ASSEMBLY

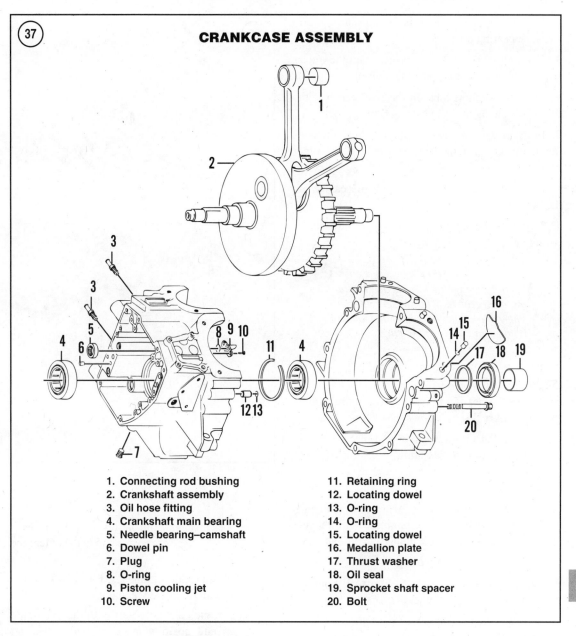

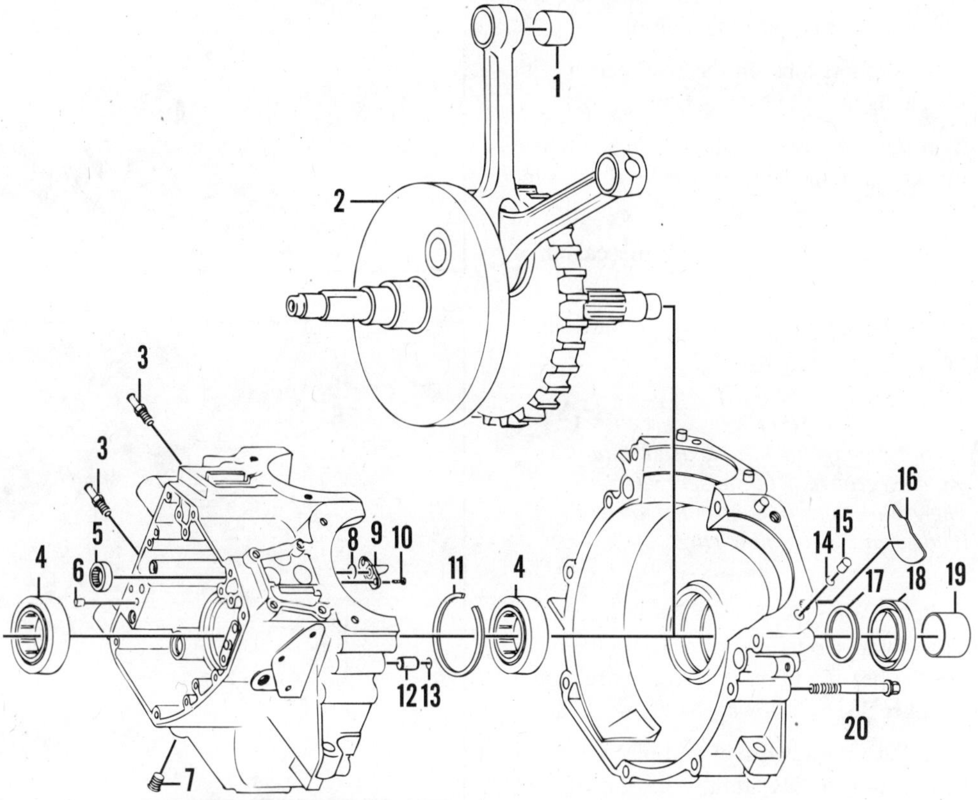

1. Connecting rod bushing
2. Crankshaft assembly
3. Oil hose fitting
4. Crankshaft main bearing
5. Needle bearing–camshaft
6. Dowel pin
7. Plug
8. O-ring
9. Piston cooling jet
10. Screw
11. Retaining ring
12. Locating dowel
13. O-ring
14. O-ring
15. Locating dowel
16. Medallion plate
17. Thrust washer
18. Oil seal
19. Sprocket shaft spacer
20. Bolt

9. Check on each side of the crankcase to make sure the bearing is centered within the receptacle. If not, reposition the bearing until it is centered correctly.

10. Spin the bearing to make sure it rotates smoothly with no binding.

Left Side Main Bearing Assembly Replacement

Refer to **Figure 37**.

The following tools or their equivalents are required to remove and install the right side main bearing:

1. Hydraulic press.
2. Crankshaft bearing support tube: (HD-42720-5).
3. Pilot/driver: (B-45655).

Bearing removal

1. Place the crankcase on the workbench with the inboard surface facing up.

2. If still in place, remove the crankshaft spacer from the bearing bore.

3. Carefully pull the thrust washer from the outer surface of the crankcase past the oil seal.

4. Place the support tube on the workbench with the A side facing up.

5. Position the crankcase with the inner surface facing up and place the bearing bore over the support tube.

6. Use a suitable size drift and tap the oil seal out of the bearing bore. Discard the oil seal.

7. Turn the crankcase over with the inner surface facing up.

CAUTION

Do not damage the crankcase retaining ring groove with the screwdriver. The groove must remain sharp to correctly seat the retaining ring.

8. The roller bearing (A, **Figure 38**) is secured in the crankcase with a retaining ring (B) on the inner surface of the bearing bore. Remove the retaining ring (B, **Figure 38**) as follows:

   a. Use a flat tip screwdriver and place it under the retaining ring. Carefully lift the edge of the retaining ring up and out of the crankcase groove.

   b. Slide the tip of the screwdriver around the edge of the bearing and continue to lift the retaining ring out of the crankcase groove.

   c. Remove the retaining ring.

9. Position the support tube (A, **Figure 39**) on the press bed with the A side facing up.

10. Position the crankcase half with the outer side facing up and position the crankshaft's bearing bore over the support tube. Correctly align the two parts.

11. Slide the pilot/driver (B, **Figure 39**) through the crankcase bearing and into the support.

12. Center the press ram (C, **Figure 39**) directly over the pilot/driver (B) and slowly press the bearing out of the crankcase.

13. Remove the crankcase and special tools from the press bed.

14. Clean the crankcase half in solvent and dry it with compressed air.

38

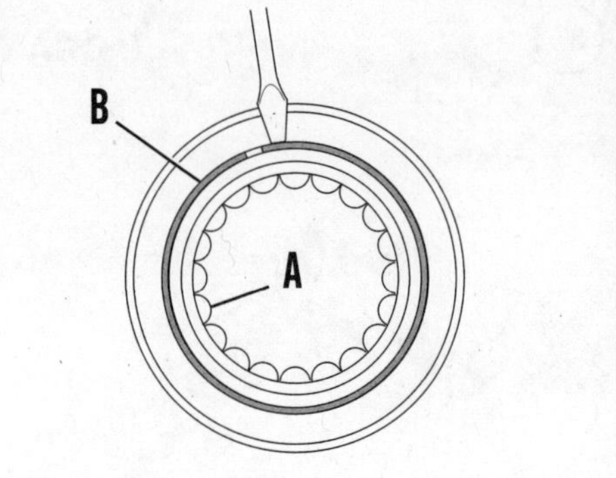

39

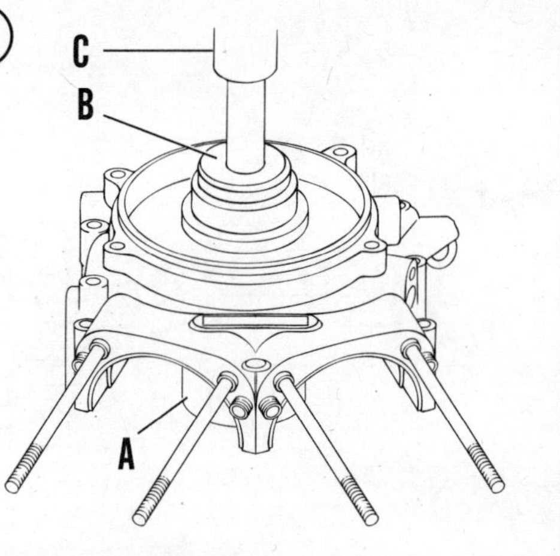

Bearing installation

1. Apply clean engine oil, or press lube, to the bearing receptacle in the crankcase and to the outer race of the *new* bearing.

2. Position the support tube (A, **Figure 40**) on the press bed with the A side facing up.

3. Position the crankcase half with the inner side facing up and position the crankshaft's bearing bore over the support tube. Correctly align the two parts.

4. Correctly position the *new* bearing (B, **Figure 40**) over the crankcase bore with the manufacturer's marks facing down.

5. Slide the pilot/driver (C, **Figure 40**) through the new bearing and the crankcase and into the support.

6. Center the press ram (D, **Figure 40**) directly over the pilot/driver (C) and slowly press the bearing into the crankcase until it *lightly* bottoms in the crankshaft bearing bore.

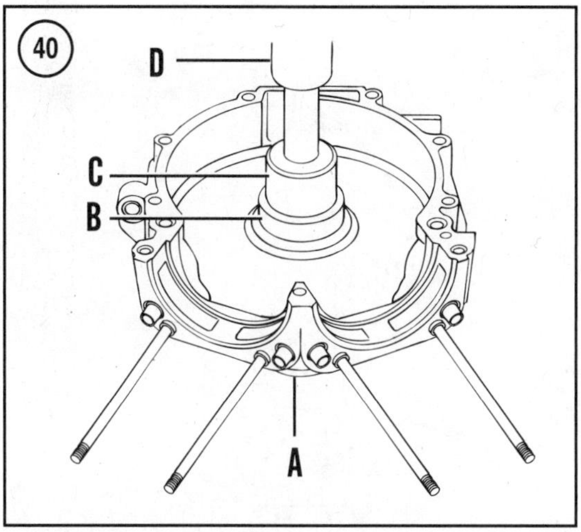

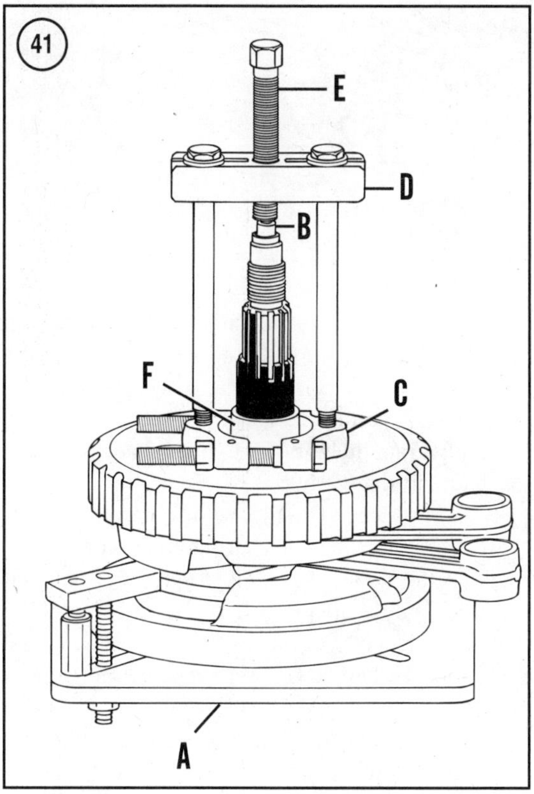

7. Remove the crankcase and special tools from the press.

8. Make sure the bearing has been pressed in past the retaining ring groove. If the groove is not visible above the bearing, repeat Steps 2-6 until the groove is visible.

9. Position the crankcase on the workbench with the inner surface facing up.

CAUTION
Do not damage the crankcase retaining ring groove with the screwdriver. The groove must remain sharp to correctly seat the retaining ring.

NOTE
If the retaining ring will not correctly seat in the crankcase groove, the bearing is not correctly seated in the crankcase bore. Repeat Steps 2-6

10. Install the bearing's *new* retainer ring as follows:

a. Work the retaining ring into the crankcase groove being careful not to damage the crankcase groove.

b. Use a flat tip screwdriver and push the retaining ring. Continue to push the retaining ring into the crankcase groove and make sure it is correctly seated in the groove.

Crankshaft End Play Inspection

All 2003-on models are equipped with assembled roller bearings and this procedure is no longer necessary.

Crankshaft Left Side Main Bearing Assembly Inner Race Replacement

Removal

1. Support the crankshaft in a support fixture (HD-44358), or an equivalent, with the bearing side facing up (A, **Figure 41**).

2. Place a hardened plug (B, **Figure 41**) between the bearing puller and the end of the crankshaft.

3. Install the bearing splitter under the bearing inner race (C, **Figure 41**).

4. Apply graphite lubricant to the bearing puller center screw, and attach a bearing puller (D, **Figure 41**) to the splitter.

WARNING
*In Step 5, **never** use the heat gun in conjunction with the penetrating oil. The heat from the gun may ignite the oil resulting in a fire.*

5A. Use an industrial heat gun and apply heat uniformly to the bearing inner race for approximately 30 seconds.

5B. If a heat gun is not available, apply penetrating oil to the inner race and crankshaft and allow the oil to penetrate for 30 minutes.

6. Make sure the bearing puller is square to the crankshaft so the bearing inner race is not out of alignment with the crankshaft shoulder.

7. Slowly tighten the center screw (E, **Figure 41**) and withdraw the bearing inner race (F) from the crankshaft shoulder.

8. Remove the bearing puller, splitter and bearing inner race from the crankshaft.

9. Remove the trust washer from the crankshaft. Discard the thrust washer, it cannot be re-used.

10. Clean the sprocket shaft with contact cleaner. Check the sprocket shaft for cracks or other damage. If it is damaged, refer service to a Harley-Davidson dealership.

Installation

The sprocket shaft bearing cone installer (HD-997225-55B) is required to install the sprocket shaft bearing inner race.

1. Support the crankshaft in a support fixture (HD-44358), or an equivalent, with the bearing side facing up (A, **Figure 42**).

2. Thread the pilot shaft (B, **Figure 42**) onto the crankshaft until it contacts the crankshaft

3. Slide the *new* thrust washer (C, **Figure 42**) over the sprocket shaft.

WARNING

In Step 4, ***never*** *use the heat gun in conjunction with the penetrating oil. The heat from the gun may ignite the oil resulting in a fire.*

4A. Place the *new* bearing race on the workbench. Use heat gun and uniformly heat the bearing race for approximately 60 seconds. Wear heavy duty gloves and install the *new* inner race (D, **Figure 42**) onto the crankshaft

42

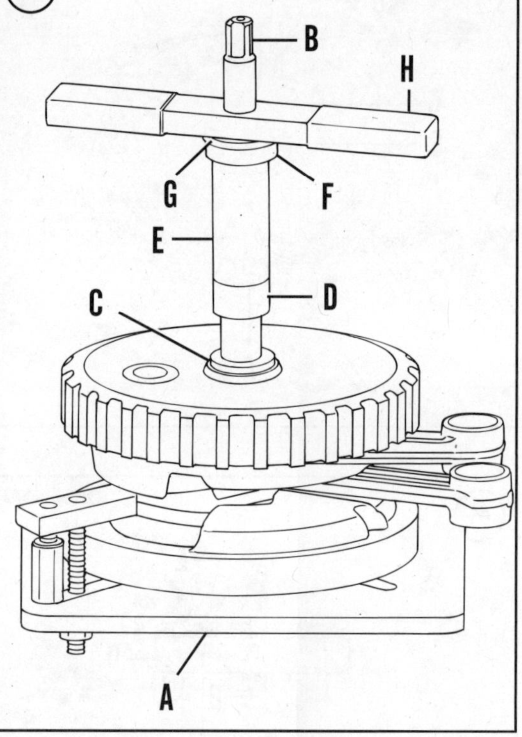

4B. If a heat gun is not available, apply penetrating oil to the inner surface of the bearing race and to the crankshaft shoulder. Install the *new* inner race (D, **Figure 42**) onto the crankshaft.

5. Apply graphite lubricant to the threads of the pilot shaft and flat washer

6. Slide the sleeve (E, **Figure 42**) onto the crankshaft until it contacts the bearing inner race.

7. Slide the new bearing (F, **Figure 42**) and flat washer (G) over the pilot shaft until it contacts the top of the sleeve.

8. Thread the handle (H, **Figure 42**) onto the pilot shaft (B).

9. Slowly tighten the handle *clockwise* until the bearing inner race bottoms on the crankshaft shoulder.

10. Unscrew and remove all parts of the special tool.

Table 6 ENGINE SERVICE SPECIFICATIONS

Item	New in. (mm)	Service limit in. (mm)
Cylinder bore		
Standard	–	3.752 (95.301)
Oversize 0.005 in.	–	3.757 (95.428)
Oversize 0.010 in.	–	3.762 (95.555)
Piston-to-cylinder clearance		
Early style piston	0.0006-0.0017 (0.015-0.043)	0.003 (0.076)
Late style piston	0.0014-0.0025 (0.036-0.064)	0.003 (0.076)
Piston pin fit in piston (2004-on models)	0.0007-0.0012 (0.018-0.030)	0.002 (0.051)
Valve stem-to-guide clearance (2005 models)		
Intake	0.001-0.003 (0.0254-0.0762)	0.0038 (0.0965)
Exhaust	0.001-0.003 (0.0254-0.0762)	0.0038 (0.0965)
Valve seat width (2005 models)		
Intake and exhaust	0.040-0.062 (1.02-1.58)	–
Valve stem protrusion (2005 models)		
Intake and exhaust	2.005-2.039 (50.93-51.79)	–
Valve spring free length (2005 models)		
Intake and exhaust	2.325 (59.06)	–
Camshaft support plate		
Camshaft chain tensioner shoe	–	0.090 (2.29)*
Camshaft bushing fit	–	0.0008 (0.0203)
Camshaft bushing inside diameter	–	0.8545 (21.704)

* 1/2 thickness of shoe.

Table 7 REAR CAMSHAFT SPROCKET SPACERS

Part No.	in.	mm
25722-00	0.287	7.29
25723-00	0.297	7.54
25721-00	0.307	7.80
25719-00	0.317	8.05
25717-00	0.327	8.31

14

Table 8 ENGINE TORQUE SPECIFICATIONS

Cylinder head bolts	Refer to text

CHAPTER FIVE

CLUTCH AND PRIMARY DRIVE

CLUTCH ASSEMBLY (2005 MODELS)

The clutch assembly is identical to prior to years with the exception of the seal on the clutch inspection cover. The O-ring has been replaced with a large gasket. Install the *new* gasket as follows:

1. Position the *new* gasket with the rubber molding and the words *Toward Engine* facing the chaincase cover.
2. Align the triangular shaped hole in the *new* gasket with the top hole in the clutch inspection cover.

CAUTION
Do not push the screw through the triangular shaped hole in the new gasket as the sealing qualities of the gasket will be damaged.

3. Insert the screw, with the captive washer, though the clutch inspection cover and carefully *thread it* it all the way through the triangular shaped hole in the new gasket.

4. Install the clutch inspection cover (**Figure 43**) and new gasket onto the chaincase cover and thread the top screw part way in.
5. Make sure the clutch inspection cover is correctly aligned with the chaincase cover and install the remaining four screws with captive washers.
6. Use a T27 Torx driver and tighten the screws in a crisscross pattern to 84-108 in.-lb. (9.5-12.2 N•m).

Table 9 CLUTCH TORQUE SPECIFICATIONS

Item	ft.-lb.	in.-lb.	N•m
Clutch inspection cover screws	–	84-108	9.5-12.2

CHAPTER SIX

TRANSMISSION

TRANSMISSION CASE (2003-ON MODELS)

Shift Arm Assembly

Inspection

The shift arm adjustment procedure is the same as on prior models with the following exceptions. The some of the shift shaft components are now an integral unit as shown in **Figure 44**.

1. Check the shift pawl for wear. Replace the shift arm assembly if necessary.
2. Check the spring for wear or damage. If the spring will not hold the pawl against the shift arm, replace it.
3. Check the shift arm shaft for wear or damage. Check the end splines for wear or damage.
4. Check the shift rod lever for wear or damage. Check the internal splines for wear or damage.

SHIFTER ADJUSTMENT (2003-ON MODELS)

The shifter arm adjustment procedure is the same as on prior models with the exception shift shaft components. Some of the shift shaft components are now an integral unit as shown in **Figure 45**.

44

SHIFT ARM ASSEMBLY

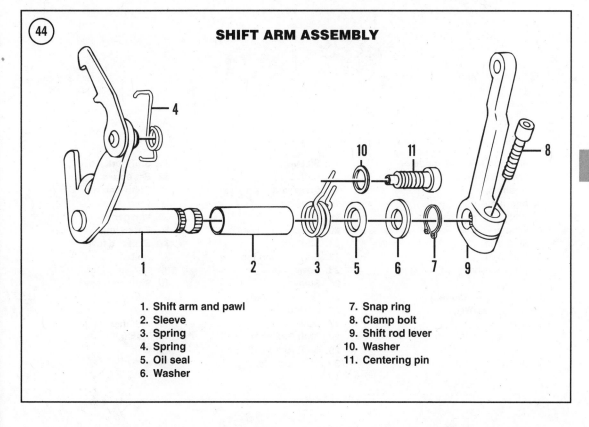

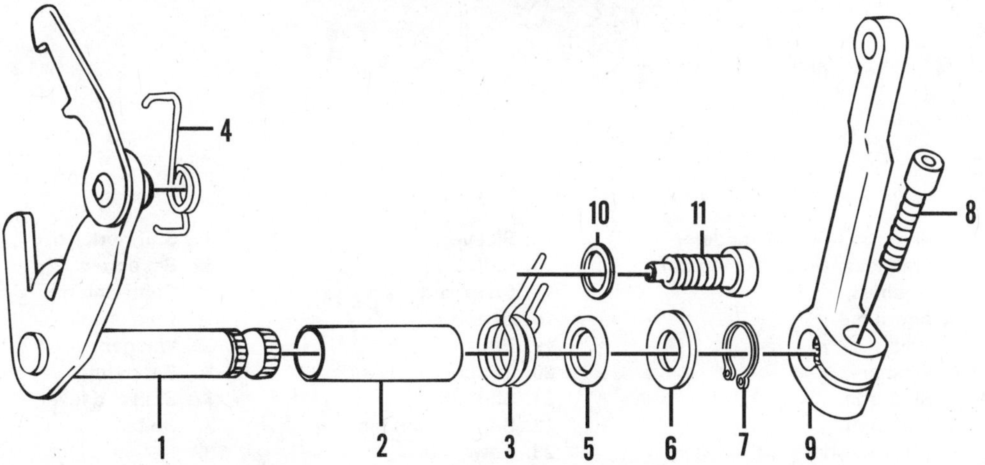

1. Shift arm and pawl
2. Sleeve
3. Spring
4. Spring
5. Oil seal
6. Washer
7. Snap ring
8. Clamp bolt
9. Shift rod lever
10. Washer
11. Centering pin

45

SHIFT ASSEMBLY

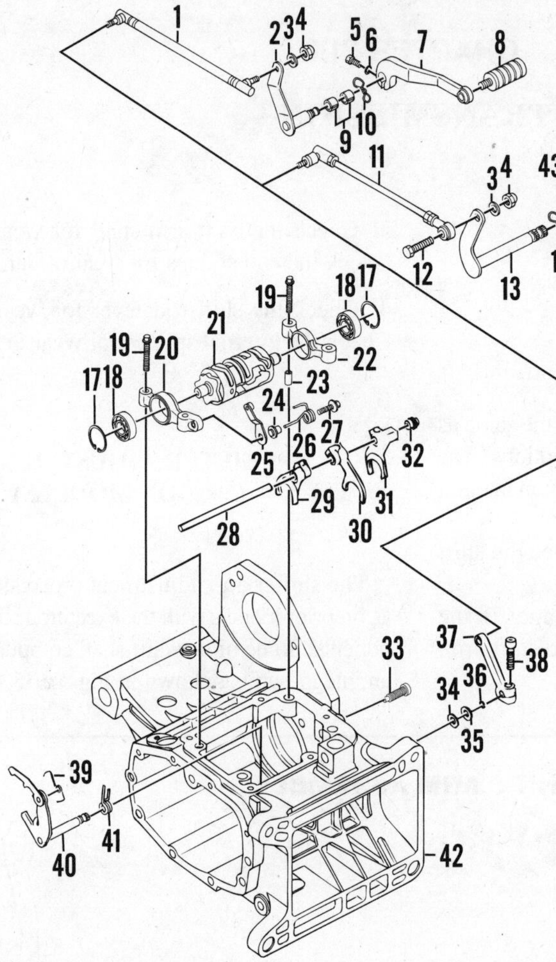

1. Shift rod (FXDWG models)
2. Shift lever (FXDWG models)
3. Washer
4. Acorn nut
5. Bolt
6. Washer
7. Shift lever
8. Shift peg
9. Wave washer
10. Wave spring
11. Shift rod (all models except FXDWG)
12. Bolt
13. Shift lever (all models except FXDWG)
14. O-ring
15. Sleeve
16. Shift lever
17. Snap ring
18. Bearing
19. Bolt
20. Support–right side
21. Shift drum
22. Support–left side
23. Dowel pin
24. Sleeve
25. Detent follower
26. Spring
27. Bolt
28. Shift fork shaft
29. Shift fork No. 3
30. Shift fork No. 2
31. Shift fork No. 1
32. Set screw
33. Centering pin
34. Oil seal
35. Washer
36. Snap ring
37. Shift rod lever
38. Bolt
39. Spring
40. Shift cam pawl
41. Spring
42. Transmission case
43. Retainer
44. Washer
45. Bolt

CHAPTER SEVEN

FUEL, EXHAUST AND EMISSION CONTROL SYSTEMS

AIR FILTER BACKPLATE

Removal/Installation (Fuel Injected Models)

Air filter backplate service is identical to carbureted models.

ELECTRONIC FUEL INJECTION (EFI)

This section describes the components and operation of the sequential port electronic fuel injection (EFI) system. The advantages of a map controlled fuel and ignition system working together are tremendous. It allows for the elimination of an inefficient cold start enrichment devise and allows for accurate control of the idle speed. Without a carburetor there is no need for periodic adjustments and altitude compensation is automatic. Improved torque characteristics are achieved, while at the same time allowing for greater fuel economy and low exhaust emissions due to the matching of the air/fuel ratio and ignition point, dependent upon load conditions. Engine performance modification is possible by installing an electronic control module (ECM) with different map characteristics.

Complete service of the system requires a Harley-Davidson Digital Technician and a number of other specialty tools. However, basic troubleshooting diagnosis is no different on a fuel-injected machine than on a carbureted one. If the check engine light comes on or there is a drivability problem, make sure all electrical connections are clean and secure. A high or erratic idle speed may indicate a vacuum leak. Make sure there is an adequate supply of fresh gasoline. If basic tests fail to reveal that cause of a problem, refer service to a Harley-Davidson dealership. Incorrectly performed diagnostic procedures can result in damage to the fuel injection system.

Electronic Control Module and Sensors

The electronic control module (ECM), mounted under electrical panel cover on the right side, determines the optimum fuel injection and ignition timing based on input from six sensors. The sensors **Figure 46** and their locations and functions are as follows:

1. The throttle position sensor (TP), located on the front of the induction module and attached directly to the throttle shaft, indicates throttle angle. The ECM calculates the air volume entering the engine based on the throttle angle.

2. The crankshaft positions sensor (CKP), located towards the front of the left crankcase, is an inductive type sensor. The ECM determines the engine speed by how fast the machined teeth on the flywheel pass by the sensor.

3. The engine temperature sensor (ET) is located on the front cylinder head. The ECM adjusts the injector opening time based on input from this sensor.

4. The intake air temperature sensor (IAT) is located inside the induction module (rear cylinder's intake runner). The ECM determines the air density and adjusts the injector opening time based on input from this sensor.

5. The manifold absolute pressure sensor (MAP) is located on top of the intake module. The MAP monitors intake manifold pressure (vacuum) and sends this information to the ECM.

6. Idle air control (IAC) valve is located on top of the induction module. The ECM controls the engine idle speed by opening and closing the IAC passage around the throttle plate.

Make sure the ECM is securely mounted within the electrical panel assembly to prevent damage from vibration. Do not tamper with the ECM; it is sealed to prevent moisture contamination.

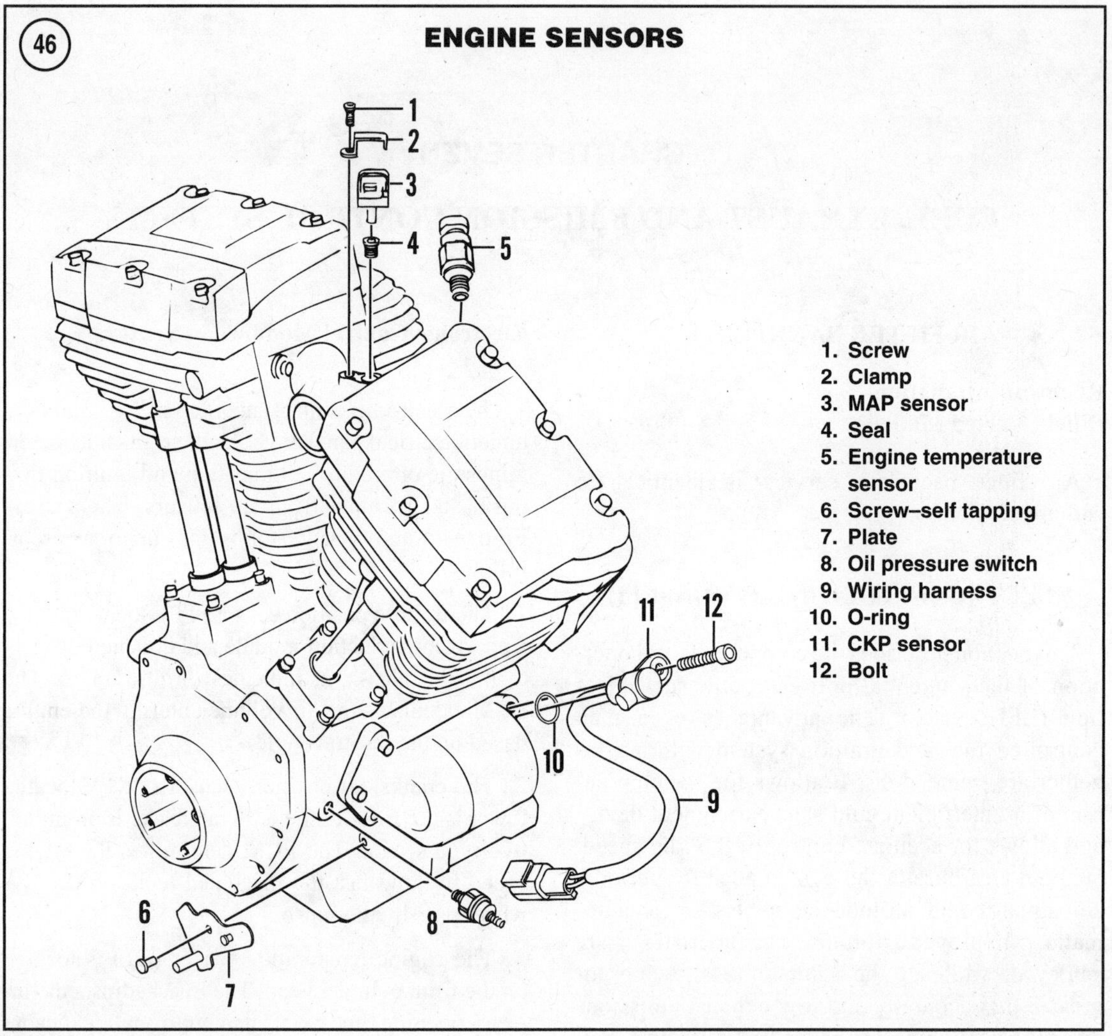

Fuel Supply System

Fuel pump and filters

The fuel pump and filter assembly is located inside the fuel tank. This assembly is part of the removable canopy attached to the top of the fuel tank. The canopy provides easy removal and installation of the attached components without having to work within the fuel tank cavity. An inlet screen on the fuel pump and the secondary fuel filter canister are located downstream from the fuel pump to provide maximum filtration before the fuel reaches the fuel injectors.

Fuel lines

The fuel line is attached to the base of the fuel tank with a quick-disconnect fittings.

The fuel supply line pressure is 55-62 psi (379-427 kPa). A check valve is located on the fuel line where it attaches to the fuel tank.

Fuel Injectors

The solenoid-actuated constant-stroke pintle-type fuel injectors consist of a solenoid plunger, needle valve and housing. The fuel injector's opening is fixed and fuel pressure is constant.

The ECM controls the time the injectors open and close.

Induction Module

The induction module (**Figure 47**) consists of the two fuel injectors, fuel pressure regulator, throttle po-

47

INDUCTION MODULE

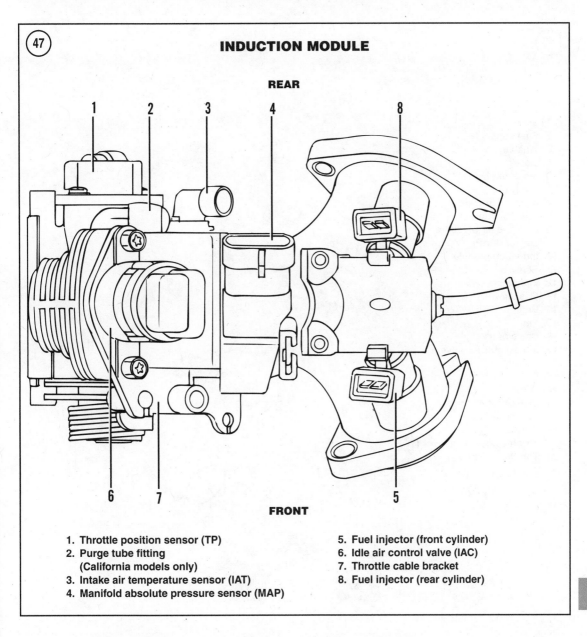

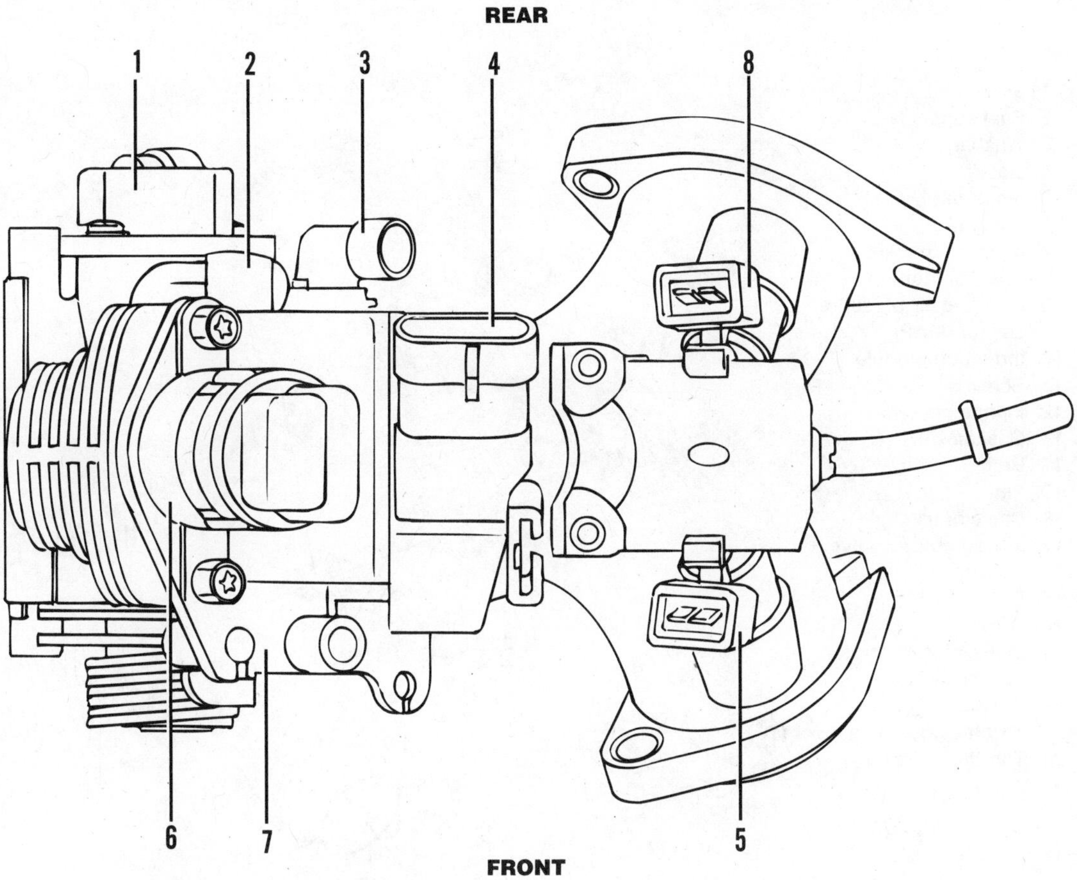

1. Throttle position sensor (TP)
2. Purge tube fitting (California models only)
3. Intake air temperature sensor (IAT)
4. Manifold absolute pressure sensor (MAP)
5. Fuel injector (front cylinder)
6. Idle air control valve (IAC)
7. Throttle cable bracket
8. Fuel injector (rear cylinder)

sition sensor, intake air temperature sensor, idle speed lever, fuel supply line fitting and the idle speed control actuator.

DEPRESSURIZING THE FUEL SYSTEM (FUEL INJECTED MODELS)

The fuel system is under pressure at all times, even when the engine is not operating. The system must be depressurized prior to loosening fittings or disconnecting fuel lines within the fuel injection system. Gasoline will spurt out unless the system is depressurized.

1. Remove the cover from the electrical panel.
2. Remove fuel pump fuse (lower left side corner).
3. Start the engine and allow it to idle until it runs out of gasoline.
4. After the engine has stopped, operate the starter for three seconds to eliminate any residual gasoline in the fuel lines.
5. After all service procedures have been completed, install the fuel pump fuse and the electrical panel cover.

(48)

INDUCTION MODULE

1. Screw
2. Fuel supply line
3. Washer
4. Gasket
5. Mounting bracket
6. Fuel rail
7. Mouring bracket
8. Fuel injector
9. Manifold air pressure sensor (MAP)
10. Induction module
11. Screw
12. Flange
13. Gasket
14. Bolt
15. Pin
16. Cable bracket
17. Idle air control valve (IAC)
18. Gasket
19. O-ring seal
20. Screw
21. Intake air temperature sensor (IAT)
22. Gasket
23. Throttle position sensor (TP)
24. Throttle housing

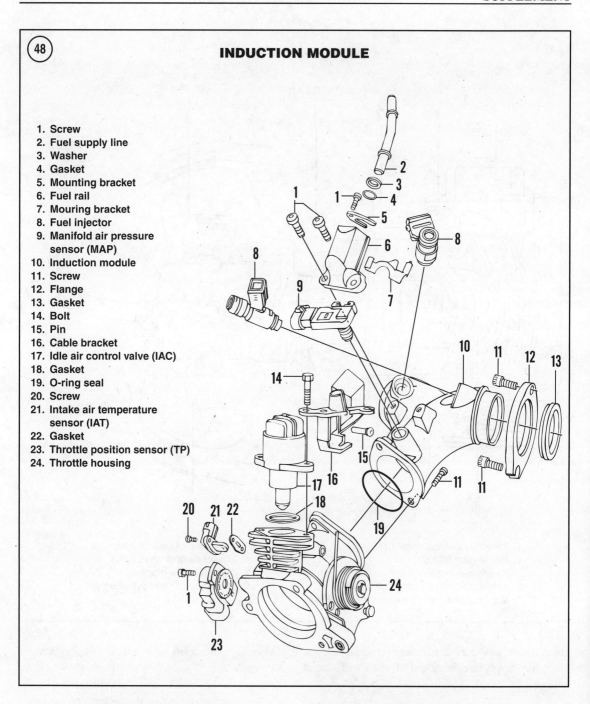

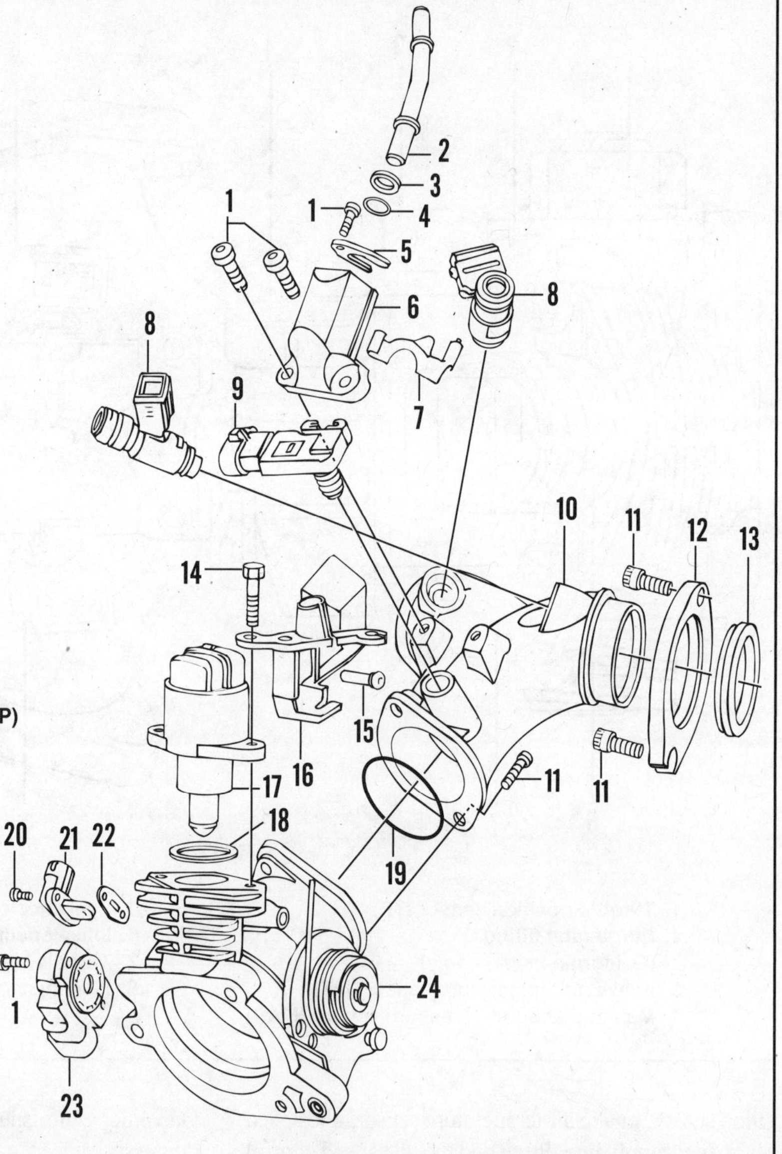

INDUCTION MODULE (FUEL INJECTED MODELS)

Removal

Refer to **Figure 48**.

1. Remove the fuel tank as described in this Supplement.
2. Remove the air filter assembly and backing plate as described in Chapter Seven.
3. On California models, disconnect the EVAP hose from the port on the induction module. Plug the end of the hose to keep out debris.
4. *Carefully* disconnect the electrical connector from each fuel injector by rocking the connector back and forth.

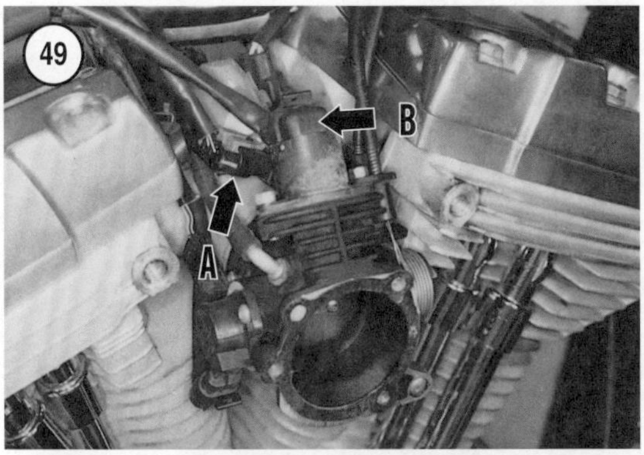

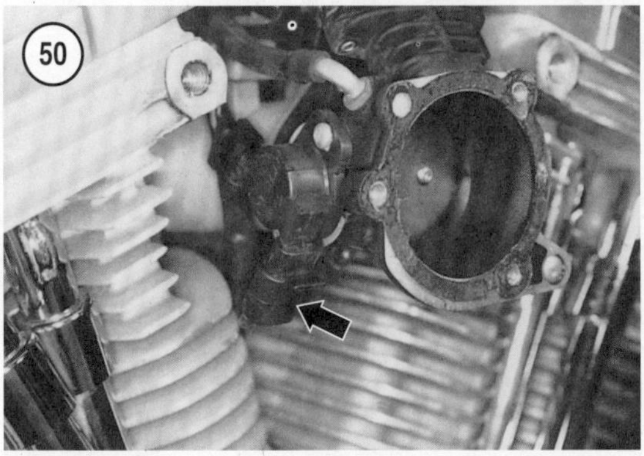

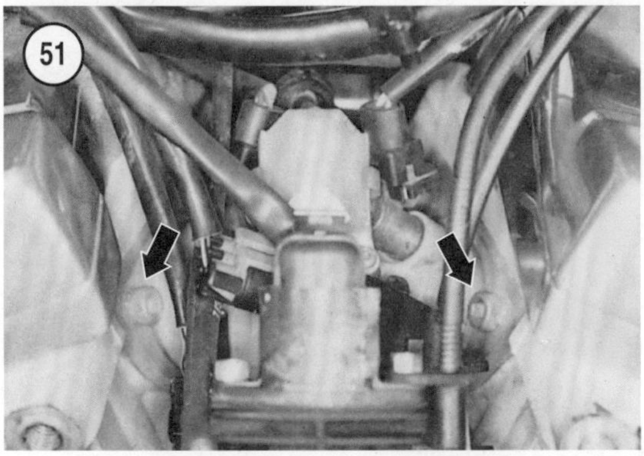

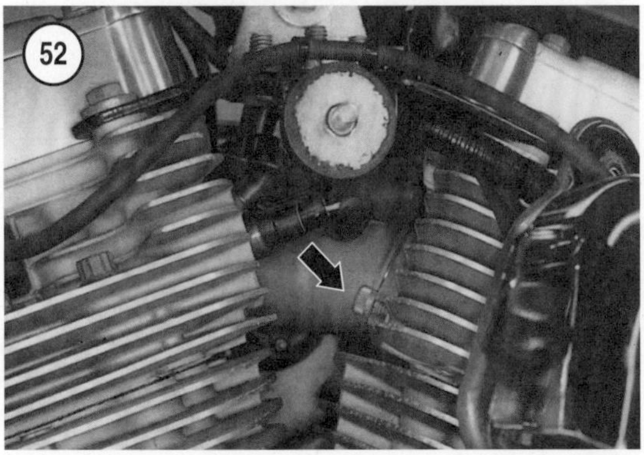

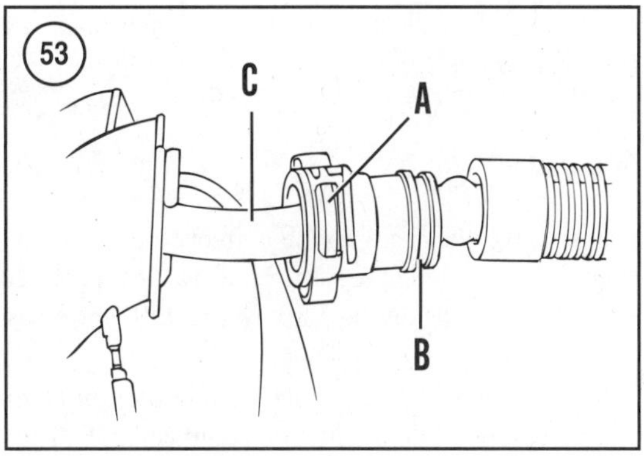

5. Disconnect the following electrical connectors from the induction module:

   a. IAT (A, **Figure 49**).
   b. Idle air control (IAC) valve (B, **Figure 49**).
   c. MAP.
   d. TP sensor (**Figure 50**).
   e. Fuel injectors.

6. Disconnect the throttle cables from the induction module as described in this Supplement

NOTE
The front and rear intake manifold flanges are different. If the flanges are not marked, label them with an F and R so they will be reinstalled in the correct locations.

7. Working on the right side of the motorcycle, loosen and remove the lower two bolts (**Figure 51**) securing the cylinder head mounting flanges to the cylinder heads. Loosen, but do not remove, the upper two bolts securing the cylinder head mounting flanges to the cylinder heads.

8. Working on the left side of the motorcycle, loosen and remove the lower two bolts (**Figure 52**) securing the cylinder head mounting flanges to the cylinder heads. Loosen, but do not remove, the upper two bolts securing the cylinder head mounting flanges to the cylinder heads.

9. Slide the induction module part way out of the cylinder head ports past the upper bolts.

10. Depress the button (A, **Figure 53**) on the fuel line fitting. Disconnect the fuel line and fitting (B, **Figure 53**) from the induction module fitting (C) and remove the induction module.

11. Remove the mounting flanges and discard the seals.

12. Inspect the induction module and fuel hoses as described in this section.

Installation

1. Install the flanges onto the correct side of the induction module with the slotted hole at the top. Refer to the marks made during *Removal*. Install *new* seals onto the induction module.
2. Partially install the induction module and fuel line assembly. Slide the fuel line connector (B, **Figure 53**) onto the induction module fitting (C) until it clicks. Gently pull on the fuel line to ensure the fitting is locked in place. Slide the induction module on the upper two bolts.
3. Connect both throttle cables to the induction module as described in this chapter.
4. Align the mounting flanges and install the two lower bolts by hand. Use the same tool set up used to loosen the bolts. Do not tighten the bolts at this time.
5. Working on the right side of the motorcycle, tighten the lower two bolts until snug, do not tighten to the final torque specification at this time. Use the same tool set up used to loosen the bolts.
6. Working on the left side of the motorcycle, tighten the upper two bolts to 97-142 in.-lb. (11-16 N•m).
7. Working on the right side of the motorcycle, tighten the lower two bolts to 97-142 in..-lb. (11-16 N•m).
8. Carefully attach the electrical connector to each fuel injector. Align the grooves in the female connector with the tabs in the male space housing. Push the connector halves together until both latches click.

NOTE

In Step 9, push the electrical connector halves together until the female latches slot connector is fully engaged with the tabs on the male space housing.

9. Connect the following electrical connectors from the induction module:
   a. Fuel injectors.
   b. TP (**Figure 50**).
   c. MAP.
   d. IAC valve (B, **Figure 49**).
   e. IAT (A, **Figure 49**).

(54) **THROTTLE CABLES**

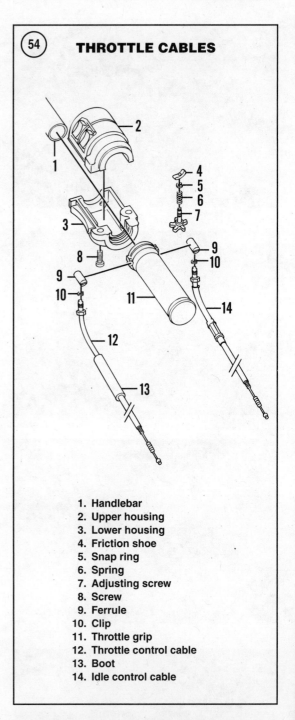

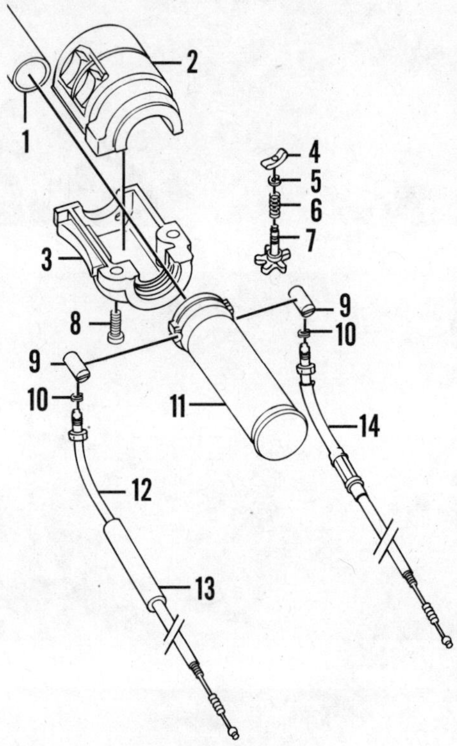

1. Handlebar
2. Upper housing
3. Lower housing
4. Friction shoe
5. Snap ring
6. Spring
7. Adjusting screw
8. Screw
9. Ferrule
10. Clip
11. Throttle grip
12. Throttle control cable
13. Boot
14. Idle control cable

10. On California models, connect the EVAP hose to the port on top of the induction module.

11. Install the air filter assembly as described in this Supplement.

12. Install the fuel tank as described in this Supplement.

55

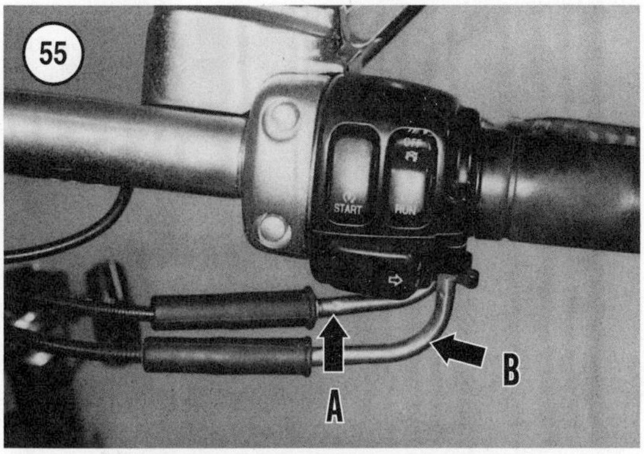

56

57

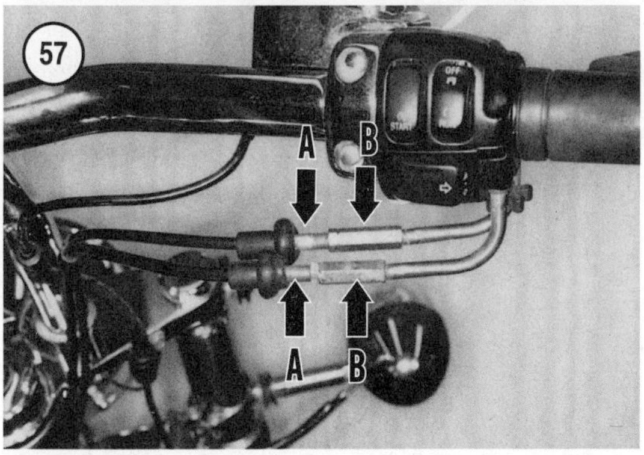

Inspection

Check the induction module assembly for wear, deterioration or other damage. Replace the seals as a set if necessary. The throttle housing is not serviceable and must be replace if damaged.

THROTTLE AND IDLE CABLES (FUEL INJECTED MODELS)

There are two different throttle cables (**Figure 54**). At the throttle grip, the front cable is the throttle control cable (A, **Figure 55**) and the rear cable is the idle control cable (B).

58

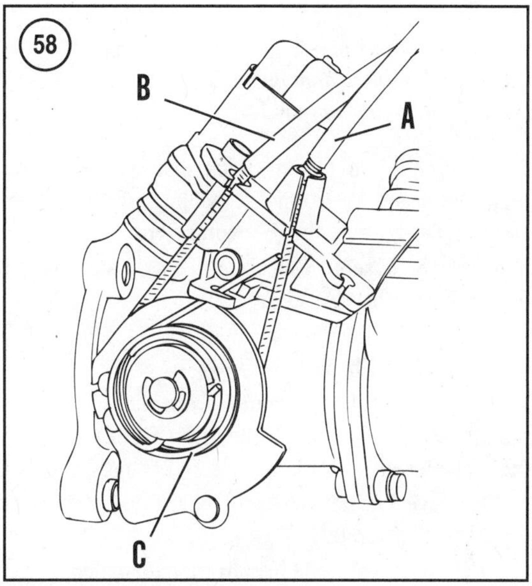

At the induction control module, the idle control cable is located at the top of the throttle wheel (A, **Figure 56**) and the throttle control cable (B) is located at the bottom.

Removal

1. Remove the fuel tank as described in this Supplement.
2. Remove the air filter and backing plate as described in Chapter Seven.
3. Make a drawing or take a picture of the cable routing from the induction module through the frame to the right side handlebar.
4. At the right side handlebar, loosen both control cable adjuster locknuts (A, **Figure 57**), then turn the cable adjusters (B) *clockwise* as far as possible to increase cable slack.
5. At the induction module, perform the following:
   a. Use needlenose pliers to disconnect the throttle cable (A, **Figure 58**) and the idle cable (B) from the throttle barrel (C).
   b. Carefully pull the throttle and idle control cables from the integral cable guides in the induction module.
6. Release the cables from the integral cable guides in the induction module.

CAUTION

Failure to install the spacer in Step 7 will result in damage to the rubber boot and plunger on the front brake switch.

7. Insert a 5/32 in. (4 mm) thick spacer between the brake lever and lever bracket. Make sure the spacer stays in place during the following steps.
8. Remove the screws securing the right side switch assembly together (A, **Figure 59**).
9. Remove the front master cylinder (B, **Figure 59**) as described in Chapter Twelve.
10. Remove the brass ferrules from the notches on the inboard side of the throttle grip (**Figure 60**). Remove the ferrules from the cable end fittings.
11. Remove the friction shoe from the end of the tension adjusting screw.
12. Remove the throttle grip from the handlebar.

NOTE

Use a rocking motion while pulling on the control cable housings in Step 13. If necessary, place a drop of engine oil on the housings retaining rings to ease removal.

13. Pull the crimped inserts at the end of the throttle and idle control cable housings from the switch lower housing.
14. Remove the cables from the frame.
15. Clean the throttle grip assembly and dry it thoroughly. Check the throttle slots for cracks or other damage. Replace the throttle if necessary.
16. The friction adjust screw is secured to the lower switch housing with a circlip. If necessary, remove the friction spring, circlip, spring and friction adjust screw. Check these parts for wear or damage. Replace damaged parts and reinstall. Make sure the circlip seats in the friction screw groove completely.
17. Clean the throttle area on the handlebar with solvent.

Installation

1. Apply a light coat of graphite to the housing inside surfaces and to the handlebar.
2. On the lower switch housing, push the larger diameter silver throttle cable insert into the larger hole in front of the tension adjust screw. Push it in until it snaps into place.

59

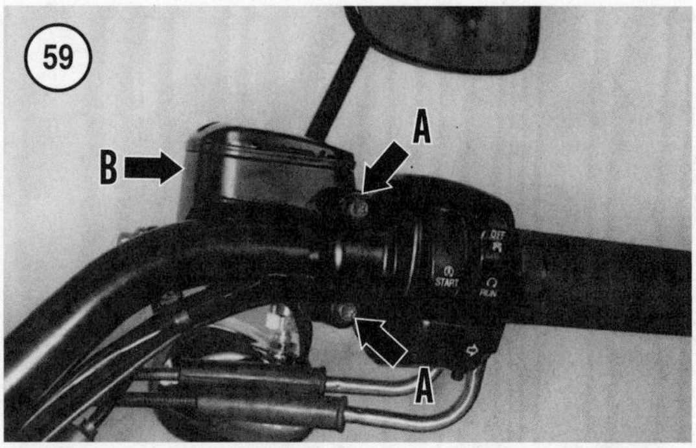

3. Push the smaller diameter gold throttle cable insert into the smaller hole in the rear of the tension adjusting screw. Push it in until it snaps into place.
4. Position the friction shoe with the concave side facing up and install it so the pin hole is over the point of the adjuster screw.
5. Install the throttle grip onto the handlebar. Push it on until it stops, and pull it back about 1/8 in. (3.2 mm). Rotate it until the ferrule notches are at the top.
6. Place the lower switch housing below the throttle grip. Install the brass ferrules onto the cables so the end fittings seat in the ferrule recess. Seat ferrules in their respective notches on the throttle control grip. Make sure the cables are captured in the molded grooves in the grip.
7. Assemble the upper and lower switch housings and the throttle grip. Install the lower switch housing screws (A, **Figure 59**) and tighten them finger-tight.
8. If it is not in place, insert the 5/32 in. (4 mm) thick spacer between the brake lever and lever bracket. Make sure the spacer stays in place during the following steps.
9. Install the front master cylinder (B, **Figure 59**) as described in Chapter Twelve.
10. Securely tighten the switch housing screws.
11. Remove the cardboard insert from the front master cylinder.
12. Operate the throttle and make sure both cables move in and out properly.
13. Correctly route the cables from the handlebar to the induction module.
14. At the induction module, perform the following:
   a. Install the idle cable (B, **Figure 58**) ball end over the top of the throttle barrel (C) and install the cable ball end into the upper hole in the throttle barrel. Make sure it is properly seated.
   b. Install the throttle cable (A, **Figure 58**) ball end under the bottom of the throttle barrel (C) and

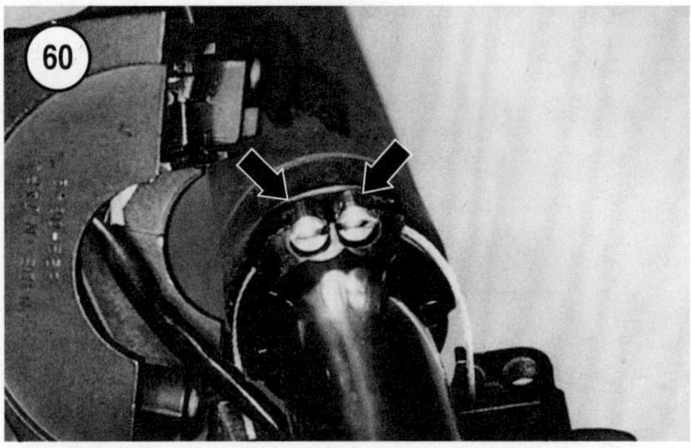

install the cable ball ends into the lower hole in the throttle barrel. Make sure they are properly seated.

c. Install the cables into the integral cable guides in the induction module.

15. At the throttle grip, tighten the cables to keep the ball ends from being disconnected from throttle barrel.

16. Operate the hand throttle a few times. Make sure the throttle barrel operates smoothly with no binding. Also make sure both cable ends are seated squarely in their cable bracket guides and in the throttle barrel.

17. Adjust the throttle and idle cables as described in Chapter Three.

18. Install the backing plate and air filter as described in Chapter Three.

19. Install the fuel tank as described in this chapter.

WARNING

Do not ride the motorcycle until the throttle cables are properly adjusted. Improper cable routing and adjustment can cause the throttle to stick open. This could cause loss of control.

20. Start the engine and allow it to idle in neutral. Then turn the handlebar from side to side. Do not operate the throttle. If the engine speed increases when turning the handlebar assembly, the throttle cables are routed incorrectly or are damaged. Recheck cable routing and adjustment.

FUEL TANK CONSOLE

Removal/Installation (FXD, FXDI, FXDX, FXDXI Models)

Refer to **Figure 61**.

NOTE

On models so equipped, always disarm the optional TSSM security system prior to disconnecting the battery or the siren will sound.

1. Disconnect the negative battery cable as described in Chapter Eight.
2. Remove the seat as described in Chapter Thirteen.

NOTE

It is not necessary to remove the five short rings since they secure the top plate trim ring to the base of the console.

3. Remove the three long screws securing the fuel cap trim ring and console to the top plate.
4. Pull the fuel cap trim ring straight up and remove it.
5. Remove the screw securing the rear portion of the console. Pull the console and trim/gasket straight up and remove it from the fuel tank.
6. If necessary, remove the fuel filler cap and O-ring from the top plate.
7. To remove the fuel gauge, perform the following:
   a. Remove the front and rear bolts, washers and acorn nuts securing the fuel tank.
   b. Raise the fuel tank. On the left side, disconnect the fuel gauge electrical connector from the main harness.
   c. Pull the fuel gauge straight and gasket up and out of the top plate.
8. Install the fuel gauge as follows:
   a. Install the fuel gauge and *new* gasket into the top plate.
   b. Connect the fuel gauge electrical connector onto the main harness.
   c. Lower the fuel gauge and install the bolts, washers and acorn nuts. Tighten the bolts and nuts to 15-20 ft.-lb. (20-27 N•m).
9. If removed, install the fuel filler cap and O-ring onto the top plate.
10. Install the trim/gasket onto the console and make sure it is correctly seated around the console perimeter.
11. Install console and trim/gasket straight onto the fuel tank. Make sure it is correctly seated, and install the screw securing the rear portion. Tighten the screw to 18-24 in.-lb. (2.0-2.7 N•m).
12. Position the slot in the fill cap trim cap over the tab on the console and install the trim cap.
13. Install the three long screws securing the fuel cap trim ring and console to the top plate. Tighten the

14

(61)

FUEL TANK CONSOLE (FXD, FXDI, FXDX, FXDXI)

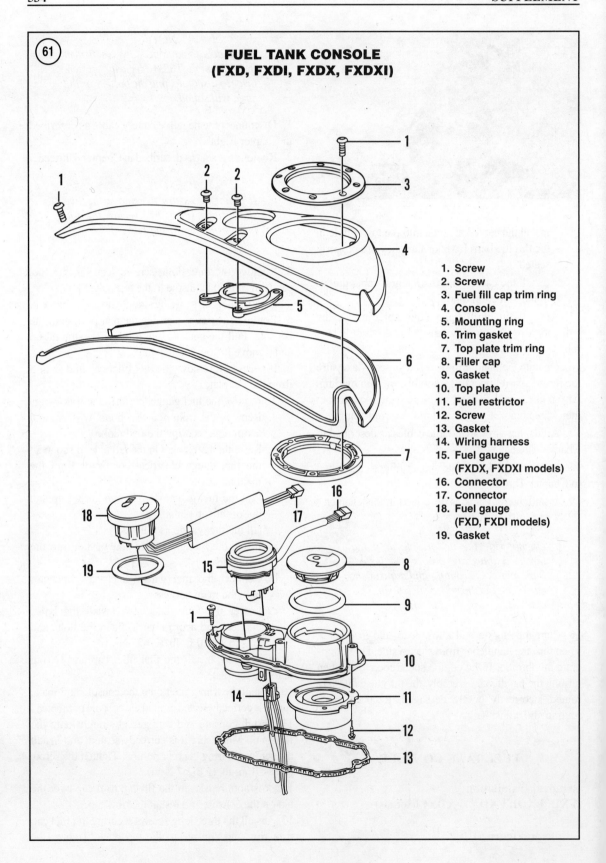

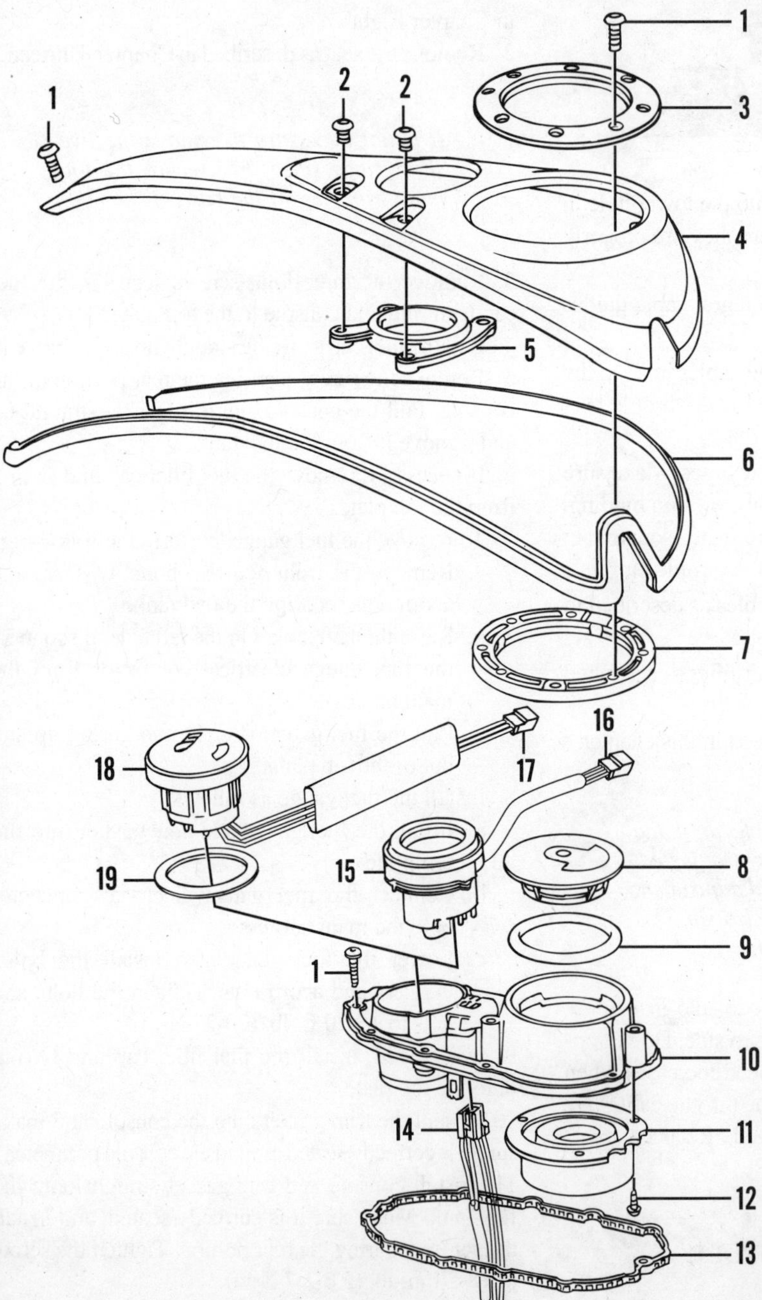

1. Screw
2. Screw
3. Fuel fill cap trim ring
4. Console
5. Mounting ring
6. Trim gasket
7. Top plate trim ring
8. Filler cap
9. Gasket
10. Top plate
11. Fuel restrictor
12. Screw
13. Gasket
14. Wiring harness
15. Fuel gauge (FXDX, FXDXI models)
16. Connector
17. Connector
18. Fuel gauge (FXD, FXDI models)
19. Gasket

screws to 18-22 in.-lb. (2.03-2.5 N•m). If the remaining five screws were removed, tighten them to 18-22 in.-lb. (2.03-2.5 N•m).
14. Install the seat as described in Chapter Thirteen.

Removal/Installation (FXDL, FXDLI Models)

Refer to **Figure 62**.

NOTE
On models so equipped, always disarm the optional TSSM security system prior to disconnecting the battery or the siren will sound.

1. Disconnect the negative battery cable as described in Chapter Eight.
2. Remove the seat as described in Chapter Thirteen.
3. Place a towel on top of the fuel tank to protect the finish.
4. Remove the three screws securing the middle and rear portion of the console. Pull the console and trim/gasket straight up and place it on top of the fuel tank.
5. Disconnect the 12-pin electrical connector from both the speedometer and the tachometer.
6. Install by reversing these removal steps. Note the following:
   a. Install the trim/gasket onto the console and make sure it is correctly seated around the console perimeter.
   b. Install console and trim/gasket straight onto the fuel tank. Make sure it is correctly seated.
   c. Install the mounting screws and tighten to 18-24 in.-lb. (2.0-2.7 N•m).

Removal/Installation (FXDWG, FXDWGI Models)

Refer to **Figure 63**.

NOTE
On models so equipped, always disarm the optional TSSM security system prior to disconnecting the battery or the siren will sound.

1. Disconnect the negative battery cable as described in Chapter Eight.
2. Remove the seat as described in Chapter Thirteen.
3. Remove the rear screw securing the leather trim panel to the fuel tank.
4. Place a towel on top of the fuel tank to protect the finish.
5. Remove the two screws securing the middle portion of the console. Pull the console and trim/gasket straight up and remove it from the fuel tank.
6. Raise the fuel tank. Disconnect the speedometer and indicator lamp connectors from the main harness.
7. Install by reversing these removal steps. Note the following:
   a. Install the trim/gasket onto the console and make sure it is correctly seated around the console perimeter.
   b. Install console and trim/gasket straight onto the fuel tank. Make sure it is correctly seated.
   c. Install the mounting screws and tighten to 18-24 in.-lb. (2.0-2.7 N•m).

FUEL TANK (2004-ON CARBURETED MODELS)

WARNING
Some fuel may spill from the fuel tank hose when performing this procedure. Because gasoline is extremely flammable and explosive, perform this procedure away from all open flames, including appliance pilot lights, and sparks. Do not smoke or allow anyone to smoke in the work area, as an explosion and fire may occur. Always work in a well-ventilated area. Wipe up any spills immediately.

WARNING
Route the fuel tank vapor hoses so that they cannot contact any hot engine or exhaust component. These hoses contain flammable vapors. If a hose melts from contacting a hot part, leaking vapors may ignite, causing a fire.

Removal/Installation

The fuel hose is secured to the fuel tank with non-reusable clamps. If the same type of clamp is going to be reinstalled, purchase new ones before servicing the fuel tank.

Refer to **Figure 64**.

62

FUEL TANK CONSOLE (FXDL, FXDLI)

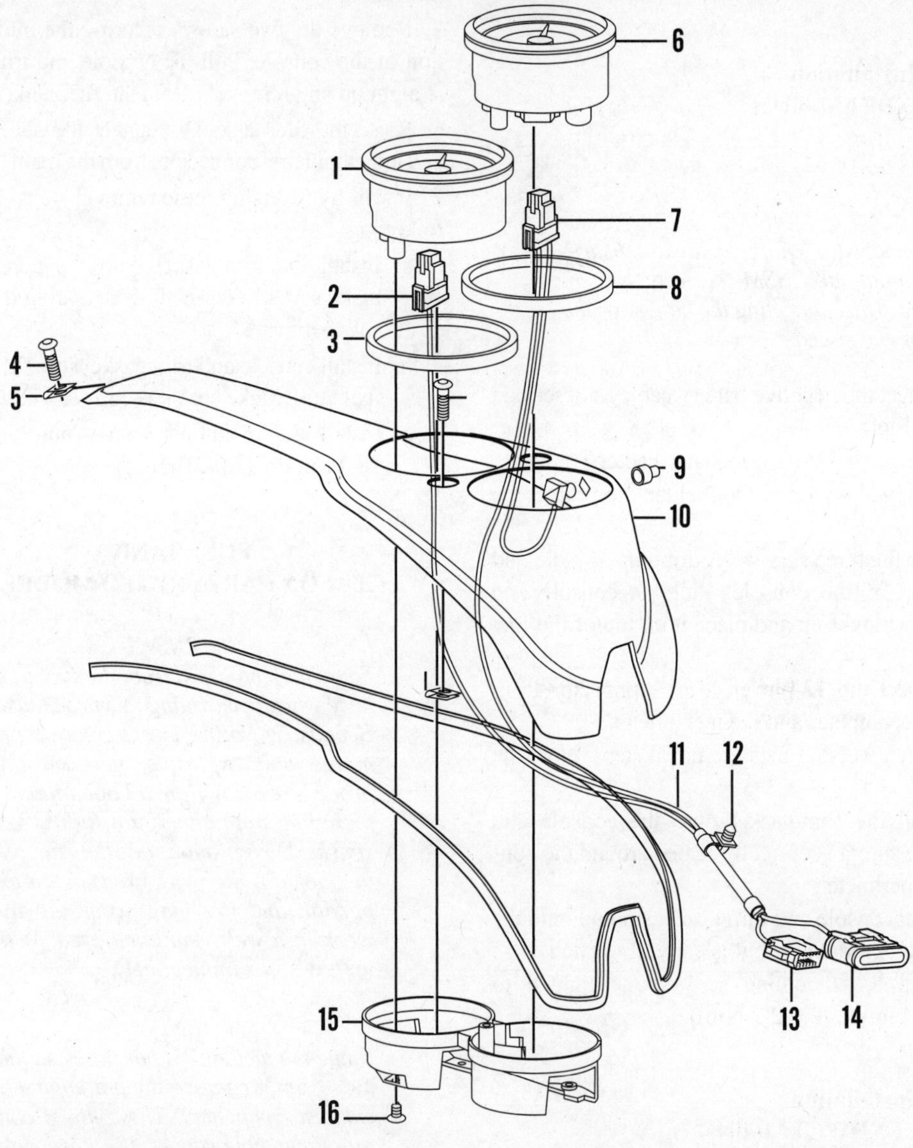

1. Tachometer
2. Socket
3. Gasket
4. Screw
5. Speed nut
6. Speedometer
7. Socket
8. Gasket
9. Reset switch rubber boot
10. Console
11. Wiring harness
12. Clamp
13. Connector (12-pin)
14. Warning light
15. Back clamp
16. Screw

63

FUEL TANK CONSOLE (FXDWG, FXDWGI)

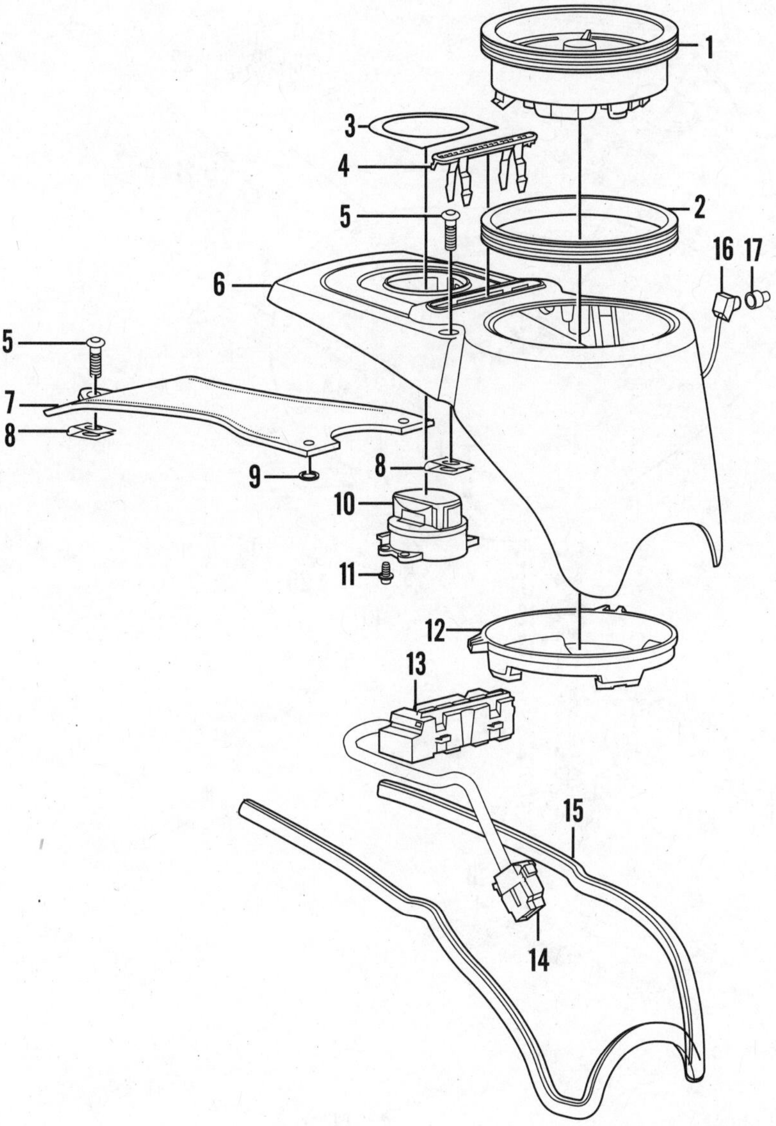

1. Speedometer
2. Gasket
3. Bezel
4. Indicator lamp bezel
5. Screw
6. Console
7. Leather trim panel
8. Speed nut
9. Push nut
10. Ignition switch
11. Screw
12. Back clamp
13. Indicator lamp assembly
14. Connector
15. Trim gasket
16. Reset switch
17. Reset switch rubber boot

(64)

FUEL TANK–CARBURETED MODELS (2004-ON)

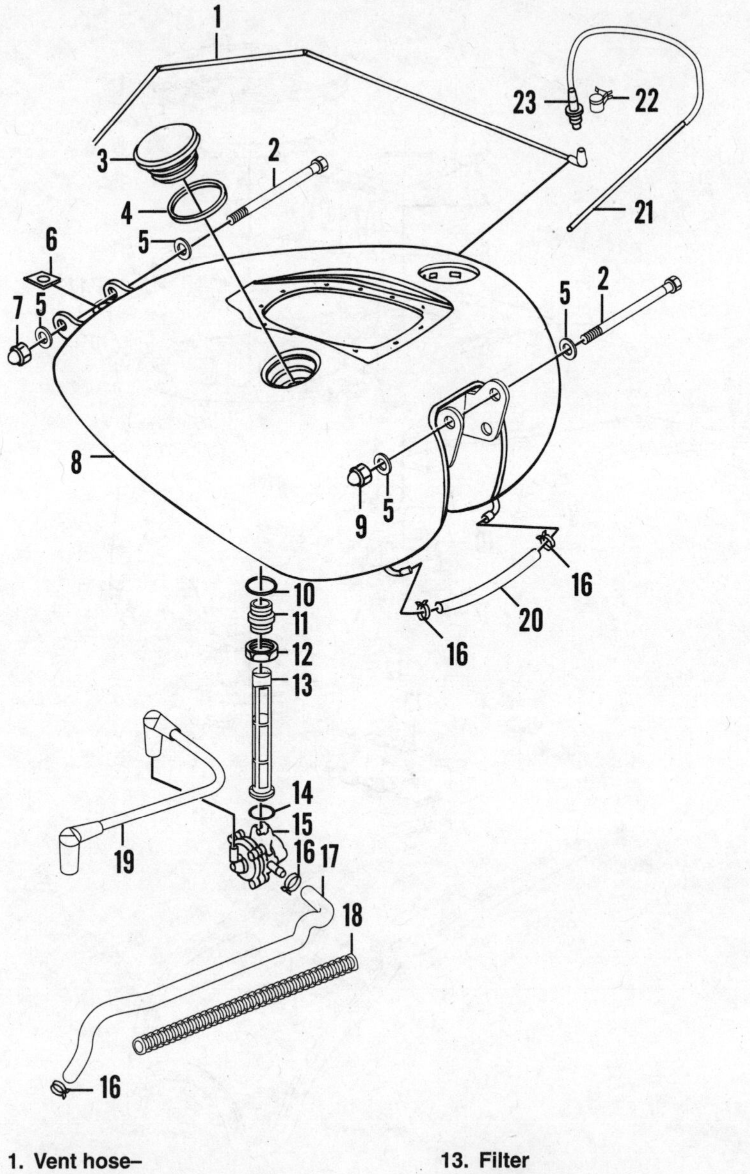

1. Vent hose–
   fuel tank-to-vapor valve
2. Bolt
3. Filler cap
4. Gasket
5. Washer
6. Clip
7. Acorn nut
8. Fuel tank
9. Acorn nut
10. O-ring
11. Adaptor
12. Nut
13. Filter
14. Gasket
15. Fuel shutoff valve
16. Hose clamp
17. Fuel hose
18. Insulator
19. Vacuum hose
20. Crossover hose
21. Vent hose–
    vapor valve-to-atmosphere
22. Clip
23. Vapor valve

65

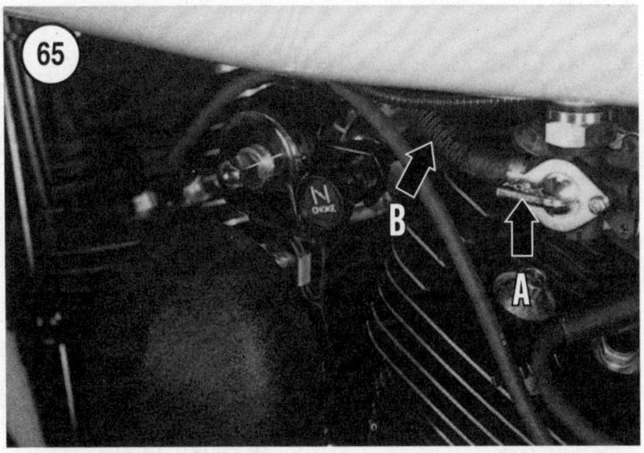

66

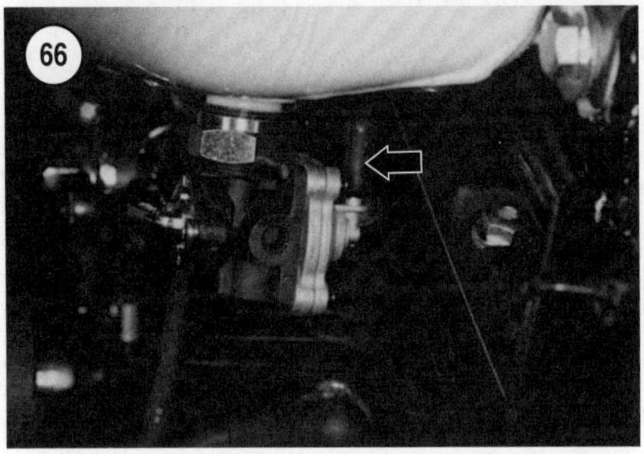

67

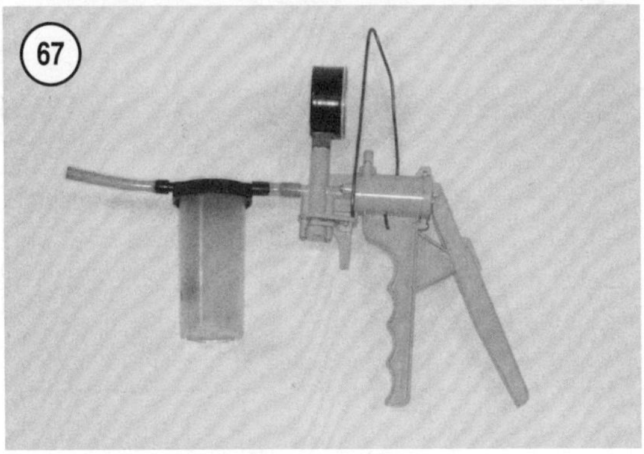

NOTE
On models so equipped, always disarm the optional TSSM security system prior to disconnecting the battery or the siren will sound.

1. Disconnect the battery negative cable.
2. Remove the fuel tank console as described in this section, if necessary.
3. Turn the fuel valve (A, **Figure 65**) to the OFF position.
4. Remove the hose clamp and disconnect the fuel hose (B, **Figure 65**) from the valve.

NOTE
A crossover tube connects the two fuel tank compartments. Drain both sides of the tank before removing the tank in the following steps.

5. Drain the fuel tank as follows:

NOTE
A vacuum-operated fuel valve is installed on all carbureted models. A hand-operated vacuum pump is required to drain the fuel tank.

   a. Connect the drain hose to the fuel valve and secure it with a hose clamp. Insert the end of the drain hose into a gas can.
   b. Disconnect the vacuum hose (**Figure 66**) from the fuel valve.
   c. Connect a hand-operated vacuum pump (**Figure 67**) to the fuel valve vacuum hose fitting.
   d. Turn the fuel valve to the RES position.

CAUTION
In the following step, do not apply more vacuum than 25 in. (635 mm) Hg or the fuel valve diaphragm will be damaged.

   e. Gently operate the vacuum pump handle and apply up to a *maximum* of 25 in. (635 mm) Hg of vacuum. Once the vacuum is applied the fuel will start to flow into the gas can.
   f. When fuel stops flowing through the hose, turn the fuel valve off and release the vacuum. Disconnect the vacuum pump and drain hose.
6. Disconnect the vent hose from the fuel tank.
7. Disconnect the crossover hose from one side of the fuel tank. Plug the tank opening and apply a hemostat to the crossover hose.
8. Remove the front and rear bolts, washers and acorn nuts securing the fuel tank to the frame.
9. If the fuel tank console is still in place, perform the following:
   a. Partially lift off and remove the fuel tank.
   b. On the left side, disconnect the fuel gauge electrical connector.
10. Lift off and remove the fuel tank.

NOTE
Store the fuel tank in a safe place away from open flames or where it could be damaged.

68

FUEL TANK–FUEL INJECTED MODELS (2004-ON)

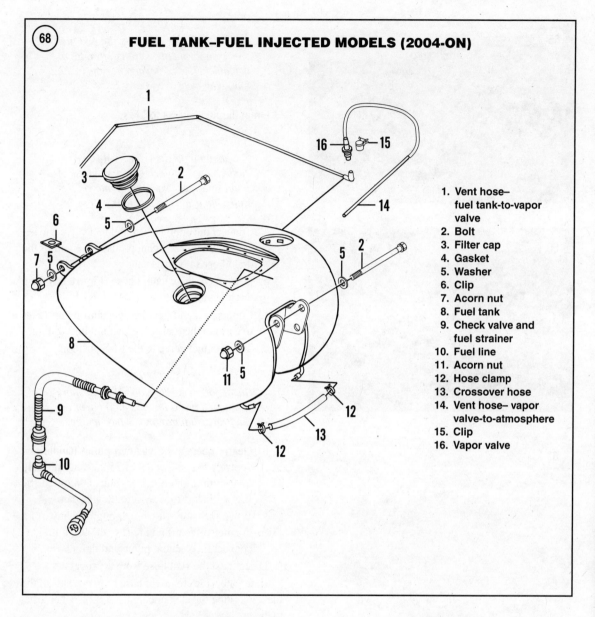

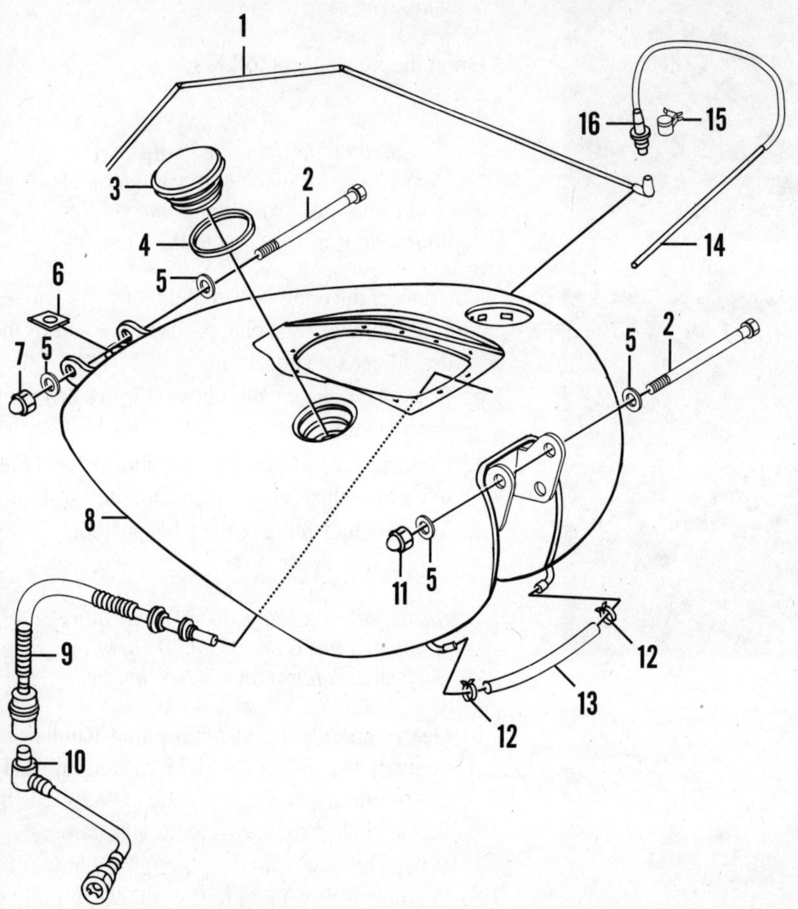

1. Vent hose–fuel tank-to-vapor valve
2. Bolt
3. Filter cap
4. Gasket
5. Washer
6. Clip
7. Acorn nut
8. Fuel tank
9. Check valve and fuel strainer
10. Fuel line
11. Acorn nut
12. Hose clamp
13. Crossover hose
14. Vent hose– vapor valve-to-atmosphere
15. Clip
16. Vapor valve

11. Drain any remaining fuel left in the tank into a gas can.

12. Installation is the reverse of these steps. Note the following:

   a. Tighten the front and rear bolts and nuts to 15-20 ft.-lbs. (20-27 N•m).

   b. Reconnect the fuel hose to the fuel valve and secure it with a *new* hose clamps.

   c. Connect the crossover hose and secure it with a *new* hose clamps.

   d. Refill the tank and check for leaks.

FUEL TANK (2004-ON FUEL INJECTED MODELS)

WARNING

Some fuel may spill from the fuel tank hose when performing this procedure. Because gasoline is extremely flammable and explosive, perform this procedure away from all open flames (including appliance pilot lights) and sparks. Do not smoke or allow anyone to smoke in the work area, as an explosion and fire may occur. Always

work in a well-ventilated area. Wipe up any spills immediately.

WARNING
Make sure to route the fuel tank vapor hoses so that they cannot contact any hot engine or exhaust component. These hoses contain flammable vapors. If a hose melts from contacting a hot part, leaking vapors may ignite, causing a fire.

Fuel Tank Draining

1. Depressurize the fuel system as described under *Depressurizing The Fuel System* in this section.
2. Make a drain hose from 5/16 in. inner diameter hose and plug one end of it. Make it long enough to go from the fuel tank crossover hose fitting to a gas can.
3. Disconnect the crossover hose from one of the fittings on the fuel tank. Immediately connect the drain hose made in Step 2 to the fuel tank fitting.
4. Place the plugged end of the drain hose into the gas can and remove the plug. Drain the fuel from that side of the fuel tank.
5. Disconnect the drain hose and reinstall the plug into one end of it.
6. Repeat for the other side of the fuel tank.
7. Plug the fuel tank crossover fittings to prevent the draining of fuel.

Removal/Installation

The crossover fuel hose is secured to the fuel tank with non-reusable clamps. If the same type of clamps are going to be reinstalled, purchase *new* ones before servicing the fuel tank.

Refer to **Figure 68**.

1. Depressurize the fuel system as described under *Depressurizing The Fuel System* in this Supplement.
2. Remove the seat as described in Chapter Thirteen.

NOTE
On models so equipped, always disarm the optional TSSM security system prior to disconnecting the battery or the siren will sound.

3. Disconnect the battery negative cable as described in Chapter Eight.
4. Remove the fuel tank console as described in this section.
5. Disconnect the fuel pump electrical connector on fuel tank top plate.

WARNING
A small amount of fuel will drain out of the fuel tank when the fuel line is disconnected from the base of the tank. Place several shop cloths under the fuel line fitting to catch any spilled fuel prior to disconnecting it. Discard the shop cloths in a suitable safe manner.

6. Pull up the chrome sleeve on the fuel line quick disconnect fitting (**Figure 69**) and disconnect the fuel supply line from the fuel tank.
7. Disconnect the crossover hose (**Figure 70**) from one of the fittings on the fuel tank. Drain the fuel tank as in this section.
8. Disconnect the vent hose from the fuel tank.
9. Remove the front and rear bolts, washers and acorn nuts securing the fuel tank to the frame.
10. Lift off and remove the fuel tank.

NOTE
Store the fuel tank in a safe place away from open flames or where it could be damaged.

11. Drain any remaining fuel left in the tank into a gas can.
12. Installation is the reverse of these steps. Note the following:
   a. Tighten the front and rear bolts and nuts to 15-20 ft.-lbs. (20-27 N•m).
   b. Reconnect the fuel line quick disconnect fitting (**Figure 69**) onto the fuel tank until it clicks into the locked position. Pull down on the fuel line to make sure it is secured to the fitting.
   c. Refill the tank and check for leaks.

FUEL TANK TOP PLATE AND FUEL GAUGE SENDING UNIT (2004-ON ALL MODELS)

Refer to **Figure 71**.

1. On fuel injected models, depressurize the fuel system as described in this chapter section.
2. Remove the seat as described in Chapter Thirteen.
3. Drain the fuel tank as described in this Supplement.
4. Remove the fuel tank console as described in this section.
5. On models so equipped, remove the fuel level gauge as described in this section.

6A. On carbureted models, disconnect the electrical connector from the top plate of the fuel level sender unit.

6B. On fuel injected models, disconnect the electrical connector from the top plate of the fuel pump/sender.

7. Disconnect the fuel tank vent hose from the top plate.
8. Remove the T20 Torx screws securing the top plate to the fuel tank. Discard the screws as they cannot be reused.
9. Rotate the top plate toward the right side until the vent tube clears the fuel tank opening.
10. On fuel injected models, perform he following:
   a. Depress the tab and remove the fuel pump/sender wiring from the top plate.
   b. Disconnect the wire harness from the fuel pump.

CAUTION
Do not bend the arm during removal of the sending unit. If bent, it will result in an inaccurate reading and must be replaced.

11. Carefully remove the top plate and sending unit while moving it back and forth and while lifting and turning it in either direction.
12. Remove the gasket from the fuel tank and discard it.
13. To remove the fuel level sender from the top plate, move the locking tab toward the rear of the top plate and disengage the sender from the top plate. Remove the sender from the top plate.
14. Install by reversing these removal steps. Note the following:
   a. Install a *new* gasket between the top plate and the fuel tank. Do not apply any type of sealant to the gasket.
   b. Use *new* T20 Torx screws and tighten in a crisscross pattern to 20 in.-lb. (2.3 N•m).
   c. Refill the tank and check for leaks.

FUEL PUMP AND FUEL FILTER (2004-ON FUEL INJECTED MODELS)

Refer to **Figure 72**.

Fuel Pump and Fuel Filter Removal/Installation

1. Remove the top plate assembly as previously described in this section.
2. Depress the tab and disconnect the fuel hose from the fuel pump assembly.
3. Disconnect the electrical connector from the fuel pump assembly.
4. Lift up on the fuel pump assembly tab, push the assembly toward the front of the fuel tank and disengage it from the fuel tank.
5. Rotate the fuel pump assembly *clockwise* and upward. Carefully remove the assembly from the left side of the fuel tank opening.
6. Install by reversing these removal steps. Note the following:
   a. Install a *new* O-ring on the fuel hose where it connects to the fuel pump assembly.
   b. Push the fuel hose onto the assembly until it clicks into the locked position. Pull on the fuel hose to make sure it is secured to the fitting.

71

FUEL TANK TOP PLATE–ALL MODELS (2004-ON)

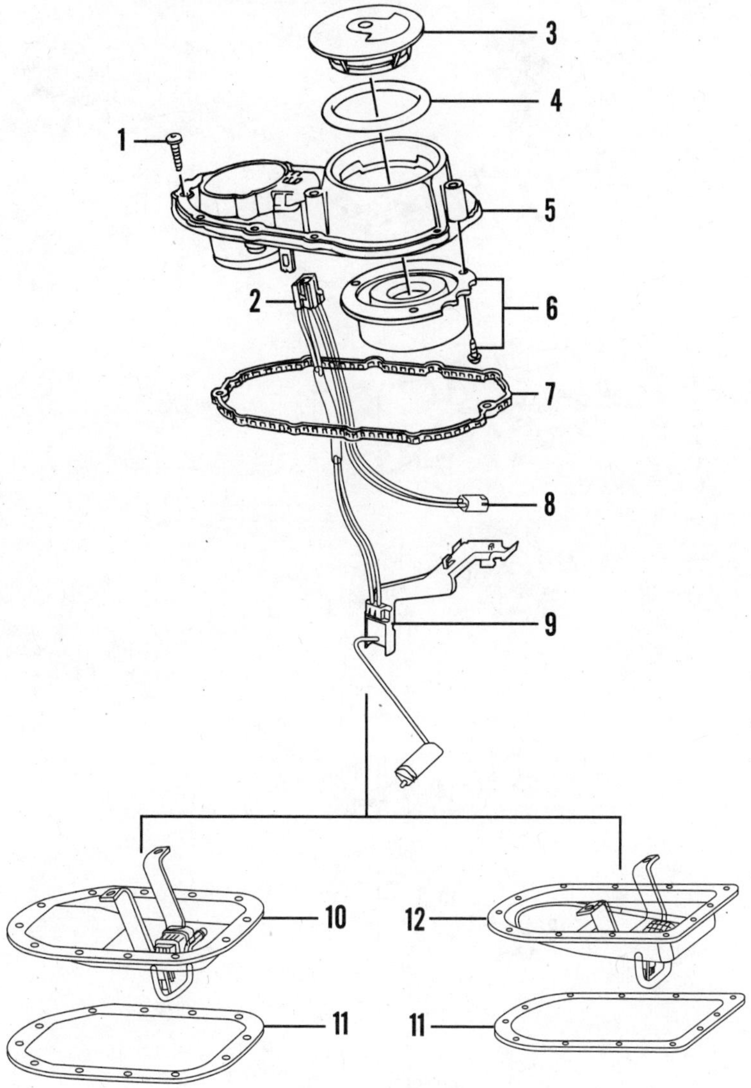

1. Screw
2. Wiring harness
3. Filler cap
4. Gasket
5. Top plate (FXD, FXDI, FXDX, FXDXI, FXDC, FXDCI)
6. Fuel restrictor
7. Gasket
8. Connector
9. Fuel level sending unit
10. Top plate (FXDWG, FXDWGI)
11. Gasket
12. Top plate (FXDL, FXDLI)

(72)

FUEL PUMP AND FILTER–FUEL INJECTED MODELS (2004-ON)

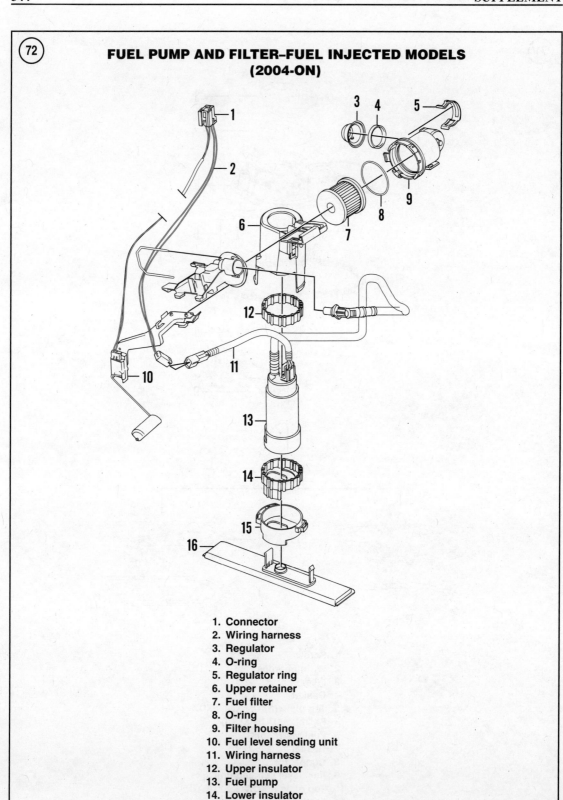

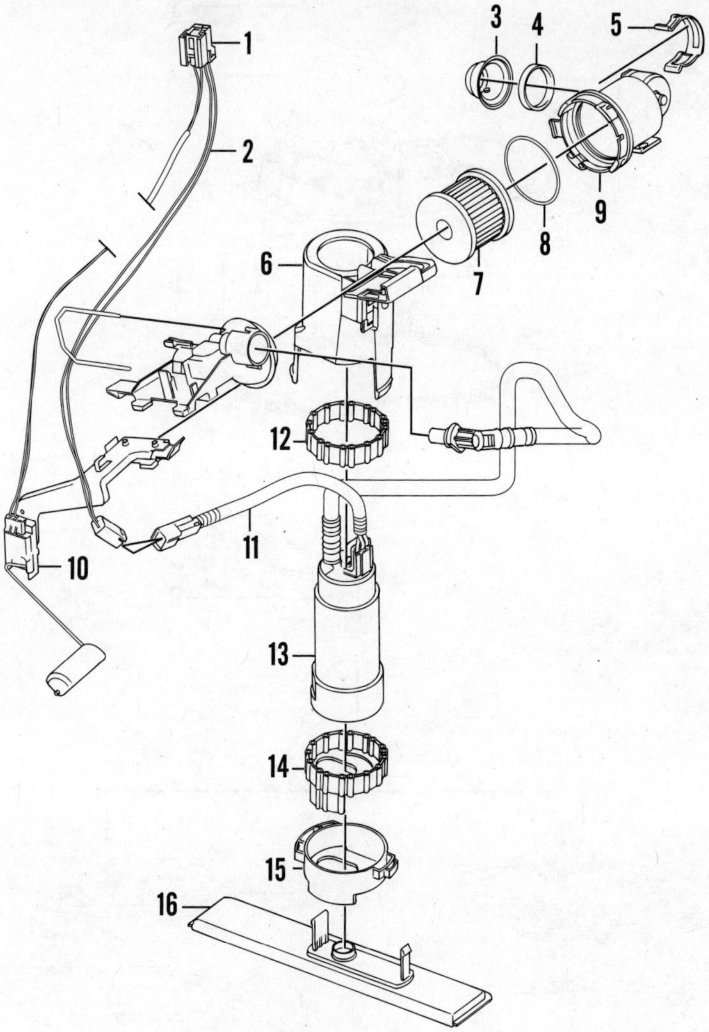

1. Connector
2. Wiring harness
3. Regulator
4. O-ring
5. Regulator ring
6. Upper retainer
7. Fuel filter
8. O-ring
9. Filter housing
10. Fuel level sending unit
11. Wiring harness
12. Upper insulator
13. Fuel pump
14. Lower insulator
15. Lower retainer
16. Inlet strainer

Fuel Filter Replacement

1. Remove the fuel pump and fuel filter assembly as previously described.
2. Depress the tabs on fuel filter housing and separate the end cap from the fuel filter housing.
3. Remove the O-ring securing the fuel filter to the housing. Remove the filter and discard it.
4. Install a *new* filter into the housing and secure it with a *new* O-ring.
5. Attach the fuel filter housing onto the end cap and push in on until the tabs click into the locked position.
6. Install the fuel pump and fuel filter assembly as previously described.

Fuel Regulator Replacement

1. Remove the fuel pump and fuel filter assembly as previously described.
2. Remove the wire terminal from the end of the regulator and filter housing.
3. Disengage the clip and remove it from the regulator.
4. Withdraw the regulator and O-ring from the filter housing. Discard the O-ring.
5. Install a *new* O-ring and regulator into the filter housing. Push in until both parts are seated.
6. Install the clip and push in on until the tabs click into the locked position.
7. Install the fuel pump and fuel filter assembly as previously described.

Fuel Inlet Strainer Replacement

1. Remove the fuel pump and fuel filter assembly as previously described.
2. Depress the tabs on the fuel inlet strainer and remove the strainer from the fuel pump and the lower retainer.
3. Install a new inlet strainer onto the fuel pump inlet receptacle and onto the lower retainer.
4. Push the inlet strainer onto the lower retainer until the tabs click into the locked position.
5. Install the fuel pump and fuel filter assembly as previously described.

Fuel Pump Replacement

1. Remove the fuel pump and fuel filter assembly as previously described.
2. Use a flat blade screwdriver and break the fuel pump locking tabs securing the fuel hose to the end cap.
3. Remove the fuel inlet strainer as previously described.
4. Disconnect the electrical connector from the fuel pump.
5. Depress the locking tabs and separate the lower retainer from the upper retainer.
6. Remove the fuel pump from the upper retainer.
7. If necessary, replace the isolators into the upper and lower retainers.
8. Install a *new* fuel pump into the upper retainer.
9. Install the lower retainer onto the upper retainer and push in on until the tabs click into the locked position.
10. Install the hose onto the end cap.
11. Connect the electrical connector onto the fuel pump.
12. Install the fuel inlet strainer as previously described.
13. Install the fuel pump and fuel filter assembly as previously described.

Table 10 FUEL SYSTEM TORQUE SPECIFICATIONS

Item	ft.-lb.	in.-lb.	N•m
Fuel cap trim ring screw	–	18-22	2.0-2.5
Fuel gauge bolts	15-20	–	20-27
Fuel tank console screw	–	18-24	2.0-2.7
Fuel tank mounting bolts	15-20	–	20-27
Fuel tank top plate screws	–	20	2.3
Induction module bolts (EFI) upper and lower	–	97-142	11-16

CHAPTER EIGHT

ELECTRICAL SYSTEM

ALTERNATOR

Refer to **Figure 73**.

Rotor Removal/Installation

The removal and installation procedure is the same as on all other models, except the washer previously used inside and outside of the rotor has been eliminated.

Stator Removal

1. Remove the rotor as described in this Supplement and Chapter Eight.

NOTE
On models so equipped, always disarm the optional TSSM security system prior to disconnecting the battery or the siren will sound.

2. Disconnect the negative battery cable as described in this Supplement.
3. Pull back the rubber boot at the plug cover. Release the locking tab and disconnect the alternator rotor electrical connector from the voltage regulator connector.
4. Insert a small screwdriver between the socket housing side of connector going to the alternator stator and the locking wedge on the socket housing. Gently pivot the screwdriver tip and pop the wedge loose.
5. Lift the terminal latches inside the socket housing and back the sockets through wire end of connector.
6. Remove the four T27 Torx screws (A, **Figure 74**) securing the stator assembly to the crankcase. New Torx screws must be used on installation.

NOTE
If necessary, spray electrical contact cleaner or glass cleaner around the wiring harness grommet to help ease it out of the crankcase boss receptacle.

7. Use an awl to carefully lift the capped lip on the grommet (**Figure 75**) from the crankcase and push it into the bore.
8. Carefully push the stator wires and grommet (B, **Figure 74**) through the crankcase bore and remove the stator assembly.
9. Inspect the stator mounting surface on the crankcase for oil residue from a damaged oil seal. Clean it off if necessary.
10. Inspect the stator wires (A, **Figure 76**, typical) for fraying or damage.
11. Inspect the rubber grommet (B, **Figure 76**) for deterioration or hardness.
12. Check the stator connector pins for looseness or damage.

Stator Installation

1. Apply a light coat of electrical contact cleaner or glass cleaner to the wiring harness grommet to help ease it into the crankcase boss receptacle.
2. Insert the electrical harness and grommet into the crankcase boss receptacle and carefully pull it through until the grommet is correctly seated.

CAUTION
New T27 Torx screws must be installed. The threadlocking compound originally applied to the Torx screws is for one time use only. If a used Torx screw is installed, it can work loose and cause engine damage.

3. Move the stator into position on the crankcase and install four *new* Torx screws (A, **Figure 74**). Tighten the screws to 55-75 in.-lb. (6.2-8.4 N•m).
4. Move the wires to the right side of the motorcycle.
5. Apply a light coat of dielectric compound to the electrical connector prior to assembling it. Reassem-

73

CHARGING SYSTEM–ALL MODELS (2004-ON)

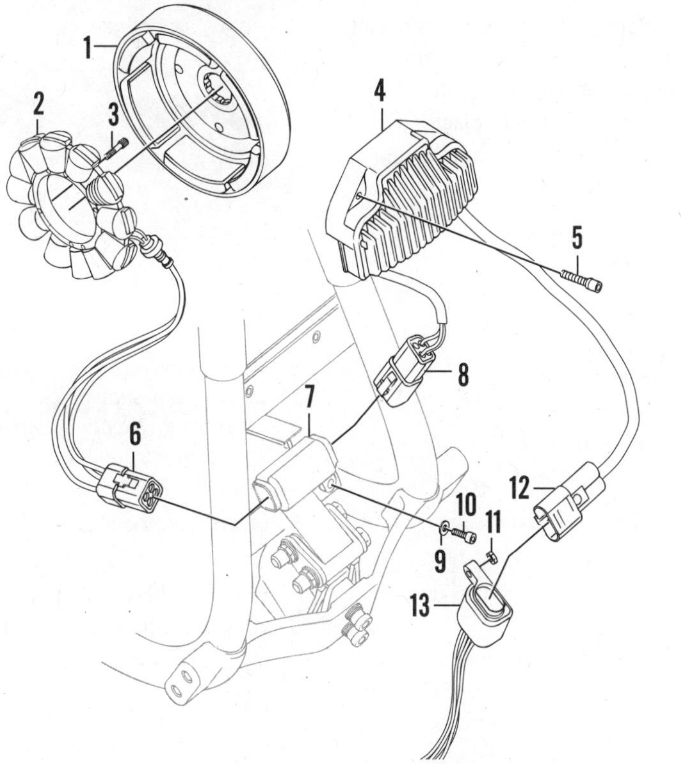

1. Rotor
2. Stator coil assembly
3. Allen bolt
4. Voltage regulator
5. Bolt
6. Connector
7. Plug cover
8. Connector
9. Washer
10. Screw
11. Nut
12. Connector
13. Connector

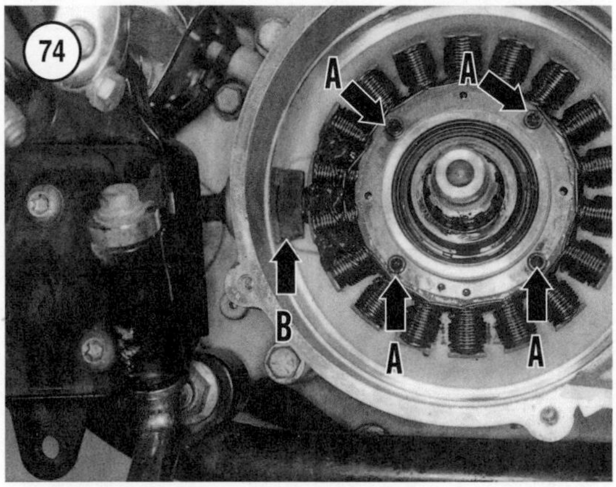

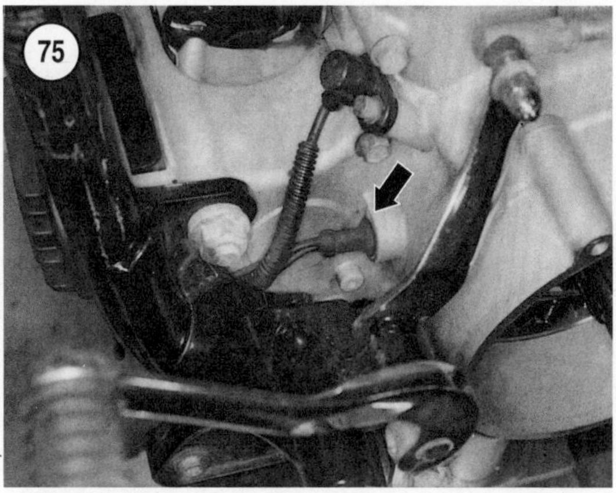

ble the electrical connector socket by reversing Steps 4 and 5 of *Removal*. Make sure it has locked together securely.

6. Connect the alternator rotor electrical connector onto the voltage regulator connector. Make sure they are push together until the tab clicks into the locked position. Pull the rubber boot back into place.

7. Install the rotor as described in this Supplement.

VOLTAGE REGULATOR

Removal/Installation

Refer to **Figure 73**.

NOTE
On models so equipped, always disarm the optional TSSM security system prior to disconnecting the battery or the siren will sound.

1. Disconnect the negative battery cable as described in Chapter Eight.
2. Pull back the rubber boot at the plug cover. Release the locking tab and disconnect the voltage regulator electrical connector from the alternator stator connector.
3. Release the locking tab and disconnect the voltage regulator electrical connector from the main wiring harness.
4. Remove the two bolts securing the voltage regulator to the frame cross member.
5. Remove the voltage regulator and related wiring from the frame.
6. Install by reversing these removal steps. Note the following:
   a. Tighten the bolts to 60-80 in.-lb. (6.8-9.0 N•m).
   b. Apply a light coat of dielectric compound to the electrical connectors prior to installing them.
   c. Connect both voltage regulator electrical connectors. Make sure they are push together until the tab clicks into the locked position. Pull the rubber boot back into place.

IGNITION SYSTEM (2004-ON MODELS)

Ignition Coil Removal/Installation

Refer to **Figure 77**.

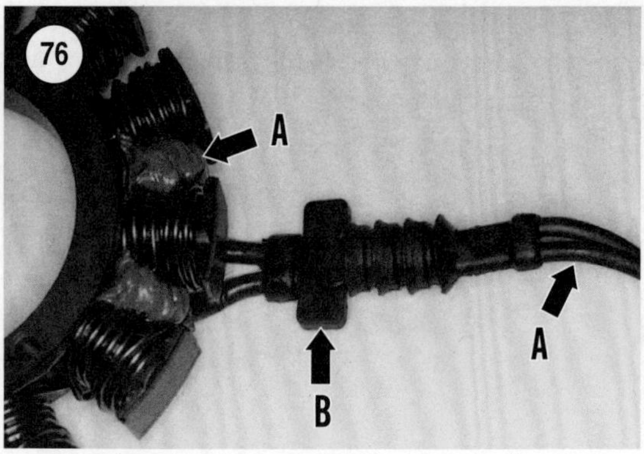

NOTE
On models so equipped, always disarm the optional TSSM security system prior to disconnecting the battery or the siren will sound.

1. Disconnect the negative battery cable as described in Chapter Eight.
2. Remove the cover from the electrical panel as described in this Supplement.
3. Disconnect the secondary lead from each spark plug (**Figure 78**).
4. Disconnect the front cylinder's secondary lead from the clip on the frame.
5. Disconnect the electrical connector from the backside of the ignition coil.

6A. On FXDL, FXDLI, FXDWG, FXDWGI, FXDC and FXDCI models, unscrew the long screw and washer securing the ignition coil cover and ignition coil. Do not lose the spacer between the cover and the ignition coil.

6B. On FXD, FXDI, FXDX and FXDXI models, unscrew the short screw securing the ignition coil.

7. Remove the ignition coil from the electrical panel.
8. Install by reversing these removal steps. Tighten the screws to 50 in.-lb. (5.6 N•m).

Ignition Control Module (2004-On Carbureted Models) and Electronic Control Module (2004-On Fuel Injected Models) Removal/Installation

Refer to the *Electrical Panel* section in this Supplment.

(77)

IGNITION SYSTEM COMPONENTS–ALL MODELS (2004-ON)

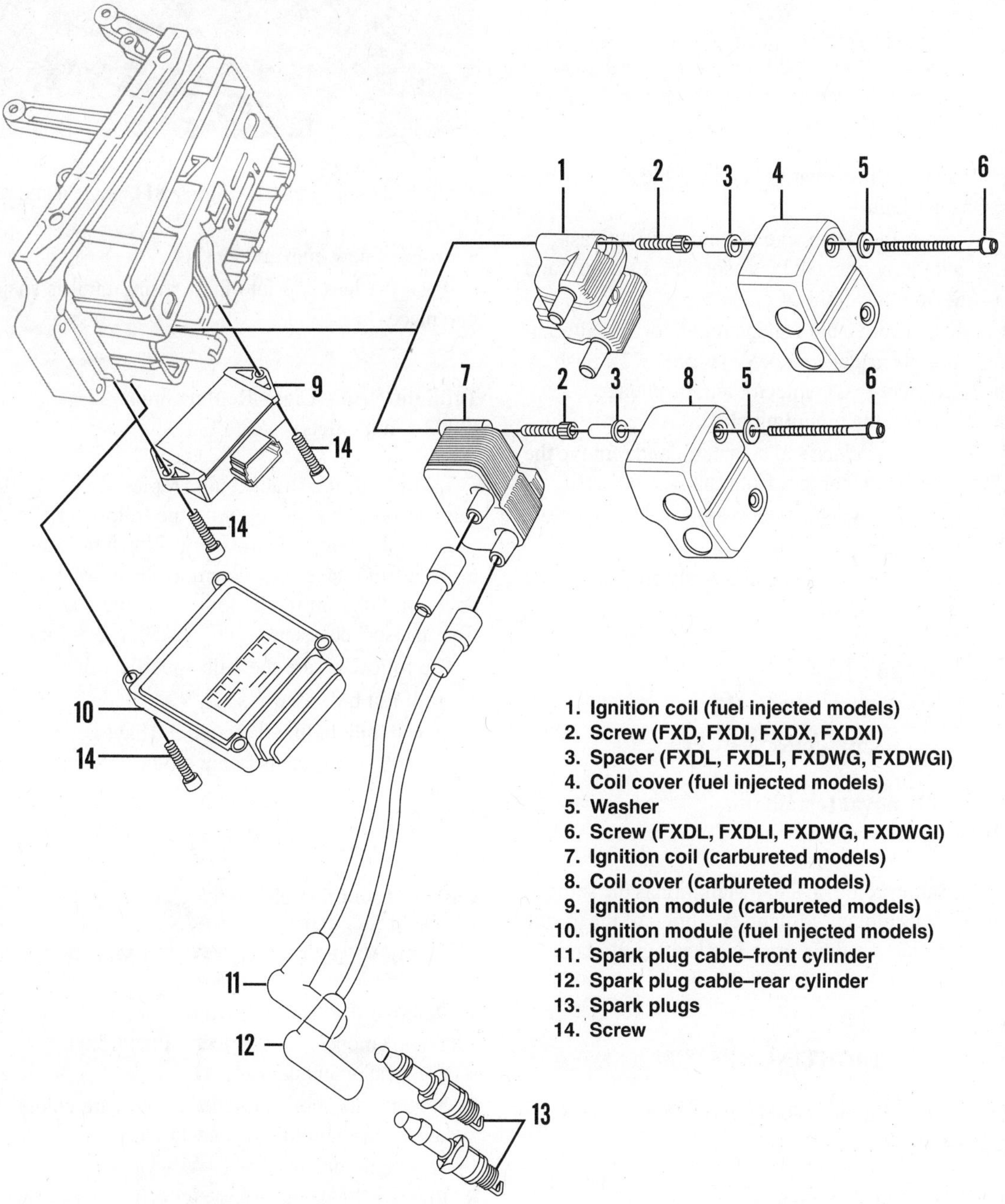

1. Ignition coil (fuel injected models)
2. Screw (FXD, FXDI, FXDX, FXDXI)
3. Spacer (FXDL, FXDLI, FXDWG, FXDWGI)
4. Coil cover (fuel injected models)
5. Washer
6. Screw (FXDL, FXDLI, FXDWG, FXDWGI)
7. Ignition coil (carbureted models)
8. Coil cover (carbureted models)
9. Ignition module (carbureted models)
10. Ignition module (fuel injected models)
11. Spark plug cable–front cylinder
12. Spark plug cable–rear cylinder
13. Spark plugs
14. Screw

Crankshaft Position Sensor (CKP) (2004-On Models)

The crankshaft position sensor (**Figure 79**) is located on the front left side of the crankcase next to the oil filter.

NOTE

On models so equipped, always disarm the optional TSSM security system prior to disconnecting the battery or the siren will sound.

1. Disconnect the negative battery cable as described in Chapter Eight.
2. Remove the Allen screws, and captive washers, and withdraw the CKP sensor (**Figure 80**) and O-ring from the crankcase.
3. Located above the voltage regulator and alternator stator electrical connector (**Figure 73**), push on the CKP electrical connector and disengage it from the T-stud on the mounting plate.
4. Separate the electrical connector and remove the CKP and wiring harness from the frame.
5. Install by reversing these removal steps. Note the following:
   a. Install a *new* O-ring and apply engine oil to it prior to installation.
   b. Tighten the Allen screws to 90-120 in.-lb. (10.2-13.6 N•m).

STARTING SYSTEM

Starter Removal/Installation (2004-On Models)

The starter removal and installation is the same as on previous models with the exception of the torque specification on the starter jackshaft bolt. Tighten the bolt to 60-80 in.-lb. (6.8-9.0 N•m).

LIGHTING SYSTEM

Front Turn Signal Bulb Replacement (2003-On Models)

1. Locate the notch in the lens cap.
2. Insert a coin into the notch and carefully twist the coin until the lens cap come off the housing (A, **Figure 81**).

3. Push in on the bulb (B, **Figure 81**), rotate it and remove it.
4. Install a new bulb and lens.
5. Push the lens cap into the housing until is snaps into place.

Taillight/Brake Light Replacement (2003-On Models)

Taillight/Brake light bulb replacement is the same as previous models with the following exception. On 2003 models, rotate the blown bulb and remove it from the socket assembly, then install a new bulb. On 2004-on models, pull the bulb straight out from the socket assembly, and install a new bulb.

The following are the bulb specifications:

1. Taillight bulb: 7 watts.
2. Brake light bulb: 2003 models (bayonet type) 27 watts, 2004-on models (wedge type) 25 watts.

SWITCHES

Ignition/Light Switch Removal/Installation (2004-On FXDWG and FXDWGI Models)

1. Remove the fuel tank console for FXDWG and FXDWGI models as described in the Chapter Seven section of this Supplement.
2. Note the location and color of the wire colors attached to the ignition switch. Disconnect the wires from the ignition switch.
3. Remove the screws securing the ignition switch to the underside of the console and remove the switch.
4. Install by reversing these removal steps. Tighten the mounting screws securely.

79

ENGINE SENSORS

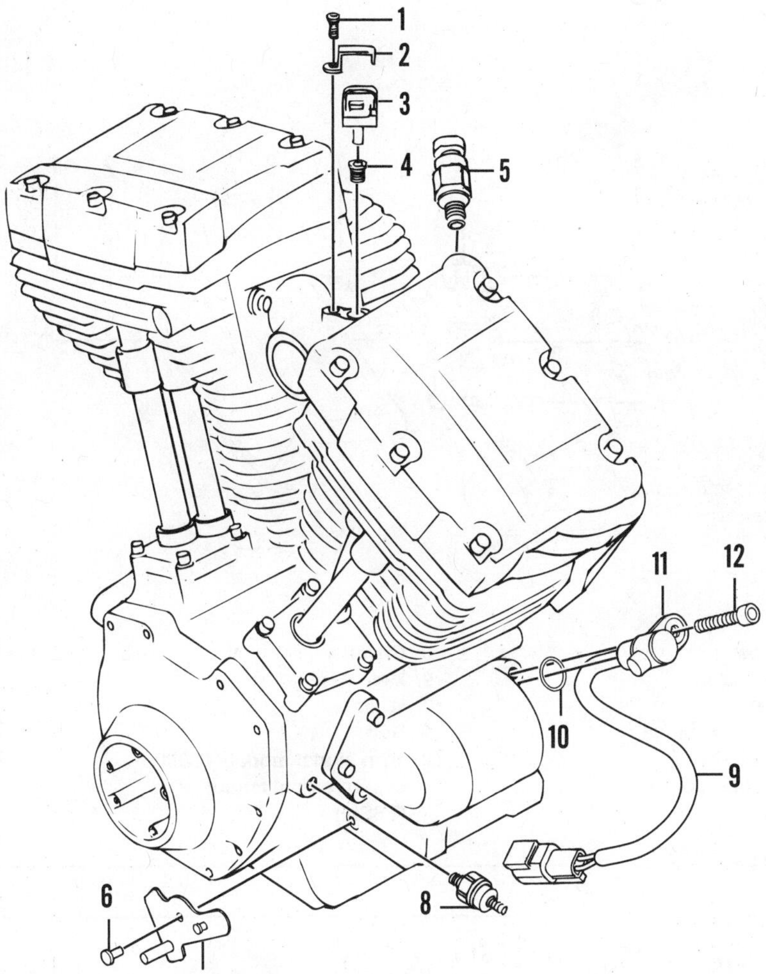

1. Screw
2. Clamp
3. MAP sensor
4. Seal
5. Engine temperature sensor
6. Screw–self tapping
7. Plate
8. Oil pressure switch
9. Wiring harness
10. O-ring
11. CKP sensor
12. Bolt

80

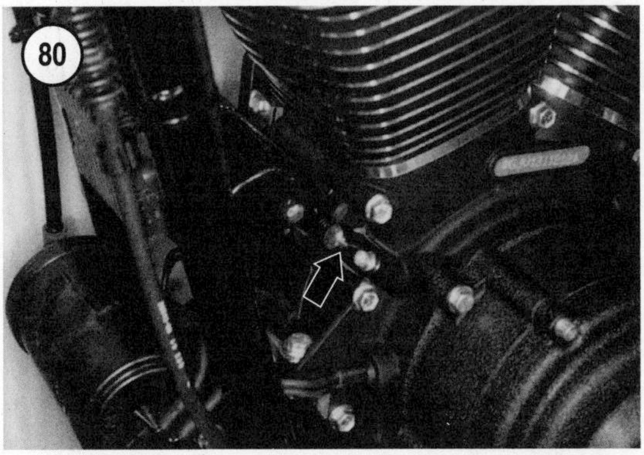

81

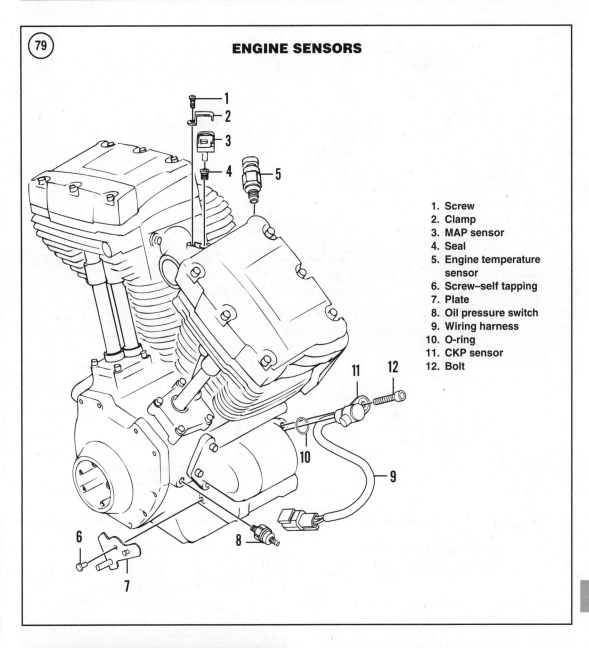

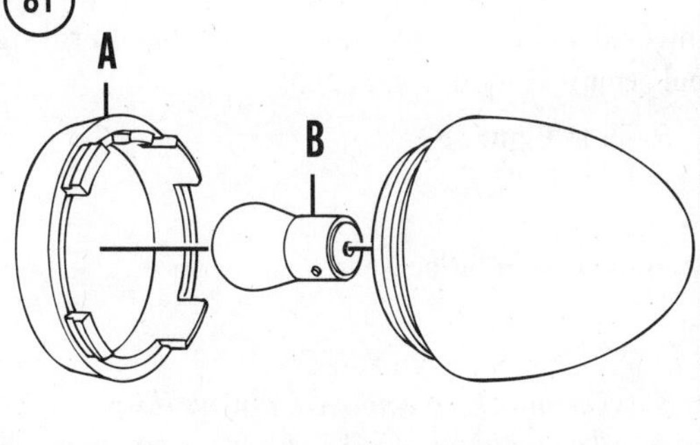

(82) **ELECTRICAL PANEL (2004-ON)**

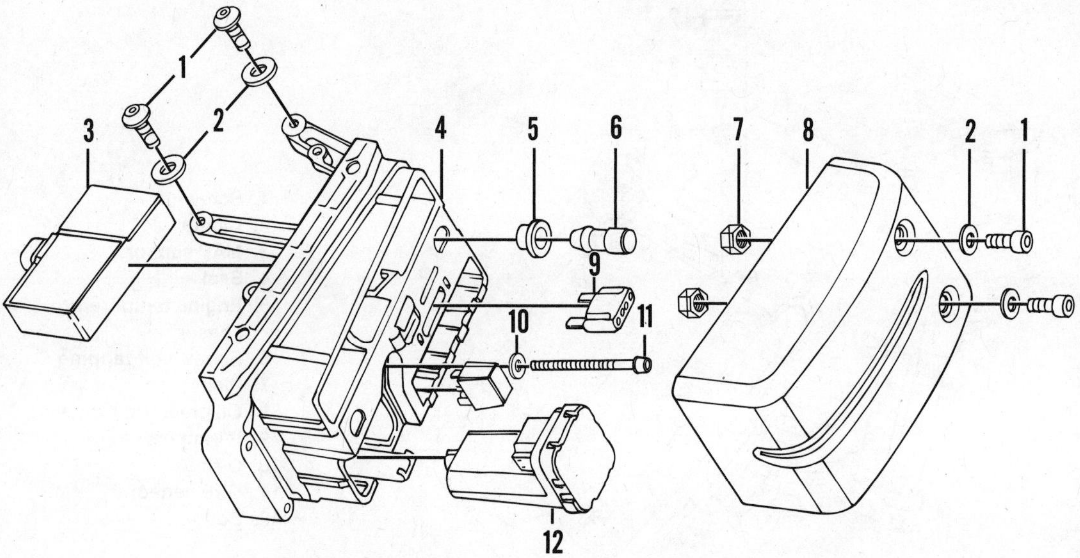

1. Screw
2. Washer
3. Siren
4. Electrical panel
5. Grommet
6. Mounting pin
7. Nut
8. Cover
9. Main fuse (40A)
10. Washer
11. Bolt
12. Turn signal module (TSM) or turn signal module (TSSM)

ELECTRICAL PANEL (2004-ON MODELS)

The electrical panel assembly mounts on the left side of the motorcycle. The panel assembly houses the fuses, ignition control module (carbureted models) or electronic control module (fuel injected models), starter relay (carbureted models), system relay (fuel injected models), turn signal canceller, turn signal/security module and siren.

Refer to **Figure 82**.

Removal/Installation

NOTE

On models so equipped, always disarm the optional TSSM security system prior to disconnecting the battery or the siren will sound.

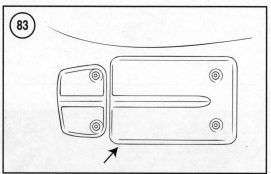

(83)

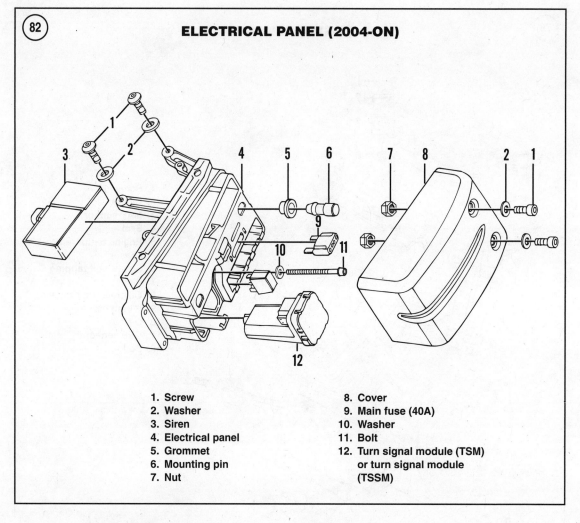

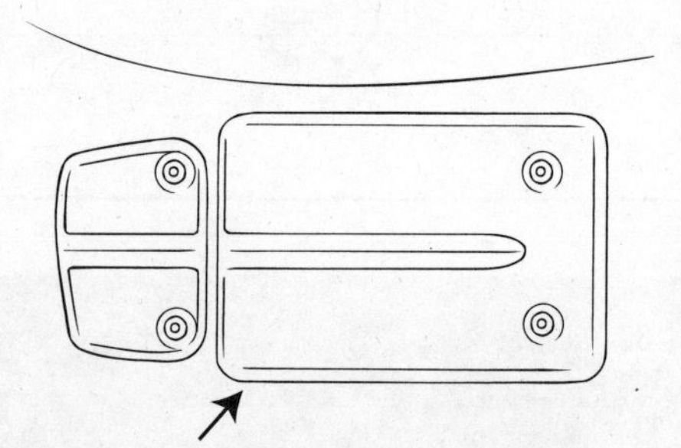

1. Remove the seat as described in Chapter Thirteen.
2. Disconnect the negative battery cable as described in Chapter Eight.

84

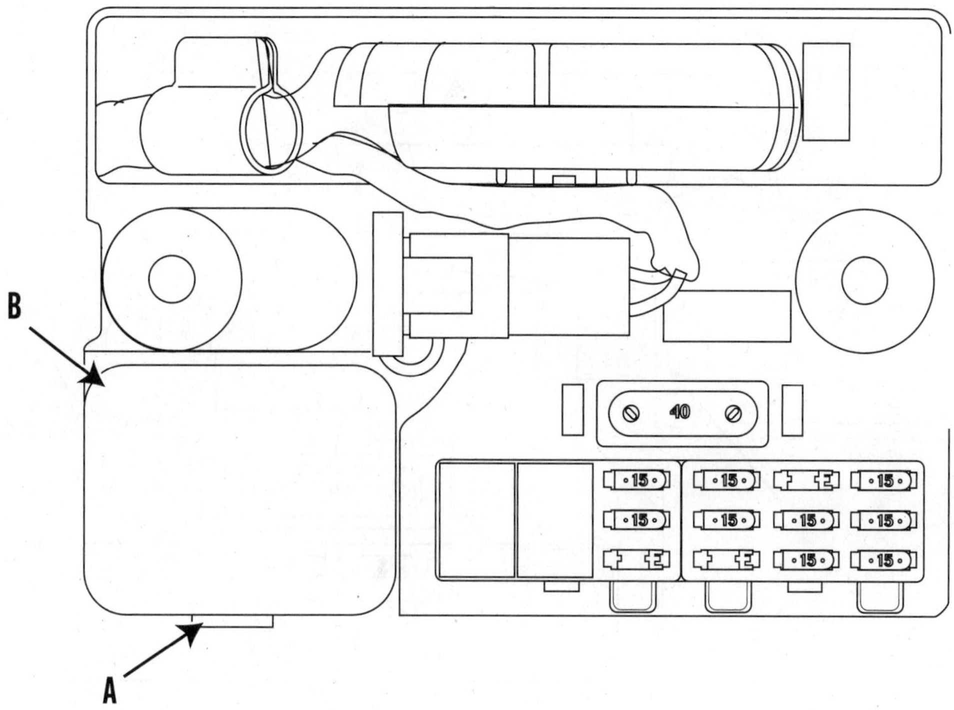

3. Hold onto both sides of the cover, pull straight out and remove the cover (**Figure 83**) from the electrical panel.
4. Remove the 40 amp main fuse from the connector.
5. Disconnect the main fuse connector as follows:
   a. Insert a small flat blade screwdriver into the slots on each side of the main fuse holder.
   b. Carefully depress the tabs on the main fuse holder connector and disengage it from the electrical panel.
6. To remove the TSM/TSSM unit, perform the following:
   a. Depress the tab (A, **Figure 84**) on the electrical panel securing the TSM/TSSM unit (B).
   b. Pull the TSM/TSSM unit from the opening in the panel, disconnect the electrical connector from unit, and remove it.
7. Slide the data link connector (A, **Figure 85**) toward the front and disengage it from the electrical panel.
8. To remove the ignition control module (ICM [2004-on carbureted models]) or electronic control module (ECM [2004-on fuel injected models]), perform the following:
   a. Carefully disconnect the 12-pin (ICM) or 36-pin (ECM) electrical connector (B, **Figure 85**) from the module.
   b. Disconnect the ignition coil four-pin electrical connector from the backside of the ignition coil unit.
   c. Disconnect the spark plug secondary wires from the ignition coil unit.
   d. Remove the front long screws and washers securing the electrical panel to the frame mount.
   e. Remove the top short screws and washers securing the frame mount.
   f. Carefully push the electrical connectors back through the opening in the electrical panel.

NOTE

On fuel injected models, note the location of the ground strap on the front mounting screw.

14

85

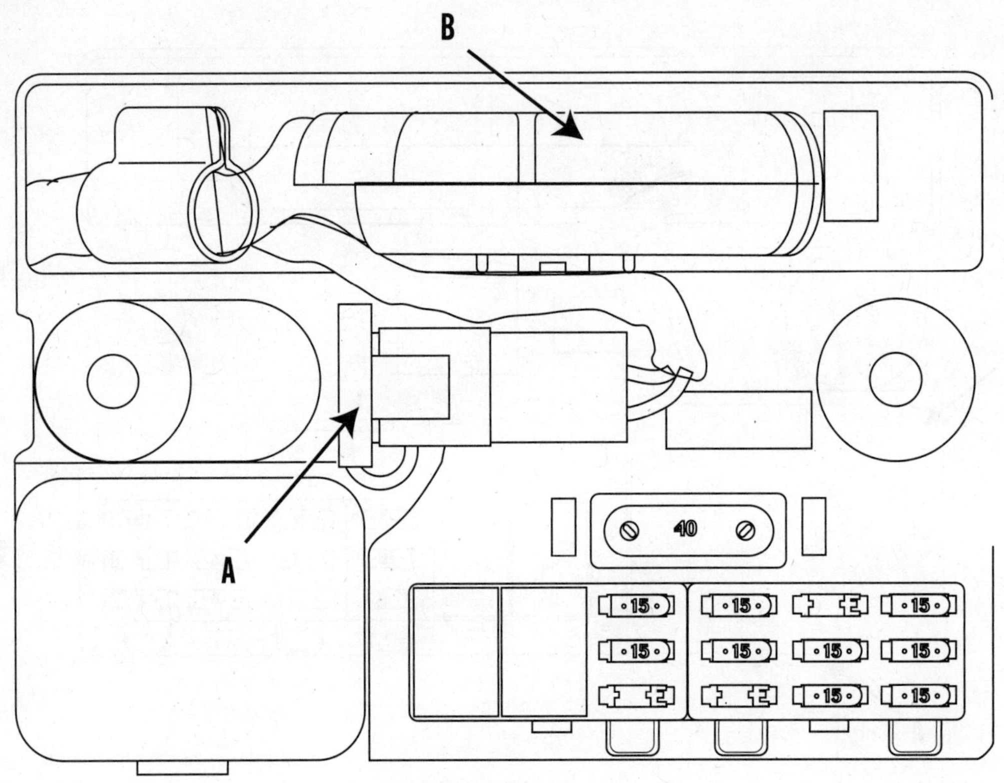

g. Remove the screws securing the ICM or ECM unit to the base of the electrical panel and remove the unit.

9. Remove the electrical panel from the frame.

10. Install by reversing these removal steps. Note the following:

a. Tighten the top short screws to 100 in.-lb. (11.3 N•m).

b. Tighten the front long screws to 50 in.-lb. (5.6 N•m).

c. Apply a light coat of dielectric compound to the electrical connectors prior to installing them.

d. Connect the electrical connectors. On connectors so equipped, make sure they are push together until the tab clicks into the locked position.

TURN SIGNAL MODULE (TSM) AND TURN SIGNAL MODULE/SECURITY MODULE (TSSM) (2004-ON MODELS)

The turn signal module and turn signal module/security module operation is the same as on prior years with the exception of the removal and installation of the unit.

Removal and installation are covered under *Electrical Panel* in this section.

STARTER RELAY REPLACEMENT (2004-ON MODELS)

NOTE

On models so equipped, always disarm the optional TSSM security system

86

FUSE PANEL (CARBURETED MODELS)

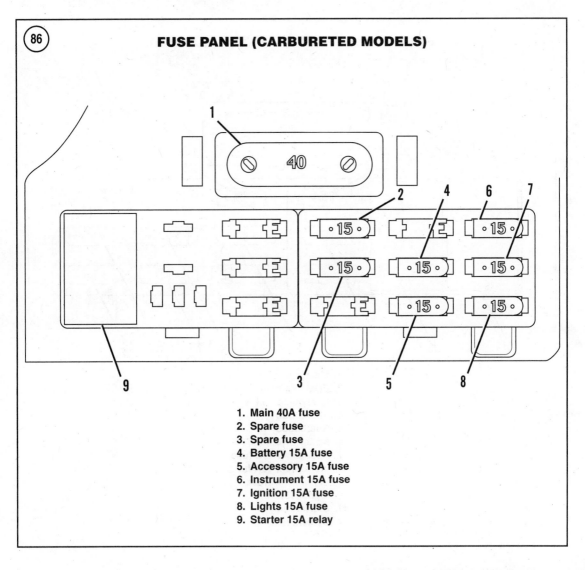

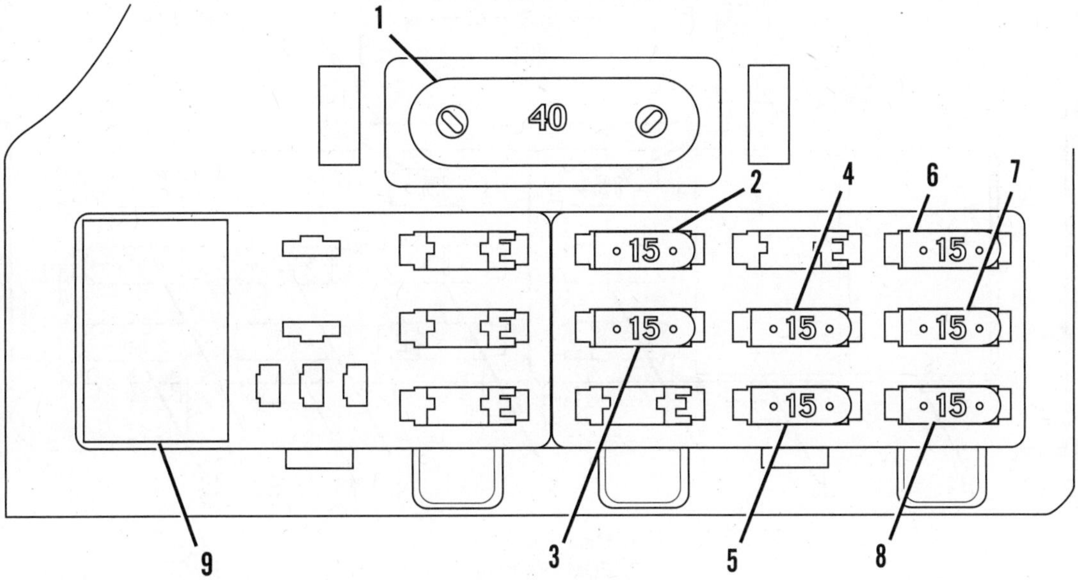

1. Main 40A fuse
2. Spare fuse
3. Spare fuse
4. Battery 15A fuse
5. Accessory 15A fuse
6. Instrument 15A fuse
7. Ignition 15A fuse
8. Lights 15A fuse
9. Starter 15A relay

prior to disconnecting the battery or the siren will sound.

1. Remove the seat as described in Chapter Thirteen.
2. Disconnect the negative battery cable as described in Chapter Eight.
3. Hold onto both sides of the cover, pull straight out and remove the cover (**Figure 83**) from the electrical panel.
4. Pull straight out and remove the starter relay from the electrical panel. Refer to **Figure 86** or **Figure 87**.
5. Install the starter relay onto the electrical panel.
6. Install the cover onto the electrical panel.

SYSTEM RELAY REPLACEMENT (2004-ON FUEL INJECTED MODELS)

NOTE

On models so equipped, always disarm the optional TSSM security system prior to disconnecting the battery or the siren will sound.

1. Remove the seat as described in Chapter Thirteen.
2. Disconnect the negative battery cable as described in Chapter Eight.
3. Hold onto both sides of the cover, pull straight out and remove the cover (**Figure 83**) from the electrical panel.
4. Pull straight out and remove the system relay from the electrical panel. Refer to **Figure 87**.

(87) **FUSE PANEL (FUEL INJECTED MODELS)**

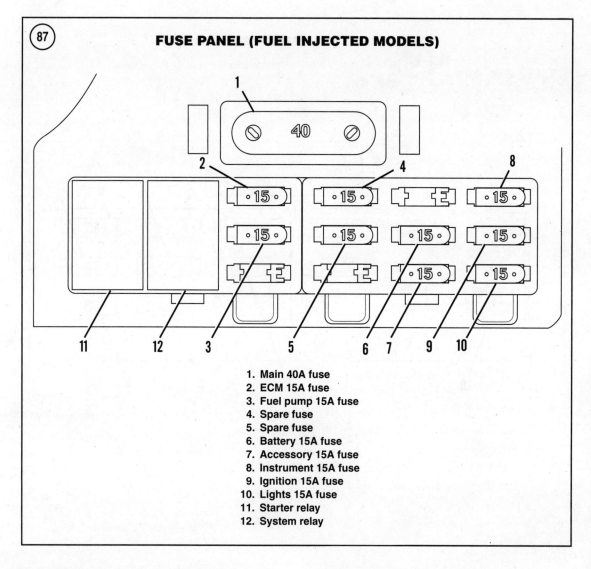

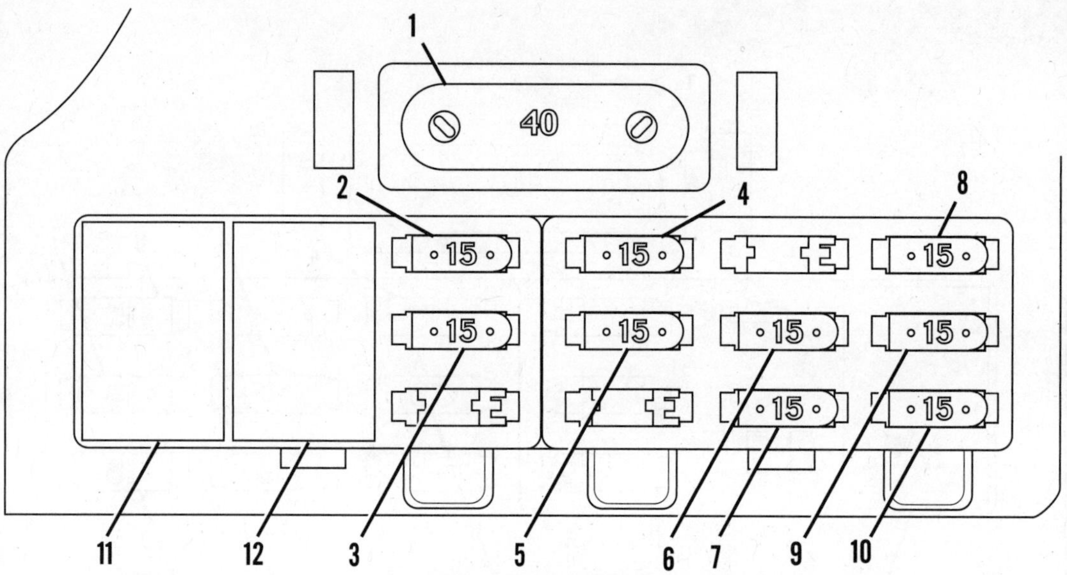

1. Main 40A fuse
2. ECM 15A fuse
3. Fuel pump 15A fuse
4. Spare fuse
5. Spare fuse
6. Battery 15A fuse
7. Accessory 15A fuse
8. Instrument 15A fuse
9. Ignition 15A fuse
10. Lights 15A fuse
11. Starter relay
12. System relay

5. Install the starter relay onto the electrical panel.
6. Install the cover onto the electrical panel.

INSTRUMENTS

Removal/Installation (2005 FXDC, FXDCI Models)

Removal and installation is the same as on prior FXD Series models with the exception of the shape of the shape of the meter housing as shown in **Figure 88**.

Removal/Installation (2004-On FXDL, FXDLI Models)

Refer to **Figure 89**.

1. Remove the fuel tank console as described in the Chapter Seven section of this chapter.
2. Unscrew and remove the reset switch rubber boot.
3. Remove the reset switch from the console.
4. Remove the screws securing the back clamp to the console.
5. Remove the back clamp and remove the speedometer and/or tachometer from the console.
6. Remove the gasket from the meter or console.
7. Install by reversing these removal steps. Note the following:
   a. If necessary, apply alcohol or glass cleaner to the gasket to ease its installation onto the meter.
   b. Tighten the back clamp screws securely. Do not pinch the wiring between the back clamp and the console.

88

INSTRUMENTS–FXDC, FXDCI (2005)

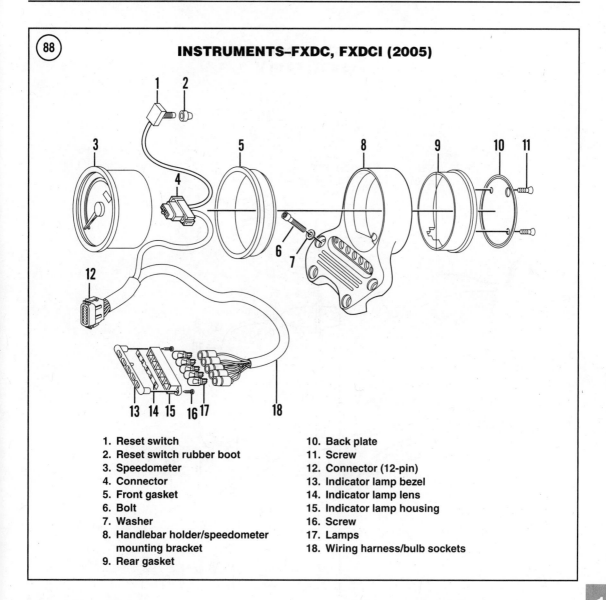

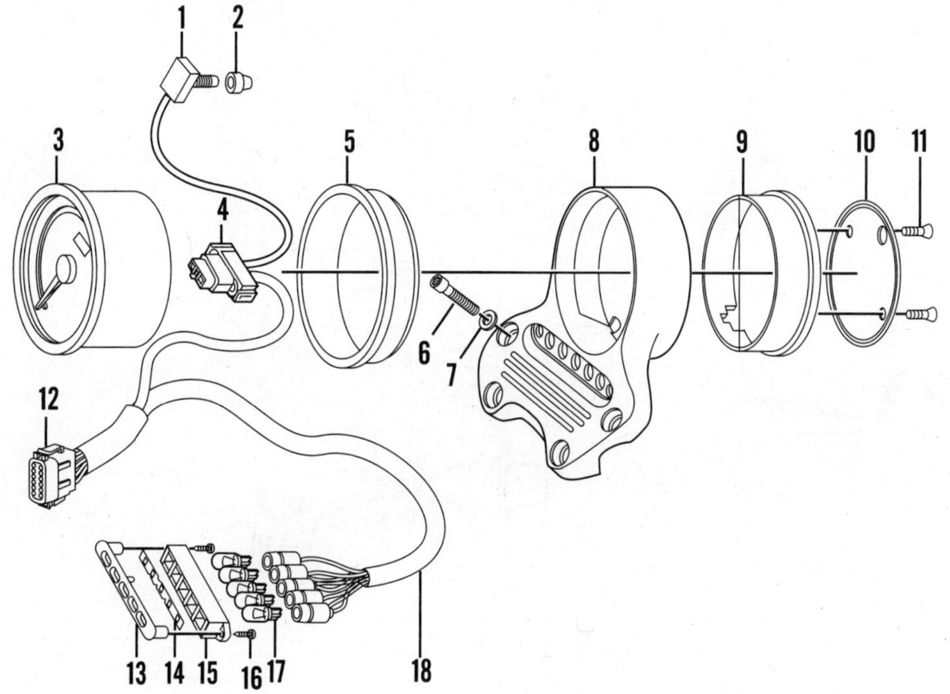

1. Reset switch
2. Reset switch rubber boot
3. Speedometer
4. Connector
5. Front gasket
6. Bolt
7. Washer
8. Handlebar holder/speedometer mounting bracket
9. Rear gasket
10. Back plate
11. Screw
12. Connector (12-pin)
13. Indicator lamp bezel
14. Indicator lamp lens
15. Indicator lamp housing
16. Screw
17. Lamps
18. Wiring harness/bulb sockets

Removal/Installation (2004-On FXDWG, FXDWGI Models)

Refer to **Figure 90**.

1. Remove the fuel tank console as described in the Chapter Seven section of this Supplement.
2. Unscrew and remove the reset switch rubber boot.
3. Remove the reset switch from the console.
4. Use a flat blade screwdriver and carefully pry between the three tabs on the back clamp and release it from the speedometer. Remove the back clamp.
5. Remove the speedometer and gasket from the console.
6. Install by reversing these removal steps. Note the following:

   a. If necessary, apply alcohol or glass cleaner to the gasket to ease its installation onto the meter.

   b. Tighten the back clamp screws securely. Do not pinch the wiring between the back clamp and the console.

FUSES AND MAXI-FUSE (2004-ON MODELS)

All models are equipped with a series fused to protect the electrical system. The number of fuses varies depending on model. The 40 amp circuit breaker used on prior models has been replaced with the 40 amp maxi-fuse. Always carry spare fuses

89

FUEL TANK CONSOLE (FXDL, FXDLI)

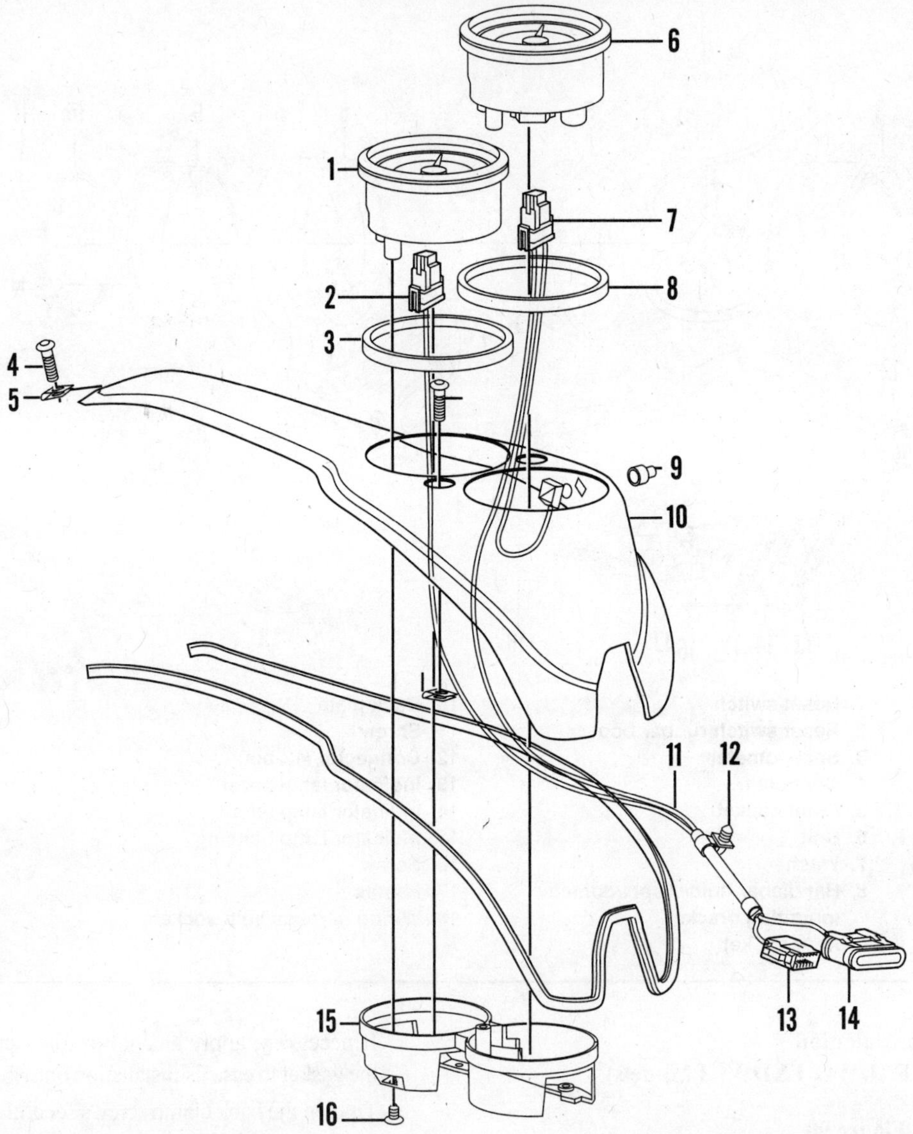

1. Tachometer
2. Socket
3. Gasket
4. Screw
5. Speed nut
6. Speedometer
7. Socket
8. Gasket
9. Reset switch rubber boot
10. Console
11. Wiring harness
12. Clamp
13. Connector (12-pin)
14. Warning light
15. Back clamp
16. Screw

(90)

FUEL TANK CONSOLE (FXDWG, FXDWGI)

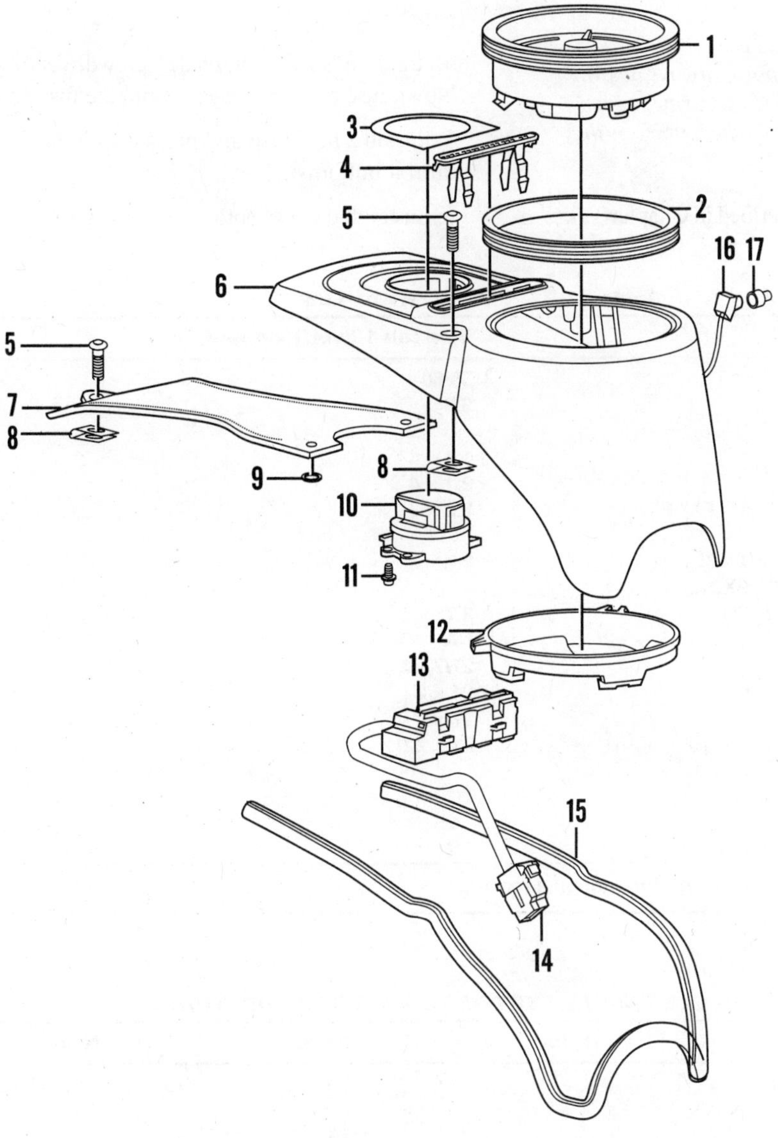

1. Speedometer
2. Gasket
3. Bezel
4. Indicator lamp bezel
5. Screw
6. Console
7. Leather trim panel
8. Speed nut
9. Push nut
10. Ignition switch
11. Screw
12. Back clamp
13. Indicator lamp assembly
14. Connector
15. Trim gasket
16. Reset switch
17. Reset switch rubber boot

The fuse ratings are identical to prior years. Refer to **Figure 86** or **Figure 87** for fuse location on the panel.

Fuse Replacement

NOTE
On models so equipped, always disarm the optional TSSM security system prior to disconnecting the battery or the siren will sound.

1. Remove the seat as described in Chapter Thirteen.
2. Disconnect the negative battery cable as described in Chapter Eight.
3. Hold onto both sides of the cover, pull straight out and remove the cover (**Figure 83**) from the electrical panel.
4. Insert a small flat blade screwdriver under the blown fuse and disengage it from the fuse panel.
5. Install a *new* fuse and press it into the fuse panel until it bottoms.
6. Install the cover onto the electrical panel.

Table 11 REPLACEMENT BULBS

Item	Size (all 12 volt) × quantity
Headlamp	55/60
Position lamp*	3.9
Indicator lamps	
FXDL, FXDLI	1.1 × 4
FXDP	2.1 × 4
All models except FXDL and FXDP	2.2 × 3
Fuel gauge	
FXDL FXDLI, FXDWG, FXDWGI	2.7
FXD, FXDI, FXDC, FXDCI, FXDX, FXDXI, FXDX-CONV, FXDXT	3.7
FXDP	NA
Front turn signal/running light	27/7 × 2
Front turn signal*	21 × 2
Rear turn signal	27 × 2
Rear turn signal	21 × 2
Tail/brake lamp	
2003	7/27
2004-on	7/25
Tail/brake lamp*	5/21

* Indicates bulb specification for HD International models.

Table 12 ELECTRICAL SYSTEM TORQUE SPECIFICATIONS

Item	ft.-lb.	in.-lb.	N•m
Crankshaft Allen screws	–	90-120	10.2-13.6
Electrical panel			
Long screws	–	50	5.6
Short screw	–	100	11.3
Ignition coil screws	–	50	5.6
Starter jackshaft bolt	–	60-80	6.8-9.0
Stator screws	–	55-75	6.2-8.4
Voltage regulator bolts	–	60-80	6.8-9.0

CHAPTER TEN

FRONT SUSPENSION AND STEERING

FRONT FORK

Front Fork Service (2002-On FXDL)

Service to the front fork is the same as on prior FXDL models with the exception of the fork oil quantity and oil level.

Assemble the front fork as described in Chapter Ten. Add 10.6 oz. (314 ml) and adjust the fork oil level so it is 6.69 in. (169.9 mm) from the top surface of the fork tube.

STEERING HEAD AND STEM

Removal/Installation (2005 FXDC and FXDCI Models)

Removal and installation of the steering stem is the same as on prior models with the exception of the handlebar holder that is also the speedometer mounting bracket (**Figure 88**).

Remove the bolts securing the handlebar holder/speedometer mounting bracket. Secure the speedometer and mounting bracket to the lower stem after removal.

Table 13 FRONT FORK OIL CAPACITY AND OIL LEVEL DIMENSION

Model	Capacity oz. (ml)	Oil level dimension in. (mm)
FXDL, FXDLI	10.6 (316)	6.69 (169.9)
FXDX, FXDXI, FXDXT	Use oil level	5.04 (128)
FXDP	NA	
NA = Information not available from the manufacturer.		

CHAPTER ELEVEN

REAR SUSPENSION

SHOCK ABSORBERS

Shock Absorber Busing Inspection and Replacement

Shock absorber inspection is the same as on prior models with the exception of the bushings. The bushings are no longer available and cannot be replaced, if worn or damaged, replace the shock absorber.

CHAPTER TWELVE

BRAKES

FRONT BRAKE PAD REPLACEMENT

Front brake pad removal and installation is the same as on previous models with the following exception.

The brake pads are not symmetrical. The pad with one tab (A, **Figure 91**) must be installed on the inboard side of the left side caliper and on the outboard side of the right side caliper. The pad with two tabs (B, **Figure 91**) must be installed on the outboard side of the left side caliper and on the inboard side of the right side caliper.

REAR BRAKE PAD REPLACEMENT

Rear brake pad removal and installation is the same as on previous models with the following exception.

The brake pads are not symmetrical. The pad with one tab (A, **Figure 91**) must be installed on the outboard side. The pad with two tabs (B, **Figure 91**) must be installed on the inboard side of the caliper.

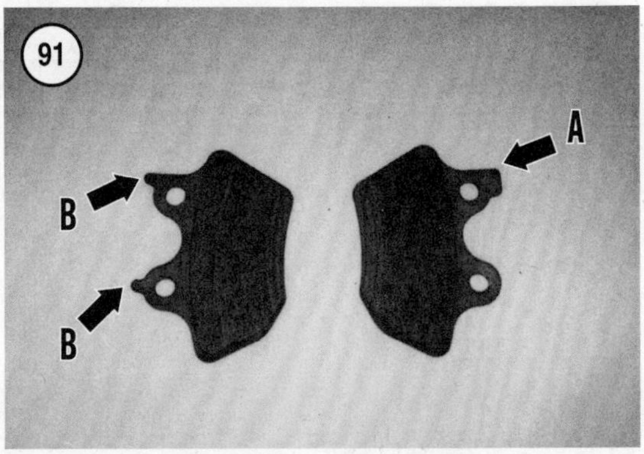

REAR BRAKE PEDAL (2003-ON FXDWG MODELS)

Removal/Lubrication/Installation

Refer to **Figure 92**.

1. Remove the exhaust system as described in Chapter Seven of the main body of this manual.

(92) **REAR BRAKE PEDAL**

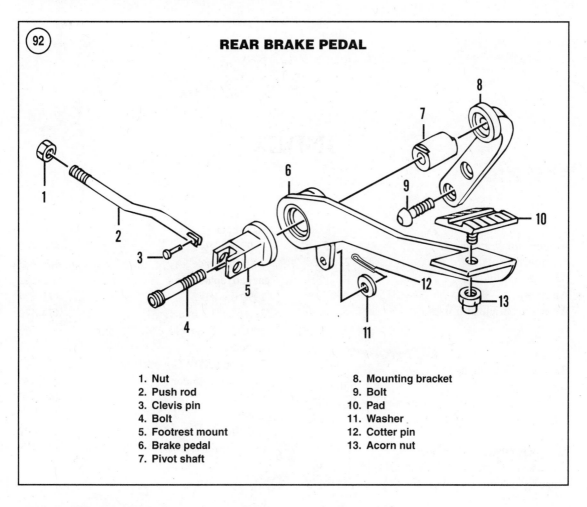

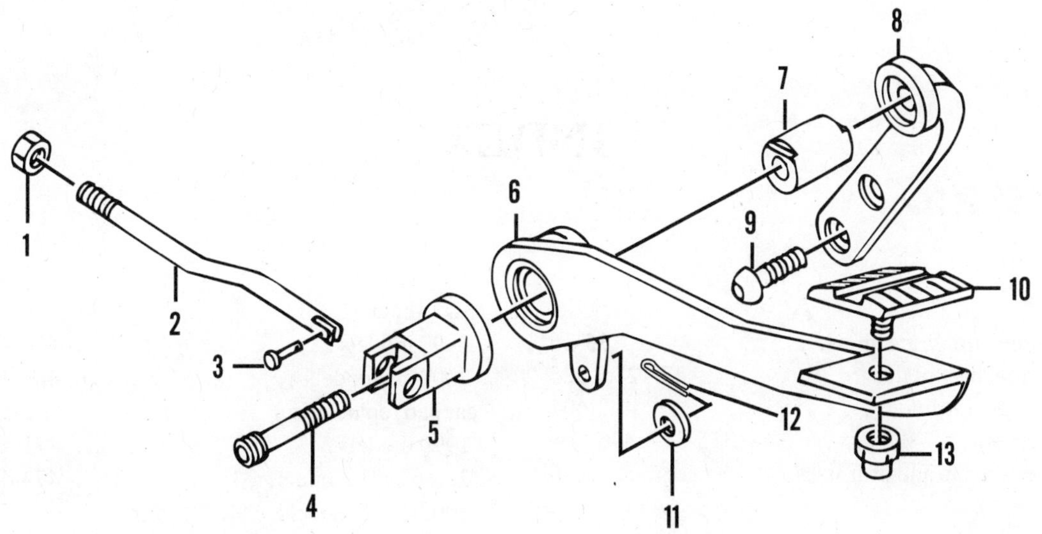

1. Nut
2. Push rod
3. Clevis pin
4. Bolt
5. Footrest mount
6. Brake pedal
7. Pivot shaft
8. Mounting bracket
9. Bolt
10. Pad
11. Washer
12. Cotter pin
13. Acorn nut

2. Remove the bolt and nut securing the footrest to the footrest mount. Remove the footrest.
3. Remove the cotter pin, washer and clevis pin securing the push rod to the brake pedal. Disconnect the pushrod.
4. Remove the bolt securing the footrest mount and the brake pedal to the mounting bracket. Remove the brake pedal.
5. If necessary, remove the bolts securing the mounting bracket to the frame and remove the mounting bracket.
6. Inspect the brake pedal for fractures or damage and replace if necessary.
7. Inspect the bushing within the pedal for wear. Replace if necessary.
8. Inspect the pivot shaft where the pedal rides for wear.
9. Lubricate the bushing and bracket shoulder with waterproof grease.
10. Install the pedal by reversing these removal steps. Note noting the following:
    a. Tighten the special bolt securely.
    b. Install a *new* cotter pin and bend the ends over completely.
    c. Adjust the rear brake pedal height as described in Chapter Three of the main body of this manual.

INDEX

D

E

15

F

T

15

V

W

WIRING DIAGRAMS

1999-2000 FXDWG MODELS

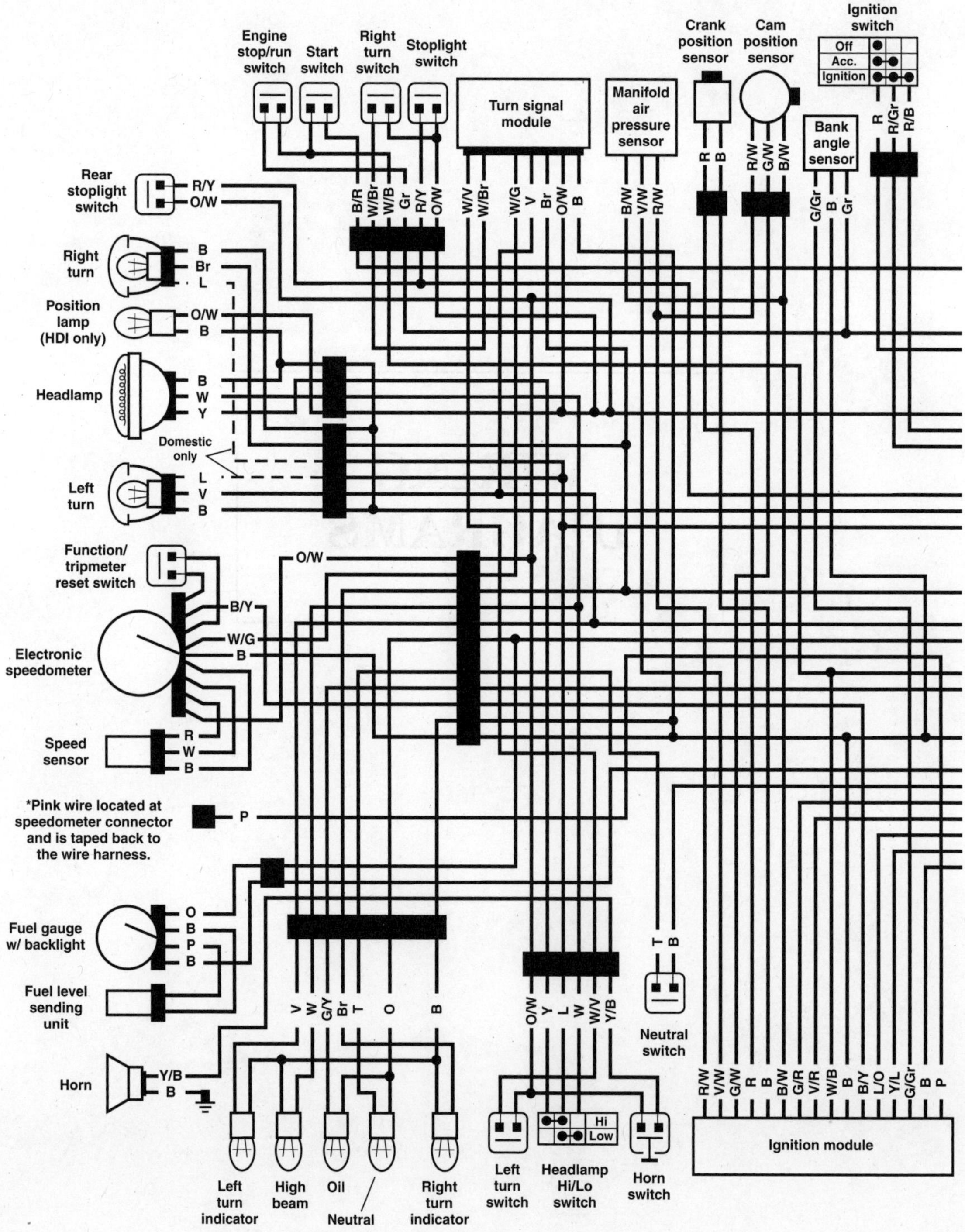

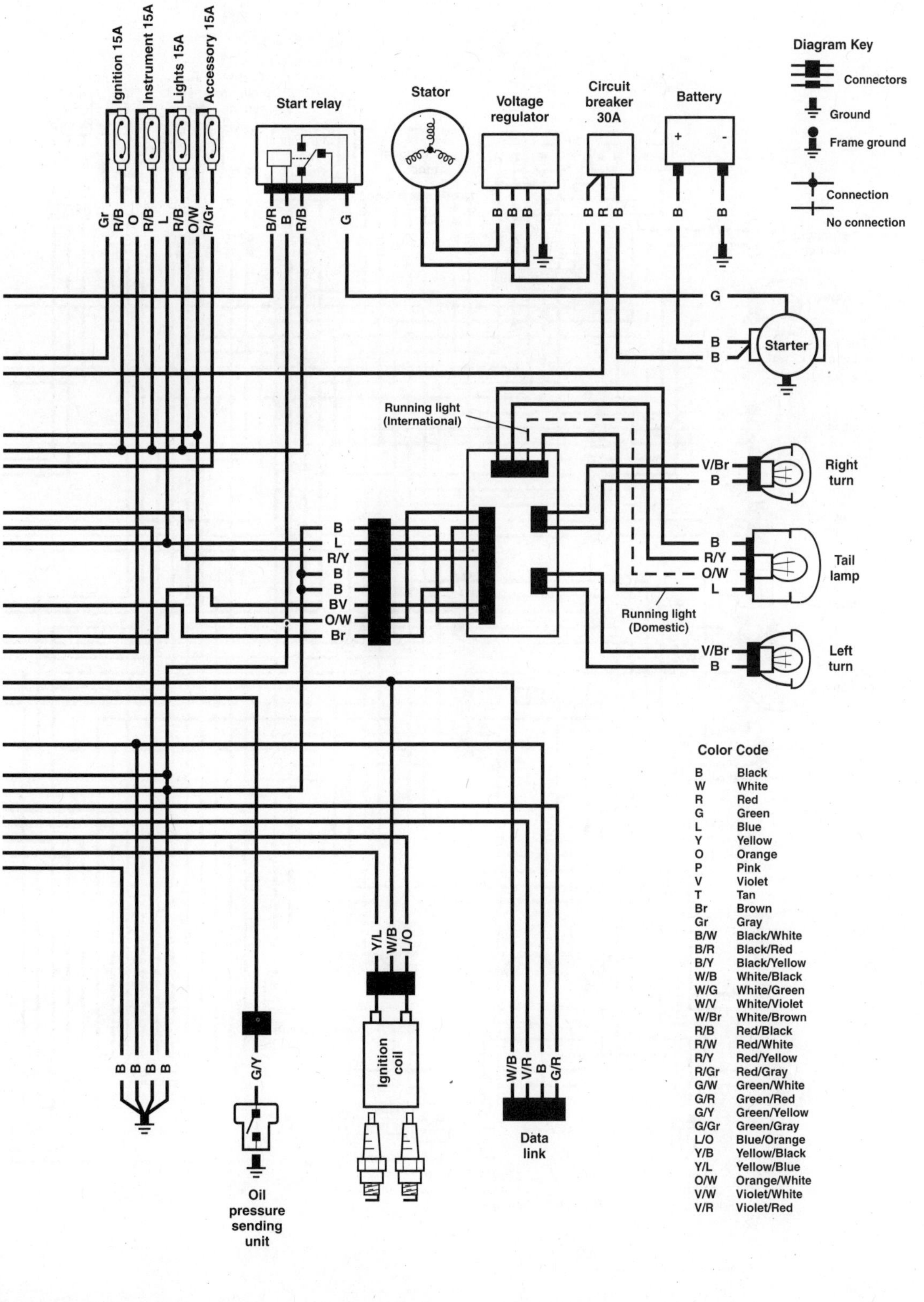
Ignition 15A
Instrument 15A
Lights 15A
Accessory 15A
Start relay
Stator
Voltage regulator
Circuit breaker 30A
Battery
+
-
Diagram Key
Connectors
Ground
Frame ground
Connection
No connection
Gr
R/B
O
R/B
L
R/B
O/W
R/Gr
B/R
B
R/B
G
B
B
B
B
R
B
B
B
G
B
B
Starter
Running light (International)
V/Br
B
Right turn
B
L
R/Y
B
B
BV
O/W
Br
B
R/Y
O/W
L
Tail lamp
Running light (Domestic)
V/Br
B
Left turn
Color Code
B Black
W White
R Red
G Green
L Blue
Y Yellow
O Orange
P Pink
V Violet
T Tan
Br Brown
Gr Gray
B/W Black/White
B/R Black/Red
B/Y Black/Yellow
W/B White/Black
W/G White/Green
W/V White/Violet
W/Br White/Brown
R/B Red/Black
R/W Red/White
R/Y Red/Yellow
R/Gr Red/Gray
G/W Green/White
G/R Green/Red
G/Y Green/Yellow
G/Gr Green/Gray
L/O Blue/Orange
Y/B Yellow/Black
Y/L Yellow/Blue
O/W Orange/White
V/W Violet/White
V/R Violet/Red
Y/L
W/B
L/O
Ignition coil
W/B
V/R
B
G/R
Data link
B
B
B
B
G/Y
Oil pressure sending unit

16

1999-2000 FXDS-CONV, FXDL, FXDX, FXD MODELS

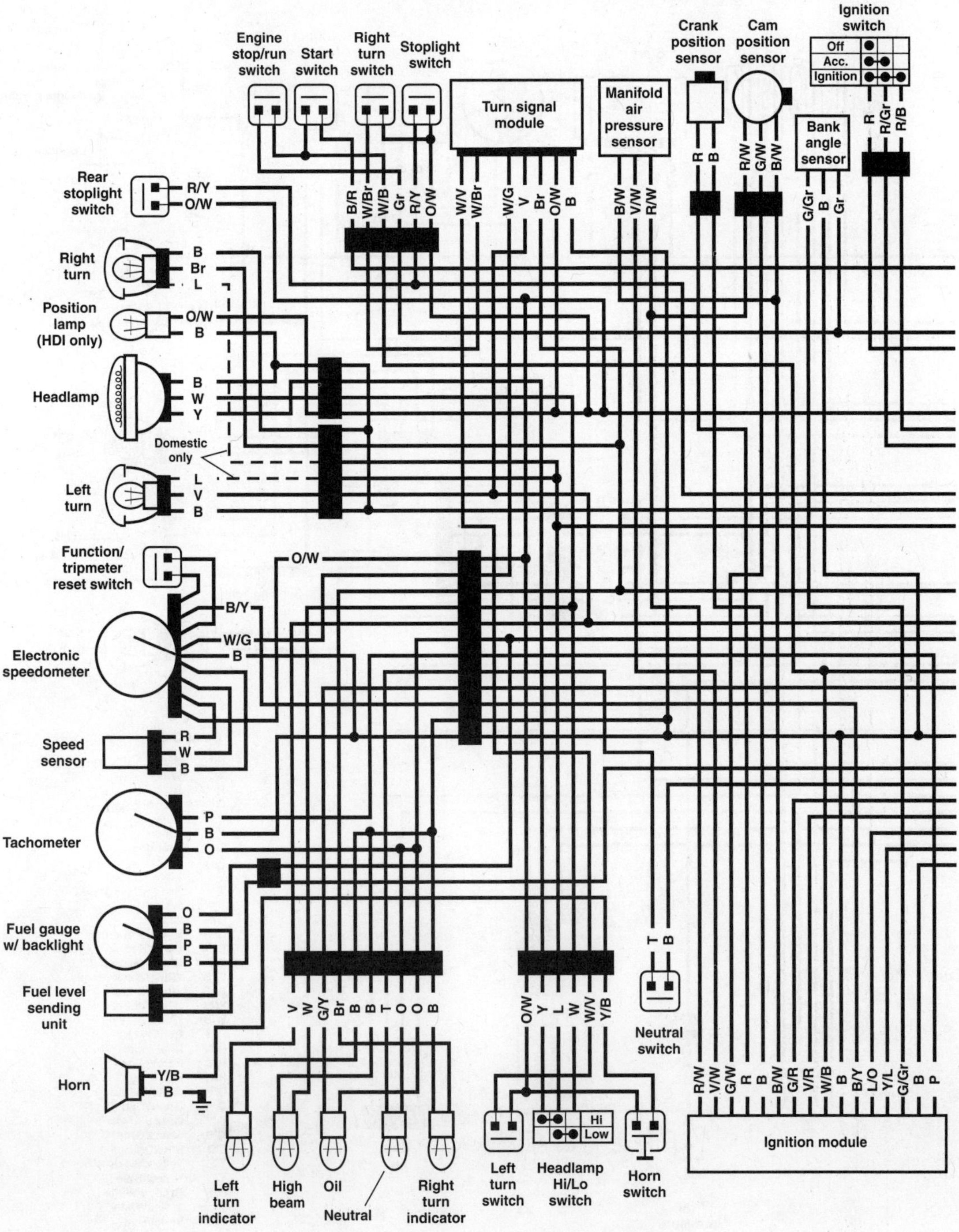

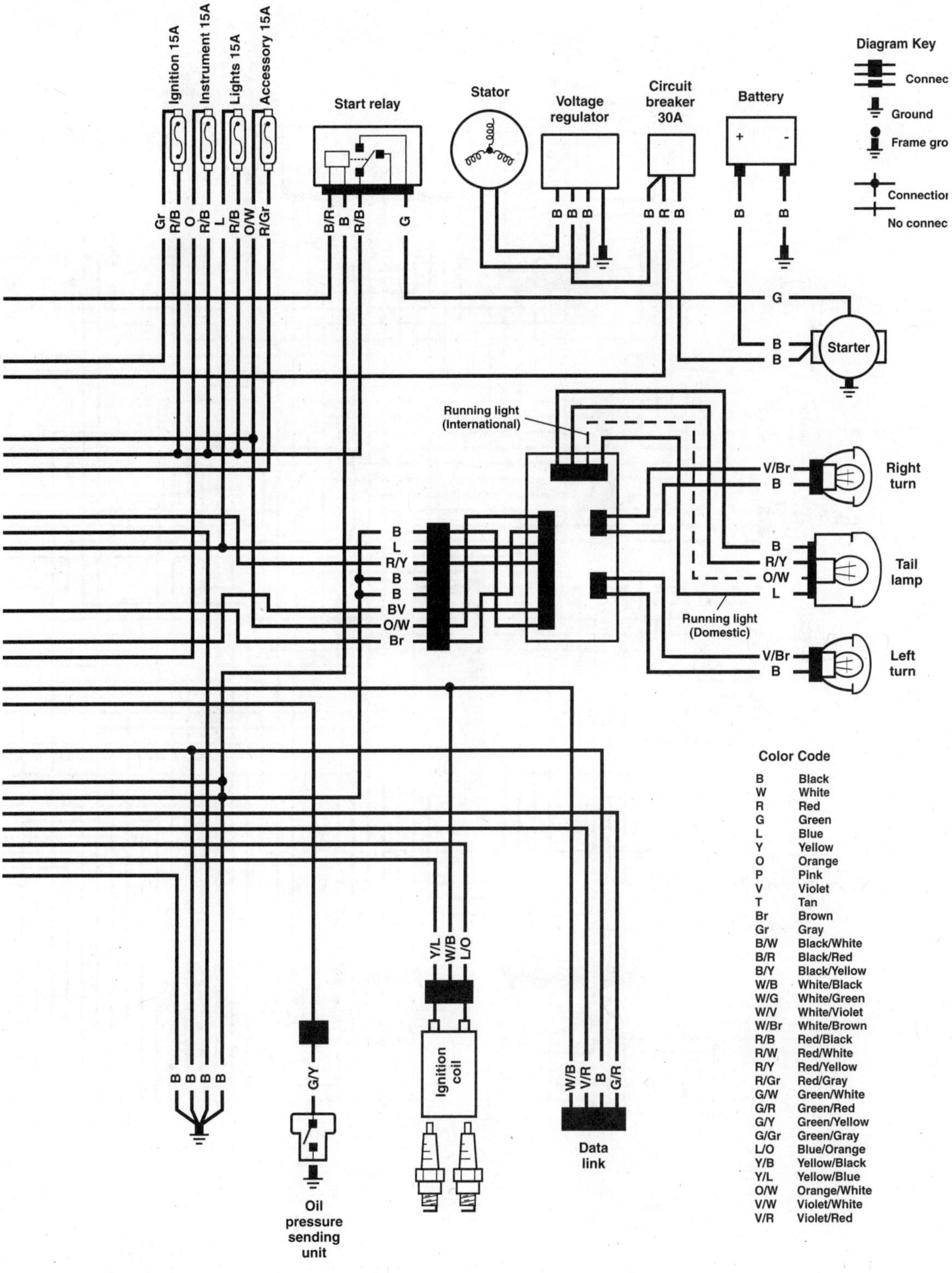

Ignition 15A
Instrument 15A
Lights 15A
Accessory 15A
Gr R/B O R/B L R/B O/W R/Gr
Start relay
B/R B R/B G
Stator
Voltage regulator
B B B
Circuit breaker 30A
B R B
Battery
+ -
B B
Diagram Key
Connec
Ground
Frame gro
Connectio
No connec
G
B
B
Starter
Running light (International)
V/Br
B
Right turn
B
L
R/Y
B
B
BV
O/W
Br
B
R/Y
O/W
L
Tail lamp
Running light (Domestic)
V/Br
B
Left turn
B B B B
G/Y
Oil pressure sending unit
Y/L W/B L/O
Ignition coil
W/B V/R B G/R
Data link
Color Code
B Black
W White
R Red
G Green
L Blue
Y Yellow
O Orange
P Pink
V Violet
T Tan
Br Brown
Gr Gray
B/W Black/White
B/R Black/Red
B/Y Black/Yellow
W/B White/Black
W/G White/Green
W/V White/Violet
W/Br White/Brown
R/B Red/Black
R/W Red/White
R/Y Red/Yellow
R/Gr Red/Gray
G/W Green/White
G/R Green/Red
G/Y Green/Yellow
G/Gr Green/Gray
L/O Blue/Orange
Y/B Yellow/Black
Y/L Yellow/Blue
O/W Orange/White
V/W Violet/White
V/R Violet/Red

2001-2003 FXDWG MODELS

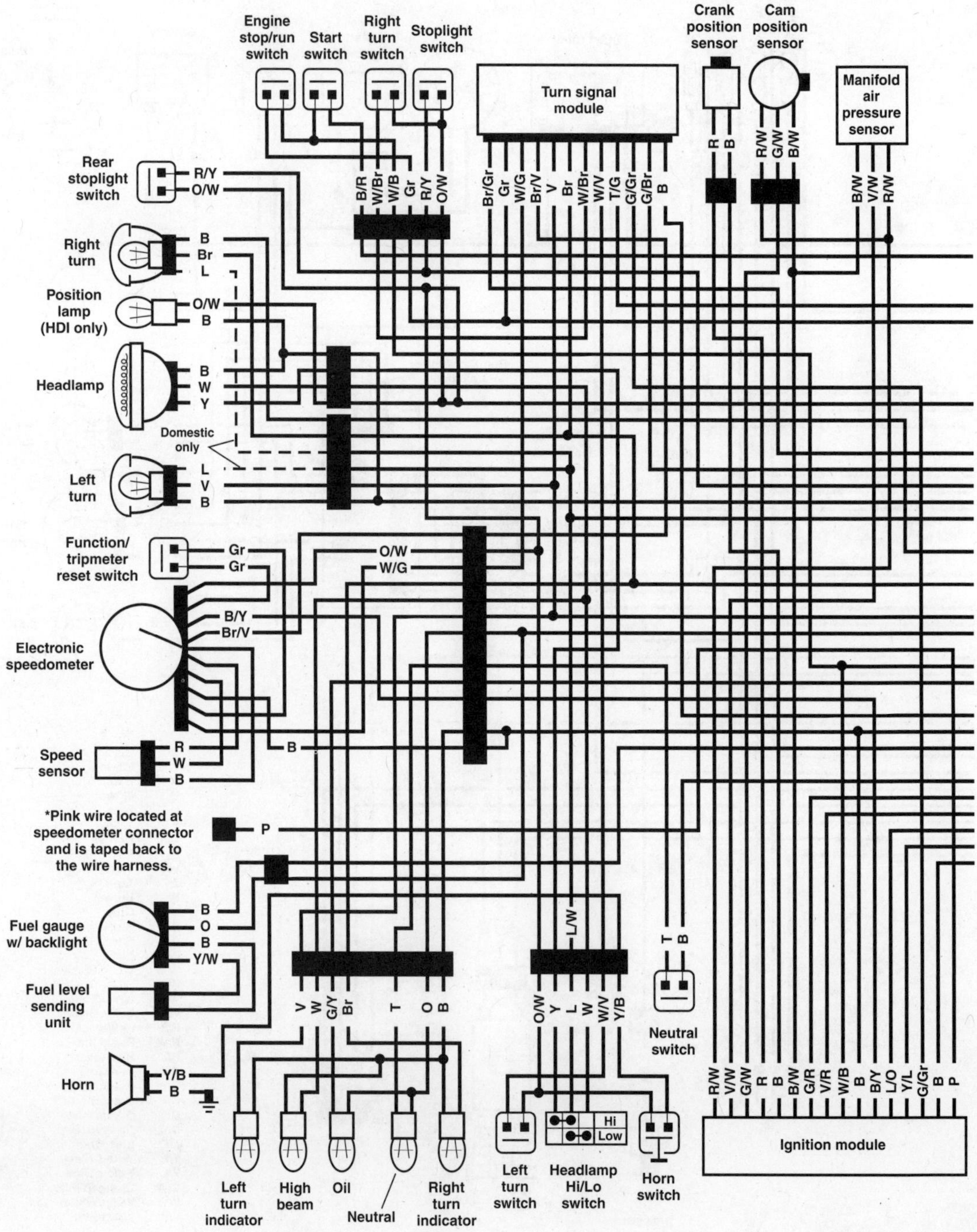

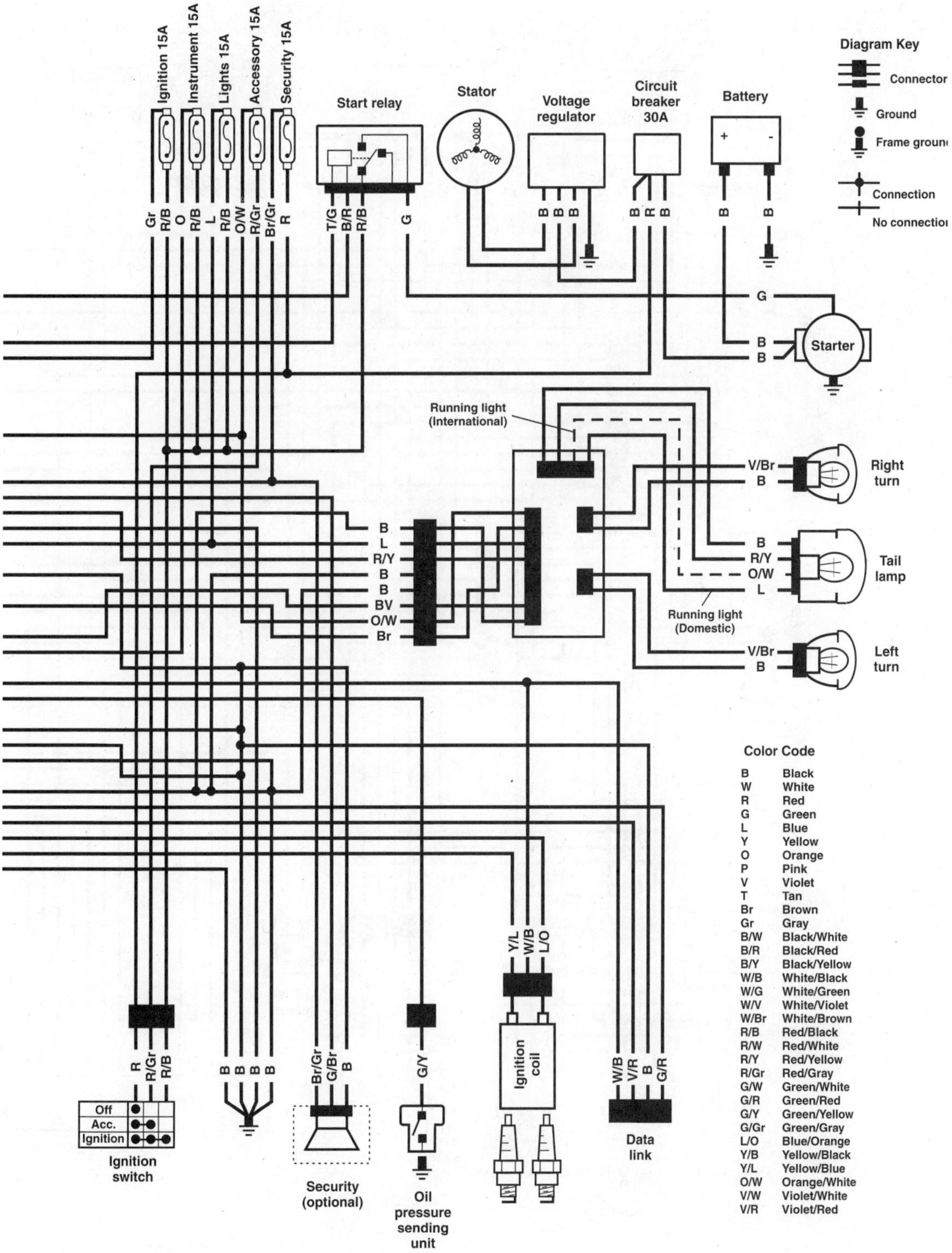
Ignition 15A
Instrument 15A
Lights 15A
Accessory 15A
Security 15A
Start relay
Stator
Voltage regulator
Circuit breaker 30A
Battery
Diagram Key
Connector
Ground
Frame ground
Connection
No connection
Gr
R/B
O
R/B
L
R/B
O/W
R/Gr
Br/Gr
R
T/G
B/R
R/B
G
B
B
B
B
R
B
B
B
G
B
B
Starter
Running light (International)
V/Br
B
Right turn
B
L
R/Y
B
B
BV
O/W
Br
B
R/Y
O/W
L
Tail lamp
Running light (Domestic)
V/Br
B
Left turn
Color Code
B Black
W White
R Red
G Green
L Blue
Y Yellow
O Orange
P Pink
V Violet
T Tan
Br Brown
Gr Gray
B/W Black/White
B/R Black/Red
B/Y Black/Yellow
W/B White/Black
W/G White/Green
W/V White/Violet
W/Br White/Brown
R/B Red/Black
R/W Red/White
R/Y Red/Yellow
R/Gr Red/Gray
G/W Green/White
G/R Green/Red
G/Y Green/Yellow
G/Gr Green/Gray
L/O Blue/Orange
Y/B Yellow/Black
Y/L Yellow/Blue
O/W Orange/White
V/W Violet/White
V/R Violet/Red
Y/L
W/B
L/O
R
R/Gr
R/B
Off
Acc.
Ignition
Ignition switch
B
B
B
B
Br/Gr
G/Br
B
Security (optional)
G/Y
Oil pressure sending unit
Ignition coil
W/B
V/R
B
G/R
Data link

2001-2003 FXDX, FXDXT, FXDL & FXD MODELS

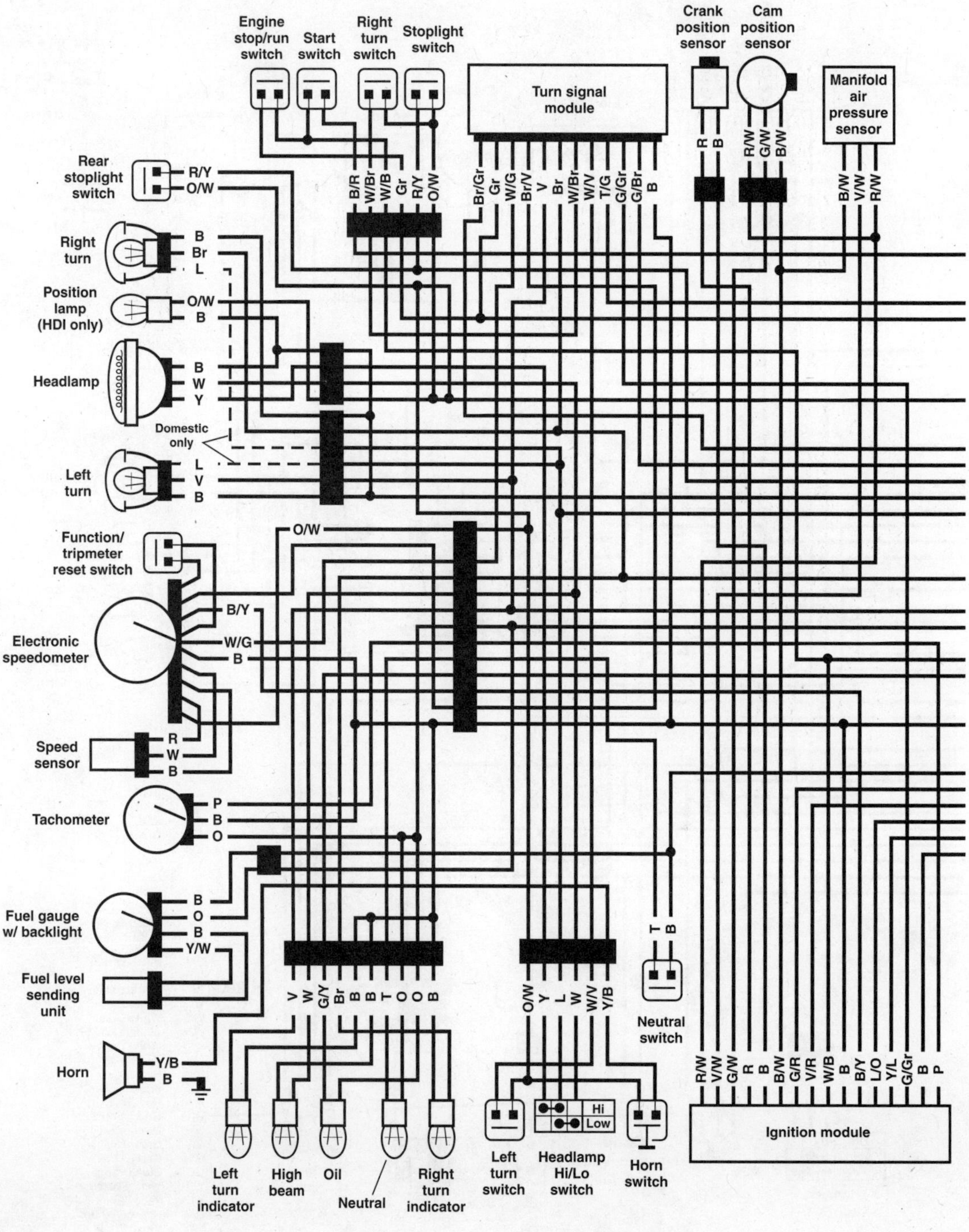

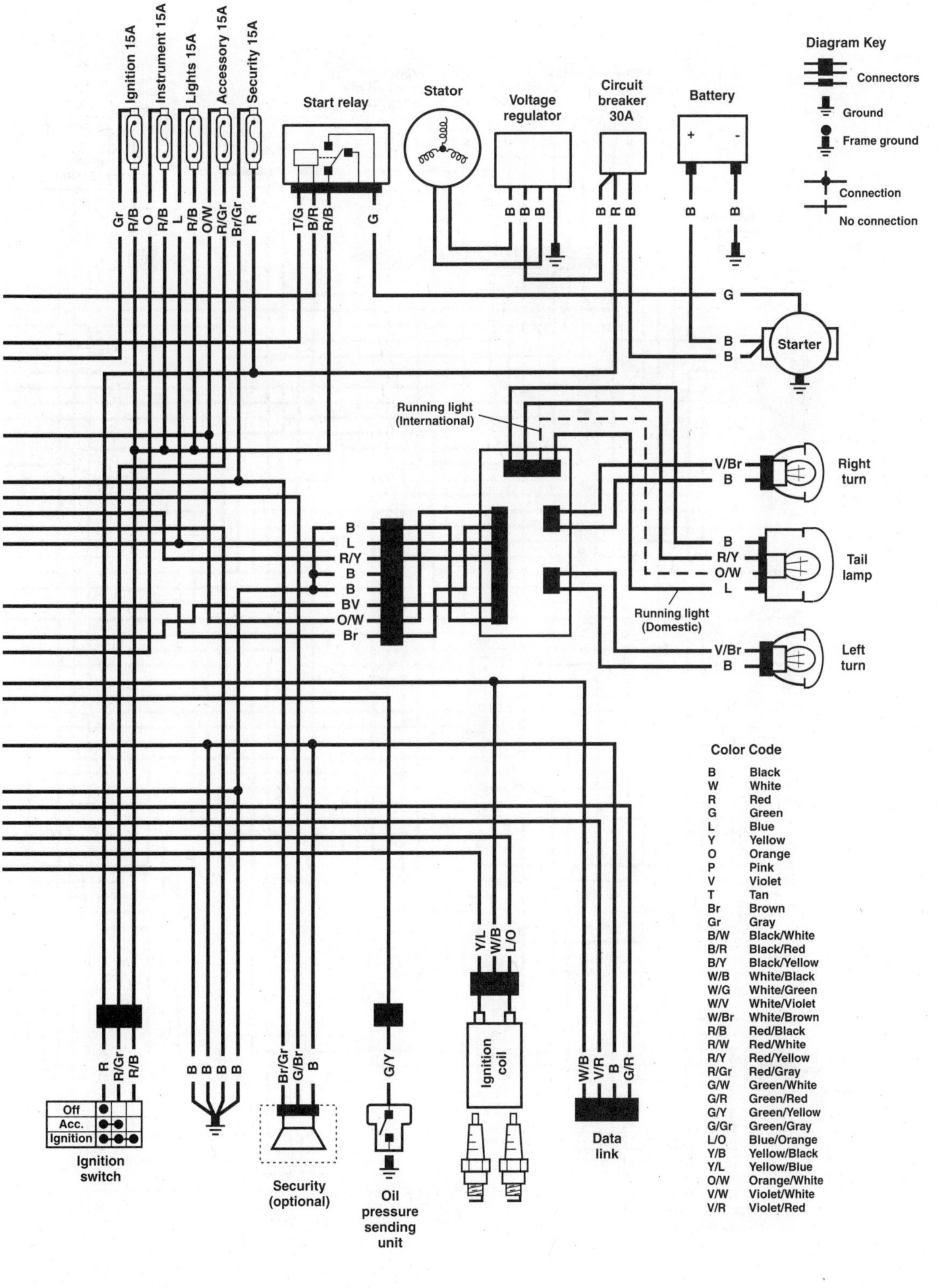
Ignition 15A
Instrument 15A
Lights 15A
Accessory 15A
Security 15A
Start relay
Stator
Voltage regulator
Circuit breaker 30A
Battery
Diagram Key
Connectors
Ground
Frame ground
Connection
No connection
Starter
Running light (International)
Right turn
Tail lamp
Running light (Domestic)
Left turn
Ignition coil
Ignition switch
Off
Acc.
Ignition
Security (optional)
Oil pressure sending unit
Data link
Color Code
B Black
W White
R Red
G Green
L Blue
Y Yellow
O Orange
P Pink
V Violet
T Tan
Br Brown
Gr Gray
B/W Black/White
B/R Black/Red
B/Y Black/Yellow
W/B White/Black
W/G White/Green
W/V White/Violet
W/Br White/Brown
R/B Red/Black
R/W Red/White
R/Y Red/Yellow
R/Gr Red/Gray
G/W Green/White
G/R Green/Red
G/Y Green/Yellow
G/Gr Green/Gray
L/O Blue/Orange
Y/B Yellow/Black
Y/L Yellow/Blue
O/W Orange/White
V/W Violet/White
V/R Violet/Red

16

2001-2004 FXDP MODELS

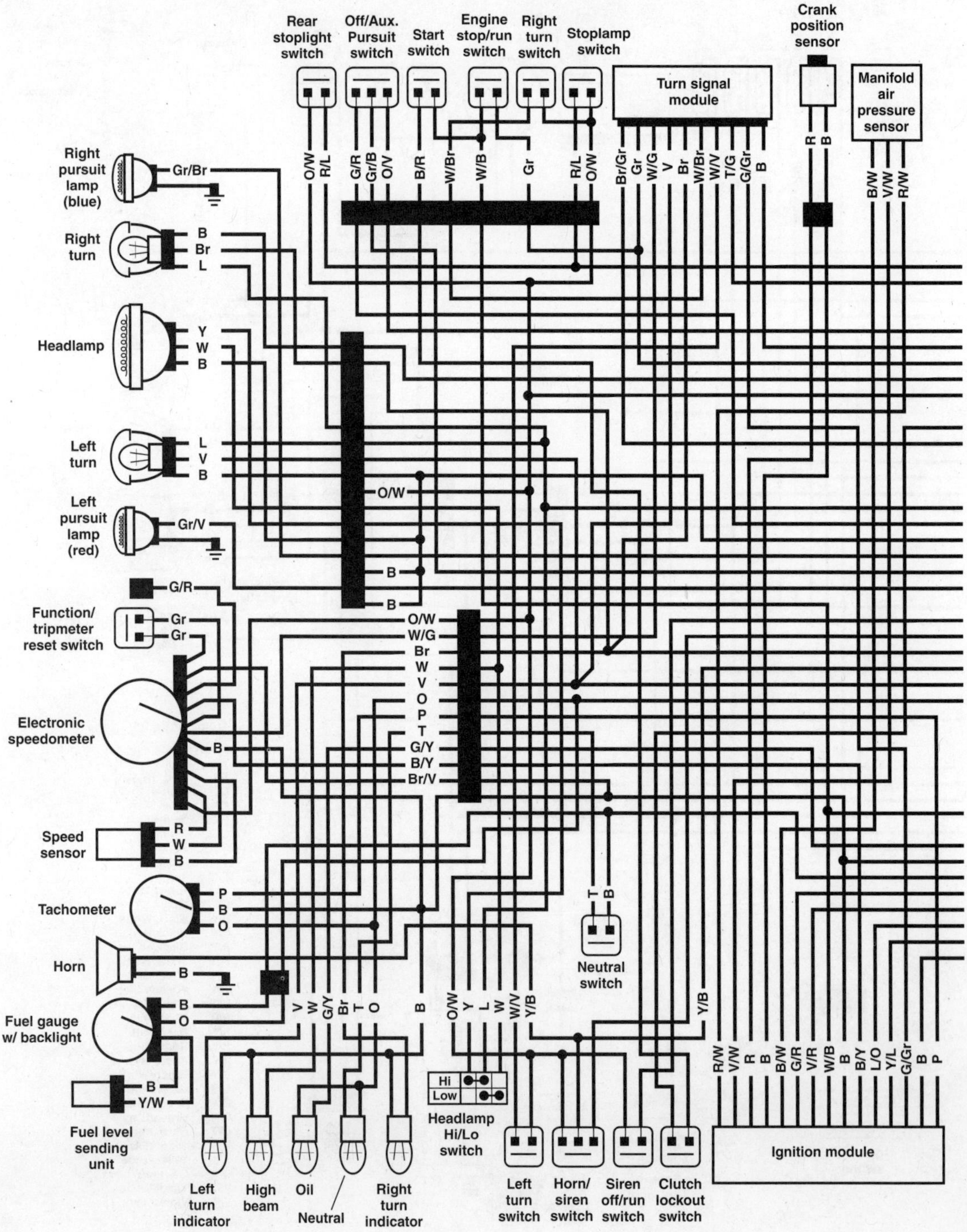

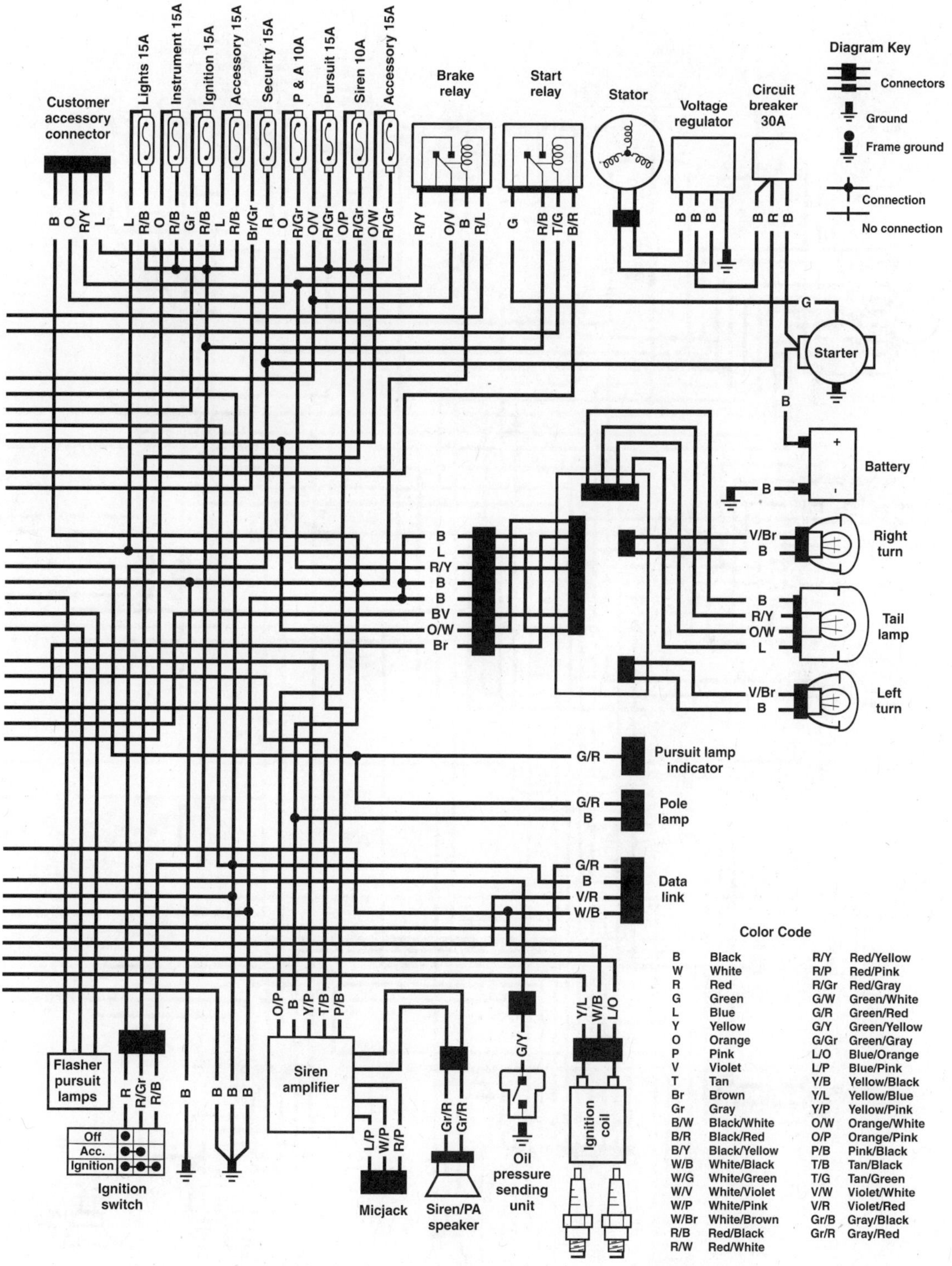

Color Code

B	Black	R/Y	Red/Yellow
W	White	R/P	Red/Pink
R	Red	R/Gr	Red/Gray
G	Green	G/W	Green/White
L	Blue	G/R	Green/Red
Y	Yellow	G/Y	Green/Yellow
O	Orange	G/Gr	Green/Gray
P	Pink	L/O	Blue/Orange
V	Violet	L/P	Blue/Pink
T	Tan	Y/B	Yellow/Black
Br	Brown	Y/L	Yellow/Blue
Gr	Gray	Y/P	Yellow/Pink
B/W	Black/White	O/W	Orange/White
B/R	Black/Red	O/P	Orange/Pink
B/Y	Black/Yellow	P/B	Pink/Black
W/B	White/Black	T/B	Tan/Black
W/G	White/Green	T/G	Tan/Green
W/V	White/Violet	V/W	Violet/White
W/P	White/Pink	V/R	Violet/Red
W/Br	White/Brown	Gr/B	Gray/Black
R/B	Red/Black	Gr/R	Gray/Red
R/W	Red/White		

2004-2005 EFI FXDWG MODELS

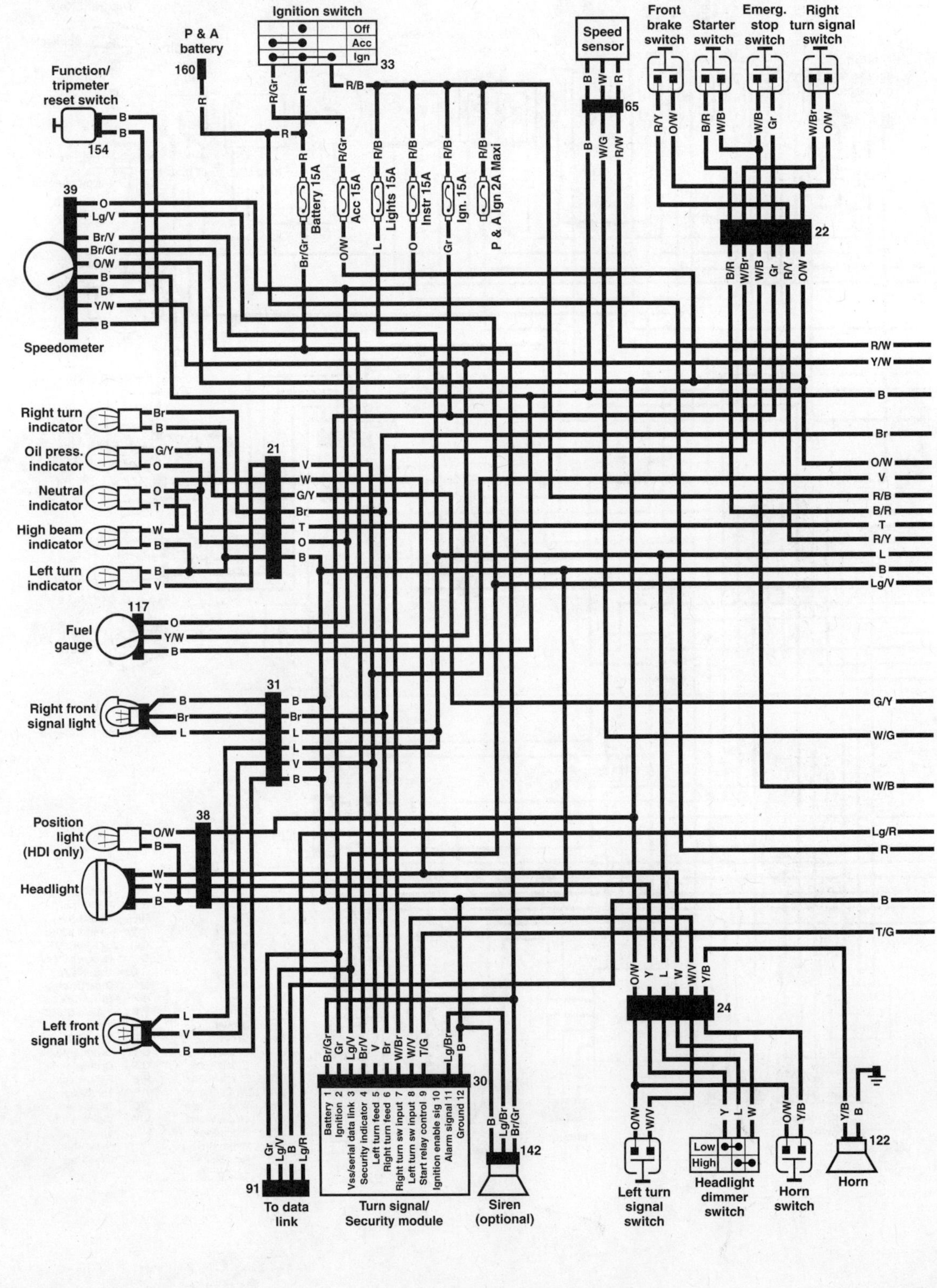

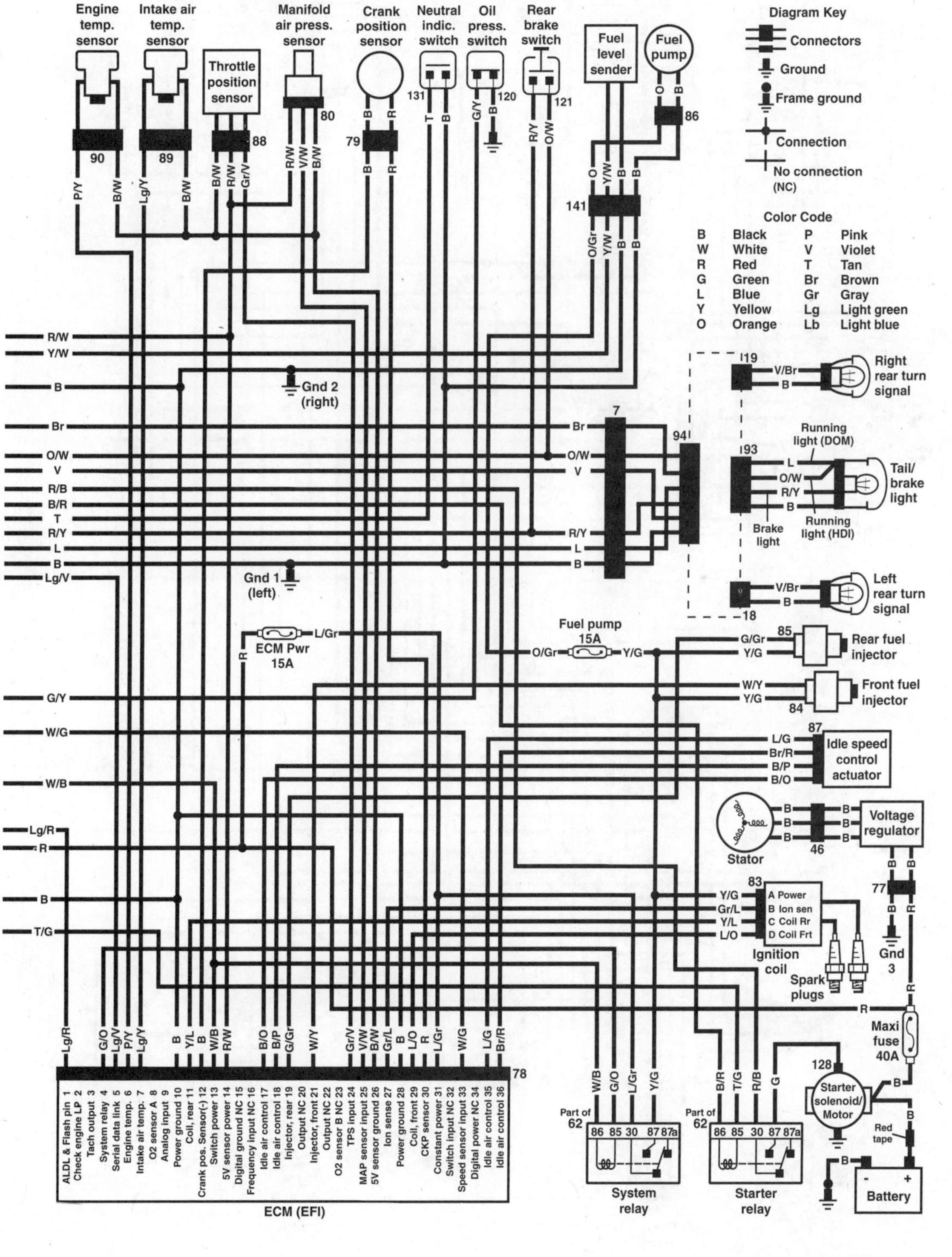
Engine temp. sensor
Intake air temp. sensor
Throttle position sensor
Manifold air press. sensor
Crank position sensor
Neutral indic. switch
Oil press. switch
Rear brake switch
Fuel level sender
Fuel pump
Diagram Key
Connectors
Ground
Frame ground
Connection
No connection (NC)
Color Code
B Black
W White
R Red
G Green
L Blue
Y Yellow
O Orange
P Pink
V Violet
T Tan
Br Brown
Gr Gray
Lg Light green
Lb Light blue
Gnd 2 (right)
Gnd 1 (left)
Right rear turn signal
Running light (DOM)
Tail/ brake light
Brake light
Running light (HDI)
Left rear turn signal
ECM Pwr 15A
Fuel pump 15A
Rear fuel injector
Front fuel injector
Idle speed control actuator
Stator
Voltage regulator
Gnd 3
A Power
B Ion sen
C Coil Rr
D Coil Frt
Ignition coil
Spark plugs
Maxi fuse 40A
Starter solenoid/ Motor
Red tape
Battery
Part of 62
86 85 30 87 87a
System relay
Starter relay
ALDL & Flash pin 1
Check engine LP 2
Tach output 3
System relay 4
Serial data link 5
Engine temp. 6
Intake air temp. 7
O2 sensor A 8
Analog input 9
Power ground 10
Coil, rear 11
Crank pos. Sensor(-) 12
Switch power 13
5V sensor power 14
Digital ground NC 15
Frequency input NC 16
Idle air control 17
Idle air control 18
Injector, rear 19
Output NC 20
Injector, front 21
Output NC 22
O2 sensor B NC 23
TPS input 24
MAP sensor input 25
5V sensor ground 26
Ion sense 27
Power ground 28
Coil, front 29
CKP sensor 30
Constant power 31
Switch input NC 32
Speed sensor input 33
Digital power NC 34
Idle air control 35
Idle air control 36
ECM (EFI)

16

2004-2005 EFI MODELS EXCEPT FXDWG

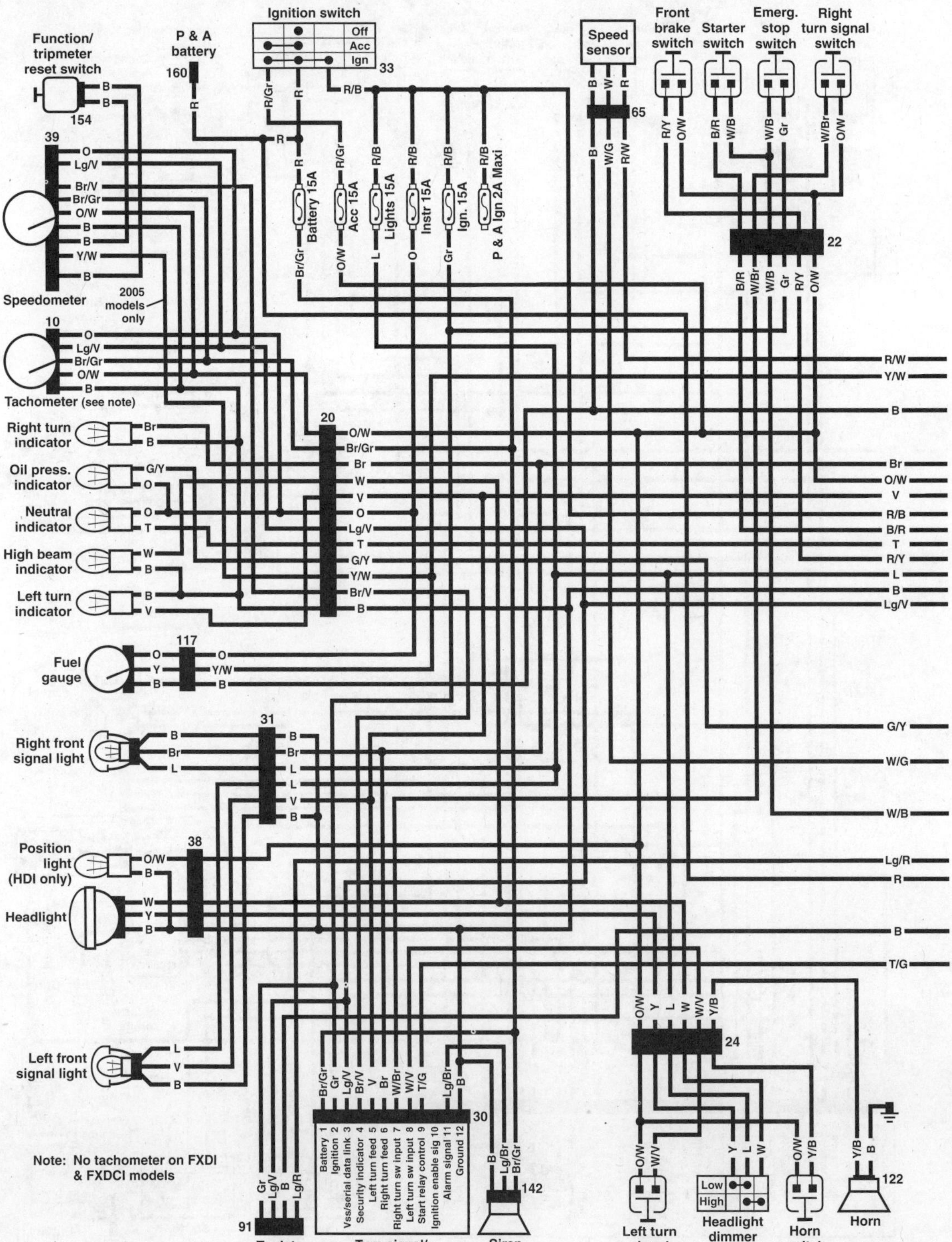

Note: No tachometer on FXDI & FXDCI models

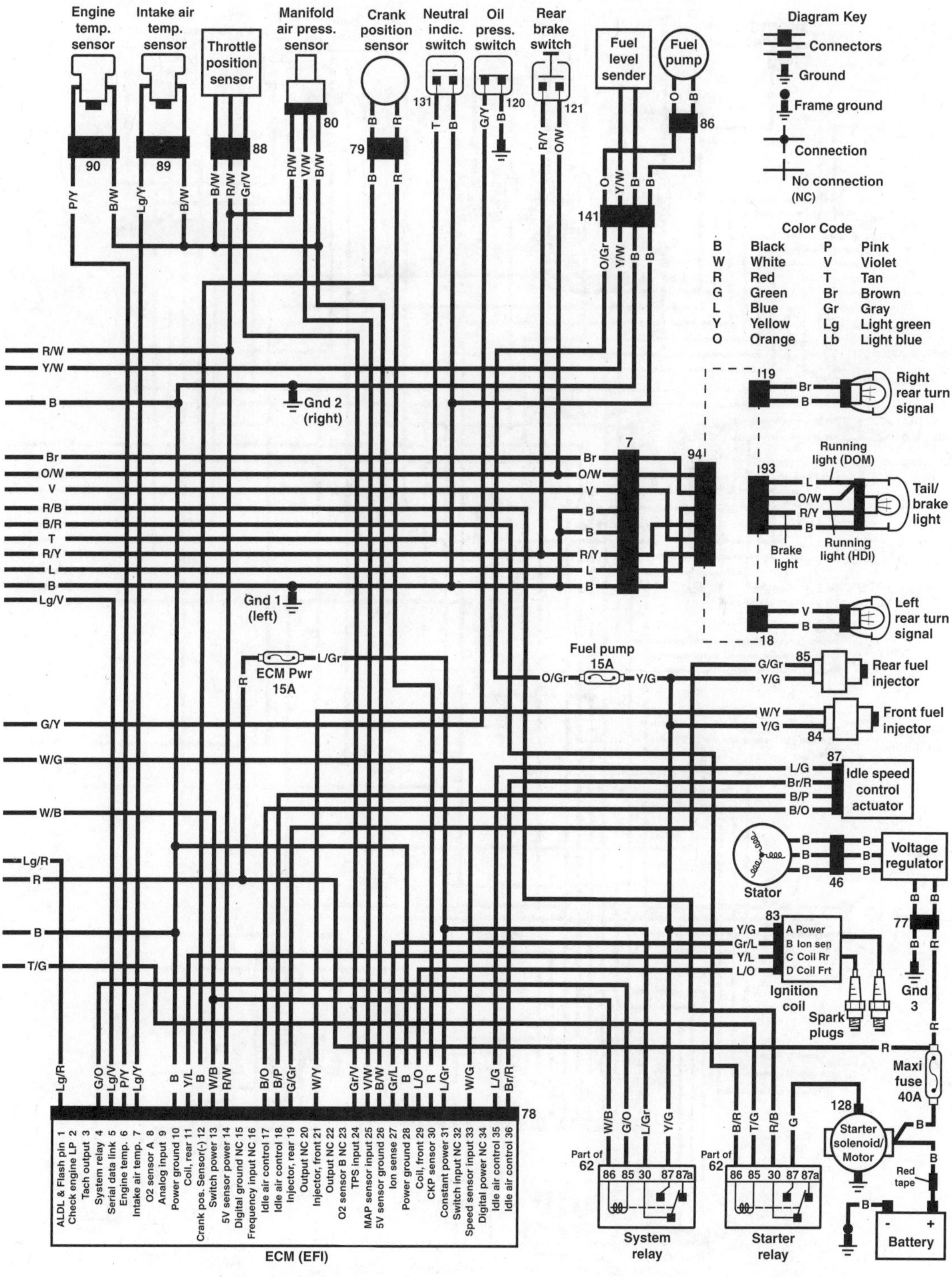

Engine temp. sensor
Intake air temp. sensor
Throttle position sensor
Manifold air press. sensor
Crank position sensor
Neutral indic. switch
Oil press. switch
Rear brake switch
Fuel level sender
Fuel pump
Diagram Key
Connectors
Ground
Frame ground
Connection
No connection (NC)
Color Code
B Black
W White
R Red
G Green
L Blue
Y Yellow
O Orange
P Pink
V Violet
T Tan
Br Brown
Gr Gray
Lg Light green
Lb Light blue
Gnd 2 (right)
Gnd 1 (left)
Right rear turn signal
Running light (DOM)
Tail/ brake light
Brake light
Running light (HDI)
Left rear turn signal
ECM Pwr 15A
Fuel pump 15A
Rear fuel injector
Front fuel injector
Idle speed control actuator
Stator
Voltage regulator
Gnd 3
A Power
B Ion sen
C Coil Rr
D Coil Frt
Ignition coil
Spark plugs
Maxi fuse 40A
Starter solenoid/ Motor
Red tape
Battery
ALDL & Flash pin 1
Check engine LP 2
Tach output 3
System relay 4
Serial data link 5
Engine temp. 6
Intake air temp. 7
O2 sensor A 8
Analog input 9
Power ground 10
Coil, rear 11
Crank pos. Sensor(-) 12
Switch power 13
5V sensor power 14
Digital ground NC 15
Frequency input NC 16
Idle air control 17
Idle air control 18
Injector, rear 19
Output NC 20
Injector, front 21
Output NC 22
O2 sensor B NC 23
TPS input 24
MAP sensor input 25
5V sensor ground 26
Ion sense 27
Power ground 28
Coil, front 29
CKP sensor 30
Constant power 31
Switch input NC 32
Speed sensor input 33
Digital power NC 34
Idle air control 35
Idle air control 36
ECM (EFI)
Part of 62
System relay
Starter relay

16

2004-2005 CARBURETED FXDWG MODELS

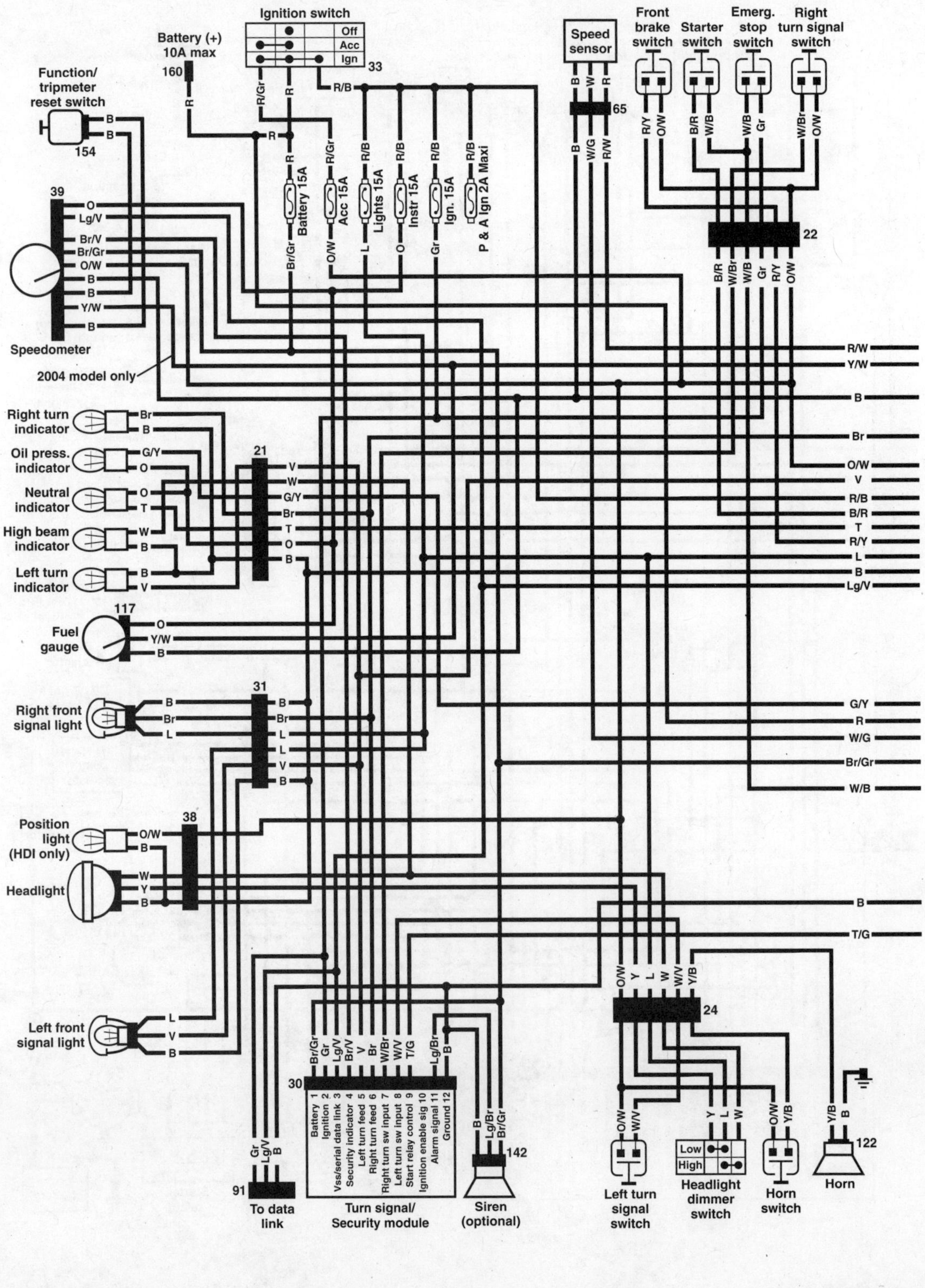

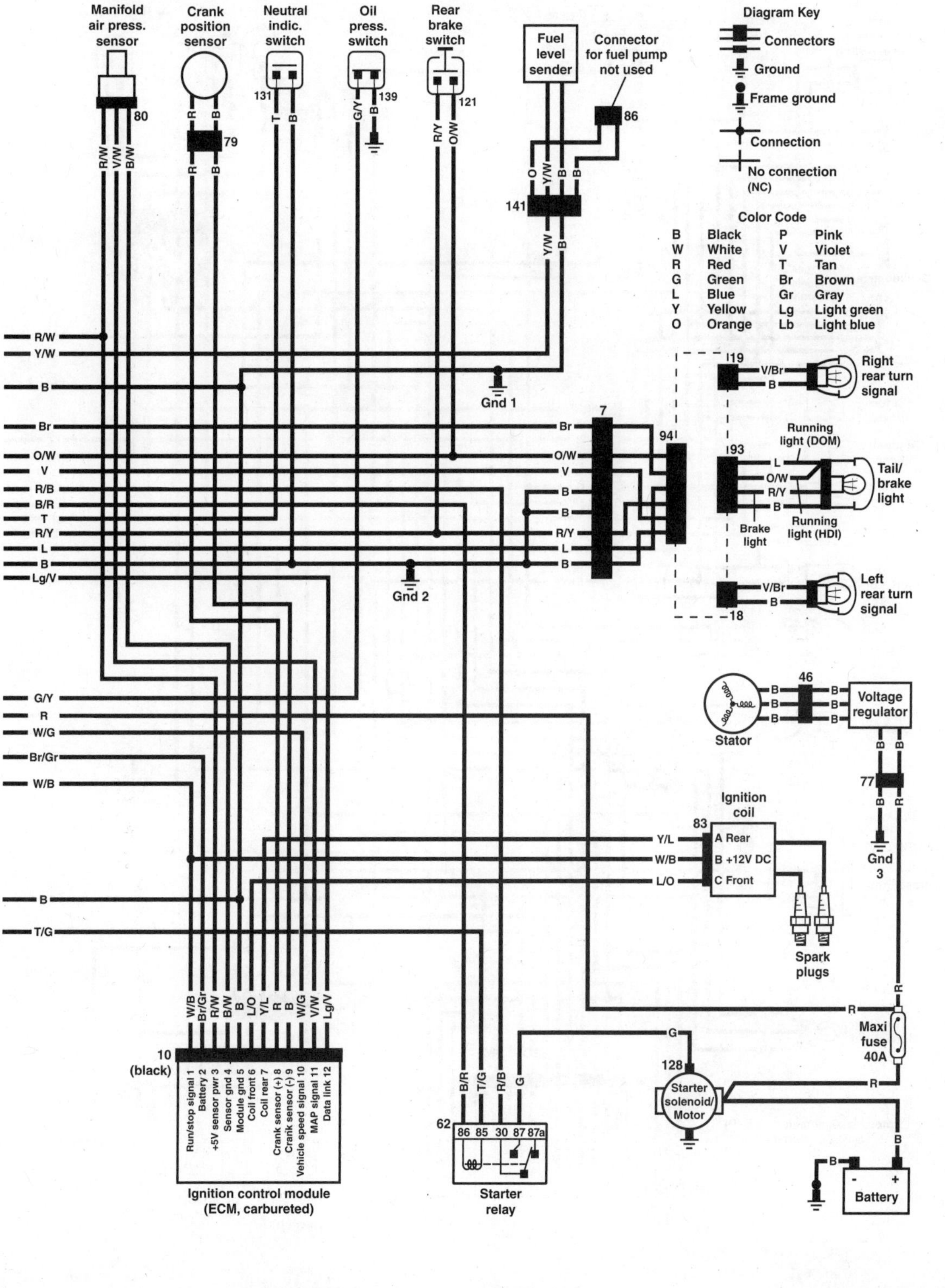
Manifold air press. sensor
Crank position sensor
Neutral indic. switch
Oil press. switch
Rear brake switch
Fuel level sender
Connector for fuel pump not used
Diagram Key
Connectors
Ground
Frame ground
Connection
No connection (NC)
Color Code
B Black
W White
R Red
G Green
L Blue
Y Yellow
O Orange
P Pink
V Violet
T Tan
Br Brown
Gr Gray
Lg Light green
Lb Light blue
Gnd 1
Gnd 2
Right rear turn signal
Running light (DOM)
Tail/ brake light
Brake light
Running light (HDI)
Left rear turn signal
Stator
Voltage regulator
Gnd 3
Ignition coil
A Rear
B +12V DC
C Front
Spark plugs
Maxi fuse 40A
Starter solenoid/ Motor
Battery
Run/stop signal 1
Battery 2
+5V sensor pwr 3
Sensor gnd 4
Module gnd 5
Coil front 6
Coil rear 7
Crank sensor (+) 8
Crank sensor (-) 9
Vehicle speed signal 10
MAP signal 11
Data link 12
10 (black)
Ignition control module (ECM, carbureted)
Starter relay
86 85 30 87 87a

2004-2005 CARBURETED MODELS EXCEPT FXDWG

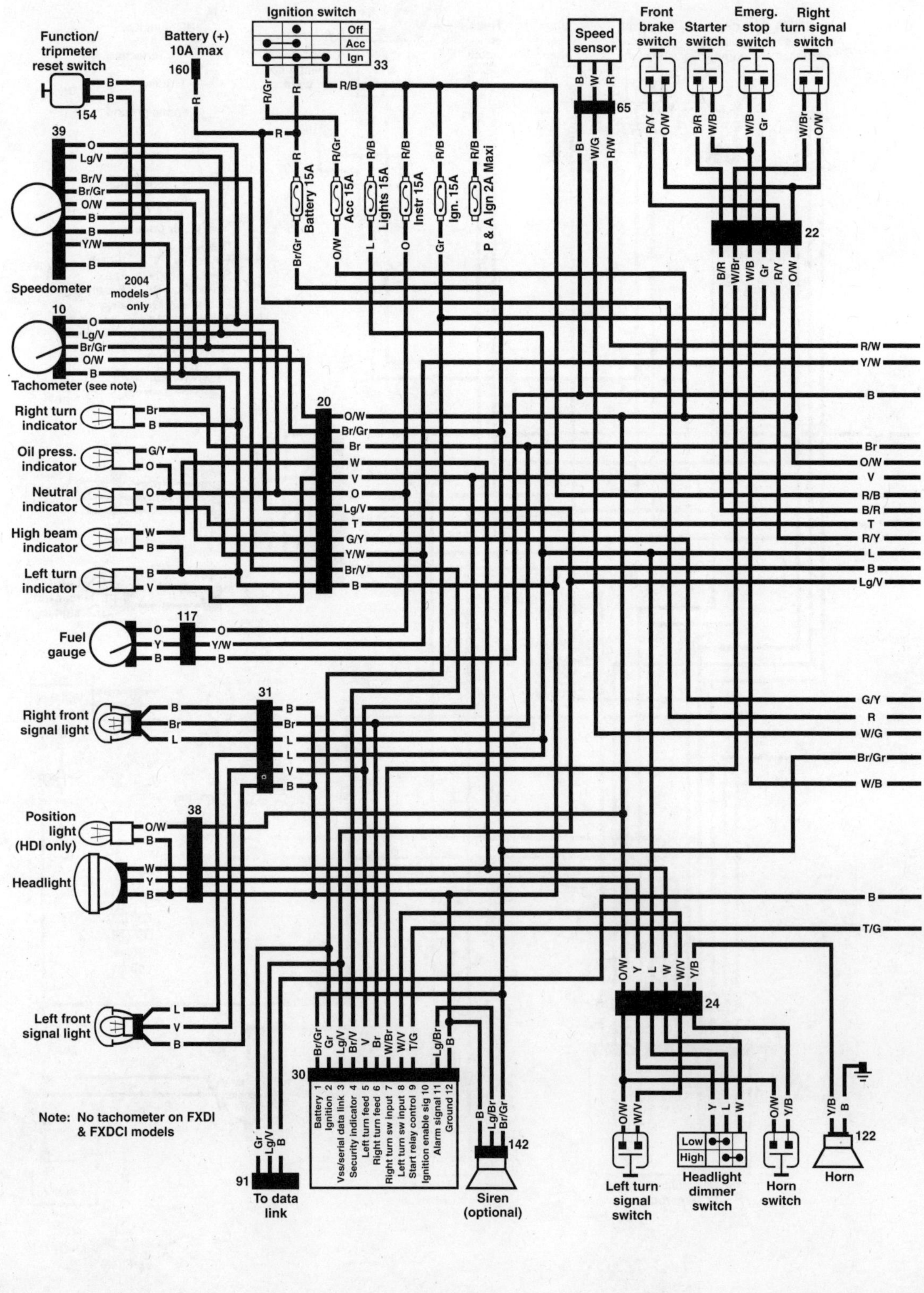

Note: No tachometer on FXDI & FXDCI models

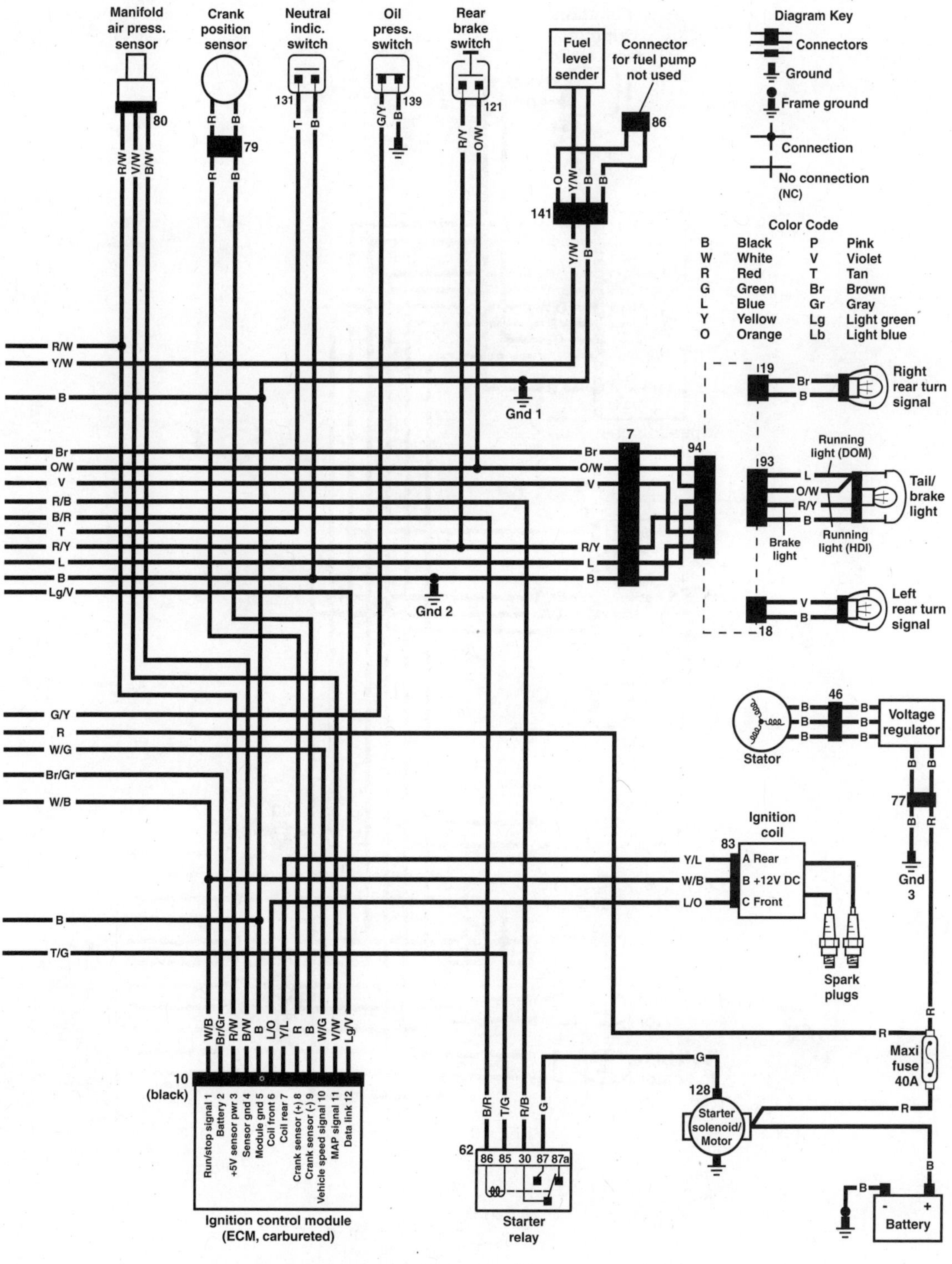
Manifold air press. sensor
80
R/W
V/W
B/W
Crank position sensor
79
R
B
Neutral indic. switch
131
T
B
Oil press. switch
G/Y
139
B
Rear brake switch
121
R/Y
O/W
Fuel level sender
Connector for fuel pump not used
86
141
O
Y/W
B
B
Diagram Key
Connectors
Ground
Frame ground
Connection
No connection (NC)
Color Code
B Black
W White
R Red
G Green
L Blue
Y Yellow
O Orange
P Pink
V Violet
T Tan
Br Brown
Gr Gray
Lg Light green
Lb Light blue
R/W
Y/W
B
Gnd 1
Br
O/W
V
R/B
B/R
T
R/Y
L
B
Lg/V
7
94
Gnd 2
119
Right rear turn signal
93
Running light (DOM)
Tail/ brake light
Brake light
Running light (HDI)
18
Left rear turn signal
G/Y
R
W/G
Br/Gr
W/B
B
T/G
Stator
46
Voltage regulator
77
Gnd 3
Ignition coil
83
Y/L
W/B
L/O
A Rear
B +12V DC
C Front
Spark plugs
Maxi fuse 40A
G
128
Starter solenoid/ Motor
Battery
10 (black)
Run/stop signal 1
Battery 2
+5V sensor pwr 3
Sensor gnd 4
Module gnd 5
Coil front 6
Coil rear 7
Crank sensor (+) 8
Crank sensor (-) 9
Vehicle speed signal 10
MAP signal 11
Data link 12
Ignition control module (ECM, carbureted)
62
B/R
T/G
R/B
G
86 85 30 87 87a
Starter relay

2004-2005 SPEEDOMETER AND TACHOMETER

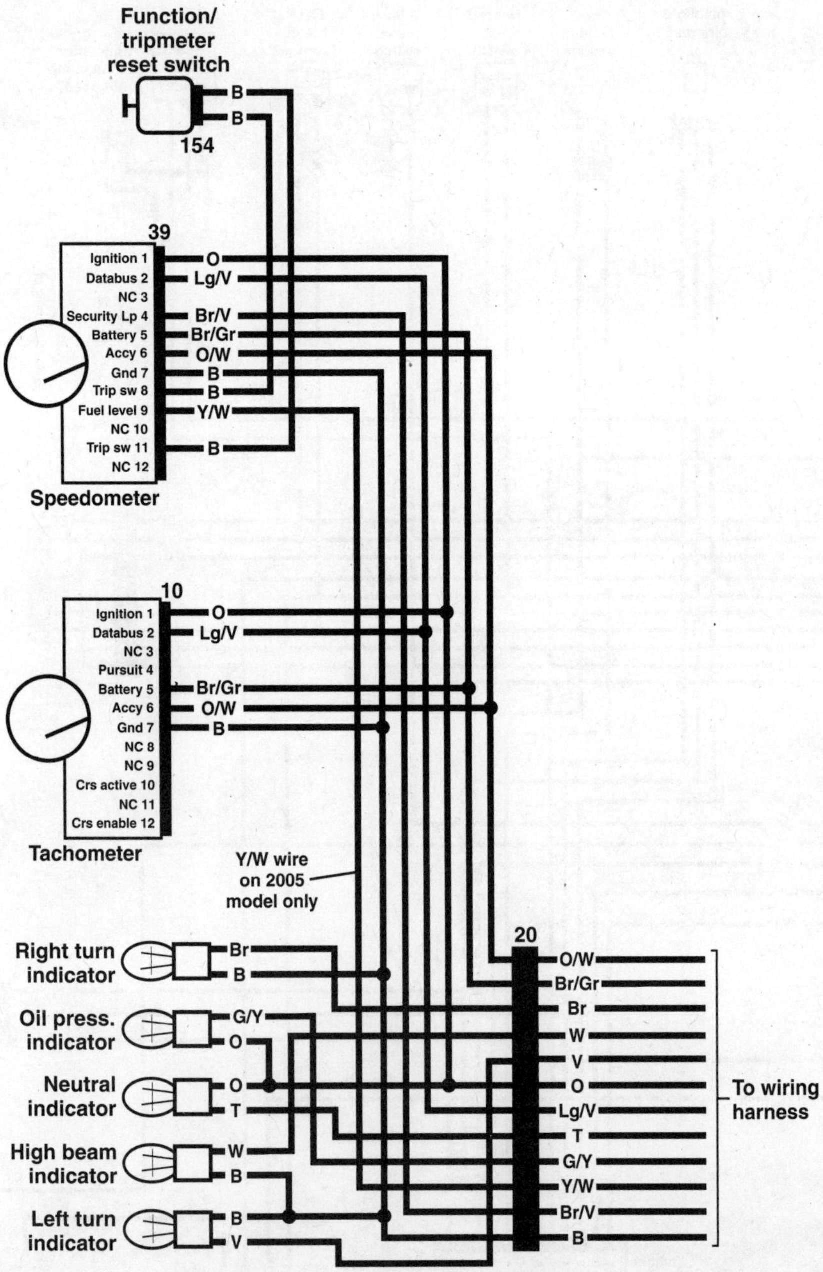

NOTES

NOTES

NOTES

NOTES

MAINTENANCE LOG

Date	Miles	Type of Service

MAINTENANCE LOG

Date	Miles	Type of Service